FOURTH EDITION

BEHAVIOR DISORDERS OF CHILDHOOD

RITA WICKS-NELSON

Rockefeller Scholar, CSEGA
Marshall University
Huntington, West Virginia

ALLEN C. ISRAEL

University at Albany
State University of New York

PRENTICE HALL

Upper Saddle River, New Jersey 07458

Library of Congress Cataloging-in-Publication Data
Wicks-Nelson, Rita
  Behavior disorders of childhood / Rita Wicks-Nelson, Allen C.
Israel. — 4th ed.
    p. cm.
  Includes bibliographical references and index.
  ISBN 0–13–083536–6
  1. Child psychopathology. I. Israel, Allen C. II. Title.
RJ499.W45 2000
618.92'89—dc21   99-30387
              CIP

TO LEONARD C. NELSON,

MARY WICKS,

THE MEMORY OF WILLIAM WICKS

RW-N

TO HELEN ISRAEL

THE MEMORY OF KARLTON ISRAEL

THE MEMORY OF ALICE ISRAEL

ACI

Editorial Director: *Charlyce Jones-Owen*
Editor-in-Chief: *Nancy Roberts*
Acquisitions Editor: *Jennifer Gilliland*
Assistant Editor: *Anita Castro*
AVP, Director of manufacturing and production: *Barabara Kittle*
Managing Editor: *Mary Rottino*
Production Liaison: *Fran Russello*
Project Manager: *Patty Donovan/Pine Tree Composition*
Manufacturing Manager: *Nick Sklitsis*
Prepress and Manufacturing Buyer: *Tricia Kenny*
Creative Design Director: *Leslie Osher*
Interior Design: *Ximena Tamvakopoulos*
Cover Designer: *Ximena Tamvakopoulos*
Cover Art: *Paul Tallinghast/SIS, Inc.*
Director, Image Resource Center: *Melinda Lee Reo*
Manager, Rights & Permissions: *Kay Dellosa*
Image Specialist: *Beth Boyd*
Photo Researcher: *Teri Stratford*
Line Art Coordinator: *Guy Ruggiero*
Electronic Art Creation: *Ximena Tamvakupoulos*
Director of Marketing: *Gina Sluss*

This book was set in 10/12 New Baskerville by Pine Tree Composition, Inc.,
and was printed and bound by R.R. Donnelley and Sons. The cover was printed by Phoenix Color
Corp.

© 2000, 1997, 1991, 1984 by Prentice-Hall, Inc.
Upper Saddle River, New Jersey 07458

Printed in the United States of America
10 9 8 7 6 5 4 3 2 1

ISBN: 0-13-083536-6

Prentice-Hall International (UK) Limited, *London*
Prentice-Hall of Australia Pty. Limited, *Sydney*
Prentice-Hall Canada Inc., *Toronto*
Prentice-Hall Hispanoamericana, S.A., *Mexico*
Prentice-Hall of India Private Limited, *New Delhi*
Prentice-Hall of Japan, Inc., *Tokyo*
Pearson Education Asia Pte Ltd., *Singapore*
Editora Prentice-Hall do Brasil, Ltda., *Rio de Janeiro*

BRIEF CONTENTS

CONTENTS

3 APPROACHES TO UNDERSTANDING AND TREATING CHILDHOOD BEHAVIOR DISORDERS   46

6 ANXIETY DISORDERS 113

7 DEPRESSION AND PROBLEMS IN PEER RELATIONS   146

8 CONDUCT DISORDERS   182

11 LANGUAGE AND LEARNING DISABILITIES 290

12 AUTISM AND SCHIZOPHRENIA 320

13 DISORDERS OF BASIC PHYSICAL FUNCTIONS 359

14 PSYCHOLOGICAL FACTORS AFFECTING MEDICAL CONDITION 388

15 EVOLVING CONCERNS FOR YOUTH   415

The passage of time is uppermost in our minds as this fourth edition of *Behavior Disorders of Childhood* nears completion and the twentieth century simultaneously winds down. What a century it has been for the study of young people and their well-being. The past one hundred years have witnessed the movement from relative ignorance to the opening of innumerable doors to knowledge about human development in general and behavioral disorder more specifically. During the lifetime of this text, we have been fortunate to participate in an expanding field characterized by progress, challenge, and excitement. We have tried in this fourth edition to continue to capture the search for understanding the behavioral problems experienced by youth and to convey both what is known and what is yet to be known.

This text shares the fundamental characteristics of previous editions. Designed as a relatively comprehensive introduction to the field of behavior disorders of childhood and adolescence, it includes central issues, theoretical and methodological underpinnings, descriptions and discussions of many disorders, clinical and research data, assessment, and treatment approaches. As is usually the case for a work of this kind, space limitation demands some selectivity of content.

Three major themes, or predilections, continue to be woven throughout the text. Their importance has become firmly established. The first is the assumption that the developmental context can contribute much to understanding childhood behavior problems. As normal developmental sequences and processes are increasingly elucidated, they are being brought to bear on identifying and explaining the growth of disordered development. The text reflects our interest in relating normal and disturbed growth.

Also obvious throughout the book is the view that behavioral problems are the result of interactions among variables. With few if any exceptions, behavior stems from multiple influences and their continuous interactions. The influences of biological structure and function, inheritance, cognition, social and emotional factors, family, peers, social class, culture, and situational settings can be expected to come into play.

Our third bias is toward empirical approaches and the theoretical frameworks that rely heavily on the scientific method. We believe that the complexity of human behavior calls for systematic conceptualization and observation, data collection, and hypothesis testing. The methods and results of research thus are critical components of virtually all chapters.

Also recognized in this text is that problems of the young are intricately tied to broad social and cultural values and practices regarding issues such as proverty, ethnicity/race, and gender as well as standards for behavior, conceptualizations of dysfunction, and treatment. Many of these issues are incorporated into discussions throughout the text, including poverty's effects, gender differences, the impact of parental divorce, the ethics of research, the use of medications in treating children, and educational mainstreaming. Discussions of such topics often make clear the importance of research in informing social and ethical choices.

The text is not formally broken into sections, but it will be apparent that the first five chapters present broad underpinnings of the field: historical context, developmental context, theoretical perspectives, research methodology, and classification/diagnosis. All of these chapters draw heavily on the psychological literature, but they also show the multidisciplinary nature of the study of the problems of youth. We assume that most readers will have some background in psychology, but we also have made an effort to serve those who may have relatively limited background and experience.

Chapters 6 through 14 discuss specific behavior disorders: anxiety, depression, conduct problems, attention deficit-hyperactivity, general and specific learning disabilities, autism, and schizophrenia to name major categories. Definition and description, prevalence, developmental course and outcome, causal hypotheses, assessment, and treatment are discussed in varying detail. The chapters are similar but not identical in organization, reflecting what is currently of most interest and what is best established. Chapter 15, the closing chapter, focuses on concerns for youth, including the need for and progress being made in preventing behavior disorders.

The thoughtful evaluations and suggestions of the following reviewers are much appreciated:

G. Leonard Burns
Washington State University
Department of Psychology

David Glenwick
Fordham University
Department of Psychology

John Grych
Marquette University
Department of Psychology

Yolanda Kaye Jackson
University of Kansas
Department of Psychology/Human Development

We extend our sincere thanks to several individuals who helped in various ways with this edition: Susan Chalmers, Helena Roderick, and George Tremblay, Ph.D. We would particularly like to acknowledge the insightful and dedicated efforts of Masha Ivanova. Her work in locating material for this volume and in various other aspects of the preparation of this manuscript were invaluable. And thanks to Daniel and Sara for their caring, support, and patience.

Finally, we note that the order of authorship was originally decided by a flip of the coin to reflect our equal contributions. In all of our work we have shared equally.

Rita Wicks-Nelson
Allen C. Israel

CHAPTER 1

INTRODUCTION

This book is written for all those concerned with behavioral or psychological problems displayed by the young. We anticipate, and hope, that you will find this field of study as satisfying as we do. It is an area of study that encompasses both humanitarian concerns for young people and scientific intrigue. Moreover, this is a particularly promising time to study behavioral dysfunction. The need for increased understanding, prevention, and treatment is substantial, and it is a need that is recognized in many parts of the world. At the same time, research into behavioral disturbance and human development is growing by leaps and bounds, with contributions from many professional disciplines. As is usually true in science, increased knowledge and improved methods have led to new questions and paradoxes. This combination—new understandings, new questions, new avenues of inquiry—gives both promise and excitement to the study of behavioral dysfunctions in young people. It is probably not exces-sively optimistic to suggest that a field of study barely defined at the beginning of the twentieth century will see remarkable progress during the new century that we are embarking upon.

DEFINING THE DISCIPLINE: WHAT IS DISORDERED BEHAVIOR?

There is no concise and simple way to define and identify disordered functioning. Behavioral reper-toires come in endless varieties. We will examine many kinds of behavioral problems throughout this book and will also see that behavioral disor-ders are evaluated and treated from several per-spectives. They are also referred to by many labels: behavioral disturbances, behavioral dysfunctions, behavioral problems, psychological problems, ab-normal behavior, maladaptive behavior, impair-ments, deficiencies, deficits, and psychopathology. Regardless of the label, however, parents and oth-ers often assume that behavioral disturbance is much like a medical disease that has a specific in-dicator, such as the presence of infection. This is overwhelmingly not the case. Rather, guidelines for identifying, or diagnosing, behavioral dysfunc-

THE FACES OF PROBLEM BEHAVIOR

Karen was a nine-year-old girl with a history of refusal to eat solid foods. Six weeks previously, she had choked on a piece of popcorn, with coughing and gagging. From that time on, she had refused to eat any solid foods and had lost about fifteen pounds. She had also developed multiple fears concerning choking. She would not brush her teeth for fear a bristle would come out and she would choke. She slept propped on pillows for fear a loose tooth would come out while she was asleep and that she would choke and suffocate. She was afraid to go to sleep and requested to sleep with her mother because of her fears. She also had frequent nightmares and vivid dreams of choking. (From Chatoor, Conley, & Dickson, 1988, p. 106)

Joe, who is eight years old, has a history of multiple problems. They include chronic hyperactivity, destructive behavior, short attention span, difficulty following verbal directions, low frustration tolerance, impulsiveness, poor interpersonal relationships, fighting, lying, stealing, disobedience, running away from school, and setting fires. His parents had discounted the importance of these behaviors, preferring to believe that little boys should be allowed to express themselves. Joe had been recommended for special education placement in the first grade, but his parents had re-

fused the recommendation. His behavior worsened in the second and third grades, and after Joe exposed himself to female peers, the school forced further evaluation. (From Rapport, 1993, pp. 284–285)

Anne was brought to a community mental health center by her mother, who feared Anne might be a Satanist. The previous evening, Anne had been discovered naked, chanting, and clutching a knife dripping with blood. She had begun to worship Satan and noted that praying to Satan brought her relief. Anne had changed in other ways. She had acquired new friends, although she spent much time alone in her room. She had dyed her blond hair black and cut one side short. Anne reported that she had difficulty falling asleep because she worried about her grades and her parents' divorce. She believed she was partly responsible for the divorce. She found it hard to concentrate in school, was irritable, and had lost 15 pounds without dieting. Anne denied any intent or plan for suicide, involvement with cults, or drug use. She no longer shops with friends, swims, or bikes, because these activities take too much energy. Anne spoke to the therapist coherently but with a slow, monotone voice. (Adapted from Morgan, 1999, pp. 35–37)

tions are based on relatively fluid judgments of what is or is not problematic.

DEVIANCE AND HARMFULNESS

Problem behavior frequently is viewed as "abnormal." "Ab" means "away" or "from," whereas "normal" refers to the average or standard. Thus ab-

normal simply means something that deviates from the average. However, common usage also assumes that the deviation is harmful in some way to the individual.

In its manual for classifying and diagnosing mental disorders, the American Psychiatric Association (1994) defines a disorder as an impairment or dysfunction of the individual that causes distress to the person or increased risk of death, pain, disability, or loss of freedom. Clearly, a disorder is viewed as "bad" for the individual. However, it can be argued that disorder is better viewed as a person's reactions to an environmental circumstance rather than as a dysfunction within the individual (Mash & Dozois, 1996). Moreover, the definition offered above leaves open the precise meaning of impairment or dysfunction.

In fact, judgments are always involved in determining whether behavior is a manifestation of dysfunction. A behavioral standard must be established for what is acceptable or healthy, and a decision made about whether the behavior of interest meets the standard. Of course, dramatic differences are easy to identify. Most of us would agree that children who cannot learn to speak or to feed and dress themselves show impairments. Less dramatic instances are harder to judge. Individuals may display behaviors that are quite common or only slightly deviant from the normal standard—and yet the behaviors appear maladaptive. In these instances, parents, teachers, other adults, and occasionally children themselves rely on numerous criteria to make the judgment that "something is wrong."

CULTURAL AND SOCIAL STANDARDS FOR BEHAVIOR

Cultural standards. The role of cultural standards, or cultural norms, perhaps the broadest basis for judging behavior, was tellingly discussed many years ago by the anthropologist Ruth Benedict. After studying widely diverse cultures, Benedict (1934b) proposed that each society selects certain behaviors that are of value to it and socializes its members to act accordingly. Individuals who do not display these behaviors, for whatever reasons, are considered deviant by the society. Deviance is always related to cultural standards. Benedict noted, for example, that the suspiciousness typically exhibited in one Melanesian culture would be considered pathological in our society. The Melanesians would not leave their cooking pots because they feared that the food would be poisoned by others (Benedict, 1934a). Further-

more, Melanesians who displayed the helpfulness, kindness, and cheerfulness that is viewed as positive in our society were considered abnormal in their culture.

Cultural standards are applied to children as well as to adults, and these standards broadly influence expectations, judgments, and beliefs about the behavior of youth. Youngsters in the United States, for example, are expected to show less self-control and less deference to adults compared with children in some other parts of the world (Weisz et al., 1995). Relative to some other cultures, then, we might be more likely to express concern about the overcontrolled, passive child. Similarly, in technologically advanced societies that value certain intellectual skills, special concern would be voiced about the child who does not measure up to these standards of intellectual development.

A study by Weisz et al. (1988) showed that culture might influence the degree to which childhood problems are considered serious. Parents and teachers in the United States and Thailand read descriptions of child problems and then answered questions about them. As Figure 1-1 shows, the Thai adults were less worried than the U.S. adults. This finding appears consistent with the teachings of Thai Buddhism that every condition changes and that behavior does not reflect enduring personality. In another study, Weisz and his colleagues (1995) found that teachers in Thailand reported more conduct problems in students than teachers in the United States, while trained observers reported just the opposite. The researchers suggested that Thai teachers may hold more demanding behavioral standards.

Culture can also influence how problem behaviors are explained, as was demonstrated in a study in which mothers of North African and Middle Eastern background living in Israel were interviewed about their children who were retarded (Stahl, 1991). Almost half of the mothers gave magic-religious causes for the condition. They believed in Fate, demons entering the body, an Evil Eye, and punishment from God. These mothers relied on magic-religious treatments accordingly: burning the child's hand to drive out demons,

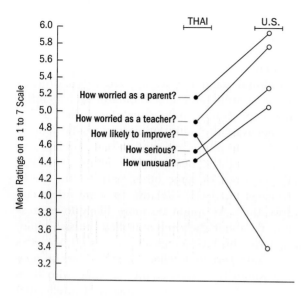

FIGURE 1-1 Thai and U.S. adults' rating of concern about childhood behavior problems.

Weitz, Suwanlet, Chaiyasit, Weiss, Walter, & Anderson, 1988.

burning a piece of cloth belonging to the person who cast the Evil Eye, praying, or getting help from a rabbi. All of this behavior is consistent with the cultural beliefs of their native countries. The study also shows that minority groups or subcultures in a heterogeneous society may have unique beliefs and standards by which they explain or judge behavior. Such subcultural differences have been described in the United States, which might be expected in such a heterogeneous nation.

Situational standards. Judgments about the deviance or normality of behavior also take into account what is expected in specific social situations or settings. Although energetic running may be quite acceptable on the playground, it would create havoc in the classroom or a dental office. And singing aloud might well be tolerated at home but rarely allowed in the library. Norms for social interaction can be quite subtle; for example, how we phrase a statement could mean the difference between a compliment or an insult. Individuals are expected to act in certain ways in certain situations—in short, to meet situational norms. When

individuals do not, questions are raised about their competency.

Gender norms. Behavioral standards are also specified according to gender. In most societies, males are expected to be relatively more aggressive, dominant, active, and adventurous; and females, to be more passive, dependent, quiet, and sensitive. These gender stereotypes guide judgments about normality. We would probably be less inclined to worry about the hypersensitive, shy girl and the excessively dominant boy than about their opposite-sex counterparts.

Changes over time. Finally, it must be noted that changes in societal values and expectations can affect judgments of behavior. For example, recent years have brought a loosening of gender norms and controversy about what should be considered "normal" male and female behavior. Evolving ideas about mental health have similarly influenced judgments about behavior. In the 1800s, masturbation was considered a sign of disturbance or a behavior that could cause insanity (Rie, 1971). Nail biting, too, was once seen as a sign of degeneration but is viewed as quite harmless today (Anthony, 1970).

DEVELOPMENTAL CRITERIA

Age, as an index of developmental level, is always of consideration in judging behavior, but it is especially crucial with youth because they change so rapidly. Judgments about behavior require developmental norms. The typical rates and sequences of the growth of skills, knowledge, and social-emotional behavior serve as developmental standards to evaluate the possibility that "something is wrong." Adults would be mistaken to worry about the one-year-old who is not yet walking, because many children of this age do not walk. However, if the same child is unable to sit without support, concern would be appropriate, because virtually all babies can sit up before their first birthdays.

However, it is not the only the delay or failure to keep up with peers that identifies psychopathology. Children sometimes "act their age" but then fail to progress. Temper tantrums might not be labeled a problem in a three-year-old but would

The behavior that is expected of or considered appropriate for a child varies across cultures.
(Laimute Druskis) (Michael Heron)

likely be seen as problematic if they persisted into the twelfth year. Children may also achieve developmental norms and then regress, or return, to behavior typically seen in younger children.

Several other normative factors are often considered. Behavior that meets age norms may still be judged disturbed if it occurs too frequently or infrequently, is too intense or insufficiently intense, or endures over too long or too short a period of time. It is not unusual for a child to display fear, for example, but fearfulness may be a problem if it occurs in an excessive number of situations, is extremely intense, and does not weaken over time. Concern might also be expressed for the child whose behaviors change, such as when a friendly, outgoing girl turns shy and solitary.

Adults are rightly concerned, too, when a child displays several questionable behaviors or seems troubled by several things.

In addition to delay, regression, atypical intensity, and unexpected change in behavior, children more rarely exhibit behaviors that appear qualitatively different from the norm. That is, they display behavior that is not at all seen in normal development. For example, most children become socially responsive to their caretakers soon after birth, but children diagnosed as autistic display atypical unresponsive behaviors. Such qualitatively different behaviors frequently indicate that there is a pervasive problem in development.

THE ROLE OF OTHERS

Children hardly ever refer themselves for evaluation, thereby declaring themselves as having a problem. Rather, the feelings and beliefs of others in the immediate environment play a role in identifying problem behaviors. The labeling of a problem is likely to occur when others become disturbed, for example, when parents worry about their child's social isolation or when a teacher is concerned about a child's inability to learn to read.

Referral of children to mental health professionals may have as much or more to do with the characteristics of parents, teachers, or family physicians as with the children themselves (Costello & Angold, 1995a; Verhulst & van der Ende, 1997). Indeed, disagreement often exists among adults as to whether a child "has a problem." Adult attitudes, sensitivity, tolerance, and ability to cope all play a role in identifying children's impairments. Research studies indicate the influence of various factors on parental descriptions and identification of children's problems (McMahon & Forehand, 1988; Mash & Dozois, 1996). For example, depressed mothers have been found to distort their children's behavior by giving overly negative descriptions (Richters, 1992).

In summary, we can see that defining, identifying, and conceptualizing behavioral or psychological disorders is a complex matter that depends on many factors. Disordered behavior is not an entity carried around in a person. It involves a judgment

that behavior is atypical and harmful—a judgment that is based on society's values, the social context, and beliefs about how youth normally develop.

DETERMINING THE EXTENT OF DISORDERS OF YOUTH

Determining the rate, or frequency, of disorders of youth is important because it suggests the extent to which prevention, treatment, and research are needed. Rates are reported in various ways. *Prevalence* refers to the number or percentage of cases of a disorder in a population at any specific time. *Lifetime prevalence* is the number or percentage of cases of a disorder in a population that have been experienced at any time in life. *Incidence* refers to the number or percentage of new cases that have appeared in a population within a specific time period, for example, during one specific year.

It is not easy to establish rates of disorders. One common method of doing this is to survey youth who have been brought to the attention of mental health services, medical facilities, schools, and so forth. These are so-called clinic cases. The obvious problem with this method is that clinic cases do not necessarily represent the entire population of youth with problems. Clinic cases may be biased in a number of ways. On the one hand, they can exclude youth who have gone unnoticed or for whom help has not been sought as a result of such factors as denial, shame, fear, or high levels of tolerance of problems by adults. Clinic cases may also underrepresent children whose parents cannot afford treatment. On the other hand, clinic cases can overrepresent children who act out or otherwise disturb others, whereas children with the same disorder who do not disturb others do not get counted.

Another method to determine rates of disorders entails surveying entire general populations, or representative samples of such populations. These so-called *epidemiological* studies are extremely useful because they also collect other information that can shed light on the disorders. Comparisons of the results of epidemiological studies are often difficult, however, because of differences in populations selected, quality of sampling, and the way that problem behavior is defined and measured. Nevertheless, investigations of unbiased populations is an important way to study behavior. (Epidemiology is further discussed in Chapter 4.)

An interesting finding from population studies is that many children show specific behaviors that may or may not be considered signs of disturbance. In one of the earliest systematic investigations, almost five hundred mothers of a sample of all six- to twelve-year-olds in Buffalo, New York, evaluated their children's behavior in detail (Lapouse & Monk, 1958). They reported, among other things, that 49 percent of their offspring were overactive, 48 percent lost their tempers twice weekly, and 28 percent experienced nightmares. This study is of historical interest, and later studies from various countries confirm that such behavioral problems are commonly reported (Cotler, 1986). Problems that are isolated or only moderately disruptive, or those that spontaneously decrease or disappear, are viewed as transient developmental crises that may or may not require professional consultation. An important task for researchers is to understand better when behavior problems will be transient crises and when they will persist or predict later disturbance (Campbell, 1995).

Many recent cross-national epidemiologic studies employed standardized scales to establish the prevalence of problems or employed criteria that would result in a clinical diagnosis. Among the twelve or so countries studied are Germany, New Zealand, Ireland, France, Thailand, and Canada (Bird, 1996; Crijnen, Achenbach, & Verhulst, 1997). Prevalence rates vary a good deal across the countries, and it is not easy to interpret the data. Although true differences probably exist, some of the variation is likely due to the different methods being used. As an example of the findings, Figure 1-2 shows data from five major studies from four different countries. Prevalence varied from about 18 percent to 26 percent (Verhulst & Koot, 1992). An estimate of 15 percent to 20 percent prevalence of clinic-level disorder for children and ado-

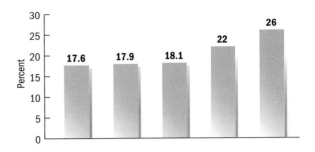

FIGURE 1-2 Percentage of population with diagnosable disorders in five community studies of children and adolescents. Data from Verhulst and Koot, 1992.

lescents is fairly widely accepted today (Costello & Angold, 1995a; Weist, 1997).

An additional point worth noting is that disorder may have increased over recent years. For example, small increases occurred in parental and teacher reports of various problems shown by youth in the United States from 1976 to 1989 (Achenbach & Howell, 1993). There were significant increases in the number of children scoring in the clinical range. In general, there is concern in the United States that changing social conditions have increased the risk of behavioral disorders because of high levels of poverty, family divorce, abuse in the family, and other adversities (Takanishi & DeLeon, 1994).

Thus it appears that substantial needs on the part of young people exist. Moreover, it is estimated that less than one-third of needy youth are receiving support and treatment sufficient to overcome their behavioral problems (Weist, 1997). One recent study of four U.S. sites shows that only 25 percent of youth with clinic-level disorder had some contact with a mental health related professional (Leaf et al., 1996).

DEVELOPMENTAL LEVEL AND ONSET OF DISORDERS

A question that has been of interest to professionals and parents alike is whether behavioral difficulties are more likely to arise during certain developmental years relative to other years. If so, parents might be more alert to the possibility of problems, adopt a "nip in the bud" strategy, and consider timely evaluation of behavior. Knowledge about the usual age of onset may also be important to understanding the causes, severity, and outcome of disorders (Giaconia et al., 1994). For instance, it has been established that drug use at an early age is associated with greater chance of severe drug dependency in adulthood.

The data are mixed with regard to whether problems generally increase or decrease across childhood and into middle adolescence. There is some suggestion that problems decrease with age in population studies and increase in clinic samples (Mash & Dozois, 1996). However, many factors affect the findings, including who reports the problems and how problems are measured.

There is a clear relationship between age of onset and *specific* problems (Cantwell & Rutter, 1994). Developmental delays in language and speech are usually seen early in life, when children are first acquiring these skills. Autism, too, arises early. Deficiencies in attention are typically diagnosed prior to school or when children begin school, as are impairments in general intelligence and ability to learn. Fears and anxieties can arise at any age, but specific fears are somewhat related to age. Aggression, noncompliance, stealing, and the like can also arise at different ages. Depression, anorexia, drug abuse, and schizophrenia often first occur with the approach of adolescence, although they may occur earlier (Kazdin, 1993a).

Recent years have seen increased interest in disorders that may arise in infancy. These include disorders of biological regulation, such as various feeding problems, and problems in establishing healthy attachments to parents or other caregivers (Lyons-Ruth, Zeanah, & Benoit, 1996). Problems at this time of life are viewed as either predictors of future disorders or as disorders in their own right.

The link between age of onset and certain dysfunctions is not coincidental, of course. Chronological age is correlated with children's developmental level. In turn, developmental level makes some behavioral problems more likely than others. For example, the cognitive and emotional levels of four-year-olds make it unlikely that preschoolers experience the thoughts and feelings that are labeled as depression at later ages. Studies of the association of specific disorders and developmental level can be productive in increasing knowledge about the underlying processes.

In some cases, the ages at which disorders seem to arise may actually be the ages at which disorders are first noticed or identified. In such instances, environmental or other factors can be expected to play a role. An example is mental retardation, which is defined as children's intellectual functioning being below that of their age-mates. More cases of retardation are identified during the school years than during preschool or postschool years (Patton, Beirne-Smith, & Payne, 1990). The demands of the classroom—and school policy to evaluate intellectual performance—identify individuals who otherwise appear to function adequately in their home environments. Thus it is important to make a distinction between actual age of onset and the age at which disorders are identified.

GENDER DIFFERENCES: WHO IS AT GREATER RISK?

A common finding about the disorders of youth is that many occur more frequently in males than in females (Cantwell & Rutter, 1994). These disorders include autism, hyperactivity, antisocial behavior, language problems, and learning disabilities. Table 1-1 shows the prevalence for twenty-one disorders of infancy, childhood, and adolescence. In all but four of these, male prevalence is higher. Anxiety, depression, and substance abuse are among the disorders not included in the table (with the exception of separation anxiety), but these disorders become increasingly important with adolescence. Overall, females outnumber males in anxiety and depression, whereas males outnumber females in substance abuse.

Gender differences in prevalence can be attributed to several developmental factors. Boys may be more biologically vulnerable than girls. They have

TABLE 1-1

Gender Prevalence for Some Disorders of Youth

Prevalence Higher in Males

Mental Retardation	Attention Deficit
Reading Disorder	Hyperactivity Disorder
Receptive Language Disorder	Conduct Disorder
Mixed Language Disorder	Oppositional Disorder
Phonological Language	Tourette's Syndrome
Disorder	Rumination
Stuttering	Encopresis
Autistic Disorder	Enuresis
Childhood Disintegrative	Stereotypic Movement
Disorder	Disorder
Asperger's Disorder	

Prevalence Higher in Females

Rett's Disorder (occurs only in girls)
Separation Anxiety Disorder
Selective Mutism

Prevalence Equal in Males and Females

Feeding Disorder

Adapted from Hartung and Widiger, 1998.

higher death rates from the moment of conception, and a variety of inherited disorders are related to the Y chromosome carried by males. Psychosocial factors undoubtedly play a role in creating differential gender prevalence. For example, gender role socialization and differential experiences may lead to greater aggression in boys and greater anxiety and depression in girls. It is possible that biological vulnerability interacts with socialization and social expectation to create gender differences in rates of disorders (cf. Earls & Jung, 1987; Jensen et al., 1990).

However, the higher prevalence of disorder in males may also be related to data collection. Prevalence data often rely on biased clinic samples. Adults, who are responsible for most clinic referrals, tend to refer children who engage in troublesome, disruptive behaviors. Because disruptive behavior occurs more in boys, clinic samples are biased toward boys. This bias is independent of other problems boys may have. For example, boys with reading problems are referred over girls with reading problems—presumably because of boys' higher rates of disruptive behaviors (Shaywitz, Fletcher, & Shaywitz, 1996). Such a referral bias would give misleadingly high rates of reading disorder in boys relative to that in girls. On the other hand, girls may experience more worry and anxiety than boys, but these difficulties do not get as much adult attention (Keenan & Shaw, 1997).

The bias in clinic samples may affect gender prevalence in another, more indirect, way (Hartung & Widiger, 1998). When more boys are seen in mental health facilities, they become the subject of more research. This outcome leads to the disorders' being described according to the way that the symptoms are expressed in boys, which may not be identical to the symptom picture in girls. When these descriptions (criteria) are used for identifying the disorder, fewer girls will fit the symptom picture and be identified. This process is depicted in Figure 1-3. In this hypothetical example, its assumed that the actual prevalence for a disorder is equal for boys and girls, but that more males with the disorder are referred to a clinic because of unruly behavior and thus studied. The hypothetical outcome of the process is that for every two boys who display the disorder, only one girl does so. Regardless of what the actual prevalence is originally, when referral is biased toward one gender and research favors one gender, descriptions of the disorder may change and affect the identification of the disorder.

Indeed, if a disorder is expressed differently in males and females, and if the criteria for the disorder favors one gender over the other, misleading gender prevalence will result. For example, it has been suggested that female rates of conduct problems are low because females act out in antisocial ways that are not recognized by the criteria. According to this line of reasoning, female prevalence would increase when the criteria include behaviors typical of female acting out.

Gender differences in prevalence is a complex and controversial topic. It is likely that true gender differences do exist, but questions remain about the degree of the differences. This issue has practi-

Diagnostic Criteria

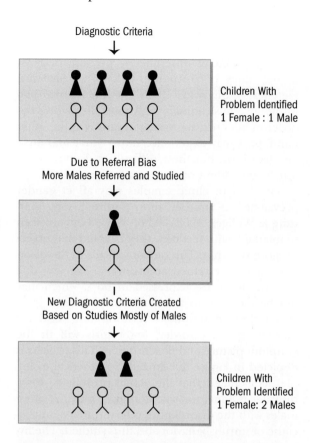

Children With
Problem Identified
1 Female : 1 Male

Due to Referral Bias
More Males Referred and Studied

New Diagnostic Criteria Created
Based on Studies Mostly of Males

Children With
Problem Identified
1 Female: 2 Males

FIGURE 1-3 Referral bias of males often leads to disproportionate study of males, which can affect criteria for the disorders. When the new criteria are used, more males will be identified than females.

cal implications for children. If a disorder is believed to be more prevalent in one gender relative to the other, children of that gender are more likely to be treated differently and to be the focus of research, treatment, and prevention efforts. Therefore, investigation of this matter is likely to continue.

We have so far seen that complexity characterizes what superficially appears to be simple issues with regard to the psychopathology of youth. Despite this complication, however, progress is being made in understanding the needs of children and adolescents. This is a relatively recent circumstance, which is illuminated in the next section.

HISTORICAL INFLUENCES

Humans have long speculated on behavioral dysfunction, but early interest focused primarily on adults. The first recordings of specific childhood problems appeared in the early 1800s (Rie, 1971). By the end of the century, a few attempts had been made to classify childhood disorders, and causes had been proposed. Mental retardation received the most attention, but psychoses, aggression, hyperactivity, and "masturbatory insanity" had all been noted. Blaming behavioral disorder on wickedness or devils had largely declined, and the dominant view about causation became genetic (Costello & Angold, 1995a). It was generally assumed that inheritance and degeneration that began in childhood led to irreversible disease, which subsequently could be transmitted to the next generation.

Then several developments radically altered how children and adolescents were viewed, how their development might go awry, and how they might be treated (Table 1-2). We will look at these major developments, many of which we will return to in later chapters.

THE INFLUENCE OF SIGMUND FREUD

As a young neurologist, Sigmund Freud collaborated with others, especially Joseph Breuer, who believed that certain disorders could be caused by psychological events. Freud was particularly interested in the idea that psychological experiences in childhood appeared connected to symptoms in adulthood, such as paralysis and blindness, for which no physical cause was evident. These problems seemed to be alleviated when the patient was able to talk emotionally about earlier experiences. Such observations set Freud on a lifelong course to construct a grand theory of development and a treatment method for disordered behavior.

On the basis of his study of adults, Freud was convinced that psychological childhood conflicts were the key to understanding behavior. He also hypothesized that all children pass through the same developmental stages, and he related these stages to later behavior. In *Three Essays on the Theory of Sexuality*, published in 1905, and in his 1909

TABLE 1-2

Some Early Historical Landmarks

1896	The first child clinic in the United States was established at the University of Pennsylvania by Lightner Witmer.
1905	Alfred Binet and Theophil Simon developed the first intelligence tests to identify feebleminded children.
1905	Sigmund Freud's *Three Essays on the Theory of Sexuality* described a startingly different view of childhood development.
1908	In *A Mind That Found Itself,* Clifford Beers recounted his mental breakdown and advocated an enlightened view of mental disorders, initiating the mental hygiene and child guidance movements.
1909	G. Stanley Hall invited Sigmund Freud to Clark University in Worcester, Massachusetts, to lecture on psychoanalysis.
1909	William Healy and Grace Fernald established the Juvenile Psychopathic Institute in Chicago, which would become the model for the child guidance clinics.
1911	The Yale Clinic of Child Development was established for child development research under the guidance of Arnold Gesell.
1913	John B. Watson introduced behaviorism in his essay "Psychology as a Behaviorist Views It."
1917	William Healy and Augusta Bronner established the Judge Baker Guidance Center in Boston.
1922	The National Committee on Mental Hygiene and the Commonwealth Fund initiated a demonstration program of child guidance clinics.
1924	The American Orthopsychiatric Association was established.
1928–1929	Longitudinal studies of child development began at Berkeley and Fels research Institute.
1935	Leo Kanner authored *Child Psychiatry,* the first child psychiatry text published in the United States.

lectures at Clark University in Worcester, Massachusetts, Freud introduced his radical ideas about the importance of childhood to adult development (Evans & Koelsch, 1985; Rie, 1971). His views were controversial from the start, but they came to provide a systematic framework for conceptualizing both child and adult behavior.

Among Freud's many contributions was the movement away from biological and towards psychological etiology, or causation. He acknowledged that humans have inherited dispositions, but he also recognized environmental influences on the origins of psychological problems (Costello & Angold, 1995a). Freud viewed the individual as a developing entity whose behavior could be transformed and who could turn out to be more or less psychologically healthy.

By the 1930s, Freud's ideas had been widely interpreted by Melanie Klein, Erik Erikson, Heinz Hartmann, and others. Freud's daughter Anna elaborated his ideas and especially applied them to children (Fine, 1985). These efforts helped to establish psychiatry as a major discipline in the study and treatment of childhood disorders. In 1935, Leo Kanner published the first child psychiatry text in the United States.

BEHAVIORISM AND SOCIAL LEARNING THEORY

While Freud was stirring up the academic and clinical world with his innovative ideas, an approach stemming from psychology was introduced in the United States that would rival Freud's ideas (Sears, 1975). Behaviorism was launched by John B. Watson's essay "Psychology as a Behaviorist Views It" (1913). Unlike Freud, Watson placed little value on describing developmental stages and on early psychological conflicts. Instead, he drew on theories of learning to emphasize that most behavior originates through learning processes. Watson thought that people's behavior, whether adaptive or maladaptive, could be explained by learning experiences. Among his most quoted words are the

Both Sigmund Freud (center) and his daughter Anna Freud (foreground) were influential in the development of the psychodynamic conceptualizations of childhood disorders.
(AP/Wide World Photos)

John B. Watson was a highly influential figure in the application of the behavioral perspective.
(The Bettman Archive)

following, which reflect his belief in the power of experience to shape children's development.

Give me a dozen healthy infants, well-formed, and my own specified world to bring them up in and I'll guarantee to take any one at random and train him to become any type of specialist I might select—doctor, lawyer, merchant, chief and yes, even beggar-man and thief, regardless of his talents, penchants, tendencies, abilities, vocations, and race of his ancestors. (Watson, 1930, p. 104)

In addition to a strong emphasis on learning and environment, Watson was committed to testing ideas by the experimental method, as were other behaviorists (Horowitz, 1992). E. L. Thorndike (1905) made an early contribution to behaviorism by formulating the Law of Effect. Simply put, this law states that behavior is shaped by its consequences. If the consequence is satisfying, the behavior will be strengthened in the future; if the consequence is discomforting, the behavior will be weakened. Thorndike considered the Law of Effect a fundamental principle of learning and teaching; later researchers substantiated his claim. Of special note is B. F. Skinner, who became widely known for investigating and writing on the application of behavioral consequences to the shaping of behavior (Skinner, 1948; 1953; 1968). Skinner can be viewed as Watson's direct descendant in his emphasis on learning, the environment, and experimental methods (Horowitz, 1992).

Behaviorism thrived in the United States during the first half of the twentieth century. Its impact on behavior disorders came gradually, as Mowrer, Bijou, Baer, and others applied learning principles to children's behavior. Albert Bandura highlighted observational learning and emphasized the role of cognition in learning (Grusec, 1992). The work of these men focused on different aspects of learning, but it emphasized the importance of the social context. The approach is thus often described as the social learning perspective. When applied explicitly to the assessment and treatment of behavior problems, it is often called behavior modification, or behavior therapy.

THE MENTAL HYGIENE AND THE CHILD GUIDANCE MOVEMENTS

Another important thread of influence was being woven in different settings. Despite the interest in adult psychopathology by the early twentieth century, much remained to be learned, and treatment often consisted of custodial hospital care. The mental hygiene movement in the United States aimed to increase understanding, improve treatment, and prevent disorders from occurring at all.

In 1908, Clifford Beers wrote an autobiographical account, *A Mind That Found Itself,* telling of the insensitive and ineffective treatment he had received as a mental patient. Beers proposed reform, and he obtained support from renowned professionals, including Adolf Meyer. Recognizing both psychological and biological causes of behavior disorders, Meyer believed that they stemmed from failure of the individual to adapt to life circumstance. He proposed a "commonsense" approach to studying the patient's environment and to counseling. Meyer also set the course for a new professional role—that of psychiatric social worker (Achenbach, 1974).

Beers's efforts also led to the establishment of the National Committee for Mental Hygiene to study mental dysfunctions, support treatment, and encourage prevention. Because childhood experiences were viewed as influencing adult mental health, children became the focus of study and guidance (Rie, 1971).

In 1896, at the University of Pennsylvania, Lightner Witmer had already set up the first child psychology clinic in the United Sates (McReynolds, 1987; Ross, 1972). This clinic primarily assessed and treated children who had learning difficulties. Witmer also founded the journal *Psychological Clinic* and began a hospital school for long-term observation of children. He related psychology to education, sociology, and other disciplines.

An interdisciplinary approach was also taken by psychiatrist William Healy and psychologist Grace Fernald in Chicago in 1909, when they founded the Juvenile Psychopathic Institute. The focus of the institute was on delinquent children, and its approach became the model for child guidance. Healy was convinced that antisocial behavior could be treated by psychological means, by helping youngsters adjust to the circumstances in which they lived (Santostefano, 1978). This approach required understanding the whole personality and the multiple causes of behavior. Freudian theory provided the central ideas for dealing with psychological conflicts, and attempts were made to gather information about family and other important relationships (Santostefano, 1978; Strean, 1970). The psychiatrist, psychologist, and social worker formed a collaborative team toward this end, meeting to discuss cases.

Healy and his wife, psychologist Augusta Bronner, continued to use this approach when they opened the Judge Baker Guidance Center in Boston. The National Committee for Mental Hygiene subsequently established several other child clinics, adopting the same approach. The cases now also included personality and emotional problems. These clinics flourished in the 1920s and 1930s.

In 1924 the child guidance movement was formally represented by the formation of the American Orthopsychiatric Association, with Healy as its first president and Bronner as its second. To this

MRS. HILLIS: IMPROVING CORN, HOGS, AND CHILDREN IN IOWA

The establishment of the Iowa Child Welfare Station was sparked by Mrs. Cora Bussey Hillis, who demonstrated how advocacy for children can go hand in hand with advocacy for science (Sears, 1975). Mrs. Hillis was the mother of several children, but she had also lost children. She believed that ignorance about children's development and health could be blamed for the deaths of her children.

Mrs. Hillis was aware of the much respected agricultural station of the college in Ames, Iowa. In her mind's eye, she could see a comparable child welfare station that would be devoted to research, teaching, and dissemination of knowledge. The work of the station would focus on problems in children's development and health. Researchers would be trained, as would professionals to work directly with children and parents. A body of knowledge would be constructed and disseminated to the public as rapidly as possible. Mrs. Hillis had faith that if research could "improve corn and hogs it could also improve children" (p. 17).

With the consultation of Carl Emil Seashore, a psychologist and dean of the graduate school at the State University of Iowa, a proposal was written. This was an unusual idea that caused squabbling in the rather conservative legislature. Eventually the concept was backed by labor unions, women's clubs, and other organizations. In 1917 the legislature appropriated $50,000 to open the station at the Iowa City campus, near the departments of medicine and education, where Mrs. Hollis had envisioned it.

day, the association includes a variety of professionals concerned about children and adolescents.

THE SCIENTIFIC STUDY OF YOUTH

It was also during the early twentieth century that systematic study of youth became widespread. A central figure in this endeavor was G. Stanley Hall. Like many others of this period, Hall knew little about the development of the young, and so he collected questionnaire data about their fears, dreams, preferences, play, and other aspects of functioning (Grinder, 1967; Sears, 1975). Some questionnaires focused on the problems of youth with the goal of understanding mental disorder, crime, social disorder, and the like (White, 1992). Hall wrote extensively on children and adolescents, and he also trained students who later became leaders. As president of Clark University, Hall invited Freud to lecture in 1909. He also helped establish the American Psychological Association, of which he was its first president.

At about the same time, an important event occurred in Europe: Alfred Binet and Theophil Simon were asked to design a test to identify children who were in need of special education (Siegler, 1992; Tuddenham, 1962). They presented children of various ages with different tasks and problems, thereby establishing age-norms by which intellectual performance could be evaluated. The 1905 Binet-Simon test became the basis for the development of intelligence tests. It also encouraged professionals to search for ways to measure other psychological attributes.

Another outstanding figure was Arnold Gesell, who meticulously recorded the physical, motor, and social behavior of young children in his laboratory at Yale University (Thelen & Adolph, 1992). He charted developmental norms, relying on structured observation, naturalistic observation, and parental report. Gesell, who was fascinated with the benefits of photography to record infant and child behavior, left a voluminous film archive. An organizing concept of his work was maturation, the intrinsic unfolding of development relatively independent of environmental influences. Gesell was also a strong advocate for children to have optimal rearing environments.

Commencing around 1920, child study began to benefit from several longitudinal research projects that evaluated youth as they developed over many years. Research centers existed at the universities of California, Colorado, Michigan, Minnesota, Ohio, and Washington; the Fels Research Institute; Columbia Teachers College; the Johns Hopkins University; and the Iowa Child Welfare Station. A body of knowledge about normal development began to accumulate that eventually was applied to the study of child and adolescent disorders.

Today, the study and treatment of disorders of youth variously reflect the diverse historical events and movements that were set into motion in the early decades of the twentieth century. Some of the early events are currently more influential than others, and newer influences have, of course, come into play. Research into all areas of childhood and adolescent development has reached new heights of sophistication and is being brought to bear on questions of pathology. Both older and more recent assumptions, conceptualizations, and knowledge are giving shape to today's theories, research, and practice regarding behavioral disturbances of young people.

CURRENT THEMES AND EMPHASES

If we had to choose one statement to capture the essence of today's approach to child and adolescent psychopathology, the statement would emphasize diversity and complexity. Thus it is at the risk of oversimplification that we highlight major themes and emphases that we believe characterize the field today. Many of these will be apparent in discussions throughout this text.

- Current study and practice of child psychopathology is multidisciplinary. Psychology, psychiatry, neurobiology, medicine, education, anthropology, and other disciplines contribute somewhat different, but often overlapping, knowledge, understandings, and interests.

- The complexity of human behavior and development calls for systematic conceptualization, observation, data collection, and hypothesis testing.

- The child is best viewed as an ever-changing psychological, social, and biological entity actively interacting with a complex environment.

- With few, if any, exceptions, behavior stems from multiple causes—psychological, sociocultural, biological—that work together. These all must be reckoned with if we are truly to understand and be able to change problem behavior.

- Normal and abnormal behavior go hand in hand, and we must study one in order to understand the other. Indeed, these areas of study are mutually enriching.

- Cross-cultural studies are enriching, and thus are needed for complete understanding of the development and problems of youth.

- Continued efforts are needed to construct treatments and to verify their effectiveness.

- Efforts toward prevention of behavior disorders are essential.

- Advocacy for the well-being of youth is an appropriate component of the study of psychopathology, particularly because young people may lack the maturity and social influence to advocate for themselves.

YOUTH AS SPECIAL CLIENTS

It is in clinical interaction, broadly defined, that various professionals come into personal contact with children and adolescents—as well as with their families—who are experiencing difficulties. Not only do youth have the needs that older clients have for competent, dependable, and respectful care, but they also have special needs.

INTERDISCIPLINARY APPROACH

It is often the case that more than one professional is involved in assessing and treating a child, among which are psychologists, psychiatrists, social workers, and special education teachers.

Most psychologists working with child and adolescent problems have specialized in clinical psychology. In addition, others may have specialized in developmental, school, or educational psychology. They usually hold the doctoral degree (Ph.D. or Psy.D.), which demands four to five years of university graduate study. Psychology has sturdy roots in the laboratory and an interest in both normal and abnormal behavior. Training in psychology thus includes psychological research, as well as direct contact in assessing and treating troubled individuals. Many psychologists have a strong background in assessing behavior by means of psychological testing.

Psychiatrists, on the other hand, hold the doctorate in medicine (M.D.); they are physicians who have specialized in the care of the mentally disturbed. Psychiatrists function in ways that are similar to those of psychologists, but they tend to view problem behavior more as a medical dysfunction. They make a unique contribution to psychopathology by conducting medical evaluations and prescribing medication when appropriate.

Social workers generally hold the master's degree (M.A.) in social work. Like psychologists and psychiatrists, they may counsel and conduct therapy, and historically their special focus has been working with the family and other social systems in which children are enmeshed.

Special education teachers, who usually have obtained the master's degree, emphasize the importance of providing needy children and adolecents with optimal educational experiences. They are able to plan and implement individualized educational programs, thus contributing to the treatment of many disorders.

Troubled youths also come to the attention of nurses, general physicians, teachers in regular classrooms, and workers in the legal system. Indeed, these professionals may be the first to hear about a problem. Therefore, interdisciplinary consultation commonly occurs and often is ideal. A good amount of coordination is necessary if this approach is to be effective. Who functions as the coordinator may depend on the type of disorder, the developmental level of the client, the first point of professional contact, and the treatment setting.

WORKING WITH PARENTS

Dealing with disorders of youth almost always involves contact with at least one parent and frequently requires working closely with parents.

Parents vary greatly in their motivation to participate in psychological or mental health evaluation and treatment for their offspring. Consultation and help are sought for many reasons. Most parents, of course, are truly concerned about the welfare of their sons and daughters and consequently seek help. Parents may also be driven to alleviate conflicts with their child or to reduce their own worries. They may even be referred by schools or the courts, sometimes against their own wishes. All these factors, and additional ones as well, can influence motivation for and success of treatment.

Parents also vary in the ability to understand, support, and carry out recommendations. The entire range of that ability exists, with some parents being superbly apt at forming a therapeutic alliance with the child and therapist. On the other hand, some accommodations often must be made for parental issues. Some parents fear that they will be blamed for their offsprings' problems (Kraemer, 1987), thus leading to defensiveness. Others may have inappropriate goals; for example, authoritarian parents may desire their child or adolescent to be excessively obedient. Parents can resent professional suggestions, be overly dependent, or expect therapists to "fix" the problem without the parents' involvement. Regardless of these attitudes, parents frequently desire and can benefit from education and training relevant to the difficulties being experienced.

The importance of the parents' role is apparent in cases in which treatment is discontinued prior to successful completion. Family rather than child variables play the dominant role (Armbruster & Kazdin, 1994; Kazdin et al., 1997). The risk of dropping out of treatment is higher with socioeconomic disadvantage, young age of mother, single-parent families, harsh child-rearing practices, parent psychopathology, and family stress. More immediate factors, such as parental perception that treatment is irrelevant or parents' having a less than satisfactory relationship with the therapist, have also been associated with discontinuance. In one study, dropping out of treatment was affected by both the referral source and parental dysfunction (Gould, Shaffer, & Kaplan, 1985). The dropout rate was especially high for families that had both disturbed parents and school referrals.

Whatever the situation, parents are vital in treatment and provide information and perceptions that no others can provide. Thus the competent and sensitive professional welcomes parental participation and works toward optimizing the quality of the child-parent relationship and successful intervention.

WORKING WITH AND FOR THE YOUNG CLIENT

Direct interaction with youth is both rewarding and demanding. Young children may be especially incapable of identifying problems and seeking treatment, and they most often enter treatment at the suggestion or coercion of adults. Sensitivity to the child's perspective and efforts to create and maintain motivation may be critical.

Attention to the child's developmental level is imperative. Such knowledge is essential in evaluating the child's problems and in judging the significance of problems. Understanding a child's developmental competencies and failures also provides guidelines for treatment. An example is training children to control their own behavior by giving themselves verbal directions in problem solving. Such a strategy can be therapeutic for particular kinds of problems. However, very young children would not be expected to do as well with this technique as would older children.

Finally, young people have basic rights that must be recognized and protected. To the extent that they are able, youth have a right to assent to treatment, participate in decisions about the goals of treatment, and to understand how the goals will be attempted. As with all treatment endeavors, young clients have a basic right to privacy and confidentiality, although age of the youth plays a role in determining the specific guidelines to be followed.

When they treat young people, mental health workers often face tough questions concerning social, ethical, and legal matters. For example, today's sensitivity to child abuse makes it of heightened concern with regard to legal rights (DeKraai & Sales, 1991). Therapists are typically required by law to report abuse. In some cases, this mandate can conflict with professional judgments about what is best for the child and the family in treatment. There are instances in which mental health workers believe that the reporting of abuse may actually hinder intervention. Nevertheless, professionals must understand and meet legal requirements, inform families of the kinds of things that must be reported, and work within the legal framework to fulfill their professional obligations to their clients. Ethical and legal dilemmas regarding behavioral disorders are not uncommon, but they are of special concern when they involve young people who are limited in speaking for themselves.

SUMMARY

■ Behaviors judged to be a problem are typically considered deviant from some standard and harmful to the individual. Standards for behavior depend on cultural values, situational and gender norms, and developmental criteria. The attitudes, sensitivities, and tolerance of adults are important in determining whether or not a child or an adolescent is viewed as having a problem.

■ The prevalence or incidence of disorders can be assessed through surveys of various clinic settings, but these samples suffer from biases. Epidemiological surveys of entire populations, or representative samples of populations, avoid bias. Comparisons of epidemiological studies are difficult, however, because of differing methodology.

■ Behaviors that may be viewed as disturbed are actually quite prevalent in the general population of youth. These behaviors may be transient, may persist, or may predict future problems. It is widely accepted that 15 to 20 percent of youth have diagnosable behavioral disorders and that most are not receiving treatment.

■ Behavioral disorders first occur at all times during childhood and adolescence, and no general age trend is clearly established. However, onset of specific disorders is related to developmental level.

■ Many disorders occur more frequently in boys than in girls, although girls show a higher occurrence of disorders such as anxiety and depression. Gender differences may be determined by biological or environmental factors or by their interaction. Differences in prevalence may be partly due to biases in clinic samples and in diagnostic criteria for the disorders.

■ Interest in behavioral disorders of youth has evolved gradually. The early decades of the twentieth century marked important influences: Freud's work, behaviorism and social learning theories, the mental hygiene and child guidance movements, and dramatic increase in the study of youth. These events and movements brought new knowledge and conceptualizations of childhood and adolescent disorders.

■ The current study and practice of childhood psychopathology is characterized by multidisciplinary and scientific efforts; recognition of the link between normal and abnormal development; a view of the child as an active developing entity; the assumption that behavior has multiple causes; and interests in cross-cultural studies, effective treatments, prevention, and advocacy.

■ Professional care of children and adolescents is interdisciplinary, involving psychologists, psychiatrists, social workers, education specialists, and several other professionals.

■ Parents' participation in the treatment of their children is often crucial. The parents' needs, motivations, and abilities cannot be ignored. When families drop out of treatment, the reasons for dropout concern family matters and parents' perception of treatment.

■ The treatment of young people requires special consideration of their motivation for treatment and their level of development. Consideration must be given to children's rights to have privacy, to assent to treatment, and to participate in decisions. Professional care of the young client raises special ethical and legal dilemmas.

CHAPTER 2

THE DEVELOPMENTAL CONTEXT

We have already acknowledged the importance of the relationship between normal and abnormal development. This relationship is the focus of the present chapter.

A few decades ago, developmental psychology, which traditionally takes normal development as its subject matter, and clinical child/adolescent psychology and psychiatry began to recognize that each had something to offer to and to gain from the other. By the 1970s, their cooperative efforts became meaningful enough to warrant recognition and a new label—developmental psychopathology (Cicchetti, 1984; 1989). Developmental psychopathology is a general framework for understanding disordered behavior in relation to normal development (Achenbach, 1990; Cicchetti & Cohen, 1995). This approach is interested not only in the origins and developmental course of disordered behavior (Sroufe, 1986) but also in individual adaptation and success.

The developmental approach makes several specific contributions to the study of the problems of youth. Perhaps the most obvious contribution is that it offers descriptions of the usual course of growth, which serve as a standard by which behavior can be judged problematic or impaired. It is important that developmental research findings and developmental theories offer facts, hypotheses, and models pertaining to the processes responsible for development, and thus how development might go awry. Since no one theory can explain all the numerous changes that take place during life, diverse accounts must be considered.

The developmental framework is also concerned with specific issues that are relevant to child and adolescent disorders. For example, developmentalists are interested in conceptualizing the variables that promote or hinder optimal development and in understanding the stability, or continuity, of behavior over time. Such matters are relevant to understanding normal as well as abnormal development.

In this chapter, we will examine the meaning of development, consider normal development as a context for behavioral problems, and examine select issues relevant to behavioral dysfunction.

What Is Development?

If we were to ask strangers passing on the street to define the term "development," many would surely offer "growth" as a synonym. And most would note that development requires time. These are sound ideas. Development does indeed include growth, and it does occur over time. For example, children gradually become physically larger and display a larger number of social responses. However, development is much more complex, and developmentalists themselves do not always agree on its characteristics and on how it proceeds. Nevertheless, the following can serve as a guide for the developmental framework (e.g., Cicchetti & Schneider-Rosen, 1986; Santostefano, 1978; Sroufe & Rutter, 1984; Hodapp, Burack, & Zigler, 1990).

1. Development refers to change over the lifespan. Change may be quantitative or qualitative. Thus the number of ways (quantity) that a child interacts with others may increase but so might the features (qualities) of the behaviors.
2. There is a common, general course of early development of the physical, cognitive, emotional, and social systems. Within each system, early, global structures and functions become more finely differentiated and then integrated. Integration occurs across systems as well.
3. Some theorists view development as occurring in distinct qualitative stages or steps that appear in the same order in all individuals. Other theorists describe development as gradual change that may or may not have a fixed ordering; they do not believe that distinct stages can be identified.
4. Development proceeds in a coherent pattern, so that for each individual, present functioning is connected to the past as well as to the future. Thus development can be thought of as proceeding along pathways of more or less complexity. In youth, pathways are open and flexi-

ble, but there is some narrowing of possibilities with age.
5. Over the lifespan, developmental change may take many forms. New and higher modes of functioning and goals are attained, but change may not always be positive.
6. Human development is malleable but there are limitations on what can change and how much change is likely.
7. Development is the result of interactions or transactions among biological, psychological, and sociocultural variables.

In the remainder of this chapter, we will see how many of the preceding considerations are applied to both normal and atypical development.

Normal Development as a Context for Behavioral Dysfunction

Normal development encompasses a wide array of complex influences and processes. Our purpose here, therefore, is a modest one: to survey aspects of early development as a broad context within which behavioral problems may occur.

Genetics and Development

Genetic contributions to behavioral development operate in complex ways, at both the species and the individual levels. Through evolutionary processes, all humans are biologically programmed for common characteristics that enhance adaptation to environmental circumstances. Normal biological development assures that children can physically manipulate the environment, take in and process information about the world, communicate with others, and form social and emotional attachments to others. In a small minority of children, basic development goes awry, resulting in problems that range from small to devastating. In addition, when development is fundamentally sound, the biological system provides considerable opportunity for individuals to vary in characteristics.

The basic genetic material, which was gradually described throughout the twentieth century, consists of chromosomes, segments of which are called genes. Chromosomes are composed of deoxyribonucleic acid (DNA), the hereditary material that directs development and cell activity. Most cells have twenty-three pairs of chromosomes. One pair, the sex chromosomes, differs in females and males: Females have two X chromosomes, and males have an X and a Y chromosome. The Y chromosome has fewer genes and is smaller and lighter.

In contrast to other cells, the ovum and sperm undergo a special maturational process, *meiosis,* that results in each having only twenty-three single chromosomes, one from each of the original pairs. Thus at conception, each prospective parent contributes half of the chromosome complement to the offspring. Prospective mothers contribute an X chromosome, whereas prospective fathers can contribute either an X or a Y.

The processes of meiosis and conception assure billions of possible chromosome combinations for any one individual. Other genetic mechanisms result in even greater variability. Chromosomes may exchange genes, break and reattach to each other, and change by mutation, which is spontaneous alteration of the DNA molecule. Environmental interactions contribute further to produce an infinite variety of humans.

Even today, hereditary influences on behavioral characteristics are often misunderstood. Genes act only indirectly by guiding the biochemistry of cells. Characteristics for which genetic influence has been established can be modified by the environment, some substantially. For example, height is genetically influenced but is affected by diet and disease. Genes are therefore best thought of as helping to set a range within which characteristics will develop. Furthermore, hereditary effects are often not set over time; in fact, genes program both change and stability. In general, then, the path between genetic endowment—the *genotype*—and observable characteristics of the individual—the *phenotype*—is much more indirect and flexible than is often believed. Genetic influences on adaptive or maladaptive behavior are critical, but they operate in conjunction with environmental influences.

PHYSICAL AND MOTOR DEVELOPMENT

Conception takes place in the fallopian tube, and within a few days, the developing cells, the zygote, attaches itself to the wall of the uterus. The zygote floats freely in the amniotic sac except for its attachment by the umbilical cord to the placenta of the prospective mother (Figure 2-1). If all goes uneventfully, birth occurs about thirty-eight weeks after conception. These weeks of prenatal growth are crucial in that the organism can be dramatically affected by biological and environmental factors. Adversities during pregnancy and birth are associated with numerous later behavioral difficulties.

From the moment of conception, growth occurs in a quite predictable manner, following general principles. Growth takes place from the head to the tail regions (cephalocaudal), so that at birth, the head is disproportionately large. Growth also occurs from the center of the body to the periphery. This process is illustrated in prenatal development by the growth of the chest and trunk prior to that of the limbs, fingers, and toes. With later development, body proportion changes.

Throughout life, different body parts develop at different rates (Tanner, 1970). For example, the skeleton, muscles, and internal organs grow rapidly during infancy and early childhood, slow down in middle childhood, and then accelerate in adolescence. In contrast, the reproductive system develops slowly until adolescence, when it grows rapidly. The notable growth that occurs at adolescence is known as the adolescence growth spurt, whereas sexual maturation more generally is referred to as *puberty*. By age twenty or so, most basic physical growth has occurred, and stability and aging characterize the physical systems during adulthood.

The nervous system. The nervous system begins to develop shortly after conception when a group of cells called the neural plate thickens, folds inward, and forms the neural tube. This tube differentiates into the nervous system, and most brain

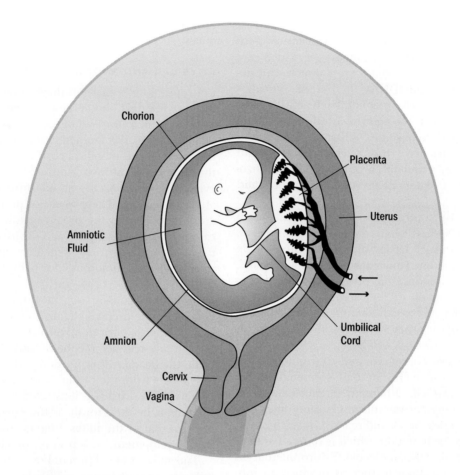

FIGURE 2-1 Schema of the developing child showing indirect contact with the mother's circulatory system.

cells are produced prenatally (Nowakowski, 1987). At birth the brain is about 25 percent of its adult weight, making it proportionately larger than most other organs.

Further growth occurs after birth. By age five, the brain reaches about 95 percent of its adult weight. Neurons (nerve cells) grow in size and in number of synaptic connections to other neurons. Myelin, a fatty cover, continues to be laid down on the axons of some neurons; myelin speeds up nerve transmission. Different parts of the nervous system develop in spurts more rapidly than others, and the pattern is related to functioning (Gree-

nough, Black, & Wallace, 1987). For example, nerves that control reflexes are well developed at birth, but areas that control voluntary movement grow substantially during the first year of life and later.

Brain development depends not only on biological programming but also on experience. Research has shown that animals which have the opportunity to explore object-filled, enriched environments develop more neurons and synapses than animals reared in simple environments (Hockfield & Lombroso, 1998). Experience also shapes early brain development by eliminating, or pruning, neurons that have few or redundant connections (Casaer, 1993). Such brain changes are linked with behavior such as increased capacity to learn and the ability to respond to specific sensory stimuli.

Motor development. Like physical growth, motor development is quite predictable. Infants display many involuntary reflexes. Some reflexes are related to vital bodily functioning, such as the blinking and sucking reflexes. However, others are of questionable value and disappear early, or perhaps are transformed into voluntary action (Thelen, 1986). The absence of reflexes at birth and the persistence of specific ones beyond certain times are signs of nervous system dysfunction. Abnormal reflexes may thus give early warnings of developmental problems.

Voluntary movement develops in a universal sequence. It generally follows the head-to-tail principle; for example, babies gain control of their arms more quickly than of their legs. Children also control the center of the body before the extremities, and large areas before small muscle groups. Therefore, when children begin to use crayons, they first use the entire arm and only gradually acquire hand control. Once control is gained over specific muscle groups, children begin to integrate many operations into complex movements. Table 2-1 shows the average age at which some of the basic motor milestones are achieved. As with reflexes, deviations from the timing and patterning of these milestones may indicate nervous system

Practice plays an important role in the development of complex motor skills. Motor development can affect other areas of functioning and influence self-concept.

(Spencer Grant, Monkmeyer)

dysfunctioning and risk for developmental problems. Between the ages of six and twelve, there is a noticeable increase in children's ability to jump rope, skate, climb, ride bicycles, and the like. Such skills often peak in the teen years.

Physical development and motor development depend on many biological and environmental factors. Biological programming is suggested by the fact that growth follows a standard sequence for almost all children. It is likely that children would sit, stand, use their hands, and walk even if the environment gave little encouragement to such behaviors. Body shape, height, and weight also are clearly influenced by inheritance. Still, environmental effects are obvious. Youth who con-

TABLE 2-1

Some Early Gross Motor Milestones

Milestone	Months
Rolls over	2 to 4
Sits without support	5 to 7
Stands holding on to furniture	8 to 9
Creeps on hands and knees	9 to 10
Stands without support	10 to 13
Walks alone	11 to 14
Walks upstairs alone, two feet per step	21 to 25

INFLUENCES OF MOTOR HANDICAPS AND PHYSICAL GROWTH ON DEVELOPMENT

The growth of motor and physical characteristics are of interest in themselves and also because they influence other aspects of development.

For example, if motor development goes awry, the child may be considerably disadvantaged in manipulating and learning about the world. Motor handicaps and slow motor development can lessen motivation for mastering the environment (Jennings, Connors, & Stegman, 1988), and they may influence how the child is perceived by others and the self.

A related influence concerns judgments of physical attractiveness (e.g., Eagly et al., 1991). Attractive people are often viewed in more positive ways than less attractive persons, for example, as smarter and more likable. Physical abnormality may often be avoided or reacted to with a mix of sympathy, curiosity, disregard, or embarrassment. Individuals may be overly polite because they are

unsure of how to respond to physical abnormality and, in turn, those with physical difficulties may be further disadvantaged because they do not receive appropriate feedback about their behavior.

Another aspects of physical growth that can influence psychosocial functioning is the timing of puberty (Dubas, Graber, & Petersen, 1991; Graber et al., 1997; Malo & Tremblay, 1997). Early-maturing boys have been reported as more popular, poised, and attractive, but they also show problem behavior. Later maturation in boys has been linked with anxiety, low self-esteem, and low social competence. In girls, early maturation has been associated with depression, anxiety, and troublesome behavior. Some of these girls select older peers, tend to break social norms, become involved in adolescent dating and drug use, or drop out of school (Stattin & Magnusson, 1990).

sume excessive calories are likely to be overweight, and those who are physically active are likely to develop muscle strength and coordination. Experience also plays a role in complex movements: Most people can readily hop and skip, but superior gymnastic and carpentry skills require much learning. Observing others, practicing the activities, and acquiring "motor programs"—mental representations of what acts follow other acts—are important processes in motor development (e.g., Pick, 1989). The growth of motor abilities and the physical systems can have wide ranging affects on youth.

COGNITION AND COMMUNICATION

Although the newborn may seem quite unaware of its surroundings and unable to profit from experi-

ence, this is far from true. Infants cannot report what they sense, but researchers can determine exactly what infants are looking at, whether their heart rates and muscle activity change in response to different odors, and the like. Such measures confirm that infants come into the world with considerable capacity to sense their surroundings. Seeing, hearing, smelling, tasting, and touching— all of which develop rapidly during the first years of life—are the basis for experiencing the environment. In the normal course of events, sensory information is accurately perceived and processed through learning and cognition.

There are many ways to conceptualize learning and cognition. Three basic learning processes are widely recognized: classical conditioning, operant conditioning, and observational learning. These processes operate at or soon after birth, enabling the infant to associate events and to soon respond with increasing variability to events. Basic processes become more complex as "higher" mental processes develop, including the abilities to select and maintain attention to stimuli, memorize information, mentally represent stimuli, form concepts, and manipulate information or think about the world.

A useful way to view higher mental processes is referred to as the information processing approach. Briefly put, a simplified information processing model assumes that information is received by the sensory systems and encoded into the brain or mind, where it is first received into short-term or working memory and then may be stored in long-term permanent memory. Information can be retrieved from long-term memory and used in thinking about or responding to the world. Important in this model are many cognitive processes, such as attention mechanisms and strategies to handle or manipulate information. In addition, the so-called executive functions of the information processing system permit the individual to select, monitor, evaluate, and revise strategies.

Another influential view of cognition is Jean Piaget's developmental theory. Piaget saw the child as a biological organism that adapts to its environment by actively organizing and interpreting experiences (Flavell, 1963; Petersen, 1982). In so doing, the child's mind first constructs quite simple mental structures, or *schemas,* and subsequently more sophisticated ones. Some experiences can be interpreted by already existing schemas; this process is referred to as *assimilation.* However, some new experiences require *accommodation;* that is, the modification and growth of schemas. Through assimilation and accommodation, the mind of the child develops increasingly advanced schemas and attains greater understanding of the world. Both biological maturation and experience are necessary for such cognitive development.

Piaget hypothesized that cognitive growth occurs in four distinct periods or stages, roughly correlated with chronological age (Table 2-2). As with all stage theories, it was assumed that the stages occur in a particular sequence and build on the preceding ones. At any one stage, intelligence is qualitatively different from what it is at any other stage. This theory has implications for how children might perceive the world at any particular stage, what they are prepared to learn, and how developmental problems might be interpreted.

Piaget's influence declined during the 1980s (Beilen, 1992). However, his theory has encouraged an enormous amount of research and has offered assumptions and concepts used by other theorists. Conceptualization of basic learning

TABLE 2-2

Piaget's Stages of Cognitive Growth

Stage	Indication
Sensorimotor: birth to 2 years	World is first known through innate sensorimotor reflexes. Behavior becomes voluntary, refined, integrated, planful. Ability develops mentally to represent the world in images and words.
Preoperational: 2 to 7 years	Broadened view of the world is achieved as concepts of space, number, color, etc., develop. World is re-created in play. Children can deal with varied situations.
Concrete operational: 7 to 11 years	Ability develops to see the world from others' viewpoints. Ability develops to understand that processes can reverse and that objects can change in form without change in mass (conservation of mass). Ability develops to simultaneously hold in mind several dimensions of a problem. There is increased understanding of relationships.
Formal operational: 12 years onward	Truly logical thinking appears: Child can better abstract, think about possibilities, form and evaluate hypotheses, deduce and induce principles.

processes and higher mental processes are essential to understanding normal and disturbed development.

Language and communication. The growth of communication skills, a dramatic process by any standard, is closely linked to learning and cognition. Among the skills required for language are the abilities to distinguish and produce sounds, to string sounds into words and words into grammatical sentences, to derive meaning from language, and to grasp the social context in which a message is being sent. Table 2-3 presents some of the widely recognized steps in early language acquisition. By the time children begin elementary school, most have mastered basic skills (Baker & Cantwell, 1991), although communication continues to be perfected for many years, even throughout adulthood for some individuals.

How language is acquired has long fascinated philosophers and scientists. Perspectives range from an extreme focus on biological programming to a focus on environmental input (Whitehurst & Valdez-Menchaca, 1988). The biological system is obviously constructed so that language is achieved, but language development relies heavily on social input. Social stimulation facilitates early language acquisition, and the child's babbling and talking attract the attention of caretakers.

Language is clearly related to intellectual functioning, and it is also a social activity. Impairments in language can result in academic problems, social interactional problems, social isolation, and low self-esteem.

EMOTIONAL DEVELOPMENT

The emotions enter into almost all human experience. Typically, several aspects of emotions are recognized. Individuals have private experiences of emotions—"feelings" of sadness, happiness, anger, disgust, and the like—that are often accom-

TABLE 2-3

Early Acquisition of Language and Communication

	Reception	Expression
Birth to 6 months	Reacts to sudden noise. Is quieted by a voice. Locates sound. Recognizes name and words like "bye-bye."	Cries. Babbles, laughs. Initiates vocal play. Vocalizes to self. Experiments with voice.
6 to 12 months	Stops activity to "*no.*" Raises arms to "*come up.*" Obeys simple instructions. Understands simple statements.	Makes sounds of the culture's language. Combines vowel sounds. Imitates adult sounds. Says first words.
12 to 18 months	Carries out two consecutive commands. Understands new words. Listens to nursery rhymes.	Uses ten words. Requests by naming objects. Connects sounds so that they flow like a sentence.
18 to 24 months	Recognizes many sounds. Understands action words like "*show me.*"	Uses short sentences. Uses pronouns. Echoes last words of a rhyme.
24 to 36 months	Follows commands using *in, on, under.* Follows three verbal commands given in one utterance.	Uses possessive, noun-verb combinations. Mother understands 90 percent of communications.
36 to 48 months	Increases understanding of others' messages and social context of communication.	Uses increasingly complex language forms, such as conjunctions and auxiliary verbs.

Based on Bryant, 1977; Whitehurst, 1982.

From their facial expressions, it appears that very young children experience basic emotions such as happiness and unhappiness.

(Courtesy of L. Wicks) (Jim Whitmer/Stock, Boston)

panied by bodily reactions, such as rapid heartbeat or a "nervous" stomach. In addition, the emotions may be outwardly expressed by smiles, scowls, or drooping shoulders.

Even very young infants show emotional expression and respond appropriately to the emotional expression of their caretakers (Harris, 1994; Izard, 1994). Of course, it is impossible to know exactly what they are experiencing. Perhaps specific facial expressions are interpreted by the brain so that infants have feelings akin to the pleasure, anger, and disgust felt by older people. It is unlikely that early emotion is identical to later emotion, though, because emotional "feelings" depend on experiences in the world and on the cognitive ability to interpret these experiences. Nevertheless, many emotions and their expression seem to be present in some form by the time children are two or three years of age.

The understanding of emotion also begins remarkably early (Harris, 1994). For example, infants appear to understand that emotion is directed at targets or objects. Thus if a caretaker expresses fearfulness in the presence of an object, the young child is less likely to approach the object. The child seems to use the caretaker as a social reference. Two- and three-year-olds are able to name and talk about basic emotions, and they recognize that emotion depends on how the individual interprets the situation to which he or she is responding. By age five or six, both the expression and the understanding of emotions are quite refined (Bullock & Russell, 1986). Humans are biologically prepared for such growth, and early emotional milestones may be universal. However, emotion is also shaped by the specific social environments encountered by infants and children (Harris, 1994; Malatesta et al., 1986).

Temperament. The word "temperament" refers to basic disposition or makeup. Although it is not synonymous with emotion, it does include emotion. The concept of temperament is an old one, going back to the classical Greek era. The present surge of interest in temperament was begun by Chess and Thomas's study of New York City children (1972; 1977). These investigators were especially interested in explaining the development of problem behaviors. They recognized environmental influences on the development of behavior, but they were struck by individual differences in how infants behaved from the first days of life. Perhaps the infants' style of behavior entered into the development of problem behavior. On the basis of parental interviews and actual observations, Chess and Thomas were able to demonstrate that young babies had distinct individual differences in temperament that were somewhat stable over time.

Chess and Thomas defined temperament in terms of nine categories of behavior (Table 2-4). They also identified three basic temperamental styles: easy, slow-to-warm, and difficult. The latter is characterized by negative mood, intense reactions to stimuli, sleep irregularities, and the like. Difficult temperament is associated with social and psychological disturbance (Caspi, Elder, & Bem, 1995; Gjone & Stevenson, 1997a).

Today temperament is generally viewed as individual differences in emotionality, activity level, and sociability (Prior, 1992). It is partly based on the biological makeup of the person and there is evidence for heredity influence (Lemery et al., 1999; Wilson & Matheny, 1986). Nevertheless, the stability of temperament over time is modest to moderate (Bates, 1987; Persson-Blennow & McNeil, 1988), and some of the instability is undoubtedly due to environmental influences.

Temperament is considered important in development because the child's way of behaving enters immediately into social interactions that, in turn, influence the general environment and the child's behavioral tendencies. Thus temperament can be expected to be transformed, and the individual's changing characteristics continue to play a role in his or her development (Kagan, Arcus, & Snidman, 1993).

Emotional regulation. Both the emotions and temperament are implicated in a variety of behavior disorders. All children must acquire regulation or control of their emotions, which entails learning to monitor, evaluate, and modify the intensity and timing of emotional reactions. This major developmental task is gradually mastered, with some youngsters having more difficulty than others in regulating their reactions (e.g., Weinberg et al., 1999; Williams et al., 1999). Inadequate emotional control can cause undue anxiety and upset, and can make it difficult for children to recover emotional calm after being stressed. Regulating anger may be particularly challenging for some youngsters. Both the quality and the intensity of the emotions play some role in most behavior difficulties, either as a central factor (such as in extreme fears) or as a side effect (such as unhappiness resulting from academic failure).

THE SOCIOCULTURAL CONTEXT

Development, whether adaptive or maladaptive, occurs in a sociocultural context that can best be considered as domains of overlapping, interacting social influences. Although there is more than one way to depict this context, the developing youngster is typically viewed as embedded within family, community, and cultural domains—all of which interact with each other and the child. It is expected that the importance of any one domain will vary, depending on the developmental level of the individual.

With this general depiction in mind, we will selectively examine the family, peers, school, social class, and culture. We will return to their influences in susequent chapters.

Family. In all societies, the family is considered a major, if not the major, arena for socialization of children (Maccoby, 1992). Family influence is dominant during childhood when malleability is high; it is especially pervasive and strong; and it may endure over the entire lifespan. It is therefore not surprising that major developmental theories

---

TABLE 2-4

The Chess and Thomas Categories of Temperament

1. Activity level
2. Regularity of biological functioning (e.g., eating, sleeping)
3. Approach/withdrawal to new stimuli; approach is positive, such as smiling; withdrawal is negative, such as crying
4. Adaptability to changing situations
5. Level of stimulation necessary to evoke a response
6. Intensity of reaction
7. Mood (e.g., pleasantness, friendliness)
8. Distractibility to extraneous stimuli
9. Attention span and persistence in an activity

Infants and their caretakers are predisposed to interact in ways that foster attachment.

(Courtesy of Penny Genbeu/Tony Stone Images)

offer views of family processes and influences and that an enormous amount of research has been conducted on the family. Early family attachments, family interactions, and family roles and structure are broad aspects of the family context within which normal and disordered behavior develop.

Early Family Attachments Virtually all infants and their caretakers seem biologically prepared to interact in ways that foster their relationship. Most parents are remarkably adept in understanding their babies' signals and needs, and they optimize social interactions. Infants, in turn, are sensitive to parental emotional-social signals. Early child-parent interactions thus flow like a dance, with each partner's behaviors coordinated with the other's (Elias, Hayes, & Broerse, 1988). Such interactions are the basis for the special social-emotional bond that is called attachment, which gradually develops and becomes evident when the child is seven to nine months of age.

Early attachment has been extensively studied with a procedure developed by Ainsworth and called the Strange Situation. The caretaker (usually the mother), infant, and a stranger interact in a comfortable room in the laboratory. The caretaker leaves and returns to the room several times on a predetermined schedule. The infant's behavior is videotaped and later analyzed. Initial research indicated that many infants could be categorized as displaying secure, ambivalent, or avoidant attachment. Later studies of children in families at risk for disturbance indicated a fourth pattern, disorganized/disoriented attachment (Lyons-Ruth, Zeanah, & Benoit, 1996). Infants who have been exposed to pathological, abusive caretaking tend to display disorganized/disoriented attachment behaviors, excessive social inhibition, or excessive sociability and attachment to relative strangers (APA, 1994). Table 2-5 summarizes these four patterns of attachment behaviors.

The development of one pattern, or quality, of attachment rather than another appears to depend on the interaction of parent behavior, child characteristics, and life circumstances (Campbell, 1988). Parental sensitivity to the infant's needs and provision of opportunity to explore the world foster secure attachment. Infant temperament and its interaction with parental characteristics have influence. The child who meets parental expecta-

TABLE 2-5

Four Patterns of Infant Attachment

SECURE

Infant stays close to caretaker and also ventures away to explore the environment

Infant may or may not be distressed at separation from the caretaker

Infant reacts positively when the caretaker returns

Infant is open to communication of affect

Infant displays few ambivalent or avoidant behaviors

AMBIVALENT

Infant communicates high distress and anger

Infant shows anger while seeking contact with the caretaker

Infant may display passivity and helplessness

Infant is not easily soothed

AVOIDANT

Infant shows little affect or distress

Infant avoids contact with caretaker

Infant attends to the environment, apparently as a way to minimize anger and interest felt toward the caretaker

DISORGANIZED/DISORIENTED

Infant displays contradictory behaviors such as sequence of contact seeking, anger, avoidance, and distress in face of needs for comfort and security

Infant shows freezing or "slow motion" of expression and movement

Infant appears apprehensive regarding caretaker

Infant may show disoriented wandering and change of affect

Adapted from Lyons-Ruth, Zeanah, & Benoit, 1996

tions, is easy to care for, and readily smiles and vocalizes is likely to foster positive feelings and behaviors in the adult. The social context also matters; for example, attachment of stressed mothers and their temperamentally difficult babies is of higher quality when the mothers feel that they are receiving support from other adults (Crockenberg, 1988).

Early attachment is considered important not only because of the immediate behaviors displayed by the infant but also because these behaviors have been shown to correlate with later behavior. Some studies indicate that secure attachment is associated with adaptive behavior in childhood and adolescence, such as competence and positive peer interactions, and that insecure attachment places

children at risk for maladaptive behaviors and problems (Dunn & McGuire, 1992; Sroufe & Fleeson, 1986). Attachment experiences are hypothesized to become internalized, that is, become a basis for the child's constructing an internal working model for subsequent adaptation and relationships. Securely attached children are thought to have confidence that their caretakers will be responsive to their needs, a trust that becomes a model for future relationships (Kerns et al., 1996). To put these data and hypotheses in perspective, however, attachment patterns can change as circumstances change and not all studies show a link between attachment and adaptive behavior.

Most studies of attachment have focused on the mother as the primary caretaker. However, children become attached to fathers, grandparents, and others early in life. With age, attachment manifests itself differently, and additional emotional bonds are established.

Family Interactions Direct observations of nuclear families (that is, parents and offspring) indicate some differences in father and mother interactions with their children. Fathers spend less time with their offspring, provide less care, and engage in more active, physical activity and play (Biller, 1993; Collins & Russell, 1991; Ninio & Rinott, 1988). Fathers also tend to treat their children in more gender stereotypic ways; for example, they encourage gender-related play and more readily accept dependency in girls. In contrast, mothers interact more around caregiving activities and tend to treat daughters and sons more alike (Lytton & Romney, 1991). These differences should not be overemphasized, however, since father and mother interactions with their children are probably more alike than different. Moreover, it is clear that both parents have influence on their offspring. Historically, mother influence has received much more attention, and only during the last two decades has extensive research been directed toward fathers. With regard to behavioral problems of youth, mothers have often been implicated, whereas the role of fathers is comparatively uninvestigated (Phares, 1992).

Family interaction studies do indicate that the nuclear family is a complex, interacting system.

		CONTROL: High	CONTROL: Low
ACCEPTANCE	High	**Authoritative** Set and enforce standards Considerate of children's needs Encourage independence, individuality	**Indulgent/Permissive** Few Demands for mature behavior Children regulate self Tolerate children's impulses
	Low	**Authoritarian** Strictly set rules which cannot be challenged Fairly severe punishment	**Neglectful** Uninvolved Little time, attention, emotional commitment given to children

FIGURE 2-2 Patterns of parental behavior.
Based in part on Maccoby and Martin, 1983.

For example, the presence of a third family member changes social interaction between two other members (Stewart et al., 1987). Patterson's (1986) work with families with an antisocial child describes how a hostile response by one family member elicits hostility in return, and other family members might also join in. On the basis of many similar research findings, the once popular view of family influence flowing only from parents to children is now rejected. It is currently well recognized not only that parents influence children and each other but that children also influence parents. This is not to say that the parent-child relationship is symmetrical, or even should be. Parents select the settings in which children develop, control access to material goods, exert physical control, and have greater knowledge than their children (Maccoby, 1992).

Such asymmetry suggests the importance of parenting styles (Dubow, Huesmann, & Eron, 1987; Maccoby, 1992). Two dimensions have been found central to how parents manage their children. One dimension is degree of control, or demand; the second is degree of acceptance, or warmth. Figure 2-2 presents the four parenting styles according to these dimensions. Particular child characteristics are thought to be associated with each style. It is generally agreed that the authoritative style is related to the most favorable child attributes. Authoritative parents assume control, set rules, expect their children to abide by the rules, follow through with consequences, and are simultaneously warm, accepting, and considerate of the needs of their children. The youngsters, in turn, tend to be independent, socially responsible, prosocial, and self-confident. Children of authoritarian parents tend to withdraw but can be aggressive and have low self-esteem. Children of indulgent/permissive parents tend to be impulsive, aggressive, dependent, and irresponsible. Neglectful parenting is associated with children's having difficulties getting along with parents and peers, displaying antisocial behavior, and having school problems (Steinberg et al., 1994).

In examining the findings about parenting styles, it is worthwhile to consider three related issues. First, although parents have more power in the family than children have, their style may in part be a response to their children's characteristics. Second, effective parenting involves consideration of each child's needs and developmental level. What would be "controlling" at one level would not necessarily be controlling at another. Third, the degree to which the analysis of parenting behavior holds for all children, cultures, or subgroups within cultures is unclear. The analysis is thus best employed as a general guideline for understanding families.

Family Roles and Structure Relatively recent changes in U.S. families have created considerable interest in, as well as some concern about, their impact on children. One of these transformations is the increase of women in paid employment. Sixty-two percent of mothers with children under age six were employed in 1995 (Scarr, 1998). It has been speculated that employment could influence parents' investment in their children, perceptions of and expectations for children's behavior, and parenting styles—and thus children's development

(Greenberger & Goldberg, 1989; Greenberger, O'Neil, & Nagel, 1994). In fact, few differences exist between two-parent families in which mothers do or do not work (Muller, 1995; Silverstein, 1991). Overall, effects depend on specific factors such as mothers' attitudes, the work situation, fathers' involvement, and child characteristics. Variables can combine to foster or hinder optimal development (Gottfried & Gottfried, 1988).

A second quite dramatic change in U.S. families has to do with how they are structured. When we consider family structure, we tend to think of the "traditional" nuclear family of two parents and their offspring. But great numbers of youth in the United States experience divorce; one in four children is affected before age sixteen (Barnes, 1994). The number of youth living in single-parent families has also increased, as a result of divorce or other reasons. It is estimated that 50 percent to 60 percent of children born in 1990 will at some time live in a single-parent family, probably headed by a mother (Hetherington, Bridges, & Insabella, 1998). More children are also living in various other family arrangements; step-families make up about 17 percent of all two-parent families with children under age eighteen. As a group, these children are at some developmental risk. However, the families vary a great deal, as do children's needs and coping abilities. It is not the structure itself that matters, but the way in which the family is able to function. Chances are that most children will do quite well when the family is characterized by authoritative parenting, warmth, harmony, and cohesion.

Finally, it is important to consider the general finding that children living in the same family grow up to be quite different from each other, partly because their experiences are different (Plomin, 1995). There are many things that cause this difference. Each child has a unique place in the family and experiences unique interactions. Particular events, whether a divorce or change of residence, occur at a different age for each child. And each child probably has a unique perspective of family events and functioning. In addition, of course, young people are shaped by forces outside the family.

Peers. When children of seven, ten, and fourteen years of age were asked to name those who were most important to them, all named close family members, but more ten-year-olds mentioned extended family, and more fourteen-year-olds added friends (Levitt, Guacci-Franco, & Levitt, 1993). Remembering our own experiences, many of us probably are not surprised by these findings. Even before we consider friends among our most important relationships, however, we have had peer contacts that have contributed to our development. Much before preschool age, children begin to distinguish between what is "adult" and what is "child." Peer relationships change over time, growing in complexity and importance throughout childhood into adolescence (Brownell, 1986; Corsaro & Eder, 1990; Hartup, 1983).

Peers can influence each other in many ways, the specific influences differing somewhat with age. In general, peers provide opportunities for the learning of social and other skills, help set social values, serve as standards against which children judge themselves, and give or withhold emotional support. Peers can reinforce or punish behavior, serve as behavioral models, protect and victimize each other, and enter into friendships or adversarial relationships.

Some children are more accepted and popular with their peers than others. Some are actively disliked and rejected. There is much evidence showing that poor peer relationships, especially rejection, are linked in complex ways to a variety of childhood and adolescent problems and outcomes (Boivin & Hymel, 1997; Parker & Asher, 1987). Thus it is important to understand the factors involved in peer status. The child's characteristics play some role. The accepted child is likely to be socially competent, friendly, helpful, and considerate (Dunn & McGuire, 1992). Rejection is related to the child's being aggressive, disruptive, or withdrawn.

Children's status with their age-mates is also related to other social domains. For example, teachers can play a role in shaping peer status (White & Kistner, 1992). Several studies also indicate that peer status is related to the family system. For example, children's perception of a secure relationship with their mother was related to more favorable peer relationships (Kerns et al., 1996). Another study found that parents of popular children were authoritative/democratic and that this style was linked to the child's positive social behavior. In contrast, parents of rejected children tended to be authoritarian/restrictive (Dekovic & Janssens, 1992). It seems reasonable to assume that what children experience in parent interaction shapes how they relate to peers. At the same time, we know that a child's characteristics enter into both peer and parent relationships, so that causal connections among these factors are probably complex.

School. The school is one of the most central contexts in children's lives. The primary function of the school is to teach intellectual skills and knowledge accumulated by society, but formal education also plays a role in socializing children to society's social and political values. The messages given about these values can act powerfully on development. Furthermore, schools operate as social systems in and of themselves. Student-teacher relationships, classroom structure, pedogogy, rules, methods of discipline, standards, and expectations all play a role in shaping individual children.

Most adults can name teachers they particularly liked or disliked and with whom they learned much or little. Indeed, the quality of child-teacher relationships is associated with various outcomes (Birch & Ladd, 1998). For example, close relationships are linked with positive outcomes such as school liking and academic competence whereas conflictual relationships are linked with unfavorable school attitudes, classroom disengagement, and poor academic performance.

There is evidence that some schools are associated more strongly than others to student achievement, regardless of the characteristics of the students who attend them. That is, certain qualities of school climate and practice foster scholastic and positive social behaviors (Eccles et al., 1993; Howlin, 1994; Rutter, 1983). Among these qualities are the following:

- Clear, agreed-on goals and values
- Fostering of positive attitudes toward education and social cohesiveness
- Opportunities for all students
- Most class time given to individualized, structured curriculum with student feedback
- Positive teacher-student relationships, and teachers who model positive behaviors
- Opportunities for students to act responsibly and to participate in running the school
- Discipline, with appropriate praise and encouragement and little use of punishment
- Good working conditions

School experiences may influence children's futures by setting into motion particular events that continue the shaping process (Rutter, 1983). By helping the child achieve academically, schools may open career doors. By instilling values, work habits, and self-esteem, schools may continue to affect learning and social development.

Indeed, a considerable amount of research now indicates that schools exert sizable influences on academic achievement, social behavior, and later employment (Sylva, 1994). Some of these influences appear to operate directly, whereas others operate indirectly by affecting students' motivation to learn, their self-concepts with regard to learning, and their cognitions about learning (such as the belief that effort leads to achievement).

Social class and culture. Social class, or socioeconomic status (SES), is determined by factors such as family income, educational achievement, and occupational level, which correlate with each other. Virtually all societies are stratified according to social class, and social class is marked by differences in many facets of life—environmental conditions, social interactions, values, attitudes, expectations, and opportunities.

With regard to child development, investigations of the effects of social class have focused on poverty. Children of poor families are at risk for many adverse outcomes (Bradley & Whiteside-Mansell, 1997; McLoyd, 1998). They are more likely to die and to suffer from disease and disability. Figure 2-3 shows the death rate of infants under one year for the total U.S. population and

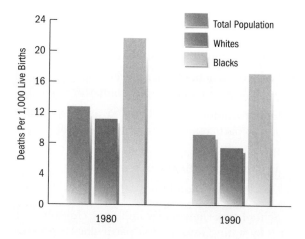

FIGURE 2-3 Death rate of infants under one year of age.
U.S. Bureau of the Census, Statistical Abstract of the United States: 1998
(118th ed.). Washington, DC, 1998.

for the white and black populations. The disadvantage of black people is due at least in part to their disproportionate rate of poverty. Birth weight—a factor in infant death, deformity, and later developmental problems—is related to poverty. Inadequate maternal and medical care probably underlies this unfortunate association. Poor children more often manifest lowered intelligence, fighting, antisocial behavior, drug use, depressive symptoms, and other behavioral problems. Poverty also works against family stability and increases stress. On reaching school, children of poor families do less well, and as adults they acquire less desirable jobs and have higher rates of unemployment. Young women are at risk for early pregnancy and single parenthood. This disadvantageous pattern often repeats itself over generations.

Although it is all too easy to cite the adversities involved in growing up poor, it is more difficult to sort out the interconnectedness of so many factors. How exactly does poverty bring about unfortunate circumstance and prevent children from reaching optimal development? Complex paths of influence are likely. Here we will point to only a few aspects of interest.

The ways in which poverty is connected to other influences work against optimal child development. Among other things, economic hardship is linked to less access to social services and a variety of social supports. Poor families tend to be more isolated. They lack help with child care, psychological support, role models, someone to help out in emergencies, and the like. Poor families who have access to support suffer less from the effects of poverty.

In addition, parenting is often noted as mediating the effects of poverty. There is evidence that lower social class parents have somewhat different goals for their children and that they hold different values (Bradley & Whiteside-Mansell, 1997). They may socialize their children in ways that they believe will ensure their children's job security and acceptance by others. Middle-class families seem to emphasize choice, intellectual challenges, and job status; they expect their children to have control over their lives and to influence others. These differences may translate into how children are managed. In fact, child-rearing practices do vary by social class. In general, lower social class mothers tend to be more restrictive, controlling, and disapproving. They talk less to their children and elicit less language from them. Research suggests that higher social class is associated with parents' giving more time, effort, and verbal attention to their young children (Hart & Risley, 1992). Differences in parenting, in turn, are related to children's cognitive and social development.

The influence of social class—and all of the other social influences we have examined—operates within some broader cultural context. A society's beliefs and values make their way into social structures, social roles, and ways of "doing business," all of which affect the socialization of children. Culture not only affects the goals toward which youth are shaped but also influences how these goals are attained. So we see, for example, that mothers and teachers in Japan and the United States interact differently with children and that this difference is linked to children's characteristics (McDermott, 1991).

Our overview of the social-cultural context of development is necessarily selective. We have tried to capture important examples and issues and to show that influences are not independent of each other. Rather, they overlap, and one social context influences others (Bronfenbrenner, 1986). The social world is complex, dynamic, and challenging. As we will see in the following section, development itself is best described in this way.

HOW DEVELOPMENT OCCURS: MULTIFACTOR, INTEGRATIVE MODELS

Today's developmentalists view growth as the result of numerous variables: biological, psychological, and sociocultural. Multifactor, or integrative, explanations of development are variously known as interactional or transactional models. They assume that many factors interact to bring about developmental change and that interaction is ongoing (transactional). Although this assumption may now seem commonsensical, there is a long history of trying to explain development in simpler ways. Perhaps the simpler approach was due partly to the difficulty of dealing with more complex explanations of behavior.

Developmentalist who employ multifactor models do so in somewhat different ways. To provide the "flavor" of this approach, we will briefly examine two examples, both of which address behavior problems (Compas, Hinden, & Gerhardt, 1995).

THE BIOPSYCHOSOCIAL MODEL

As its name implies, the biopsychosocial model presumes that development is a function of interacting biological and psychosocial variables. In past times, the dichotomy was made between biological and psychosocial (environmental) determinants of development. Some had argued that biological influences, especially genetic programming, primarily determined how children would "turn out." Others had argued that environmental experiences and learning played the critical role in development. Today this nature-nurture dichotomy is rejected on the basis of empirical evidence. For example, research with animals shows

that optimal development of the brain and visual system depends on both genetic programming and stimulation from the environment (e.g., Aoki & Siekevitz, 1988).

An especially telling example of the interplay of biology and environment in humans is provided by children born prematurely or suffering medical complications just before or after birth (Greenberg & Crnic, 1988; Sameroff, 1990). Overall, these individuals have more neurological and intellectual difficulties later in life than full-term infants. Still, it was discovered that many do well and that it is difficult to predict developmental outcome on the basis of the severity of pregnancy and birth complications. When children are severely biologically damaged, the outcome is likely to be poor. But for most cases, an important predictor of outcome is social class/home environment. When family and cultural factors enhance development, children with even severe birth complications can become indistinguishable from those who suffered no birth complications. It is now commonly acknowledged that the development of children born with adverse medical experiences requires a multifactor explanation that considers biological and psychosocial variables.

THE "GOODNESS-OF-FIT" MODEL

Earlier in this chapter, we referred to the research on temperament. Recall that Chess and Thomas identified individual differences in temperament early in life. These investigators found that some children could be classified as temperamentally "difficult": They displayed negative mood, high-intensity reactions, irregularities of sleep, and the like. These children were more likely to have behavioral problems. However, Chess and Thomas recognized that final outcome depended partly on how the children "fit" or matched their environments. If the parents of a difficult child downplayed the difficulties and optimally managed them, behavior problems were less likely to develop. In other words, development depended on how well the person and environment fit each other.

This basic conceptualization of match or mismatch is central in the work of Eccles and her colleagues (1993), which deals with early adolescence. In the United States, the adolescent years are widely viewed as a time of biological and psychosocial transition, which is successfully negotiated by most individuals. However, 15 percent to 30 percent of adolescents drop out of school, regularly consume alcohol and drugs, and get into legal trouble. Many of the problems begin in early adolescence. Eccles and her colleagues hypothesized that this situation results from a mismatch between the needs of developing adolescents and the opportunities provided by the school and the family. We will look at one of their specific hypotheses.

The researchers found that teachers and adolescents agreed that there was less opportunity for students to participate in decision making in the seventh grade (junior high) than in the sixth. However, the adolescents also reported that they desired increased participation during this time of their lives. Thus a mismatch between the social environment and adolescent needs was revealed—and was hypothesized to breed problems.

It is noteworthy that the more physically mature females (who were reaching adolescence earlier) perceived the mismatch as greater than did girls who were less physically mature. Eccles and her colleagues found this difference especially interesting because other studies had shown that early-maturing girls report engaging in more school truancy and misbehavior compared with less mature girls as they moved into junior high school.

All these findings suggested that a mismatch between adolescent need for autonomy and the school environment might help explain the development of problems. In this developmental analysis, physical maturation interacts with the social environment to bring about a poor person-environment fit. Such a multifactor, interactional analysis has much to offer as we seek to better understand the development of behavior problems.

We will see in our discussions of specific behavior disorders that multifactor models are often required to explain the development of a disorder. It is not unusual to see elaborate explanations of several variables working together to bring about adaptive or maladaptive behavior or outcomes.

CONCEPTUALIZING DEVELOPMENTAL INFLUENCES

Conceptualizing all the variables that underlie development simply as biological, psychological, and sociocultural is only a first step in thinking about developmental influences. There are several other useful ways to view developmental factors or influences.

NORMATIVE AND NONNORMATIVE INFLUENCES

A distinction can be made between normative and nonnormative influences (Gerrity, Jones, & Self, 1983). Normative influences happen to most people in some more or less predictable way. Normative age-graded influences affect most all individuals at similar times of life. For example, puberty occurs for most people between the ages of eleven to fourteen, and entrance into elementary school between five and seven years. Normative history-graded influences affect most all people of the same generation, or cohort. Examples are the experience of war or economic depression or a civil rights movement.

In contrast, nonnormative influences, although not necessarily unusual in themselves, may occur only to certain persons, perhaps at unpredictable times and in atypical circumstances. Examples are severe illness and premature death of a parent. Nonnormative events are the chance events that affect development.

We would expect the content of normative and nonnormative influences to vary somewhat across cultures, but in any case there is value in recognizing both types of influence when examining development. It is generally thought that nonnormative events are more likely to result in heightened stress or challenge. For example, a child's experiencing very late puberty or severe illness presents challenges to adaptation.

Necessary and/or Sufficient Causes of Behavior Problems

In noting that behavior has multiple influences, it is useful to make a distinction between necessary and sufficient causes. A necessary cause must be present in order for the disorder to occur. However, a necessary cause may or may not be sufficient to produce the disorder. As an example, consider schizophrenia, an often debilitating dysfunction that can affect youth. Although causation is not completely understood, many investigators believe that some genetic abnormality must exist, that is, is necessary for the occurrence of the problem. But it also appears that at least in some cases, the presence of genetic abnormality does not result in the disorder; that is, it is not sufficient to produce the disorder.

The distinction between necessary and sufficient causes is useful in that it recognizes that the many factors that may play a role in development do not necessarily play the same or equal roles. We must also keep in mind that it is possible that for some disorders, no one factor is clearly necessary. Here, different influences may add or multiply and reach a threshold to produce an adverse outcome.

Direct and Indirect Influences

It is fruitful to recognize that influences on development may be direct or indirect. When a direct effect operates, variable X leads straight to outcome Y. Indirect effects are operating when X influences one or more variables that, in turn, lead to Y. It is usually more difficult to establish indirect effects because a pathway of influence exists that may be complex.

The Timing of Influences

An important idea in developmental psychopathology is that events and experiences may have different influences, depending on the developmental level of the individual. The time at which something happens can make a difference. There are several reasons for this outcome (Rutter, 1989b). The nervous system may be affected differently depending on its developmental status. The effects of experience also depend on the psychological processes that emerge at different times. Thus separation from a parent due to death is probably less impactful for children at five months of age than at twenty-four months because attachment is less formed at five months. The influence of experience may also be related to the timing of social factors. For example, nonnormative events can be stressful because they are "off time" and put the individual "out of sync" with social expectations and supports.

Developmentalists have been especially interested in the influence of early experience on the origin of behavior problems. Research with animals indicates that early experiences can indeed be especially impactful to the brain and behavioral development. Theoretical propositions have also argued for the importance of early influence. Freud (1949) regarded the infant's love for its mother as the prototype for all later love relationships and thus crucial for social-personality development. His idea was in part responsible for early interest in attachment between infants and their mothers. Social learning theorists have suggested that early learning might be especially important because it is the basis for later learning.

The extreme position about early experience argues that the first few years of life are critical in that they set later development. Much research indicates that this extreme critical period hypothesis is unfounded for most human functions. The more moderate and accepted view asserts that early life may be an especially sensitive but not an absolutely critical period, that few, if any, experiences set an irretrievable path through life (e.g., Ramey & Campbell, 1987; Rutter & Garmezy, 1983). Humans are malleable, most developmental outcomes are determined by many variables, and later experience can often moderate what has gone before. This position argues (1) that strong efforts should be made to provide children with early optimal environments and (2) that continuing positive experiences are important. Indeed, empirical studies of early prevention and intervention programs show that an early "dose" of positive experience is often not enough, that developing children require ongoing positive input appropriate to their changing abilities (e.g., Ramey & Ramey, 1998).

RISK AND RESILIENCY

There is enormous interest today in understanding the factors that make it more or less likely that a child will develop disordered behavior. Such information might increase knowledge about etiology and might be valuable in preventing problems. The concepts of risk and resiliency are central to developmental psychopathology.

Risk factors, or risks, are variables that increase the chance of behavioral difficulties or impairments. In the presence of risk, some individuals are adversely affected (are vulnerable), whereas others maintain healthy functioning, that is, are resilient. *Resilience* implies protection from risk factors, or the ability to bounce back in the face of life's adversities (Smith & Prior, 1995).

RISK

Researchers have identified many risk factors. Table 2-6 shows one way to conceptualize risk. Some risk factors can be viewed as stemming from individual disposition to respond maladaptively to life experiences. Disposition may arise through biological mechanisms or life experiences, or the combination of these. Difficult temperament is an example of a dispositional risk factor. Risk is also based in life adversities or events that bring stress or strain (Garmezy, 1994; Garmezy & Masten, 1994). Stress factors can be acute, occurring suddenly and perhaps calamitously, or they can be chronic (e.g., poverty). Some life events, such as parental divorce, may appear on the surface to be acute and limited, but they hold the potential for chronic demands and strains.

Research has gone beyond the simple identification of risk factors. Current understanding of risk includes the following findings (Kopp, 1994; Lambert, 1988; Liaw & Brooks-Gunn, 1994; Rutter, 1987).

TABLE 2-6

Some Developmental Risk Factors

Constitutional
  Hereditary influences; gene abnormalities
  Prenatal, birth complications
  Postnatal disease, damage
  Inadequate health care, nutrition

Family
  Poverty
  Abuse, neglect
  Conflict, disorganization, psychopathology, stress
  Large family size

Emotional and Interpersonal
  Psychological patterns such as low self-esteem, emotional immaturity, difficult temperament
  Social incompetence
  Peer rejection

Intellectual and Academic
  Below average intelligence, learning disability
  Academic failure

Ecological
  Neighborhood disorganization, crime
  Racial, ethnic, gender injustice

Nonnormative Stressful Life Events
  Early death of a parent
  Outbreak of war in immediate environment

Based in part on Coie et al., 1993.

---

1. Some risk factors are strongly associated with developmental problems (e.g., some specific chromosome abnormalities), whereas outcome is more variable for others.
2. There is some connection between risk factors and specific disorders. For example, risk factors may be somewhat different for intellectual deficits than for behavioral difficulties. The same may hold for levels of dysfunction within a disorder; for instance, genetic and prenatal factors are relatively strong risks for severe mental retardation compared with mild retardation.
3. It is likely that youth are more vulnerable to risk at certain times in development, for example, during early prenatal growth and during adolescence. Moreover, at any one time, youth may be more affected by certain risk factors than others.

RISK IN INDIGENOUS POPULATIONS

We have variously recognized culture as a determinate of standards for behavior and as an influence on development. Culture can be a risk factor in certain situations. It has been shown, for example, that children and adolescents who belong to indigenous, or native, cultural groups have higher rates of behavioral dysfunction than youth of dominant populations (Kvernmo & Heyerdahl, 1998). These native groups include American Indians, Maoris in New Zealand, Inuits in Canada, and Sami in Norway. Depression, anxiety, substance abuse, and school failure are among the reported problems. Although methodological factors might partly explain higher rates of disorder in indigenous groups, acculturation is thought to play a role in creating behavioral dysfunction.

Acculturation refers to changes in culture resulting from different cultures coming into contact with each other (Kvernmo & Heyerdahl, 1998). Acculturation is a dynamic process set into motion by voluntary action, such as voluntary immigration, or by situations that force cultural change, for example, by one cultural group forcing its dominance over another. Indigenous youth are thought to be at risk for acculturative problems because the situation is often involuntary, the dominant group may wish to change the culture of the indigenous group, and the indigenous group must frequently deal with prejudice and discrimination—all of which can create practical hardship and raise issues of cultural identity. In addition, indigenous people are often socially and economically disadvantaged. For instance, the American Indian population has high rates of birth, infant mortality, unemployment, and poverty relative to the general population of the United States (Beals et al., 1997).

4. The number of risk factors present is important. A single factor may certainly have an impact, but multiple risk factors have been shown to be especially deleterious. As the number increases, so does negative outcome.
5. Risk may accumulate over time to set up pathways of risk; that is, the impact of a risk factor may increase the likelihood of future risks. Such pathways may be complex and may well be different for specific disorders or even for different outcomes within a disorder.

Researchers are interested in examining the processes that underlie risk. The distinction may be made between *distal* and *proximal* variables. Take, for instance, the risk factor of low social class. This is a distal variable, a description of the environment that can be considered as background, or some distance from the individual. But social class is associated with or mediated by variables that operate in the immediate context, such as lack of social support or parental rearing style associated with social class. It is such proximal variables that are likely to tell us more about the processes of risk (e.g., Bendersky & Lewis, 1994).

RESILIENCY

In the presence of risk factors, why do some individuals succumb, whereas others appear to rise above threat, to be resilient? There is a tendency to think of resiliency as existing within the individual, perhaps because of the apparent perseverance and courage that may seem to characterize children who suffer hardship and rise above it. Indeed, children's characteristics are a component of resiliency, but protection also resides in the environment.

One of the first notable studies of resiliency was conducted on the Hawaiian island of Kauai (Garmezy & Masten, 1994; Werner & Smith, 1982). The participants, who were studied over many years, were at potential risk because of chronic adversities associated with poverty and family variables. Although most of the participants developed problems, one-third were successfully negotiating their lives in late adolescence. The investigators summarized the reasons for resiliency in three broad categories. One category concerned personal attributes; those who enjoyed success were, for example, intelligent, sociable, and socially competent. Second, family strengths existed in that families provided affection and support in times of stress. Third, support outside the family, from individuals and institutions such as the school and church, appeared to foster self-worth and self-efficacy in the children. The resilient children apparently had been exposed to less actual risk and to more protection.

Resiliency is often conceptualized as arising from the child's competence and adaptability. Masten and Coatsworth (1998) suggest that competence in youth is manifested in how well major tasks of adaptation are met. These tasks are assumed to apply to most children and to change with development. Table 2-7 indicates widely agreed-on developmental tasks.

Research has identified intelligence and other personal attributes as minimizing the impact of risk. For example, self-understanding and the ability to think and act independently appear to protect adolescents from the negative effects of their parents' psychiatric disturbance (Beardslee & Podorefsky, 1988). Other personal attributes that may provide protection in specific situations include self-esteem, an easygoing temperament, self-discipline, and social skills (Luthar, 1993).

Nevertheless, as we have already recognized, protection is also afforded by certain environmental variables. Family factors can be crucial. For example, children facing the stress of parental divorce can be protected by a close relationship with one parent. Support from the wider social envi-

TABLE 2-7

Examples of Developmental Tasks

Age Period	Task
Infancy to preschool	Attachment to caregiver(s) Language Differentiation of self from environment Self-control and compliance
Middle childhood	School adjustment (attendance, appropriate conduct) Academic achievement (e.g., learning to read, do arithmetic) Getting along with peers (acceptance, making new friends) Rule-governed conduct (following rules of society for moral behavior and prosocial conduct)
Adolescence	Successful transition to secondary schooling Academic achievement (learning skills needed for higher education or work) Involvement in extracurricular activities (e.g., athletics, clubs) Forming close friendships within and across gender Forming a cohesive sense of self: identity

From Masten and Coatsworth, 1998.

ronment—from teachers, peers, and others—can also make a critical difference. Table 2-8 summarizes factors thought to be important in resilience.

As with risk, there is a need to better understand the complexities of resiliency and the mechanisms that underlie it. For example, do personal attributes and factors in the social environment interact to produce protection? If so, how and when? The competent, self-assured girl may protect herself, for example, by rejecting self-blame, or alternatively, she may understand the need for social support and be especially effective in obtaining it. Perhaps several mechanisms are likely. Current research on resiliency is focusing on understanding such underlying processes.

Ultimately, of course, it is hoped that research into risk and protection will contribute strongly to

TABLE 2-8

Factors Involved in the Resilience of Children and Adolescents

Source	Characteristic
Individual	Good intellectual functioning
	Appealing, sociable, easygoing disposition
	Self-efficacy, self-confidence, high self-esteem
	Talents
	Faith
Family	Close relationship to caring parent figure
	Authoritative parenting: warmth, structure, high expectations
	Socioeconomic advantages
	Connections to extended supportive family networks
Extrafamilial context	Bonds to prosocial adults outside the family
	Connections to prosocial organizations
	Attending effective schools

From Masten and Coatsworth, 1998.

TABLE 2-9

Rutter's Description of Four Protective Mechanisms

Reduction of Risk Impact

The impact of risk can be reduced by
providing the child with practice in coping;
reducing demands of the risk factor;
preparing the child for the situation;
exposing the child when he/she can cognitively handle the situation; and
decreasing exposure to the risk factor.

Reduction of Negative Chain Reactions

Exposure to risk often sets up a chain of reactions that perpetuates risk effects into the future. Interventions that prevent such chains are protective.

Development of Self-Esteem and Self-Efficacy

People's concepts and feelings about their social environments, their worth, and their ability to deal with life's challenges are important. Positive development results from satisfying social relationships and success in accomplishing tasks.

Opening of Opportunities

Many events, particularly at turning points in people's lives, reduce risk by providing opportunities for adaptive growth. Examples are changes in geographic location, chance to continue one's education, shifts in family roles.

Adapted from Rutter, 1987

prevention and amelioration of behavior disorder. Table 2-9 is taken from Rutter's (1987) description of four general ways in which young people might be protected. Rutter sees these ways as operating at key turning points in people's lives, when risk can be redirected. Continued research in this area is bound to lead to better knowledge of why and how vulnerable youth succumb to risk in varying degrees, whereas resilient youth react in constructive ways—even in the face of seemingly overwhelming adversity.

CHANGE AND CONTINUITY IN BEHAVIOR DISORDERS

Developmentalists have considerable interest in understanding change and continuity over time. Development is defined in terms of change, and humans certainly are malleable. But there are limits to malleability, so that both change and continuity would be expected (Lerner, 1987). This process is exemplified in physical aging. When someone reaches old age, the person's face is both different from and similar to its appearance at age ten, twenty, and forty. However, it may be quite difficult to predict the exact appearance at older age and to describe how the transformation occurred. This example can be applied to psychological functioning. In a general way, we can anticipate both change and continuity as individuals travel along life's pathways, although much is yet to be learned about transformation.

When the issue of change or continuity is applied to the study of behavior disorders, a central question is, Do behavior problems at earlier times in life carry over to, or predict, the same or different disorders in later life? This question is important for understanding the development of behavior problems, and it also has implications for treatment and prevention. Early behavior problems are always of concern to the degree that they cause discomfort and unhappiness and close the door of opportunities for growth. When such problems continue over time in some fashion, they have even graver implications.

It is important to note that it is often quite difficult to trace the course of a disorder over time. At different developmental levels, behaviors that appear different from each other may actually express the same underlying disturbance. To take a simple example, a five-year-old may demonstrate aggression by pushing a playmate, whereas an adolescent is more likely to use subtle sarcasm. The term "*heterotypic continuity*" refers to the continuance of a behavior in which the form of the behavior changes with development or over time. Efforts to understand the link between early and later disorders must deal with this phenomenon.

What is known about the continuity of disorders? It is no surprise that we see both change and continuity. Some problems are quite transitory. For example, the presence of enuresis (bed-wetting past four or five years of age) drops considerably after childhood. Child aggression and antisocial behavior can be relatively stable over time. Specific links between early and later problems in mood, such as depression, have become better established than they once were. Moreover, some disorders are notably stable, such as severe mental retardation and autism.

In addition to determining whether and in what forms a disorder may continue over time, developmental psychopathologists seek to understand the processes responsible for change or continuity. As an example, we will look at the study conducted by Caspi and colleagues (1987), in which the continuity of behavior of eight- to ten-year-olds was traced across thirty years. The behavior examined was an ill-tempered interactional style, represented in childhood by temper tantrums (biting, kicking, striking) and verbal explosions (swearing, screaming, shouting). For males, an association was found between childhood ill-temper and adult moodiness and irritability, as well as lower levels of behavior control, de-

pendability, production, and ambition. The men experienced erratic work patterns and downward occupational mobility, and they were likely to divorce. For females, childhood tantrums were related to marriage to men of low occupational status, unhappy marriage and divorce, and ill temperedness as mothers.

In an effort to address underlying processes, the researchers suggested two processes by which maladaptive behavior is maintained over time. *Cumulative continuity* stems from children's channeling themselves into environments that perpetuate the maladaptive style. The ill-tempered boy may limit opportunity by dropping out of school, thereby creating frustrating situations, to which he responds with more irritability, undercontrol, and the like. *Interactional continuity* originates in the transaction between the person and the environment. The person acts, others respond accordingly, and the person reacts to this response. It is assumed that the coercive, ill-tempered style of the child pays off in the short run, so that through reinforcement it is maintained, only eventually to be destructive.

Caspi and his colleagues make no explicit assumption that ill-temperedness has genetic origins, but other research indicates that both experience and biological variables may play a role in linking early and later behaviors. This line of investigation increasingly describes developmental pathways by which early and later behaviors are linked.

PATHWAYS OF DEVELOPMENT

From our discussion of the many variables that contribute to development, it is obvious that it is difficult to predict the developmental path of any one individual. Nevertheless, researchers have begun to conceptualize and describe a number of general developmental pathways, some of which indicate change and others of which indicate stability.

Figure 2-4 indicates five trajectories that map development across the adolescent years in terms of adaptation (Compas et al., 1995). Path 1 is char-

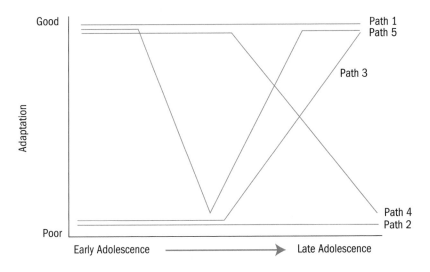

Path 1 Stable Adaptation
Few behavior problems; good self-worth.
Low risk exposure.

Path 2 Stable Maladaptation
Chronic adversities; little protection.
Example: aggressive, antisocial behavior maintained.

Path 3 Reversal of Maladaptation
Important life change creates new opportunity.
Example: military career affords opportunity.

Path 4 Decline of Adaptation
Environmental or biological shifts bring adversity.
Example: family divorce contributes to maladaptation.

Path 5 Temporal Maladaptation
Can reflect transient experimental risk taking.
Example: use of illegal drugs.

FIGURE 2-4 Five developmental pathways during adolescence.
From Compas, Hinden, and Gerhardt, 1995.

acterized by stable adaptation, that is, positive self-worth and lack of problems. Path 2 indicates stable maladaptation. Path 3 shows maladaptation at the beginning of adolescence that turns into positive outcome. Path 4 shows adaptation at the beginning that turns into decline. Path 5 indicates a temporary decline in adolescence but a bouncing back to adaptive behavior.

Two aspects of this work are of interest to us, in light of our pervious discussions. One aspect is that descriptions of the pathways include risk and protection factors for populations of youth who, as a group, show these various trajectories.

The second concerns the relationship of the pathways to outcome. Specifically, Paths 1, 3, and 5 all lead to positive adaptation, and Paths 2 and 4 lead to poor adaptation. These relationships exemplify the principle of *equifinality,* that diverse factors or paths can be associated with the same outcome (Cicchetti & Cohen, 1995). Equifinality is observed or hypothesized with regard to numerous behavioral disorders of childhood and adolescents.

Another important principle, which is not apparent in Figure 2-4, is referred to as *multifinality.* This is the principle that a factor may function dif-

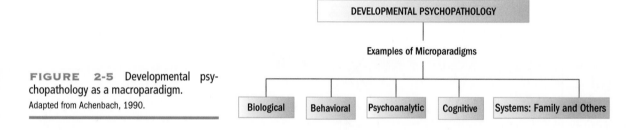

FIGURE 2-5 Developmental psychopathology as a macroparadigm.
Adapted from Achenbach, 1990.

ferently depending on a host of considerations and thereby may lead to different outcomes. For example, insecure attachment in infants may lead to several different outcomes, depending on the context of the infants rearing environments and their competencies.

The principles of equifinality and multifinality are additional reflections of a common theme in the development of behavior, including disturbed behavior: the theme of enormous complexity that we can address only in terms of what is likely to happen along life's pathways.

DEVELOPMENTAL PSYCHOPATHOLOGY AND OTHER APPROACHES

We began this chapter by describing developmental psychopathology as a broad framework for relating normal and abnormal development and behavior. As Achenbach (1990) and others have made clear, the approach adopts general developmental principles and findings but does not impose specific theoretical explanations. Achenbach views the developmental approach as a way of integrating other approaches and theories around a core of developmental issues and questions. He thus labels it a "macroparadigm," a broad perspective that subsumes other perspectives, or "microparadigms." Figure 2-5 presents this idea in schematic form. Each microparadigm in this schema offers a specific view of behavior disorders. Each makes its own assumptions, offers theoretical concepts, asks specific questions, and adopts certain methods to answer questions. It is to such perspectives that we turn in the next chapter of this text.

SUMMARY

◼ The developmental approach to the study of behavior disorders offers developmental norms, hypotheses, and a broad framework within which to understand problems of youth.

◼ Development refers to change over the lifespan that proceeds in a coherent manner along various pathways. Although change can take many forms, it has limits. Developmental change is a product of transactions among biological, psychological, and sociocultural variables.

◼ The genetic basis of development is the chromosomes, which direct the biochemistry of the body. Hereditary influence, which is complex and indirect, sets a range within which normal and dysfunctional behaviors develop.

◼ Early physical and motor growth occur in universal, orderly sequences. The nervous system is relatively well developed at birth, and further development depends on both biological and environmental influences. Motor development, the timing of maturation, and physical attractiveness can influence psychosocial growth.

◼ From birth, children have the capacity to perceive the environment and to learn. Basic learning processes become more sophisticated as higher mental processes and thinking develop gradually. Information processing models conceptualize many cognitive processes. Piaget's theory proposed that through assimilation and accommodation, children develop increasingly sophisticated schemas of the world in four distinct stages.

■ By age five, basic language skills are acquired. The capacity for language clearly is programmed into the human species, but interaction with others shapes development. Language skill has implications for both intellectual and psychosocial functioning.

■ The rudiments of emotion are present from early life, and by age five or six, children show considerable ability to express emotion and to interpret others' emotions. Temperament refers to biologically based, somewhat stable individual differences in emotionality, activity, and sociability. The regulation of both emotion and temperament are important factors in behavioral problems.

■ The social context of development consists of overlapping, interacting domains of influences that include family, peers, school, social class, and broad cultural influences.

■ Attachment, the early socioemotional bond between infants and their caretakers, is influenced by parental sensitivity, infant temperament, and the social context. Insecure attachment is associated with maladaptive behavior.

■ Family interaction is complex, with each person affecting others. Studies of parenting styles suggest that an authoritative, warm style fosters favorable development. Today's analyses of family life consider the many changes in family structures and roles.

■ Peers influence each other in many ways. Some children are readily accepted by their peers; others are rejected. Poor peer relationships are associated with childhood and later problem behavior.

■ Schools that promote positive academic and social behaviors appear to have certain characteristics. Development is influenced by knowledge and skills acquired in school and also by the values, work habits, and self-concepts that schools encourage.

■ Low SES disadvantages children because of poverty, less than optimal health care, higher family stress, and lower school achievement. The impact of social class operates in part through family socialization practices that vary with social class. Social class and other social influences operate within a larger cultural context of beliefs and values.

■ Today's multifactor, integrative models of development assume that biological and psychosocial variables continuously interact to bring about development. The biopsychosocial and goodness-of-fit models are important examples.

■ There are several useful ways to conceptualize developmental factors or influences. Development is affected by normative and nonnormative factors. With regard to behavior problems, it is useful to distinguish necessary versus sufficient causal factors and direct versus indirect influences. The timing of experiential influences is an important consideration.

■ There is increasing understanding of the factors that put children at risk for developing dysfunctional behavior or that provide protection from risk. Both risk and resiliency reside in the individual and the environment. Researchers are examining the processes by which risk and resiliency operate.

■ The issue of change and continuity of behavior is a central concern of developmental psychopathologists. Both change and continuity are seen in disturbed behavior. Among the processes by which maladaptive behavior is maintained are cumulative continuity and interactional continuity.

■ The concept of developmental pathways is another important conceptualization in the study of behavioral problems. Several general paths of adaptation-maladaptation through the adolescent years have been suggested by research studies. The principles of equifinality and multifinality reflect the complexity of development.

■ Developmental psychopathology serves as a framework, or macroparadigm, for organizing other approaches or perspectives of behavioral disorder.

CHAPTER 3

APPROACHES TO UNDERSTANDING AND TREATING CHILDHOOD BEHAVIOR DISORDERS

T he millions of youngsters who each year are in need of mental health services present with a variety of behavioral, emotional, social, learning, and physical problems. Very often youngsters have more than one difficulty. Our goal is to come to understand the problems experienced by these youngsters and their families and the variety of treatment approaches taken in assisting them. As you have probably already come to realize, there are a variety of influences and circumstances that contribute to the development, maintenance, identification, referral, evaluation, and treatment of these difficulties. In addition, a variety of professionals are likely to be called on in the process of working with these youngsters and their families. Given the complexity and heterogeneity of this picture, it is necessary to be able to consider a variety of influences.

In Chapter 2, we examined developmental processes and the way that a developmental perspective can help us to understand behavior disorders of childhood and adolescence. We also saw

that within this broad developmental paradigm, one can identify a number of different views or microparadigms. Each view highlights some of the influences that contribute to a developmental perspective on behavior disorders (Achenbach, 1990).

At one time, the approach to behavioral disorder and other psychological phenomena was characterized by "big," all-encompassing theories that sought to explain all the phenomena of interest within a singular theory. Currently, however, it is more common to find "smaller" theories that seek to explain particular phenomena. It is also the case that rather than an emphasis on a singular explanation being adequate, current explanations of a particular child and family problem often appreciate the interplay of a number of influences. Indeed, there is an increasing appreciation of an ongoing problem-solving process approach to understanding and treating behavior disorders of childhood and adolescence. Central to engaging in this process are a conceptual framework to

46

guide efforts and a reliance on well-established research findings. In this chapter we examine several of these microparadigms, or perspectives. Each one addresses a particular variety of influence that contributes to the complex interplay of influences that are the mosaic of child and adolescent behavior disorders. Before turning to particular viewpoints, however, let us look at the meaning of terms such as "perspective" and "paradigm."

TAKING DIFFERENT PERSPECTIVES

Much of what we now know about behavior problems comes from applying the objective methods of science. However, the writings of Thomas Kuhn (1962) and others have made us increasingly aware that science is not a completely objective endeavor. To understand this point it is best to remember that scientists, like all of us, must think about and deal with a complex world. To do this they make assumptions and form concepts. When a set of such assumptions is shared by a group of investigators, Kuhn refers to them as a paradigm. Here we employ the terms perspective, paradigm, and view interchangeably to refer to this perceptual/cognitive "set" that the scientist takes in order to study and understand phenomena.

What are the implications of adopting a particular perspective? Perspectives help us make sense of a puzzling and complex universe. They enable us to view new information in the context of previous experience and to have a basis for reacting to it. Taking a perspective is thus adaptive and functional. At the same time, perspectives limit us as well. They guide us in "selecting" the issues chosen for investigation, but may preclude us from asking certain questions. Once a question is selected for investigation, a decision must be made: What will be observed in order to answer this question? All things are not observed, just some things. Perspectives influence this choice and also how observations are done. In turn, particular methods and instruments help in detecting certain phenomena

but result in our missing others. Once information is collected, the adoption of a paradigm affects the interpretation we make of the "facts" we have collected. Overall then, perspective-taking strongly organizes how a problem is approached, investigated, and interpreted.

BIOLOGICAL INFLUENCES

The conjecture that psychopathology is due to a defective or malfunctioning biological system can be traced in the Western world to Greek culture. Hippocrates (460–370 B.C.), who is considered the father of medicine, was an advocate of somatogenesis ("soma" refers to "body," "genesis" means "origin"). He postulated that proper mental functioning relied on a healthy brain and that deviant thinking or behavior was thus the result of brain pathology.

The biological perspective initially assumed that biology directly causes abnormal behavior. The original psychiatric classification system developed by Kraeplin in the late 1800s, which was the forerunner of current systems, was clearly based on this assumption. Early discoveries of biological causes for particular behavioral problems (for example, the revelation that a spirochete bacterium caused syphilis and the mental deterioration of syphilis's late stages) led to the hope that similar causes would be found for all abnormal behavior. With limited exception, this has not proven to be the case. Today the predominant view is that although biological influences are of importance, these are likely to be part of a complex transaction among biological and various psychological and sociocultural influences.

As we saw in Chapter 2, the influence of biological factors on a child's behavior can occur through a variety of processes and mechanisms. Here we will examine three topics: the structure of the brain, the nervous system and its biochemical functioning, and genetic influences.

THE STRUCTURE OF THE BRAIN

The structural integrity of the nervous system, particularly the brain, is one of the biological influences that has been examined (Nelson & Bloom,

1997; Rutter, 1998). A cross-section of the human brain is illustrated in Figure 3-1. The brain is typically described as being divided into three major subsections: the hindbrain, the midbrain, and the forebrain. The hindbrain, which regulates basic body functions such as sleeping, breathing, heart rate, and body movements, includes the cerebellum, pons, and medulla. The midbrain contains much of the reticular activating system, although this extends into the pons and medulla as well. The reticular activating system regulates sleep and waking. The midbrain also coordinates communication between the hindbrain and the forebrain. The forebrain consists of the two cerebral hemispheres connected by the corpus callosum. Each hemisphere has four regions, or lobes. The frontal lobes are located near the front of the brain, and the temporal lobes are located near the temples on the side of the brain. The parietal lobes are located near the top rear of the brain, and the occipital lobes are located at the rear of the head.

The cerebral hemispheres are involved in a wide variety of activities, such as sensory processing, motor control, and higher mental functioning, including information processing, learning, and memory. The thalamus and hypothalamus are structures that lie below the cerebral hemispheres, between the forebrain and the midbrain. The thalamus is involved in processing and relaying information between the cerebral cortex and other parts of the central nervous system. The hypothalamus regulates basic urges such as hunger, thirst, and sexual activity. The multi-structured limbic system, which includes parts of the cerebral hemispheres, the thalamus, and the hypothalamus, through its regulation of the endocrine glands and the autonomic nervous system (discussed later), plays a central role in the regulation of emotions and biological urges.

Abnormal development or actual damage to the biological system may produce a variety of intellectual and behavioral difficulties. Known or

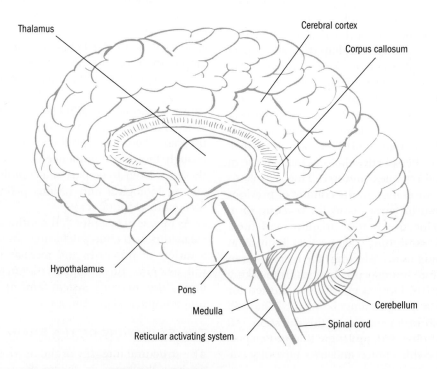

FIGURE 3-1 Cross-section of the human brain.

presumed damage may occur during pregnancy (prenatal), at about the time of birth (perinatal), or during later development (postnatal).

Prenatal influences. Damage to the developing fetus by toxic substances receives a great deal of public and professional attention. At one time, it was believed that the placenta protected the fetus from harmful substances that might enter the mother's bloodstream. We now know that a variety of teratogens appear to be related to fetal death, disease, malformation, or functional/behavioral effects (Hogan, 1998; Singer et al., 1997). The effects of drugs such as thalidomide, alcohol, tobacco, cocaine, heroin, and methadone on prenatal development have received a great deal of study. The potential negative effects of radiation and environmental contaminants, such as polychlorinated biphenyls (PCBs), are also well known. In addition, many maternal diseases (e.g., rubella, syphilis, gonorrhea) are known to have harmful effects. Acquired Immune Deficiency Syndrome (AIDS) is a growing threat to newborn babies that is of particular current concern (Armistead et al., 1998).

Clearly, many of the findings produce much controversy because they are related to sensitive economic, social, and political issues. Indeed, caution is appropriate, since ethical considerations do not permit research that would provide clear conclusions, such as studies in which pregnant women would be intentionally exposed to any of these conditions. We thus must rely on animal studies, the results of which may not hold for humans, and on investigations of humans under natural (uncontrolled) conditions. Interpretation of the impact of particular teratogens in such instances is difficult, because exposure to any one teratogen can be associated with exposure to others, as well as to other potentially harmful effects such as poor prenatal care, malnutrition, and other factors, like maternal stress, that are associated with substance abuse and poverty (Hogan, 1998; Singer et al., 1997). These other factors can influence outcome both prenatally and during the child's subsequent development.

Since a wide variety of potential teratogens exist (Kopp & Kaler, 1989), it may not be entirely possi-

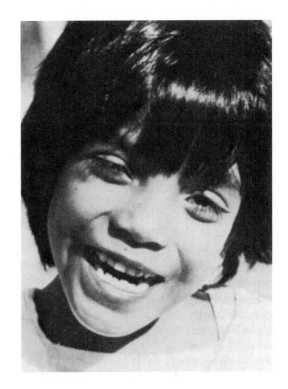

The girl pictured here is one of two daughters born to an alcoholic mother, since deceased. On the basis of history, mental deficiency, and physical findings, both daughters were diagnosed as having *fetal alcohol syndrome.* Several key features of the syndrome are visible in this girl, including narrow eye openings, underdeveloped-thin upper lip, flattening or absence of the usual indentation under the nose, and possible drooping of the upper eyelids. Behavioral deficits are also implicated in this syndrome.

(Courtesy of March of Dimes Birth Defects Foundation)

ble to avoid exposure. Indeed, as women increasingly enter the workplace, they raise their risk of exposure to toxic agents. However, a pregnant woman does have some control over her environment; she can take special care not to expose herself to disease and to obtain treatment if a disease is contracted. In addition, prenatal adversities might be minimized by recognizing and addressing other variables associated with negative outcome, such as age of the mother and maternal stress (Kopp, 1994).

Perinatal and later influences. It is important to note that nervous system damage may also occur during or after birth. At birth, experiences such as excessive medication given to the mother, unusual delivery, and anoxia (lack of oxygen) may result in damage to the newborn. There is evidence to suggest that the frequency of some perinatal complications is greater in lower SES children. Furthermore, as noted in Chapter 2, perinatal complications and SES factors have an interactive effect on the infant's subsequent development (Liaw & Brooks-Gunn, 1994).

Postnatal damage may occur as a result of experiences such as accident, illness, malnutrition, or accidental poisoning. Exposure of children to lead, even at relatively low levels, is one example of accidental poisoning that has received considerable attention and would appear to have negative impact on processes such as attention and cognitive development (Fergusson, Horwood, & Lynskey, 1993; Tesman & Hills, 1994).

Regardless of when biological insult occurs, both the site and the severity of brain damage help determine the nature of the difficulties. A precise description of the relationship between damage and dysfunction cannot always be made, however. Thus the link between brain damage and psychopathology is often unclear and awaits continued developments in both basic and clinical brain research (Fletcher & Taylor, 1997; Rakic & Lombroso, 1998).

One of the major concerns of those who work with children is whether problems arising from brain damage can be remediated. A controversial issue is whether the child's immature central nervous system is highly "plastic," that is, more likely to recover after injury, than is the adult system. The issue is a complex one (Huttenlocher, 1994; Nelson & Bloom, 1997; Thatcher, 1994). Timing of injury is only one factor affecting recovery. Size, location, and progression of the lesion, severity of the insult, secondary complications such as infection, and type and degree of environmental stimulation are some other factors. An emphasis on plasticity encourages efforts to develop lost or unachieved functioning, but it may have some negative consequences. Frustration for the child, parent, and teacher may result when complete plasticity is assumed but is not realized. The assumption that the young brain is highly plastic

Many head injuries are the result of accidents. The use of helmets for bicycling and other activities can appreciably reduce the number of head injuries.
(Courtesy of A.C. Israel)

may lead also to imprecise forms of intervention. On the other hand, identification of loss and realistic expectations for recovery can lead to advances in our understanding and to improved remediation.

NERVOUS SYSTEM FUNCTIONING AND BIOCHEMISTRY

Much of both early and current thinking about the role of biological influences on disordered behavior implicates imbalances in body chemistry. Hippocrates speculated that adequate mental functioning relied on a proper balance of the four bodily humors: blood, phlegm, yellow bile, and black bile. Thus, for example, excessive black bile was thought to produce melancholia, or what we would today label as depression.

Although specific mechanisms for specific disorders are often questioned, there is fairly broad agreement that biochemistry in some form contributes to disturbed behavior. The biochemistry of neurotransmitters and central nervous system functioning have become important foci of biology's contribution to the study of behavior disorders.

The nervous system has billions of neurons, which conduct the electrochemical impulses by which communication occurs. Neurons have three major parts: a cell body; dendrites that branch out from the cell body and can receive messages from other cells; and axons that transmit messages to other cells. These messages must cross the gap between neurons (the synaptic gap, or cleft). When an impulse reaches the end of the axon, neurotransmitters are released that cross the synaptic gap and communicate with other cells through receptor sites on those cells (Figure 3-2).

Neurotransmission can go awry in a number of ways. For example, too much or too little of a particular neurotransmitter can be released. Problems can also exist in reuptake—the process by which the neuron reabsorbs the neurotransmitter for subsequent transmissions. Also, the density and sensitivity of receptors to a particular neurotransmitter or the presence or absence of other chemicals, which are known as blocking agents, at the receptor sites can affect neurotransmission. A number of different neurotransmitters have been identified as playing a role in various forms of abnormal behavior, such as depression and Attention Deficit Hyperactivity Disorder (Emslie et al., 1994; Pliszka, McCracken, & Maas, 1996). Norepinephrine, serotonin, dopamine, acetylcholine, and gamma amibutyric acid (GABA) are some of the major neurotransmitters that have been studied.

How the biochemistry of the body reacts to situations that an individual may encounter is also part of the biological perspective on behavior disorders. The autonomic nervous system, which helps to regulate one's emotional state, consists of two branches. The sympathetic nervous system mediates increased arousal, preparing the body for action. The parasympathetic nervous system, on the other hand, works to slow arousal and to conserve the body's resources. One of the ways the autonomic nervous system operates is through stimulation of the endocrine system, a collection of glands that release hormones into the bloodstream. Research on neuroendocrine functioning is an important part of the study of a variety of child and adolescent disorders. For example, differences in autonomic reactivity in Panic Disorder, neurohormonal dysregulation in Obsessive-Compulsive Disorder, and the role of growth hormone regulation in depression have received attention (Dummit & Klein, 1994; Emslie et al., 1994; Leonard et al., 1994).

GENETIC INFLUENCES

The study of genetic influences on human behavior is extremely complex and is currently expanding in several directions (Hewitt et al., 1997; Pike & Plomin, 1996; Plomin & Rutter, 1998). Application to child and adolescent disorders is comparatively underresearched, but this situation is changing. Genetic research can tell us subtle things about etiology, for example, whether all or only some cases of a disorder are likely to have a genetic component. Genetic research can even confirm the role of environment in causation and can point to characteristics of the environment that might be especially important (Hewitt et al., 1997; Pike & Plomin, 1996).

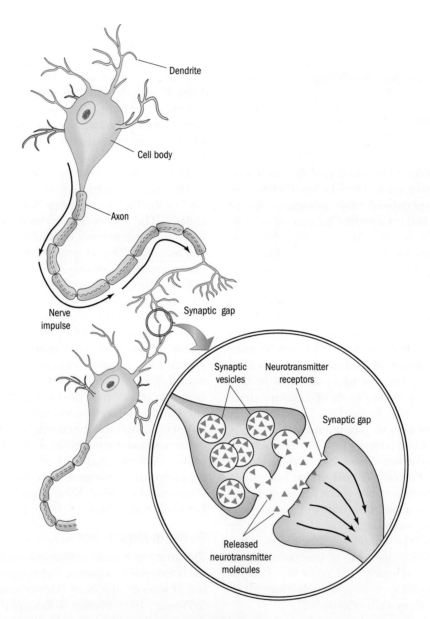

FIGURE 3-2 Impulses are transmitted from one neuron to another, across a synaptic cleft or gap, through the release of neurotransmitters.

A complete discussion of genetic influence on childhood disorders is not possible here. The topics selected for examination are intended to introduce this area and to facilitate understanding of later discussions of the genetics of specific behavior disorders.

Inheritance through single genes. Beginning with the work of Gregor Mendel, scientists have sought to describe inheritance of certain characteristics influenced by one gene pair. Mendel correctly hypothesized that each parent carries two hereditary factors (later called genes) but passes on only one to the offspring. He also noted that one form of the factor is dominant, in that its transmission by either parent leads to the display of that form of the characteristic. The other form, the recessive, displays itself only when it is transmitted by both parents. Both of these patterns, as well as the sex-linked pattern described later, are involved in the inheritance of many human attributes and disorders.

Huntington's chorea is an example of a disease transmitted by a dominant gene. This disease causes death but does not show up until adulthood, when limb spasms, mental deterioration, and perhaps dementia become evident. Many people know of this inherited disease because it was the cause of the death of Woody Guthrie, a well-known folk singer and the father of Arlo Guthrie.

Tay-Sachs disease provides an example of a disorder carried by one gene pair and transmitted recessively. A degenerative disease of the nervous system, it usually results in progressive deterioration of mental abilities, motor capacities, and vision, and then death by the age of one to three. An estimated 60 to 90 percent of all cases of Tay-Sachs is found among children of Ashkenazic Jewish heritage.

The sex-linked pattern of inheritance involves genes on the sex chromosomes. Of special interest is the situation in which the relevant gene is recessive and is carried on the X chromosome, such as in red-green color blindness, hemophilia, and Lesch-Nyhan syndrome. The latter is a rare, untreatable disorder that results in unusual motor development, mental retardation, and extreme self-mutilation in children. The disorder is found only in males, who die early and thus do not have offspring. The Lesch-Nyhan child has a normal father and a mother who carries the disorder, having one normal X chromosome and one affected X chromosome. Sons receive their only X chromosome from their mothers. Those who receive the recessive defective gene will develop the disorder, since the Y chromosome transmitted from the father carries no gene at all to offset the defective gene. Daughters receive one X chromosome from each parent. If a girl receives the defective recessive gene from her mother, it is usually offset by the dominant normal gene from her father; the

girl has no affliction herself but could transmit Lesch-Nyhan to her son.

Researchers continue to explore the effects of single gene pairs or other relatively simple genetic etiology on specific behavior disorders. Such research and research concerning more complex genetic inheritance have been facilitated by new molecular genetic methods (Flint, 1996; Lombroso, Pauls, & Leckman, 1994). Molecular genetics is concerned with the search for the genes involved in the development of a disorder or of a characteristic that increases the risk for disorder. There are two major strategies for finding genes: linkage and association (Plomin & Rutter, 1998). Linkage analysis explores whether the pattern in which a specific disorder appears among family members is the same as for genetic markers. The approximate chromosome location is known for the genetic markers. For example, inherited disorders, such as color blindness, that are known to be linked to a particular chromosome have been used as markers. If the behavior disorder and color blindness appear in family members in the same pattern, then it can be presumed that the genes that control them are close neighbors on the same chromosome. Association analysis involves the correlation between a gene and some trait among unrelated individuals. Individuals with a particular form of a gene (allele) differ on a trait from individuals with a different form of that gene. For example, individuals with a long-repeat (a segment of the gene varies in the number of times it repeats 2 to 8 times) allele of the gene DRD4 have higher novelty-seeking scores than those without a long-repeat allele (Plomin & Rutter, 1998).

The efforts of Nancy Wexler and a team of research scientists in searching for the gene responsible for Huntington's disease is an example of recent advances. Through the use of linkage analysis techniques, the disorder had been mapped to an area on chromosome 4, and Wexler's group was able to identify the gene responsible for Huntington's disease (Huntington's Disease Collaborative Research Group, 1993).

Investigating the effects of multiple genes. In contrast to the effects due to a single gene pair, most of the behaviors we are concerned with in studying child and adolescent behavior disorders are thought to involve many genes as well as environmental influences. Such multifactorial inheritance is much more difficult to trace than single gene effects. Accordingly, the study of genetic influences on human behavior relies on a combination of evidence from a variety of research methods. We will now look briefly at the major research methods of behavior genetics.

The three major research strategies of behavior genetics that have been applied to behavior disorders are the family, twin, and adoption methodologies (Plomin, 1994b). These methods are employed to assess heritability, a statistic that indicates the degree to which genetic influence accounts for variance in behavior among individuals in the population studied. The contribution of environmental influences is also obtained.

Youth with behavior disorders often have parents, siblings, and other family members with similar problems. However, such aggregation of behavior problems in families does not necessarily mean that a genetic influence is operating. Family environment may also be operating.

In family studies, the relatives of an individual identified as exhibiting a certain behavior or disorder (the proband) can be examined to determine whether or not the relatives exhibit the same behavior or problem. Identical twins are 100 percent genetically related. The average genetic relatedness of first-degree relatives (parents and their offspring and siblings) is 50 percent. Half-siblings and other second-degree relatives are 25 percent genetically related. Third-degree relatives, such as cousins, are only 12.5 percent genetically related. If there is a genetic influence on a disorder, family members who are genetically more similar to the proband should be more likely to exhibit the same or related difficulties. Statistical estimates of heritability can be calculated from family studies.

The essence of twin designs is a comparison of identical twin resemblance (concordance) to fraternal twin resemblance. Identical or monozygotic (MZ) twins have identical genes. Fraternal or dizygotic (DZ) twins are, on average, only 50 percent alike genetically; in fact, they are no more alike genetically than any other two siblings. In its most basic form, the twin method points to genetic influence if there is greater concordance among identical twins than among fraternal twins. That is, genetic influence is suggested when a disorder occurs more frequently in both members of MZ twin pairs than it does in both members of DZ twin pairs (Edelbrock et al., 1995).

Adoption studies are designed to evaluate the relative contributions of genetics and environment by studying adopted and nonadopted individuals and their families. One strategy is to start with adopted children who display a particular behavior disorder and to examine rates of that disorder in members of the children's biological families compared with rates in their adoptive families. Another strategy is to start with biological parents who exhibit a particular disorder and to examine the rate of disorder in offspring separated from the parent in early childhood and then raised in another household. Rates of disorder in these children can then be compared with a number of comparison groups (e.g., siblings who were not given for adoption and were raised by the biological parent). Also, associations between risk factors, such as family conflict, and behavior problems can be compared in adopted and nonadopted youngsters. Adoption strategies can thus help reveal complex relations between genetic and environmental influences (Braungart-Rieker et al., 1995).

All behavior genetic methods have limitations and potential confounds. For example, in adoption studies, prenatal as well as genetic factors are part of the biological parent's "contribution." Thus greater rates of disorder among biological relatives than among adoptive relatives could be due to prenatal influences. Combinations and refinement of methods, and more sophisticated quantitative analyses, seek to address many of the shortcomings of individual methods. These advances also permit evaluation of hypothetical models of genetic transmission and of the interaction of genetic and environmental influences (Eaves et al., 1997; O'Connor et al., 1998; Plomin, 1995).

Results from behavior genetic research suggest that heritability estimates for behavioral dimensions or disorders rarely exceed 50 percent and that heritability is often appreciably lower than this (Plomin, 1994b). This finding means that substantial variation in behavior is attributable to nongenetic influences. In this way, behavior genetic research has provided evidence for the importance of environmental influence. Influences of family environment that are shared by siblings and that contribute to their development can be revealed (Gjone & Stevenson, 1997b; O'Connor et al., 1998). Behavior genetic research has also highlighted the importance of environmental influences that are not shared by children growing up in the same family. These influences, known as nonshared environment, make children in the same family different from one another. They are also important to the development of behavior disorders (Pike & Plomin, 1996).

Chromosome abnormalities. Approximately 40 percent of spontaneously aborted fetuses are known to have chromosomal abnormalities. Among live births, it has been estimated that 3.52 infants per 1,000 are born with an abnormal number of chromosomes and that 2.23 infants are born with structural abnormalities of the chromosomes (Gath, 1985).

Chromosomes that are aberrant in either number or structure are known to cause death or a variety of deficiencies. These "accidents" are often not inherited, so that they influence only the specific developing embryo. A large number of different chromosomal anomalies have been described. Mental retardation is commonly associated with many of them (Simonoff, Bolton, & Rutter, 1996). Perhaps the most widely recognized disorder attributed to a chromosome aberration is Down syndrome. Characterized by mental deficiency, it is usually caused by an extra #21 chromosome. A group of abnormalities that results from sex chromosome aberrations has also been discovered. These disorders are often characterized by below-average intelligence, atypical sexual development, and other difficulties.

Newer methods of chromosomal analysis, such as staining methods, allow detection of quite subtle abnormalities in size, shape, and other characteristics of portions of chromosomes. Also, the dis-

covery of a group of structural features known as fragile sites has proven helpful in understanding the origins of certain disorders. For example, the fragile X syndrome is due to a fragile site on the X chromosome. This condition is thought to be responsible for many cases of mental retardation (Lombroso et al., 1994; Simonoff et al., 1996).

THE PSYCHODYNAMIC PERSPECTIVE

The psychoanalytic theory of Sigmund Freud was the first modern systematic attempt to understand mental disorders in psychological terms. Trained as a physician and neurologist, Freud drew on his knowledge of biology and the natural sciences to formulate proposals about psychological functioning. He proposed a grand theory of universal principles to explain both normal and abnormal behavior. Freud's ideas went through several transitions during his lifetime, and are now referred to as classical psychoanalytic theory (Kessler, 1988; Wolman, 1972). Only a brief description of this complex and highly systematized theory will be given here.

Although Freud recognized the importance of social influences, he emphasized intrapsychic, or mental, processes in behavioral development. Moreover, he proposed that critical mental processes were unconscious, that is, inaccessible to rational awareness. According to Freud, the mind, or personality, consisted of three mental "structures"—the id, the ego, and the superego—and a fixed amount of psychological energy. His theory described a dynamic process of transfer of this energy among the structures of the mind.

THE STRUCTURES OF THE MIND

The id, present at birth, is the source of all psychic energy. Operating entirely at an unconscious level, the id irrationally seeks immediate and unconditional gratification of all instinctual urges. These instinctual, or biological, impulses are sexual and aggressive in nature. The other psychic structures, the ego and superego, evolve from the id and must obtain their energy from it. The ego is primarily conscious, and its principle task is to mediate between instinctual urges and the reality of the outside world. The mature ego employs its rational, cognitive, decision-making functions to do so. The superego develops when the immature ego cannot handle all conflicts. In order to deal with some of these, the ego incorporates societal standards, and this is the beginning of a separate superego. The superego sets ideal standards for behavior and is the conscience, or self-critical part, of the individual. In trying to satisfy the id's instinctual urges, the ego must consider not only reality but also the ideals of the superego. The psychodynamics of the Freudian perspective arise out of the attempts of these three systems to achieve their frequently conflicting goals. Unconscious conflicts are central to psychological functioning.

PSYCHOSEXUAL STAGES

The psychoanalytic perspective relies on a stage theory of development. As the child develops, the focus of psychic energy passes from one bodily zone to the next, leading the individual through five fixed stages of psychosexual development. Each stage derives its name from the bodily zone that is the primary source of gratification during the period.

The oral stage extends from birth through approximately the first year of life. The mouth is the center of pleasure and the infant is highly dependent on the mother for nurturance. Thus, the central themes of this stage are oral pleasure and interpersonal dependency. The crisis that ends this period is weaning, when the infant must give up some oral pleasures and dependencies.

During the second and third years of life the locus of satisfaction shifts to the anal zone. The retention and expulsion of feces are the major sources of stimulation and pleasure during this anal stage, and toilet training is the major crisis for this period. The period has several themes; primary among them are holding back and giving, which may be reflected, for example, in an ungenerous or generous personality.

During the next period, the phallic stage, the genitals become the focus of pleasure. The chief conflict of this period is the desire to possess the opposite-sex parent and the fear of retaliation

from the same-sex parent. For the boy this conflict is called the Oedipus complex; for the girl it is known as the Electra complex. The resolution of the Oedipal and Electra complexes is central to both sex-role and moral (superego) development.

At about age six, the child enters the latency stage, in which sexual and aggressive impulses are subdued. With puberty, however, these impulses are revived, and the adolescent enters the genital stage, during which heterosexual interests predominate. This stage continues for the remainder of the individual's life. The latency and genital stages are less important to the understanding of behavioral disorders, since Freud suggested that the basic personality structure is laid down by the end of the phallic stage.

According to Freud, the child is hindered in development by not more-or-less resolving the crises or conflicts at any one stage. Failure to reach resolution results in the individual becoming psychologically fixated at the stage. Fixation adversely affects development at all subsequent stages.

ANXIETY AND THE DEFENSE MECHANISMS

From the psychoanalytic perspective, the concept of anxiety is crucial to the development of disordered behavior. Anxiety is the danger signal to the ego that some unacceptable id impulse is seeking to gain consciousness. To protect itself from anxiety, the ego creates defense mechanisms such as repression, projection, displacement, and reaction formation. These mechanisms mostly function to deny or distort unacceptable impulses. Although they may be adaptive, defense mechanisms may also generate psychological symptoms. (See "Little Hans . . .".)

CRITICISMS AND MODIFICATIONS OF PSYCHOANALYTIC THEORY

Classical psychoanalytic theory has been modified by a number of workers. Probably the best known of these are the so-called neo-Freudians who minimized the importance of sexual forces and stressed the importance of social influences; they include Karen Horney, Erich Fromm, Harry Stack Sullivan, and Erik Erikson. Others, such as Freud's daughter Anna, remained more loyal to the ortho-

LITTLE HANS: A CLASSIC PSYCHOANALYTIC CASE

One of Freud's most frequently cited cases, the case of "Little Hans," illustrated both Freud's conceptualization of symptoms as arising from defense mechanisms and of the phallic stage of development. The case has served as a model for the psychoanalytic interpretation of childhood phobias even though Freud saw Hans only once, and worked primarily through the boy's father (Freud, 1909–1953).

Hans was very affectionate toward his mother and enjoyed spending time "cuddling" with her. When Hans was almost five, he returned from his daily walk with his nursemaid frightened, crying, and wanting to cuddle with his mother. The next day, when the mother herself took him for the walk, Hans expressed a fear of being bitten by a horse, and that evening insisted on cuddling with his mother. He cried about having to go out the next day and expressed considerable fear concerning the horse. These symptoms, which continued to get worse, were interpreted by Freud as reflecting the child's sexual impulses toward his mother

and his fear of castration by the father. The ego began its defenses against these unacceptable impulses by repressing Hans's wish to attack his father, his rival for his mother's affection. This was an attempt to make the unacceptable impulse unconscious. The next step was projection: Hans believed that his father wished to attack him, rather than that he wished to attack his father. The final step was displacement. The horse was viewed as dangerous, not the father. According to Freud, the choice of the horse as a symbol of the father was due to numerous associations of horses with Hans's father. For example, the black muzzle and the blinders on the horse were viewed as symbolic of the father's mustache and eyeglasses. The fear Hans displaced onto the horse permitted the child's ambivalent feelings toward the father to be resolved. He could now love his father. In addition, thinking of horses as the source of anxiety allowed Hans to avoid anxiety by simply avoiding horses (Kessler, 1966).

---

dox tradition, but elaborated and emphasized the role of the ego in development.

Despite the many modifications of Freud's original theory, this general perspective has been severely criticized on both conceptual and methodological grounds. For example, psychoanalytic formulations rest primarily on the impressions and recollections of clinical cases. They also involve large inferential leaps from what is observed to what is interpreted as existing. In addition, the mechanisms Freud postulated are intrapsychic and often unconscious and are therefore difficult, if not impossible, to investigate. Thus, much of the criticism of psychanalytic theory has rested on its

untestability. However, criticism has come on other grounds as well.

Those working within the psychoanalytic tradition today have attempted to expand their methodologies. For example, the use of systematic observation has been attempted. Some workers in this tradition have also attempted to incorporate recent research findings on infant and child development into their conceptualizations (Shapiro & Esman, 1992; Zeanah et al., 1989).

Psychoanalytic theory was the dominant approach to childhood psychopathology during the first half of the twentieth century, and activity continues based on the conceptualizations and treatments derived from this viewpoint (Bemporad, 1991; Target & Fonagy, 1994). Although its influence has waned, among its contributions is drawing attention to the importance of mental processes, anxiety and other emotions, infant and early childhood experiences, and child-parent relationships.

THE BEHAVIORAL/SOCIAL LEARNING PERSPECTIVE

The central concept of the behavioral/social learning perspective is that childhood disorders are learned in the same way that other behaviors are learned. As indicated in Chapter 1, the publication of John B. Watson's essay "Psychology as a Behaviorist Views It" (1913) set into motion a perspective that would serve as the major rival to the psychoanalytic position. Although this perspective was also a broad one, it differed from the psychoanalytic paradigm in a number of key ways. Unlike Freud, Watson emphasized observable events rather than unconscious intrapsychic conflicts. Developed in the psychological laboratory rather than in a clinical setting, the behavioral perspective heavily emphasized objective empirical verification. Learning and the influence of the environment were seen as the appropriate focus of study. Furthermore, development was viewed as a continuous process rather than as a fixed sequence of

stages. The assumption was made that learning continues throughout the life span and therefore that "personality" is not set by a certain age. Finally, unlike classical psychoanalytic theory, the behavioral perspective did not develop as a single comprehensive theory aimed at explaining all behavior. Rather, a number of theories, often employing similar language but each describing a different aspect of the learning process, were suggested.

CLASSICAL CONDITIONING

Pavlov's demonstrations of dogs learning to salivate to previously neutral stimuli served to focus attention on the process of classical conditioning. Two early studies based on this model stand out because of the great impact they had on the application of classical conditioning to human problems. Watson and Rayner's (1920) now famous case of Little Albert was an early illustration of the conditioning of fear. Albert, an eleven-month-old child, initially showed no fear reactions to a variety of objects, including a white rat. He did, however, exhibit fear when a loud sound was produced by the striking of a steel bar. Watson and Rayner attempted to condition fear of the white rat by producing the loud clanging sound each time Albert reached for the animal. After several of these pairings, Albert reacted with crying and avoidance when the rat was presented without the noise (see Figure 3-3). Thus it appeared that fear could be

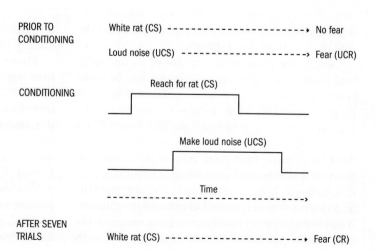

FIGURE 3-3 Watson and Rayner's case of Little Albert. The repeated pairing of an unconditioned stimulus (noise) that produced fear with a previously neutral stimulus (rat) resulted in the rat itself producing a conditioned response of fear.

learned through classical conditioning. Needless to say, there are significant ethical difficulties with conducting studies such as Watson and Rayner's, and therefore behavioral researchers have tended to focus their attention on applying classical conditioning principles to the treatment of disorders.

The second landmark study was Mary Cover Jones's (1924) demonstration that the principles of classical conditioning could be applied to the removal of fearful responses. Peter, a boy of two years and ten months, exhibited a fear of furry objects. Jones first attempted to treat Peter by placing him with a rabbit, along with children who liked the rabbit and petted it. The treatment appeared to be working but was interrupted when Peter became ill for nearly two months. Just prior to his return to treatment, he was also frightened by a large dog. With Peter's fear back at its original level, Jones decided to treat Peter with a counterconditioning procedure, which involved allowing Peter to eat some of his favorite foods while the animal was moved progressively closer, thus pairing the feared stimulus with pleasantness. The procedure was apparently successful in reducing the boy's fears, and he was ultimately able to hold the animal by himself.

This case demonstration lacks sufficient control, and we cannot draw conclusions regarding the effectiveness of the procedures derived from classical conditioning. Of additional concern is Jones's inclusion of nonfearful children in treatment sessions. Did the presence of the children, like that of the food, make the situation pleasant, or did they also serve as models for nonfearful behavior? Despite these limitations, Jones's contribution was important and stimulated the development of numerous treatments based on the principles of classical conditioning.

OPERANT CONDITIONING

The approach to learning set forth in Thorndike's Law of Effect and in the work of B. F. Skinner and his followers is probably the behavioral perspective most extensively applied to children's disorders. Operant, or instrumental, conditioning emphasizes the consequences of behavior. Behavior is acquired or reduced, and it is emitted in some circumstances but not in others, through reinforce-

ment, extinction, punishment, and other learning processes (see Table 3-1). As for classical conditioning, the majority of efforts derived from operant conditioning have focused on the treatment rather than the etiology of disordered behavior.

The principles of operant conditioning have increasingly been applied to a broad range of difficult and complex problems, and the treatment procedures themselves have become more varied and complex. The specific applications of these procedures will be discussed throughout the succeeding chapters of this book. The applications all share the assumption that problem behavior can be changed through a learning process and that the focus of treatment should be on the consequences of behavior. Central to this approach also is the concept of functional assessment. In Chapter 5 and throughout the book, we will see that there are many ways to assess problem behavior (e.g., interview, observation, self-report). Functional assessment asks, "What is the function of the child's problem behavior within her or his environment?" The same behavior problem may serve different functions in the same or different children. For example, a child's refusing to go to school can serve a number of different functions (Kearney & Silverman, 1996). It may serve to

1. avoid stimuli that provoke negative affective responses (e.g., classrooms, teachers, buses);
2. escape from aversive social/evaluative situations (e.g., public speaking, peer interactions);
3. gain attention (e.g., through tantrums, noncompliance, clinging); and/or
4. allow access to tangible rewards (watching television, special foods).

Functional assessment seeks to gain an understanding of what leads to the behavior and what contributes to its recurrence. This understanding provides insight into the function that the behavior problem is serving and suggests possible treatment interventions.

OBSERVATIONAL LEARNING

The investigator most widely associated with observational learning, or modeling, is Albert Bandura, who, along with his associates, has conducted a

TABLE 3-1

Some Fundamental Operant Conditioning Processes

Term	Definition	Example
Positive reinforcement	A stimulus is presented following a response (*contingent upon the response*), increasing the frequency of that response.	Praise for good behavior increases the likelihood of good behavior.
Negative reinforcement	A stimulus is withdrawn contingent upon a response, and its removal increases the frequency of that response.	Removal of mother's demands following a child's tantrum increases the likelihood of tantrums.
Extinction	A weakening of a learned response is produced when the reinforcement that followed it no longer occurs.	Parents ignore bad behavior, and it decreases.
Punishment	A response is followed by either an unpleasant stimulus or the removal of a pleasant stimulus, thereby decreasing the frequency of the response.	A parent scolds a child for hitting, and the child stops hitting; food is removed from the table after a child spits, and the spitting stops.
Generalization	A response is made to a new stimulus that is different from, but similar to, the stimulus present during learning.	A child is fearful of all men with mustaches like that of a stern uncle.
Discrimination	The process by which a stimulus comes to signal that a certain response is likely to be followed by a particular consequence.	An adult's smile indicates that a child's request is likely to be granted.
Shaping	A desired behavior that is not in the child's repertoire is taught by rewarding responses that are increasingly similar to (*successive approximations of*) the desired response.	A mute child is taught to talk by initially reinforcing any sound, then something that sounds a little like the word, and so on.

large number of studies that bear on the genesis and treatment of childhood disorders. It has been demonstrated that children can acquire a variety of behaviors—aggression, cooperation, delay of gratification, sharing—by watching others perform them. These studies suggest how observational learning can lead to both the acquisition and the removal of problem behaviors.

Studies by Bandura and his colleagues on children's imitation of aggressive behavior illustrate how a problem behavior may be acquired through the observation of a model. In one well-known experiment, Bandura (1965) showed nursery school children a five-minute film in which an adult exhibited a number of unusual, aggressive behaviors toward a Bobo doll. The behaviors were also accompanied by distinctive verbalizations. One group of children saw a final scene in which the model was rewarded for aggression; another group saw a final scene in which the model was punished; and the remaining group did not see any final scene. Later each child was left alone to play in a room containing the Bobo doll and other toys. The child could engage in imitative aggressive behavior or in nonimitative behavior. As you might expect, the children who had seen the model punished exhibited fewer imitative aggressive responses in the playroom. The experimenter then reentered the room and told each child that for each aggressive behavior like the model's that he or she could reproduce, a treat would be given. All three groups now showed the same high level of imitative aggression. The study demonstrated that acquisition of the aggressive behavior had occurred and, moreover, that its performance depended on certain environmental "payoffs."

Although the phenomenon of observational learning seems straightforward and simple, it is actually quite complex. Numerous variables influence the imitative process. For example, multiple models, conflicting models, and attributes of the models themselves can affect whether imitation will occur. In addition to direct imitation of modeled behavior, observation can lead to generalized inhibition or disinhibition of behavior. For example, a child who observes another child's being scolded for running about may become quieter in other ways (inhibition). Observing a great deal of shooting and fighting on television, in contrast, may lead a child to exhibit other forms of aggression, such as verbal abuse and physical roughness, with peers (disinhibition). In neither case is the exact behavior of the model imitated; rather, a class of behaviors becomes less or more likely to occur because of observation of a model.

Whether imitation is specific or generalized, complex processes are required for observational learning to occur (Bandura, 1977b). Such learning relies on the child's attending to the salient features of the model's behavior. The child must also organize and encode this information and remember it. The acquired behavior must then be performed when it is anticipated that it will meet with desired consequences. The process of learning by observation is viewed by Bandura and others as more than a simple mimicking of behavior. The social learning perspective that has developed from this and other research has placed increasing emphasis on cognitive processes such as attention, memory, and problem solving (Rosenthal, 1984).

COGNITIVE INFLUENCES

Cognitive processes are an important aspect of contemporary psychology and of conceptualizing the behavior problems of children and adolescents. The tendencies to think negatively, misperceive social cues, make faulty attributions regarding the causes of events and behavior, and fail to enact adequate problem solving are examples of cognitive processes hypothesized to be related to behavioral disorders. For example, thinking negatively about the self, the world, and the future

(Beck, 1976) and viewing oneself as helpless (Abramson, Seligman, & Teasdale, 1978) are examples of cognitive views of depression that have influenced current thinking. Cognitive models of how disorders develop and are maintained, as well as interventions based on cognitive views, have continued to evolve (Beck, 1993; Mahoney, 1993; Spence, 1994). One particular perspective influenced by the cognitive trend in psychology that has contributed to the understanding and treatment of child and adolescent problems is the cognitive-behavioral perspective.

As indicated earlier, behaviorally oriented clinicians such as Bandura began to suggest that increased attention be paid to the role of cognitive processes (Kendall, 1993; Meichenbaum, 1993). This integrated model, which came to be known as the cognitive-behavioral perspective, is integrative in that it appreciates that a number of influences operate in an interactive manner. The cognitive-behavioral approach incorporates and emphasizes behavior, cognition, affect, and social factors in understanding behavior problems and their treatment (Kendall et al., 1997). From this perspective, behaviors are learned and maintained by interacting systems of external events and cognitions, and cognitive factors influence whether environmental events are attended to, how events are perceived, and whether these events affect future behavior. The cognitive part of this interaction is based on the assumption that maladaptive cognitions contribute to maladaptive behavior. As an example of support for this hypothesis, maladaptive thoughts and beliefs have been found among phobic and anxious children. For example, in test situations, test-phobic youngsters frequently report more off-task thoughts, more negative self-evaluations, and fewer positive self-evaluations (Ollendick & King, 1998).

Bandura's (1977b) examination of imitative learning, Camp's "Think Aloud" program applying a mediational approach to decrease aggressive behavior and increase prosocial behavior in aggressive boys (Camp et al., 1977), and Meichenbaum and Goodman's (1971) training program to teach impulsive children to "think before they act," are some early examples of these efforts. The sequence of steps in Meichenbaum and Goodman's self-instructional training and an example of the instructions that the child was taught to verbalize illustrate this approach.

1. While the child watches, an adult model self-instructs aloud while performing the desired task.
2. The child performs the task as the adult instructs aloud.
3. The child self-instructs aloud while performing the task.
4. The child whispers the instructions while doing the task.
5. The child uses private speech to guide performance.
6. The number of self-statements employed by the child is then enlarged over several training sessions.

Okay, what is it that I have to do? You want me to copy the picture with the different lines. I have to go slow and be careful. Okay, draw the line down, down, good; then to the right, that's it; now down some more and to the left. Good. I'm doing fine so far. Now back up again. No. I was supposed to go down. That's okay. Just erase the line carefully . . . Good. Even if I make an error I can go slowly and carefully. Okay, I have to go down now. Finished. I did it. (Meichenbaum & Goodman, 1971, p. 117.)

Kendall (1991; Kendall et al., 1997) suggests that the various and complex cognitive functions hypothesized to contribute to the development, maintenance, and treatment of behavior disorders can be organized in terms of four components: cognitive content, cognitive processes (operations), cognitive products, and cognitive structure. Kendall also suggests that a further way of distinguishing cognitive functioning is to differentiate between cognitive deficiencies and cognitive distortions. These concepts are described and defined in Table 3-2. Various illustrations of the ways in which cognitive influences contribute to the development and treatment of child and adolescent behavior disorders are presented throughout the book.

A SYSTEMS APPROACH

The child or adolescent is often viewed as imbedded within a number of systems, such as the peer group, the school, the neighborhood, and the

---

TABLE 3-2

Cognitive Terms and Concepts

Cognitive structures. Sometimes also referred to as schema, these are the internal organization and the manner in which information is represented in memory. Anxious children and adolescents, for example, may have a dominant schema of threat and may be prone to see impending danger, loss, criticism, and the like.

Cognitive content. This refers to the specific self-talk and information that is stored in memory.

Cognitive process. This refers to how experiences are perceived and interpreted. Descriptions of procedures used by aggressive children in processing information, such as encoding of cues, interpretation of those cues, selection of goals, constructing a response, evaluation and expectation of response, and enactment of behavior, are examples of cognitive process.

Cognitive products. These are the results of the structure, content, and process. Attributions and the way that the child explains the causes of behavior are examples of cognitive products. The tendency of aggressive children to attribute hostile intent to their peers is a specific example of a cognitive product.

Cognitive deficiencies. These refer to an absence of thinking. The lack of forethought and planning that was targeted in the self-instructional program for impulsive children by Meichenbaum and Goodman is an example.

Cognitive distortions. These refer to thought processes that are dysfunctional. Depressed children viewing themselves as less capable than their peers even though others do not is an example of cognitive distortion.

---

larger societal context. A systems approach views the youngster and these systems as being involved in an ongoing reciprocal relationship—the youngster, for example, is both influenced by and influences the peer group; the peer group is both influenced by and influences the school, and so on. These relationships can be conceptualized in a number of ways. Figure 3-4 illustrates some potential systems and one potential way in which this notion of reciprocal and ongoing system influences might be depicted. Another aspect of the notion of systems is that the "problem" is not necessarily "owned" by the child but rather can be viewed as a system that is not functioning adaptively with respect to the goals for that particular youngster. A youngster with problems may drift into a peer group that supports antisocial behavior and poor

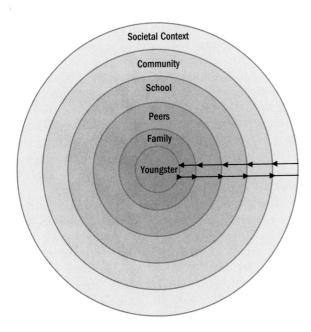

FIGURE 3-4 The youngster is embedded in a number of systems that influence and are influenced by each other. Such reciprocal influence may occur between any number of these systems and the youngster.

academic functioning. A school system with a large number of problem youngsters may decide that it needs to group them together in classes and may thereby help to sustain the problematic behavior. Such a perspective suggests the importance of studying not only individual variables but also aspects of the systems themselves. The family is the system that has probably received the greatest attention.

THE FAMILY SYSTEM

Virtually all approaches to behavior disorders acknowledge the family as having a major impact, and we shall see throughout the book how family factors contribute to behavior problems in children and adolescents. The focus in the majority of these approaches, however, has remained on the designated child. In contrast, if the family is viewed from a systems perspective, the family unit, rather than the individual, is the appropriate "organism" to study and treat.

There are a number of different family systems perspectives that have informed clinical work with the families of children and adolescents (Johnson, Rasbury, & Siegel, 1997), but a review of these is beyond the scope of this chapter. Most of these perspectives, however, have developed within the context of treatment, and thus they have focused on family themes or styles of communication that are to be addressed in therapy. For example, families of antisocial youngsters have been viewed as coercive. The family has developed a coercive style of relating and it is this pattern of interaction that contributes to the development and maintenance of the problematic behavior of the designated youngster. Treatment should then have as a focus modifying this coercive style of relating among family members. A number of concepts that describe family systems have been developed (e.g., cohesion, control, organization, conflict), and families' ways of relating are described in these terms. A particular way of relating and the flexibility of that style may or may not be adaptive regarding goals for a youngster's development and functioning. High levels of cohesion and a hierarchical pattern of control may be adaptive with younger children but may be less adaptive as an adolescent desires to balance time between family and friends and seeks greater autonomy. Higher levels of organization and greater control may be needed in a family with a diabetic youngster faced with a complex and precise pattern of medical regimen than is optimal for her or his nondiabetic peer. The study of such family systems variables, their interaction with other influences, and the value of viewing the family as a system, have proven informative in the study of child and adolescent behavior disorders.

THE SCHOOL AND EDUCATIONAL SYSTEM

Like the family, the school is a system that the child must encounter on a daily basis, and thus the school is also an important arena for intervention and prevention services for children (Durlak, 1997; Weist, 1997). Also, like the family, the school/educational system has a long-standing history as an important influence on youth. Much of this influence has focused on working with youngsters in an educational context and is sometimes referred to as a psychoeducational approach.

The term "special education" has also been used to describe the efforts of educators to deal with the problems of atypical children. That the vast majority of children receive extended formal education as a right rather than as a privilege is a given in today's society. This has not always been the case, nor has education always been assigned an important role in dealing with children's problems (Fagan, 1992).

Lilly (1979c) has provided an overview of the history of special education. The initial view of the special education approach, particularly for the mentally retarded, was optimistic. Residential treatment centers were developed to prepare handicapped individuals to return to the community. Residential schools evolved, however, into permanent residences for the more severely handicapped children. Moreover, little attention was given to persons whose problems were milder. Compulsory education laws then forced the educational systems to provide services for the less severely handicapped.

Another development—the construction of general tests of intelligence—had a long-lasting and far-reaching impact on special education. These tests defined a new group of mildly handicapping conditions. The presence of children with "milder" conditions in the school systems led to the development of special classes. With expansion of services, legislation for mandatory special education, and the development of university-based research and training programs, special educational services experienced rapid growth beginning in the 1950s.

Subsequent changes in special education occurred as a result of court cases and legislation. Many of these changes initially arose out of concern for the mentally retarded (MacMillan, 1982). However, the principles evolved have been extended to other problems. In 1975 the delivery of special services was dramatically affected by P.L. 94–142, The Education for All Handicapped Children Act. This influential law and the application of the psychoeducational perspective will be dis-

cussed in more detail later in the book. However, it is appropriate to recognize here two matters that have been of particular importance (Lilly, 1979a; MacMillan & Kavale, 1986). One point is that special educators have been prominent in questioning the need to employ traditional categories or special labels with children. Special educators have often led the fight against the use of categorization and for the recognition of the role of social and environmental factors in the etiology of childhood problems.

The second matter is the issue of whether children should be placed in special classes (Sylva, 1994). Although special classes were originally developed to help children who were not succeeding in regular classrooms, a number of educators began to question their efficacy (Dunn, 1968). Whether children with problems should be placed in special classrooms or instead included or "mainstreamed" into the regular school system remains a complex and controversial question with far-reaching implications. Drawing attention to this concern is one of the continuing contributions of the psychoeducational approach.

MODES OF TREATMENT

As we indicated earlier, the perspective that a therapist adopts affects the style of the therapy offered. Thus, for example, a professional with a behavioral or social-learning perspective is likely to offer treatments that are action oriented, focus on present problems, and assume that therapy is a learning process governed by principles common to all learning situations.

Another approach to conceptualizing treatments is by means of what we will term the mode of treatment, that is, how services are delivered. For example, as we indicated previously, therapists operating from a variety of theoretical perspectives advocate for the inclusion of the family in treatment. Thus working with the family is a mode of treatment employed by therapists from a variety of perspectives. Treatment of children is delivered in a variety of other modes as well. Indeed, particu-

Working with children in an educational context and a commitment to education as a means of intervention characterize the psychoeducational approach.

(Courtesy of A.C. Israel)

larly as child and adolescent disorders come to be seen as arising out of a combination of influences, any one therapist is likely to employ several different modes of treatment, and in treating a particular child, the therapist may use a combination of these modes (e.g., Tuma & Pratt, 1982).

Therapists may see the young client in individual one-to-one sessions. These sessions may resemble the verbal interchanges of adult sessions; or particularly with young children, play may be the primary mode of interaction between the therapist and the child. But therapists may also spend relatively little time with the child and may focus instead on training the parents to work with the child. Such parent training may have the added benefit of providing general parenting skills that will be useful in other situations or with other children. Sometimes various members of the family are seen in separate individual treatment. Alternatively, the therapist may choose to work with the family as a unit. Often consultation is given to significant other adults who work with the child—a teacher, for example. In addition, various forms of

treatment may be delivered in a group rather than in an individual format. Medications may also be employed in the treatment of children and adolescents.

The modes indicated here are only some of the forms of treatment employed in working with youth. In this section, we will briefly present an overview of some of the most commonly used modes of treatment. In later chapters, we will present specific examples of these modes as they are employed with particular problems.

INDIVIDUAL AND GROUP PSYCHOTHERAPY

The typical view of psychotherapy is that it is a one-to-one verbal experience. With adults this is the most common mode of treatment. However, treatment in groups has also been offered by therapists from a variety of theoretical perspectives. The same assumptions and methods that guide individual therapies may be used, but in a group format. Although the group format may be selected in order to offer services to larger numbers of children and adolescents, there are other rationales for this choice (Johnson, Rasbury, & Siegel, 1997). Groups offer the opportunity for socialization experiences not present in the individual mode. Also, group treatment may be more appealing to the child or adolescent because it is less threatening, demonstrates that peers have difficulties, and often includes opportunities for activities not likely to occur in one-to-one relationships with an adult therapist.

Whether in individual or group format, treatments that would be described as verbal forms of psychotherapy are a major form of intervention, particularly with older children and adolescents. However, the need to alter treatment procedures to fit the child's level of cognitive and emotional development is one factor that has produced nonverbal modes of working with children.

PLAY THERAPY

A common mode is the use of play as a therapeutic vehicle. This use is consistent with the importance of play in the development of young children (Rubin, Fein, & Vandenberg, 1983; Smith, 1988). Play as a mode of therapy is, for many therapists, a solution to the lesser verbal abilities of the child. Rather than relying exclusively on abstract verbal interactions, the therapist uses play to help concretize communications. As a means of communication, play is used in therapy by most practitioners. However, using play itself as a therapeutic vehicle and play therapy as a more structured and distinct approach to treatment also exists (Russ, 1995; Ablon, 1996). The two most well-known perspectives on play therapy are derived from the psychodynamic and the client-centered perspectives.

Play therapy was the focus of a controversy between two of the principal and early developers of child treatment from a psychoanalytic perspective. Early analysts agreed that change was needed in analytic techniques in order effectively to treat children. This idea led to the use of play as a mechanism for children to express their thoughts and feelings. However, among the controversies that arose was whether to view children's play as the equivalent of verbal free association that is central in adult therapy. Also, there was disagreement over the psychoanalytic interpretation of children's play.

Melanie Klein (1932) was one of the first therapists to emphasize play in the treatment of children, and her ideas gained wide popularity. She used the term "play therapy" to refer to the process whereby the child's play was used as the basis for psychoanalytic interpretation, much as verbal free association was used in the psychoanalysis of adults. Anna Freud (1946) disagreed with the emphasis and significance given to play by Klein and others. Anna Freud viewed play as only one potential mode of expression. Moreover, she felt that although the child did express emotions and thoughts through play, these should not be cognitively equated with the purposeful production of free association by adults.

The two women also disagreed on the interpretation of the material derived from play. Klein placed a heavy emphasis on symbolic interpretation of play and gave it a prominent role throughout the psychoanalytic process. Anna Freud, in contrast, gave less emphasis to play interpretation and did not see it as always symbolizing conflict. She, for example, disagreed with Klein that a child's opening a lady's handbag symbolically expresses curiosity regarding the contents of the mother's womb. Rather, the child may be responding to an experience on the previous day when someone brought a present in a similar receptacle (A. Freud, 1946). The contemporary psychoanalytic position tends to favor Anna Freud's positions on play and other issues (Johnson et al., 1997). Indeed, the term "play therapy" as it is used today refers to child treatment in which play is the major mode of expression, regardless of the therapist's orientation, rather than to Melanie Klein's more narrow definition.

Another major influence on the evolution of play therapy was the work of Virginia Axline, who developed her approach from the client-centered perspective associated with Carl Rogers. The basic principles outlined by Axline (1947) remain the guidelines for contemporary client-centered play therapy (Johnson et al., 1997). The principles of the client-centered approach are the same for adults and children of varying ages. The therapist

The use of play as a mode of therapy is common with younger children. Play allows for the establishment of rapport, but it also provides a means of communication more age-appropriate than verbal forms of therapy.

(David Young-Wolf/PhotoEdit)

makes adjustments in communication style to create the appropriate accepting, permissive, and nondirective therapeutic environment. The use of play with young children helps to create such an environment.

PARENT TRAINING

Many professionals have taken the position that change in the child's behavior may best be achieved by producing changes in the way that the parents manage the child. This viewpoint is consistent with the observation that it may often be the parent's perception, along with the child's actual behavior, that results in children being referred for treatment.

Parent training procedures have been applied to a wide variety of childhood problems. A number of approaches have emerged, and a number of popular books appear on the shelves of bookstores everywhere. However, in terms of systematic applications and research, most work has come from the social learning/behavioral approach.

Behavioral parent training has received a great deal of clinical and research attention, and a number of reviews and discussions have appeared (Dangel & Polster, 1984; Kazdin, 1997; McMahon & Wells, 1998). Original efforts focused on teaching parents to manage the consequences, or contingencies, that they applied to children's behavior. More recent approaches include a wider variety of skills, such as skills in verbal communication and expression of emotion. In addition, investigators have found that stressors such as socioeconomic disadvantage, single parent status, social isolation, and maternal depression are related to poorer outcome of parent training (Forehand, Furey, & McMahon, 1984; Israel, Silverman, & Solotar, 1986; Wahler & Dumas, 1984; Webster-Stratton, 1985). This finding has led to the examination of a variety of modifications to existing programs (Webster-Stratton, 1994). In addition, parent training is frequently employed as part of a multifaceted approach to treatment. Other components may include additional therapeutic work with the parent, direct work with the child, or work with the teacher and the school.

TREATMENT IN RESIDENTIAL SETTINGS

Residential treatment is usually considered a mode of intervention for severe behavior problems (Johnson et al., 1997). The problems may be so difficult to treat that working with the youths on an outpatient basis does not provide enough contact or control. Also, there may be a concern that children may harm themselves or others and, therefore, that closer supervision is necessary. The child may also be removed from the home because circumstances there are highly problematic, suggesting that successful interventions could not be achieved at home. Unfortunately, the lack of availability of alternative placements can result in children's being institutionalized when interventions in less restrictive environments, like group or foster homes, might be successful. On the other hand, treatment in residential settings is often undertaken when other modes of intervention have not proven successful.

Residential treatment may occur in group homes, child psychiatry units in medical hospitals, units in nonmedical settings, and juvenile facilities that are part of the legal/judicial system. Treatment in such settings usually involves a variety of services, including therapeutic, educational, and vocational interventions. Because programs differ so much in what the actual content is, they have been difficult to evaluate, and therefore we know less than we would like about their effectiveness (Johnson et al., 1997; Kazdin, 1985).

PHARMACOLOGICAL TREATMENT

Pharmacological treatments (medications) are part of the interventions employed for a variety of childhood and adolescent behavior disorders (Johnson et al., 1997; Werry & Aman, 1999). Psychopharmacological agents are often employed in combination with other modes of treatment. Medications that affect mood, thought processes, or overt behavior are known as psychotropic or psychoactive, and thus the term "psychopharmacological treatment" is often employed. Examples of some of the pharmacological agents frequently employed in the treatment of children and adolescents include stimulants (e.g., methylphenidate—Ritalin) for Attention Deficit Hyperactivity Disorder; antipsychotics (e.g., clozapine, risperidone) for schizophrenia; and selective serotonin reuptake inhibitors (SSRIs, e.g., clomipramine) for Obsessive-Compulsive Disorder.

Psychotropic drugs produce their therapeutic effects by their influence on the process of neurotransmission. Poling, Gadow, and Cleary (1991) describe some of the ways that these medications can affect neurotransmission:

1. By altering the body's production of a neurotransmitter.
2. By interfering with the storage of a neurotransmitter.
3. By altering the release of a neurotransmitter.
4. By interfering with the inactivation of a neurotransmitter or the reuptake of a neurotransmitter.
5. By interacting with receptors for a neurotransmitter.

For some psychoactive drugs, there is a specific and clearly hypothesized mechanism for their action, whereas for others, the specific reasons for their effectiveness are unknown. The action of certain drugs in producing antipsychotic effects is an example of a mechanism of action that has been specified. A lock-and-key analogy can be employed to describe how these drugs act by blocking receptors for the neurotransmitter dopamine (Poling et al., 1991). The molecules of the neuroleptic (antipsychotic) drug and dopamine are similar, but not identical, keys. The receptor is the lock. The dopamine key fits the receptor lock perfectly and can unlock it and affect transmission to the neuron on which the receptor is located. The neuroleptic key, in contrast, will enter the dopamine receptor lock but will not unlock it. This imperfectly fitting key does, however, prevent dopamine from entering the receptor. Thus dopamine molecules are prevented from combining with receptors and affecting neurotransmission. Blocking dopamine's function is thus the mechanism by which certain antipsychotic agents are presumed to have their therapeutic action.

The use of psychoactive drugs, support for their effectiveness, and their presumed mechanisms of action will be discussed in later chapters dealing with specific disorders.

SUMMARY

■ This chapter introduces the major views or perspectives that have guided investigators of behavior disorders in youth. Rather than there being grand theories competing against each other, it is currently appreciated that a complex interplay of a variety of influences is involved in the development of behavior disorders in children and adolescents.

■ The biological perspective has addressed a number of influences. The structural integrity of the brain, the biochemical functioning of the nervous system, and genetic influences are being investigated.

■ The role of teratogens has been of particular interest regarding prenatal damage to the nervous system. Perinatal and later influences are also important.

■ Neurotransmitters and the neuroendocrine system are critical aspects of the role of nervous system functioning in the development of behavior disorders.

■ Hereditary influences on behavior disorders are likely to involve multiple genes. Molecular genetics seeks to find specific genes that influence behavior disorders. Methods such as linkage and association are employed in this effort. The methods of behavior genetics (family, twin, adoption studies) have been employed to estimate heritability of behavioral disorders, but they also suggest the importance of the environment. A number of disorders, such as Down syndrome, are attributable to chromosomal abnormalities.

■ The role of learning is central to the behavioral/social learning perspective. This approach involves a number of learning theories. Principles of classical and operant conditioning and observational learning have all contributed to the application of this perspective to problems displayed by young people.

■ Investigation of the influences of cognition has emphasized how cognitive structures, content, processes, and products have informed our approach to understanding and treating behavior disorders.

■ A systems approach emphasizes that a youngster is embedded in a number of systems that reciprocally influence each other and the youngster.

■ The influence of the family on the child and on the adolescent is broadly acknowledged. Viewing the family as a system emphasizes how the family maintains behavior problems and therefore should be a focus of intervention.

■ The psychoeducational perspective highlights how aspects of education affect child and adolescent disorders. Mandatory education, special education, and issues such as mainstreaming/inclusion have been central themes of this perspective.

■ Various modes of treatment for children, adolescents, and their families are available. Individual therapy, group therapy, play, parent training, residential placement, and psychopharmacological treatments are all modes of treatment that have been applied to a variety of child and adolescent problems.

CHAPTER 4

RESEARCH: ITS ROLE
AND METHODS

I n preceding chapters, we saw how the developmental approach and theoretical perspectives of psychopathology provide frameworks for the investigation of problem behaviors. An enormous amount of research is being conducted to test various hypotheses and otherwise to study dysfunction in young people. This chapter discusses the role of research and major methods of investigation. Basic research designs and strategies are described, and examples of their applications are provided. Research methods vary along several dimensions, but all aim to go beyond commonsense speculation to objective, reliable knowledge.

THE NATURE OF SCIENCE

The word "science" comes from the Latin word for "knowledge," or to know, but refers to knowledge gained by a particular method of inquiry. The application of the scientific method to human behavior is a relatively recent historical event. Humans have long considered themselves special creatures,

too complicated and mysterious for scientific study. Even today we hear that scientific inquiry might be inappropriate or perhaps even dangerous when applied to humans. For the most part, though, we have come to value the products of science, such as e-mail and lifesaving medicines, and what science can tell us about ourselves and the world. Psychology and related disciplines are committed to the view that the scientific method can provide the most valid information about human functioning, behavior, and development.

The overall purpose of science is to describe phenomena and to offer explanations for them. The investigators of behavioral disturbance ask a melange of questions about normal and problem behaviors. Consider the variation of important questions reflected in the following list, as brief as it is.

- What percentage of children are at risk for developing behavior disorders?

- Is parents' use of physical punishment as a means of disciplining their children related to the development of childhood behavior problems?

- Are there ways in which the classroom can be enriched so as to help children with learning disabilities?

- Does child abuse make it more likely that children will have emotional problems in adulthood?
- What causes depression?
- Do gender differences exist in psychopathology?

Sometimes it is necessary only to count or to describe cases to answer such questions. At other times, it is necessary to determine the exact conditions under which a phenomenon occurs and its relationship to other variables. Often we want to determine cause-and-effect relationships to understand better and to be able to predict behavior.

Researchers rarely, if ever, simply pose and try to answer questions in an intellectual vacuum. Rather, they call on theories to guide their endeavors. A *theory* is an integrated set of propositions to explain phenomena. Theoretical concepts and assumptions guide research goals, choice of variables, procedures, analyses, and conclusions. In the early stage of research, theoretical concepts may be little more than hunches or guesses based on informal observations, whereas later they may be more developed and specific. Some subjectivity and creativity are always involved in generating research questions and in deciding how best to seek answers.

It is common to try to test specific *hypotheses*—tentative assumptions—derived from theory. Hypothesis testing is valuable in that it tends to build knowledge systematically rather than haphazardly. Any one investigation rarely proves that a hypothesis is either correct or incorrect; instead, it provides evidence for or against the hypothesis. In turn, a hypothesis that is supported serves as evidence for the accuracy and explanatory power of the underlying theory. A failed hypothesis, in contrast, serves to disprove, limit, or redirect the theory. Thus observations and theories work together to advance scientific understanding.

Just as researchers ask a variety of questions, they work in a variety of settings, ranging from the natural environments of the home or school to the more controlled laboratory. Similarly, different methods and designs are used, depending on the purposes of the research—and on ethics and practicality, too. In all cases, however, observation and measurement, reliability, and validity are important considerations.

OBSERVATION AND MEASUREMENT

At the heart of scientific endeavors are observation and measurement. The scientific method thus can be applied only to aspects of the world for which these processes can be used. Both observation and measurement are challenging for behavioral scientists. It is relatively simple to observe and to measure overt action, but thought and emotion, which are intricately entwined with action, are more elusive. Typically the scientist must *operationalize* the behavior or concept being studied. That is, some observable and measurable operation must be selected to define the behavior or concept. To take a few examples, aggression might be operationalized as the frequency with which children actually push or strike their playmates. Depression might be operationalized by the degree to which a person reports feelings of sadness and hopelessness.

In the attempt to tap all sources of information, behavioral scientists make many kinds of observations and measurements. They directly observe overt behavior with or without special apparatus; record physiological functioning of the heart, brain, or sense organs; ask people to report or rate their own behavior, feelings, and thoughts; and collect the reports of others about the subject of investigation. Such endeavors may be conducted either in the laboratory or in natural settings, and confidence in them and importance accorded to them vary.

RELIABILITY

In addition to assuming that knowledge can be gained by observation, the scientific method also assumes that events repeat themselves, given identical or similar conditions; consequently, the events can be observed again by others. If the same events are not reported under similar conditions, the original finding is considered unreliable or inconsistent and therefore remains questionable. The need for *reliability* of results places a burden on researchers to conceptualize clearly and concisely, observe, measure, and communicate their findings so that others may replicate and judge their work. Science must be open to the scrutiny and evaluations of others.

VALIDITY

Whereas reliability refers to the consistency or repeatability of results, *validity* refers to the correctness, soundness, or appropriateness of scientific findings. Validity is a complex matter and in general must be judged in terms of the purpose of the research and the way that the results are used. The concepts of internal and external validity are central to understanding validity.

Internal validity refers to the extent to which explanations for phenomena are judged to be correct or sound. Or to put it in another way, it refers to the degree to which alternative explanations can be ruled out (Campbell & Stanley, 1963). The more certain we are that alternative explanations can be ruled out, the more confidence we have in the offered explanation.

Internal validity is closely tied to the notion of control in research. It is maximized by research designs and procedures that build control over the variables that could affect the findings of the investigation. By controlling the procedures, the researcher limits the conditions that can explain the results. By controlling extraneous factors, the researcher optimizes the likelihood of being able to attribute the findings to specific factors. As we shall see, it is only the "true" experiment that approaches such control. This fact does not mean, of course, that other methods are useless; each method has its strengths as well as its weaknesses.

External validity asks the question of generalizability: To what populations and situations can the results of an investigation be generalized (Campbell & Stanley, 1963)? Researchers are virtually always interested in this question. Generalizability cannot be assumed, however. It cannot automatically be concluded, for example, that research findings based on a particular population of preschool girls hold for older girls or for boys. Similarly, the results of laboratory studies may or may not generalize to the world outside the laboratory.

The question of generalizability is rarely, if ever, completely answered, although evidence increases as various populations and settings are tested. It is ironic that attempts to increase internal validity may decrease external validity, because the former requires controls that may create artificial situations. This dilemma is one of several that must be taken into account in the selection of a research method.

BASIC METHODS OF RESEARCH

In the following discussion, several basic research methods are described. As will be obvious, each has both weaknesses and strengths, and each may be more suitable in some situations than in others.

THE CASE STUDY

This method is commonly used in investigations of behavioral disorder. It focuses on an individual, describing the background, present and past life circumstances, and characteristics of the person. Case studies can tell us about the nature, course, causes, correlates, and outcomes of behavior problems.

The following is an abbreviated version of a case report of a boy who was considered at risk for a serious disorder, childhood schizophrenia.

Max was a seven-year-old boy when he was first referred for psychiatric evaluation by his school principal ... Long-standing problems such as severe rage outbursts, loss of control, aggressive behavior, and paranoid ideation had reached crisis proportions.

Max was the product of an uncomplicated pregnancy and delivery, the only child of a professional couple. There was a history of "mental illness" in the paternal grandmother and two great aunts. Max's early development was characterized by "passivity" ... He used a bottle until age three. Verbal development was good; he spoke full sentences at one year. Toilet training was reportedly difficult ...

Max was clumsy and had difficulty manipulating toys, his tricycle, and his shoelaces. When he began nursery school, he was constantly in trouble with other children ... Max "developed a passion for animals" ... At age five Max acquired an imaginary companion, "Casper—the man in the wall" who was ever present. Max insisted that he could see him, although no one else could. Casper's voice, he said, often told him he was a bad boy.

Max's behavior was so unmanageable during the first and second grade he was rarely able to remain in the classroom ... Max described animals fighting and killing people ... The psychologists noted a schizoid quality because of the numerous references to people from outer space, ghosts, and martians, as well as the total absence of human subjects ... Despite his high intelligence (IQ 130), Max was experiencing the world as hostile and dangerous. The psychologist considered Max to be at great risk for schizophrenia, paranoid type. (Cantor & Kestenbaum, 1986, pp. 627–628)

The case study continues, telling of Max's enrollment in special schools and his psychotherapy. A major focus of treatment was to reduce Max's anxiety, which was thought to cause his aggression and bizarre behaviors. Parental involvement, rewards for appropriate behavior, and medication were all employed. Despite some quite disturbed behaviors, improvement occurred, and Max eventually was able to attend a university engineering program.

The primary goal of this case report was to illustrate a therapeutic approach to treating seriously disturbed children and to emphasize that treatment must be tailored to each child's needs. Case studies can well meet such a goal, for one of the strengths of case studies is the power to illustrate. They can richly describe phenomena, even phenomena that are so rare that they would be difficult to study in other ways. They can provide hypotheses to be tested and can clinically examine results produced by other methods.

The weaknesses of the case study concern reliability and validity. The descriptions of life events often go back in time, and the accuracy and completeness of such retrospective data are often suspect. Thus reliability of the data is in question. When case studies go beyond description to interpretations, there are few guidelines to judge the validity of the interpretations. External validity also is weak in the case study method: Since only one person is examined, the findings cannot be generalized confidently to others. There are ways to increase reliability and validity, however. For example, several case studies demonstrating the same principle can increase generalizability.

Despite their shortcomings, case studies have played a critical role in the development of clinical psychology and psychiatry (Chess, 1988; Wells, 1987). Clinicians consider them "do-able" and relevant to their concerns (Morrow-Bradley & Elliot, 1986).

SYSTEMATIC NATURALISTIC OBSERVATION

Systematic naturalistic observation consists of directly observing individuals in their "real world," at times simply to describe naturally occurring behavior, and at other times, to answer specific questions or to test hypotheses.

An example of an investigation to test hypotheses is a study by Dadds (1992) and colleagues. They were interested in the development or maintenance of childhood depression. The researchers compared parent-child interaction in families that had a child who was clinic-referred for either de-

Direct observation allows the researcher systematically to measure behavior as it is occurring.
(Courtesy of A.C. Israel)

pression, conduct disorder, or depression/conduct disorder. On the basis of past research, it was hypothesized that parents in all the clinic families would display aversive behaviors toward the clinic-referred children and their siblings but that only the conduct disordered children (with or without depression) would reciprocate with aversive behavior. The families, as well as a comparison group of nonclinic families, were videotaped during a typical evening meal. The tapes were then coded by independent observers who were trained to use the Family Observation Schedule, an observation instrument that provides twenty categories for parent and child behaviors. Table 4-1 shows some of the categories. Reliability of the coding was checked by a different observer, who coded one-third of the tapes. All observers were unaware of the family's group status and of the hypotheses being tested.

For the sake of brevity, we will focus on the main findings, which partially supported the hypotheses. Parents with clinic-referred children did indeed show more aversive behaviors compared with control parents. And the conduct disordered children who were not depressed acted in negative, coercive ways. All the other children did not display anger and did not show aversive behaviors. Thus, differences existed in the interactions of families with children referred for different kinds of child problems.

This research is a sophisticated study that utilized trained observers who were blind to the status of the families, a carefully constructed coding system, and a reliability check on the observations. It permitted many statistical comparisons and testing of hypotheses on the basis of behavior in a natural setting. On the other hand, analyses were limited to the selected categories of behavior, as is generally true for this method. The degree to which naturalistic observations can be generalized depends on the way that subjects are selected and other factors.

CORRELATIONAL METHODS

Correlational methods determine whether a relationship exists between or among variables. The variables may be measured in the natural environ-

---

TABLE 4-1

Examples of Behavior Categories Used in the Dadds et al. (1992) Study

Parent-Child Categories

Smile: Facial movement conveying happiness

Frown: Facial movement conveying anger, sadness, disapproval

Praise: Specific praise offered the child by the parent

Question: Nonaversive request for information from the child

Aversive Question: Request for information deemed aversive because of content or tone of voice

Instruction: Nonaversive verbal command that specified a clear behavioral action

Aversive Instruction: Verbal command that specified a clear behavioral action, presented aversively

Child Behavior Categories

Smile: Facial movement conveying happiness

Frown: Facial movement conveying anger, sadness, disapproval

Noncompliance: Refusal to initiate compliance with specific instruction within five seconds

Complaint: Verbal complaint involving whining, screaming, protest, temper

Aversive Mand: Aversive or unpleasant directive by the child to another person (e.g., "Fix my dinner now!")

Physical Negative: Actual or threatened physical attack or damage to another person or destruction of an object

From Dadds, Sanders, Morrison, & Rebetz, 1992.

ment or in the laboratory in a variety of ways. Researchers then calculate a correlation coefficient, which is a quantitative measure of the existence, direction, and strength of the relationship.

Correlational research can be extremely helpful. It is useful when initial exploration is the goal of research. Here the investigator may first want to determine whether any relationships exist among variables before specific hypotheses are advanced.

Correlational studies can also be helpful when ethical considerations preclude manipulation. Suppose, for example, that an investigator seeks knowledge about the impact of child abuse, poor nutrition, or family conflict on children's behaviors. It would be ethically impossible to manipulate these factors by exposing children to them. However, unfortunate as it is, some children are exposed to these situations in the naturally occurring environment, and correlational research can then determine whether these situations are related to children's behavior. Such knowledge can suggest hypotheses. Moreover, when a relationship is revealed, it is possible to predict one variable from the other.

Correlational analyses can involve many variables in complex research designs. Here we take a simple example in order to describe basic aspects of the method. In its simplest form, the question asked in correlational research is, Are factors *X* and *Y* related, and, if so, in what direction are they related, and how strongly? The first step of the research is to select a sample that represents the population of interest. Next, two scores must be obtained from each participant, one a measure of variable *X* and the other a measure of variable *Y*. Statistical analysis of these data must then be performed. In this case, the Pearson product-moment coefficient, *r*, could be computed.

The value of Pearson *r*,* which always ranges between +1.00 and −1.00, indicates the direction

and the strength of the relationship. Direction is indicated by the sign of the coefficient. The positive sign (+) means that high scores on the *X* variable tend to be associated with high scores on the *Y* variable, and that low scores on *X* tend to be related to low scores on *Y*. This relationship is referred to as a positive, or direct, correlation. For example, a positive relationship exists between children's age and body weight: Older children usually weigh more. The negative sign (−) indicates that high scores on *X* tend to be related to low scores on *Y*, and that low scores on *X* tend to be related to high scores on *Y*. An example of a negative correlation (also called an indirect, or inverse, correlation) is adult age and lung capacity: As adults increase in age, their lung capacity tends to decrease.

The strength or magnitude of a correlation is reflected in the absolute value of the coefficient. Thus a correlation of +.55 is equally as strong as one of −.55. The strongest relationship is expressed by an *r* of +1.00 or −1.00, both of which are considered perfect correlations. As the coefficient value decreases in absolute value, the relationship becomes weaker. A coefficient of 0.00 indicates that no relationship exists at all. In this case, the score on one variable tells us nothing about the score on the other variable.

Let us consider a hypothetical example of correlational research. Suppose that an investigator expected that children's self-concept and performance on a certain achievement test are positively related. After obtaining an appropriate sample of children, the researcher would obtain two scores for each child—one score a measure of self-concept and one a measure of achievement. The hypothetical data might appear as in Table 4-2. Pearson *r* for these data would be calculated, and its value found to equal +.82. How would this finding be interpreted? Obviously, a correlation exists, and the positive sign indicates that children who scored high on the measure of self-concept tend to score high on the achievement test. Moreover, the magnitude of the coefficient indicates that the relationship is strong (since +1.00 is a perfect positive relationship). Thus the researcher's hypothesis is supported by the correlational analysis.

*Pearson *r* is just one of several correlation coefficients that could be calculated, depending on the nature and complexity of the study. The general procedures and interpretations described here apply to other correlation coefficients.

TABLE 4-2

Self-Concept and Achievement Scores

Data from a Hypothetical Study of Children's Self-Concept and Performance on an Achievement Test. The Pearson r value is +0.82, which indicates a strong positive relationship between the variables.

Child	Variable X Self-Concept Score	Variable Y Achievement Test Score
Daniel	2	5
Nicky	3	4
Sara	4	12
Beth	7	16
Jessica	9	10
Alia	11	22
Brent	13	18

The degree to which correlational research is reliable depends mainly on the reliability of the measures used. The degree to which the study gives valid information about the relationship of the variables depends on how well it was conducted. However, a common mistake is to automatically draw cause-and-effect conclusions from the results. Causal links cannot be validly assumed from correlational analyses; two problems of interpretation exist.

The problem of directionality and other variables. One problem is that cause may flow in either direction. The other is that some other variable(s) may be responsible for the revealed correlation. In the preceding hypothetical example, it is possible that self-concept causes achievement scores or that achievement causes self-concept scores. Or perhaps other variables, such as general intelligence or family dynamics, produce the correlation between self-concept and achievement.

There are, however, a few things that can be done to indicate what causal relationship might exist. For one, the nature of the variables can be examined for a suggestion of cause and effect. If a positive correlation were found between diet and school performance in children, for example, it would seem more likely that diet influenced schoolwork than vice versa.

However, other variables could be responsible for the relationship between diet and school performance, perhaps social class factors. If there were good reason to suspect some role for social class, a partial correlation statistical procedure could be useful. This method partials out, or removes, the effects of other variables, allowing the investigator to determine whether the two original variables are still correlated. The trouble with partialing, however, is that one can never be sure that all possible causative variables have been examined.

Techniques such as structural equation modeling, too complex to discuss here, do permit researchers to have more confidence in their hypotheses about cause and effect. Our discussion of correlational research has focused on the basics of the method, but we shall have further opportunity throughout the text to see how the techniques are used in research.

THE EXPERIMENTAL METHOD

The "true" experiment comes closest to meeting the rigorous standards of the scientific method. Regardless of its particular purpose, the experimental method is characterized by the following:

1. An explicitly stated hypothesis
2. Subjects appropriately selected and assigned to groups that are exposed to different conditions or manipulations
3. Two or more conditions or manipulations selected by the investigator (the independent variable)
4. Observation and measurement (the dependent variable)
5. Control of the procedures by the investigator
6. Comparison of the effects of the manipulations

Control is of utmost importance. The experiences of the subjects are prearranged and meticulously presented, with the different groups being exposed to different conditions. This procedure permits final judgment about the causes of the findings of the study.

To illustrate the experiment, we draw on a study of the Abecedarian Project by Ramey and Campbell (1984). These investigators tested the hypothesis that early education prevents intellectual retardation in at risk children. On the basis of past research, they believed that such children would benefit from a child-centered, intellectually stimulating environment provided as part of a daycare service.

Potential participants were identified through prenatal clinics and the local social service department. Each family was then surveyed with the High Risk Index to determine parental education, income, presence or absence of fathers and relatives, children's intellectual performance, and the like. Families meeting a criterion score were considered at risk. Final selection was made after the mother was interviewed and given an intelligence test. Participants were chosen either before or soon after the birth of the subject child.

Families then were paired according to similarity on the High Risk Index, and the children from each pair were randomly assigned to either the treatment or the control group. Such matching and random assignment were crucial to the experiment because these procedures aimed to create groups that were approximately equal in relevant characteristics.

The *independent variable* in this study was the provision of the educational program. All the children in the treatment group began day care by three months of age, and their development was tracked until they reached fifty-four months. The day-care center operated five full days a week, for fifty weeks of the year. The educational program included language, motor, social, and cognitive components, varying somewhat with the child's age. Special emphasis was given to the development of communication skills. Thus a good deal of attention was paid to verbal exchanges, and children were read to each day. Reading, mathematics, and social skills programs were used.

Control-group children did not attend the day-care center and were not exposed to the educational program. Efforts were made otherwise to equate their experiences with those of the treatment group: They were given similar nutritional supplements, pediatric care, and supportive social services.

To assess the possible influence of the independent variable, all children were tested twice annually with standardized developmental or intelligence tests. These measures were the *dependent variable*. The examiners were randomly assigned to the testing sessions.

The test results revealed that beginning at eighteen months, children in the treatment group scored significantly higher than children in the control group, and the group difference was statistically significant.* Figure 4-1 shows one way of examining the findings. It indicates that at twenty-four, thirty-six, and forty-eight months, the educationally treated children were much less likely to obtain intelligence scores at or below 85 than were the control children. The researchers thus concluded that the educational program resulted in intellectual benefits for the treated at risk youngsters.

Is this conclusion justified; that is, does the study have internal validity? The method by which the subjects were selected and assigned makes it unlikely that the results simply reflect group differences that existed before the study was conducted. Moreover, efforts were made to treat the experimental and control groups similarly except for the independent variable. To the degree that this was accomplished, it can be confidently concluded that the study is internally valid and that the results are due to the treatment. With regard to this issue, caution is appropriate, however. When research is conducted in the laboratory, it is relatively easy to control the experiences of the groups. In field experiments such as Ramey and Campbell's, the degree of control and thus internal validity is less clear. An additional issue concerns the actual collection of data. It appears that

---

*Statistical significance refers to the statistical probability that a finding is a chance result. The accepted rule is that a significant finding would occur by chance five times or less were the study to be repeated one hundred times. (This level of probability, the .05 level, is indicated in research by the term $p < .05$.) Thus we are reasonably sure that the result is not a chance finding.

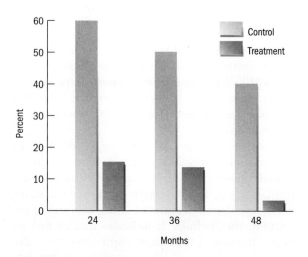

FIGURE 4-1 Percentage of Stanford-Binet IQ scores at or below 85 at three ages for treatment and control subjects. From Ramey & Campbell, 1984.

those who gave the standardized tests may have known the group to which each child had been assigned, raising the question of bias in data collection. At the same time, possible bias of the individual testers was offset by their being randomly assigned to testing sessions.

What about external validity, or generalizability, of the findings? As mentioned earlier, this matter is rarely completely settled, but validity is enhanced in the Ramey and Campbell study by its being done in a setting in which such training might eventually occur. To the extent that other day-care settings would be similar to the original setting, external validity could be expected. External validity would also be anticipated when the children in a new study resembled Ramey and Campbell's original sample. The findings appear to apply to both sexes, because no differences were found between girls' and boys' scores. [Although our purpose here is to evaluate Ramey and Campbell's study as an experiment, we note that subsequent followup indicated that the benefits of early intervention can be observed several years later (Campbell & Ramey, 1994).]

The Ramey and Campbell study is one variation on the experimental method. Other experiments might, for example, be conducted in the laboratory, select subjects in somewhat different ways, include more groups, or collect data at only one time. Although specific statistical analyses might vary, their purpose would be the same: to determine whether group differences go beyond what might be expected by chance. When a significant statistical difference is found and when the experiment is rigorously designed and conducted, a causal connection between the independent and dependent variables can be assumed. Thus the experiment is a powerful tool for explanation.

SINGLE-SUBJECT EXPERIMENTS

The typical experiment, described in the previous section, is conducted with groups of people, and with one or more control groups serving to help rule out alternative explanations of the findings. A strategy akin to this sort of experiment is to conduct an experiment with a single or a few individuals, provided that some control to rule out alternative explanations is employed. This approach is sometimes referred to as single-case designs (Kratochwill & Levin, 1992) or as time-series studies because measurements are taken across time periods. With careful control, internal validity is possible. External validity is not strong, because generalization from single subjects cannot be made with confidence. However, external validity can be increased by repeating the study with different subjects.

The ABA' design. Single-subject designs are frequently used to evaluate the influence of a clinical intervention. One way to control the possibility for alternative explanations is to use what is known as the ABA' design. The problem behavior is carefully defined and measured across time periods, during which the subject is exposed to different conditions. During the first period (A), measures are taken of the behavior prior to any intervention. This baseline measure serves as a standard against which change can be evaluated. In period B, the intervention is carried out while the behavior is measured in the identical way. The intervention is then removed for a period of time known as the reversal period (A').

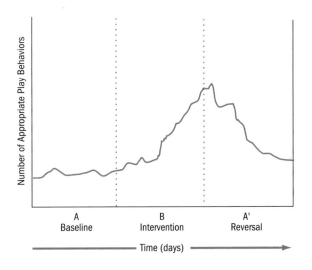

FIGURE 4-2 Hypothetical example of the ABA′ design.

Multiple baselines designs. When ABA′ designs are inappropriate, alternative designs with multiple baselines may be appropriate. In one multiple baseline design, two behaviors are recorded across time. After baselines are established for both, the intervention is made for only one behavior. During the next phase, intervention is applied to the other behavior as well. For example, a clinician may hypothesize that a child's temper tantrums and throwing of objects are maintained by adult attention to these behaviors. Withdrawal of attention would thus be expected to reduce the behaviors. Support for the hypothesis can be seen in Figure 4-3, a hypothetical graph of the frequency of both behaviors across time periods. Because behavior change follows the pattern of the treatment procedure, it is likely that withdrawal of attention and not some other variable caused the change.

In another type of multiple baseline design, treatment is given to more than one person, following different time lines. For example, Koegel, O'Dell, & Koegel (1987) evaluated the effects of a new treatment to enhance language development in autistic children. As Figure 4-4 shows, two children began the old treatment (Teaching Method I) at the same time, and individual baselines were

Figure 4-2 gives a hypothetical example of the ABA′ design. Appropriate play behavior occurs at low frequency during the baseline, increases during the treatment phase B, and decreases when the intervention is removed in the A′ phase.

In studies in which behavior improves during intervention, particularly if clinical treatment is the aim, a fourth period (B′), during which the successful intervention is reintroduced, must be added. Typically the relevant behaviors show improvement again.

Nevertheless, the ABA′ design is limited in that the intervention may make reversal (A′) unlikely. For example, when treatment results in increased academic skill, the child may not display decreases in the skill when intervention is removed. From a treatment standpoint, this is a positive outcome; from a research standpoint, however, there is no way to demonstrate that the intervention caused the positive behavior. The ABA′ design also has an ethical problem in that the researcher may hesitate to return to baseline conditions once a manipulation is associated with positive change. And again, although the manipulation may appear responsible for the change, without a return to baseline condition, a definite demonstration of its effects is lacking.

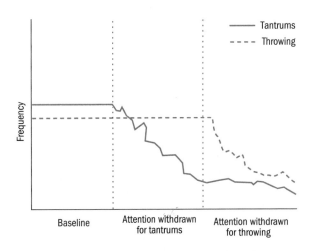

FIGURE 4-3 Frequency of tantrums and throwing across the phases of a hypothetical multiple baseline, single-subject experiment.

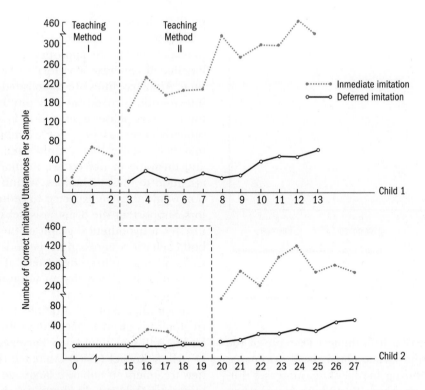

FIGURE 4-4 Number of correct verbal imitations across months during Teaching Methods I and II.
From Koegel, O'Dell, and Koegel, 1987.

recorded. Child 1 was then provided the new treatment, and Child 2 followed several months later. Data were recorded in the clinic for two kinds of verbal imitation. The demonstration of similar patterns of change for both children that occurs only when the new treatment is introduced increases confidence that the treatment actually caused improvement (internal validity). Moreover, external validity is enhanced by the fact that the effect held across two persons.

In addition to reversal and multiple baseline procedures, other methods of control and statistical analyses have been developed for single-subject studies (Barlow & Hersen, 1984; Kratochwill & Levin, 1992). All these designs permit the researcher-clinician to test hypotheses while working with one or a few subjects and, in the case of treatment, to focus on the child of immediate concern.

CONTROLLED OBSERVATIONS AND MIXED DESIGNS

In studying behavior disorders, researchers often use designs that involve what are referred to as classificatory variables. Subjects are selected who differ on some characteristic (classification) and are compared. For example, youth who are considered delinquent or nondelinquent are measured in some way under controlled conditions and compared. There may or may not be manipulations of other factors.

Consider, for example, a finding in the research literature that children who are diagnosed with Attention Deficit Hyperactivity Disorder (ADHD) are more rejected by their peers than are children with no behavioral disorder. It might be concluded that there is something about ADHD that causes rejection—perhaps the excessive motor activity or impulsive behavior that is symptomatic of ADHD. Although this conclusion is partly true, the interpretation turns out to be more complex. Rejection is also due to the aggression that characterizes many boys with ADHD. A factor that is associated with ADHD, not only the ADHD itself, underlies rejection. As this example demonstrates, when research participants are selected on the basis of a classificatory variable, interpretation of the findings must be cautiously made.

Caution is also required in interpreting the results of mixed designs. In mixed designs, research groups are chosen on the basis of classificatory factors, and then a manipulation occurs (Davison & Neale, 1996). Take the hypothetical case in which both boys with ADHD and normal boys (the classificatory factor) are given two kinds of attention tasks (a manipulation). Suppose the ADHD group does well with one task but not the other, whereas the normal group does well with both tasks. The problem of interpretation still exists despite the manipulation: It is not clear that hyperactivity itself rather than some associated feature caused the results.

To summarize, the research methods we have discussed in this section varied in several ways, and each had weaknesses and strengths. The experiment and single-subject experiment, in which manipulation occurs in controlled situation, best meet the standards of internal validity and best permit causal inferences to the drawn. Nonetheless, the choice of research method depends on the purpose of the investigation, as well as practical and ethical considerations. Scientific endeavors are enriched by the availability of various methods.

QUALITATIVE RESEARCH METHODS

Throughout this century, psychology has been largely committed to the belief that truth or scientific knowledge must be grounded in direct obser-

vation (Krahn, Hohn, & Kime, 1995). An intricate part of this commitment is placing high value on *quantitative* measurement done by *objective investigators* in *controlled situations*. Most of the methods discussed in this chapter fall under the rubric of quantitative research methods. They represent the positivistic or empirical paradigm that underlies much of the scientific progress made in modern times (Ely, 1991).

In recent years, however, interest has grown in diverse approaches captured by the term "qualitative methods." These approaches include in-depth interviews, life histories, memoirs, some case descriptions, and ethnographies (narratives of cultures). Diaries, letters, and other written records may be examined. Naturalistic observation is also important, with situations being recorded initially in narration rather than with a restrictive coding of categories of behavior. Moreover, the data may be seen as more credible when the observer becomes a participant in the setting, thereby optimizing understanding (participant observation). Regardless of the specific method, though, the following are among the characteristic of qualitative research (Ely, 1991).

■ It is assumed that events can be adequately understood only when they are observed in context.

■ The contexts of inquiry are not contrived; they are natural.

■ It is assumed that human behavior and development are best understood from a personal frame of reference. Thus individuals are given the opportunity to speak for themselves about their beliefs, attitudes, and experiences.

■ There is an attempt to understand the reported experience as a unified whole rather than in terms of separate variables.

It is not unusual to collect large amounts of written data in qualitative research. Once collected, the narrative data are then conceptualized, analyzed, and interpreted (Strauss & Corbin, 1990). This process entails coding or categorizing statements or written observations. What gets coded, how the coding is accomplished, and how data are interpreted vary with the approach and aims of the study. Some researchers make relatively few interpretations, allowing the participants to speak for themselves. Among the uses of the data are the development of basic knowledge, illustration and enrichment of quantitative findings, and evaluation of programs. Qualitative research can also be used to create hypotheses and theories.

EXAMPLES OF QUALITATIVE RESEARCH

Recent qualitative research in psychology has examined, among other topics, life satisfaction in the elderly, stress related to loss of jobs, parents' perception of child psychotherapy, parents' adjustment to the birth of a handicapped child, and parents' experiences with regard to their child's life-threatening illness (Fiese & Bickman, 1998; Krahn et al., 1995).

As an example of the approach, we take a recent study of parents' experiences as participants in a support program called Parent to Parent (Ainbinder et al., 1998). The specific purpose of the program is to provide support for parents who have a child with disabilities, such as mental retardation, cerebral palsy, or chronic illness. Each parent is matched with a supporting parent who has a child with a similar disability. The supporting parent, who receives training for the helping role, provides information and emotional support, usually by telephone. In addition to a quantitative survey evaluation, the program was evaluated by qualitative, semistructured interviews that explored the impact and meaning of having a supportive parent. The transcribed telephone interviews were coded and categorized according to themes that emerged from the conversations. Among the themes were these: the way that the program was helpful, reasons for failure, skills and information learned, availability and mutuality of support, and personal growth. Here are examples of interview text that reflect three of the themes.

Learning
I wanted some reassurance that [our daughter] is likely to have most of the same things everybody else has, as far as you know, going to school and having friends, going out and doing things. And [our supporting parent's] daughter's involved in a lot of things. She's got a good life. And that gave me a great deal of hope about the future of our daughter, that she can have a good life, too. (Ainbinder et al., 1998, p. 104)

Personal Growth (emotional well-being)
I think it really lifted my spirits. I'd get off the phone and I'd just really feel good. Even if things had been going smoothly, I felt myself even higher. And if it has been tough, if I'd had a situation that has been kind of exasperating or trying, just talking about it to somebody who understood, I feel better and I could stop beating myself up a lot. (Ainbinder et al., 1998, p. 105.)

*Failure of the Program
(supporting parents' child was "worse off")*
And the other thing I've found with her, her baby is not doing very well sometimes . . . She asks how my baby is and he has been doing very healthy, thank God. I don't want to say "doing great" . . . We don't share a lot about our children, actually, which is kind of what I would like . . . I find the only time I really want to call her is if I have a problem because then I don't feel bad about saying "I have this problem and what do you think I should do?" (Ainbinder et al., 1998, p. 106)

Overall the data indicated how talking, sharing, comparing, and learning with others who are perceived as similar can enhance coping and adaptability. The qualitative analysis of Parent to Parent provided understanding of the strengths and weaknesses of the program in a way that the quantitative data did not.

WEAKNESSES OF QUALITATIVE METHODS

Qualitative methods have several shortcomings. Sample size is often small, huge amounts of data can be difficult and costly to analyze, and guidelines for analysis need to be better established. Also problematic is the subjective nature of the data. Serious issues are raised about reliability and validity. How is science to find "the truth" when it is assumed that the truth springs from and can be different for individuals? Guidelines are being offered to address these questions. One way to increase validity is to combine qualitative and quantitative approaches. The qualitative procedures allow flexible, broad-scope investigation, whereas the quantitative procedures allow more traditional data collection and hypothesis testing. The data sets, obtained in different ways, also serve as a check on each other. This strategy, known as triangulation, can extend the scope of the findings and increase confidence in them.

CROSS-SECTIONAL, LONGITUDINAL, SEQUENTIAL STRATEGIES

In addition to the basic methods already described, research studies can also be categorized as either cross-sectional or longitudinal, or as a combination of these strategies known as sequential designs.

CROSS-SECTIONAL STRATEGY

In the cross-sectional strategy, different groups of subjects are observed at one point in time. For example, the peer relations of fourth-, sixth-, and ninth-graders can be compared. The strategy is relatively inexpensive and efficient, and it can provide much information. It is thus a popular approach.

However, tracing developmental change with cross-sectional research is problematic. For example, someone interested in whether the frequency of aggression changes with development may measure aggression in five-, ten-, and fifteen-year-olds. If the younger children displayed more aggression, it might be concluded that aggression decreases as children develop. However, this conclusion may not be warranted. Age *difference* is not necessarily age or *developmental* change. Perhaps specific experiences of the different age groups, due to societal changes over time, are responsible for the findings. Younger children might have watched more violent television or received more reinforcement for aggression during an era characterized by greater violence and aggression. Thus the finding may reflect societal change rather than the developmental course for aggression. To make matters more complex, the same societal changes can influence different age groups differently, making it extremely difficult to interpret cross-sectional data.

LONGITUDINAL STRATEGY

In longitudinal research, the same subjects are evaluated over time, with repeated observations or tests. This strategy "sees" development as it occurs. One of the first such studies was Lewis Terman's

investigation of intellectually gifted children, who were tested several times over many decades beginning in 1921 (Cravens, 1992; Sears, 1975). Terman's research was followed by other now-classic studies that traced the growth of intellectual, social, and physical abilities.

The longitudinal strategy is unique in its capacity to answer questions about the nature and course of development. Does an early traumatic event, such as the death of a parent, play a role in the origin of childhood psychopathology? To what extent does adolescent aggression carry over into adulthood? Can early intervention prevent later problems in infants who experience prenatal difficulties? The longitudinal method can be extremely helpful in answering these kinds of questions (Verhulst & Koot, 1991).

Still, this method has serious drawbacks. Longitudinal studies are extremely expensive and require the investigators to commit themselves to a project for many years. It is also difficult to retain subjects over long periods of time, and the loss of participants can bias the subject sample. For example, those who drop out may be more transient, less psychologically oriented, or less healthy than the subjects who continue. Another problem in longitudinal research is the repeated testing of participants, who may become test-wise. Efforts to change or improve the testing instruments make it difficult to compare earlier and later findings. Finally, subjects are not the only ones who change over the years; so may society. Thus, for example, if individuals were followed from birth to age twenty from 1930 to 1950, their development might be different from that of persons of the same age span followed from 1970 to 1990, because of historical variables. The 1930 to 1950 group would likely have had different experiences than would the 1970 to 1990 group (e.g., in health care, educational environments). Thus these possible generational, or cohort, effects must be considered in interpreting longitudinal studies.

SEQUENTIAL DESIGNS

To overcome some of the weaknesses of the cross-sectional and longitudinal strategies, researchers interested in developmental change can combine the two approaches in a variety of sequential designs (e.g., Farrington, 1991). Take, for example, a hypothetical study in which groups of children of different ages are studied over a relatively short time span. At Time I, children aged three, six, and nine years are examined in a cross-sectional study. Similar examination of the same groups of children occurs again three years later at Time II, and again another three years later at Time III. Figure 4-5 depicts the study. As can be seen by reading down the columns of the figure, cross-sectional comparisons can be made at three different times. In addition, as can be seen reading from left to right across the figure, the children (A, B, and C) are studied longitudinally over a six-year period (2000–2006). The age range in the investigation is thus twelve years (from three to fifteen years), although the study is completed in six years.

Various comparisons can provide a wealth of information from such a sequential design. To take a simple case, if aggression were found to increase with age at Times I, II, and III (cross-sectional analyses) and also across time for each group of children (the longitudinal analyses), evidence would be strong for developmental change over the entire age range. Moreover, by comparing aggression at age six, or nine, or twelve (as shaded in the figure), the impact of societal conditions

could also be evaluated. It might be found, for example, that aggression at age nine increased from the year 2000 to 2003 to 2006. Since only one age is involved, this increase is not developmental and likely indicates a change in societal conditions during the years under investigation. Thus, sequential designs can be powerful in separating age differences and developmental changes, while taking generational effects into consideration.

RISK RESEARCH

We have already seen that the concept of risk is important in understanding, predicting, and potentially reducing behavior problems. For this reason, we will explore risk research more extensively.

The cross-sectional strategy can help identify possible risk factors. We could, for example, study children with learning disabilities at one point in time to determine whether parental discord is a strong correlate. If so, the hypothesis could be made that parental discord puts children at risk. However, we would want to determine whether parental discord operated earlier so as to affect the child. There are two basic ways to approach this task: retrospective and prospective studies.

In *retrospective designs,* youth are identified, some of whom display the problem of interest and others of whom serve as comparison controls. Then information is collected about their earlier characteristics and life experiences. The purpose of this follow-back method is to seek hypotheses about the relationship of early variables and the later-observed characteristics. One obvious weakness of this method concerns the reliability of the data. Old records and memories of the past may be sketchy, biased, or mistaken. Another obvious limitation of the method is that the discovery of a relationship between the past and the present does not establish causation. Nevertheless, this kind of study is relatively easy to conduct, and it can help form hypotheses about risk factors. When a control group is not used, the results are not as useful.

Prospective designs investigate risk longitudinally, observing subjects at certain time intervals.

Age Group	Time		
	I (2000)	II (2003)	III (2006)
A	3	6	9
B	6	9	12
C	9	12	15

FIGURE 4-5 Schema of a sequential research design in which children of different ages are examined cross-sectionally and longitudinally.

As time passes, some of the subjects may show problem behaviors. The researcher can then examine the data to determine what variables are linked to the occurrence of the disorder. Prospective studies have the drawback of all longitudinal research (e.g., expense, loss of subjects). In addition, when researchers begin these demanding investigations, they must select the variables that will be observed along the way. Selection is often based on educated guesses, and relevant variables can be missed. Another serious drawback is that the number of youth who eventually develop a disorder of interest may be quite small, so that data must be collected on large numbers of participants. Despite these difficulties, the prospective design is invaluable in identifying risk factors and is commonly employed (e.g., Kopp, 1994).

Furthermore, there is a way to enlarge the number of participants who may eventually display behavioral dysfunction. This method entails selecting subjects who are known to be at risk because of a factor already associated with the disorder. Such prospective longitudinal research is called *high-risk research.*

A well-known example of this approach involves children who are at high risk for developing schizophrenia because of their having a parent with schizophrenia. Mednick and Schulsinger (1968) were among the first to use this strategy when they followed 207 high-risk adolescents and a low-risk, matched control group. None of the participants had been diagnosed as schizophrenic when the study began. A major evaluation was conducted when the subjects averaged twenty-five years and again when they averaged forty-two (Parnas et al., 1993). Several similar investigations were also initiated (Erlenmeyer-Kimling et al., 1990; Marcus et al., 1993). In addition to confirming that having a parent with schizophrenia increases risk for the disorder, this research has shown several other factors to be variously associated with the development of schizophrenia. These include prenatal and pregnancy complications, childhood and adolescence attention and cognitive deficits, neurological problems, psychosocial factors, and structural and functional brain abnormalities. It would be misleading not to point out that high-risk research is demanding and expensive. In the case of schizophrenia, it has contributed to knowledge about the disorder.

EPIDEMIOLOGICAL RESEARCH

Epidemiological research has its basis in medicine and initially focused on investigating infectious diseases. It is assumed that disease or disorder can best be understood and dealt with by viewing individuals in the context of the physical and social environments in which disorder develops (Costello et al., 1993; Costello & Angold, 1995a). As mentioned in Chapter 1, the method entails the collection of data from large general populations or representative samples of the populations. ("The Isle of Wight . . ." briefly describes a classic epidemiological investigation that has provided much valuable information.)

A main goal of epidemiology is to establish the prevalence or incidence of disorders in a population. However, the goals are much more extensive than this. Epidemiology also seeks to understand how a disorder is distributed in the population, what factors are correlated with the disorder, what are the causes and modes of transmission, what groups of people are at high risk, and how the disorder can be reduced. Thus the quests for scientific knowledge and healthier populations are intricately linked.

Within this framework, researchers interested in behavioral disorders of youth have begun to apply the developmental perspective. For example, they are particularly interested in the continuity and discontinuity of disorders, in the processes that link early and later behaviors, and in the risk factors that might operate at different ages.

Assessment of behavior to determine disorder is always an issue in epidemiology. In the highly respected Isle of Wight study, clinicians did extensive assessments of children (Verhulst & Koot, 1992). But both expense and time limitations can preclude that sort of procedure. More recently, standardized structured or semistructured interviews have been increasingly employed. In addition to being more efficient, standard instruments

THE ISLE OF WIGHT EPIDEMIOLOGICAL STUDIES

Michael Rutter and his colleagues initiated the Isle of Wight studies in the 1960s, in a small rural island off the south coast of England (Costello & Angold, 1995a; Rutter, 1989a). These studies are now famous for being the first large-scale population investigations of prevalence of behavioral disorders in children. Parents and teachers of all children, ages ten and eleven, completed questionnaires about the children's emotional and behavioral difficulties. On the basis of cutoff scores, a high-risk group of children was identified, and prevalence for all approximately two thousand children was estimated. Parents, teachers, and the high-risk children themselves were interviewed. Diagnoses of disorders were made through a semistructured interview that was used in London, at the Maudsley Hospital, where Rutter and many of the colleagues practiced. Psychiatrists and other clinicians conducted the interviews. The overall prevalence rate of children deemed to have disturbances serious enough to require treatment was between 6 percent and 7 percent. Four years later, the survey was repeated with similar methods. The estimated prevalence for these fourteen- to fifteen-year-olds was now 21 percent.

Early in the 1970s, another survey was completed comparing children on the Isle of Wight with children from a poor inner-city area of London. These youth were ten years of age. The methodolgy was somewhat different, notably in that parents but not the children were interviewed. Prevalence was estimated at 12 percent on the Isle of Wight and 25 percent in the London area.

In addition to presenting prevalence data, these studies provided valuable information about many correlates of disorder and the utilization of mental health services. In the original survey, 7 percent of the children were considered to be in need of treatment, and the overall treatment rate was 1 percent. In the 1970s study of the Isle of Wight population, 12 percent of adolescents were considered in need of treatment, and 2 percent overall were in treatment (16 percent of those with a disorder). Although prevalence data vary over time and studies, this pattern of a greater number of youth in need of treatment than the number who receive treatment has not changed.

are designed with the goal of diagnosis in mind, and the findings from different studies can be readily compared. At the same time, these instruments can limit the questions that might otherwise be asked by sensitive clinicians. The development of assessment techniques for epidemiology is an ongoing effort.

Correlational methods are often used in epidemiological studies to determine relationships among variables. The cross-sectional strategy can

be useful. For example, data collected from a community sample of youth can indicate the prevalence of disorders and the correlates of the existing disorders. However, longitudinal data are needed to understand developmental patterns of disorders (Costello, 1990; Costello et al., 1993).

Epidemiology provides valuable information. Numerous studies provide data on the rates of disorders and on the way that the disorders are distributed in populations (e.g., by sex, social class, race). This knowledge is crucial for prevention and the delivery of optimal mental health services. Identification of correlates makes possible the formulation of hypotheses about risk and causation, and it helps rule out other considerations (e.g., Offord & Fleming, 1991). For instance, population studies have failed to show a link between autism and social class, thus ruling out social class variables as risk or causal factors in this dysfunction. As epidemiological research becomes more advanced, increased benefits will be reaped. In the United States, this is an exciting time in epidemiology, because the federal government has committed major funding for the study of youth (Costello et al., 1993).

ETHICAL ISSUES

Scientific research is enormously beneficial, but it brings concern about the welfare and rights of participants. Underlying such concern is sensitivity to individual rights, both legal and ethical, and to past documented abuse of research subjects. One well-known instance in which the problem of abuse was raised involved research into the natural course of hepatitis. From the 1950s to the 1970s, children with mental retardation who resided in the Willowbrook school in the state of New York were deliberately infected with hepatitis in order to study the disease (Glantz, 1996). Abuse in social science research probably has not been as dramatic as in biomedical research, but ethical issues constantly arise.

For many years the American Psychological Association has published a manual of ethical guidelines for research. The Society for Research in Child Development publishes similar guidelines, which specifically address research with children. Table 4-3 summarizes these guidelines. Psychological research also falls under guidelines offered by the Department of Health and Human Services and Department of Education regulations may apply to research conducted in schools (Porter, 1996).

Following ethical guidelines is a mandate for all researchers. Although doing as mandated may seem quite simple, ethical concerns are often complex. Thus researchers are often advised to consult with colleagues when in doubt about an issue. In any event, though, research projects are judged prior to their being conducted by federally mandated institutional review boards (IRBs) that consider such issues as the scientific soundness of the research, the risk/benefits ratio, and privacy

When a youngster participates in research, informed consent by a parent or guardian, and possibly by the youth, should be obtained. What constitutes informed consent by a youngster is a complex issue.

(Courtesy of A.C. Israel)

TABLE 4-3

Ethical Standards for Research with Children

Principle 1: Non-harmful Procedures. No research operation that may physically or psychologically harm the child should be used. The least stressful operation should be used. Doubts about harmfulness should be discussed with consultants.

Principle 2: Informed Consent. The child's consent or assent should be obtained. The child should be informed of features of the research that may affect his or her willingness to participate. In working with infants, parents should be informed. If consent would make the research impossible, it may be ethically conducted under certain circumstances; judgments should be made with institutional review boards.

Principle 3: Parental Consent. Informed consent of parents, guardians, and those acting in loci parentis (e.g., school superintendents) similarly should be obtained, preferably in writing.

Principle 4: Additional Consent. Informed consent should be obtained of persons, such as teachers, whose interaction with the child is the subject of the research.

Principle 5: Incentives. Incentives to participate in the research must be fair and not unduly exceed incentives the child normally experiences.

Principle 6: Deception. If deception or withholding information is considered essential, colleagues must agree with this judgment. Participants should be told later of the reason for the deception. Effort should be made to employ deception methods that have no known negative effects.

Principle 7: Anonymity. Permission should be gained for access to institutional records, and anonymity of information should be preserved.

Principle 8: Mutual Responsibilities. There should be clear agreement as to the responsibilities of all parties in the research. The investigator must honor all promises and commitments.

Principle 9: Jeopardy. When, in the research, information comes to the investigator's attention that may jeopardize the child's welfare, the information must be discussed with parents or guardians and experts who can arrange for assistance to the child.

Principle 10: Unforeseen Consequences. When research procedures result in unforeseen, undesirable consequences for the participant, the consequences should be corrected and the procedures redesigned.

Principle 11: Confidentiality. The identity of subjects and all information about them should be kept confidential. When confidentiality might be threatened, this possibility and methods to prevent it should be explained as part of the procedures of obtaining informed consent.

Principle 12: Informing the Participants. Immediately after data collection, any misconceptions that might have arisen should be clarified. General findings should be given the participants, appropriate to their understanding. When scientific or humane reasons justify withholding information, efforts should be made so that withholding has no damaging consequences.

Principle 13: Reporting Results. Investigators' words may carry unintended weight; thus, caution should be used in reporting results, giving advice, making evaluative statements.

Principle 14: Implications of Findings. Investigators should be mindful of the social, political, and human implications of the research, and especially careful in the presentations of findings.

Summarized from the Report from the Committee for Ethical Conduct in Child Development Research, *SRCD Newsletter* (Winter 1990). Society for Research in Child Development, Inc.

(Glantz, 1996; Langer, 1985). Special consideration is given to cases involving young subjects, who are viewed as requiring special protection.

DO NO HARM AND DO GOOD

A basic ethical principle is that no serious harm, physical or psychological, be done to participants. Research with children has sometimes involved procedures in which the participants were made uncomfortable, for example, by waiting alone in a room (Cozby, Worden, & Kee, 1989). Studies investigating aggression have engaged children in aggressive acts or have exposed them to aggressive live or filmed models. Children have also served as subjects in research on the effects of medications, which can entail complex ethical dilemmas.

RISKS AND BENEFITS IN MEDICATION RESEARCH

A study was conducted to evaluate the effects of the medication fenfluramine on hyperactivity in mental retardation (Hoagwood, Jensen, & Fisher, 1996). Children five to thirteen years of age exhibiting these disorders were each exposed to five conditions: placebo, three different doses of fenfluramine, and one dose of a comparison drug, Ritalin. Each condition lasted for two weeks, and the order of the conditions varied across children. The order of medications was unknown to all individuals in contact with the children. Several ethical dilemmas were apparent in this investigation.

The use of fenfluramine raised the issue of more than minimal risk to the participants. Fenfluramine is somewhat controversial because animal studies suggested that it could cause long-lasting change in the brain. This potential demanded that the investigators do a careful literature search of the drug and weigh the risks against the potential benefits. Copies of the relevant research were presented to the Institutional Review Board, along with statements as to why the investigators believed that participants would not be exposed to unacceptable harm (e.g., animal study results were inconsistent). In addition, the investigators argued that fenfluramine could be helpful to children who did not respond to Ritalin. This risk-benefit analysis was accepted by the IRB, which agreed that potential benefits outweighed the probability of harm. The IRB required the investigators to warn of possible harm to the children in the informed consent form presented to the parents.

In turn, another ethical issue unexpectedly arose. It appeared that the warning of risk was interpreted by parents as indicating that the medication was powerful enough to bring benefits when all other drugs failed. Thus the researchers felt ethically compelled to protect parents from this unintended effect. This was done by informing parents that there was no evidence that fenfluramine is more powerful than other drugs nor that any drug is likely to bring permanent improvement in mental retardation.

Managing possible aversive side effects of the medication was necessary in this study and conflicted with the need for researchers to be unaware of the order in which each child was receiving the medications. Parents were given written information about possible side effects and telephone numbers of selected staff in case of emergency. These staff members had sealed envelopes with a medication code for each child. Depending on the seriousness of parents' reports, the staff offered assurances, requested that the child be seen, or suspended medication.

Finally, it was judged ethically appropriate to report the results to parents and, with their permission, to professionals caring for the child. Each child could benefit directly by the finding as to which condition was most effective for him or her. Even when a child did not profit from either medication, such information could be useful. Furthermore, the principal investigator was in the position to suggest alternatives, while making it clear that alternatives had not been evaluated in the study. In this way, benefits could be maximized for children whose participation potentially contributed to others' welfare.

Clearly, there is potential for harm that must be guarded against. Moreover, ethical guidelines based on the idea of respect for each individual require that benefits be maximized. It is not always possible for individuals to benefit personally from the investigation that they participate in, but a risk-benefit ratio needs to be considered (Porter, 1996). In general, risk of harm can ethically be greater when greater benefit is likely. Obviously there are limits to this principle in that risk of serious harm is usually unacceptable.

VOLUNTARY INFORMED CONSENT

Another fundamental ethical consideration is that individuals must be free to refuse to participate in research, given that they understand the investigation. The principle of *informed consent* requires that subjects consent to participate and be provided information to understand reasonably the risks and benefits involved (Frankel, 1978; Levine, 1991; Weithorn, 1987). This requirement includes understanding the purpose of the research, the role of the subjects, procedures, and possible alternatives to participation. Clearly, young children often cannot understand these issues, but in any event parents must consent for their child because children are not of legal age.

It is still recommended that young people have the opportunity to assent. What constitutes informed consent for children? It is suggested that adolescents be given the same information as adults and be asked to sign consent forms (e.g., Ferguson, 1978; Langer, 1985). The same procedure can be used for the school-age child, but researchers need to convey information in more concrete terms, with personal consequences spelled out. At the very least, children as young as seven years should be asked whether they assent to participate. With infants and toddlers, informed consent is not a reasonable expectation, and parental or guardian consent is usually sufficient for a child's participation. Such proxy consent has problems, however, because parent and child needs are not always identical.

A component of informed consent is that it be given freely, or voluntarily. The line between voluntariness and coercion can be subtle. For in-

stance, take the situation in which the child may be promised undue rewards for participation. Does that condition meet the standards for voluntariness? Parents too can be coerced by social and economic pressures into permitting their child's participation. For example, if research participation is desired by an agency that offers therapeutic care, the parents of a child who needs care may be afraid to refuse permission.

BALANCING IT ALL

In the final analysis, judgments about what is ethical often come down to balancing several factors. The individual's competence to understand and voluntarily consent, the risk of harm, and the possibility of benefit all play a crucial role in guiding ethical standards. The ways in which these factors are balanced can be demonstrated by considering whether a child's participation is in a therapeutic (beneficial) or nontherapeutic procedure (Levine, 1991). In some situations, the child's assent to participate may not be binding, and parental consent may be sufficient. For instance, the child's refusal to participate may be disregarded when the research risk is minimal and the child may directly benefit. In nontherapeutic research, the child's consent may be considered of utmost importance—for example, when risk is greater than minimal and the research is unlikely to directly benefit the child.

The ethics of research, like other ethical concerns, can never be a completely settled matter. Ongoing discussion and tension are appropriate. The prevailing emphasis on human rights and the recognition of past abuse have led to quite stringent surveillance and guidelines. It is important that reasonable balance be maintained, however, so that beneficial research goes forward (e.g., Arnold et al., 1995).

SUMMARY

■ Knowledge of human behavior is gained by scientific methods that vary with regard to settings, procedures, methods, and purpose.

■ The aim of science is to describe phenomena and offer explanations for them. Theoretical concepts guide all aspects of research, including the hypotheses advanced. Hypothesis testing builds knowledge systematically and is tied to the advancement of theory.

■ Observation and measurement are at the heart of science. The assumption that events repeat themselves, given the same or similar conditions, places importance on the reliability, or consistency, of research findings. Also crucial is the issue of validity, the soundness or correctness of findings. Internal validity refers to the degree to which alternative explanations for results can be confidently ruled out. External validity refers to generalizability of findings to other populations and settings.

■ Basic research methods include the case study, systematic naturalistic observation, correlational studies, the experiment, single-subject experiments, and controlled observations and mixed designs. Each of these has weaknesses and strengths.

■ Interest in qualitative methods of research has increased. These methods place high value on individuals' perception of their experiences in their natural environments. Data are collected through in-depth interviews, life histories, and the like. Reliability and validity can be problematic.

■ Research can also vary regarding whether a cross-sectional or a longitudinal strategy is adopted. Cross-sectional studies examine groups of people at one time. These studies are efficient and economical, and they can establish age differences. The longitudinal strategy is much better for tracing development; however, it is expensive and lengthy, and it may suffer from subject loss and repeated measurement. In addition, longitudinal data may reflect generational, or cohort, effects.

■ Sequential designs combine the longitudinal and cross-sectional strategies to permit examination of developmental change, age differences, and the influence of generational (historical) variables.

■ Retrospective (follow-back) studies and prospective longitudinal research of individuals with behavior disorders are useful in identifying risk and possible causal factors. High-risk research follows the development of persons believed to be at risk for a disorder.

■ Epidemiological research aims to establish the rates and distribution of disorders in a population, the factors correlated with disorders, and risk and causal variables. Because this type of research has a basis in medicine, it is interested in the prevention and the treatment of disorders.

■ Ethical issues in research are addressed by several government and professional agencies. Respect for individuals mandates that participants in research not be harmed and that they freely and knowledgeably consent to be subjects. Concern for research participants must be weighed with the potential benefits derived from studying human behavior.

CHAPTER 5

CLASSIFICATION AND ASSESSMENT

T his chapter is concerned with how childhood and adolescent behavior disorders are defined, grouped, and evaluated. The terms *classification,* or *taxonomy,* and *diagnosis* are used to refer to the process of description and grouping. By classification and taxonomy we mean delineating major categories or dimensions of behavior disorders. This can be done for either scientific or clinical purposes. Diagnosis usually refers to the process of assigning an individual to a category of a classification system. Assessment refers to an ongoing process of evaluating youngsters, in part to assist the processes of classification and diagnosis. These entwined processes thus are intricately related to the scientific and clinical aspects of child and adolescent disorders.

CLASSIFICATION AND DIAGNOSIS

A classification system is a way to systematically describe a phenomenon. Biologists have classification systems for living organisms, and physicians classify physical dysfunction. Similarly, systems

exist to classify behavioral disorders. These systems describe categories or dimensions of problem behaviors. A category is a discrete grouping, for example, a category of anxiety disorder or conduct disorder. In contrast, the term "dimension" implies that a behavior is continuous and can occur to various degrees. Thus, for example, a child may exhibit high, moderate, or low levels of anxiety.

Any classification system must have clearly defined categories or dimensions. In other words, the criteria for defining a category must be explicitly stated. Clear and explicit definitions allow for good communication among professionals. Next, it must be demonstrated that the category or dimension exists. That is, the features used to describe a category or dimension tend to occur together regularly—in one or more situations or as measured by one or more methods.

Classification systems must also be reliable and valid. These terms were applied to research methods in Chapter 4. When applied to classification or diagnosis, the terms retain the general meanings of consistency and correctness but are used in somewhat different ways.

With regard to reliability, interrater reliability refers to whether different diagnosticians use the same category to describe a person's behavior. For example, it addresses the question, Is Billy's behavior called separation anxiety by two or more professionals who observe it? Test-retest reliability asks whether the use of a category is stable over some reasonable period of time. For example, is Mary's problem again diagnosed as learning disability when she returns for a second evaluation?

To be valid, diagnostic groupings must be clearly discriminable from one another. Questions of the validity of current diagnostic systems have largely focused on their utility. A diagnosis must provide us with more information than we had when we originally defined the category. Thus diagnoses should give us information about the etiology of a disorder, the course of development that the disorder is expected to take, response to treatment, or some additional clinical features of the problem. Does the diagnosis of conduct disorder, for example, tell us something about this disorder that is different from other disorders? Does the diagnosis tell us something about what causes this problem? Does it tell us what is likely to happen to youngsters having this disorder and what treatments are likely to help? Does it tell us additional things about these young people or their backgrounds? The question of validity is thus largely one of whether we know anything we did not already know when we defined the category. The clinical utility of a classification system is also judged by how complete and useful it is. A diagnostic system that describes all the behavioral disorders that come to the attention of clinicians in a manner that is useful to them is more likely to be employed.

Finally, another important aspect of validity is whether our description of a disorder is accurate. Is the way we have described and classified this disorder the way it actually exists in nature?

CLINICALLY DERIVED CLASSIFICATION SYSTEMS

Clinically derived classification systems are based on the consensus of clinicians that certain characteristics occur together. Historically the classification of abnormal behavior focused primarily on adult disorders. Until relatively recently there was no extensive classification scheme for child and adolescent behavior disorders.

DSM. The most widely used classification system in the United States is the American Psychiatric Association's Diagnostic and Statistical Manual of Mental Disorders (DSM). The Tenth Revision of the International Classification of Diseases (ICD) developed by the World Health Organization (WHO, 1992) is an alternative system that is widely employed and Diagnostic Classification: 0–3 is a system developed to classify mental disorders of very young children (Zero to Three, 1995). Since the DSM system is the dominant system in the United States, we will focus our discussion on it.

The DSM is a categorical approach to classification and thus accepts a view that the difference between normal and pathological is one of *kind* rather than one of *degree*. It also says that distinctions can be made between *qualitatively* different types of disorders.

The DSM is an outgrowth of the original psychiatric taxonomy developed by Kraeplin in 1883, from which children's disorders were omitted. DSM-I contained only two categories of childhood disorders: Adjustment Reaction and Childhood Schizophrenia (American Psychiatric Association, 1952). By the 1960s it had become obvious that a more extensive system was needed. DSM-II added the category of Behavior Disorders of Childhood and Adolescence, which was subdivided into six kinds of disorders (American Psychiatric Association, 1968). The next two revisions, DSM-III and III-R, expanded appreciably the number of categories specific to children and adolescents. As in the past, some adult diagnoses could also be used for youth. These two revisions and the most recent revision, DSM-IV, also involved some changes in the organization of particular categories (American Psychiatric Association, 1980; 1987; 1994).

In DSM-IV all disorders are classified in one of two major groups called axes. On Axis I the clinician indicates any existing clinical disorder (e.g., Conduct Disorder) or other condition that may be a focus of treatment (for example, an academic problem). On Axis II, Mental Retardation or a Personality Disorder, if present, is indicated. These two axes represent the diagnostic categories that are the core of the DSM system. In addition to these two axes, it is recommended that each individual be evaluated in three other arenas, so that a fuller picture is created. Any current medical conditions that are relevant to understanding or treating the youngster are indicated on Axis III. Axis IV is used to indicate any psychosocial or environmental problems that may affect diagnosis, treatment, or prognosis (e.g., death of a family member, housing problems). Axis V is for reporting the clinician's judgment of the child's or the adolescent's overall level of functioning.

Table 5-1 presents the major DSM-IV diagnostic categories described as "usually first diagnosed in infancy, childhood, or adolescence." Each category is further divided into subcategories. A clinician may give a youngster any of these diagnoses, or a diagnosis from elsewhere in the DSM-IV can also be employed. Some of the other diagnostic categories that might be employed for youngsters are psychoactive substance use disorders, schizophrenia, mood disorders, anxiety disorders, eating disorders, and psychological factors affecting medical condition.

The current DSM handling of child and adolescent disorders is considerably more complex and provides more specific subcategories than did earlier versions. Although this was intended to cor-

rect the limited attention to childhood problems in earlier versions, the outcome has been controversial. One issue is whether the existence of specific subcategories is justified by empirical evidence. Another issue is that the more specific subcategories may threaten the reliability of a system. In earlier attempts at diagnosing adult disorders, agreement among diagnosticians was considerably lower for subgroups than for larger categories (Beck et al., 1962). Two-thirds of these disagreements between diagnosticians resulted from inadequate criteria for making a diagnosis. Thus efforts were made in DSM-III, DSM-III-R, and DSM-IV to improve reliability by replacing general descriptions of disorders with clear and more delineated diagnostic criteria. To make a diagnosis of Separation Anxiety Disorder, for example, the following requirements must be met: (1) the child must exhibit three or more of eight specific symptoms for at least four weeks; (2) the onset of these symptoms must occur before the age of eighteen (an inclusion criterion); and (3) the disturbance does not occur exclusively during the course of Pervasive Development Disorder, Schizophrenia, or other psychotic disorder (an exclusion criterion).

There have also been efforts to examine the validity of the DSM approach to classification. Typically these have focused on issues of clinical utility. For example, during the development of DSM-IV, the validity of describing three subtypes of Attention Deficit Hyperactivity Disorder was examined (Lahey et al., 1994). Several differences were found among children who met the criteria for the three subcategories. Not only did they display different behaviors, but the groups also differed in age, sex ratio, academic impairment, and peer acceptance. Therefore, knowing whether a child meets the diagnostic criteria for one and not another subcategory also imparts additional information that did not enter into the diagnostic process. These findings thus support the validity of the three diagnostic subcategories. Nevertheless, despite evidence for the validity of some diagnostic categories, there is still considerable concern regarding the validity of many of the DSM child and adolescent categories, even among those who are,

---

TABLE 5-1

DSM-IV Disorders Usually First Diagnosed in Infancy, Childhood, or Adolescence

Mental Retardation

Learning Disorders

Motor Skills Disorder

Communication Disorders

Pervasive Developmental Disorders (e.g., Autistic Disorder)

Attention Deficit and Disruptive Behavior Disorders

Feeding and Eating Disorders of Infancy or Early Childhood

Tic Disorder

Elimination Disorders

Other Disorders of Infancy, Childhood, or Adolescence (e.g., Separation Anxiety Disorder, Selective Mutism)

in large part, sympathetic to the system's approach to classification (Cantwell, 1996).

There is broad agreement that starting with DSM-III and DSM-III-R, and continuing with DSM-IV, improvements have been made, such as the increased use of a structured set of rules for diagnosis and greater comprehensiveness. Also, in developing DSM-IV, work groups attempted to draw on empirical data in a more consistent fashion (Widiger et al., 1991). The system, however, is not without its critics, and substantial conceptual and political issues remain unresolved (Follette & Houts, 1996; Nathan, 1994).

For example, it is usually argued that changes begun with DSM-III have increased interclinician agreement in diagnosis to higher levels. This strategy for improving reliability has been successful, but it is still the case, as would be expected, that reliability is good for some disorders and poorer for others. The reliability of diagnoses of childhood anxiety disorders is consistent with this general description (Werry, 1994). Under certain circumstances, moderate to strong reliability can be achieved. Even here, however, reliability varies depending on the specific anxiety disorder, the source of information (parent, child), and the child's age and sex (Rapee et al., 1994). Research on the diagnostic reliability of the DSM has thus yielded mixed results. Furthermore, evidence of higher levels of reliability have typically been obtained under research conditions in which diagnosticians are given special training and employ information-gathering procedures different from those likely to be used in typical clinical practice. The reliability of typical clinicians may not be as high (Sonuga-Barke, 1998).

It is also argued that research has focused on pragmatic aspects of reliability and validity. Questions regarding the clinical utility of the system have been the primary focus. Although this focus is clearly of importance, it ignores the separate question regarding diagnostic categories: Does DSM-IV provide an accurate representation of the nature of disorders? Whether a system is useful or helpful for clinicians is a different question from whether it is a good description of the true nature of clinically significant differences in psychological

functioning (Sonuga-Barke, 1998). For example, earlier we presented evidence that supported the validity of describing three subtypes of Attention-Deficit Hyperactivity Disorder (ADHD). However, research by Hudziak and his colleagues (Hudziak et al., 1998), seeking to validate DSM-IV criteria for ADHD, conducted structured diagnostic assessments of a community sample of over 1,500 pairs of adolescent female twins. Their findings again support the existence of these subtypes *but* suggest that the subtypes are best conceptualized as three *continua* (continuously distributed between clinical and nonclinical levels) rather than disease categories.

Another concern with the current system is the problem of "comorbidity." This term is used to describe the situation in which youngsters meet the criteria for more than one disorder. The use of this term is controversial and has been questioned (Lillienfeld, Waldman, & Israel, 1994). The term implies the simultaneous existence of two or more distinct disorders in the same individual. While the issues involved are complex, clearly one alternative view is that it is a mistake to conceptualize these disorders in distinct categorical terms. However, even if one accepts the value of retaining distinct categories, there are multiple ways to conceptualize a child's or an adolescent's meeting the diagnostic criteria for more than one disorder (Carson & Rutter, 1991). It may be, instead, that many disorders have mixed patterns of symptoms. For example, mood disorders may be characterized by a mixture of depression and anxiety. Another alternative is that there are shared risk factors: Some of the same risk factors lead to the problems used to define both disorders. Or perhaps the presence of one disorder (or set of problems) creates an increased risk for developing the other disorder. A related idea is that the second set of problems is a later stage in a developmental progression where earlier problems may or may not be retained, even as additional difficulties develop. For example, it has been suggested that for some children and adolescents, anxiety and depression are related in this kind of developmental sequence (Brady & Kendall, 1992). These are only some of the possible hypotheses to explain "co-

CO-OCCURRENCE: A COMMON CIRCUMSTANCE

Children and adolescents who are evaluated by professionals in clinic or school settings often present with a number of different problems. It frequently occurs that these youngsters' problems are viewed as fitting the criteria for a number of different disorders and thus clinicians often decide to give these children or adolescents more than one diagnosis. How to best conceptualize these instances of co-occurrence or comorbidity is an ongoing concern. The case of Samuel is an example of this common circumstance of co-occurrence of behavior disorders.

Samuel, an 11-year-old child, was referred to a clinic for attempted suicide after he had consumed a mixture of medicines, prescribed to his mother, in an attempt to kill himself. Samuel had slept at home for almost two days, when he was finally awakened by his mother and brought to the hospital.

Samuel lived in an inner-city neighborhood and since second grade had been in repeated trouble for stealing and breaking into empty homes. He

had academic difficulties, was assigned to a special reading class, and was truant from school on a number of occasions. His mother may have experienced several major depressive episodes, sometimes drank heavily, and may have relied on prostitution for income. Samuel's father had not been in contact with the mother since Samuel was born.

At his interview, Samuel appeared sad and cried at one point. He reported having severe "blue periods," the most recent of which had been continuous for the past month. During these periods he thought that he might be better off dead. Samuel also reported that he had recently started to wake up in the middle of the night and had been avoiding his usual neighborhood "gang."

Samuel was given a diagnosis of Major Depressive Disorder and a diagnosis of Dysthymia (a milder but more chronic form of depression) was also considered. In addition he received a diagnosis of Conduct Disorder, Childhood Onset Type and a diagnosis of Reading Disorder. (Adapted from Rapoport & Ismond, 1996)

morbidity." At present the solution to this issue remains unclear. For these reasons, and others, some prefer the term "co-occurrence" to the term "comorbidity."

Epidemiological research indicates that co-occurrence of child and adolescent disorders is quite high; indeed, it may be the norm rather than the exception (Nottelmann & Jensen, 1995) (See "Co-occurrence: A Common Circumstance"). This finding has led some to question the categorical system of DSM-IV on a number of grounds. For example, from the perspective of clinical utility, is this a useful way for clinicians to approach youngsters' problems? Also, there is the question of an accurate representation of the nature of disorder:

Is it best to think of these multiple diagnoses given to a single youngster as distinct and separate disorders? We will further explore the issue of "comorbidity" in later chapters.

There has also been concern expressed about the proliferation of categories and the very comprehensiveness of the DSM system. Although some of the concern is based on conceptual issues (Folete & Houts, 1996), the motivation for and wisdom of making such a wide variety of youngsters' behaviors classifiable as mental disorders has also been questioned (Harris, 1979; Schacht & Nathan, 1977). Designating as mental disorders problems in academic skill areas such as reading and mathematics is an example of this concern. Also, although DSM-IV was probably more open to diverse views than were earlier versions, there were still relatively few nonpsychiatrists, members of various racial and other minority groups, or women participating in its development (Nathan, 1994).

Some observers accept that the DSM system is a dominant reality in the present zeitgeist. Indeed, a classification system, like anything else, is viewed as being influenced by the general social atmosphere within which it exists. Despite its acceptance and use, however, the system is in some ways fundamentally inconsistent with some approaches to children's problems (Scotti, 1996; Valla et al., 1994). For example, DSM does not employ situational variability to moderate diagnostic labels. This omission may be problematic for a behavioral perspective in which situational factors and functional relationships are presumed to influence behavior. Furthermore, some have argued that the DSM promotes a disease/medical model that emphasizes biological etiology and treatment, that deemphasizes environmental factors and the cultural context, and that views disorder as being within the child rather than resulting from the interaction of the child and the environment (Sonuga-Barke, 1998; Sroufe, 1997).

EMPIRICAL APPROACHES TO CLASSIFICATION

The empirical approach to classifying child and adolescent behavior problems is an alternative to the clinical approach to taxonomy. This approach employs statistical techniques to identify patterns of behavior that are interrelated. The general procedure is for the respondent to indicate the presence or absence of specific behaviors in the youngster. The information from these responses is quantified in some way. For example, a "0" is marked if the child does not exhibit a certain characteristic, a "1" is given if a moderate degree of the characteristic is displayed, and a "2" is indicated if the characteristic is clearly present. To develop a taxonomy, such information is obtained for a large number of youngsters. Statistical techniques are then employed to indicate which behaviors tend to occur together. Factor analysis and

cluster analysis are the primary statistical techniques employed in these studies. These procedures are based on correlations among items. The correlation of every item with the others is calculated, and groups of items that tend to occur together are thus identified (Achenbach, 1998). These groups are referred to as factors or clusters. The term "syndrome" is also often employed to describe behaviors that tend to occur together, whether identified by empirical or clinical judgment procedures. Thus, rather than relying on clinicians' views as to which behaviors tend to occur together, empirical and statistical procedures are employed as the basis for developing a classification scheme.

There have been multiple efforts to develop empirically defined syndromes. This research has involved different instruments, responded to by different kinds of adult caregivers, evaluating different populations of youth, who are seen in different settings. The results are quite consistent (Achenbach, 1985; Quay, 1986a).

Substantial evidence exists for two broadband, or general, clusters of behaviors or characteristics. One of these clusters has been given the various labels of externalizing, undercontrolled, or conduct disorder. Fighting, temper tantrums, disobedience, and destructiveness are some of the characteristics frequently associated with this pattern. The second grouping has been variously labeled internalizing, overcontrolled, or anxiety-withdrawal. Descriptions such as anxious, shy, withdrawn, and depressed are some of the characteristics associated with this grouping.

Among the instruments used to derive the two broad-band clusters just described is the Child Behavior Checklist (CBCL), which can be completed by the parents of children four to eighteen years of age (Achenbach, 1991b). The Teacher Report Form (TRF) is a parallel instrument completed by teachers of children five to eighteen years old (Achenbach, 1991c), and the Youth Self-Report (YSR) is designed to be completed by youths from eleven to eighteen (Achenbach, 1991d). Research with these instruments has also identified eight empirically defined less general, or "narrowband," syndromes common to the three instruments. Three of these syndromes fall within the broader category of Internalizing, two fall within the Externalizing grouping, and three are neither clearly Internalizing nor clearly Externalizing (Achenbach, 1991a). These syndromes are described in Table 5-2. Every child who is evaluated receives a score on each of the syndromes, and a profile of syndrome scores for a particular child can be described (see Figure 5-1). This approach to classification evaluates each youngster on several dimensions.

Thus this approach to classification differs from the clinical approach of the DSM in at least two ways. The first difference between the two approaches is in how groupings are defined and formed (empirically versus clinical consensus).

The second difference is that the empirical approach to classification views problems as dimensional rather than categorical. It suggests that differences between individuals are quantitative rather than qualitative and that the difference between normal and pathological is one of degree rather than one of kind.

Empirically based classifications also employ data from normative samples as a frame of reference for judging the problems of an individual youngster. For the CBCL, TRF, and YSR, for example, there are two sets of norms available against which to compare an individual child's or adolescent's scores. A youngster's scores can be compared with norms for nonreferred children or adolescents or with norms based on young people referred for mental health services. There are separate norms for each sex in particular age ranges, as rated by each type of informant. Thus there are separate parent informant CBCL norms for boys four to eleven, boys twelve to eighteen, girls four to eleven, and girls twelve to eighteen and separate similar norms for teacher and for youth informants (Achenbach, 1991b, c, d). In evaluating the behavior problems of an eleven-year-old boy named Scott, for example, one could compare Scott's scores on the empirically based syndromes derived from each of his parents' reports with two sets of norms: norms of parent reports for nonreferred eleven-year-old boys and norms of parent reports for clinic-referred eleven-year-old boys. Scores based on Scott's teacher's responses to the TRF could be compared with similar norms of teachers' reports for eleven-year-old boys. And scores based on Scott's own responses to the YSR could be compared with norms of nonreferred and clinic-referred responses of boys his age.

Reliability and validity. Reliability studies of empirically derived systems generally indicate that problem scores are quite reliable. The pattern of reliability is both interesting and informative (Achenbach, 1991a).

Test-retest correlations from two ratings by the same informant are often in the .80 and .90 range. So, for example, correlations for mothers' ratings on the CBCL taken one week apart ranged from

---

TABLE 5-2

Eight Syndromes Common to the CBCL, TRF, and YSR—with Sample Items

Internalizing Syndromes		
Withdrawn	**Somatic Complaints**	**Anxious/ Depressed**
Would rather be alone	Overtired	Cries a lot
Shy, timid	Aches, pains	Fearful, anxious
Withdrawn	Stomachaches	Unhappy, sad, depressed

Mixed Syndromes		
Social Problems	**Thought Problems**	**Attention Problems**
Acts too young	Hears things	Can't concentrate
Gets teased	Sees things	Can't sit still
Not liked by peers	Strange ideas	Impulsive

Externalizing Syndromes		
Delinquent Behavior	**Aggressive Behavior**	
Lacks guilt	Mean to others	
Bad companions	Destroys others' things	
Steals at home	Fights	

Adapted from Achenbach, 1991a.

.82 to .95 for different syndrome scores. Agreement between different raters observing the child in the same situation is also quite good, although lower than for two evaluations by the same person. Agreement of mothers and fathers on the CBCL, for example, varied depending on syndrome, and ranged between .48 (Thought Problems) and .79 (Attention Problems). If one averages parent agreement across syndromes, the interparent correlation also varied by the age and gender of the child and ranged from .65 to .75. Level of agreement, however, is notably lower between raters who observe youngsters in distinctly different situations. The average correlation between parents and teachers for the CBCL and TRF Total Problem Score, for example, was .44. Degree of agreement varied as a function of youngster's age and sex. Finally, children's self-ratings on the YSR were significantly, but modestly, related to parents' ratings (.36 for boys, .40 for girls) and teachers' ratings (.27 for boys, .25 for girls). These lower correlations may reveal something about young people's behavior, rather than just about the reliability of the approach to classification. There may be aspects of a youngster's behavior that are consistent across time and situations, but a youngster's behavior may vary considerably with different individuals and in different situations. Also, certain attributes may be more or less evident to different individuals or to other persons as compared with the youngsters themselves (e.g., aggression versus feelings of loneliness). Such findings alert us to the possible limitations and bias of any one rater's perspective whether obtained by responses to a particular instrument or by clinical interview (Achenbach, McConaughy, & Howell, 1987; Hewitt et al., 1997; Rowe & Kandel, 1997). Figure 5-1 illustrates the differences in responses of a young girl's mother and father to the Child Behavior Checklist. Differing perceptions of two informants may provide important information to a clinician.

The validity of empirically derived classification systems is indicated by a variety of studies. The findings described earlier, which indicate that the same broadband syndromes have emerged in a variety of studies employing different instruments, different types of raters, and different samples, suggest that the categories reflect valid distinctions. Cross-cultural studies that find similar syndromes (deGroot, Koot, & Verhulst, 1996) add further support. Also, Achenbach (1991b) reports on comparisons of the Child Behavior Checklist and other commonly employed checklists, completed by the same sample of parents. Correlations were significant for total problem scores, the broadband syndromes (internalizing and externalizing), and almost all of the comparable narrowband syndromes. It is important to remember that these significant correlations emerged even though the instruments and their categories often consist of different items. The findings show that the syndromes are valid ones because they emerge under a variety of conditions.

Another way of examining validity is to investigate whether differences in scores relate to other criteria. Comparison of youngsters referred for outpatient mental health services with a sample of nonreferred young people matched for SES, age, and gender indicated that the clinical sample differed significantly from the nonreferred sample on all scores and that this finding was true for all sex/age groups (Achenbach, 1991b). Differences among youngsters scoring high on different syndromes also address the validity of empirically identified syndromes. For example, empirical efforts have identified separate aggressive (overtly aggressive behaviors) and delinquent (lying, stealing, truancy) syndromes (see Table 5-2). Although both kinds of problems are combined in the DSM-IV criteria for a diagnosis of Conduct Disorder, empirical evidence suggests different correlates for the two syndromes. For example, research suggests stronger biochemical correlates and heredity and greater developmental stability for the Aggressive than for the Delinquent syndrome (Achenbach, 1998; Eley, 1997). Scores on these empirical syndromes have also been shown to predict outcomes such as future syndrome scores, academic problems, use of mental health services, and police contacts six years later (Achenbach et al., 1995b; Stanger et al., 1996). Findings such as these support the validity of the empirical and dimensional approach to classification.

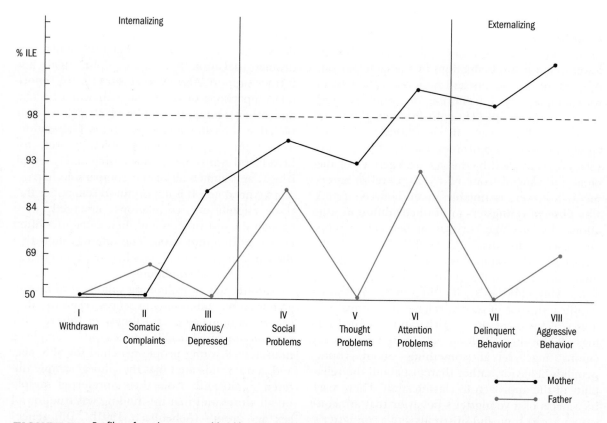

FIGURE 5-1 Profiles of an eleven-year-old girl based on Child Behavior Checklists completed by her mother and father.

THE IMPACT OF LABELS

As we have already noted, classification and diagnosis are intended to facilitate understanding and treatment of behavior disorders. As scientists we can study groups of young people to seek common etiologies. As clinicians we can benefit from previous knowledge in our approach to new cases. However, categories, may also limit the information we seek or the interpretations we make of events. This is one reason why there is concern about applying a category to an individual young person and transforming it into a label.

Although classification is intended as a scientific and clinical enterprise, it can be seen as a social process. The diagnostic label becomes a social status, which carries implications for how people are thought of and treated. If this impact is negative, the label actually detracts from the original purpose of categorizing—that of helping young people (Kliewer & Biklen, 1996).

Formal classification has as its stated intent the categorization of disorders, not persons. Indeed, Cantwell, one of the creators of the current DSM approach, notes: "Any classification system classifies psychiatric disorders of childhood; it does not classify children. Thus it is correct to say, 'Tommy Jones has infantile autism.' It is incorrect to say 'Tommy Jones, the autistic' . . ." (Cantwell, 1980, p. 350). Often ease of communication is the reason for a particular phrasing. For example, the term "autistic children" may be employed rather than repeating the phrase "children receiving the diagnosis of autism." Thus it is realistic to expect the use of terms such as "autistic children" or "depressed children," despite the intent to avoid misplacement of labels. In light of such practices, it is important to be aware of the potential negative effects of the labeling process.

Attention to the potential negative impact of labels is based on information suggesting that they can lead to stigmatization and to even further behavior problems and social difficulties (Milich, McAninch, & Harris, 1992). Expectations regarding a child may be based not only on his or her actual behavior but also on biased perceptions resulting from a label. The child may respond to others' reactions in ways that maintain or exacerbate problem behaviors.

The potential negative perceptions that labels may produce is illustrated in a study by Foster and Salvia (1977). Teachers were asked to view a videotape of a boy and to rate his academic work and social behavior. The tape displayed age- and grade-appropriate behavior in all cases, but some teachers were told that the boy was learning disabled, whereas others were told that he was normal. Teachers watching the "learning disabled" boy rated him as less academically able and his behavior as more socially undesirable than did teachers watching the "normal" child. Furthermore, the negative expectation that may be transmitted by labels is suggested by the findings of a study by Briggs et al. (1994). Adults read vignettes of a six-year-old child engaged in aggressive behavior on a school playground. The stories varied regarding the family history of the child (normal, mother dying of cancer, sexually abused). After reading the vignette, the adults completed a questionnaire about their expectations regarding the behavior of the child. Results indicated that adults had different expectations regarding the sexually abused child; for example, the adults expected the sexually abused child to have more behavior problems and lesser achievement than either of the other two children.

Labels may not always produce negative expectations. Some suggest that labels provide an "explanation" for the child's problematic behavior. The adult is provided with an understanding of why the child is behaving in this manner, thus re-ducing the likelihood of negative reactions and creating more appropriate expectations of what a child can be expected to do. That labels do not always lead to negative expectations is illustrated in a study by Wood and Valdez-Menchaca (1996). Adults interacted with four children, one of whom had previously been diagnosed with an expressive language disorder (ELD). These adults were randomly assigned to one of two conditions: The first was a nonlabel condition in which the child with ELD was not identified, and the second was a label condition in which the child with ELD was identified. Adults in the nonlabel group ranked the child with ELD as significantly less likable, less productive, and less academically competent than the other children. Adults in the label group, in contrast, did not rank the children as different on these attributes. Observations by the adults indicated that adults in the label group did observe the same inappropriate behaviors as those in the nonlabel group but that they appear to have been "more accepting" of such behavior. It is, of course, not clear under what conditions expecting or not expecting children with difficulties to meet the expectations set for other children is helpful or detrimental.

The use of labels may also invite other difficulties. The danger of overgeneralization is one concern: It may incorrectly be assumed that all youngsters labeled with Attention Deficit Hyperactivity Disorder, for example, are more alike than they actually are. Such an assumption readily leads to neglect of the individual child or adolescent. It is also possible that if people react to the youngster as a member of a category, then the youngster may behave in a manner consistent with the expectations of the label.

Finally, Lilly (1979b) and others also suggest that traditional diagnostic categories ignore the fact that a youngster's problems "belong" to at least one other person—the one who is identifying or reporting the problems. As Algozzinne (1977) has noted, the young person may not be inherently "disturbed" but is labeled deviant because of the reactions of others to his or her behavior. Algozzine modified the instructions for the Behavior Problem Checklist. Adults were asked "how disturbing" particular items would be in working with children. The responses of adults to this "Disturbing Behavior Checklist" were submitted to a factor analysis. It is interesting that behavior rated as to degree of disturbingness seemed to cluster in much the same way as in previous studies of disturbed behavior. As we shall see throughout this book, there is much evidence that supports the notion that how a youngster is described and viewed may reflect as much on who is doing the describing as it does on the behavior of the child or adolescent.

Many experts involved in the study and treatment of children or adolescents are concerned about the problems of categorical labels, and these experts advocate to reduce the possible harmful effects. It is acknowledged, however, that categorization is embedded in our thinking and contributes to the advancement of knowledge. Completely discarding categorization is neither desirable nor possible. Thus it is important to strive to improve our classification system and at the same time to be sensitive to social factors inherent in the use of categories, the social status imparted by a label, and the impact of labels on the young person and others (Adelman, 1996; Hobbs, 1975).

ASSESSMENT

Evaluating child and adolescent problems is a complex process. By the time a youngster comes to the attention of a clinician, the presenting problem is usually, if not always, multifaceted. Also, since assessment is the first part of any contact, the professional's knowledge of the problem will be limited. Both of these factors, as well as common sense and caution, argue for a broad and comprehensive assessment process. The best interests of the young person are most likely served by a comprehensive assessment of multiple facets of the youngster and his or her environment.

A COMPREHENSIVE ASSESSMENT

As we shall see throughout our discussion, behavior disorders in youngsters are complex, often containing a variety of components rather than a single

problem behavior. Furthermore, these problems are typically best understood as arising out of and being maintained by multiple influences. Such influences include biological factors, various aspects of the youngster's behavioral, cognitive, and social functioning, and influences of the family and other social systems such as peers and school. Thus an assessment must be comprehensive in evaluating a variety of potential presenting problems, measuring a variety of aspects of youngsters themselves, and assessing various contexts and other individuals. Moreover, information must be obtained from a variety of sources (e.g., the youngster, parents, teachers). These multiple sources are required to assess problems that may vary by context or be displayed differently in interactions with different individuals. A child may behave differently at home, in school, or in playing with his or her peers. Also, different persons may view the same or similar behaviors differently. A mother who is depressed and experiencing a variety of life stresses may be less able to tolerate minor deviations from expected behavior. Such differences in perception may be important both in coming to understand the presenting problems and in planning interventions. Assessment thus requires the use of multiple and varied methods as well as familiarity with assessment instruments for individuals of many different ages. The process requires considerable skill and sensitivity.

Assessment is best accomplished by a team of clinicians carefully trained in the administration and interpretation of specific procedures and instruments. Because assessment is usually conducted immediately on contact with the young person or family, it demands special sensitivity to anxiety, fear, shyness, manipulativeness, and the like. If treatment ensues, assessment should be a continuous process, so that new information can be gleaned and the ongoing effects of treatment can be ascertained. In this way, the clinician remains open to nuances and can avoid rigid judgments about a multifaceted and complex phenomenon.

THE INTERVIEW

The general clinical interview is clearly the most common form of assessment (Watkins et al., 1995). Information on all areas of functioning is obtained by interviewing the youngster and various others in the child's or adolescent's social environment. The fact that behavior is likely to vary according to the situation or to be viewed differently by various observers argues for interviewing a variety of individuals who have contact with the youngster (for example, parents, siblings, or teachers).

Whether the youngster will be interviewed alone will probably vary with age. The older child generally is more capable and is more likely to provide valuable information than is a younger child. Nevertheless, clinicians often elect to interview even the very young child in order to obtain their own impressions. Preschool and grade school children can provide valuable information if appropriate developmental considerations are involved in tailoring the interview to the individual child (Bierman & Schwartz, 1986). For example, an adultlike face-to-face interview may be intimidating for a young child. This difficulty may be reduced if the interview is modeled after a more familiar play or school task. Alternatively, some professionals recommend that the assessment of preadolescent children begin with more structured aspects of the evaluation (e.g., rating scales, structured interviews) rather than the relatively unstructured general clinical interview (Kamphaus & Frick, 1996).

Most clinicians seek information concerning the nature of the problem, past and recent history, present conditions, feelings and perceptions, attempts to solve the problem, and expectations concerning treatment. The general clinical interview is used not only to determine the nature of the presenting problem and perhaps to formulate a diagnosis but also to gather information that allows the clinician to conceptualize the case and to plan an appropriate therapeutic intervention.

A recent development in the interviewing of children and adolescents is the use of structured interviews. The general clinical interview, discussed above, is usually described as open-ended or unstructured. Because such interviews are most often conducted in the context of a therapeutic interaction and are employed along with a variety of other assessment instruments, it has been difficult

to evaluate the reliability and validity of the interview itself. Structured interviews have arisen in part to create interviews that are likely to be more reliable. They also have been developed for the more limited purpose of deriving a diagnosis based on a particular classification scheme such as the DSM or for use in screening large populations for the prevalence of disorders. Table 5-3 lists several of the structured interviews used with children and adolescents. These interviews can be conducted with the youngster and with his or her parent(s).

In the unstructured general clinical interview, there are no particular questions that the clinician must ask, no designated format, and no stipulated method to record information. That is not to say that there are no guidelines or agreed-on procedures for conducting an effective interview. In-

---

TABLE 5-3

Some Structured Interviews Used in Diagnosing Child and Adolescent Disorders

Anxiety Disorders Interview for Children (ADIS-C)
  Developed for differential diagnosis of anxiety disorders in children. (Silverman and Eisen, 1992)

Child Assessment Schedule (CAS)
  A conversational format modeled after traditional child clinical interview—relatively low in structure. (Hodges, Cool, & McKnew, 1989)

Diagnostic Interview for Children and Adolescents (DICA)
  A highly structured interview with separate versions for younger and older children. (Welner et al., 1987)

Diagnostic Interview Schedule for Children (DISC)
  A highly structured interview with questions organized diagnostically. (Shaffer et al., 1996)

Interview Schedule for Children (ISC)
  Low in structure, with primary aim being assessment of affective symptoms and associated problems. (Kovacs, 1985)

Schedule for Affective Disorders and Schizophrenia in School-Aged Children (K-SADS)
  Intermediate in structure and, despite title, assesses a wide range of childhood disorders. (Kaufman et al., 1997)

deed, there is an extensive literature on effective interviewing (Cox & Rutter, 1985; Nietzel, Bernstein, & Milich, 1994). However, unstructured interviews are intended to give the clinician great latitude. In contrast, structured interviews consist of a set of questions that the interviewer asks the youngster. In addition, rules are provided for how the interview is to be conducted, and explicit guidelines are provided for how the youngster's responses are to be recorded and scored.

The investigation of the reliability of interviews must take into account many variables. This necessity is illustrated in a study by Edelbrock and his colleagues (Edelbrock et al., 1985). The Diagnostic Interview for Children, a structured interview that covers a broad range of symptoms and behaviors, was administered to 242 children and their parents. The children had been referred for inpatient or outpatient mental health services. Interviews were conducted twice, with both children and parents, approximately nine days apart. Of interest is that the test-retest reliability based on the child reports was lower for younger than for older children, whereas the reliability based on parent reports was higher for the younger children. The authors suggest that these findings are related to the cognitive development of the children, on the one hand, and to shifts in parents' perceptions and awareness of their child's behavior, on the other.

The validity of interviews, like any other assessment instrument, needs to be evaluated as well. This requirement is particularly difficult for structured interviews designed to achieve a diagnosis, since the validation of the interview is inevitably affected by the validity of the diagnostic system on which it is based. As we have seen, diagnostic systems like the DSM are still evolving, and knowledge of their validity is still being studied. An additional complication in investigating validity is that there is no "gold standard" or ultimate criterion to serve as the basis of comparison. Is the comparison to be made with clinician judgment, parent report, or the Child Behavior Checklist?

Most efforts have focused on how to improve structured interviews for diagnostic and research uses. The questions of what their potential is for

more general clinical practice and what impact they will have on the typical clinician remain unclear.

PROJECTIVE TESTS

At one time the most common form of psychological test employed to assess children was the projective test. These tests are less commonly used today, in large part because of the continuing lack of empirical evidence regarding norms, reliability, and validity (Anastasi & Urbina, 1997; Knoff, 1998).

Projective tests were derived from the psychoanalytic notion of projection as a defense mechanism: One of the ways in which the ego deals with unacceptable impulses is to project them onto some external object. It is assumed that the impulses cannot be expressed directly. Therefore, an ambiguous stimulus is presented, allowing the youngster to project "unacceptable" thoughts and impulses, as well as other defenses against them, onto the stimulus. Projective tests are also used by some clinicians in a manner that involves less psychodynamic inference. This type of analysis examines formal aspects of the test response, for example, the distance between human figures that the child draws. Interpretations are then made on the basis of this response style rather than on the basis of the content of the response.

In the Rorschach test, the youngster is asked what he or she sees in each of ten ink blots (Figure 5-2). The most commonly used methods for scoring and interpretation are based on characteristics of the response, such as the portion of the blot responded to (location), factors such as color and shading (determinants), and the nature of what is seen in the blot (content) (Exner & Weiner, 1995). The Human Figure Drawing, or Draw-a-Person test (Koppitz, 1984; Machover, 1949), requires the youngster to draw a picture of a person and then a second person of the opposite sex. The House-Tree-Person technique (Buck, 1992) asks the child to draw a house, a tree, and a person. In the Kinetic Family Drawing technique (Burns & Kaufman, 1970), the child is asked to draw a picture of everyone in the family, including himself or herself, "doing something." Typically the clinician then asks questions about the drawings. Mur-

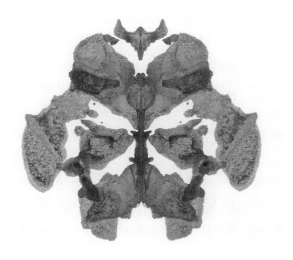

FIGURE 5-2 Inkblot designs, similar to the one pictured here, are employed in the Rorschach test.

ray's (1943) Thematic Apperception Test (TAT), the Children's Apperception Test (CAT) (Bellak & Bellak, 1949; Bellak, 1993), and the Roberts Apperception Test for Children (McArthur & Roberts, 1982) provide the youngster with pictures for which he or she is asked to make up a story. Figure 5-3 presents pictures similar to those used in the CAT.

OBSERVATIONAL ASSESSMENT

Early attempts to observe children's behavior made use of diaries or continuous observations and narrations that were deliberately nonselective (Wright, 1960). From this tradition evolved observations of a more focused, pinpointed set of behaviors that could be reliably coded by observers (Bijou et al., 1969). Such observations are similar or even identical to those done in research studies.

Recent observational methods have come largely from workers with a behavioral/social learning perspective. The observations are fre-

FIGURE 5-3 Drawings similar to those employed in the CAT.

quently made in the child's natural environment, although sometimes planned situations are created in clinic or laboratory settings to approximate naturally occurring interactions. Observations range from single, relatively simple, and discrete behaviors of the child, such as the occurrence of toileting, to observations of the child and peers, to complex systems of interactions of family members (Kolko, 1987; Israel, Pravder, & Knights, 1980; Reid, 1978). Clearly, ongoing interactions are more difficult to observe and code than are the behaviors of a single individual; however, they are likely to be theoretically and clinically relevant.

The first step in any behavioral observation system involves explicitly pinpointing and defining behaviors. Observers who are trained to use the system then note whether a particular behavior or sequence of behaviors occurs. Most coding systems have been inspected for reliability. Indeed, behavioral/social learning studies commonly report on the reliability of the observations employed, even if a reliability check is not the major purpose of the research.

The aspect of reliability most frequently reported is interrater reliability. Two or more observers independently observe the same behavior, and then the degree of agreement is calculated. Research indicates that a number of factors affect reliability as well as validity and clinical utility (Hops, Davis, & Longoria, 1995). For example, the complexity of the observational system and changes over time in the observers' use of the system (observer drift) are two factors known to affect observation. Careful training and periodic monitoring of observers' use of the system are recommended for reducing distortions in the information obtained from direct observation.

The issue of reactivity is often cited as the greatest impediment to the utility of direct observation. Reactivity refers to whether the knowledge that one is being observed changes one's behavior. Thus introducing a trained observer or videotaping equipment into a situation may cause those in the situation to react to this novel stimulus and so to behave in a different manner than usual. A number of strategies are recommended to help reduce reactivity. One is to use persons already in

the situation (e.g., teachers) as observers. Doing this is likely to reduce the artificial and novel aspects of observation. A second approach is to arrange for observers to be present for some period of time prior to data collection, so that their presence is less artificial and no longer novel.

Behavioral observations are the most direct method of assessment and require the least inference. The difficulty and expense involved in training and maintaining reliable observers is probably the primary obstacle to their common use in nonresearch contexts. Since direct observation has long been considered the hallmark of assessment from a behavioral perspective, attempts have been made to create systems that are more amenable to widespread use. For example, experienced observers may be asked to make global ratings on the basis of observation of behavior rather than recording specific behaviors. Direct observation is, however, just one aspect of a multimethod approach to behavioral assessment that can include self-monitoring of behavior, interviews, ratings and checklists, and self-report instruments.

PROBLEM CHECKLISTS AND SELF-REPORT INSTRUMENTS

Problem checklists and rating scales were described in our discussion of classification (pp. 97–100). There are a wide variety of these instruments. Some are for general use, for example, the Revised Behavior Problem Checklist (Quay & Peterson, 1983) and the Child Behavior Checklist (Achenbach, 1991b), and others are used with particular populations. The Revised Conners Parent Rating Scale (Conners et al., 1998b), for example, can be used when Attention Deficit Hyperactivity Disorder needs to be assessed. The considerable empirical literature suggests that these instruments may be valuable tools for clinicians and researchers.

For example, the parent-reported problems and competencies of 2,600 youth (fourteen- to sixteen-years old) assessed at intake into mental health services and 2,600 demographically matched nonreferred youngsters were compared (Achenbach et al., 1991). Checklist scores clearly discriminated between the clinic and nonreferred children regarding both behavior problems and social competencies. Furthermore, referral status accounted for greater differences in behavior than did factors such as age, SES, and gender. Figure 5-4 illustrates the differences between clinic and nonreferred children.

A general rating scale may thus help a clinician judge the parent's view of the child's adjustment against norms for referred and nonreferred populations. This procedure can help in evaluating the appropriateness of the referral. Once a particular presenting problem is identified, the use of a more specific rating scale might also be part of the clinician's assessment strategy.

Furthermore, rating scales completed by different informants may help the clinician gain a fuller appreciation of the clinical picture and of potential situational aspects of the child's problem. For example, there is a Teacher Report Form (Achenbach, 1991c) that can supplement a parent's report on the Child Behavior Checklist (CBCL), and there is a Revised Teacher Rating Scale (Conners et al., 1998a) to go along with the Revised Conners Parent Rating Scale. The availability of the CBCL, TRF, and YSR in the Achenbach instruments, makes it possible to compare multiple informants' reports about the child with respect to a common set of problem items and dimensions. For exam-

ple, when two or more respondents using these instruments describe a child, a statistic can be computed indicating the degree of agreement. This degree of agreement for a particular child can then be compared with the degree of agreement between comparable informants for a large representative sample. Thus it is possible to know whether the degree of agreement between Tommy's mother and his teacher is less than, similar to, or greater than the average mother-teacher agreement about boys in Tommy's age range.

In addition, the clinician or researcher may also draw on a wide variety of instruments to assess the youth's own report (Reynolds, 1993). Here, too, there are general measures, for example, the Youth Self-Report (Achenbach, 1990), and more specific measures. There are self-report measures specific to problems such as anxiety and depression and also instruments to assess constructs related to adjustment such as control beliefs and self-concept (Connell, 1985; Harter, 1985; Kovacs, 1992; Reynolds & Richmond, 1985). Many of these measures will be described in later chapters that focus on particular child and adolescent problems.

Parents and other adults can also be asked to complete self-report instruments about themselves. These instruments may assess specific prob-

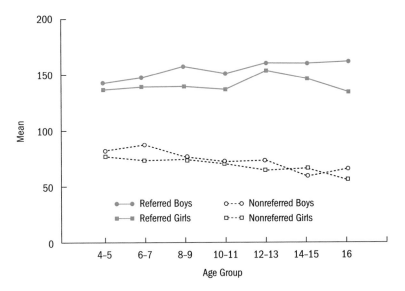

FIGURE 5-4 Mean total problem scores for referred and nonreferred children of each sex at each age.

(From Achenbach et al., 1991.)

lems for these adults; for example, a parent's own anxiety or depression might be assessed. However, a wide variety of aspects of these adults' functioning can be of importance. For instance, the feelings, attitudes, and beliefs of these adults, particularly with respect to the child or adolescent, may also be assessed (e.g., the Parenting Stress Index-Abidin, 1995); or aspects of the family environment may be measured (e.g., the Family Environment Scale-Moos & Moos, 1986; and the Parent-Adolescent Relationship Questionnaire-Robin, Koepke, & Moye, 1990). Such assessment can provide important information about the youngster's social environment and factors that may contribute to problem behavior and thus facilitate conceptualizing the presenting problem and planning intervention.

INTELLECTUAL-EDUCATIONAL ASSESSMENT

The evaluation of intellectual-academic functioning is an important part of almost all clinical assessments. Intellectual functioning is a central defining feature for disorders such as mental retardation and learning disabilities, but it may also contribute to and be affected by a wide variety of behavioral problems. Compared to most other assessment instruments, tests of intellectual functioning tend to have better established normative data, reliability, and validity. Although our present discussion of these instruments is brief, additional information will be presented in later chapters.

Intelligence tests. By far the most commonly employed assessment devices for evaluating intellectual functioning are tests of general intelligence. In fact, they probably constitute the most frequently employed assessment device other than the interview. The Stanford-Binet–Fourth Edition (Thorndike, Hagen, & Sattler, 1986); the Wechsler tests—the Wechsler Preschool and Primary Scale of Intelligence–Revised (Wechsler, 1989) and the Wechsler Intelligence Scale for Children–Third Edition (Wechsler, 1991); and the Kaufman Assessment Battery for Children (Kaufman & Kaufman, 1983) are some of the intelligence tests widely used in clinical settings. All are individually administered and yield an intelligence

(IQ) score. The average score is 100, and an individual score reflects how far above or below the average person of his or her age an individual has scored.

Intelligence tests have long been the subject of heated controversy. Critics have argued that the use of IQ scores has resulted in intelligence being viewed as a real thing rather than as a concept. Furthermore, this use has led to intelligence being viewed as a rigid and fixed attribute rather than as something complex and subtle. Critics also claim that intelligence tests are culturally biased and have led to social injustice (cf. Kamin, 1974; Kaplan, 1985). Although intelligence tests are popular and useful in predicting a variety of outcomes, these criticisms and continued concern with legal, ethical, and practical issues demand that they be used cautiously and that continued attention be paid to test improvement and monitoring of appropriate usage (Perlman & Kaufman, 1990; Kamphaus, 1993).

Developmental scales. Assessment of intellectual functioning in very young children, and particularly in infants, requires a special kind of assessment instrument. A popular measure is the Bayley Scales of Infant Development (Bayley, 1969; 1993). The original version extended from two to thirty months of age. The revised version expanded that range from one to forty-two months. Performance on developmental tests yields a developmental index rather than an intelligence score. Unlike intelligence tests, which evaluate language and abstract reasoning abilities, developmental scales emphasize sensorimotor skills and simple social skills. For example, the Bayley examines the ability to sit, walk, place objects, attend to visual and auditory stimuli, smile, and imitate adults. The Bayley includes a Motor Scale, a Mental Scale, and a Behavior Rating Scale that assesses aspects of the child's behavioral style (e.g., attitude, interest). Perhaps because intelligence tests and developmental scales tap different abilities, there is only a low correlation between performance on them (Sattler, 1988).

Ability and achievement tests. In addition to assessing general intellectual functioning, it is often necessary or helpful to assess functioning in a particular area. A variety of tests have been developed for this purpose (Katz & Slomka, 1990; Sattler, 1988). The Wide Range Achievement Test (Jastak & Wilkinson, 1984) and the Woodcock Mastery Tests (Woodcock, Mather, & Barnes, 1987), for example, are two measures of academic achievement that are administered to an individual youngster. Tests such as the Iowa Test of Basic Skills (Hoover et al., 1996) and the Stanford Achievement Test (Harcourt Brace Education Measurement, 1997) are group-administered achievement tests employed in many school settings. Specific ability and achievement tests are particularly important in working with children with learning and school-related problems.

ASSESSMENT OF PHYSICAL FUNCTIONING

Assessment of physical functioning can provide several kinds of information valuable to understanding disordered behavior. Family and child histories and physical examinations may reveal genetic problems that are treatable by environmental manipulation. For example, phenylketonuria (PKU) is a recessive gene condition that is affected by dietary treatment. Avoidance of phenylalanine in the child's diet prevents most of the cognitive problems usually associated with the condition. In addition, diseases and defects may be diagnosed that affect important areas of functioning either directly (for example, a urinary tract infection causing problems in toilet training) or indirectly (for example, a sickly child being overprotected by parents). Also, signs of atypical or lagging physical development may be an early indication of developmental disorders that eventually influence many aspects of behavior.

The assessment of the nervous system is considered particularly important to understanding a variety of problem behaviors, but especially mental retardation, autism, learning disabilities, and attention deficit disorders. Brain and other neurological dysfunction, measurable in various ways, is thought to be associated with abnormal physical reflexes, motor coordination problems, and sensory and perceptual deficits.

Currently assessment of presumed neurological dysfunction in children usually consists of a combination of direct neurological approaches and indirect neuropsychological assessment. Such assessment requires the coordinated efforts of neurologists, psychologists, and other professional workers.

Neurological assessment. There are a number of procedures that directly assess the integrity of the nervous system (Teodori, 1993). The computer has revolutionized neurological assessment, and new techniques have become the primary mode of evaluation. The electroencephalograph (EEG) is a procedure with a long history that has been improved by the availability of computers (Kuperman et al., 1990). The EEG and the Event-Related Potential (ERP) require placing electrodes on the scalp that record activity of the brain cortex in general or during a time when the individual is engaged in information processing. Individual differences in EEG activation patterns have been found in studies of fearful and inhibited children and in infants of depressed mothers, and the ERP has been used to study learning and language disorders (Dawson et al., 1997; Nelson & Bloom, 1997).

New technologies such as brain imaging techniques have vastly improved our ability to assess and localize damage or abnormalities in brain structure and have begun to be employed in research and clinical work with children and adolescents (Zametkin, Ernst, & Silver, 1998). For example, computerized tomography, or the CT scan (also referred to as computerized axial tomography—CAT scan), allows tens of thousands of readings of minute variations in the density of brain tissue, measured from an X-ray source, to be computer processed so that a photographic image of a portion of the brain can be obtained. The resulting image can reveal subtle structural abnormalities of the brain. Positron emission tomography (PET) scans determine the rate of activity of different parts of the brain by assessing the use of oxygen and glucose, which fuel brain activity. The more active a particular part of the brain is, the more blood carrying glucose flows to this area. After a small amount of radioactive substance has been injected into the bloodstream, amounts of radiation appearing in different areas of the brain are measured while the person engages in some particular task. Many images are taken of the brain, and a computer-produced color-coded picture is created that indicates different levels of activity in different parts of the brain. Newer developments allow PET scans to estimate the production of brain neurotransmitters. Functional magnetic resonance imaging (fMRI) is a noninvasive procedure that produces sharp images, by tracking subtle changes in oxygen in different parts of the brain. Particular parts of the brain are called on to perform some task, and these regions receive increased blood flow and thus increased oxygen. By placing the person inside a circular magnet, the MRI scanner detects these changes and produces pictures of the brain that indicate areas of activity. Related magnetic resonance techniques permit the study of various brain chemicals. These relatively new assessment tools are becoming increasingly important in individual assessment and research.

Neuropsychological assessment. Neuropsychological assessment employs tests that contain learning, sensorimotor, perceptual, verbal, and memory tasks. From the individual's performance on these tasks, inferences are made about central nervous system functioning. Neuropsychological assessment is thus an indirect means of assessing brain function.

Neuropsychological assessments originally were employed in the hope that they could detect the presence or absence of brain damage. The development of direct methods of assessing the integrity of the central nervous system and the failure to find evidence of brain damage in suspected populations have resulted in a shift of focus. The emphasis is currently more likely to be on distinguishing groups of behavioral and learning disorders that are presumed to have a neurodevelopmental etiology. For example, any test that discriminates learning disabled from normal learners might be considered neuropsychological in this sense (Taylor, 1988b). Interest also exists in assessing changes arising out of alterations in the

central nervous system, for example, evaluating recovery from head injury.

The current interest in neuropsychological assessment is attributable, at least in part, to increased sensitivity to the needs and legal requirements of providing services to children with handicapping conditions—some of whom exhibit problems presumed to have a neurological etiology. Also, advances in medicine have resulted in increasing numbers of children who survive known or suspected neurological trauma. The increase in survival rates of infants born prematurely is one example. Children with acute lymphocytic leukemia who receive treatment that includes methotrexate injected directly into the spinal column and radiation to the head are yet another example.

Neuropsychological assessment appreciates the need for broadly based assessment. Two of the most widely used collections of instruments are the Halstead-Reitan Neuropsychological Test Battery for Children (Reitan & Wolfson, 1993) and the Luria-Nebraska Neuropsychological Battery–Children's Revision (Golden, Purisch, & Hammeke, 1985). As the term "battery" implies, these instruments consist of several subtests or scales, each intended to assess one or more abilities. The use of a broad spectrum of tests is the usual strategy employed in neuropsychological approaches to assessment (Fletcher & Taylor, 1997). The spectrum may be designated or fixed batteries like the preceding, or flexible batteries based on combinations of other existing tests (e.g., the Wechsler Intelligence Scales, achievement tests, the Bender Visual-Motor Gestalt Test; see Figure 5-5), or indeed some combination of these approaches.

Neuropsychological assessment in children is still a relatively young field, and continued development of instruments that derive from evolving research on cognitive development, neurological development, and brain-behavior relationships is ongoing. Research is also being directed toward developing strategies that more clearly specify impairment and guide rehabilitation.

One other issue that needs to be addressed is the often subtle assumption that the behaviors that are assessed and the neuropsychological as-

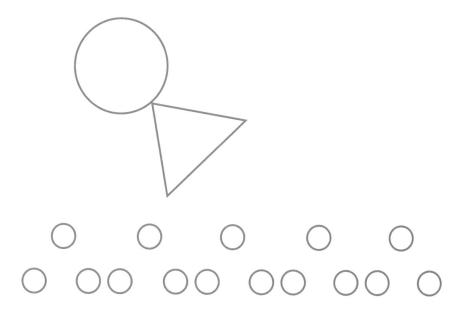

FIGURE 5-5 The Bender-Gestalt, a neuropsychological test, consists of designs, similar to those here, which the child is asked to copy.

sessments themselves are free from social and environmental influences. There is little empirical justification for this assumption. For example, brain damage is correlated with social class and family variables that are disadvantageous to social adjustment and physical health (Rutter, Graham, & Yule, 1970; Sameroff & Chandler, 1975). These sociofamilial variables may themselves underlie both the brain damage and the observed behavioral or learning problems.

SUMMARY

■ Clinically derived classification relies on consensus among clinicians regarding disorders and their definition. The DSM, the clinically derived system most likely to be employed in the United States, is a categorical approach to classification.

■ The recent versions of DSM include an increased number of categories of child and adolescent disorders, provide more highly structured rules for diagnosis, use a multiaxial system to assess various aspects of functioning, and have drawn on research data in a more consistent fashion.

■ Although reliability of the DSM has been improved by more structured diagnostic rules, there is still considerable variation across categories. The validity of some of the diagnostic categories has received considerable attention, but the validity of others is still questioned. Despite improvements, DSM is still criticized by some on clinical, scientific, ethical, and social-political grounds.

■ The problem of "comorbidity,"—youngsters' meeting the criteria for more than one disorder—presents particular challenges.

■ Empirical approaches to classification rely on behavior checklists and statistical analyses, and tend to be associated with dimensional rather than categorical approaches to classification.

■ Achenbach's Child Behavior Checklist, Teacher Report Form, and Youth Self-Report are examples of checklists employed in the empirical approach. There is good support for two broad syndromes—an undercontrolled, externalizing, conduct disorder syndrome and an overcontrolled, internalizing, anxiety-withdrawal syndrome—and support for subcategories within each general syndrome.

■ Information from multiple informants suggests sensitivity to the possible influence of situational differences on behavior and to differences due to the respondent's perspective.

■ Critics of diagnostic systems remind us of the possible dangers of labeling children and adolescents. To the extent that such labels reduce our effectiveness as scientists and clinicians, they do not serve the young person's best interest.

■ Conducting a comprehensive assessment is necessary, not only for classification and diagnosis but also for planning and executing appropriate interventions. The complex process of assessment requires a multifaceted approach.

■ The general clinical interview is the most common form of assessment. Structured interviews are organized so as to provide information for a DSM diagnosis.

■ Projective tests are probably less widely used than was once the case as a result of questions concerning their reliability and validity.

■ Observation of behavior is central to a behavioral/social learning approach and is a direct method of assessment. The practicality of implementing current observation systems in general clinical practice is an impediment to their widespread use.

■ Problem checklists can be employed to sample a wide range of behavior problems or those problems particular to a specific disorder. These checklists may enable the clinician to compare a child to appropriate norms and to examine issues such as situational aspects of a child's behavior and the perceptions of various informants.

■ Self-report measures are available for both the youngster and the relevant adults in the youngster's life. These instruments can be used to assess constructs directly related to the presenting problem (e.g., anxiety, depression) or related constructs of potential interest (e.g., self-concept, control beliefs, parenting stress, family environment).

■ Intellectual-educational assessments are conducted for a wide variety of presenting problems. General intelligence and developmental levels are evaluated, as well as specific abilities and achievement. Although intelligence tests are popular, they are in many ways controversial. Given that they present a variety of concerns, they should be used cautiously.

■ Assessment of physical functioning, especially of the nervous system, is important for many behavior problems. Methods include case histories, medical examinations, the EEG, and several newer techniques, such as the CT scan, PET scans, and MRIs. Much attention has also been given to neuropsychological testing as a means of indirectly assessing known or suspected problems in central nervous system functioning.

CHAPTER 6

ANXIETY DISORDERS

With this chapter we begin an examination of specific behavior disorders. The children and adolescents discussed in this and the next chapter are variously described as anxious, fearful, withdrawn, timid, depressed, and the like. They seem to be very unhappy and to lack self-confidence. These youngsters are often said to have emotional difficulties that they take out on themselves; thus the term "internalizing disorders" is often employed to describe such problems.

AN INTRODUCTION TO INTERNALIZING DISORDERS

A variety of evidence supports the existence of an empirically defined broadband internalizing syndrome (see Chapter 5). Although there is widespread acceptance of this broad syndrome, the existence of reliable and valid subcategories is far less clear (Daugherty & Shapiro, 1994).

For clinically defined classifications, the problems now under discussion were broadly referred to as neuroses, a term that is now employed less frequently. More specific terms such as phobias, obsessions and compulsions, anxiety disorders,

and depression are employed in much of the current literature and in current clinical practice. The next two chapters of this text are organized around these frequently employed terms.

However, the use of these more specific clinical diagnostic categories, such as the various anxiety and depressive disorders described in the DSM system, is also often questioned, partly because of the difficulty often encountered in achieving adequate interrater reliability. Even with the use of structured diagnostic interviews that were developed to improve reliability, results are best described as uneven (Silverman, 1994).

In addition to the issue of reliability, considerable evidence indicates that a given child or adolescent often meets the criteria for more than one of the different subcategories or disorders (Nottlemann & Jensen, 1995b). In Chapter 5 it was suggested that one of the criteria for a good classification system is that categories be distinct and not overlap. Thus one issue that needs to be addressed for these subcategories is overlapping attributes and diagnostic criteria (Clark & Watson, 1991; Malcarne & Ingram, 1994; Shaffer et al., 1989).

The phenomenon of an individual's meeting the criteria for more than one disorder, which is often termed "comorbidity," was discussed in Chapter 5. The dilemma is an appreciable one. Children who receive an anxiety disorder diagnosis frequently also meet the criteria for one or more other diagnoses. Keller et al. (1992), for example, found that 38 (14 percent) of the 275 youngsters they studied received an anxiety disorder diagnosis. Many of the children receiving an anxiety disorder diagnosis also met the criteria for other disorders. For example, 37 percent of the youngsters receiving an anxiety disorder diagnosis also received a diagnosis for a depressive disorder. Similarly, Cohen et al. (1993b) assessed for the presence of three different internalizing disorders (depression, separation anxiety, and overanxious disorder) and found that 20 percent of the youngsters with an internalizing disorder met the criteria for more than one of these disorders. The problem becomes even more complex when one also considers noninternalizing disorders such as disruptive behavior disorders. In the Keller et al. study, for example, of the children receiving an anxiety disorder diagnosis, 16 percent also met the diagnostic criteria for Attention Deficit Disorder, and 16 percent were diagnosed with Conduct Disorder. In the Cohen and colleagues study, 36 percent of the youngsters with an anxiety disorder also met the criteria for one of these disruptive behavior disorders.

With these considerations in mind, let us turn to an examination of internalizing disorders. In this chapter we examine anxiety disorders, and in Chapter 7 we discuss the problems of depression and social withdrawal.

DEFINITION AND CLASSIFICATION OF ANXIETY DISORDERS

There is general agreement on a definition of the phenomenon of anxiety or fear (Barrios & O'Dell, 1998; Lang, 1984). Anxiety or fear is defined as a complex pattern of three types of reactions to a perceived threat. This tripartite model describes overt behavioral responses (e.g., running away, trembling voice, closing eyes), physiological responses (e.g., changes in heart rate and respiration, muscle tension, stomach upset), and subjective responses (e.g., thoughts of being scared, self-deprecatory thoughts, images of bodily harm). Much as with the

situation for the larger category of internalizing disorders, however, there is considerable disagreement as to whether and how anxiety disorders should be subcategorized. It is argued that at present, there is insufficient information to make any particular classification scheme clearly the most valid or useful (Barrios & Hartmann, 1997; Silverman, 1993). Because the DSM classification is the approach most commonly used in recent literature, much of this chapter is organized using this system. In the following section, we briefly describe the DSM and the empirical approaches to classification of youngsters' fears and anxieties.

THE DSM APPROACH

DSM-IV describes one type of anxiety disorder that is "usually first diagnosed in infancy, childhood, or adolescence." Separation Anxiety Disorder is characterized by the child's excessive distress when separated from persons to whom there is a strong attachment and by the avoidance of situations that require separation. In addition to this disorder, a child or an adolescent can be diagnosed with many of the other anxiety disorders. Phobic disorders are characterized by fear or avoidance of specific objects or situations other than separation or involvement with strangers. Panic Disorder is characterized by sudden attacks of intense anxiety. These attacks do not occur only in response to a particular phobic stimulus or threatening situation. Generalized Anxiety Disorder is characterized by frequent and excessive anxiety or worry about a number of activities or events rather than anxiety being focused on particular objects or situations. Obsessive-Compulsive Disorder is characterized by recurrent unreasonable thoughts or urges and by repetitive and irrational behaviors. Appreciable anxiety occurs when these obsessive-compulsive rituals are resisted. Posttraumatic Stress Disorder involves anxiety that is linked to a catastrophic event (e.g., rape, assault, earthquake, airplane crash). The youngster persistently reexperiences the event, avoids stimuli associated with the event, and experiences persistent symptoms of increased arousal. We will expand on the DSM definitions as we turn to a discussion of each disorder.

THE EMPIRICAL APPROACH

Empirical systems that are based on statistical procedures have also yielded subcategorizations that are related to anxiety disorders. Within the broad category of internalizing disorders, for example, Achenbach (1991a) describes an anxious/depressed syndrome (see Table 6-1). There is not, however, a separate anxiety syndrome or other narrower syndromes that correspond to the specific anxiety disorders of the DSM, suggesting that in youngsters, the various anxiety and depression symptoms tend to occur together. Other internalizing syndromes, such as "somatic complaints" (e.g., feeling dizzy, having stomachaches) and "withdrawn" (e.g., refusing to talk, feeling withdrawn), also contain symptoms that are likely to be related to anxiety problems.

TABLE 6-1

Behavior Problems Included in the Anxious/Depressed Syndrome

Lonely

Cries a lot

Fears impulses

Needs to be perfect

Feels unloved

Feels persecuted

Feels worthless

Nervous, tense

Fearful, anxious

Feels too guilty

Self-conscious

Suspicious

Unhappy, sad, depressed

Worries

Harms self

Thinks about suicide

Overconforms

Hurt when criticized

Anxious to please

Afraid of mistakes

From Achenbach (1991a).

SPECIFIC PHOBIAS

Youngsters with phobias try to avoid the situation or object that they fear. For example, children who have an extreme fear of dogs may refuse to go outside. When confronted with a large dog, they may "freeze" or run to their parent for protection. In crying out for help, the youngster may describe feelings of tension, panic, or even fear of death. Nausea, palpitations, and difficulty in breathing may also occur. These reactions may occur even when contact with the feared situation is merely anticipated. Thus, not only is the youngster restricted in his or her activities, but fears of encountering dogs are also likely to change the lifestyle and activities of the family as a whole.

DEVELOPMENTAL CHARACTERISTICS OF CHILDREN'S FEARS

Knowing about normal fears is important to understanding children who require clinical attention. Many investigators have explored the development of fears, and a number of trends are suggested by their data.

General prevalence. Several classic studies of general populations indicate that children exhibit a surprisingly large number of fears. Jersild and Holmes (1935) reported that children aged two to six years had between four and five fears and exhibited fearful reactions once every four-and-a-half days. MacFarlane, Allen, and Honzik (1954), in their longitudinal study of children from age two through fourteen, found that specific fears were reported in 90 percent of their sample. Forty-three percent of the six- to twelve-year-olds studied by Lapouse and Monk (1959) had seven or more fears. An interesting aspect of the latter study is the suggestion that mothers may underestimate the prevalence of fears in their children. Mothers reported 41 percent fewer fears than indicated by the children's own reports.

Although it appears that fears are quite common among children, the prevalence of intense fears is less clear. In one investigation in the United States, fewer than 5 percent of mothers indicated that their children exhibited extreme fear, as opposed to nor-

Fears are quite common in children. It is only when these fears are persistent, are intense, interfere with functioning, or are developmentally inappropriate that they may require clinical attention.
(Tamara Reynolds/Tony Stone Images)

mal (5 to 15 percent) or no (84 percent) fear reactions (Miller, Barrett, & Hampe, 1974). This finding is consistent with Rutter, Tizard, and Whitmore's (1970) Isle of Wight study, in which serious fears were reported in only seven per thousand of the ten- and eleven-year-olds studied. In contrast, however, Ollendick's (1983) sample of children between the ages of three and eleven averaged between nine and thirteen extreme fears, and Kirkpatrick's (1984) sample of adolescents between the ages of fifteen and seventeen averaged between two and three intense fears. Other epidemiological data also suggest that extreme fears may be more prevalent (Rutter, 1989a). In addition, the use of semistructured interviews with nonreferred children (Bell-Dolan, Last, & Strauss, 1990) indicates that anxiety disorder symptoms are common. Between 10.7 and 22.6 percent of children endorsed symptoms of phobias. (Phobias, clinical level fears, are described later).

Sex and age differences. Most research suggests that girls exhibit a greater number of fears than boys (King et al., 1989; Kirkpatrick, 1984; Ollendick, 1983). Some studies suggest a greater fear intensity in girls as well (Graziano, DeGiovanni, & Garcia, 1979). Findings of sex differences probably should be interpreted with caution since it is quite possible that gender-role expectations are, in part, responsible for differences between boys and girls in displaying and admitting to fears.

It is most commonly reported that both the number and the intensity of fears experienced by children decline with age (King et al., 1989; Lapouse & Monk, 1959; MacFarlane et al., 1954). Figure 6-1, in general, illustrates this pattern. It is also usually reported that certain fears appear to be more common at particular ages: for example, fear of strangers at six to nine months, imaginary creatures during the second year, fear of the dark among four-year-olds, and social fears and fear of failure in older children (Miller et al., 1974). Bauer (1976) found similar trends and suggested that developmental changes in children's perception can inform our understanding of their fears. For example, increasing differentiation of internal

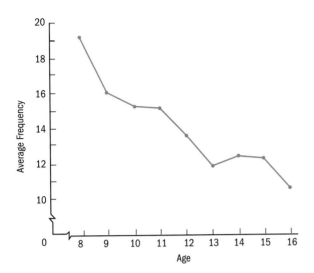

FIGURE 6-1 Frequency of fears across age.
From King, Ollier, Iacuone, Schuster, Bays, Gullone, & Ollendick, 1989.

reality from objective reality may help explain why younger children fear ghosts and monsters, whereas older children have more realistic fears of physical danger or injury. Social expectations and the acceptability of expressing certain fears at a particular age must also be considered. Older children, for instance, may be socialized to believe that bedtime fears are inappropriate, and they therefore may not express them. Age combined with gender-role expectations may produce similar effects. For example, although equal proportions of younger boys and girls indicated that they had frightening dreams, 10 percent of sixth-grade boys as opposed to 70 percent of same-age girls reported this experience (Bauer, 1976).

In a study of American and Australian children and adolescents, Ollendick, King, and Frary (1989) also found that the number and intensity of fears decreased with age. However, when the kinds of fears reported were examined, eight of the ten most feared objects or situations were the same regardless of age (Table 6-2). Additional fears, however, were consistent with age differences in the content of fears. Among seven- to ten-year olds, "getting lost in a strange place" (43.6 percent) and "being sent to the principal" (42.9 percent) were among the ten most endorsed fears. For eleven- to thirteen-year-olds, "having my parents argue" (36.7 percent), and for fourteen- to sixteen-year olds, "failing a test" (29.9 percent), were among the ten most common fears.

Should youngsters' fears receive clinical attention? Mild fear reactions and those specific to a developmental period might be expected to dissipate quickly. However, if the fear, even though short-lived, creates sufficient discomfort or interferes with functioning, intervention may be justified. Most authorities would not usually view age-appropriate fears as requiring clinical attention unless they were quite intense or continued longer than expected. "Phobia" is the term usually employed to describe fears that are exaggerated in these ways.

DSM CRITERIA

The essential feature of the DSM-IV diagnosis of Specific Phobia is a marked and persistent fear of a specific object or situation that is excessive or unreasonable. In addition, the diagnosis requires that exposure to the phobic stimulus almost invariably provokes an immediate anxiety response. In children this anxiety may be expressed by crying, tantrums, freezing, or clinging. A third criterion for adults and adolescents is that the person must recognize that his or her fear is excessive or unreasonable; however, this feature may be absent in children. Fourth, the child or adolescent must avoid the phobic situation(s) or must endure exposure with intense anxiety and distress. Finally, the fear must produce marked distress or must interfere significantly with the youth's normal routine, academic functioning, or social relationships.

DSM-IV suggests that specific phobias be further subcategorized into five types: animal, natural environment (e.g., heights, storms, water), blood-injection-injury, situational (e.g., airplanes, enclosed places), and other (e.g., in children, avoidance of loud sounds or costumed characters).

TABLE 6-2

The Ten Most Common Fears Reported by Age

| | | Percent of Youth Reporting Fear | | |
| | | Age | | |
Item	Total	7–10	11–13	14–16
Being hit by car/truck	54.7	62.2	52.8	48.4
Not being able to breathe	52.7	56.9	50.6	50.4
Bombing attack/being invaded	48.5	51.6	47.2	46.6
Fire—getting burned	45.4	52.1	43.0	40.8
Falling from high place	43.1	48.9	39.4	41.0
Burglar breaking into house	41.0	46.1	39.9	36.7
Earthquake	40.5	48.6	40.3	31.4
Death—dead people	36.6	41.1	36.7	31.1
Getting poor grades	33.8	33.6*	33.9	34.0
Snakes	33.1	35.3*	33.4*	29.7*

* Indicates that this fear was not one of the top ten for this particular subsample.
From Ollendick, King, & Frary, 1989.

EPIDEMIOLOGY AND DEVELOPMENTAL COURSE

Specific phobias are among the most commonly diagnosed anxiety disorders in children and adolescents. Although estimates of prevalence vary somewhat, reviews suggest that an average of about 5 percent of the youngsters exhibit "excessive worries or fears" or phobias. Specific phobias are typically described as more prevalent in girls than in boys, but this gender difference is not consistently reported (Anderson, 1994; Costello & Angold, 1995b; Silverman & Ginsberg, 1998).

There is not a great deal of research information on the natural course of specific phobias, but there is often the impression that children's phobias are relatively benign and that improvement will occur over time with or without treatment. However, there is reason to question this perception and to think in terms of continuity over time (King & Ollendick, 1997). Reports of phobic adults, although limited by their retrospective nature, suggest that specific phobias are likely to begin in childhood and may for some individuals persist into adulthood (Kendler et al., 1992b). Furthermore, the age of onset reported by adults with phobias can give us some suggestion of the course of different phobias. Öst (1987), for example, found variations in reported age of onset among adults referred for treatment who received six different DSM-III diagnoses: agoraphobia (anxiety about being in a situation where escape might be difficult or embarrassing), social phobia, and four subgroups of specific phobias. The results shown in Figure 6-2 illustrate that, with the exception of claustrophobia, specific phobias appear to have the earliest age of onset and to occur during childhood. A reasonable suggestion, therefore, is that specific phobias are likely to begin during childhood and that for at least some individuals, they may persist over time.

Youngsters with specific phobias are also likely to meet the criteria for other diagnoses. For example, Last, Strauss, and Francis (1987) found that among youngsters who were referred to an anxiety disorders clinic with a primary diagnosis of specific

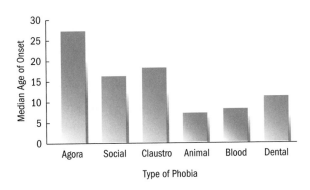

FIGURE 6-2 Median age of onset for various phobias. Adapted from Öst, 1987.

phobia, the majority met criteria for one or more other disorders. Additional diagnoses included other anxiety disorders, depression and mood disorders, and externalizing disorders such as Oppositional Defiant Disorder. Treatment studies of phobic children also suggest that many experience co-occurring disorders (King & Ollendick, 1997).

SOCIAL PHOBIA

Louis, a twelve-year-old white male, was referred by his school counselor because of periodic episodes of school refusal, social withdrawal, and excessive need for reassurance. Louis had few friends and rarely participated in social activities. Louis found parties, eating in public, and using public restrooms particularly difficult. Spanish class was also particularly difficult for him because there were regular assignments to read aloud or to carry on conversations with classmates. Louis's mother described him as always having been excessively fearful, timid, scared of everything, and needing constant reassurance. The mother herself had a history of anxiety problems, was fearful of meeting new people, and had little social contact. (Adapted from Silverman & Ginsburg, 1998)

The second category of phobia specified by DSM-IV is Social Phobia (or Social Anxiety Disorder). Louis received this diagnosis, as well as the diagnosis of Generalized Anxiety Disorder (described later). The diagnosis of social phobia, compared with specific phobias, is a newer one,

and the disorder has received less systematic attention in children and adolescents (Beidel & Randall, 1994).

DESCRIPTION

Youngsters with social phobia fear social situations. They are afraid to meet and talk with people. Because these youngsters try to avoid social situations, they may miss school and may be unlikely to participate in recreational activities. For example, younger children may not attend birthday parties or participate in Boy Scout or Girl Scout meetings. Adolescents' social development may be interfered with, since these youngsters are not likely to attend school events such as club meetings or dances, or to date. Even everyday and seemingly mundane activities, such as eating in public, may be avoided. Albano, Chorpita, and Barlow (1996) describe a teenage girl who spent every lunch period in a bathroom stall so as to avoid the school cafeteria. Youngsters such as this are likely to have concerns about being embarrassed or negatively evaluated. Their thoughts are likely to focus on negative attributes that they perceive in themselves and to be self-deprecatory. Complaints of illness and stomachaches are common, especially in younger children.

Children and adolescents with social phobias may experience distress in a variety of social situations (Beidel & Randall, 1994). For youngsters in the eight to twelve age range, the most commonly identified situations involve public speaking (reading aloud, giving a book report, giving a speech). Distress in these situations was reported by 88 percent of socially phobic children. Other situations identified included eating in public, writing in public, going to parties, using public restrooms, speaking to authority figures, and informal interactions with peers, parents, and friends. Although public speaking was the distressful situation encountered by the largest number of youngsters, it was not the stressful situation that occurred most often in a youngster's day. Diaries kept over a two-week period suggested that informal peer interactions occurred most frequently, accounting for 42.9 percent of distressful situations encountered by a youngster.

SELECTIVE MUTISM

A young kindergarten girl, Amy, does not speak in school or with her peers. She has been this way since beginning preschool. Children like Amy might be given a diagnosis of Selective Mutism.

Youngsters with Selective Mutism do not talk in specific social situations. These social situations, such as the classroom or play activities, are ones in which their peers typically do talk or in which talking is important to their development. This behavior occurs despite the fact that they do speak in other situations. For example, they may speak easily with family members if no one else is present. The onset of this disorder is described as usually occurring before age five. These youngsters are also often described as shy, withdrawn, fearful, and clinging (American Psychiatric Association, 1994).

Selective Mutism is classified in DSM-IV among "other disorders of infancy, childhood, and adolescence," but recently it has been suggested that it might better be conceptualized as a type of social phobia. Black and Uhde (1995) found that 90 percent of thirty children with Selective Mutism met the criteria for social phobia in other ways than reluctance to speak. Similarly, Dummitt and his colleagues (1997) found that all of the fifty selectively mute children that they evaluated met the criteria for either Social Phobia or Avoidant Disorder (an earlier diagnosis that is subsumed under Social Phobia in DSM-IV) and that about half had an additional anxiety disorder. Thus it may be useful to view Selective Mutism as a type of Social Phobia.

The development of the Social Anxiety Scale for Children–Revised (La Greca & Stone, 1993) suggests that social anxiety in elementary-school-age children can be grouped into three factors: fear of negative evaluation from peers, social avoidance and distress in new situations, and generalized social avoidance and distress (Table 6-3). Research also suggests that social anxiety is associated with less social acceptance by peers, lesser feelings of self-worth, and more negative interactions with peers (Ginsburg, La Greca, & Silverman, 1998).

CLASSIFICATION

DSM-IV describes social phobia as a marked and persistent fear of acting in an embarrassing or a humiliating way in social or performance situations. The fear occurs in situations in which the person is exposed to unfamiliar people or to scrutiny by others. In applying this criterion to children, it must be demonstrated that they have the capacity to engage in age-appropriate social relationships with familiar people—that the difficulties are not due merely to absence of appropriate social skills. Furthermore, the social anxiety must occur in peer settings, not just in interactions with adults. In children this anxiety may be expressed by crying, tantrums, freezing, or shrinking from social situations with unfamiliar people.

The criteria for social phobias are similar to those for specific phobias:

1. Exposure to the feared situation almost invariably provokes anxiety.
2. There must be a recognition by the adolescent that the fear is excessive or unreasonable (this may be absent in children).

TABLE 6-3

Examples of Items from the Three Factors of the Social Anxiety Scale for Children–Revised

Fear of Negative Evaluation from Peers

I worry about what other kids think of me.

I'm afraid that other kids will not like me.

I feel that kids are making fun of me.

Social Avoidance and Distress—New Situations

I feel shy around kids I don't know.

I feel nervous when I'm around certain kids.

Social Avoidance and Distress—General

I feel shy even with kids I know very well.

It's hard for me to ask other kids to play with me.

By permission of author Annette M. La Greca.

3. The feared situations are avoided or are endured with intense distress.

To meet diagnostic criteria, this anxiety must also interfere with academic functioning or social relationships, or must produce marked distress about the phobia.

Adolescence is a developmental period during which social anxieties are quite common; therefore, the distinction between normal and abnormal social anxiety may be particularly difficult. Interpretation of severity, defined in the DSM diagnostic criteria by phrases such as "almost invariably," "marked distress," "intense anxiety," and "interferes significantly," becomes particularly important in this age group (Clark et al., 1994).

Since there are limited empirical data regarding social phobia in children and adolescents, the exact nature of the disorder is unclear. Also, a large proportion of youngsters diagnosed with social phobia meet the criteria for other anxiety disorders and for depression (e.g., Last et al., 1992). The task of clarifying distinctions among Social Phobia, anxiety disorders such as Generalized Anxiety Disorder, and social relational constructs such as behavioral inhibition and shyness must, therefore, also be addressed. (These other anxiety disorders and related social relations constructs are discussed later and in Chapter 7.)

EPIDEMIOLOGY

Social phobia is estimated to occur in approximately 1 percent of children and adolescents (e.g., Kashani & Orvaschel, 1990; Lewinsohn et al., 1993a; McGee et al., 1990). In terms of the prevalence in clinic populations, 14.9 percent of youngsters assessed at an anxiety disorders clinic were given a primary diagnosis of social phobia, and 32.4 percent had a lifetime history of the disorder (Last et al., 1992). On the basis of reports of children seen in clinics and retrospective reports, the age of onset is typically described as middle to late adolescence (Öst, 1987; Strauss & Last, 1993). The disorder is most frequently diagnosed in adolescents; however, it can occur earlier but is rarely diagnosed in children under ten years old (Beidel & Randall, 1994; Vasey, 1995). It is probably the case that prevalence increases with age, and in view of discrepancies with adult rates, the disorder may be underrecognized, particularly in adolescents (Albano & Barlow, 1996; Clark et al., 1994). At present it is not clear whether there are gender differences in the prevalence of social phobias. Most youngsters with social phobia also meet the criteria for another anxiety disorder, and adolescents may also meet the criteria for a major depressive disorder.

SEPARATION ANXIETY AND SCHOOL REFUSAL

Kenny, a ten-year-old boy, lived with his parents and his two half-siblings from his mother's previous marriage. He was brought to an anxiety disorders clinic by his parents because he was extremely fearful and had refused to go to school during the past several months. Kenny was also unable to be in other situations in which he was separated from his parents (playing in the backyard, a Little League practice, staying with a sitter). When separated from his parents, Kenny cried, had tantrums, or threatened to hurt himself (e.g., jump from the school window). Kenny also exhibited high levels of anxiety, a number of specific fears, significant depressive symptomatology (e.g., sad mood, guilt about his problems, occasional wishes to be dead, and periodic early awakening). Kenny's separation problems appear to have begun about a year earlier when his father was having drinking problems and was away from home for prolonged periods of time. Kenny's separation problems gradually worsened over the year. (Adapted from Last, 1988)

DESCRIPTION

Anxiety concerning separation from a primary caregiver is part of the normal developmental process in infants. Children, from the first year of life through the preschool years, typically exhibit periodic distress and worry when they are separated from their parents or other individuals to whom they have an attachment. Indeed, the absence of any distress on separation may be indicative of an insecure attachment. Even in older children, it is not uncommon for expectations, beliefs, and prior separation experiences to lead to feelings of homesickness when separated from parents (Thurber & Sigman, 1998). It is only when distress on separation persists beyond the expected age or is excessive that such separation anxiety is viewed as problematic.

Young children experiencing separation anxiety may be clingy, following their parents around. They may express general fear or apprehension, experience nightmares, or complain of somatic symptoms (e.g., dizziness, headaches, stomachaches, nausea). Older children may complain about not feeling well, may think about illness or tragedy that might befall them or their caregivers, become apathetic and depressed, and be reluctant to leave home or to participate in activities with their peers.

Separation-anxious children may threaten to harm themselves. This threat is usually viewed as a means to escape or avoid separation. Serious suicidal behavior is rare in children with Separation Anxiety Disorder.

Historically the term "school phobic" was employed to describe children who exhibited anxiety regarding school attendance. Severe anxiety and somatic symptoms such as dizziness, stomachaches, and nausea that "keep" the child at home were described. The parents, concerned with the child's health and anxiety, were often reluctant to force attendance. It was not clear, however, that in all cases the child actually feared the school situation. Thus some workers questioned the use of the term "school phobia" to describe the disorder. Indeed, many cases of school phobia appeared instead to be due to a fear of separation from the mother and home. This theme, that avoidance of school may be just one manifestation of the larger fear of separation, has long been popular. Therefore, some workers suggested the more comprehensive term "school refusal" (Hersov, 1960), and this term has since become common. However, this term may be taken to imply a conscious decision by the child to refuse to go to school, a perspective that does not seem applicable to all cases. Thus there is still much conceptual disagreement and terminological confusion in the literature (Blagg & Yule, 1994; Kearney & Silverman, 1996).

As suggested before, it is best not to view all cases of school refusal as being similar or as having a unitary cause. The most common conceptualization of school refusal in children, however, does attribute the problem to separation anxiety. Psychodynamic explanations describe the child's insistence on remaining at home as satisfying both the child's and the mother's needs and conflicts concerning separation. The basic notion is that strong attachment leads the child to fear that something may happen either to the self or to the mother during separation. In the latter instance, the child may have aggressive wishes toward the parent that the child fears will be fulfilled (Kessler, 1988). There is little information about the father's role in this process.

Behavioral explanations of school refusal as separation anxiety presume that the child has learned an avoidance response because of some association of school with an existing intense fear of losing the mother. Once avoidance behavior occurs, it may be reinforced by attention and other rewards, such as toys and special foods, that the child receives while at home.

Clinical reports suggest that onset of the disorder often follows some life stress (death, illness, change of school, move to a new neighborhood), but to date there is limited empirical support for such a connection.

CLASSIFICATION

The DSM-IV category of Separation Anxiety Disorder (SAD) is intended to describe children with excessive anxiety regarding separation from a major attachment figure and/or home. Diagnostic criteria include eight symptoms involving worry or distress and related sleep and physical problems. These symptoms (Table 6-4) are associated with concerns of separation from or worry of harm befalling major attachment figures. Three or more of these symptoms must be present for at least four weeks. The problems must be present prior to age eighteen and must result in significant distress or impairment in social, school, or other areas of functioning.

Reluctance or refusal to go to school is one of these eight symptoms; however, a child need not exhibit this behavior to receive the diagnosis since

---

TABLE 6-4

Symptoms Used in DSM-IV to Diagnose Separation Anxiety Disorder

1. Recurrent excessive distress when separation from home or major attachment figures occurs or is anticipated

2. Persistent and excessive worry about losing, or about possible harm befalling, major attachment figures

3. Persistent and excessive worry that an untoward event will lead to separation from a major attachment figure (e.g., getting lost or being kidnapped)

4. Persistent reluctance or refusal to go to school or elsewhere because of fear of separation

5. Persistent and excessive fear or reluctance to be alone or without major attachment figures at home or to be without significant adults in other settings

6. Persistent reluctance or refusal to go to sleep without being near a major attachment figure or to sleep away from home

7. Repeated nightmares involving the theme of separation

8. Repeated complaints of physical symptoms (such as headaches, stomachaches, nausea, or vomiting) when separation from major attachment figures occurs or is anticipated

---

only three of the eight symptoms need to be present to receive the diagnosis. Thus not all children with separation anxiety disorder exhibit school refusal. In addition, as suggested by the term "school phobic," not all school refusers need to show separation anxiety. Some children, for example, may fear some aspect of the school experience. This latter group might be diagnosed under the specific phobia or social phobia categories. For example, children may fear going to school because of anxiety regarding evaluation, speaking in public, or meeting new people. Studies of clinic-referred children support a distinction between separation-anxious and phobic school refusers (Kearney, Eisen, & Silverman, 1995; Last & Strauss, 1990).

School refusal is often also differentiated from truancy. Truants are usually described as absent on an intermittent basis, often without parental knowledge. The school refuser, in contrast, is usually absent for continuous extended periods, during which time the parents are aware of the child's being at home. Also, truants are often described as poor students who exhibit other conduct problems such as stealing and lying. However, the considerable co-occurrence of anxiety and conduct disordered problems in children has led some to suggest that the refuser/truant distinction may not be a useful one (Russo & Biedel, 1994).

We have chosen to describe school refusal and separation anxiety together, since much of what has been written about the problem of school refusal and its etiology has derived from a separation anxiety perspective. In addition, given that compulsory education laws require all children to attend school, it seems likely that many children with separation anxiety would also have problems with school attendance. To the extent that school refusal is related to a phobic reaction to some aspect of the school situation, the considerations regarding specific and social phobias would apply.

EPIDEMIOLOGY AND DEVELOPMENTAL COURSE

Separation anxiety disorder is probably one of the most common anxiety disorders in children. Estimates of prevalence in community samples typically

Refusing to go to school and/or to be separated from parents is a common reason for referral for psychological services.

(Ed Lettau/Photo Researchers, Inc.)

percent of children with Separation Anxiety Disorder were given one or more other diagnoses, with the most common being Generalized Anxiety Disorder, present in about 33 percent of these children (Last, Strauss, & Francis, 1987).

Almost all children appear to recover from Separation Anxiety Disorder; however, many appear to develop some later disorder, with depression being particularly common (Last et al., 1996). In older adolescents, separation anxiety may be the precursor of more serious problems (Blagg & Yule, 1994; Tonge, 1994). As adults, such individuals may be at risk for a number of problems, including depression. Large-scale longitudinal studies are clearly needed to clarify hypothesized relationships, particularly in girls, to adult disorders such as Agoraphobia and Panic Disorder.

School refusal is usually estimated to occur in .4 percent to 1.5 percent of the general population (e.g., Grannel de Aldaz et al., 1984; Ollendick & Mayer, 1984). It is interesting, however, that some reports suggest that as many as 69 percent of referrals for any kind of child phobia are for school refusal, and the problem is seen in approximately 3 percent to 8 percent of clinic-referred children (Last & Strauss, 1990; Miller et al., 1972; Smith, 1970). Miller and others have suggested that this tendency may be due to the fact that the problem creates considerable difficulty for parents and school personnel.

School refusal, unlike SAD, can be found in children of all ages. There is the suggestion that in younger children, the problem is likely to be related to separation anxiety, but children in middle-age groups and early adolescence are likely to have complex and mixed presentations of anxiety and depressive disorders. Prognosis seems best for children under the age of ten years and successful treatment seems to be particularly difficult with older children (Berg & Jackson, 1985; Blagg & Yule, 1994; Miller et al., 1974). If left untreated, serious long-term consequences seem possible.

In working with school refusers, the majority of clinicians of all orientations stress the importance of getting the youngster back to school (Blagg & Yule, 1994; King, Ollendick, & Gullone, 1990). Successful strategies take an active approach to the

range from about 3 to 12 percent of children, the average being about 5 percent. Among children referred to clinics for anxiety disorders, approximately 12 percent to as much as one-third receive a primary diagnosis of Separation Anxiety Disorder (Albano et al., 1996; Silverman & Ginsburg, 1998). The prevalence declines after early childhood, and the disorder is probably uncommon in adolescence (Clark et al., 1994). Some studies report a greater prevalence of SAD among girls as compared with boys, but others report no gender differences (Albano et al., 1996). Children with Separation Anxiety Disorder often also meet diagnostic criteria for other disorders. At an outpatient clinic, about 80 problem—finding a way of getting the youngster back to school even if this is difficult or requires the threat of legal intervention.

GENERALIZED ANXIETY DISORDER

Phobias, school refusal, and separation anxiety represent relatively focused anxiety disorders. However, anxiety is sometimes experienced in a less focused manner. Clinicians frequently describe children and adolescents who worry excessively and exhibit extensive fearful behavior. These disturbances are not focused on any particular object or situation but rather occur in a number of situations and are not due to a specific recent stress. Such youngsters seem excessively concerned with their competence and performance, and they exhibit nervous habits (e.g., nail biting), sleep disturbances, and physical complaints such as stomachaches.

CLASSIFICATION

Prior versions of the DSM employed the diagnosis of Overanxious Disorder of Childhood and Adolescence (OAD) to recognize this clinical entity. With DSM-IV, however, this diagnosis was eliminated. Instead, children and adolescents would now be considered, along with adults, under the category of Generalized Anxiety Disorder (GAD). We will use both terms here since much of the literature has employed the term "overanxious disorder."

Generalized Anxiety Disorder is characterized by frequent excessive anxiety and worry about a number of different events or activities. The youngster finds it difficult to control this worry, and the anxiety and worry are accompanied by other symptoms. The youngster must exhibit one or more of six additional symptoms, which are presented in Table 6-5. Symptoms must be present most days and be present for at least 6 months. These symptoms must also cause significant distress or impairment in important areas of the youngster's functioning. The following description captures the clinical picture.

TABLE 6-5

Symptoms Used in DSM-IV to Diagnose Generalized Anxiety Disorder

Excessive anxiety or worry

Difficulty controlling worry

1. Restlessness or feeling on edge
2. Fatigue
3. Difficulty concentrating
4. Irritability
5. Muscle tension
6. Disturbed sleep

Like his mother, John had a very low opinion of himself and his abilities . . . and found it difficult to cope with the "scary things" inside himself. His main problem had to do with the numerous fears that he had and the panic attacks that overtook him from time to time. He was afraid of the dark, of ghosts, of monsters, of being abandoned, of being alone, of strangers, of war, of guns, of knives, of loud noises, and of snakes. . . . Like his mother again, he had many psychosomatic complaints involving his bladder, his bowels, his kidneys, his intestines and his blood. . . . He also suffered from insomnia and would not or could not go to sleep until his mother did. . . . He was also afraid to sleep alone or to sleep without a light, and regularly wet and soiled himself. He was often afraid but could not say why and was also fearful of contact with others. (Anthony, 1981, pp. 163–164)

PREVALENCE AND DEVELOPMENTAL COURSE

Epidemiological studies of nonclinic samples suggest that Generalized Anxiety Disorder is a relatively common problem in younger children. However, exact estimates vary from 2.9 to 14 percent (Anderson et al., 1989; Cohen et al., 1993b; Costello, 1989). The disorder is usually reported to be more common in girls, and the median age of onset is estimated to be about ten years of age (Keller et al., 1992). The rates of the disorder are generally stable across the period from childhood to adolescence (Strauss, 1994). However, there are exceptions to this finding. Cohen et al. (1993b), for example, found a strong linear decline in rates of overanxious disorder for boys between the ages of ten and twenty, but very little decline for girls during this same age period.

Generalized Anxiety Disorder is probably the most common anxiety disorder among adolescents (Clark et al., 1994). However, estimates of rates in the general population of adolescents vary ranging from 3.7 to 7.3 percent (Kashani & Orvaschel, 1990; McGee et al., 1990; Whitaker et al., 1990). The findings of Cohen et al. (1993) indicate a rate of about 14 percent for girls in both the fourteen to sixteen and the seventeen to twenty age ranges, but a prevalence of about 5 percent for boys in both of these age groups.

The disorder is a common presentation among youngsters seen in clinical settings. Keller and colleagues (1992), for example, report that 85 percent of the youngsters with an anxiety disorder were diagnosed with Overanxious Disorder. Although other estimates are not quite this high, the disorder is commonly diagnosed (Albano et al., 1996). Furthermore, the disorder does not seem transitory. For example, Keller and colleagues (1992) report a mean duration of four-and-a-half years for episodes of Overanxious Disorder. Persistence may be particularly likely for those with more severe symptoms. Cohen, Cohen, and Brook (1993a) found that 47 percent of youngsters with the most severe symptoms continued to meet diagnostic criteria for Overanxious Disorder two-and-a-half years later. Greater impairment also seems to be associated with the presence of more severe overanxious symptoms, and increased impairment is seen among adolescents (Clark et al., 1994; Strauss, 1994).

Indeed, an examination of developmental differences in children and adolescents provides some interesting information (Strauss et al., 1988). The criteria for OAD were met by 55 of the 106 cases of anxiety disorders examined in this investigation. In order to examine developmental differences, two groups were formed by dividing children under and over twelve years of age. Strauss and her colleagues found that the two groups did not differ in terms of the prevalence of the OAD diagnosis or sociodemographic characteristics. Both groups also showed similar rates of specific OAD symptoms. Older children, however,

presented with a greater number of symptoms than did younger children and also reported higher levels of anxiety and depression. Table 6-6 illustrates the percentage of children in each age group who also met the diagnostic criteria for other disorders. Within the anxiety disorders, young children were significantly more likely to receive a concurrent diagnosis of Separation Anxiety Disorder, and older children a concurrent diagnosis of Simple Phobia (Specific Phobia). Older children were also significantly more likely to receive a concurrent diagnosis of Major Depression, and younger children a concurrent diagnosis of Attention Deficit Disorder. These findings suggest a developmental difference in how generalized anxiety is experienced. However, it should also be noted that many other diagnostic categories were represented in one or both of the age groups. Youngsters who meet the diagnostic criteria for OAD or GAD also are likely to meet the diagnostic criteria

---

TABLE 6-6

Concurrent DSM-III Diagnoses for Younger versus Older Children with Overanxious Disorder

	Age Groups	
DSM-III Diagnoses	**<12 years (Percent)**	**≥12 years (Percent)**
Anxiety disorders		
Separation Anxiety Disorder	69.6	21.9*
Avoidant Disorder	13.0	25.0
Simple Phobia	8.7	40.6*
Social Phobia	8.7	9.4
Agoraphobia	0	6.3
Panic Disorder	0	15.6
Obsessive-Compulsive Disorder	4.3	9.4
Major Depression	17.4	46.9*
Oppositional Disorder	17.4	6.3
Conduct Disorder	8.7	0
Attention Deficit Disorder	34.8	9.4*

* Statistically significant difference.

Adapted from Strauss, Lease, Last, & Francis, 1988.

for other disorders (Cohen et al., 1993b; Strauss, 1994), and these youngsters appear to meet the criteria for more additional disorders than youngsters with other diagnoses (Silverman & Ginsburg, 1998). Indeed, using the older Overanxious Disorder diagnosis, some have questioned whether OAD is a distinct disorder. Alternatively, what is now considered a separate disorder might instead be viewed as indicating a general constitutional vulnerability toward anxiety or emotional reactivity, with help sought for youngsters on the basis of the presence of other anxiety or internalizing disorders (Beidel, Silverman, & Hammond-Laurence, 1996).

PANIC ATTACKS AND PANIC DISORDER

While falling asleep, Frank often experienced discrete episodes of his heart beating quickly, shortness of breath, tingling in his hands, and extreme fearfulness. These episodes lasted only fifteen to twenty minutes, but Frank could not fall asleep in his bedroom and began sleeping on the living room couch. His father brought him back to his bed once he was asleep, but Frank was tired during the day, and his schoolwork began to deteriorate. (Adapted from Rapoport & Ismond, 1996)

Intense, discrete experiences of extreme fear that seem to arise quickly and often, without any clear cause, are known as panic attacks and are another way that adolescents and children experience anxiety.

DEFINITION AND DIAGNOSIS

A distinction is made between panic attacks and Panic Disorder. A panic attack is a discrete period of intense fear or terror that has a sudden onset and reaches a peak quickly—ten minutes or less. DSM-IV describes thirteen somatic or cognitive symptoms, four or more of which must be present during an episode (see Table 6-7). There are three different categories of panic attacks, defined by the presence or absence of triggers. Unexpected (uncued) panic attacks occur spontaneously or "out of the blue" with no apparent situational trigger. In contrast, situationally bound (cued) panic attacks occur on almost all occasions when the

---

TABLE 6-7

Symptoms of a Panic Attack According to DSM-IV

1. Palpitations, pounding heart, or accelerated heart rate
2. Sweating
3. Trembling or shaking
4. Sensations of shortness of breath or smothering
5. Feeling of choking
6. Chest pain or discomfort
7. Nausea or abdominal distress
8. Feeling dizzy, unsteady, lightheaded, or faint
9. Derealization (feelings of unreality) or depersonalization (being detached from oneself)
10. Fear of losing control or going crazy
11. Fear of dying
12. Paresthesias (numbness or tingling sensations)
13. Chills or hot flushes

---

person is exposed to or anticipates a feared object or situation (e.g., a dog). Situationally predisposed panic attacks occur on exposure to a situational cue, but not all of the time; that is, they do not occur invariably, and they may occur following exposure rather than immediately.

Panic attacks are not themselves a diagnosis within the DSM system, but rather they may occur in the context of several different anxiety disorders. One of these disorders is Panic Disorder. To meet the diagnostic criteria for a Panic Disorder, the youngster must experience recurrent *unexpected* panic attacks. In addition, at least one of these attacks must be followed by at least a month of one or more of the following consequences: (1) persistent concern about additional attacks, and/or (2) worry about the meaning of the attacks (e.g., "I'm having a heart attack, "I'm going crazy"), and/or (3) an appreciable change in behavior related to the attacks.

More severe cases of panic may lead to the youngster's becoming terrified of leaving home for fear of being alone or as a way to avoid certain circumstances where the youngster might have a panic attack that he or she can't control or might be embarrassed by. This pattern of avoidance is know as agoraphobia.

DESCRIPTION AND PREVALENCE

Although there is an established literature regarding panic attacks and Panic Disorder in adults, it is only more recently that the occurrence of panic in children and adolescents has received attention (Kearney et al., 1997; Ollendick, Mattis, & King, 1994). This discrepancy was, in part, due to controversy as to whether there was sufficient evidence of the existence of panic attacks and Panic Disorder in youngsters (Kearney & Silverman, 1992; Klein et al., 1992). Much of the controversy revolved around whether children experienced both the physiological and cognitive symptoms of panic, and if so, whether these were experienced as spontaneous (uncued).

Although methodological criticisms suggest caution (Kearney & Silverman, 1992), reviews of research indicate the presence of panic attacks and Panic Disorder in adolescents and, to a lesser degree, in prepubertal children (Ollendick, 1998). Many adults who experience panic attacks or Panic Disorder, for example, report that onset had occurred during adolescence or earlier. Also, both community samples and clinic-based studies indicate the presence of panic attacks and Panic Disorder in adolescents. Evidence regarding preadolescents is less well established, and the occurrence of spontaneous (uncued) prepubertal panic may be rare (Klein et al., 1992).

Panic attacks do not appear to be uncommon in adolescents. For example, 16 percent of youngsters between the ages of twelve and seventeen in a community sample of Australian youth reported at least one full-blown panic attack (four or more of the thirteen symptoms) in their lifetime (King et al., 1997). Other community samples report even higher lifetime rates of panic attacks among adolescents (Ollendick, 1998). Regarding Panic Disorder, Whitaker and colleagues (1990) report a lifetime prevalence for panic disorder of 0.6 percent in a general adolescent sample of fourteen- to seventeen-year-olds. The prevalence reported in clinical samples of adolescents is higher—about 10 to 15 percent (e.g., Alessi, Robbins, & Dilsaver, 1987; Last & Strauss, 1989). Estimates of the exact prevalence vary, depending on how information is gathered (Clark et al., 1994). Both panic attacks and Panic Disorder are reported more frequently in girls than in boys.

With regard to how panic is experienced, studies of adolescents seen in clinics indicate that these youths evidence both the physiological and cognitive symptoms of panic. For example, Bradley and Hood (1993) found that seven of the physiological symptoms were reported by more than 50 percent of their sample. Cognitive symptoms were reported less frequently: "going crazy" was reported by 32 percent, and fear of dying by 25 percent. Whether panic attacks are cued or spontaneous is less clear. Psychosocial stressors (e.g., family conflict, peer problems) were reported as possible precipitants by twenty-six of the twenty-eight adolescents in this study. Some studies, however, report that for some youngsters, the panic attacks are judged to be spontaneous—"out of the blue." There is a problem in judging the spontaneous nature of panic attacks in youngsters, who are probably less insightful than adults and therefore may report an attack as spontaneous if the youngsters are not specifically and carefully questioned about cues. This problem is particularly true in relation to younger children.

In comparison with adolescents, not much normative information is available regarding panic in children. Although both panic attacks and Panic Disorder are reported in clinical samples of children, they are less frequent than in adolescent samples, and their expression may differ somewhat from the presentation in adolescents and adults (Ollendick, 1998).

Adolescents who experience panic attacks do experience considerable distress. Few, however, seem to seek treatment. Intensity and frequency of attacks do not seem related to seeking treatment. It may be the case that adolescents do not seek treatment until agoraphobic avoidance develops (Ollendick, 1998).

Youngsters with panic attacks or Panic Disorder who do present at clinics are likely to have a family history of panic attacks or other severe anxiety symptoms. These youngsters are also likely to present with a variety of other symptoms, and many of these youngsters meet the criteria for additional diagnoses (Ollendick et al., 1994). In addition to meeting the criteria for anxiety disorders, youngsters frequently also meet criteria for a diagnosis of depression. The high proportion of youngsters who report a history of separation anxiety has led to the suggestion that Separation Anxiety Disorder is a precursor to Panic Disorder. This hypothesis requires further investigation. Mattis and Ollendick (1997), for example, have proposed a developmental model of panic. This model incorporates the experience of separation, which is conceptualized as a source of stress, an initial vulnerability related to the child's temperament (e.g., tendency to be biologically overreactive to stress), and an insecure-ambivalent attachment (leading to reduced ability to regulate arousal). These factors contribute to a developmental pathway where the repeated stresses of separation lead to the development of a panic disorder. Such models represent a potential source of research hypotheses. It seems likely that Separation Anxiety Disorder would be only one of many possible paths to the development of panic disorder.

REACTIONS TO TRAUMATIC EVENTS

How do youngsters react to experiencing natural disasters such as hurricanes, the violence of a sniper attack, kidnapping, or other disasters such as fires or ship sinkings? Until relatively recently there had been little systematic study of children's reactions to such traumatic events.

Trauma is usually defined as an event outside everyday experience that would be distressing to almost anyone. Early descriptions of children's exposure to such trauma suggested that reactions would be relatively mild and transient, and thus these experiences were not given a great deal of attention. However, reports began to emerge of more severe and long-lasting reactions. These reports also became more salient with the introduc-

tion of a specific diagnostic category of Posttraumatic Stress Disorder (PTSD). In addition, information began to be gathered from the youngsters. Parents were found to report significantly lower levels of anxiety and other PTSD symptoms in their children than were reported by the youngsters themselves (Udwin, 1993; Vogel & Vernberg, 1993).

Terr's (1979; 1983) description of the reactions of twenty-six children kidnapped from their Chowchilla, California, school bus in 1976 is one study that influenced how children's posttraumatic responses were understood. The children and their bus driver were held for twenty-seven hours. At first they were driven around in darkened vans and then moved to a buried tractor trailer, where they remained until some of the victims dug themselves out. Terr interviewed the child victims and at least one parent of each child within five to thirteen months of the kidnapping. She found all of the children to be symptomatic, with 73 percent showing moderately severe or severe reactions. Assessments two to five years after the kidnapping also revealed that many symptoms persisted, including fears among all the children.

DEFINITION AND DIAGNOSIS

The diagnostic category of PTSD was introduced in the third version of the DSM, and in DSM-III-R some symptoms specific to children were added. The diagnosis of PTSD according to DSM-IV requires that the person be exposed to a traumatic event that includes a threat of death, serious injury, or physical integrity to the self or others, and in which the person's response involves fear, helplessness, or horror. In children this reaction may be expressed instead as disorganized or agitated behavior. In addition, the youngster must experience three categories of symptoms for more than one month: reexperiencing of the traumatic event, persistent avoidance of stimuli associated with the trauma, and persistent symptoms of increased arousal. Examples of these three kinds of symptoms are presented in Table 6-8. The disturbance must also cause significant interference in important areas of the youngster's functioning.

TABLE 6-8

Symptoms Used in DSM-IV to Diagnose Posttraumatic Stress Disorder

Reexperiencing the Traumatic Event (1 or more)[a]

1. Recurrent distressing recollections (in young children may be trauma-related play)
2. Recurrent distressing dreams
3. Acting or feeling as if event were recurring
4. Intense distress to cues that symbolize the event
5. Physiological reactivity to cues that symbolize the event

Persistent Avoidance of Trauma-Related Stimuli and General Numbing (3 or more)[a]

1. Avoidance of trauma-related thoughts, feelings, or conversations
2. Avoidance of activities, places, or people associated with the trauma
3. Inability to recall important aspects of the trauma
4. Diminished interest in significant activities
5. Feelings of detachment from others
6. Restricted range of affect
7. Sense of foreshortened future

Persistent Symptoms of Increased Arousal (2 or more)[a]

1. Sleep difficulties
2. Irritability, anger outbursts
3. Difficulty concentrating
4. Hypervigilance
5. Exaggerated startle response

[a] Numbers in parentheses indicate the number of symptoms required in each category.

DESCRIPTION OF YOUNGSTERS' REACTIONS

The reactions of youngsters to traumatic events may vary considerably. Many youngsters exhibit symptoms without meeting the criteria for a diagnosis of PTSD. These children may still experience considerable distress and interference with functioning. It is also common for youngsters to exhibit additional problems (e.g., depression) or to meet the criteria for additional diagnoses (Pfefferbaum, 1997).

Most youngsters become upset at reminders of the trauma, and they experience repetitive, intrusive thoughts about the event. This is true of children experiencing even mild levels of exposure to life-threatening disasters. Among preschool and school-age children, reenactment in play of aspects of the disaster is frequently reported. Initially such play may be part of the reexperiencing symptoms, but if play progresses, it may be a useful part of the recovery process as well. Saylor, Powell, and Swenson (1992), for example, report that after Hurricane Hugo occurred in South Carolina, children's play progressed from blowing houses down to acting out the role of roofers during rebuilding.

Youngsters may also exhibit increased frequency and intensity of specific fears. These occur to stimuli directly related to or associated with the experience, but not to unrelated stimuli. Thus adolescent British girls on a school trip who experienced the sinking of their cruise ship *Jupiter* developed fears of swimming, of the dark, or of boats and other forms of transportation, but they did not show elevated levels of unrelated fears when compared with schoolmates who did not go on the trip or with girls from a comparable school (Yule, Udwin, & Murdoch, 1990).

Separation difficulties and clingy, dependent behaviors are also common. These behaviors may be exhibited in reluctance to go to school or in a desire to sleep with parents. Other sleep problems, such as difficulty in getting to sleep, nightmares, and repeated dreams related to the traumatic event, are also common. A sense of vulnerability and loss of faith in the future have also been reported. In adolescents this may interfere with planning for future education and careers; moreover, school performance is reported to suffer. Other commonly reported symptoms include depressed mood, loss of interest in previously enjoyed activities, irritability, and angry or aggressive outbursts. Guilt about surviving when others have died can also occur.

DEVELOPMENTAL COURSE AND DETERMINANTS

In general, symptoms of PTSD decline over time, but substantial numbers of youngsters continue to report symptoms. For example, La Greca and her colleagues (1996) examined the symptoms of posttraumatic stress in third- through fifth-grade children, during the school year after Hurricane Andrew occurred in Florida. Symptoms of avoidance and general numbing decreased over time, being present in about 49 percent of the children at three months and about 24 percent of the children at ten months. Similarly, the number of children with symptoms of arousal decreased from 67 to about 49 percent in the same time period. However, substantial numbers of children continued to report reexperiencing symptoms—approximately 90 percent at three months and 78 percent at ten months.

Not all children and adolescents experience the same pattern or intensity of symptoms, and reactions may vary in how long they persist and may fluctuate over time. A number of factors seem to influence reactions. La Greca, Silverman, and Wasserstein (1998) describe a model of posttraumatic stress reactions (Figure 6-3) that includes four factors: exposure to trauma, child characteristics, child's coping, and access to social support.

Degree of exposure to the traumatic event is an important influence. Pynoos and his colleagues (1987), for example, studied 159 California schoolchildren who were exposed to a sniper attack on their school in which one child and a passerby were killed and thirteen other children were injured. Children who were trapped on the playground showed much greater effects than those who had left the immediate vicinity of the shooting or were not in school that day. At a fourteen-month follow-up, for example, among the most severely exposed children, 74 percent still re-

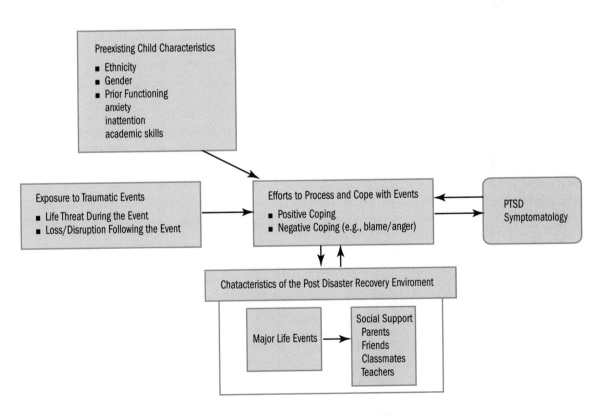

FIGURE 6-3 Conceptual model for predicting children's reactions to a natural disaster.
From LaGreca, Silverman, & Wasserstein (1998).

ported moderate to severe PTSD symptoms, whereas 81 percent of the nonexposed children reported no PTSD (Nader et al., 1991). Although level of exposure to this life-threatening trauma was an important factor, reactions did occur among children who did not experience a high degree of exposure. Subjective experience of threat and greater knowledge of the child who was killed were associated with increased reactions among less-exposed children.

Individual differences that existed prior to a traumatic event (e.g., anxiety level, ethnicity) are also likely to influence the youngster's reaction. For example, African-American ethnicity and predisaster anxiety predicted children's reactions to Hurricane Andrew (La Greca et al., 1998). Children's initial attempts at coping may also affect the course of their reactions. Children's use of negative coping strategies (e.g., blaming others, screaming) may contribute to persistent symptoms (La Greca et al., 1996). The reactions of children and adolescents to traumatic events are also related to the reactions of their parents and others in their environment. If the parents themselves suffer severe posttraumatic stress or for some other reason are unable to provide an atmosphere of support and communication, their children's reactions are likely to be more severe.

These findings naturally lead to the question of how best to intervene when children and adolescents are exposed to traumatic events. Because there has been relatively little evaluation of interventions, clear recommendations are difficult to make; however, clinical consensus suggests certain key components (AACAP, 1998b; Pfefferbaum, 1997; Vernberg & Vogel, 1993; Yule, 1994). Within a short time of the disaster, debriefing groups are usually employed to encourage youngsters and their families to share their feelings and open channels of communication, to prepare them for possible reactions in the future, and to help them realize that such reactions are normal reactions to abnormal events. Additional group work or individual cognitive-behavioral interventions may be necessary for some youngsters. These interventions should involve exploration of the trauma, should train youngsters in the use of specific stress

management techniques, should address thoughts and attributions, and should include parents in the treatment. (Anxiety reduction interventions are described later in the chapter.) Treatments that include these components may help in coping or alleviating symptoms and may help to enhance a sense of control and mastery.

OBSESSIVE-COMPULSIVE DISORDER

DEFINITION AND DIAGNOSIS

Obsessions are unwanted, repetitive, intrusive thoughts, while compulsions involve repetitive, stereotyped behaviors that the child or adolescent feels compelled to perform. The disorder involves either obsessions or compulsions, or in a majority of youngsters, both (March & Mulle, 1998). The definitions employed in DSM-IV to characterize obsessions and compulsion are presented in Table 6-9. Beyond defining the nature of obsessions and compulsions, DSM-IV criteria for Obsessive-Compulsive Disorder (OCD) indicate that the person realizes that the thoughts and behaviors are unreasonable. This particular feature is not required for the diagnosis of OCD in children but may become part of the clinical picture in older children and adolescents. The disorder is known to occur in children under the age of seven (Swedo et al.,

---

TABLE 6-9

DSM-IV Definitions of Obsessions and Compulsions

Obsessions: Intrusive, persistent thoughts, impulses, or images that

1. cause anxiety or distress
2. are not simply excessive real-life worries
3. the person attempts to ignore, suppress, or neutralize
4. are recognized as products of one's own mind

Compulsions: Repetitive behaviors or mental acts that

1. the person feels driven to perform
2. are unrealistic attempts to prevent or reduce distress or dreaded situation

1989c). Among these very young children, odd repetitive acts may be seen as strange even by the child. However, children may initially have their own explanations. For example, seven-year-old Stanley indicated that he had seen a show in which Martians contacted humans by putting strange thoughts in their heads. Stanley explained his compulsion to do everything in sequences of four as a sign that he had been picked as the Martians' contact on earth. After two years of no contact, Stanley gave up this explanation but not his ritual (Rapoport, 1989). The child may thus come to recognize that the ideas or behaviors involved are unreasonable but still feel the need to repeat them.

Another part of the criteria for the diagnosis of OCD is that the obsessions or compulsions are highly time-consuming and that they result in considerable interference with normal routines, academic functioning, and social relationships. Rapoport's (1989) description of Sergei illustrates the nature and consequences of the disorder.

Sergei is a 17-year-old former high school student. Only a year or so ago Sergei seemed to be a normal adolescent with many talents and interests. Then, almost overnight he was transformed into a lonely outsider, excluded from social life by his psychological disabilities. Specifically, he was unable to stop washing. Haunted by the notion that he was dirty—in spite of the contrary evidence of his senses—he began to spend more and more of his time cleansing himself of imaginary dirt. At first his ritual ablutions were confined to weekends and evenings and he was able to stay in school while keeping them up, but soon they began to consume all his time, forcing him to drop out of school, a victim of his inability to feel clean enough. (p. 83)

PREVALENCE

Obsessive-Compulsive Disorder is probably not as rare as was once believed (March & Leonard, 1996). Low estimates were due to several considerations, including attempts by the persons to hide their difficulties, lack of public awareness, and limited availability of treatment. An epidemiological study of nonreferred adolescents suggests a prevalence rate of 1 percent and a lifetime prevalence rate of 1.9 percent in the general adolescent population (Flament et al., 1988). Most estimates also

Keeping things in certain specific locations and order is common among children. It is only when these kinds of behaviors interfere with normal functioning that they should cause concern for clinicians and other adults.
(Courtesy of A.C. Israel)

suggest that at younger ages, boys outnumber girls, but that by adolescence, the genders are equally represented (March & Mulle, 1998). Among a sample of seventy consecutive child and adolescent cases seen at the National Institute for Mental Health (NIMH), seven had an onset prior to the age of seven years, and the mean age of onset was ten years of age. The onset of obsessive-compulsive symptoms in boys tended to be prepubertal (mean age nine), whereas in girls, the average onset (mean of eleven years) was around puberty (Swedo et al., 1989c).

DESCRIPTION AND DEVELOPMENTAL COURSE

Behavior with obsessive-compulsive qualities occurs in various stages of normal development (Leonard et al., 1990). For example, very young children may have bedtime and eating rituals or may require things to be "just so." Disruption of these routines often leads to distress. Also, young children are often observed to engage in repetitive play and to show a distinct preference for sameness. Benjamin Spock (Spock & Rothenberg, 1992), in his widely read book for parents, notes that mild compulsions—such as stepping over cracks in the sidewalk or touching every third picket in a fence—are quite common in eight-, nine-, and ten-year-olds. Such behaviors that are common to the child's peer group are probably best viewed as games. Only when they dominate the child's life and interfere with normal functioning is there cause for concern. The specific content of OCD rituals generally does not resemble these common developmental rituals, and the OCD rituals have a later stage of onset. It is not clear at present whether developmental rituals represent early manifestations of obsessive-compulsive disorder in some children (Leonard et al., 1990).

Judith Rapoport and her colleagues at NIMH conducted a series of studies that increased the attention given to obsessive-compulsive behavior in youngsters. Initially, like most clinicians, Rapoport saw few cases of childhood Obsessive-Compulsive Disorder. Indeed, when she began her work, she did not know whether or not she would find enough cases to complete the initial research. From the initial series of cases, the NIMH group began to get a sense of the obsessions and compulsions that were common in this population (e.g., Swedo et al., 1989c). Table 6-10 indicates the most common obsessions and compulsions among these children and adolescents.

Subsequent reports have corroborated these findings (Henin & Kendall, 1997). Compulsive rituals are reported more frequently than obsessions; this may be different than reports concerning adults, in which obsessions and compulsions are reported at fairly equivalent rates. There appear to be two broad themes: the first theme is a preoccupation with cleanliness, grooming, and averting danger; and a secondary theme is a pervasive doubting—not knowing when one is "right." Washing, repeating, and checking rituals are the most common. Obsessions involving dirt, germs, contamination, or fear of something terrible happening are the most frequently reported.

OCD is described as following a course of the emergence and fading of various symptoms over time. Multiple obsessions and compulsions are usually present at any one time, and usually the symptoms change over time, although no clear progression is identified (Rettew et al., 1992).

TABLE 6–10

Obsessions and Compulsions among Children and Adolescents Receiving the Diagnosis of Obsessive-Compulsive Disorder

	Percent Reporting Symptom
Obsessions	
Concern with dirt, germs, or environmental toxins	40
Something terrible happening (fire, death, or illness of self or loved one)	24
Symmetry, order, or exactness	17
Scrupulosity (religious obsessions)	13
Concern or disgust with bodily wastes or secretions (urine, stool, saliva)	8
Lucky or unlucky numbers	8
Forbidden, aggressive, or perverse sexual thoughts, images, or impulses	4
Fear of harming others or oneself	4
Concern with household items	3
Intrusive nonsense sounds, words, or music	1
Compulsions	
Excessive or ritualized handwashing, showering, bathing, toothbrushing, or grooming	85
Repeating rituals (going in or out of a door, up or down from a chair)	51
Checking (doors, locks, appliances, emergency brake on car, paper route, homework)	46
Rituals to remove contact with contaminants	23
Touching	20
Measures to prevent harm to self or others	16
Ordering or arranging	17
Counting	18
Hoarding or collecting rituals	11
Rituals of cleaning household or inanimate objects	6
Miscellaneous rituals (such as writing, moving, speaking)	26

Note: Percentages total more than 100 percent because many youths had more than one symptom. Adapted from Rapaport, 1989.

Most youngsters diagnosed with OCD also meet the criteria for at least one other disorder (Hanna, 1995). For example, in the seventy consecutive cases at NIMH previously described, only 26 percent had no other diagnosis (Swedo et al., 1989c). Multiple anxiety disorders, depression, and eating disorders are commonly reported (Henin & Kendall, 1997). OCD also often occurs with Tourette's Syndrome (a chronic disorder with a genetic and neuroanatomical basis characterized by motor and vocal tics and related urges) and other tic disorders (Leckman et al., 1997).

Research also suggests that the disorder is likely to follow a chronic course (Leonard et al., 1994). Even research that was conducted during a period when recommended treatments were available suggests that the problems persist. Leonard and her colleagues (1993) followed fifty-four youngsters who had received pharmacological treatment and were reevaluated two to seven years later. The group as a whole had improved, in that only 19 percent were unchanged or worse. However, 70 percent were still taking medication, 43 percent still met the diagnostic criteria for OCD, and only 11 percent exhibited no obsessive-compulsive symptoms.

ETIOLOGY OF ANXIETY DISORDERS

The causes of anxiety disorders in children and adolescents are by no means clear, and much of the information that is available represents a downward extension from the adult literature. It is likely that anxiety disorders are influenced by multiple factors that interact with each other in complex ways. One issue regards the specificity of the influences. It is possible that different anxiety disorders result from different combinations of influences. Alternatively, the influence of a particular factor or combination of factors may contribute to the development of anxiety disorders in general rather than to a specific anxiety disorder. For example, are the children of parents with panic disorder at risk for panic disorder or for anxiety disorders in general? Finally, there may be multiple paths and different combinations of risk factors toward the same outcome. Youngsters may experience different combinations of influences yet meet the criteria for the same disorder.

BIOLOGICAL INFLUENCES

Multiple sources indicate that anxiety disorders occur in families (Rutter et al., 1990b; Silverman & Ginsburg, 1998). The degree to which such familial aggregation results from genetic or environmental influences remains unclear (Thapar & McGuffin, 1995). However, findings from family aggregation and twin studies are consistent with a genetic contribution to anxiety disorders.

One type of family study indicates that children whose parents have an anxiety disorder are at risk for developing an anxiety disorder. For example, Beidel and Turner (1997) assessed children of parents with anxiety disorders, depressive disorders, mixed anxiety/depressive disorders, and no disorder. Children of parents in the three "at risk" groups were significantly more likely to have a disorder or to an anxiety disorder than children of parents with no disorder. However, there were no significant differences between the children of the three parental diagnostic groups. These findings suggest a familial influence on internalizing disorders, but not more specifically for anxiety disorders, or for a particular anxiety disorder. In an additional comparison, the authors compared the percentage of children in each at risk parental group (1) who had an anxiety disorder *only* with (2) those who had a nonanxiety diagnosis or had an anxiety disorder diagnosis plus a second nonanxiety disorder. Among youngsters who had one or more disorders, 90 percent of the offspring of anxious parents had anxiety disorders only, compared with 44 percent of the offspring of depressed parents and 53 percent of the offspring of mixed anxious/depressed parents. Thus children of anxious parents primarily had anxiety disorders, whereas children of parents in the two other risk groups were more likely to have a variety of disorders.

Family aggregation of anxiety disorders is also indicated by research that shows that parents whose children have anxiety disorders are themselves likely to have anxiety disorders. For example, Last et al. (1991) interviewed family members of children with anxiety disorders, Attention-Deficit Hyperactivity Disorder, and no disorder. Parents of children with anxiety disorders had significantly higher rates of anxiety disorder diagnoses than parents of children in the other two groups.

A more specific examination of the influence of inheritance indicates that genetic influences seem to be suggested for anxiety disorders (Kendler et al., 1992b; Torgersen, 1993). Twin studies do indicate higher rates of concordance for monozygotic as compared with dizygotic twins. In the Virginia Twin Study of Adolescent Behavioral Development (Eaves et al., 1997), heritability estimates for anxiety tended to be lower than for other disorders. Heritability estimates were also higher for measures of a general anxiety construct than for specific anxiety disorders. These findings are consistent with other reports (King & Ollendick, 1997; Thapar & McGuffin, 1995) and suggest that genetic factors may play a limited role in the development of some anxiety disorders and that what may be inherited is a general tendency, such as emotional reactivity and behavioral responsivity to stimuli (Gray, 1985). The Virginia Twin Study findings also suggested that the genetic contribution to anxiety disorders may be greater for girls than for boys. Finally, these findings indicate a substantial contribution of shared environment (those environmental influences shared by siblings) to anxiety disorders.

It should be noted that there is evidence of genetic influence for Obsessive-Compulsive Disorder (Leonard et al., 1994). As a function of their work with youngsters with OCD, many workers came to believe in a biological basis for Obsessive-Compulsive Disorder (March & Mulle, 1998). The disorder was found to be more prevalent among youngsters with a first-degree relative with obsessive-compulsive behavior than among the general population, and many parents of youngsters with the disorder met diagnostic criteria for OCD or exhibited obsessive-compulsive symptoms (Lenane et al., 1990; Riddle et al., 1992; Swedo et al., 1989c). In addition, a number of studies have reported that both OCD and Tourette's syndrome (or less severe tic

disorders) occur in the same persons at higher than expected rates and have also found a familial association between the two disorders (Leonard et al., 1994). These findings were viewed as suggesting a possible genetic cause for OCD.

Further support for a biological basis for OCD came from findings of an association between obsessive-compulsive symptoms and certain known neurological disorders. Also, brain imaging studies suggested that OCD was linked to the anatomy of the basal ganglia, a group of brain structures lying under the cerebral cortex (Luxenberg et al., 1988; Swedo et al., 1989a; Swedo et al., 1989b). There has also been the suggestion that some cases, which have a sudden onset or exacerbation of OCD symptoms and tics, may be triggered by streptococcal infection—"strep throat" (Allen, Leonard, & Swedo, 1995a). This effect is believed to result from an autoimmune reaction produced when antibodies formed by the body against the strep cells react with and cause inflammation in cells of the basal ganglia.

Biological factors may contribute to the development of anxiety disorders in other ways. When exposed to unfamiliar settings or people, children with an early constitutional/temperamental style described as inhibited, may display signs of physiological arousal, avoid or withdraw, or display dependent, clinging behavior. These are similar characteristics to those displayed by anxious youngsters. Also, these temperamentally inhibited children have been shown to be more likely to develop anxiety disorders (Biederman et al., 1993; Kagan, 1997). This temperamental style will be discussed further in Chapter 7.

PSYCHOSOCIAL INFLUENCES

Children may develop anxiety problems as a result of exposure to some traumatic event such as being attacked by a dog. In addition, families may also influence the development of anxiety through other environmental paths. For example, children may "learn" to be anxious from their parents, and families may "create" environments that place youngsters at risk for the development of anxiety problems (Ollendick & King, 1991). Exposure to frequent and/or highly stressful events and observation of anxious adults' styles of coping with such experiences seem likely to contribute to similar patterns of difficulty in the children of such families.

The contributions of some of these environmental influences can be examined in the context of phobias. Watson and Rayner's (1920) demonstration of conditioning of fear in Little Albert (see Chapter 3) was an early suggestion of the role of traumatic experience in the development of phobias. However, traumatic experiences are not always reported in the etiology of children's phobias.

Rachman (1977) postulated three different environmental paths by which, alone or in combination, phobias might be acquired: (1) direct experience/conditioning (e.g., a child is attacked by a dog); (2) indirect experience/vicarious exposure-modeling (e.g., a child observes a fearful parent); and (3) transmission of information (e.g., a child hears stories about traumatic experiences from others). Although there is little research investigating the contributions of these various pathways to the development of phobias in youngsters, there is some suggestion of the importance of indirect experiences. Ollendick, King, and Hamilton (1991) asked a large sample of Australian and American youngsters (nine to fourteen years of age) to report retrospectively on the sources of their fears. They found that the development of ten highly prevalent fears were most frequently attributed to informational and modeling factors. Similarly, a majority of parents of dog-phobic youngsters indicated that modeling was the most significant influence on the development of their children's phobias (King, Clowes-Hollins, & Ollendick, 1997). However, it is likely the case that youngsters' fears are multiply determined. Indeed, these indirect sources of fears were often combined with direct conditioning experiences, and therefore the potential influence of such direct associative learning should not be ignored (Forsyth & Chorpita, 1997).

In addition to modeling anxious behavior or relating stories of fearful and traumatic experiences, parents may influence the development of anxiety through their parenting styles. For example, Dadds and his colleagues (1996) videotaped families with children from seven to fourteen years old while the families were discussing and developing a plan for hypothetical threatening situations. Parents of anxious children listened less to their children, pointed out fewer positive consequences of adaptive behavior, and were more likely to respond to a child's solutions that were avoidant. In contrast, parents of nonclinic children were more likely to listen to and agree with their children's plans that were neither aggressive or avoidant. Following the family discussion, children from both groups were asked for their plan for the situation. Anxious children offered more avoidant solutions, and the children's choice of plans was associated with those behaviors that differentiated parents of anxious children from those of nonclinic children.

Parents of anxious children have also been described as intrusive and overprotective. Dumas, LaFreniere, and Serketich (1995) videotaped and coded interactions between mothers and their preschool children. Mothers of children who were classified as anxious, as compared with those classified as competent or aggressive, exhibited the highest levels of aversive control (e.g., criticism, intrusions) and the lowest levels of compliance and responsivity to their child. The authors propose that such interactions may limit the development of prosocial behaviors and of adaptive coping styles in anxious children.

These kinds of parenting styles may contribute to the child's failure to develop a sense of control over events. This failure, in turn, may contribute to a vulnerability to develop anxiety and other internalizing disorders (Chorpita & Barlow, 1998; King, Mietz, & Ollendick, 1995). Also, specific cognitions may develop, for example, the perception of situations as hostile or threatening, that may place the youngster at risk for developing or maintaining anxiety problems (Bell-Dolan, 1995).

An additional indication of the contribution of parenting to the development of anxiety disorders comes from the literature concerning the impact of attachment (Main, 1996). Insecure mother-child attachments have been shown to be a risk factor for the development of anxiety disorders (Bernstein, Borchardt, & Perwein, 1996). For example, Warren et al. (1997) reported on the adolescent outcome of a group of youngsters who, as infants, had been assessed using Ainsworth's Strange Situation Procedure. At 12 months of age, these youngsters had been classified as either securely attached, avoidantly attached, or anxiously/resistantly attached. When they were 17.5 years old, they were assessed, through a structured interview, for current or past anxiety disorders. Raters did not know the child's past attachment status. Fifteen percent of the adolescents had at least one past or current anxiety disorder. Fifty-one percent of the adolescents had a disorder other than an anxiety disorder. More youngsters with anxiety disorders were, as infants, classified as anxious/resistant, and more children with other (nonanxiety) disorders were classified as avoidant. Also, 13 percent of children who were not anxiously/resistantly attached as infants developed anxiety disorders, whereas 28 percent who were anxiously/resistantly attached developed anxiety disorders. Furthermore, anxious/resistant attachment was found to contribute to the development of anxiety disorders even after maternal anxiety and measures of infant temperament were accounted for. Thus a specific kind of insecure attachment may contribute to the development of anxiety disorders.

ASSESSMENT OF ANXIETY DISORDERS

OVERVIEW

A comprehensive assessment of a youngster presenting with anxiety will likely involve a variety of assessment needs, be sensitive to developmental issues, and allow problems of clinical concern to be differentiated from normal fears and worries (March & Albano, 1998). Thus initial and ongoing assessment presents a considerable challenge.

As is usually the case, a general clinical interview is likely to yield information that is valuable to the clinician in formulating an understanding of the case and in planning an intervention. Structured diagnostic interviews (both general and more specific to anxiety disorders) are available and may be employed to derive a clinical diagnosis

(Silverman, 1994). Assessment of anxiety disorders is often guided by the tripartite model of anxiety discussed earlier. Thus assessment methods will address one or more of the three response systems (behavioral, physiological, subjective). Various methods exist (Barrios & Hartmann, 1997). However, as was also discussed earlier, how best to subcategorize anxiety disorders remains unclear. Therefore, in addition to diagnosis or a three response system approach, assessment may be guided by empirical findings of how anxiety problems in youngsters can be conceptualized. For example, March and his colleagues (1997) have developed the Multidimensional Anxiety Scale for Children (MASC). The MASC is a self-report instrument that can be completed by the youngster and parent(s). It yields scores on four empirically defined factors: physical symptoms, social anxiety, harm avoidance, and separation anxiety. This allows examination of the various aspects of anxiety presentation in a single instrument.

Given that youngsters with anxiety disorders often present with a variety of other problems as well, more general empirically derived instruments, such as the Achenbach behavior checklists, may also be employed to help in describing a range of behavior problems and various people's perspectives.

It is likely that aspects of the environment may contribute to the anxiety difficulties and therefore the youngster's environment will need to be assessed as well. For example, it may be desirable to assess the specific environmental events that are associated with heightened anxiety, to evaluate patterns of family interactions and communication, to assess the reactions of adults or peers to the youngster's behavior, and to assess the existence of problems in other family members. The assessment of multiple aspects of the problem and the use of multiple informants, including the child or adolescent, are likely to yield valuable information.

ASSESSING THE THREE RESPONSE SYSTEMS

Methods for assessing the overt behavioral aspects of children's and adolescents' fears and anxieties make use of direct observation (Dadds, Rapee, &

Barrett, 1994). Behavioral avoidance tests require the youngster to perform a series of tasks involving the feared object or situation. The child or adolescent is directed to approach the feared stimulus situation in planned graduated steps. Thus the youngster might be asked to move closer and closer to a feared dog and then increasingly to interact with the dog.

Alternatively, rather than exposing the youngster to a planned graduated series of steps, observations can be made in the natural environment where the fear or anxiety occurs. Trained observers may use a specific observational system to record the youngster's behavior, in predefined categories, as it is happening. Checklists may also be employed wherein the observer checks off the specific behaviors that are exhibited. Recording is usually done a short time after the behavior has occurred. Finally, global ratings of the youngster's fearful behavior are often obtained. For example, someone rates on a five-point scale the degree to which the child or adolescent approached a feared object or situation. Self-monitoring procedures require the youngster to observe and to systematically record his or her own behavior. A daily diary of each observation may be obtained as part of an initial assessment and is also often part of treatment efforts.

Assessing the subjective component of anxiety relies heavily on judgments of emotional discomfort. It may be difficult for adults to reliably identify the existence of such discomfort in children. In addition, children may have difficulty in labeling and communicating their subjective feelings, thus creating a considerable assessment challenge.

The subjective component of the youngster's anxiety can be evaluated by a variety of self-report measures (James, Reynolds, & Dunbar, 1994). Global self-ratings of degree of anxiety or of fear are often obtained. Youngsters may report how anxious they are, overall or in a specific situation, by choosing from a series of facial expressions, by indicating a number on a drawing of a fear thermometer, or by selecting a number on a scale. The choice of method depends, in part, on the child's developmental level.

Observations of the child's behavior in the natural environment can be made as the child takes gradual steps in encountering the feared situation.
(Joel Gordon)

There are also self-report instruments that assess overall subjective anxiety such as the State-Trait Anxiety Inventory for Children (Spielberger, 1973) and the Revised Children's Manifest Anxiety Scale (Reynolds & Richmond, 1978), which contains items such as "I have trouble making up my mind" and "I am afraid of a lot of things."

There are also instruments to assess specific aspects of anxiety disorders. For example, there are instruments to assess a variety of specific fears. The Revised Fear Survey Schedule for Children (Ollendick, 1983) asks youngsters to respond to each of eighty items by indicating their level of fear ("none," "some," or "a lot"). And social anxiety may be assessed by the Social Anxiety Scale for Children–Revised (La Greca & Stone, 1993) and the Social Phobia and Anxiety Inventory for Children (Beidel, Turner, & Morris, 1995).

The physiological component of anxiety is assessed by measuring parameters such as heart rate, skin conductance, and palmar sweat. Practical difficulties often inhibit the obtaining of these measures. The development of portable and inexpensive recording devices has greatly facilitated such recording. However, the physiological aspects of anxiety in children and adolescents are assessed less frequently than the other two response systems (Barrios & Hartmann, 1997; King, 1994).

TREATMENT OF ANXIETY DISORDERS

The treatment of anxiety in children and adolescents has a long history. However, research regarding effective treatments is less extensive than for adults.

PHARMACOLOGICAL TREATMENTS

Pharmacological treatments for anxiety disorders in children and adolescents have made use of a variety of medications. Selective serotonin reuptake inhibitors (SSRIs), tricyclic antidepressants, and anxiolytics, particularly the benzodiazepines, have been most frequently suggested for treating children and adolescents. However, in general, there are limited studies of the effectiveness of medication in treating anxiety disorders in children and adolescents, and many of these have methodological shortcomings. Systematic study is needed to establish safety and efficacy (Allen, Leonard, & Swedo, 1995b). Thus, in practice, the use of pharmacological treatment for anxiety in youth is probably not the treatment of first choice. If medication is employed, it is likely to be as an adjunct to psychological interventions, and the relative contributions of these two components requires investigation (AACAP, 1997; Kearney & Silverman, 1998; Popper & Gherardi, 1996).

The treatment of obsessive compulsive disorder is an area where there does seem to be support. The serotonin reuptake inhibitor (SRI) chlomipramine and various SSRIs, such as fluoxetin (Prozac), sertraline (Zoloft), paroxetine (Paxil), and fluvoxamine (Lurox), have been shown to be effective in treating OCD in children and adolescents (AACAP, 1998a; Popper & Gherardi, 1996).

PSYCHOLOGICAL INTERVENTIONS

Much of the research on psychological interventions with children and adolescents has been directed at the treatment of fears and phobias and has been largely from a behavioral or cognitive-behavioral perspective. However, these investigations suffer from a number of limitations (King, 1993; Morris & Kratochwill, 1983). For example, the vast majority deal with the treatment of fears and anxieties of mild to moderate intensity, leaving the effectiveness of treatment of severe problems less well explored. It does seem clear, however, that exposure to feared stimuli is an essential element of successful fear-reduction programs. Thus it seems reasonable to conceptualize many of the treatments as various ways of facilitating exposure to the feared object or situation.

Systematic desensitization. One of the most widely used behavioral treatments is systematic desensitization and its variants. In imaginal desensitization, a hierarchy of fear-provoking situations is constructed, and the youngster is asked to visualize scenes, starting with the least and progressing to the most fear-producing. These visualizations are presented as the youngster is engaged in relaxation or some other response that is incompatible with fear. This process is repeated until the most anxiety-provoking scene can be comfortably visualized. In "in vivo" desensitization, the actual feared object or situation is employed rather than using visualizations. A third variant, emotive imagery, uses an exciting story involving the child's favorite hero, instead of relaxation, as the anxiety inhibitor. Items from the fear hierarchy are woven into the story. Research involving imaginal and in vivo desensitization suggests that they are probably effective in treating children's fears and phobias (Ollendick & King, 1998).

Modeling. A commonly employed behavioral procedure is modeling. The work of Bandura and his colleagues (e.g., Bandura & Menlove, 1968) was the impetus for more recent research. In all modeling therapies, the child observes another person interacting adaptively with the feared situation. The model can be live or symbolic (e.g., film or slides). In numerous experimental studies, modeling procedures have been demonstrated to be superior to control conditions and to be effective over a fairly wide age range. Participant modeling, in which observation is followed by the fearful child joining the model in making gradual approaches to the feared object, is one of the most potent treatments (Ollendick & King, 1998).

Lewis's (1974) often cited treatment of fear of the water illustrates the use of modeling, and participant modeling in particular. Forty boys between the ages of five and twelve were assigned to one of four treatment conditions. Children in a modeling-plus-participation condition observed a film of three boys of similar age performing tasks such as those in a swimming test. These coping models initially exhibited fear but gradually increased their competency in dealing with the tasks; eventually they were shown playing together happily in the water. Immediately following observation of the film, the children were taken by a second experimenter to the pool for a ten-minute participation phase. They were encouraged to engage in the activities involved in the swimming test and were given social reinforcements for attempting these activities. When the behavioral swim-

ming test was repeated the next day, a control group showed no change. Boys in modeling-only and participation-only conditions exhibited significant improvement, but the most effective treatment was the combination of modeling and participation. A follow-up evaluation of twenty-five of the boys five days later suggested that the gains had been maintained and had generalized to a different pool and different swimming instructor. Once again the modeling-plus-participation boys seem to have fared the best.

These findings and others indicate that modeling treatments can be highly effective. However, it is not clear what is responsible for the success. Treatments such as Lewis's (1974) often involve other components, such as the social reinforcement given to the boys for swimming activities.

Contingency management. Modeling and systematic desensitization and its variants are treatments that were developed as ways of reducing a child's fear or anxiety. The assumption was that the child's anxiety or fear had to be reduced or eliminated before he or she could approach or function in the problematic situation. Contingency management procedures that are based on operant principles do not make this assumption. Rather, the child's avoidant/anxious behavior is addressed directly by altering the contingencies for such behavior—ensuring that positive consequences follow exposure to the feared stimulus, that positive consequences do not follow avoidance of the feared stimulus, and that the child is rewarded for improvement. These procedures are also sometimes described as reinforced practice. In the studies that have employed contingency management or reinforced practice as a separate treatment, these procedures have been shown to be effective in treating children's fears and phobias (Ollendick & King, 1998).

Cognitive-behavioral treatments. Cognitive-behavioral treatments include a variety of strategies designed to alter the thoughts, beliefs, and perceptions of anxious children. These procedures are based on the assumption that modifying the child's maladaptive cognitions will lead to changes in the child's anxious/avoidant behavior. Some investigators have examined the self-management of children's beliefs or cognitions as a treatment strategy. Children are taught to use positive self-statements through modeling, rehearsal, and social reinforcement. Kanfer's cognitive self-control approach to fear of the dark is an early example of the successful application of this coping strategy (Kanfer, Karoly, & Newman, 1975). Five- to six-year-old children were assigned to one of three conditions. Those in the competence group were to self-instruct with phrases such as "I am a brave boy(girl). I can take care of myself in the dark." Children in the stimulus control group were taught to say phrases such as "The dark is a fun place to be. There are many good things in the dark." In the neutral group, children recited nursery rhymes. The competence condition was superior to the other two groups in reducing the children's fear of the dark.

Subsequent studies, employing similar cognitive self-management strategies, have explored the treatment of fears of a clinical magnitude. Graziano's home-based program for nighttime fears is one example (Graziano & Mooney, 1982). Graziano and his associates combined self-talk with various other elements (relaxation training, pleasant imagery, and contingency management) to treat long-standing fear of the dark. Two to three years after treatment, improvement was maintained in almost all of the cases. Like Graziano's approach, many treatments actually combine multiple procedures.

The development and evaluation of such broad-based cognitive-behavioral treatment for children with anxiety disorders has been enhanced by the work of Kendall and his colleagues (Kendall et al., 1997). The sixteen to twenty week treatment program educates children about and teaches them how to use four cognitive components of their anxiety: (1) recognizing the physiological symptoms of anxiety, (2) challenging and modifying anxious talk, (3) developing a plan to cope with the situation, and (4) evaluating the success of coping efforts and utilizing self-reinforcement. Behavioral strategies such as modeling, in vivo exposure, role play, relaxation training, and contingency management are utilized in the treatment

sessions and in getting the children to apply what they have learned in actual anxiety-provoking situations. Youngsters (ages nine to thirteen) diagnosed with one of three DSM-III-R anxiety disorders (Overanxious Disorder, Separation Anxiety Disorder, Avoidant Disorder) were randomly assigned either to the treatment group or to a waiting list control group. At the end of treatment, children in the treatment group fared better on a number of measures. Furthermore, significant reductions in measures of distress and anxiety in treated children put these children in the normal range on these measures. In addition, 64 percent of the treated youngsters no longer met diagnostic criteria for an anxiety disorder as compared with 5 percent (one case) in the control condition. Follow-up assessments at one year and three years following treatment indicated that these treatment gains were maintained (Kendall, 1994; Kendall & Southam-Gerow, 1996).

Dadds and his colleagues in Australia (Barrett, Dadds, & Rapee, 1996) have extended the cognitive-behavioral approach by including a family involvement component. In the family component, the child and parents were treated in small family groups. In addition to the cognitive-behavioral procedures for the child's anxiety, the family program included training for the parents in child management, anxiety management, and communication and problem-solving skills. Youngsters (ages seven to fourteen) who met diagnostic criteria for Separation Anxiety Disorder, Overanxious Disorder, or Social Phobia were randomly assigned to either a cognitive-behavioral therapy, cognitive-behavioral plus family management therapy, or waiting list control group. Both treatments proved superior to the control group, and at both the end of treatment and at a one-year follow-up, the combined treatment exceeded the treatment that focused primarily on the child. For example, about 96 percent of the youngsters in the combined condition no longer met diagnostic criteria for an anxiety disorder at follow-up compared with about 70 percent of the youngsters in the group that was primarily child-focused. In an additional study, this group demonstrated that the training of parents in parental anxiety management improved the outcome for anxious children if one or more of their parents were anxious but that it did not enhance the effectiveness of child-focused cognitive behavioral therapy among children whose parents were not anxious (Cobham, Dadds, & Spence, 1998).

Treating Obsessive-Compulsive Disorder. OCD differs in a number of ways from the other anxiety disorders we have reviewed (e.g., known and suspected etiological factors, patterns of "comorbidity," support for pharmacological treatment). We will therefore provide a brief separate discussion of treatment for this disorder.

Two kinds of intervention, alone or in combination, seem to be the current treatments of choice for OCD (Leonard et al., 1994; van Balkom et al., 1994). As indicated earlier, serotonin inhibitors (SRIs and SSRIs) have been demonstrated as effective pharmacological treatments for children and adolescents with OCD. Clomipramine (an SRI) is the medication most extensively studied. Cognitive-behavioral interventions are the other treatment recommended. The treatment typically involves education about OCD, training in modifying cognitions to resist obsessions and compulsions and to enhance change, and contingency management and self-reinforcement. The central aspect of cognitive-behavioral approaches, however, is exposure with response prevention (March & Mulle, 1998). The youngster is exposed to the situation that causes anxiety, and the compulsive ritual is prevented by helping the youngster resist the urge to perform it. Stanley's (1980) clinical report describes an early use of response prevention in the treatment of an eight-year-old girl and her family.

Amanda was referred by her G.P. because of her excessive checking behaviour. Three months prior to this referral Amanda's parents became increasingly worried as more and more of her time was involved in carrying out her rituals, e.g., she was taking at least 20 minutes to dress in the morning instead of the 5 minutes which had been more than ample previously. The symptoms had first become noticeable 6 months before.

The rituals had begun slowly following the family's move to their present home. This had been the second major move made by the family in three years involving a change of house, school, geographic area and father's job. . . . Both Amanda and her younger sister had coped reasonably well with the moves, and the parents did not think these had any connection with Amanda's symptomatology. No satisfactory reason for the development of the symptoms was identified. . . . At interview Amanda presented as an alert, bright eight-year-old whose face fell at the mention of her "fussiness." . . . There was no evidence of obsessional symptoms in her school work and the teacher had not noticed anything unusual in her affect or behaviour.

Amanda was able to talk about her symptomatology as though it were a thing apart from herself. She saw it as an intrusion on her previously happy life and felt depressed by the restrictive elements of her ritual. She found her peer relationships were affected by no longer being able to invite friends home in case they disturbed her ornaments, toys, etc. . . . The family appeared to be functioning very cohesively, which may explain how each person had become involved in Amanda's symptomatology.

At the time of referral Amanda's symptoms included the following. . . .

(1) Every night she closed the curtains, turned down the bed and fluffed up her pillow three times before beginning to undress. Any disruption of this routine caused great distress.
(2) The top bedcover had to be placed with the fringes only just touching the floor all around.
(3) At night Amanda removed her slippers slowly and carefully, she then banged them on the floor upside-down, then the right-way-up, three times and nudged them gently and in parallel under the bed.
(4) Before going to sleep Amanda had to go to the toilet three times. She often woke up in the middle of the night and carried out the same performance.
(5) Before carrying out a ritual Amanda sang:

"One, two, three, Come dance with me, Tra la la, Tra la la."

(6) All dressing and undressing had to be done three times. This included pulling up her pants three times after every visit to the toilet.
(7) All Amanda's toys had special places which had to be checked and rechecked before leaving the bedroom.
(8) The ornaments on top of the piano had special places. These positions were so precise that Amanda's mother found dusting and polishing almost impossible. (pp. 86–87)

The family was instructed not to give Amanda special attention and to treat her as a girl who did not have compulsive urges. The parents were also trained to initiate response prevention procedures. Starting with the least upsetting situation, the parents prevented Amanda from engaging in her rituals. Once she had coped with a situation, the next step up the hierarchy was taken. After the first two days, in which Amanda experienced considerable anxiety, she gradually began to relax. After two weeks, all her symptoms had disappeared. No new or additional problems arose, and Amanda was still symptom free at the one-year follow-up.

Clinical recommendations are often given for a combined cognitive-behavioral and pharmacological approach to treating children with OCD. However, there are no large controlled studies comparing cognitive-behavioral therapy, medication, and their combination. In a small pilot study comparing the two treatments alone, both cognitive-behavioral therapy and clomipramine were found to be effective in treating youngsters (ages eight to eighteen), with some results favoring the cognitive-behavioral treatment (DE Haan et al., 1998).

SUMMARY

■ A variety of evidence supports the existence of a broad category of child and adolescent internalizing problems. The existence and definition of valid subcategories are, however, more controversial.

■ Anxiety or fear is generally defined as a complex pattern of three response systems: overt behavioral, physiological, and subjective responses.

■ DSM-IV describes one anxiety disorder within the "usually first evident in infancy, childhood, or adolescence" grouping: Separation Anxiety Disorder. A youngster can also receive other anxiety disorder diagnoses.

■ The empirical approach to classification describes subcategories of internalizing disorders. The existence of a single anxious/depressed syndrome suggests that these problems tend to co-occur.

■ Fears are quite common in children. There also seem to be age- and gender-related variations in numbers and content of fears. Phobias, as dis-

tinguished from normal fears, are judged to be excessive, persistent, or nonadaptive.

■ Specific phobias are among the most commonly diagnosed anxiety disorders in children and adolescents. They are likely to begin in childhood and may persist over time. Youngsters with this diagnosis, as with other anxiety disorders, frequently have other co-occurring disorders.

■ Children and adolescents with social phobias are likely to be concerned about being embarrassed or negatively evaluated. Avoidance of social situations interferes with development. Prevalence probably increases with age. Social anxieties are quite common during adolescence making the interpretations of prevalence and degree of disturbance difficult.

■ Youngsters with selective mutism do not talk in selected social situations. This disorder may be a type of social phobia.

■ Separation anxiety is a common problem among children but becomes less common by adolescence.

■ "School refusal" describes children whose anxieties keep them from school. This term accommodates cases of both separation anxiety and phobias related to aspects of the school situation. School refusal in adolescence is likely to be complex.

■ Treatment of school refusal is most successful if begun early, and it probably needs to be tailored to the specific kinds of school refusal exhibited.

■ Youngsters diagnosed with Generalized Anxiety Disorder (GAD) exhibit excessive worry and anxiety that is not focused on any particular object or situation. GAD is a relatively common problem and is probably the most common anxiety disorder among adolescents. GAD is common among youngsters seen in clinical settings, and the disorder may persist. The question of overlap with other diagnoses is of concern.

■ Panic attacks may be cued or uncued, and they may occur in the context of several anxiety disorders. Panic Disorder is associated with recurrent unexpected panic attacks. The presence of panic in adolescents seems suggested, but the existence, particularly of uncued panic, in younger children is less clear. Family histories of panic and severe anxiety are commonly reported, as are the presence of other anxiety symptoms and depression.

■ The diagnosis of Posttraumatic Stress Disorder requires reexperiencing of a traumatic event, avoidance of stimuli associated with the trauma, and symptoms of increased arousal. Not all youngsters experience the same pattern, intensity, or persistence of PTSD symptoms, and reactions may fluctuate over time. In general, symptoms decline over time, but substantial numbers of youngsters continue to report symptoms. Degree of exposure to the trauma, preexisting child characteristics and coping abilities, and reactions of parents are among the influences that may determine a youngster's reaction to a trauma.

■ Obsessive-Compulsive Disorder (OCD) is characterized by repetitive and intrusive thoughts and/or behaviors. Washing, repeating, and checking rituals are the most common. Obsessions involving contamination or fear of something terrible happening are most frequently reported. OCD is more common than once thought and often appears to follow a chronic course. Researchers have come to believe that there is a biological basis for the disorder.

■ The development and maintenance of anxiety disorders are influenced by multiple factors that interact in complex ways.

■ There is a familial aggregation for anxiety disorders.

■ Genetic factors may play a role, but for many disorders, what may be inherited is a general tendency toward emotional reactivity. Evidence for a genetic and biological basis seems strongest for Obsessive-Compulsive Disorder.

■ Psychosocial influences play a considerable role in the development of anxiety disorders. Associative learning, imitation, information transmission, and styles of parenting are some of the mechanisms of influence.

■ Assessment of anxiety is typically guided by the three response systems: overt behavior, subjective responses, and physiological responses. In the context of a general and comprehensive assessment, various methods exist for assessing anxiety.

■ Direct observation and behavioral approach tests are employed to assess overt behavioral aspects. The subjective aspects of anxiety are assessed through a variety of self-report measures. Physiological aspects of anxiety are less frequently assessed than the other two response systems.

■ Various perspectives on the youngster's problem, information about a full range of problems, and information about the youngster's environment should be obtained.

■ In general, the most support exists for psychological treatments for anxiety problems in youngsters. Pharmacotherapy, if employed, is usually an adjunct to such treatment. Treatments based on exposure to the feared stimulus have proven effective, as have contingency management and cognitive-behavioral interventions.

■ Cognitive-behavioral treatments involving exposure and response prevention and pharmacological treatments employing serotonin reuptake inhibitors have been shown to be effective in treating Obsessive-Compulsive Disorder.

CHAPTER 7

DEPRESSION AND PROBLEMS IN PEER RELATIONS

I n this chapter we will examine the problems of depression and peer relations. In isolating each of these as separate categories, we confront many of the same problems that we found in examining anxiety disorders. For example, children and adolescents who meet the criteria for a diagnosis of depression are often also given other diagnoses. Similarly, the social withdrawal that one might associate with internalizing problems is part of a more general concern with deficits in peer relations and social skills. Such social deficits are characteristic of youngsters with a number of different disorders. Thus the designation of each of these problems as distinct entities is not without controversy. Nonetheless, examining depression and peer relations makes sense in terms of how the research and the treatment literature are organized.

CHILD AND ADOLESCENT DEPRESSION

Until relatively recently depression in children and adolescents had not received a great deal of attention. However, there has clearly been an increase in interest, which can be traced to a number of influences. Promising developments in the identification and treatment of mood disorders in adults have played a role. In addition, improvements in diagnostic practices have facilitated the application of diagnostic criteria to children and adolescents. The emergence of a number of measures of depression has also allowed researchers to examine the phenomenon in clinic and normal populations of youngsters. Furthermore, the new perspective of developmental psychopathology focused additional attention on depression in young people.

THE EXPERIENCE OF DEPRESSION

In everyday usage, the term "depression" refers to the experience of a pervasive unhappy mood. This subjective experience of sadness, or dysphoria, is also a central feature of the clinical definition of depression. Descriptions of youngsters viewed as depressed suggest that they experience a number of other problems as well. Irritability, loss of the experience of pleasure, social withdrawal, lowered self-esteem, inability to concentrate, poor school-work, alterations of biological functions (sleeping, eating, elimination), and somatic complaints are often noted.

These youngsters also frequently experience other psychological disorders. Both internalizing and externalizing difficulties are reported. Anxiety disorders, such as Separation Anxiety Disorder, are probably the most commonly noted additional disorders. Conduct Disorder and Oppositional Defiant Disorder also occur among depressed youth. Among depressed adolescents, alcohol and substance abuse disorders are also common additional diagnoses.

The case of a fifteen-year-old boy, Nick, described by Compas (1997), illustrates many of these features as well as some of the factors that contribute to the development and course of depression.

Nick lives with his mother. His father left before Nick was born. Nick was born with a curvature of the spine as a result of which he walks awkwardly and is limited in his physical abilities. The incident that resulted in Nick being brought to the clinic was his arrest for shoplifting. However, his mother reports that this was just the "straw that broke the camel's back." A number of things have led her to be concerned about Nick for the past year. She reports that Nick is irritable and sullen much of the time, that they are constantly fighting and arguing. Even the slightest thing seems to send Nick into a fit of anger. Nick's outbursts have escalated recently, including occasions when he has thrown things and punched holes in walls and doors. Nick's mother also reports that he seems unhappy and is withdrawn spending increasing amounts of time at home and alone.

During the initial interview Nick is sullen and aloof and shows little emotion. Over the course of the interview Nick reveals that he is very unhappy, has few things in his life that give him pleasure, and feels hopeless about things improving for him. He is self-conscious about his appearance, his peers tease him and he feels that he is disliked, and he hates himself.

Nick's mother leaves for work early and he is expected to get himself up and off to school. Nick is absent from school more days than not. Nick's typical day is described as: "He wakes up early in the morning after having stayed up late the night before watching television, but he lies in bed until 9:00 or 10:00 A.M. He then

Sad affect, or dysphoria, is the central characteristic of most definitions of depression.
(Penny Tweedie/Tony Stone Images)

spends much of the day at home alone playing video games or watching television." Nick has gained considerable weight and he reports that he is having trouble controlling his appetite. Nick snacks and eats junk food all day long. Nick's mother returns home from work late in the afternoon. They often argue about his having missed another day of school. They eat dinner together silently while watching television. The rest of the evening is filled with arguments about Nick's homework, school attendance problems, and his refusal to go to bed before midnight. (pp. 197–198).

RECENT HISTORY

A brief look at recent history may aid our understanding of current views of childhood depression. As we noted earlier (Chapter 3), the dominant view in child clinical work for many years was the orthodox psychoanalytic perspective. From this perspective, depression was viewed as a phenomenon of the superego and of mature ego functioning (Kessler, 1988). It was argued, for example, that in depression, the superego acts as a punisher of the ego. Since the child's superego is not sufficiently developed to play this role, it is impossible, within this perspective, for a depressive disorder to occur in children. It is not surprising, therefore, that depression in children received little attention.

A second major perspective on childhood depression added to the controversy regarding the existence of a distinct disorder. The concept of masked depression represented an interesting view. This view held that there is a disorder of childhood depression. However, it was proposed that there are numerous instances when the dysphoric mood and other features that are usually considered essential to the diagnosis of depression are not present. It was held that an underlying depressive disorder does exist but that the youngster's depression is "masked" by other problems (depressive equivalents), such as hyperactivity or delinquency. The "underlying" depression itself is not directly displayed but is inferred by the clinician. Some workers, indeed, suggested that masked depressions were quite common and may have resulted in childhood depression being underdiagnosed (Cytryn & McKnew, 1974; Malmquist, 1977).

The notion of masked depression was clearly problematic. There was no operational way to decide whether a particular symptom was or was not a sign of depression. Indeed, the symptoms that were suggested as masking depression included virtually the full gamut of problem behaviors evident in youngsters. The concept of masked depression was, therefore, quite controversial.

The concept of masked depression was important, however. It clearly recognized depression as an important and prevalent childhood problem. The central notions of masked depression—that depression in children does exist and that youngsters may display depression in a variety of age-related forms and in ways that may be different from adult depression—are still widely held. The concept that depression is manifested differently in children and adults contributed, in part, to the evolution of a developmental perspective.

Early in the evolution of a developmental perspective, some workers suggested that behaviors that led to the diagnosis of depression might be only transitory developmental phenomena—common among children in certain age groups (Lefkowitz & Burton, 1978). The classic Berkeley survey, for instance, found that 37 percent of girls and 29 percent of boys at age six exhibited insufficient appetite (a problem often thought to be associated with depression). By age nine, these figures had dropped to 9 percent and 6 percent, respectively, and 14 percent of both sexes at age fourteen had insufficient appetites (MacFarlane, Allen, & Honzik, 1954). Thus insufficient appetite should probably not be considered a deviant behavior among six-year-olds. However, if insufficient appetite is present at age nine, especially in boys, it might be considered atypical. Other behaviors, such as "excessive reserve," occur too often in children of all ages to be considered abnormal. Other investigators (Lefkowitz, 1977) suggested that substantial proportions of children in the normal population may possess symptoms judged characteristic of depressive disorder in clinical samples.

Thus it was suggested that depression in childhood may not exist as a clinical entity different from common and transient developmental phenomena. Lefkowitz and Burton (1978) suggested that perhaps one of the reasons why clinicians gave the diagnosis of childhood depression was the mistaken belief that behaviors (symptoms) such as insufficient appetite or excessive reserve are rare and, therefore, are important when manifested.

A developmental perspective on depression has continued to evolve and will be described throughout this chapter. This early position, however, drew attention to the need to differentiate transient episodes of sadness and negative affect, which may be common reactions among children, from more long-lasting expressions of such emotions. Also, the distinction between depression as a symptom and depression as a syndrome is important to consider here. One or two "depressive" behaviors of a child may be viewed as typical of that developmental stage. However, it is different to suggest that a cluster of such behaviors accompanied by other problems and impaired functioning is also likely to occur in a large number of children (Kovacs, 1997). Awareness of normative and developmental patterns, in any case, is clearly important and might change clinical impressions, leading to changes in diagnostic practices. The developmental perspective has become an important element in the study of depression (Cicchetti & Toth, 1998; Schwartz, Gladstone, & Kaslow, 1998).

DEFINITION AND CLASSIFICATION

Understanding depression in children and adolescents is a complex task. The phenomenon itself involves a complex interplay of influences and a complex clinical presentation. In addition, as suggested above, there have been a variety of perspectives on depression in young people and a variety of ways in which depression has been defined.

A study by Carlson and Cantwell (1980) illustrates this point. A sample of 210 children was selected at random from over 1,000 children between the ages of seven and seventeen seen at the UCLA–Neuropsychiatric Institute. Three different criteria were employed to define depression. At intake the presence of depressive symptoms among the presenting problems was noted, and this served as one criterion. The youngsters were also

administered a version of the Children's Depression Inventory (a paper-and-pencil measure), a second criterion. Finally, as a third criterion, separate interviews with 102 of the youngsters and their parents were conducted to assess the presence of a DSM affective disorder. The use of the presence of depressive symptoms at intake as a criterion led to the largest number of children being designated as depressed, the depression inventory led to fewer, and DSM diagnosis led to the least. However, it is also clear that the results were not simply a matter of using more or less stringent criteria. Rather, there appear to be some differences in definition. For example, not all children designated as depressed by the depression inventory were designated as depressed using the depressive symptom criterion as would be expected if the former were just a more stringent definition. Similarly, not all DSM affective disorder children were designated as depressed using the criterion of depression inventory score.

These and other findings indicate that different groups of youngsters may or may not be designated as depressed, depending on how depression is assessed (Kaslow & Racusin, 1990). Such variations may be due to differences in method employed (e.g., depression inventory versus DSM diagnostic criteria) or to the informants selected (e.g., youngster versus parent). As we have mentioned previously, different informants are likely to give quite different views of children's emotional and behavioral problems.

This difference is illustrated in a study by Kazdin (1989b). DSM diagnoses of 231 consecutive child admissions to an inpatient psychiatric facility were made on the basis of direct interviews with the children and their parents. This method of diagnosing depression was compared with criteria that were based on exceeding a cutoff score on the Children's Depression Inventory (CDI). Both the children and their parents completed the CDI. In addition, children and/or their parents completed a number of other measures to assess attributes reported to be associated with depression. Consistent with the findings of Carlson and Cantwell described above, different groups of children appeared to be designated as depressed depending on the criteria employed. In addition, characteristics associated with depression varied depending on the method used to designate the presence of depression. Some of these results are illustrated in Table 7-1. Defining depression as a high self-report score on the CDI indicated that depressed children were more hopeless; had lower self-esteem; made more internal (as opposed to external) attributions regarding negative events; and on the basis of a locus of control (IE) scale, were more likely to believe that control was due to external factors rather than themselves. Depressed and nondepressed children defined by the other two criteria (parent CDI and DSM) did not differ from each other on these characteristics. Employing the parent CDI criterion, children with high depression scores appear to be more problematic across a wide range of symptoms (as measured by the Child Behavior Checklist—CBCL) than those with very low depression scores. Depression as designated by the other two criteria did not appear to be associated with this wide range of problems. Thus conclusions regarding correlates of depression may be affected by the criterion and informant employed to designate youngsters as depressed.

It is not possible at this point to make definitive statements about the "correct" definition or classification of depression. It is probably fair, however, to state that the dominant view is that childhood depression is a syndrome or disorder and that the most often employed definition is that offered by the DSM.

The DSM approach. In DSM-IV, depression is included in the category of Mood Disorders. There are no separate diagnostic categories for mood disorders in children or adolescents. The criteria employed to diagnose mood disorders are the same for children, adolescents and adults. Mood disorders are sometimes described as unipolar (one mood, either depression or mania) versus bipolar (both moods).

Major Depressive Disorder (MDD) is the primary DSM category for defining depression. This disorder is described by the presence of one or more Major Depressive Episodes. The symptoms required for the presence of a Major Depressive Episode are the same for children, adolescents, and adults (with one exception), and these are listed in Table 7-2. The one exception is that in children or adolescents, irritable mood can be substituted for depressed mood. Indeed, some reports suggest that a majority of depressed youths (over 80 percent) exhibit irritable mood (Goodyer & Cooper, 1993; Ryan et al., 1987). The presence

---

TABLE 7-1

Mean Characteristic Scores of Depressed and Nondepressed Children as Designated by Different Criteria for Depression

Measures	Children's Depression Inventory (by Child)		Children's Depression Inventory (by Parent)		DSM Diagnosis	
	High	**Low**	**High**	**Low**	**Depressed**	**Nondepressed**
Hopelessness	7.3	3.3	5.3	5.0	5.4	4.8
Self-esteem	22.7	38.9	28.2	30.8	29.2	30.9
Attributions	5.4	6.5	5.8	5.8	6.0	6.0
Locus of Control	9.8	6.8	8.2	8.7	7.9	8.4
Total behavior problems (CBCL)	75.8	75.3	81.6	69.0	76.5	75.0

Adapted from Kazdin (1989).

TABLE 7-2

Symptoms Used by DSM-IV to Diagnose a Major Depressive Episode

1. Depressed or irritable mood
2. Loss of interest or pleasure
3. Change in weight or appetite
4. Sleep problems
5. Motor agitation or retardation
6. Fatigue or loss of energy
7. Feelings of worthlessness or guilt
8. Difficulty thinking, concentrating, or making decisions
9. Thoughts of death or suicidal thoughts/behavior

of five or more of the symptoms is required. One of these symptoms must be either depressed (or irritable) mood or loss of pleasure. The symptoms must be present for at least two weeks and must cause clinically significant distress or impairment in important areas of the youngster's functioning (e.g., social, school).

Dysthymic Disorder is the other principal depressive disorder included in DSM-IV. It is essentially a disorder in which many of the symptoms of a Major Depressive Episode are present in less severe form but are more chronic—that is, they persist for a longer period of time. Depressed mood (or in children and adolescents, irritable mood) is present for at least one year along with two or more of the following symptoms: (1) poor appetite or overeating, (2) sleep disturbance, (3) low energy or fatigue, (4) low self-esteem, (5) concentration or decision making problems, and (6) feelings of hopelessness. Again, the symptoms must cause clinically significant distress or impairment. The term "double depression" is sometimes employed to describe instances in which both dysthymia and a major depressive episode are present. Dysthymia typically occurs prior to a Major Depressive Episode.

Youngsters who are depressed can also be given a diagnosis of Adjustment Disorder With Depressed Mood. This is viewed as a response to a stressor in which depressive symptoms do not meet the criteria for other depressive disorders.

The other mood disorders included in DSM-IV, Bipolar Disorders and Cyclothymia, involve the presence of mania (persistently elevated, expansive, or irritable mood) as well as depressive symptoms. In addition to the presence of mania, at least three or more other symptoms must be present in order to meet the criteria for a Manic Episode. These symptoms are described in Table 7-3. Individuals diagnosed with bipolar and cyclothymic disorders experience both mania and depression. In comparison with depression, less is known about these disorders in children and adolescents (Nottelmann & Jensen, 1995a).

As was indicated before, the view inherent in the DSM approach is that mood disorders found in youngsters are the same as those found in adults. There is some research consistent with this perspective. Many of the cognitive attributes, biological correlates, and behaviors found in depressed adults have also been reported to occur in children and adolescents (e.g., Kaslow, Rehm, & Siegel, 1984; Kazdin et al., 1985; Puig-Antich, 1983). However, differences have also been found, and this finding has led many workers to conclude that it is premature to accept the use of the same criteria for depressive disorders across all age groups (Nurcombe, 1994; Poznanski & Mokros, 1994). They suggest that research is not sufficient

TABLE 7-3

Symptoms Used by DSM-IV to Diagnose a Manic Episode

1. Persistent elevated, expansive, or irritable mood
2. Inflated self-esteem
3. Decreased need for sleep
4. Being more talkative than usual
5. Feeling of thoughts racing
6. Distractibility
7. Increased goal-directed activity or psychomotor agitation
8. Excessive pleasurable activity that can lead to negative consequences (e.g., buying sprees, sexual indiscretions)

and that certain findings require explanation. The gender ratio in prevalence is one example (Compas, Hinden, & Gerhardt, 1995; Nolen-Hoeksema & Girgus, 1994). There is a greater prevalence of depression among adult females than adult males, whereas in youngsters, prevalence differences between the genders are not usually reported until sometime during adolescence. In addition, some of the serious concomitants of adult depression are less evident in children, and some biological correlates appear to differ as well (Kazdin & Marciano, 1998). Also, antidepressant medications have not been demonstrated to have the same effectiveness in children and adolescents as they have in adults (Johnston & Fruehling, 1994). Finally, the high rates of additional disorders found in youngsters diagnosed as depressed also suggest continued attention to developmental differences in the expression of depression. The association of depression with other difficulties may hold important information regarding both the development of depression and its treatment (e.g., Anderson & McGee, 1994; Kovacs et al., 1984; Lewinsohn et al., 1993a).

Empirical approaches. Syndromes that involve depressive symptoms have also been identified by empirical approaches to taxonomy. This is illustrated by the syndromes that emerge in research employing Achenbach's instruments (see Chapter 5). The syndrome that includes depressive symptoms that regularly occur together also includes symptoms characteristic of anxiety. Thus this research does not find a syndrome that includes symptoms of depression alone. The problems that define this anxious/depressed syndrome were described in Chapter 6 (p. 115). This syndrome of mixed depression and anxiety features has emerged consistently in research with children and adolescents, and again highlights the issue of whether depression in youngsters manifests itself the same way as it does in adults.

How best to define and classify depression in children and adolescents remains a focus of ongoing research. One issue is determining developmentally sensitive criteria. In light of this evolving perspective, many workers have chosen to concern themselves with youngsters who exhibit constellations of depressive symptoms whether or not they meet DSM criteria for a mood disorder. The focus is on youngsters who experience relatively extreme levels of symptoms of depression, however measured or defined. This approach makes sense in that a variety of methods and measures are employed in defining depression in existing research. Furthermore, it is not clear that diagnostic criteria are the critical cutoff. Many youngsters who fall short of meeting diagnostic criteria may still exhibit impairment in their everyday functioning (Kazdin & Marciano, 1998).

EPIDEMIOLOGY

Estimates of the prevalence of depression vary considerably, reflecting, in part, differences in how depression is defined and diagnosed (Reynolds & Johnston, 1994; Schwartz et al., 1998). In addition, there are developmental considerations that complicate getting accurate estimates. The difficulty of administering similar assessments to youngsters of different ages is one consideration. Also, widely employed assessment tools, such as interviews, require that the youngster think in terms of psychological constructs and effectively communicate what is remembered. Such processes clearly depend on developmental level.

Major Depressive Disorder (MDD) is by far the most prevalent form of affective disorder among children and adolescents (Lewinsohn, Rhode, & Seeley, 1998). Bipolar disorders occur in less than 1 percent of community samples of adolescents. Among youngsters with unipolar disorders, about 80 percent experience MDD, 10 percent dysthymia without MDD, and 10 percent "double depression." In community surveys, reported prevalence rates for MDD in children range between 0.4 and 2.5 percent, and between 0.4 and 8.3 percent in adolescents. The epidemiology of Dysthymic Disorder is less well studied. Reported prevalence rates among children range between 0.6 and 1.7 percent, and among adolescents between 1.6 and 8.0 percent (Birmaher et al., 1996a).

These prevalence rates probably underestimate the scope of the problem. For example, lifetime prevalence rates, rather than prevalence rates at any one point in time, indicate that episodes of clinical depressions may be quite common, particularly among adolescents. In the Oregon Adolescent Depression Project (OADP), a large prospective epidemiological study of a representative community sample of adolescents ages fourteen to eighteen, Lewinsohn and his colleagues (Lewinsohn et al., 1998) estimate that by age 19, approximately 28 percent of adolescents will have experienced an episode of MDD (35 percent of young women and 19 percent of young men). Other information also suggests lifetime prevalence rates of diagnosable depressive disorders among the general population as high as 20 to 30 percent (Compas, Ey, & Grant, 1993; Lewinsohn et al., 1993a). This finding would mean that about one out of four youngsters in the general population experiences a depressive disorder sometime during childhood or adolescence. Also, 40 to 50 percent of the OADP youngsters scored above the criteria for depression "caseness" on a standard self-report depression questionnaire (the Center for Epidemiologic Studies Depression Scale). The comparable finding in adults is 16 to 20 percent. Finally, youngsters who exhibit depressive symptoms but who do not meet diagnostic criteria are not included in the prevalence estimates cited above. These youngsters may, however, exhibit impairments in their academic, social, and cognitive functioning and also are at greater risk for future disorders than are youngsters who do not exhibit these depressive symptoms (Kazdin & Marciano, 1998; Lewinsohn et al., 1998).

Gender and age are clearly relevant to estimates of the prevalence of depression in young people. Usually no gender differences are reported for children ages six to twelve (Angold & Rutter, 1992; Fleming, Offord, & Boyle, 1989). When differences are reported, depression is more prevalent in boys than in girls during this age period (Anderson et al., 1987). Yet among adolescents, depression is more common among girls and begins to approach the 2:1 female to male ratio usually reported for adults (Lewinsohn et al., 1994). This age-gender pattern is illustrated in Figure 7-1. It is worth noting that for adolescents of both sexes, there is a greater prevalence of depression than exists for younger children (Angold & Rutter, 1992; Cohen, Cohen, Kasen et al., 1993; Lewinsohn et al., 1993a; Whitaker et al., 1990). The OADP findings and other information (Nolen-Hoeksema & Girgus, 1994) suggests that the gender difference in MDD levels probably emerges between the ages of twelve and fourteen. Consistent with this picture are findings from the Dunedin Multidisciplinary Health and Development Study, a large epidemiological study conducted in New Zealand (Hankin et al., 1998). Rates of clinical depression (Major Depressive Episode or Dysthymic Disorder) in these youngsters was assessed at a number of points between the ages of eleven and twenty-one. At age eleven, males showed a tendency to have higher rates of depression than females; at thirteen, there were no gender differences; and females had higher rates of depression at ages fifteen, eighteen, and twenty-one. Gender differences were greatest between fifteen and eighteen, and rates of depression began to level off after age eighteen. Again, these findings are illustrated in Figure 7-1. Findings of other investigators suggest that gender differences in depression may be more pronounced among youngsters referred for mental health services than in a nonreferred sample (Compas et al., 1997).

Several reports suggest that the rates of major depression may be increasing (Birmaher et al., 1996a). This trend has been reported for youngsters as well as for adults. Lewinsohn and his colleagues (1993b) reported on a community sample of adolescents divided into two cohorts: those born from 1968 to 1971 and those born from 1972 to 1974. The greater rate of depression in the more recent age-cohort is illustrated by the fact that by fourteen years of age, 7.2 percent of the more recent cohort had an episode of MDD as compared with 4.5 percent in the earlier cohort. The cumulative rates of depression through the adolescent years in the two groups are presented in Figure 7-2. Kovacs and Gatsonis (1994) report similar trends in a clinical sample of three cohorts

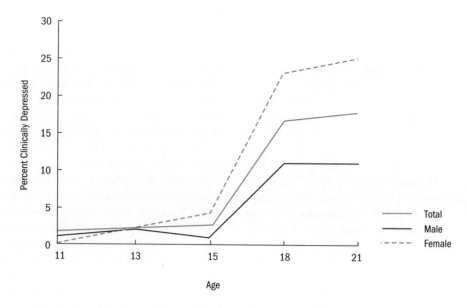

FIGURE 7-1 The development of clinical depression by age and gender.
From Hankin, Abramson, Moffitt, Silva, McGee, & Angell (1998).

of depressed youngsters. For example, children born from 1969 to 1970, 1970 to 1971, and 1973 to 1975 were on average 11.6, 11.0, and 9.9 years old, respectively, when they experienced their first episode of MDD.

Finally, youngsters who are depressed typically experience other problems as well. This finding is indicated in research examining DSM diagnoses. These investigations indicate that 40 to 70 percent of youngsters diagnosed with MDD also meet the criteria for another disorder and that 20 to 50 percent have two or more additional disorders (Birmaher et al., 1996a). The most common additional nonmood disorders are anxiety disorders, disruptive behavior disorders, and substance abuse disorders (Harrington, Rutter, & Fombonne, 1996; Kovacs, 1996, Lewinsohn et al., 1998).

DEVELOPMENTAL COURSE

It is interesting to ask, How is depression manifested, and what is the prevalence of depression at different developmental periods? Although the di-

agnostic criteria in DSM-IV are largely the same for children, adolescents, and adults, there is an appreciation that depression may be manifested differently in children and adolescents than in adults.

Schwartz, Gladstone, and Kaslow (1998) describe the phenomenology of depression at different developmental stages. Infants and toddlers lack the cognitive and verbal abilities necessary to self-reflect and report depressive thoughts and problems. It is difficult, therefore, to know what the equivalent to adult depressive symptoms may be in this age group. Given cognitive, language, and other developmental differences, it is likely that depressive behavior in this age group may be quite different than in adults. However, the description of deprivation reactions in infants separated from their primary caregivers in many ways seems similar to that of depression (Bowlby, 1960; Spitz, 1946). These and other distressed infants and infants of depressed mothers have been observed to exhibit behaviors such as lethargy, feeding and sleep problems, irritability, sad facial ex-

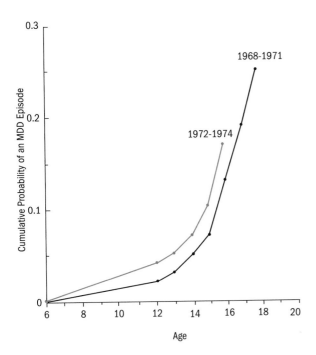

FIGURE 7-2 The cumulative rates of depression through the adolescent years in two cohorts of depressed youngsters. From Lewinsohn, Rohde, Seeley, & Fischer (1993).

pression, excessive crying, and decreased responsivity—behaviors often associated with depression.

Depression in preschoolers is also difficult to assess. Again, many of the symptoms associated with later depression have been noted in youngsters in this age group (e.g., irritability, sad facial expression, changes of mood, feeding and sleep problems, lethargy, excessive crying). Differences in cognition and language, as well as limited information, make it difficult to know how these behaviors are related to the experience of depression and depressive syndromes in older individuals and whether or not these represent stable patterns.

For the period of middle childhood (six to twelve years), there is more evidence that a prolonged pattern of depressive symptoms may emerge. Younger children in this age group typically do not verbalize the hopelessness and self-

deprecation associated with depression. However, nine to twelve-year-olds who exhibit other symptoms of depression may verbalize feelings of hopelessness and low self-esteem. Still, in youngsters in this age group, depressive symptoms may not be a distinctive syndrome but may occur with a variety of symptoms usually associated with other disorders. So, for example, as mentioned before, a mixed depressed/anxious syndrome rather than a separate depressed syndrome emerges in empirical taxonomies (Achenbach, 1991a).

During the early adolescent period, the manifestation of depression is in many ways similar to that of the childhood period. Over time, however, probably in relation to shifts in social and cognitive development, the presentation of depression in older adolescents starts to resemble more closely the symptoms of adult depression. In their community sample of adolescents, Lewinsohn and his colleagues (1998) report a median age of onset for MDD at 15.5 years. As part of their longitudinal research and their effort to examine the relationship of age of onset and familial contributions to depression, Harrington and his colleagues (1997) compared a group of prepubertal onset depressed youngsters to a group of youngsters whose onset of depression was postpubertal. Rates of depression in relatives of youngsters in the two groups did not differ. There were, however, other differences in the families of the two groups. Manic disorders tended to be higher among relatives of the postpubertal-onset group, and relatives of the prepubertal depressed youngsters had higher rates of criminality, and there were higher rates of family discord in this group as well. This evidence is consistent with viewing prepubertal onset depressive disorders as distinct from postpubertal onset depression. These authors also report that the continuity to major depression in adulthood was lower among prepubertal onset youngsters than among those with postpubertal onset of depression. This finding is also consistent with viewing depression with onset in adolescence as more similar to adult forms of the disorder and different from earlier onset depression.

Adolescence thus appears to be a period when depressive syndromes similar to adult depression have their onset. As noted before, there is a significant increase in the prevalence of depression in adolescence, and prevalence may reach adult levels in late adolescence. What, then, is the clinical course of depression during adolescence and into adulthood? How long does an episode of major depression last? Are there future episodes?

In the OADP community sample (Lewinsohn et al., 1998), the median duration of an episode of MDD was 8 weeks, the range was from 2 to 520 weeks, and earlier onset of depression (at or before the age of fifteen) was associated with longer episodes. The recurrent nature of depression is illustrated by the finding that among adolescents who recovered from their first episode, 5 percent experienced another episode within six months, 12 percent within a year, and 33 percent within four years. Kovacs (1996), in her review of studies of clinically referred youngsters, found a median duration of MDD episodes of seven to nine months. It was found that about 70 percent of these clinically referred youngsters had recurrences of MDD episodes when followed up for five or more years. Thus the duration of episodes in clinical samples may be more than three times the duration in community samples, and the likelihood of recurrence of a major depressive episode twice as great. Episodes of depression in adolescents may last for an appreciable period of time and for some youngsters may present a recurring problem. A sample of participants in the OADP project were interviewed after their twenty-fourth birthday. Those who prior to age nineteen had met criteria for MDD or Adjustment Disorder With Depressed Mood were more likely to meet criteria for MDD during young adulthood than their peers with a nonaffective disorder or no disorder prior to age nineteen (Lewinsohn et al., 1999). In addition, follow-up studies suggest that some adolescents with MDD develop bipolar disorder (periods of depression and mania) within five years after the onset of depression, but the percentage of such outcomes is not clear (Birmaher et al., 1996a; Kovacs, 1996; Lewinsohn et al., 1999).

Regarding bipolar disorders, Lewinsohn, Klein, and Seeley (1995) examined the course of bipolar disorder in a large community sample of adolescents (ages fourteen to eighteen). The median duration of the most recent manic episode for these youngsters was 10.8 months. The youngsters with a diagnosis of bipolar disorder (eighteen adolescents, 1 percent of the sample) had an earlier age of onset for their affective disorder. Their first affective episode was earlier (mean age = 11.75 years old) than for adolescents with a history of major depression with no periods of mania (mean age = 14.95 years old). The total amount of time with an affective disorder was longer for these youngsters as well. The estimated mean duration of affective disorder for these youngsters with bipolar disorder was 80.2 months compared with a mean duration of 15.7 months for youngsters in the OADP sample with MDD.

The youngsters with bipolar disorder also met the criteria for other nonaffective disorders. Anxiety disorders (especially Separation Anxiety Disorder), disruptive disorders (especially Attention-Deficit Hyperactivity Disorder), and substance abuse disorders were the most common other diagnoses. These youngsters had also developed significant impairment in school, social, and family functioning.

INFLUENCES ON THE DEVELOPMENT OF DEPRESSION

Biological influences.   Biological views of depression in children and adolescents focus on genetic and biochemical influences. These views derive largely from the adult literature, since there are less data available on children and adolescents (Emslie et al., 1994; Rutter et al., 1990b).

Genetic Influences   Genetic influences are generally thought to play a role in depression in children and adolescents. This view derives from a number of findings. For example, the data based on twin, family, and adoptive studies of mood disorders in adults suggest a heritability component in adult depressive disorders (Kendler et al., 1992; Weissman, Kidd, & Prusoff, 1982; Wender et al., 1986). Also, if onset of depression occurred before twenty years of age, greater rates of depression were found among family members (Klein et al.,

1995; Puig-Antich et al., 1989; Weissman et al., 1988). In addition, first-degree adult relatives of depressed children and adolescents have been found to have greater than expected rates of depressive disorders (Birmaher et al., 1996a; Kovacs et al., 1997). Findings that children of parents with major depressive disorder are at increased risk for major depression (discussed later) can also be seen as consistent with a genetic influence.

Although a genetic contribution seems possible, even research that suggests a heritability component in adult depression also indicates the importance of environmental influences. For example, O'Connor and his colleagues (1998), using behavioral genetic methods, examined a sample of same-sex adolescent siblings between the ages of ten and eighteen years of age. The sample included monozygotic (MZ) and dizygotic (DZ) twins, full siblings, half siblings, and unrelated siblings. Results indicated an appreciable genetic component to depressive symptoms. However, there were significant influences of shared and nonshared environment as well. Further investigation is needed to clarify the contribution of genetics to the development of depression in children and adolescents.

The complexity of these issues is illustrated in a study by Rende and his colleagues (1993). These investigators examined depressive symptomatology in a general (unselected) sample of 707 pairs of adolescent siblings. By comparing MZ twins, DZ same-sex twins, and same-sex full siblings from nondivorced families, as well as full, half, and unrelated same-sex siblings from step families, the authors were able to make use of twin and adoption study methodologies to examine genetic and environmental influences on depression. A significant genetic influence was found when the depressive symptomatology of the full sample was examined. However, surprisingly, a significant genetic influence on depression was not found if only youngsters with high levels of depression were considered. Instead, there was a significant influence of shared environment, that is, nongenetic influences shared by both siblings in a family. The authors suggest that one possible explanation for these findings is that genetic influence operates on personality and temperamental factors, such as emotionality and sociability, that affect the full range of depressive symptomatology. The expression of extreme depressive symptomatology, however, may result, against this background of moderate genetic influence, from environmental experiences that are shared by siblings in a family. Several psychological variables have been implicated in the development of depression that may operate in this manner. For example, being raised in a family in which a parent is depressed has received considerable attention. The influence of parental depression is discussed later.

Biochemistry of Depression The study of the biochemistry of depression in adults has highlighted the role of neurotransmitters such as norepinephrine, serotonin, and acetylcholine. The impetus to study these neurotransmitters came largely from findings that the effectiveness of certain antidepressant medications with adults was related to levels of these chemicals or receptivity to them. For example, an early suggestion, the catecholamine hypothesis, proposed that low levels of norepinephrine were created by too much reabsorption by the neuron releasing it or by too efficient a breakdown by enzymes. This was thought to result in too low a level of norepinephrine at the synapse to fire the next neuron. Current research continues to explore the role of neurotransmitters; however, the mechanisms of action are clearly very complex, involving not only the amounts of neurotransmitters available but also the complex interaction among neurotransmitter systems and receptors.

Studies of the neuroendocrine systems (connections between the brain, hormones, and various organs) add complexity to this picture. Dysregulation of the neuroendocrine systems involving the hypothalamus, pituitary gland, and the adrenal and thyroid glands is thought of as a "hallmark" of adult depression (Emslie et al., 1994). These systems are also regulated by neurotransmitters. Thus the picture regarding depression is likely to be a complex one. Although there is significant promise for this line of research regarding child and adolescent depression, the rapid biological changes during this period (e.g., hormonal activity during puberty) offer a particular challenge.

Research on the biological aspects of depression suggests that during the earlier developmental periods of childhood and adolescence, the neuroregulatory system is not equivalent to that in adulthood. Biological indicators later in development, for example in older adolescents who are more severely depressed, may be more similar to those for depressed adults. Thus although many workers still find evidence for a biological dysfunction in childhood depression, a simple translation of the adult findings is not sufficient (Ivanova, 1998; Puig-Antich, 1986).

For example, disturbances of sleep are associated with clinical levels of depression. Research has indicated that EEG patterns during sleep are strong biological markers of major depressive disorders in adults (Gillin et al., 1979; Kupfer & Reynolds, 1992). But many of the sleep findings reported in adults are not characteristic of children diagnosed with major depressive disorders (Birmaher et al., 1996a). Some research does suggest, however, that some abnormalities related to the rapid eye movement (REM) stage of sleep (e.g., a shortened period of time before REM sleep begins) may be present particularly in depressed adolescents. Also, adults with major depression hypersecrete basal levels of cortisol, a stress hormone produced in the adrenal glands. Investigations of youngsters with major depression have failed to find cortisol hypersecretion. Indeed, the opposite, hyposecretion (less cortisol produced), has been found among depressed youngsters (Goenjian et al., 1996). Increased cortisol levels, similar to those for depressed adults, may occur among older and more severely depressed adolescents (Rao et al., 1996).

Findings regarding biological correlates of depression in children and adolescents are limited and sometimes contradictory. Also, the understanding of findings requires comparison with normative data on these functions. Such normative data are not readily available (Emslie et al., 1994). In general, differences in biological markers of depression might suggest that the child and the adult disorders are different. Alternatively, such differences in biological markers may represent age-related differences in the same disorder.

Social-Psychological Influences. Despite increased interest in recent years, much of the thinking regarding social and psychological influences on child and adolescent depression is still based on theories derived from work with depressed adults. We will examine several of the social-psychological influences and provide illustrations of work based on children and adolescents.

Separation and Loss A common psychological explanation of depression is that it results from separation or loss. Psychoanalytic explanations of depression, following from Freud, emphasize the notion of object loss. The loss may be real (parental death, divorce) or symbolic. Identification with and ambivalent feelings toward the lost love object are thought to result in the person's directing hostile feelings concerning the love object toward the self. Some psychodynamic writers emphasize loss of self-esteem and feelings of helplessness that result from object loss, and they minimize the importance of aggression turned inward toward the self (Kessler, 1988).

Some behaviorally oriented explanations also involve separation and loss. Both Ferster (1974) and Lewinsohn (1974) emphasized the role of inadequate positive reinforcement in the development of depression. Loss of or separation from a loved one is likely to result in a decrease in the child's sources of positive reinforcement. However, inadequate reinforcement may also result from factors such as not having adequate skills to obtain desired rewards.

Past support for the theory that separation played a role in the genesis of depression came from several different sources. For example, a fairly typical sequence of reactions of young children to prolonged separation from their parents was described by a number of investigators (e.g., Bowlby, 1960; Spitz, 1946). In this so-called anaclitic depression, the child initially goes through a period of "protest" characterized by crying, asking for the parents, and restlessness. This is followed

The theme of separation-loss is a central concept in many theories of depression. The loss may be real or imagined.

(Courtesy of A.C. Israel)

shortly by a period of depression and withdrawal. Most children begin to recover after several weeks.

High rates of early parental loss or separation among children referred for treatment of a variety of psychological problems have also been cited. Seligman et al. (1974), for example, reported that among one hundred consecutive adolescent referrals, 36.4 percent had experienced loss of one or both parents. In contrast, in public school and medical clinic control samples, only 11.7 percent and 16.6 percent, respectively, had experienced such loss. Differences between the treatment and control samples were particularly high for parental loss between three to six years of age and twelve to fifteen years of age. Another comparison involving depressed and nondepressed children between the ages of five and sixteen indicated that 50 percent of the depressed group but only 23 percent of the nondepressed group experienced parental separation prior to the age of eight (Caplan & Douglas, 1969).

The connection between loss and depression has been examined in regard to adult depression. For a long time, the widely held view was that such early loss puts one at high risk for later depres-sion—especially women. More recent examinations of this issue question this view, in part because most studies were plagued with methodological problems (Finkelstein, 1988; Tennant, 1988). The current view is that early loss is not in and of itself pathogenic. The link between such loss and later depression is not direct. Rather, it is hypothesized that such loss, as well as other circumstances, can set in motion a chain of adverse circumstances such as lack of care, changes in family structure, and socioeconomic difficulties that put the individual at risk for later disorder (Bifulco, Harris, & Brown, 1992; Saler & Skolnick, 1992).

Much of the research on the association between loss and depression has relied on the retrospective reports of adults. Recently investigations of the impact of loss on children themselves has received attention (Tremblay & Israel, 1998). For example, Sandler and his colleagues found support for a model consistent with the indirect effects of loss (West et al., 1991). Among a sample of ninety-two families who had lost a parent within the previous two years, depression in youngsters (ages eight to fifteen) was not directly linked to the loss. Rather, the level of parental demoralization, family warmth, and stable positive events following the loss mediated the effects of parental death on depression in these youngsters.

Cognitive-Behavioral Perspectives Many of the conceptualizations derived from behavioral, cognitive, and cognitive-behavioral perspectives contain related and overlapping concepts (Hammen, 1992; Kaslow, Brown, & Mee, 1994). Influences such as interpersonal skills, cognitive distortions, views of self, control beliefs, self-regulation, and stress are the focus of these perspectives on child and adolescent depression.

As indicated earlier, writers such as Ferster (1974) and Lewinsohn (1974) suggested that a combination of lowered activity level and inadequate interpersonal skills plays a role in the development and maintenance of depression. Thus it is suggested that depressed individuals do not elicit positive interpersonal responses from others. Indeed, there is evidence that depressed youths display deficits in social functioning and that they are viewed as less likable by others (Kaslow, Brown, & Mee, 1994; Schwartz, Gladstone, & Kaslow, 1998). For example, Bell-Dolan, Reaven, and Peterson (1993) obtained self, peer, and teacher reports of both depression and social functioning for 112 fourth- to sixth-graders. Negative social behavior (aggression and negative support seeking), social withdrawal, and low social competence were all related to higher ratings of depression.

A learned helplessness explanation of depression (Seligman & Peterson, 1986) suggests that some individuals, as a result of their learning histories, come to perceive themselves as having little control of their environment. This learned helplessness is in turn associated with the mood and behaviors characteristic of depression. Separation may be a special case of learned helplessness: The child's attempts to bring the parent back may result in the child's thinking that personal action and positive outcome are independent of each other. As indicated before, the concept of helplessness as an element in depression is held by some psychodynamic workers as well.

Helplessness conceptualizations emphasize how the person thinks about activity and outcome—a person's attributional or explanatory style. An explanatory style in which one blames oneself for *negative events* (internal) views the causes of the event as being stable over time (stable) and generalizable across situations (global) is thought to be characteristic of depressed individuals. The opposite style, external-unstable-specific attributions for *positive events*, may also be viewed as part of this depressed style. In recent revisions of this perspective the interaction of stressful life events with cognitive style is given greater emphasis (Abramson, Metalsky, & Alloy, 1989). This revision is referred to as the hopelessness theory of depression. Attributional style (a diathesis) acts as a moderator between negative life events that the person sees as important (a stress) and hopelessness. Hopelessness, in turn, leads to depression. A number of studies have reported maladaptive attributional styles in depressed youngsters (Gladstone & Kaslow, 1995) and the diathesis-stress notions of hopelessness theory have received some support (Nolen-Hoeksema, Girgus, & Seligman, 1992). However, additional attention needs to be given to inconsistencies in findings, investigation of developmental patterns, and a clearer articulation of the relationship of attributional style and life events (Kaslow, Brown, & Mee, 1994).

The role of cognitive factors in depression is also the major emphasis of other theorists. Beck (1967; 1976), for example, assumes that depression results from negative views of the self, others, and the future. Depressed individuals, Beck hypothesizes, have developed certain errors in thinking that result in their distorting even mildly annoying events into opportunities for self-blame and failure. Research studies have found evidence in depressed youngsters of the cognitive distortions suggested by Beck's theory (Kendall, Stark, & Adams, 1990; Leitenberg, Yost, & Carroll-Wilson, 1986). The nature of the cognitive distortion-depression link, however, requires further clarification (Hammen, 1992). For example, cognitive distortion may not be general but instead may be limited to certain kinds of situations, such as those that are interpersonal and emotional. It is also not clear whether these cognitions play a causal role in depression as an underlying vulnerability or whether they are associated with depression in some other way, perhaps co-occurring with depression or being a consequence of depression.

The dimension of control, part of a helplessness perspective discussed before, has also been the focus of additional consideration. Deficits in one or more specific self-control behaviors (self-monitoring, self-evaluation, and self-reinforcement) are hypothesized to contribute to the development of depression. According to this self-control model (Rehm, 1977), depressed individuals selectively focus on negative rather than positive events and on immediate rather than delayed consequences of behavior, set overly stringent self-evaluative criteria, and provide themselves with little positive reinforcement and excessive punishment. Depressed children, for example, despite similar performance, exhibit lower evaluations of their performance and punish themselves more than do nondepressed peers (Meyer, Dyck, & Petrinack, 1989). There is a growing body of literature suggesting self-control deficits in depressed youngsters. Thus it may be worthwhile to examine the self-regulatory behavior that is modeled or encouraged by parents of depressed youngsters (Kaslow, Brown, & Mee, 1994). With this observation in mind, we turn to the influences of parental depression on youngsters.

The Impact of Parental Depression A major area of research on childhood depression has been an examination of children of depressed parents. There are several reasons for the proliferation of such research. Because family aggregation of mood disorders in adults was known to exist, it was presumed that examining children of parents with mood disorders would reveal a population likely to experience childhood depression. Such a high-risk research strategy has the potential to be a more efficient means of investigating a problem than a random sampling of the population would be. In addition, such research might provide information on the continuity between child, adolescent, and adult mood disorders.

Numerous studies have found that youngsters from homes with a depressed parent are at increased risk for developing a psychological disor-

der. Such youngsters may also be four times more likely to develop an affective disorder than children of parents with no psychological disorder (Beardslee, Versage, & Gladstone, 1998). A number of longitudinal studies have been particularly informative. Hammen and her colleagues (1990) compared the long-term effects of maternal depression and maternal chronic medical illness. Over the course of a three-year period, with evaluations at six-month intervals, children of both depressed mothers and medically ill mothers exhibited elevated rates of psychological disorder as compared with children of non-ill mothers. Rates of disorder were higher for children of depressed mothers than for those with medically ill mothers.

Weissman and her colleagues (Weissman et al., 1997) followed the offspring of two groups of parents over a ten-year period. At the time of the follow-up, the offspring were in late adolescence or were adults. Parents and offspring were assessed with a structured diagnostic interview. Offspring for whom neither parent had a psychological disorder (low risk) were compared with offspring for whom one or both parents had a diagnosis of Major Depressive Disorder (high risk). The offspring of the depressed parents had increased rates of MDD, particularly before puberty. The high-risk group also had increased rates of other disorders, including phobias and alcohol dependence. These results are illustrated in Table 7-4. In addition, more serious depression was experienced by offspring of depressed parents as compared with depression experienced by offspring of nondepressed parents. However, the depressed offspring of depressed parents were less likely to receive treatment when they were depressed. More than 30 percent of the depressed offspring of depressed parents never received any treatment.

Beardslee and his colleagues have examined the question of the impact of parental depression in a non–clinically referred population (Beardslee et al., 1996, 1998). Families were recruited from a large health maintenance organization. Assessments, including a structured diagnostic interview, were conducted initially and four years later. Families were divided into three categories: parents with no diagnosis, parents with a nonaffective dis-

TABLE 7-4

Percentage of Youngsters with Disorders among Offspring of Parents with MDD and with No Diagnosis

	Parental Diagnosis	
Diagnosis in Offspring	MDD	None
Any mood disorder	85	38
MDD	56	25
Any anxiety disorder	42	15
Phobias	21	8
Panic disorder	13	0
Alcohol dependence	22	7

Adapted from Weissman, Warner, Wickramaratne, Moreau, & Olfsen, 1997.

TABLE 7-5

Risk Factors Predicting the Experiencing of Affective Disorders in Youngsters During Follow-up Period

Risk Factor	Percentage of Youngsters with Affective Diagnosis
Parent Nonaffective Diagnosis	
Absent	12
Present	32
Parent MDD	
Absent	18
Present	34
Earlier Child Diagnosis	
Absent	16
Present	30
Number of Risk Factors Present	
None	7
1	18
2	25
3	50

Adapted from Beardslee, Keller, Seifer, Lavori, Staley, Podorefsky, & Shera, 1996.

order, and one or both parents with an affective disorder. Parental nonaffective disorder, parental MDD, and the number of diagnosed disorders that the child experienced prior to the first assessment predicted whether the youngster experienced a serious affective disorders in the time between assessments. The percentage of diagnoses associated with each of these risk factors and with the number of risk factors present is illustrated in Table 7-5.

The findings presented here suggest that the risk associated with parental depressions may not be specific. Children with a depressed parent appear to be at risk for a variety of problems, not just depression. Also, children of parents with other diagnoses or with chronic medical conditions may also be at risk for depression. It may be that various disorders that youngsters experience share common risk factors, whereas some risk factors are specific to depression. It is also possible that there are disruptions to effective parenting that are common to parents with various disorders and also that there are disruptions to parenting that are more likely to occur among parents with a particular disorder.

There may be a variety of mechanisms whereby depressive mood states in parents might be associated with dysfunction in their children. Much of the research on the link between parental depression and child adjustment has focused on depression in mothers, and relatively little is known regarding the role of depressed fathers (Cummings & Davies, 1994; Kaslow, Deering, & Racusin, 1994). As suggested before, shared heredity may play a role in the link between parental and child depression. However, parental depression may have an impact through a variety of nonbiological pathways. For example, parents can influence their child through parent-child interactions, through coaching and teaching practices, and by arranging their child's social environment.

As indicated before, both depression in adults and depression in young people have been associated with certain characteristic ways of thinking and cognitive styles (Alloy, Lipman, & Abramson, 1992; Beck, 1976; Hammen, 1990). It is possible that depressed parents transmit these styles to their children. These maladaptive ways of thinking may also impact the general manner in which the depressed adults manage and parent their offspring (Nolen-Hoeksema et al., 1995).

Parental depression may result in disruption of effective parenting. For example, the depressed parents' absorption in their own difficulties may make them less attentive and aware of their children's behavior. Monitoring of a child's behavior is a key element in effective parenting. Depressed parents may also perceive behaviors to be problematic that other parents do not. This difference in perception is important, since being able to ignore or tolerate low levels of problematic behavior is likely to lead to less family disruption. In addition, studies involving direct observation of families with a depressed parent or child indicate that interactional patterns in these families may serve to maintain the depression in the parent or child (Dadds et al., 1992; Ge et al., 1995; Hops et al., 1987). Depressed behavior by one family member may be maintained because it serves to avoid aggressive and conflictual behavior with and among other family members. Indeed, an association between marital conflict and parental depression is frequently reported, and these two variables are in turn related to problematic outcomes in children and adolescents (Cummings & Davies, 1994; Downey & Coyne, 1990).

In addition to marital discord, families with a depressed parent may experience high levels of stressful life events (e.g., health and financial difficulties). These stressful life events in turn are likely to exacerbate a parent's depressive episodes and contribute to disruptions in parenting. For example, high levels of stress may restrict the parent's ability to involve the child in activities outside the home and may limit the family's social networks. Thus the child may have limited opportunity to interact with other adults outside the family or to have access to other sources of social support.

Finally, the link between parent and child depression has been viewed in the context of attachment (Cicchetti & Toth, 1998; Teti et al., 1995). The parental emotional unavailability and insensitivity that may be associated with depression have been shown to be strong and reliable predictors of insecure parent-child attachments. Attachment theory holds that children's internal working models or representations of the self and the social world are importantly influenced by early attachments. It is in these early relationships that the child first experiences and learns to regulate intense emotions and arousal, experiences the social world, and develops a concept of the self. In other words, working models that guide future experiences are thought to be first developed in these early attachment relationships. In children with insecure parent-child attachments, the cognitive and emotional contents of these working models have been described as remarkably similar to the cognitive and emotional patterns characteristic of depression (Cummings & Davies, 1994). Insecure attachments, for example, may interfere with the child's developing capacity to regulate affect and arousal and may be associated with poorer self-concept and less trust in the availability and responsiveness of the social world.

It is clear that from very early on, infants are affected by their mother's or caregiver's behavior. Infants of depressed mothers may develop a depressed mood style that generalizes to their reactions to others and that may persist (Field, 1992). A study by Murray (1992) illustrates the relationship between maternal depression and attachment. A large sample of women were screened for depression after childbirth. Women with no previous history of depression and no depression since delivery (control group) were compared with women with no previous history of depression but who were depressed following delivery; with women with a previous history of depression but with no depression since delivery; and with women with a previous history of depression who were also depressed following delivery. These women were followed for eighteen months. At this time, mother-child attachment was assessed, and the infants were assessed on a number of other measures. Infants of postnatally depressed mothers were more likely to be insecurely attached than those of control mothers. These results are illustrated in Figure 7-3. Infants of mothers who had a previous history of depression but were not postnatally depressed were not significantly more

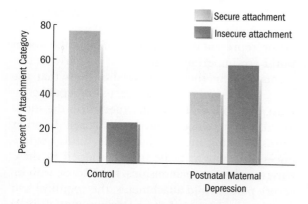

FIGURE 7-3 Securely and insecurely attached infants as a function of postnatal maternal depression.
Adapted from Murray, 1992.

likely to be insecurely attached than infants of control mothers; however, there was a trend in this direction. The relationship of maternal depression to other variables was also illustrated. For example, the adverse effect of lower social class on infant cognitive development was found primarily when mothers had experienced their first onset of depression following childbirth.

Although it seems clear that children of depressed parents are at increased risk for a number of difficulties, it needs to be made clear that not all children of depressed parents experience these adverse outcomes. Many children with a depressed parent form secure parent-child attachments with that parent, experience good parenting, and do not develop disorders (Beardslee et al., 1998; Kaslow, Deering, & Racusin, 1994). Furthermore, there are likely to be age and gender differences regarding the effects of parental depression (e.g., Hops, 1995; Tarullo et al., 1995).

SUICIDE

Suicide is often mentioned in discussions of depression. The rate of completed suicide is relatively low among youngsters as compared with adults. The prevalence of completed suicides is increasing, however (see "Suicide Among Children..."). Moreover, suicidal behavior includes not only com-

pleted suicide but also suicide attempts and suicidal ideation. When this entire range of suicidal behavior is considered, it is suggested that this class of psychopathology is prevalent, particularly among adolescents and, to a lesser extent, among children. Based on a prospective longitudinal study of approximately 1,500 adolescents between fourteen and eighteen years of age by Lewinsohn and his colleagues (1996), the prevalence of adolescent suicidal behavior can be described. A total of 19.4 percent of these adolescents had a history of suicidal ideation. Suicidal ideation was more prevalent in young women (23.7 percent) than in young men (14.8 percent). More frequent suicidal ideation was predictive of future suicide attempts. However, even mild and relatively infrequent suicidal thoughts increased the risk for a suicide attempt.

Suicide attempts had occurred in 7.1 percent of this community sample. Girls (10.1 percent) were more likely than boys (3.8 percent) to attempt suicide. Suicide attempts before puberty were uncommon. The majority of attempts made by girls consisted of either ingestion of harmful substances (55 percent) or cutting themselves (31 percent). Boys employed a wider variety of methods—ingestion (20 percent), cutting (25 percent), gun use (15 percent), hanging (11 percent), and other methods, such as shooting air into one's veins and running into traffic (22 percent). Some adolescents attempted suicide more than once. The first three months after an attempt were a period of particularly high risk for a repeated attempt. Reattempts were made by approximately 27 percent of the boys and 21 percent of the girls. The likelihood of a suicidal attempt remained above the rates expected in the general population for at least two years. At twenty-four months, 39 percent of the boys and 33 percent of the girls had reattempted.

Suicide is often thought of as a symptom of disorders such as depression. Indeed, depression is related to suicide among children and adolescents (Flisher, 1999; Lewinsohn et al., 1996), and constructs such as hopelessness that are associated with depression have been found to be predictive of suicidal behavior (Levy, Jurkovic, & Spiro, 1995). For example, in a longitudinal study, Ko-

SUICIDE AMONG CHILDREN AND ADOLESCENTS: REASON FOR CONCERN

There is increasing public concern about suicide in young people. This is, of course, in part due to sadness at the death of any young person and the sense of lost potential. However, there is another basis for the concern. Several reports cite statistics that are quite dramatic regarding the rates of suicide among young people (Centers for Disease Control and Prevention,1995; National Center for Health Statistics, 1998).

In the period from 1994 to 1996, the number of deaths due to suicide in the United States among persons of all ages was approximately 11 persons per 100,000. This rate was slightly less than the 1980 rate of 11.4 per 100,000. Children's suicide during the 1994–1996 period remained a rare event, with 0.8 youngsters per 100,000 between the ages of 5 and 14 dying as a result of suicide. However, in 1980 the rate was 0.4 per 100,000—an increase of 100 percent. Comparable rates for fifteen to twenty-four-year-olds were 12.3 and 13.0 per 100,000—an increase of about 6 percent. As can be seen in the accompanying table, risk is greatest for white males. However, from 1980 to 1992, suicide rates for black males between ten and fourteen years old rose from 0.5 to 2.0 per 100,000, an increase of 300 percent!

An increased use of guns appears to be one of the factors contributing to this grim situation. Among people under twenty-five, 64.9 percent of the suicides in 1992 were firearm-related. And among fifteen- to nineteen-year-olds, firearm-related suicides accounted for 81 percent of the increase between 1980 and 1992 in the overall rate of suicide. Since suicide *attempts* among younger persons have not increased, the rise in completed suicides may be due, in part, to the use of more lethal means.

The Centers for Disease Control and Prevention (1995) has identified the following strategies to improve the prevention of suicide among young persons: (1) training school personnel and community leaders to identify youngsters at highest risk; (2) educating youngsters about suicide; (3) implementing screening and referral services; (4) developing peer-support programs; (5) establishing suicide crisis centers and hotlines; (6) restricting access to highly lethal methods; (7) and intervening after a suicide to prevent other youngsters from attempting suicide.

Rate[a] of Suicide Among Youngsters by Age Group: 1980 to 1992

Race/Age Group	Male			Female		
	1980	1992	Percent Change	1980	1992	Percent Change
White						
10–14	1.4	2.6	+86	0.3	1.1	+233
15–19	15.1	18.4	+22	3.3	3.7	+12
Black						
10–14	0.5	2.0	+300	0.2	0.4	+100
15–19	5.6	14.8	+164	1.6	1.9	+19
Other[b]						
10–14	0.0	1.1	Undefined	0.0	0.2	Undefined
15–19	18.6	17.5	−6	3.0	5.0	+67

[a]Per 100,000 persons.
[b]Data for other racial groups were limited and therefore combined.

vacs, Goldston, and Gatsonis (1993) found that a significantly greater proportion of youngsters with depressive disorders attempted suicide than did youngsters with other disorders. However, suicidal behavior may be associated with a variety of disorders, and the presence of two or more disorders appreciably increases the risk of suicidal attempts (Fergusson & Lynskey, 1995; Lewinsohn, Rhode, & Seeley, 1995). Conduct disorder and substance abuse diagnoses are common among completed suicides. Indeed, some research suggests considerable diagnostic heterogeneity among young suicide completers, and depression may not always be the most common diagnosis. Shaffer et al. (1988), for example, reported the following prevalence rates among male adolescent suicide completers: major depression (21 percent), substance abuse (37 percent), antisocial behavior (67 percent). The rates for female adolescent suicide completers were major depression (50 percent), substance abuse (5 percent), and antisocial behavior (30 percent). Therefore, although depression is an important risk factor, the presence of a depressive disorder is neither necessary nor sufficient for the occurrence of suicidal behavior. It is probably important to be aware that some workers indicate that the presence of problems (e.g., problem behavior such as aggression and impulsivity in combination with and independent of depression) at levels below criteria for any diagnosis of disorder also increase the risk of suicidal behavior (King et al., 1992).

There are multiple factors that likely contribute to an increased risk for suicide (Birmaher et al., 1996a; Wagner, 1997). At the level of the individual, risk factors include physical illness and psychological disorders that include attributes such as depression, hopelessness, impulsivity, and aggression. Family factors (such as abuse and poor communication) and family disruption are also frequently cited as risk factors. Although these are possible contributing factors, improved research is needed before conclusions regarding particular family risk factors can be made (Wagner, 1997). Other factors such as high levels of stress in school and social relations, and sociocultural influences, including the ready availability of firearms, are also thought to contribute to increased risk. Young people are often thought to be particularly vulnerable, since their problem solving and self-regulatory skills and their abilities to cope with stressful circumstances may be limited. Some youngsters may be faced with circumstances that cause considerable stress that they may view as beyond their control. These youngsters may also have limited understanding that undesirable situations can and often do change.

As illustrated in Figure 7-4, the variables that on the basis of research are thought to be significant contributors to suicidal risk cluster into four constructs: psychopathology, physical illness, environment (e.g., parental divorce/separation, death of a parent or relative, poor family support, daily hassles), and interpersonal problems. These four constructs were thought to have both a direct effect on suicidal behavior and an indirect effect, which is mediated through the adolescents' cognitive/coping styles. The arrows in Figure 7-4 indicate the effects on suicidal behavior that were found to be significant. Psychopathology, physical health, and environment had direct effects on suicidal behavior. Interpersonal problems did not have a direct effect on suicidal behavior. In addition, all four constructs had indirect effects on suicidal behavior that were mediated by the adolescents' cognitive/coping styles, which in turn had impact on the suicidal behavior.

Most analyses of suicidal risk in young people have looked at particular variables in isolation. On the basis of research findings with adolescents, Lewinsohn and his colleagues have attempted to develop a more comprehensive model of suicidal risk, illustrated in Figure 7-4, that combines these relevant variables (Lewinsohn et al., 1996). In this model, suicidal behavior is conceptualized as existing along a continuum. We can get an idea of the prevalence of various degrees of suicidal behavior by looking at the percentage of youngsters along this dimension:

No suicidal thoughts/behaviors (77.9 percent)

Thoughts of death (2.5 percent)

Wishing to be dead (3.3 percent)

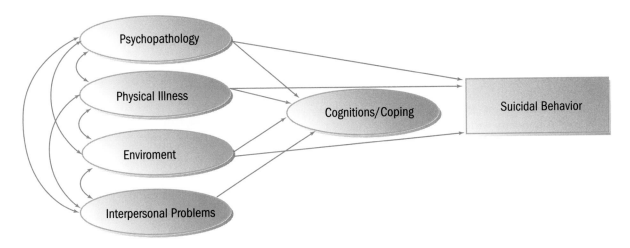

FIGURE 7-4 A model of the relation of risk factors to suicidal behavior. Curved arrows to left of diagram indicate that these risk constructs are related to each other.
Adapted from Lewinsohn, Rhode, & Seeley, 1996.

Suicidal ideation (5.7 percent)

Suicide plan (3.5 percent)

Less serious suicide attempt (1.8 percent)

Multiple suicide attempts (2.8 percent)

ASSESSMENT OF DEPRESSION

The assessment of depression is likely to involve a number of strategies and to sample a broad spectrum of attributes. As we have seen, depression may manifest itself in a number of ways throughout development. In addition, youngsters who experience depression are also likely to experience a number of other difficulties. Moreover, since a variety of influences may contribute to the development of depression, assessing the parents, family, and social environments of the youngster, as well as individual characteristics of the youngster is likely to prove informative.

A general clinical interview and the use of a general dimensional instrument like the Child Behavior Checklist are common. Interviews intended to yield a DSM diagnosis and a variety of measures that focus more specifically on depression and related constructs have been developed (Compas, 1997; Hodges, 1994; Reynolds, 1994). These inter-

views and assessment devices have greatly facilitated research on depression in children and adolescents.

Of the measures of depression that have been developed, self-report instruments are among the most commonly employed. They are particularly important, given that many of the key problems that characterize depression, such as sadness and feelings of worthlessness, are subjective. The Children's Depression Inventory (CDI) (Kovacs, 1992) is probably the most commonly used measure of this type. It is an offspring of the Beck Depression Inventory, a commonly used inventory for adults. The CDI asks youngsters to choose which of three alternatives best characterizes them during the past two weeks. Twenty-seven items sample affective, behavioral, and cognitive aspects of depression. Research on gender and age differences, reliability, validity, and clinically meaningful cutoff scores has been conducted for the CDI (Reynolds, 1994). Other self-report measures include two developed by Reynolds that have been reported to have good psychometric properties (Reynolds, 1994): Reynolds Child Depression Scale for use with children eight to thirteen (Reynolds, 1989) and Reynolds Adolescent Depression Scale for use with youngsters twelve to eighteen (Reynolds, 1987).

Many self-report measures are also rephrased so that they can be completed by significant others such as the child's parents (Clarizio, 1994). Measures completed by both the child and the parent often show only low levels of correlation, and agreement may vary with the age of the youngster (Kazdin, 1994; Renouf & Kovacs, 1994). These results suggest that information provided by different sources may tap different aspects of the child's behavior. For example, the children's self-reports of depression, but not their parents' reports, correlate with hopelessness and suicidal thoughts (Kazdin, Rodgers, & Colbus, 1986). Parents' reports of depression in their child, on the other hand, correlate with the child's mood-related expression and social behavior (Kazdin et al., 1985).

Instruments may also be completed by other adults such as teachers and clinicians (Clarizio, 1994). Ratings by peers can likewise provide a unique perspective. The Peer Nomination Inventory of Depression (Lefkowitz & Tesiny, 1980) asks children to nominate peers who fit certain descriptions. Table 7-6 presents questions regarding depression, happiness, and popularity to which the peers are asked to respond. A child's score is the sum of the nominations received for all the depression items.

Measures of constructs that are related to depression have also been developed, and there are many characteristics that might be assessed. For example, measures of attributes such as self-esteem (e.g., Harter, 1985) and perceived control over events (e.g., Connell, 1985) are likely candidates for assessment. In addition, assessing various cognitive processes such as hopelessness (Kazdin et al., 1986), attributional style (Seligman & Peterson, 1986), and cognitive distortions (e.g., Leitenberg, Yost, & Carroll-Wilson, 1986) have been and are likely to be helpful for both clinical and research purposes.

TREATMENT OF DEPRESSION

Less is known regarding the treatment of depression in youth compared with knowledge regarding interventions for adults. That little systematic re-

---

TABLE 7-6

Peer Nomination Inventory for Depression Items

Who often plays alone? (D)

Who thinks they are bad? (D)

Who doesn't try again when they lose? (D)

Who often sleeps in class? (D)

Who often looks lonely? (D)

Who often says they don't feel well? (D)

Who says they can't do things? (D)

Who often cries? (D)

Who often looks happy? (H)

Who likes to do a lot of things? (H)

Who worries a lot? (D)

Who doesn't play? (D)

Who often smiles? (H)

Who doesn't take part in things? (D)

Who doesn't have much fun? (D)

Who is often cheerful? (H)

Who thinks others don't like them? (D)

Who often looks sad? (D)

Who would you like to sit next to in class? (P)

Who are the children you would like to have for your best friends? (P)

Note: D = items that are included in depressed score
       H = items in happiness score
       P = items in popularity score

Adapted from Lefkowitz & Tesiny.

---

search exists is not surprising given the recency of attention to the problem of child and adolescent depression. Treatments that have been attempted with depressed youngsters have largely been adaptations of interventions that seem to be successful in treating depression in adults. Pharmacotherapy and cognitive-behavioral treatments will be examined briefly.

Pharmacological treatments. The practice of prescribing antidepressant medication for children and adolescents is still controversial, since the effectiveness and safety of pharmacotherapy with depressed youngsters remains unclear (American Academy of Child and Adolescent Psychiatry,

1998; Birmaher et al., 1996b). Tricyclic antidepressants such as imipramine, amitriptyline, nortriptyline, and desipramine have been the most widely studied medications. Selective serotonin reuptake inhibitors (SSRIs) such as fluoxetine (Prozac) and other compounds such as bupropion have also been employed with depressed children and adolescents. The use of such medications is for the most part based on clinical trials or on a small number of controlled studies. This research does not clearly support the superiority of these drugs over placebo in either prepubertal children or adolescents. At present it is difficult to know whether these medications, many of which are reported effective in treating adult depression, are ineffective for youth or whether adequately designed research is lacking. These medications are widely employed, however, and these or other pharmacological agents may ultimately prove to be effective, alone or in combination with other treatments. However, since antidepressant medications are principally developed and marketed for adults, there are less well established guidelines for their administration and little systematic data on their safety. Issues of safety and side effects are of particular concern, since there are appreciable biological differences between children and adults and since little is known regarding the long-term impact of these medications on development, particularly in young children.

Cognitive-behavioral treatments. Most psychological interventions for depression in children and adolescents derive from a cognitive behavioral perspective. Cognitive aspects of these treatments confront, educate, and modify the youngster's maladaptive cognitions (e.g., problematic attributions, excessively high standards, negative self-monitoring). Behavioral aspects of treatments focus on goals such as increasing pleasurable experiences; increasing social skills; and improving communication, conflict resolution, and social problem-solving skills.

Although, in general, findings are positive, there is little established information about the psychological treatment of depression in children and adolescents, particularly in cases involving clinical levels of depression (Kaslow & Thompson, 1998; Kazdin & Marciano, 1998; Kendall & Panichelli-Mindel, 1995). Much of the literature involves clinical reports. In addition, interventions suggested for youngsters have been based on downward extensions of interventions employed with adults. Although this was a reasonable way to begin to explore effective treatment, there are limitations to such an approach that need to be addressed (Hammen et al., 1999; Stark, Rouse, & Kurowski, 1994). For example, the lives of depressed youngsters differ from those of adults. Children and adolescents will likely have ongoing daily contact with parental influences that may contribute to the problem of depression. Also, youngsters are exposed on a daily basis to the potential negative consequences of social skill difficulties and the impact of peer relation difficulties. Adults, on the other hand, may arrange their lives to avoid familial and social contacts. As we develop a better understanding of the social-psychological factors that contribute to depression in children and adolescents, treatments that differ from those employed with adults and that address relevant developmental experiences of depressed children and adolescents are likely to be the most effective.

Even though they are the most commonly researched psychological interventions, there are few controlled outcome studies of cognitive-behavioral treatments. Several of these studies are described here to illustrate interventions deriving from a cognitive-behavioral perspective.

Butler and her colleagues evaluated the relative effectiveness of role play, cognitive restructuring, an attention-placebo condition, or no treatment (Butler et al., 1980). Fifth- and sixth-grade children were identified as depressed through self-report measures and teacher referral. Role play consisted of teaching interpersonal skills as well as problem-solving techniques. Cognitive restructuring focused on altering maladaptive cognitions. The results favored the role-play intervention; however, the differences between groups were not clear-cut.

Stark, Reynolds, and Kaslow (1987) compared self-control, behavioral problem solving, and a waiting list (no treatment) control in treating nine- to twelve-year-olds defined as moderately to severely depressed using the Children's Depression Inventory. The self-control treatment focused on teaching children self-management skills such as self-monitoring, self-evaluation, and self-reinforcement. Behavioral problem solving emphasized education, self-monitoring of pleasant events, and group problem solving directed toward improving social behavior. Both treatments resulted in improvements and were superior to the control group. The two treatments, however, did not differ from each other.

Weisz and his colleagues (1997) compared a cognitive-behavioral intervention based on the relationship between perceived control and depression to a no treatment control condition. The children, in grades three to six, exhibited mild to moderate depressive symptoms. They were treated in small groups during school hours. The eight-session program emphasized control skills that helped identify and develop activities that the child found mood enhancing and that the child valued; that identified and modified depressogenic thoughts; that fostered cognitive techniques for mood enhancement; and that aided relaxation and positive imagery. At the end of treatment and at a 9-month follow-up, the treatment group showed significantly greater decreases in depressive symptoms than did the control group, as indicated by scores on the Children's Depression Inventory (CDI) and the Revised Children's Depression Rating Scale (CDRS-R). These results are illustrated in Figure 7-5.

A study by Lewinsohn and his colleagues (1990; 1998) suggests the effectiveness of a cognitive-behavioral treatment for depressed adolescents. Youngsters aged fourteen to eighteen who met diagnostic criteria for depression were randomly assigned to one of three conditions: adolescent-and-parent, adolescent-only, and wait-list control. Treatment was a cognitive-behavioral group intervention known as the Coping with Depression Course for Adolescents (a skills-training, multicomponent intervention meant to address areas thought to be problematic for depressed adolescents). Adolescents attended sixteen two-hour sessions, twice a week, that focused on teaching

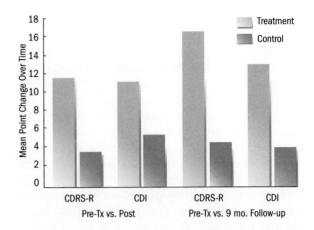

FIGURE 7-5 Change in Revised Children's Depression Rating Scale (CDRS-R) and Children's Depression Inventory (CDI) scores from pretreatment to posttreatment and from pretreatment to nine-month follow-up.

From Weisz, Thurber, Sweeney, Proffitt, & LaGagnoux, 1997.

methods of relaxation, increasing pleasant events, controlling irrational and negative thoughts, increasing social skills, and teaching conflict resolution (communication and problem-solving) skills. In the parent involvement condition, parents met for nine weekly sessions. They were provided with information on the skills being taught to their teenagers and were taught problem-solving and conflict resolution skills.

As compared with the wait-list control, treatment groups improved on depression measures. For example, at the end of treatment, only 52.4 percent of the adolescent-and-parent youngsters and 57.1 percent of the adolescent-only youngsters, as compared with 94.7 percent of control youngsters, still met diagnostic criteria. The teenagers in the treatment conditions were followed for two years after the end of treatment, and their treatment gains were maintained. Control participants were not available for follow-up, since they were offered treatment at the end of the treatment period. Figure 7-6 illustrates the findings of this study at pretreatment, at posttreat-

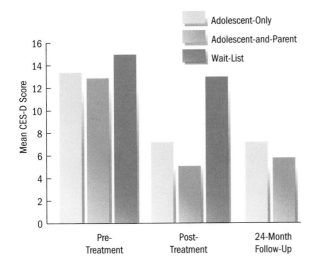

FIGURE 7-6 Response to cognitive-behavioral group treatment by depressed adolescents.

Adapted from Lewisohn, Clarke, Hops, & Andrews, 1990.

ment, and at the twenty-four-month follow-up for one of the measures employed (the adolescents' report on the Center for Epidemiological Studies Depression Scale—CES-D).

Treatments that are derived from a cognitive-behavioral perspective and treatments that address interpersonal and family aspects of depression in children and adolescents are promising. However, it is clear that additional large-scale controlled treatment studies are needed (Kazdin & Marciano, 1998). Successful treatment strategies will need to include components capable of addressing multiple aspects of depression and of the social and family environments of depressed youngsters.

Prevention. Finally, several aspects of depression in children and adolescents suggest the potential value of preventive interventions (Birmaher et al., 1996b; Kazdin & Marciano, 1998). At-risk youngsters might be identified by factors such as familial risk (e.g., depressed parents), peak periods of incidence (adolescence), and early episodes of subclinical levels of depression. Also, because depression is often characterized by recurrence of

episodes, early intervention in childhood may affect the long-term course of the disorder. Although few studies of prevention of depression in youngsters have been reported, there is some suggestion that this approach holds some promise. Clarke et al. (1995) screened 1,652 adolescents and identified youngsters who experienced depressive symptoms but who did not meet the criteria for a diagnosis of depression. These adolescents were randomly assigned either to a "usual care" control condition or to a fifteen-session cognitive-behavioral intervention. Both groups were also allowed to pursue whatever outside sources of care they desired. There was a significant difference in the incidence of Major Depression or Dysthymia at twelve-month follow-up—14.5 percent in the treated group versus 25.7 percent in the control group. Jaycox et al. (1994) identified youngsters between ten and thirteen years of age who had elevated scores on the Children's Depression Inventory and reported that high levels of parental conflict existed in their families. The children were assigned either to a group receiving treatment that involved cognitive interventions and social problem-solving training or to a no-treatment control condition. Children receiving treatment experienced significantly greater relief and prevention of depressive symptoms at the end of treatment and at six-month and two-year follow-ups. Indeed, differences between the two conditions increased over time (Gillham et al., 1995).

PROBLEMS IN PEER RELATIONSHIPS

There are several reasons why peer relations have become the focus of increasing attention (Putallaz & Dunn, 1990). Seminal papers, such as those by Hartup (1970; 1989), emphasized the unique developmental context provided by a youngster's peer group. These efforts and others also highlighted the influence of peers on immediate and long-term social and cognitive growth (Dunn, 1996; Parker et al., 1995). At the same time, there was a decline in the prevalence of Freudian theory, which had heavily emphasized parent-child relationships. This change allowed for the recogni-

tion of the importance of other socialization influences. Finally, a variety of social and economic
conditions increased the opportunities for youngsters to interact with their peers. For example, the
increase in the number of working parents has resulted in a rise in the number of children in day
care and in the amount of time youngsters spend
with peers. Such changes have provided both an
impetus and an opportunity to study children's social relations.

PEER RELATIONS AND DEVELOPMENT

The literature on development indicates the importance of peer relationships. Such relationships
provide the opportunity for learning specific skills
that may not be available in other social relationships. Hartup (1989) suggests that two major kinds
of relationships seem necessary to the child's development. Vertical relationships to individuals
who have greater knowledge and social power,
usually adults, provide the child with protection
and security, and they are the contexts within
which basic social skills emerge. In addition, children must experience horizontal relationships,
which are relationships with individuals, such as
peers and siblings, who have the same amount of
social power as the children themselves. Some of
the ways in which peer interactions may play a
unique and essential role include the development of sociability and intimacy, elaboration of cooperation and reciprocity, negotiation of conflict
and competition, control of aggression, socialization of sexuality and gender roles, moral development, and development of empathy. Of course,
this does not mean that peer social development is
independent of child-adult interactions. Indeed,
early parent-child socialization seems related to
later peer interactions (e.g., Park & Waters, 1989;
Parke & Ladd, 1992; Rubin, 1994; Youngblade &
Belsky, 1992), and relationships with both peers
and adults are necessary for optimum growth
(Hartup, 1989).

STUDYING PEER RELATIONSHIPS

The study of peer relationships and the notion of
social competence that underlies it are complex
processes. As attention to social relations with

Peer interactions provide a unique and essential opportunity to
develop certain skills.
(Courtesy of A.C. Israel)

peers has increased, there has been developing appreciation of the multifaceted nature of such relationships. Early efforts, as well as much of the research literature that we have available to us,
focused on the child's overall status in the peer
group (group acceptance/popularity). More recently it has been suggested that additional attention be paid to the role of friendships and the
characteristics and attitudes of a youngster's
friends (Hartup, 1996). For example, although
popularity and having a close friend may be related, the concept of friendship is different from
that of peer status or popularity (Newcomb & Bagwell, 1995). If youngsters have a close friend, the
resulting friendship can affect how they feel regardless of their peer status. Also, having a close
friend may buffer some of the effects of being rejected or neglected by peers or, conversely, may increase the likelihood of problematic outcomes
(Bierman & Welsh, 1997; La Greca, 1993). As development proceeds, close friendships may take
on increasing importance, and the nature of these
relationships and the characteristics of the peers
in a youngster's social network are likely to be of
greater influence.

The study of peer relationships, however, has focused primarily on group acceptance and relied heavily on the use of two forms of sociometric measures. For example, the nomination format requires children to name classmates liked most or liked least. The rating format requires that children rate each of their classmates along some dimension(s), such as how much they like to play with each child.

Early research made use of sociometric measures to evaluate a youngster's peer status as popular or unpopular. More recently, a number of different peer status groups (popular, rejected, neglected, controversial, and average) have been articulated within a two-dimensional approach to classifying peer status. The dimension of social preference reflects the extent to which children are liked or disliked by their peers. Social impact, on the other hand, refers to the degree to which children are noticed by their peers or to their social salience. Table 7-7 illustrates how the preference and impact dimensions are defined and employed to derive peer classifications. Such assignments are often employed in research on the relationship between adjustment and peer relations.

What we know is limited in a number of ways. Much of the literature addresses the issues of peer rejection and of aggressive behavior. However, peer rejection is associated not just with aggression; it can also be associated with social withdrawal. One must be aware, too, of developmental changes. For example, social withdrawal becomes more clearly related to rejection and also associated with internalizing problems as children get older (Dunn & McGuire, 1992; Rubin et al., 1995). Most research on peer relations has focused on the childhood period. There needs to be greater attention given to developmental status and to the period of adolescence in particular. Furthermore, gender differences also deserve greater attention (Bierman & Welsh, 1997; Inderbitzen, 1994).

PEER RELATIONS AND ADJUSTMENT

A dramatic example of the potential contribution of peer relations to a youngster's adjustment is provided in a case described by Hartup (1996):

Delano, a 14-year-old boy, and his best friend ambushed and killed his mother on her way home. In a newspaper account, the mother was said to have had "difficulties" with her son and the family's home contained guns. Delano was described as having attention deficit disorder and learning disabilities. He had a long history of difficulties and recently had gotten into trouble with a step brother for wrecking a car and bringing a gun into a movie theater.

Delano was also described as "a lonely and unliked kid who was the frequent victim of schoolmates' taunts, jeers, and assaults. . . . He was often teased on the bus and at school because of his appearance and abilities. . . . He got teased bad. Every day he got teased. He'd get pushed around. But he couldn't really help himself. He was kind of skinny. . . . He didn't really have that many friends."

There were actually two good friends. The first was relatively well adjusted, but Delano took a gun safety

TABLE 7-7	
Peer Classifications	
Social Preference (SP)	The difference between number of liked most (LM) and liked least (LL) nominations
Social Impact (SI)	The sum of number of liked most (LM) and liked least (LL) nominations
Popular	High SP score with higher than average LM and lower than average LL
Rejected	Low SP score with lower than average LM and higher than average LL
Neglected	Low SI score with no LM votes from peers
Controversial	High SI score with both LL and LM scores higher than average
Sociometrically Average	All other children

Adapted from Kupersmidt and Patterson, 1991.

course for hunting with this friend. Delano and the second youngster described themselves as the "best of friends" and spent a great deal of time together. This friend was not as well adjusted and it was this friend with whom the murder was committed. The boys admitted to planning the ambush and it seems relatively certain that the murder would not have likely occurred if these two friends had not encouraged each other to do it. (1996, p. 1)

Peer relations and later adjustment. One of the most commonly cited reasons for interest in children's peer relationships is their association with later adjustment. Early reports cited an association between poor peer relations and high rates of juvenile delinquency (Roff, Sells, & Golden, 1972), dropping out of school (Ullmann, 1957), and bad conduct discharges from the army (Roff, 1961). Cowen and his colleagues found an association with later psychiatric referrals (Cowen et al., 1973). In a series of studies, they screened large numbers of children for signs of disturbance. Low peer status in the third grade was a better predictor of later psychiatric problems than traditional adjustment indices including IQ, academic achievement, and ratings by teachers and other school personnel.

The association of peer status and later adjustment is clearest for children with low peer acceptance and for those who exhibit aggression towards peers. The link between early shyness/withdrawal and later maladjustment is not as clear, since this relationship has been less studied (Parker & Asher, 1987). However, data do suggest that some rejected children are not aggressive but rather are socially withdrawn (French, 1988; 1990). This group of rejected children and other withdrawn and socially isolated children may also be at risk for later adjustment difficulties (Biederman et al., 1993; Asendorpf, 1993; Newcomb et al., 1993; Rubin, Stewart, & Coplan, 1995).

An examination of archival data from the original Berkley Guidance Study (MacFarlane, Allen, & Honzik, 1954) illustrates the developmental stability of a shy-withdrawn style and its long-term impact (Caspi, Elder, & Bem, 1988). Ratings of shyness and excessive reserve when the children were

eight to ten years old were significantly correlated with teacher ratings of withdrawal and related behaviors when the youngsters were preadolescents. Also, significant positive correlations were obtained between childhood shyness and shyness evaluated when the participants were about forty. Furthermore, shy boys were more likely to delay entry into marriage, parenthood, and stable careers, and they also exhibited less occupational achievement and stability. In contrast, shy girls from this cohort, born in the late 1920s, were more likely than their peers to follow what the authors term a conventional pattern of marriage, childbearing, and homemaking. These results do not relate early shyness to "pathological" outcomes. However, they do show a pattern of stability regarding how the individual approaches key life transitions that require social initiation and interaction. The participants did not exhibit an extreme of shyness and were drawn from a relatively homogeneous sample. In a differently defined sample, more adverse consequences might have occurred.

Peer relations and childhood problems. Problems with peers are frequently reported for both children and adolescents in the general population. Even though such problems are quite common, reports of difficulties with peers discriminate youngsters referred for psychological services from nonreferred youngsters (Achenbach, 1991b). Indeed, problems with peers are one of the most frequently mentioned problems in referrals to mental health centers. Problems in social relationships are also part of the diagnostic criteria for a wide variety of disorders (e.g., autistic disorder, attention-deficit hyperactivity disorder, conduct disorder, social phobia). In addition, social relationship problems are associated with both externalizing and internalizing disorders in children (Parker et al., 1995). Successful peer relations, on the other hand, may help ensure the development of social competence in the face of multiple adverse factors. They may thereby serve a preventive function and reduce the likelihood of disorder (Cicchetti, Toth, & Bush, 1988).

A study by Kupersmidt and Patterson (1991) illustrates the relationship between peer status and adjustment. The sociometric status of a sample of second, third, and fourth graders was assessed through nominations for being liked most and liked least. Social preference, social impact, and peer status group were determined for each child following the guidelines described in Table 7-7. Children were designated as popular, rejected, neglected, controversial, or sociometrically average. Two years later when the children were in the fourth through the sixth grade, a number of assessment instruments were completed, including a modified version of the Achenbach Youth Self-Report (YSR). As an index of a negative outcome, the authors examined whether a child had scores in the clinical range in one or more specific problem areas (the narrowband syndromes of the YSR). Figure 7-7 illustrates the relationship between sociometric status and this index of adjustment difficulties. Rejected boys and girls exhibited higher than expected rates of clinical-range difficulties. In addition, girls with neglected peer status had even higher levels of clinical-range difficulties.

In addition to this nonspecific indicator of adjustment, the authors examined the relationship between peer status and each of the more specific problem areas defined by the various narrowband behavior problem scores. There was no relationship between peer status and any specific behavior problem for boys. However, a finding of particular interest to us in this chapter emerged for girls. For girls, the base rate for depression scores in the clinical range was 6.1 percent. Sociometrically average, popular, and controversial girls were below this base rate. Rejected girls (11.9 percent), however, were more than twice as likely to report high levels of depression than these other three groups. Furthermore, neglected girls (27.3 percent) were more than twice as likely as rejected girls and more than five times as likely as the other groups of girls to report depression problems.

There has also been increasing evidence that a shy/withdrawn style may be more stable than was once thought (Kagan, Reznick, & Snidman, 1990; Kerr et al., 1994). The complexity of this style is indicated by the variety of terms (e.g., shyness, social withdrawal, social isolation, social avoidance, so-

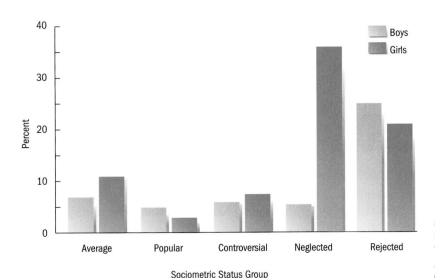

FIGURE 7-7 Percentage of boys and girls in clinical range for one or more specific behavior problems as a function of sociometric status.

Adapted from Kupersmidt, & Patterson, 1991.

cial inhibition) that have been used to refer to an unusual lack of social interaction with peers. What is known suggests the value of distinctions within this general category (Asendorpf, 1993; Coplan et al., 1994). We turn now to a brief description of an interesting body of research that has addressed the stability of one possible form of a socially withdrawn style.

Behavioral inhibition to the unfamiliar. Jerome Kagan and his colleagues (Kagan, 1997) have identified a temperamental quality that they describe as "behavioral inhibition to the unfamiliar." This style is characterized in general as withdrawn with a tendency not to approach unfamiliar objects or situations. This disposition, present at a very young age, is viewed as a persistent attribute in some portion of children. However, the quality may be displayed in different forms at different ages. In young children, one to two years of age, "these dispositions appear most often to unfamiliar persons, contexts, and objects, and the withdrawal is often accompanied by crying and/or seeking a target of attachment." By the time the child is three, the "feature of withdrawal is considerably more subtle. When an unfamiliar person enters a room, the temperamentally inhibited child, who would have retreated to the mother at one year of age, will cease playing and talking and show a prolonged latency to approach the adult. A year later, when in an unfamiliar room with an unfamiliar child, the inhibited child will fail to initiate play for the first ten to twenty minutes, remaining quiet and close to the mother." Children who remain behaviorally inhibited until age seven "will be quiet with an unfamiliar adult, will play apart from peers in a group context like school, will display a serious facial expression, and will become stressed by mild challenge or occasional failure" (Kagan et al., 1990, p. 220).

Kagan's findings are based on longitudinal research of children who are identified as extreme with respect to the probability of their withdrawal or approach to unfamiliar people or events. The children are assessed at several points in their development, and the stability and correlates of behavioral inhibition are examined.

Of particular interest is the development of internalizing problems in these inhibited children. At five-and-a-half years of age, children who were originally classified as inhibited had developed more fears than had uninhibited children. Furthermore, fears in the uninhibited children could usually be related to a prior trauma; this finding was not true for the inhibited children (Kagan et al., 1990). Other research suggests that inhibited children are at risk for the development of clinical disorders and of anxiety disorders in particular. A collaborative effort between Kagan and his colleagues and Joseph Biederman and his colleagues, for example, examined two samples: Kagan's original sample and a sample of high-risk offspring of parents with panic disorder/agoraphobia and other disorders (Biederman et al., 1993). Significant differences between inhibited and not inhibited children were observed. Inhibited children were more likely to meet the criteria for four or more disorders, for two or more anxiety disorders, and for specific anxiety disorders (Avoidant Disorder, Separation Anxiety Disorder, and Agoraphobia). Furthermore, the rates of anxiety disorders for inhibited children increased over the three-year period that they were followed. Thus in terms of our discussion of peer relations, it may be that some portion of shy withdrawn children have the temperamental style that Kagan has described as behaviorally inhibited. These children may be at risk for the development of multiple disorders and would seem to be at particular risk for the development of anxiety disorders.

TREATMENT OF THE WITHDRAWN CHILD

Given this chapter's focus on internalizing disorders, we emphasize the withdrawn or shy child rather than the aggressive child in our discussion of treatments. Many programs have been designed to improve the social skills and peer relations of children. A thorough review of this material is beyond the scope of this section. Several reviews provide a good summary and critique of this literature (Beelmann, Pfingsten, & Losel, 1994; Bierman, 1989; La Greca, 1993; McFadyen-Ketchum & Dodge, 1998; Schneider, 1992). These reviews suggest that interventions to improve children's social competencies have focused on the development of specific social skills and/or the cognitive processes presumed to underlie the peer difficulties. Social skills approaches can be grouped as either molecular or molar in focus (La Greca, 1993). Molecular approaches emphasize the training of discrete skills such as eye contact, responding positively to peers, and initiating interactions. A molar focus might train skills such as participation in group activities, cooperation, and sharing. Social cognitive approaches stress training in social problem solving, taking another's perspective, self-control, and the like. Increasingly, interventions have stressed more complex, multimodal approaches (Beelmann et al., 1994). Interventions seem reasonably successful in producing changes; however, the long-term effects and generalization outside the intervention setting are less clear. In the following sections, we describe examples of these successful interventions and also suggest avenues for improving generalization across time and setting.

Reinforcing increased peer interaction. Some workers have focused on the antecedents and consequences of low rates of peer interactions. Indeed, the effectiveness of reinforcement in increasing peer contact was the focus of some of the early work on social skills interventions (Allen et al., 1964; Walker et al., 1979). It was soon realized, however, that reinforcement of high rates of interaction may not always produce positive outcomes. It may also lead to unacceptable rates of aggressive behavior (Kirby & Toler, 1970) and thereby to being unpopular (Conger & Keane, 1981). In addition, there is some disagreement regarding whether rate of interaction is an appropriate treatment target for socially withdrawn children. For example, it has been argued that little support exists for the notion that overall rate of peer interaction is an indicator of current social incompetence or of risk for later difficulties (Dodge, 1989). However, others point to evidence that if children with very low rates of interaction are selected for study, important and valid differences are found (Hops & Greenwood, 1988).

Imitation, coaching, and instruction. Exposure to filmed models has been demonstrated to affect

positively the behavior of preschool isolates (e.g., O'Connor, 1969; 1972). However, it is unclear whether effectiveness is due to observation of a model or to other variables, such as coaching and instruction (Conger & Keane, 1981). Several investigators have explicitly employed coaching-instructional techniques. These interventions use a variety of procedures, including instruction in social skills knowledge and concepts, modeling and rehearsal with classmates, and reinforcement and encouragement of generalization (e.g., Bornstein, Bellack, & Hersen, 1977; Gottman, Gonso, & Schuler, 1976; La Greca & Santogrossi, 1980; Oden & Asher, 1977). For example, Ladd (1981) selected third-grade children low on peer acceptance who were also observed to be deficient in the three areas to be targeted. The latter criterion is important, since it matches specific interventions to pretreatment deficiencies—something that is often lacking in treatment studies. Children were assigned to either a skill training treatment, attention control, or nontreatment control condition. Training consisted of instructions, guided and self-directed rehearsal, and feedback plus training in self-evaluation. Three verbal skills were targeted: asking questions, leading (offering useful suggestions and directions), and offering support to peers. Differences in both behavioral observations and sociometric ratings in favor of the treatment condition were obtained. It seems likely that the finding of both improvement in targeted behavior and actual social acceptance is due to the selection of intervention targets. In this study, behaviors that the children were deficient in, rather than general skills, were targeted. Thus it is likely that these behaviors were related to the children's original unpopular status.

The use of peers in treatment. Although most interventions for improving children's social abilities are implemented by adults, an interesting approach is the use of peers as helping agents. Peers can provide appropriate models for desired behavior. They are also already present in the setting where the relevant behavior occurs and can provide natural consequences that continue to maintain behavior over time. Indeed, a variety of peer-

A withdrawn or socially isolated child may need assistance in developing appropriate social skills and in increasing peer interactions.

(Kate Connell/Tony Stone Images)

mediated interventions have been demonstrated to improve the social behavior of withdrawn children (Odom & Strain, 1984).

Furman, Rahe, and Hartup's (1979) program employing peers to assist socially withdrawn children is particularly intriguing. Furman and colleagues identified preschool children who engaged in peer interactions during less than 33 percent of observations and who were at least 10 percentage points below their class means. Twenty-four such social isolates were assigned to unstructured play sessions with a "therapist" who was twelve to eighteen months younger, to play sessions with a same-age "therapist," or to no treatment. Exposure to a younger peer was highly effective in increasing the social activity of withdrawn children. Both groups of children exposed to "therapists" showed improvement, whereas the control group did not. However, seven of the eight isolates exposed to a younger partner increased their social behavior at least 50 percent, whereas only three of the eight withdrawn youngsters exposed to a same-age partner exhibited comparable increases. The principal effect of the treatments

was to increase rates of positive behaviors but not of neutral and punishing acts. The authors hypothesize that the effectiveness of the peer play sessions, particularly with younger children, was due to an increased opportunity to successfully practice initiating and directing social activity.

Additional evidence for the importance of using peers as part of the process of intervention is provided in a treatment that employed the more common adult-directed training. Bierman and Furman (1984) assigned children who were identified as unaccepted by their peers and deficient in conversational skills to one of four treatment conditions. In the individual condition, the targeted child received coaching in conversational skills in the context of making a film. In the group experience condition, the targeted child, along with two nontargeted peers, was involved in making the same film, but without any coaching in conversational skills. In a combined coaching and group condition, the child, along with the two peers, received coaching in the context of making the film. The remainder of the children were assigned to a no-treatment control condition. At the end of treatment, targeted children who had received skills training, compared with those who had not, had superior conversational skills. Whether training was received in an individual or a group context did not significantly affect this outcome. This difference persisted at the follow-up assessment. Thus skills training, whether done in an individual or a group context, produced sustained improvements in conversational skills.

The results regarding peer acceptance are also quite interesting. Ratings of peer acceptance were obtained by averaging the ratings given by all the child's same-sex classmates. Children who were involved in group conditions had higher posttreatment acceptance scores than those not involved in group conditions. This difference, however, did not persist at follow-up. The presence or absence of skills training did not affect these findings. That is, peer acceptance was affected only by the group experience variable.

For the children involved in the two group conditions, an additional partner sociometric measure was available—a rating of acceptance of the target child by *peers actually involved in the training* with them. When the judgments of these peers were considered, children who received group skills coaching were more liked than those who received only the group experience. This finding was true both at the end of treatment and at follow-up. Thus it would appear that group involvement alone can improve peer status, but this effect may be short-lived. Sustained peer acceptance may require more than a structured group experience. Skills training that involves peers from the child's social environment may be an essential component of long-term success.

Inclusion of peers is probably only part of developing effective interventions that are sensitive to the multiple aspects of the social world of the child. It is probably important not only to include peers in training but also perhaps to address more directly the perceptions of peers regarding the rejected or ignored child. Bias in such perceptions may make peer reputation slow to change even when there are real changes in the targeted youngster's social behavior. Also, much of the attention to date has been on enhancing overall peer acceptance, while there has been little effort to develop interventions that promote peer friendship. Both are likely to be important, and as a youngster progresses from preschool to adolescent years, close friendships are likely to take on increasingly significant roles.

Much of the research on interventions has occurred in a school context. Inclusion of teachers in intervention planning is important because of their potential role in monitoring peer behaviors and providing appropriate consequences. Teachers can also provide interventions such as peer-pairing or cooperative group assignments that have the potential to foster the social integration of a child (La Greca, 1993; Malik & Furman, 1993). It is important also to remember that parents play an important role in a youngster's peer relations. Parents, for example, arrange opportunities for peer interactions, and they monitor and supervise peer contacts. The role that parents can play is illustrated in a study by Vernberg et al. (1993). Strategies employed by parents to help adolescents establish new friendships after relocation to a new community were found to cluster into four groups: meeting other parents, enabling proximity to peers, talking to the adolescent, and encouraging activity. On the basis of three home interviews with each of 138 mother-adolescent pairs, the authors found that more frequent use of these strategies predicted greater companionship and intimacy with new friends among these adolescents. Interventions that include attention to improving and directing parent involvement in ways that encourage and enhance their children's social skills can be part of a multicomponent intervention. This strategy seems particularly important for clinicians working with a youngsters outside a school setting.

SUMMARY

■ The experience of pervasive sadness is a central feature of most conceptualizations of depression. Irritability, loss of the experience of pleasure, social withdrawal, lowered self-esteem, inability to concentrate, poor schoolwork, alterations of biological functioning, and somatic complaints are often noted.

▪ The psychoanalytic theory of depression suggested that the problem would not exist in children.

▪ The concept of masked depression, although problematic, resulted in greater attention to the problem and highlighted developmental issues. Data supporting the importance of a developmental perspective in understanding issues such as prevalence and symptom patterns are continuing to emerge.

▪ The view that childhood depression is a disorder with the same essential features as its adult counterpart is probably the dominant view at present. This view is the approach taken by the DSM system. Research findings suggest both similarities to and differences from the adult disorder.

▪ Major Depressive Disorder, Dysthymic Disorder, and Adjustment Disorder With Depressed Mood are DSM diagnoses typically given to depressed youngsters. Other mood disorders involve the presence of mania as well as depression.

▪ Major Depressive Disorder is the most prevalent form of affective disorders among children and adolescents.

▪ Episodes of clinical depression are quite common among adolescents. Depression is more prevalent among adolescents than children and among girls during adolescence.

▪ Youngsters with depression are also likely to experience other problems.

▪ Much of the thinking about the determinants of child and adolescent depression is based on theories or information derived from adults.

▪ Research suggests a genetic component to depression in youngsters, but this research also suggests a considerable influence of shared and nonshared environment.

▪ Research on the biochemistry of depression suggests that during childhood and early adolescence, the biological aspects of depression differ from adult cases. Older adolescents who are more severely depressed are more likely to resemble adult cases.

▪ Separation/loss has been a major theme in many theories of depression. Cognitive and behavioral theories also suggest other contributions to the development of depression.

▪ A learned helplessness perspective suggests that a learned perception of lack of control leads to a cognitive style and behaviors characteristic of depression. Recent revisions of this perspective—hopelessness theory—emphasize the interaction of stressful life events and cognitive style. Cognitive theories such as Beck's and self-control models of depression have also received attention.

▪ Maternal depression appears to be related to childhood dysfunctions, but this relationship does not seem to be either specific to childhood depression or inevitable. Various mechanisms such as heredity, modeling, ineffective parenting, stress, and attachment may link maternal depression and child dysfunction.

▪ Most contemporary views of depression in children and adolescents suggest a model that integrates multiple determinants.

▪ Although completed suicide among youngsters is relatively rare, increased prevalence has caused considerable concern. The range of suicidal behavior is more prevalent. Suicidal behavior is related to depression but is related to other problems as well.

▪ The causes of suicidal behavior are often multiple (e.g., psychopathology, physical health, family environment, interpersonal relations) and complex.

▪ Assessment of depression is likely to sample a broad spectrum of attributes and to involve a number of strategies. Obtaining information from a variety of informants and with a variety of measures seems important.

▪ Assessment has been facilitated by the development of structured diagnostic interviews. In addition, self-report measures, such as the Children's

Depression Inventory, are frequently employed and have received considerable research attention. Instruments available to assess attributes associated with depression (e.g., hopelessness) add to our ability to conduct a thorough assessment.

■ Less is known regarding the treatment of depression in youth than in adults, and most treatments are largely adaptations of interventions for adults.

■ The prescription of antidepressant medications for children and adolescents is widespread and may be an important component of treatment for some youngsters. However, the use of medications continues to be controversial, since effectiveness and safety remain unclear. Tricyclic antidepressants and SSRIs are most commonly employed.

■ Treatments derived from behavioral and cognitive-behavioral perspectives and treatments that address interpersonal and family aspects of depression in youngsters seem promising. However, continued development of treatments that are sensitive to multiple aspects of the psychological, social, and family influences on depressed youngsters are needed, as well as additional large-scale treatment and prevention studies.

■ Peer relationships provide the opportunity for learning certain skills that may not be available in other social relationships.

■ The definition and measurement of peer relations and social competence requires continued attention. Problems with peers are one of the most frequently mentioned reasons for referrals for psychological services. Successful peer relations, on the other hand, may protect the child from the impact of adverse factors and thereby decrease the likelihood of disorder.

■ Poor peer relations have been of interest because of their association with current and later adjustment difficulties. Although the link between shyness, withdrawal, rejection, and peer relations needs to be explored further, emerging evidence suggests a potential link to adjustment.

■ The work of Kagan and his colleagues is an example of one variation of a shy/withdrawn style, its stability, and its relationship to adjustment.

■ Many programs have been designed to improve the social skills of children. Reinforcing increased rates of peer interactions, interventions combining imitation, coaching and instruction, and the use of peers in treatment have all been demonstrated to contribute to successful interventions.

■ There should be continued development of and research on multifaceted treatments, particularly those addressing the complexity of peer relations and the potential contribution of parents and teachers.

CHAPTER 8

CONDUCT DISORDERS

C linicians commonly hear complaints of a youngster's noncompliant, aggressive, and antisocial behavior. Such concerns are voiced by parents, teachers, other adults, and peers. These behaviors are also problematic for parents and teachers of youngsters who have not had contact with clinical or legal systems. At some time or another, most parents have problems with their child's fighting, lying, destroying property, or repeatedly failing to follow directions.

The fact that these problems are common and disruptive makes them a topic of concern for parents and for those who work with children. However, extreme and persistent forms of these behaviors cause a degree of disturbance and destruction well beyond the common experience. Thus they are of serious concern not only for the family but also for institutions such as the school and for society at large. The seeming persistence of these behaviors over time for some individuals—perhaps from early childhood through adult life—also contributes to their importance. This chapter deals

with young people to whom labels such as conduct disorder, oppositional defiant disorder, and juvenile delinquency are often applied.

DESCRIPTION AND CLASSIFICATION

The complexity and heterogeneity of the disruptive, negative, and antisocial behaviors exhibited by children and adolescents are increasingly being appreciated. The various terms employed to describe such behavior (e.g., acting out, disruptive, externalizing, undercontrolled, oppositional, antisocial, conduct disorder, or delinquent) reflect the variety of ways that this behavior is described. Although there is a general understanding of this broad category, attempting to refine and subcategorize such behavior is a continuing goal. Among disruptive behavior problems, a distinction has often been made between inattention, hyperactivity, and impulsivity on the one hand, and aggression, oppositional behaviors, and more serious conduct problems on the other (Waldman, Lillienfeld, & Lahey, 1995). The behaviors in the first grouping are discussed in greater detail in the next chapter, which is on Attention Deficit Hyperactivity Disorder (ADHD). The oppositional and conduct disordered behaviors of the second grouping are considered here. In our discussion, the term "conduct disorder" is used to describe severe levels of this general group of aggressive-antisocial behaviors, whereas the proper noun "Conduct Disorder" specifically refers to a diagnostic category such as that defined by DSM-IV.

The following description of Doug illustrates many of the features that characterize youth who exhibit persistent aggressive and antisocial behavior.

Doug is an eight-year-old white male who was brought for treatment by his mother because of his unmanageable behavior at home. The specific concern was with Doug's aggressive behavior, especially aggression toward his eighteen-month-old brother. When Doug is angry he chokes and hits his younger brother and constantly makes verbal threats of physical aggression. In the months immediately before his referral to treatment, Doug's behavior became more out of control, and his mother felt she was unable to cope. Apart from his aggression in the home, Doug has played with matches and set fires over the last three years. These episodes have included igniting fireworks in the kitchen of his home, setting fires in trash dumpsters in the neighborhood, and starting a fire in his bedroom, which the local fire department had to extinguish.

At school his behavior has been disruptive over the last few years. His intellectual performance is within the normal range (WISC-R full scale IQ = 96) and his academic performance is barely passing. His aggressive behavior against peers and disruption of class activities have led to his placement in a special class for emotionally disturbed children. Even so, his behavior is not well controlled. The school has threatened expulsion if treatment is not initiated.

Doug currently lives with his mother and two brothers. He is second born. For the first few years of Doug's life, there was considerable disruption in the home. Doug's father frequently abused alcohol. When drunk, he would beat his wife and children. The mother and father separated on a number of occasions and eventually were divorced when Doug was five years old. After the divorce, the mother and children moved in with the maternal grandfather who also drank excessively and physically abused the children. Less than two years ago, the mother had another child by her former husband. With the stress of the new child, the death of her father with whom she was living, and Doug's continuing problems, the mother became depressed and began to drink. Although she is not employed, she spends much of her time away from the home. She leaves the children unsupervised for extended periods with a phone number of a neighbor for the children to call if any problems arise with the baby. (Kazdin, 1985, pp. 3–4)

EMPIRICALLY DERIVED SYNDROMES

An empirically derived syndrome involving aggressive, oppositional, destructive, and antisocial behavior has been identified in a wide variety of studies. This syndrome has been given a variety of names, including undercontrolled, externalizing, or conduct disorder. It would appear that this syndrome is a robust one in that it emerges employing a variety of measures, reporting agents, and settings.

There have also been efforts to distinguish narrower groupings within this broad externalizing/conduct disorder syndrome. Achenbach (1993), for example, has described two syndromes, aggressive behavior (e.g., fights, destroys things, is explosive) and delinquent behavior (e.g., lies, steals, is truant), within the broader externalizing syndrome. The behaviors characteristic of these two narrow syndromes based on the Achenbach instruments (Child Behavior Checklist-CBCL; Teacher Report Form-TRF; Youth Self-Report-YSR) are listed in Table 8-1. Children may exhibit only one or both types of problems.

The validity of this distinction is supported by a variety of research findings (Achenbach, 1998). For example, research has suggested a higher degree of heritability for the aggressive than the delinquent syndrome (Edelbrock et al., 1995). There also would appear to be developmental differences in the two syndromes. In a longitudinal analysis, Stanger, Achenbach, and Verhulst (1997) found that the average scores in the population of the two syndromes declined between ages four and ten. After age ten, however, the scores on the aggressive syndrome continued to decline, whereas scores on the delinquent syndrome increased. These findings are illustrated in Figure 8-1. These same authors also found that the stability (the similarity of a particular individual's behavior at two points in time) was higher for the aggressive than for the delinquent syndrome. These and other findings suggest that it is important to distinguish between types of externalizing/conduct disorder problems.

TABLE 8–1

Behaviors from the Aggressive and Delinquent Syndromes[a]

Aggressive Behavior	Delinquent Behavior
Argues	Lacks guilt
Brags	Bad companions
Mean to others	Lies
Demands attention	Prefers older kids
Destroys own things	Runs away from home
Destroys others' things	Sets fires
Disobedient at school	Steals at home
Jealous	Steals outside home
Fights	Swearing, obscenity
Attacks people	Truancy
Screams	Alcohol, drugs
Shows off	Thinks about sex too much
Stubborn, irritable	Vandalism
Sudden mood changes	Tardy
Talks too much	
Teases	
Temper tantrums	
Threatens	
Loud	
Disobedient at home	
Defiant	
Disturbs others	
Talks out of turn	
Disrupts class	
Explosive	
Easily frustrated	

[a] Items listed are summaries of the actual content (wording) of items on the instruments. Some items are included in the CBCL, TRF, and YSR versions of these syndromes, whereas others are specific to one or two of these instruments. Adapted from Achenbach (1993).

Empirical approaches to classifying conduct disorders have also suggested other ways of grouping problem behaviors within this broad category. These approaches are not mutually exclusive and indeed do overlap with the aggressive/delinquent distinction and with each other. Some approaches suggest a distinction based on *age of onset* (Hinshaw, Lahey, & Hart, 1993): a later- or adolescent-onset category consisting principally of nonaggressive and delinquent behaviors, and an early-onset category that includes these behaviors as well as aggressive behaviors. Two other approaches to subcategorizing that have been described are the salient symptom approach and the overt-covert dimension (Kazdin, 1989a). The *salient symptom* approach is based on the primary behavior problem being displayed. Distinguishing antisocial children whose primary problem is aggression from those whose primary problem is stealing is an example. Aggressive behavior may be particularly important to single out in this way. There is support for distinguishing aggression from other conduct disordered behavior in terms of its social impact, correlates, gender differences, and developmental course (Loeber & Stouthamer-Loeber, 1998).

Expansion of this distinction suggests a broader distinction between *overt* confrontational antisocial behaviors (e.g., arguing, fighting, temper tantrums) and *covert* or concealed antisocial behaviors (e.g., fire setting, lying, stealing, truancy). The reliability and validity of the overt-covert distinction are supported by evidence that problem behaviors do tend to cluster together in these groupings and that different outcomes are associated with such clusters (Loeber & Schmaling, 1985; Loeber & Stouthamer-Loeber, 1998). A further expansion of this distinction suggests grouping conduct problems by employing two dimensions: an overt-covert distinction and a *destructive-nondestructive* dimension of behavior (Frick, 1998). This approach and the clusters of behaviors based on it are illustrated in Figure 8-2. There may be a developmental progression in which the clusters of these conduct problem behaviors emerge. These kinds of distinctions continue to be explored in the context of an empirical and developmental approach to understanding conduct-disordered behavior. The developmental approach is further discussed in the next section.

THE DSM APPROACH

Within the category of Attention Deficit and Disruptive Behavior Disorders, DSM-IV includes the diagnostic categories of Attention Deficit Hyperactivity Disorder (discussed in Chapter 9) and two

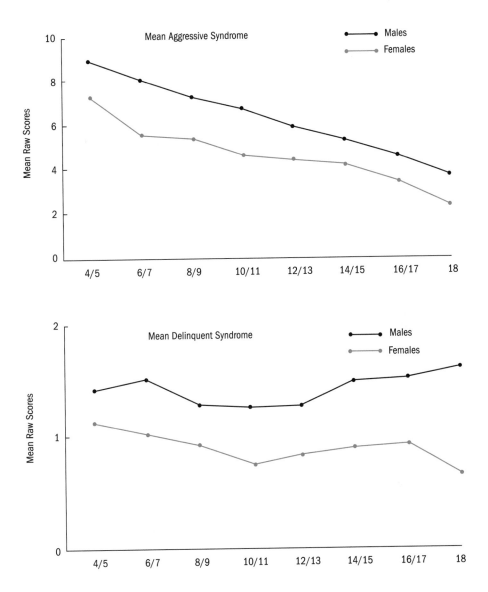

FIGURE 8-1 Mean aggressive and delinquent syndrome scores by age for males and females.

Adapted from Stanger, Achenbach, & Verhulst, 1997.

other diagnoses: Oppositional Defiant Disorder and Conduct Disorder.

Young children are often stubborn, do not comply with requests or directions from adults, and in a variety of ways, exhibit oppositional behavior. Not all such behavior is indicative or pre-

dictive of clinical problems. Indeed, appropriate and skilled assertions of autonomy may be desirable and may facilitate development (Johnston & Ohan, 1999). It is the less skilled and excessive oppositional and defiant behavior that may indicate present or future problems.

DESTRUCTIVE

COVERT-PROPERTY
DESTRUCTIVE

Steals
Firesetting
Vandalism
Lies

AGGRESSION

Cruel to Animals
Spiteful
Cruel
Assault
Fights
Bullies

COVERT ← → OVERT

STATUS OFFENSES

Runs Away
Truancy
Uses Substances
Swears

OPPOSITIONAL

Temper Tantrums
Argues
Annoys Others
Stubborn
Angry
Defies Adults
Touchy

NONDESTRUCTIVE

FIGURE 8-2 Clusters of conduct disorder behavior defined by the two dimensions of overt to covert and destructive to nondestructive.
From Frick, 1998.

TABLE 8-2
Behaviors Used by DSM-IV to Define an Oppositional Defiant Disorder
Loses temper.
Argues with adults.
Actively defies or refuses to comply with adult requests or rules.
Deliberately annoys others.
Blames others for own mistakes or misbehavior.
Is touchy or easily annoyed.
Is angry and resentful.
Is spiteful or vindictive.

Oppositional Defiant Disorder (ODD) is described as a pattern of negativistic, hostile, and defiant behavior lasting at least six months. The behaviors used to define oppositional-defiant problems are listed in Table 8-2. In order to receive a diagnosis of Oppositional Defiant Disorder, at least four of these behaviors must be present. To distinguish the behaviors from expected levels of opposition and assertiveness, any behavior must be judged to occur more frequently than is typical for a child of comparable age.

Oppositional and noncompliant behavior is clearly a common problem. It is prevalent among nonclinic children. However, it is also one of the most frequently reported problems of children referred to clinics (Achenbach, 1991a; Rey, 1993) and is more common among clinic referred children than nonreferred children (e.g., Achenbach et al., 1991; Griest et al., 1980). It is unclear whether DSM-IV's approach of having a separate category of Oppositional Defiant Disorder is the best way to group these problem behaviors (Frick

et al., 1993; Russo et al., 1994). However, it is clear that noncompliance represents a practical problem for parents, teachers, and clinicians. Also, noncompliant, stubborn, and oppositional behavior may represent for some youngsters the earliest steps on a developmental path of persistent antisocial behavior (Hinshaw et al., 1993; Loeber et al., 1993).

The essential feature of the diagnosis of Conduct Disorder (CD) is a repetitive and persistent pattern of behavior that violates the basic rights of others as well as the major age-appropriate societal norms. The list of symptoms and the groupings that DSM-IV suggests in describing Conduct Disorder are presented in Table 8-3. The diagnosis of Conduct Disorder requires that three or more of these behaviors be present during the past twelve months, with at least one present in the past six months. Two subtypes, Childhood-Onset and Adolescent-Onset, are specified on the basis of whether one or more of the criterion behaviors had an onset prior to age ten years.

PATTERNS OF CO-OCCURRENCE

Youngsters who receive one of the disruptive disorder diagnoses also frequently experience other difficulties and receive other diagnoses. In considering the issue of the overlap between the two diagnoses themselves, DSM-IV stipulates that a youngster cannot receive both diagnoses. If a youngster meets the criteria for both Conduct Dis-

TABLE 8-3

Behaviors Used by DSM-IV in Diagnosing Conduct Disorder

Aggression toward People and Animals

Bullies, threatens, or intimidates

Initiates physical fights

Has used a weapon

Is physically cruel to people

Is physically cruel to animals

Has stolen while confronting a victim

Has forced someone into sexual activity

Destruction of Property

Has deliberately engaged in fire setting with the intention of causing serious damage

Has deliberately destroyed others' property (other than by fire setting)

Deceitfulness or Theft

Has broken into house, building, or car

Often lies to obtain goods or favors or to avoid obligations

Has stolen items of nontrivial value without confronting a victim

Serious Violations of Rules

Stays out at night despite parental prohibitions, beginning before age thirteen

Has run away from home overnight at least twice (or once without returning for a lengthy period)

Is often truant from school, beginning before age thirteen

order and Oppositional-Defiant Disorder, he or she is given only the Conduct Disorder diagnosis. However, the question remains of how these two disorders relate (Frick, 1998; Johnston & Ohan, 1999). Are they, for example, separate disorders, or is ODD a developmental precursor to CD?

Most youngsters who receive the diagnosis of CD also meet the criteria for ODD. In the Developmental Trends Study of clinic-referred boys 7 to 12 years old, 96 percent of those who met criteria for CD also met criteria for ODD. The reported average age of onset was about six years for ODD and about nine years for CD, suggesting that among boys with Conduct Disorder, this is pre-

ceded by behaviors characteristic of Oppositional-Defiant Disorder and that these behaviors are "retained" as additional antisocial behaviors emerge. On the other hand, ODD does not always result in CD. Of the boys with ODD (but no CD) at the initial assessment, 75 percent had not progressed to CD two years later. About half of the boys with ODD at Year 1 continued to meet the criteria for ODD at Year 3, and about one-quarter no longer met the criteria for ODD. Thus, although most cases of Conduct Disorder meet the criteria for Oppositional-Defiant Disorder, most youngsters with Oppositional-Defiant behaviors do not progress to a conduct disorder (Hinshaw, Lahey, & Hart, 1993).

There is considerable co-occurrence of ODD and CD with Attention Deficit Hyperactivity Disorder (ADHD). Among children diagnosed with ADHD, it is estimated that between 35 and 70 percent develop ODD, and between 30 and 50 percent develop CD (Johnston & Ohan, 1999). When these disorders co-occur, ADHD seems to precede the development of the other disorders. It might be speculated that impulsivity, inattention, and overactivity present a particular parenting challenge. In instances where weaknesses in parenting exist, a pattern of noncompliant and aversive parent-child interactions may be set in motion. The challenges of parenting an ADHD child may thus play a role in the early onset of ODD behaviors and continue over the course of development to maintain and exacerbate ODD/CD behaviors. Parent-child relationships are only one of the potential mechanisms whereby the presence of ADHD may increase the risk for ODD/CD. It would appear, however, that the inattention, impulsivity, and overactivity associated with ADHD seems to be one possible path toward more persistent and more severe conduct disorders (Fergusson & Horwood, 1998; Loeber & Stouthamer-Loeber, 1998; Maughan & Rutter, 1998).

In addition to the frequent co-occurrence of other disruptive behavior disorders, youngsters with conduct disorders commonly experience a variety of other difficulties. Younger aggressive children are frequently rejected by their peers (Newcomb, Bukowsi, & Pattee, 1993). Youngsters with

FIRE SETTING

Much of the information that we describe in this chapter addresses what can be termed overt conduct disordered behavior (e.g., oppositional-defiant behavior, aggression). Fire setting represents a behavior that would be described as covert.

Juvenile fire setting produces serious damage in terms of loss of life, injury, and property damage. It is also associated with serious difficulties for the child, family, and community (Barnett & Spitzer, 1994; Kolko, 1985).

Fire play probably emerges as a part of normal development for many children as well as for those who become fire setters (Kolko, 1985). Fire play occurs in a very large proportion of preschool children. However, this early interest, along with the early presence of models to imitate, may then be followed by additional later models and/or easy access to materials. This situation provides a possible context and the beginnings for the fire-setting problem.

What other factors may distinguish those children who actually set fires? One factor that is frequently reported on the basis of clinical experience is the lack of social competence and difficulties in interpersonal situations. Indeed, a comparison of inpatient fire setters and other children hospitalized for a psychological disorder indicates that the fire setters possess fewer social skills (Kolko, Kazdin, & Meyer, 1985). Some workers view this deficiency as resulting in an inability to express anger effectively. It is recognized that fire setters are probably a heterogeneous group. One distinction that is often made is between those who set fires as a form of aggression and those who set fires without an awareness of the consequences (e.g., because of curiosity).

It has also been suggested that for many youngsters, fire setting is part of a cluster of covert antisocial behaviors that include destruction of property, stealing, lying, and truancy. Among inpatients, it was found that fire setters engaged in more of these kinds of behaviors than did non–fire setters. In contrast, the two groups were not different in aggressive behaviors (Kuhnley, Hendren, & Quinlan, 1982).

Family difficulties related to fire setting resemble those that have been described for conduct disorders in general (Barnett & Spitzer, 1994; Kolko, 1989). For example, Kazdin & Kolko (1986) examined parental psychological adjustment and marital satisfaction in a clinical sample of youngsters. In this sample, twenty of the twenty-seven fire setters received a primary or secondary diagnosis of conduct disorder, compared with only eleven of twenty-seven nonsetters. Significantly higher scores of overall psychological difficulties, and depression in particular, were found among the mothers of fire setters compared with mothers of nonsetters. These differences were not found on the basis of the presence or absence of a conduct disorder diagnosis. Similarly, it was only the presence or absence of fire setting that appeared to be associated with poor marital adjustment. Thus even in a sample of families all of whom have a severely disturbed child, families of fire setters appear to differ from those of nonsetters.

These and similar findings have led some workers to suggest a particular conceptualization of many fire-setting children. In this conceptualization, fire setting represents a later stage of progression of antisocial symptoms to those that are more extreme (cf. Forehand et al., 1991; Kolko & Kazdin, 1986).

persistent conduct disorders are also frequently described as having certain cognitive impairments and lower school achievement (Caspi & Moffitt, 1995; Maughan & Rutter, 1998). Lower IQ, particularly verbal deficits, have been reported among juvenile delinquents, and tests of executive function (higher order cognitive functions that permit one to process information and problem-solve) suggest deficits in this area for conduct disordered youngsters. How these other difficulties and conduct disorders relate to each other is a complex question (Caspi & Moffitt, 1995; Hinshaw et al., 1993; Maughan & Rutter, 1998). In what ways do cognitive and language difficulties contribute to the development of conduct disorders? What is the relationship between these deficits, conduct disorder, and poor academic performance? To what extent are some of these deficiencies related to ADHD—are they characteristic of only the subset of youngsters with conduct disorder who also have ADHD? These issues, which are beyond the scope of our current discussion, remain to be resolved.

Internalizing disorders such as anxiety and depression also occur at higher than expected rates among youngsters with conduct disorders (Loeber & Keenan, 1994; Nottelmann & Jensen, 1995b). Estimates of the rate of co-occurrence of conduct problems and anxiety disorders vary widely from 19 to 53 percent (Nottelmann & Jensen, 1995b). This pattern of co-occurrence may be more likely to occur in boys during preadolescence into adolescence, but in young women, from adolescence into adulthood (Lewinsohn, Rohde, & Seeley, 1995; Zoccolillo, 1992). The impact of the co-occurrence of anxiety with conduct disorders may also differ by age, the impact being worse in older children. Younger, prepubertal boys with both conduct and anxiety disorders have been reported to be less aggressive than those with conduct disorder alone; however, older boys with both disorders were more aggressive than the conduct disorder only boys (Hinshaw, Lahey, & Hart, 1993). A related body of research on shy/withdrawn children who also display conduct problems suggests that they may have worse outcomes than youngsters with only conduct problems (Serbin et al., 1991).

Kerr et al. (1997) differentiated between the concepts of behavioral inhibition and social withdrawal (see Chapter 7). They found that in aggressive boys, behavioral inhibition was a protective factor against delinquency, whereas withdrawn-disruptive boys remained at risk. Thus the protective aspects of anxiety/withdrawal may come from behavioral inhibition rather than lack of social contact.

The co-occurrence of depression and conduct disorder in community samples has been estimated to be between 12 and 25 percent (Loeber & Keenan, 1994; Nottelmann & Jensen, 1995b). However, among a community sample of older adolescents, Lewinsohn and his colleagues (1995) found that a major depressive disorder co-occurred in 38 percent of youngsters with a disruptive behavior disorder (CD, ODD, or ADHD). In clinical samples, approximately 33 percent of children and adolescents have a co-occurrence of conduct and depressive disorders (Dishion, French, & Patterson, 1995). In both community and clinic populations, boys seem to be overrepresented in regard to the co-occurrence of conduct and depressive disorders (Dishion et al., 1995; Lewinsohn et al., 1995). Depression does not seem to affect the severity of conduct problems (Loeber & Keenan, 1994). For example, Capaldi (1992) found that for two groups of boys, those with conduct problems and depression and those with conduct problems only, psychosocial correlates (e.g., parenting practices, associating with deviant peers, academic skills deficits) were the same. Finally, there appear to be a number of factors that may help account for the frequent co-occurrence of conduct problems and depression. In most cases, it appears that the onset of conduct problems precedes the onset of depression. It may be that frequent failures and conflict experiences (e.g., with peers and school) contribute to depression in youngsters with conduct problems (Dishion et al., 1995). Another potential cause of the co-occurrence of these problems may be common genetic influences. In a behavior genetic study of twins and related and nonrelated nontwin siblings, approximately 45 percent of the covariation between depressive and antisocial symptoms could be attributed to a common genetic liability, the remainder being explained by shared and nonshared environmental influences (O'Connor et al., 1998).

DELINQUENCY

In addition to empirical and DSM approaches to classifying antisocial and conduct-disordered behavior, it is important to consider the notion of delinquency. The term "delinquency" is primarily a legal rather than a psychological one. As a legal term, it refers to a juvenile (usually under eighteen) who has committed an index crime or a status offense. An index crime is an act that would be illegal for adults as well as for juveniles (e.g., theft, aggravated assault, rape, or murder). A status offense is an act that is illegal only for juveniles (e.g., truancy, association with "immoral" persons, violation of curfews, or incorrigibility). It is important also to make a distinction between delinquent behavior and what might be called official delinquency.

This distinction is important because some behaviors described as delinquent are quite common. Surveys based on adolescent self-reports show that as many as 80 to 90 percent of youths report involvement in delinquent activity before reaching the age of eighteen. In contrast, if one examines official records (e.g., police, courts), a much lower rate of delinquency is suggested—15 to 35 percent for males and 2 to 14 percent for females. The estimate of rate varies with the stringency of the definition of "official record" (Moore & Arthur, 1989).

It is important to recognize that whether an act by a juvenile gets classified as official delinquency may depend as much on the actions of others as it does on the youth's behavior. The norm violation must, of course, be noticed by someone and must be reported to a law-enforcement official. A police officer then can either arrest the youth or merely issue a warning. If the youth is arrested, he or she may or may not be brought to court. Once in juvenile court, only some individuals receive the legal designation of delinquent; others may be warned or released in the custody of their parents. Various definitions of delinquency can be used anywhere

in this process. And then, of course, many individuals apparently commit offenses but don't get caught.

Subtypes of delinquency. Distinctions have been made between subtypes of delinquency. One distinction that has received a great deal of attention is that between the socialized and the unsocialized delinquent. This distinction is based on the results of factor analytic studies and other kinds of research, as well as on clinical observations (Quay, 1986b; Rutter & Giller, 1984). The socialized, or subcultural, subgroup describes youths who associate with a delinquent peer group and accept the values of that subculture. This category is defined by characteristics such as

1. having bad companions;
2. stealing in company with others;
3. belonging to a gang; or
4. staying away from home and school.

Socialized delinquents are also described as experiencing little distress or psychopathology, and little difficulty in relating to peers. The second category—unsocialized, or psychopathic—applies to delinquents who do not seem to be part of a delinquent peer group. Furthermore, this subcategory is often thought to distinguish a form of delinquency in which emotional or behavioral disturbance is present.

THE USE OF ALCOHOL AND OTHER DRUGS

The use of illicit substances, once considered an adult problem, is now common among adolescents and preadolescents. In addition to concern regarding illegal drugs such as marijuana, cocaine/"crack," hallucinogens (e.g., LSD), and heroin, there is concern regarding abuse of "legal" substances. Alcohol, nicotine, psychoactive medications (e.g., stimulants, sedatives), over-the-counter medications (e.g., sleep aids and weight reduction aids), and inhalants (e.g., glue, paint thinner) are accessible and potentially harmful. They may also play a roll in starting some young people on a course of long-term and increased substance abuse (Bailey, 1989; Cambor & Mill-

Association with a peer group that supports the use of alcohol and other drugs is clearly a contributing influence to the development of substance use and abuse.

(Courtesy of A.C. Israel)

man, 1996). Those working with youngsters are faced with the challenge of discriminating between normal patterns of experimentation and abuse that may have serious short- and long-term consequences. What constitutes misuse or abuse? One extreme definition views any use of alcohol by a minor as abuse since such use is illegal. Less extreme and more prevalent are definitions that address drinking patterns and related negative consequences (e.g., difficulties with school, legal authorities, peers, or family).

Alcohol is the most commonly used drug among all age groups, including the young (National Institute of Drug Abuse, 1992). Reports suggest that the use of other drugs occurs together with the use of alcohol. Lynskey, Fergusson, and Horwood (1998) suggest that a common or shared vulnerability to substance use may help explain the correlation between use of different drugs. They examined the correlation between the use of alcohol, tobacco, and cannabis among a group of sixteen-year-old New Zealand youngsters. Their results suggested a model in which affiliation with delinquent or substance-using peers, novelty seeking, and parental illicit drug use contributed to a common vulnerability to substance use. Figure 8-3 illustrates this model. The model suggests that the correlation between use of different substances in adolescents, a frequent observation, is due to the fact that there are shared risk factors that create a common or shared vulnerability. This vulnerability then leads to increased likelihood of using various substances.

This model might be contrasted to stage models that posit a developmental sequence (Kandel, 1982). The use of legal drugs such as alcohol and tobacco precede the use of illicit drugs. It is virtually never the case that a nonuser goes directly to the use of illegal drugs. Participation in one stage does not necessarily mean that the young person will progress to the next stage. Only a subgroup at each stage progresses to the next level of use. The earlier the youngster begins one stage, the greater is the likelihood of other drug use (Windle, 1990). Thus the earlier that legal drugs are used, the greater the likelihood of illicit drug use (Kandel & Yamaguchi, 1993). Also, heavier use at any stage seems to be associated with "progress" to the next stage. Findings that alcohol and drug use are beginning early, even before the teenage years (e.g., Huizinga, Loeber, & Thornberry, 1993), are particularly disturbing in the context of a developmental stage model.

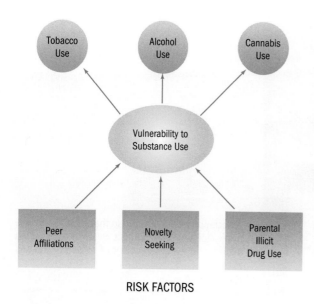

RISK FACTORS

FIGURE 8-3 Risk factors contributing to a common vulnerability that helps explain why there is use of multiple substances by adolescents.

Adapted from Lynskey, Fergusson, & Horwood, 1998.

A variety of theories have been offered and risk factors suggested to explain the origins and maintenance of alcohol abuse. No single explanation has received clear acceptance.

One variety of explanation views adolescence as a period of transition (e.g., Jessor & Jessor, 1977). Certain behaviors mark this transition. Use of alcohol is an example of such a behavior, since it is deemed appropriate for adults but not for adolescents. Individual differences and environmental variables are assumed to affect the rate at which an individual makes the transition to adulthood and thereby the age of onset of these behaviors. This transitional notion is consistent with findings that not all adolescents who are problem drinkers abuse alcohol as adults.

Social learning explanations of alcohol or other substance abuse emphasize exposure and consequences. Exposure to others who drink or abstain is assumed not only to provide an impetus toward certain behaviors but also to influence attitudes toward drinking. At greatest risk is the child of an alcoholic or other substance abuser (Bailey, 1989; Chassin et al., 1996). The anticipation of positive or negative consequences for drinking is also a central aspect of such explanations.

The importance of teenagers' expectancy regarding the effects of alcohol is illustrated in a study of the development of drinking behavior (Smith & Goldman, 1994; Smith et al., 1995). Over a two-year period during which many of the youngsters first began to drink, expectations that drinking would facilitate social interactions predicted initiation into drinking. Those who expected social facilitation also drank more over the two-year period, and future expectations regarding the effects of drinking were not reduced, but rather became more positive.

Adolescent substance use has also been viewed within the context of a stress and coping model (Wills & Filer, 1996). Youngsters facing greater negative life events and perceived stress are more likely to use alcohol and other substances. These substances serve a coping function for the adolescent, or at least they are perceived to do so. Among youngsters who have fewer available adaptive-active coping mechanisms (e.g., seeking information, considering alternatives, taking direct action), there is a greater likelihood of use of avoidant coping mechanisms (e.g., distraction, social withdrawal, wishful thinking) and of alcohol and other substances as ways of dealing with stress.

There is no single factor that can easily explain which youths start or stay on this substance use path. Explanations must include an array of variables—biological, psychological, and social—that affect development over time. However, early conduct problems are associated with later substance use, regardless of other variables (Lynskey & Fergusson, 1995). In addition, high rates of delinquency, sexual intercourse, and pregnancy are found to occur with substance use (Huizinga et al., 1993). Furthermore, the presence of these kinds of externalizing problems in children of alcoholic and antisocial parents may explain, in part, why those youngsters are more likely to engage in heavy alcohol use than their peers (Hussong, Curran, & Chassin, 1998). Thus prevention and treatment programs for substance use need to address multiple influences, be aware of developmental issues, and be comprehensive in scope.

EPIDEMIOLOGY

Aggression, as well as antisocial, oppositional, and similar behaviors, certainly are some of the most common childhood problems. Disobedience, tantrums, demanding, and whining are among the most common concerns expressed by parents of young children seen in primary health care settings (Schroeder & Gordon, 1991). Many of these behaviors are also reported by parents of children not referred for problems (Achenbach, 1991a). Prior to preschool, boys and girls do not differ in the level of conduct problems displayed, but by about age four, boys exhibit greater physical aggression and other externalizing behavior problems than do girls (Keenan & Shaw, 1997).

Conduct problems are also one of the most frequent reasons for referral to child and adolescent treatment services (Kazdin, 1995a). The exact prevalence of conduct disorders is difficult to establish, and a number of factors contribute to this difficulty, including the informant employed (e.g., parent or child), age, and gender. The prevalence estimates available are also based on earlier versions of the DSM, and diagnostic criteria have changed considerably. Studies of prevalence in community samples often report rates of between 2 and 10 percent, with estimates of 6 to 10 percent for Oppositional-Defiant Disorder and 2 to 9 percent for Conduct Disorder (Costello, 1990; Earls, 1994). Conduct disorders are more commonly diagnosed in boys than in girls; a ratio of about 4:1 is typically cited (Earls, 1994). There also appears to be a relationship between gender and age in the prevalence of conduct disorders. For example, Offord et al. (1987) reported a prevalence of conduct disorder for boys of 6.5 percent in the four to eleven age group and 10.4 percent in the twelve to sixteen age range. The corresponding increase was greater for girls, from 1.8 to 4.1 percent.

Delinquent behavior that is not as serious and that does not persist over time is common among adolescents (White, Moffitt, & Silva, 1989). Such behavior is not usually considered by professionals as an indication of persistent psychological or social difficulties, but is more likely to be thought of as within the normal range of adolescent experimentation. It is persistent or chronic delinquent behavior that is of greater concern. Indeed, it would appear that approximately half of official delinquents commit only one offense. The probability of future delinquent acts rises dramatically, however, with each additional offense, continuing into adulthood. Individuals with repeated offenses (recidivists) account for a vast majority of juvenile offenses (Moore & Arthur, 1989). As Table 8-4 illustrates, there is little doubt that juvenile crime is a serious problem (U.S. Bureau of the Census, 1998). Chronic delinquency appears to start early. For example, Tolan (1987) reported that committing a first juvenile offense before the age of twelve was the single best predictor of the seriousness, number, and variety of future offenses.

Issues of definition and methodology can readily be seen when one examines the research on delinquency. Official records often indicate greater delinquency among lower-class and minority youths and boys. However, confidential reports of behavior by the youths themselves are less likely to show these differences (Moore & Arthur, 1989). This finding led some to conclude that reported differences in rates of delinquency based on social class, race, and gender were due to selection of

TABLE 8-4

Number of Cases Disposed by Juvenile Courts for Youths Ages Ten to Seventeen

Reasons for Referral	Year		
	1985	**1990**	**1995**
Violent offenses	67,000	97,000	142,000
Property offenses	489,000	565,000	623,000
Delinquency offenses (e.g., vandalism, drug law violations)	555,000	658,000	949,000

From U.S. Bureau of the Census, *Statistical Abstract of the United States: 1998* (118th ed.). Washington, DC, 1994.

certain groups for prosecution. Subsequent reviews, however, suggested that such bias was not as strong as originally proposed (Moore & Arthur, 1989; Rutter & Giller, 1984; West, 1985). Self-report studies may have given too much weight to minor and occasional misbehavior, which may be quite widespread. These findings suggest that although it is likely that certain advantaged youngsters probably do avoid the legal designation of delinquent, this avoidance is probably not sufficient to explain differences in delinquency among certain social groups. Real associations between delinquency and social class probably do exist; however, they are probably more moderate than was once contended.

DEVELOPMENTAL COURSE

STABILITY OF CONDUCT DISORDERS

An important aspect of conduct problems is their reported stability over time (Fergusson, Lynskey, & Horwood, 1996; Olweus, 1979; Stanger et al., 1996; Tolan & Thomas, 1995). Early presence of conduct disordered behavior appears to be related to later aggressive and antisocial behavior and to a range of psychological and social-emotional difficulties later in life (Caspi, Elder, & Bem, 1987; Farrington, 1995; Hafner, Quast, & Shea, 1975; Robins et al., 1971; Roff & Wirt, 1984).

However, like most issues related to behavior disorders in children and adolescents, the question of the stability or continuity of antisocial/conduct disordered behavior is a complex one (Loeber & Stouthamer-Loeber, 1998; Maughan & Rutter, 1998). The measurement of aggressive behavior or of more broadly defined externalizing behaviors that is taken at separate times several years apart do result in relatively high correlations. For example, Olweus (1979) reported average correlations of around .60 for measures of aggression over ten-year age spans. Similarly, correlations were .58 for scores on both the broad externalizing and the narrower aggressive syndromes of the Child Behavior Checklist that were measured an average of six years after initial assessment (Stag-

ner et al., 1996). These substantial correlations do suggest a stability of aggressive, externalizing behavior from preschool into adolescence. However, it is also important to remember what these correlations indicate—that the relative positions of individuals regarding these behaviors remains somewhat stable between Time 1 and Time 2. This stability of relative position does not mean that the level of aggression or conduct disordered behavior remains the same. Thus if the levels of aggression in most children decreased about the same amount over time, this decrease would still produce a high correlation between the two measures of aggression. Indeed, we saw earlier (Figure 8-1) that the scores on the aggressive behavior syndrome of the CBCL decreased with age.

Findings that there is continuity of aggressive and antisocial behavior does not also mean that all individuals who exhibit early conduct disordered behavior continue to do so. Only some portion of youngsters continue to exhibit aggressive and antisocial behavior. Although change can occur at any time, preschool and adolescence appear to be particular times when desistance of externalizing problems occurs. Campbell and her colleagues (Campbell, 1997) found that whereas there was stability of externalizing behaviors from the ages of four to six, only 30 to 50 percent of preschoolers identified as hard to manage met the criteria for externalizing problems at school entry. Loeber and Stouthamer-Loeber (1998) report that among a community sample of inner-city boys, the prevalence of physical fighting started to decrease by age fifteen. The challenges are to describe patterns of both continuity and desistance of aggressive and antisocial behavior and to identify those variables that influence the course of antisocial behavior over time.

DEVELOPMENTAL PATHS

Much attention has been given to the developmental aspects of conduct disorders and to the conceptualization of developmental progressions (e.g., Farrington, 1986; Loeber et al., 1993; Patterson, DeBaryshe, & Ramsey, 1989; Robins, 1978). Loeber (1988) proposed a model that can serve to illustrate some of the attributes that might characterize the developmental course of conduct disorders. The model suggests that at each level, less serious behaviors precede more serious ones but that only some individuals progress to the next step at each level. Progression on a developmental path is characterized by increasing diversification of antisocial behaviors. Youngsters who progress evidence new antisocial behaviors, and previous behaviors may also be retained rather than replaced. Individuals may differ in their rate of progression, or innovation rate, which is defined as the number of novel categories of antisocial behavior during a time period.

Age of onset is probably the most mentioned aspect of the development of conduct disordered behavior. Many studies have found that early age of onset is related to more serious and persistent antisocial behavior (Earls, 1994; Tolan & Thomas, 1995). A number of authors have proposed two distinct developmental pathways leading toward antisocial behavior, one with a childhood onset and the other with an adolescent onset (Hinshaw et al., 1993; Moffitt, 1993a).

The adolescent onset pattern is the more common developmental pathway. There is little oppositional or antisocial behavior exhibited during childhood. During adolescence many youngsters begin to engage in illegal activities, and although most exhibit only isolated antisocial acts, some engage in enough antisocial behavior to qualify for a diagnosis of Conduct Disorder. Youngsters following this pathway tend to exhibit less severe antisocial behaviors and to be less aggressive. They are also less likely to persist in their antisocial behaviors beyond adolescence—leading Moffitt (1993a) to suggest the term "adolescence-limited antisocial" behavior.

An example of the support for this adolescent-onset pathway comes from the Dunedin Multidisciplinary Health and Development Study (McGee et al., 1992). Prospective examination of a birth cohort of New Zealand youngsters revealed a large increase in the prevalence of nonaggressive conduct disorder but no increase in aggressive conduct disorder at age fifteen compared with age eleven. These youngsters were clearly exhibiting problem behavior; for example, they were as likely to be arrested for their delinquent offenses as were childhood-onset delinquents. However, their offenses were less aggressive, and the adolescent-onset cases included slightly more females than males, in contrast to the predominance of males among conduct disorder cases at age eleven. This rather common emergence during adolescence of nonaggressive antisocial behavior that is not likely to persist beyond adolescence is contrasted to early-onset antisocial behavior.

The childhood-onset developmental pathway fits with the notion of the stability of conduct disordered behavior. Indeed, Moffitt (1993a) terms this pattern "life-course persistent antisocial behavior." Retrospective studies of antisocial adults are consistent with this picture of stable conduct disordered behavior. It must be remembered, however, that a substantial number of children with an early onset of antisocial behavior do not persist on this pathway. Many youngsters, for example, who are aggressive as preschoolers are not aggressive as adolescents, nor do they exhibit high levels of other antisocial behaviors. The early-onset pathway is less common than the adolescent-onset pattern, with estimates of about 3 to 5 percent of the general population (Hinshaw et al., 1993; Moffitt, 1993a). Youngsters following this pattern are also more likely to exhibit other difficulties, such as Attention Deficit Hyperactivity Disorder, learning disabilities, and academic difficulties. Indeed, problems of hyperactivity/inattention are hypothesized to contribute to the persistence of conduct disordered behavior in at least a subgroup of these youngsters (Loeber & Stouthamer-Loeber, 1998; Maughan & Rutter, 1998).

Even though there is stability of problematic behavior for children entering this pathway, among some of these individuals, the antisocial behaviors exhibit qualitative change in the course of development. Hinshaw and colleagues (1993) describe the features of this heterotypic continuity of antisocial behavior:

The preschooler who throws temper tantrums and stubbornly refuses to follow adult instructions becomes the child who also initiates fights with other children and lies to the teacher. Later, the same youth begins to vandalize the school, torture animals, break into homes, steal costly items, and abuse alcohol. As a young adult, he or she forces sex on acquaintances, writes bad checks, and has a chaotic employment and marital history. (p. 36)

Studies employing DSM diagnostic categories also offer support for the existence of an early onset persistent developmental pattern. The first problem behaviors to emerge in the childhood-onset path may be the oppositional and defiant behaviors characteristic of Oppositional-Defiant Disorder (ODD). Later behaviors characteristic of the Conduct Disorder (CD) diagnosis may emerge, but the vast majority of these CD youngsters still meet the criteria for ODD. They have "retained" the early antisocial behaviors. It is also important to note, however, that most youngsters with an ODD diagnosis do not progress to CD (Hinshaw et al., 1993).

Figure 8-4 is a hypothetical illustration of the changing prevalence of antisocial behavior with age. The figure illustrates how there are a smaller number of "life-course persistent" individuals with a longer duration on their developmental path.

There are also a larger number of "adolescent-limited" individuals who contribute to the increase in prevalence of antisocial behavior during adolescence.

Loeber has proposed a view of the development of conduct disorders that expands on the notion of these two "age of onset" types (Loeber & Stouthamer-Loeber, 1998; Loeber et al., 1993). In examining the development of aggression and violence, Loeber suggests that there are three developmental types:

1. a life course-type,
2. a limited-duration type, and
3. a late-onset type.

The late-onset type is added to account for a minority of violent adults who do not have a history of aggression earlier in their lives. The life-course type is also subdivided into those with a preschool onset and those whose onset is later in childhood or adolescence. Loeber also suggests that rather than a single pathway, a multiple pathways concep-

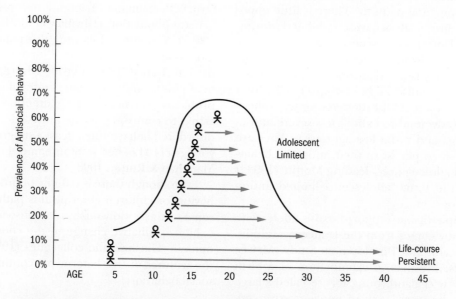

FIGURE 8-4 Hypothetical illustration of the changing prevalence of participation in antisocial behavior across the life course. (The solid line represents the known curve of crime over age. The arrows represent the duration of participation in antisocial behavior by individuals.) From Moffitt, 1993.

tualization best describes the development of an individual's antisocial behavior. On the basis of a longitudinal study of inner-city youth and following from the idea of distinguishing between overt and covert behaviors described earlier, Loeber proposed a triple-pathway model (see Figure 8-5):

1. an overt pathway starting with minor aggression, followed by physical fighting, followed by violence;
2. a covert pathway starting with minor covert behaviors, followed by property damage, and then moderate to serious delinquency; and
3. an authority conflict pathway prior to age twelve, consisting of a sequence of stubborn behavior, defiance, and authority avoidance.

The last of these pathways is based on disobedience and conflict with authority. Authority conflict behaviors are related to but separate from both overt and covert conduct disordered behavior. Individuals may progress along one or more of these pathways. As illustrated in Figure 8-5, entry into the authority conflict pathway typically begins earlier than entry into the other two pathways, and not all individuals who exhibit early behaviors on a pathway progress through the subsequent stages. The percentage of youngsters exhibiting behaviors characteristic of later stages is less than those exhibiting earlier behaviors on a pathway.

Investigators continue their efforts to describe the developmental pathways of antisocial, conduct disordered behavior. At the same time, they also

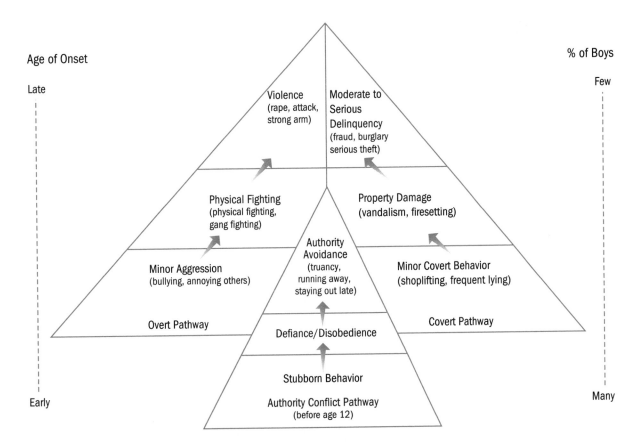

FIGURE 8-5 Three pathways to boys' problem behavior and delinquency.
From Loeber & Hay, 1994.

seek to identify the influences that first put young-sters on those pathways and that determine whether the antisocial behavior will continue or desist.

ETIOLOGY

The development of conduct-disordered and anti-social behavior may be affected by a variety of in-fluences. Figure 8-6 illustrates potential multiple influences. This model, which is described by Dishion, French, and Patterson (1995), is an adap-tation of Bronfenbrenner's (1989) view of a hier-archy of nested systems. Intrapersonal factors are characteristics of individuals that interact with the environment in the development of antisocial be-havior. Relationship processes are the immediate context in which this development occurs. Behav-ior settings are the physical settings in which these relationships occur, and community contexts are larger social influences. Each system directly and indirectly affects the development of antisocial be-havior. Here we will give primary attention to in-trapersonal factors and relationship process influ-ences, but the larger contexts in which these occur should not be ignored.

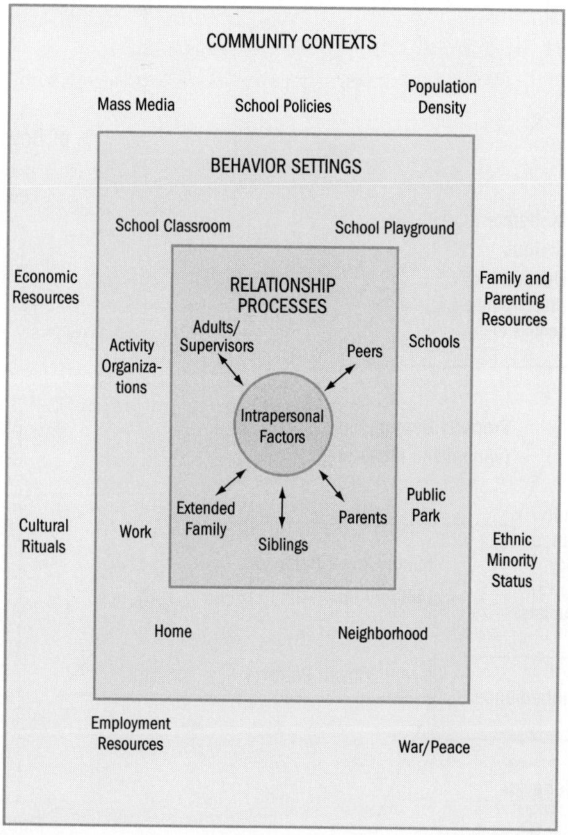

AGGRESSION AS A LEARNED BEHAVIOR

Aggression, which is a central part of the defini-tion of conduct disordered behavior, is often sug-gested as a basis for differentiating among con-duct disordered youth. Aggression is also a common difficulty among nonreferred children. Children clearly may learn to be aggressive by being rewarded for such behavior (Patterson, 1976b). For example, Patterson, Littman, and Bricker (1967) found that among nursery school children, aggressive acts that were followed by "positive" consequences (e.g., passivity or crying by the victim) were likely to be repeated, whereas "negative" consequences (e.g., retaliation or telling the teacher) resulted in the aggressor's switching either behaviors or victims. Another in-teresting finding emerged from this study. Chil-dren who were initially passive and unassertive were frequently victimized. Some, however, even-tually exhibited aggressive behaviors, were rein-forced by positive consequences, and increased their frequency of such behavior. While illustrat-ing the importance of reinforcement for aggres-sion, this study also suggests another source of learning—imitation of aggressive models.

A great deal of attention has focused on how children learn through imitation of aggressive models. Bandura's (1965) work with nursery school children demonstrated that children imi-tated an aggressive filmed model. The conse-quences experienced by the model affected the performance, but not the learning of aggression. Thus in one set of circumstances, a young boy may

FIGURE 8-6 A hypothetical ecological model for the study of antisocial behavior, illustrating how antisocial behavior may be influenced by a variety of factors.

From Dishion, French & Patterson, 1995.

RELATIONAL AGGRESSION

It is frequently reported that boys exhibit significantly higher levels of aggression than do girls. Is this because girls are less aggressive?

Aggression has generally been defined in terms of overt physical or verbal behaviors intended to hurt or harm others (e.g., hitting or pushing, threatening to beat up others). Perhaps nonphysical forms of aggression that are relevant to young females have been ignored rather than there being real gender differences in levels of overall aggression (Crick & Grotpeter, 1995).

It has been suggested that aggression in girls may focus on relational issues—behaviors intended to damage another child's feelings or friendships. Examples of such *relational aggression* include the following:

Purposefully leaving a child out of some play or other activity.

Getting mad at someone and excluding the person from a peer group.

Telling lies about someone so that the other kids won't like the person.

Telling someone you will not like him or her unless the person does what you say.

Saying mean things about someone so that others will not like the person. (Crick & Grotpeter, 1996)

Research has indicated that relational aggression can be distinguished from overt/physical aggression and is found even at an early (preschool) age. Girls are more relationally aggressive than boys and more likely to be among extreme groups of relationally aggressive youngsters. Relational aggression was also found to be associated with peer rejection and feelings of loneliness, depression, and isolation (Crick & Grotpeter, 1995; Crick, Casas, & Mosher, 1997). Also, youngsters who engaged in gender nonnormative forms of aggression (i.e., overtly aggressive girls and relationally aggressive boys) exhibited a greater number of behavior problems than those who engaged in gender normative aggression or were nonaggressive (Crick, 1997).

not perform aggressive behavior that he has learned. However, at another time, when the boy anticipates positive consequences for aggression, the behavior will be performed. It has also been demonstrated not only that children may learn new and novel aggressive responses following observation of an aggressive model but also that aggressive responses already in the child's repertoire are more likely to occur—disinhibition of aggression.

Children certainly have ample opportunity to observe aggressive models. Parents who physically punish their children serve as models for aggressive behavior. In fact, children exhibiting excessive aggressive or antisocial behaviors are likely to have siblings, fathers, and even grandparents with records of aggressive and criminal behavior (Farrington, 1987; Huesmann et al., 1984; West, 1982) and to have observed especially high rates of aggressive behavior in their homes (Kashani et al., 1992; Patterson, DeBaryshe, & Ramsey, 1989). Aggression is also ubiquitous in television programs and in other media.

FAMILY INFLUENCES

The family environment can be a principal arena for the learning of aggressive behavior. However, family influences are not limited to the acquisition of aggression or to the mechanisms of family influence described above. Indeed, family influences play an important role in the genesis of various conduct disordered behaviors. A high incidence of deviant or criminal behavior has been reported in families of delinquents and young children with conduct problems (Kazdin, 1985; Rutter & Giller, 1984; West, 1982). Longitudinal studies, in fact, suggest that such behavior is stable across generations (Glueck & Glueck, 1968; Huesmann et al., 1984). It seems, then, that conduct disordered children may be part of a deviant family system. Numerous family variables have been implicated, including family socioeconomic status, family size, marital disruption, poor-quality parenting and parental neglect, and parental psychopathology (Frick, 1994; Patterson, Reid, & Dishion, 1992). We will highlight a few of these influences.

Parent-child interactions and noncompliance. The manner in which parents interact with their children contributes to the genesis of conduct disordered behavior. For example, parental involvement and supervision and parental discipline practices are related to conduct problems.

Defiant, stubborn, and noncompliant behaviors are often among the first problems to develop in children. Given that noncompliance occurs in both clinic and nonclinic families, what factors might account for the greater rate of noncompliance in some families? One possible factor is suggested by evidence that parents of clinic and nonclinic children differ in both the number and the types of commands that they give. Parents of clinic-referred children issue more commands, questions, and criticisms, and they also issue commands that are presented in an ineffective, angry, humiliating, or nagging manner (Delfini, Bernal, & Rosen, 1976; Forehand et al., 1975; Lobitz & Johnson, 1975). Such parental behavior has been shown to be associated with deviant child behavior (Griest et al., 1980). Consequences that parents deliver also affect the child's noncompliant behavior. A combination of negative consequences (ignoring the child and verbal reprimands) for noncompliant behavior and rewards and attention for appropriate behavior seems to be related to in-

creased levels of compliance (Forehand & McMahon, 1981).

The work of Patterson and his colleagues. Gerald Patterson and his colleagues have developed an intervention program for families with aggressive children that is based on a social learning perspective (Patterson et al., 1975; Patterson et al., 1992). Patterson developed what he refers to as coercion theory to explain how a problematic pattern of behavior develops in children who are labeled as aggressive. Observations of referred families suggested that acts of physical aggression were not isolated behaviors. On the contrary, such acts tended to occur along with a wide range of noxious behaviors that were used to control family members in a process labeled as coercion. How and why does this process of coercion develop?

One factor is parents who lack adequate family management skills. According to Patterson (1976b; Patterson et al., 1992), parental deficits in child management lead to an increasingly coercive interaction within the family. Central to this process are the notions of negative reinforcement and the reinforcement trap. Here is an example:

■ A mother gives in to her child's tantrums in the supermarket and buys him a candy bar.

■ The short-term consequence is that things are more pleasant for both parties.
  ■ The child has used an aversive event (tantrum) to achieve the desired goal (candy bar).
  ■ The mother's giving in has terminated an aversive event (tantrum and embarrassment) for her.

■ Short-term gains, however, are paid for in long-term consequences.
  ■ The mother, although receiving some immediate relief, has increased the probability that her child will employ tantrums in the future.
  ■ The mother has also been provided with negative reinforcement that increases the likelihood that she will give in to future tantrums.

In addition to this negative reinforcement trap, coercive behavior may also be increased by direct

A child may engage in aversive behaviors in order to get something that he or she wants. If the parent repeatedly gives in, this capitulation may contribute to coercive patterns of interaction in the family.
(Michael Newman/PhotoEdit)

positive reinforcement. Aggressive behavior, especially in boys, may meet with social approval. However, escape-conditioning is even more important. The child uses aversive behaviors to terminate (escape) aversive intrusions by other family members (Patterson, 1982).

The concept of reciprocity adds to our understanding of how aggression may be learned and sustained. As indicated earlier, children as young as nursery school age can learn in a short time that attacking another in response to some intrusion can terminate that intrusion. In addition, the victim of the attack may learn from the experience and is more likely to initiate attacks in the future. The eventual victim of escalating coercion also provides a negative reinforcer by giving in, thereby increasing the likelihood that the "winner" will start future coercions at higher levels of intensity and thus get the victim to give in more quickly.

This process is exacerbated by the ineffectiveness of punishment. The finding that in problem families, punishment does not suppress coercive behavior but may serve to increase it has been re-

ferred to as punishment acceleration. The ineffectiveness of punishment may be due to the strong reinforcement history for coercive behavior and to inconsistent use of punishment in these families (Patterson, 1982).

The description of a coercive process and ineffective parenting has served as the basis for Patterson's intervention project and for his evolving developmental model (Patterson et al., 1989; Patterson et al., 1992). In addition to describing the "training" of antisocial behavior in the home, Patterson has described a relationship between antisocial behavior in boys and poor peer relationships, academic incompetence, and poor self-esteem. It is suggested that ineffective parenting produces the coercive, noncompliant core of antisocial behavior, which in turn leads to these other disruptions. Furthermore, it is hypothesized that each of these outcomes serves as a precursor to subsequent drift into deviant peer groups.

The perspective of Patterson and his coworkers has expanded to include a wide array of variables that affect the family process. Their efforts have also attended to problems such as poor peer relations, school failure, low self-esteem, and depression, which are associated with antisocial behavior. However, at the core of this complex theoretical model is the parent training model (see Figure 8-7) that has proven to be so robust that Patterson and his colleagues call it basic black; "it is simple, elegant and seems appropriate for more than one setting" (Patterson et al., 1992, p. 62).

The constructs of parental discipline and parental monitoring are described as contributing to and being influenced by the child's antisocial behavior. Parental discipline is defined by an interrelated set of skills: accurately tracking and classifying problem behaviors, ignoring trivial coercive events, and using effective consequences when necessary to back up demands and requests. Parents of problem children as compared with other parents have been found to be overinclusive in the behaviors that they classify as deviant. Thus these parents differ in how they track and classify problem behavior. These parents also "natter" (nag, scold irritably) in response to low levels of coercive behavior or behavior that other parents see as neutral. Other parents are able to ignore these behaviors in their children. Parents of antisocial children fail to back up their commands when the child fails to comply, and they also fail to reward compliance when it does occur. These parents, therefore, also differ in the consequences that they apply to their child's behavior.

Parental monitoring of child behavior is also important to the development and persistence over time of antisocial behavior. The amount of time a child spends unsupervised by parents increases with age. The amount of unsupervised time has also been found to be positively correlated with antisocial behavior. Patterson describes his treatment families as having little information as to where their children are, whom they are with, what they are doing, or when they will be home. This situation probably arises from a variety of considerations, including the repeated failures that these parents have experienced in controlling their children even when difficulties occurred right in front of them. Also, requesting information would likely lead to a series of confrontations that the parents prefer to avoid. These parents have low expectations regarding the likelihood of positive responses to their involvement either from their own children or from social agencies such as schools (Patterson et al., 1992).

Extrafamilial influences and parental psychopathology. The question of why some families and not others exhibit inept management practices has received some attention. Patterson (Patterson et al., 1992) posits that any number of variables may account for changes over time in family management skills. Patterson's own findings and those of other investigators (Wahler & Dumas, 1989) support the relationship between extrafamilial stressors (e.g., daily hassles, negative life events, financial problems, family health problems) and parenting practices. In addition, the handing down of faulty parenting practices from one generation to the next seems to help explain the problematic parenting characteristics of anti-

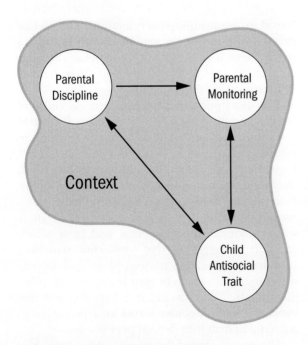

FIGURE 8-7 The parent training model.
From Patterson, Reid, & Dishion, 1992.

social families. Social disadvantage and living in neighborhoods that require a very high degree of parenting skills also place some families at risk. Finally, various forms of parental psychopathology are associated with poor parenting practices. Parents with antisocial difficulties have been particularly implicated in the parenting practices associated with the development of conduct disordered behavior, such as low levels of parental involvement (Capaldi & Patterson, 1991). Also, heavy drinking by parents may be associated with inept monitoring of the child and less parental involvement (West & Prinz, 1987). Figure 8-8 illustrates a model of how a variety of influences may lead to disruption of effective parenting and to child antisocial behavior.

Marital discord. There appears to be a clear association between marital discord and behavior problems in children of these families (Davies & Cummings, 1994; O'Leary & Emery, 1985). Parental conflict and divorce have frequently been cited in homes of delinquents and children with conduct disorders (Kazdin, 1985; Rutter & Giller, 1984). It would appear that the conflict leading to and surrounding the divorce are principle influences in this relationship and that less conflict and greater cooperation are associated with fewer problems in children (Amato & Keith, 1991; Hetherington, Bridges, & Insabella, 1998). If aggression between the parents is also present, childhood disorder seems even more likely than would be expected on the basis of marital discord alone (Jouriles, Murphy, & O'Leary, 1989).

The relationship between marital conflict and conduct disorders can be explained in a number of ways. Parents who engage in a great deal of marital conflict or aggression may serve as models for their children. Perhaps such parents direct high rates of conflictual and aggressive behavior at others as well, including the child. The stress of marital discord and the adjustment of the single parent to divorce may also interfere with parenting practices and the ability of the parent to monitor the child's behavior. The relationship between discord and conduct problems may also operate in the opposite causal direction; that is, the child's disruptive behavior may contribute to marital discord. Alternatively, conduct problems and marital discord may not be causally related. Rather a "third variable," such as the presence of parental antisocial disorder, may explain this relationship (Lahey et al., 1988). Indeed, there are high rates of antisocial personality disorder (APD) among conduct-

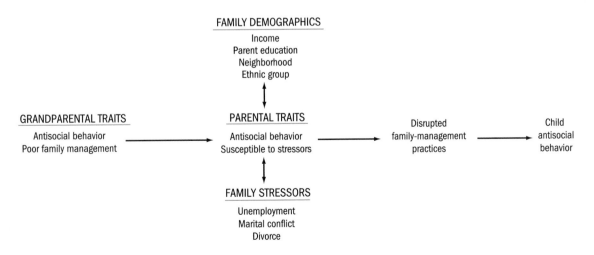

FIGURE 8-8 Disruptors of effective parenting.
From Patterson, DeBaryshe, & Ramsey, 1989.

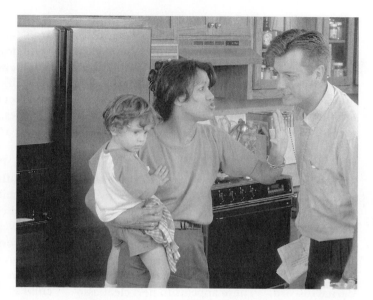

Marital discord and aggression between parents can contribute to the development of conduct disordered behavior in children.

(B. Daemmrich/The Image Works)

disordered youngsters, and APD is associated with high rates of marital instability (Frick, 1994).

It is appropriate to emphasize that much of this research describes only group differences and is correlational in nature. It is often assumed that parental behavior causes childhood conduct disorders. The relationship, however, may be at least reciprocal. Anderson, Lytton, and Romney (1986) found that mothers of conduct problem boys and mothers of normal boys both interacted more negatively with conduct problem boys than with normal boys. They suggested that the child's behavior is the influence in these interactions, not the mother's. In addition, we have also suggested that it may be inappropriate to assume that fundamental deficiencies in parenting skills account for conduct problems in children. These problems exist in a larger context. It may be that a high level of environmental stress (related to family and community/neighborhood factors) that is experienced by the parents, and not the level of parenting skills alone, contributes to parenting difficulties (McLoyd, 1990; Paschall & Hubbard, 1998; Patterson et al., 1992; Wahler & Dumas, 1989).

PEER RELATIONS

It is important to note briefly that peer relations play a role in the development and maintenance of aggressive and antisocial behavior. For example, we saw that Patterson and his colleagues (Patterson et al., 1992) have found that aggressive boys often experience rejection by their peers and that this rejection, in combination with other influences, leads to a drift into deviant peer groups.

Difficulties in interpersonal relations have repeatedly been found among conduct disordered youth (Baum, 1989). Research indicates that aggressive children are frequently rejected by their peers (Coie, Belding, & Underwood, 1988). Not all aggressive children are rejected, and not all rejected children are aggressive. However, these rejected aggressive children suffer immediate social consequences, and they are also at risk for negative long-term outcomes such as delinquency, adult criminality, educational failure, and a variety of indices of adult psychological maladjustment (Parker & Asher, 1987). Thus the combination of aggression and peer rejection clearly places these youngsters at risk.

Beyond the fact that not all aggressive young-sters are rejected, rejected youngsters may not be without friends. In late childhood and into adolescence, conduct disordered and delinquent young-sters have friends who also engage in aggressive and antisocial behaviors. Research has shown that these deviant peer associations play a role in the initiation and maintenance of antisocial behavior (Fergusson & Horwood, 1996; Keenan et al., 1995). Fergusson and Horwood (1998) report on the linkages between early conduct problems and outcomes at age eighteen in a group of New Zealand children studied longitudinally since birth. They found that conduct problems at age eight were associated with poorer outcomes, such as leaving school by age eighteen without appropriate educational qualifications and a period of three months or more of unemployment. Among the factors that mediated the relationship between early aggression and later poor outcomes was the youngsters' peer affiliations. Youngsters who between the ages of fourteen and sixteen had reported having friends who were delinquent or who used substances (e.g., alcohol, cannabis) were at greater risk for these negative outcomes.

SOCIAL-COGNITIVE INFLUENCES

Youngsters with conduct disorders have been described as thinking about social interactions in ways that influence the development and persistence of their aggressive and antisocial behavior. For example, they may attribute hostility to another child's actions, may not be able to take another person's perspective, may not use social problem-solving skills, may not think before they act, or may not use self-verbalizations to control their behavior.

Kenneth Dodge and his colleagues (Crick & Dodge, 1994) have proposed a model of thought processes that are presumed to occur in appropriate social interactions but that are distorted or absent in problematic social interactions. They suggest a social cognitive process that begins with encoding (looking for and attending to) and then interpreting cues, and then includes searching for possible alternative responses, selecting a specific response, and finally enacting the selected response. Investigations based on this model have revealed that aggressive youngsters have poorer social problem-solving skills and display deficits and distortions in the various parts of this process. For example, aggressive youngsters make use of fewer social cues and misattribute hostile intent to their peers' neutral actions. They also generate fewer responses and ones that are less likely to be effectively assertive and more likely to be aggressive solutions. They may also expect that aggressive responses will lead to positive outcomes.

Dodge and Somberg's (1987) examination of attributional biases among aggressive boys is an example of how such social-cognitive influences may operate. Aggressive-rejected and nonaggressive-adjusted boys, eight to ten years old, viewed video-recorded scenes involving different pairs of boys in play activity. In each vignette, one boy engaged in a behavior that led to a negative outcome for the second boy. The intention of the child varied across the scenes (either hostile, accidental, prosocial, or ambiguous). Subjects were asked two questions about each vignette: Which of the four intents did the boy have, and how would they respond if the provocation happened to them (get mad, tell the teacher, ask the peer why it happened, forget it and keep playing)? Each subject saw scenes and responded under two circumstances, relaxed and threat conditions. The threat condition was created when the boys "accidentally" overheard a conversation in the next room between the experimenter and another boy. This prepared conversation led the subject to believe that he would soon have to do a task with this other boy who disliked both him and the experimenter and that this boy would likely get into a conflict with the subject. As expected, aggressive subjects were more likely to attribute hostile intent to the boys in the vignettes and to indicate more aggressive responses to perceived hostility. The hypothesis that hostile attributions would be exaggerated under conditions of threat was also supported. These findings are illustrated in Figure 8-9.

Dodge and his colleagues (Dodge, 1991; Schwartz et al., 1998) have also made a distinction between two types of aggressive behavior: reactive

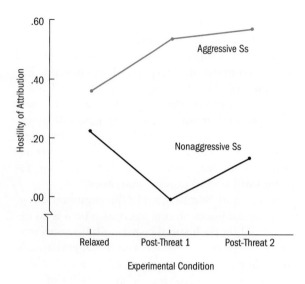

FIGURE 8-9 Attributions of hostility to ambiguous provocations by aggressive and nonaggressive boys under both relaxed and threatening conditions.
From Dodge & Somberg, 1987.

aggression and proactive aggression. Reactive aggression is an angry ('hot-blooded") retaliatory response to a perceived provocation or frustration. Proactive aggression, in contrast, is generally not associated with states of anger or aggression and is oriented to specific goals or supported by positive environmental contingencies. These different types of aggression are associated with different social-cognitive deficiencies. Reactively aggressive youngsters display deficiencies in early stages of the social-cognitive process; for example, they underutilize social cues and attribute hostile intent to others. Proactively aggressive youngsters display deficiencies in later stages of the process; they are likely to positively evaluate aggressive solutions and to expect that they will lead to positive outcomes. The two types of aggression also seem to be related to different outcomes. Reactively aggressive boys were found to display higher rates of other problems and to have an earlier onset of such difficulties than were proactively aggressive

boys (Dodge et al., 1997). Reactively aggressive boys also seem more likely to be the targets of negative peer attitudes and behaviors (Schwartz et al., 1998).

BIOLOGICAL INFLUENCES

The idea that antisocial and criminal behavior has strong biological roots has a long history. As early as the late-nineteenth century, the Italian physician Lombroso wrote of the "stigmata of degeneration." Law violators were described as a distinct physical type at birth, with distinct physical features such as long earlobes, fleshy and protruding lips, and abundant wrinkles. Females were said to commit fewer crimes because their lesser intelligence and sexual coldness overcame their naturally jealous and vengeful nature (cited in Empey, 1978). This conceptualization had an extensive impact on criminology and social policy for over a third of a century, but current-day scientists have accumulated sufficient evidence to reject it.

Genetics. Contemporary versions of genetic contributions to antisocial behavior do exist. However, it is realized that linkages between biology and conduct disorders or criminality will be nowhere as direct as implied in earlier theories (Susman, 1993).

Until recently there was little or no direct evidence regarding genetic contributions to childhood conduct problems, and there was limited evidence regarding the role of genetics in adolescent delinquency. These findings suggested a lesser genetic component for adolescent delinquency than for adult criminal behavior. How might this difference be explained? The childhood-onset versus adolescent-limited distinction discussed earlier may be germane. Conduct disordered behavior and delinquent behavior are quite common during adolescence, and in many cases, they do not persist into adulthood. It might, therefore, be reasonable to hypothesize an increased genetic component in antisocial behavior that persists from childhood into adult life (Rutter et al., 1999).

Early findings from a number of longitudinal behavior genetic studies of children and adoles-

BULLIES AND THEIR VICTIMS

Many people are familiar with the problem of bullying either through personal experience or through literature, television, or movies. The most extensive research on this topic has been conducted in Scandinavia by Olweus (1993; 1994), who reports that approximately 15 percent of youngsters between the ages of seven and sixteen are involved in bullying either as bullies or as victims (approximately 9 percent as victims, 7 percent as bullies, and 1.6 percent as both victim and bully) and that similar or larger percentages are reported in various countries. The percentage of youngsters who report being bullied decreases with age during the elementary years, whereas bullying itself is more stable. A larger percentage of boys than girls engage in bullying and are victims of bullying.

A youngster is being bullied when he or she is repeatedly exposed to the intentional negative actions of another youngster who is either physically or psychologically more powerful than the victim. Boys are exposed to more direct open attacks then are girls. Less visible, indirect bullying can occur in the form of spreading of rumors, manipulation of friendship relationships, and social isolation. Girls are exposed to a greater extent to this more subtle form of bullying than to open attacks. Boys, however, are exposed to this indirect bullying at rates comparable to that of girls.

The typical bully is described by Olweus (1994) as being highly aggressive to both peers and adults; having a more positive attitude toward violence than students in general; being impulsive; having a strong need to dominate others; having little empathy towards victims; and, if a boy, being physically stronger than boys in general. Not all highly aggressive youngsters are bullies, and differences between bullies and other aggressive youngsters remain to be clarified.

The typical victim is described as more anxious and insecure than other students, cautious, sensitive, quiet, nonaggressive, and suffering from low self-esteem. If victims are boys, they are likely to be physically weaker. In general, victims do not have a single good friend in their class. These so-called passive or submissive victims are most common, and this submissive, nonassertive style seems to precede being selected as a victim (Schwartz, Dodge, & Coie, 1993).

It is clearly important to address the bully/victim problem. Bullying can be viewed as part of a more general antisocial, conduct disordered behavior pattern, and thus these youngsters are at risk. Indeed, Olweus (1994) reports that 60 percent of boys classified as bullies in grades 6 to 9 were convicted of at least one officially registered crime by age twenty-four and that 35 to 40 percent of former bullies had three or more convictions by this age as compared with only 10 percent of control boys.

The consequences for the victims of bullying also suggest the importance of intervening early. The victims of bullying form a large group of youngsters who are, to a great extent, ignored by the school and whose parents may be relatively unaware of the problem. One can imagine the effects of going through years of school in a state of fear, anxiety, and insecurity. Some portion of these youngsters' self-esteem is so poor and their hope for change so low that they view suicide as the only possible option (Olweus, 1994). A case described by Olweus illustrates the pain that youngsters may suffer.

Henry was a quiet and sensitive 13-year-old boy in grade 7. For several years he had been harassed and attacked occasionally by some of his classmates ... During the past couple of months, their attacks had become more frequent and severe, for one reason or another.

(continued)

Henry's daily life was filled with unpleasant and humiliating events. His books were pushed from his desk all over the floor, his tormentors broke his pencils and threw things at him, they laughed loudly and scornfully when he occasionally responded to the teacher's questions. Even in class, he was often called by his nickname, the "Worm."

As a rule, Henry did not respond, he just sat there expressionless at his desk, passively waiting for the next attack. The teacher usually looked in another direction when the harassment went on. Several of Henry's classmates felt sorry for him but none of them made a serious attempt to defend him.

A month earlier, Henry had been coerced, with his clothes on, into a shower which had been turned on.

His two tormentors had also threatened him several times to give them money and steal cigarettes for them at the supermarket. One afternoon, after having been forced to lie down in the drain of the school urinal, Henry quietly went home, found a box of sleeping pills in the bathroom and swallowed a handful of pills. Later on the same afternoon Henry's parents found him unconscious but alive on the sofa in the living room. A note on his desk told them that he couldn't stand the bullying any more, he felt completely worthless, and believed the world would be a better place without him. (Olweus, 1993, pp. 49–50)

cents do suggest a genetic component to conduct disordered/externalizing behavior. The Virginia Twin Study of Adolescent Behavioral Development (Eaves et al., 1997; Hewitt, et al., 1997), for example, examined genetic and environmental influences in a sample of 1,412 Caucasian twin pairs ages eight to sixteen. On the basis of symptom counts derived from semistructured interviews with both twins and with both parents and on self-report measures completed by parents, children, and teachers, there is evidence for a considerable genetic influence. However, there is also considerable variability in the findings, depending on the informant (e.g., mother or father) and the source of information (interview versus questionnaires). There is also support for the effects of shared environment in the findings. The Nonshared Environment and Adolescent Development Project examined a sample of 720 same-sex adolescent siblings (monozygotic and dizygotic twins, full siblings, half-siblings, and unrelated siblings) between the ages of ten and eighteen years of age. On the basis of a brief version of the Child Behavior Checklist, there was evidence for moderate genetic influence

on externalizing behavior scores and also evidence for the impact of shared environment (Deater-Deckard et al., 1997). Composite measures, which were based on adolescent and parent reports and observational measures, suggested that approximately half of the variability in antisocial behavior and depressive symptoms was due to genetic influences and that shared and nonshared environmental influences were also significant. It was also concluded that if one examined the co-occurrence of antisocial behavior and depressive symptoms, approximately 45 percent of the covariation of the two could be explained by a shared genetic liability (O'Connor et al., 1998).

Conclusions regarding the nature of genetic contributions to antisocial/conduct disordered behavior must be made with caution. Findings are preliminary and far from unequivocal. Also, Rosenthal's (1975) hypothesis that what is inherited is certain characteristics (for example, body build, sensitivity to alcohol) that make an individual prone to antisocial behavior in response to environmental pressures seems reasonable. Although genetic influences may play some role, they inevitably interact in complex ways with environmental influences, such as social conditions, family variables, and certain social learning experiences that are the major factors in determining etiology (Rutter et al., 1999).

Neurophysiological influences. Psychophysiological variables have also frequently been hypothesized to be related to antisocial behavior. The antisocial personality has been viewed as an individual with chronic underarousal who is thus motivated to provide additional arousal. Some support for this notion came from studies that found that the performances of delinquents and younger conduct disordered children were affected by the novelty and complexity of tasks (DeMyer-Gapin & Scott, 1977; Orris, 1969; Skrzypek, 1969; Whitehill, DeMyer-Gapin, & Scott, 1976). However, the interpretation of these results as stimulation-seeking is controversial (Rutter & Giller, 1984). Findings of differences in heart rate and electrodermal responding (SCRs: skin conductance responses) also seem consistent with the hypothesis of low arousability. Raine and Venables's (1984) review of the literature found support for the existence of lower resting heart rate among antisocial youths. These findings are difficult to interpret, however, because of the relationship of resting heart rate with other variables such as SES, physical fitness, and larger body size. Differences between antisocial/conduct disordered youths and nonantisocial controls in SCRs to stimulation have also been reported (e.g., Borkovec, 1970; Delamater & Lahey, 1983; Schmidt, Solanto, & Bridger, 1985).

Quay (1993) hypothesized a biological foundation for aggressive, life-course persistent conduct disorders. He suggested that a combination of heart rate and SCR findings, such as those described above, can provide a more specific hypothesis than general arousability. This hypothesis is based on Gray's (1987) theory of brain systems: a Behavioral Inhibition System (BIS) and a Behavioral Activation System (BAS) that have distinct neuroanatomical and neurotransmitter systems. The BIS is related to the emotion of anxiety and tends to inhibit action in novel or fearful situa-

tions or under conditions of punishment or nonreward. The BAS tends to activate behavior in the presence of reinforcement and is the reward seeking component of behavior. An imbalance between the BIS and BAS systems is hypothesized to create a predisposition that in combination with adverse environmental circumstances produces behavior problems. Figure 8-10 depicts how an imbalance between the two systems might contribute to either externalizing (antisocial) or internalizing (anxious/depressed) behavior. Quay (1993) suggests that an overactive reward system (BAS; e.g., reflected in heart rate) combined with an underactive behavioral inhibition system (BIS; e.g., reflected in skin conductance) may be implicated in the genesis of persistent aggressive conduct disorders.

Deficits in neuropsychological functioning have also been suggested as contributing to the development of conduct disorders. The idea that brain dysfunction is among the causes of antisocial behavior is not new, but the scientific investigation of these influences is relatively recent. Moffitt's (1993b) review suggests that neuropsychological tests reveal deficits particularly in verbal and executive functions (e.g., sustaining attention, abstract reasoning, goal formation, planning, self-awareness). Neuropsychological measures were related to indications of poor outcomes, such as early onset of conduct disorder, stability over time, aggressiveness, and the presence of Attention Deficit Hyperactivity Disorder symptoms. Moffitt argues for further study of neuropsychological variables as causal factors for conduct disorder, and proposes a developmental model.

This model hypothesizes early differences in the infant nervous system that may be due to factors such as prenatal or postnatal exposure to toxic agents. Compromised neurological functioning affects a variety of areas, including temperament. This effect, in turn, may set in motion a chain of problematic parent-child interactions, particularly under conditions of family adversity. Conduct disorder is thus viewed as evolving from early individual differences in neuropsychological functioning that may be perpetuated and exacer-

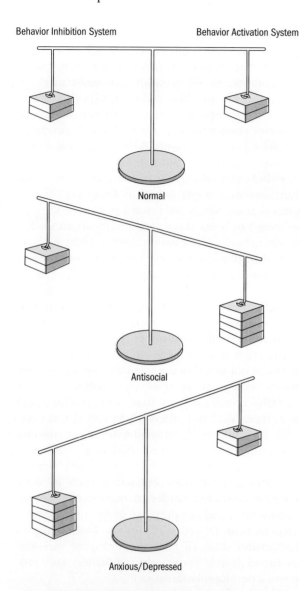

Behavior Inhibition System   Behavior Activation System

Normal

Antisocial

Anxious/Depressed

FIGURE 8-10 An imbalance between the BIS and BAS system is hypothesized to create a predisposition towards the development of a particular kind of behavior problem.
From Dishion, French, & Patterson, 1995.

bated by transactions with the social environment. It is also possible that early neurological damage may directly produce conduct disordered behavior rather than its being produced through the transaction mechanisms described by Moffitt (Pennington & Bennetto, 1993). Neuropsychological con-

ceptualizations of conduct disorder development may apply to only some conduct disordered youngsters. Refinements of theoretical concepts are needed, as is additional research that expands the populations studied and that makes use of other methods of assessing neurological functioning, such as brain imaging techniques.

ASSESSMENT

As is the case for most child and adolescent problems, assessment of conduct disordered behavior is likely to be a complex and multifaceted process. Multiple informants, including the youth, parents, other family members, teachers, and peers, are likely to be valuable sources of information. The various manifestations of conduct disordered behavior and other problem domains, such as attentional deficits, hyperactivity, impulsivity, and depression will need to be evaluated. Furthermore, given the appreciable involvement of family, peers, and school, these environments and individuals may also need to be evaluated. Below we describe those assessment procedures that address conduct and other problem behaviors and the interactions of these youngsters with others. However, it should be recognized that assessment may extend to the problems of other individuals, to measurement of others' attitudes and skills (e.g., parenting), and to ongoing life stressors.

INTERVIEWS

A general clinical interview with the parents is typically conducted, and older children and adolescents themselves can be interviewed. An interview with younger children may not be as easily conducted or be a reliable source of information; however, the opportunity to interact with the young child may be helpful to the clinician in formulating hypotheses and in establishing rapport. An interview with the entire family may also provide valuable information. In addition, an interview with the teacher or school personnel is frequently part of the assessment process and can provide important information about certain spheres of functioning. For the purposes of diagnosis, structured interviews with the youngster and parent are often conducted.

BEHAVIORAL RATING SCALES

There are a number of behavioral rating scales that assess the youngster's behavior, which are completed by adults or by the youngster. Several of these have been recommended for use with youngsters with conduct problems (McMahon & Estes, 1997). The Achenbach (1991a) instruments—Child Behavior Checklist, Youth Self-Report, and Teacher Report Form—can provide information about a broad array of problem areas, including those of an externalizing nature. Information from multiple sources can be compared, and comparisons of each informant's response to age and gender appropriate norms are possible. The Behavioral Assessment System for Children (BASC) (Reynolds & Kamphaus, 1992) is another behavioral rating scale system that allows assessment of a broad array of problems through the reports of multiple informants.

Behavioral rating scales that focus more specifically on conduct problems are also available. The Eyberg Child Behavior Inventory (ECBI) and the Sutter-Eyberg Student Behavior Inventory (SESBI) are examples (Eyberg, 1992). The ECBI is completed by parents and can be used for youngsters ages two to sixteen. The items describe conduct problems, and two scores can be obtained: the number of problems present and an intensity score based on the frequency of occurrence. There are normative data and recommended clinical cutoff points for scores on the ECBI. The SESBI is completed by teachers, is identical in format, and yields the same to scores. Although described as measures of conduct problems, the instruments do contain items sampling the range of "disruptive behavior" problems that correspond to DSM diagnoses of Oppositional Defiant Disorder and Attention Deficit Disorder, as well as Conduct Disorder. Although the majority of items represent conduct problems rather than ADHD, children who exceed the cutoff may represent a heterogeneous group of children with disruptive behavior problems (McMahon & Estes, 1997).

The Self-Report Delinquency Scale (SRD) (Elliott, Huizinga, & Ageton, 1985) is probably the most widely used youth self-report measure of conduct problems. It consists of items derived from the Uniform Crime Reports and includes index offenses (e.g., theft, aggravated assault), other delinquent behaviors, and drug use, and it is intended for use with youngsters eleven to nineteen years old. Self-report measures are less commonly used with younger children because of concern with their ability to accurately report conduct problems.

BEHAVIORAL OBSERVATIONS

Behavioral observation systems have long been a part of the assessment of conduct problems. There are a large number of systems designed for use in clinic, home, and school settings (McMahon & Estes, 1997). Some observational systems have been employed in more than one setting. Behavioral observations are viewed as desirable because of the potential bias of reports based on interviews and questionnaires.

The Behavioral Coding System developed by Forehand and his colleagues (Forehand & McMahon, 1981) and the Dyadic Parent-Child Interaction Coding System II (Eyberg et al., 1994) are two similar observational systems for assessing parent-child interactions in the clinic. Both place the parent and the child in situations that vary from free-play/child directed to adult directed activities. Various child and parent behaviors are observed and scored. Many of these focus on parental commands (antecedents) and consequences for child compliance or noncompliance. The Interpersonal Process Code (Rusby, Estes, & Dishion, 1991) is another observational system designed for clinic use that is an outgrowth of observational systems developed by Patterson and his colleagues. It was developed to encompass previous systems and to be used in a variety of settings (e.g., home, school) and with various participants (e.g., peers, teachers).

The three observational systems described here have also been used in home settings, and these and other systems have been employed in the schools, e.g., The Fast Track School Observation

Program (Conduct Problems Prevention Research Group, 1992). Observation in natural settings is desirable, since this is the setting where many of the conduct problem behaviors and interactions occur. Such use, however, for practicing clinicians is rare. The systems are complex and require extensive periods of training and the use of trained observers. The observations themselves are lengthy, and coordination with times when relevant behaviors are occurring "naturalistically" in the homes or schools represents a significant scheduling challenge.

An alternative to using trained observers in the home or other natural environments is to train adults in the child's environment to record and observe certain behaviors. An additional advantage of this approach is the opportunity to observe and record behaviors that occur at low rates (e.g., stealing or fire setting) and that would likely be missed by trained observers making occasional visits. The Parent Daily Report (PDR) (Chamberlain & Reid, 1987) is one widely used measure of this kind. During brief telephone interviews, the parent is asked whether any of the targeted behaviors occurred during the past twenty-four hours. The Daily Telephone Discipline Interview (Webster-Stratton & Spitzer, 1991) was developed as an extension to the PDR to provide more information about parental interventions surrounding child behaviors reported on the PDR.

Most of the observational systems described here are targeted for children and their parents, teachers, and peers. There are also observational systems available for coding parent-adolescent conflict, problem solving, and communication (Foster & Robin, 1997).

TREATMENT

Many different treatments have been attempted with conduct-disordered youth. Only a portion of these have received careful empirical evaluation regarding their effectiveness. Here we will briefly describe treatments that have been shown to be effective or promising (Brestan & Eyberg, 1998; Kazdin, 1997).

PARENT TRAINING

A variety of parent training programs have been implemented, and studies evaluating these interventions indicate that parent training is among the most successful approaches to reducing antisocial and aggressive behaviors in youth (Brestan & Eyberg, 1998; Kazdin, 1997). These parent training programs have a number of features in common (Kazdin, 1997).

1. Treatments are conducted primarily with the parents.
   a. The therapist teaches the parents to alter interactions with their child so as to increase prosocial behavior and to decrease deviant behavior.
   b. Young children may be brought into sessions to train both the parents and child in how to interact. Older youths may participate in negotiating and developing behavior change programs.
2. New ways of identifying, defining, and observing behavior problems are taught.
3. Social learning principles and procedures that follow from them are taught (e.g., social reinforcement, points for prosocial behavior, time out from reinforcement, loss of privileges).
4. Treatment sessions are an opportunity to see how techniques are implemented and to practice using techniques. Behavior change programs implemented in the home are reviewed.
5. The child's functioning in school is usually incorporated into treatment.
   a. Parent-managed reinforcement programs for school and school-related behavior are often part of the behavior change program.
   b. If possible, the teacher plays a role in monitoring behavior and providing consequences.

One example of parent management training comes from work on noncompliant behavior. Forehand and his colleagues developed a treatment program for noncompliant children (four to seven years old) and their families (Forehand & McMahon, 1981). Parents are taught to give direct, concise commands (alpha commands), allow the child sufficient time to comply, reward compliance with contingent attention, and apply negative contingencies to noncompliance. The effectiveness of this program has been investigated in a number of studies, and behavioral improvement has been shown to occur (McMahon & Wells, 1998). Forehand and his colleagues have also demonstrated that following treatment, parents of clinic children perceived their offspring to be as well adjusted as parents of nonclinic children perceived their offspring (Forehand, Wells, & Griest, 1980). Successful treatment of noncompliance also seems to reduce other problem behaviors, such as tantrums, aggression, and crying (Wells, Forehand, & Griest, 1980). In addition, untreated siblings increase their compliance, and it seems likely that this outcome is due, at least in part, to the mother's use of her improved skills with the untreated child (Humphreys et al., 1978). Finally, research demonstrates that training in a variety of tasks enhances generalization across a range of situations and from clinic to home (Powers & Roberts, 1995).

There are ethical issues involved in reducing noncompliance in children. Compliance is not always a positive trait, and the child's ability to say "no" to certain requests is something that seems desirable to either train or retain. In this regard, it is important to assure that parents do not expect 100 percent compliance, which is neither the norm nor a desirable quality in our society. A quiet, docile child should not be the treatment goal.

As we have seen, Patterson's conceptualization of the development of antisocial behavior evolved in the context of treating these children and their families. The importance of parenting skills in Patterson's formulation led to the development of a treatment program that focused on improving these skills (Patterson et al., 1975; Patterson et al., 1992). Patterson's program is another illustration of the social-learning approach. The program teaches parents to pinpoint problems, to observe and record behavior, to more effectively use social and nonsocial reinforcers for appropriate or prosocial behavior, and to more effectively withdraw reinforcers for undesirable behavior. Families can be introduced to these procedures by studying a programmed text (Patterson, 1975; 1976a). Each family also attends clinic and home sessions and has regular phone contact with a therapist, who helps develop interventions for particular targeted behaviors and who models desired parenting skills. Problematic behaviors in the school setting are also targeted, and interventions involve both the parents and school personnel. Active treatment is terminated when both the therapist and family believe that a sufficient number of problematic behaviors have ceased, appropriate behavior has stabilized, overall family functioning has become more positive, and the parents have become able to handle additional problems with little, if any, assistance (Patterson, Chamberlain, & Reid, 1982).

Webster-Stratton and her colleagues (1984; 1990; 1994; Webster-Stratton, Hollinsworth, & Kolpacoff, 1989) have developed a videotape/group discussion program for young children (three to eight years old) with conduct problems, including Conduct Disorder and Oppositional Defiant disorder. The program is based on many of the same social learning principles described earlier. A standard package of videotaped programs of modeled parenting skills has been developed. These videos, which contain 250 vignettes of about two minutes each, include examples of parents interacting with their children in both appropriate and inappropriate ways. They are shown to groups of parents, and following each vignette there is a therapist-led discussion of the relevant interactions. Parents are also given homework assignments that allow them to practice parenting skills at home with their children.

The treatment program has been evaluated in a number of studies in which it has been compared with waiting-list control groups and with alternative parenting interventions. Parents completing the program have rated their children as having fewer problems than have control parents and themselves as having better attitudes and more confidence regarding their parenting role. Observations in the home have also shown these parents to have better parenting skills and their children to have greater reductions in problem behavior.

These improvements were maintained at one- and three-year follow-up evaluations. Webster-Stratton (1996; Webster-Stratton & Spitzer, 1996) has also expanded the BASIC program to include enhancement of parents' interpersonal skills, the child's social problem solving skills, and the social support that the family members receive.

COGNITIVE PROBLEM-SOLVING SKILLS TRAINING

Parent training approaches focus on family aspects of conduct disordered behavior. Other treatments focus more specifically on aspects of the child's functioning. Among these interventions are those that derive from the interpersonal and social-cognitive aspects of conduct disordered behavior that were described earlier. These interventions address social-cognitive deficiencies and distortions among conduct disordered youngsters (Kazdin, 1993c; Kendall & Panichelli-Mindel, 1995). There have been a number of problem-solving skills training programs, but they share a number of features in common (Kazdin, 1997).

1. The emphasis is on the thought processes involved in the child's approach to interpersonal situations.
   a. In step-by-step approaches, the child is taught to solve interpersonal problems.
   b. The child makes statements to himself or herself that direct attention to the aspects of problems that lead to effective solutions.
2. Solutions (behaviors) that are selected are important as well.
   a. Prosocial behaviors are fostered (e.g., modeling, direct reinforcement).
3. Through games, academic activities, and stories, use is made of structured tasks to teach cognitive problem-solving skills.
   a. As treatment progresses, these skills are increasingly applied to real-life situations.
4. Therapists usually play an active role. They
   a. model cognitive processes by making verbal self-statements,
   b. apply a sequence of statements to problems,
   c. provide cues to prompt appropriate skills, and
   d. apply feedback and praise for correct skills.
5. Treatment usually combines several different procedures, including modeling and practice, role playing, and consequences for the skills displayed.

Kazdin, Siegel, and Bass (1992) compared three different interventions applied to youngsters ages seven through thirteen who were referred for severe antisocial behavior: a cognitive problem-solving skills treatment (PSST), like those described above, a parent management training (PMT) modeled after Patterson's work; and a combined PSST plus PMT condition. Both the PSST and PMT conditions led to significant improvements in functioning at home, at school, and in the community both immediately after treatment and at a one-year follow-up. The combined treatments, however, had significantly greater therapeutic effect than either of the treatments alone on the youngsters' functioning and on parental stress and functioning. In addition, the combined treatments resulted in a greater proportion of the youngsters' falling within normative levels of functioning. These findings suggest the value of interventions that address the multiple influences operating in conduct disordered youth and their families. Knowing which treatments or combinations of treatments will be effective for which youngsters and families, however, remains a considerable challenge (Kazdin, 1995b).

Problem-solving skills training has been demonstrated to be an effective intervention, and ongoing research regarding the cognitive processes involved in aggression and other conduct disordered behavior should continue to inform treatments. However, questions still remain regarding whether or what changes in cognitions are responsible for the changes in conduct problems and what other family and individual factors influence outcome. It has been suggested that problem-solving approaches should be more effective with older youngsters because of their more fully developed cognitive abilities. The effectiveness for youngsters of different ages, however, remains unclear.

FUNCTIONAL FAMILY THERAPY

In general, the kinds of interventions that have been described as successful with younger conduct disordered children, such as parent training, have been far less successful with adolescents and chronic juvenile delinquents (Kazdin, 1993c; McMahon & Wells, 1998). A treatment program for delinquents and their families, called functional family therapy (FFT), has been developed by Alexander and his colleagues (Alexander & Parsons, 1982; Morris, Alexander, & Waldron, 1988). This program integrates behavioral-social learning, cognitive-behavioral, and family systems perspectives (Alexander, Holtzworth-Munroe, & Jameson, 1994). The problem behavior of the youngster is assumed to serve a function—it is the only way that some of the interpersonal functions of the family can be met. Specific interventions drawn from the findings of parent management training discussed earlier are included. Treatment, however, focuses also on the interpersonal processes of the family system. The goals of therapy are to improve the communication skills of families; modify cognitive sets, expectations, attitudes, and affective reactions; and establish new interpretations and meanings of behavior. For example, families of delinquents have been reported to be more defensive in their communications, to be more blaming and negative in their attributions, and to show lower levels of mutual support than nondelinquent families (Kazdin, 1997). Improving family functioning in these areas is a treatment goal in FFT.

Treatment sessions focus on directly altering communication patterns in the family. Therapists employ a variety of techniques: modeling, prompting, shaping and rehearsing effective communication skills, and feedback and reinforcement for positive changes. In addition, contracts are created to establish reciprocal patterns of positive reinforcement that may have broken down or that rarely existed in these families. For example, a contract regarding a privilege for a certain family member also specifies that person's responsibilities for securing those privileges and provides bonuses for all parties for compliance with the contract.

Evidence supporting this approach has been reported (Alexander, 1973; Alexander and Parsons, 1973; Alexander et al., 1976; Alexander et al., 1989). The program has been demonstrated to improve significantly the interactions of families of status offenders who were arrested for running away or possessing alcohol. In addition to improved interactions, significantly lower rates of recidivism were also obtained six to eighteen months following treatment (Alexander & Parsons, 1973; Parsons & Alexander, 1973). Klein, Alexander, and Parsons (1977) also demonstrated a preventive impact for the treatment program. Examination of juvenile court records for siblings of initially referred delinquents indicated that siblings from this behavioral-family systems treatment had significantly lower rates of court referrals than siblings from control groups. Although this treatment has been primarily applied to families of status offenders, one report has replicated positive outcomes with families of youths who have committed more serious and repeated offenses (Barton et al., 1985).

COMMUNITY-BASED PROGRAMS

Institutionalization might be considered a traditional and perhaps obvious approach to intervention with delinquents. Reform schools, training schools, and detention centers may include some therapeutic, educational, or rehabilitative programming or may only provide custodial care. Evidence that incarceration reduces recidivism has not been encouraging (Griffin & Griffin, 1978; Mulvey et al., 1993). It is likely that persistence of appropriate behavior upon release has as much or more to do with the environment to which the youth returns as it does with the nature of institutional programming. Furthermore, placing youths in such institutions may expose them to a pervasive and sophisticated delinquent subculture in which deviant behaviors may be learned and reinforced. These concerns and the success of some community-based programs have led to attempts to deal with delinquency outside of institutional programs.

One approach has been labeled "diversion" (Lemert, 1971). The goal is to divert youthful offenders away from the juvenile justice system and to provide services for them through a variety of different agencies (for example, educational, job training). It was hoped that by providing adequate skills and avoiding stigmatization and labeling, recidivism would be reduced. There seems to be justification for minimal and community-based intervention (Mulvey et al., 1993). Given that a large number of delinquents are not destined for careers of crime, even less intensive interventions would appear to be the best strategy for first or minor offenses. However, it must be recognized that some portion of youthful offenders will require additional intervention. In such cases, community-based programs that remove the youth from the juvenile justice system seem recommended.

The examination of treatment alternatives by Davidson and his colleagues is an example of findings that support such a conclusion (Davidson & Basta, 1989). In one investigation, several different forms of intervention were provided to 213 male juvenile offenders averaging 14.2 years of age. Youths were randomly assigned to treatments that differed in content; however, all had a college student volunteer who worked with them six to eight hours per week in the community. The various treatment conditions that took place entirely outside the juvenile justice system did not differ in terms of their effectiveness and resulted in lower rates of recidivism than for a control group of youths not given treatment but routinely processed by the court. Treatment with a juvenile justice system component, however, did not result in lower recidivism than for this nontreated control group. The results of this intervention program have been replicated in other locations and with the use of other kinds of volunteers and paid staff (Davidson & Basta, 1989). The search for effective alternatives to institutionalization has led to several other approaches.

The Teaching Family Model (TFM) developed at Achievement Place is an oft-cited example of a community-based program for delinquent youth and an example of many behaviorally based (largely operant) interventions. Achievement Place is a home-style residential treatment program begun in 1967 by the faculty and students of the Department of Human Development at the University of Kansas (Fixsen, Wolf, & Phillips, 1973; Phillips, 1968). Adolescents who have legally been declared delinquent or who are dependent neglect cases live in a house with two trained teaching parents. The youths attend school during the day and also have regular work responsibilities. The academic problems, aggression, and other norm-violating behaviors exhibited by these adolescents are viewed as an expression of failures of past environments to teach appropriate behaviors. Accordingly, these deficits are corrected through modeling, practice instruction, and feedback. The program centers on a token economy in which points and praise are gained for appropriate behaviors and are lost for inappropriate behaviors. Points can be used to purchase a variety of privileges that are otherwise unavailable. If a resident meets a certain level of performance, the right to go on a merit system and thus avoid the point system may be purchased. This process is seen as providing a transition to usual sources of natural reinforcement and feedback, such as praise, status, and satisfaction. The goal is gradually to transfer a youngster who is able to perform adequately on merit to his or her natural home. Teaching-parents help the natural parents or guardians to structure a program to maintain gains made at Achievement Place.

One of the outstanding features of the TFM approach is the large quantity of research that the program has produced (Willner et al., 1978). Numerous single-subject design experiments have evaluated the components of the program, thereby suggesting cause-and-effect relationships. The effectiveness of TFM has been evaluated by both its developers and independent investigators (Kirigin et al., 1982; Weinrott, Jones, & Howard, 1982). These evaluations suggest that the TFM approach is more effective than comparison programs while the adolescents are involved in the group home setting. However, once they leave this setting, differences disappear.

Difficulties in transitions back to the youths' own families and long-term effectiveness are common in all interventions with delinquent populations. Given this consideration, the developers of TFM have suggested a "long-term supportive family model" in which specially trained foster parents would provide care for a single adolescent into early adulthood (Wolf, Braukmann, & Ramp, 1987).

There seems to be general consensus that many programs are limited in their effectiveness (cf. Borduin, 1994; Henggeler, 1994). Interventions with antisocial youth are likely to require the coop-

eration of multiple human service agencies. Often the coordination of such services is difficult to achieve, and individualizing such efforts to fit the needs of youngsters and their families is even more challenging. Recent approaches, which are known as individualized care or wraparound services, employ interdisciplinary teams to develop a plan that is both individualized and comprehensive (Borduin, 1994; Burchard & Clark, 1990). Also, the logic of early intervention and prevention is compelling, and here, too, programs that include multiple components that address the child, family, and school are most likely to be ef-

---

FAMILY NAME: Maggie _____   **DATE OF ADMISSION:** _____

STRENGTHS   **NEEDS**

Individual

STRENGTHS	NEEDS
Athletic, enjoys sports. Attractive and likeable. Average intelligence. Takes care of siblings. Antisocial behavior limited to aggression. Cares deeply for her mother and wants things to be better at home and school. She responds well to praise.	History of school and community aggression. Physically fights mother. Victim of child sexual abuse.

Family

STRENGTHS	NEEDS
Extended family lives close by and are concerned about M's behavior and home life. Gradmother and aunts willing to do "whatever it takes." Mother is seriously concerned about her drug use and M's school and home behavior. Children's basic needs are met by the mother—she is a survivor. Strong family bond.	Maternal crack cocaine dependence. Poor monitoring. High conflict, crowded living conditions. Low financial resources. Mother feels hopeless about changing her and M's behavior. Mother has minimal parenting skills. Family is socially isolated. Grandmother has cancer.

Peers

STRENGTHS	NEEDS
Prosocial peers in grandmother's neighborhood.	Aggressive and antisocial peers. Peers have little commitment to school.

School

STRENGTHS	NEEDS
Athletic programs. A counselor has a close relationship with Maggie and wants her to do well.	Limited resources. Policy of zero tolerance for threatening teachers. View behavior problems as moral flaw. Quick to expel students. Poor relationship to surrounding community. History of conflict with the family.

Neighborhood/Community

STRENGTHS	NEEDS
Several churches located in the neighborhood.	Drug infested. Criminal subculture. Minimal prosocial outlets.

FIGURE 8-11 A sample of results from an initial assessment that describes strengths and needs in the various systems considered by MST.

From Henggeler, Schoenwald, Borduin, Rowland, & Cunningham, 1998.

fective (Conduct Problems Prevention Research Group, 1992).

MULTISYSTEMIC THERAPY

Maggie is a thirteen-year old white seventh-grader who lives with her unemployed, crack-addicted mother, mother's live-in boyfriend, two sisters (ages ten and eight years), and a daughter of one of her mother's crack-addicted friends. Maggie was referred because she was physically violent at home (e.g., she was arrested several times for assaulting family members), at school (e.g., she beat a classmate with a stick and threatened to kill a teacher), and in the neighborhood (e.g., she was arrested twice for assaulting residents of her housing development). Many of Maggie's aggressive actions followed all-night binges by her mother. Maggie primarily associates with delinquent peers, was placed in a special class, and was recommended for expulsion from school. The family resides in a high crime neighborhood, and the only source of income is welfare benefits. (Adapted from Henggeler et al., 1998, p. 23)

Multisystemic therapy (MST) (Henggeler & Borduin, 1990; Henggeler et al., 1998) is a family-systems-based approach; however, the child is considered to exist in a number of systems, including family, peers, school, neighborhood, and community—a social ecology (Bronfenbrenner, 1989). MST uses treatment strategies derived from family systems therapy and from behavior therapy to treat serious juvenile offenders and their families. The approach seeks to preserve the family and to maintain the youths in their homes. MST addresses not only the family system but also skills of the offender and extrafamilial influences, such as peers, school, and neighborhood. Figure 8-11 is a sample of the results of an initial assessment regarding Maggie, which describes both strengths and needs in the various systems considered by MST. Family sessions, which are conducted in the home and community settings, are flexible and individualized for each family.

Henggeler, Melton, and Smith (1992) report on a comparison of MST to the usual services offered by a Department of Youth Services to serious juvenile offenders and their families. These youths were viewed as at imminent risk for out-of-home placement. They averaged 3.5 previous arrests, 54 percent had at least one arrest for a violent crime, and 71 percent had been incarcerated previously

for at least three weeks. The findings of this study (illustrated in Figure 8-12) indicate that MST was significantly more effective than the usual services. In addition, families receiving the MST intervention reported increased family cohesion, whereas reported cohesion decreased in the other families. Also, a composite measure showed that aggression with peers decreased for MST youths but that it remained the same for the youths receiving usual services. Several other reports by Henggeler and his colleagues suggest the usefulness of MST with a variety of populations and suggest the long-term effectiveness of this approach (Henggeler et al., 1998).

The difficulties in treating adolescents with serious and persistent conduct disorders has led some to suggest a change in the way in which conduct disorders are conceptualized. The suggestion is that the disorder be viewed as "social disability" (Wolf et al., 1987) or as analogous to a chronic physical disease such as diabetes (Kazdin, 1987; Mulvey et al., 1993). These kinds of models suggest not single and short-term treatments, but rather multiple interventions throughout the youngster's life—perhaps into early adulthood. The multidetermined nature of antisocial behavior and the potential stability of conduct disor-

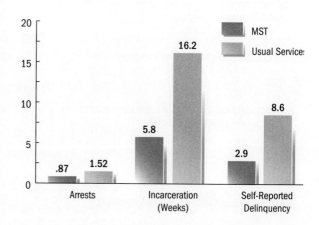

FIGURE 8-12 A comparison of multisystematic therapy (MST) to usual services for serious juvenile offenders. Adapted from Henggeler, Melton, & Smith, 1992.

dered behavior certainly suggest early, multifaceted, flexible, and ongoing interventions.

SUMMARY

■ Aggression, oppositional behavior, and other antisocial behaviors are among the most common problems among referred youngsters as well as in the general population.

■ Empirical approaches have consistently identified a syndrome of aggressive, oppositional, antisocial behaviors. This syndrome has been labeled undercontrolled, externalizing, or conduct disorder. Two narrow syndromes have been described within this broad syndrome and have been designated as aggressive behavior and delinquent behavior. Etiological and developmental differences between the two support the validity of this distinction. Other ways of distinguishing among groupings of conduct disordered behavior, such as age of onset, an overt versus covert distinction, and a further destructive-nondestructive distinction, have also been suggested.

■ DSM-IV contains a grouping of disorders that includes Oppositional Defiant Disorder (ODD) and Conduct Disorder (CD), along with Attention Deficit Hyperactivity Disorder. ODD is described as a pattern of negativistic, hostile, and defiant behavior. CD is described as a repetitive and persistent pattern of behavior that violates both the basic rights of others and societal norms. Two subtypes, childhood onset and adolescent onset, are indicated.

■ Youngsters who receive one of the preceding diagnoses are also likely to experience other difficulties. One specific issue is whether ODD is a precursor of CD. A high rate of co-occurrence of ODD/CD with ADHD is also found. ADHD appears to be a risk factor for the other two disorders. Youngsters with ODD/CD may also exhibit cognitive and academic difficulties and problems such as anxiety and depression.

■ Delinquency is largely a legal term rather than a psychological one. The term refers to a youth who has committed an index crime or a status offense.

■ The use of alcohol and illegal drugs by youngsters is a particularly widespread concern. A variety of theories, models, and risk factors have been suggested to explain such substance use. No single explanation has received clear acceptance.

■ Prevalence rates in community samples of between 6 and 10 percent for ODD and 2 and 9 percent for CD are reported. Conduct disorders are more commonly diagnosed in boys. Serious delinquent behavior is a clear societal problem. There are probably associations between rates of delinquency and variables such as social class and gender.

■ An important aspect of conduct problems is their reported stability over time. However, the issue of stability is a complex one that includes conceptualizations of stability and individual differences.

■ Conduct disordered behavior has been conceptualized in terms of developmental progressions or paths. There are a number of attributes that describe an individual's progression along a developmental path. Age of onset is probably the most mentioned aspect. An adolescent onset path is the most common, and antisocial behavior among such youngsters is less likely to persist beyond adolescence. Pathways characterized by overt, covert, and authority conflict behaviors have also been described.

■ Conduct disordered behavior likely develops through a complex interaction of influences. A variety of influences have received attention, including the learning of such behavior through imitation and the consequences that such behavior receives. Family influences also occur through degree of parental involvement and parenting practices. The work of Patterson and his colleagues has contributed to our knowledge in this area. The parents' own psychological difficulties, marital discord, and extrafamilial/community influences are also noted.

■ Peer relations both contribute to and are consequences of conduct problems. Characteristics of the youngster, such as social information-processing skills and interpersonal problem-solving skills, are also thought to contribute to the development of conduct disordered behavior. Biological influences, such as genetics and neuropsychophysiological influences, may also play a role.

■ Assessment of conduct problems is likely to be complex and multifaceted. Interviews, behavioral rating scales, and behavioral observations are among the methods employed.

■ A variety of interventions have been attempted with conduct-disordered youngsters. Parent training, which focuses on the parenting processes involved in conduct problems, is among the most successful approaches. Interventions employing cognitive problem-solving skills training focus more specifically on aspects of the youngster's functioning.

■ Functional Family Therapy integrates cognitive-behavioral and family systems approaches to work with delinquent youth and their families. Community-based programs such as the Family Teaching Model are among the approaches to working with youthful offenders. Multisystemic Therapy is a systems-based intervention that addresses the child, family, peers, school, neighborhood, and community, and that has shown some promise.

■ The persistent nature of conduct disorders in some youth suggest the need for the development of long-term, individualized, and multifaceted interventions.

CHAPTER 9

ATTENTION DEFICIT HYPERACTIVITY DISORDER

e never sits still; he's always into something.

She doesn't pay attention to what I say.

He doesn't think before he acts.

In school, she's up and out of her seat in a flash.

He's not doing well in school and is behind his peers.

These kinds of concerns, voiced by parents and teachers, are the main presenting problems for children who receive the diagnosis of Attention Deficit Hyperactivity Disorder (ADHD).

Only a few disorders of youth garner as much public interest and have been so surrounded by controversy as ADHD. Most of the general public has at least passing knowledge of the disorder, which is widely referred to as "attention deficit disorder" or "hyperactivity." These terms reflect the changing conceptualizations of the disorder. Controversy about ADHD has focused on both its nature and the pharmacological treatment that was widely introduced in the late 1960s.

HISTORICAL BACKGROUND

What we now refer to as ADHD has traveled a long and tortuous road of conceptualizations (Barkley, 1996). Important early accounts of the disorder include that of the English physician George Still, who described a group of boys with a "defect in moral control" as inattentive, impulsive, overactive, lawless, and aggressive, among other things. In the United States, a 1917–1918 encephalitis epidemic aroused interest in the individuals who suffered this brain infection and who were left with similar attributes. A comparable clinical picture was also noted in children who had suffered head injury, birth trauma, and exposure to infections and toxins.

Early conceptualizations emphasized the overactivity or motor restlessness of these children, and the terms "hyperkinesis," "hyperkinetic reaction," and "hyperkinetic syndrome" were variously applied (Barkley, 1989). Today we are inclined to use the term "hyperactivity" to refer to this excessive motor activiity.

Nevertheless, several other behavioral problems were recognized as being associated with hyperactivity, especially attention deficits and impulsivity. In time, attention deficits took center stage, and hyperactivity was downgraded in importance. This shift in conceptualization was reflected in DSM-III

(1980), which recognized attention deficit disorder with hyperactivity (ADDH) or without hyperactivity.

This was far from the end of the road, however. In DSM-III-R (1987), the disorder was relabeled Attention Deficit Hyperactivity Disorder (ADHD), and the category of attention deficit without hyperactivity was effectively dropped. Children were diagnosed on the basis of displaying eight of fourteen behaviors, which could be different mixes of inattention, hyperactivity, and impulsivity. That is, ADHD was viewed as unidimensional, so that any mix of symptoms met the criteria. Along with changing criteria, ideas about etiology shifted and included brain damage, minimal brain damage, and to a lesser extent, environmental influences.

CURRENT CLASSIFICATION AND DIAGNOSIS

A central problem in defining ADHD has been the relationship of inattention, hyperactivity, and impulsivity. Are they best viewed as part of a single dimension? As co-occurring but independent of each other? Might two of them be alike but different from the third? On the basis of factor analytic research designed to understand better the nature of ADHD, the disorder was again reconceptualized in DSM-IV (1994). Attention Deficit/Hyperactivity Disorder, as it is now called, is viewed as having two factors, inattention and hyperactivity/impulsivity. The two factors compose three subtypes: Predominantly Inattentive, Predominantly Hyperactive/Impulsive, and a Combined Type. The major symptoms for ADHD and the subtypes appear in Table 9-1. There is research support for the validity and usefulness of the DSM-IV subgrouping (Bauermeister et al., 1995; Hudziak et al., 1998; Lahey & Carlson, 1991; Lahey et al., 1994). Symptoms tend to cluster according to these types, and other characteristics also differentiate the three subgroupings. It is the combined type that most often has been described and investigated in the past.

TABLE 9–1

DSM-IV Symptoms of Attention-Deficit/Hyperactivity Disorder

A. Symptoms of Inattention

Fails to attend to details or makes careless mistakes in school work or other activities.

Has difficulty in sustaining attention.

Does not seem to listen when spoken to.

Does not follow through on instructions or duties.

Has difficulty organizing tasks and activities.

Avoids, dislikes tasks requiring sustained mental effort.

Often loses things necessary for tasks or activities.

Is distracted by extraneous stimuli.

Is forgetful in daily activities.

B. Symptoms of Hyperactivity–Impulsivity

Hyperactivity

Fidgets with hands or feet or squirms.

Leaves seat inappropriately.

Runs about or climbs inappropriately (in adolescents or adults, may only be feelings of restlessness).

Has difficulty playing quietly or in quiet activities.

Is often "on the go" as if "driven by a motor."

Talks incessantly.

Impulsivity

Blurts out answers before questions completed.

Has difficulty awaiting turn.

Interrupts or intrudes on others.

Requirements for Diagnosis

ADHD Predominantly Inattentive Type: Six or more symptoms of A

ADHD Predominantly Hyperactive-Impulsive Type: Six or more symptoms of B

ADHD Combined Type: Six or more symptoms of both A and B

Diagnosis of ADHD demands onset before age seven and the display of symptoms for at least six months. Because the criterion behaviors appear to some degree in normal children and may vary with developmental level, a diagnosis is given only when symptoms are at odds with developmental level. In addition, symptoms must be pervasive; that is, occur in at least two settings (e.g., home and school). The requirement of pervasiveness is new in DSM-IV and merits further comment.

Behavioral manifestations of ADHD depend somewhat on the settings in which they are observed. Some children appear pervasively inattentive, hyperactive, or impulsive with parents, teachers, or peers. Others appear to show disturbed behavior in only one setting and are said to show situational ADHD. Evidence exists that pervasiveness is linked to severity of the disorder and other correlates. The ICD diagnostic system has long required that symptoms be displayed pervasively; thus, DSM and ICD are now in agreement on this point. Nevertheless, concern is expressed that the requirement of pervasiveness may fail to identify cases with relatively mild symptoms (August & Garfinkel, 1993).

In the following sections, we will discuss the primary difficulties of ADHD and then examine other problems often associated with the syndrome. We use the general label Attention Deficit Hyperactivity Disorder (ADHD) to refer to youth displaying these problems.

PRIMARY CLINICAL CHARACTERISTICS

INATTENTION

Attention problems are noted in various ways by adults who come into contact with children with ADHD. Parents and teachers report that the children, compared with most of their peers, skip rapidly from one activity to another, do not pay attention to what is said to them, are easily distracted, do not concentrate, do not stick to a task, daydream, or lose things. Formal observations also show that children and adolescents with ADHD pay less attention to their work than learning disabled or normal controls (Barkley, 1998a). One baffling aspect of adults' reports is that children appear in some situations as unable to concentrate or to pay attention but in other situations as sitting for hours playing a game, drawing, or building with blocks. Thus attention can be focused and sustained when the child is interested or otherwise motivated. Inattention is a problem mostly in repetitious, boring, routine situations, such as household chores and uninspiring homework.

Although the reports of adults provide reasonably good global descriptions of ADHD, controlled research has been conducted in the attempt to elucidate some primary deficit in attention. In the laboratory, children with ADHD do less well than control children on many tasks that demand attention. Such poor cognitive performance could be due to other variables, however, such as motivation or comprehension. To isolate attention itself, researchers have manipulated attention and then examined the specific effects. Attention consists of several elements, and selective and sustained attention have especially been examined.

Selective attention is the ability to attend to relevant environmental stimuli or not to be distracted by irrelevant stimuli. Some studies indicate that the introduction of irrelevant stimuli does distract children with ADHD (Leung & Connolly, 1996). For example, boys with ADHD were more distracted from television watching by the presence of toys than were control boys (Milich & Lorch, 1994). It appears that distraction is more likely to occur when the irrelevant stimuli are novel or salient or embedded in the task at hand (Douglas, 1983). Distraction is also more likely when the tasks are boring, distasteful, or difficult. Nevertheless, there have been many accounts of distractibility being no greater than that of normal children, so that strong support for a basic deficit in selective attention has been seriously questioned by some investigators (Taylor, 1994; 1995). Moreover, attempts to alleviate ADHD by placing children in environments that restrict irrelevant stimuli do not appear effective. In some cases, irrelevant stimuli even enhance performance (van der Meere & Sergeant, 1988).

Sustained attention refers to paying attention to a task over a period of time. Off-task behavior in school and at home could reflect problems in sustained attention. In the laboratory, sustained attention often has been tested with a continuous performance test (CPT). Although several versions exist, the fundamental task is for the person to push a button to identify a target stimulus, such as a letter when it appears in a series of letters consecutively projected onto a screen (e.g., when *t* follows *r*). Errors can be made by not reacting to the target (which shows inattention or lack of vigilance) and by reacting to nontarget stimuli (which may show failed inhibition). Children with ADHD often make more of both errors and are slower than normal children and children with other diagnoses (Losier, McGrath, & Klein, 1996; Taylor, 1995). However, a true deficit in sustained attention would lead to a worsening of performance as the length of the task increases. Research does not consistently show this result, casting some doubt on the primacy of a deficiency in sustained attention (Taylor, 1995; van der Meere, Wekking, & Sergeant, 1991).

What can be made of these rather confusing findings? It appears that sustained attention is often acknowledged as a problem, whereas more doubt exists about selective attention. It is important to recognize, however, that the research has mostly been conducted with children who displayed hyperactivity and impulsivity or what DSM-IV now calls ADHD, Combined Type. The research findings have led many investigators to conclude that something other than inattention is the central impairment in this disorder.

HYPERACTIVITY AND IMPULSIVITY

Hyperactivity. Children with ADHD often are described as always on the run, restless, fidgety, and unable to sit still. These children squirm, wiggle, tap their fingers, and elbow their classmates (Greenhill, 1991; Whalen, 1989). All too often, they have minor mishaps, such as spilling drinks and knocking over objects, as well as more serious accidents that result in bodily harm. The quality of the motion often seems different from ordinary activity by being excessively energetic, haphazard, disorganized, and lacking in goals. Hyperactive children appear to have difficulty in regulating

their actions according to the wishes of others or to the demands of the particular situation.

Much of the information about activity problems comes from parent and teacher reports. More objective assessment can be made with direct observations and with small devices worn by the child (actometers, pedometers) that measure movement. These objective devices demonstrate the excessive movement of children with ADHD compared with normal controls. However, there is a good deal of individual variation and hyperactivity also depends on the situation at hand.

Situational specificity was shown in a study that used a recording device to monitor motor activity continuously for one week (Porrino et al., 1983). Hyperactive boys were more active than controls overall, but especially during reading and mathematics in school, playing on the weekends, and sleeping. Figure 9-1 shows some of the results. In general, motor excess and restlessness are more likely in sedentary or highly structured situations, such as sitting in school and church, than in relaxed settings with fewer external demands (Greenhill, 1991).

Impulsivity. The essence of impulsivity is a deficiency in inhibiting behavior, which appears as "acting without thinking." The child may jump in and try to solve a problem before figuring out the first step, heedlessly engage in dangerous behaviors, cut in line in front of others, or take shortcuts when performing a task. Given a choice of a small immediate reward or waiting for a more substantial reward, the reward at hand is often preferred. Games that require patience or restraint are not well negotiated and the child may also interrupt others or blurt out socially inappropriate or hurtful verbalizations. In short, there is an inability to hold back, inhibit, and control behavior. This kind of behavior, reported by parents and teachers and seen in objective observations, often leads others to judge the child as careless, irresponsible, immature, lazy, or rude (Barkley, 1998a).

In the laboratory, impulsivity has been assessed in different ways that indicate deficits in ADHD. A commonly used task is the Matching Familiar Fig-

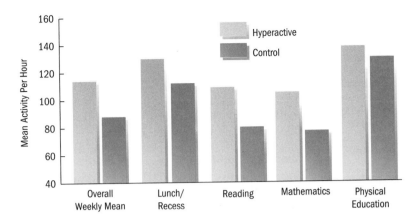

FIGURE 9–1 Activity scores over four days for twelve hyperactive and twelve control children. There were significant group differences in overall activity and during reading and mathematics.

Adapted from Porrino, Rapoport, Behar, Sceery, Ismond, & Bunney, 1983.

ures Test (MFFT). Children are presented with a standard picture and six additional ones, all but one of which vary slightly from the standard. Children are asked to select the picture that matches the standard. Relatively fast selection and errors in matching are taken as indicators of impulsivity. These indicators, and especially errors in matching, can discriminate ADHD from normal children, although not unfailingly (Whalen, 1989).

Another popular task is referred to as the Stop—Signal task (Schachar & Logan, 1990). An *X* or *O* is presented on a screen, and the child is told to press one of two buttons that correspond to the letters as they come on the screen. Button presses are to be withheld when a special signal also comes on so that the child must sometimes rapidly inhibit (stop) the response. Deficits on the Stop—Signal task have been shown in several studies with ADHD children (Oosterlaan, Logan, & Sergeant, 1998). This finding, in conjunction with the results of other research, makes clear that inhibition of motor responses is an important aspect of attention deficit hyperactivity disorder.

CASE DESCRIPTION OF ADHD, COMBINED TYPE

Although children diagnosed as ADHD are heterogeneous with regard to symptoms, the most frequently seen type is the combination of inattention, hyperactivity, and impulsiveness. The following case description illustrates the combined type of ADHD shown in a child of almost seven years of age.

Jimmy was not seen as a "bad" child by his parents; he was not ill tempered, oppositional, or aggressive. But he was in constant motion, and often wandered off, sometimes getting into dangerous situations such as running into the road without looking and putting keys in an electric socket. Jimmy frequently did not follow through on his parents' requests, although this did not appear to be deliberate. Rather it seemed that Jimmy got sidetracked by things he found more interesting. He had constantly to be reminded to stay on task. His parents adopted an active style of dealing with him—monitoring him, reminding him, using immediate reinforcement and punishment.

When Jimmy was enrolled in preschool, his inattentive, overactive, and impulsive behaviors led his parents to withdraw him from one program and his being asked to leave a second program. Among the difficulties were talking out of turn, dropping out of group activities, distracting others, and engaging in too much imaginative play. Similar kinds of behaviors were reported in kindergarten, where he had problems focusing attention, being too active, and being unable to work independently. An evaluation at that time showed Jimmy to have high average intelligence but achieving at somewhat lower levels.

By first grade, Jimmy's impulsivity began to interfere with his social relationships. He was described as immature and silly. His peers complained of his bothering them, grabbing them, and pulling them, and although Jimmy was friendly he was unable to maintain friendships. His behavior, more acceptable at early ages, was no longer accepted by peers. Teachers too had complaints. The coach noted an inability to participate in organized sports and that Jimmy was off-task and silly. In the classroom he failed to follow instructions, often did not complete work in time, and disrupted others by constant activity and noise making. The teacher used behavior modification with minimal success to help him stay on task.

A subsequent evaluation indicated that Jimmy was above average in intelligence, with deficits in sustained attention on a continuous performance test, and with a history of chronic and pervasive inattention and hyperactivity-impulsivity. These problems impaired his social relationships and his academic work. No other psychiatric disorder was apparent. (Paraphrased from Hathaway, Dooling-Litfin, & Edwards, 1998, pp. 313–316)

This description of Jimmy's behavior shows not only the primary characteristics of ADHD but also hints at how the disorder more broadly affects functioning.

ASSOCIATED CHARACTERISTICS

In addition to the core problems of ADHD, youth with the disorder are reported to experience more than their share of difficulties in diverse areas of functioning. These characteristics are of considerable clinical and theoretical interest.

INTELLIGENCE, LEARNING DISABILITIES, ACADEMIC PERFORMANCE

Intelligence and learning disabilities. As a group, children with ADHD perform slightly lower on general intelligence tests than normal control subjects and their own normal siblings (Anastopoulos & Barkley, 1992; Barkley, 1998a). Intellectual impairment has been linked to hyperactivity in children as young as three years of age (Sonuga-Barke et al., 1994). However, many children fall into the normal range, and the entire range of intelligence is found, including giftedness (August & Garfinkel, 1989; Schachar, 1991). It is unclear whether ADHD interferes with test taking behav-

ior, whether it directly interferes with intellectual functioning, or whether only subgroups of ADHD children manifest lowered intelligence. However, it is established that children with ADHD are at risk for specific learning disabilities (LD). They have impairments in reading, mathematics, spelling, and other academic areas, which are not due to lowered general intelligence.

Academic problems. Academic failure is striking among youth with ADHD. It is evidenced by achievement test scores, school grades, failure to get promoted in school, and placement in special education classes (Anastopoulos & Barkley, 1992; Dulcan, 1989). Children with ADHD often do not appear to achieve what they seem capable of learning. As many as 30 percent may repeat a grade at school, 30 percent to 40 percent may experience at least one special education placement, and as many as 56 percent may need academic tutoring (Barkley, 1998a). Moreover, from 10 percent to 35 percent may fail to graduate high school. Academic problems may be obvious in the first few years of school (Lahey et al., 1998). This general picture has been shown in several countries in addition to the United States. For the majority of children with ADHD, the classroom is characterized by requirements that are not readily met.

EXECUTIVE FUNCTIONS

Various basic cognitive deficits are inconsistently associated with ADHD (e.g., in verbal memory and visual-spatial abilities). There is better evidence for deficits in executive functions (Pennington & Ozonoff, 1996; Tannock, 1998) that involve planning and organizing actions, inhibiting responses, mentally representing a task, switching strategies, and self-regulation. Many different kinds of tasks are used in evaluating executive functions, including the Matching Familiar Figures Test and the Stop—Signal test. Tasks that require the child to inhibit a response are especially affected in ADHD. This finding relates to what we have already seen: Children with ADHD are impulsive and have difficulty in holding back and regulating their actions.

Children diagnosed with ADHD display hyperactivity, impulsivity, and a level of intensity that can be disagreeable to others.

(Monmeyer/Kopstein)

SOCIAL AND CONDUCT PROBLEMS

Social difficulties are reported in high percentages of cases of ADHD. Such troublesome behavior may lead adults to seek professional help for the child even more than may the primary problems of the disorder. How do many children with ADHD actually behave that so upsets others? Consider the following (Whalen & Henker 1985; 1998).

Children with ADHD have high social impact. They are talkative and socially busy; they often initiate social exchanges. They tend to be louder, faster, and more forceful than peers. Their vigor, intensity, and emotionality is out of keeping with the social situation and the needs of others.

Their behavior is often bothersome, intractable, disruptive, noncompliant, and disagreeable. Annoying actions may seem unintentional, and the child may even desire to be altruistic—as in the case of a ten-year-old who, in trying to help a man in a wheelchair while at the same time balancing a carton of milk, succeeded in dribbling more and more milk on the man. Such an isolated incident would not in itself be disastrous, but children with ADHD all too often get into "trouble" and disrupt the normal flow of social interaction. A subset of the children are highly aggressive.

At least in some situations, the basis of social problems does not appear to be lack of understanding of the situation. The children are able to think through situations and know what is appropriate. Rather, they are unable to enact the proper behavior, especially when excited or provoked. There is also evidence that they sometimes have social goals that could be expected to create problems. For example, they may prefer fun and trouble even at the expense of breaking rules (Melnick & Hinshaw, 1996).

Peers and teachers. Given this profile of social behaviors, it is not surprising that children with ADHD have trouble making and keeping friends and are often judged negatively. Other youngsters view many of them as troublesome, noisy, and unhappy, and they tend to dislike and reject them (Flicek, 1992). When working with ADHD children, peers tend to rapidly become directive and controlling. Rejection and dislike apply mostly to the children who are impulsive and hyperactive, whereas children with only attention problems tend to be ignored or neglected (Hinshaw, 1998).

Teacher reaction to ADHD is similarly problematic. For example, in one study, teachers of young children associated all types of ADHD with lowered prosocial and cooperative behaviors, and hyperactivity/impulsivity with disruptive and less self-controlled behavior in young children (Lahey et al., 1998). Teachers also tend to be more directive and controlling with children with ADHD.

Family relationships. As might be expected, ADHD also takes a toll on family well-being and interaction, with parents being excessively directive and intrusive (Barkley, 1998a; Hechtman, 1991). Mothers are particularly negative, quarrelsome, and unrewarding, especially with sons. There is also good evidence for the following:

- Negative mother-child interactions occur as early as the child's preschool years and may be especially strong at that time.

- Conflicts are strongly associated with the child's being oppositional.

- Negative interactions appear to stem largely from the child's behavior and then, at least with older children, become reciprocal.

- Father-child interactions are less problematic but still affected and sibling-child interactions are characterized by high conflict.

Broader indices of family malfunctioning are also associated with ADHD. They include excessive parenting stress; lowered sense of parenting competence; decreased contact with the extended family; increased alcohol use; and increased marital conflict, separation and divorce (Barkley, 1998a). Again, this profile is especially associated with the child's being oppositional or displaying conduct problems. Although conflicted parent-child interaction may often have a basis in the child's behavior, parental characteristics cannot be completely discounted as a cause of family dysfunction. As we will see, the parents themselves are at genetic risk for a variety of problems, including the kinds of behaviors displayed by their children. In addition, of course, family members influence each other in complex ways.

ACCIDENTS AND INJURY

Compared with control groups, children with ADHD suffer more accidental injury. For example, it was found that 7 percent suffered an accidental poisoning and 23 percent had bone fractures, compared with 3 percent and 15 percent in controls (Szartmari et al., 1989). Among individuals who experience accidents such as bicycle misfortunes, a greater number than would be expected appear to be hyperactive, impulsive, or defiant. Older youth with ADHD may be at greater risk for automobile accidents and for driving offenses such as speeding. Although it appears reasonable that inattention, hyperactivity, and impulsivity could account for heightened accident rates, aggressiveness that can co-occur with ADHD may also play a role.

ADAPTIVE FUNCTIONING

In recent years, some effort has been made to evaluate ADHD in terms of general adaptiveness (Hinshaw, 1998). Despite generally normal intelligence, deficits have been found. Deficiencies in self-care and independence are sometimes at the level that would be expected with much greater cognitive impairment. Thus many of the children seem capable of more mature behavior, but they do not enact it. Greater monitoring by parents and other adults is required than what might otherwise be anticipated.

DSM-IV SUBTYPES OF ADHD

We have seen that DSM-IV recognizes three subtypes of ADHD: predominantly inattentive (PI), predominantly hyperactive/impulsive (HI), and the combination of these types (ADHD-C). So far there is relatively little research on HI. It has been suggested, but not established, that HI may appear earlier, and at least in some cases, it may develop into ADHD-C.

Children displaying only attention deficits have been of interest. Indeed, the category of Attention Deficit Disorder without Hyperactivity that was included in the DSM-III is essentially again recognized with the new name of ADHD, Predominantly Inattentive Type. Renewed interest is based on stronger evidence that it is a distinct and valid subgroup.

For subtypes of a disorder to be valid, they must be different in symptoms and also in other important ways. Children with predominantly attention problems are characterized as sluggish, lethargic, daydreamy, more socially withdrawn, and more anxious (Barkley, 1998a). This is a very different clinical picture than that of the restless, on-the-go, disruptive, and often noncompliant behaviors of the hyperactive/impulsive child. The contrast is captured in the following portrayal of Tim. For comparison we recommend that you review the case description of Jimmy that appears on p. 225.

Tim was a quiet, somewhat introverted child who easily faded into the crowd. His early development was unremarkable, and he was not a behavior problem.

In elementary school, Tim's behavior and academic performance were adequate. But he did not volunteer information, often appeared in a daze, and often did not catch what teachers said when they called upon him. He could read but had difficulty staying with a train of thought, which created comprehension problems. Approaching third grade, Tim began to have increased difficulties in school, including completing his work on time, but he was not found eligible for special services. Teachers commented on his daydreaming, attentional lapses, poor focusing, and being "spacy." His grades became less consistent, ranging from Bs to Ds. Tim's attentional problems and poor study habits took a larger toll in high school, and academic failures resulted in a transfer to vocational education.

Despite academic problems, Tim made and kept friends, although he was reserved and indifferent to organized recreational activities. His academic performance was a source of strain and conflict with his mother, who reported that Tim was often irritable, talked back, and blamed others for his mistakes. He was, however, compliant in other ways. Based on assessment when he was almost eighteen years of age, Tim was described as presumably of average intelligence, with a chronic history of inattentiveness, distractibility, and underachievement. (Paraphrased from Hathaway, Dooling-Litfin, & Edwards, 1998, pp. 329–330)

There seems little doubt that the behavioral profile of PI stands out relative to other types of ADHD. Progress is being made in illustrating additional ways in which it is different from hyperactivity/impulsivity. It has been suggested that PI is associated with slower information processing, greater distractibility, more academic problems, and more anxiety and depression (Faraone et al., 1998). It also appears that children with predominantly inattentive symptoms have fewer behavior problems than children with the combined type of ADHD, especially fewer conduct problems. It is still difficult to draw firm conclusions from the findings, however, and further studies are needed. Nevertheless, PI appears to be a valid subtype of ADHD. At the same time, the distinctiveness of PI suggests to some that it might better be considered a unique disorder, not a subtype of ADHD at all. Barkley (1998a) argues in just this way and suggests that central to PI are deficits in selective attention and slow cognitive processing. In contrast, the basic deficit in hyperactivity/impulsiveness is viewed as an inability to inhibit behavior. Further research is clearly needed on this issue.

CONCEPTUALIZATIONS OF ADHD

Despite an enormous amount of interest and investigation, ADHD is still somewhat of an enigma. Whereas there is general agreement about the primary difficulties of the disorder, there is less consensus about how to conceptualize them. Several theories have proposed specific basic deficits in ADHD. These theories tend to focus on youth who display hyperactivity/impulsivity, not solely inattention. Recent conceptualizations can be categorized as focusing on deficits in motivation or self-regulation and inhibition.

MOTIVATIONAL DEFICITS

Motivational theories emphasize that children with ADHD require especially strong or salient reinforcers. These children have been shown to do poorly when there are partial schedules of reinforcement and when reinforcers are scarce in tedious situations. They also prefer immediate small reward to delayed larger reward. It has been suggested that ADHD involves lowered sensitivity to reinforcement, so that rewards must be increased or made more salient in some way to control the child's behavior (Barkley, 1990). Assuming this to be the case, it can be reasoned that weak or inconsistent reinforcement could be the basis of the child's failure to pay attention, persist on tasks, or comply with others' requests or directives.

Sonuga-Barke (1994) has analyzed the child's heightened tendency for immediate reinforcement. He suggests that motivation regarding delay might explain many behaviors that characterize ADHD. According to this analysis, the child has an aversion to delay and thus acts rapidly to avoid delay in specific situations. An impulsive style of behaving thereby is adopted.

Although there are data showing that children with ADHD may act somewhat differently from normal youth with regard to reinforcement, the data are inconsistent (Barkley, 1998a). In testing boys with ADHD on a variety of tasks, Aman, Roberts, & Pennington (1998) argued that motivational deficits were unlikely. Although the children had difficulty on some tasks, they did very well on others, a finding that argues against a general motivational problem. In addition, the boys expressed disappointment when they performed poorly and often corrected themselves when the task allowed for correction. This anecdotal interpretation does not prove the lack of a motivational deficit, of course, but other conceptualizations of ADHD behaviors are being given more weight.

DEFICITS IN SELF-REGULATION AND INHIBITION

Among the most widely cited conceptualizations of ADHD is Douglas's (1988) theory of self-regulation (Whalen & Henker, 1998). Douglas used this broad concept, which encompasses high-order information processing, to explain facets of the hyperactivity, impulsivity, and inattention of ADHD.

She proposed that central to self-regulation are deficits in inhibition, problems in modulating arousal, and atypical responses to the consequences of behavior. These aspects of behavior appear in many accounts of ADHD. Of them, deficits in response inhibition has moved to the forefront in explanations of ADHD. We will look at Quay's (1997) and at Barkley's (1998a) theories of inhibition.

Quay based his conceptualization on Gray's neurobiological model of brain functioning (Oosterlaan et al., 1998). This model proposes two brain system that work in opposition to each other. The Behavioral Inhibition System is related to anxiety and tends to inhibit behavior in situations that are novel, fear eliciting, or characterized by punishment or nonreward (see p. 209). The Behavioral Activation System is sensitive to rewards, and activates responding in the presence of reinforcement. Quay has hypothesized that the Behavioral Inhibition System is underactive in ADHD, so that inhibition is deficient.

Barkley's (1998a) conceptualization broadly links behavioral inhibition to executive functions and self-regulation. It applies only to cases in which hyperactivity/impulsivity are observed. A schema of the model is shown in Figure 9-2.

Behavioral inhibition is central in this model in that it is critical to the performance of other executive functions. These other executive functions, in turn, influence the motor control of behavior. Behavioral inhibition consists of three abilities. First is the ability to inhibit likely responses from occurring in the situation; second is the ability to inhibit ongoing responses. These two inhibitory functions assure a span of time during which the executive functions can be employed for self-regulation. The third inhibitory ability then comes into play, which is the ability to protect the executive functions against interference from other events so that they can operate. In these ways, behavioral inhibition facilitates the workings of the executive functions.

Barkley proposes four executive functions, each of which has several elements. They are briefly noted as follows:

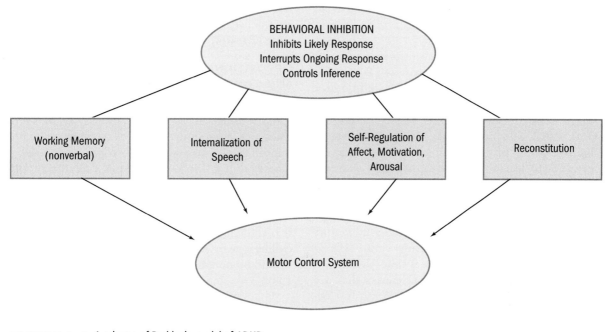

FIGURE 9–2 A schema of Barkley's model of ADHD.

■ Working memory allows information to be held in mind so that it may be considered.

■ Internalization of speech facilitates mental reflection on rules and instructions to guide behavior.

■ Self-regulation of affect and motivation allows control of the emotions and motivations, and makes it possible for them to be redirected.

■ Reconstitution permits analysis and synthesis of experiences and creative thinking.

These executive functions provide the means for the individual to self-regulate his or her behavior. When inhibition is disordered, self-regulation is adversely affected. On the basis of evidence about brain functioning, Barkley proposes that a disturbance in the frontal areas of the brain is responsible for inhibitory abnormality. This elaborate theory requires substantiation and potentially can serve as a framework for further understanding of ADHD.

ADHD AND CO-OCCURRING DISORDERS

A striking fact about ADHD is the degree to which it coexists with other diagnosable behavioral disorders. Perhaps half of children with ADHD also have another behavioral disturbance. Rates of co-occurrence do vary considerably depending on the specific disorders, criteria for diagnosis, samples selected, and other factors. Unsurprisngly, co-occurrence is higher in clinic than population samples and is related to greater impairment (Whalen & Henker, 1998).

LEARNING DISABILITIES

Co-occurrence of ADHD and LD is widely reported, although the rates vary considerably (Faraone, Biederman, & Kiely, 1996). In epidemiological studies, a range of 9 percent to 11 percent has been reported; in clinic populations, the range is much higher, perhaps 20 percent to 50 percent (Anastopoulos & Barkley, 1992; Robins, 1992).

From a clinical point of view, it is important to know whether early ADHD leads to LD, or vice versa, since such knowledge could lead to better prevention or intervention. In fact, several links are possible (McGee & Share, 1988; Pennington et al., 1993; Stevenson et al., 1993). As shown in Figure 9-3, the primary deficits of ADHD may interfere with learning to the degree that warrants diagnosis of LD. Or learning difficulties may create an inattentive, impulsive behavioral style that is diagnosed as ADHD. Alternatively, perhaps some common biological and/or environmental factors simultaneously but independently cause ADHD and LD. Another possible link is that ADHD and learning disabilities have distinct causes that are correlated with each other. The relationship between these disorders could also be reciprocal in that they build on each other. As helpful as it

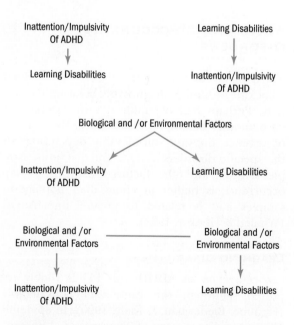

FIGURE 9–3 Possible links between ADHD and learning disabilities.

would be to understand the developmental pathways between ADHD and LD, present data are unclear (Barkley, 1998a).

OPPOSITIONAL DEFIANT DISORDER AND CONDUCT DISORDER

Children with ADHD frequently have difficulty in social interaction, as we have already recognized. They are frequently reported as noncompliant, oppositional, annoying, and argumentative—behaviors that fall into the DSM-IV category of Oppositional Defiant Disorder (ODD). Furthermore, ODD may lead to Conduct Disorder (CD), which involves aggression, deceit, and violations of rules. It is estimated that between 35 and 70 percent of children with ADHD develop ODD and between 30 and 50 percent develop CD (Johnston & Ohan, 1999).

The similarity of ADHD, ODD, and CD is reflected in their being grouped together in DSM-IV as "attention-deficit and disruptive behavior disorders." Given this similarity and their high co-occurrence, it is reasonable to ask, Are these disorders actually only one common disorder? Researchers have considered this issue and answered "no." Epidemiological and clinic studies in different countries indicate that the disorders have distinct features (e.g., Fergusson, Horwood, & Lloyd, 1991; Leung et al., 1996; Pillow et al., 1998). ADHD generally is more strongly associated with cognitive impairment and neurodevelopmental abnormalities. Conduct problems are more strongly related to adverse family factors and psychosocial disadvantage.

Furthermore, important differences exist between children having only ADHD, only oppositional/conduct problems, and the combination of these. Children displaying the combination show greater levels of aggression, lying, cheating, and stealing (Barkley, 1998a; Jensen, Martin, & Cantwell, 1997). They more often believe that others have hostile intent towards them, and they are more rejected by peers. They may also have lower IQs and more learning disabilities, although these effects are not always found. Overall, though, children who display both sets of problems appear more disturbed, are more likely to be pervasively

CO-OCCURRING DISORDERS AND RISK FOR SMOKING

That children with ADHD and co-occurring disorders are at greater developmental risk than youth with ADHD alone is shown in many specific findings. Consider the study by Milberger (1997) and her colleagues in which the association between ADHD and cigarette smoking was examined in a follow-up assessment of a large sample of six- to seventeen-year-old boys. (The sample excluded youth from the lowest social class.) The frequency of smoking was determined by self-report from the older boys and from mother report for the younger boys. Smoking was defined for younger boys as any amount of smoking every day, providing that the duration was at least one month. For older participants, smoking was defined as one pack or more daily at least four times a week.

According to these definitions, 19 percent of the ADHD participants were smokers compared with 10 percent of the non-ADHD comparison group. Adolescents with ADHD also began to smoke at earlier ages. Of those who smoked, 25 percent began before age fifteen, and about 70 percent were smoking by the time they reached age seventeen. In the comparison group, the comparable figures were 9 percent before age fifteen and 23 percent by age 17.

The investigators then examined the data for ADHD participants in terms of co-occurring conduct, mood, and anxiety disorders. As Figure 9-4 indicates, rates of smoking increased with the number of co-occurring disorders. Higher rates occurred in all groups of ADHD plus a co-occurring disorder, and it was significantly higher in the ADHD plus conduct disorder group.

The medical risks of smoking are, of course, well established. Cigarette smoking is also gener-

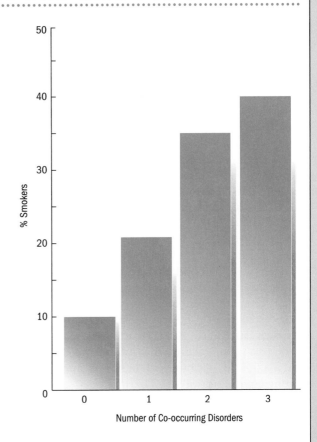

FIGURE 9–4 Relationship between number of co-occurring disorders and cigarette smoking in youth with ADHD.
Adapted from Milberger, Biederman, Faraone, Chen, & Jones, 1997.

ally associated with drug abuse and in this study, the odds of drug abuse were five times greater in smokers than in nonsmokers.

hyperactive, and are more likely to have continuing problems (McArdle, O'Brien, & Kolvin, 1995). The combination of ADHD and other disruptive behaviors is generally more strongly related to parental antisocial behavior, marital conflict, maternal stress, and negative adolescent-parent communication and conflict (e.g., Barkley, Anastopoulos, et al., 1992). Knowing whether a child with ADHD also has conduct problems tells us much about risks to the child. The several differences between ADHD with and without conduct problems have led some investigators to suggest that it may be valid to view the combined disorder as a subcategory of ADHD (Jensen, et al., 1997).

As has been previously noted (p. 187), questions have been raised about the causal link between ADHD and conduct/oppositional problems. It appears that the hyperactivity and impulsivity of ADHD precede and predict conduct disorder symptoms but that the opposite is not true (Loeber et al., 1995). The appearance of ADHD prior to conduct disorder might be expected simply because a criterion for ADHD demands impairment before age seven and some manifestations of conduct problems are unlikely at an early age. Early ADHD symptoms may affect child-parent interactions that in turn put the child on a path to oppositional behavior and subsequent conduct disorder. There is also some evidence that genes that influence hyperactivity also influence conduct problems in young children (Silberg et al., 1996). It appears, then, that these coexisting problems might be linked in several ways and through complex pathways.

ANXIETY AND MOOD DISORDERS

Relatively little is known about ADHD and the internalizing disorders. However, about 25 percent of youth with ADHD also have anxiety disorders (Barkley, 1998a; Jensen et al., 1997). Along with the disruptions of ADHD, they experience the fears, worries, and other discomforts of anxiety. These children appear somewhat less hyperactive and impulsive than ordinarily found in ADHD, and they may display fewer conduct problems. The co-occurrence of ADHD and depression is also found, with perhaps somewhat smaller rates than for anxiety disorders (e.g., Biederman et al., 1996).

As with other disorders that coexist with ADHD, the reasons for the association are unclear. Family stress and adversity are related to the ADHD child having anxiety or depression. In addition, a child's risk for one of the disorders is related to risk among family for the other disorder. This family pattern suggests that some connection between the disorders "runs in the family," but it does not clarify the connection.

EPIDEMIOLOGY

The prevalence of attention-deficit hyperactivity disorder is frequently estimated at about 3 to 5 percent of the school-age population (APA, 1994). This figure is based on clinic cases. When parents and teachers provide data in population studies, prevalence is variable and reaches as high as 20 percent (August & Garfinkel, 1989; Taylor, 1994). What accounts for this discrepancy? Population studies are typically based solely on parents' or teachers' completing rating scales, whereas clinic cases use additional criteria, such as age of symptom appearance and pervasiveness of symptoms.

Age is related to prevalence in that there appears to be a decline from childhood to adolescence, especially for boys (Schaughency et al., 1994).

More boys than girls consistently receive the diagnosis of ADHD, with the ratio of perhaps four to nine boys to one girl (APA, 1994). Community-based studies indicate a smaller gender ratio, making the degree of gender differences questionable (Achenbach et al., 1995a; Taylor, 1994). Any gender difference may partly be due to a referral bias. ADHD in girls is at times described as different from ADHD in boys, for example, as involving less overall hyperactivity and, in clinic samples, more impaired intellectual functioning (Gaub & Carlson, 1997). Further study is needed in this area because gender differences may not be substantial (Sharp et al., 1999).

The relationship of prevalence and social class is unclear. We know that ADHD appears in all social classes and higher rates are sometimes associated with low social class or psychosocial adversity (e.g., Szatmari 1992). Less definitive is whether the latter finding can be explained by other factors, such as social class differences in conduct disturbance (Barkley, 1998a).

Cross-cultural prevalence data are particularly interesting. To begin with, the gender difference and ADHD's association with learning and conduct problems as observed in the United States are reported in other countries (Whelan & Henker, 1998). Quite striking, however, is the variation in overall prevalence. Differing clinical practices undoubtedly account partly for this finding (Taylor, 1994). For example, the United Kingdom, which has used more stringent criteria for diagnosing ADHD than the United States, reports lower prevalence. When standard questionnaire ratings of behavior are employed, however, a difference is not found. Nevertheless, differing cultural standards might also influence rates of prevalence. Ratings in the United Kingdom and China showed that almost three times as many Chinese boys were identified. On closer examination, it was revealed that the Chinese boys were actually more attentive and less active than the U.K. boys. Consider further a study in which clinicians from China, Indonesia, Japan, and the United States were asked to rate the behaviors of boys presented in video vignettes. Ratings of hyperactivity and disruptive behaviors were higher for the Chinese and Indonesian than for the Japanese and U.S. mental health workers (Tao, 1992). These findings suggest that cultural expectations and values play a role in interpreting what is "abnormal."

ETIOLOGY

The search for causes of ADHD implicates several variables, many of which are biological or are thought to affect biological functioning. As was noted in the beginning of this chapter, actual brain damage or injury was once considered the primary cause of hyperactivity. When it became evident that brain damage could not be identified in most children who showed such difficulty, it was assumed that some undetectable "minimal brain dysfunction" existed. By the late 1950s and early 1960s, the need for better empirical evidence was recognized. Theories of brain dysfunction subsequently became more closely tied to empirical evidence.

Of course, even if one assumes abnormalities of the brain, the question of what causes brain dysfunction remains. In a small percentage of cases, perhaps 5 percent, brain damage from vehicle accidents, falls, and other trauma is related to symptoms of ADHD (Barkley, 1998a; Max et al., 1998). But what explains the majority of cases? Is the cause genetic, or is it due to disease, poor diet, environmental teratogens? What role does the psychosocial environment play? As we examine etiology, we will see that all these and other questions have been posed.

BRAIN STRUCTURE AND ACTIVITY

Various parts of the brain have been hypothesized as the site of dysfunction in ADHD, but most interest has focused on the frontal lobes and the related striatal areas (Semrud-Clikeman et al., 1994). Damage to the frontal lobe has long been associated with the symptoms found in ADHD. Of importance is that the frontal areas are also thought to be involved in attention, executive functions, and motor functions. Figure 9-5 depicts the brain, with a hemisphere partly cut away to allow a view of the inner striatal midbrain area. The prefrontal lobe region that controls motion and behavior more generally is linked to the underlying striatal structures.

Various measures point to brain abnormalities in ADHD. Although obvious structural damage is usually not evident, more subtle anomalies have emerged. For example, the corpus callosum (fibers by which the two hemispheres communicate with each other) and the cerebellum (involved in motor coordination and certain kinds of memory) are sometimes smaller than average (Tannock, 1998). However, the most consistent and telling abnormality is the smaller than average size of the right frontal area, the caudate nucleus,

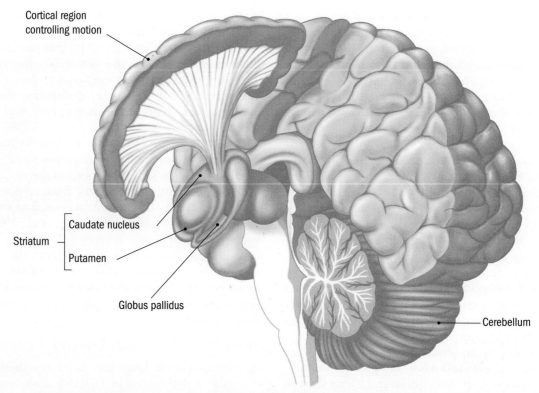

Cortical region
controlling motion

Caudate nucleus

Striatum

Putamen

Globus pallidus

Cerebellum

FIGURE 9–5 Drawing of the brain indicating some of the hemisphere structures implicated in ADHD.
Adapted from Youdin and Riederer, 1997.

and the globus pallidus (Barkley, 1998a; Tannock, 1998). In some cases, these areas are equal in size on both sides of the brain, in contrast to the normal brain, which is asymmetrical, the right side being somewhat larger than the left. Moreover, abnormality of these brain areas is associated with poor response inhibition in children with ADHD (Casey et al., 1997).

Abnormal functioning of the frontal-striatal areas also has been found. Brain scans show that children with ADHD have decreased blood flow and decreased glucose utilization, which are signs of underactivity. This finding extends to parents of ADHD children who themselves displayed symptoms of hyperactivity: They too showed lowered metabolism in the frontal area (Hechtman, 1991; Taylor, 1994; Zametkin & Rapoport, 1986).

In addition, children with hyperactivity show abnormal electrophysiological responding (Hecht-

man, 1991; Taylor, 1994). Measures of electrical activity such as heart rate and skin conductance sometimes indicate underarousal (Barkley, 1998a). A substantial minority of children have abnormal EEGs, although these anomalies vary and are difficult to interpret. In addition, electrical responses to specific events (evoked response potentials) do give some evidence for underreaction to stimuli. The findings implicate the prefrontal area of the brain and also attention and inhibition.

Another focus of research is the biochemistry of the brain. Most emphasis has been given to norepinephrine, dopamine, and serotonin (Hechtman, 1991; Taylor, 1994). One approach has examined levels of neurotransmitters whereas another approach has examined the behavioral effects of drugs known to influence the relevant neurotransmitters. Although consistent differences between ADHD children and controls have not been found on many measures, the best evidence implicates dopamine and norepinephrine. These neurotransmitters are considered important in the functioning of the frontal-striatal and related areas of the brain (Anastopoulos & Barkley, 1992). It has been suggested that dopamine, norepinephrine, and epinephrine all play an intricate role in ADHD, which is hypothesized to involve the frontal and parietal lobes and several other brain structures (Pliszka, McCracken, & Maas, 1996). Although this proposal requires testing, it would not be surprising to find complex relationships among several neurotransmitters and brain structures.

What can be concluded from investigations of the brain? First, we must note that research findings are not always consistent. Second, abnormalities have been shown in the frontal-striatal areas, which are involved in functions that seem deficient in ADHD. Third, other brain areas are likely involved; indeed, we have noted abnormalities of the corpus collosum and cerebellum and a hypothesized role for the parietal lobes. Fourth, underarousal of the brain is implicated. Fifth, much effort is still needed to understand what brain network underlies ADHD, how brain functioning has gone awry, and what has caused the malfunctioning.

GENETIC FACTORS

It is not unusual for a parent with a hyperactive youngster to come into a clinic expressing the belief that the child inherited hyperactivity from his father or perhaps from some other relative. Is such an impression accurate? It may well be, because there is clear evidence for genetic transmission.

For many years, numerous studies have shown that the families of children with ADHD have higher rates of psychopathology, including ADHD, than would be expected (Barkley, 1998a; Tannock, 1998). The more recent and higher-quality research has consistently found higher rates of ADHD in first-degree family members of male probands and has extended the findings to girls with ADHD, second-degree relatives, and adult probands with ADHD. Between 10 percent to 35 percent of first-degree family members are

likely to have ADHD, and children of parents with ADHD have a high risk of the disorder.

Twin studies provide clearer evidence of inheritance. They indicate an average heritability of .80. Preliminary data suggest that both inattention and hyperactivity/impulsivity are heritable. The finding of substantial heritability is supported by limited adoption studies.

The mode of inheritance is not established (Neuman et al., 1999; Pennington & Ozonoff, 1996). Some evidence exists for a single gene with complex dominant transmission. Molecular genetic studies are focusing on several genes related to dopamine, but the findings are so far not definitive. It may be that several genetic mechanisms operate.

PREGNANCY AND BIRTH COMPLICATIONS

The idea that ADHD is sometimes traceable to pregnancy and birth complications is supported, although inconsistently, by research studies. Studies of children born prematurely and of very low birthweight indicate risk for attention problems and hyperactivity/impulsiveness (Schothorst & van Engeland, 1996; Sykes et al., 1997). These difficulties persist into childhood and adolescence in some portion of the children.

Prenatal maternal alcohol consumption and tobacco smoking also put children at risk. In an extensive U.S. study that followed women from pregnancy to the time their offspring were fourteen years old, prenatal alcohol use was linked to activity level, attention deficits, and difficulties in organizing tasks (Streissguth et al, 1984; 1989; 1995). Research conducted in Germany also indicates that hyperactivity associated with prenatal alcohol exposure persists over time into childhood and to a lesser extent into adolescence (Steinhausen, Willms, & Spohr, 1993). Milberger (1996) and colleagues demonstrated the risk of maternal tobacco smoking and showed that it was not explained by the mothers' own symptoms of ADHD.

The fact that children with ADHD show a higher than usual incidence of minor physical abnormalities (MPAs) has suggested prenatal causation. These slight abnormalities—such as low-seated ears and whorls of hair on the back of the head—develop during early pregnancy and are thought to be due to early developmental factors or genetic transmission (Deutsch et al., 1990). These abnormalities are also found in heightened numbers in behavioral disorders such as mental retardation and autism. However, clear evidence is lacking about if and how MPAs are connected to the etiology of ADHD (Barkley, 1998a; Weiss, 1991).

Interpreting the correlational data on pregnancy and birth complications is usually not an easy task. For example, women who are more likely to have children with ADHD may also have greater risk for alcohol and tobacco abuse because of greater risk for psychiatric disorders (Barkley, 1997). What, then, would account for ADHD in the children? Moreover, we would not necessarily expect a strong link between pregnancy/birth complications and persistent ADHD because of the well-known modifying effects of the social environment. Indeed, Chandola et al. (1992), who found a link between ADHD and length of labor and hemorrhage, reported that the predictive value of their findings was "disappointingly low." Nevertheless, pregnancy and birth complications may account for some cases of ADHD.

Diet's Role in ADHD

The belief that diet causes hyperactivity has been commonly held by the general public but is not strongly accepted by the professional community (Taylor, 1994; Anastopoulos & Barkley, 1992). Controversy about dietary influences has occurred, perhaps most strongly with regard to the Feingold diet. The history of this controversy exemplifies the need for continuing empirical investigations into the etiology of ADHD and effectiveness of treatment. (See Accent "Challenges to Reported. . . .")

The effects of dietary sugar have been of considerable interest. Anecdotal reports of some parents of clinic and nonclinic children indicate their belief that sugar intake causes their offspring to become hyperactive and disorganized. A limited number of correlational studies has shown a link between sugar consumption and behaviors that characterize ADHD (Prinz & Riddle, 1986), but more recent meta-analysis of the experimental research indicates that neither the behavior nor the cognitive functioning of children is influenced by sugar (Wolraich, Wilson, & White, 1995).

The overall evidence suggests that diet does not play a strong role in the etiology of ADHD but may affect a small number of children, most likely those who are intolerant to certain foods (Richters et al., 1995; Taylor, 1994).

Environmental Lead

It is widely recognized that exposure to lead is dangerous to humans. High levels of lead have been associated with serious deficits in biological functioning, cognition, and behavior (Tesman & Hills, 1994). Low levels of exposure over long periods of time also adversely affect children.

A number of correlational studies have examined lead levels and attention and activity levels. Lead levels of blood typically have been examined and also occasionally the amount of lead in the dentine of children's deciduous ("baby") teeth. Major studies sensitive to methodological issues have found significant but small links (Fergusson, Horwood, & Lynskey, 1993; Silva et al., 1988; Thomson et al., 1989). Perhaps no more than 4 percent of the variance in ADHD symptoms can be attributed to lead in children with high lead levels (Barkley, 1998a). And most children with ADHD do not have high levels of lead.

Thus, it is likely that decreases in environmental lead would probably not substantially affect the prevalence of ADHD. This likelihood does not mean that caution should be thrown to the wind, because lead can be poisonous. Exposure to lead can come from lead-based paints, automobile emissions, leaded crystal and ceramic dishes, and solder on old copper pipes. Thus the Centers for Disease Control and Prevention and the U.S. Environmental Protection Agency disseminate information about the prevention of lead poisoning.

Psychosocial Factors

Although psychosocial variables are not considered primary in the etiology of ADHD, they do play a role.

Goodman and Stevenson's (1989) study of twins found an association of ADHD behaviors

CHALLENGES TO REPORTED DIETARY EFFECTS ON ADHD

In 1975, Feingold, a physician researcher interested in allergies, published a book, *Why Your Child Is Hyperactive*, which inspired both controversy and investigation into dietary effects on hyperactivity. Feingold asserted that food containing artificial dyes and flavors, certain preservatives, and naturally occurring salicylates (for example, in apricots, prunes, tomatoes, cucumbers) was related to hyperactivity. He claimed that 25 percent to 50 percent of hyperactive–learning disabled children responded favorably to diets that eliminated these substances (Harley & Matthews, 1980; Tryphonas, 1979). On the other hand, it was claimed that when children on the diet ingested a prohibited food, hyperactivity occurred dramatically and persisted for two to three days.

This position received pervasive media coverage and was rapidly espoused by many parents, who reported impressive anecdotes about behavioral improvement in their children on Feingold's diet. Some of the fanfare undoubtedly was due to the fact that Feingold advocated the diet for mental retardation, delinquency, learning problems, and autism, as well as for hyperactivity. Evaluation by skeptical committees called for well-designed research to examine the efficacy of the Feingold diet.

Conners and his colleagues were among the first to examine hyperactive children while they were on a special diet and while they were on a control diet. Teachers, but not parents, found the diet more effective. Subsequently, three "challenge" studies were run in which children who were on the Feingold diet and had shown improvement were "challenged" by a cookie with food dyes or a cookie with no dyes. The results were ambiguous but, for the most part, did not support Feingold's claims (Conners, 1980). Other research is consistent with this finding (Gross et al., 1987; Harley & Matthews, 1980; Spring, Chiodo, & Bowen, 1987).

---

with seven adverse family variables, including parental malaise, marital discord, coldness to the child, and criticism of the child. The link with family adversity—such as family dysfunction, single parenting, and urban status—has been found in other studies as well (e.g., McGee et al., 1991; Stormont-Spurgin & Zentall, 1995).

Campbell (1987) studied parental ratings of their three-year-olds when the children were referred for help. When the children were age six, those who had received the more negative ratings of ADHD behaviors had families that had experienced more stress and were lower in social status. An unfavorable mother-child relationship also predicted stability of the problems. Stormont-Spurgin & Zentall (1995) found that families of preschoolers with ADHD and aggression were more restrictive and aggressive than families whose preschoolers displayed ADHD alone.

Studies of hyperactive school-age children indicate that their parents are less consistent, more impatient, and more authoritarian (Campbell, 1995; Woodward, Taylor, & Dowdney, 1998). Nigg and Hinshaw (1998) found that boys with ADHD with or without antisocial behavior more likely had mothers with a history of depression and/or anxiety and fathers with a childhood history of ADHD. All these findings implicate family variables.

Nevertheless, family correlates of ADHD need to be regarded cautiously (Barkley, 1996). To begin with, genetic twin studies indicate that all nongenetic factors combined account for only about 20 percent of the variation in ADHD symptoms. Psychosocial effects are thus likely to be quite small. Furthermore, poor child management by parents can be a reaction from the child's disturbed behavior, not a cause of it. In addition, since parents themselves are at genetic risk for ADHD, their behavior may stem from their own genetic disposition.

On the other hand, it is not unreasonable that at least for some children, ADHD results from a biological predisposition for the relevant behaviors that then interacts with psychosocial variables. Organized and regular routines, rules that are authoritatively enforced, quiet activities, and the like may be especially crucial for children vulnerable to ADHD. The controlling, intrusive parental style that is associated with ADHD may worsen the child's behavior (Hechtman, 1991).

It is also possible that teacher behaviors might play a role in shaping a child's attentiveness and reflectivity. How a classroom is organized and how activities are structured can influence academic achievement, perhaps especially for children predisposed to ADHD behaviors (Whalen, 1989). As with parents, teacher perception and tolerance of student behavior may influence daily social interactions.

Few researchers and clinicians believe that parents or teachers are a primary cause of ADHD. However, psychosocial variables, particularly family factors, provide the critical context within which the disorder develops (Barkley, 1996; Taylor, 1994); therefore, it seems likely that they shape the nature and the severity of the disorder. This may be particularly true for cases that involve the combination of ADHD and oppositional/conduct disorders.

Overall, it is quite striking that after much research, the etiology of ADHD remains uncertain. Establishing causation has been hindered by practices that have often been troublesome, such as the use of different criteria to identify cases of ADHD for investigation. Etiology may also be heterogeneous and may vary with different subgroups of ADHD. For example, ADHD with and without conduct disorder may have somewhat different developmental pathways and may involve a combination of several factors. Nevertheless, some progress is being made in establishing genetic contributions to etiology, in understanding how brain functioning may be related to the symptoms of the disorder, and in recognizing how psychosocial influences may shape and maintain the problem behaviors.

DEVELOPMENTAL COURSE AND OUTCOME

Until relatively recently, clinical description and research of ADHD focused on school-age children, mostly boys. Undoubtedly this was the case because the disorder is especially notable when children enter school and must conform to the requirements of attentive, "good" deportment. Nevertheless, the importance of studying attention deficit hyperactivity disorder across developmental levels has become evident. Since ADHD is believed to emerge by age seven, examination of the earlier years of life can be critical to understanding the development of the disorder. At the same time, we now know that children do not necessarily "outgrow" ADHD, as was once believed. Follow-up studies are thus important to describe the developmental course of the disorder, help predict outcome, and suggest intervention and prevention.

INFANCY AND THE PRESCHOOL YEARS

It is believed that at least some cases of ADHD begin in infancy, but this possibility is not easily established. How would ADHD manifest itself so early in life? It seems reasonable that the temperamental traits of high activity level and inattention might indicate the disorder. Sanson et al. (1993) reported that a group of children who were hyperactive and aggressive at age eight had early difficult temperament. By age three to four, the children were more active and less cooperative and manageable, as was a group that later displayed only hyperactivity. It appears that hyperactivity/

impulsivity may arise earlier than inattention (Barkley, 1998a).

Other investigations also show that by preschool age, inattention and restless behavior can be identified (Campbell, 1990; 1995; McGee et al., 1991). In most cases the problems will cease. When they do not, parents complain of stress with regard to managing the overactivity and noncompliance of their offspring. Inadequate caregiving and family adversity are noted (Carlson, Jacobvitz, & Sroufe, 1995). The child's early temperament and continuance of difficult behavior, as well as a family history of ADHD, seem important in predicting whether disturbance will further continue (Barkley, 1998a). In a minority of children destined to be diagnosed as ADHD, the primary manifestations of the syndrome as well as some secondary problems are evident very early.

MIDDLE CHILDHOOD

By age six, over 90 percent of children with ADHD are identified (Barkley, 1998a). Once the behaviors of ADHD are exhibited, they often remain stable and may increase throughout childhood. These are the years that have been best documented. As we have seen, in addition to the primary behaviors of ADHD, for many children, social relationships are far from satisfactory, peer rejection becomes obvious, school becomes a punishing place, and academic achievement falls. Negative feedback about school performance and other behaviors can accumulate to adversely affect self-concept and motivation. In addition, clinical-level oppositional behaviors and conduct problems can become apparent.

ADOLESCENCE AND ADULTHOOD

Continuity of ADHD or associated problems is obvious in many adolescents. The range of affected youth varies from 30 percent to 80 percent (Barkley, 1998a; Hansen, Weiss, & Last, 1999). The primary deficits of ADHD, especially hyperactivity, may lessen in a substantial number of cases, so that the diagnosis of ADHD may no longer apply. Even in these cases, however, other difficulties may exist: poor school performance, conduct problems, antisocial behavior, substance use or abuse, social problems, low self-esteem, and emotional problems (Fischer et al., 1993; Slomkowski, Klein, & Mannuzza, 1995).

Studies that follow ADHD children into young adulthood indicate that perhaps 50 percent to 65 percent still variously demonstrate some of the primary deficits and/or impaired social relationships, depression, anxiety, low self-concept, antisocial behavior, drug use, and educational and occupational disadvantage (Barkley, 1990; Mannuzza et al., 1993, 1998; Weiss & Hechtman, 1986). Perhaps 25 percent are chronically antisocial. There is also evidence for risky sexual behavior, indicated by a high number of sexual partners, smaller probability of using birth control methods, fatherhood at younger age, and greater likelihood of sexually transmitted diseases (Barkley, 1998a; Hansen et al., 1999). Most of these young adults are employed, although their work history is somewhat unstable, and job status is on the low end.

Studies of outcome in middle and late adulthood are so far unavailable. However, evidence that ADHD or residual problems carry over into adulthood comes from adults who were never diagnosed with the disorder as children but appear to have had early symptoms. Barkley (1998a) has described adults who presented themselves at a clinic for adult ADHD. As a group, they had problems in attention, inhibition, and self-regulation, as well as in social, emotional, and work life. Although further research is needed, the diagnosis of ADHD might validly apply to these individuals.

VARIATION AND PREDICTION OF OUTCOME

In reviewing the data on outcome for ADHD, it is important to consider some aspects of the overall picture. First, with development comes a change in the kinds of difficulties experienced; that is, heterotypic continuity is observed. Second, the percentage of youth who continue to have problems varies a good deal from study to study. This variance could be an accurate reflection of real differences in samples, but the rates seem also to depend on who is doing the reporting, as well as on other methodological factors. Third, despite the long list of difficulties that can exist into later years, the general trend is for continuity of prob-

TABLE 9–2

Some Predictors of Adolescent and Adulthood ADHD

Academic performance

Aggression and conduct problems

General intelligence

Parents' ADHD and psychiatric disorder

Parents' child-rearing practice; parent-child interaction

Peer relationships

lems to weaken over time. Certainly not all children with ADHD experience maladaptations in later years. Indeed, many overcome earlier problems and are reasonably adjusted in adulthood. This fact leads to the fourth point, the question: What factors predict outcome?

Table 9-2 lists some of the factors that predict adolescent or adult problems. However, it turns out that no factor strongly predicts later outcome. In addition, different factors seem more related to outcome in some areas of functioning than in other areas (Campbell, 1995; Fischer et al., 1993; Fergusson, Lynskey, & Horwood, 1997; Lambert, 1988). For example, educational outcome appears especially associated with earlier deficits in attention, intelligence, and academic skill, as well as in family social class and child-rearing practices. In contrast, adolescent and adult antisocial behavior is linked to several early factors including family disturbance and the occurrence of previous aggression and conduct problems. As is usual, behavior develops from complex transactions between the child's characteristics and the psychological and social contexts.

ASSESSMENT

Whether the purpose of assessment is diagnosis, planning for treatment, or both, several aspects of ADHD are useful guidelines (Barkley, 1990; 1997; Hinshaw & Erhardt, 1993).

■ Since ADHD is best conceptualized as a biopsychosocial disorder, assessment must be *broad-based and include various procedures* to evaluate the primary and secondary manifestations of the disorder, family functioning, and biological functioning.

■ Since ADHD may be situationally specific, evaluation must include *different settings* such as the home and school.

■ Since ADHD is *developmental,* a developmental history is important, and assessment will vary somewhat with developmental level.

■ Since ADHD has high rates of co-occurrence with other behavioral disorders, assessment requires careful distinctions.

The following discussion will emphasize the psychological and social factors most important in childhood ADHD. The approach of Barkley (1990; 1997) and his colleagues is heavily drawn on. Interviews, rating scales, and direct observation are the major components that are discussed.

INTERVIEWS

Parents are the chief source of information in most cases of attention deficit hyperactivity disorder. Standard structured or semistructured interviews can be used. Information needs to be obtained about the child's and the family's history, the school, and the child's behavioral problems and strengths.

It is important to assess specific parent-child interactions, not only for diagnosis but also for treatment planning. Barkley asks parents specific questions about particular situations that are problematic (Table 9-3). Details about situations identified as troublesome are obtained. For example, questions are asked about what the child does, how the parents respond, and how often problems occur in the situation. Table 9-4 illustrates this question format for one situation: when visitors are in the home. Note that noncompliance is quite evident and that interaction becomes increasingly aversive. This is a common pattern in child-parent exchanges.

TABLE 9-3

Interview Format Suggested by Barkley

Questions	Situations
1. Is this a problem area?	Overall interactions
2. What does the child do in this situation?	Play alone
3. What is your response?	Play with others
4. What will the child do next?	Mealtimes
5. If the problem continues, what will you do next?	Dressing in morning
6. What is usually the outcome of this interaction?	Washing and bathing
7. How often do these problems occur in this situation?	Parent on telephone
8. How do you feel about these problems?	During television
9. On a scale of 0 to 10 (0 = no problem, 10 = severe problem), how severe is this problem to you?	Visitors at home
	Visiting others' homes
	In public places
	While mother is occupied
	Father at home
	Chores
	Bedtime
	Other situations

Barkley, 1981.

The youth being assessed should also be interviewed. The nature and length of this interview depend on the age and the ability of the person. With younger children, the interview may simply be a time for getting acquainted, establishing rapport, and observing the child's appearance and behavior. Observations of behavior must be interpreted cautiously, however, because children with ADHD are known to act more appropriately during office visits than they are reported to act in other settings. Older children and adolescents are more able to report reliably on their functioning, family dynamics, school performance, peer relationships, and the like.

Teacher interviews are of consequence because next to parents, teachers probably spend the most time with youth and can directly address difficulties in the school setting. Although contacts may initially be by telephone, direct interview is valuable. The focus is on learning and academic problems and on peer interaction. In addition, information can be obtained about parent-school interaction and cooperation, as well as school services. Under the Individuals with Disabilities Education Act and other legal mandates or policies, some youth with ADHD have rights to special evaluation and educational services (see p. 283).

RATING SCALES

Parent and teacher rating scales and checklists, which are popular tools for assessing ADHD, can provide much information with relatively little time and effort. Some useful rating scales are broadband and thus not only identify ADHD but also its co-occurrence with other disorders. In general, these scales can help determine whether behavior is deviant from the norm and different from behaviors displayed by other diagnostic groups. Several of them suggest cutoff scores to identify ADHD. The Child Behavior Checklist is an example of a widely used broadband instrument. Narrowband scales are useful in assessing

---

TABLE 9-4

Illustration of Interview Format Suggested by Barkley

....

EXAMINER: How does your child generally behave when there are visitors at your home?

MOTHER: Terrible! He embarrasses me tremendously.

E: Can you give me some idea of what he does specifically that is bothersome in this situation?

M: Well, he won't let me talk with the visitors without interrupting our conversation, tugging on me for attention, or annoying the guests by running back and forth in front of us as we talk.

E: Yes? And what else is he likely to do?

M: Many times, he will fight with his sister or get into something he shouldn't in the kitchen.

E: How will you usually respond to him when these things happen?

M: At first I usually try to ignore him. When this doesn't work, I try to reason with him, promise I'll spend time with him after the visitors leave, or try to distract him with something he usually likes to do just to calm him down so I can talk to my guests.

E: How successfully does that work for you?

M: Not very well. He may slow down for a few moments, but then he's right back pestering us or his sister, or getting into mischief in the kitchen. I get so frustrated with him by this time. I know what my visitors must be thinking of me not being able to handle my own child.

E: Yes, I can imagine it's quite distressing. What will you do at this point to handle the situation?

M: I usually find myself telling him over and over again to stop what he is doing, until I get very angry with him and threaten him with punishment. By now, my visitors are making excuses to leave and I'm trying to talk with them while yelling at my son.

E: And then what happens?

M: Well, I know I shouldn't, but I'll usually grab him and hold him just to slow him down. More often, though, I may threaten to spank him or send him to his room. He usually doesn't listen to me though until I make a move to grab him.

E: How often does this usually happen when visitors are at your home?

M: Practically every time; it's frustrating.

E: I see. How do you feel about your child creating such problems in front of visitors?

M: I find myself really hating him at times (*cries*); I know I'm his mother and I shouldn't feel that way, but I'm so angry with him, and nothing seems to work for me. Many of our friends have stopped coming to visit us, and we can't find a babysitter who will stay with him so we can go out. I resent having to sacrifice what little social life we have. I'm likely to be angry with him the rest of the day.

Barkley, 1981.

---

specific aspects of ADHD, such as school behavior. Parent and teacher versions are available for several of these instruments, as are some self-report versions useful particularly for adolescents. Many of the rating scales are of good quality, but their appropriateness, reliability, and validity must always be examined. We will look at an example of the widely employed scales.

The Conners parent and teacher scales are employed for initial screening. On the Conners scales, children are rated on whether they display each behavior (0) not at all, (1) just a little, (2) pretty much, or (3) very much. Both the parent and the teacher scales exist in longer and abbreviated forms, they are easy to use, and there is good evidence for their validity (Edelbrock & Rancurello, 1985). In addition, both scales have recently been revised. Among other things, the purposes of the revisions were to extend the normative base of each scale and to update items to reflect current knowledge about ADHD. Table 9-5 shows the seven major factors of the Conners Parent Rating Scale–Revised and examples of the forty-five items as they are distributed across the factors (Conners et al., 1998a). The Conners Teacher Rating Scale–Revised has thirty-eight

TABLE 9-5

Seven Factors of the Revised Conners Parent Rating Scale, with Examples

1. Cognitive Problems
   Trouble concentrating
   Careless mistakes
   Arithmetic problems

2. Oppositional
   Loses temper
   Irritable
   Defies adults

3. Hyperactivity-Impulsivity
   Always on the go
   Restless
   Excitable

4. Anxious-Shy
   Timid
   Many fears
   Clings to parents

5. Perfectionism
   Everything just so
   Has rituals
   Sets high goals

6. Social Problems
   Does not make friends
   Doesn't get involved
   Feels inferior

7. Psychosomatic
   Aches and pains
   Complains
   Seems tired

Adapted from Conners, Sitarenios, Parker, and Epstein, 1998b.

important, along with behaviors such as "out of seat," aggression, disruption, and inattention. Several observational coding procedures for ADHD behaviors exist, for example, for the structured classroom and clinic playroom (Jacob, O'Leary, & Rosenblad, 1978; Roberts, 1990). More general procedures may also be appropriate, such as the Parent-Adolescent Interaction Coding System (Robin & Foster, 1989).

OTHER PROCEDURES

Additional assessment methods are often necessary and/or useful. Among these are standardized tests of intelligence, academic achievement, and adaptive behavior. Procedures to evaluate inattention and impulsivity have been developed, and several continuous performance tests seem promising. However, their use in assessment is limited (Barkley, 1998a; Rapport, 1993).

Since the family plays a role in the maintenance and developmental course of ADHD, questionnaires that describe family functioning can be essential. Measures of peer relationships can also be useful.

Biological assessment reasonably includes a medical/developmental history, a medical examination that entails neurological examination, and in rare cases, perhaps an EEG or brain scan. Medical evaluation does not usually identify ADHD, but it can be worthwhile when biological factors are highly suspect. It might then provide information potentially useful in treatment or in understanding the disorder.

items and six factors similar to those of the revised parent scale (Conners et al., 1998a). It is anticipated that the revised scales will replace the older ones.

DIRECT OBSERVATIONS

Direct observation can be extremely useful in assessing ADHD, but it is time-consuming and expensive. Barkley (1990) recommends it whenever it can reasonably be accomplished. Observations have typically focused on interpersonal and school functioning (Rapport, 1993). In the home, compliance and stimulus-consequence patterns are important. In the school, social interaction is equally

TREATMENT

A variety of treatments have been applied to attention deficit hyperactivity disorder. They include individual counseling, parent training, academic remediation, cognitive therapy, social skills training, and insight therapies (Whalen & Henker, 1998). Traditional psychotherapy is not considered especially helpful, and the effectiveness of some other treatments such as play therapy and individual counseling is not documented (DuPaul et al., 1991; Pelham, Wheeler, & Chronis, 1998). Pharmacotherapy and behavioral interventions are the treatments of choice. For a period of time, it was thought that cognitive-behavioral interventions would be suitable for ADHD, but this has not proven to be the case.

PHARMACOLOGICAL TREATMENT

A report by Bradley in 1937 is usually cited as the first instance of the treatment of behavior disordered children with stimulant medication (Barkley, 1998b). Many pharmacological agents have been used for ADHD since then, including stimulant, antidepressant, and anticonvulsant drugs (Table 9-6). Stimulant medications are by far the treatment of first choice, and they are the most popular treatment in the United States for attention deficit hyperactivity disorder.

The most commonly employed stimulants are methylphenidate (Ritalin), dextroamphetamine (Dexedrine), pemoline (Cylert), and the relatively new Adderal. It is estimated that over 2 percent of all school-age children receive these medications. These drugs have been extensively researched, with methylphenidate, the most used, being the most studied.

Although much controversy surrounds the use of stimulants, it is not, in the view of most profes-sionals, due to their failure to alleviate rapidly the primary deficits of ADHD. An estimated 75 percent of medicated children show increased attention and reduced impulsivity and activity level, both in the laboratory and in the structured, natural environments that elicit ADHD behaviors (Whalen & Henker, 1998). This general finding is exemplified in Figure 9-6. Stimulant medications can also reduce co-occurring aggressive, noncompliant, oppositional behaviors (Hinshaw et al., 1989). An impressive amount of data supports the claim for efficacy across settings and measures (Swanson et al., 1995; Whalen & Henker, 1998). Perhaps not surprising, then, is that parents and teachers interact more positively and use fewer controlling behaviors with ADHD children who are benefiting from medications (Gadow & Pomeroy, 1991; Murphy, Greenstein, & Pelham, 1993). Thus pharmacological treatment may benefit children not only directly but also through improving social relationships.

Since it became evident that many children do not "outgrow" ADHD, adolescents have been treated with medications. Reductions in inattention/impulsivity and noncompliance, as well as enhancement of cognitive functioning, have been demonstrated in this population, although continuing research is needed (Campbell & Cueva, 1995; DuPaul, Barkley, & Connor, 1998).

The stimulants used to treat ADHD increase the arousal and activity of the central nervous system and may mimic the action of dopamine and norepinephrine. On the surface, it once seemed strange that increased arousal from stimulants would benefit ADHD, and the effects were thus said to be paradoxical. This notion of paradoxical effects is now discounted (Taylor, 1994). In fact, stimulants influence normal children and adults, as well as those with ADHD, by focusing attention and the like. Still to be established definitively is where these effects occur in the brain, but it is likely in the midbrain or frontal cortex (DuPaul et al., 1998).

The effects of most stimulants are rapid but wear off within a few hours. They are therefore commonly given two or three times a day. Slow-release medications that can be taken less often

---

TABLE 9-6

Medications Most Commonly Used to Treat ADHD

Stimulants: Medications of First Choice

Ritalin (Methylphenidate)

Dexedrine (Dextroamphetamine)

Cylert (Pemoline)

Adderall (Combined Amphetamine and Dextroamphetamine)

Antidepressants: First Alternative Choice

Tricyclics (e.g., Desipramine, Imipramine)

Other antidepressants

Less-Used Medications

Anticonvulsants

Antihypertensives

Antipsychotics

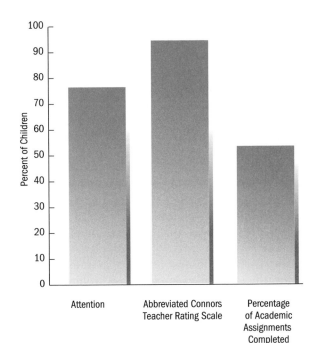

FIGURE 9-6 Percentage of children with ADHD showing improved or normalized classroom behaviors on various measures when treated with methylphenidate.

Adapted from Rapport, Denney, DuPaul, and Gardner, 1994.

are also available. Monitoring of treatment is important, especially because individuals respond differently to medications and to specific dosages. In addition, a medication of certain dosage can affect different target behaviors differently.

Concerns about medication. Despite the benefits of stimulant medication, several concerns and criticisms have been expressed.

One concern is the failure of medication. Approximately 20 percent to 30 percent of children do not benefit from stimulant medication. Children under the age of four years may benefit the least and also suffer more adverse side effects (Barkley, 1990). When ADHD combines with significant problems in anxiety or depression, re-

sponse to stimulant medication is likely to be poor, and response to antidepressants to be more favorable. Even with children who benefit, evidence is lacking for long-lasting efficacy (DuPaul et al., 1998). This situation is somewhat surprising regarding academic performance because short-term improvement in the core deficits of ADHD, on laboratory learning tasks, and in school performance might be expected to affect longer-term academics.

A second concern about treatment with stimulants is possible adverse biological side effects. Most common are insomnia and anorexia, but stomach pain, headaches, irritability, rashes, and involuntary muscle movement also occur (DuPaul et al., 1998; Gadow & Pomeroy, 1991). These side effects are often mild and may diminish in two or three weeks or after a reduction in dosage. Suppression of growth is also reported, but when drug treatment is stopped, growth rebounds. Because stimulants may worsen motor and vocal tics and perhaps even occasionally cause them, they are not recommended for the small percentage of children with these symptoms. In general, stimulants are considered relatively safe drugs for most children, and adverse effects can be reversed with adjustment in dosage or change to another stimulant. As a precautionary measure, medications are sometimes halted on weekends and over school vacations, but even this step is usually not considered necessary. Monitoring is always essential, however, as a minority of children cannot tolerate stimulants.

At one time, concern was expressed that pharmacological treatment might result in children's experiencing undue worries and detrimental cognitions, for example, worries that they would become "hyper" without medications or beliefs that their behavior is controlled by external forces rather than by their own efforts. However, there is little evidence for this concern, and children may actually gain feelings of competence and self-control (Milich, 1994; Whalen & Henker, 1998). This is an area that requires sensitive assessment because individual children and adolescents report a variety of attitudes about taking medications.

The use of medications in treating ADHD has caused a firestorm of controversy over the years, fueled by considerable media coverage. For example, the November 30, 1998, issue of *Time* magazine ran a cover story, "The Age of Ritalin," in which it discussed the dilemmas of ADHD, noting that Ritalin production had increased sevenfold in the previous eight years and that 90 percent of production is consumed in the United States. Media attention that serves to educate is beneficial, of course. Unfortunately, concerns about medications have sometimes been expressed in emotionally charged and exaggerated ways by parents, professionals, and organized groups (Barkley, 1990; Swanson et al., 1995). According to Barkley (1998a), a destructive antimedication campaign based on uncritically published and alarming stories was conducted by the Church of Scientology, which also filed a lawsuit against the American Psychiatric Association for fraud in developing diagnostic criteria for ADHD (the case was dismissed). Two national groups, the Attention Deficit Disorder Associations (ADDA) and Children with Attention Deficit Disorder (CHADD), have influentially voiced their criticisms as well as provided education about ADHD. In addition to the concerns we have already discussed, some critics have argued that children are misdiagnosed or overdiagnosed and then prescribed medication that cannot help them but could harm them. Some critics believe that medication is overused because it is a "quick fix" for the schools and for some parents. Several government agencies and professional groups have been involved in studying the treatment of ADHD and in promulgating guidelines and regulations for medication use (Swanson et al., 1995). Although extreme emotional reaction and exaggeration can hardly be helpful, professionals who recognize the benefits of stimulants also point to their limitations and warn against their misuse or overuse.

BEHAVIORAL INTERVENTION

Despite the short-term success of pharmacological treatments, there are many reasons for psychosocial interventions. Medications may not be an option for every child because they may be ineffective, cause intolerable side effects, or simply be refused. Then too, behavioral, academic, or social

difficulties often remain even with medication use. Behavioral interventions are the most well developed and the most documented alternative treatments. They are applied to a wide range of problems, are either limited or broad in scope, and are combined with other treatments.

Behavior modification emphasizes the importance of consequences of behavior in controlling attention, impulsivity, rule adherence, academic effort, and social interaction. Because of the nature of ADHD, powerful salient external reinforcers are often needed over long periods of time (Barkley, 1998b). Reinforcers typically include not only tokens or points that can be traded for a variety of rewards but also social consequences such as praise. Even so, positive reinforcement alone may be insufficient, for example, in controlling behavior in the classroom (Hinshaw & Erhardt, 1993). Thus negative consequences are often given in the form of time-out or response cost; that is, the child loses opportunity for reinforcers or must give up a portion of the tokens or points previously earned.

Behavioral interventions have been conducted in special settings, such as special classrooms, or in the clinic. These interventions can improve behavior but benefit is more likely when contingencies are applied in other settings as well. The need to build in generalization to "real world" settings is recognized. For example, when training ADHD children in social skills in the clinical setting, Frankel et al. (1997) also trained parents to facilitate their children's newly acquired social behavior in the natural environment. It can be argued that the most effective treatments are conducted in the child's natural environments and many behavioral interventions are conducted in the home or school, or with parents or teachers who work directly with the child.

Parent training. Managing a child with ADHD can be stressful for families, and perhaps even more so in the presence of co-occurring conduct problems. Parents tend to become worn down and overly directive. They may also begin to view themselves as lacking the normal skills of parenting (Anastopoulos, Smith, & Wien, 1998). These facts coupled with the obvious influence that parents have on their children's behavior make families a natural focus of intervention.

As an example of an extensive parent training program, we turn to an approach that emphasizes the management of noncompliance and defiance in children three to eleven years of age (Anastopoulos et al.,1998; Barkley, 1997). This focus is consistent with the view that ADHD involves a deficit in self-regulation and frequently involves oppositional defiant behavior. The program consists of ten steps, that are covered in weekly parent training sessions. The behavioral aspects are evident in brief descriptions of the steps.

1. **Why Children Misbehave.** The causes of defiant behavior are discussed in terms of child characteristics, parent characteristics, situational consequences and parenting style, and stressful family events.
2. **Pay Attention.** Parents are trained to attend to their children's behavior and are advised to increase attention to appropriate behavior and to ignore inappropriate behavior.
3. **Increasing Compliance and Independent Play.** Positive parental attention is extended to independent play situations. Parents are taught to use brief commands and to reinforce compliance.
4. **When Praise Is Not Enough: Poker Chips and Points.** Parents are asked to set up a home token economy to provide external reinforcers to activities not intrinsically motivating, such as home chores.
5. **Time-Out! and Other Disciplinary Methods.** The home economy system is monitored, and parents are trained to use time-out and response cost for noncompliance with rules or requests.
6. **Extendng Time-Out to Other Misbehavior.** The techniques that parents are using in child management are reviewed, especially punishment techniques. Parents are also encouraged to extend time-out and response cost to other home situations as needed.
7. **Anticpating Problems: Managing Children in Public Places.** Management procedures are extended to misbehavior in public places such as stores and restaurants.
8. **Improving School Behavior: Daily School Behavior Report.** School issues are addressed, especially modification of the child's immediate classroom environment. A daily report is sent from the teacher to the parents; appropriate school behavior is reinforced at home.
9. **Handling Future Behavior Problems.** A general review is provided, and discussion is held about how parents might use their newly acquired management skills in the future.
10. **Booster Session and Follow-Up Meetings.** About one month after, a "booster" session is typically held to evaluate progress and to review and refine the intervention procedures. Additional sessions can be scheduled if desired.

This parent training program is often an integral part of a broader clinical approach to ADHD. Whether it is recommended depends on its appropriateness to the individual case. For example, parents may resist the program or may require marital counseling first, or the child's difficulties may center primarily on the school setting.

In general, limited data suggest that parent interventions can result in improvement of children's functioning, reduction of parental stress, and strengthening of self-esteem with regard to parenting (Anastopoulos et al., 1998). However, there is a serious question as to whether these programs, when combined with pharmacological treatment of the children, provide any improvement beyond the effects of medications. This issue will be addressed shortly.

Classroom management. School-based behavioral intervention is effective in producing improvement with regard to attention, disruptive behavior, and academic performance. Most commonly the teacher administers the intervention. The procedures include token reinforcement, punishment, and contingency contracting. In the latter technique, the child and the teacher sign a written agreement specifying how the child will behave and the contingencies that will accrue (Table 9-7). Teachers typically receive training and consultation to conduct these programs.

TABLE 9-7

Hypothetical Child-Teacher Contingency Contract

I agree to do the following:

1. Take my seat by 8:10 every morning.
2. Remain in my seat unless Ms. Duffin gives permission to me or the class to leave seats.
3. Not interrupt other students when they are speaking to class.
4. Complete morning written work as assigned before lunch break.
5. Complete afternoon written work as assigned before gym or recess in the afternoon.

I agree that when I do the above, I will:
. . . earn extra time in the computer corner
. . . earn extra time to do artwork
. . . earn extra checkmarks that I can trade for art supplies

I agree that if I do not do 1–5 above each day, I will:
. . . not be able to participate in recess activities

Based on DuPaul, Guevrement, and Barkley, 1991

In addition, parents and teachers can work together to improve behavior in the classroom. Typically, goals and reinforcers for the child are individually decided on. Teachers help the child to achieve these goals, monitor the child's behavior, and consistently send home specific reports, often in the form of a simple checklist. Contingencies are managed by the parents, with the child having the opportunity to earn an array of reinforcers.

Research suggests that classroom structure and organization may be important to enhancing learning in children with ADHD (Pfiffner & Barkley, 1998). Increasing stimulation within the task—for example, by the use of color, shape, or tape recordings—might increase attention to the task. Keeping the length of the task within the child's attention span and using timers to pace performance might be of benefit. Rules that are written and clearly displayed also may help guide the child. Placing the child's desk away from other children and near the teacher can reduce peer reinforcement of inappropriate behavior and can also facilitate teacher monitoring and feedback.

Teacher variables have largely been neglected with regard to the success of classroom management of ADHD (Greene, 1995). Yet teachers have considerable control in setting up the learning environment and differences among teachers are expected. It thus is important to understand better which teachers would be most accepting of and effective in implementing behavioral programs. Moreover, as Greene notes, teacher-student compatibility might be important. Variables such as the teacher's flexibility, tolerance for the disruptions common in ADHD, and interactional style are worthy of investigation.

There seems little doubt that behavioral methods can help many ADHD children in the short run. Empirical investigations show that on-task, attentive, appropriate behaviors can be shaped and academic improvement made by school-based treatments. However, questions remain about whether training in one situation carries over to others and about the durability of effects. In addition, behavioral programs often require much effort and time, sometimes beyond what is feasible for teachers and parents. Finally, improvement, although notable, is smaller than improvements found for treatment with medication.

COGNITIVE-BEHAVIORAL INTERVENTION AND SELF-REGULATION

Although cognitive-behavioral treatment has not proven itself successful, it is discussed here because it has been of interest. Central to this approach is enhancement of self-control or self-regulation, which would seem a natural target in treating ADHD. Moreover, self-control can increase generalization and maintenance of appropriate behavior, because the behavior would not solely depend on external cues and contingencies in new situations.

Several techniques have been employed to enhance self-regulation. Self-monitoring involves having individuals learn to observe and record their own behaviors. For example, they may record the frequency of on-task behavior. This step is often followed by self-reinforcement for the desired behavior. Another technique, self-instruction, involves children being trained to make statements to themselves to help focus and guide their behaviors on a task. The self-statements may include questions that help clarify the task, answers to the questions, and self-guidance (e.g., "slow down," "the next step is . . ."). The verbalizations usually are combined with modeling, reinforcement, and other procedures.

Despite a rationale for cognitive-behavioral interventions, findings from many studies consistently demonstrate the lack of improvement in behavior and academic performance in children with ADHD (Hinshaw, Klein, & Abikoff, 1998; Pelham et al., 1998). There is only limited suggestion that some cognitive-behavioral interventions—such as social skills training—may be helpful when they are combined with intensive behavioral treatments. In addition, teaching self-regulation might enhance maintenance and generalization of learned behavior when cognitive-behavioral techniques are used with intensive behavioral treatments. Research on this possibility would be worthwhile.

COMBINED AND MULTIMODAL TREATMENTS

There is no doubt that pharmacotherapy is most effective in bringing about short-term improvement in ADHD but also that it has several drawbacks. Although the behavioral approach has had its successes, it is not sufficiently effective and is demanding of caretakers. Since no one approach offers long-term improvement, the combination of the two treatments has been employed, as well as multimodal interventions that include a wider range of therapies.

Is the combination of medication and behavioral treatments effective? Several studies failed to show more positive outcome for combinations of treatments than for single treatments (Anastopoulos & Barkley, 1992). More specifically, medication alone was as effective as when it was combined with other approaches. Nonetheless, the door was left open as to whether combined treatments might have some benefits. For example, a study by Ialongo and colleagues (1993) indicated that a combined approach was important in maintaining treatment benefits over time. Favorable outcome was also reported for multimodal treatment em-

ployed for serious antisocial behavior in boys with ADHD (Satterfield, 1994; Satterfield et al., 1987). This individualized intervention combined medication, child therapy, family therapy, marital therapy, and tutoring.

Such findings, in conjunction with the lack of long-term effectiveness of any treatments, resulted in the National Institutes of Mental Health initiating a six-center investigation of lengthier, more intensive multimodal treatment (Richters et al., 1995). Results from only one of these efforts are available to date (Abikoff & Hechtman, 1996; Hinshaw et al., 1998). This study assigned boys to medication alone; medication plus parent, child, and teacher intervention; and medication with an intervention to control attention. Among the psychosocial components were tutoring, social skills training, organizational training, parent training, counseling, and limited contingency management. Intensive intervention was provided for one year, and maintenance intervention for the second year. Improvement was found in all outcome measures, but psychosocial treatment did not supplement gains from medication. In addition, when children were taken off medication, their behavior rapidly deteriorated. (It should be pointed out that this investigation did not include a psychosocial-alone treatment.) Several ongoing NIH studies are yet to be completed, and some of them include novel components. Thus, as Hinshaw and colleagues (1998) note, we can look forward to hearing from the most rigorous efforts undertaken to ameliorate the course of ADHD.

At the present time, clinicians take various stances with regard to treatments. Medication is widely employed, but some clinicians prefer to try behavioral techniques initially, to see whether medications might be avoided. Others believe that a combination of treatments might be the best approach for many children, since different treatments might address different deficits. In addition, parent training in managing their youngsters with ADHD is judged important, as is treating disorders that co-occur with ADHD. The requirement for treatment to be tailored to individual needs is apparent, even as these needs may change as the child develops.

SUMMARY

....

■ Inattention and hyperactivity/impulsivity are core problems of ADHD. DSM-IV recognizes three subtypes of ADHD, Predominately Inattentive, Hyperactive/Impulsive, and the combination of these. Diagnosis demands the presence of disturbance by age seven and impairment in at least two settings.

■ The core problems of ADHD, which occur more in structured situations, are widely observed by parents and teachers. Measures such as the Matching Familiar Figures Test, continuous performance tests, and the Stop-Signal task are used to evaluate these deficits.

■ As a group, youth with ADHD experience several additional difficulties, including somewhat lowered intelligence, learning disabilities, academic failure, problems in executive functions, social and conduct problems, and increased accidents/injury.

■ The DSM-IV subtype Predominantly Inattentive is characterized by sluggish, daydreamy, more socially withdrawn, and more anxious behavior than the subtypes involving hyperactivity/impulsvity. The question has been raised as to whether it should be considered a unique disorder.

■ Current theories of ADHD emphasize deficits in motivation that are reflected in the need or preference for strong, salient, immediate reinforcers. Even more dominant are theories emphasizing deficits in inhibition and behavioral regulation.

■ ADHD co-occurs at high rates with other behavioral disorders, especially learning disabilities, oppositional and conduct problems, and anxiety and depression. Co-occurrence with ODD/CD is most common and is associated with more severe problems, less favorable outcome, and perhaps different developmental pathways.

■ About 3 percent to 5 percent of the school population is estimated to show ADHD. Boys are diagnosed more frequently than girls, perhaps partly because of referral bias. Prevalence appears somewhat higher in lower social classes. Notable cross-national differences probably reflect, in part, differences in diagnostic and cultural standards.

■ Brain dysfunction is considered likely in ADHD. There is special interest in the frontal/striatal area of the brain, and in the neurotransmitters norepinephrine and dopamine. Metabolic rates, abnormal EEGs, and diminished physiological reactions suggest underarousal.

■ Substantial genetic transmission of ADHD is indicated by family and twin studies. Medical conditions and pregnancy/birth complications are linked to ADHD. Diet and lead poisoning appear to have only small influence.

■ ADHD is associated with family factors, including poverty, stress, and negative family interactions. The psychosocial environment plays a role in shaping and maintaining ADHD behaviors.

■ Hyperactivity and impulsivity can begin by age three or four. Symptoms often remain stable or increase during childhood, while academic, social, and conduct problems become obvious. A substantial number of cases continue into adolescence, and some into adulthood. The primary symptoms decrease, but associated difficulties exist. Continuity of problems is linked to several variables.

■ The identification of ADHD requires broad-based assessment that takes into account developmental level, situational specificity, and co-ocurrence with other disorders. A comprehensive model includes interviews with the children, parents, and teachers; standardized rating scales; direct observation; medical examinations; intelligence testing; and other procedures.

■ Stimulant medication is the most common treatment for ADHD. It relieves both the primary and many secondary manifestations in about 75 percent of cases. Several concerns are expressed about pharmacotherapy, which remains controversial.

■ Behavioral interventions emphasize consequences for attention, rule adherence, academic effort, socially appropriate behaviors, and parent and teacher training. Effectiveness has been documented. Cognitive-behavioral treatments are not shown to be effective.

■ There is no evidence that any treatment shows long-term efficacy. Combinations of treatments hardly seem more powerful than medication alone. A major research effort is under way to study further the effects of multimodal treatments.

CHAPTER 10

MENTAL RETARDATION

From the beginning of history, even in simple societies, some individuals have been considered intellectually disabled and socially incapable (Clarke & Clarke, 1985). However, until about 1700, mental retardation (MR) was little understood and scarcely recognized as different from other disorders (Reschly, 1992). In the early 1800s, the concept of mental retardation more firmly took root as involving deficient mental functioning and handicaps in the daily tasks of living. Beliefs and concepts continued to evolve and are evolving even today.

The labels applied to the condition also changed over time. The terms *idiot,* from the Greek meaning "ignorant person," *imbecile,* from the Latin meaning "weakness," and *moron,* meaning foolish or having deficient judgment, were all once employed in the professional literature (Potter, 1972; Scheerenberger, 1983). These terms took on increasingly negative connotations, and changes in terminology were partly an attempt to substitute more positive labels. The current trend

to use "mental handicap" or "intellectually challenged" continues this effort. However, as long as we denigrate and are insensitive to mental retardation, any label applied to it might eventually carry negative meaning.

Perhaps more strongly than most other behavioral disorders, mental retardation has been viewed as a trait of the individual. Biological dysfunction has often been assumed. Nevertheless, for some time, formal definitions of retardation have avoided etiological assumptions. It is important that the many ways in which the environment causes and impacts mental development now are being given more than passing attention.

DEFINITION AND CLASSIFICATION

Mental retardation is recognized by all major classification systems. We present the definition offered by the American Association on Mental Retardation (AAMR), which has led efforts to understand and ameliorate MR. Founded in 1876 (and once called the American Association on

Mental Deficiency), this organization has long provided definitions of mental retardation that have been adopted by others, including the DSM. In its latest publication manual *Mental Retardation: Definition, Classification, and Systems of Support,* AAMR modified its definition of mental retardation, claiming a paradigm shift.

AAMR'S PARADIGM SHIFT

The following is the definition currently offered by AAMR:

> Mental retardation refers to substantial limitations in present functioning. It is characterized by significantly subaverage intellectual functioning, existing concurrently with related limitations in two or more of the following applicable adaptive skill areas: communication, self-care, home living, social skills, community use, self-direction, health and safety, functional academics, leisure, and work. Mental retardation manifests before age 18. (Luckasson et al., 1992, p. 5)

In this definition, subaverage intellectual functioning refers to scores of approximately 70 to 75 or below on a general test of intelligence, such as the Stanford-Binet and the Wechsler scales. This IQ range is roughly two or more standard deviations below the mean on these tests. Limitations in adaptive skills are viewed as related to intellectual limitations, rather than to other circumstances, for example, cultural background. The age criterion signifies that mental retardation is seen as a developmental disorder. Age eighteen approximates when individuals in our society usually assume adult roles and when crucial psychosocial development and brain development have typically occurred.

The current definition of mental retardation reflects the long history of how the condition has been conceptualized and identified. At first primarily considered a medical disorder, MR had been diagnosed on the basis of physical examinations and global, ill-defined judgments of everyday competence. The construction of more objective general tests of intelligence, along with greater recognition of nonmedical factors, then resulted in an emphasis on intelligence test performance. Perceived limitations and abuse of these tests, in turn, resulted in greater attention to adaptive behavior. Thus individuals who fall into the retarded range on intelligence tests but otherwise get along adequately at home, school, or work are not now judged as mentally retarded according to more recent definitions. Deficits in adaptive behavior without poor performance on intelligence tests also do not warrant the diagnosis of retardation.

Defining MR in terms of intellectual and adaptive skills and recognizing it as a developmental disorder are not new to AAMR. Why, then, does AAMR claim a "paradigm shift" in its definition? Briefly put, the shift has to do with a stronger rejection of mental retardation as an absolute trait of the individual and a greater emphasis on environmental interactions that influence how the person is functioning.

Figure 10-1 indicates that these ideas are critical to how mental retardation is conceptualized. The individual is viewed as functioning in complex ways in a sociocultural context. The diagnosis of MR depends on how the individual is actually functioning in the environment; if functioning

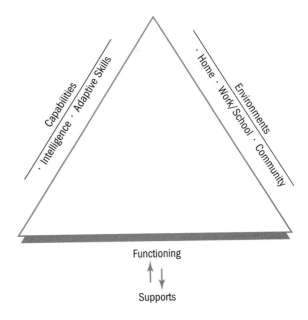

FIGURE 10-1 AAMR's model of mental retardation. Luckasson et al., 1992

changes, so might the diagnosis. Functioning is related to capabilities (shown on the left side of the figure), which interact with the environments in which individuals live, learn, play, work, and socialize (shown on the right side). This model also indicates that functioning and supports provided to the individual are reciprocally related. It is assumed that personal strengths exist along with deficits and that functioning will generally improve with appropriate supports.

CLASSIFYING MENTAL RETARDATION

AAMR's paradigm shift has affected the way in which individuals with retardation are classified into subgroups. It has been long recognized that great variability exists in the abilities and behaviors of people with mental retardation. It thus seems reasonable that classification according to severity of retardation might be helpful in intervention and research. Following this line of reasoning, AAMR once employed four levels of retardation: mild, moderate, severe, and profound. Individuals were assigned to a level according to their intelligence test scores. This approach has been widely employed by other classification systems.

Nevertheless, AAMR's new model eliminates classifying people by IQ levels and instead classifies by needed environmental supports. For each person, descriptions are to be given of strengths and weaknesses with regard to four aspects:

- intellectual functioning and adaptive skills;
- psychological and emotional functioning;
- physical functioning and health; and
- the person's current environment and the environment that would be optimal for continued growth.

Then a profile is developed of needed supports across the four aspects. The profile stipulates, for each aspect, a level of support required: intermittent, limited, extensive, or pervasive. Table 10-1 defines these levels. Thus instead of a broad diagnosis based on IQ, such as "severe mental retardation," the diagnosis might be "a person with mental retardation with extensive supports needed in the areas of social skills and self-direction" (Luck-

TABLE 10-1

AAMR's Levels of Needed Support

Intermittent	Support on "as needed" basis. Person needs sporadic supports or short-term supports during life-span transitions or crises (e.g., during job loss or acute medical crisis). Supports may be high or low intensity.
Limited	High or low intensity supports are needed consistently for only a limited time (e.g., time-limited employment training).
Extensive	Supports characterized by regular involvement (e.g., daily) in at least some environments (e.g., work or home) and are not time-limited (e.g., long-term home living supports).
Pervasive	Supports characterized by constancy and high intensity across environments. Potentially life sustaining in nature. Typically involve more staff members and intrusiveness.

Luckasson et al., 1992.

asson et al., 1992, p. 34). This approach recognizes that needs for support might be different in one area of functioning from another. It also indicates AAMR's concept of mental retardation as dynamically linked to the environment rather than being viewed as a static quality of the individual.

CONTROVERSY OVER DEFINITION

Although AAMR's new definition is endorsed by many professionals, it also has raised considerable controversy (Jacobson & Mulick, 1996; MacMillan & Reschly, 1997). One concern is that the new definition raises the upper limits of the IQ criterion to 75, from the previous limit of 70, meaning that more people might be declared mentally retarded, arguably not in their best interest. To put this matter in broader perspective, this is not the first time that controversy has existed with regard to the IQ criterion. In 1959, AAMR employed a definition that allowed individuals to be diagnosed with MR when they scored one or more standard deviations below the mean on intelligence tests. (See Figure 10-2.) Those who scored in the approximate range of 69 to 85 were considered to be retarded at the

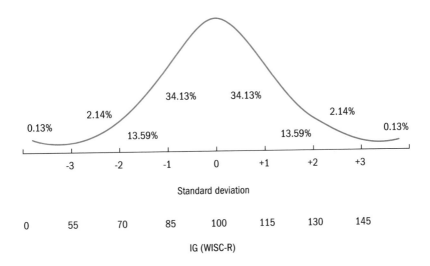

FIGURE 10-2 The distribution of scores on the WISC-R test of general intelligence fitted to the normal distribution. Standard deviation units indicate how far above or below a score is from the mean of 100. The standard deviation for the WISC-R is 15 points. When MR is defined by one or more standard deviations below the mean, approximately 16 percent of the population are mentally retarded. When MR is defined by two or more standard deviations below the mean, 2 to 3 percent of the population are mentally retarded.

borderline level. By this definition, about 16 percent of the population could be diagnosed as mentally deficient. Arguments ensued about the unreasonableness of the criterion, especially because certain socially disadvantaged groups were disproportionately labeled borderline mentally retarded. In 1973, AAMR shifted the IQ criterion to approximately 70 or below, where it remained until 1992.

A second criticism of the new definition revolves around the criterion for adaptive functioning, which previously had been defined as limitation across a combination of several domains of functioning and which now requires limitations in two of ten specific domains. The new criterion requires assessment methods that can reliably identify limitations in all ten specific domains; however, such methods do not exist. Finally, many professionals criticize the classification of MR by levels of support. Currently there is no reliable method for measuring levels of support, so classification by levels is likely to be flawed. In fact, DSM-IV is now at odds with AAMR in that it continues to classify MR by intelligence levels.

Table 10-2 shows the four levels employed by DSM-IV and a general description of functioning for each level. Also indicated is the comparable classification used by educators in the United States, which consists of three subgroups based on expectations for learning: educable, trainable, and severely/profoundly handicapped. Although recent changes in educational policy and practices regarding exceptional students have made this classification less relevant, it guided the management of intellectually handicapped students for many years and is still sometimes employed.

It is useful to keep in mind that about 85 percent of all cases are of mild retardation, about 10 percent of moderate, 3 to 4 percent of severe, and 1 to 2 percent of profound retardation (American Psychiatric Association, 1994). The many persons with mild retardation are viewed as quite different in functioning and in other important ways from

TABLE 10-2

Levels of Mental Retardation According to DSM-IV

Level	IQ Range	Percent of MR Population	Functioning
Mild (Educable)	50–55 to about 70	85	Social and communication skills usually develop in preschool years Have minimal sensorimotor deficits Can acquire about sixth-grade academic skills by late teens Usually achieve adult vocational and social skills for self-support May need guidance, assistance, supervised living, but often live successfully in the community
Moderate (Trainable)	35–40 to 50–55	10	Communication skills usually develop in early childhood Attend to personal care, with support Are unlikely to progress beyond second-grade academic skills Can benefit from social and occupation skills training and do supervised unskilled or semiskilled work Adapt well to supervised community living
Severe (Severely or profoundly handicapped)	20–25 to 35–40	3–4	May learn to talk and minimally care for self at school age Have limited ability to profit from preacademic training In adulthood, may perform simple tasks with supervision In most cases, adapt well to community living with family or in group homes
Profound (Severely or profoundly handicapped)	below 20–25	1–2	In most cases, have a neurological condition Have sensorimotor impairments in childhood With training, may show improvement in motor, self-care, communication skills May do simple supervised tasks For optimal development, require structure, constant supervision with individual caretaker

Based on APA 1994; and Singh, Oswald, & Ellis, 1998.

persons classified at the other three levels. Thus a distinction is commonly made between mild retardation and more severe retardation, with the IQ of about 50 marking the boundary. This distinction will be relevant to later discussion.

Changes in and controversy about the definition of mental retardation demonstrate the degree to which MR is a socially constructed category. AAMR's paradigm shift can be beneficial in that it encourages the view that human functioning at any level of intelligence is influenced by an individual's interactions with the environment. However, only future developments will tell whether and how AMMR's present definition will stand the test of time.

EPIDEMIOLOGY

The prevalence of mental retardation is estimated at about 2 to 3 percent of the general population when IQ is taken as the criterion, as it often is (Singh, Oswald, & Ellis, 1998). This figure roughly coincides with what would be expected from the theoretical distribution of IQ scores, as Figure 10-2 shows. When mental retardation is defined by both IQ and adaptive behavior, as recommended, prevalence drops to under 1 percent (Scott, 1994). This difference might reflect the fact that about half of those with mild retardation are not identified because their behavior is sufficiently adaptive in their environments.

Prevalence data are especially interesting when age and severity of retardation are inspected. Preschool youngsters are only rarely identified, and most have IQs below 50, apparently because the more severe cases are obvious and therefore elicit attention. But a dramatic shift occurs when children enter school. Prevalence increases as more mild retardation is identified, probably because the children are unable to meet the new demands in this situation. Then a decline occurs in adulthood, perhaps due partly to death or to the unavailability of adults to be tested and counted. In addition, with the demands of school gone, essentially unchanged adults may successfully engage in unskilled jobs and may function adequately in society, while others may continue to learn into adulthood and thus meet various demands (Clarke & Clarke, 1985).

Other variables are important when prevalence is examined (Crnic, 1988; Scott, 1994). Low socioeconomic groups account for a disproportionate number of cases, especially of mild retardation and MR is also more prevalent in some minority groups. In addition, it appears more among males than females. The usual kinds of explanations are offered for these data; that is, group differences might be due to biological or social variables or to a combination of these.

Mental retardation is associated with a high prevalence of physical disorders (Singh et al., 1998). Up to 20 percent of persons with MR and 50 percent of those with MR and cerebral palsy have a seizure disorder. Other problems include motor impairments, blindness, and deafness. Impairments tend to rise with increasing severity of retardation.

The epidemiology of mental retardation is an interesting reminder that prevalence varies with many factors, including the demands of different environments and the likelihood of cases being identified. By current definition, a person should not be identified as mentally retarded until his or her competence fails to meet standards for intelligence and adaptive functioning. In the next sections, we will further examine the concepts of intelligence and adaptive behavior.

THE NATURE OF TESTED INTELLIGENCE

What is intelligence? Most of us have some intuitive idea about its general nature and could identify individuals whom we believe are "very smart" or "not so smart." We might agree, as have theorists, that intelligence involves the knowledge possessed by a person, the ability to learn or think, or the capacity to adapt to new situations. Beyond these general definitions, however, we might run into disagreements. Indeed, theorists themselves disagree about the precise nature of intelligence and have proposed various theories and measurements of intelligence. Although we cannot do justice to this topic, a bird's-eye view of two central approaches indicates what is evaluated by tests of general intelligence.

Modern intelligence testing goes back to the work of Alfred Binet and his colleagues at the beginning of the twentieth century. Their approach—referred to as the traditional psychometric approach—focused on individual differences and on the idea that underlying abilities explained differences in intellectual functioning (Beirne-Smith, Ittenbach, & Patton, 1998). Most psychometricians believe that intelligence consists of both a general ability, called g, and numerous specific abilities (for example, motor and verbal abilities). They measure intelligence by presenting the examinee with various tasks that tap both general and specific abilities. This psychometric approach is sometimes described as examining the products of these abilities rather than the processes involved in the abilities.

In more recent years, information processing theories have come to the fore. They focus on the processes by which individuals perceive sensory stimuli, store information, manipulate information, and perhaps act on it. Different theorists have somewhat different ways of conceptualizing these processes, but in any case, intelligence is measured according to how well a person performs on processing tasks. For example, the abilities to plan, attend, and simultaneously deal with several bits of information might be measured (Anastasi & Urbina, 1997). The various information processing theories contribute much to the understanding of mental retardation. However, the psychometric approach largely shaped views of intelligence throughout most of the twentieth century and was basic to the Stanford-Binet and the Wechsler scales, which have been the most popular intelligence tests. Thus the earlier psychometric view is central to our immediate discussion.

EARLY TEST CONSTRUCTION AND ASSUMPTIONS ABOUT HEREDITY

When Binet and his colleague Simon were asked by the Minister of Public Instruction in Paris to find a way to identify children who needed special educational experiences, they approached their task in a practical way: They tested children of different ages on brief tasks relevant to classroom academic learning. In 1905 Binet and Simon published their first intelligence scale consisting of sets of tasks that average children of various ages

passed. Age-ordering of tasks reflected the belief that mental development increases with age throughout childhood. On the basis of their performance, children were assigned a mental age (MA), which is the age corresponding to the chronological age (CA) of children whose performance they equaled. Thus a seven-year-old who passed the tests that average seven-year-olds passed was assigned an MA of seven; a seven-year-old who passed the tests that the average six-year-old passed obtained an MA of six. Binet's work reflected concern for scientific integrity. Reliability of the tests over time was checked by testing groups of children and then retesting them later. Validity was established by comparing children's test scores with their actual school performance.

Binet made several assumptions about intelligence (Siegler, 1992). He believed that intelligence encompassed many complex processes. He also believed that atypical performance was best understood by comparisons with standard (average) performance. Binet viewed intelligence as malleable within limits, rather than fixed, and influenced by the social environment. As an advocate for children as well as a theorist, Binet feared that children could be inaccurately evaluated and he argued that carefully constructed standardized tests were necessary to minimize this possibility. Moreover, he and his colleagues devised methods to improve intellectual functioning, and they recommended that educational programs be fitted to each child's special needs and be conducted in small-sized classes (Tuddenham, 1962).

Intelligence testing was brought to the United States when Henry Goddard translated and used the Binet scales with residents of the Vineland Training School in New Jersey. Then in 1916, about five years after Binet's death, Lewis Terman—working at Stanford University—revised the early scales into the Stanford-Binet test. He adapted the items to the U.S. population and tested a relatively large number of children. Terman also adopted the idea of the intelligence quotient (IQ) as the ratio of an individual's mental age to chronological age, multiplied by 100 to avoid decimals. The ratio IQ enabled direct comparison between children of different ages. Today

Alfred Binet (1856–1911), a French psychologist, helped develop the first intelligence tests.
(Corbis/New York Public Library collection)

the major intelligence tests employ statistical comparison, so that what is often referred to as IQ is no longer a quotient but a score that nevertheless denotes age comparison. (See Table 10-3 for various measures relevant to intelligence tests.)

Goddard and Terman made some markedly different assumptions from those of Binet about the nature of intelligence. They assumed that the tests measured inherited intelligence that would remain stable over the life of the individual (e.g., Cravens, 1992). They also saw the need for *eugenics*, the improvement of the human species by control of inheritance. These beliefs had broad social implications. At the time, with the passage of compulsory education laws, the public schools had begun to place children with academic problems into ungraded classes, and there also was interest in "feebleminded" youth (MacMillan & Reschly, 1997). These children were disproportionately from immigrant and low social class homes. The assumptions that intelligence was fixed by inheritance eventually caused serious conflicts about the nature of intelligence and about the use of intelligence tests, especially with populations of lower social class. Although overly simple hereditary arguments are not popular today among professionals, such arguments have been a controversial part of the measurement of intelligence and of the identification of mental retardation.

IS INTELLIGENCE STABLE OR CHANGING?

Related to the arguments about heritability is the issue of whether measured intelligence is stable over time. The issue, which has long been debated, can be examined by studying a group of people longitudinally and comparing their earlier IQ scores with later IQ scores. When such test-retest measurements are made after preschool age, IQ scores are quite stable for groups of normal functioning individuals (e.g., Matarazzo, 1990). In general, correlations between sets of scores are stronger when the time between testings is shorter.

It is important to note that these correlational analyses examine groups of people. However, individual scores can also be examined over time. Earlier in this century it was widely held that individual IQ scores could not change but information gradually emerged to challenge this view. McCall, Applebaum, & Hogarty (1973), for example, concluded from their own and other data that IQ changes of thirty and forty points occur fairly often. Conditions such as illness, fatigue, the family situation, educational opportunity, social adjustment, and mental health have all been associated with change in individual IQ (Robinson & Robinson, 1976).

Do these findings apply to individuals with mental retardation? In general, the IQs of mentally handicapped persons are more stable than those of persons with average and superior scores, and the lower the scores, the greater is the stability (Berger & Yule, 1985). But, again, change can occur. For example, Silverstein (1982) tested mildly retarded children for four consecutive years, starting at about age eleven. Almost 12 percent of the children showed ten to twelve points change in either direction. More dramatic change has been documented when the social environment has been deliberately improved (Clarke & Clarke, 1984).

WHAT DO IQ TESTS TELL US ABOUT A PERSON?

Another central issue about intelligence is the question of what an IQ score tells us about a person. This is, of course, a question about the valid-

---

TABLE 10-3

Measures Relevant to Tests of Intelligence

CA	Chronological age.
MA	Mental age. The age score corresponding to the chronological age of children whose performance the examinee equals. For the average child, MA = CA.
IQ (ratio)	The ratio of mental age to chronological age multiplied by 100. IQ = MA/CA x 100.
IQ (deviation)	A standard score derived from statistical procedures that reflects the direction and degree to which an individual's performance deviates from the average scores of the age group.

ity of the test employed. Recall that Binet and Simon sought to measure academic ability and produced some evidence for the validity of their scale. Indeed, if intelligence is defined as ability that relates to school performance, evidence exists for validity. Perhaps this finding is unsurprising, because intelligence tests measure various abilities but mostly emphasize verbal abilities, which are important in academics. After age five, the correlations of IQ with school grades and reading, spelling, and mathematic achievement scores are moderately high, generally in the range of .40 to .75 (Berger & Yule, 1985; Matarazzo, 1992). Moreover, the relationship between IQ and academic performance appears even stronger for individuals whose IQ scores fall into the below average range.

Intelligence test scores also relate to a variety of out-of-school achievements, but the correlations are relatively low (Baumeister, 1987). In fact, various limitations of intelligence tests have been recognized. Binet and Wechsler themselves believed that intelligence tests did not assess all factors that might contribute to intelligence (Siegler, 1992; Wechsler, 1991). Cooperation, social responsiveness, and motivational variables such as expectancy for success and failure may influence test scores and everyday intelligence, but their influence is not well discriminated on intelligence tests (Scarr, 1982). In addition, intelligence tests are given in highly controlled situations with highly structured questions, so that IQ does not adequately reflect the everyday world that requires various strategies to solve problems in various situations (Fredericksen, 1986; Sternberg et al., 1995). IQ scores thus can be expected to be more valid in some situations than in others and validity may vary for groups of people to the extent that these groups function in different environments (Garcia, 1981).

In summary, caution is necessary in interpreting measured intelligence and in using scores to categorize people as mentally retarded. IQ scores are relatively stable, but they are not cast in stone. They provide important information about individual functioning but cannot tell us everything. Scores need to be interpreted within the context of the individual's life, including how the person

functions in different environments and with supports. Overall, IQ tests are an important tool but are inadequate as an exclusive tool for identifying retardation and making decisions about treatment, education, and other aspects of individuals' lives.

THE NATURE OF ADAPTIVE FUNCTIONING

Working at the Vineland Training School several decades ago, Edgar Doll emphasized the importance of social adequacy and the ability of persons with retardation to manage their lives. He published a scale to measure what he called social competence, a forerunner of the present concept of adaptive behavior (Myers, Nihara, & Zetlin, 1979). In 1959, AAMR first included deficits in adaptive functioning as a criterion for mental retardation. Subsequently AAMR offered the following definition:

Adaptive behavior refers to the quality of everyday performance in coping with environmental demands. The quality of adaptation is mediated by level of intelligence; thus, the two concepts overlap in meaning. It is evident, however, from consideration of the definition of adaptive behavior, with its stress on everyday coping, that adaptive behavior refers to what people do to take care of themselves and to relate to others in daily living rather than the abstract potential implied by intelligence. (Grossman, 1983, p. 42)

Research has shown a moderate relationship between adaptive behavior and intelligence. There is an overlap between these concepts, but measures of adaptive behavior also tap factors other than the mental functioning tapped by IQ tests (DeStefano & Thompson, 1990).

Over the years, many definitions of adaptive behavior have been offered, recognizing several domains of functioning. The ideas of social responsibility and personal independence appear central to the concept (Luckasson et al., 1992). Behaviors associated with sensorimotor, communication, self-help, and primary socialization skills are emphasized in early life whereas during later childhood and adolescence, reasoning and judgments about the environment and social relationships increase in importance. Moreover, adaptiveness might vary across cultures that hold different expectations for behavior, can vary with situations, and can depend on the match between the individual and the immediate situation (Scott, 1994). For example, in so-called "six-hour retardation," the child appears retarded in functioning while at school but functions adequately at home and in the neighborhood.

Research demonstrates the importance of daily living skills to persons with mental retardation. For example, maladaptive behaviors such as temper tantrums or being destructive are associated with individuals' being placed in institutions. Moreover, a connection between adaptive behavior and later adjustment in the community is being established (McGrew, Bruininks, & Thurlow, 1992). Success and satisfaction in life are surely influenced by competence in everyday functioning.

DEVELOPMENTAL COURSE AND CONSIDERATIONS

Inherent in any consideration of MR are developmental issues and questions concerning cognitive and adaptive skills. Development typically goes awry early in life, frequently prior to birth, and it is often associated with abnormalities in the growth of perceptual, motor, emotional, and behavioral systems. Nevertheless, the developmental approach has only recently come into its own with regard to MR (Hodapp & Zigler, 1997). We will recognize three issues relevant to the approach.

The first concerns the rate or pattern of intellectual development. Does cognition grow slowly over time in individuals with retardation, become permanently arrested at a specific time, or change through a series of spurts and lags? This question is far from answered. However, different courses of development appear associated with different specific syndromes of retardation.

A second issue is whether cognition in MR is qualitatively different from normal cognition and whether it follows the normal sequence of growth. Normal cognitive processes might exist and develop in the normal order, although growth might be delayed and stop relatively early in the sequence (Hodapp & Zigler, 1997). Alternatively, cognitive processes might be qualitatively different and the sequence of development might be disturbed. These ideas have been tested with a variety of tasks, as will be detailed later in the chapter. Although the research is not exhaustive, it appears that both accounts apply to mental retardation.

A third developmental issue concerns the prognosis for MR. Mental retardation is mostly considered chronic, especially the more severe levels. However, there is evidence for improvement in some cases.

ETIOLOGY

Although mental retardation is associated with hundreds of specific medical and genetic conditions, as well as with psychosocial disadvantage, causation is not clearly identified in an estimated 20 to 30 percent of cases of severe retardation and in 50 to 60 percent of mild retardation (Gillberg, 1997; Luckasson et al., 1992).

Historically there was a tendency to view MR as falling into two categories: that caused by biological factors and that caused by psychosocial factors (Luckasson et al., 1992). This account has been replaced by more complex explanations, which recognize, however, that in any single case, one factor may contribute more than others. It is nevertheless useful to categorize causation or risk in some way, and we follow Scott (1994) in recognizing three kinds of influences that have been widely discussed: organic risk factors, polygenic inheritance, and psychosocial/cultural influences.

ORGANIC RISK FACTORS

Attributing mental retardation to organic risk implies that biological conditions account for disordered brain function and intellectual deficiency. Empirical evidence supports this idea. Major pathological causes are known and believed to be primary in about 25 percent of MR cases (Scott & Carran, 1987). Organic problems are associated with all levels of MR but especially with more severe retardation. For example, known pathology exists in an estimated 55 to 75 percent of children with severe retardation but in only 10 to 25 percent with mild retardation (Scott, 1994).

Zigler and his colleagues have emphasized that although IQ scores are said to be normally distributed in the general population, they actually fall into a distribution that resembles the normal curve except for a "bump" at the low end (Burack, 1990; Zigler, Balla, & Hodapp, 1984). This excess of low scores, they suggested, is accounted for by individuals who have suffered major biological impairment that overwhelms the normal distribution of intelligence (Simonoff, Bolton, & Rutter, 1996). In fact, there is evidence for a group of more severely retarded individuals, coming from all social classes, who show an excess of genetic abnormalities, multiple congenital anomalies, clear evidence of brain dysfunction such as cerebral palsy, and reduced life expectancy. Biological impairment, regardless of the level of retardation with which it is associated, may be due to abnormal genetic mechanisms, prenatal or birth variables, or postnatal circumstances.

Genetic abnormalities. A variety of genetic aberrations, both inherited and noninherited, are associated with specific syndromes of mental retardation. The exact way in which these abnormalities cause lowered intelligence is not understood, and brain studies of intelligence are still relatively sparse (Thompson, 1997). A few genetic syndromes account for a relatively large number of cases of MR. Our discussion highlights three syndromes, which demonstrate different genetic abnormalities and distinct clinical features.

Down Syndrome Aberrations in the number and structure of chromosomes are the single most common cause of severe retardation (Simonoff et al., 1996). Down syndrome, the most common single disorder of mental retardation, occurs in approximately one in a thousand births (Thapar et al., 1994). This condition accounts for an estimated 5 percent of mild retardation and 30 percent of more severe cases (Gillberg, 1997).

Down syndrome was described in 1866 by Langdon Down, a British physician. For several years, it was noted that concordance in monozygotic twins approached 100 percent, which implicated a genetic process (Rainer, 1980). In 1959, only three years after human chromosomes were fully described, Lejeune and others discovered trisomy #21 in persons with Down syndrome. As shown in Figure 10-3, the #21 chromosome appears in a triplet instead of a pair. Ninety-five percent of all cases are attributed to this abnormality. (The remainder are caused either by translocations of chromosome #21, in which part of the chromosome breaks off and attaches to another chromosome, or by mosaicism, in which only some body cells have abnormal chromosomal makeup, often involving #21.)

The occurrence of trisomy #21 increases with maternal age. Advancing maternal age is apparently related to failure of the chromosome pairs to divide in meiosis, with trisomy #21 being a result. However, the extra chromosome has been traced to fathers in a minority of cases (Evans & Hammerton, 1985; Holmes, 1978). Younger women who have a child with trisomy #21 have a small risk for having another child with Down syndrome (Simonoff et al., 1996).

Children with Down syndrome are born with a variety of physical abnormalities that results in a common resemblance. Most characteristic is the epicanthal folds at the corners of the eyes and the upward slant of the eyes, which gave rise to the now outdated name "mongolism." Other features include facial flatness, fissured and thick tongues, broad hands and feet, and poor muscle tone (Aman, Hammer, & Rojahn, 1993). There is risk of serious health problems, such as heart defects and hearing impairment. Although life expectancy is below normal, it has climbed substantially in recent years (Carr, 1994).

Tested intelligence typically ranges in the moderate to profound levels of retardation and is occasionally higher (Szymanski & Kaplan, 1991). Developmental deficits are usually evident during the first few years of life, and amidst many spurts and regressions, the rate of development progressively

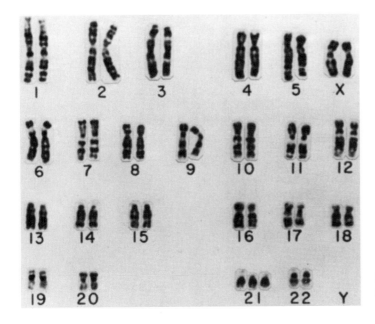

FIGURE 10-3 The chromosome complement of a female with trisomy # 21.

Courtesy of the March of Dimes Birth Defects Foundation.

slows throughout childhood and adolescence (Bregman & Hodapp, 1991; Carr, 1994). The relative impairments and strengths associated with Down syndrome are becoming better understood. Language functioning is typically delayed and relatively weak, and there is weakness in scanning details of the environment to extract information (Laws, 1998; Rossen et al., 1996). Social skills are relatively high; these children generally cooperate with others and respect social rules. At the same time, their emotional development is slowed, and the emotions seem muted (Whitman, O'Callaghan, & Sommer, 1997).

As with all children, the home environment is important to development. A disproportionately high percentage of infants and toddlers with Down syndrome are insecurely attached to their caretakers (Atkinson et al., 1995). Mother-child interaction may be subtly different from the normal by the first or second year (Berger, 1990; Landry & Chapieski, 1989). This factor may have some basis in the children's behavior, as they tend to be less socially responsive and to give less predictable and appropriate social signals (Roach et al., 1998). Mothers, in turn, appear to be more directive and controlling. It has been suggested that this maternal style is detrimental to the child's development; however, this is not necessarily so. Mothers can simultaneously direct their child's behavior and show support, for example, by making it easier for the child to succeed and by appropriately praising the child. The combination of parental directiveness and sensitive support has been linked to positive child outcome.

Fragile X Syndrome This condition is one of many specific syndromes associated with mental retardation that are inherited in Mendelian single-gene patterns. Many of the syndromes involve defective metabolism in which handicaps gradually worsen. Recessive genes are often implicated, although sex-linked and dominant gene patterns are found. Treatment, when it exists, often involves a diet to reduce the biochemical substance that is inade-

TABLE 10-4

Examples of Metabolic Disorders Associated with Mental Retardation

Disorder and Mechanism	Metabolic Disturbance	Manifestation	Treatment
Phenylketonia			
recessive inheritance	Inability to convert the amino acid phenylalanine due to deficient liver enzyme	Retardation, hyperactivity, unpredictable behavior, convulsions, eczema can occur.	Diet low in phenylalanine, if begun early, can prevent or reduce retardation.
Maple Syrup Urine Disease			
recessive inheritance	Abnormal metabolism of amino acids—leucine, isoleucine, valine	Infants develop rigidity, seizures, respiratory irregularities, hypoglycemia. Most die in few months if untreated or are severely retarded.	Diet low in leucine, isoleucine, valine is used.
Schilder's Disease			
sex-linked inheritance	Decrease in fats in CNS resulting in demyelination of cerebral white matter	Onset more common in older children and adults. Personality and behavioral changes. Paresis; cortical blindness and deafness; convulsions; dementia.	No established treatment; may respond to steroids.
Galactosemia			
recessive inheritance	Inability to convert galactose (carbohydrate) to glucose	After a few days of milk intake, jaundice; vomiting; diarrhea; failure to thrive. Leads to rapid death or mental retardation.	Early galactose-free diet permits normality.

Based on Cytryn and Lourie, 1980.

quately metabolized or to add a missing biochemical. Table 10-4 lists a few of these known disorders. Such conditions account for only a small proportion of mental deficiency; nevertheless, it is encouraging that advances in genetics hold promise for prevention and specific treatments.

In contrast to many inherited conditions, fragile X syndrome is of particular interest because, although discovered relatively recently, it is second to Down syndrome as a cause of retardation, affecting about 5 percent of cases of more severe retardation and 5 percent of cases of mild retardation (Gillberg, 1997). It acquired its name from an abnormal "fragile" site on the X chromosome. Although genetic transmission was apparent early on, much investigative work was necessary to track down the unusual X-linked pattern (Simonoff et al., 1996; Thapar et al., 1994). Fragile X syndrome involves, in the area of the FMR-1 gene, repeats of a triplet of DNA nucleotides (cytosine, guanine, guanine). Persons in the general population have between six and fifty of these repeats. Male and female carriers of fragile X syndrome have fifty to two hundred repeats; this condition is known as the premutation. It is unstable and tends to expand to the full mutation of over two hundred repeats, in which case the FMR-1 gene is not expressed. This mutation is the full-blown fragile X syndrome. An interesting aspect is that only when females transmit the premutation does it expand to the full mutation. It is inconclusive as to whether women with the premutation are developmentally affected, but they pass the condition to offspring, with the possibility of a full mutation occurring. Sons are affected more than daughters by this X-linked condition.

Males with fragile X syndrome tend to have distinctive long faces, large ears, and oversized testicles. Nearly all have mental retardation, usually mild to moderate but sometimes severe. There is a notable and predictable decline in IQ from about ten to fifteen years of age (State, King, & Dykens, 1997). A distinct profile has emerged of relative strength in verbal long-term memory and relative weaknesses in short-term memory, visual-motor coordination, sequential processing, mathematics, and attention. Many of these individuals also display relative strength in adaptive behavior, but gains are less evident after age ten. Behavioral difficulties include hyperactivity, stereotypies, and poor peer relations.

Nowhere near as many females with fragile X syndrome display mental retardation, and when they do, it tends to be mild although similar to the male profile. Learning disabilities are common in females with one affected X chromosome, as well as various behavior problems and social impairments.

Williams Syndrome This syndrome is a rare disorder associated with a gene deletion on chromosome 7 (State et al., 1997). It is characterized by a distinctive "elfinlike" face, growth deficiency, cardiac and kidney problems, and abnormal calcium metabolism. The syndrome is typically associated with mild to moderate retardation, with the mean IQ being in the middle fifties (Howlin, Davies, & Udwin, 1998). Deficiencies exist in abilities such as general knowledge, abstract conceptualization, and problem solving (Rossen et al., 1996). Especially intriguing is a discrepency between nonlingusitic and linguistic abilities (Hodapp & Zigler, 1997).

Performance IQ tends to be significantly lower than verbal IQ. Visual-spatial skills are below what would be expected in keeping with the children's mental age. Furthermore, the deficits appear distinct and are striking (Rossen et al., 1996). Even at adolescence, there is an inability to perceive gross differences in spatial orientation and to copy simple stick figures. Selective attention is given to details rather than to whole configurations, an example of which is provided in Figure 10-4. Here we see that participants with Williams syndrome focused on the local feature (Y) in their drawings, whereas those with Down syndrome focused on the global feature (D). Despite such visual-spatial deficits, some individuals with Williams syndrome show remarkable ability to discriminate and remember faces.

At the same time, even with notable verbal deficits, children and adults with Williams syndrome have sometimes been described as having a relatively sophisticated vocabulary and ability to employ it. Their communication style has been described as coherent, fluent, and "pseudo-mature" (Hodapp & Zigler, 1997; State et al., 1997). In addition, although research describes behavior problems such as anxiety, hyperactivity, and stubbornness, case studies report charming and friendly personality. Here is a description capturing both the engaging abilities and the deficiencies of Williams syndrome.

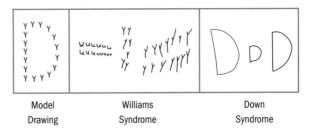

Model Drawing   Williams Syndrome   Down Syndrome

FIGURE 10-4 When copying drawings such as the Model Drawing, adolescents with Williams syndrome copy the local feature (Y) in arrangements that do not resemble the global feature (D). Adolescents with Down syndrome do the opposite. Adapted from Rossen, Klima, Bellugi, Bihrle, & Jones, 1996.

In describing her future aspirations, Crystal, a 16-year-old adolescent, states: "You're looking at a professional book writer. My books will be filled with drama, action, and excitement. And everyone will want to read them. I'm going to write books, page after page, stack after stack . . . I'll start on Monday." Crystal describes a meal as "a scrumptious buffet," an older friend as "quite elegant," and her boyfriend as "my sweet petunia"; when asked if someone could borrow her watch, she replies "My watch is always available for service." Crystal can spontaneously create stories—she weaves a tale of a chocolate princess who changes the sun color to save the chocolate world from melting; she recounts with detail a dream in which an alien from a different planet emerges from a television. Her creativity extends to music; she has composed the lyrics to a love song. . . . In view of her facility with language, proclivity for flowery, descriptive terms, and professed focus on drama and action, her aspiration may seem plausible; but in fact, Crystal has an IQ of 49, with an IQ equivalent age of 8 years. (Rossen et al., 1996, p. 367)

Case descriptions like that of Crystal, in conjunction with other research, firmly establish that among genetic syndromes, specific genetic mechanisms, developmental course, and attributes of mental retardation can be strikingly different.

Prenatal and birth complications. Organic risk factors associated with prenatal development and/or perinatal events are commonly encountered in cases of mental retardation (Gillberg, 1997). Prenatal exposure to disease, chemicals, drugs, radiation, poor nutrition, and Rh incompatibility may jeopardize the intellectual development of the child. In recent years, much attention has been given to maternal use of alcohol and illegal drugs such as cocaine.

Low birth weight and prematurity are also associated with neurological and intellectual deficits (Bregman & Hodapp, 1991). Preterm infants who show neurological insults on ultrasound assessments (e.g., hemorrhage in the brain) are more likely to show later disability than preterm babies without such neurological indicators.

Complications occurring at birth, such as head injury, seizures, and anoxia, can also take a toll. Anoxia occurs in about five of one thousand births; about 20 percent of the infants are adversely affected, and cerebral palsy with mental retardation can follow (Scott, 1994). It is now thought that birth complications often reflect pre-existing conditions, which may be the basis for both difficult birth and retardation. In such cases, birth complications in themselves may contribute relatively little to the etiology of MR.

Postnatal factors. Mental retardation may also be caused postnatally by a variety of variables, including seizures, malnutrition, diseases such as encephalitis and meningitis, lead poisoning, and head injuries from auto, bicycle, and other accidents. All these factors can interfere with nervous system functioning and development. Sometimes causation appears relatively clear, as when intellectual decrements are traced to disease of the brain. However, it is not always easy to establish clear causation; for example, malnutrition that affects the brain may be confounded with other variables. Nevertheless, many postnatal circumstances undoubtedly put the child or adolescent at organic risk.

POLYGENIC INFLUENCES

The organic influences just discussed are assumed to cause mental retardation through abnormal brain development or brain damage. In this sense, they are pathological. In contrast, polygenic influences derive from multiple genes whose effects combine to produce variation in intelligence in normal populations. Mental retardation is viewed as representing the lower scores in this nonpathological polygenic variation.

The argument that inheritance influences intelligence and mental deficiency is an old one that in past times was often based on flimsy or flawed "proof." For example, in his influential study of the Kallikak family, Goddard (1912) traced the quite distinct genealogical lines of Martin Kallikak. One line originated from Kallikak's liaison with a barmaid, the second from later marriage to a woman of "better stock." From information on several hundred of Kallikak's descendants, Goddard found a pronounced difference in the two families, namely, that the first liaison had resulted in more mental deficiency, criminality, alcoholism, and immorality. Obvious weaknesses existed in this study, most notably the questionable accuracy of the data. Moreover, the results were taken as evidence that mental deficiency was inherited, although family environment could just as well have played a role.

Current understanding of hereditary influence on tested intelligence has a firm base in behavior genetic research. Intelligence test performance of identical twins is overall more similar than that of fraternal twins (McGue et al., 1993). This finding holds even on specific intellectual tasks. When identical twins are reared apart, similarity decreases but is still high. Studies of families and adopted children lend support to the twin findings. In general, it is estimated that about 50 percent of the variation in tested intelligence in populations is due to genetic transmission of multiple genes (Plomin, DeFries, & McClearn, 1990). Most of this research has been conducted with nonretarded persons. However, the few studies with individuals with retardation similarly implicate polygenic inheritance (Thompson, 1997). For example, two investigations indicate greater similarity for identical twins than for fraternal twins.

Research studies also suggest that polygenic influences vary with the level of retardation. Earlier we pointed to evidence that pathological organic factors are more strongly associated with the more severe levels of retardation. The opposite appears to hold for polygenic influences. Thus, one family study revealed that the IQs of siblings of children with severe retardation averaged 103, hinting that severe retardation did not "run in families" and that some specific organic factor caused retardation in the affected child. In contrast, the IQs of siblings of children with mild retardation averaged 85, suggesting general family influence, perhaps polygenic inheritance, psychosocial effects, or a combination of these (Broman et al., 1987; Scott, 1994).

This is not to say, of course, that pathological organic factors never cause mild retardation. It is also possible that biological advances will eventually reveal specific organic abnormalities that cannot now be detected. However, multiple explanations seem likely for mild retardation, as we will see as we turn to psychosocial risk factors.

PSYCHOSOCIAL/CULTURAL INFLUENCES

Interest in psychosocial and cultural factors is historically tied to what was once called cultural-familial retardation (Crnic, 1988). The terms "garden variety" and "undifferentiated" also were used, reflecting the large number of cases of MR that were not readily distinguished from one another. Individuals who were assigned such labels had no identifiable organic etiology and usually appeared normal. Their IQ scores fell into the 50 to 70 range, and they possessed relatively good adaptive skills. They were often first identified on entering school, and as adults, they often blended into the general population. Their family members were frequently described in similar ways.

A typical example is the description of six-year-old Johnny, who achieved a Stanford-Binet score of 67 (Robinson & Robinson, 1976). The family had eight children, several of whom were recognized as slow in school, and lived in a crowded, run-down, and disorganized home. The parents worked at unskilled jobs. Johnny's mother reported that he was a good child and that she was surprised that his teacher perceived any problem. In school Johnny could not master kindergarten reading readiness tasks and had problems in handling a pencil, folding paper, coloring within lines, and differentiating one symbol from another. He seemed to have a short attention span. He liked the other children, but they tended to ignore him and exclude him from play.

It has been observed for many years that mild retardation that "runs in families" occurs disproportionately in the lower socioeconomic classes—and some minority groups—and could be caused by psychosocial/cultural disadvantage. Many psychosocial variables correlated with social class put children at risk, such as parental education, parental attitudes, social support, and stressful life events (Sameroff, 1990). The more risk factors present, the higher is the risk.

MILD RETARDATION:
ARE INTELLIGENCE TESTS BIASED?

The issue of bias in intelligence testing is almost invariably raised with regard to mild retardation and psychosocial/cultural influences. Are intelligence tests constructed and administered in such ways that they handicap those of low social class and of certain racial/ethnic background? Children of poor families and of some minority families (e.g., African-American, Hispanic, and Native American) perform relatively poorly on these tests, on average. In interpreting this fact, it should be recognized that social class is often confounded with racial/ethnic background and that their independent effects have not been adequately examined (e.g., Helms, 1992).

The group differences just cited have resulted in serious concerns about intelligence testing. One concern has been that minority students have been disproportionately labeled mildly or educably retarded and thus have been placed in special education classes in the public schools. Many people believed that group differences on test performance (and subsequent school placements) reflect test bias rather than true differences in intelligence. Confrontations with the educational system, some of which reached the courts, ensued over a variety of testing practices and test fairness issues (MacMillan, Keogh, & Jones, 1986). Questions were raised about bilingual students' being assessed with standard English tests, about the content of tests not relating well to the subcultures in which students were being reared, and about the qualities of the tests being used.

Legal outcomes often, but not always, favored plaintiffs for the minority groups. The influential *Larry P. v. Riles* case, a class action suit in which the plaintiffs were black people, resulted in severe restrictions on the use of intelligence tests for identifying and placing black children into special education programs in California. On the other hand, the California ruling in *PASE v. Hamilton* judged that Wechsler and Stanford-Binet items were not biased against black children when these tests were used with other criteria for placement. In a later legal suit in California, black parents claimed discrimination on the basis that their children were denied the opportunity to take the tests, which could aid in assessment (Turkington, 1992). Some accommodation was made to these parents. Overall, educational systems have been forced to monitor stringently the use and administration of intelligence tests.

School placement is only one area of controversy in a long line of concerns about bias in intelligence testing. Historical accounts describe how IQ tests played an important role in establishing immigration quotas for people of southern European background and in introducing laws for the sterilization of mentally deficient individuals (Patton, Beirne-Smith, & Payne, 1990; Gould, 1981). Inherent in such uses and abuses of tests was the assumption that measured intelligence is a stable, biologically programmed characteristic of individuals. The more accepted view today is that intelligence tests assess important, circumscribed behaviors that result from the interaction of heredity and environment and that at least to some degree the behaviors can be changed throughout life by environmental factors.

Specific associations have been demonstrated between home environment variables, social class, and children's intellectual development. One study found, for instance, that IQ at age three was related to lower social class and parental practices, that is, interacting with the child, talking to the child, and being actively interested in what the child did (Hart & Risley, 1992). It appears that as a group, educationally and economically deprived parents may lack skills, or otherwise be unable to stimulate children's language and cognitive development. The investigators of this study and their colleagues have for many years been engaged in the Juniper Gardens Children's Project, an intervention and research program for disadvantaged preschool children (Greenwood et al., 1992; 1994). They have proposed a model for the development of retardation that reaches across generations. Accordingly, young children, because of limited parental interactions, begin to fall behind intellectually. On reaching school, this situation combines with school practices that lead to low educational motivation, exposure, and achievement—resulting in a high rate of school drop-out. In turn, when these children become parents, they are unable to contribute optimally to the cognitive growth of their offspring.

The adverse effects of psychosocial variables may operate through one or more pathways. Inadequate stimulation may hinder early brain development, especially the growth of synaptic networks. Behaviors conducive to success in the classroom and other learning environments may not be acquired. Attitudes and motivation favorable to achievement may be inadequately established.

Nevertheless, it is difficult to pinpoint any one cause of MR in disadvantaged children. This population is also at risk for major inherited abnormalities, prenatal and birth adversities, postnatal malnutrition, disease, and other adversities that can affect the developing brain. Variation due to polygenic inheritance is not ruled out. Given what is known about the intricacies of development, multifactor explanations might frequently apply.

LEARNING AND COGNITIVE CHARACTERISTICS

Investigators of various theoretical beliefs have been interested in demonstrating learning processes in MR and the kinds of deficits that are likely or unlikely to exist. Such information is not only of theoretical interest; it also tells us whether and what kinds of training might overcome intellectual and adaptive difficulties. Nevertheless, this is a complex area to study. There is immense variability across persons diagnosed with mental retardation and cognitive processes may vary with levels of retardation and across etiological groups. In addition, children with retardation frequently have language problems, are less familiar with research tasks that are control group children, and may be less motivated to perform well (e.g., Hodapp & Zigler, 1997). All these factors can confound the research results. Given these cautions, our discussion considers some of the contributions made by the learning theories, Piagetian, and information processing approaches. Most of the research has been conducted with children of mild or moderate retardation.

LEARNING THEORIES

Early investigations of classical and operant conditioning aimed at showing that learning is possible in those with mental retardation (Haywood, Meyers, & Switsky, 1982). Both kinds of learning were demonstrated at even severe and profound levels of retardation. Over the years, operant conditioning has been of special interest. In general, operant conditioning principles are applicable to MR (Matson & Coe, 1991). New behaviors can be shaped by successive approximations; desirable behaviors can be maintained and undesirable behaviors weakened by consistent application of appropriate contingencies. Obviously, extensive shaping is required when retardation is severe. Also, reinforcement effects can be inconsistent, and extinction of learned behaviors can easily occur. Overall though, operant learning is an effective and important approach to intervention.

PIAGETIAN THEORY

According to Piagetian theory, the mind of the child qualitatively changes through assimilation and accommodation as adaptation to the environment occurs (p. 24). The capacity of the mind to integrate information and to think in more complex ways indicates that growth is occurring. This developmental stage framework suggests ways in which the mental apparatus might go awry.

Piagetians proposed that retarded children follow the same universal sequence of stages as other children but that they advance more slowly and fall short of full mental growth. Piaget's colleague, Inhelder, was the first to study retardation from this perspective (Woodward, 1979). She found evidence that in profound retardation, development reaches only the sensorimotor stage; in moderate retardation, only the beginning of preoperations; in mild retardation, no more than concrete operations. Subsequent research indicated that those with retardation do progress through the same Piagetian and other sequences as do nonretarded children, although they do so more slowly and ultimately do not progress as far (Hodapp & Zigler, 1997). The subjects of this research were children with retardation for which there was no clear organic cause and children with Down syndrome.

This finding suggested to some investigators that mental retardation with these populations is best characterized as quantitatively different from normal development but not qualitatively different. This view was referred to as the *developmental position*. The alternative view—the *deficit position*—argued that retardation involves deficits or defects, that is, qualitative differences. Research subsequently addressed this issue with different kinds of learning tasks. It was shown that children with retardation with no identifiable organic cause exhibited the same basic reasoning processes as nonretarded children of the same mental age. However, those with Down syndrome displayed specific deficits in certain areas, compared with nonretarded children of the same mental age, for example, problems in attention.

It is generally accepted today that on some tasks, individuals with retardation (especially less severe) simply appear delayed but that specific cognitive deficits are explicable in other cases (Bregman & Hodapp, 1991). Determining underlying deficits is an ongoing endeavor. Moreover, there is increasing focus on relative strengths and competencies so that a more complete picture can be constructed (Bray, Fletcher, & Turner, 1997). Currently, the information processing framework is dominant in this work.

INFORMATION PROCESSING

Relatively early research, stemming from learning theories, examined cognitive processes such as attention and memory. The information processing approach subsumes these and other processes. For this discussion, Figure 10-5 presents a relatively simple information processing model. Accordingly, the sensory register receives information through the senses and passes it to short-term memory or storage. Short-term memory is viewed as limited in size so that it typically can deal with only a limited amount of information for a limited time. However, short-term memory can retain information somewhat longer while it employs strategies to prepare it for long-term memory, or can work on information that it receives from long-term memory. Thus it is known as working memory. Long-term memory permanently stores information, which can be retrieved with varying degrees of ease. Information can be retrieved directly from long-term memory, or it can be routed back to short-term memory, where it might be used with other information in problem solving or other thinking.

This information processing model also includes executive functions (or metacognition), which involve the ability to select, monitor, evaluate, and revise information processing strategies, depending on the situation. Part of executive functions is metamemory, which is the understanding of one's own memory system and the way that it works with specific information processing tasks (Haywood et al., 1982).

In general, individuals with mental retardation demonstrate difficulties on memory tasks. It is believed, however, that long-term memory operates

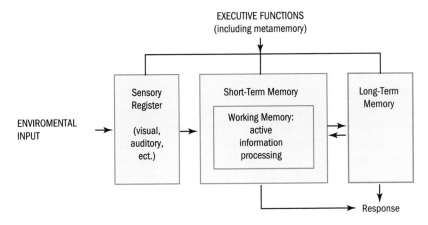

FIGURE 10-5 A general model of information processing.
Adapted from Atkinson and Shiffrin, 1968; and Swanson, 1987.

about as well as it does for nonretarded persons (Bray et al., 1997). That is, once something is learned and placed into long-term store, it is retained reasonably well. It is believed that difficulties exist in short-term, or working, memory. Many processes appear to be involved, including attention, strategy use, generalization, and executive functions.

Attention is crucial at various stages of information processing, and several deficiencies have been shown. For example, at the sensory register stage, persons with retardation are less able to orient and select stimuli (Tomporowski & Tinsley, 1997). Attentional deficits are also apparent in working memory when tasks require effortful processing. As a general rule, when processing demands increase, attention problems increase more for mentally retarded persons than they do for nonretarded persons.

Much research has been conducted on the strategies used in working memory. Successful strategies include rehearsing material, organizing material, and elaborating and transforming material so that it fits with what is already stored. Some of these strategies obviously demand complex thinking. Developmental progression has been charted for normal children, showing increases in both the use of strategies and their complexity.

With retardation there can be failure to employ effective strategies or to use them effectively (Borkowski & Cavanaugh, 1979; Borkowski, Johnston, & Reid, 1987; MacMillan et al., 1986). In some cases, performance improves when children are taught effective strategies and/or are instructed to use them. For example, in paired associate learning, a pair of stimuli (usually words or pictures) is first presented, and then the child is given one of the stimuli and is asked to provide the other. By age five or six, most normal children are able to produce and employ mediators that help them associate the paired stimuli. They may, for instance, connect the stimuli "snow" and "ice cream" by thinking the word "cold" or by imagining mounds of a white substance. However, children with retardation do not easily generate and use mediators in paired associate learning. When they are provided mediators by experimenters or are instructed to use mediators, their performance often improves (Borkowski & Cavanaugh, 1979).

To some extent children with retardation can even continue to use acquired strategies later on with tasks identical to the training tasks. However, they do not easily generalize strategies to new tasks, thus seriously curtailing training effects (Borkowski et al., 1987; Glidden, 1985). Problems in generalization appear related to deficits in executive functions and metamemory. That is, children with retardation inadequately select and monitor strategies, and they develop metamemory more slowly than nonretarded children (MacMillan et al., 1986).

Despite the various processing deficits observed in MR, Bray, Fletcher, and Turner (1997) point out that there is greater cognitive competence than once supposed. For example, competence has been displayed in visual recognition memory and long-term memory on many tasks. These investigators also note strengths in strategy use; for example, rehearsal of information is spontaneously employed and it increases with age. Nevertheless, Bray and colleagues recognize that strategy competence is fragile, which they hypothesize is due to limitations in the capacity of working memory.

SOCIAL CHARACTERISTICS AND BEHAVIOR PROBLEMS

Since 1980 or so, there has been increased interest in studying the social functioning of people with mild and moderate retardation (Greenspan & Love, 1997). Social skills are obviously essential for making friends and being successful in school, the workplace, and the community (Bradley & Meredith, 1991). These skills are of great importance in light of the relatively recent trend to facilitate more normal life experiences for those with retardation. In fact, for those with mental retardation, social competence may be even more important than it is for normal children. Nonretarded children often hold negative attitudes about their retarded peers and reject them. However, negative attitudes are less likely in the presence of appropriate and socially competent behavior (Siperstein & Bak, 1985).

SOCIAL SKILLS AND SOCIAL UNDERSTANDING

People with mental retardation often show deficits in social skills crucial to personal relationships (Davies & Rogers, 1985). Impairment is indicated in many ways, for example, in inappropriate facial expression and body contact, lack of verbal greetings and small talk, inappropriate comments, and lack of empathy in responding to others. Social cognition is also impaired, for example, the understanding of others' perspectives and of social situations and social cues. These deficits are not surprising: We would expect the general intellectual deficits of MR to interfere directly with the development of social competence. However, it is also likely that mental retardation leads to experiences that hinder social growth or increases problem behaviors.

A limited amount of research indicates a developmental lag in children with MR but also suggests gradual progress in such abilities as taking others' perspectives and resolving interpersonal conflicts. It appears that the acquisition of social cognitive skills may develop in the same order as they do for nonhandicapped children (Greenspan & Love, 1997).

In recent years, social skills training has been provided in various settings for individuals of various ages. Most training programs are behaviorally based and include instruction, modeling, role playing, and reinforcement (Marchetti & Campbell, 1990). Normally developing peers have been shown to facilitate social interaction, and specific environmental features have been shown to be linked to social interaction (Handen, 1998). Curricula for the teaching of social skills are available. In addition to these treatments, everyday activities can enhance social development. For example, preliminary study of participation in the Special Olympics by persons with mental retardation linked this experience with social competence (Dykens & Cohen, 1996).

BEHAVIOR PROBLEMS

Social adaptiveness of individuals with mental retardation is hindered by the various behavior problems they exhibit. Some of these problems are sufficiently severe to meet criteria for clinical diagnoses. Studies of community, clinic, and institutionalized samples indicate that prevalence is relatively high, although estimates vary. From epidemiological research, Bregman (1991) concluded that between one-third and two-thirds of

Special Olympics is an example of community programs that attempt to normalize the lives of retarded persons and to provide them with success experiences and a sense of self-worth.

(Joel Gordon)

those with mental retardation show significant psychopathology, a rate much higher than for control groups. Scott (1994) notes that the retarded population shows three to four times more problems than the general population. These rates apply to children and adolescents as well as adults. There is some indication that the number of youth with problems increases with age (Handen, 1998). In addition, behavior problems increase as retardation becomes more severe.

The kinds of disturbances exhibited in youth and adults are similar to those shown in the general population. Aggression, anxiety, depression, attention problems, hyperactivity, obsessive-compulsive disorder, schizophrenia, autism, stereotypies, and self-injury have all been reported (Bregman, 1991). Standard diagnostic criteria apparently apply well when IQ is about 50 or higher, but not as well otherwise (Handen, 1998). It is more difficult to identify some problems (e.g., depression), particularly in more severe retardation.

What accounts for high rates of psychopathology in MR? Neurological factors no doubt explain some disturbed behavior, e.g., seizures and head trauma are associated with behavioral problems (Bregman, 1991). Biological factors are perhaps more strongly causal in severe and profound retardation. In addition, a connection exists between specific genetic syndromes and specific problem behaviors; for example, fragile X syndrome is associated with high rates of attention deficits and hyperactivity (Handen, 1998).

Nevertheless, it would be mistaken to ignore psychosocial factors as causal. Social isolation curtails exposure to appropriate behavioral models; educational failure and the stigma of labeling can lead to feelings of incompetence. Certain kinds of institutional care and even the use of medication may also be associated with behavior problems. And obviously, the home environment is important. For example, instability in families and caregiving was found to be related to behavior disturbance in mildly retarded young adults (Richardson, Koller, & Katz, 1985).

In earlier times, social and behavioral problems were simply considered a part of mental retardation. Since these problems were taken for granted, they were not adequately described, counted, and studied. This situation has changed. There is greater recognition that social and behavioral disorders may or may not be an inherent part of mental retardation, and that in either case, they warrant attention. Such dysfunctions lower the quality of life for persons with retardation, interfere with community adjustment, and correlate with institutionalization (Aman et al., 1993; Scott, 1994).

FAMILY REACTIONS AND ADJUSTMENT

The birth of a child with any kind of handicap is likely to be a traumatic event. Most parents expect that their children will be attractive, smart, and socially successful. Parents thus grieve for unfulfilled expectations, as well as face other psychological, social, and economic stress (e.g., Gunn & Berry, 1990). Reactions to having a handicapped child have been studied by the questioning and observing of families. Many common themes emerge from the data.

It has been suggested that family reaction/adjustment occurs in three stages (Blacher, 1984). On first hearing of their child's condition, parents often experience shock and denial. When abnormalities are not obvious, families are more likely to deny the diagnosis. Looking back on the event, parents with handicapped children believe that families benefit by being told the truth as early as possible, receiving information about the disorder, and being treated sympathetically (Quine & Rutter, 1994). When the diagnosis is better accepted and the child's special needs become recognized, a second stage occurs. Chronic sadness, low self-esteem, hopelessness, guilt, disappointment, and anger are reported. Parent-child attachment may be delayed, although some parents become especially attached to their handicapped child. Eventually a third stage is usually reached, characterized by emotional reorganization, adjustment, and further acceptance. Parents reconstruct the needs of the entire family and become more comfortable with their situation. They actively seek services and may become advocates for individuals with handicaps.

Although families do report the experiences just described, a stage model is probably too simple a portrait and families may continually adjust and readjust in more complex patterns. Some family members may be more affected than others. For example, mothers often bear a disproportionate burden of care (Scott, 1994). Siblings, especially sisters, similarly engage in more caretaking, although research only inconsistently shows adverse effects on siblings (Boyce & Barnett, 1993; Cuskelly & Dadds, 1992; Eisenberg, Baker, & Blacher, 1998). Overall, some members and some families do better than others. It is thus important to ask, What factors are linked to family capacity to adjust?

FACTORS RELATED TO ADJUSTMENT

One variable that affects how families function is the severity of their child's retardation. Moderate and severe levels demand not only much immediate care but also planning for lifetime care and supervision; mild retardation can mean a long period of uncertainty about the existence of deficits. Other influential factors include parental beliefs and coping skills, marital interaction, parental intellectual functioning, and siblings' perception of differential treatment by parents, social class variables, professional services, and social support (e.g., Atkinson et al., 1995; Flynt, Wood, & Scott, 1992; Sloper et al., 1991; Wolf et al., 1998). These numerous factors—child characteristics, family characteristics, and social variables—create a complex picture. For instance, one study showed that mothers are more affected by the child's behavior and fathers by variables external to the child, such as unemployment and financial strain (Sloper et al., 1991).

PLACEMENT DECISIONS

Many families face the decision of whether to keep their child at home or to arrange for the child to live elsewhere, perhaps in some sort of institution or group home. Several factors enter into the decision. Table 10-5 shows some of the reasons that families in one study gave for placing their child with severe handicaps (Bromley & Blacher, 1991). Many of these reasons have been cited in other re-

TABLE 10-5

Factors Reported by At Least 40 Percent of Parents as Strongly or Very Strongly Influencing the Decision for Out-of-Home Placement

Factor	Percent
Day to day stress	81
My child's level of functioning and potential for future learning	75
My child's behavior	60
Feelings of my nonhandicapped children	55
My spouse's attitude toward placement	48
Medical or physical problems of my handicapped child	48
Availability of respite care	46
Availability of babysitters	43
Advice from professionals	41

Adapted from Bromley and Blacher, 1991.

search. From this we can surmise that reducing the child's problems and daily stress could impact the placement decision. Family members prosper from social support, breaks from caregiving, and freedom to pursue their own interests (Botuck & Winsberg, 1991; Joyce, Singer, & Isralowitz, 1983). Assistance can be provided by in-home or out-of-home respite care for youth with disabilities. In-home care involves having trained caregivers coming to the home on a part-time schedule. Out-of-home programs entail the child's traveling to some other place for care; for example, the child may live at home during the week and stay at a hospital or foster home on weekends. Mothers receiving respite care report that they feel relief and greater well-being, experience less depression, have more time for personal care and for other family members, enjoy leisure activities, and relate in a more positive way to their child with disabilities.

Although the decision about their child's living arrangement must often weigh heavily on parents, Eisenberg, Baker, and Blacher (1998) found that families come to terms with their choice. They appear to choose what they believe will benefit all family members. Families that chose to place their child out-of-home cite numerous positive consequences and few regrets. Families that chose to keep their child at home—and most do—see negative consequences of placement and report positive experiences related to their decision. For instance, Jason Konidaris (1997) reported that he "infinitely" gained from his relationship with his handicapped brother—that he became a more complete person who balances compassion, discipline, and responsibility. Other siblings have reported that they benefited by acquiring increased empathy, maturity, patience, honesty, acceptance of differences, ability to help others and to cope with stress, and appreciation for health and family (Eisenberg, Baker, & Blacher, 1998). In many families, siblings appear to be considerate of and kind to the child with handicaps, thus showing qualities that could be forerunners of altruism and humanistic concerns in adulthood (Dunn, 1988).

Fortunately, greater recognition is now being given to family needs. Efforts are being made to provide economic assistance, medical care, child and family therapy, training in child management, and training of parents as teachers for their handicapped children. Research indicates that helping families obtain services from community resources rather than solely from professional agencies can be especially advantageous (Handen, 1998). Nevertheless, provision of needed supports can wax and wane with society's broader economic and social concerns, and families can experience high levels of burnout, financial struggles, and insecurity about future services. Support for families has always been important but is especially crucial now that the philosophy of treatment for retardation strongly encourages family involvement and home care.

ASSESSMENT

Our discussion of the assessment of mental retardation draws heavily on Handen's (1997) recent review. Assessment may serve several purposes. Diagnosis may be required for school placement or for obtaining special services. It is fairly common for parents to seek a second opinion about their child's functioning or they may seek help in facilitating the diagnosed child's development or managing behavior. Thus, employing a standard battery of assessment instruments or methods will not appropriately serve every child. Rather, the purpose of the evaluation can best determine the comprehensiveness of the assessment and the procedures and instruments used. Assessment of intelligence, adaptive behavior, and academic achievement, along with a developmental history, may be more than sufficient for diagnosis (e.g., Gillberg, 1997). If an important goal is testing hypotheses about the cause of already-diagnosed retardation, evaluation could reasonably include extensive physical examinations and medical tests.

Assessment of intelligence, adaptive behavior, behavior adjustment and problems, academic progress, family functioning, and medical concerns are all appropriate, depending on the case. We will detail two of these areas, general intelligence and adaptive skills, which are central to diagnosis and which rely on standardized tests. However, intelligence and adaptive skills tests are criticized for not being sufficiently prescriptive, that is, for not providing information adequate to guide intervention (Detterman & Thompson, 1997; Scotti et al., 1996). Thus our discussion will also include functional assessment and curriculum-based assessment, which are more intricately linked to treatment after diagnosis.

TESTS OF GENERAL INTELLIGENCE

Standardized, individually given intelligence tests are the single most important instruments to diagnose mental retardation. The Stanford-Binet and Wechsler tests have proven themselves reasonably reliable and valid; some newer tests developed from a stronger theoretical rationale do not yet have as firm a research base. For infants, toddlers, or children with severe deficiency, developmental tests substitute for the more advanced intelligence tests.

Developmental tests. Several standardized, individually given developmental scales exist. Among the most popular is the Bayley Scales of Infant De-

velopment-II, which covers age one month to forty-two months (Bayley, 1969/1993). Performance on this test is termed developmental quotient (DQ), since it evaluates different abilities than do tests for older children. Infant scales give greater emphasis to sensorimotor functioning and less emphasis to language and abstraction. This feature may partly account for the fact that performance on infant tests is not highly correlated with later IQ.

Developmental tests administered during the first few years of life cannot be solely relied on to predict later intellectual performance for most children. However, they may be better predictors of mental deficiency, especially of severe retardation, than of average or superior intelligence. They may also be especially helpful when used in conjunction with histories and neurodevelopmental assessments (Bregman & Hodapp, 1991). Thus, for example, if an infant's performance is substantially behind that of age-mates, if a history of perinatal damage exists, and if there are signs of nervous system dysfunction, a diagnostician might strongly suspect mental retardation.

Stanford-Binet. The Stanford-Binet (S-B) is now in its fourth edition and is notably different from prior editions (Thorndike, Hagen, & Sattler, 1986). Items are grouped into fifteen subtests (e.g., vocabulary, copying, memory for objects), with the items increasing in difficulty. Four cognitive areas are assessed for individuals from two to twenty-three years of age: verbal reasoning, abstract/visual reasoning, quantitative reasoning, and short-term memory. Each person achieves a Standard Age Score (SAS) for each of the four areas and for the entire scale. The SASs are compared with performance of a standard norm group of the same chronological age. The average SAS is statistically set at 100. Thus a person who scores higher than 100 has performed better than average for his or her age; an obtained SAS less than 100 means a less-than-average performance. These SASs are what most people would call an IQ.

Wechsler tests. Immensely popular for assessing MR are the Wechsler Intelligence Scale for Children (WISC-III) for six-to-sixteen-year-olds, and the Wechsler Preschool and Primary Scale of Intelligence (WPPSI-R) for the age range of 4 to 6 years (Wechsler, 1989; 1991). They consist of different subtests—such as vocabulary, puzzles, and arithmetic problems—each of which contains items that become increasingly difficult. The subtests are designated as either verbal tasks or performance tasks. The former emphasize verbal skills, knowledge of the environment, and social understanding. Performance subtests emphasize perceptual-motor skills, speed, and nonverbal abstraction. The Wechsler scales permit the calculation of three deviation IQs: a verbal IQ, a performance IQ, and a full-scale IQ that combines verbal and performance scores. As with the S-B, performance is compared with a norm group of similar age, and the average performance is 100.

Kaufman tests. The Kaufman Assessment Battery for Children (K-ABC) is a relatively new, well-respected test that has predictive validity similar to that of the Wechsler child test (Anastasi & Urbina, 1997). It is designed for children from age two-and-a-half to twelve-and-a-half. The K-ABC evaluates two fundamental information processing abilities (Kaufman & Kaufman, 1983). Sequential processing is assessed with subtests that require step-by-step processing of verbal, numerical, and other content. Simultaneous processing is assessed with subtests that require integrating several pieces of visual-spatial information at the same time. The child achieves a score for Sequential Processing, a score for Simultaneous Processing, and a Mental Processing Composite score that is based on nonverbal subtests from the sequential and simultaneous processing tasks. An Achievement score is also derived from performance on six subtests, such as arithmetic and word knowledge, that resemble S-B and Wechsler subtests. The average score for each of these four scales is 100. Newer than the K-ABC is the Kaufman Adolescent and Adult Intelligence Scale (KAIT), designed for ages eleven to eighty-five or older (Kaufman & Kaufman, 1993). Based on several theories of intelligence, it appears psychometri-cally sound but still lacks a history of use and research (Anastasi & Urbina, 1997).

ASSESSING ADAPTIVE BEHAVIOR

Adaptive behavior can be assessed through interviews with families or caretakers, direct observation, and self-report in some cases. Several standardized scales have also been constructed, and attention is being given to reliability and validity.

If adaptive behavior scales are to be useful at all, they must accurately reflect current functioning. Whether they do or not often depends on the accuracy of reports from parents and caregivers. Ratings of specific questions are more likely to be accurate than ratings of general and vague questions (e.g., Can the child count to ten? versus Can the child count?). At the least, caretakers must be sensitive and have opportunities for observing behavior.

Vineland Adaptive Behavior Scales. The Vineland Adaptive Behavior Scales were originally constructed by Edgar Doll at the Vineland Training School. The latest revision of Doll's test was published in 1984 by Sparrow, Balla, and Cicchetti. Three versions exist. Two versions are semi-structured interviews for parents and other caretakers, which can be used with youth from birth to age eighteen and with low-functioning adults. The third version consists of items for teachers of three- to twelve-year-olds. All versions cover four major behavioral domains: communication, daily living skills, socialization, and motor skills. Additionally, there is an optional domain of maladaptive behavior (except in the teacher's version). Scores from the separate domains and an overall score can be compared with scores earned by a normal standard group and also with the performance of smaller special groups such as mentally retarded, emotionally disturbed, and hearing-impaired persons.

AAMR's Adaptive Behavior Scales. For several years, AAMR has published adaptive behavior scales to be employed in the community and in the schools. The recent revisions are called the Adaptive Behavior Scales—Residential and Com-

The ability to perform everyday adaptive behaviors is an important criterion in evaluating mental retardation.
(Paul Conklin/PhotoEdit)

munity (ABS-RC:2) and the Adaptive Behavior Scales-School Edition (ABS-S:2).

The ABS—Residential and Community scale is based on the performance of persons with development disabilities living in U.S. communities or institutions (Nihira, Leland, & Lambert, 1993). It examines a wide range of behaviors in persons from age three to adulthood. Table 10-6 lists many domains of functioning tested by this instrument. Statistical analyses show that five factors are tapped: personal self-sufficiency, community self-sufficiency, personal-social responsibility, social adjustment, and personal adjustment.

The ABS—School Edition is similar in behavioral domains and the information it provides (Lambert, Leland, & Nihira, 1993). It is designed for children ages three through sixteen, primarily for students with mild and moderate levels of retardation (DeStefano & Thompson, 1990). Its norm group consists of persons with developmental disabilities attending public schools in the United States, and nondisabled students.

FUNCTIONAL ASSESSMENT

Recall that functional assessment can provide hypotheses about how a targeted behavior is presently functioning for the individual; that is, what variables are reinforcing or otherwise contributing to maintaining the behavior (Durand, 1993a). Functional assessment aims to answer the question, Why is this person engaging in this behavior, in this setting, at this time? The information can then be used to construct effective intervention, because knowing what maintains a behavior can facilitate its modification. Several methods can be employed in functional assessment. Interviews, rating scales, checklists, and direct observations can be useful. A type of functional assessment that has become prominent is functional analysis, which entails a demonstration of the events hypothesized as responsible for the behavior's occurring or not occurring (Iwata et al., 1994).

Functional assessments of various types can be extremely helpful to interventions for behavior

TABLE 10-6

Many Domains of Functioning Are Assessed by the ABS-RC:2

Independent functioning
Physical development
Economic activity
Language development
Domestic activity
Violent and antisocial behavior
Untrustworthy behavior
Self-direction
Responsibility
Socialization
Numbers and time
Prevocational/vocational activity
Rebellious behavior
Stereotyped and hyperactive behavior

problems such as aggression and self-injury. Scotti and colleagues (1996) emphasize that functional analysis can also be applied to enhancing behavioral skills, and that more of this needs to be accomplished. They view functional assessment as consonant with both the behaviorists' view of the importance of the environment in influencing behavior and AAMR's focus on the environment as facilitating or hindering development and well-being.

CURRICULUM-BASED ASSESSMENT

Curriculum-based assessment goes hand in hand with programmatic intervention. Typically it is geared to a specific curriculum, so that assessment measures a child's individual progress, which in turn guides teaching or treatment. The curriculum-based approach is increasingly employed for severe and profound retardation, partly because norm-referenced intelligence tests lack sensitivity to developmental change in children within this range of intelligence (Handen, 1997).

Several specific approaches are described by Handen (1997). Some of the instruments apply to preschoolers. Of these, some have been constructed for the general population of developmental disabilities, and the assessment instruments are developmentally sequenced. An example is The Carolina Curriculum for Preschoolers with Special Needs: It has twenty-five sequences for children ranging from two to five years of age (Johnson-Martin, Attermeier, & Hacker, 1990). Other curricula and assessments were constructed for special subgroups of children. For example, the Oregon Project Curriculum for Visually Impaired and Blind Preschool Children is suited for children from birth to seventy-two months of age who have visual and other impairments (Brown, Simmons, & Methvin, 1986). Programs also exist for older children. An example is the Community Living Assessment and Teaching System, which has three instruments for school-age children and adolescents with significant cognitive deficiency (Slentz et al., 1982). Skills are assessed in the areas of self-help, social-emotional behavior, language, and motor functioning.

TREATMENT

Treatment for mental retardation must take into account not only intellectual and adaptive functioning but also interpersonal and behavioral problems. In a substantial number of cases, particularly involving severe retardation, medical conditions must be attended.

BEHAVIOR MODIFICATION

The single most important innovation in treating retardation has been the application of behavioral techniques. In the 1960s, advocates of behavior modification began to work in institutions that provided custodial care but little training or education (Whitman, Hantula, & Spence, 1990). Over the next decades, behavior modification became dominant, and an enormous amount of research was conducted. A wide range of behaviors at all levels of handicap was targeted. There was a thrust to eliminate maladaptive behaviors as well as to enhance skills in language, self-help, imitation, academic study, and work. The acquisition of daily living skills was recognized as crucial (Danforth & Drabman, 1990; Taras & Matese, 1990). Children and adolescents who cannot dress and feed themselves, or otherwise take care of their basic needs, are often limited from participating in educational and social activities. Those who are unable to shop, order food in restaurants, swim, or bowl can hardly enjoy independence in community living. Thus self-help programs have targeted the gamut of behaviors. In more recent years, training in social skills and self-control have been common, especially for mild and moderate retardation (e.g., Matson & Coe, 1991). Such training often includes cognitive components.

During the last decades, behavioral techniques have progressed notably. Guidelines have been established for various methods, and precision in teaching and generalization of learned skills have been advanced (Handen, 1998). An important distinction has been made between *discrete-trial learning* and *incidental learning*, both of which are guided by operant principles. In discrete-trial learning, the clinician selects the task to be learned and provides simple clear directives, prompts, and consequences for appropriate behavior. Teaching is usually conducted in a quiet place, away from distractions. In incidental learning, the teaching situation is informal, less structured, and more natural. It is more likely to be initiated by the child, amidst everyday contexts; for example, the child's asking for a toy is used as an opportunity for teaching. Both discrete-trial and incidental learning have been shown to be effective, and incidental learning is believed to be especially effective for generalization of learning.

Consistent with the behavioral approach, efforts have also been made to train caregivers, whether the setting is the home, community programs, or residential institutions (e.g., Whitman et al., 1990). Training can focus on general principles or on management of a specific child and it may be delivered to groups or to individual families. Training courses and curricula have been developed to disseminate information to caretakers. Evaluation of outcomes has been conducted, with attempts to establish the value of programs to the everyday activities of the child (Kiernan, 1985). Parent training has been shown to be effective, and parents can profit from ongoing contact with professionals (Handen, 1998).

Overall, behavior modification has had considerable success in serving young people with retardation, who so often in past times had been viewed as unable to learn. This is not to say that the application of behavioral techniques is simple; in fact, it requires skill, effort, and perseverance. But enormous gains have been made.

PHARMACOLOGICAL TREATMENT

Medications are not known to strengthen intellectual functioning in cases of retardation but are widely employed for medical and behavioral symptoms. Singh and colleagues (1998) report that 2 to 7 percent of children living in the community receive psychotropic drugs, and this number rises to 19 to 33 percent when antiseizure medications are considered. Drug treatment increases as the number and severity of behavioral problems increase. Medication use is higher also for those living in institutions, and particularly for those in larger institutions or institutions with restrictive environments. This trend suggests that the environments of institutions may be responsible for increased medication use; however, individuals who are institutionalized are more likely to have behavioral problems to begin with.

The management of medication in MR requires special consideration. The competent clinician is aware that accurate diagnosis of problems is made difficult because language impairments in retardation interfere with or prevent precise reporting of behavior or emotions. There could also be some differences in how nonretarded and retarded individuals respond to medication (Gadow, 1992). Good practice requires especially careful supervision, which includes determining drug efficacy and possible side effects, since some clients are unable to provide a clear picture of how they are being affected by medication. Inappropriate use of drugs and overdosing have been documented, resulting in close government monitoring.

A wide range of medications are employed to treat behavioral problems that co-occur with mental retardation (Singh et al., 1998). There is some evidence for the efficacy of psychopharmacology but the lack of controlled research is striking. This problem is, of course, not unique to MR, but it seems particularly worrisome given the prevalence of medication use and the difficulty of evaluating effects.

PSYCHOTHERAPY

Some children and adolescents with retardation can benefit from psychotherapies that aim to reduce behavioral/psychological problems (Szymanski & Kaplan, 1991). Mild and moderate intellectual deficits do not preclude individual "talking" therapies, although modifications may be required (Bregman, 1991; King et al., 1997). Certainly, psychotherapeutic techniques must be adapted to the developmental level of the client. It is probably best that therapists be directive and set specific goals. Language must be concrete and clear, and nonverbal techniques need to be used in the face of communication difficulties (e.g., play or other activities). Short, frequent sessions may be necessary.

EDUCATION

Educational services are the most extensive and common interventions for mental retardation (Handen, 1998). The amount, types, and goals of services offered have been influenced by how mental retardation has been viewed. (See Accent, "Changing Views of MR.")

The last several decades have been marked by favorable attitudes and service models. Factors responsible for this positive era include better diagnosis and intervention and studies indicating that many individuals with MR can do quite well. In addition, the 1960s brought renewed, widespread interest in the rights of poor, handicapped, and minority populations.

The concept of *normalization*, first popularized in Scandinavia, became a framework for how people with mental deficiency would be treated. The central idea of normalization is that treatment should aim at producing behaviors that are as nor-

mal as possible and should accomplish this goal by methods as culturally normal as possible (Mesibov, 1992; Thompson & McEvoy, 1992; Wolfensberger, 1980). Each person is seen as having the right to experiences that are as normal and as least restrictive as possible. The philosophy of normalization has been widely applied to the lives of people with handicaps and has influenced educational services and living arrangements for persons with MR.

IDEA AND SPECIAL EDUCATION

In the United States, educational services for persons with disabilities have evolved dramatically over the past thirty years. Both the federal government and the individual states enacted relevant legislation and provided limited funding. By the early 1970s most states had done so (Martin, Martin, & Terman, 1996). Nevertheless, the laws had loopholes—one being that they applied to children who could "benefit from education." Educational mandates were not always enforced, and funding was often inadequate. By 1971 to 1972, every school district in the country had some type of special education, but in most states, less than half of all children with disabilities received public education. Parents and other advocates turned to the courts to address the matter.

Two legal cases were especially influential in the early 1970s (Martin et al., 1996). *Pennsylvania Association for Retarded Children v. Commonwealth of Pennsylvania* challenged the state for denying services to children who had not attained a mental age of five years by the time that they would ordinarily begin first grade. Pennsylvania agreed to provide access to a free and appropriate public education to persons with MR up to age twenty-one. In the second legal case, *Mills v. Board of Education*, the District of Columbia was sued for refusing school enrollment or expelling seven children with a variety of mental or behavioral disabilities. The public school district allowed that over 12,000 children with disabilities would not be served that year because of funding inadequacies. The court did not accept this argument and ruled that under the Fourteenth Amendment, children with disabilities could not unfairly bear the burden of lack of funding.

CHANGING VIEWS OF MR

Attitudes about mental deficiency have reflected the general beliefs of the times and have prescribed how those with retardation would be treated by the societies in which they lived (Cytryn & Lourie, 1980). Roman laws permitted extermination of those with retardation; medieval Europe looked upon them as jesters or creatures of the devil. In the United States, the twentieth century was marked by periods of more or less favorable attitudes toward MR (Table 10-7).

We can trace modern attitudes to the late 1700s, to the case of the "Wild Boy of Aveyron," otherwise known as Victor. The boy was first seen running naked through the woods, searching for roots and acorns to eat. He was captured and assigned to a medical officer, Jean M. Itard, at the National Institute for the Deaf and Dumb in Paris. Victor's senses were underdeveloped; his memory, attention, and reasoning were deficient; and his ability to communicate was almost nil (Itard, as cited in Harrison & McDermott, 1972). Although it is unclear what diagnosis would be applied to Victor's behavior today, a parallel was drawn with children afflicted with "idiocy." Itard attributed the boy's deficits to lack of contact with civilized people but treatment largely failed and Victor remained in custodial care until his death.

Despite this unfortunate outcome, efforts to treat Victor did much to stimulate interest in the "feebleminded" or "retarded" (Rie, 1971). By the middle to the late 1800s, a favorable climate existed toward mental retardation and special education. Itard's student Sequin was a leader in this optimistic era, and promising ideas spread rapidly across the United States. Residential schools opened to educate children with retardation and then to return them to the community (Szymanski & Crocker, 1985). This enlightened view was marked in 1876 by the formation of AAMR.

However, optimism was gradually overcome by several developments. Increased interest in biology as a cause of MR, the rise of psychoanalysis, and the misuse or misunderstanding of IQ tests strengthened the belief that persons with retardation could not be helped and were a detriment if not a danger to society. This led to widespread institutionalization and custodial care rather than treatment, with institutions growing in number and size throughout the first half of the twentieth century. Several subsequent developments then brought renewed optimism and improved conditions.

TABLE 10-7

Attitudes toward Mental Retardation

Period	Society's Attitudes
Middle to late 1800s	Optimism, belief in education, "moral training" in special schools to return the person to society.
Late 1800s–Early 1900s	Focus on neuropathology; retardation seen as incurable defect; protection of retarded persons from society.
Early to middle 1900s	Introduction of intelligence tests, which "discover" mild retardation; assumption of link with antisocial behavior; custodial institutionalization; sterilization. "Tragic Interlude."
Middle 1900s–Present	Recognition of rights of retarded persons to public education, treatment, and life in community; the concept of normalization. Implementation of right of all handicapped children to education; deinstitutionalization and community living.

Adapted from Szymanski & Kaplan, 1991.

Adding to the general discontent with educational services was criticism of special education. Children with mental handicaps were typically assigned to special classes or schools, and this policy was criticized for drastically limiting their social contacts. Other policies, especially as they applied to mildly retarded children, were attacked in several ways (MacMillan et al., 1986). First, it was argued that minority group students were disproportionately labeled as mentally handicapped largely on the basis of biased IQ tests. Second, it was claimed that special education did not seem to benefit children. Third, it was asserted that individualized programming could be accomplished within the regular classroom, so that there was no need to segregate students with disabilities.

These and other criticisms, legal decisions, and a growing social commitment to the rights of handicapped children to appropriate education eventually resulted in a sweeping legal reform: Public Law 94-142, the Education for All Handicapped Children Act of 1975. Other federal regulations strengthened the thrust of this law by extending opportunity and rights to all handicapped people. Public Law 99-457 amended the Education for All Handicapped Children Act, extending provisions to developmentally delayed three- to five-year-olds and creating voluntary intervention for infants. In the early 1990s, the Education for All Handicapped Children Act was expanded under the title the Individuals with Disabilities Education Act (IDEA). In addition, The Vocational Rehabilitation Act of 1973 and the Americans with Disabilities Act of 1990 legally ensured access to education and jobs and broad opportunities.

The purpose of what is now called IDEA is to assure that all students with handicaps obtain an appropriate free public education; to guarantee the rights of these students and their parents; to assist states and localities in providing education; and to assess and assure the effectiveness of educational efforts. These purposes and mandates have been refined in several legal cases (e.g., Osborne, 1992). Appropriate education essentially means educational experiences tailored to each child's needs. An individualized education plan (IEP) is constructed for each student receiving special education. IEPs must consider the child's present functioning, educational objectives, long-term goals, educational services to be provided, expected duration of services, and procedures for evaluations. The programs must be reviewed annually by a committee and the child's parents. Furthermore, students with disabilities must be educated with nonhandicapped children to the maximum extent that is appropriate; that is, they must be placed in the least restrictive environment possible and in programs as close to home as possible.

Overall, IDEA has strengthened individualized programming, increased parental participation in the education of their handicapped youngsters, and encouraged maintenance of youth with disabilities in their local communities and in regular schools. Under the policy of *mainstreaming*, many more children are integrated with their peers in the schools. A variety of placements are possible. Table 10-8 shows one way of organizing these options along a continuum of integration: regular class-based, special class-based, special school-based, and nonschool-based programs. These placements provide increasing levels of support, and proper placement requires matching the child with appropriate support. More recently, the Regular Education Initiative has called for *inclusion* of students, which goes beyond mainstreaming by implying that most children with disabilities can best be educated in regular classrooms (Hocutt, 1996). "Full inclusion" means that all children would be so educated, so that special education as we know it today would hardly exist.

Regardless of the successes of IDEA, the effectiveness of special education is still questioned. This is not an easy matter to settle because research must address all kinds of disabilities, a variety of severity of disability, and many alternative programs. Even within a type of placement, the activities, quality of teaching, and support services vary a good deal. A child in one classroom, whether special education or not, may have very different experiences from a child in another classroom.

Thus it is not surprising that divergent opinions exist on the overall effectiveness of special educa-

TABLE 10-8

Alternative Educational Placements for Students with Retardation, According to Needs for Support and Program Integration

Children with intermittent or limited support needs	*Regular class-based programs* Special materials and equipment Special consultation Visiting supplemental services Resource room with special education teacher Diagnostic-prescriptive teaching center
Children with limited or extensive support needs	*Special class-based programs* Special education class Part-time in regular class Full-time in special class
Children with extensive or pervasive support needs	*Special school-based programs* Special day school Special residential school
Children with pervasive support needs	*Nonschool-based programs* Hospital instruction Homebound instruction

Adapted from Beime-Smith, Ittenbach, & Patton, 1998.

tion, and that some opinions are strongly held. A considerable amount of research has not clearly supported anticipated academic and social benefits, and criticism abounds (Howlin, 1994; Detterman & Thompson, 1997). Specific to our immediate interest, it has been argued that students with mild mental handicap can be disadvantaged by being placed into contained special classrooms or resource rooms rather than spending time in regular classrooms (Ysseldyke et al., 1991). However, Hocutt's (1996) analysis of recent studies presents a somewhat more optimistic picture. Academic and social outcomes for educable mental retardation can be predicted by classroom variables such as teaching style and activities promoting student interaction. Students with severe retardation can be successfully integrated into local schools, and integration is associated with increased social interaction. No adverse effects were shown for non-

handicapped students, and they appeared to profit in increased social development and awareness of the needs of disabled students. Hocutt emphasizes that no available intervention eliminates disabilities, that instructional and other classroom features matter more than placement itself, and that effective interventions require considerable investment of resources, time, effort, and teacher support.

Howlin (1994) notes several strong arguments for integration of students with mild or moderate difficulties. Placement in regular classrooms can avoid stigmatization, at least in principle, and can also encourage the modeling of academic and social skills. Integration in regular school settings can also put the child on a path to playing a full role in society in adulthood. Howlin's implied concern about what happens to children with retardation when they reach adulthood is shared by most professionals and advocates of the handicapped. Indeed, there is considerable emphasis today on the goals of lifelong community integration and productive adulthood, particularly for those with mild to moderate retardation. The Hawaii Transition Project is an example of a program designed to achieve these goals (Patton et al., 1990). This multiyear project prepares adolescents for post–high school roles by identifying future opportunities, assessing and matching students to community roles, and adapting school programming to support the student's transition to a new role and setting. The transition is facilitated with the help of adult service providers, resulting in the student's being enrolled in an appropriate postsecondary educational or work setting.

Unfortunately, only an insufficient number of programs are designed to actively and systematically promote productive adulthood in the community for the mentally handicapped. Indeed, Polloway and his colleagues (1991) argue that educational curriculum from elementary school onward should be geared toward long-range planning for adult integration into the community. Although present efforts are far from ideal, it is promising that mental retardation is increasingly viewed in terms of supports required for optimal development rather than inherent deficiencies of the individual.

DEINSTITUTIONALIZATION AND INTEGRATION INTO THE COMMUNITY

There is no doubt that persons with retardation are now integrated into communities, in comparison to their treatment in earlier times in the twentieth century when institutionalizaton was more common. The philosophy of normalization played a role in the movement to deinstitutionalize persons with retardation. Convincing arguments were made against public institutions, many of which were large and poorly staffed. It was argued that the residents did not receive individualized training and medical care, much less adequate human interaction. In fact, it was believed that residents often learned damaging behaviors, such as excessive dependency.

These arguments—along with concern over the costs of maintaining institutions, the creation of funding for alternatives, and other considerations—led to change. In the United States, the number of persons in large public residential institutions began to decline in the late 1960s, as did the number of institutions, paralleling changes in education (Braddock & Heller, 1985; Craig & McCarver, 1984). Moreover, fewer younger individuals were placed in institutions; from 1977 to 1989, the percentage of residents younger than age twenty-one decreased from 36 percent to 11 percent. (Beirne-Smith, Ittenbach, & Patton, 1998).

Along with these transformations came the rise of community settings as alternatives for traditional institutional living (Bruininks, Hauber, & Kudla, 1980; Emerson, 1985). These included small regional centers, small group homes, and foster homes, which interface with the larger community and provide a more homelike atmosphere and greater opportunity for privacy and independence. Such placements can fall short of ideal, of course, and they can have negative qualities observed in traditional institutions, such as social iso-

lation, regimentation, fostering of dependency, and lack of power of the residents (Landesman, 1990; Lord & Pedlar, 1991). Nevertheless, there is consensus that alternative living arrangements are likely to provide more normal and more positive experiences.

Although most families choose to rear their child with retardation at home, there are now more acceptable alternatives should these be required or desired. Moreover, alternatives may be increasingly important as the child reaches adulthood or as parents become elderly. Most children with retardation will continue to have disabilities, but many with mild deficiencies can become relatively independent and most can benefit from a variety of settings that support integration into their communities.

SUMMARY

■ AAMR defines mental retardation as subaverage intellectual functioning with concurrent deficits in adaptive skills manifested before age eighteen. Subaverage intellectual functioning refers to performance of 70 to 75 or less on individual standardized tests of intelligence. Deficits in adaptive skills must be evident in at least two areas of functioning. This definition proposed a paradigm shift in its greater emphasis on the interaction of the individual and the environment and is somewhat controversial.

■ AAMR now classifies MR by levels of environmental supports needed by individuals, but the DSM-IV continues to classify MR by four IQ levels: mild, moderate, profound, and severe.

■ The prevalence of mental retardation in the general population is about 2 to 3 percent based on IQ scores and about 1 percent based on IQ and adaptive skill deficits. Rates are disproportionately high in persons of school age, low social class, and male gender.

■ Modern intelligence testing began with the work of Binet and Simon, who assumed that intelligence is somewhat malleable. Goddard and Terman, who used and adapted the early Binet scales in the United States, assumed that intelligence was fixed and inherited. The Stanford-Binet and Wechsler scales are widely used to identify MR. Measured intelligence is relatively stable for most people and correlates reasonably well with academic performance. Several limitations of IQ tests have been noted.

■ Adaptive behavior refers to domains of everyday behavior. Social responsibility and personal independence are central to adaptive skills, which develop over time. Judgments of adaptive skills need to consider cultural expectations and specific situations.

■ Developmental issues are central in MR but require more investigation. Data do show that the rate and the pattern of intellectual development vary across etiological groups. Cognitive growth can occur similarly to that of normal development (although it proceeds more slowly and reaches a lower ceiling) or can be qualitatively different than normal. MR is typically considered chronic, although improvement can occur.

■ Mental retardation has many causes. Organic risk factors are associated with disordered brain function; they include genetic abnormalities, prenatal and birth complications, and various postnatal influences. Polygenic inheritance and psychosocial influences are also implicated in etiology.

■ Organic risk is more closely associated with moderate and severe levels of retardation, whereas polygenic and psychosocial etiology are more closely associated with mild MR and what was once called cultural-familial retardation.

■ Mild retardation especially has been discussed with regard to the cultural bias of IQ tests. Legal decisions have forced the stringent monitoring of intelligence testing in the public schools.

■ Research into learning and cognition indicates that learning principles apply to MR. Although development occurs in Piagetian stages, it is slow, and advanced stages are not achieved. Analyses of information processing demonstrate deficits in several components (such as attention, strategy use, generalization, executive functions), and also relative strengths.

■ Youth with retardation show deficits in social skills and social cognition, as well as rates of behavioral disturbances much higher than for the general population. These difficulties may be directly related to the characteristics of MR, but may also be caused by the life experiences of persons with retardation.

■ Family adjustment to having a child with retardation is influenced by child characteristics, family characteristics, and social variables. Many families face the decision of whether to place the child out-of-home; most keep the child at home and report benefits.

■ Assessment of MR is best guided by its goals and can include evaluation of intelligence, adaptive behavior, academic achievement, family functioning, and biological status. Standardized IQ tests and adaptive behavior scales are central in assessment, and relatively well constructed tests are available. Functional assessment and curriculum-based methods are especially valuable in guiding intervention.

■ Treatment of MR includes behavior modification, medication, and psychotherapies. Behavioral techniques to shape and strengthen appropriate skills and to weaken maladaptive behaviors are especially effective. Psychopharmacology, which requires particular sensitivity because of the nature of MR, can be effective in treating medical and behavioral disturbances but controlled outcome studies are scarce. "Talking" psychotherapies have a limited usefulness in mild or moderate retardation.

■ Attitudes toward retardation have varied over time and have been associated with quality of treatment. Since the mid-1900s, the concept of normalization and concern for the rights of disabled people have served as a framework for treatment and education. P.L. 94-142 (now titled the Individuals with Disabilities Education Act) and related laws have brought several changes to the educational system. Children and adolescents with retardation are now more integrated in schools, although many questions remain about the effects of mainstreaming, inclusion, and special education.

■ Paralleling changes in education has been the movement for deinstitutionalization and alternative living arrangements, which also aims to integrate persons with disabilities into their communities.

CHAPTER 11

LANGUAGE AND LEARNING DISABILITIES

As we saw in Chapter 10, mental retardation is a developmental disorder that broadly affects intellectual functioning at various levels of severity. But intellectual impairments are not always general; they can appear in some specific areas and not others. This chapter is about youth who display specific language and/or learning impairments but otherwise normal intellectual and physical abilities. Mental retardation and obvious perceptual and medical conditions are not present, nor are environmental factors that might explain the impairments. It is generally assumed that disturbance occurs in normal developmental processes, so that the specific disabilities are apparent relatively early in life.

Specific disabilities can vary from being very subtle to severe, with concomitant effects on academic performance. They thus can cast a shadow of failure over the child during the school years. They may interfere with innumerable daily activities that require speaking, reading, writing, or dealing with numbers. Peers may often respond negatively to a child's inability to learn or communicate as others do, and parents and teachers may attribute impairments to the child's laziness or lack of motivation. Continuing problems can adversely affect social relationships in adulthood and occupational success. Indeed, it could be argued that learning disabilities have had increasing impact on individual lives because of escalating demands for certain kinds of learning in our industrial and technologically sophisticated world.

HISTORICAL BACKGROUND AND DEFINITION

HISTORICAL CONTEXT

Language and learning disorders (LLDs) have been recognized for a long time. Two major themes ushered in the field as we know it today (Lyon, 1996a). One theme was an interest in understanding adults and children who displayed unusual combinations of strengths and weaknesses in language or intelligence. Individual cases played an important role in portraying such discrepancies. For example, the abilities of a ten-year-old boy with reading problems were described in this way:

He was apparently a bright and in every respect an intelligent boy. He had been learning music for a year and had made good progress in it. . . . In all departments of his studies where the instruction was oral he had made good progress, showing that his auditory memory was good. . . . He performs simple sums quite correctly, and his progress in arithmetic has been regarded as quite satisfactory. He has no difficulty in learning to write. His visual acuity is good. (Hinshelwood, 1917, pp. 46–47)

Many similarly puzzling cases were presented by physicians, giving the field a medical orientation. The work of the physician Paul Broca is well known in this regard. Broca documented the inability of his patients to express themselves verbally while maintaining the ability to comprehend what others said. He traced the problem to an area in the left hemisphere of the brain, which now carries the name *Broca's area*. It became widely documented that brain injury or damage in adults led to a variety of such behavioral symptoms, as speech problems, learning difficulties, and inattention (Hammill, 1993). Similar problems in children were thus hypothesized to be caused by brain dysfunction of some sort, perhaps too subtle to be identified. Thus, as for attention-deficit hyperactivity disorder, the label "minimal brain damage" or "dysfunction" was applied.

The second major theme of recent interest in specific learning problems sprang from concern that a select group of children had educational needs that were not being met by the schools. Until the 1960s, children whose school performance was below their general ability were often referred to as "underachievers" (Kessler, 1988). Attention was given to their psychosocial behavior, motivation, anxiety, and family functioning. It was also recognized that some of these children had specific learning problems, such as in reading and arithmetic, and some were said to have "minimal brain damage." Many parents and professionals believed that the needs of these children were not being satisfied. Meanwhile, behavioral scientists had begun to recommend ways in which learning disorders might be remediated (Lyon, 1996a).

In 1963 representatives from several organizations met at a symposium sponsored by the Fund for Perceptually Handicapped Children. Samuel Kirk, a well-respected educator, addressed the conferees, noting that the children of their concern exhibited a variety of deficiencies that were assumed to be related to neurological dysfunction, especially learning difficulties, perceptual problems, and hyperactivity. Kirk suggested that the term *learning disabilities* would be suitable for all of these children and also would avoid the need to establish nervous system dysfunction in identifying the youngsters. Importantly, he thought that the term could encourage and guide the assessment and educational intervention so needed by these children. That evening the conferees organized into the Association for Children with Learning Disabilities (Hammill, 1993).

Learning disabilities (LD) was not a new term, but Kirk's presentation marked the creation of a new field (Hallahan & Kauffman, 1978; Taylor, 1988a). The term gradually became widely accepted by professional groups and parents, and a field of study grew around it. Educators and parents henceforth played an important role in an area previously dominated by physicians and psychologists. Parents whose children might otherwise have been labeled mentally retarded were given hope that the problem was limited and could be treated. Teachers were relieved of the suspicion that they were to blame for the failure of certain students. School administrators and other concerned professionals were provided with a label that could make children eligible for special services. Thus from the beginning, children labeled with learning disabilities constituted a heterogeneous group and the social context for labeling these youngsters was a complex one involving advocacy (Senf, 1986).

PROBLEM OF DEFINITION

The definition of learning disability given by Kirk's group became extremely important because it was adapted by the federal government in mandating special education for learning disabled children. It was incorporated into Public Law 94-142, The Education for All Handicapped Children Act of 1975 (now IDEA). The definition used by the federal government states the following:

Specific learning disability means a disorder in one or more of the basic psychological processes involved in understanding or in using language, spoken or written, in which the disorder may manifest itself in an imperfect ability to listen, think, speak, read, write, spell, or to do mathematical calculations. The term includes such conditions as perceptual handicaps, brain injury, minimal brain dysfunction, dyslexia, and developmental aphasia. The term does not include children who have learning problems which are primarily the result of visual, hearing, or motor handicaps, or mental retardation, or emotional disturbance, or of environmental, cultural, or economic disadvantage (U.S. Office of Education, 1977, p. 65083)

This definition became the guideline for the way that state departments of education define and identify learning-disabled students (Mercer, King-Sears, & Mercer, 1990). It is critical to how learning disabilities are thought about and how research samples on learning disabilities are chosen. Nevertheless, ongoing dissatisfaction is still expressed about several important issues.

Operationalizing the definition. One of the criticisms of the definition is that it is conceptual and lacks specific guidelines to identify a learning disability. Is it necessary to establish dysfunction in basic psychological processes? If so, how is this to be done, and what criteria should be used, especially since these basic processes are not well established? What criteria are to be used to decide that language, reading, writing, arithmetic, and other skills are below expectations for the child? These questions have not been easy to answer, and different methods have been generated to identify developmental learning disabilites (Morris, 1988; Stanovich, 1991). These methods grew out of criteria set by the Office of Education; however, they most often do not directly target the psychological processes assumed to be deficient.

One method identifies children with learning disabilities as performing below expected grade or age level in at least one academic area. Variations occur in the specific criterion, although it is often set in the range of one-half to two years below expectations. Thus with the two-year criterion, a

sixth-grader who is achieving at the fourth-grade level in arithmetic can be labeled as learning disabled, providing that certain other factors do not account for the performance. One obvious problem in this approach is that a large discrepancy would seem more serious for a younger child than for an older child. Being two years behind is more serious for a third-grader than for a sixth-grader. This problem can be reduced by setting the criterion, for example, at one year deficiency for younger children and two years for older children. Of course, judgments still must be made as to what the criterion should be at each grade level. Different criteria are used by different state departments of education.

The other more common way to identify LD is by a discrepancy between general intellectual ability and specific achievement level. It is assumed that performance on measures of general ability will exceed performance on measures of the hypothesized specific impairment. Comparisons are typically made between IQ tests and achievement tests that tap the suspected domain, be it reading, writing, arithmetic, so forth. However, there is no absolute agreement on how large a discrepancy between intelligence and achievement scores is needed to define a learning disability. In practice, the size of any found discrepancy is statistically compared with the discrepancy between intelligence and achievement that would be expected in the general population to which the child can be reasonably compared. If the found discrepancy is significantly larger than what would be expected, a learning disability is said to exist. However, state education departments, which usually determine the standards, set different standards about the size of the discrepancy that is considered significantly large (Mercer et al., 1990). This situation has obvious implications for the number of children who will be identified as learning disabled and receive special education.

Still other problems exist with the IQ-achievement discrepancy approach. The strategy assumes that IQ and achievement are independent and that a learning disability will not affect IQ (Siegel, 1989). Nonetheless, intelligence tests measure most of the abilities considered deficient in LD, and learning disabilities may cause a decrease in IQ (Stanovich, 1986; 1991). In fact, for most LD groups, the average IQ is about 90 (Taylor, 1988a).

Exclusionary criteria. The definition of learning disabilities clearly excludes some children from being considered learning disabled. Indeed, it is sometimes said that LD is defined more by what it is *not* than by what it is. By definition the disabilities cannot be primarily due to visual, hearing, or motor problems, mental retardation, emotional disturbance, or environmental, cultural, or economic disadvantage. All of these factors can hinder children's communicating and learning, causing them to fall behind their peers. But problems caused primarily by any of these conditions do not fit the concept of specific language or learning disabilities. There is considerable concern about this exclusion. For one thing, it is not always easy to determine the primary cause of a disability. For example, an emotional disturbance may be primary (that is, cause learning problems) or secondary (that is, result from learning problems). It may also be difficult to distinguish some cases of learning disabilities from underachievement due to lack of motivation, cultural disadvantage, and other factors (Stanovich, 1986). Moreover, several investigations, especially of reading problems, indicate that general learning problems may not differ much from specific disabilities (Rispens & van Yperen, 1997). This finding challenges the concept of specific disabilities and the exclusion of children with general learning problems from educational interventions that might be beneficial.

Other dissatisfactions. Other dissatisfactions with the definition have been expressed. It is argued that the term "learning disabilities" is much too broad and does not fully recognize how heterogeneous LDs are. In fact, it is necessary to define disabilities in terms of specific domains, such as reading or mathematics, and this approach is commonly employed by the educational system and the major psychiatric classification systems.

Because the federal government definition is overly general and unsatisfactory, various groups have offered modified definitions. The definition used by The National Joint Committee for Learning Disabilities more clearly states that "learning disabilities" refers to a group of disorders and it makes no reference to "basic psychological processes." Federal guidelines have, in fact, never spelled out criteria for such processes (Hammill, 1993). Unlike the federal government definition, the NJCLD definition does state that learning disabilities are presumed to be due to central nervous system dysfunction and may occur over the life span.

Overall, definitions continue to be vague and exclusionary (Lyon, 1996a). This state of affairs has serious implications. Different definitions and criteria have led to confusion, difficulties in establishing prevalence rates, clinical practices with little rationale, and incomparability of groups chosen for research purposes. In addition, because different states have adopted differing criteria for identifying LD, different standards determine the number of children receiving special education and whether any individual child will or will not receive special education.

On a more optimistic note, it can be argued that attempts to conceptualize learning disabilities, with all the shortcomings, has called attention to a real problem (Taylor, 1988a). Considerable effort is being made to describe and identify children with learning disabilities, to understand their functioning, and to maximize their achievements.

LANGUAGE DISABILITIES

Language disorders have historically been referred to as "aphasia," a term that means loss of language due to brain damage or dysfunction. Since this meaning does not accurately fit developmental impairments in children, the terms "developmental aphasia" and "developmental dysphasia" have been used instead. More commonly employed in the United States and elsewhere are the terms "specific language disorders" (SLD) or "specific language impairments" (SLI). We will use these terms interchangeably and will also use the terms "language disorders" and "language disabilities" to refer to specific disabilities. We begin discussion with an overview of normal language development to provide a framework for understanding disordered communication.

NORMAL LANGUAGE DEVELOPMENT

As was briefly noted in Chapter 2, basic language skills develop rapidly in sequence so that most six-year-old children are amazingly adept in language use. Table 11-1 defines the basic components of language that must be mastered. In addition, the distinction between reception and expression of language is important. Reception has to do with the comprehension of communications sent by others; expression concerns the production of language. Reception is developmentally acquired earlier than expression (as anyone who has tried to learn a second language knows).

Infants come into the world geared to hear language: they have an amazing capacity to distinguish sounds and the rhythm of language. Within a few months, the cooing and babbling of speech sounds are well under way, and the stops and starts and rhythm of the language infants are hearing make their way into the sounds that the infants are producing. By their first birthdays, most infants are saying a few words. Some speech sounds are more difficult than others, and individual differences in articulation become obvious. Even before this time, infants have begun to understand the speech of others. The receptive and expressive skills that begin to develop during the first year are basic to language development. They require that infants distinguish *phonemes*, the basic sounds of their language. (English has forty-four phonemes represented by twenty-six letters of the alphabet and letter combinations.) It is fascinating that for a period of time during the first year, infants can produce and distinguish many sounds that are not part of their language, and then this ability contracts to the sounds of their language. In other words, infants seem to come into the world with a general ability to process language sounds, and then this ability narrows and is refined. Some combination of biological predisposition and experience allows infants to begin to acquire the phonology of the language that they hear and to connect meaning to the sounds.

By two years of age, most children have gone from saying single words, to two-word utterances, to longer strings of words placed into meaningful phrases or sentences. Vocabulary increases dramatically, different parts of speech are acquired, the ability to arrange words properly improves, and comprehension grows. Progress continues at a rapid rate and includes understanding the social "rules" of language, for example, taking turns and speaking more loudly to someone who cannot hear well. By age seven, much of the basics of language are acquired, although development continues into adolescence and even into adulthood.

CLASSIFICATION OF LANGUAGE DISABILITIES

From even a brief review of language development, it is obvious that a variety of impairments might occur; problems can exist in phonology, syntax, semantics, and so forth. It is possible, then, to classify disabilities in several ways. The critical importance of phonology and of the distinction between expressive and receptive language is widely recognized. The DSM-IV classifies disabilities as phonological, expressive, and receptive-expressive disorders. Table 11-2 provides a summary of the diagnostic criteria for these categories, which are referred to as Communication Disorders. The category of Mixed Receptive–Expressive Disorder reflects the fact that receptive problems do not typically occur alone. All diagnoses require

---

TABLE 11-1

Basic Components of Language

Phonology	Sounds of a language and rules for combining them
Articulation	Actual production of speech sounds
Morphology	Formation of words, including the use of prefixes and suffixes (e.g., un, ed, s) to give meaning
Syntax	Organization of words into phrases and sentences
Semantics	Meanings in language
Pragmatics	Use of language in social contexts

TABLE 11-2

DSM-IV Criteria for Three Communication Disorders

Phonological	Expressive	Receptive-Expressive
A. Failure to use age-appropriate and dialect-appropriate speech sounds (e.g., use of substitutions and omissions)	A. Scores from standardized measures of expressive language are substantially below scores for nonverbal intelligence and receptive language	A. Scores from standardized measures of both receptive and expressive language are substantially below those for nonverbal intellectual capacity

B. The difficulties interfere with academic or occupational achievement or with social communication.

C. If mental retardation, a speech-motor or sensory deficit, or environmental deprivation is present, the language difficulties are in excess of those usually associated with these problems.

that some kind of discrepancy be observed. For Phonological Disorder to be diagnosed, the child must perform below that of age-peers. Diagnosis of Expressive Disorder or Receptive-Expressive Disorder requires the use of standardized, individually given language and intelligence tests. In all cases, language impairments must be severe enough to interfere with daily functioning. Furthermore, the impairments cannot be accounted for by general intellectual or sensorimotor deficits, nor by insufficient environmental stimulation. (See Table 11-3.)

CLINICAL DESCRIPTION

Phonological disorder has to do with the misproduction of speech sounds. The child makes errors, distortions, substitutions, and omissions in producing speech. For example, incorrect sounds

TABLE 11-3

Description of Language Disorders

Type of Disorder	Time of Appearance	Deficits
Phonological	Severe cases apparent by 3 years; others by age 6	Age-appropriate speech sounds incorrectly made; some sounds omitted or some substituted by other sounds.
Expressive Language	Severe cases apparent before 3 years; less severe may become apparent as late as adolescence	Impairment in expressed language: small vocabulary, vocabulary errors, short sentences, simplified grammar, unusual word order, slow rate of language development, etc.
Receptive-Expressive Language	Typically apparent before age 4; less severe cases not until age 7 or older	Impairment in language comprehension; in mild cases, difficulty with meaning of particular kinds of words (e.g., spatial) or statements (e.g., if-then); in severe cases, inability to understand basic vocabulary and simple sentences. In addition, expressive language deficits exist.

(phonemes) may be used in the place of more difficult ones, as in the use of *wabbit* for *rabbit*. Or difficult phonemes may be omitted, as when *bu* is used instead of *blue*. Because most children display some misarticulation as they acquire speech, developmental norms are important in diagnosis. A distinction can be made between simple misarticulations and a broader problem in the child's understanding of the sound structure of the native language (Whitehurst & Fischel, 1994). The latter is manifested in inability to complete rhymes or to identify the separate sounds in a word.

Expressive language disorder involves the production of speech with regard to vocabulary, sentence structure, and other aspects of language output. Thus, for example, children with expressive problems may have a limited vocabulary and may speak in extremely short, simple sentences. However, they understand speech and age-appropriate concepts, and thus they can correctly obey simple commands or point to objects in response to others' communications.

Receptive-expressive language disorder involves difficulties in comprehending the communication of others. The child may fail to respond to speech, seem deaf, respond inappropriately, or be uninterested in television. Single words, phrases, the multiple meanings of a word, past tense, or word order may all be problematic. Thus deficits in expression and less often in articulation are present. It is not surprising, then, that receptive language dysfunction is generally the most severe language impairment.

In general, many language difficulties seem to be delays in the use of normal language (Miller & Tallal, 1995). Still, abnormal features, such as the use of jargon, may be present, especially in the case of a receptive disorder. There is also considerable variation in the severity of disorder. Imagine, if you will, the difference between the child who is struggling (albeit more than peers) only to articulate the difficult sounds of words versus the child who has serious difficulties in understanding what parents are trying to communicate. Both may be frustrated, but the child with comprehension problems is at much greater developmental risk.

EPIDEMIOLOGY

The prevalence of SLD is not well established, because of differences in diagnostic practices, assessment instruments, and other factors. DSM-IV estimates that childhood prevalence for each type of SLD does not exceed 5 percent (APA, 1994). However, prevalence varies with age and also with severity and type of disorder. The expressive type is more common than the receptive type (Whitehurst & Fischel, 1994). Simple phonological problems (misarticulations) decrease throughout childhood and are uncommon in adolescence. Since language use develops rapidly in early life, disorders are often evident prior to the child's going to school. However, milder impairments may not be evident until schoolwork places greater cognitive demands on the child.

In clinic populations, prevalence of SLD is much greater, running as high as 71 percent (Cohen, 1996). Perhaps most striking is the high percentage of cases of specific language impairments in children who had been referred for other problems, not language difficulties. For example, one study of children referred to mental health centers in Canada for a variety of reasons found that 62 percent had a language impairment and that the impairment had not previously been suspected in 34 percent of these cases.

Boys are widely reported as having higher rates of SLD than girls (APA, 1994; Whitehurst & Fischel, 1994). However, there is no gender difference in phonological deficits (Lyon, 1996a). It is also possible that higher rates for boys reflect a bias due to their being more likely also to display behavior disorders that attract attention.

UNDERLYING PSYCHOLOGICAL DEFICITS

Children with SLD show a variety of underlying cognitive deficits, some of which have been proposed as being central to SLD. Bishop (1992b) evaluated six hypotheses that targeted various deficits to explain language disorders, including deficits in learning and in the ability to use symbols to represent the world. Two of the hypotheses were favored: impairment in the processing of rapid or brief sounds, and limited capacity to process information that slows down the processing of large amounts of information. Bishop suggested that the combination of these problems might explain some cases of SLD. If information processing is slow, auditory information would be especially affected because sound signals are very brief. In turn, language would be affected because it depends on rapid processing of sound. There is evidence that language impaired children have difficulty in identifying very fast sounds embedded in speech (Miller & Tallal, 1995).

Deficits in short-term memory for sounds has also been related to specific language disorders. Gathercole (1998) reviewed a model of this memory system. Auditory short-term memory can be evaluated by saying aloud a string of words and asking the person to repeat them back. The number of words repeated is a measure of short-term memory. This task is handled by phonological memory, which in turn has two components. One is the short-term phonological store, which holds sound information for only two seconds. The other component is subvocal rehearsal, that is, a quiet repeating of the words (which can be indicated by movements of the lips or throat). Subvocal rehearsal allows the individual to maintain the sounds of the words for a longer period of time in the phonological store. It also permits visual information to enter storage by recoding it into sound. When people read they often move their lips or throat muscles and through such subvocalizing the printed material is recoded into auditory information. In normally developing children, subvocal rehearsal does not develop until about seven years of age and is related to improvement in phonological memory. Children's phonological memory is related to the acquisition of vocabulary and speech production.

Children with SLD have extremely poor phonological short-term memory. Even when matched on language ability with other children, they display greater deficits in phonological short-term memory. Of interest is that findings from a twin study of SLD indicate heritability of this process (Bishop, North, & Donlan, 1996).

Although progress is being made in understanding the processes that underlie language and that might go awry in SLD, there is much research yet to be done. Given the heterogeneity of language impairments, it seems reasonable to expect that several important deficits might be involved (Bishop, 1992b; Whitehurst & Fischel, 1994).

LEARNING DISABILITIES

The term "learning disabilities" usually refers to developmental problems in reading, writing, and arithmetic—the "three Rs" of the classroom that are essential to learning as well as to everyday functioning. These disorders are also respectively termed "dyslexia," "dysgraphia," and "dyscalculia." They are recognized not only by the educational system but also by both DSM and ICD. DSM previously referred to them as academic skill disorders and now calls them Learning Disorders.

Table 11-4 provides a summary of the DSM-IV criteria for diagnosis of Reading Disorder, Disorder of Written Expression, and Mathematics Disorder. Diagnosis is based on a substantial discrepancy between measures of achievement or ability and the individual's intelligence, age, or education. The disturbance must interfere significantly with academic achievement or daily living. Moreover, it cannot be accounted for by a sensory deficit. These criteria are in keeping with the definition of learning disabilities used by the Individuals with Disabilities Education Act.

We will discuss each of these disorders in turn, examining their clinical manifestations and underlying psychological deficits. Discussion will focus more heavily on reading disorders because the vast majority of children with LD have reading problems and because reading has been more intensively investigated.

CLINICAL CHARACTERISTICS AND DEFICITS OF READING DISABILITIES

Children with reading problems may struggle to pronounce words correctly when reading orally, read excessively slowly or haltingly, have limited

TABLE 11-4

DSM-IV Criteria for Disorders of Reading, Written Expression, and Mathematics

A. Achievement or ability is measured by standardized tests, is substantially below that expected given the person's age, measured intelligence, and age-appropriate education.

B. The disturbance significantly interferes with academic achievement or activities of daily living that require the ability.

C. If a sensory deficit is present, the difficulties are in excess of those usually associated with the sensory deficit.

vocabulary, be able to read but not understand what they have read, or not remember what they have read.

Earlier we examined the elements of language that must be acquired for normal language development. The best way to understand the difficulties of poor readers is to inspect what the process of normal reading entails. At the least a reader must:

■ discriminate printed letters or combinations of letters (graphemes);

■ understand that graphemes are related to language sounds;

■ discriminate words and understand that they are composed of sounds;

■ use vocabulary, that is, words and their meanings;

■ understand the basic ways in which words are combined into phrases and sentences;

■ extract meaning from words, punctuation, and sentences; and

■ put extracted meaning into memory store.

What cognitive abilities are involved in reading and reading problems? In the earlier decades of the twentieth century, Samuel Orton's hypotheses about reading disabilities became extremely influential. Orton (1937) put visual deficits at the heart of the problem, and this hypothesis remained cen-

tral for some years to come. Orton noted that among other difficulties, visual deficits caused dyslexic children to reverse letters (*d* for *b*: *saw* for *was*) and even to write in mirror images (Vellutino, 1979). Other theorists suggested that dyslexia was caused by eye defects that led to impairments in scanning or tracking visual stimuli or by deficits in the processing of form, pattern, and spatial organization in visual stimuli. These theories suggested that defects, which distorted visual stimuli, occurred at the early sensory stage of visual processing. Such deficits were inferred from the accuracy and speed with which children matched stimuli, drew figures, and the like. They were thought to be caused by brain abnormalities or dysfunctions.

Despite the popularity of the visual-perceptual hypothesis, it was gradually challenged by contrary evidence. It is presently believed that although visual processing may cause reading problems for some children, it is not central in most cases (Silver, 1991; Snowling, 1991). The prevalent view emphasizes that reading disorder is a complex language deficiency.

In one simple demonstration of this view, Vellutino (1987) asked poor readers in the second through sixth grades to copy words and other stimuli after a brief visual presentation. They then were requested to name the words. Poor readers correctly copied the word—vision did not appear problematic—but they then had difficulties in naming the words. For instance, they copied *was* correctly, and even correctly named the letters as *w, a, s*. However, they named the word *saw*. The incorrect naming thus appeared to be a language problem rather than a visual defect.

Since reading involves the recoding of language, the child who has weak language skills could be expected to be at risk for reading disabilities (Vellutino, 1979). In fact, reading deficits are more common in children who have language delays (Bashir & Scavuzzo, 1992; Mann & Brady, 1988). Comprehension of written material appears to reflect a global deficit in language (Stothard & Hulme, 1995). Poor readers do worse than excellent readers on many language tasks but not on nonverbal tasks.

Considerable research now indicates that central to reading disorder is a deficit in phonological processing, that is, in using the sound structure of language to process written material. Before they can learn to read, children must recognize that spoken words can be segmented into sounds, an ability referred to as "phonological awareness." For example, they must realize that the word *Dad* has three sounds. This task can be a relatively difficult one for children because the sounds in spoken words tend to overlap rather than to be segmented: *Dad* is said as one unit of sound. Nevertheless, by the time they reach seven years of age, most children have acquired the ability to segment words by sound. The 15 percent to 20 percent who persist in having difficulties are at risk for reading problems (Fletcher et al., 1994; Lyon, 1996a).

To read requires another crucial component of phonology: the understanding that language sounds are represented by letters of the alphabet or by a combination of letters. Then sound can be mapped to letters and words. Young children who are aware of the sounds of their native language and who can map sounds to letters and words become the better readers. In contrast, children with phonological deficits have difficulty in naming actual words and artificial "words." They also typically recall fewer items from lists of linguistic material than do good readers—whether the lists are composed of letter, words, nonsense syllables, sentences, digits, or nameable objects and whether the lists are heard or seen (Mann & Brady, 1988). The problem in short-term memory for linguistic material may involve deficits in using or retrieving sounds to represent the verbal items, and so phonological deficits may underlie the memory problem (Hulme & Roodenrys, 1995).

At the same time, memory problems in reading may also be due to other deficiencies. Poor readers use fewer strategies that promote memory, such as rehearsal, organization, and elaboration (Bauer, 1987; Bauer & Newman, 1991). They also use strategies less often and less efficiently. For example, in learning lists of words, rehearsal is used less, and so is organization of the words by meaning (Pressley & Levin, 1987). In more complex tasks, such as the learning of prose, poor readers do not elaborate or add context to facilitate their learning, and they do not as efficiently select cues from the text that would aid the retrieval of information from memory. At least in some cases, poor readers are capable of using the strategies but do not do so.

It is also likely that deficits in executive functions affect reading. In general, children with LD lack knowledge about when, why, and how to use the strategies that they possess (Pressley & Levin, 1987; Torgesen, 1986). They fail to notice what a specific task requires and to monitor how well they are doing. Moreover, when they realize that they are having difficulty, they give up instead of switching strategies and trying harder, as efficient learners do. Whereas giving up has to do with motivation, it is clear that metacognition is inadequate in some cases.

Several processes appear critical in the enormously complex ability to read. Phonological processing is especially important in the early stages of learning to read, but not all poor readers have deficits in this area. Children who have comprehension problems without phonological difficulties have been identified. Nevertheless, the evidence that most early-occurring reading disabilities stem from deficits in phonological processing is compelling (Stanovich, 1994). Several investigators suggest that these deficits may be a marker for dyslexia.

CLINICAL CHARACTERISTICS AND DEFICITS OF WRITTEN EXPRESSION

Although research with regard to written expression lags behind that of reading, there is a consensus that writing disabilities are multidimensional (Culbertson, 1998).

Problems in the mechanics of writing are obvious in some cases of dysgraphia. Smooth, rapid, and clear handwriting develops gradually and with effort in normally developing children. In the presence of specific disabilities, the task of producing letters and words on paper goes slowly and is laborious. Children with dysgraphia have difficulty in keeping up with written school assignments, may be last to hand in papers, and may sit for hours over homework. Even with time and effort, the quality of their handwriting is poor (see Figure 11-1). Perception, especially visual-motor coordination, is implicated.

Good writing requires more than mechanically producing characters on paper, however, and deficits also exist in language-based skills. Spelling errors, misordered and awkward placement of words, poor sentence construction, and poor punctuation are common. In addition, there is a problem of creating meaning in written material. Some of this problem is related to difficulties in word usage and sentence construction. However, higher-order cognitive and metacognitive skills are also involved (Lyon, 1996a; Wong et al., 1997). That is, disabled writers lack skill in understanding the goal of their writing, developing a plan, organizing the points to be made, linking ideas, and the like. Figure 11-2 provides an example of the work of a learning disabled adolescent assigned to write a compare-and-contrast essay. The essay is comprehensible but demonstrates weaknesses in sentence construction, awkward phrasing, lack of paragraphing, and deficits in organization. (This student's writing greatly improved through an intervention program aimed at teaching cognitive and metacognitive skills.)

CLINICAL CHARACTERISTICS AND DEFICITS OF MATHEMATICS DISABILITIES

The clinical descriptions of children with mathematics disorder indicate an array of deficits including problems in accurately reading numbers, simple addition and subtraction, understanding arithmetic terms and symbols, paying attention to arithmetic signs, spatial organization, and memory for number facts. As in reading and writing, arithmetic consists of several aspects that require different abilities as children take on more complex tasks. A distinction can be made between arithmetic calculation (Figure 11–3) and reasoning.

Some of the cognitive understandings required for mathematics begin during the first few years of life. Even the simple calculations accomplished by very young children require some conceptual understanding of amount, size, and number. Developmental milestones reached during age three to six are thought to play a role in success in arith-

metic (Semrud-Clikeman & Hynd, 1992). Among these milestones are arranging objects by size, counting to ten, copying numbers and block designs, sorting objects by a particular characteristic, and understanding the concepts of long-short, some-few, big-small, and more than–less then.

Visual-spatial, language, and reading abilities all play a part in children's success in arithmetic. Visual imagery has been shown to be important in certain types of problems (Semrud-Clikeman & Hynd, 1992). A child who can mentally "see" a group of six apples and a group of three apples is thereby aided in solving the problem "How many apples would you have if you started with six and took away three?" Visual discrimination, memory for visual sequences, and visual-motor coordination correlate with success in arithmetic. As arithmetic problems move from relatively simple drill and calculation to more complex word problems, language and problem solving come into play. Thus with increasing age, verbal skills and higher-level reasoning are correlated with success.

VARIATION IN CLINICAL PROFILES

Although learning disabilities can be described as if they are "pure" reading, writing, or mathematics difficulties, deficits often occur in combinations. Most children with LD have reading problems, but many have additional learning difficulties. In the classroom, teachers report that these children confuse one word with another, fail in simple arithmetic computations, rapidly forget too much of what they have learned, or struggle to write neatly (Taylor, 1989).

Variation is also seen within a disorder. Some children may show quite isolated deficiencies within an academic area, but the deficits tend to be broader. Thus mathematics deficits may exist in only some or all of the needed computational, visual-spatial, memory, and mathematical reasoning skills. In reading, deficits may exist in only some or all of the required skills for associating sound with symbols and recognizing and remembering written words. The heterogeneity of the clinical picture means that each child's abilities must be carefully assessed to maximize intervention.

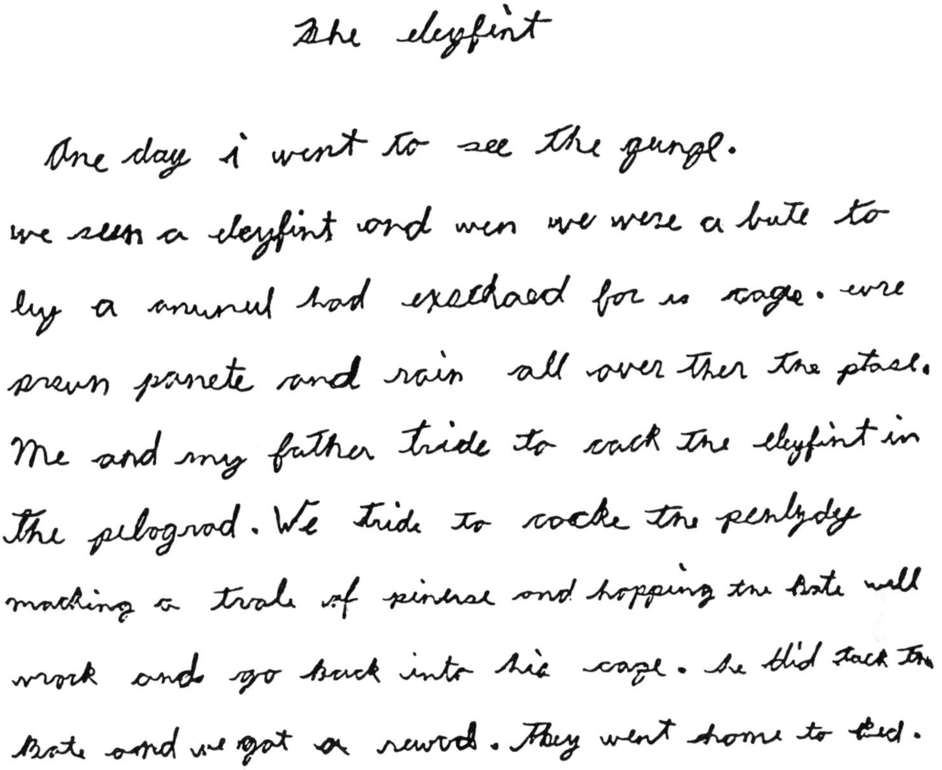

the elefint

One day i went to see the jungl.
we seen a elefint and wen we were a bute to
ly a anunul had esethaed for is cage. ewe
srewn panete and rain all over ther the ptasl.
Me and my father tride to eack the elefint in
the pelogrod. We tride to cocke the penlydy
mathing a trale of sindrse and hopping tru bate well
work and go back into his cage. he thid tack tm
Bate and we got a rewrd. They went home to bed.

The Elephant
One day I went to see the jungle. We seen a elephant and when
we were about to leave an animal escaped from his cage. Every
person panicked and ran all over the place. Me and my father tried
to catch the elephant in the playground. We tried to catch the
elephant by making a trail of peanuts and hoping the bait would
work and he would go back into his cage. He did take the bait and
we got a reward. Then we went home to bed.

FIGURE 11-1 The writing of an eleven-year-old boy and the probable translation. The writing shows imagination, a rich vocabulary, and a basic grasp of storytelling. There also are misspellings of common and uncommon words, added and missing words in sentences, poorly formed letters, and retracing of letters that suggest difficulty in the mechanics of writing.
From Taylor, 1988a.

Hokey and basketball are two sports they both have comparesions they both sports, they contrast in many ways like in hokey you use a stick and a puck, but in basketball you use one ball and your hands.They also compare in that when you play them the goal is to get the puck or basketball into a goal or net.Another contrast is that hokey is played on ice and basketball is played on courts.When you play hokey or basketball you noticed that the puck and ball both touch the ground that is another way to compare.In hokey the goal.net is placed on the ground and in basketball the net is on a backboard in the air that is another contrast.If you have ever been to a hokey or basketball game there is always quaters or periods in a game so that the players can take a break,in that way they compare. Basketball has four quarters and Hockey has three periods to a game and they are different in that way.But the best comparisions in hokey and basketball is the fans,many people love hockey and basketball that's why they are one of most played and favored sports in the world.

FIGURE 11-2 A compare-and-contrast essay written by an adolescent with learning disabilities.
From Wong, Butler, Ficzere, and Kuperis (1997).

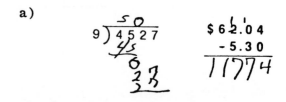

FIGURE 11-3 Arithmetic computation errors made by (top) a twelve-year-old boy and (bottom) a ten-year-old girl with learning disabilities.
From Taylor, 1998a.

SUBTYPING LEARNING DISABILITIES

There have been many efforts to discover whether the variety of learning and language disabilities can be accounted for by more basic subtypes (Culbertson, 1998). Well over one hundred studies have been conducted in the last thirty-five years just to subtype reading disabilities. As an example, consider the early work of Mattis, French, and Rapin (1975). They gave a group of reading-disabled children a battery of neuropsychological tests and concluded from the results that three subgroups existed. The largest group showed language disorder, the second group had visual-spatial deficits, and the third group had problems in articulation of language and motor problems. Subsequent investigations indicated that a small percentage of the children showed a combination of two of the subtypes. In reviewing the extensive work on reading, Culbertson (1998) concludes that language/auditory processing underlies one major subtype of reading and that visual-spatial deficits underlie a second major subtype. However, Lyon (1996a) has concluded that the processing of sound, the processing of written characters, and memory span are central to subtypes of reading.

Compared with earlier studies, research on subtyping now employs more sophisticated computer and statistical methods. Nevertheless, methodological weaknesses in this work are noted. In addition, an overwhelming number of different subtypes have been generated by various investigators, and different conclusions have been drawn. However, this line of research has contributed to the understanding of LLD, and the effort to reveal valid categories is worthwhile.

EPIDEMIOLOGY

Prevalence rates reported for LD vary considerably. The use of different definitions is one reason that estimates vary across community samples. Prevalence rates are also obtained from the educational system, which not only employs varying definitions but also responds to sociopolitical demands for special education. Thus, for example, between 1977 and 1987, the number of learning disabled children served by special education just about doubled (Kirk & Gallagher, 1989). It is debatable whether actual prevalence increased or whether more children were being placed into the LD category. Given these considerations, DSM-IV reports that prevalence of learning disabilities among U.S. school-age children ranges from 2 percent to 10 percent (APA, 1994).

Data on the prevalence of each type of disability are scant. DSM-IV gives the figure of 4 percent of school-age children with reading disorder and 1 percent with arithmetic disorder. Writing disorder is said to be rare unless it is associated with other learning disabilities. However, estimates of 8 percent to 15 percent have been given for writing disorder, with no gender difference (Lyon, 1996b). Vague definitions of the disorder cast doubt on the validity of estimated prevalence.

Boys have been more often identified than girls, perhaps three to five times as often. However, this gender difference is now questioned, at least concerning reading disorder. The findings from the Connecticut Longitudinal Study are particularly interesting (Shaywitz, Fletcher, & Shaywitz, 1996). Randomly selected children were individually assessed for reading disability when they were second- or third-graders. No gender difference was found. However, when these same children were evaluated by the school system, more boys than girls were identified as reading disabled. Other analyses showed that (1) boys are more likely to receive higher ratings on intrusive behaviors such as high activity level and aggression and (2) reading disabled children with behavior problems are more likely to be identified than reading disabled children without behavior problems. This finding suggests that at least in the early grades, girls may be underidentified (and thus not obtain needed educational services).

Prevalence rates regarding social class and cultural groups are also related to school practices and to sociopolitical issues (Kessler, 1988). White middle-class children compared with black chil-dren were once disproportionately placed in learning disabilities classes, and black children disproportionately placed in classes for the educably mentally retarded. Indeed, learning disabilities were said to be middle-class disorders (Senf, 1986). However, by the early 1980s, group differences had been substantially reduced in learning disabilities classrooms, apparently because of increased enrollment of black students (Chinn & Hughes, 1987). Survey data collected in 1990 by the Office of Civil Rights show that 5 percent of all African-American students were given the diagnosis of learning disability, the same as for white students (Reschley, 1996). Such change probably reflects pressure to recognize standardized tests as discriminatory towards certain groups, to avoid the stigma of mental retardation, and to obtain school placements that would optimize learning. In any event, though, school practices and sociopolitical issues have implication for prevalence rates.

PSYCHOSOCIAL AND BEHAVIOR PROBLEMS OF LLD

Although academic and learning deficiency is clearly the main concern of learning disabilities research, social behavior is of considerable interest. Many, perhaps most, children with disabilities appear to do well in this regard, but risk operates. Psychosocial and behavioral problems have often been interpreted as a consequence of LLD. This interpretation may make intuitive sense, but other causal possibilities exist.

SOCIAL RELATIONSHIPS AND SOCIAL COMPETENCE

The social relationships of at least some children with LLD are less than satisfactory. Peers, teachers, and parents describe various difficulties in interacting with these children and tend to display negative attitudes towards them (Gresham & Elliott, 1989; Margalit, 1989; Rourke, 1988). Teachers associate learning disabilities with a variety of annoying and otherwise problematic behaviors. Among these behaviors are anxiety, immaturity, disrup-

Social interaction and motivational factors play an important role in the development of learning and learning difficulties.
(Courtesy of A.C. Israel)

tiveness, and hyperactivity (e.g., Heavey et al., 1989). Children with learning disabilities have received lower ratings than nondisabled youngsters on cooperation, organization, coping, tactfulness, responsibility, and other such attributes. Not only do parents recognize their handicapped children's academic problems, but they also note difficulty in managing their children.

The unpopularity of children with disabilities is shown in several investigations in which youngsters rated classmates or nominated classmates who, for example, would make a good president or who would not be welcomed at their birthday party (Pearl, Donahue, & Bryan, 1986). Children with learning disorders were often rated as less popular than nondisabled peers, and they were more rejected or neglected. Figure 11-4 represents the general finding, which has been shown in a meta-analysis of the research (Ochoa & Palmer, 1995). Risk for social rejection can begin prior to first-grade referral to special education and continue into young adulthood (Bryan, 1997). This finding does not mean, of course, that all disabled children are rejected or otherwise have poor relationships; Bryan (1997) reports that risk varies from approximately 35 percent to 60 percent.

One of the factors that may underlie difficult relationships is social competence. Research sug-

gests that children with learning disorders are less socially competent than non-LD peers, as measured by inventories and laboratory tasks (Ritter, 1989; Rourke & Fuerst, 1995; Toro et al., 1990). This deficiency is manifested in difficulty in identifying the emotional expression of others, misreading of social situations, errors in guessing how other children feel in particular situations, and deficits in social problem solving. It is again important to note that not all of the children show social deficits. Moreover, situational influences may be quite strong in determining whether a child behaves competently or not.

BEHAVIOR PROBLEMS

There is also a higher than average risk for a variety of behavioral disturbances, both internalizing and externalizing problems (Beitchman et al., 1996; Rourke & Fuerst, 1995; Rutter, Maywood, & Howlin, 1992). An association with attention problems and hyperactivity is well established, with the overlap of LD and ADHD estimated in the range of 20 to 25 percent (Culbertson, 1998). Risk for behavior problems holds for clinic and nonclinic samples.

Specific language impairments have been associated with a variety of behavior problems; approximately 50 percent of the children display some

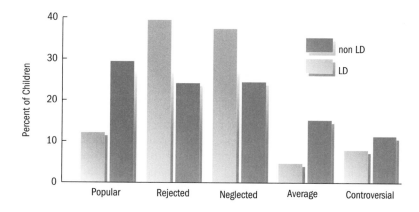

FIGURE 11-4 Percentage of disabled learners and nondisabled learners selected by classmates into each social category. All children were in regular fourth-through sixth-grade classrooms.

Data from Stone and LaGreca, 1990.

type of difficulty (Stevenson, 1996). In young children, overactivity and behavioral immaturity (such as dependency and bowel control) were especially common. In older children, internalizing problems were more common.

Reading disorder has frequently been associated with conduct disorder, and the causal connection has received much consideration. Three major causal possibilities readily come to mind. The first, that conduct disturbance causes LD, has not received much attention. In fact, it is excluded by the definition of LD as *not* being due to emotional disturbance (e.g., Rourke & Fuerst, 1995). The second hypothesis, that learning problems increase the likelihood of behavioral problems, seems quite reasonable. Children with LLD might well react to academic failure and social rejection with frustration, anger, and acting-out behaviors. The third causal hypothesis, that reading and conduct problems co-occur but that some other factor (or factors) is responsible for the relationship, has also been seriously examined. We will look further at this issue.

Antisocial behavior is correlated with both concurrent and later reading difficulties (Fergusson & Lynskey, 1997). The study we are about to describe supports this finding. It draws on an exten-

sive longitudinal investigation of children born in New Zealand in 1977. At age six, a small percentage of this population was identified as reading delayed on the basis of their scoring one standard deviation below the mean on a standard reading test. At age eight, scores on the Wechsler Intelligence Scale for Children were used in conjunction with the reading scores to classify children as having a specific reading disability. Two groups were thus formed, a general reading delay group and a specific reading disability group. Conduct problems were assessed at ages ten, twelve, fourteen, and sixteen years, using maternal, teacher, and self reports. Demographic and family data were also collected (e.g., maternal education, social class).

The overall results showed that children with reading problems were rated with more conduct disturbance than children without reading problems. The link was stronger for the reading delay group than for specific reading disability. An important outcome is that reading problems were also associated with many other factors, including the children's early conduct and attention problems and several family factors. When the influence of these factors was taken into account, the relationship between reading disability and con-

SOCIAL DEFICITS AND NONVERBAL LEARNING DISABILITIES (NVLD)

Social deficits have been described in a group of children who are thought to display a unique profile of functioning. As early as 1967, Johnson and Myklebust described children who had deficits in understanding the actions, gestures, and facial expression of others. They had problems in perception, but their verbal functioning was relativity spared (Culbertson, 1998). Subsequently these children were studied by others.

Rourke and his colleagues have described the group through subtyping studies. The disorder has been given various names, including "nonverbal learning disability," "social-emotional learning disabilities," and "right hemisphere deficit syndrome." NVLD is characterized by a set of complex strengths and weaknesses in perceptual, psychomotor, attention, and problem-solving skills. These underlying characteristics are hypothesized to lead to relative strengths in verbal abilities and deficits in both mathematics and social competence (Rourke & Fuerst, 1995). For example, visual-spatial deficits are thought to be responsible for the problems in interpreting other people's fa-

cial expressions, gestures, and other nonverbal signals. Similarly, deficits in problem solving are thought to hinder good social judgment. NVLD is also associated with the development of internalizing behavioral symptoms. It is proposed that NVLD is a distinct subtype of learning disabilities that explains some cases of poor psychosocial functioning. Since the prevalence of NVLD is small, however, it can account for only a small number of cases.

Rourke and Fuerst (1995) hypothesize that NVLD is caused by abnormal development of or damage to the white matter of the brain that implicates the right hemisphere. The characteristics displayed in NVLD have been associated with disease or damage to the right hemisphere, which is more involved in spatial skills and less involved in language functions than the left hemisphere. Thus, the psychosocial difficulties in NVLD may have a different basis from the social and behavioral problems linked to language-based disabilities.

duct problems disappeared. Especially influential were conduct problems at age six, which explained much of the association of reading and behavioral disturbance. This finding supports the hypothesis that the link between reading disability and conduct problems is established early and that the development of reading disability is not directly responsible for conduct disturbance. This general conclusion is supported by other investigations (Williams and McGee, 1996). This study does not explain why conduct disorder at age 6 predicted later reading problems, however. Do the behavior problems interfere with the child's ef-

forts to read? Is there some underlying abnormality that affects behavior and also interacts with the tasks of reading that become important when the child begins school? As is often the case, the developmental pathway appears to be complex.

MOTIVATIONAL FACTORS IN LLD

There is considerable interest in the motivational behavior of children with learning disabilities, since effort is essential for their academic success. Yet their motivation may be adversely affected by the difficulties and failure that are part and parcel of LLD.

Evidence exists that some older children with learning disabilities have lowered self-esteem with regard to their academic performance. Research has also shown that children's beliefs about school performance can affect their actual school performance (Stetsenko et al., 1995; Little & Lopez, 1997). Consider the following:

■ Children hold certain beliefs about five factors thought to influence school performance: effort, ability, luck, teachers, and unknown factors. A developmental pattern exists across several cultures pertaining to these beliefs. Younger children tend to believe that the five factors play about an equal role in bringing about school achievement and in avoiding school failure. By later childhood, effort and ability are believed to be more important than the other factors.

■ The degree to which a person believes that he or she has access to these factors is related to school performance. This perception is referred to as *agency*. A child who believes that he or she has ability, for example, is said to have agency with regard to this factor.

■ The degree to which a person has a sense of generally being able to produce desirable outcomes is related to school performance. This perception is referred to as *control*.

Given these considerations, some children appear to enter a vicious cycle of academic failure and low motivation that works against them (Licht & Kistner, 1986). As a result of academic failure, they come to doubt their intellectual abilities and believe that their efforts to achieve are futile. This results in their being frustrated and giving up easily in the face of difficulty. In turn, further failure is experienced, which reinforces their belief in lack of ability. It appears that a sense of agency and of control has suffered (see Figure 11-5).

There is evidence that this cycle operates. Studies show that children with learning disabilities tend to have lower expectations for success than other children. They are less likely to credit suc-

FIGURE 11-5 Learning disabled children may experience a vicious cycle of academic failure and low motivation.

cess to their ability and are more likely to attribute failure to inadequate ability. In addition, learning handicapped children tend to believe that their efforts will not improve the situation and that the situation is controlled by external variables (e.g., Allen & Drabman, 1991; Tarnowski & Nay, 1989). Although these beliefs may have some reasonable basis, they also tend to contribute to the difficulties.

Not all students who have difficulties in school respond in the same way, of course; situational and other factors lead some children to be more adaptive than others. Licht and Kistner (1986) note several factors that play a role in creating individual differences. One factor is the degree of failure experienced: Less failure is associated with more adaptive motivation. Children's developmental level may also be influential. Research indicates that children under age seven generally have high opinions of their abilities, and even when they do not, motivational problems may not appear. By age ten, social comparison becomes more significant and older children may thus be more susceptible to negative feedback about their failure (Bjorklund & Green, 1992).

Teacher feedback may also influence children's self-perceptions. Although feedback can be negative, especially when the child is difficult to manage, teachers may also try to encourage low-achieving students by giving less criticism and more praise, even following quite poor performance. However, praise for performing easy tasks that require little effort probably is not beneficial in the long run, when children must persist in the face of difficulty (Light & Kistner, 1986). A general guideline is that praise should depend on effortful work and should provide specific information as to how the child might improve performance.

Parents certainly could be expected to play a role in determining children's self-perceptions and motivation. The belief that their parents accept and love them is related to children's self-esteem (Morvitz & Motta, 1992). Whereas parental denial of their children's learning problems is not helpful, realistically encouraging the child's sense of agency and control (e.g., by encouraging effort) can be supportive. Parents (as well as teachers) are also in the position to build confidence in areas in which the child may already have some confidence, which can contribute to general positive self-regard (cf. Grolnick & Ryan, 1990).

To put this discussion of motivation into proper perspective, it should be noted that it may apply to many children, not just to those who have learning disabilities. It is reasonable to assume that youth who experience academic failure are at greater risk for motivational problems. Thus regardless of the etiology of learning disorders, the role that motivation might play in academic achievement should be considered.

ETIOLOGY OF LLD

The assumption that neurological damage or dysfunction underlies language and learning disabilities has been a dominant hypothesis. This perspective was obvious among early theorists, who linked brain disorder to children of average intelligence who displayed learning, perceptual, language, and behavioral problems such as hyperactivity .

How has the hypothesis of biological etiology fared? Brain damage and learning handicaps are certainly associated (Bigler, 1987). There are learning disabled children with histories of neurological disorders such as cerebral palsy, epilepsy,

nervous system infections, and head injury (Taylor, 1988a). Specific learning disabilities are associated with prenatal alcohol use, neurological delays, neurological soft signs, and immune system dysfunction (e.g., Taylor, 1989; Snowling, 1991). Nevertheless, these findings were often not compelling until more recent technological advances strengthened the notion that some kind of biological dysfunction underlies specific developmental disorders (Bryan, 1991).

GENETIC INFLUENCE

Genetic influence on learning disabilities has been suspected for some time and is now more firmly established (DeFries & Gillis, 1993; Maughan & Yule, 1994). Language dysfunctions are known to "run in families" (Bishop, 1992a), and limited research indicates that the parents and siblings of children with spelling disability are at risk (Schulte-Korne et al., 1996). A twin study has shown greater concordance in identical over fraternal pairs for language disabilities (Bishop, North, & Donlan, 1996).

There is a greater amount of research on the genetics of reading disabilities. Between 35 percent and 40 percent of first degree relatives of reading disordered children have reading problems, much higher than the general population risk (Beitchman & Young, 1997). Twin comparisons also indicate heritability. For example, data from the Colorado Reading Project show 68 percent concordance for identical twins and 40 percent for fraternal twins (DeFries & Light, 1996). Moreover, hereditary influence has been found for phonological processing and single-word reading. This is a particularly interesting finding given the importance of these processes in the development of language and reading.

Some progress is being made in identifying the specific chromosomes and mechanisms that might be responsible for reading disorders (DeFries & Light, 1996; Smith et al., 1990). Chromosomes 15 and 6 have been implicated in some cases; that is, inheritance is linked to one of these genes in some families and the other gene in other families. Both polygenic and single-gene effects are suspected. In fact, there is considerable evidence that reading disabilities are transmitted through several different genetic mechanisms. Since the disabilities themselves may be heterogeneous, it is tempting to speculate that different genetic mechanisms may underlie different reading disabilities. However, it is too early to draw this conclusion.

BRAIN ABNORMALITIES

Some of the most exciting investigations of etiology concern brain abnormalities. Specific cerebral structures have been known for a very long time to subserve language functions. In the 1860s, it was demonstrated that a small area of the left frontal lobe, Broca's area, was associated with speech production, and an area in the temporal lobe, Wernicke's area, was soon associated with language comprehension. In recent times, brain scans have enabled researchers to observe the brain as individuals participate in language and reading tasks. These scans and other research methods have revealed the importance of several brain structures in language and reading functions (See Figure 11-6).

Earlier investigators of language and reading disabilities did not, of course, have the advantages of modern technology, but they nevertheless hypothesized various brain dysfunctions as causing disabilities. Studying dyslexia in the late 1930s, Orton proposed that visual information was processed by both hemispheres of the brain but that the right hemisphere held visual stimuli in reversed form and order (Vellutino, 1979). For most children, it was proposed, this arrangement was not a problem because the left hemisphere became dominant over the right. In dyslexia, left hemisphere dominance was considered flawed, so that the right hemisphere gained some control and its reversed patterns were expressed in a variety of ways. Orton's proposal is not given credence today, but interest in the hemispheres continues largely on the basis of evidence that the left hemisphere is specialized for processing language and the right for processing spatial information. Current hypotheses include the possibilities that the left hemisphere develops more slowly than it should or that the hemispheres do not properly communicate with each other (Maughan & Yule, 1994).

An interesting finding, which come from brain scans and postmortem brain studies, implicates the planum temporale (Hynd, Marshall, & Gonza-

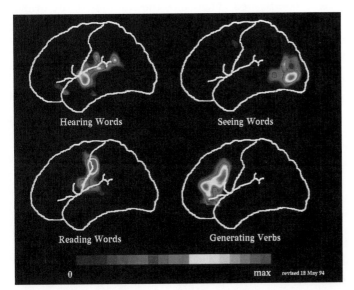

FIGURE 11-6 PET scans of the human brain as it processes language. These scans actually spotlight the areas of the brain most active in hearing, seeing, reading, and speaking.

Adapted from Morris and Maiston, 1998.

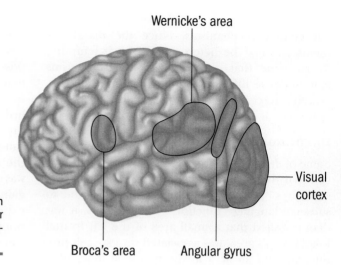

Wernicke's area

Visual cortex

Broca's area

Angular gyrus

FIGURE 11-7 Major areas of the brain involved in reading. The visual cortex receives visual input; the angular gyrus transforms visual input into sound information; Wernicke's area is involved in comprehension.

lez, 1991; Hynd & Semrud-Clikeman, 1989a,b; Peterson, 1995). This is a triangular-shaped region on the upper surface of the temporal lobe extending to the lower surface of the parietal lobe. In normal brains, the left side of the planum temporale is usually larger than the right side. In individuals with dyslexia, this asymmetry is absent. In addition, abnormal cell structure has been found, as well as abnormal activation and metabolism.

The planum temporale is thought to be involved in phonological processing. A limited number of studies shows that functioning of the planum temporale is different in individuals with or without dyslexia when they are engaged in phonological and other reading processing tasks. It is speculated that abnormalities of the planum temporale may be present during the first six months of prenatal development, possibly because of genetic factors.

Shaywitz and colleagues (1998) recently used functional magnetic resonance imaging as adult dyslexic and normal readers engaged in increasingly demanding phonological tasks. The dyslexic readers showed relative underactivation in the visual cortex, angular gyrus, and Wernicke's area

and relative overactivation around Broca's area. These findings are further evidence for phonological difficulties in reading disorder (Figure 11-7).

As informative and interesting as these neurological findings are, caution is needed (e.g., Peterson, 1995). The research samples are often small, and measurements of brain areas are not easily accomplished. Then too, the findings of abnormal brain structure and function are not always consistent; for example, there are individuals with abnormal symmetrical temporal lobes who show no reading problems. In addition, studies of adult samples, raise the question of how well the findings apply to children. Not only is there a need to replicate findings with children, but longitudinal studies would be ideal in tracing the development of language and learning skills in normal and disabled individuals.

ROLE OF PSYCHOSOCIAL AND ENVIRONMENTAL FACTORS

Although biological variables appear to be critical causes of LD, environmental influences also operate. In fact, the importance of psychosocial and motivational effects on learning is well recognized by professionals and parents. Several variables are known to influence the development of language and learning (Beitchman et al., 1997). Early vocabulary growth is predicted by the number of words the child hears from its mother, and vocabulary benefits as well from having others read to the child. Among the factors that can influence learning are family interactions, parental attitudes toward learning, child management practices, social class, and cultural values (Taylor, 1988a). Stevenson and Fredman (1990) found that large family size and certain aspects of mother-child interaction were linked to reading problems, and they noted that family involvement in the child's learning may be especially influential in early reading acquisition. Whitehurst & Fischel (1994) believe that family verbal interaction is not the root of specific language disorders but that once verbal interactions become abnormal—probably as a result of the child's deficits—they can play a role in maintaining the deficits. Child characteristics such as motivation and temperament, along with the matching of expectations for the child to the child's ability, may also play some role in at least maintaining disabilities.

Although most conceptualizations of learning disabilities assign environmental causation a secondary role, not everyone agrees with this emphasis. A general argument put forth is that only some of the children identified as LLD have neurological dysfunction that may interfere with learning and academic achievement (Coles, 1989). Individual biological differences in learners are recognized, but social, cultural, political, and economic influences are viewed as fundamental in creating or preventing learning problems. Thus, when a child fails to learn in school, the cause of failure must be explored not only by examining child-teacher interaction but also by looking at broader factors, such as how the school's structure and attitudes might be causing failure. It is therefore important to identify social, economic, and political variables that affect the child, teacher, and school. This position has been criticized for ignoring the fact that some children display learning problems even when provided good opportunity to learn, for ignoring evidence for a brain abnormalities,

and for broadening the definition of learning disabilities to include poor achievers not ordinarily labeled as LD (Galaburda, 1989; Rourke, 1989; Stanovich, 1989). A more moderate position would view some learning handicaps as originating from both neurological and environmental variables (e.g., Adelman, 1989). This interactional approach emphasizes the importance of knowing more about environmental factors, including instructional methods, that might influence whether and how specific learning handicaps might occur or be maintained.

DEVELOPMENTAL COURSE AND OUTCOME OF LLD

As is true for many issues pertaining to LLD, the use of varying standards for defining disorders makes it difficult to interpret research findings on their developmental course. Another confound is that some of the investigated samples include both specific disabilities and general disabilities without distinguishing these groups.

Language disabilities, if moderate to severe, are manifested in the preschool years; mild difficulties may not be identified until later; especially mild problems in comprehension. Whitehurst and Fischel (1994) reviewed research with regard to specific language impairments that were identified during the early preschool years. The language abilities of the vast majority of the children were in the normal range by five years of age, although language and reading skills were weak relative to other areas of development. Even so, a minority of the children were at risk for subsequent language and reading difficulties, and the longer the initial language impairments continued, the greater the risk. Moreover, risk for later problems increased from articulation problems to expressive problems to receptive-expressive problems. This hierarchy of risk has been noted by others (e.g., Baker & Cantwell, 1989; Rutter, Mayhood, & Howlin, 1992). Children who display only misarticulations appear to be at low risk. In contrast, many children with receptive difficulties may eventually acquire language comprehension only after traveling a long and difficult path, and some may never develop completely normal comprehension of language.

It is noteworthy that language impairment has been related to subsequent social and behavioral problems (Baker & Cantwell, 1987; Beitchman et al., 1996). For example, in a population study of children with speech and language impairments at age five, those with the more severe disabilities manifested both internalizing and externalizing problems at a seven-year follow-up.

In reviewing the prognosis for reading disorders, Maughan (1995) points to the shortcomings of the data, such as inappropriate comparison groups. Analyses of outcomes for reading disabilities also tend to focus on general rather than specific reading problems. Given this, relatively well-designed studies do indicate that reading problems tend to persist during the school years into adolescence and adulthood. However, much individual variation is seen, including improvement (Williams & McGee, 1996). Some children with very poor reading skills at age seven have been reported as catching up with their peers by preadolescence, and improvement can occur from adolescence into early adulthood. General intelligence, initial severity of reading problems, and reading ability of the mother have been found to predict outcome. Continued practice and experience with literacy materials may also play a role when reading comprehension and word recognition improve. An interesting finding is that phonological processing does not improve much in dyslexic children or adults. Since reading failure is so prevalent among those with learning disabilities, it appears that at least for some, LD is a chronic condition (Silver, 1989; Spreen, 1988).

As we have already seen, early reading problems are linked to concurrent and later internalizing and externalizing problems. However, the casual path is indirect, with early behavior disorder and family factors playing a role (Fergusson & Lynskey, 1997; Williams & McGee, 1996). Only some reading disabled children will have later social difficulties and boys appear more at risk than girls.

A recent national study provides an interesting profile of students with various types of handicap-

ping conditions, including LD, MR, emotional disturbance, and other conditions (Wagner & Blackorby, 1996). These youth were of the first generation to go entirely through elementary school under The Education for All Handicapped Children Act. Approximately 40 percent of all students dropped out of the educational system before completing high school. Of the students in the learning disabilities category who finished high school, close to one-third had enrolled in postsecondary education at some time three to five years after they had left school. This contrasted with about two-thirds of the comparable general population of youth. About 70 percent of LD students were employed three to five years after leaving school, a rate about equal to that for the general population. Employment was related to graduation from high school, to a concentration of vocational classes in high school, and to being male and white. Wages tended to be low, however—with women, African American youth, and youth from economically disadvantaged homes earning the least. How all of these individuals will do in future years remains to be seen. In fact, there is little research on how LLD students fare during the adult years.

ASSESSMENT FOR LLD

When language disorders are suspected in preschoolers, parents seek assessment from a variety of professionals. Later-occurring or more subtle language problems and learning handicaps are most often evaluated in the educational system, following procedures set for compliance with IDEA. Teachers typically have the critical role of seeking consultation for the child, most likely having already spoken to the parents about the child's problems. School psychologists do much of the actual assessment; they gather information from the teacher and often are the persons who observe the child in the classroom (Bryan & Bryan, 1986). In some cases, the child may be evaluated in mental health settings, and the school subsequently will do an assessment and then will arrange a meeting among school professionals, parents, and other relevant individuals to discuss the evaluation and to plan for intervention. Guidelines set by the state must be followed if services are sought for the child.

Adequate assessment requires an interview with the parents and seeks information about the child's prenatal, developmental, and medical history; the child's behavioral and social functioning; family background; and family functioning and concerns.

Of critical importance in identifying learning disabilities and understanding the child's deficits are psychological tests that establish the child's academic achievement, general intelligence, and specific language, cognitive, perceptual, or motor skills. The focus of academic assessment is usually on reading, spelling, and arithmetic skills, although tests are available to examine other areas, such as social studies knowledge. It is important to

evaluate components of academic domains (Beitchman & Young, 1997). Evaluations for reading, for example, might include measures of sounding out words, recognizing sounds for letters, and comprehending written material. The child may also be given cognitive tests that evaluate specific visual, auditory, motor, language, and thinking skills. It is important that difficulties be described in detail, since they can take several forms and involve several cognitive components (Taylor, 1988a). Strengths also need to be assessed.

A large number of tests are available for these purposes (Whitehurst & Fischel, 1994). Among the many tests employed are the Wide Range Achievement Test (Jastak & Wilkinson, 1984), the Peabody Individual Achievement Test (Dunn & Markwardt, 1970), and the Woodcock-Johnson

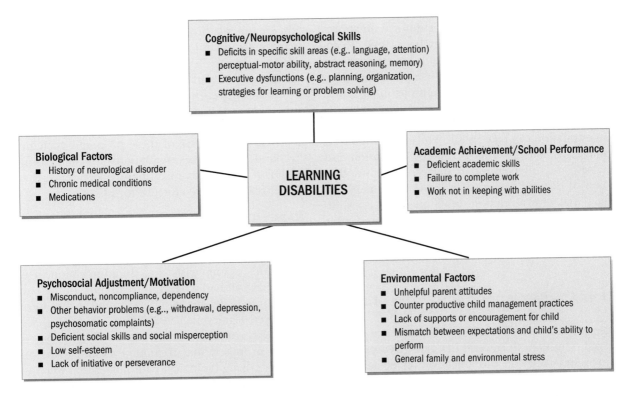

FIGURE 11-8 Taylor's model for comprehensive assessment of LD.
From Taylor, 1998a.

PsychoEducational Battery (Woodcock & Johnson, 1978). Selection of tests should, of course, take into consideration reliability and validity, as well as possible cultural bias.

When it is relevant, the evaluator should also discuss the child's study habits, motivations, self-esteem, and concerns (e.g., Byran, 1997). Because learning disabilities are essentially defined in terms of achievement and cognition, there is probably a tendency to assess inadequately the behavioral, social, and motivational contexts in which the child is operating. Taylor (1988a) has provided a model for comprehensive assessment of LD. As shown in Figure 11-8, it includes the child's psychological adjustment. It also takes into account environmental factors that can promote or have adverse influence on the child's functioning. For example, evaluation of parental attitudes, environmental stress, and the match between the child's abilities and others' expectations are important aspects of assessment.

Finally, assessment should be done at an appropriately early time (Satz & Fletcher, 1988). Reading problems can be predicted in kindergarten or first grade (Lyon & Cutting, 1998). Yet most children are not referred for learning problems until after they have experienced several years of academic failure. Unnecessary and inappropriate delay in evaluation can take its toll. The child and family may experience a lengthy time of frustration and upset, and intervention is delayed. The implication of delayed treatment is made obvious by the fact that severe reading disabilities are very difficult to overcome when they are diagnosed after eight years of age.

TREATMENT APPROACHES TO LLD

Despite the fact that biological factors are considered dominant in causing LD, most treatment approaches focus on the amelioration of academic and learning problems. Our discussion follows this focus. Before doing so, however, we point out that an optimal treatment approach considers the child within a larger framework.

Children and families can profit from individual therapy, family counseling, and more general supports. Intervention may be appropriate for the social and behavioral problems that sometimes co-occur with learning problems. Stimulant medications may be considered. In the presence of Attention-Deficit Hyperactivity Disorder, stimulants can decrease problems of inattention, impulsivity, and disruptive noncompliant behaviors, and can improve classroom productivity and short-term academic performance. When stimulants have been employed with learning disabilities without ADHD, the results are similar. More classroom work may be produced, although there is little sustained improvement on achievement tests (Gadow & Pomeroy, 1991). The risk of adverse medical side effects must be evaluated, of course. Other medical treatments might be warranted in unusual cases when there is a history of neurological dysfunction or damage (Taylor, 1989).

As with other areas of behavioral disorders, certain treatments are viewed with skepticism by researchers and clinicians. For example, recommendations have been made with regard to antihistamines and diet, including massive doses of vitamins, specific elements such as copper and zinc, sugar, and the Feingold diet that reduces food additives and preservatives (Silver, 1987; Wilsher, 1991). Some of these proposals go hand in hand with recommendations for decreasing ADHD. Overall, there is little or no evidence that these treatments are effective for LLD.

EARLY TREATMENT APPROACHES

Intervention for LD has reflected the mutidisciplinary nature of the field. Psychologists, physicians, educators, optometrists, and communication therapists have all had a hand in treatment. In the late 1960s and 1970s, many different approaches were employed (Hammill, 1993). They reflected three models (Lyon & Cutting, 1998). The biological model proposed that treatment should focus on the underlying biological pathologies that were assumed to cause LD. The psychoeducational model (also known as the diagnostic-remedial approach) assumed that treatment must relieve psychoneurological deficits thought to underlie LLD. The behavioral model made no assumptions about underlying etiology or deficits, and directed treatment towards improving academic skills through learning principles.

The psychoeducational model was particularly popular (Hammill, 1993). Various underlying perceptual and cognitive processes were targeted for improvement. Training programs that involved practice in eye-hand coordination, spatial relationships, and other perceptual-motor behaviors were offered by some of the best educational specialists. Other methods targeted language and the way it is received and expressed through the senses (Bryan & Bryan, 1986). Fernald's multisensory method, for example, presented academic material through sight, touch, hearing, and kinesthetic (muscle) cues—assuming that learning is facilitated by multisensory experiences. Still other programs identified the modes through which the learning disabled child best learned and then taught in that mode. Thus, a child who learned more effectively with visually presented material was encouraged to learn by seeing; the child who processed auditory information better than written information was given oral tests.

Many of the early treatments based on the biological and psychoeducational models fell by the wayside in the 1970s, primarily because they had not been proven successful in either remediating academic performance or in reducing the proposed underlying deficits of LD (Hammill, 1993; Taylor, 1989). These models are reflected in current neuropsychological approaches, which retain the idea that intervention should aim at underlying deficits and which attempt to link deficits to brain functioning. Nevertheless, the behavioral model has enjoyed more success and continues to play a role in the interventions that are favored today (Lyon & Cutting, 1998).

BEHAVIORAL, DIRECT INSTRUCTION, COGNITIVE APPROACHES

The traditional behavioral approach aims at identifying academic or social skill deficits and modifying them through contingency management, feedback, and modeling. The goal may be to increase the number of completed arithmetic problems, strengthen comprehension of written material, or improve handwriting. Reinforcement can include verbal praise, tokens, or desired activities. In practice, such behavioral techniques are often combined with direct instruction and cognitive approaches.

Direct instruction pinpoints academic learning tasks and teaches to them. That is, if the child has a disability in reading, then exercises and practice are provided with letters, words, and other literary materials (Hammill, 1993). This is very different from previous approaches to train perceptual-motor skills to overcome LD. The tasks typically are analyzed into components. Among other things, direct instruction entails selecting and stating goals, presenting new material in small steps and with clear and detailed explanations, incorporating student practice, guiding students, and monitoring student understanding (Lyon & Cutting, 1998). Some direct instruction programs are highly organized with regard to content and teacher behavior. An example is the work of Englemann and colleagues. Teacher-student interactions and lessons are tightly structured as teachers follow lessons that have been previously scripted and field-tested. Teachers present questions at a rapid pace to students in a group, and student responses are provided with feedback and reinforcement. This method has proven itself effective with high-risk students (Morrell, 1998).

The cognitive approach tends to emphasize the remediation of metacognition and executive functions in information processing. That is, students are taught to understand better their own cognitive processes and to regulate cognitive activity (Palincsar & Brown, 1986). They are encouraged to be active problem solvers. Instruction emphasizes increasing awareness of task demands, using appropriate strategies, monitoring the success of the strategies, and switching to another strategy when necessary. The approach has been applied to reading comprehension, mathematics, written expression, memory skills, and study skills (Lyon & Moats, 1988; Maccini & Hughes, 1997; Wong et al., 1997).

The cognitive-behavioral approach is closely aligned to the cognitive approach, but it places special emphasis on students' monitoring and directing their own learning. They do so by assessing, recording, and self-reinforcing their own behavior.

EDUCATIONAL ISSUES AND LLD

Of all youth eligible for special education in the United States, about 50 percent are identified as having specific learning disabilities (Reschley, 1996). This number constitutes approximately 5 percent of the general school-age population. Table 11-5 compares the percentage of students diagnosed with LD with students in other categories of disability. It is striking that the combined categories of LD and speech/language impairment constitute almost 75 percent of all eligible students. Despite the fact that various criteria are used in diagnosing disabilities, it is obvious that as a group, children with these disorders are greatly influenced by the quality of special education.

Consistent with IDEA's mandate for the least restrictive placement, several school options are available for learning disabled students. Overall, about one-third of all students in special education spend 80 percent or more of the school day in general education classrooms, and another one-third spend 40 percent to 80 percent in general

TABLE 11-5

Percentage of School-Aged Population Diagnosed with Disabilities

Disability Category	Percent of IDEA-Eligible Population	Percent of General Population of Youth
Learning disability	51	5.2
Speech or language impairment	23	2.3
Mental retardation	11	1.1
Seriously emotionally disturbed	8	.9
Other	7	.7

Adapted from Reschley, 1996.

education (Hocutt, 1996). Most students with learning or language disabilities are in regular classrooms, in the combination of the regular classroom and the resource room, or in self-contained special classrooms (Lerner, 1989).

If the regular classroom teacher has no training in learning disabilities, a special education teacher may act as a consultant, provide materials, or actually teach the child in the regular classroom. In the resource room, the teacher typically has special education training and teaches to small groups. It is important that experiences in the resource room be integrated with those of the regular classroom. Self-contained special classrooms usually serve the most severely handicapped students. Teachers typically have special training, and class size is small so that instruction can be better individualized.

The question of the effectiveness of special education for LD students has often been raised. In general, the findings from older studies were inconsistent. Studies conducted from 1980 indicate slightly better academic outcomes for students in special education (Hocutt, 1996). These students, more than LD students in regular classrooms, also believe themselves more academically competent. It is likely that it is not placement as much as the quality of instruction that influences outcome.

The Regular Education Initiative (REI) has substantial implication for LD students, who, as a group, tend to have mild disabilities and at least outwardly can easily fit into regular classrooms. Recall that REI is a movement to advance the idea that most children with disabilities can be best served in the regular classroom setting (Carnine & Kameenui, 1990). It is part of the broader movement to integrate people with handicaps into regular education and society in general (Hammill, 1993).

REI has been controversial (e.g., Maloney, 1994/1995; Keogh, 1988). Quality of instruction is central to concerns about REI. Good teachers in regular classrooms rely on several principles of instruction that apply to most students (See Accent). At issue is whether teachers will have the knowledge, support, and motivation to maintain optimal teaching strategies while also accommodating stu-

GENERAL PRINCIPLES OF INSTRUCTION

The following are among the principles of instruction that are likely to enhance learning in a variety of settings and with students who have learning disabilities (Taylor, 1989).

1. Academic competence is related to the amount of time devoted to students' being actively engaged in academic work. As commonsensical as this may seem, research shows that class time often is not spent on academics.
2. Academic competence also is related to the teacher's actively instructing, modeling, directing, and guiding learning. Learning handicapped children do not usually benefit from discovery learning; they require structure and feedback.
3. Some degree of individualized instruction is helpful. This principle is related to the idea of mastery learning: that a fixed minimum level of achievement be set and the child be provided with instruction and practice to reach that level.
4. Generalization of learning across tasks and time usually must be deliberately built into instruction. For example, after a child learns a particular arithmetic technique, practice in using the technique on slightly different problems can be given.
5. Incentives are usually helpful, and they should be tied to specific goals (e.g., number of words spelled correctly).
6. Training is best focused on remediating all deficiencies rather than focusing on a single one, because improvement in one skill often is not related to improvement in another (e.g., accuracy in reading and comprehension in reading). In addition, mastery of lower-order skills and knowledge is necessary for higher-order abilities.

dents with special needs. Teachers in regular classrooms do not have some of the advantages of special education classrooms, which are characterized by small class size that lends itself to slower pace of instruction, encouragement of individualized goals set by Individual Education Plans, and close student monitoring (Hocutt, 1996). Many teachers do not have the specialized training to adapt curricula for learning disabilities and to deal with behavior problems.

Concern over REI has resulted in The Learning Disabilities Association of America's formally advocating for the availability of alternative settings. This organization notes that placement of all children with LLD into regular classrooms can violate federal mandates and children's rights as much as placement of all children into separate classrooms (Maloney, 1994/1995; The Link, 1995). Hammill

(1993) has warned that REI can lead to students not having to be diagnosed which, in turn, could lead to reduced funding, reduced training of special education teachers, and fewer organizations devoted to concerns about learning disabilities.

Advocates of REI point to meta-analytic research showing that inclusion of handicapped students into regular classrooms results in small-to-moderate benefits to academic achievement and social outcomes (Baker, Wang, & Walberg, 1994/1995). That is, students do better on standardized achievement tests and in relating to others as rated by peers, teachers, observers, and themselves. Outcomes for nonhandicapped students in these classrooms are also favorable (Staub & Peck, 1994/1995). Advocates believe that concern should be directed not towards *whether* inclusive education should be provided but towards *how* it should be implemented.

The issue is not likely to be settled quickly, but inclusion is being implemented, in part or fully, in many school districts.

SUMMARY

■ Specific learning disabilities refer to deficits in psychological processes manifested in language, reading, writing, listening, thinking, and the like. Learning disabilities are not due primarily to sensory or motor handicaps, mental retardation, emotional disturbance, or environmental disadvantage. Children are identified on the basis of language or academic achievement being lower than expected for age, grade, or general intelligence. Several dissatisfactions are expressed with this definition, but it remains influential.

■ Prevalence of learning disabilities ranges from 2 to 10 percent of U.S. schoolchildren, with rates for boys higher than for girls. Prevalence has been affected by school practices regarding the identification of LD.

■ Some students with LLD have relationship problems and deficits in social competence. Nonverbal learning disabilities (NVLD) is a subtype of LD that is characterized by deficits in social competence, perception, and mathematics.

■ Youth with LLD are at risk for interalizing and externalizing problems, including ADHD and conduct disturbance. It is unlikely that reading problems directly cause conduct problems and that any casual path is complex.

■ Motivation factors in LD are worthy of consideration because problems in learning may lead to a negative motivational cycle that includes a sense of failure and lack of control.

■ Specific language disabilities fall into three categories: phonological, expressive, and receptive-expressive. These are defined respectively with regard to speech sounds, to expression of a full range of language forms, and to comprehension of language.

■ The prevalence of language disorders is estimated at 2 to 5 percent in the general population and much higher in clinical samples. Prevalence varies with age and with type and severity of disorder.

■ Of the several psychological deficits considered central in language disorders, of particular interest are deficits in rapid processing of auditory signals and phonological memory.

■ Youth with learning disabilities show an array of reading, writing, and mathematics problems; most are reading disabled.

■ In the recent past, much importance was given to visual-perceptual deficits in reading, but greater emphasis is currently given to language processing deficits. Phonological processing deficits are considered critical to beginning reading. Writing disorders involve impairments in handwriting, language-based skills, and metacognition. Mathematics depends on visual-spatial abilities as well as language and reading skills.

■ Language and learning disabilities have been subtyped into numerous categories, including several for reading and nonverbal learning disabilities.

■ Evidence is growing for several kinds of genetic transmission of language and reading disabilities. Also especially interesting is the association of abnormalities of the planum temporale with dyslexia and phonological processing. Research suggests, too, that disabled readers may not use the same brain pathways as normal readers.

■ Environmental variables undoubtedly play some role in specific language and learning disabilities, but they are mostly assigned a secondary role. However, it is argued by some that LLD should be more broadly defined, and that more serious consideration should be given to environmental influence.

■ Many preschoolers with language articulation problems are doing well by school age; children with expressive and receptive language deficits are at greater developmental risk for later academic and behavioral difficulties. Reading disabilities often persist into adolescence and adulthood, and severity of early problems, intelligence, and mothers' reading ability predict continuity.

■ Identification and assessment of learning disabilities most often occur in the educational system, as part of IDEA's mandate. The teacher and the school psychologist play critical roles. Tests of academic achievement, intelligence, and cognitive processes are central in identifying learning disabilities. Broad assessment is ideal, however, as is early identification.

■ Treatment of learning disabilities has included several disciplines. Today's treatments emphasize direct instruction in academic skills, the training of metacognition and learning strategies, enhancement of self-control, and the use of behavioral methods to enhance academic skills and behavior.

■ In the schools, most children with LLD are served in regular classrooms, and in resource rooms and contained special education classrooms. The effectiveness of one placement over another is argued. General principles of good instruction can be applied in various settings, but concern is expressed about the feasibility of accommodating students with special needs in regular classrooms. Advocates of REI emphasize that effort should be spent on implementation instead of discussion of drawbacks.

CHAPTER 12

AUTISM AND SCHIZOPHRENIA

T his chapter focuses on youth who are given the diagnosis of autism or schizophrenia. Although these disorders are now widely considered independent from each other, they have a history of being intricately connected. Both involve pervasive and often continuing problems in social, emotional, and cognitive functioning. Development may lag and be qualitatively different from normal development in ways that have compelled an enormous amount of interest and investigation. Indeed, it could be argued that efforts to describe, understand, and treat these developmental disturbances constitute one of the more intriguing journeys in the discipline of developmental psychopathology.

HISTORIC LINK OF AUTISM AND SCHIZOPHRENIA

Despite the longtime recognition of the disorders that we are about to discuss, their description and classification have been confusing and controversial (Newsom, Hovanitz, & Rincover, 1988). These disorders have been termed as or associated with adult psychoses, that is, severely disruptive disturbances implying abnormal perceptions of reality and the need for supervision and protection (Prior & Werry, 1986; Volkmar, 1996).

Adult psychotic disturbances were noted in the early twentieth-century classifications of mental disorders (Goldfarb, 1970). Kraepelin, who set the basis for modern classification, termed a group of psychotic disturbances "dementia praecox." "Dementia" reflected his belief that progressive deterioration occurred; "praecox" indicated that the disorders began early in life. Bleuler later applied the term "schizophrenias" to the disorders. He argued that deterioration was not inevitable and that time of origin was more varied. In fact, both Kraepelin and Bleuler noted a small number of cases that had begun in childhood (Cantor, 1988).

Ideas about such adult disturbance were soon extended to children. For example, early in the twentieth century, Theodore Heller described children who suffered severe set-backs after brief normal development, and the relationship of the condition to schizophrenia was debated (Volkmar et al., 1997a). Other investigators described select groups of children as having early onset of schizophrenia, and still others pointed to syndromes that appeared similar, but not identical, to schizophrenia. Various diagnostic terms were applied, including "disintegrative psychoses" and "childhood psychoses." Beginning around 1930 and for several years afterward, "childhood schizophrenia" served as a general label, while numerous subcategories were employed (Volkmar, 1987; Rutter & Schopler, 1987).

In 1943, Leo Kanner described what he called "early infantile autism," arguing that it was different from other cases of severe disturbance, which often had later onset. Supporting the idea of a distinct syndrome of early autism was information showing that severe disturbances were age related. Data from several different countries indicated a large number of cases before age three, remarkably low prevalence in childhood, and increased prevalence in adolescence (Kolvin, 1971; Rutter, 1978). This pattern suggested that different syndromes might underlie the earlier-occurring and later-occurring disturbances. It was argued by some that children whose problems appeared early were different from those whose problems came later, not only in behavior but also in social class, family history, and other factors (Dawson & Castelloe, 1992).

Over the years, subsequent investigations led to different conceptualizations of what once was considered psychoses of youth. Today, autism and schizophrenia are viewed as distinct disorders; moreover, only the latter is considered a psychotic disorder that can affect youth. As we shall see, however, several knotty classification issues still exist with regard to both disorders.

AUTISTIC DISORDER

Kanner's 1943 descriptions of eleven of the severely affected children whom he examined were comprehensive and, with some important exceptions, have stood the test of time (Mesibov & Bourgondien, 1992; Volkmar, Klin, & Cohen, 1997b). Kanner concluded that of particular importance were communication deficits, good but atypical cognitive potential, and behavioral problems such as obsessiveness, repetitive actions, and unimaginative play. Kanner emphasized, however, that the fundamental disturbance was an inability to relate to people and situations from the beginning of life. He quoted parents as referring to their disturbed children as "self-sufficient," "like in a shell," "happiest when left alone," and "acting as if people weren't there" (1973, p. 33). To this extreme disturbance in emotional contact with others, Kanner applied the term *autistic*, which means an absorption in the self or subjective mental activity.

Most of the characteristics originally described by Kanner were subsequently observed by others, and autism eventually was recognized by the major classification systems as a distinct syndrome of severe disturbance that arises in infancy or early life. Autism subsequently became one of the most investigated disorders of youth.

Leo Kanner offered the first description of infantile autism and is considered a pioneer in the study of this disorder.
(The Johns Hopkins Medical Institutions)

CLASSIFICATION AND DIAGNOSIS

Since 1980 DSM has recognized autism as a subcategory of Pervasive Developmental Disorders (PDD), which are characterized by early occurring, severe impairments that are qualitatively deviant relative to the person's developmental level (American Psychiatric Association, 1994). Both DSM-IV and ICD-10 recognize several such disorders, which have symptoms similar to autism and have historically been difficult to distinguish from autism and from each other. Individuals with autism exhibit impaired social interaction, disturbed communication, and restricted, repetitive behaviors and interests—which are sometimes referred to as the triad of primary difficulties. Table 12-1 indicates DSM-IV descriptions of these diagnostic features for what DSM now calls Autistic Disorder. Diagnosis requires a total of six items or more, with all three features present and with social interaction impairments more heavily weighted. Onset must occur prior to age three.

EPIDEMIOLOGY

Lotter's (1966) pioneering population study showed the frequency of autism to be 4.5 per 10,000 children. A recent review of twenty epidemiological studies conducted over thirty years in several countries confirms that autism is quite rare; the median prevalence was 4.8 per 10,000 (Fombonne et al., 1997).

However, high rates are reported, sometimes going well into double digits (Bryson, 1997; Howlin, 1998). How can such a discrepancy be accounted for? One factor may be differences in the manner in which the research populations were ascertained. Higher rates may also indicate better detection of autism. Probably of most importance, increased prevalence appears to reflect the use of broader diagnostic criteria, which increases the number of children receiving the diagnosis.

Boys quite consistently display autism more often than girls, with the ratio of three to five boys to one girl (American Psychiatric Association, 1994; Klinger & Dawson, 1996). There is some evidence that autism in females is associated with lower IQ scores and less favorable course.

Kanner's (1943) early descriptions noted that autism typically occurs in the upper social classes. However, large population studies now indicate no social class difference (Fombonne et al., 1997; Gillberg, 1992). Perhaps early samples were biased in that families of higher social class were more likely to receive professional services.

CLINICAL DESCRIPTION

In this section, the behavioral manifestations of the triad of problems of autism are described, as well as associated characteristics. Descriptions focus more heavily on preschool and school-age children, who have been most studied. It is worth noting that there is much variation in the clinical picture, both in specific symptoms and in the severity of problems, with the result that general descriptions may not well illustrate individual cases.

Social interaction. Descriptions of autism among infants rely heavily on retrospective reports of parents; however, an additional source is provided by home movies recorded by families before autism was recognized in their children, as well as by clini-

---

TABLE 12-1

Major DSM-IV Features for Autistic Disorder

1. Qualitative impairment in social interaction manifested by:
   impaired nonverbal behaviors
   failure to develop age-appropriate peer relationships
   lack of spontaneous sharing of enjoyment or interests
   lack of social or emotional reciprocity

2. Qualitative impairment in communication manifested by:
   delay or lack of spoken language
   impairment in initiating or sustaining conversation
   stereotyped, repetitive, or idiosyncratic language
   lack of age-appropriate, spontaneous make-believe or
      imitative play

3. Restrictive, repetitive, stereotyped behavior, interests, or activities manifested by:
   preoccupation with stereotyped restrictive interests
   inflexible adherence to nonfunctional routines or rituals
   stereotyped repetitive motor mannerisms
   persistent preoccupation with parts of objects

cal observation. These studies indicate that problems of social interaction can begin very early (Adrien et al., 1993; Borden & Ollendick, 1992; Gillberg et al., 1990; Stone, 1997). Even when very young, many of the children are socially unresponsive, fail to track people visually, avoid eye contact, exhibit an "empty" gaze, fail to respond to others with emotional expression and positive affect, and show little interest in being held. Figure 12-1 demonstrates these findings with data from a laboratory study that observed mothers and their four-year-olds with autism or Down syndrome or no disorder. Children with autism gazed less and smiled less at their mothers, and they rarely shared objects of interest (Dissanayake & Crossley, 1996).

Such behaviors might well be expected to interfere with the establishment of social bonds, and the clinical literature sometimes suggests an inability to form social attachment. However, this is probably too strong a statement (Sigman et al., 1997). For example, in the Dissanayake and Crossley (1996) investigation just cited, the children with autism approached their mother, sat on her lap, and initiated physical contact such as touching and kissing. Research shows that children with autism respond to their caregiver's departure and direct more social behavior to their caregiver than to a stranger, much as do normal children (Sigman et al., 1997). It appears, then, that many of these children have a special relationship with their caregivers. At the same time, they display a variety of atypical, deficient, and delayed social behaviors, thus causing many parents to perceive that something is wrong (Volkmar et al., 1997a).

Although social deficits may change in form with development, they rarely disappear, and the level of social skills is below that expected on the basis of tested intelligence. During childhood, aloofness and disinterest are notable, as are a variety of social deficits such as lack of understanding of social cues and inappropriate social actions. Thus the child may ignore others, fail to engage in cooperative play, or seem overly content to be alone (Volkmar et al., 1997a). These impairments often lessen with time, but even higher-functioning adolescents and adults may seem "odd" and

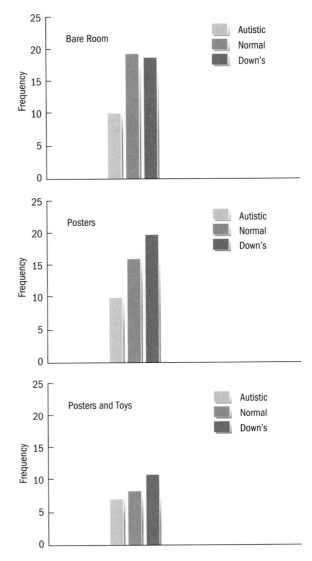

FIGURE 12-1 The mean frequency at which infants gazed at their mothers. The laboratory setting varied: The room was bare except for furniture; or wall posters were added; or wall posters and toys were added.

Adapted from Dissanayake and Crossley, 1996.

have difficulty in forming friendships as they move through life. Some older individuals may desire social contact but still have problems with the subtleties of interaction and probably feel incompetent and isolated. It is unsurprising, then, that people with autism rarely marry.

Communication. Disturbed communication—both nonverbal and verbal—is a second element of the triad of difficulties in autism.

Humans typically "speak" to each other nonverbally by gesture, bodily posture, and facial expression. Even before speech develops, children both understand some of these messages and use gestures to communicate. Such nonverbal communication correlates with language development and other competencies (Lord & Paul, 1997).

Children with autism show atypical or deficient nonverbal communication. Even though these deficits may be subtle, they strongly suggest a specific problem in understanding social and emotional stimuli, such as the emotional expressions on the faces of other people. Similarly, children with autism use fewer nonverbal signals and may project an expressionless "woodenness" (Attwood, Frith, & Hermelin, 1988). Disturbed eye contact and lack of the social smile and other emotional expressions are widely noted. Deficits in *joint attention interactions* are also striking. These interactions involve gestures such as pointing and eye contact that focus the child's and caretaker's attention on an object, presumably for sharing an experience. In typical development, joint attention is present by twenty-four months, and its precursors (such as following the gaze of another person) emerge by nine to twelve months (Corkum & Moore, 1998; McEvoy, Rogers, & Phllips, 1993). In addition, when youth with autism use simple instrumental gestures that point to something or communicate "come here" or "be quiet," more complex gestures that express feelings (e.g., putting arms around someone to express friendship) may be lacking, even into adolescence (Attwood et al., 1988). Some of these deficits may be specific to autism.

As with nonverbal communication, both comprehension and expression of spoken language are problematic. The comprehension of language has been less studied but has sometimes been found to be delayed compared with controls with specific language disorders (Lord & Paul, 1997). About 50 percent of children with autism do not develop useful speech. They remain mute or rarely say more than words or simple phrases. Babbling and verbalizations may be abnormal in tone, pitch, and rhythm, and these deficits may persist into adolescence and adulthood (Tager-Flüsberg, 1993). In those who acquire language, development is delayed and often abnormal. Grammar and syntax may be less affected than other aspects of language (Lord & Paul, 1997). The use of odd words or phrases is common (e.g., "cuts or bluesers" for "cuts or bruises"), as is the use of excessively concrete speech. Echolalia and pronoun reversal are also common.

In *echolalia* the person echoes back what another has said, either immediately or at a future time. This behavior is not unique to autism: It can be a passing feature of normal development, and it is also seen in dysfunctions such as language disorders, schizophrenia, and blindness. Why echolalia occurs in autism is not known, but it appears to occur more frequently when settings and tasks are unfamiliar, aversive, or fearful (Charlop, Schriebman, & Kurtz, 1991). Perhaps it serves a communicative function—such as an attempt to make a request—or perhaps it serves as desired self-stimulation.

Confusion about the use of pronouns is also more common in autism than in other disorders or normal development. The child may refer to others as *I* or *me,* and to the self as *he, she, them,* or *you.* And so the child may request a drink of milk for herself by saying, "She wants milk." *Pronoun reversals* may stem from echolalia, for example, when an adult verbalizes, "You can play ball," and the child echoes this statement. However, it seems likely that there is a more general deficit—perhaps failure to understand that different people have different perspectives or that language requires different forms to refer to different persons (Lord & Paul, 1997; Oshima-Takane & Benaroya, 1989; Tager-Flüsberg, 1993).

The most notable impairment of language concerns pragmatics, the social use of language (Baron-Cohen, 1988; Klinger & Dawson, 1996). Individuals with autism include irrelevant details in conversations, interrupt, shift inappropriately to another topic, and overall fail to develop conversation. In more severe cases, language is mostly simple statements, requests, and commands (proto-imperatives), with little commentary to enrich conversation (protodeclaratives). In higher-functioning autism, children can do somewhat better. Some are able to tell stories and may communicate more effectively when given prompts or models of conversation (Loveland & Tunali-Kotoski, 1997). Some children are able to read; in fact, they may read at a higher level than would be expected ("hyperlexia"). However, the comprehension of what they read is below normal (Lord & Paul, 1997).

Restricted, repetitive behavior and interests. The third major impairment of autism is atypical and sometimes bizarre behaviors that are described as restricted, rigid, obsessive, repetitive, or stereotyped activities and interests.

Stereotyped motor behaviors commonly reported by parents include rocking, toe-walking, whirling, and arm, hand, or finger flapping (Klinger & Dawson, 1996). More subtle forms include rubbing hands along surfaces and sniffing. It is unknown whether or how these behaviors are related to repetitious motor behavior that occurs in normal infancy (Newsom, 1998). Some investigators believe that the repetitive behavior may provide sensory/perceptual stimulation that is especially reinforcing to persons with autism.

More elaborate routines are also displayed, even in less severe cases. These routines usually include repetitious motor behavior, restricted interests, and ordering of objects and events (Charlop, Schreibman, & Kurtz, 1991). Children may appear obsessed with specific toys, a vacuum cleaner, or numbers. They may hoard worthless objects or may talk ceaselessly about an object and be upset if it is lost. These preoccupations may either change abruptly or last for years. In addition, play behavior may be rigid and lacking in social imitation and imagination. Children with autism often do not pretend when they play, nor use symbols or themes (Baron-Cohen, 1993). They may simply re-

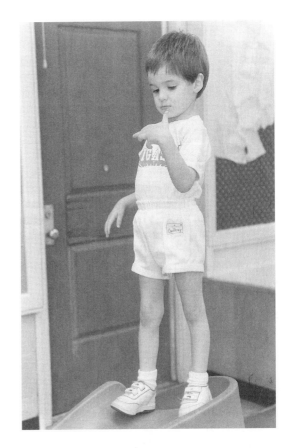

Stereotyped hand movements commonly occur in autism.
(Carl Glassman)

peat behaviors over and over, such as lining up items. It is common for them to adopt rigid routines that must be followed. Changes in the environment, such as rearrangement of furniture or schedules, may cause them to react with considerable upset.

Sensory and perceptual deficits. The sensory organs are intact in autism, but abnormal responses to stimuli make sensation and perception suspect (e.g., Ornitz, 1985; Prior, 1986). Indeed, many investigators believe that these abnormalities are fundamental to autism, even though they are only an associated feature of autism in DSM-IV (Newsom, 1998).

Both oversensitivity and undersensitivity to stimulation are reported (Klinger & Dawson, 1996). In oversensitivity the child is disturbed by moderate stimulation, for example, moderate noise. Thus the child may dislike, fear, or avoid sensory input. Undersensitivity, which is perhaps more common, is reflected in many ways. Children may fail to show the startle response or otherwise not respond to verbal communications and sounds, may not react to the sight of others, may walk into objects, or may let objects fall from their hands. Undersensitivity may lead them to seek stimulation by scratching surfaces or engaging in abnormal movements (Adrien et al., 1987). Other anomalies involving perception and attention are documented in laboratory studies, and we will later examine some of the findings.

Intellectual performance. Although intelligence is not a diagnostic criterion for autism, it is important in clinical description. Kanner originally described children with autism as of at least average intelligence, and some of those children with special abilities. It is possible for autistic individuals to be at this ability level, but it is now known that at least 75 percent of all cases show mental retardation, with most exhibiting moderate or severe deficiency (Newsom, 1998; Sigman, 1998). Largely on the basis of measured intelligence, the distinction has been made between individuals functioning at a higher or a lower level (IQ 70 or less).

It is noteworthy that the test profiles of persons with autism who show mental deficiency are less uniform than profiles typically seen in mental retardation (Minshew, Sweeney, & Bauman, 1997; Newsom, 1988). There are greater deficits on tasks that involve abstract and conceptual thinking, language, and social development. Nonverbal skills appear better developed, for example, as shown on the block design task that involves visual perceptual-motor skills (Happe, 1994b; Volkmar et al., 1997b; Shah & Frith, 1993). The findings have been interpreted as suggesting deficits on a variety of complex tasks or in late information processing (Minshew et al., 1997).

Amidst this general picture, a small minority of the children have special cognitive skills—splinter

skills—that are inconsistent with their general intelligence. A smaller proportion show quite amazing savant abilities. Spectacular memory, mathematics, calendar calculations, word knowledge, and music and art talents are displayed (e.g., O'Conner & Hermelin, 1990; Pring & Hermelin, 1993). Some of these abilities are indeed spectacular (Treffert, 1988). One individual needed only 1.5 minutes to calculate the number of seconds in seventy years, seventeen days, and twelve hours, even considering the effects of leap years. And one five-year-old, despite limited language and retarded daily living skills, had perfect music pitch, a classical piano repertoire, and the ability to improvise music. There is no established explanation for savant abilities, although they tend to be related to repetitive and obsessive behaviors (Pring, Hermelin, & Heavey, 1995). These abilities often emerge early in life, without training and without obvious inheritance.

Behavior problems. Children with autism display various behavior problems—aggression, outbursts, temper tantrums, and hyperactivity. Their moods may shift unpredictably, and inappropriate or excessive fears and anxiety are common. A particularly compelling problem is self-injurious behavior (SIB), such as head banging, biting of the hands, scratching, eye gouging, and hair pulling (Schreibman & Charlop-Christy, 1998). None of these behavior problems are specific to autism, but they interfere with learning and adaptation, and require good management.

BLAMING AUTISM ON FAILED PARENTING

Over a long period of time, many proposals have been put forth to account for the clinical features of autism. Dominant among the early proposals was the idea that parents played a critical role. Kanner described the parents of autistic children as highly intelligent and professionally accomplished people who were preoccupied with scientific, literary, and artistic concerns, and who treated their offspring in a coldly mechanical way (1943; Kanner & Eisenberg, 1956). Inadequate, "refrigerator" parenting became implicated in causing autism, even though Kanner also hypothesized an innate social deficit. In part, this view was due to the influence of psychoanalytic theory, which emphasized that childhood problems might be rooted in parental behavior.

Bettelheim's (1967a,b) theory was the most influential of the psychoanalytic explanations (Mesibov & Van Bourgondien, 1992). He hypothesized that autism is caused by parental rejection or pathology that results in the young child's retreating into an autistic "empty fortress." Bettelheim recommended removing children from their parents and placing them in an environment that would encourage them to reach out safely to the world and to let go of autistic withdrawal. The treatment at the residential program at the Orthogenic School in Chicago assumed that the child would gain trust as more normal relationships were experienced with therapists.

A less influential psychogenic explanation that emphasized parenting focused on operant learning. Ferster (1961; 1966) proposed that the parents of autistic children failed to properly shape the behavior of their offspring through reinforcement and punishment. The children thus lacked support for a normal behavioral repertoire. Furthermore, self-stimulation and other primitive actions were strengthened by the reinforcements they received. Such failed parenting was thought to be related to parental depression, preoccupation with other activities, rejection of the child, and the like. According to this formulation, new learning might best remediate autism.

Despite very different theoretical stances, Ferster and Bettelheim shared the view that the early parent-child relationship is a critical psychological factor underlying autism. Today neither theory is given much weight. Bettelheim's ideas suffered from the dwindling influence of psychoanalytic theories, and analyses of therapeutic effectiveness cast doubt on psychoanalytic treatments. In addition, empirical studies of the 1970s and 1980s gave little support for parental deviancy (Klinger & Dawson, 1996; Mesibov & Van Bourgondien, 1992). Parents of autistic children do not, for the most part, appear different in personality and adaptive behaviors from either parents of normal children or parents of children with other behav-

ioral problems. And parent-child interaction hardly seems adequate to explain the severity and oddness of some autistic behaviors, especially when aberrations begin so early in life. In addition, disturbed social interactions could be substantially related to the child's characteristics (Borden & Ollendick, 1992).

Placing the burdens of autism on parents is now viewed as blaming them for something largely out of their control, and interest has shifted to other concerns. Current efforts to understand autism center on determining its unique psychological and neurological abnormalities and on seeking causes of these anomalies. Our discussion will consider these topics in turn.

PSYCHOLOGICAL DEFICITS

Hermelin and O'Conner's (1970) pioneering studies of autistic children's psychological functioning encouraged careful laboratory investigation. Autistic children were increasingly compared with normal children and other control groups in order to more completely describe functioning and to identify some fundamental psychological deficit that might account for the features of the disorder. Research efforts have been extensive and productive. We will overview four of the important proposals that have grown from the research.

Affective-social deficit. Kanner early proposed that the fundamental deficit in autism is an affective-social failure that results in disturbed interpersonal relations. The everyday behaviors of autistic persons suggest this: the lack of social smile and eye gaze, failure to engage in joint attention interactions, and so forth. Research on the processing of human faces and emotional expression also indicates deficits. For example, compared with controls, school-age autistic children showed impaired recognition of human faces to which they had been previously exposed (Boucher, Lewis, & Collis, 1998). In another study, control group children attended to and sorted photographs of people on the basis of facial expressions such as happy and sad, but children with autism sorted according to the type of hats the people wore (Hobson, 1993). In still another study, autistic children looked less at and showed less concern for an adult who simulated hurting himself with a hammer (Charman et al., 1997). Such findings indicate impairment in recognizing, comprehending, and responding to socioemotional stimuli.

In view of such evidence, Hobson (1993; Hobson & Lee, 1998) has proposed a basic biological disturbance in interpersonal relations. He argues that normal development requires children to understand that persons exist, and that they themselves are both like and different from other persons. Such knowledge arises from interactions with others, and Hobson emphasizes that affect plays a critical role in interpersonal understanding. He points out that affect is fundamental to human functioning: The expression and comprehension of basic emotions are universal and appear very early in life. In autism, affect is disturbed, and social processing is defective. Therefore, individuals with autism do not understand how others experience and think about the world, and social behavior, communication skill, and symbolic thinking are all adversely influenced. This proposal puts an innate affective-social defect as primary in autism.

Social cognitive deficits. Other theories emphasize social cognition as a primary deficit in autism. Central to these theories is a disturbance in the ability to mentalize, or mentally represent, the world. There has been extensive study of *theory of mind*—the ability to infer mental states in others and in one's own self (Perner et al., 1989). Having a theory of mind means that we understand that mental states (desires, intentions, beliefs, feelings) exist and that they are connected to action. For example, if we observe another person being exposed to a situation, we assume that the person's mind has knowledge of the situation, holds certain beliefs about the situation, and perhaps has certain emotions about the situation—all of which may help determine how the person behaves. Theory of mind can be thought of as the ability to read others' minds, which guides our interaction with others. If we infer that someone is sad, we may be especially kind; if we infer that someone is only faking sadness, we are probably less inclined to be kind.

The several aspects of theory of mind can be evaluated with different tasks and questions. Consider, for example, a procedure to test the understanding that another person can hold a false belief. In the Sally-Ann test, the child is told that Sally places a marble in a basket and exits the room. Ann then transfers the marble to a box, and Sally returns to the room. The child is asked where Sally will look for the marble. To answer correctly, the child must understand that Sally falsely believes that the marble is still in the basket where she had placed it and that this belief will guide her action.

Theory of mind typically develops gradually and by three to four years is fairly well under way (Wellman, 1993). Table 12-2 shows some first-order abilities that are acquired, at least partly, by age four. At about age six, children use second-order abilities, that is, they can think about another person's thinking about a third person's thoughts (Baron-Cohen et al., 1997).

There is strong evidence that the ability to mentalize is either delayed or lacking in autism (Baron-Cohen & Swettenham, 1997). First-order tests are failed by a majority of the children, and a greater number fail second-order tests. Impairments exist in understanding complex causes of emotion, as well as in spontaneous play that involves the mental state of "pretend." Moreover, deficits may first appear very early, even in the precursors of theory of mind, exist across age, and be present in higher-functioning persons.

Baron-Cohen and others believe that impairment in theory of mind underlies many of the social and language deficits of autism—for example, failure to understand facial expression, relate to others, acquire the pragmatics of language, and engage in pretend play (Tager-Flüsberg, 1997; Baron-Cohen & Swettenham, 1997; Waterhouse & Fein, 1997).

Executive dysfunctions. The proposal that deficits in executive functions are fundamental in autism is being given much consideration. Children and adults with autism perform more poorly than control groups on tests of executive functions (McEvoy, Rogers, & Pennington, 1993; Ozonoff,

TABLE 12-2

Some Aspects of Theory of Mind Understood Early in Life

	Example
Mental states exist apart from the physical world.	Bill's mental image of a cookie is different from an actual cookie.
People's mental states are private.	Linda "sees" a cat in her mind, but Claire cannot directly experience this imaged cat.
People have knowledge of something when they have observed it.	Nicky saw Nancy drive off in a van, so he knows Nancy is gone.
People can hold false beliefs.	Lise believes it is raining, even though it is not.
People's beliefs, accurate or false, are linked to behavior.	Alia put on her heavy coat because she believed it was cold outside.
People have desires, which can be linked to behavior.	Jack wants the auto to be neat, so he cleans it.
People have emotions, which can be linked to behavior.	Mary is smiling and jumping up and down, so she is feeling happy.
People have intentions, which can be linked to future behavior.	Rick says he will go shopping; he has this planned action in mind.

Based on Wellman, 1993.

1997). For example, they do less well on the Tower of Hanoi task, which calls for planning ahead to rearrange loops on pegs according to certain rules. The evidence points to deficits in planning ahead, in switching to a new rule, and in disengaging from a salient stimulus that leads to error (e.g., Bailey, Phillips, & Rutter, 1996). However, poor performance can be difficult to interpret because executive functions involve so many underlying operations. For example, attention is an important component, and, indeed, problems in attention have been observed (Burack et al., 1997; Courchesne et al., 1994). Nevertheless, the executive dysfunctions of autism involve an inflexibility that might account particularly for the rigid stereotypies of autism and some communication problems.

Weak central coherence. Yet another proposal suggests that weak central coherence explains certain manifestations of autism (Happe, 1994a). It is proposed that in normal cognition, individuals use context to weave together what would otherwise be fragmented bits of information to make a whole, to give global meaning. This process is referred to as central coherence. Individuals with autism are believed to be weak in central coherence; that is, they tend to focus on the parts of stimuli and fail to integrate information into wholes.

Performance on many perceptual tasks can be interpreted in this way (Baron-Cohen & Swettenham, 1997). For example, when asked to identify a face in a photograph of either the entire face or only parts of the face, normal children do better with the entire face. In contrast, children with autism do equally well with the entire face or only a part of the face. In an important study, Shah and Frith (1993) investigated the quite striking superior performance that persons with autism show on the Block Design task on the Wechsler intellligence test. Not only do they perform well compared with what they do on other tasks, but they also outperform matched mentally retarded and normal groups. Shah and Frith argued that superior ability to break the design into segments helps on this task. Also, autistic children generally perform better than controls on embedded figure tasks, which call for recognizing a part of the stimulus figure that is embedded within a larger picture (Jolliffe & Baron-Cohen, 1997).

The hypothesis of weak central coherence has also been applied to reading tasks in which it is important to consider the whole context. For example, the correct pronunciation of "tear" is greatly aided by context, as in "There is a *tear* in her eye" versus "There is a *tear* in her dress" (Baron-Cohen & Swettenham, 1997). Deficits on this task have been demonstrated with individuals with autism, suggesting difficulty with extracting global meaning (Happe, 1996).

All these findings suggest that processing is more analytic and less global and integrative than it normally is, which can lead to exceptional performance on some tasks but is also disadvantageous. Still, investigations of central coherence are limited, and the question remains of whether weak central coherence exists at relatively early stages of perception or at higher-level processing, as shown in reading tasks (Happe, 1996). Nonetheless, weak central coherence is of interest, since it might underlie the unusual perception, special abilities, and some communication difficulties of autism.

Is there a basic psychological deficit? Investigators have long sought to identify a fundamental psychological deficit that might underlie and explain the features of autism. At the least, any fundamental impairment would have to (1) explain the varied aberrations displayed in autism, (2) be present in all cases, and (3) be specific to autism (Ozonoff, Pennington, & Rogers 1991). How do the deficits that we have described measure up to these requirements?

It appears that all of the proposed deficits explain some features of autism better than others (Bailey et al., 1996; Baron-Cohen & Swettenham, 1997). For example, affective-social deficits and theory-of-mind deficits reasonably account for autism's social impairments and pragmatic communication problems but do not account for the stereotyped behaviors and restricted interests. In contrast, executive dysfunctions and weak central coherence do not easily explain autism's social features but do account more strongly for other features.

Do all persons with autism exhibit the underlying deficits under discussion? Although more research is needed, deficits in understanding affective-social stimuli, in theory-of-mind, and in executive functions are at least widespread in the autistic population (Bailey et al., 1996). Data on weak central coherence are still limited.

Finally, we need to ask whether the deficits are specific to autism. If a deficit is specifically linked to a disorder, it is easier to conclude that it might account for the features of the disorder. The evidence is not clearly supportive. Problems in affect and face perception are reported in other disorders, such as schizophrenia, although these problems may be somewhat different (Bailey et al., 1996). Evidence that theory-of-mind deficits are specific to autism has been considered fairly compelling, but recent meta-analyses show these deficits in mental retardation (Yirmiya et al., 1998). Deaf children also exhibit difficulties in understanding mental states, although this difficulty is undoubtedly a *result* of not being able to converse with others, whereas in autism, mentalizing deficits are said to *cause* communication problems (Russell et al., 1998). Executive dysfunctions are found in many disorders, including schizophrenia and ADHD, making it unlikely that they alone can explain autism (Baron-Cohen & Swettenham, 1997). With regard to how specific weak central coherence is to autism, much more data are required before any conclusion can be reached (Bailey et al., 1996).

Overall, then, the claim that any one fundamental psychological deficit can explain the features of autism is not well supported. Of course, the possibility exists that a crucial fundamental deficit has yet to be discovered. Another possibility is that specific deficits might be responsible for different features of autism. This possibility could help explain the wide variation in the symptoms of the disorder: the clinical picture would depend on which particular deficit—or combination of deficits—is present.

As efforts to understand the psychological deficits of autism continue, it is important to show how, or even if, the psychological deficits actually bring about autistic symptoms. There is also a need to more strongly link psychological deficits to brain functioning, a link that any neurological explanation of the disorder requires (Bailey et al., 1996).

NEUROLOGICAL ABNORMALITIES

Diverse evidence exists for neurological abnormalities in autism. Although the neurological examination itself often indicates no abnormality, some cases do show signs such as motor clumsiness, tremor, and abnormalities of gait, posture, and reflexes (Minshew et al., 1997; Tsai & Ghaziuddin, 1991). In addition, higher than average head circumference and brain volume have been found (Piven et al., 1996a). Lainhart and colleagues (1997), for example, studied 91 cases, mostly children under the age of sixteen. Fourteen percent had a head circumference greater than the ninety-seventh percentile of normal circumference, and many others had relatively large heads. Specific known disorders did not account for head size. Moreover, large head size did not exist at birth, suggesting some developmental process. This is an intriguing finding because it is more typical to find reduced brain size in mentally handicapped persons. Studies indicate increased volumes of the parietal, temporal, and occipital lobes but not of some other brains parts (Minshew et al., 1997).

Many brain structures have been examined with imaging or postmortem techniques. Abnormalities are found in only a small number of cases and in various locations. The most consistent support is for microscopic abnormalities of the cerebellum and limbic system structures (Minshew et al., 1997; Pennington & Welsh, 1997). These tend to show reduced number of cells and/or reduced cell density. Some of the findings suggest that malformations may develop during the prenatal period.

In brain functioning, the association of autism with epilepsy and abnormal EEGs was one of the earliest indications of biological dysfunction (Minshew et al., 1997). Epilepsy can develop at any age, but onset is more common in childhood and in adolescence than earlier. This relatively late onset is different from what occurs in mental retardation (Bailey et al., 1996). By young adulthood, prevalence of epilepsy ranges from 20 percent to 35 percent. Brain dysfunction is also suggested by abnormal EEGs in about 50 percent of cases.

Epilepsy and abnormal EEGs may be more common in severe cases.

Brain PET scans indicate some disturbance, but the findings have been contradictory and are not easily interpreted (Bailey et al, 1996; Pennington & Welsh, 1997). Brain functioning has also been studied by measuring responses to specific stimuli, for example, measuring electrical responses or eye movement. This approach indicates abnormalities in information processing in high-level auditory, visual, and somatosensory pathways (Minshew et al., 1997).

Extensive biochemical analyses are being conducted. The most dependable finding is that blood levels of serotonin are high in 25 percent to 50 percent of cases of autism (Anderson & Hoshino, 1997; Bailey et al., 1996; Klinger & Dawson, 1996). It is interesting that serotonin reportedly plays a critical role in nervous system development. Attention also has been given to the opiates (endorphins) because they are suspected of being involved in symptoms such as decreased pain and self-injurious behavior, repetitive behavior, and poor social relationships. Support for opiate abnormalities is far from clear, however. Limited evidence implicates other substances as well, but many biochemical findings are inconsistent and complex.

What can be concluded from the diverse neurological investigations so far conducted? There is increasing evidence that a highly localized abnormality will not account for autism. Rather, it is more likely that abnormalities exist at the neural system level or in multiple brain parts, with the cortex being involved (Minshew et al., 1997). It appears that brain development characterized by abnormal growth of neurons, excessive tissue in some areas, and too little tissue in other areas, affects several cognitive functions including those involved in emotional and social interaction.

ETIOLOGY

Identifying the psychological and neurological abnormalities of autism takes us far in understanding the condition. But we must still ask the question, What causes anomalies in the first place?

Little support exists for psychosocial or other environmental causation, but evidence has mounted for biological causation.

Medical conditions. Autism has been associated with several known medical conditions. Could these and their underlying causes account for the disorder?

Known genetic disorders are linked to autism. Fragile X syndrome (p. 256) is found in an estimated 2.5 percent of cases of autism (Rutter et al., 1997). This association was initially described as stronger, suggesting that the fragile X syndrome might be a strong etiological factor in autism. Although this is unlikely, it is possible that some cases of autism are an expression of this abnormal X condition.

Epidemiologic studies generally indicate that .4 percent to 2.8 percent of cases of autism are diagnosed with the genetic disorder of tuberous sclerosis, a higher rate than in the general population (Dykens & Volkmar, 1997). This disorder occurs from spontaneous mutations and is transmitted through dominant genes, with a gene on chromosome 9 and on chromosome 16 having been identified (Harrison & Bolton, 1997). The affected individuals have variable phenotypes involving benign tumors of the brain and many other organs, which were described as "potato-like tubers" and which gave rise to the name "tuberous sclerosis." Seizure disorders are common, and between 50 percent and 60 percent of all cases show mental retardation. When autism and tuberous sclerosis are linked, most cases are associated with mental retardation and seizures, suggesting that the autism stems from brain pathology accompanying tuberous sclerosis (Bailey et al., 1996). Again, perhaps autism is one of many expressions of the abnormal genes (Baker, Piven, & Sato, 1998).

Additional medical conditions associated with autism include PKU and other genetic abnormalities, cerebral palsy, known infections such as meningitis, hearing impairment, and epilepsy. However, the strength of the overall connection to autism is argued. On the basis of population studies in Sweden, Gillberg (1992) concluded that 37 percent of cases were linked to identifiable medical conditions, and Gillberg and Coleman (1996) proposed a rate of 25 percent. From a review of research, Rutter et al. (1994) estimated a much lower rate of about 10 percent. The lower estimate appears more widely accepted (e.g., Newsom & Hovanitz, 1997). Apparently, medical conditions are found more when mental retardation is part of the clinical picture of autism. Nevertheless, it is unclear whether medical conditions should be viewed as directly causing autistic symptoms or as coexisting with autism for reasons yet unknown. Perhaps both alternatives apply, depending on the specific medical condition. In any event, only a small minority of cases of autism are likely due to known medical conditions.

Inheritance. Genetic transmission (independent of known genetic conditions) is thought to be more influential. For several years, inheritance was given little consideration, but Folstein and Rutter's (1978) first systematic twin study changed this situation. Thirty-six percent of the monozygotic and none of the dyzygotic pairs were concordant for autism. Subsequent major studies confirmed and strengthened these findings. One study found twin rates of 69 percent versus 0 percent, whereas another found rates of 91 percent versus 0 percent (Bailey et al., 1995; Steffenburg et al., 1989).

The twin investigations suggest that what may actually be inherited is a more general cognitive/linguistic/social disability. In the original Folstein and Rutter (1978) research, 82 percent of identical and only 10 percent of fraternal twins were concordant for cognitive/linguistic problems. In the Bailey et al. (1995) study, this same pattern was revealed, and the identical twins also showed social impairments that continued into adulthood. Thus autism could be a severe manifestation of a broader cognitive/linguistic/social inherited disturbance.

Family studies of autism are generally consistent with this view. The rate of autism in siblings of autistic children is 3 percent to 7 percent, and about 8 percent of extended families have an additional autistic member (Bailey et al., 1996; Newsom, 1998). With a few exceptions, family studies also indicate that nonautistic siblings and parents of children with autism have subtle cognitive, linguistic, and social problems (Piven & Palmer, 1997; Rutter et al., 1993; Tsai & Ghaziuddin, 1991). Again, this finding suggests a broad genetic predisposition that may lead to either autism or milder related disorders.

The mode of genetic transmission is unknown. Some investigators favor several interacting genes (e.g., Simonoff, Bolton, & Rutter, 1996), whereas others see evidence of autosomal and sex-linked inheritance (Newsom & Hovanitz, 1997). It is possible that different modes of transmission may operate in different cases.

Genetic heterogeniety may also operate in autism. For example, different genes may influence different features (language deficits, social deficits, etc.), or different mixes of genes may produce variations in the clinical picture (Le Couteur et al., 1996). Alternatively, different genes could produce different subgroups of autism (e.g., low or high functioning). Resolution of this issue awaits further investigation.

Prenatal and birth complications. Prenatal and birth insults to the brain have been suggested as causing autism, especially when autism occurs extremely early in life (Tsai & Ghaziuddin, 1991). Many pregnancy and birth variables have been identified, including prenatal rubella and influenza, low birth weight and prematurity, older age of mothers, breech delivery, respiratory distress, and maternal bleeding (e.g., Bryson, Smith, & Eastwood, 1988; Levy, Zoltak, & Saelens, 1988). However, the birth complications are relatively minor, and autism is not always associated with prenatal/birth factors (Piven et al., 1993). It is possible, of course, that prenatal and obstetric adversities cause only some cases. However, pregnancy and birth complications could result from, rather than cause, an abnormal fetus (Bolton et al., 1997; Bailey et al., 1996).

Overall, then, no one biological factor or process has been identified as responsible for autism. Medical conditions and prenatal/birth complications may account for a small minority of cases and in the absence of support for other factors, genetic transmission is currently given an important role in etiology. Different factors may be involved in different cases or subgroups of autism, and causal factors may work alone or in combination to adversely affect the developing brain. What parts of the brain are involved, how brain functioning is disturbed, and how brain abnormalities bring about the psychological deficits and symptoms of autism are not established. However, it is believed that early neurodevelopmental problems underlie most, if not all, cases of autism, and research continues at a brisk pace.

DEVELOPMENTAL COURSE AND OUTCOME

The scarcity of longitudinal studies of autism means that knowledge about its developmental course is not as complete as we would like it to be. Nevertheless, it is clear that symptoms often appear during the first or second years of life. Reliable diagnosis can be made by age three but frequently occurs during the later preschool years when language and cognitive deficits are more evident (Stone, 1997). Variations in onset are reported. Some children always seemed different to their parents, whereas others appeared to develop normally for a while and then failed to maintain developmental milestones, or regressed and displayed qualitatively different development. An erratic course of development may occur, with spurts and lags, and both typical order and atypical order of behavioral development have been described (Burack & Volkmar, 1992; Snow, Hertzig, & Shapiro, 1987).

In many but not all cases, childhood brings a lessening of social and communicative disturbance (e.g., Piven et al., 1996b; Sigman, 1998; Volkmar et al., 1997a). However, development still lags and shows deviances relative to control groups. Adolescence can be relatively uneventful, can show improvement that may persist into adulthood, or can be marked by a variety of behavior problems, such as increased aggression, self-destructiveness, and sexual curiosity that can lead to socially inappropriate behavior (Mesibov & Handlan, 1997; Tsai & Ghaziuddin, 1991). In perhaps 30 percent or more cases, adolescence brings serious deterioration from which the individual may never recover

(Gillberg, 1992; Klinger & Dawson, 1996). Although onset of seizures occurs in some of these cases, it is unclear what underlies the worsening of symptoms. In young adulthood, some cases of autism show behavioral and social improvements (Lord & Rutter, 1994).

In general, though, eventual outcome usually is not favorable. Lotter's (1974) review of three independent studies concluded that 61 to 74 percent of cases were judged as having poor or very poor status by adolescence. Sigman (1998) concluded that 45 to 75 percent of child cases have poor/very poor outcomes in adolescence. Other studies confirm that the majority of children with autism continue to have difficulties into adolescence and adulthood (Rumsey et al., 1985; Tager-Flüsberg, 1993).

Children's intellectual level and the development of communicative language by age five predict outcome. Szatmari and colleagues (1989) found one of the better outcomes in their follow-up of sixteen high-functioning children: as young adults, 31 percent lived independently, and half had completed or attended college and were employed. On an optimistic note, the academic skills of persons with autism may be benefiting from the improved education and training that is now more widely available to them (Klinger & Dawson, 1996; Venter, Lord, & Schopler, 1992). (See the Accent for Temple Grandin's account of growing up with autism to become a successful person with a professional career.)

ANOTHER LOOK AT CONCEPTUALIZING AND CLASSIFYING AUTISM

Early in this chapter, we mentioned problems that remain in classifying autism. One problem is the variability across cases. Some investigators have proposed subgroups based on characteristics such as language problems, social functioning, or nervous system dysfunction (Volkmar et al., 1997b). One widely recognized distinction is between higher and lower functioning autism, the former usually defined by an IQ of 70 or above. Among other differences, higher functioning persons generally have less severe symptoms, distinct educational needs, and better prognosis (Wing, 1997).

Nevertheless, no formal subclassification exists for persons diagnosed with autism.

Another issue is that youth display disorders that appear similar, but not identical, to autism. The major classification systems include them with autism under the general category of Pervasive Developmental Disorders. Table 12-3 describes three of these syndromes, which garner considerable interest today. Two are characterized by early normal development. Rett's Disorder, found only in females, involves regression during the first year of life and several severe impairments. In Childhood Disintegrative Disorder, development appears quite normal until at least two years of age; then prior to age ten, regressions result in behaviors similar to those of autism. The validity of the third disorder, Asperger's Disorder, is especially controversial in that it is often viewed as a mild form of autism, of higher-functioning autism, or autism without retardation. Many children with apparently related symptoms still do not fit the clinical profile for any of these disorders, and the reliability and validity of the pervasive developmental disorders are still debated (e.g., Mahoney et al., 1998).

ASSESSMENT

Assessment of autism is demanding because of the variability among cases and the need to evaluate several areas of functioning (Wakschlag & Leventhal, 1996). Medical and neuropsychological assessments can be valuable in helping to identify autism, investigate its causes, and treat associated conditions such as seizures. The neurological exam, neuropsycholgical battery, visual and hearing examinations, brain scans, EEGs, and other tests are relevant. However, the extent of such assessments can be expected to vary with individual cases. Psychological and behavioral assessments are critical for diagnosis as well as treatment. They typically include interviews with parents and other significant adults, as well as testing and behavioral observation of the client.

Interviews and clinical observation. Several interview protocols, checklists, and behavioral procedures have been developed to aid assessment.

A Personal Account of Autism

At middle age, Temple Grandin is a professor of animal science at Colorado State University, a designer of animal equipment and stockyards, and a writer. One topic of her writings is her firsthand experience with autism.

Ms. Grandin (1997) attributes a good part of her success to educational opportunity and mentors. At thirty months, she began structured nursery school and language training; she was mainstreamed from kindergarten through sixth grade; and she then attended boarding school before enrolling in a small liberal arts college. She had wise mentors. Her mother taught her to read in the third grade, an aunt constructively guided her, teachers encouraged her interest in science, and people in industry hired her and helped her develop her abilities.

For those who find it difficult to imagine the experiences of autism, Ms. Grandin's descriptions are instructive. For example, Ms. Grandin notes her "horrible oversensitivity" to sound and touch. As a child, someone's touch brought "an overwhelming, drowning wave of stimulation." She responded to hugs by stiffening and pulling back. At the same time, she yearned for touch and crawled under sofa cushions to obtain it. At age eighteen, she was even more innovative: she built a pressure machine that applies the pressure of foam-padded panels against her body.

Ms. Grandin describes difficulties in memory and in learning verbally. She relies heavily on images that she has stored in her mind, and she thinks in pictures. Concepts are visualizations of many examples. For instance, she has no general or abstract concept of a boat, just images of several boats she has seen. Any one boat image is linked to other memories; her father's boat is linked to fishing and to picnics. To think about boats, she must search her visual memory for specific boats and then find associated images. Thinking in pictures is slower than verbal thinking; it does, however, lend itself to the task of designing equipment.

Ms. Grandin reports that she has become better at handling social interactions. For common social interactions, she uses prerehearsed responses. For example, she has stored images of previous encounters with jealous engineers and of effective responses. Depending on logic rather than emotion, these responses are employed. In fact, Ms. Grandin characterizes her functioning by intellectual more than emotional intensity. And she speaks of the motivations and balances in her life in this way:

Many people with autism become disillusioned and upset because they do not fit in socially and they do not have a girlfriend or boyfriend. I have just accepted that such a relationship will not be part of my life. Learning the complex social interactions that would be expected is too complicated . . . I think I will stick to writing and equipment design . . . It is important to me that I do work that is of value to society. I want to be appreciated for the work I do. I am happiest when I am doing something for fun, like designing an engineering project, or something that makes a contribution to society. (Grandin, 1997, p. 1039)

TABLE 12-3

Pervasive Development Disorders

Rett's Disorder (Described by Andreas Rett, 1966, in Austria)

Disorder reported only in girls

Normal development until about six months

Head growth deceleration

Hand skills deterioration; stereotypic hand-washing movement

Abnormal gait and trunk movement

Severe language impairment; muteness

Disorder usually associated with mental retardation

Diminished interest in social environment

Childhood Disintegrative Disorder (Heller's Syndrome) (Described by Theodore Heller, 1908, in Austria)

Normal development until about two years

Multiple regression in language development, social behavior, play, and motor skills

Qualitative impairment in social interaction and communication

Stereotyped activities and motor behavior

Asperger's Disorder (Described by Hans Asperger, 1944, in Austria)

Sustained social impairments but not withdrawal

Impairments in nonverbal communication

Unusual, restrictive behavior, activities, interests

Motor clumsiness

No general delay in spoken language but deficits in pragmatics, voice rhythm

No general delay in cognitive or adaptive skills

Verbal IQ perhaps higher than performance IQ

Based in part on APA (1994); Van Acker (1997); and Volkmar, Klin, and Cohen (1997b).

These instruments focus on the child's behavior, and some of them inquire into prenatal, family, and other variables. Ratings are based on actual observation of the child, impressions of the child's past or present behavior, or records. The degree to which reliability and validity has been established varies across the instruments, and efforts in this area need to continue as new tools are constructed. We will detail three of the instruments.

The Childhood Autism Rating Scale (CARS) consists of fifteen items on which the child is rated during or immediately after observation, usually by professionals. The items cover many areas of functioning, including emotional response, imitation, social relations, communication, perception, and intelligence (Schopler et al., 1980; Schopler, Reichler, & Renner, 1988). Over half of the variation in scores is due to the items that cover social and communication behaviors (Newsom & Hovanitz, 1997). Directions are provided to create situations for observation of specific behaviors. For example, to observe social relationships, the evaluator engages the child in toy play or other activities, varying the amount of intrusion. On the basis of observation and reports from parents and others, each item is rated on a seven-point scale indicating the extent to which the behavior deviates from normal behavior. According to a summary of the ratings, children are considered severely autistic, mildly to moderately autistic, or nonautistic. Interrater reliability is adequate, and validity checks show CARS to be useful in screening children and older persons for autism. It is one of the most widely employed instruments.

Also widely used is the Autism Behavior Checklist (ABC), which consists of fifty-seven items placed in five categories: sensory, relating, body and object use, language, social and self-help skills (Krug, Arick, & Almond, 1978). The ABC was constructed to identify severely handicapped persons who display high levels of autistic behaviors, and it is part of a larger assessment instrument aimed at educational planning (Newsom & Hovanitz, 1997; Volkmar et al., 1988). Each yes/no item is assigned a weight from one to four according to how well it predicts autism. For example, "has no social smile" is rated two; "has pronoun reversal" is rated three. Children are rated on the basis of how well each item describes them. Profiles for different age groups are provided, as well as comparisons with other handicapping conditions. Adequate interrater reliability and validity have been found (Newsom & Hovanitz, 1997; Vostanis et al., 1994). The ABC is probably most useful in screening young children who may be autistic and require further evaluation.

The Autism Diagnostic Observation Schedule (ADOS) consists of eight semistructured tasks to assess individuals six to eighteen years of age with a mental age of at least three years (Lord et al., 1989; Newsom & Hovanitz, 1997). The ADOS is based completely on formal observation, and administration requires twenty to thirty minutes. Constructed primarily for higher-functioning, verbal, autistic persons, it emphasizes social behavior and language. There are two sets of materials for most tasks, so that clients of different developmental levels can be evaluated. Performance on each task is rated, and exact responses are described. Ratings are given in four domains: social interaction, communication, stereotyped behavior, and mood and nonspecific abnormal behavior. The ratings are made on a three-point scale, from normal to autism. Studies of reliability and validity have been reported for the ADOS, as well as for its downward extension for children below developmental level of three years (PL-ADOS). These instruments require additional research, are being further developed, and appear promising.

Intelligence and adaptive behavior tests. The use of intelligence tests in autism can be problematic, since they emphasize language and require cooperation and motivation. However, obtained scores are moderately stable over time and can be helpful in several ways (Newsom & Hovanitz, 1997). For example, they can help predict academic achievement and classroom placement, especially for higher-functioning children, and can aid in evaluating the outcome of intervention.

The Stanford-Binet and the Wechsler scales are widely used, but also helpful are tests that rely less on verbal and more on performance tasks. For example, the Leiter International Performance Scale and the Ravens's Coloured Progressive Matrices are employed with autistic persons who are mute, deaf, or minimally verbal. For assessing young or very low-functioning children, developmental scales are appropriate, such as the Bayley Scales of Infant Development.

Adaptive behavior scales can aid in both differentiating autism and planning treatment. They are employed most often with older children and adolescents (Newsom & Hovanitz, 1997). AAMR's Adaptive Behavior Scale is especially useful in identifying deficits in many practical domains and in evaluating educational outcomes. Scores on the Vineland Adaptive Behavior scales indicate greater social deficits with autism than with other developmental disabilities (Newsom & Hovanitz, 1997; Volkmar et al., 1987). Deficits are greater than would be predicted from IQ scores.

Behavior and skill analysis. More than the assessment techniques already described, behavior and skill analysis emphasizes the needs of the client in particular environmental settings and the shaping of behavior to meet those needs. These assessments are usually employed when behavioral and educational treatments are anticipated. Although they often require much time and meticulous observation and implementation, they can be enormously useful for selecting and monitoring intervention.

Assessment focuses on understanding environmental demands and any mismatch between the client's behavior and these demands (Newsom & Hovanitz, 1997). Therefore, assessment involves careful examination of both the environmental setting and the client's skills and responses. An example of this approach is summarized in Table 12-4 (Brown et al., 1979; cited in Newsom and Hovanitz, 1997). First, the environment in which the child will function and the specific skills required are determined. Next, for each activity in which the child is expected to engage, the skills normally required are ascertained. In some cases, the determination may be made to adapt the task to the client's abilities.

As is always the case, behavioral assessment determines the specific behaviors that require modification and identifies the variables that guide and influence behaviors. In autism it is often necessary to assess behaviors that interfere with the child's being productive, such as self-stimulation, self-injury, and high activity level. Functional assessment that examines how a problem behavior functions for the client can be beneficial (Schreibman, 1997).

Family assessment. The families of a child with autism experience many of the emotions of parents of other developmental disordered children.

TABLE 12-4

Guidelines to Assessment in Natural Environments

Steps to Evaluate the Environment

1. Determine the important environments in which the child functions (e.g., home, restaurant, supermarket).
2. Divide these environments into subenvironments (e.g., home into kitchen, bedroom, etc.).
3. Identify the most important activities in each subenvironment (e.g., cooking, washing dishes).
4. Identify specific skills needed for child's partial or full participation in the activities (e.g., cutting potatoes, stacking dishes).

Steps to Evaluate Specific Skills Needed by an Activity

1. Analyze skills used by normal persons in the activity.
2. Determine the skills the child can perform by observing the child in the environment or in a simulated environment.
3. Compare the child's performance with that of normal person to identify missing skills.
4. Consider possible adaptations of skills, materials, rules, etc. (e.g., teach a mute child to order restaurant foods with pictures).

Adapted from Newsom, Hovanitz, and Rincover, 1988.

It has been suggested, however, that the social-emotional isolation of autism may make it particularly difficult for families to cope (Siegel, 1997). The more that is understood about the stresses, the greater the chance of enhancing family well-being. Although parents have always been major caregivers for their autistic offspring, they have increasingly become a critical part of the therapeutic team. Thus family assessment has implications for facilitating the treatment of autism. Everyone can benefit from balancing family needs and the child's need for intensive care (Wakschlag & Leventhal, 1996).

Family assessment depends mostly on interviews and questionnaires that evaluate stress, child management, attitudes, coping, conflict, financial status, motivation, and skills for participation in treatment. Among the instruments employed are the Family Environment Scale (Moos & Moos, 1986) and the Parenting Stress Index (Abidin, 1995).

TREATMENT

The extensive efforts to alleviate autism have been motivated by the compelling needs of children with autism and, in more recent years, by family and societal advocacy for treatment. Early efforts frequently were based on the psychoanalytic formulation that failed parenting caused autism. As this assumption became suspect, clinicians increasingly turned to other interventions. Some interventions focused on changing specific behaviors or meeting specific needs of clients; others aimed toward more comprehensive improvement in the functioning of individuals with autism (Rogers, 1998).

Today a large array of treatments are offered, including many unconventional approaches. There is increased awareness of the need to demonstrate efficacy through rigorous scientific evaluation. Indeed, concern is expressed about possible harm being done by unconventional and inadequately evaluated treatments, some of which make excessive therapeutic claims (Klin & Cohen, 1997). Although no treatment approach claims to cure autism, noteworthy progress has been achieved in pharmacological, behavioral, and educational interventions.

Pharmacological treatment. Medications are best seen as adjuncts in the treatment of autism. Many kinds have been explored. We review a few of the currently important medications, with a focus on their effects on brain chemistry.

The antipsychotic medications are of first choice. Haloperidol (Haldol), a dopamine antagonist, is one of the best studied and most effective (Campbell et al., 1996; McDougle, 1997). In general, antipsychotic medications can reduce agita-

UNCONVENTIONAL TREATMENTS FOR AUTISM

Klin and Cohen (1997) are among those who recognize that many unconventional treatments for autism have not been adequately studied or proven effective. They note that over a dozen unconventional treatments are offered within a hundred-mile radius of their clinic. Such approaches include megavitamins, hugging therapy, auditory training, visual training, physical exercise, allergy desensitization, and psychomotor skills patterning. In some instances, advocates of unconventional therapies aggressively market their approaches and are hostile toward evaluations by independent investigators. Treatments have sometimes been touted as almost miraculous breakthroughs, resulting in false hopes for parents, wasted resources, and worst of all, inappropriate intervention.

Facilitated Communication (FC) is an example of a controversial intervention. Rosemary Crossley developed the technique in which the client types messages on a keyboard while the client's hand or arm is guided by a facilitator-therapist. FC, which was brought from Australia to the United States by Douglas Biklen, received much attention from Biklen's article in the *Harvard Educational Review* (Mulick, 1994; Schopler, 1994). Media attention became widespread and included programming on television's popular *Primetime.*

Claims of FC's success appeared quite remarkable. Children with autism and other severe disabilities who previously had little or no ability to communicate were reported as sending complex and poetic messages. In some cases, intelligence test scores were said to have dramatically risen. But not everyone was comfortable with these claims, since FC had not been adequately evaluated. In addition, a number of facilitated communications implicated family and professionals in physical and sexual abuse. Discomfort eventually led to the systematic research of FC (e.g., Perry, Bryson, & Bebko, 1998; Simon, Toll, & Whitehair, 1994). It now seems quite clear that the messages that are sent in facilitated communications largely originate with the facilitator-therapists, who seem unaware that their help has gone beyond guidance.

Nevertheless, loyalty to FC continues among some parents and therapists, who claim the technique to be effective for their children or clients. Putting aside personal gain that could operate in a few instances, what might account for loyalty to FC or other unconventional approaches that appear to contradict what is known about autism? Allegiance might be sustained by hope for a cure. And perhaps the philosophy underlying FC—respect for and belief in the competence of persons with autism—might help sustain loyalty to the method (Mundy & Adreon, 1994; Routh, 1994a). This humanistic philosophy is understandably appealing; however, the need for rigorous research on the effectiveness of interventions is obvious. FC might reasonably encourage some clients to use alternative communication techniques (Durand, in press), but when viewed as a panacea, it can be harmful.

tion, aggressiveness, stereotypies, social withdrawal, emotional instability, and self-injurious behavior (Dawson & Castelloe, 1992). Not all persons are helped, however, and adverse side effects occur over time in a minority of patients. Of particular concern are motor problems, including tardive dyskinesia (involuntary repetitive movements of the tongue, mouth, and jaw). In one study, such side effects occurred in 33 percent of the patients (Campbell et al., 1997).

Risperidone, an atypical antipsychotic medication that is antagonistic to dopamine and serotonin, can reduce aggression, overactivity, and stereotypies across all ages (Kumra et al., 1997; Nicolson, Awad, & Sloman, 1998). Of special importance is that risperidone may avoid the adverse motor side effects of the typical antipsychotic medications. Weight gain and sedation are commonly reported, and abnormal liver function has been observed in a few children. Risperidone appears promising, but well-controlled research is needed to substantiate both its beneficial and its adverse effects.

Substances that reduce brain serotonin are of interest because 25 to 50 percent of autistic children show high blood serotonin levels—and high levels are associated with greater intellectual and stereotypic impairments. Numerous studies have been conducted on fenfluramine. Early investigations reported various benefits, but later controlled studies contradicted this finding (Aman & Kern, 1989; Campbell, 1988). There is concern about anorexia, weight loss, sedation, impaired learning ability, irritability, and toxic effects on the brain. Presently, fenfluramine is not widely recommended. Several other medications that reduce serotonin show promise and appear to be well tolerated (McDougle, 1997).

Another class of medications employed is antagonistic to the opiates (endorphins). Opiate levels could be related to insensitivity to pain and self-injury, attention deficits, and other behavioral problems (e.g., Campbell et al., 1993; Sahley & Panksepp, 1987). Naltrexone is one of the drugs examined in several studies. The findings indicate that it sometimes reduces hyperactivity and restlessness/irritability but has no significant affect on

the core symptoms of autism or on self-injurious behavior (Buitelaar, Willemsen-Swinkels, & Van Engeland, 1998; Kolmen et al., 1998; McDougal, 1997).

Overall then, some medications show some efficacy in reducing problem behaviors, thereby facilitating behavioral and educational interventions. However, much is yet to be known about the effects of pharmacotherapy, which range from improvement to worsening of behavior. Dosage level and age of the client are always important variables. Furthermore, it is particularly difficult to prescribe and monitor effects on very young children. Thus the need for well-controlled investigations is substantial.

Behavioral intervention. Behavioral treatments have been especially effective, many have been described in detail, and many have been rigorously studied. The approach is dominant in teaching specific positive behaviors—such as those related to language, social interaction, and self-care—and in reducing specific undesirable behaviors—such as aggression, self-stimulation, and self-injury. The usual behavioral techniques have been employed—reinforcement, punishment, extinction, shaping, fading, generalization techniques, and so forth—and there has been a strong thrust to train parents and other caregivers in behavioral techniques.

In addition, important advances have occurred (Schreibman, 1997). In the 1960s, in response to the lack of any successful treatments and to their belief that operant learning could ameliorate autism, behaviorists presented simple demonstrations of behavior change in clients with autism. Early efforts enjoyed some success but were also challenged by failures. Too often, newly learned behavior did not generalize, punishment appeared necessary to modify some behaviors, and other behaviors were not readily modified at all. Refinements and advances were required to meet these challenges. In addition, it became obvious that intensive, comprehension programs would be necessary to bring about substantial improvement in the lives of individuals with autism. We will track some of the progress in behavioral treatment as we first discuss examples of interventions that focus on specific behaviors and then comprehensive behavioral intervention.

Desirable Behavior: Language Acquisition Lovaas and his colleagues at the University of California at Los Angeles were among the first to teach speech to autistic children, and with modifications their techniques are still relevant. Acquisition was conceptualized as the learning of receptive and expressive speech (Lovaas, Young, & Newsom, 1978).

Receptive labeling is typically an effective first step (Newsom, 1998). Here, the child is presented with preferred food or an object, the therapist verbally refers to the food in some way, and the child is expected to respond nonverbally. For example, a cup of juice is presented and the therapist says "touch the cup". If the child does so, a reward is forthcoming, preferably related to the task, so the child might be permitted to drink the juice. If the child does not respond a prompt is given: the therapist may move the child's hand toward the cup and then repeat the procedure. The prompt is later faded. Generalization of learning is also built in. Several examples of the same class of words are presented (for example, different cups), and training is presented by different people in different settings.

The acquisition of *expressive speech* entails the therapist's naming an object as a prompt for the child to produce the verbalization (Lovaas & Newsom, 1976; Newsom, 1998). If necessary, the child is reinforced for approximations until the correct response is shaped. As several labels are acquired, new objects are presented with already learned objects to teach discrimination. Subsequently, simple requests (e.g., "I want——" or "Gimme——") are taught. Generalization is facilitated by the presentation of different objects in the same class and by different requests. Speech sounds, words, and phrases are gradually programmed so that the child acquires a repertoire of language through modeling and reinforcement. With progress, language itself becomes reinforcing, and external rewards and prompts are faded. More advanced forms are gradually taught, such as pronouns, ad-

jectives, verb tenses, and plurals. Some children can eventually learn to generate sentences and to respond to an array of verbalizations, although considerable training time and effort are required. Others do less well, but some can profit from learning a combination of speech and sign language, or sign language alone.

As is obvious, the procedures include methods to facilitate generalization. Indeed, operant learning has been strengthened by more effective procedures to promote generalization and to encourage more natural communication (Koegel et al., 1998). The need for such procedures became apparent when children failed to use acquired speech out of the learning setting, lacked spontaneous speech, and did not use speech functionally. For example, the child might respond to someone's comment but not spontaneously initiate conversation, nor use speech to engage in everyday activities. Training with different objects, in different settings, in different situations, and by different teachers can help overcome generalization problems (Durand & Carr, 1988). However, incidental learning is also employed so that the child's behavior comes more under the control of the natural environment (Schreibman, 1997). For example, teaching the child to request verbally a desired item makes it likely that language will be used to obtain reinforcements in everyday settings (Newsom, 1998). Permitting the child to select objects for training and using reinforcers tied naturally to the object (e.g., labeling a doll is reinforced with playing with the doll) give the child some control of training and create a "real world" situation.

Reducing Maladaptive Behavior Self-stimulation, bizarre speech, tantrums, aggression, and self-injury are among the behaviors that interfere with social relationships, learning, and educational placement and that even directly harm individuals with autism. A variety of techniques have been employed to reduce these behaviors, and success has been documented with single-subject research designs. We will discuss self-injury as an example, although much of what is said can apply to other behaviors as well.

Repetitious self-injurious behavior (SIB), which usually disappears in normal children by school age, is observed in perhaps 15 percent of developmentally disabled youngsters (Durand & Carr, 1985). It varies in form, and intensity ranges from minor to life-threatening damage. SIB weakly correlates with other repetitious stereotypic behaviors (Rojahn, Tasse, & Morin, 1998).

It is widely thought that biological or environmental factors—or a combination of the two—underlie the behavior (Mace et al., 1998). The association of SIB with Lesch-Nyhan and other genetic syndromes, as well as with middle ear infection, suggests an abnormal organic need for sensory stimulation that self-injurious behavior might provide. Even so, SIB is also influenced by environmental factors.

The history of treating SIB shows that it can be relatively difficult to change (Bregman & Gerdtz, 1997). Medications have achieved only some success, and early behavioral interventions often were not successful. When self-injury threatened the child and interventions were ineffective, punishment was sometimes employed. Punishments included lemon juice squirted into the mouth and contingent electric shock. Although such aversive consequences can be effective, they raised serious ethical questions (Public Interest, 1989; Shopler, 1994). Those who oppose aversive treatment see it as inhumane and painful, as well as potentially the cause of physical side effects, stress, and death. Supporters argue that aversive treatment is an acceptable last resort for extreme self-abuse, no worse than commonly used aversive medical treatments that bring about long-term gain. In 1989 The National Institutes of Health recommended, among other things, that aversive treatment be employed only in brief interventions for severe cases, and only after review and consent (Bregman & Gerdtz, 1997). Ongoing efforts to find more effective and acceptable procedures were strengthened and renewed.

These efforts include more comprehensive analysis of variables that can influence self-injury. Figure 12-2 presents a schema for organizing such influences (Newsom, 1998). Treatment can focus on any of the three classes of variables or on some combination of them. *Setting events* are background variables that can change the probability that a behavior will occur. For example, a child's fatigue can make it more likely that the child will respond with SIB in certain situations. *Antecedent*

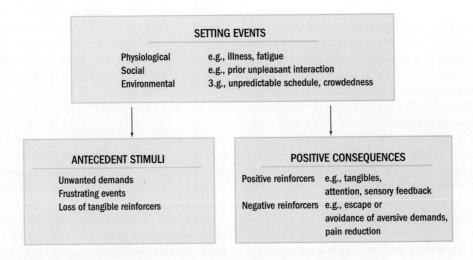

FIGURE 12-2 A schema of variables that influence problem behaviors.
Adapted from Newsom, 1998.

stimuli occur just prior to self-injury and precipitate the behavior. *Positive consequences* for SIB are also critical. Self-injury can be reinforced with tangibles such as food, toys, and activities, or attention from others. It is only natural for caretakers to comfort, distract, or verbally dissuade a child from engaging in self-injury; however, this attention can actually increase SIB. SIB also can be negatively reinforced; for example, when unwanted demands are made on a child, self-injury may occur. Caregivers confronted with such a situation might understandably cease to make the demands, thereby negatively reinforcing SIB.

Analysis of self-injury provides a general guide to intervention. Modification of setting events and antecedent stimuli can prevent SIB from occurring at all. Modification of reinforcement contingencies can reduce already-occurring behavior. However, with so many variables possibly influencing self-injury, functional assessment is crucial to determine which specific factors are operating in the situation (Durand, 1993b). Naturalistic observations of the child, interviews with caregivers, and rating scales are helpful. The Motivation Assessment Scale is a convenient rating scale used to determine the influence of attention, tangibles reinforcement, escape, and sensory feedback on SIB (Durand & Crimmins, 1988). In addition, functional analysis can be conducted, in which the client is actually exposed to different conditions while the rate of SIB is observed, in order to determine the variables that are influencing the behavior.

As an example of the general approach, we consider the work of Durand (1990) and his colleagues, who have shown that SIB and other maladaptive behaviors are often used intentionally as a way to communicate needs or desires. They analyze how SIB is functioning and then train more adaptive communication that can substitute for self-injury. The approach, which is called Functional Communication Training, is exemplified in the case of Tim, a twelve-year-old boy diagnosed with autism and moderate mental retardation (Durand & Carr, 1991). Tim easily became frustrated and hit himself several times a day, therefore periodically requiring medical attention. A

functional assessment suggested that self-injury was being reinforced by allowing Tim to escape from undesirable situations when he injured himself. Next, a baseline observation of SIB was conducted, during which the teacher was either to ignore the SIB or to block the more severe behaviors that might cause injury. Tim was then taught, with modeling and prompting, to request assistance with tasks that he might desire to escape by simply saying "Help me." Training took place in the classroom, and several different trainers were deliberately used with two different tasks. The recording of Tim's SIB and verbal requests showed his progress (Figure 12-3). Further observation also revealed that the trained behaviors endured when Tim returned to school in two subsequent years. On the basis of such demonstrations, as well as on other research, Durand and Carr (1991; 1992) not only believe that Functional Communication Training is effective but also that it generalizes to other situations and endures over time. Functional Communication Training has been successful in the home, residential settings, and schools. Overall, substantial progress is being made in treating SIB and other maladaptive behaviors in individuals with autism.

Comprehensive Treatment: Lovaas's UCLA Project So far, our discussion has emphasized treatment of specific targeted behaviors. We now turn to an intensive behavioral program aimed at generating multiple positive outcomes for children with autism. In 1970 Lovaas and his colleagues developed a program involving graduate students, parents, and teachers (Lovaas, 1987; Lovaas & Smith, 1988). Very young children were chosen because it was assumed that their learning of new behaviors would more easily generalize to other environments. It was also believed that desirable school inclusion would be more easily accomplished in preschools rather than later in elementary schools.

To be accepted into the study, children had to have been independently diagnosed as autistic, be less than forty-six months of age, and have a specified mental age. Nineteen subjects were assigned to intensive training (Group I), and nineteen were assigned to a minimal training control condition

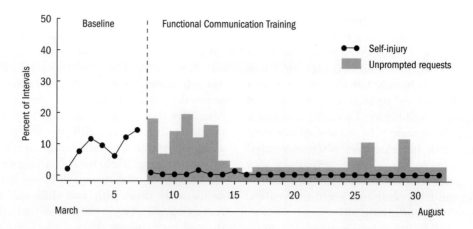

FIGURE 12-3 The occurrence of SIB and unprompted verbal requests for help as a function of intervention. Each point on the graph represents data from each observation day across several months.

Adapted from Durand and Carr, 1991.

(Group II). Group I had a mean IQ of 53, and Group II, an IQ of 46. Comparison was also made with Group III, an outside group of autistic children that received no training in the project. All three groups were very similar.

Treatment lasted for two or more years. Children in Group I worked one-to-one with their parents and student therapists for more than forty hours each week. Operant techniques were the basis of training. Initially treatment focused on reducing maladaptive behaviors, compliance to simple verbal commands, imitation, appropriate play, affectionate behaviors, and extending training in the family. The second thrust emphasized language growth, interactive play, and teaching children to function in the preschool. The third phase emphasized emotional expression, preacademic skills, and learning by observation of other children. Effort was made to place children in regular preschools where teachers would help in training. Children in Group II received almost the same treatment but with less than ten hours of interaction per week.

At initial follow-up, the experimental children averaged seven years of age. They had significantly higher educational placement and IQ than the control groups, which did not differ from each other. Table 12-5 shows specific results. Prior to the study, only two Group I children had scored in the normal range of IQ, whereas eleven had scored in the severely retarded range; seven had been echolalic, and eleven had been mute.

A second follow-up when Group I children averaged thirteen years of age showed that they had maintained improvements over Group II (McEachin, Smith, & Lovaas, 1993). School placement, with little exception, remained the same. Group I children achieved significantly higher average IQ scores (85 versus 55) and Vineland Adaptive Behavior scores (72 versus 46). Personality test scores were borderline for both groups. Overall, eight of nine Group I children who had done well at the first follow-up were holding their own in regular classrooms and approached normal functioning.

The UCLA program has been criticized on several counts (Mundy, 1993; Rogers, 1998; Schopler, Short, & Mesibov, 1989). For example, children were not assigned randomly to groups, the amount of training that individual children received was not reported, and concerns were expressed about assessment. Also, intensive treat-

TABLE 12-5

Educational Placement and Mean IQ Score at Initial Follow-up in the UCLA Project

	Percent of Children Completing Regular First Grade		Percent of Children in Language Handicapped and LD Class		Percent of Children in First Grade for Autistic-Retarded	
Group I	47	IQ: 107	42	IQ: 70	11	IQ: 30
Group II	0		42	IQ: 74	58	IQ: 36
Group III	5	IQ: 99	48	IQ: 67	48	IQ: 44

Adapted from Lovaas, 1987.

ment still failed for some children. Despite shortcomings, the project has been cited as having a stronger scientific design than most other treatment studies (Rogers, 1998). Subsequent investigations that followed in the project's footsteps indicate some benefits, although the studies do not adequately replicate the UCLA work. The findings offer hope that intensive behavioral treatments may make a difference in the lives of at least some children with autism. Overall, these results, combined with the many successes to modify specific behaviors, have made the behavioral approach a leading treatment option.

TEACCH: Comprehensive Educational Treament. TEACCH, which stands for **T**reatment and **E**ducation of **A**utistic and related **C**ommunication handicapped **CH**ildren, is the only university-based statewide program mandated by law to provide services, research, and training for autism and related disorders (Schopler, 1997). TEACCH has evolved over thirty years as an alternative to a psychoanalytic-based approach used in the 1960s at the University of North Carolina. From the beginning, families played a critical role in developing TEACCH. Priority was given to three areas: home adjustment, education, and community adaptation. A clear philosophy and set of values emerged over the years, as shown in Table 12-6. In addition, evaluations were conducted, and the findings were used to improve the program.

TEACCH now operates regional centers at six locations near branches of the University of North Carolina, a Developmental Evaluation Center, and an Area Health Education Center. Each of the regional centers is directed by a psychologist and has a staff of five to seven therapists who trained in various disciplines such as special education, speech and hearing, child development, and vocational therapy. The regional centers provide individual assessment, training for parents to serve as cotherapists for their children, family support, consultation, professional training, and collaboration with other relevant agencies.

TABLE 12-6

Shared Values of the TEACCH Treatment Program

Characteristics of autism are understood from observation rather than through professional theory.

Parent-professional collaboration is vital.

The child's adaptation is improved through teaching new skills and making environmental accommodations to deficits.

Assessment for individualized treatment occurs through formal instruments or informal observation.

Priority is given to cognitive and behavior theory.

Enhancement of skills and acceptance of deficits go hand-in-hand.

A holistic orientation deals with the whole situation.

Lifelong community-based services are crucial.

Based on Schopler, 1997.

TEACCH affiliates with 265 North Carolina classrooms and is involved in selecting and training the teachers. Students are enrolled in the classrooms after they are assessed by TEACCH and receive an Individualized Educational Plan. Many of the children continue to receive other services at the regional centers; in addition, many of the parents are trained to conduct home teaching with their children.

Parents and professionals also collaborate on educating the wider community about autism and on developing additional community services. Over the years, these services have involved summer recreation, respite care, services for adolescents, group homes, vocational initiatives for older clients, and, more recently, preschool services. Parents, who are organized at the regional centers and classrooms, are affiliated with the Autism Society of America.

TEACCH has been evaluated in various ways (Schopler, 1994; 1997). For example, a comparison of highly structured operant learning sessions and nondirective and psychoanalytic play therapy indicated the superiority of the structured approach. Other evaluations demonstrated the effectiveness of parent training and positive parental attitues toward TEACCH. Outcome studies showed that only 7 percent of the TEACCH students required resticted living placements in adulthood compared with 39 to 78 percent of the general autistic population. More recently, short-term gains have been reported for a TEACCH-based home intervention for preschool children (Ozonoff & Cathcart, 1998). TEACCH has been recognized for excellence and implemented across the United States and in Europe. Nevertheless, methodological weaknesses in outcome studies, including lack of controls, have been noted (Smith, 1999).

Educational opportunities. Autism is among the disabilities included in the Individuals with Disabilities Education Act (IDEA). Indeed, most persons with PDD meet the criteria or are eligible because of mental retardation, language or learning deficits, or emotional disturbance (Berkman, 1997). Thus, the states and school districts are obliged to identify children with autism, provide services from birth, include families in evaluation and intervention, and deliver appropriate educational programs.

The commitment to the least restrictive alternatives and school inclusion has diminished institutionalization and has increased educational opportunities. However, issues have been raised (Klin & Cohen, 1997). For example, behavioral treatment can conflict with the ideal of the least restrictive environment. Also, the effects of school inclusion are debated. It is not surprising that opinions run the gamut from advocacy for a strict policy of inclusion to arguments for the need for more varied educational settings (Burack, Root, & Zigler, 1997). Unfortunately, we do not have adequate research to resolve the issue. Limited investigations indicate that some children with autism can benefit academically and socially from classroom interaction with normal peers. However, inclusion without support is likely to fail. Factors such as adaptation of curricula, social skills training, teacher attitude, and encouragement of peer interaction make a difference. Nevertheless, the marked differences in abilities in persons with autism suggest the need for alternative educational settings.

Educational opportunity appears to have brought improvement in the functioning of autistic youth (Venter et al., 1992). In addition, environments that prepare the individual for future employment hold promise for independent living and increased quality of life. Experiences that emphasize such things as task completion, self-management, and specific vocational training can be helpful. Making a gradual transition from school to the work environment and building on the interests and talents of the individual to create job skills can be crucial (Grandin, 1997).

Improvement in the lives of individuals with autism is the result, in part, of both rigorous research and commitment and advocacy of professionals and the families themselves. A telling account of one woman's experience as a parent of a son with autism, an advocate, and a professional is provided by Sullivan (1997). She founded the Autism Services Center in Huntington, West Virginia, an agency that plays a critical role in delivery of services in the state. Among other things, Sullivan describes the development of her son, who with assistance held a job in the local library, was declared "Client of the Year" by the state rehabilitation services, and served as a model when Dustin Hoffman created the role of a man with autism in the film *Rainman*.

SCHIZOPHRENIA

As noted early in this chapter, both Kraepelin and Bleuler identified a small percentage of cases of schizophrenia in which onset occurred in childhood. By the 1930s, the first studies of childhood schizophrenia had appeared (Cantor, 1988). During subsequent decades, many efforts were made to conceptualize the nature of the condition. Because youth who were classified with childhood schizophrenia varied a great deal from each other, attempts were made to identify subgroups or syndromes. It was on this landscape that Kanner argued for a distinct syndrome of autism, and autism and various other pervasive developmental disorders became differentiated from schizophrenia and schizophrenia-like disorders.

CLASSIFICATION AND DIAGNOSIS

Nevertheless, issues remained about the classification and nature of schizophrenia itself. Central to our discussion is the relationship of childhood-onset schizophrenia to later-onset schizophrenia. Are there different age-related disorders, or is there a basic disorder manifesting itself at different times of life? By 1980 some consensus was reached that the essential features of schizophrenia hold across age, so that the same basic diagnostic criteria can be applied to individuals of all ages. This approach appears to be working reasonably well, although some dissatisfaction exists, and the issue of continuity across age is not completely settled. In keeping with the clinical and research literature, we will often make distinctions among childhood schizophrenia (with onset by age twelve or so) and schizophrenia that first occurs during adolescence or during adulthood.

Table 12-7 indicates DSM-IV's major diagnostic features for schizophrenia. The first three of these features—delusions, hallucinations, and disorganized speech—are typically considered reflections of psychosis, that is, to indicate a break with reality.

Delusions, or erroneous beliefs, and *hallucinations*, or erroneous perceptions, are often considered the hallmarks of schizophrenia. But *disorganized speech*, which reflects disordered thinking, has often been viewed as a critical feature. *Disorganized behavior* is manifested in many ways: inappropriate silliness, unexpected agitation and aggression, lack of self-care, and the like. *Catatonic behaviors* are motor disturbances, such as decreased or excessive motor reactivity, and rigid and strange bodily postures. All the behaviors so far described are referred to as positive symptoms. However, people with schizophrenia also display negative symptoms, that is, a lack of normally occurring behaviors. Thus they may exhibit little emotion, their speech may consist of brief replies that do not seem to convey much information (alogia), or they may neither initiate nor maintain goal-directed actions (avolition).

Schizophrenic behaviors obviously disrupt normal adaptation and relationships. Thus young people so diagnosed must have previously shown a higher level of functioning or failure to reach normal levels of achievement. Diagnosis also requires continuous disturbance for at least six months, to rule out transient conditions.

Although youth can be successfully diagnosed, the strong reliance on positive psychotic symptoms

TABLE 12-7
Major DSM-IV Features for Schizophrenia

1. Delusions
2. Hallucinations
3. Disorganized speech
4. Disorganized or catatonic behavior
5. Negative symptoms: diminished affect, speech content, and goal-directed activities

for diagnosis has implication for very young children. Early developmental level may not lend itself to these psychotic manifestations or to their being reported by the child. Thus current diagnostic systems cannot identify schizophrenia if it occurs very early. In fact, it is difficult to diagnose schizophrenia until age seven or eight (Gooding & Iacono, 1995).

The DSM-IV and other classification systems include subcategories for schizophrenia, such as paranoid and disorganized schizophrenia. However, the reliability and validity of the subcategories are debated with regard to adult cases, and subgroups have not been systematically applied to children.

EPIDEMIOLOGY

Data on the prevalence of childhood schizophrenia are limited because of the low frequency of the disorder in youth. One review puts prevalence estimates at twenty or fewer cases per ten thousand (.2 percent or less), compared with the adulthood rate of 1 percent (Gooding & Iacono, 1995). Prevalence is age related, however. It is thought to be extremely low before ages five to six (lower than for autism), to increase somewhat during childhood, and then to rise rapidly during adolescence to reach the adult rate (McClellan & Werry, 1994/1997).

At early ages, schizophrenia has often, but not always, been reported as more frequent in males than in females (Asarnow & Asarnow, 1996).

Schizophrenia in children may occur at higher rates in less educated and less professionally successful families (Volkmar, 1991), and this social class difference has been cited as one way in which schizophrenia differs from autism. However, the data are mixed and may be biased by a strong reliance on hospital samples (Werry, 1992). In adulthood, schizophrenia is more prevalent in the lower social classes. It is also observed in cultures all over the world.

CLINICAL DESCRIPTION

The core psychotic features of schizophrenia are striking; however, associated characteristics are important considerations. We will first focus on the

psychotic features and then on the associated characteristics shown by youth. (For a case description, see p. 72).

Hallucinations. Hallucinations are false perceptions that occur in the absence of identifiable stimuli. Individuals experiencing hallucinations report hearing, seeing, or smelling things that others do not hear, see, or smell. Such perceptual abnormalities can vary in content and in complexity. For example, simple hallucinations are indistinct shapes or sounds, whereas complex hallucinations are more organized, such as identifiable figures or voices (Volkmar et al., 1995).

Table 12-8 shows some of the characteristics of four samples of children diagnosed with schizophrenia, including the hallucinations they reported. Hallucinations occurred at high rates and with remarkable consistency across the samples. Auditory hallucinations were by far the most common. Visual hallucinations were reported fairly often, whereas those involving touch and smell were quite rare. These findings are consistent with other studies of children and adults with schizophrenia (Kemph, 1987; Volkmar et al., 1995).

Table 12-9 details the variety of hallucinations reported by children in the study by Russell, Bott, and Sammons (1989), as well as the percentage of children who experienced each type. It was not uncommon for a single child to report several types, but in this sample, nonauditory hallucinations never occurred without auditory hallucinations. The following are examples of the children's reports of their experiences:

Auditory: The kitchen light said to do things and "shut up."

Command: A man's voice said "murder your stepfather" and "go play outside."

Visual: A ghost with a red, burned, and scarred face was seen several times in different places

Religious: God said, "Sorry D., but I can't help you now, I'm helping someone else."

Persecutory: Monsters said child is "stupid" and that they will hurt him.

TABLE 12-8

Some Characteristics of Childhood Schizophrenia in Four Studies

		Mean Age	**Male: Female**	**Mean IQ**	**Percent of Cases Showing Symptoms**			
					Auditory Hallucinations	**Visual Hallucinations**	**Delusions**	**Thought Disorder**
Kolvin et al., 1971	N = 33	11.1 (est.)	2.66:1	86	82	30	58	60
Green et al., 1992	N = 38	9.58	2.17:1	86	84	47	55	100
Russell et al., 1989	N = 35	9.54	2.2:1	94	80	37	63	40
Volkmar et al., 1988	N = 14	7.86 (est.)	2.5:1	82	79	28	86	93

Adapted from Green et al., 1992; Russell et al., 1989; and Volkmar et al., 1991.

Delusions. Delusions are false beliefs that are maintained even in the face of realistic contradiction. They vary in content. For example, *delusions of persecution* involve beliefs of impending harm from someone, whereas *delusions of reference* involve inaccurate beliefs that certain events or objects have particular significance. Delusions can also be simple or complex, and fragmentary or systematized. As shown in Table 12-8, delusions occurred relatively frequently and with consistency across the research samples of children. Table 12-9 indicates the many types of delusions that children report, and some children report several types. The following are examples:

Persecutory: A child believed his father had escaped jail and was coming to kill him.

Somatic: One child believed that a boy and a girl spirit lived inside his head.

Bizarre: A boy was convinced he was a dog and growing fur. One time he refused to leave the veterinarian's office unless he got a shot.

Grandiose: A boy had the firm belief that he was different and able to kill people. He believed that when God "zoomed" through him, he became strong.

Thought disorder. Delusions are a disturbance in the content of thought, but the form of think-ing is also distorted in schizophrenia. Formal thought disorder involves difficulties in organizing thoughts and is reflected in disorganized speech. Several indications of thought disorder are recognized. The person may display *loose associations*, that is, jumping from topic to topic with no obvious connection between topics and without awareness of the problem. Speech may be *illogical* and quite *incoherent* and incomprehensible to others. It may also have *impoverished* content, conveying little information because it is vague, too abstract or concrete, or repetitive. It may include *neologisms*, words that are meaningless to others. Loose associations and incoherence are demonstrated in this excerpt from an interview with a seven-year-old boy:

I used to have a Mexican dream. I was watching TV in the family room. I disappeared outside of this world and then I was in a closet. Sounds like a vacuum dream. It's a Mexican dream. When I was close to that dream earth I was turning upside down. I don't like to turn upside down. Sometimes I have Mexican dreams and vacuum dreams. It's real hard to scream in dreams. (Russell et al., 1989, p. 404)

Table 12-8 shows high percentages of thought disorder in the four samples of children studied, but it also reveals a large variation across the samples. Although these differences may indeed be real, they may also be due to difficulty in identifying thought disorder in children and to differences in how it is defined (McKenna, Gordon, et al., 1994).

TABLE 12-9

Percentage of Children with Hallucinations and Delusions

Types of Hallucinations	Percent
Nonaffective auditory	80
Command	69
Visual	37
Conversing voices	34
Religious	34
Persecutory	26
Commenting voices	23
Tactile	17
Olfactory	6
Somatic	6

Types of Delusions	Percent
Persecutory	20
Somatic	20
Bizarre	17
Reference	14
Grandiose	11
Thought insertion	11
Control/influence	9
Mind reading	9
Thought broadcasting	6
Thought control	3
Religious	3

From Russell, Bott, & Sammons, 1989.

Associated features. Among the characteristics associated with childhood schizophrenia are motor abnormalities that include awkwardness, delayed milestones, poor coordination, and peculiar posture (Cantor, 1988; Eggers, 1978; Watkins, Asarnow, & Tanguay, 1988). Emotional and social disturbances also occur. The children often show lack of emotion, or they laugh, cry, or show anger when the situation does not warrant such a response (e.g., Green et al., 1992). Coldness, moodiness, anxiety, and depression have been reported

(Eggers, 1978; Prior & Werry, 1986). Although there is little systematic study of social behavior, the difficulties include social withdrawal and isolation, inability to initiate social interactions, and ineptness (Bettes & Walker, 1987; Watkins et al., 1988).

Basic language skills are not as deficient as in autism, but impaired communication is observed in childhood and adolescent samples (Jacobsen & Rapoport, 1998; Prior & Werry, 1986; Watkins et al., 1988). Speech obviously reflects thought disorder, and many atypical features do occur, such as echolalia, neologisms, and decreased use of conjunctions to connect ideas (Caplan, Guthrie, & Komo, 1996).

Performance on intelligence tests is somewhat deficient in childhood schizophrenia. Many of the children score at borderline to average levels. Scores in the mentally retarded range are nowhere as evident as in autism. Perhaps 10 to 20 percent of cases show low IQ scores (McClellan & Werry, 1994/1997). There are few studies of IQ subtest performance, but relative deficits may exist on verbal tasks and tasks requiring short-term information processing (Asarnow et al., 1987; Green et al., 1992). Preliminary data suggest that intelligence declines during at least the first few years after psychotic symptoms appear (Jacobsen & Rapoport, 1998).

DEVELOPMENTAL COURSE AND OUTCOME

The occurrence of schizophrenia in childhood can be sudden but is more likely to be gradual or insidious (Asarnow & Asarnow, 1996; McClellan & Werry, 1994/1997). Nonpsychotic symptoms occur prior to psychotic symptoms and diagnosis. These nonpsychotic disturbances include delays and aberrations in language, and in motor, sensory, and cognitive functions, as well as social withdrawal, school problems, and "odd" personality (e.g., Watkins et al., 1988). Psychotic symptoms— and thus diagnosis—become more likely at school age. Table 12-10 reflects this developmental course for thirty-eight children hospitalized with schizophrenia.

The quality of hallucinations and delusions also shows a developmental trend (Eggers, 1978; Rus-

TABLE 12-10

Children's Ages at Onset of Symptoms and Diagnosis of Schizophrenia

Age (approximate years)	Percent Showing Onset of Nonpsychotic Symptoms	Percent Showing Onset of Psychotic Symptoms	Percent Diagnosed
0–3	8	0	0
3–5	18	0	0
5–7	45	18	5
7–9	13	42	29
9–11	13	29	37
11–12	3	11	29

Adapted from Green, Padron-Gayol, Hardesty, and Bassiri, 1992

sell et al., 1989). The themes of childhood make their way into children's psychotic experiences. Early hallucinations are likely to include animals, toys, and monsters, and to be simple. Similarly, when delusions first appear, they are quite simple (e.g., a monster wants to kill me), and then they gradually become more elaborate, complex, abstract, and systematized. These changes are in keeping with cognitive and socioemotional development (Volkmar, 1996).

The way in which schizophrenia begins in adolescence is less clear. Many diagnosed adolescents do have histories of attention, motor-perceptual, and other neurodevelopmental problems as well as worry, shyness, moodiness, and aggression. Nonetheless, onset is perhaps not as insidious, appearing more commonly with a sudden outbreak of disturbance (King & Noshpitz, 1991). Stress associated with this time of life may play a role. This picture seems more similar to adult schizophrenia, as do the psychotic symptoms of adolescent onset. For example, persecutory and grandiose delusions are more common than in childhood cases, and delusions are more complex and systematized (Volkmar et al., 1995).

What eventually happens to youth who are diagnosed with schizophrenia? In general, it appears that, as in adult schizophrenia, some individuals have a chronic condition, others experience episodes of difficulties that come and go, and still others recover. Eggers and Bunk (1997) found that 50 percent of childhood cases showed poor outcome and that 25 percent were recovered. Asarnow and Asarnow (1996) reported that 67 percent showed continuing schizophrenia or a related disorder. Two studies of adolescent schizophrenia indicated that about 78 percent and 50 percent of cases were not doing well (Gillberg, Hellgren, & Gillberg, 1993; Krausz & Muller-Thomsen, 1993).

It appears, then, that outcome is often unfavorable but nevertheless variable. Good adjustment before onset, sudden onset, and identifiable precipitants are related to better outcome. In other words, the child or adolescent who seems to be getting along reasonably well and then is taken with acute symptoms associated with specific events has a better chance of recovery. Early age of onset has been reported as predicting poor outcome (Werry, 1992), suggesting that childhood schizophrenia is an ominous form of the disorder. We must wait for future investigations to tell us more about the course and outcome of schizophrenia in youth.

NEUROLOGICAL FACTORS

Over the years, it has become increasingly apparent that later-occurring schizophrenia involves neurological abnormalities. Evidence comes from studies that pinpoint psychological deficits (such as in attention) and studies that indicate anomalies in parts of the brain that are thought to correspond to the psychological deficits. Most of the data come from adults diagnosed with schizophrenia and from the records of children at high risk who were diagnosed in adolescence or adulthood. However, findings have begun to accumulate for childhood schizophrenia. Although limited, they are notably similar to what has been revealed about later-occurring schizophrenia.

Neurological dysfunction is suggested by general characteristics of children with schizophrenia, such as perceptual deviations, motor delay, coordination problems, and other soft neurological signs (Cantor, 1988; Jacobsen & Rapoport, 1998). Neurological signs have also been reported as childhood symptoms of persons diagnosed in adulthood.

Structural abnormalities of the brain have been demonstrated across age, although not universally (Jacobsen & Rapoport, 1998; Schulz et al., 1998). The initial method used to examine the brain was postmortem studies, and brain imaging now more clearly identifies structural abnormalities. Among the most common findings is slight enlargement of the ventricles (fluid-filled spaces), which suggests underdevelopment or loss of brain tissue. Indeed, gray matter of the brain appears reduced. Reduced volume is found in the temporal-limbic area (e.g., hippocampus, amygdala) and the frontal area, and this finding has been associated with poor adjustment before diagnosis and neuropsychological deficits (e.g., Gur et al., 1998). There are some data that structural change progresses in childhood schizophrenia. In addition, neurons in the brain are abnormal and in abnormal locations (Weinberger, 1994).

Disturbances are demonstrated in other ways as well, and many implicate the frontal and temporal-limbic areas. A well-established finding is that a subset of adults with schizophrenia has difficulty in visually tracking a continuously moving stimulus; limited data show the same in adolescents and children. Tracking problems may be related to frontal lobe dysfunction (Gooding & Iacono, 1995). Neuropsychological testing indicates various deficits in attention and information process-

ing, such as verbal memory, abstraction, language, and executive functions (Asarnow & Asarnow, 1996; Cannon et al., 1994). The frontal and temporal lobes are involved in such functions. PET scans indicate that the prefrontal area of the brain is underactive when engaged in processing tasks (Gershon & Rieder, 1992). In addition, low reactivity of the autonomic nervous system, which might involve the hippocampus, has been widely reported for a subgroup of adults with schizophrenia (Ohman & Hultman, 1998). A study of child patients shows abnormalities in autonomic functioning that resemble anomalies seen in chronic adult patients (Jacobsen & Rapoport, 1998).

For many years dopamine has been implicated in schizophrenia. The antipsychotic medications that were first available appear to alleviate symptoms by blocking dopamine. Conversely, substances that increase dopamine, such as amphetamines, can increase psychoses. Moreover, dopamine is important in several cerebral pathways, including the temporal-limbic and frontal areas. However, dopamine's role in schizophrenia is not simple. Dopamine levels do not differ in persons with or without schizophrenia, and the typical antipsychotic medications help only some patients, and they improve positive but not negative symptoms. Furthermore, newer "atypical" antipsychotic medications affect serotonin and other neurotransmitters (Weinberger, 1994). These facts do not suggest that dopamine is unimportant in schizophrenia; rather, they indicate that the complex ways in which neurotransmitters affect one another and their functioning must be taken into account.

Current research on neurotransmitters and on other neurological factors in schizophrenia is extensive (indeed, our discussion is only a brief overview). The findings are promising but also complex, and sometimes even puzzling; they have yet to reveal a coherent portrait of schizophrenia.

ETIOLOGY

The etiology of schizophrenia is thought to involve multiple factors.

Genetic factors. A limited number of studies indicate higher than expected occurrence of schizophrenia or schizophrenia-like disorders in the first-degree relatives of children with schizophrenia (Asarnow & Asarnow, 1996; Jacobsen & Rapoport, 1998). Chromosome abnormalities have been revealed in a few children, but it would be premature to draw conclusions about this work.

However, the general finding of genetic influence is consistent with extensive research conducted in several countries on adult schizophrenia. The risk for adult schizophrenia rises as one's genetic relationship to a schizophrenic person increases (Gottesman, 1993). For example, risk is about 13 percent for children of a schizophrenic parent but only 2 percent for first cousins. (This risks compares with a 1 percent risk in the general population.) Identical twins have greater concordance than fraternal twins (48 percent versus 17 percent), and adoption studies also evidence a role for genetic transmission. Estimates of heritability are high (Cannon et al., 1998). As with autism, the genetic vulnerability may express itself in disorders similar to and less severe than schizophrenia (Cannon et al., 1994).

Researchers are working to determine the gene(s) and mode(s) of genetic transmission. So far there are no conclusive findings. Linkage analyses that have identified several possible chromosomes require follow-up research, since the findings from linkage studies have often failed replication (e.g., Buchanan et al., 1998). Single-gene effects may operate in some instances, but most cases are thought to involve multiple genes. The genetic data are impressive, but they do not tell the entire story. It is noteworthy that identical co-twins of adults with schizophrenia are about as likely not to have schizophrenia as to have it. Thus nonheredity influence apparently is involved in producing adult-onset schizophrenia.

Pregnancy and birth complications. Although prenatal and birth complications have not so far been linked to childhood schizophrenia, they have been linked to the condition in adults (Ohman & Hultman, 1998). Included are variables such as early birth and low birth weight, multiple births, infections, physical trauma, lack of oxygen, and convulsions (Gooding & Iacono, 1995). Structural brain deficits have sometimes been associated with these complications. Particularly interesting findings came from a study of Finnish people who had been exposed prenatally to influenza virus during an epidemic (Mednick et al., 1988). Those exposed during the second trimester of pregnancy but not during other trimesters had a greater risk for eventually developing schizophrenia, suggesting a critical prenatal period. The association of prenatal infections has been shown in other but not all studies.

Research by Cannon (1993) and his colleagues indicates that etiology can be complex. Their results came from high-risk research in which Danish children with schizophrenic parents were followed over several years. Not only were pregnancy/birth complications and genetic risk independently associated with adult-onset schizophrenia in the offspring, but also these variables acted together to contribute to the development of schizophrenia. Furthermore, risk was related to brain abnormalities.

Social and psychological factors. Life events, that is, adverse happenings or demands for change that are stressful, are among the possible environmental influences on adult-onset schizophrenia. Such events increase in the weeks prior to symptoms (Fowles, 1992). Although acute stress is not ruled out as the sole cause of symptoms in some cases, it is more likely that stress interacts with other factors to contribute to etiology. The degree to which stress plays a role in childhood cases is not established.

Family characteristics have long been suspect as causal in schizophrenia. It was early hypothesized that childhood schizophrenia was caused by family factors such as immature mothering and passive fathering, inability of the child to separate from the mother, and reactions to pathological family dynamics (Alanen, 1960; Goldfarb, 1970). Indeed, the phrase "schizophrenogenic mothering" was once used to capture the idea that pathological parenting was the basic cause of the condition. Families with a member diagnosed with schizophrenia were described as having deviant interactions (e.g., Mishler & Waxler, 1965). However, there were difficulties with this early research: replications failed, no one deviant interaction was consistently found, and deviant interaction could be the result, rather than the cause, of having a dysfunctional family member.

Today there is renewed interest in the family. One series of studies has examined communication deviance (CD), which is defined as vague and distorted communication that indicates dysfunction in thinking and attention (Asarnow, 1994). Among the findings is that CD was higher in parents of children with schizophrenia or a related condition than it was in parents of children showing depression or a related condition (Asarnow, Goldstein, & Ben-Meir, 1988). Moreover, in families that had children with schizophrenia, high CD was related to greater impairment in the children. High parental expression of hostility, criticism, and emotional overinvolvement (high EE) also has sometimes been associated with schizophrenia. High EE was linked in one investigation to the eventual diagnosis of schizophrenia (or related disorders) in high-risk adolescents (Valone, Goldstein, & Norton, 1984). In adult-onset schizophrenia, this measure of family environment is correlated with return of symptoms after remission (Butzlaff & Hooley, 1998).

The possible influence of family climate is shown in the Finnish Adoption Study, which followed adopted children of mothers with schizophrenia and a control group (Tienari et al., 1990). Overall, maladjustment of the adoptees was related to disturbed family relationships. Adoptees whose biological mothers had schizophrenia and who themselves were eventually so diagnosed had also been reared in families rated as having disturbed relationships. Moreover, the adopted offspring of schizophrenic parents who had rates of schizophrenia at about the general population rates had experienced healthy rearing environments. This finding suggests that family disturbance played a role in etiology.

The findings from family research is often interpreted as suggesting that vulnerable children who experience certain kinds of family interactions or disturbances are especially stressed and that this combination of variables increases the risk for schizophrenia. Although this view is not unreasonable, we must be cautious about accepting this interpretation (Asarnow & Asarnow, 1996). The research has methodological weaknesses and is not entirely consistent. And other interpretations are reasonable. Perhaps adverse family interactions are shaped by the characteristics of dysfunctional members rather than the other way around. Or family genetic influence might account for some of the findings.

Multifactor models of schizophrenia. Present knowledge about schizophrenia (mostly later-onset) has led to the proposal that etiology involves multiple factors. A diathesis-stress model is often invoked as a general etiological framework. It assumes that an organismic vulnerability or diathesis, probably genetic, interacts with some kind of stress to produce schizophrenia. The stress has its basis in the environment and could include prenatal/birth complications, adverse life events, family dynamics, or other factors, the influence of which could accumulate. The nature of the vulnerability and of the environmental input, as well as the extent to which each influence is involved, might vary and produce somewhat different outcomes.

Neurodevelopmental hypotheses are especially dominant today in accounting for later-onset schizophrenia (Buchanan et al., 1998). The association of prenatal/birth insults and schizophrenia suggests early damage, as do the cognitive, neurological, and social disturbances often shown by individuals prior to diagnosis of schizophrenia. Weinberger (1987; 1994) is among those who believe that a multifactor neurodevelopmental explanation best fits the data. He hypothesizes that early development of the cortex of the brain goes awry. The decreased amount of gray matter and mislocations of neurons in the brain are among the supportive evidence for this idea. The prenatal period of development is implicated, since cells migrate to their normal sites during this time. Brain disturbance, it is hypothesized, causes disorganization in function, which the brain may try to compensate for. In any event, the damage does not manifest itself until the brain further matures and interacts with stress to produce psychotic features. The fact that the prevalence of psychotic behavior increases in adolescence fits well with the fact that the frontal lobe of the brain matures relatively late into adolescence.

It is unclear to what degree current models of schizophrenia apply to onset in childhood. In fact, the relationship of later-onset to child-onset schizophrenia is not firmly established. Nevertheless, evidence appears to be growing for similarity in psychotic symptoms (aside from some development-related differences), neuropsychological deficits, brain abnormalities, and genetic underpinnings. These similarities, in conjunction with the insidious onset and severity of some of the symptoms, have led to the proposal that childhood schizophrenia may be a severe form of later-onset schizophrenia (Jacobsen & Rapoport, 1998).

ASSESSMENT

Broad assessment of a child or an adolescent suspected of schizophrenia is important, possibly requiring several sessions and multiple informants. The following categories have been suggested as a guide for comprehensive assessment (McClellan & Werry, 1994/1997; Volkmar, 1996).

- Historical information, including pregnancy complications, early development, age of onset, medical and family history.

- Assessment for the positive and negative symptoms of schizophrenia, and associated features.

- Psychological assessment, including intelligence, communication, and adaptive skills testing.

- Physical and neurological examinations. EEG, brain scans, and other medical tests are best limited to cases in which medical etiology is suspect (Adams et al., 1996).

- Consultation with the school and social services as necessary.

Concern has been expressed about evaluating the psychological manifestations of childhood schizophrenia. Standardized rating scales and semistructured interviews are helpful—such as the

several versions of the Kiddie-SADS, the Schedule for Affective Disorders and Schizophrenia for School-aged Children (Asarnow, 1994; Kaufman et al., 1997). Nevertheless, the emphasis on psychotic symptoms in diagnosing the disorder in young children is problematic because psychosis tends to occur only after nonpsychotic symptoms.

In addition, it is sometimes difficult to identify true hallucinations and delusions in young children (McKenna, Gordon et al., 1994). Brief hallucinations may be reported but do not necessarily signal schizophrenia. Children may also report distorted perceptions that reflect no more than vivid imaginations that may be difficult to distinguish from true hallucinations. Similarly, it may be especially difficult to tell whether bizarre ideas, obsessions, and preoccupations reported by the young should be considered delusions that indicate schizophrenia. This circumstance is especially true in children younger than five or six years, who are still limited in thinking logically and in distinguishing reality from fantasy (Volkmar et al., 1995).

The identification of thought disorder is also influenced by developmental level. Because language skills are crucial in assessing thought disorder, evaluation might well be affected by the level of these skills. In addition, it is reasonable to assume that what is considered abnormal thinking might vary with development level. In this regard, Caplan's (1994) study of children's thinking is noteworthy. Employing both a standardized scale and an interview that elicited children's responses to stories, she detected that loose associations are rare in normal children past age seven and that illogical thinking decreases. Among the interesting findings is that loose associations may be a particularly strong indicator of childhood schizophrenia.

Assessment of adolescents, especially older adolescents, seems less problematic than that of children. Because psychotic symptoms appear more similar to those observed in adult-onset schizophrenia., assessment scales and procedures for adults are more useful. Nevertheless, psychotic symptoms in adolescents (or adults) do not always indicate full-blown schizophrenia. Studies show that 2 to 30 percent of youth, either at risk or in clinical groups, report hallucinations and delusions that are not severe enough for the diagnosis of schizophrenia (Altman, Collins, & Mundy, 1997).

TREATMENT

As with other aspects of childhood and adolescent schizophrenia, there is a lack of systematic research on treatment; therefore, to some extent we must generalize from what is known about treatment of adults. The treatment of schizophrenia has a long history that somewhat parallels the history of patients with mental retardation. As attitudes changed, so did treatment approaches, which ranged from pessimistic, negligent, and sometimes abusive treatments, to optimistic and kinder interventions. With the advent of antipsychotic medications and the philosophy of normalization, community living increased markedly during the last several decades.

Treatment can vary substantially, depending on the severity of the case, the phase the case is in, opportunity for treatment, community/family support, and the perspective of the therapist. Some severely disturbed youth remain at home and attend special schools; others are placed in hospitals and other residential settings for periods of time. Hospitalization is more likely to occur during the first episode of disturbance (Clark & Lewis, 1998). Early intervention is desirable, since it is associated with fewer symptoms in the immediate future, and the best treatment strategy employs multiple methods to alleviate the multiple problems frequently encountered.

Pharmacological treatment. Although electroconvulsive shock (ECS) therapy was once widely used to treat schizophrenia, at least in adults, its popularity has plummeted. It is rarely used with children and adolescents, because of debatable effectiveness and fear of brain damage from the seizures that it induces (Bertagnoli & Borchardt, 1990; Moise & Petrides, 1996). In the United States, a few states have legally banned the use of ECS with youth. Today, for schizophrenic patients of all ages, the medical treatment of choice is antipsychotic medications that reduce dopamine. In adults such medications can alleviate hallucinations, delusions, thought disturbance, and other symptoms, but they do less to relieve negative symptoms. Limited research shows modest improvement for children and adolescents (McKenna, Gordon, & Rapoport, 1994). However, these medications may be less effective for youth than for adults, and they do have adverse side effects such as dyskinesia and other motor abnormalities.

These weaknesses have led to interest in the newer, atypical antipsychotic drugs. Recent research indicates that risperidone and especially clozapine may be effective for youth (Kumra et al., 1997). These medications, which affect serotonin and dopamine, do not have the side effects of the typical antipsychotics, and they may relieve both positive and negative symptoms. On the other hand, they too have some adverse side effects, and clozapine is associated with seizures and impairment of the immune system. Thus even newer antipsychotic medications, such as olanzapine, are being tested for children (Kumra et al., 1998).

Psychoanalytic treatment. Psychoanalytic therapy has focused on the young person's being dominated by id impulses, having poor ego function, and being unable to separate from the mother. In past times, there was often no distinction made between autism and childhood schizophrenia, so that Bettelheim's approach, for example, was likely used with both syndromes (p. 327). The role of the therapist, depending somewhat on the client's age, is to help the child establish a separate self, interpret the world, distinguish reality from fantasy, develop a sense of mastery, and find more adaptive defenses (Cantor & Kestenbaum, 1986; Ekstein et al., 1972). For adolescents there is a focus on the developmental tasks of this time of life, for example, on identity formation and physical maturation. Regardless of age, an intense, warm, and trusting relationship is critical. This approach has its advocates but has been deemphasized in recent years (King & Noshpitz, 1991).

Behavioral treatment. Operant and cognitive-behavioral methods are the dominant behavioral techniques for treating later-onset schizophrenia.

Operant treatment has been employed for many years in hospitals and other institutions, especially to encourage self-care and other daily living habits. The underlying aim is to help maintain clients as active agents in their own lives and to facilitate their leaving hospitals for less restrictive environments. Interventions often meet these goals. Now that most individuals with schizophrenia are living in the community for long periods of time, the behavioral approach is applied in many different settings and is often a component of family interventions.

Both maladaptive, bizarre behaviors that interfere with functioning and adaptive behaviors are targeted. Thus, for example, psychotic behavior may be ignored while social interaction skills are modeled and reinforced. Indeed, enhancement of social skills has been targeted with some success, although learned skills may weaken over time (e.g., Bellack & Mueser, 1993).

Family approaches. It is generally recognized that appropriate family involvement and support is critical to clients and that family members themselves can benefit from counseling and training. Family treatment, therefore, is a popular approach. The intervention of Falloon and his colleagues is particularly interesting. Their aim was to reduce levels of expressed emotion—of hostile emotional involvement—because high EE has been correlated with high rates of relapse (Falloon et al., 1985, cited in Davison and Neale, 1998). Families were informed of the biological nature of schizophrenia and of the importance of compliance with medication treatment. In the home, they were provided with behavioral and cognitive training on how best to express feelings and on how to solve problems. Comparison with a control group receiving individual psychotherapy indicated that this family intervention was beneficial.

It is clear that a comprehensive approach and a generally supportive environment are needed in treating later-onset schizophrenia. For example, a recent meta-analysis indicates that the combination of pharmacotherapy and psychosocial treatments is more effective than only medications (Mojtabai, Nicholson, & Carpenter, 1998). Medication, behavioral intervention, family therapy, individual therapy, the teaching of specific academic or developmental skills, and occupational considerations need to be considered. Support is crucial across different phases of schizophrenia, not just during the acute phase, although treatment components may certainly vary with the specific phase. Less obvious, however, is optimal treatment for children with schizophrenia. Medications are somewhat effective, and it is likely that other components of adult treatments apply well to young people. However, research on the treatment of children is especially needed.

SUMMARY

■ Severe childhood disorders similar to adult psychoses have been difficult to conceptualize and classify. Autism is now recognized as a nonpsychotic pervasive developmental disorder that is independent of the psychotic disorder of schizophrenia.

■ Autism is diagnosed by impaired social interaction, impaired communication, and restricted preoccupations and stereotyped behaviors. DSM-IV diagnosis requires the occurrence of symptoms by age three. In addition to varied manifestations of its primary symptoms, at least 75 percent of cases show mental retardation, with deficits in perception, abstraction, information processing, and theory of mind.

■ Autism is rare, occurs more in boys than girls, and is unrelated to social class.

■ Inadequate parenting was once viewed as central in autism, but efforts have more recently focused on the psychological deficits and neurological abnormalities of autism. Deficits in social-affective functions, theory of mind, executive functions, and central coherence are among the psychological deficits considered central in autism. No one of these deficits completely accounts for all autistic symptoms, however.

■ Considerable evidence exists for neurological abnormalities: soft neurological signs, large head circumference, brain abnormalities, an association with epilepsy and abnormal EEGs, and high blood levels of serotonin. It is most likely that autism involves multiple brain areas or systems.

■ In autism, genetic etiology is heavily weighted today; different modes of transmission are possible, as well as genetic heterogeniety. Associated medical conditions and prenatal/birth complications may play some causal role.

■ The developmental course of autism appears variable, with cases showing both improvement and deterioration. Thirty percent of cases may deteriorate in adolescence. Outcome is often unfavorable and is best predicted by early intelligence and language development. Some individuals do lead reasonably successful lives.

■ No formal subgrouping exists for autism, although higher and lower functioning is informally recognized. Current study of other pervasive developmental disorders is of considerable interest today.

■ Comprehensive assessment methods are useful in autism, including social, behavioral, intellectual, and medical evaluations. Useful rating scales, checklists, and interviews are available. Behavior and skill analysis is especially helpful for guiding intervention. Family assessment has taken on greater importance as families increasingly are therapeutic agents.

■ Phamacological treatment is an adjunct to behavioral/educational approaches. Progress in behavior modification is notable; the comprehensive UCLA Project reports some of the most favorable outcomes. TEACCH, which has several components, is employed in the educational system in North Carolina and elsewhere. Children with autism are entitled to services under the Individuals with Disabilities Educational Act.

■ Schizophrenia in childhood and adolescence is diagnosed with the same criteria used for adults. The hallmarks are hallucinations, delusions, and thought disorder. These are referred to as positive symptoms, along with disor-

ganized behavior and catatonia. The negative symptoms are a lack of typical behaviors, such as minimal emotional response and speech. Associated abnormalities have also been noted in motor behavior, language, cognition, and social behavior.

■ The prevalence of schizophrenia is extremely small in early childhood, increases somewhat in middle childhood, and escalates notably in adolescence. Prevalence may be higher in males and in lower social class families.

■ In children, onset of schizophrenia appears more insidious than it does for older persons, and nonpsychotic symptoms occur before psychotic symptoms. Hallucinations and delusions show developmental change. The course of schizophrenia varies, but outcome is often unfavorable. Good adjustment prior to onset and acute onset predict better outcome.

■ Neurological abnormalities in schizophrenia are evidenced in many ways, for example, in neurological soft signs, structural abnormalities of the temporal-limbic and frontal brain areas, and deficits in attention and memory. Genetic influence, pregnancy/birth variables, and psychosocial factors are implicated in later-onset etiology. Multifactor explanations, including neurodevelopmental models, are suggested. Relatively less is understood about childhood schizophrenia, but evidence is accumulating that it is a severe form of the later-onset condition.

■ As with autism, comprehensive assessment is ideal. Identifying psychotic symptoms in childhood can be problematic.

■ Guidelines for intervention for schizophrenia are largely based on treatment of later-onset cases, although research shows that the antipsychotic medications can reduce positive symptoms in children. A multimethod approach is recommended, and intervention would be expected to vary somewhat, depending on the specific case and its phase.

CHAPTER 13

DISORDERS OF BASIC PHYSICAL FUNCTIONS

Problems of physical functioning and health are discussed in this chapter and the next. In many ways, these problems represent the interface between psychology and pediatrics. The term "pediatric psychology" is often applied to this field of research and practice. For many of the problems discussed, parents first turn to their pediatrician for help (Roberts & Lyman, 1990). For example, early problems with the feeding of infants and toddlers, starting and managing toilet training, and difficulties in getting children to sleep are among the problems brought to pediatricians (Gross & Drabman, 1990). Also, the problems discussed here involve issues of physical functioning that require collaboration between psychologists and physicians. The life-threatening starvation of anorexic adolescents and the problem of enlarged colons in encopretic children are two examples.

It is common for children to exhibit some difficulty in acquiring appropriate habits of eating, elimination, and sleep. Both the child's ability to master these relevant tasks and the parents' ability to train the child are important to the immediate well-being of both. Parents and others may judge their adequacy as parents by how they manage these early child-rearing tasks. Also, how these tasks are handled can set the foundation for later difficulties. Problems may occur in the same area (for example, the later eating disorder of anorexia nervosa) or in more general ways (for example, problems with authority figures). Although parents solve many early difficulties themselves, professional assistance is also frequently sought (Schroeder & Gordon, 1991). In this chapter, attention is given to some commonly encountered difficulties that are part of normal development. The principal focus, however, is on problems that are serious enough to make them of clinical concern.

DISORDERS OF EATING

A wide range of problems having to do with eating and feeding are commonly reported (Budd & Chugh, 1998; Hertzler, 1983a,b). These include

359

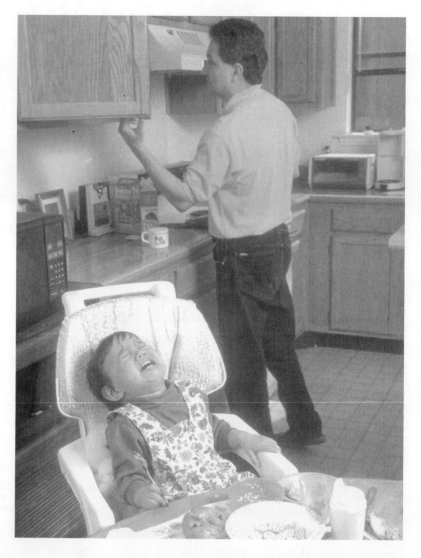

Young children often exhibit feeding and eating problems. This difficulty may result in disruption and cause their parents considerable distress.

(B. Daemmrich/The Image Works)

undereating, finicky eating, overeating, problems in chewing and swallowing, bizarre eating habits, annoying mealtime behaviors, and delays in self-feeding. Many of these problems can cause considerable concern for parents and appreciable disruption of family life. For example, O'Brien (1996) found that approximately 30 percent of a sample of parents of infants and toddlers reported that their children refuse to eat the foods presented to them. Adequate nutrition and growth are clearly a concern, but restricted eating is also often accompanied by other behavioral problems such as tantrums, spitting, and gagging. Severe cases of food refusal may be associated with even more difficult social and psychological problems and may result in medical complaints and malnourishment. Indeed, some cases of failure to thrive (life-threatening weight loss or failure to gain weight) can be conceptualized as a special case of such refusal (Kelly & Heffer, 1990; Kerwin & Berkowitz, 1996). Thus some eating problems may actually endanger the physical health of the child. The clinical disorders discussed in the following sections are some that have attracted attention from researchers and clinicians.

RUMINATION

Rumination (or mercyism), first described in 1687, is a syndrome with a long history (Kanner, 1972). It is characterized by the voluntary and repeated regurgitation of food or liquid in the absence of an organic cause. When infants ruminate, they appear deliberately to initiate regurgitation. The child's head is thrown back, and chewing and swallowing movements are made until food is brought up. In many instances, the child initiates rumination by placing his or her fingers down the throat or by chewing on objects. The child exhibits little distress; rather, pleasure appears to result from the activity. If rumination continues, serious medical complications can result, with death being the outcome in extreme cases (American Psychiatric Association, 1994).

Rumination is most often observed in two groups, infants and individuals who are diagnosed as mentally retarded. Among children who are developmentally normal, rumination usually appears during the first year of life. In mentally retarded individuals, a later onset is often observed, and the incidence of the disorder seems to increase with greater degrees of mental retardation. In both groups, rumination appears to be more prevalent in males (Kerwin & Berkowitz, 1996; Mayes, 1992).

Etiology and treatment. Rumination in infants is often attributed to a disturbance in the mother-infant relationship (Mayes, 1992). The mother is described either as having psychological difficulties of her own that prevent her from providing the infant with a nurturant relationship or as experiencing significant life stress that interferes with her ability to attend to the infant. Rumination is sometimes seen as the infant's attempt to provide this missing gratification. Alternatively, others view the act as habitual in nature. The pattern may start, for example, with the normal occurrence of spitting up by the infant. The behaviors may then be reinforced by a combination of pleasurable self-stimulation and the increased attention from

adults that follows (e.g., Kanner, 1972; Linscheid, 1978). It is possible to integrate these various explanations by hypothesizing that the learning of rumination may be more likely in circumstances in which the mother does not provide adequate stimulation and attention. Rumination among individuals diagnosed as mentally retarded is commonly viewed as a learned habit.

A wide variety of treatments have been suggested for rumination (Mayes, 1992). Satiation and aversive procedures have been employed with mentally retarded individuals. In satiation procedures, the individual is fed large quantities of food, often three to six times normal meal portions. Aversive procedures most often involve the administration of unpleasant-tasting substances or a mild shock contingent on the child's initiating the behaviors that lead to rumination. Since both professionals and parents are particularly reluctant to apply aversive procedures to infants, they prefer to find nonaversive alternatives. Treatments emphasizing contingent use of social attention have been successful, and there is some suggestion that with infant ruminators, noncontingent stimulation and attention are also effective (Mayes, 1992). These procedures have the advantage of being easily implemented by the parents in the home and of being acceptable to them. However, sufficiently controlled evaluations of interventions, particularly with infants, are lacking.

PICA

"Pica" is the Latin term for magpie, a bird known for the diversity of objects that it eats. This disorder is characterized by the habitual eating of substances usually considered inedible, such as paint, dirt, paper, fabric, hair, and bugs.

During the first year of life, most infants put a variety of objects into their mouths, partly as a way of exploring the environment. Within the next year, they typically learn to explore in other ways and thus come to discriminate between edible and inedible materials. The diagnosis of pica is therefore usually made when there is a persistent eating of inedibles beyond this age, and pica is most common in two- and three-year-olds.

Information regarding the prevalence of pica is limited but is reported to be particularly high among mentally retarded individuals (e.g., McAlpine & Singh, 1986). Pica can lead to a variety of damage, including parasitic infection and intestinal obstruction due to the accumulation of hair and other materials. Also, pica appears to be related to accidental poisoning (American Psychiatric Association, 1994; Halmi, 1985).

Etiology and treatment. A number of causes for pica have been postulated (Kerwin & Berkowitz, 1996). Because youngsters have been observed eating strange substances when food is unavailable, it has been proposed that pica is an attempt to satisfy nutritional deficits. Parental inattention, lack of supervision, and lack of adequate stimulation have also been proposed. Several findings suggest cultural influences.

Millican and Lourie (1970) found, for the black children whom they studied, that most of the families had migrated from the southeastern United States, where eating of earth containing clay and laundry starch is a frequent custom among pregnant women. Certain superstitions are reported to govern this behavior. An interesting observation is that the mothers of children with pica were found to have a higher frequency of the behavior than mothers of children without pica. And young black children, who might be strongly affected by cultural acceptance of pica, exhibited a lower rate of psychological difficulties than did older children and white children displaying pica.

Educational approaches aimed at informing mothers of the dangers of pica and at encouraging them to discourage the behavior may be somewhat successful. However, there is the need to supplement such interventions with more intensive therapeutic endeavors in some cases. Behavioral interventions that address antecedents and consequences of pica behavior have been suggested (Bell & Stein, 1992). Interventions vary from less intrusive procedures, such as reinforcement of behaviors incompatible with pica, to more intrusive aversive procedures, such as contingent squirts of water to the child's face and restraining the child. These procedures are often combined with rein-

forcement for appropriate behavior and increased attention to the child. In general, less intrusive procedures should be attempted prior to employing more aversive interventions.

OBESITY

Sean, a ten-year-old, who was 50 percent overweight for his height and age, enrolled in a treatment program for obese children and their families. Sean's pediatrician described a history of steady, greater than expected weight gains with extreme increases in the last three years. Sean's father was normal weight, but his mother was about 40 percent overweight and had made numerous unsuccessful weight-loss attempts. Neither of Sean's two siblings was overweight. Sean snacked frequently on large amounts of high-calorie food, with most of his calories consumed after school while his parents were at work. His mother often found candy wrappers in Sean's room and clothes' pockets. Sean's parents reported that as Sean gained weight, his physical activity had decreased and most of his leisure time was spent watching television. They were concerned with his frequent shortness of breath. Sean had no close friends and was something of a loner. He was teased about his weight at school and by his siblings. Although the parents indicated that they were committed to Sean's losing weight, there were indications of some family "sabotage." Much of the family's activities revolved around food, and food was used as a reward. Sean's father described himself as a gourmet cook, and his high-calorie, high-fat meals were "family times." Sean spent considerable time at his grandmother's, who took pleasure in providing him with food and snacks. (Adapted from Israel & Solotar, 1988)

Obesity is an important health problem and is among the most prevalent nutritional diseases in children and adolescents. Several aspects of the prevalence data point to obesity as a significant health problem. Prevalence increases with age (Aristimuno et al., 1984; Garn & Clark, 1976; Huse et al., 1982), and with age there is also an increase in the percentage of obese children who will become obese adults (Garn et al., 1986; Rolland-Cachera et al., 1987). What is perhaps most striking are reports that indicate that the prevalence of childhood obesity is increasing (Campaigne et al., 1994; Gortmaker et al., 1987). Dietz (1988), comparing national health survey data over a fifteen-year period beginning in the mid-1960s, found that the prevalence of obesity increased 54 percent among six- to eleven-year-old children and 39 percent among twelve- to seventeen-year-old adolescents.

Obesity in childhood is associated with numerous physical health problems, particularly those related to risk of heart disease (Aristimuno et al., 1984; Dietz, 1995). In addition, there are associations with social and psychological difficulties (e.g., Melbin & Vuille, 1989; Pierce & Wardle, 1993). Indeed, a National Institutes of Health panel concluded that "obesity creates an enormous psychological burden. In fact, in terms of suffering, this burden may be the greatest adverse effect of obesity" (NIH, 1985, p. 4).

An example of research illustrating the psychological problems associated with obesity is a study by Israel and Shapiro (1985). Parents of overweight children who were enrolled in a weight-loss program completed Achenbach's Child Behavior Checklist prior to treatment. The behavior problem scores of these children were significantly higher than the norms for the general population. However, they were significantly lower than the norms for children referred to clinics for psychological services. These findings are illustrated in Figure 13-1. Thus it would appear that overweight

children attending a weight-loss program experience psychological difficulties to a greater extent than do members of the general population but that the overweight children's problems are not as severe in most areas as those exhibited by children receiving psychological assistance for other behavioral problems. Clearly, it cannot be determined from this study whether these problems contribute to or result from being overweight.

The obese child's social interactions may be adversely affected by negative evaluations. Because children hold negative views of obesity, those children who are perceived as overweight are ranked as less liked. Children who are as young as six describe silhouettes of an obese child as "lazy," "stupid," "cheats." Furthermore, the reduction of activity and dexterity that often accompanies obesity makes social isolation and rejection even more likely. These effects appear to continue throughout development. College acceptance rates were lower for obese adolescent girls than for nonobese girls with comparable academic credentials (Dietz, 1995; Stunkard & Sobel, 1995).

The etiology of obesity. The causes of obesity are certainly multiple and complex. Any explanation must include biological, psychological, and social/cultural influences (Krasnegor, Grave, & Kretchmer, 1988; Leibel & Hirsch, 1995).

Biological influences include genetic factors (Price, 1995; Siervogel, 1988) and the metabolic effects of dieting and exercise (Dietz, 1988; Saris, 1995). An example of a potential mechanism is provided by the finding of leptin deficiencies in severely obese children (Montague et al., 1997). Leptin is a protein that is believed to be involved in signaling the brain to end eating; also, a gene identified in mice appears to control the production of leptin. However, genetic contributions themselves are likely to be complex rather than simple. Of course, biological influences are not independent of environmental influences; rather, these influences interact.

The influence of psychosocial factors on the development of obesity is acknowledged by most major workers in the field. Both logic and research suggest that obese children have food in-

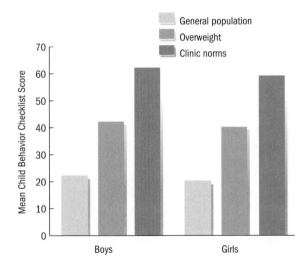

FIGURE 13-1 Mean total behavior problem scores for general population norms, overweight children, and clinic norms.
Adapted from Israel and Shapiro, 1985.

take and activity behaviors that are in need of change (Klesges & Hanson, 1988; Schlicker, Borra, & Regan, 1994). Problematic food intake and inactivity are presumed to be affected by environmental influences and to be learned in the same manner as any other behavior. Children, for example, observe and imitate the eating behavior of their parents and others around them and are reinforced for engaging in that style of eating (Klesges & Hanson, 1988). Eating and inactivity may also become strongly associated with physical and social stimuli, so that they become almost automatic in some circumstances. Moreover, people may learn to use food to overcome stress and negative mood states, such as boredom and anxiety. The treatment of obesity that has been developed from a social learning perspective seeks to break these learned patterns and to develop more adaptive ones.

Society's view of obesity is an important cultural influence. Television provides a striking example of how the larger society might contribute to the development of weight problems in children. American children watch a great deal of television, on average about two to three hours each day (Scarr, Weinberg, & Levine, 1986). In addition to the negative effects of inactivity associated with television watching, children's diets are probably adversely influenced (Jeffrey et al., 1979). Indeed, a significant association between time spent watching television and the prevalence of obesity has been reported (Dietz & Gortmaker, 1985).

Behavioral treatment. Multifaceted programs that emphasize behavioral interventions and education have been the most effective treatments for childhood obesity. The work of Israel and his colleagues (Israel & Solotar, 1988; Israel et al., 1994) illustrates the general approach. Children and parents attend meetings during which the following four areas are regularly addressed: intake, which includes nutritional information, caloric restriction, and changes in actual eating and food preparation behaviors; activity, which includes both specific exercise programs and increasing the energy expended in daily activities, for example, walking to a friend's house rather than being dri-

ven; cues, which identify the external and internal stimuli associated with excessive eating or inactivity; and rewards, which provide positive consequences for progress by both the child and the parent. Homework assignments are employed to encourage the families to change their environments and to practice more appropriate behavior.

Research supports the effectiveness of the behavioral approach to children's weight reduction (Epstein et al., 1995; Israel, 1990; Israel & Zimand, 1989). However, there is still a need for improved interventions that produce greater, more consistent, and more long-lasting weight loss. The importance of certain treatment components, including parental involvement, have been emphasized. Israel, Stolmaker, and Andrian (1985), for example, provided parents with a brief course in the general principles of child management. The parents then participated with their children in a behavioral weight-reduction program during which the application of the general parenting skills to weight reduction was emphasized. Another group of parents and children received only the behavioral weight-reduction program. At the end of treatment, both groups achieved a significantly greater weight loss than the control children who were not receiving treatment. One year following treatment, children whose parents had received separate child-management training had maintained their weight losses better than other treated children.

These results and others suggest the importance of changing family lifestyles and of providing parents with the skills necessary to maintain appropriate behavior once the treatment program has ended (Israel, 1988). This is a particularly important issue in light of repeated evidence that individuals frequently regain the weight they have lost. In addition to parental involvement, the importance of increased activity, particularly when it is part of the family's lifestyle, and various other family factors have been shown to be related to treatment outcome (Foreyt & Goodrick, 1993; Israel, Silverman, & Solotar, 1986).

Parallel to the need to improve parental involvement, the value of enhancing the child's self-regulatory skills has also been suggested (Israel et al., 1994). Children receiving a multidimensional treatment program, comparable to the four-area program described earlier, were compared with children receiving a similar intervention plus enhanced training in comprehensive self-management skills. The results of this study are presented in Figure 13-2. In the three years prior to treatment, children in the two conditions had shown comparable patterns of increasing percentage of overweight. Both treatment conditions resulted in comparable reductions in the percentage of overweight during treatment. However, whereas children in the standard condition appeared to return to pretreatment trends in the three years following treatment, children in the enhanced self-regulation condition did not.

ANOREXIA NERVOSA AND BULIMIA NERVOSA

Anorexia nervosa and bulimia nervosa are eating disorders that involve maladaptive attempts to control body weight, significant disturbances in eating behavior, and abnormal attitudes about body shape and weight. Until relatively recently these disorders were considered quite rare. The number of cases reported, as well as the "subclinical" levels of these problems, has increased (Lucas & Holub, 1995; Phelps et al., 1993). This increase may be due to actual increases in eating disorders and/or to greater awareness and reporting of these problems. Revelations of anorexic and bulimic behavior among celebrities such as Karen Carpenter, Jane Fonda, and Princess Diana also increased popular interest.

There has been considerable debate regarding the best way to define eating disorders and the degree to which disorders overlap. When distinctions between eating disorders are considered or when attempts to subcategorize a particular disorder are made, several dimensions are usually considered. An individual's weight status is one such consideration. A person with an eating disorder may be underweight, within the normal weight range, or overweight.

A second consideration is whether the individual engages in binge-eating. A binge is usually defined by a person's (1) eating a larger amount of food during a discrete period of time (e.g., one

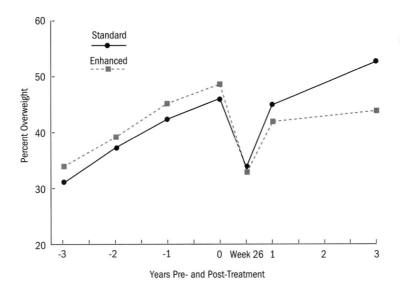

FIGURE 13-2 Mean percentage overweight from three years prior to treatment through three years following treatment.

From Israel, Grule, Baker, & Silverman, 1994.

Grammy award singer Karen Carpenter, who died at age thirty-two of heart failure, had suffered from the effects of anorexia nervosa for many years.

(Schiffman/Gamma-Liaison)

Description and diagnosis. Weight status, the presence or absence of binge-eating, and the method employed to control one's weight, therefore, are important considerations in thinking about eating disorders. We turn now to how these dimensions are involved in describing eating disorders.

Anorexia Nervosa Those individuals with eating disorders whose body weight is well below expected levels (15 percent below or more) are likely to be given the diagnosis of Anorexia Nervosa (AN). A drive for extreme thinness and a fear of gaining weight are characteristics of individuals with this diagnosis. Anorexia Nervosa is a serious disorder, and a substantial proportion of young women with the disorder have poor outcomes (Steinhausen, 1997). The extremeness of weight loss in AN can lead to significant medical complications (e.g., anemia, hormonal changes, cardiovascular problems, dental problems), and although there is no predictable long-term course for Anorexia Nervosa, the disorder may be life-threatening. It has been reported that over 10 percent of cases end in death, half of which may result from suicide (American Psychiatric Association, 1994; Pike, 1998; Steiner & Lock, 1998). The seriousness of this extreme weight loss is also illustrated by Bruch's (1979) classic description of one of her clients:

... she looked like a walking skeleton, with her legs sticking out like broomsticks, every rib showing, and her shoulder blades standing up like little wings. Her mother mentioned, "When I put my arms around her I feel nothing but bones, like a frightened little bird." Alma's arms and legs were covered with soft hair, her complexion had a yellowish tint, and her dry hair hung down in strings. Most striking was the face—hollow like that of a shriveled-up old woman with a wasting disease, ... Alma insisted that she looked fine and that there was nothing wrong with her being so skinny. "I enjoy having this disease and I want it." (pp. 2–3)

The criteria employed to diagnose Anorexia Nervosa are presented in Table 13-1. The criterion of less than 85 percent of expected weight can be the result of the youngster's refusal to gain weight or if the youngster is still growing, the failure to gain enough weight to meet the 85 percent crite-

hour) than most people would be expected to eat during that time and (2) feeling that he or she lacks control of eating during this episode (Fairburn & Wilson, 1993).

A third consideration is the method that the person uses to control her or his weight. A distinction is often made between restricting and purging strategies. The first strategy refers to a person's severely restricting food intake and/or engaging in highly vigorous exercise. The second strategy involves purging oneself of unwanted calories through methods such as vomiting or the misuse of laxatives, diuretics, or enemas.

TABLE 13-1
Criteria Used by DSM-IV to Diagnose Anorexia Nervosa
1. Body weight less than 85 percent of expected weight
2. Intense fear of gaining weight
3. Disturbance in perception of body weight and shape or denial of seriousness of low body weight
4. Absence of three consecutive menstrual cycles in post-menarcheal females

TABLE 13-2
Criteria Used by DSM-IV to Diagnose Bulimia Nervosa
1. Recurrent episodes of binge-eating
2. Recurrent inappropriate compensatory behavior to prevent weight gain
3. Occurrence of items 1 and 2 at least twice a week for three months
4. Self-evaluation unduly influenced by body shape and weight

rion. Other definitions of the disorder also include the characteristics of low body weight, fear of weight gain, and disturbance in body perception in their description of the disorder. However, some definitions have stressed that psychological variables, such as a sense of personal inadequacy, are central to defining the disorder (Bruch, 1973; 1986; Yates, 1989).

DSM-IV distinguishes between two subtypes of AN. This distinction is based on whether or not the person binges. Binge-eating/purging anorexics exhibit a persistent pattern of binge-eating and purging. In contrast, restricting anorexics achieve their weight loss by fasting and/or exercise and do not binge-eat. These subgroups have been found in large clinical samples, and the two groups are reported to differ on a number of individual and family characteristics (DaCosta & Halmi, 1992; Humphrey, 1989; Strober & Humphrey, 1987).

Bulimia Nervosa In contrast to Anorexia Nervosa, those individuals with eating disorders whose body weight is not below expected levels are likely to be given the diagnosis of Bulimia Nervosa (BN). In general, BN is characterized by recurrent binge-eating. A persistent overconcern with body shape and weight is also exhibited. This of course means that the bulimic individual needs to employ some method of compensating for eating binges. The most frequently cited method is purging by vomiting or the use of laxatives.

The DSM-IV criteria used to diagnose Bulimia Nervosa are presented in Table 13-2. In order to receive this diagnosis, the symptoms must not occur exclusively during episodes of Anorexia Nervosa—a person who displayed these symptoms as part of anorexia nervosa would not receive both diagnoses.

The issue of subtyping has also arisen in diagnosing BN. The principle consideration is whether or not purging is employed to compensate for binge-eating. Thus there are two subtypes of Bulimia Nervosa in DSM-IV: a purging type in which the person regularly induces vomiting or misuses laxatives, diuretics or enemas; and a nonpurging type in which the person fasts and/or exercises excessively but does not regularly purge.

One of the issues that is faced in diagnosing bulimia as a disorder is the high frequency of bulimic behavior reported in the general population of late adolescents and young adults and the high prevalence of concern about body shape and weight among females. These statistics and the relative newness of bulimia as a diagnosable disorder make it difficult to estimate the real incidence of the disorder.

DSM-IV also includes a category of "Eating Disorder Not Otherwise Specified." This diagnosis may be applied to individuals with mild eating disorders that would not meet the criteria for either AN or BN.

Prevalence. Eating disorders typically begin in late adolescence or early adulthood, and thus prevalence estimates, ranging from approximately 1 to 4 percent, are largely based on samples that combine adolescents and young adults (American Psychiatric Association, 1993; 1994). These disorders occur predominantly in young women, and young white women from middle- to upper-class backgrounds appear to be at greatest risk (Connors, 1996). Females represent over 90 percent of all cases. Anorexia Nervosa is reported to occur in 0.5 to 1.0 percent of females in this age group. Although the average age of onset is late adolescence, there may be peaks at ages fourteen and eighteen. Cases of earlier onset are rare but do exist (Gowers et al., 1991; Lask & Bryant-Waugh, 1992). Bulimia Nervosa is more commonly diagnosed, occurring in 1 to 3 percent of adolescent and young adult females. Lewinsohn et al. (1993) reported a lifetime prevalence rate of approximately 1 to 1.5 percent in a random sample of high school females, and this finding seems consistent with other estimates of prevalence in the general population of adolescent females (Wilson, Heffernan, & Black, 1996). The rate of occurrence in males is about one-tenth that in females.

These numbers may actually underestimate the prevalence of eating disorders, because individuals with these disorders may be overrepresented among those who do not cooperate with prevalence studies (Wilson et al., 1996). Perhaps of more importance, the stated prevalence rates are based on individuals' meeting full diagnostic criteria for AN or BN. There are many other individuals who exhibit various aspects of disordered eating and disturbances of body image. Of these individuals, many may meet the criteria for an "Eating Disorder Not Otherwise Specified," and this diagnosis may be more common than AN or BN in youngsters (Steiner & Lock, 1998). These cases are also sometimes described as "subclinical." However, they may still be of concern, given the widely held view that eating disorders are the extreme of a continuum that begins with more "normative" weight concern, body dissatisfaction, and dieting (Shisslak, Crago, & Estes, 1995). Furthermore, extreme dieting in adolescent girls may itself be associated with high levels of anxiety and depression (Patton et al., 1997). Of particular interest is the finding that these concerns with weight and shape and unusual eating behaviors are increasingly common among younger adolescents and even preadolescent girls.

Thus although eating disorders that meet full diagnostic criteria typically occur in late adolescence, disordered eating behaviors and attitudes are appearing in younger children and at an increasing rate. These problems may be possible precursors of more serious eating disorders.

There is some suggestion that by the fourth grade, girls are worried about being or becoming overweight and desire to become thinner. Mellin, Irwin, and Scully (1992), for example, found that approximately 31 percent of nine-year-old girls reported a fear of fatness and that approximately 46 percent of them reported restrained eating/dieting. In ten-year-olds, approximately 55 percent reported fear of fatness, and 81 percent reported restrained eating/dieting. In this sample of girls aged nine to eighteen, distortion of body image peaked (38 percent) at age eleven. Fifty-eight percent perceived themselves to be overweight, whereas only 15 percent were overweight by objective standards. Such concerns seem more prevalent in girls even at this young age. Thelen et al. (1992), for example, report no gender differences for second-graders. However, although there was no increase in concerns for boys, fourth- and sixth-grade girls were more concerned than second-graders with becoming overweight and were dissatisfied with their body image. Also, Shapiro, Newcomb, and Loeb (1997) found that youngsters in the third grade were afraid of becoming fat and that particularly for girls, wished they were thinner. Evidence also suggests that extreme weight concern in these young girls is predictive of the emergence of eating disorder symptoms and diagnoses (Killen et al., 1994b).

Among middle-school children, these problems remain prevalent, and more extreme weight control behaviors seem to be employed by an appreciable number of children. Gender differences also remain. The information in Table 13-3 (adapted from Childress et al., 1993) is based on a survey of the responses of over three thousand children in grades five to eight to the Kids' Eating Disorders Survey (KEDS). The percentage of youngsters endorsing these items illustrates the prevalence of these problems as well as gender differences.

TABLE 13-3

Percentage of Girls and Boys Endorsing Eating Disorder Items

KEDS Items	Percent Endorsing	
	Girls	Boys
Felt looked fat*	54.4	27.8
Was afraid of weight gain*	32.5	13.0
Dieted*	42.6	19.7
Fasted*	11.2	6.0
Vomited to lose weight	5.6	3.9
Used diet pills*	3.6	1.1
Used diuretics	2.2	0.8
Binged*	6.5	26.3

* Indicates a significant gender difference.

Adapted from Childress et al., 1993.

The prevalence of these problems seems to have increased over time. In 1984, 1989, and 1992, Phelps and colleagues (1993) surveyed all female students enrolled in middle school and high-school in a suburban school district. The rates of specific weight-control procedures employed by high school girls did not exhibit significant change over time or even decreased (e.g., use of diet pills). However, the percentage of middle-school girls using diet pills increased over time (0.8 percent, 1.7 percent, and 6.1 percent, respectively). There was a similar pattern over time for the percentage of middle-school girls deliberately vomiting in an effort to lose weight (3.8 percent, 3.3 percent, and 11.4 percent, respectively).

The presence and perhaps increase of problematic eating behaviors and attitudes in young girls poses a risk for the development of diagnosable eating disorders. In addition, these eating behaviors and attitudes appear to be associated with greater depression, lowered self-esteem, and feelings of inadequacy and personal worthlessness (e.g., Killen et al., 1994a; Lewinsohn et al., 1993). Indeed, such feelings may, in turn, lead to increased concern with weight and shape among girls who already place great personal value on these physical attributes (Cohen-Tovee, 1993).

Etiology. A variety of causal mechanisms have been proposed to explain the development of eating disorders. However, no definitive explanation exists. Indeed, it is not necessary to presume that there is a single causal explanation. It may be that these problems result from a variety of different patterns of causal factors. Furthermore, it is most likely that both AN and BN are multiply determined disorders—that is, no single cause is sufficient to explain their development (Bryant-Waugh & Lask, 1995; Williamson, Bentz, & Rabalais, 1998). Indeed, most current explanations incorporate multiple influences into conceptualizations of how eating disorders may develop. What are some of the influences that have been considered?

Clinical reports mention early feeding difficulties, and there is some support for this position. For example, Marchi and Cohen (1990) longitudinally traced maladaptive eating patterns in a group of children ages one to ten, over a ten-year span. Their findings suggested that early childhood pica was a risk factor and that picky eating was a protective factor for bulimic symptoms in adolescence. On the other hand, picky eating and digestive problems in early childhood were risk factors for elevated symptoms of Anorexia Nervosa in adolescence. Certainly, more research is needed to clarify the relationship between early eating/feeding difficulties and later eating disorders. It is not clear that early eating problems are more frequent in children who later develop eating disorders.

A frequently considered influence is the impact of previous weight history. Did a genuine history of overweight exist prior to the onset of eating disorder symptoms? There is much debate about the idea that the self-starvation that is characteristic of anorexia begins as an attempt to control genuine obesity. For the anorexic, for example, comments that the young girl is "getting plump" may stimulate normal dieting, which evolves into anorexic refusal to eat. The role of a history of being overweight in the development of Anorexia Nervosa remains unclear, and the frequency of dieting among adolescent girls raises the question of why some girls who begin this common social ritual persist well beyond the point of socially desired slimness.

Similar considerations have been discussed regarding bulimia, and there does seem to be evidence that supports the role of a personal and family history of overweight as a risk factor for the development of Bulimia Nervosa (Wilson et al., 1996). Thus the young woman who becomes bulimic may have been somewhat overweight. Her problematic behaviors may have begun as more typical attempts to reduce her weight. In this context, bulimia has been viewed in several ways. These explanations, rather than being conflicting, stress different aspects of a multifaceted cognitive-behavioral approach (Wilson & Fairburn, 1993). One explanation hypothesized is that bulimic behavior develops as a faulty weight-control method among individuals who have had poor self-control patterns modeled for them (Orleans & Barnett, 1984). Another view describes individuals who have abnormal attitudes and beliefs about weight regulation, who evaluate their self-worth in terms of their body shape, and who thus become preoccupied with weight control (Fairburn, 1985).

Research by Fairburn and his colleagues (Fairburn et al., 1997) is consistent with this view. Three groups of participants were recruited from a community sample: a group with Bulimia Nervosa, a group with other disorders (depression and anxiety), and a group of healthy controls. The groups were compared on a number of putative risk factors for bulimia nervosa. Whereas participants with Bulimia Nervosa experienced a significantly greater exposure to most risk factors as compared with healthy controls, there were very few differences in risk exposure for the bulimia group as compared with the participants with other disorders. A history of childhood obesity and negative self-evaluation were two of the risk factors to which the Bulimia Nervosa group experienced greater exposure; therefore, these factors would appear to increase the risk for developing the specific disorder of Bulimia Nervosa.

Research by Killen and his colleagues (1996) also supports the notion that extreme weight concerns contribute to the development of eating disorders. A community sample of high-school-age girls was followed over a four-year period. Four percent (thirty-six girls) developed a "partial syndrome eating disorder." These girls, even though they might not have met diagnostic criteria for AN or BN, exhibited binge-eating episodes, compensatory behavior to prevent weight gain, and overconcern with body weight and shape, or lack of control of eating during a binge. A baseline measure of weight concerns was significantly associated with the onset of the partial syndrome eating disorder. Whereas girls in the top quartile on the measure of weight concerns had the highest incidence of the syndrome, none of the girls in the lowest quartile developed eating disorder symptoms.

Independent of the question of weight history, dissatisfaction with weight and body shape has come to be viewed as part of the defining characteristics of eating disorders and one of the early aspects of the development of such problems. In response, pictorial instruments that graphically assess body dissatisfaction in young children have been developed as part of a comprehensive assessment of eating disorders (Childress et al., 1993; Collins, 1991). Use of such instruments (see Figure 13-3) has contributed to the view that body dissatisfaction and other problematic beliefs and behaviors are common and are present even in very young children.

The notion that eating disorders evolve out of a response to levels of stress for which existing skills seem inadequate is also common (Bruch, 1973; Foreyt & McGavin, 1989). Since eating disorders generally begin during the adolescent years, stresses associated with this period—such as the onset of puberty, expectations of greater autonomy and responsibility, and increased social demands—are implicated (Levine et al., 1994). For example, anorexia has been viewed as an avoidant coping response: Stringent dieting prevents the appearance of a mature body and also results in menstruation being avoided or reversed. This behavior is consistent with the view that the anorexic's fear of weight gain is related to concerns about psychosexual maturity (Crisp, 1984). In this way, the anorexic girl's behavior is negatively reinforced, since it allows her to avoid negative thoughts, feelings, and fears. The behavior is also positively reinforced, in that the young

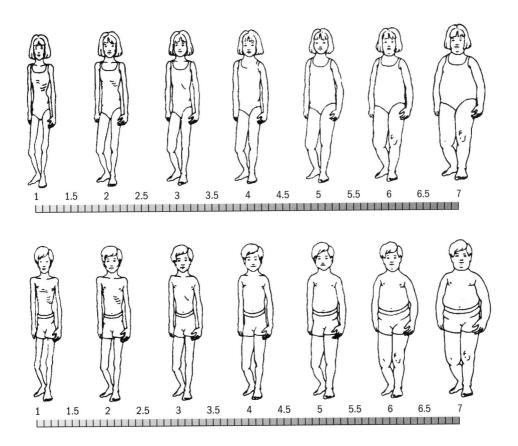

FIGURE 13-3 Pictures like these are employed to assess children's body perception.
Adapted from Collins, 1991.

woman may feel a sense of mastery, self-control, or virtue (Garner & Bemis, 1985). The feasibility of similar considerations regarding Bulimia Nervosa is supported by findings of early menarche as a risk factor for development of the disorder (Fairburn et al., 1997).

Reports based on clinical cases have also suggested early sexual abuse as a cause of eating disorders, particularly Bulimia Nervosa. However, empirical support is lacking. A study of community-based samples of women with bulimia nervosa in several countries failed to find higher rates of childhood sexual abuse in these women than was found in the general population of each country (Pope et al., 1994). Furthermore, these women did not experience higher rates of severe or pro-

longed abuse, and those bulimic women who had experienced abuse did not display more severe eating disorders than the nonabused bulimic women. This finding, of course, does not mean that childhood sexual abuse does not contribute to the development of eating disorders in some young women. However, sexual abuse would appear to be a risk factor for psychopathology in general, rather than a specific risk for the development of eating disorders (Fairburn et al., 1997; Levine, Smolak, & Striegel-Moore, 1996).

Many explanations regarding the development of eating disorders have emphasized family variables. Bruch's (1979) description of an anorexic girl is a classic example. The girl is described as the object of much family attention and control who is trapped by a need to please. Anorexia, according to Bruch, is a desperate attempt by the child to express an individual identity.

She enjoyed being home but missed the fuss they had made about her in the past, when everybody was acutely concerned about her ... Even as a child, Ida had considered herself not worthy of all the privileges and benefits that her family offered her, because she felt she was not brilliant enough. An image came to her, that she was like a sparrow in a golden cage, too plain and simple for the luxuries of her home, but also deprived of the freedom of doing what she truly wanted to do. (pp. 23–24)

It is difficult, however, to determine whether any pattern observed in a family subsequent to the onset of a disturbance is a cause or an effect. This is especially the case in anorexia, in which family observations have frequently followed the offspring's life-threatening refusal to eat. Reviews of research on family characteristics do suggest that family patterns are associated with eating disorders; however, there is no single pathway of influence. Such families tend to have a higher incidence of weight problems, affective disorder, and alcoholism or drug abuse. Also, aspects of the family environment, such as periods of low parental contact and high parental expectations, are implicated as risk factors (Fairburn et al., 1997). Families of eating-disordered young women have also been described as exhibiting controlling, interdependent family relationships, together with parental discord (Kog & Vandereycken, 1985; Strober & Humphrey, 1987). How and when family variables come into play is complex and difficult to determine (Dare et al., 1994; Thienemann & Steiner, 1993).

In investigating family variables, mother-daughter relationships have been a particular focus. Pike and Rodin (1991), for example, compared mothers whose adolescent daughters reported clinical levels of disordered eating to mothers of daughters with low levels of eating disturbances. Mothers of daughters with disordered eating viewed their daughters as less attractive and were more likely to think their daughters should lose more weight. These mothers were also more dissatisfied with the functioning of

their family system. In addition, these mothers were themselves more eating-disordered and had different dieting histories than other mothers. Mothers with eating disorders may in fact adversely influence their child's eating behaviors from early in the child's life. Stein et al. (1994) observed the interactions of two groups of mothers with their twelve- to fourteen-month-old infants. Compared with control mothers who had no eating disorder, mothers who had experienced an eating disorder during the year since their child's birth were more intrusive with their infants during both mealtime and play. These mothers also expressed more negative emotion toward their infants during mealtimes. The infants of eating-disordered mothers tended to weigh less than controls, and infant weight was inversely related to both the amount of mealtime conflict and the extent of the mother's concern about her own body shape.

Several types of biological influences have also been suggested as contributing to the development of eating disorders. Because eating and the biological mechanisms behind it are complex, the biological mechanisms that have been studied are numerous. Since eating behavior can both be influenced by and effect changes in neurobiological and neuroendocrine systems, determining causal relationships can be difficult. Thus it has been difficult to determine whether a particular biological difference found in young women with eating disorders is an individual difference that places the individual at initial risk for developing an eating disorder or is a change in the biological system that results from disordered eating.

For example, faulty hormonal regulation is suggested by the nature of some of the symptoms associated with Anorexia Nervosa (e.g., amenorrhea) and the fact that onset is frequently around puberty. However, many of the physical abnormalities that have been found in anorexics seem to result from starvation rather than to cause it (Fairburn, 1995; Pirke & Platte, 1995). These abnormalities are also found in nonanorexic individuals who have reached starvation weight and in whom hormonal indicators typically return to normal when adequate weight is gained. Another possible influence is suggested by reports of abnormalities in brain neurotransmitters among individuals with Anorexia Nervosa and Bulimia Nervosa (Kaye, 1995: Kaye & Weltzin, 1991). For example, serotonin plays a major role in the inhibition of feeding, and it is observed that there is decreased serotonin activity in bulimic individuals. It remains unclear, whether initial dieting is due to decreased serotonin activity, or whether problematic eating leads to changes in serotonin levels that then help sustain bulimic behavior.

A genetic contribution to eating disorders has also been suggested (Kendler et al., 1995; Rutter et al., 1990b). Both twin and family studies indicate a genetic component in eating disorders.. Higher than expected rates of eating disorders among family members suggest family aggregation of eating disorders. Moreover, twin studies indicate higher rates of concordance for MZ than DZ twins. Some genetic explanations of both anorexia and bulimia link them to internalizing disorders and family patterns of mood disorders. For example, episodes of depression have been reported in individuals diagnosed as anorexic and bulimic. Also, unusually high incidences of major mood disorders are reported in relatives. Nevertheless, there continues to be disagreement regarding the extent to which the data on depression and other internalizing disorders in eating-disorder patients and their families is indicative of a shared genetic etiology (Kendler et al., 1995; Rutter et al., 1990b; Strober, 1995; Wilson et al., 1996). The manner in which genes contribute to eating disorders remains unclear, but the mechanisms may involve complex contributions to personal styles, such as rigidity/obsessionality, or to biological processes involved in the regulation of eating behavior.

Any discussion of the development of eating disorders would be incomplete without a clear acknowledgment of potential cultural influences. Our society's emphasis on and valuing of slim and young bodies, particularly for women, likely contributes to the development and prevalence of such disorders (Mirkin, 1990; Wilfley & Rodin, 1995). These cultural messages are probably carried by family, peers, and the media. Guillen and

Barr (1994), for example, examined the messages contained in articles, advertisements, and other materials in *Seventeen* magazine between the years 1970 and 1990. In this magazine for adolescent women, the primary reasons presented for following a nutrition or fitness plan were to lose weight and become more attractive. Body shapes of models were less curvaceous than those in adult women's magazines, and the hip:waist ratio of models decreased over the years studied. Thus one perspective on the development of eating disorders emphasizes contemporary social influences on young women that place too great an emphasis on physical appearance and create a "culture of thinness" (Gilbert & Thompson, 1996).

Some authors remind us that these unusual eating styles are not recent phenomena. An appreciation of history can assist us in carefully examining our conceptualization of these eating disorders (Attie & Brooks-Gunn, 1995). There were, for example, a group of women living in the High Middle Ages (thirteenth through sixteenth centuries) who exhibited extreme restrictions of eating and what might be viewed as bizarre and pervasive behaviors and images regarding eating and food (Bell, 1985; Brumberg, 1986). Descriptions of the behavior of these women bear a remarkable similarity to contemporary eating disorders. The most interesting "twist" to this tale, however, is that these women were later canonized as saints. Bell (1985) chose the term "holy anorexia" to describe the condition of these women and to call attention to the cultural dimension that is often lost in current diagnostic efforts. Questions such as why a set of behaviors at one time is viewed as pious and at another as a disease force us to address important issues. To say that anorexia merely went undiagnosed in the past fails to appreciate that behaviors that appear similar may have very different origins, meanings, and functions. For example, Habermas (1992) has suggested that if fear of becoming overweight is considered as essential in defining eating disorders, then both anorexia and bulimia should be considered historically new syndromes (late nineteenth and early twentieth centuries). This is just one of the many complexities presented when one includes a cultural perspective in thinking about eating or other kinds of disorders.

Treatment. Anorexia Nervosa and Bulimia Nervosa have proven to be complex and difficult to treat. Furthermore, because treatments specific to the needs of children and younger adolescents have received far less attention, recommendations are currently based on downward extensions of controlled studies with older adolescents and adults (Robin, Gilroy, & Dennis, 1998). It is generally agreed that eating disorders derive from and are maintained by a variety of influences. Indeed, there is also considerable heterogeneity among individuals exhibiting these eating disorders. There are not, at present, treatments that are effective for all individuals, nor can we predict which treatments will work for particular individuals. Thus treatments that address multiple influences need to be developed. Here we briefly highlight some treatment approaches.

Although case reports suggest that different pharmacological treatments can be successful with eating-disordered patients, controlled research, particularly regarding children and adolescents, is either lacking or presents a somewhat more cautious picture (Heebink & Halmi, 1995; Hendren & Berenson, 1996; Walsh, 1995). There seems to be little support available for the effectiveness of pharmacological approaches to the treatment of Anorexia Nervosa. In controlled studies with adults, antidepressant medication is reported to be effective for treating Bulimia Nervosa (Werry & Aman, 1999). This effectiveness may be limited to a minority of patients. The reason for the effectiveness of antidepressants is not clear, however, since they do not appear to work via their antidepressant properties. The role of antidepressants in treating Bulimia Nervosa in youngsters thus remains unclear. With the use of any medication, caution regarding side effects with individuals who are already physiologically at risk is indicated (Yates, 1990).

Family therapy for eating disorders derives from the observation by clinicians of varying persuasions that the families are intimately involved in the maintenance of this behavior. The use of family therapy in the treatment of eating disorders is widespread in clinical practice, but research support is more limited, with some support for the effectiveness of family interventions for adolescents with Anorexia Nervosa (Dare & Eisler, 1997; Steiner & Lock, 1998). There are a variety of approaches to therapy with families of eating-disordered young women. The family systems approach, represented by Minuchin and his colleagues, is one well-known approach. This perspective views the family context as central to many disorders involving somatic symptoms, including Anorexia Nervosa (Minuchin, Rosman, & Baker, 1978). These investigators criticize other perspectives for continuing to view the locus of pathology as within the individual and for emphasizing the past. Minuchin does employ behavioral procedures to produce weight gain during brief hospitalization or on an outpatient basis.

The families of anorexics, according to Minuchin, can be described as enmeshed. The members of the family do not have distinct identities. Rather, there are diffuse boundaries among family members—they are highly involved in each other's lives. These families are also overprotective and exhibit a high degree of communication of concern. In this kind of family, the child learns to subordinate the self (individuality) to family loyalty. In turn, the child is protected by the family, and this protection further weakens the child's autonomy. This highly enmeshed family is a tightly woven system in which questioning of the system is not permitted. In such a family—which is described as rigid—even the usual kind of individual life change threatens its equilibrium. Adolescence may produce a particularly difficult crisis in the family. The child's overinvolvement with the family prevents the individualization that is necessary at this time of life, the view of one's self as independent of the family is blurred at best, and peer experience is lacking.

The anorexic's family has also always had a special concern with eating, diet, and rituals pertaining to food. The anorexic adolescent begins to challenge the family system, and rebellion is exhibited through refusal to eat. The family comes to the "protection" of the child—and maintains its stability—by making the child a sick, incompetent person who requires care. The sick role is reinforced, and the child is both protected and scapegoated. It follows from this conceptualization that the entire family system must be treated. The specific techniques employed vary with the age of the identified patient and the structural characteristics of the family. Although controlled research is lacking, Minuchin and his colleagues (1978) report that 86 percent of the fifty-three cases they treated recovered from both the anorexia and its psychosocial components.

It is not clear that there is empirical support for the hypothesized differences in anorexic families that serve as the basis for approaches to family therapy (Dare & Eisler, 1997; Vandereycken, 1995). However, the logic of family systems therapy seems compelling, and incorporation of family issues into treatment has become part of many approaches to intervention (Robin et al., 1998).

Cognitive-behavioral treatment of Bulimia Nervosa is widely accepted and is the intervention for which there is the best controlled research support (Compas et al., 1998; Robin et al., 1998). Treatment involves a multifaceted program that is based on the rationale that cognitive distortions and a loss of control over eating are at the core of the disorder (Fairburn, 1997). According to this view, cognitions regarding shape and weight are the primary features of the disorder, and other features of the disorder, such as dieting and self-induced vomiting, are secondary expressions of these concerns. In the initial stage of treatment, the patient is educated regarding Bulimia Nervosa, and the cognitive view of the disorder is made clear. During this early stage, behavioral techniques are also employed to reduce binging and compensatory behaviors (e.g., vomiting) and to establish control over eating patterns. These techniques are supplemented with cognitive restructuring techniques, and as treatment progresses, there is an increasingly cognitive focus on targeting inappropriate weight-gain concerns and on training self-control strategies for resisting binge-eating. Next, additional cognitively oriented interventions address inappropriate beliefs concerning food, eating, weight, and body image. Finally, a maintenance strategy to sustain improvements and to prevent relapses is also included.

Controlled research has shown the cognitive-behavioral approach to treatment to be superior to no treatment and to alternative treatments, including pharmacotherapy and a variety of other psychotherapies (Compas et al., 1998; Wilson, Fairburn, & Agras, 1997). Interpersonal therapy, which focuses on interpersonal problems involved in the development and maintenance of the disorder, has also proven to be an effective intervention (Fairburn et al., 1995). On the basis of these findings and on interpersonal concerns in the lives of bulimic patients, a focus on interpersonal problems has been suggested as a potential expansion of cognitive-behavioral therapy for Bulimia Nervosa (Wilson, et al., 1997).

Treatment of anorexia from a cognitive-behavioral perspective has often been conceptualized as consisting of two phases: intervention to restore body weight and to save the patient's life; and subsequent extended interventions to ameliorate long-standing adjustment and family difficulties and to maintain normal weight (Fremouw, Seime, & Dainer, 1993). Behavioral interventions have tended to focus on the first phase and to rely almost exclusively on operant learning principles to promote weight gain (Touyz & Beumont, 1997). These interventions have successfully employed positive and negative consequences contingent on weight change to produce weight gain in a relatively brief period of time. Most interventions have focused on treating hospitalized patients at a fairly critical point in their illness, and their effectiveness at this life-threatening point is an obvious contribution. However, there has been less success regarding both the long-term maintenance of weight gain and the social-emotional adjustment of patients after they have left the hospital. Behavioral investigators themselves called for the development of more broadly based cognitive-behavioral strategies that addressed both phases of treatment. Although there have been a number of case reports indicating that cognitive-behavioral therapy is effective in treating anorexia, there is a lack of controlled research to support this claim (Garner, Vitousek, & Pike, 1997).

DISORDERS OF ELIMINATION

Toilet training is an important concern for parents of young children (Mesibov, Schroeder, & Wesson, 1977; Schroeder & Gordon, 1991). Parents may view control of elimination as a developmental milestone for the child. Furthermore, entry into day care or another program may depend on achievement of appropriate toileting. For the child, pleasing the parent, a sense of mastery, and the feeling of no longer being a "baby" may all contribute to the importance of achieving toileting control.

The usual sequence of acquisition of control over elimination is nighttime bowel control, daytime bowel control, daytime bladder control, and finally, nighttime bladder control. Although there is considerable variation as to when children are developmentally ready to achieve control over elimination, bowel and daytime bladder training usually are completed between the ages of eighteen and thirty-six months.

Parents also differ as to when they feel it is appropriate to begin daytime training. Much of this decision is related to cultural values, attitudes, and the real-life pressures on the parent (e.g., day-care requirements, other siblings). An example of how day-to-day considerations probably affect this decision is illustrated by the advent of the disposable diaper. Ready availability of disposable diapers reduced many parents' inclinations toward the desirability of starting training early.

There are probably several factors that contribute to successful training. Being able to determine that the child is developmentally ready to begin training is certainly of importance. Also, correctly judging when the child has to go to the toilet can lead to important early success experiences. Adequate preparation, such as using training pants rather than a diaper, having the child in clothes that are easy to remove, and having a child-size potty seat available are also helpful. Finally, the common practice of providing praise and positive reinforcement (e.g., stickers, raisins) for appropriate toileting behavior, and doing so in a relaxed manner, has been demonstrated to be effective (O'Leary & Wilson, 1987; Schroeder & Gordon, 1991).

ENURESIS

Jay, a seven-year-old, had never achieved nighttime continence but had been continent during daytime for several years. He wets his bed an average of four days per week. No other significant behavior problems are present except for mild academic difficulties, and Jay's developmental history is unremarkable except for mild oxygen deprivation at birth and a delay in acquiring speech. Jay's biological father wet the bed until age nine.

Jay's mother and stepfather disagree in how they view his bedwetting. His mother feels he will grow out of it. His stepfather views Jay's bedwetting as laziness and removes privileges following episodes of enuresis. Both parents change the sheets when they are wet and attempt to restrict Jay's fluids prior to bedtime. They see the enuresis as a significant source of distress for the family and the conflict over how to handle it as exacerbating the problem. (Adapted from Ondersma & Walker, 1998)

About 50 percent of two-year-olds in the United States display daytime bladder control; this figure rises to 90 percent for four-year-olds. Nighttime bladder control is achieved more slowly. It is achieved by approximately 70 percent of three-year-olds and 90 percent of eight-year-olds (Erickson, 1987).

The term "enuresis" comes from the Greek word meaning "I make water." It refers to the repeated voiding of urine during the day or night into the bed or clothes when such voiding is not due to a physical disorder (e.g., diabetes, urinary tract infection). The lack of urinary control is not usually diagnosed as enuresis prior to the age of five (Doleys, 1989). Also, a certain frequency of lack of control is required before one would make a diagnosis of enuresis, and this frequency varies with the age of the child. Ordinarily, at least two such events per month is the criterion for children five to six years of age, with less frequent wetting required for the diagnosis of enuresis in older children.

A distinction is often made between the more common nocturnal enuresis (nighttime bed-wetting) and diurnal (daytime) enuresis. Enuresis is also referred to as "primary" if the child has never demonstrated bladder control and as secondary when the problem is preceded by a period of urinary continence. About 85 percent of all cases of enuresis are of the primary type (Walker, Kenning, & Faust-Campanile, 1989).

Estimates of the prevalence of nocturnal enuresis generally indicate that approximately 15 to 20 percent of five-year-old children have episodes at least once per month and that by seven years of age, approximately 7 to 15 percent of children are enuretic at that frequency. By the midteens, the prevalence of enuresis decreases to about 1 percent (Ondersma & Walker, 1998).

The causes of enuresis. A number of factors have been proposed as causes of enuresis, but no definitive cause has been established. At one time, the view that enuresis was the result of emotional disturbance was widely held (e.g., Gerard, 1939). More recent evidence does not support this view (Christophersen & Edwards, 1992). When emotional difficulties are also present in a child with enuresis, they most commonly are a consequence of enuresis rather than a cause. Enuretic children, especially as they become older, are very likely to experience difficulties with peers and other family members. It would not be surprising if the child's self-image suffered (Wagner, Smith, & Norris, 1988). It may also be the case that enuresis and emotional problems occur in the same children because similar factors contribute to the development of both. For example, a chaotic home environment may contribute to both inadequate toilet training and behavior problems.

It is frequently suggested that sleep abnormalities contribute to the development of enuresis. Many adults, for example, assume that nocturnal enuresis occurs because the child is an unusually deep sleeper. Indeed, parents often spontaneously report difficulty in arousing their enuretic children during the night. However, research regarding the role of sleep and arousal is inconsistent (Doleys, 1989). It appears that wetting can occur in any of the stages of sleep, not just in "deep

sleep." This and other evidence raises doubts about viewing all or most cases of enuresis as a disorder of sleep arousal (King & Noshpitz, 1991; Walker et al., 1989).

Another biological pathway that has been suggested is a lack of normal nocturnal increases in antidiuretic hormone (ADH). A lack of a normal nocturnal increase in ADH might lead to a higher production of urine. Among evidence for this hypothesis is the fact that some enuretic children respond well when an antidiuretic medication (a hormone analog) is administered. However, other evidence raises doubts concerning this explanation (Ondersma & Walker, 1998). Some research failed to find higher levels of urine production among enuretics, and not all children who produce high amounts of urine are incontinent. This and other evidence is not consistent with viewing low levels of ADH as the only or the primary cause of enuresis.

Family histories of enuretics frequently reveal a number of relatives with the same problem (Christophersen & Edwards, 1992). In a study of Israeli kibbutz children, there was a markedly greater incidence of bed-wetting among the siblings of enuretic children than among siblings of dry children. This association existed even though each sibling had been toilet trained by a separate caretaker in a different communal house (Kaffman & Elizur, 1977). Also, higher rates of concordance for enuresis among monozygotic than dizygotic twins have been reported (e.g., Bakwin, 1971). These results strongly suggest that at least some portion of enuretic children may have an organic predisposition toward enuresis. This as yet unspecified risk factor may or may not result in the development of enuresis, depending on various experiential factors, such as parental attitude and training procedures.

The central tenet of behavioral theories of enuresis is that wetting results from a failure to learn control over reflexive wetting. This failure can result from either faulty training or other environmental influences that interfere with learning (e.g., a chaotic or stressful home environment). Many behavioral theories incorporate some maturational/physical difficulty, such as bladder capacity or arousal deficit, into their explanation.

Treatment approaches. Prior to beginning any treatment, the child should be evaluated by a physician to rule out any medical cause for the urinary difficulties. Also, if a parent seeks treatment for a very young child, a discussion of developmental norms may be helpful. Finally, if treatment for enuresis is to be initiated, careful preparation and ensuring of parental cooperation are necessary.

A variety of pharmacological agents have been used in the treatment of enuresis. Imipramine hydrochloride (Tofranil), a tricyclic antidepressant, is probably the most commonly employed. Improvement that is achieved using imipramine does not seem to be due to the drug's antidepressant properties or to its effect on sleep. Although the mechanism for the drug's action is not entirely clear, the pathway of action may be through inhibiting norepinephrine reuptake at the postsynaptic cleft and thereby facilitating relaxation of muscles surrounding the bladder. A number of studies have demonstrated that imipramine is superior to placebos; however, the effect seems to rely on the child's continuing to take the medication. Moreover, there is reason for concern regarding possible side effects (Ondersma & Walker, 1998; Shaffer & Waslick, 1996).

Another medication, desmopressin, may have less risk of side effects. Desmopressin has been suggested as a treatment on the basis of its ability to control high urine output during sleep. Results comparable to those with imipramine have been reported. However, like imipramine, relapse occurs if the drug is discontinued (Shaffer & Waslick, 1996).

Behavioral treatments for nocturnal enuresis have received considerable research attention (Doleys, 1989; Houts, Berman, & Abramson, 1994). The most well-known of these methods is the urine-alarm or bell-and-pad system. This procedure was originally introduced by the German pediatrician Pflaunder in 1904 and was adapted and systematically applied by Mowrer and Mowrer (1938). Since then the device and the procedures have been refined by a number of investigators.

The basic device consists of an absorbent bedsheet between two foil pads. When urine is absorbed by the sheet, an electric circuit is completed that activates an alarm that sounds until manually turned off. Newer models use a system that is attached to the child's underpants and to the nightclothes or a small wristwatch-type alarm (see Figure 13-4). The parents are instructed to awaken the child when the alarm sounds. The child is taught to turn off the alarm and to go to the bathroom to finish voiding. The bedding is then changed, and the child returns to sleep. Usually records of dry and wet nights are kept, and after fourteen consecutive nights of dryness, the device is removed.

According to the Mowrers, the procedure is based on classical conditioning. Tension of the full bladder (the conditioned stimulus) is paired with the alarm (unconditioned stimulus) to produce awakening (the conditioned response) and inhibition of urination. Eventually the child wakens in response to a full bladder prior to wetting and setting off the alarm. Lovibond (1964) pro-

FIGURE 13-4 A urine alarm for treatment of enuresis. The child wears a urine sensor in the underclothes attached to an alarm worn on the nightclothes or wrist.

posed an alternative theoretical explanation—avoidance learning. He suggested that the child learns to inhibit urination in order to avoid the aversive consequences of being awakened by the alarm.

Research conducted on the urine-alarm system indicates that it is successful in a clear majority of cases, with treatment durations of between five and twelve weeks (Doleys, 1989; Houts et al., 1994). However, relapse has been reported to occur in about 40 percent of cases. Reinstituting training often results in a complete cure, however (Christophersen & Edwards, 1992).

Two modifications of the standard urine-alarm procedures have been found to reduce relapses (Walker et al., 1989). In the intermittent alarm procedure, the alarm sounds subsequent to some percentage of wettings rather than to each wetting (continuous alarm procedure). With the overlearning procedure, once the initial criterion for dryness is met, the child's intake of liquids prior to bedtime is increased, and the urine-alarm procedure is continued for some period of time.

A multifaceted and low-cost treatment developed by Houts, Liebert, and Padawar (1983) illustrates the way in which behavioral interventions have been combined in the treatment of nocturnal enuresis. Full Spectrum Home Training was designed to build on the success of behavioral treatments such as the urine-alarm in achieving initial treatment success. It was also designed to reduce relapse and to decrease the rate at which families dropped out of treatment. The procedure, which is cost effective, is a treatment manual-guided package that includes bell-and-pad; cleanliness training (having the child change his or her bed and night clothes); a procedure to increase bladder capacity, which is known as retention control training; and overlearning. The training program is delivered in a single one-hour group session, and a contract is then completed by parents and children to complete the training at home with regular calls from the treatment staff as the only additional contact.

A study by Houts, Peterson, and Whelan (1986) illustrates the program's success and examines the contribution of the components to reducing relapse. Participating families received one of three treatment combinations: Group 1 received bell-and-pad plus cleanliness training (BP), Group 2 received these two components plus retention control training (BP-RCT), and Group 3 received these three components plus overlearning (BP-RCT-OL)—the full package. A control group of children was followed over an eight-week period. No spontaneous remission of wetting occurred in control children, and they were then randomly assigned to one of the three treatment conditions.

The findings of this study indicate that although the proportion of success versus failure plus dropouts was slightly greater in the BP-RCT condition, these differences were not statistically significant. The three conditions were also equivalent in terms of the number of dry nights during training. At three-month follow-up, relapse was significantly less in the BP-RCT-OL group than in the other two groups. These results suggest the importance of overlearning in preventing initial relapse.

Table 13-4 summarizes Houts, Berman, and Abramson's (1994) findings regarding various treatments for enuresis. Research indicates that children who receive either psychological or pharmacological treatment are more likely to stop bedwetting than those left untreated. This finding suggests that parents probably should not simply wait for their child to outgrow the problem. It would also appear that behavioral interventions that in-

TABLE 13-4

Percentages of Children Who Ceased Bed-Wetting Following Different Types of Treatment

Group	Posttreatment	Follow-up
Psychological		
With urine alarm	66	51
Without urine alarm	31	21
Imipramine	43	14
Desmopressin	46	22
Placebo controls	12	8
Nontreatment controls	10	2

Adapted from Houts, Berman, and Abramson, 1994.

clude a urine alarm procedure are likely to be the most effective, particularly in the long run.

ENCOPRESIS

Susan, a six-year-old, has been soiling at least once per day since birth. The frequency of soiling had not decreased despite nearly constant attempts to convince her to use the toilet. Following careful medical examination, Susan's physician was certain that all medical causes for her condition had been ruled out. Tests, however, did reveal a considerable amount of fecal matter in her colon. During the course of the assessment, Susan's mother indicated that both she and her daughter were becoming very frustrated. It was also revealed that Susan was experiencing significant anxiety and pain with toileting. It appeared that Susan had learned to retain stools and fear toileting following early experiences with large and painful bowel movements. The toileting problems had begun to impact Susan's social functioning and self-esteem. (Adapted from Ondersma & Walker, 1998)

Functional encopresis refers to the passage of feces into the clothing or other unacceptable area when this is not due to physical disorder. The diagnosis is given when this event occurs at least once a month in a child of at least four years of age (American Psychiatric Association, 1994). The primary distinction regarding subtypes of encopresis is based on the presence or absence of constipation. The vast majority of encopretic children are chronically constipated and are classified as having constipation with overflow incontinence (or retentive encopresis).

Less writing and less research have been done concerning encopresis than concerning enuresis. Estimates of the prevalence of encopresis average about 2 to 3 percent of seven- to eight-year-old children. Percentages appear to decrease with age, being very rare by adolescence, and the problem occurs more frequently in males (Ondersma & Walker, 1998). Pediatricians, who are likely to see unselected populations of children, argue that the majority of encopretics have no associated psychopathology, a position supported by other workers (Christophersen & Edwards, 1992; King & Noshpitz, 1991). However, since encopresis occurs during the day more often than at night, it is more socially evident than enuresis and also is more likely to carry a social stigma. Consequently, enco-

presis is likely to be a source of considerable distress to both parents and children and may therefore be associated with more behavior problems, particularly among referred samples. For example, in the Worcester Encopresis Study (Young et al., 1996), children with encopresis who had been referred to a pediatric gastroenterology clinic were reported to have higher Total Behavior Problem and lower Social Competence scores on the Child Behavior Checklist than children without toileting problems. Following treatment these children had fewer behavior problems and improved social skills. To the extent that associated psychological difficulties do exist, they may be a consequence rather than an antecedent of the encopresis, or both may be related to common environmental factors (e.g., stressful family circumstances).

The causes of encopresis. Most theories acknowledge that encopresis may result from a variety of causative mechanisms. Initial constipation/soiling may be influenced by factors such as diet, fluid intake, medications, environmental stresses, or inappropriate toilet training. The rectum and colon may become distended by the hard feces. The bowel then becomes incapable of responding with a normal defecation reflex to normal amounts of fecal matter.

Medical perspectives on the problem tend to stress a neurodevelopmental approach (Doleys, 1989). Encopresis is viewed as more likely to occur in the presence of developmental inadequacies in the structure and functioning of the physiological and anatomical mechanisms required for bowel control. These organic inadequacies are viewed as temporary.

A behavioral perspective on encopresis stresses faulty toilet training procedures. Primary encopresis is largely explained by a failure to apply appropriate training methods consistently. Secondary encopresis is accounted for by avoidance conditioning principles. Pain or fear avoidance reinforces retention. Positive consequences may also maintain soiling, and inadequate reinforcement may be given for appropriate toileting (Doleys, 1989). These various learning explanations are not incompatible with physiological explanations.

For example, insufficient physiological-neurological mechanisms may be compounded by poor child training.

Treatment approaches. Most treatments for encopresis combine medical and behavioral management (Fireman & Koplewicz, 1992; Houts, Mellon, & Whelan, 1988). After the parent and the child have been educated about encopresis, the first step usually consists of an initial cleanout phase using enemas or high fiber intake to eliminate fecal impactions. Next, parents are asked to schedule regular toilet times and to use suppositories if defecation does not occur. Modifications in diet, laxatives, and stool softeners are employed to facilitate defecation. Positive consequences, such as a shared activity chosen by the child, are used to reward unassisted (no suppository) bowel movements in the toilet, as well as clean pants. If soiling occurs, children may be instructed to clean themselves and their clothes. Use of laxatives and suppositories is withdrawn. Research suggests that such treatment is highly effective, with success rates up to 100 percent and low relapse rates (Ondersma & Walker, 1998).

SLEEP DISORDERS

Parents often report that their children have problems involving sleep. It is common for parents to complain of difficulties in getting their young children to go to sleep and to sleep through the night. Nightmares are another concern that parents commonly report. To understand these common childhood sleep problems, as well as more serious sleep disorders, and to help parents judge whether and how their child's sleep is problematic, it is necessary to understand the variations in what is normal sleep for children.

At all ages, there is considerable individual variability in what would be considered a normal sleep pattern. Furthermore, patterns of sleep change with development (Horne, 1992; Stores, 1996). For example, the average newborn infant sleeps about sixteen hours per day. However, variations of four hours more or less are not uncommon. By

the time that children are one year old, the average amount of sleep has fallen to twelve hours. The typical ten- or eleven-year-old sleeps about eight hours each day. In addition to the number of hours of sleep, other aspects change as well. For example, newborns distribute their sleeping equally between day and night. Fortunately for parents, by about eight weeks, infants begin to develop signs of the day-night pattern typical in adults, and by eighteen months, sleep patterns are usually more stable.

There are two broad phases of sleep: rapid eye movement, or REM, sleep; and nonrapid eye movement, or NREM, sleep. NREM sleep is divided into four stages. Stages 3 to 4 are the deepest part of sleep and are characterized by very slow waves in the EEG and are thus sometimes referred to as slow wave sleep (SWS). The brain cycles through these stages of sleep throughout the night. The time spent in different stages of sleep also varies and changes with development. In the first year of life, for example, active REM sleep changes from about eight hours to about half this amount, thus also reducing the proportion of time spent in REM relative to other phases of sleep. The sequencing, or patterns in which the various stages of sleep occur, also changes. The phases of sleep are intermixed in irregular patterns in infants. However, as the child develops, regular patterns of light NREM, deep NREM, and REM sleep are gradually established. Figure 13-5 illustrates the pattern of sleep stages that may be characteristic for an older child or an adolescent and also indicates the stages of sleep during which some of the disorders that will be described would occur.

In this context, then, what are the most common complaints regarding children's sleep, and how are disorders of sleep defined? During the first year of life, the parents' most frequent complaint is that the child does not sleep through the night. A reluctance to go to sleep and nightmares often occur during the second year, and the three- to five-year-old presents a variety of problems, including difficulty in going to sleep, nighttime awakenings, and nightmares. Surveys suggest that approximately 25 percent of one- to five-year-olds experience some form of sleep disturbance (Min-

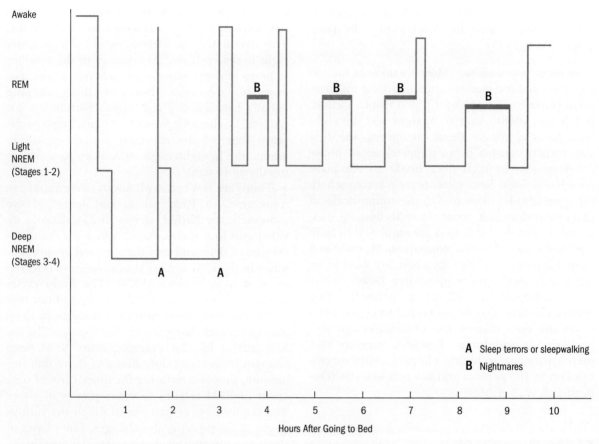

FIGURE 13-5 Sleep stage patterns typical of an older child and the points at which some sleep disorders might occur.
Adapted from Stores, 1996.

dell, 1993). Even in adolescence, complaints regarding sleep are common, particularly the need for more sleep and difficulty in falling asleep. Indeed, whereas many might think of sleep problems as being associated with young children, about one-third of adolescents in a general population sample reported at least one sleep problem that occurred at least four times per week (Morrison, McGee, & Stanton, 1992). Sleep problems seem to persist as well. Across age groups, follow-ups of one to three years suggest that the child's sleep problems continue to occur (Kataria, Swanson, & Trevathan, 1987; Morrison et al., 1992; Pollock, 1994).

Sleep difficulties are experienced by many children and are not necessarily associated with other psychological or behavioral difficulties. Indeed, if a sleep problem does not cause the child significant distress or result in impairment in social, educational, or other important areas of functioning, then it would not be considered a diagnosable mental disorder (DSM-IV). However, in some instances, sleep difficulties may be associated with or predictors of other behavioral problems (e.g., Pollock, 1994).

One reason that sleep difficulties and other childhood problems may occur together is that they may be two manifestations of a common set

Establishing a predictable bedtime routine is helpful in reducing children's sleep problems.
(Ken Karp)

of etiological mechanisms. Garland and Smith's (1991) description of the case of a nine-year nine-month-old boy illustrates this possibility:

The boy was well until he began experiencing partial awakenings approximately two hours after sleep onset. These were accompanied by a fearful appearance, a "racing heart," sweating, crying out, motor agitation, and mumbled fragments of sleep talking. The boy eventually returned to sleep without full awakening and had no memory of the event or its content. This sleep difficulty is often referred to as night (or sleep) terrors and is described below. Within a couple of weeks of the onset of these nightly attacks, the boy began experiencing spontaneous daytime panic attacks. Within four months these panic attacks were occurring several times per day and led to the boy being repeatedly sent home from school. As the frequency of the attacks increased, anticipatory anxiety and overanxious symptoms also developed involving worries about school performance despite "A" grades, and fears about the safety of family members, earthquakes, or accidents. The child's pediatrician found no physical cause for the episodes, but the persistence and severity of the problems resulted in a psychiatric consultation being sought. Interviews indi-

cated a family history of anxiety difficulties. In addition, over time, several precipitants of the child's problems were revealed. Severe marital problems, including extramarital affairs on the part of the child's father and an in-home separation of the parents, not discussed with the children, were revealed. The boy had also experienced a hockey accident that damaged his teeth, and intense competition among several friends for school grades was reported.

A combination of imipramine, education regarding the nature of the disorders, relaxation techniques, and parent counseling regarding the potential role of marital stressors are reported to have been highly effective. The sleep problem, panic attacks, and other anxiety problems ceased, the boy returned to school and all activities, and his self-confidence was restored. The authors hypothesized that both night terrors and panic attacks involve a similar constitutional vulnerability related to dysregulation of the brainstem alerting systems. (Adapted from Garland & Smith, 1991)

There are many types of sleep disorders that are of concern to clinicians working with infants, children, and adolescents (Anders & Eiben, 1997; Stores, 1996). The sleep disorders that are of primary concern are usually classified into two major categories: dyssomnias, or difficulties in initiating and maintaining sleep or of excessive sleepiness; and parasomnias, or disorders of arousal, partial arousal, or sleep-stage transitions (American Sleep Disorders Association, 1990).

DYSSOMNIAS

The problems that parents commonly report of difficulty in getting children to sleep and having them sleep through the night, if severe and chronic enough, fall into this category. These sleep and waking problems are indeed common and often occur together. They frequently are viewed as manifestations of the child's neurophysiological development and therefore are expected eventually to clear up. However, child, parental, and environmental factors do seem to play a role in a substantial number of cases. For example, a comparison of poor sleepers and good sleepers, between twelve and thirty-six months of age, revealed some surprising findings (Minde et al., 1993). Mothers' sleep diaries indicated more night wakings for the poor sleepers. However, filmed recordings indicated no differences in the actual number of wakings for the two groups. The poor sleepers were unable or unwilling to go back to sleep and woke their parent. In contrast, good sleepers were able to return to sleep on their own either by looking around and falling asleep or by quieting themselves, for example, by hugging a toy animal or sucking their thumbs. Whatever the cause, these problems may persist over many years, and they can result in considerable distress to the families involved (Stores, 1996).

It is often difficult to discriminate between "true" cases of these sleep difficulties and attention seeking. Does the child call to the parent "I can't sleep" or "I woke up" to get parental attention, or is he or she experiencing genuine sleep difficulties? Perhaps some genuine sleep problems go unreported because they are dealt with as "attention needs," or, in contrast, perhaps what are viewed as sleep problems are not really that. Before working with a family, it is important for the parents to feel secure that the sleep problem is not due to some "genuine" cause such as colic, sleep

apnea (obstruction of the airways causing breathing difficulties), or real fears on the child's part. Also, infants' and young children's difficulties may be associated with feeding practices. Sleep difficulties may be caused by the child's being accustomed to nighttime feedings or large nighttime feedings leading to wetting or discomfort. Milk intolerance may also account for some sleep difficulties. In such cases, removal of milk products from the diet should result in normalization of sleep after a relatively short period of time (Horne, 1992).

The child's level of cognitive development is also a factor. In order for children to recognize a sleep problem, they must be able to conceptualize difficulties in initiating and maintaining sleep as such (Wilson & Haynes, 1985). In older children, sleep problems may also be associated with reports of worrisome cognitions—concerns about school or peers, ruminations about past or anticipated experiences, or fears. In addition, adolescents may have difficulty in establishing good sleep habits in the context of their changing lifestyle. All these possibilities suggest the need for a careful and thorough assessment that includes evaluation of sleep habits and the sleep difficulty itself, medical and dietary factors, the child's functioning in other domains, and the family environment and parental expectations (Durand et al., 1998).

Pharmacological agents have been among the most widely used treatments; however, there is not good support for their effectiveness, and there is concern regarding negative side effects and recurrence of sleep disturbances with discontinuation of treatment. Given such concerns, behavioral interventions are usually recommended for most problems prior to the use of pharmacological treatments (e.g., Anders & Eiben, 1997; Shaffer & Waslick, 1996). Behavioral approaches to the problems of initiating and maintaining children's sleep have included a variety of procedures. But especially for young children, these interventions have focused on the consequences applied to the child's behaviors and on techniques of stimulus control (Bootzin & Chambers, 1990). For example, attention given to the child after saying goodnight can be withdrawn, praise and/or star charts for desired behavior can be given, and a distinct bedtime routine that makes clear the signs for going to sleep can be developed. Similar procedures can be applied to nighttime wakenings (Durand & Mindell, 1990; Minde, Faucon, & Faulkner, 1994).

PARASOMNIAS

Several of the childhood sleep disorders that cause concern for parents fall in the second category, parasomnias. These include sleepwalking, sleep terrors, and nightmares.

Sleepwalking. Sleepwalking (somnambulism) begins with the child's sitting upright in bed. The eyes are open but appear "unseeing." Usually the child leaves the bed and walks around, but the episode may end before the walking stage is reached. An episode may last for a few seconds or thirty minutes or longer. There is usually no later memory of the episode. It was once believed that the sleepwalking child was exceptionally well coordinated and safe. This belief has proven to be a myth, and although physical injury is rare, it is a danger of the disorder.

Approximately 15 percent of children between the ages of five and twelve have isolated experiences of walking in their sleep. Sleepwalking disorder, that is, persistent sleepwalking, is estimated to occur in 1 to 6 percent of the population. Somnambulism usually persists for a number of years but then disappears by adolescence (American Psychiatric Association, 1994).

The vast majority of sleepwalking episodes occur in the first one to three hours following sleep onset (see Figure 13-5). The fact that sleepwalking occurs during the later stages of NREM sleep (deep sleep) appears to invalidate the idea that sleepwalking is the acting out of a dream, since dreams occur in REM sleep. A characteristic EEG pattern has been found to precede each episode. This EEG pattern exists in 85 percent of all children during the first year of life but is present in only 3 percent of seven to nine-year-olds. Thus it has been suggested that central nervous system immaturity is of significance in sleepwalking disorder, and knowledge that the disorder is

usually outgrown is consistent with that conceptualization. This view does not, however, rule out psychological or environmental factors. Frequency of sleepwalking has been reported to be influenced by the specific setting, stress, fatigue, and physical illness (American Psychiatric Association, 1994; Mindell, 1993). Greater concordance rates for sleepwalking among monozygotic twins than among dizygotic twins and family patterns of sleepwalking have also been reported, leading some to propose a genetic component to the disorder. Unlike the case for adults, the presence of sleepwalking in children has not been found to be associated with psychological disturbance (Dollinger, 1986; Stores, 1996).

Sleep terrors and nightmares. Both sleep terrors and nightmares are fright reactions that occur during sleep. Sleep terrors, also known as night terrors or pavor nocturnus, are experienced by from 1 to 6 percent of children and are more common in males. Sleep terrors typically occur between the ages of four and twelve. Nightmares and sleep terrors are often confused, but they differ in a number of ways (see Table 13-5).

Sleep terrors occur during deep, slow-wave sleep and at a fairly constant time, usually about two hours into sleep (see Figure 13-5). The sleep terror is quite striking in that the still-sleeping child suddenly sits upright in bed and screams. The face shows obvious distress, and there are signs of autonomic arousal, such as rapid breathing and dilated pupils. In addition, repetitive motor movements may occur, and the child appears disoriented and confused. Attempts to comfort the child are largely unsuccessful. The child most often returns to sleep without full awakening and has little or no memory of this event the next morning. The conceptualization of the causes of sleep terrors is similar to that previously described for sleepwalking, and, indeed, they occur in the same part of the sleep cycle.

In many cases of sleep terrors and sleepwalking, intensive treatment may not be indicated, since the episodes usually disappear spontaneously, so that education and support may be sufficient. However, a number of treatments have been sug-

TABLE 13-5

Characteristics Differentiating Nightmares and Sleep Terrors

Nightmares	Sleep Terrors
Occur during REM sleep	Occur during Non-REM sleep
During middle and latter portions of the night	During first third of night
Verbalizations, if any, are subdued	Child wakes with cry or scream and verbalizations usually present
Only moderate physiological arousal	Intense physiological arousal (increased heart rate, profuse sweating, pupils dilated)
Slight or no movements	Motor activity, agitation
Easy to arouse and responsive to environment	Difficult to arouse and unresponsive to environment
Episodes frequently remembered	Very limited or no memory of the episode
Quite common	Somewhat rare (1 to 6 percent)

Adapted from Wilson and Haynes, 1985.

gested. These include response interruption, contingency management, instructional procedures, and anxiety reduction procedures (Dollinger, 1986). Because the literature consists of case studies, one cannot say whether these treatments were responsible for reported changes. Drug treatments of both disorders have also been reported; however, these medications may actually produce effects that set the stage for recurrences of these disorders, and side effects are a concern (Shaffer & Waslick, 1996).

Nightmares are the other fright reaction that occurs during sleep and are common in children between the ages of three and six years (American Sleep Disorders Association, 1990). These dreams occur during REM sleep (see Figure 13-5). It is frequently thought that the dreams are a direct manifestation of anxieties that the child faces. It has been suggested that children typically extinguish their fears by gradually exposing themselves during daytime hours to the feared stimulus (Kellerman, 1980). Some events, such as parental protectiveness, however, might restrict the child's ability to engage in such exposure, and thus the anxieties and the associated nightmares continue or are exacerbated.

No single theoretical framework has proven successful in explaining the development of nightmares, and explanations allowing for multiple causality (e.g., developmental, physiological, and environmental factors) are most likely to have the greatest utility. Consistent with anxiety being viewed as the basis for nightmares, the majority of treatments have involved anxiety reduction techniques. However, no treatment strategy can be stated as most effective, nor are the active components of the various treatments known.

SUMMARY

■ A number of eating disorders have received attention from researchers and clinicians. Of these, obesity and anorexia/bulimia have probably generated the most interest.

■ The development of obesity is influenced by a complex interaction of psychosocial and biological influences. The learning of adaptive eating and activity patterns is the basis of behavioral treatment programs. This approach to treatment is probably the most successful; however, greater weight loss and better maintenance results still need to be achieved.

■ The appropriate way to classify and conceptualize the eating disorders of anorexia and bulimia has received considerable attention. Anorexia Nervosa is a serious, life-threatening disorder characterized by extreme weight loss, an intense fear of becoming fat, and disturbance in the perception of body weight and shape. A number of other physical and psychological problems are present as well. A distinction is made between restricting and bulimic anorexics.

■ Bulimia refers to a repeated pattern of binge-eating followed by some inappropriate compensatory mechanism. Increasing prevalence of eating-disordered behavior and attitudes among young girls has been noted.

■ Explanations that incorporate multiple influences are most likely needed to understand the development of eating disorders, but no particular explanation is clearly supported. The role of a history of weight problems and attempts to control weight are often considered along with dissatisfaction with body shape and weight. There is also support for the role of stress in combination with inadequate coping skills.

■ Many explanations of the development of eating disorders have emphasized family variables, such as family history of weight problems, affective disorders and substance abuse, parental involvement and expectations, and marital discord. Mother-daughter relations have been a particular focus of investigations.

■ Although several types of biological influences are suggested for eating disorders, determining cause and effect is difficult. Hormonal regulation, neurotransmitter abnormalities, and genetic influences have been considered.

■ The importance of cultural influences must be considered in any explanation of eating disorders.

■ Anorexia and bulimia have proven complex and difficult to treat. The effectiveness of pharmacological treatments with children and adolescents is unclear. The use of family therapy or family involvement in treatment is widespread in clinical practice, although further empirical support is required. Cognitive-behavioral treatment is the intervention for bulimia nervosa, for which there is the best controlled research support. The treatment of anorexia has been conceptualized as a two-phase process—resumption of eating with associated weight gain and maintenance of improvement and treatment of associated problems. Anorexia has proven difficult to treat.

■ Enuresis and encopresis are disorders of elimination that seem best explained by a combination of biological predisposition and failure to train and/or learn bodily control. The use of imipramine or desmopressin are the most popular and best-supported medically oriented procedure for treating enuresis. Behavioral interventions (which include a urine alarm procedure) based on classical conditioning and operant learning theories have reported high success rates and low rates of remission, and they seem to be the treatments of choice at present. Encopresis, which has received considerably less attention, is probably best dealt with through a combination of medical (for example, enemas) and behavioral (for example, reinforcement) procedures.

■ Difficulties in initiating and maintaining sleep (dyssomnias) are most effectively dealt with by establishing bedtime routines and the appropriate cues for sleep. Sleep disorders such as sleepwalking and sleep terrors (parasomnias) are probably best conceptualized as resulting from a combination of nervous system immaturity and environmental factors. At present the effectiveness of various treatments remains unclear.

CHAPTER 14

PSYCHOLOGICAL FACTORS AFFECTING MEDICAL CONDITION

This chapter continues the discussion of the problems of physical conditions and health. The topics discussed here would in the past have come under the heading of psychosomatic disorders. The main focus of interest was on actual physical conditions, such as asthma, headaches, ulcers, and nausea. These disorders were known or presumed to be affected by psychological factors. The terminology for describing these disorders has undergone a number of changes in the last few decades. The term Psychosomatic Disorders was replaced in DSM-II by Psychophysiological Disorders, and in DSM-III and III-R with the term Psychological Factors Affecting Physical Condition. Most recently the term has been modified in DSM-IV to Psychological Factors Affecting Medical Condition.

HISTORICAL CONTEXT

The uncertainty over terminology reflects a long-standing controversy over the nature of the relationship between mind and body, the psyche and the soma. One of the most influential statements concerning the mind-body problem is found in the writing of René Descartes, the early seventeenth-century French philosopher. Descartes, influenced by strong religious beliefs, viewed human beings as part divine and as possessing a soul (mind) that somehow must affect the mechanics of the body. The point of contact between the two systems was presumed to be the pineal gland, located in the midbrain. This version of mind-body dualism was part of a long history of shifting opinion about whether or how spiritual or psychological factors affected bodily conditions.

During the twentieth century, interest in the impact of psychological processes on the body resulted in the development of the field of psychosomatic medicine. Early workers began to accumulate evidence and to develop theories of how psychological factors played a causative role in specific physical disorders (Alexander, 1950; Grace & Graham, 1952; Selye, 1956). As this field developed, several trends emerged. An increasing number of physical disorders were seen to be related to psychological factors. Even the common cold was thought to be affected by emotional factors. The question therefore arose as to whether it was fruitful to identify a specific group of psychosomatic disorders or whether psychological factors were operating in all physical conditions. In addition, the focus began to shift from psychogenesis, that is, psychological cause, to multicausality, the idea that social and psychological (as well as biological) factors all contribute to both health and illness at multiple points. The latter view is holistic, assuming a continuous transaction among influences. This broad scope and interactive perspective has continued to develop (Eiser, 1994; Maier, Watkins, & Fleshner, 1994; Wood, 1994).

With this shift in thinking, the field began to expand considerably. The ongoing role of social and psychological factors in medical conditions; the social, psychological, and developmental consequences of medical conditions; the role of psychological treatments for physical disorders; social and psychological aspects of medical treatments; and the role of social and psychological variables in prevention and health maintenance all began to receive increased attention (Drotar, 1981; Routh, Schroeder, & Koocher, 1983; Winett, 1995). Indeed, the concept of psychosomatic disorders as physical conditions caused by emotional factors became inadequate to encompass this expanded perspective (Tuma, 1982). Writers began to suggest other definitions (Wright, 1977), and various other terms came into existence, such as behavioral medicine, health psychology, and the term most commonly used in reference to children, pediatric psychology.

This chapter is in keeping with these changes. However, it is clearly not possible to survey this rapidly expanding field completely. Whole volumes have been dedicated to the topic or segments of it (LaGreca et al., 1992; Roberts, 1995), and several scientific journals have emerged to deal exclusively with research in this area (e.g., *Journal of Pediatric Psychology, Behavioral Medicine, Health Psychology*). In this chapter, we will examine some of the specific medical problems of children that have received the attention of psychologists and some other selected topics of interest. This examination will allow us to illustrate the changes that have occurred and the current status and diversity of this field.

ASTHMA

In this section, we will look at information on asthma in order to illustrate the changing nature of the interface between psychology and pediatric medical problems. This examination of asthma will begin to allow us to see how thinking about the role of psychological variables in physical illness has changed and expanded.

Asthma is an example of a disorder for which the early focus was on psychological causation. Here we will see how this idea has been transformed. However, before beginning our discussion, it would also be wise to remember that interest is not limited to a particular issue and a single disorder. Our understanding of other disorders has also gone through transformations, and other issues that are dealt with elsewhere in the chapter—for example, compliance with treatment recommendations—are relevant to asthma as well. It is important to keep this overlap and complexity in mind and to understand that a simple one-to-one matching of disorders and issues is not a reality. Rather, the grouping of issues and disorders is a convenience that we have employed to organize information.

DESCRIPTION OF ASTHMA

Loren is a twelve-year-old boy with moderate to severe asthma. For the fourth time in a year, he was hospitalized because of asthma. At hospital rounds, Loren's physician pointed out that his asthma could be controlled if he avoided triggers of his asthma, including exercise-induced attacks, and if he complied with his medication regimen. It was also pointed out that Loren did not use his nebulizer properly. Instead of alleviating his respiratory distress, most of the medication was wasted because of inappropriate inhaler use. Lack of quick relief frustrated Loren. As a result he tended to become angry, a behavior that only exacerbated his asthma. It was decided to (1) teach Loren to identify and avoid triggers of his asthma, (2) review his medication and adjust the regimen if possible, (3) improve his compliance to his medical treatment regimen, (4) teach him how to use his nebulizer correctly, and (5) teach him skills to control his frustration. (Adapted from Creer, 1998, p. 411)

The definition and description of asthma is complex and remains an ongoing process (National Institutes of Health, 1997). Asthma is a disorder of the respiratory system that is characterized by hyperresponsiveness of the trachea, bronchi, and bronchioles to a variety of stimuli. This hyperresponsiveness results in inflammation and narrowing of air passages, and air exchange is impaired, particularly during expiration. Intermittent episodes of wheezing and shortness of breath (dyspnea) result. Within the same individual, as well as across individuals, attacks may vary in severity. Thus asthma is an illness that is quite unpredictable, a problem for both research and management of the disorder. Severe attacks, known as status asthmaticus, which are life-threatening and require emergency medical treatment, are another challenge in treating asthmatic children. The fear of not being able to breathe and the danger of severe attacks are likely to create appreciable anxiety in the young person and in family members.

PREVALENCE AND PROGNOSIS

Asthma is the most common chronic disease in young people (Newacheck & Taylor, 1992). Approximately 10 percent of youngsters are asthmatic, and minority and poor children are overrepresented (Creer, 1998; Gergen, Mullally, & Evans, 1988). Asthma is a potentially reversible disorder, but the impact of the disease on the youngster is considerable. In addition to hospitalization and emergency room use, many school days are lost because of asthma (Weiss, Gergen, & Hodgson, 1992).

Clearly, the greatest threat is loss of life, and all measures used to treat the physical symptoms of asthma—daily medication to prevent wheezing, environmental control of potential irritants, desensitization to allergens, avoidance of infection, and emergency treatment to stop wheezing—are geared to prevent death. Although much has been done to improve the treatment of asthma, reports of increasing prevalence as well as increases in medical costs, hospitalization, and mortality rates, despite improved medical treatments, are reasons for continuing concern (Creer, 1998; Wilson et al., 1993).

ETIOLOGY

The causes of asthma are complex, and there is a considerable history of controversy concerning etiology. Indeed, the exact cause remains unknown (Creer, 1998). However, it is broadly acknowledged that genetic or other factors place some youngsters at risk for developing asthma. Figure 14-1 presents a simplified schematic description of the asthmatic process. Some cause or variety of causes produces a hypersensitivity of the air passages. Once established, this hypersensitivity results in the youngster's responding to various irritants more easily than would a nonasthmatic individual. The resulting wheezing and shortness of breath may have additional psychological consequences. Anxiety and fear may occur in anticipa-

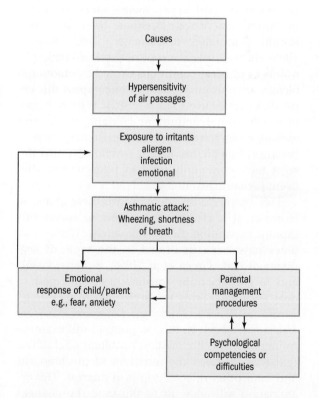

FIGURE 14-1 Schematic diagram of a general model for the development of asthma and its concomitant psychosocial effects.

tion of attacks or during them. This occurrence in itself may be a contributing irritant that increases the probability or intensity of attacks. A second class of possible psychological consequences is dependency, isolation from peers, and other behavior problems that may result from the management of the asthmatic youngster's physical symptoms.

Whatever its etiology, individuals with highly sensitive and labile respiratory tracts are potentially exposed to a second set of factors that influence whether or not asthmatic attacks occur. This second set of influences has come to be thought of as trigger mechanisms or irritants, rather than as causes of asthma. It is widely held that a variety of agents can trigger wheezing in different individuals or on different occasions for the same individual (Creer, 1998).

Repeated respiratory infection may play a role in the development of asthma, and respiratory viral infections can set off or worsen the severity of an attack. It has been recognized that viral infections are transmitted through some type of close contact, for example, from the nasal mucosa to the hand and then to the hand of another. The fact that such infections are likely transmitted to individuals via modifiable behaviors has led some investigators to develop behavioral interventions designed to modify directly such behaviors (Corley et al., 1987).

Allergies may also be related to the development and occurrence of asthmatic attacks. Allergies may exist to inhaled substances such as dust, the dander of a pet, pollen, or to ingested substances such as milk, wheat, or chocolate. Physical factors such as cold temperatures, tobacco smoke, pungent odors, and exercise and rapid breathing may also contribute to wheezing. Furthermore, psychological stimuli and emotional upset are often considered important triggers of asthma attacks (Creer, 1998; Miller & Wood, 1994).

Indeed, it is virtually impossible to assess and analyze asthma without recognizing the multiple psychological factors involved (Williamson, Head, & Baker, 1993), as powerfully illustrated in an early description by Alexander of the young asthmatic patient:

The early-onset asthma patient and his or her family face some very severe hardships … They face both peers and adults who are variously overindulgent, or lacking in understanding of their difficulties … At home their asthma may become the sole focus around which all family activities and concerns come to revolve. Their parents may feel responsible, guilty, and helpless; and at other times resentful and angry. Certainly, an asthma sufferer can learn to manipulate others with the disorder, or use it to avoid unpleasant activities or situations. It is also often difficult for the patient to sort out clearly what he or she can really do, from what is accomplished in the face of asthma. Many maladaptive and inappropriate behavior patterns can develop, as patient and family struggle with the ravages of this disorder. Such patterns can severely cripple family life and retard the social and psychological development of the child. Often, the undesirable behavior patterns affect the course of the disorder substantially. Asthma is, of course, potentially life-threatening, and many patients have experienced bouts of status asthmaticus, which on occasion may have brought them close to death. Such experiences often generate enduring anxiety responses which can manifest themselves in fears of death, hospitals, and treatment. Some patients develop conditioned fear responses, which can begin at even the first signs of wheezing. The frantic, worried behavior of parents and those treating the patient can exacerbate the young patient's fears. Moods, too, vary with the severity of symptoms and also in relation to medication taken. (Alexander, 1980, p. 274)

EARLY VIEWS

Although we have come to view the causes of asthma differently, in much of the early literature asthma was viewed primarily as a disease with psychological causes. Probably the earliest and most widely known psychosomatic explanation of asthma was the psychoanalytic explanation originally offered by French and Alexander (1941). Asthma was hypothesized to arise from an excessive, unresolved dependence on the mother and a resultant fear of separation. The symptoms of wheezing and shortness of breath were viewed as "a suppressed cry for the mother," brought on because crying, and the desire for the mother that it represents, become intolerable to the parent. French and Alexander were clearly influenced by their psychoanalytic training, and much of the support for this theory came from other psychoanalysts and from individual case studies. Research studies designed to evaluate the hypothesis often suffered from serious methodological flaws (Freeman et al., 1964) or failed to demonstrate the hypothesized relationships (McLean & Ching, 1973). It is probably important to examine the specifics of this hypothesis and its validity, however, since as Creer (1982) has pointed out, French and Alexander's ideas about psychological factors and asthma had as much impact as anything previously written. Moreover, these ideas were applied to other disorders.

Renne and Creer (1985) have summarized the basic aspects of the explanation and the information concerning its validity. The four major conclusions offered by French and Alexander are that (1) in asthmatic patients, a universal conflict exists between an infantile dependent attachment to their mothers and other emotions (particularly sexual wishes) that are incompatible with this dependent attitude; (2) asthma attacks are related to an inhibited suppressed cry for the mother; (3) there is a unique personality pattern characteristic of asthmatic patients; (4) psychoanalysis will alleviate the asthmatic symptoms. Reviews of research conducted since the publication of the original monograph by French and Alexander suggest that there is little, if any, support for their conclusions (Renne & Creer, 1985). No unique relationship appears to exist between asthmatic children and their mothers. To the extent that asthmatic children cry less, this behavior is more likely due to the realization that crying may trigger an attack. Furthermore, there is no evidence for a personality pattern unique to asthma, and asthmatic patients would seem to be as psychologically healthy as other people. Finally, psychotherapy has not been effective in alleviating the disorder.

All in all, there is little, if any, convincing evidence that psychological factors play a significant role as an original cause of the reduced respiratory capacity characteristic of asthma. However, there is evidence that psychological factors may play an important role in precipitating or triggering asthmatic attacks in at risk youngsters.

Like many other investigators, Purcell and his colleagues (1969)—working at the Children's Asthma Research Institute and Hospital (CARIH) in Denver—observed that some children became free of symptoms fairly soon after being sent away from their parents for treatment. Indeed, in the 1950s, "parentectomy" was suggested as the treatment of choice for some children (Peshkin, 1959). Were these effects due to changes in the emotional environment or the physical environment? What other variables accounted for this reaction?

An interesting study on separation suggested some answers to these questions (Purcell et al., 1969). Prior to the beginning of the study, parents of asthmatic children were interviewed and asked about the degree to which emotions precipitated asthmatic attacks. Children for whom emotions were important precipitants were expected to respond positively to separation from their parents (predicted positive), whereas children for whom emotions played less of a role were not expected to show improvement. Twenty-five asthmatic children participated in four two-week periods labeled (1) qualification, (2) preseparation, (3) separation, and (4) reunion. During the qualification period, the families were aware that the project involved a careful evaluation of asthma in children but were unaware of possible separation. During the second phase, preseparation, the idea of separation was introduced. In the third phase, the children had no contact with their families but continued their normal daily routines at home under the care of substitute parents. In the fourth phase, the children were reunited with their families. A postreunion evaluation was also conducted.

For the predicted positive group, all measures of asthma improved during the separation period. Figure 14-2 illustrates this finding for the peak expiratory flow rate (PEFR) measure, which is a measure of the maximum expiration of air possible. The children who were not predicted to respond to separation exhibited no differences across phases on any measure.

The findings of this research study, and of others like it, led investigators to view changes in the psychological atmosphere as the basis for improvement in asthmatic symptoms. However, over time both the investigators at CARIH and other investigators came to view such findings somewhat differently. It was recognized that although the magnitude of changes reported might be statistically

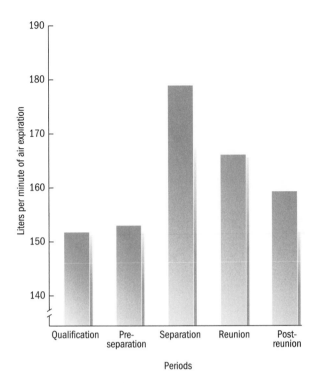

FIGURE 14-2 Mean daily peak expiratory flow rate for predicted positive group during each period of study.
From Purcell, Brady, Chai, Muser, Molk, Gordon, & Means, 1969.

significant, they were not clinically significant. Obtained changes might have been due to increased compliance with prescribed medical regimens when the substitute parents moved in and the children's parents lived in a hotel. Even though a high percentage of children treated at CARIH in the early years exhibited rapid remission of their symptoms, this percentage decreased rapidly over the years, probably as a result of several factors. For example, with increasing information and improved medications available, milder cases of asthma came to be treated by the home physician (Ellis, 1988). Thus only more severe cases were sent to the facility. Also, the diagnostic criteria used to confirm asthma shifted over time. In fact, it is questionable that children diagnosed as asth-

matic with current diagnostic procedures would exhibit a remission of symptoms as a result of being separated from their parents (Renne & Creer, 1985).

These findings and considerations, of course, do not mean that psychological factors and family functioning play no role in asthma. There seems little doubt that family functioning and psychological factors, in general, do play a role (Klinnert, Mrazek, & Mrazek, 1994). For example, home environment (e.g., dust, animal dander), activities of family members (e.g., smoking, outdoor activities), and stress (e.g., family fights, divorce) may act as triggers for asthmatic attacks. Beyond the anxiety that parents experience, the youngsters' asthma may have consequences for the parents (e.g., days lost at work because of their child's illness, medical costs) and siblings (e.g., loss of attention, restrictions in choice of family activities). Also, family members will likely have to assist in the management of the disease, especially for younger children. It is therefore not surprising that psychological interventions have focused on the triggers of asthma attacks, on the consequences of asthma, and on helping youngsters and their families manage the disease (Creer, 1991; 1998).

We have seen, then, how the focus on psychological and family factors has shifted from the cause of asthma to an interest in how parents and family may influence the frequency and severity of the symptoms and may manage the disorder (Hamlett, Pellegrini, & Katz, 1992; Miller & Wood, 1991; Wilson et al., 1993). This is one example of how those who study and work with asthmatic children have shifted and broadened their focus of interest. An interest in the psychological consequences of chronic illness such as asthma is another example (MacLean et al., 1992).

ADJUSTMENT TO CHRONIC ILLNESS

We now turn to a more extended discussion of how illness may affect the development and adjustment of a young person and of other family members. The effects of any chronic illness are likely to

Parental concern over precipitating a symptomatic attack may often lead children with chronic illnesses, such as asthma, to spend appreciable time isolated from their peers.

By permission of U.S. Department of Health and Human Services–Public Health Service (ADM, 77–497).

be pervasive, particularly if the illness is life-threatening. Stress and anxiety experienced by the youngster is likely to be substantial. In addition, limitations due to illness often place obstacles in the way of normal development. For example, contact with peers may be limited, or school attendance may be disrupted.

Of course, the family, too, needs to cope with the illness, its treatment, and its effects over long periods of time. Such long-term demands are bound to be difficult to handle, and the consistency required by treatment regimens is stressful in its own right. Thus the entire family may experience considerable anxiety and have appreciable stress placed on its daily routines.

Research on chronic illness has become a priority for pediatric psychologists (Lemanek, 1994). One frequent question is, Does chronic illness lead to poor adjustment? The answer would appear to be not necessarily, but these illnesses and related life experiences probably place the child at increased risk for behavior problems (Eiser, 1994; Friedman & Mulhern, 1992; Lavigne & Faier-Routman, 1992). For example, among youngsters with chronic medical problems, ratings of depressive symptoms exceeded averages for control subjects, and rates of depressive disorders in this population exceeded rates typically reported in community samples. However, these findings also suggest that while depression is a problem, the majority of young people with a chronic illness are not depressed (Bennett, 1994). This is consistent with other findings that although the prevalence of adjustment problems is higher among children with chronic illnesses, only a minority appear poorly adjusted (Wallander & Varni, 1998).

In addition to comparing chronically ill youngsters with controls, it may be informative to compare them with their healthy siblings. One such investigation compared the adjustment of ninety-three juvenile rheumatic disease patients with that of their healthy siblings as well as with demographically matched healthy controls (Daniels et al., 1987). The patients and their siblings had more adjustment problems than did the controls, but patients and siblings did not differ from each other. This finding suggests that adjustment difficulties are not necessarily a direct result of having a chronic disease. It is possible, however, that having a child with a chronic disease creates stress in the family environment. It is also important to remember that families with an ill child are not immune to the other considerable stresses experienced by all families, including serious illness or death of another family member or a friend, occupational changes, and financial problems (Kalnins, Churchill, & Terry, 1980). The stress placed on some families may affect the adjustment of both the patient and other children. Indeed, siblings and parents of youngsters with chronic illness do themselves seem to be at increased risk for adjustment problems. However, the findings, much like those for the chronically ill children themselves, is that the majority of family members do not have serious adjustment problems.

Furthermore, measuring adjustment at any one time is unlikely to provide a complete picture. Adjustment for the youngster and family members is likely to be an ongoing process, beginning at diagnosis and continuing through treatment, treatment completion, perhaps relapse, and the long-term course that is inherent in a chronic illness (Friedman, Latham & Dahlquist, 1998).

Thus, although some youngsters with chronic illness and their families experience significant and persistent adjustment difficulties, not all do. How might we best understand such variation in reactions among young people and their families? In an attempt to understand the process, research has examined variables such as the particular disease and its status and aspects of family functioning. Increasingly, pediatric psychology has conducted research guided by theories that suggest variables that might influence psychological outcomes (Drotar, 1994; Wallander & Varni, 1998).

Several models are available to guide research, many of which view chronic illness as an ongoing chronic stressor to which the youngster and family must continue to adapt and continue to develop appropriate coping mechanisms (Thompson et al., 1994; Wallander & Varni, 1998). Adjustment to chronic illness is best thought of as a complex function of a number of variables, each of which requires continued investigation. Characteristics of the young person would seem likely to contribute to the adjustment of both the youngster and the family; for example, the child's existing competencies and the types and variety of coping skills that the youngster possesses are likely to be important in this process. A second category of variables is disease factors, such as severity, degree of impairment, and the functional independence of the youngster. In addition, the youngster's environment (e.g., family, school, health care) are likely to be a factor in variations in adaptation. An appreciation of the complexity of the problem is illustrated by the model offered by Wallander, Varni, and their colleagues (Wallander & Varni, 1998) (see Figure 14-3).

In the following sections we examine two of the categories of influences on adjustment to chronic illness that have received considerable research attention: illness parameters and family functioning.

ILLNESS PARAMETERS AND ADJUSTMENT

The type of disease, the severity of the illness, and the degree of impairment of functioning produced by the illness are among the variables that have been examined as linking medical conditions to psychological adjustment. Of course, it is not always possible to analyze these dimensions separately. For example, certain illnesses are more severe than others, and severity is likely related to

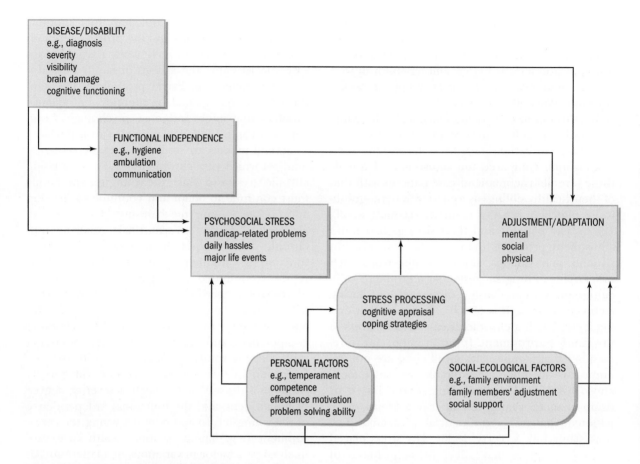

FIGURE 14-3 A conceptual model of child adjustment to chronic illness or disorder. Square-corner boxes indicate risk factors; round-corner boxes indicate resistance factors.

From Wallander and Varni, 1998.

greater restrictions in normal functioning. However, each of these variables seems important.

Disease-related parameters, such as type of disease and severity of illness, have not consistently been demonstrated to be related to adjustment. In a review of studies of depression among young people with chronic medical problems, Bennett (1994) found that youngsters with asthma, recurrent abdominal pain, and sickle cell anemia appeared to be more at risk for increased depressive symptoms than did those with cancer, cystic fibrosis, and diabetes. However, as Bennett indicates, the relatively small number of studies and methodological concerns suggests that these patterns be

interpreted with caution. In addition, research findings are not consistent with regard to adjustment differences among illness. Steinhausen (1988), for example, in contrast to the preceding findings, reported poorer adjustment in youngsters with cystic fibrosis than in those with asthma, both diseases affecting the lungs.

What, then, might be the impact of severity of the medical problem? In addition to the cystic fibrosis and asthma finding just described, Steinhausen (1988) also reported that poorer adjustment was associated with more severe illness in both of these groups, as well as in Crohn's disease and ulcerative colitis (both affecting the colon). In a similar finding, youngsters suffering from severe forms of arthritis had more behavior problems than healthy children, but children with milder or inactive forms of the disease did not (Billings et al., 1987). However, more severe forms of a disorder are not always associated with poorer adjustment (Wallander & Varni, 1998).

Investigators have found that adjustment may be associated with the degree of functional limitation caused by the condition, for example, the number of absences from school or limitations in relationships with friends (Eiser et al., 1992; Ireys et al., 1994). The degree to which the illness is controlled also appears to be important. For example, more emotional and behavioral problems are found when diabetes is poorly controlled (Mazze, Lucido, & Shannon, 1984). While these results suggest that anxiety, depression, and the like are outcomes of poor control, investigators acknowledge that the direction of causation is not clearly established. It is possible that anxiety, depression, and the like may contribute to poor metabolic control (Wiebe et al., 1994).

Ethically, we cannot manipulate emotional conditions or illness severity, nor can we randomly assign children to diseases. Thus, interpreting the impact of the dimensions of illness is inevitably difficult. Furthermore, while illness factors may help predict adjustment, their predictive ability does not appear to be that strong. Integrating illness factors into a more normative approach, one that combines these factors with the stress, risk, and resilience factors included in etiological models for youngsters without chronic medical disorder seems suggested (Timko et al., 1992). Such an approach would also allow for identification of factors relatively unique to chronic illness, as well as those common to other youngsters and families. Among the variables that might be the focus of such a normative approach, family functioning is one that has received some attention.

FAMILY FUNCTIONING AND ADJUSTMENT

Lisa L. is a fourteen-year-old with a four-year history of insulin-dependent diabetes mellitus and a variety of behavior and health status problems. Her mother reports problems with Lisa's diabetes management since diag-

nosis. These have gotten worse recently, resulting in ten hospitalizations in the past twelve months. Lisa's insulin dose has been raised but her glucose levels have failed to stabilize.

Lisa is the only adopted child in a family of four youngsters. She has three brothers, aged twenty years, two years, and one month. The oldest brother, age 20, is out of the home attending college. The two-year-old was born seriously ill and required several operations, although he is now in good health.

During the assessment process, Mrs. L did all the talking. Mr. L responded only to direct questions. Mrs. L openly expressed her hostility toward Lisa and privately expressed dissatisfaction with her husband because of his lack of assistance with child-care demands. Both parents view Lisa as openly hostile toward her father. She always involves herself in family arguments in which she sides with her mother. In contrast to their view of Lisa, the oldest son is seen as perfect. Mrs. L is also exceptionally nurturant towards her two younger sons. The two younger boys have never been left with a sitter.

The births of the two younger brothers have clearly changed Lisa's role in the family from youngest child and the focus of Mrs. L's nurturance, to sibling caretaker. Mrs. L is feeling increasingly stressed and recently left work to care for the two boys. She is angry at her husband for his passive stance, but this remains largely unexpressed. The oldest son's decision to leave home for college leaves her without any male support. Mrs. L directs much of her anger towards Lisa. Lisa is angry also, and this is directed primarily toward her father. It is possible that she may be receiving subtle encouragement from her mother for this. At the same time, Lisa's difficulties draw her parents together. Lisa's behavior and repeated hospitalizations also shift the family focus of attention away from her brothers and toward her. (Adapted from Johnson, 1998, pp. 428–429)

As we have seen in previous chapters, family functioning has frequently been linked to young people's adjustment. It is therefore not surprising that family functioning is related to the psychological adjustment of chronically ill youngsters as well (Kell et al., 1998). Without denying the particular risks and stressors associated with chronic conditions, it is reasonable as a starting point to assume that some of the family influences that are related to adjustment of other children and adolescents, such as parental depression and marital conflict, will also be related to the adjustment of young people with chronic illness. Indeed, this seems to be the case (Lavigne & Faier-Routman, 1993).

Timko and her colleagues (Timko et al., 1993), working with youngsters with juvenile rheumatic disease, examined how parental risk and resilience factors predicted disease-related functional disabilities (e.g., gripping things, doing routine household chores), pain, and psychosocial adjustments four years following initial contact with a hospital-based clinic. After the age of the youngster and initial levels of the youngster's functioning were controlled for, mothers' and fathers' personal strain and depressed mood and fathers' drinking were associated with poorer adjustment in the youngsters four years later. Better parental social functioning, the mothers' involvement in social activities, and the fathers' number of close relationships, on the other hand, seemed to facilitate the child's adjustment. Given that attention has concentrated on the contribution of maternal risk and resilience factors, it is interesting to note that the fathers' risk and resilience factors contributed to the children's functioning and adjustment beyond what was already accounted for by maternal factors and other influences.

In their comparison of diabetic youngsters and matched controls with acute illness, Wertlieb, Hauser, and Jacobson (1986) found that whereas overt expression of family conflict was related to greater problem behavior in both groups, other factors differentiated the groups. One particularly interesting finding involved differences in attempts to control and maintain the family system. Among the acutely ill youngsters, a greater control orientation in the family was strongly related to a greater probability of behavior problems. In contrast, low levels of family organization were associated with high levels of behavior problems among the diabetic youth. Families with a diabetic child have appreciable demands placed on them to organize daily routines involved in the management of the illness. Successful management of the diabetes probably requires appreciable organization and structure, as well as overtly dealing with issues of control. Structured and controlling family environments are found among youngsters with diabetes. This kind of family environment may be associated with better metabolic control of the diabetic condition, but the relationship of family environment to adjustment relationships is likely to be complex (Seiffge-Krenke, 1998; Weist et al., 1993).

Wysocki (1993) studied conflict in families with a diabetic youngster. The families of 115 adolescents with insulin-dependent diabetes mellitus completed the Parent-Adolescent Relationship Questionnaire (PARQ) (Robin, Koepke, & Moye, 1990). Consistent with the findings of Wertlieb et al., described above, and others, the families of diabetic adolescents and a normative group of families were not different regarding conflicts or other dimensions. However, scores on a PARQ scale measuring family communication and conflict resolution skills showed a clear relationship to the teens' adjustment to diabetes. These results suggest that at least some families with a diabetic adolescent might benefit from interventions aimed at reduced conflict through improved adolescent-parent communication skills.

Cohesion is another family variable that seems to be important. It is often reported that a life-threatening illness frequently draws family members closer together. Increased cohesion, although not a universal reaction to illness, has been observed in families coping with a variety of illnesses (Ross et al., 1993; Wood et al., 1989). Level of cohesion is frequently associated with the adjustment of the child or adolescent patient (Brown, Doepke, & Kaslow, 1993; Lavigne & Faier-Routman, 1993). A study of adolescent cancer survivors illustrates the importance of cohesion; however, it too suggests that relationships are likely to be complex (Rait et al., 1992).

Eighty-eight adolescents who had previously been treated for leukemia, Hodgkin's disease, or non-Hodgkin's lymphoma and who were currently in remission participated in the study. The participants were twelve to nineteen years old at the time of the assessment, with an average age of 15.6 years. Given the literature on chronic illness and family functioning, the authors hypothesized that the experience of cancer would result in greater family cohesion and that cohesion would be associated with the psychosocial adjustment of these cancer survivors.

The adolescents completed a standard measure of family adaptability and cohesion. Their scores were compared with a set of normative values on this measure that had been derived from a large community sample. The cancer survivors did differ from the normative group, but not in the predicted direction. The adolescents who had survived cancer described their families as less cohesive than the community sample. There was, though, the expected relationship between cohesion and adjustment. Greater cohesion was associated with better posttreatment psychological adjustment. However, an interesting complexity was suggested. Among "recent" survivors (treatment completed a year or less ago) and "long-term" survivors (treatment completed more than five years ago) there was the described strong relationship between family cohesiveness and adjustment. For "intermediate" survivors (treatment completed between one and five years ago), however, the association between family cohesiveness and adjustment was dramatically decreased.

In a related finding, Varni and his colleagues (Varni et al., 1996) examined the predictive effects of family functioning on the adjustment of children newly diagnosed with cancer over the first nine months after diagnosis. Higher levels of family cohesion and expressiveness were predictive of better adjustment. However, family functioning was more predictive of concurrent adjustment than of later adjustment. Thus family cohesion at one time was more closely related to adjustment at the same time than it was to adjustment six months later.

These findings illustrate the importance of studying adjustment as a process over time. The child's condition may change, and the impact of the illness on the family may not be static. Furthermore, changes in the youngster and in the illness may require changing styles of family involvement. In addition, since youngsters with chronic childhood illnesses have a greater chance of survival than ever before, these findings suggest the need for continued exploration concerning how the time since treatment, current age, age at time of diagnosis, and other such variables may be related to the association of family environment and the surviving youngster's psychological adjustment.

As more youngsters survive chronic illnesses such as cancer, the complexities of studying long-

term adjustment become clear (see From "Dying From" to "Living With" Cancer). Are perceived deficiencies (e.g., lower achievement), when found, due to poorer adjustment or to reasonable life choices about what is important? Rather than asking about better disease adjustment, it may be more reasonable to ask, "How does the experience of chronic illness affect individual development?" (Eiser, 1998).

PSYCHOLOGICAL INFLUENCES ON MEDICAL TREATMENT

Attempts to provide psychological treatment that would improve a patient's medical condition have long been one of the aspects of the interface between psychology/psychiatry and medicine. The vast majority of early attempts sought to provide the patient with psychotherapy as a means of reducing physical symptoms or curing illness. Such direct assaults on illness through psychotherapy proved to be largely ineffective (Werry, 1986). More recent efforts have taken a somewhat different approach to integrating a psychological perspective into the treatment of medical problems. Although a comprehensive review of these efforts is beyond the scope of the present chapter, a few important illustrations follow.

ADHERENCE TO MEDICAL REGIMENS

The terms "adherence" and "compliance" are most commonly used to describe how well a youngster or family follows recommended medical treatments. Diabetes provides an excellent opportunity to illustrate the way psychologists have increasingly attempted to understand the complex tasks encountered by families facing chronic childhood disorders (Krasnegor et al., 1993).

A description of diabetes mellitus. Diabetes is the most common endocrine disorder and one of the most common chronic diseases in youngsters, affecting approximately 1.8 youth per 1,000 (Gortmaker & Sappenfield, 1984). It is a chronic, lifelong disorder that results from the pancreas's producing insufficient insulin. Type I, also known as

FROM "DYING FROM" TO "LIVING WITH" CANCER

The preceding title describes a shifting emphasis regarding childhood cancer (Eiser, 1994; 1998). Cancer has long been viewed as a fatal and little understood disease. Although this frightening image still remains, it is not as accurate as was once the case. With increasing survival rates, it may now, for many youngsters, be more appropriate to view cancer as a chronic condition rather than a fatal disease. For example, in 1960 acute lymphocytic leukemia, the most common form of childhood cancer, had a survival rate of 1 percent five years after diagnosis. Current survival rates are in the order of 73 percent.

However, treatments are often lengthy, highly invasive, stressful, and accompanied by considerable pain. Also, the long-term concerns of these youngsters and their families are appreciable. Working with this population presents multiple and complex challenges. In addition to the initial task of helping the youngster and family understand and come to accept the illness, it is important to assist them in coping with a long and stressful treatment regimen and the additional stressors that the illness and its treatment place on them. For example, advice regarding the youngster's school, teacher, and peer group is likely to be important during treatment and afterward. Also, concerns regarding the longer-term impact of the disease are considerable and are probably related to developmental period. For adolescents the disease may interfere with the development of autonomy as a result of increased dependence on family and medical staff, and it may impose restrictions on social life and the development of close interpersonal relationships. Such outcomes, however, are not inevitable. The provision of ongoing and intensive psychosocial services to families throughout this process may buffer the impact of this experience and allow these youngsters to develop and function much like their peers (Noll et al., 1993).

One must also be aware that the very treatments that have resulted in longer survival may contribute to the long-term challenges. Central nervous system prophylactic treatment, for example, is one of the principle factors responsible for the increased life expectancy of youngsters with leukemia. Injection of methotrexate directly into the spinal column and irradiation of the spinal column and cranium reduce the probability of relapse, but they may have their own costs. Although the immediate and long-term impact of these treatments on cognitive and neurobehavioral functioning are not entirely clear, it appears that impairment does occur in areas such as attention, learning, and academic achievement. This disadvantage is particularly true for younger children (Brown et al., 1998; Lockwood, Bell, & Colegrove, 1999).

The shift to coping, adjusting, and adapting to cancer is clearly a more optimistic view. However, while we continue to attempt to understand this process and assist young people and families, it is also necessary to monitor these youngsters for long-term side effects of treatment. In addition, relapse remains possible, and there is an increased risk for secondary cancers. Maintaining such vigilance without creating additional and undue anxiety, while at the same time promoting an optimistic and adaptive attitude, presents a considerable challenge.

insulin-dependent diabetes mellitus (IDDM), re-quires daily replacement of insulin by injection because of the failure of the pancreas to produce insulin. Because the onset of IDDM typically occurs in childhood, this form of diabetes is often referred to as a childhood or juvenile diabetes. In Type II, non-insulin-dependent diabetes mellitus (NIDDM), some insulin is produced by the pancreas. NIDDM is an adult onset disorder; patients may or may not have to take insulin, and weight reduction and careful diet can often help to control this form of diabetes.

Onset of IDDM occurs most often around puberty. However, the onset of the disease can occur at any time from infancy to early adulthood. Although the exact etiology of IDDM is unclear, genetic factors appear to be involved. Diabetes is thought to be an autoimmune disease in which the body attacks its own pancreatic cells (Johnson, 1998).

Diabetes is characterized by free fatty acids (ketones) in the blood as well as increased sugar in the blood (hyperglycemia) and urine (glycosuria). Overt symptoms include excessive thirst, increased urination, weight loss, and fatigue. If the disorder is not controlled, a condition known as ketosis, or ketoacidosis, may occur. This is a very serious condition that can lead to coma and death (Johnson, 1998).

The youngster and family face a complex treatment regimen, which includes dietary restrictions, daily injections of insulin, monitoring of urine, and testing of blood glucose levels using small samples of blood obtained from a finger stick (see Table 14-1). On the basis of the daily tests for level of sugar and consideration of factors such as timing of meals, diet, exercise, physical health, and emotional state, the daily dosages of insulin must be adjusted. This is a complex therapeutic regimen, and even under the best of circumstances, "insulin reactions" occur often. Thus the youngster must be sensitive to the signs and symptoms of both hyperglycemia (excessively high levels of blood glucose) and hypoglycemia (excessively low blood glucose). These reactions involve irritability, headache, shaking, and—if not detected early enough—unconsciousness and seizures. The task

TABLE 14-1
Some Activities Required of Diabetic Children and Families
Inject insulin regularly
Test blood regularly
Exercise regularly
Avoid sugar
Check for symptoms—low
Check for symptoms—high
Be careful when sick
Shower regularly
Wear diabetes ID
Watch weight
Eat meals regularly
Adjust diet to exercise
Carry sugar
Test blood as shown
Change injection site
Inject insulin as shown
Watch dietary fat
Take care of injuries
Eat regular snacks
Control emotions
Inspect feet

Adapted from Karoly and Bay, 1990.

of identifying these states is made more complicated by the fact that symptoms are different for different youngsters and are subjectively experienced; consequently, it is possible for families to be misinformed about such reactions. Parents and youngster are therefore faced with a difficult, often unpredictable, and emotion-laden therapeutic program. Management of the regimen and its integration into daily life presents a considerable challenge (Delamater, 1986; Johnson, 1998).

Management of the diabetic condition. The first task in treatment is for the team of professionals to gain and maintain control of the diabetic condition. As this task is achieved, insulin requirements often decrease, and the initial fears and concerns of the youngster and family are often reduced. This has come to be known as the "honeymoon period." This period of partial remission may terminate gradually and often ends about one to two years after initial diagnosis. A self-management program with families during the first few months after diagnosis may avoid this deterioration in metabolic function (Delamater et al., 1990). This is but one example of the fact that diabetes is not a static disease. Adolescence is another time period during which management of diabetes often deteriorates (Johnson, 1995; LaGreca, 1987). Transferring control for management of the disease from the professional to the family and adolescent, as well as requiring maintenance of such control over long periods of time, is one of the challenges of working with chronic illness.

Adherence to the diabetic regimen. The concept of adherence is multifaceted (Johnson, 1993). Probably the initial step addressed in most programs is to educate the youngster and family about the disease. While such efforts are regularly made, it is also a common observation that adequate knowledge cannot be assumed (Delamater, 1986). Therefore, efforts have been made toward developing methods to assess knowledge. Behavioral observational methods have been employed to assess whether the youngster knows how to execute necessary skills such as urine and blood glucose testing (Harkavy et al., 1983). Questionnaires are frequently used to measure knowledge of the disease and the application of that knowledge to different situations (e.g., the role of insulin, and adjusting diet based on blood sugar readings). An example of such an instrument is the Test of Diabetes Knowledge: General Information and Problem Solving (Johnson, 1984). Some of the items included in this test are presented in Table 14-2. Even these few examples illustrate the difficulty and complexity of the information that youngsters and families must know. However, adherence is not just a matter of accurate information and knowledge. The young person and family must actually carry out the prescribed tasks accurately and consistently.

TABLE 14–2

Sample Items from Test of Diabetes Knowledge and Problem Solving

General Information

When giving insulin injections, you should
  (a) Inject into the same area.
  (b) Inject into different areas every time.
  (c) Inject only in the leg.
  (d) I don't know.

Ketones in the urine of a person with diabetes are
  (a) A warning sign of an insulin reaction.
  (b) A warning sign of acidosis.
  (c) A warning sign of hypoglycemia.
  (d) I don't know.

Problem Solving

You are trying out for your school's swimming team, and practice is midafternoon. Your blood sugar is usually 80-180. You should
  (a) Not take your insulin the days you practice.
  (b) Eat a big lunch that day and keep a snack handy.
  (c) Increase your insulin to give you more energy that day.
  (d) I don't know.

You take 30 units of NPH insulin each morning. One day your blood sugar at 10:00 A.M. is 300. Your urine has large ketones. In this situation, you should
  (a) Eat less today.
  (b) Eat more to counteract the ketones.
  (c) Drink extra fluids and check your blood and urine before lunch and again in one hour or two.
  (d) I don't know.

Adapted from Johnson (1984).

There are a number of reasons why it is important to know whether adherence to prescribed regimens occurs. For the clinician working with a particular youngster, effective treatment relies on the patient actually completing the necessary tasks. In a larger sense, it is impossible to assess the effectiveness of treatments without such information. Interventions conducted outside the hospital or doctor's office cannot be evaluated unless we know whether patients are adhering to recommendations. Is a treatment ineffective in controlling diabetes, or was that treatment not followed adequately?

In this chapter, it is not possible to examine all aspects of adherence. However, several important variables can be highlighted. Developmental level is an important variable affecting adherence (Iannotti & Bush, 1993; Johnson, 1993). In general, knowledge and skills seem to increase with age. For example, children under nine years may have difficulty accurately measuring and injecting insulin. Control is often gradually transferred to the youngster, and parental participation often ceases by age fifteen. However, it may be unwise, even with adolescents, for parents to withdraw from participation (Johnson, 1998).

Johnson et al. (1986) interviewed 168 diabetic children and adolescents and their parents concerning their diabetes-relevant behavior during the previous twenty-four hours. These interviews were conducted on three occasions for each family. The correlations between the reports of the youngsters and their mothers were, in general, statistically significant and moderate to strong (.42 to .78). However, the age of the youth seemed to affect mother-child agreement. On measures involving time (e.g., injection-meal timing, exercise duration), correlations were poorer for younger children. The young child's lesser sophistication regarding time is probably responsible. Youngsters in the nine to twelve and thirteen to fifteen age groups had the most consistent parent-child agreement across the thirteen behaviors assessed. Older adolescents (sixteen to nineteen years) had highly variable correlations across behaviors. For example, the correlation for injection interval was quite high (.91), whereas agreement on injection regularity was extremely low (-.04). Also, the fact that older patients are likely to be less frequently monitored by parents suggests different treatment challenges.

Adolescence appears to be a period of adherence difficulties. Despite better problem-solving abilities, adolescents with IDDM may show decreased adherence, particularly in social situations (Thomas, Peterson, & Goldstein, 1997). Social and emotional concerns, such as acceptance and greater participation in peer activities, are certainly an issue. Youngsters with diabetes may wish to avoid appearing different. The unusual behaviors required (e.g., injections, glucose testing) and dietary demands of eating frequently (when others are not) and avoiding high fat foods and sweets (when others are eating junk food) make conformity difficult. The example of vignettes used to assess social problem solving among diabetic youth that is presented in Table 14-3 illustrates some of these social challenges. Conflicts with parents over issues of independence are also likely to be present. These social and interpersonal issues most likely combine with actual physical changes, like those associated with delayed puberty, to increase management and compliance difficulties (Brooks-Gunn, 1993; Johnson, 1998).

Whereas increasing cognitive development potentially allows the adolescent to understand better the illness and to manage a complex routine, there are other aspects of cognition that may interfere with adherence. Murphy, Thompson, and Morris (1997) examined the cognitive appraisal

---

TABLE 14–3

Examples of Vignettes to Evaluate Social Problem-Solving in Diabetic Youth

Glucose Testing

Your friends ask you to go to a video arcade, and it's almost time for you to test your glucose. You don't have your test materials with you, and your friends are impatient to leave. If you stop and test, they will leave without you.

Diet—Sweets

You are invited to your best friend's birthday party, where they are going to serve cake and ice cream at a time when you are supposed to have a snack. But cake and ice cream would not fit into your diet plan at all, since you are supposed to have a snack that is low in sugar and fat.

Diet—Time of Eating

Your friends invite you out for dinner at your favorite restaurant, but they want to go really late, a lot later than you would normally eat.

Alcohol

Your friends invite you to a big party. You go there, and you find out that almost everyone is drinking beer. Your friends offer you some beer and seem to expect that you will drink it just as everyone else did.

Adapted from Thomas, Peterson, and Goldstein, 1997.

processes of twelve to eighteen-year-olds with diabetes. They found that adolescents who (1) have a negative perception of their bodies, (2) perceive little control over health when ill, and (3) have an external attributional style for negative events were at greatest risk for poor adherence.

Another major concern is the accuracy of adherence efforts. For example, it has often been observed that youngsters may be inaccurate in reading their glucose level tests (Gross, 1990). The majority of such errors are likely errors of knowledge or skill, but the actual faking of results, so as to avoid restrictions or the need for additional treatment, must also be considered. Interventions need to be planned that address both forms of inaccuracy.

Attention to the role of the primary health care provider (pediatrician, nurse) has also been examined as an important aspect of the adherence process (Dunbar-Jacob, 1993). There is a considerable discrepancy between what primary providers have recommended and what is recalled by patients and their families (Page et al., 1981). It also seems that health care providers may not be sufficiently aware of the child's level of cognitive development and so treat youngsters of varying ages as essentially the same. Thus younger children's understanding is likely to be overestimated, while the cognitive abilities of older children is underestimated (Perrin & Perrin, 1983). Also, the physician is likely to judge adherence by the youngster's health status rather than by actual behavior, and adherence may be defined as 100 percent compliance with medical recommendations.

Doctors and patients also may not share the same goals for treatment, as illustrated by a comparison of the goals of physicians treating youngsters with diabetes and the goals of the children's parents. Significant differences were found. The parents' goals were more focused on the short-term consequences of diabetes (e.g., hypoglycemia), and the physicians' on more long-term threats (complications). Youngster's diabetic control was more related to the parents' goals (Marteau et al., 1987).

It is clear that many other problems regarding adherence are worthy of continued attention. For example, it is important to anticipate environmental obstacles to compliance. Creating interventions that help adolescents deal with peers concerning their diabetes, for instance, may greatly facilitate compliance with recommendations (Gross et al., 1983). The realization that the immediate consequences of diabetes management are often negative and, therefore, more consistent with nonadherence than with adherence, may also help to anticipate difficulties. For example, the immediate consequence of injections is discomfort, and the effects of skipping injections is not immediate. Thus interventions that reduce the immediate negative effects of compliance may be of value (Schafer, Glasgow, & McCaul, 1982).

PSYCHOLOGICAL MODIFICATION OF PHYSICAL FUNCTIONS

The Eastern mystic who walks on hot coals, voluntarily slows the heart, and by the power of the mind closes a wound has always fascinated inhabitants of the Western world. Fascinating, too, are the shaman's cures by removal of evil spirits, the miracles of faith healers, and cures of medical ailments by inert placebos (Ullmann & Krasner, 1975). These phenomena highlight in a dramatic fashion the possible role of psychological interventions in the treatment of medical disorders. Each phenomenon suggests that psychological procedures can directly affect physical functioning. The systematic and scientific study of how psychology can be used to directly treat physical symptoms has become part of the shifting emphasis in understanding mind-body relationships.

Experimental research demonstrated that responses of the central nervous system could be modified by classical and operant conditioning (Kotses et al., 1976; Miller, 1969). This finding suggested that procedures such as relaxation and biofeedback could be employed to train a person to control body systems that are involved in a particular physical disorder. Indeed, a variety of psychological interventions have been applied to children's physical disorders. The research is promising but also limited, and strong conclusions regarding effectiveness cannot be drawn (Andrasik & Attanasio, 1985; Williamson, Baker, & Cubic, 1993).

The use of relaxation and biofeedback to treat children's headaches is one example of attempts to directly modify physical functioning through psychological interventions. Headaches are usually classified as tension, migraine, or a combination of the two. Tension headaches, as the name implies, are presumed to result from muscular tension (contraction) and reduced blood flow to the muscles. Migraine headaches are presumed to be a vascular disorder—vasoconstriction and vasodilation (narrowing and expansion) of the blood vessels in the head produce pounding and throbbing (Labbé, 1998; Williamson et al., 1993). Although migraines are less common, families are more likely to seek assistance for their treatment. These headaches, which produce very intense pain, are often accompanied by nausea and vomiting. This suffering and the desire to avoid potential negative aspects of existing drug treatment led to the exploration of nonpharmacological approaches (Andrasik, Blake, & McCarran, 1986; Masek & Hoag, 1990).

Biofeedback refers to a procedure in which some device gives immediate feedback to the person about a particular biological function. Feedback is usually provided by a signal such as a light or tone or by some graphic display. Such feedback to teach children to warm the temperature of their hands (skin temperature biofeedback), some form of relaxation training, or a combination of the two have been employed to treat children's migraines. The youngster learns to warm his or her hands without the assistance of the biofeedback machine and is instructed to practice at home. The mechanism whereby controlling hand temperature effects vasodilation is not clear. However, relaxation and biofeedback procedures seem promising in producing clinically meaningful levels of improvement in children's headaches (Andrasik et al., 1986; Holden, Deichmann, & Levy, 1999; Labbé, 1998).

Osterhaus and her colleagues (1993), for example, treated a group of school-aged youngsters (twelve to nineteen) with migraine headaches by using a combination of relaxation training, tem-

perature biofeedback, and cognitive training (to challenge irrational thoughts and to replace them with more rational thoughts that might produce pleasant feelings and less stress). The treatment was a school-based, after-school program of four group and four individual sessions. Regular home practice was also required. Youngsters in the experimental group were compared with a waiting list control group who received the same treatment after the experimental group had completed treatment. By the end of treatment, the experimental group had improved more than the control group on measures of headache frequency and duration, as well as on a weekly headache index of the duration and intensity of every single headache attack. However, groups did not differ significantly regarding headache intensity. At a seven-month follow-up evaluation, the experimental group experienced significant further post-treatment reductions in the duration and intensity of headaches as well as in the headache index. The youngsters in the control group were no longer available for comparison since, because of ethical considerations, they now were receiving treatment for their headaches. The results are illustrated in Figure 14-4. Employing a 50 percent reduction in headache activity as a criterion for clinically significant improvement, 45 percent of the experimental group, as compared with 11 percent of the control group, achieved clinically meaningful reductions in the headache index.

FACILITATING MEDICAL TREATMENT

Psychological factors also influence the effective delivery of medical treatments for physical disorders. Developing psychologically based procedures for enhancing the effectiveness of medical treatment is another important and growing area of interest. Procedures for dealing with pain and discomfort and for preparing for hospitalization illustrate this potentially important contribution.

Pain and distress. Despite its seeming simplicity, pain is a complex phenomenon that is difficult to assess. It is difficult, for example, to separate the pain or discomfort that the person is suffering from the anxiety that the person is experiencing

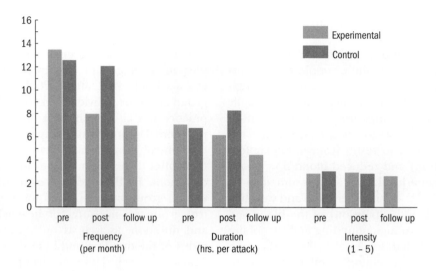

FIGURE 14-4 Mean frequency, duration, and intensity of headache attacks.
Adapted from Osterhaus Passchier, vander Helim-Hylkema, de Jong, Orlebeke, de Grauw, & Dekker, 1993.

while undergoing a painful medical procedure. This difficulty has led some to use the term "distress" to encompass pain, anxiety, and other negative affect (Jay, 1988; Varni, Katz, & Waldron, 1993). Whatever term is employed, three different response systems need to be assessed: behavioral, physiological, and cognitive-affective (Johnson & Rodrigue, 1998).

Self-report measures of the cognitive-affective component of pain are the most frequently employed measures. This is probably an intentional choice. Because pain is a subjective experience, assessing the youth's experience of pain is important. In addition, the greater accessibility of this component and the relative ease of measurement are certainly factors. However, measurement of this component is not without its difficulties. For example, the youngster's developmental level will play a large role in selecting a self-report measure. Since older children may be able to describe pain in semantic terms, interviews and questionnaires may be employed. Younger children need to rely on concrete and visual methods. The use of a pain thermometer that visually represents degrees of pain in numerical terms is one procedure that has

been employed (see Figure 14-5). In very young children who may not have the number concepts and discriminations required by this method, different measures can be employed. In that instance, faces with expressions from broad smiles to severe frowns, along with colors to indicate intensity of pain, may be useful.

The behavioral component of children's distress (for example, behaviors that require the child to be physically restrained) can often interfere with effective medical treatment. Observational methods are often used to assess children's distress behaviors. Structured behavioral observations employing a system of defined behaviors and trained observers have been employed in a variety of contexts (Blount et al., 1991; Elliot, Jay, & Woody, 1987). Because such procedures can be expensive and time-consuming, global ratings of distress by parents or nurses are often used to assess the behavioral component.

Assessment of the physiological aspect of pain is far less common. Melamed and Siegel's (1975) measurement of palmar sweat before and after youngsters underwent elective surgery is one of the earliest reports using physiological measures

PREVENTING CHILDHOOD INJURY

The role of psychological and social variables in prevention and health maintenance is another aspect of current pediatric psychology efforts. The prevention of injury to children is an example of this aspect of ongoing efforts at the interface of psychology and physical health.

Each year millions of children are injured. In the United States approximately 16 million require emergency room treatment, approximately 30,000 are permanently disabled, and more than 22,000 are killed. This represents a considerable threat to the well-being of children. Clearly the loss of life and function is tragic and the medical costs considerable.

Tremblay and Peterson (1999) describe this overwhelming loss of life and function and present a framework for understanding the clinical and policy challenges that exist. One obstacle in mobilizing injury prevention efforts is how the injury is perceived. Serious injuries are often mistakenly assumed to occur infrequently. There is also the frequent assumption among parents, and occasionally even health care workers, that most injuries are chance events and, therefore, unavoidable. Such assumptions do not encourage an active effort to prevent childhood injury. Professionals working in the area of childhood injury have therefore come to suggest abandoning the common term "accident" in favor of "unintentional injury," a term that acknowledges that the event, though not deliberate, might have been avoided.

Another challenge to injury prevention efforts is the variety of modes of injury and thus potential interventions. As Tremblay and Peterson point out, "a toddler mastering the operation of the gate blocking access to the swimming pool, a 7 year-old riding a bicycle without a helmet, and a 16 year-old driving with peers who ridicule him when he stays within the speed limit, are all candidates for a variety of potential interventions to prevent drowning, head injury, and motor vehicle injuries, respectively."

A basic contribution of psychology to these efforts is the perspective that there are important behavioral antecedents to injury prevention and that behavioral responses play a critical role in maintaining those conditions. The risk, for example, of a child ingesting household poisons is influenced by creation of a setting where the poisons are accessible, where there is not constant supervision by a caretaker, and where the child is old enough to explore his or her environment but still young enough to impulsively ingest a substance.

Prevention efforts can involve tactics directed at the entire population (multimedia campaigns), particular subsets of the population (bicycle safety programs for families with young children), or at certain milestones (well baby visits to the pediatrician) and can involve a variety of methods and targets. Changes in the environment can be created by law, for example, by mandating child resistant caps on medication. However, there is still an active component here that needs to be addressed—properly replacing the cap after each use. Education efforts about the seriousness and extent of childhood injuries in general or about specific injuries is part of the effort. However, more specific interventions aimed at modifying risk behaviors and perhaps altering the contingencies for behavior are also likely to be needed.

Attention to contingencies is often overlooked. Even in best case situations and ones in which the family is strongly committed to the best interests of the child, the combination of the low probability of injury in any particular instance, and the additional underestimation of the risk by most adults, leads to the need for additional contingencies for injury-related behavior. Use of child safety restraints in automobiles is now mandated by law in all fifty of the United States. Efforts to train parents in proper use of equipment, providing safe equipment to those who cannot afford it, and monitoring appropriate use by personnel at preschools are likely to be helpful. However, it may

also be necessary to provide and implement contingencies such as provision and enforcement of penalties for not properly restraining a child. Such contingencies can be part of a multiple component prevention program that also includes incentives for appropriate injury prevention behavior.

along with self-report and behavioral observation. However, the sophisticated equipment necessary and the difficulty involved in reliably obtaining measures such as heart rate, blood pressure, and skin conductance, result in such measures typically not being employed.

Measurement difficulty is but one aspect of the complexity of evaluating pain. The three response

systems are far from perfectly correlated. It is also the case that different measures within a single response system often show less than desirable levels of correlation. To complicate the issue further, developmental level may affect the relationship between the different response systems (Jay, 1988). Also, developmental issues may interact with aspects of the pain situation. It has been suggested, for example, that younger, more conceptually concrete children may exhibit greater distress when experiencing a more obvious but relatively minor injury (e.g., a small cut) than when they are subject to internal pain related to a more serious condition, such as arthritic joint pain (Johnson, 1988a).

Helping the child cope. Procedures have been developed to assist youngsters in coping with the pain associated with their disease or disorder (Janicke & Finney, 1999; Walco et al., 1999) or with the treatments they receive. Many of the medical treatment procedures used to assess and treat children with chronic disorders are aversive. It is commonly agreed that preparation of the youngster for an aversive procedure is the first step in helping the youngster cope and in reducing distress (Peterson & Mori, 1988). The basic rationale for preparation is that unexpected stress is worse than predictable stress. From the simple statement that preparation is good follows the complex question of how this is best achieved for each young person. Research provides some guidelines and suggests certain procedures (Powers, 1999).

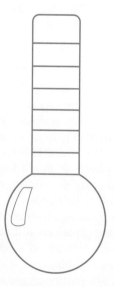

FIGURE 14-5 A child's subjective pain experience must be assessed in a developmentally appropriate manner. A pain thermometer like the one pictured is one way of concretizing differences in pain experience for young children.

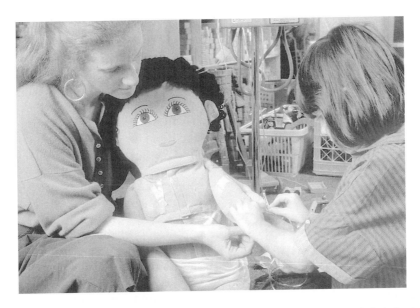

It is common for children to exhibit distress during medical procedures. Particularly for children who must undergo frequent treatment, techniques that reduce distress can facilitate good medical care.

(Will & Denl McIntyre/Photo Researchers Inc.)

Children's distress and experiences of pain during medical procedures are related to the behavior of their parents. When parents use strategies to distract the child or to direct the child to use coping techniques, the child exhibits less distress. In contrast, when parents attempt to comfort the child by reassuring statements or apologies, the techniques are associated with greater child distress (Friedman et al., 1998; Harbeck-Weber & Peterson, 1996).

The behavior of the medical practitioner is also likely to affect the youngster. An interesting finding is that information presented in a reassuring manner may reduce child distress (Dahlquist, Power, & Carlson, 1995). It may be that youngsters respond differently to parents and staff and that a combination of distraction/direction and reassurance, respectively, from these two sources may be most beneficial to the youngster (Friedman et al., 1998).

Some recommendations regarding coping strategies have been made on the basis of suggestions by youngsters themselves (Ross, 1988). Many of these suggestions cluster around the perception of being in control (Carpenter, 1992), and many involve the youngster controlling the environment during the aversive treatment procedure. The following comment by a ten-year-old boy undergoing emergency room burn treatment illustrates this phenomenon:

I said, "How about a hurting break?" and he (intern) said, "Hey, man, are you serious?" And I said, "Sure. Even when ladies are having babies they get a little rest between the bad pains." And they (the pediatric emergency room personnel) all laughed and he said, "OK, you get a 60-second break whenever you need it," and then it was much, much better, like you wouldn't believe it. (Ross, 1988, p. 5)

Although children may be capable of generating their own strategies for coping with pain and distress, procedures for teaching effective stress management/coping skills are also needed (Manne et al., 1993) and have received considerable attention (Dahlquist, 1992; Harbeck-Weber & Peterson, 1996; Kazak et al., 1996). Most current interventions consist of a variety of coping strategies derived from behavioral and cognitive-behavioral perspectives. Table 14-4 lists some of the skills included in such programs.

The work of Jay and her colleagues on reducing the stress of youngsters undergoing bone marrow aspirations is a good example of such efforts (Jay et al., 1987; 1991). Bone marrow aspirations (BMA) must be routinely conducted for youngsters with leukemia in order to examine the marrow for evidence of cancer cells. The procedure, in which a large needle is inserted into the hip bone and the marrow is suctioned out, is very painful. An injection of lidocaine is given to anesthetize the skin surface and bone, but it does not lessen the excruciating pain that is experienced with the suctioning of the marrow. The use of general anesthesia is avoided because of medical risks and expense. Intramuscular injections of sedatives are relatively unpopular, not only because they are painful but also because there is concern regarding substantial side effects.

The intervention package developed by Jay and her colleagues consists of the following five major components:

- Filmed modeling
- Breathing exercises
- Emotive imagery/distraction
- Positive incentive
- Behavioral rehearsal

TABLE 14-4

Some Skills Taught to Assist Children in Coping with Medical Procedures

Deep breathing exercises (deep inhalation and slow exhalation)

Distraction (e.g., counting ceiling tiles)

Emotive imagery (reconceptualizing the setting or pain)

Relaxing imagery

Behavioral or imaginal rehearsal (of the medical procedures)

Progressive muscle relaxation (relaxing muscle groups)

Rewards for using coping strategies

Adapted from Dahlquist, 1992.

The intervention package is administered on the day of the scheduled BMA, about thirty to forty-five minutes prior to the procedure. In the first step, youngsters are shown an eleven-minute film of a same-age model. While undergoing the BMA, the model, on a voice overlay, narrates the steps involved in the procedure, as well as his or her thoughts and feelings at crucial points. The model also exhibits positive coping behaviors and self-statements. The film is based on a coping rather than a mastery model. The child in the film exhibits a realistic amount of anxiety but copes with it rather than having exhibited no anxiety and distress at all. Next, the youngsters are taught simple breathing exercises, which are intended as active attention distracters but may also promote some relaxation.

The youngsters are then taught imagery/distraction techniques. Emotive imagery (Lazarus & Abramavitz, 1962) is a technique in which images are used to inhibit anxiety. A child's hero images are ascertained in a discussion with the child. They are then woven into a story that elicits positive affect that is presumed to be incompatible with anxiety, that transforms the meaning of the pain, and that encourages mastery rather than avoidance of pain. One girl's emotive imagery resembled the following story:

She pretended that Wonderwoman had come to her house and asked her to be the newest member of her Superpower Team. Wonderwoman had given her special powers. These special powers made her very strong and tough so that she could stand almost anything. Wonderwoman asked her to take some tests to try out these superpowers. The tests were called bone marrow aspirations and spinal taps. These tests hurt, but with her new superpowers, she could take deep breaths and lie very still. Wonderwoman was very proud when she found out that her superpowers worked, and she made the Superpower team. (Jay et al., 1985, p. 516)

Another imagery distraction technique involves teaching the youngster to form a pleasant image that is incompatible with the experience of pain (e.g., a day at the beach). The youngster chooses either the emotive or incompatible strategy and is given guidance during the bone marrow procedure to help in forming the images.

The positive incentive component of the intervention consists of a trophy presented as a symbol of mastery and courage. The youngster is told she can win the trophy if she does "the best that she can possibly do." The situation is structured so that every youngster can be successful in getting the trophy.

During the behavioral rehearsal phase, younger children "play doctor" with a doll, while older children are guided in conducting a "demonstration." The youngsters are instructed step-by-step in the administration of the BMA. As the youngster goes through the procedure, the doll is instructed to lie still and do the breathing exercises and imagery.

Jay et al. (1987) compared this cognitive behavioral package with a low-risk pharmacological intervention (oral Valium) and a minimal treatment-attention control condition. Each youngster experienced each of these interventions during three different BMAs. Which of the six possible orders of these interventions a youngster received was randomly determined. When in the cognitive-behavioral intervention condition, youngsters had significantly lower behavioral distress, lower pain ratings, and lower pulse rates than when they were in the control condition. When youngsters were in the Valium condition, they showed no significant differences from the control condition except that they had lower blood pressure scores.

The findings of this study represent one example of interventions that will help youngsters and families cope with the distress associated with certain medical procedures. The incorporation of parents to assist in promoting coping skills will likely improve the maintenance of child coping and will improve the cost-effectiveness of interventions that otherwise might require a great deal of professional time (Manne et al., 1993; Powers et al., 1993). Such interventions hold the promise of making delivery of effective medical treatment more likely.

Hospitalization. Youngsters suffering from chronic illness often require periodic hospitalization to stabilize their functioning. Normal youngsters, too, often need to enter the hospital for minor surgery. In the mid-1950s, the importance of the child's psychological reaction to early hospitalization and surgery began to be recognized. Researchers noted that a majority of children experienced mild to extreme stress reactions during and following hospitalization and that many demonstrated behavioral problems following surgery (Prugh et al., 1953). A particularly notable finding was Douglas's (1975) examination of the long-term effects of early hospitalization. Follow-ups were conducted on a sample consisting of one out of every four children born in Great Britain during a particular week. Approximately 20 percent of the children who were later hospitalized before the age of five seemed to experience some immediate adverse effect. Adolescent conduct disorders and reading difficulties seemed to occur more frequently among some small proportion of those children who had experienced early hospitalization. Early research thus seemed to indicate that at least some aspects of hospitalization could be damaging to children.

Improvements have occurred since the 1950s and 1960s, when much of this research was conducted. For example, in 1954 most New York hospitals allowed parental contact only during two visiting hours per week. In contrast, Roberts and Wallander (1992), describing a 1988 survey of 286 hospitals in the United States and Canada, found that 98 percent of the hospitals had unrestricted visiting for parents and that 94 percent allowed parent rooming-in.

Most hospitals now also offer prehospital preparation for both the child and the parents (Roberts & Wallander, 1992). Nevertheless, the procedures that are used are not always those best supported by research (Peterson & Mori, 1988). One well-supported method of preparation involves the use of models who, although apprehensive, cope with the hospitalization stresses. Melamed and Siegel's (1975) film, *Ethan Has an Operation*, showed a seven-year-old boy prior to, during, and after surgery. The child narrates the story and shows realistic but adaptive reactions to the procedures. The film has been shown to be an effective means of preparation for hospitalization and surgery (Melamed & Siegel, 1980; Peterson et al., 1984). This is but one example of the use of modeling. Other films and the use of puppets have been shown to be effective as well (Peterson et al., 1984), and interventions often combine modeling with explicit training of coping techniques. Current efforts are directed at preparation procedures that are cost-effective and therefore likely to be used and that are matched to individual characteristics of the child, parent, and family (Peterson & Mori, 1988; Peterson et al., 1990).

Despite the improvements in hospitalization, children are still faced with stressors related to their hospitalization. Spirito, Stark, and Tyc (1994), for example, found that 50 percent of the chronically ill youngsters whom they asked to name a stressor since they had been in the hospital, described a specific aspect of hospitalization (e.g., noises preventing sleep, rude staff, slow service). By way of comparison, only 33 percent and 17 percent, respectively, indicated pain-related concerns or an illness-related problem (e.g., side effects of treatment, problems or limitations caused by their illness). In contrast, the percentages of youngsters hospitalized for acute illness or injuries who indicated hospital, pain, or illness-related stressors were 39 percent, 51 percent, and 10 percent, respectively. This finding highlights the potential differing needs of children with prior hospitalization experiences. Hospital stressors require attention, since improvements in these areas are likely to enhance the mood state and adjustment of youngsters, particularly those who are chronically ill and may require frequent hospitalizations.

THE DYING CHILD

Clearly, one of the most distressing aspects of working with severely ill youngsters is the prospect of death. Even though much progress has been made at increasing survival rates, the numbers still fall short of 100 percent. Increased survival rates may make the death of a child even harder to bear when it does occur (Eiser, 1994). Several important questions are raised:

■ What is the child's understanding of death?

■ How can we best prepare the youngster and the family?

■ How do we prepare people for death while sustaining their motivation for treatment?

■ Can we help the family begin to accept the child's impending death but prevent the family from premature distancing from the child?

■ What do we do after the youngster dies?

■ How is the helper affected by working with the dying child?

These are difficult questions.

It does appear that children's conceptions of death are influenced by their parents' views and change during development (Candy-Gibbs, Sharp, & Petrun, 1985). Cognitive development plays a role in the evolving conceptualization of death (Ferrari, 1990). Young children may think of death as being less alive and assume it to be reversible. At about five years of age, an appreciation of the finality of death may be present, but death still does not seem inevitable. An understanding of death as final and inevitable and of personal mortality emerges at about age nine or ten. Although developmental differences in cognitive understanding exist, it must also be appreciated that children may be aware of death and be worried about their fatal illness even if they do not have a fully developed concept of death. Fatally ill youngsters' concepts of death do not appear to be more advanced than those of physically well youth (Jay et al., 1987).

What of family members? They too must certainly be made aware of the seriousness of the youngster's illness. However, an appropriate balance between acceptance of death and hope for life is probably adaptive. It is a genuine challenge to prepare parents for the death of their child yet enable them to help the child emotionally and assist with the treatment regimen. This undertaking requires mental health staff who are knowledgeable and sensitive. As our ability to lengthen survival—and perhaps to raise hopes of some future cure—increases, the problem will become even more difficult. Integration of support services into the total treatment program and immediate availability and access are important in delivering needed help. Once a point is reached where the child's death is likely, the focus of intervention must shift. Information and support are still needed, but the focus must change to helping the child and family to be most comfortable and to make the best use of the remaining time. Moreover, the family should not be abandoned after the young person's death. Continued assistance and support should be a part of the total treatment (Friedman et al., 1998).

Caregivers, too, are not immune to the effects of observing a youngster dying. Koocher (1980) suggests that efforts must be made to reduce the high cost of helping: the inevitable stress, feelings of helplessness, and the likelihood of burnout. These are not trivial matters. The helpers' adjustment and efficiency are not the only concern, since the potential impact of their behavior on the family and youngster is also significant. In *Who's Afraid of Death on a Leukemia Ward?* Vernick and Karon (1965) offered poignant anecdotes to this effect. One describes the impact of helpers' behavior on a nine-year-old patient who, after taking a turn for the worse, received some medical treatment and began to show improvement:

One day while she was having breakfast I commented that she seemed to have gotten her old appetite back. She smiled and agreed . . . I mentioned that it looked as if she had been through the worst of this particular siege. She nodded in agreement. I went on to say that it must have been very discouraging to feel so sick that all she could do was worry—worry about dying. She nodded affirmatively. I recognized that the whole episode must have been very frightening and that I knew it was a load off her mind to be feeling better. She let out a loud, "Whew," and went on to say that except for me, nobody really talked with her. "It was like they were getting ready for me to die." (p. 395)

Certainly, one of the most difficult decisions is what to tell the dying youngster. A protective approach or "benign lying" was once advocated. The youngster was not to be burdened, and a sense of normalcy and optimism was to be maintained. Most professionals now feel that this approach is not helpful and probably is doomed to failure anyway. The stress on the family of maintaining this deception is great, and the likelihood that the youngster will believe the deception is questionable. Some balance must be struck that takes into

consideration the child's developmental level, past experiences, timing, and an understanding of the family's belief system (Dolgin & Jay, 1989a). An example of such a balance is illustrated in the following excerpt:

A child with a life-threatening illness should be told the name of the condition, given an accurate explanation of the nature of the illness (up to the limit of his ability to comprehend), and told that it is a serious illness of which people sometimes die. At the same time, however, the child and family can be told about treatment options and enlisted as allies to fight the disease. An atmosphere must be established in which all concerned have the opportunity to ask questions, relate fantasies, and express concerns, no matter how scary or far fetched they may seem. When the patient is feeling sick, weak, and dying, there is no need to [be reminded] of the prognosis. If a family and patient know a prognosis is poor but persist in clinging to hope, one has no right to wrest that from them. The truth, humanely tempered, is important, but we must be mindful of the patient and how [the patient's] needs are served. To tell the "whole truth" or a "white lie" for the benefit of the teller serves no one in the end. (Koocher & Sallan, 1978, p. 300)

SUMMARY

■ Attempting to determine the role of psychological factors in physical disorders is part of a long tradition of trying to understand the relationship between mind and body.

■ The current view that psychological factors are relevant to physical disorders in a number of different ways represents a shift from the earlier, more limited view of psychosomatic diseases caused by emotional factors.

■ Current conceptualizations of the role of psychological factors in asthma illustrate many of the changes that have occurred. For example, there is not support for the idea that psychological factors play a role in causing reduced respiratory capacity. Psychological influences, however, are one of a variety of possible trigger mechanisms that can bring on an asthmatic episode.

■ The appreciable social and emotional consequences of chronic illness have received increasing attention. For juvenile diabetes and other chronic illnesses, there is likely to be considerable individual variability in how youngsters and families cope, and adjustment is likely to be an ongoing process.

■ Researchers have sought to determine the impact of parameters of the illness, such as severity, and of aspects of family functioning, such as conflict, on the chronically ill child's or adolescent's adjustment.

■ Psychology can contribute to effective treatment of medical conditions in a number of ways.

■ Medical treatment is often rendered ineffective because of failure of the patient and family to adhere to prescribed treatment regimens. Adherence is a complex process. Attempts to improve adherence require attention to multiple dimensions such as the youngster's developmental level, family patterns of interaction, and the role of the health-care professional.

■ Psychological treatments (for example, relaxation and biofeedback) may be able to modify physical functioning directly. These interventions are likely to be adjuncts to medical treatment.

■ Psychology may also facilitate the delivery of medical interventions. Treatment programs to reduce the distress felt by youngsters who are undergoing medical procedures not only make the youngster more comfortable but also make easier the task of medical personnel.

■ Despite increasingly high survival rates, the prospect of death is one of the most distressing aspects of working with some chronically ill youth. Psychological contributions to understanding the child's conception of death and the mechanisms of coping with this possibility can be an aid in effective and caring treatment. Attention must also be given to the continuing needs of family members. The impact of death on the professional who is working with these youngsters is profound and will affect that person's ability to help.

CHAPTER 15

EVOLVING CONCERNS FOR YOUTH

This final chapter focuses on concerns for the well-being of young people. It is a truism that the future of every society depends on its youth, and concerns for youth are frequently expressed. In both the United States and other countries, policy and actual practice have not always been consistent with voiced concerns. The welfare of the young is tied to economic conditions, so that it is not surprising that basic care and opportunity are especially problematic in developing countries. However, because resources and implementation of programs devoted to the development of youth also depend on social and political attitudes, care can vary enormously even when resources are adequate.

Concerns for youth have long been expressed in the United States. Some of the current concerns hark back to the 1960s and 1970s, when much emphasis was placed on the rights of individuals deemed disadvantaged and powerless in society. The economic and sociopolitical changes of the more recent years have brought new con-

cerns. The lives of youth are affected by what is happening in the personal lives of their parents, the value assigned to the young, the priorities given to health care and education, the state of the economy, and a host of other factors. Sensitive and caring adults are looking at these influences with an eye toward better care for youth.

Progress in understanding human development has also stimulated efforts toward optimizing the potential of the young. Although no one would deny that knowledge about development is incomplete, we have come far from viewing the young simply as little adults. Their unique needs are better known; the general course of physical, intellectual, and social growth is well on the way to being mapped; and developmental influences, including risk and protective factors, are increasingly understood. Child specialists and others are enthusiastic about using this knowledge to reduce behavioral disorder, enhance development, and enrich lives. Thus both societal and professional factors are shaping concerns for youth and the ways in which these concerns are manifested in programs and policies.

Our discussion in this chapter is necessarily selective. Focusing on behavioral and psychological issues, we recognize many interacting influences, as is consistent with our general view of development. Although we also focus on the United States, we conclude the chapter by acknowledging concerns for youth growing up in circumstances that can be very different from those in the United States. We seek not only to discuss developmental risk but also to point to the future with some optimism. One of the themes of this chapter is the progress being made in preventing disorders, and we begin there. In turn, we will look at issues concerning the family, child maltreatment, youth services, and international matters.

PREVENTION

In the United States, interest in prevention can be traced to the early-twentieth-century writings of Clifford Beers, the mental hygiene movement, and the creation of the child guidance clinics (Heller, 1996). However, progress did not come easily. Neglect and actual resistance were common responses to arguments for preventive interventions. Several reasons accounted for this situation. The mental health disciplines have traditionally focused on treatment: professionals are trained for treatment, and they are financially rewarded for treatment. Then too, it has always been difficult to deflect funding from the obvious needs of those already displaying problems, a need that is never completely met. As a result, prevention has not been well funded. In addition, doubts have existed about the basis for prevention. Disorders with known etiology are clearly preventable, at least in principle. If we know that an infection of the brain causes disturbed behavior, we can work towards

finding ways to prevent the infection. But the etiology of behavioral disorder is rarely known and is likely to be multifactorial. Thus it was argued that prevention was hardly feasible. It was also pointed out that evidence for the efficacy of prevention was far from compelling.

More recently, there has been increased interest in prevention. Some of the arguments for preventive efforts are beginning to hold sway. It can hardly be disputed that, at least in the abstract, prevention is superior to treating conditions that already exist. From a humanitarian point of view, prevention clearly is more desirable: It averts discomfort and suffering. Practical considerations also argue for prevention. We have seen that population surveys often identify about 15 percent to 20 percent of youth as having clinic-level problems. Treatment is often costly and sometimes unavailable for groups of needy people. As it is, perhaps only 5 percent of youth with diagnosable conditions receive any kind of mental health care (Costello et al., 1993). Even with treatment, it is difficult to undo certain disturbances once they set in.

In addition, the considerable amount of research on behavioral disorders and prevention is beginning to have an impact. Although the etiology of most disturbances is not completely understood, research has identified risk factors and protective factors for many specific disorders and more generally. Thus there is now a firmer basis for selecting populations for preventive efforts and for designing interventions. Finally, substantial evidence for the effectiveness of prevention is beginning to mount (Durlak & Wells, 1997; Munoz, Mrazek, & Haggerty, 1996). Overall, this is an optimistic time with regard to prevention.

CONCEPTUALIZING PREVENTION

Prevention has not always been viewed in the same way. A three-prong approach based on Caplan's (1964) work has served as a general framework for thinking about prevention. In this approach, prevention is viewed as primary, secondary, or tertiary. Primary prevention, which attempts to stave off disorders in the first place, involves both general health enhancement and prevention of specific dysfunction. Secondary prevention is usually defined as the effort to shorten the duration of existing cases through early referral, diagnosis, and treatment. It is a "nipping in the bud" strategy. Tertiary prevention aims to reduce problems that are residual to disorders. Thus it might seek to minimize the negative impact of labeling a child as learning disabled or to rehabilitate a person who has suffered a severe mental disorder. Tertiary prevention is clearly worthwhile but is an after-the-fact strategy that reduces dysfunction.

Recent conceptualizations tend to define prevention in terms of primary interventions that occur prior to the full onset of disorders or problems. Variations exist in the specific ways in which primary interventions are conceived. Figure 15-1 shows one way to depict primary prevention. In the figure, prevention is set apart from treatment and from aftercare that might reduce additional dysfunction, and it has three components.

■ Universal preventive interventions are targeted to entire populations for which greater than average risk has not been identified. Ideally, cost of the interventions is low, the interventions are acceptable to the population, and risk of adverse outcome from the interventions is also low (Munoz et al., 1996). An example is advertising to convince a general population to avoid the use of harmful addictive drugs.

■ The second component, high-risk interventions, targets individuals who are at higher than average risk for disorder. Thus intervention might be directed toward individuals with biological risk, high stress, family dysfunction, or poverty.

■ The third component is targeted to high risk individuals who show minimal but detectable symptoms or signs forecasting a disorder, or who have biological markers that predispose a

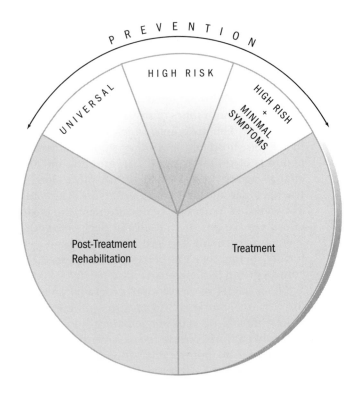

FIGURE 15-1 A conceptualization of prevention.

disorder. These persons do not meet the criteria for the disorder.

The wellness goal. One of the more notable ways in which definitions of prevention vary has to do with acceptance or rejection of the goal of wellness. A recent report of the Institute of Medicine (chartered by the National Academy of Science) accepts reduction of risk and increased protection as part of prevention but rejects promotion of optimal states of wellness (Munoz et al., 1996). In other words, it defines prevention in terms of preventing illness or disorder but rejects going beyond that to optimal functioning. In contrast to this narrow definition, Landsman (1994) likens primary prevention to the work done by architects, who attempt to build healthy and aesthetic surroundings by working with large populations of people and the way in which they interact with their surroundings. Albee (1986; 1996), an influential advocate for a broad definition of prevention, notes that many mental disorders are linked to poverty, sexism, racism, and other social ills. He thus desires broad social change and building individual competence, security, and optimism as protection from disease and disorder. For Albee, achieving social equality should be a part of prevention programs.

Cowen (1991; 1995) also argues for wellness, or health promotion, defining it as going beyond the absence of malfunction to having a sense of such things as belongingness, purpose, control, and satisfaction with oneself and one's life. Cowen (1995) cites five major elements as central to wellness:

- Forming wholesome early attachments
- Acquiring age-appropriate competencies
- Experiencing life in environments that favor healthy development
- Having a sense of control over one's fate
- Coping positively with stress.

These elements are viewed as similar to inoculations, that is, as protection against possible later adverse outcomes. Moreover, Cowen argues that all people can benefit from this approach. Intervention would take many pathways—working with

individuals, settings, communities, society's structures, and social policy to promote the well-being of the many. It would require input from diverse fields, such as mental health, human development, community planning, social policy, and the like.

Although most prevention targets at-risk populations, prevention programs aimed at enhancing general mental health also exist. For example, some interventions teach children problem-solving strategies, which may increase their overall competence to deal with the challenges and opportunities of their daily lives. It has been suggested that the narrower definition of prevention, which emphasizes disease or disability reduction, and the broader definition, which more generally promotes mental health, are both legitimate and complementary (Cowen, 1997; Riess & Price, 1996).

EXAMPLES OF PREVENTION PROGRAMS

Prevention programs for youth vary tremendously in focus and setting. Table 15-1, which summarizes 177 primary prevention programs for children, gives some idea of this variation (Durlak & Wells, 1997). The programs focused on modifying either the environment or children's learning or behavior. Affective education and interpersonal problem solving were among the areas targeted. Some interventions also targeted life transitions, since these can be both times of stress and opportunities for growth. The programs, which were conducted in schools, hospitals, and other settings, involved children of different racial background, and the change agents were mental health professionals, teachers, parents, and college students. The table also indicates a measure of effectiveness, the mean effect size. To put the findings in perspective, the average participant in a prevention program performed better than 59 percent to 82 percent of control group participants.

Other kinds of prevention programs include, for instance, working with parents of low birth weight infants or with single-parent adolescents. Still other efforts encourage positive lifestyles, as in fostering an unfavorable attitude toward risky sexual behavior. Early screening of general intelli-

TABLE 15-1

Primary Prevention Programs for Children

Type of Program	*n*	Mean effect[a]
Environment-Centered		
School-based	15	0.35
Parent training	10	0.16
Transition Programs		
Divorce	7	0.36
School entry/change	8	0.39
First-time mothers	5	0.87
Medical/dental procedure	26	0.46
Person-Centered Programs		
Affective education		
Children 2 to 7	8	0.70
Children 7 to 11	28	0.24
Children over 11	10	0.33
Interpersonal problem solving		
Children 2 to 7	6	0.93
Children 7 to 11	12	0.36
Children over 11	0	–
Other person-centered programs		
Behavioral approach	26	0.49
Nonbehavioral approach	16	0.25

[a] All means differ significantly from zero except for Parent training.
Adapted from Durlak and Wells, 1997.

gence, reading deficits, attention deficits, school maladjustment, and other problems is often crucial for identifying youth who are at risk for developing problems.

Many prevention programs target young people affected by poverty. In a country as wealthy as the United States, between 20 percent to 25 percent of children live below the federal guidelines for poverty (McLoyd, 1998; Routh, 1994b). Moreover, poverty rates for children have been higher than for other age groups since 1975. Poverty is disproportionately high among minority groups and mother-headed households. Although a complex of factors has created increasing poverty among children, it is nevertheless appalling that child poverty is higher in the United States than in similar industrialized countries (Dubow & Ippolito, 1994; Pollitt, 1994). Figure 15-2 represents this

general finding. Of course, it is well known that poverty puts children at risk with regard to diet, health, developmental delay, behavior problems, teenage pregnancy, exposure to drugs, family stress, educational achievement, and occupational opportunity.

A considerable number of well-designed and well-evaluated preventive programs currently exist. We will now detail a few of these efforts, two that are family or community based and two that are school based.

Mother-infant programs. These programs target the development of low birth weight or premature infants. The association of low birth weight with a variety of adverse outcomes is well established. Except for cases of extreme physical damage, adverse effects can be reduced or overcome by a high quality of care, which appears related to parents' attitudes and skills, family resources, and social support (e.g., Greenberg & Crnic, 1988; Sameroff, 1990). The transactional model of development frequently has been used to explain this finding. Complex, ongoing interactions among the child, parents, and larger social environment produce various developmental paths that differentially affect infant growth. Extraordinary medical intervention is often critical to favorable outcome, but so too is the quality of care given to the infants.

There are many examples of successful infant-mother programs. The Mother-Infant Transactional Program (MITP) is one. Its purpose was to assist mothers in adjusting to the care of their low birth weight infants and to enhance infant development (Achenbach et al., 1990; Rauh et al., 1988). A fundamental assumption was that confident, knowledgeable, and effective parenting would reduce the probability of infant developmental problems. Each mother worked with a supportive, specially trained nurse for three months in order to (1) appreciate better her infant's unique characteristics, (2) recognize the infant's communications, and (3) appropriately respond to these signals. The eleven sessions included the infants and, when possible, the fathers. Techniques entailed direct instruction, demonstration, modeling, and practical experience in handling

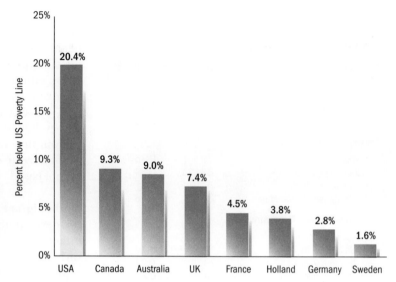

FIGURE 15-2 Child poverty rates in selected Western industrialized countries in the mid-1980s.

Note: Children include those under eighteen years of age. This figure is based on data presented in Smeeding (1992).

From McLoyd, 1998.

the infant. The nurse encouraged parental feelings of comfort and confidence.

Infants in the MITP intervention were compared with low birth weight infants randomly assigned to no-treatment and to normal birth infants. It was demonstrated that for the most part, mothers in the intervention group expressed more self-confidence and satisfaction with the mothering role and perceived their infants as less difficult temperamentally. Infant cognitive status was measured at several times. As Figure 15-3 shows, treated infants became different from the low birth weight controls and more similar to the full-term controls.

Other research indicates the efficacy of intervention for low birth weight or premature infants (Olds & Kitzman, 1993). The Infant Health and Development Program consisted of a three-year pediatric follow-up, family education and support, and educational day care (Bradley et al., 1994). It was conducted at several sites. Evaluations showed positive effects on infant health and development that went beyond the effects of pediatric care.

Mother-infant programs often entail several components, which are delivered in the home, at centers, or in both settings. They often target families with multiple stressors due, for instance, to poverty or single-parenting. Intervention can be successful in spite of multiple stressors, although stress and minimal protection take their toll. More research is needed as to the long-term effectiveness of infant-mother intervention. Nevertheless, these programs clearly show that preventive efforts are feasible and worthwhile. Early intervention can help create a more positive pathway for future development.

Preschool intervention. Among the most important of interventions designed to reduce the risks of poverty are early school programs. An initial assumption was that brief interventions might put poor children on equal footing with more economically fortunate youngsters. It was assumed that early experience is especially important for brain, intellectual, and social growth and that preschool intervention could put children on a path to acade-

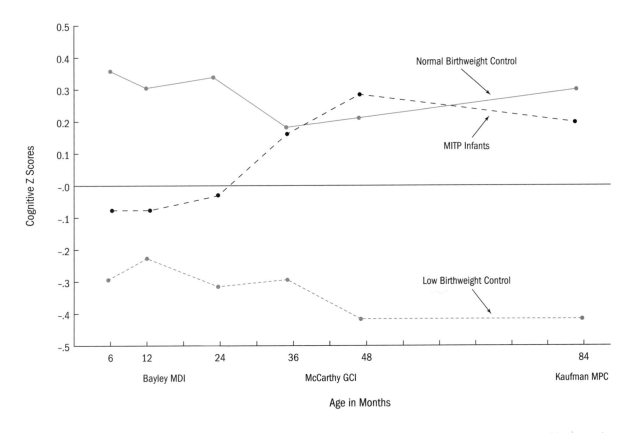

FIGURE 15-3 Cognitive test scores at different ages for the MITP infants, low birth weight controls, and normal birth weight controls.
From Achenbach et al., 1990.

mic achievement that, in turn, could boost their chances of attaining self-worth, decent jobs, and healthy, fulfilling lives. The intent was well captured in the name Head Start, which was given to the federally funded program that was designed for poor children and that also included children with special disabilities. (See Accent.)

Innumerable early intervention programs exist for children of low income families and other high risk children. (See also the Abecedarian project, p. 77). They are funded by private, local, and other federal agencies. Over a thirty-year period, the effectiveness of early school interventions, including Head Start, has been studied. This large

literature is in fundamental agreement on many points (Guralnick, 1998; Ramey & Ramey, 1998; St. Pierre & Layzer, 1998). The following are among the conclusions that have been drawn.

1. High quality interventions show positive effects on cognitive and social development.
2. Greater effects are seen in programs that enroll children early and continue for longer periods of time.
3. Greater benefits are associated with greater intensity of the program (that is, positive experiences tightly packed into time).

A HEAD START FOR CHILDREN AT RISK

Head Start was federally funded in 1964 by the Economic Opportunity Act, as part of the federal government's War on Poverty. From the beginning, it was conceptualized as a comprehensive developmental program to enhance cognitive, social, and emotional growth; health; and family and community relationships (Zigler & Styfco, 1993). Head Start thus encompassed several major components.

■ *Education.* The educational component places children into classes with a high teacher-student ratio. The ethnic and cultural characteristics of the community are considered. For example, when a majority of the children are bilingual, some of the staff speak the children's native language.

■ *Health.* Physical and mental health are emphasized. Nutritious meals are served, and parents are offered education in nutrition. Medical examinations include hearing, vision, and dental checkups; follow-up medical treatment is provided when appropriate. A mental health professional is available to evaluate special needs and to provide training in child development for staff and parents.

■ *Parent Involvement.* Community involvement is fundamental to Head Start. Parents participate in decisions about the program, many serve as volunteers or employees, and many participate in workshops related to the welfare of their children or the family.

■ *Social Services.* Head Start families often have needs for other services; it is the task of the Head Start social service coordinator to help obtain these services. The object is to strengthen the family unit so that it may do the best job possible in rearing children and supporting its adult members.

The program barely got off the ground when it was concluded that it did not result in intellectual advancement for preschoolers (e.g., Cronbach, 1975; Jensen, 1969). However, the test of time favors the conclusion that Head Start can be beneficial in ways similar to other preschool interventions. Woodhead (1988) has described the process like a relay race: A burst of cognitive and school readiness fades, but not before the baton has been given to other runners on the team—teacher expectations, self-confidence, school promotions, avoidance of special education, parental aspirations, and so forth. Nevertheless, vigilance is required to maintain the quality of Head Start programs, and demands have been made for performance standards and careful monitoring (Kassebaum, 1994).

Head Start legislation has continuously funded preschool programs and, in addition, Parent and Child Centers, the Comprehensive Child Development Programs, and programs for infants and toddlers (Ramey & Ramey, 1998). In 1996, Head Start served over 750,000 children, 68 percent of whom were four to five years of age, and at least 10 percent of whom had disabilities.

4. Programs that provide more comprehensive services have greater benefits.
5. Some children benefit more than others, and benefits appear related to initial risk status.
6. Initial benefits on standardized intellectual tests fade over time, especially when learning and motivation are not supported by the social environment.
7. Longer-term benefits can be observed in the school environment. These include reduced grade retention and special education placement, and increased rates of high school graduation. Some studies also show higher employment rates and reduction of antisocial behavior.

These findings indicate that quality programs can make a difference in the lives of many children disadvantaged by poverty and special disabilities. Nevertheless, there is agreement that preschool programs by themselves are insufficient to overcome the effects of poverty. It could hardly be expected that even high-quality programs could ameliorate continuing poverty and adversity. Moreover, many poor children, especially those in urban communities, are experiencing unsurpassed violence, fear, and despair in their communities (Takanishi & De Leon, 1994). Early inventions must be linked to welfare reform, community development, and training for adults for a global economy.

The Rochester Primary Mental Health Project (PMHP). This project, initiated in 1957 by Cowen, Zax, and their colleagues, took the school as its focus for preventive efforts (Cowen et al, 1975; Zax & Cowen, 1967). The school was selected not only because it is the setting for much socialization and learning but also because children were experiencing school maladjustment. Teachers complained that several children were demanding a disproportionate amount of time and energy. These students were not being well served, the rest of the class was being disrupted, and teacher morale was suffering. Mental health

A critical component of Head Start is preschool experience that offers multiple activities and a high teacher to child ratio.
(Paul Conklin/PhotoEdit)

services for these children were either unavailable, or it was assumed that troubles would disappear with time. They did not (e.g., Cowen et al., 1966).

Although PMHP has evolved over the years, its continuing thrust has been systematic early identification and prompt preventive intervention for school maladjustment. What follows is a brief description of the principal aspects of the program. More extensive descriptions are available elsewhere (e.g., Cowen & Hightower, 1989a, 1990).

One of the innovative aspects of PMHP is mass screening of youngsters soon after they begin school. Screening methods have consisted of parental interviews, psychological testing, teacher reports, and direct observations. Diverse kinds of data are collected concerning developmental and health history, school problem behaviors and competencies, and factors in the children's life situations that may relate to school adjustment. Information is obtained from multiple informants.

Children identified in PMHP as already manifesting maladjustment, or as likely to do so in the future, become the recipients of special treatment by nonprofessional child aides. Conversation, books, games, and media provide a framework for interaction with the child. The child is encouraged to deal with problem areas and feelings, and enhancement of self-esteem is considered important. Specific activities depend on the needs of the individual child. The utilization of minimally paid nonprofessionals as child aides is a noteworthy dimension of PMHP. Many of these are mothers with relatively modest formal education. They receive some training at the project, but personal qualities are also considered a potent treatment resource. Although the use of nonprofessional child aides was initially justified on the basis of professional shortages and financial austerity, the child aides are now seen as an asset of the program rather than a compromise (Cowen & Hightower, 1989b; Hightower & Braden, 1991).

The general model of the PMHP can thus be characterized by its (1) focus on young children; (2) use of active, systematic screening for early school maladjustment; (3) expansion of services through the use of nonprofessional aides; and (4) use of professionals in activities such as training, supervision, consultation, and research/program evaluation. The program has been flexibly applied so as to meet the demands of particular situations.

Research has been an essential component of the PMHP; from the start, it was designed to improve the program and to demonstrate possible benefit. Research has been conducted, for example, on assessment instruments to initially screen children and to evaluate their progress (e.g., Gesten, 1976; Hightower et al., 1987). Evaluation of the program's effectiveness has been extensive. Examination of several hundred children who participated in PMHP at some time during 1974 to 1981 suggested reductions in acting out, shyness, and learning problems, as well as gains in sociability, assertiveness, and tolerance of frustration (Weissberg et al., 1983). However, the raters knew that the children were PMHP participants, and the study had no control group.

Although the realistic constraints of doing research in schools has often limited the rigor of research designs, the large number of evaluations over the years do suggest that the program has been effective. And an important step is that research findings have been fed back into the program to structure improvements (Cowen & Hightower, 1989b; Hightower & Braden, 1991). For example, not all the findings over the years have been positive; some data indicated that those most helped were the shy-anxious children, and greater efforts then were made to facilitate the aides' effectiveness with acting-out and learning-disabled students (Cowen, Gersten, & Wilson, 1979; Lorion, Cowen, & Caldwell, 1974).

PMHP began as a single demonstration project, but by 1983, twenty PMHP projects were operating in the Rochester, New York, area. Through active dissemination efforts, the program was also adopted elsewhere, and an estimated 350 school districts around the world implemented the project (Cowen & Hightower, 1989b).

On the basis of their experiences in PMHP, Cowen and his colleagues more recently developed the Rochester Child Resilience Project (RCRP). This project is rooted in understanding the impact of chronic life stress on children and the resilience of some children experiencing monumental adverse circumstances. The project was designed to investigate the correlates and antecedents of resilient outcomes among highly stressed fourth- to sixth-grade urban children (Cowen et al., 1990). Early results from RCRP have begun to identify variables that differentiate stress-affected and stress-resilient children and their parents (Cowen et al., 1990; Cowen et al., 1994). Some of these are child variables, such as an internal and realistic sense of control, problem-solving skills, coping strategies, and self-esteem. Other variables involve the parent-child relationship and the caregiver's sense of being an effective parent. This research is an example of how investigations of resiliency can be useful to those concerned with enhancing the wellness of children and families at risk because of highly stressful environments (Cowen, 1994).

The School Transitional Environment Project (STEP). STEP is designed to avert future difficulties for students who are functioning adaptively in their schools (Felner & Adan, 1988; Felner et al., 1993; Hightower & Braden, 1991). The focus is on a normative life event—the transition into middle, junior, or high school. School transition can be a risky time for youngsters; it is associated with diminished academic performance, substance abuse, delinquency, and school dropout. Transition is considered riskier in schools that provide little social support and that have complex organization (e.g., students feeding in from many other schools, many new social demands). Therefore, STEP targets such schools.

Central to STEP is the creation of units in which a group of students is assigned to a homeroom and to academic classes as well. STEP homerooms are placed in physical proximity, so that cohesion is increased and complexity of the large school decreased. In addition, homeroom teachers take on new tasks in guidance and monitoring. For example, they assist students in selecting classes, provide brief counseling, and oversee attendance and truancy. Teachers receive training in these areas. Coordination is structured through regular teacher meetings to discuss student functioning, needs for referral, and problems. In this way, STEP units simulate small schools by creating small units in which groups of people are in close contact and responsible to each other. The intervention largely focuses on modifying the environment.

Evaluations have shown STEP's effectiveness. Compared with control students, STEP students attended school at higher rates, had higher grades, and rated the school environment favorably. A five-year follow-up found significantly higher grades, a 55 percent lower school dropout rate, and reduced levels of problems such as depression and substance abuse (Durlak, 1997). This favorable outcome has generally held in subsequent STEP programs, which have serviced students from working, semiskilled, and blue-collar families in both urban and rural settings.

FAMILIES IN TRANSITION

The importance of family influences on child and adolescent development has been evident throughout this book. In this section, we will highlight three family topics that illustrate how contemporary change in the family is part of evolving concerns for the child.

The current state of the family and its future is a common topic in the media and of conversations at social events, over the dinner table, in shopping malls, and, indeed, wherever people meet. It is also a politically salient topic. Although it is often assumed that the issue is the decline of the traditional family, it need not, and indeed should not, be articulated in this way. Scholars who have studied the history of the American family have argued that we are suffering from the "mystique of the traditional family"—a first-time married couple living with their biological children in a father-headed family (Bahr, 1988; Emery & Kitzmann, 1995). These scholars challenge the idea that the family has decayed from some past idyllic form, and they point out that various family forms have always existed in sizable numbers. Research, too, has led us away from a focus on the traditional family *structure* with findings that it is family *processes* (warmth, communication) that are of greatest importance for child development, not family structure. In drafting the Convention on the Rights of the Child, the United Nations also moved away from the concept of family structure and chose instead to employ the term "family environment" in its attempt to protect the child's right to family (Melton, 1996). The term "family environment" stresses family functioning over its structure and recognizes the diversity of definitions of family.

Several factors have caused us to rethink our definitions of family. Among these are the increasing number of children raised in single-parent homes and the new family relationships created by remarriages (Hetherington, Bridges, & Insabella, 1998; Schroeder, 1989; U.S. Bureau of the Census, 1998). The number of women working outside the home also influences contemporary conceptualizations of family.

MATERNAL EMPLOYMENT AND CHILD CARE

Social and economic influences have resulted in the majority of mothers being employed outside the home. Among two-parent families with school-aged children, the rate of maternal employment is approximately 68 percent (U.S. Bureau of the Census, 1998). Table 15-2 illustrates this pattern in the years between 1975 and 1997. Increases occurred for mothers with children of all ages. The percentage of mothers employed outside the home was up about 4 percent between 1993 and 1997. It is notable that by 1985, the majority of

mothers of children below school age were working outside the home.

Considerable attention has been given to the impact of maternal employment on the women themselves, on marital relations, and of course on the development of their children (Hoffman, 1989; Scarr, Phillips, & McCartney, 1989). The apprehension that is felt regarding care of children by someone other than their mother is reflected in the fact that the U.S. Labor Department considers care by a child's own father as "other relative care" (Scarr, 1998). Nevertheless, there are generally few differences between two-parent families in which the mothers do or do not work (Harvey, 1999; Muller, 1995; Silverstein, 1991). The impact of maternal employment depends on a host of factors, including the child's age; the amount of time parents spend at work; the way that remaining time is used by the family; the quality of child-care arrangements; parental attitudes toward work and their various roles; family structure; and other psychological, social, and economic variables (Gottfried & Gottfried, 1988; Harvey, 1999; Hoffman, 1989; Scarr et al., 1989). Indeed, the question of maternal employment could be framed in terms of what variables affect families in general and what conditions should be provided to maximize the functioning of all families (Scarr, Phillips, & McCartney, 1990; Silverstein, 1991).

Child care. Increased maternal employment outside the home has focused attention on the need for a variety of child-care arrangements (Clarke-Stewart, 1992; Scarr, 1998; Schroeder, 1989). The term "child care" is used to refer to any nonmaternal care of children who reside with their parent(s) or close family members. There are two, somewhat conflicting, goals of child care: maternal employment and child development. From the perspective of the workplace, the goal is quantity of affordable child care, whereas from the perspective of the child's needs, the goal is high-quality (likely expensive) care that enhances development (Scarr, 1998).

Historically, children of working mothers were most commonly cared for by family members or neighbors. There are currently a variety of child-

TABLE 15-2

Percentage of Mothers in Two-Parent Families in the Labor Force by Age of Own Youngest Child

Age of Child	1975	1985	1997
Under 3	32.7	50.5	61.3
3 to 5	42.2	58.4	67.0
6 to 13	51.8	68.2	76.5
14 to 17	53.5	67.0	80.1
Total	44.9	60.8	71.1

Adapted from U.S. Bureau of the Census, *Statistical Abstract of the United States: 1998* (118th ed.). Washington, DC, 1998.

care arrangements. In addition to care by relatives, children may be cared for by nonrelatives in either the child's own home or another's home, and a substantial proportion attend some type of organized child-care facility (e.g., day-care center, preschool program, early childhood education program). Of the over 21 million children under the age of six in the United States in 1995, 40 percent were cared for regularly by their parent(s), and 60 percent were in some form of child-care arrangement (U.S. Bureau of the Census, 1998). The proportions of these children in various nonparental care arrangements are shown below. (The data add to over 60 percent because some children experienced more than one type of care.)

■ Organized child-care facilities—31 percent

■ Care by a relative—21 percent

■ Care by a nonrelative—18 percent

There are economic and ethnic/racial differences in the proportions of young children in various nonparental care situations. For example, whereas nearly half of children from families below the poverty threshold are cared for by relatives, similar arrangements exist for a little less than one-third of children from families at or above the poverty level. About half of white non-Hispanic and black children are in an organized child-care facility, whereas only a little over one-third of Hispanic children are cared for in this kind of arrangement (Federal Interagency Forum on Child and Family Statistics, 1998).

The impact of early care arrangements has been the topic of much debate among professionals and in the public press (Scarr, 1998). Parents are often concerned about finding arrangements that can provide the kinds of care they desire and that help shape their children's development in a manner consistent with their own values. The effects of early child care are likely to depend on the quality of care provided, and there is considerable variability in available child care. Quality of care is, of course, a complex concept. Scarr (1998) describes the dimensions used to define quality child care.

■ Health and safety requirements

■ Responsive and warm interaction between staff and children

■ Developmentally appropriate curricula

■ Limited group size

■ Age-appropriate caregiver:child ratios

■ Adequate indoor and outdoor space

■ Adequate staff training

Quality of care is difficult to measure. Also, the care selected is correlated with attributes of the parent, family, and child, thus increasing the difficulty in interpreting any effects on the child as due to type of child care (Fuller, Holloway, & Liang, 1996). Although it would seem logical that the quality of child care that youngsters experience would affect their development, research does not show that it has a major impact on the development of children from ordinary homes. The effects on children from disadvantaged homes may be stronger in that child care may provide elements that are less available in their lives (Scarr, 1998).

Care of school-age children. There is concern as well for children of school age. Some older children have no formal provisions for care. These are the so-called "latchkey" children, who must use a key to let themselves into their empty homes after school. Less value-laden terms, such as "children in self-care" have increasingly been advocated to describe this situation. Accurate estimates of the prevalence of self-care are hard to come by; however, data suggest an increasing likelihood of self-care throughout the elementary school years (Riley, 1997). Estimates of the number of children in self-care range from 7.2 percent to 15 to 20 percent of early elementary and 45 percent of late elementary school-age children (Peterson & Magrab, 1989).

Attention to self-care is relatively recent, and although the developmental implications for children are uncertain, they should not be ignored. Of course, the impact will not be the same for all children. The amount of time in self-care, parental attitudes, the child's developmental level, other family

Many children return to empty homes after school. The impact of such "self-care" requires further study.

(Courtesy of A.C. Israel)

the child is adequately prepared. Peterson (1989) suggests that three major areas need to be considered in preparation: injury risk, emotional difficulties, and selection of activities. Preparation has several components, including discussion with the child and arranging for a contact person if the child feels help is needed. It is also essential that the child have a safe and secure environment.

SINGLE PARENTING

Many of the issues raised about the impact of maternal employment in two-parent families apply to children being reared in single-parent homes. Parenting is a difficult task even when undertaken by two parents, and a single parent takes on the responsibilities on her or his own.

The growing number of children being reared in single-parent homes in the United States and elsewhere has made the issue an important one (Hernandez, 1994). Figure 15-4 illustrates the increasing percentage of homes headed by a single parent. Thirty-two percent of all U.S. families and 64 percent of all African-American families with

influences, and available social supports are likely to influence an individual child's reaction.

One question regarding self-care focuses on its potential impact on cognitive and academic functioning. Does self-care preclude after-school interactions with an adult that enhance cognitive development and assure the completion of school assignments? Perhaps these needs are met later in the evening, since working parents appear to participate in child-centered activities by attending less to homemaking chores (Scarr et al., 1989). Much has also been written about the possibility that self-care has negative emotional effects on children. However, there is little carefully conducted research to support the hypothesis of adjustment difficulties among latchkey children (Lovko & Ullman, 1989).

It may be that self-care, even if not ideal, is an alternative arrangement for some children. When self-care is employed, it is necessary to ensure that

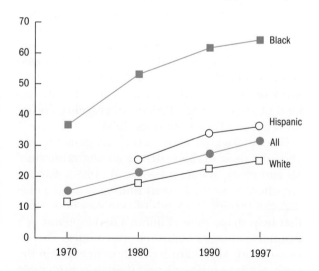

FIGURE 15-4 Percentage of single-parent families by race and Hispanic origin, from 1970 to 1997.

Adapted from U.S. Bureau of the Census, *Statistical Abstract of the United States: 1998* (118th ed.). Washington, DC, 1998.

LATCHKEY TO CHILD CARE

Community programs that target prevention or amelioration of childhood problems often raise questions about the relationship of professionals to members of the community and about who is to have power to guide the goals and implementation of the programs. In a bottom-up approach, the community has a good deal of control, which takes advantage of community knowledge, resources, and talent, and perhaps strengthens the community's sense of competence. In addition, programs in which the participants have input are thought to be more successful.

David Riley (1997) has described his experiences with regard to programs for latchkey children. When Riley began talking to parents about the potential problems of unsupervised care of children, the initial response was that few children were in this situation. Riley then began to collect data, a project that was done in close collaboration with communities. The data showed a pattern that beginning in second grade and continuing throughout middle childhood, increasing numbers of children spent some days unsupervised or caring for a younger sibling. The number of families needing after-school care also was reported.

The findings spoke for themselves in showing the need for child care.

As the number of data collection projects increased, Riley was forced by lack of time and funding to take a backseat. Community members became the major researchers. As it turned out, the planning committees "were unable to let their reports sit on the shelf." Seven years later, Riley found that 69 reports had been issued in communities around the state of Wisconsin, 92 child care program sites had been established, and 6,750 children had been served.

The School-Age Child Care project has been replicated in twelve other states. With replication has come adaptation to the needs or desires of the communities. In one community, Riley's colleague Mary Peters interviewed native-speaking Cherokee and Creek-Muscogee Indians about their needs. In sharing the data with the tribal elders, she asked them whether an after-school program in which children learned the traditional stories, dances, and crafts of their Indian culture might be beneficial. The ensuing program both provided child supervision and strengthened the indigenous culture of the community.

children were headed by a single parent in 1997. Single-parent households include many children born to unmarried teenage mothers. In 1996 about 55 of every 1,000 adolescent girls between the ages of fifteen and nineteen gave birth to a child (U.S. Bureau of the Census, 1998). These children, in particular, have been reported to encounter developmental problems in preschool (Furstenberg, Brooks-Gunn, & Chase-Lansdale, 1989). Many young single mothers live in poverty, a situation that likely contributes to these findings (Brooks-Gunn & Duncan, 1997).

Not all single-parent homes are headed by never-married mothers, however. Many are created by divorce. Professionals have also been concerned about the impact of divorce on children and adolescents.

DIVORCE AND REMARRIAGE

That many marriages end in divorce is well documented. The divorce rate in the United States more than doubled between 1970 and 1981 (Guidubaldi & Perry, 1985). Although this trend has leveled off and perhaps declined in recent years, large numbers of children will experience their parents' divorce (U.S. Bureau of the Census, 1998; Hernandez, 1994). However compelling, statistics do not completely capture the impact of the problem. Many children experience more than one divorce. Some experience periodic separation and discord in families where divorce petitions are filed and withdrawn. Thus divorce and remarriage are not static events, but a series of family transitions that modify the lives of children (Hetherington, Stanley-Hagan, & Anderson, 1989; Wallerstein, 1991).

A lengthy review of the literature on the effects of divorce and remarriage is beyond the scope of our discussion. Reviews of this extensive literature are available (Emery & Kitzmann, 1995; Grych & Fincham, 1999; Hetherington et al., 1998). It is generally agreed that children and adolescents from divorced and remarried families, in comparison with those from two-parent nondivorced families, are at increased risk for developing adjustment problems. Those who have undergone multiple divorces are at greater risk.

For the most part, the adjustment of youth from divorced and remarried families are similar. Difficulties occur in a broad array of areas of functioning. Children experience academic difficulties, externalizing behavior, internalizing problems, lower self-esteem, lower social competence, and social relationship difficulties. Adolescents exhibit some of the same problems and, in addition, are more likely to drop out of school and be unemployed, to be sexually active at an earlier age, to have children out of wedlock, and to be involved in delinquent activities and substance abuse (Amato & Keith, 1991; Hetherington et al., 1998). However, research findings suggest that the adjustment differences between youngsters from divorced and remarried families and those from nondivorced families are small in magnitude and that the vast majority of children from divorced and remarried families function in the normal range of development (Amato & Keith, 1991; Emery & Forehand, 1994; Emery & Kitzmann, 1995). However, these findings should not lead us to ignore the clinical significance of the adjustment problems experienced by some youngsters

from divorced families (Grych & Fincham, 1999). What, then, accounts for increased risk for those youngsters who do develop adjustment difficulties and the resilience of those who do not?

Hetherington and her colleagues (1998) suggest a model, based on a set of interrelated risks, to explain the links between divorce and remarriage and a youngster's adjustment (see Figure 15-5). The adjustment of children and adolescents to marital transitions is the result of a complex interaction among a large number of influences. This complex process also must be considered in the context of an ongoing developmental process. While the process of family transitions is occurring, neither the youngster nor the developmental tasks to be faced remain static. Finally, ethnic and cultural influences are salient in this process, but much of what we know is based on the experiences of European-American families. With such complexities in mind, we turn to an examination of some of the influences likely to impact the adjustment of children and adolescents to marital transitions.

One of the influences that contributes to a youngster's adjustment to marital transitions is preexisting individual factors, which contribute to exposure and vulnerability. Adult (parent) characteristics (e.g., antisocial behavior, depression) place some parents at risk for marital discord and multiple marital transitions, and therefore their children are also more likely to be exposed to marital transitions. A youngster's prior level of adjustment is likely to contribute to her or his reaction to divorce or remarriage. Indeed, when a youngster's prior level of adjustment is taken into account, differences due to the marital transitions are greatly reduced. However, the youngster's prior level of adjustment may have resulted in part from the marital disruption and family discord that contributed to the divorce. In turn, the challenges of parenting a difficult child may have contributed to the marital transition. In addition, the individual parent difficulties that contributed to divorce, as well as the behavior problems in their children, may be influenced by common genetic contributions (Jockin, McGue, & Lykken, 1996; McGue & Lykken, 1992). For example, genetics may contribute to a characteristic that increases

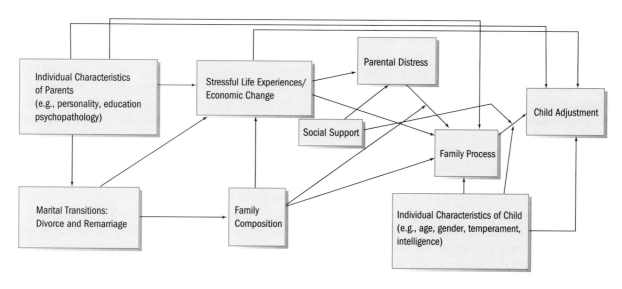

FIGURE 15-5 A transactional model of the predictors of children's adjustment following divorce and remarriage.
From Hetherington, Bridges, and Insabella, 1998.

the likelihood of both parent antisocial behavior (a risk for divorce) and externalizing behavior problems in children and adolescents. Clearly, even this part of the picture is complex.

Other individual characteristics of the youngster may also contribute to adjustment to marital transitions. Children with an easy temperament may be better able to cope with the disruptions associated with marital transitions. Youngsters with a difficult temperament may be more likely to elicit negative responses from their stressed parents and to have greater difficulty adapting to parental negativity and marital transitions. They may also be less capable of eliciting the support of other people around them (Hetherington et al., 1998).

In addition, the youngster's gender may affect adjustment to marital transitions. Earlier reports suggested that boys were more affected by divorce and girls by remarriage. More recent studies, however, find less pronounced and less consistent gender differences. Improvements in research methodology may in part be responsible. Also, some of these differences may be due to changes in custody and visitation arrangements that may have increased father involvement. It is likely that

the impact of gender will be complex, depending on the aspect of adjustment studied, gender-related differences in patterns of development, timing of marital transitions, and other such factors (Emery & Kitzmann, 1995; Hetherington et al., 1998).

Ethnic differences may be another consideration. For example, some research suggests that black adolescents benefit more from living in stepfamilies than white adolescents do. McLanahan and Sandefur (1994) suggest that the improved income, supervision, and role models provided by stepfathers may be more advantageous to black children because they are more likely to live in neighborhoods with fewer resources and social controls.

The youngster's age at the time of divorce is another variable that has received considerable attention. Some research had suggested that preschool-age children's adjustment was more affected by divorce; however, findings have been mixed (Amato & Keith, 1991). Again, this is likely to be a complex issue (Emery & Kitzmann, 1995; Grych & Fincham, 1999). If one is interested in ongoing adjustment over time, age at divorce is confounded with time since divorce and current age (reflecting developmental level and developmental transitions being faced). These confounded time-related issues must also be considered in the context of viewing adjustment to divorce as an ongoing developmental process.

The impact of family composition on adjustment has largely been viewed from the perspective that any deviation from traditional structure is problematic and research has largely been focused on parental absence. This perspective is, in general, not well supported. There is some evidence that the well-being of boys may be enhanced by the presence of a father. However, effects of family composition/parent absence are not simple and are likely modified by factors such as parent availability, quality of family relationships, and the child's gender (Hetherington et al., 1998). Furthermore, there are cultural and ethnic differences in how family is defined. The presence of extended family in the household, for example, is more likely among African-American families than among European-American families, as is a wide informal network of kin (including longtime friends as well as relatives) available in a "parent" role (Emery & Kitzmann, 1995).

The impact of economic changes and associated life stress on children and adolescents who experience marital transitions has received considerable attention. The distress (anger, depression, loneliness, anxiety, etc.) experienced by the parents is also acknowledged as an important influence. The contribution of these variables to the youngster's adjustment are thought to be largely mediated by their impact on family processes. Economic stress and parental upset contribute to dysfunctional family relations (e.g., conflict) and interfere with effective parenting (Hetherington et al., 1998).

MALTREATMENT OF YOUTH

Although child maltreatment has probably existed since the beginning of civilization, recent concern is usually dated to the early 1960s (Cicchetti & Olsen, 1990). Especially influential was an article by pediatrician C. Henry Kempe and his colleagues, in which the term "battered child syndrome" was coined (Kempe et al., 1962). Their efforts were stimulated by alarm at the large number of children at pediatric clinics with nonaccidental injuries. Subsequent efforts resulted in all fifty states adopting mandated child abuse reporting laws by the year 1970. In 1974 the U.S. Congress passed the Child Abuse Prevention and Treatment Act (Public Law 93-247) to give some national focus to the problem and to prescribe actions that states should take.

Since the late 1970s, the problem has become a major public concern. For example, in 1976 only 10 percent of the population thought abuse was a serious problem, compared with over 90 percent in 1983 (Magnuson, 1983). Between 1982 and 1991, the number of cases of alleged maltreatment doubled (National Center for Child Abuse and Neglect, 1993). According to the U.S. Bureau of the Census (1998), over 2 million reports of child abuse or neglect were filed in 1996, involving over 3 million children. If one considers only substantiated and indicted cases, there were well over 900 thousand cases in 1996.

DEFINING MALTREATMENT

There is agreement that child abuse and neglect are serious and prevalent problems. What is not as clear is an agreed on definition of what constitutes maltreatment and the prevalence of the problem. Although federal guidelines exist, the specifics of defining maltreatment fall to the states, and definitions vary considerably. This situation obviously creates difficulties for research, interventions, and legal practice (Cicchetti, 1994; English, 1998). Four types of maltreatment are typically described in the literature: physical abuse, sexual abuse, neglect, and emotional abuse. The definitions of the four major types of maltreatment are presented in Table 15-3 .

When most people hear the widely used term "child abuse," they assume that it refers to physical assault and serious injury. However, the general legal definition that has evolved over several decades includes both the commission of injuries and acts of omission, that is, failure to care for and

TABLE 15-3

Definitions of the Major Forms of Maltreatment

1. **Physical abuse:** An act of commission by a caregiver that results or is likely to result in physical harm, including death of a child. Examples of physical abuse acts include kicking, biting, shaking, stabbing, or punching of a child. Spanking a child is usually considered a disciplinary action, although it can be classified as abusive if the child is bruised or injured.

2. **Sexual abuse:** An act of commission, including intrusion or penetration, molestation with genital contact, or other forms of sexual acts in which children are used to provide sexual gratification for the perpetrator. This type of abuse also includes acts such as sexual exploitation and child pornography.

3. **Neglect:** An act of omission by a parent or caregiver that involves refusal or delay in providing health care; failure to provide basic needs such as food, clothing, shelter, affection, and attention; inadequate supervision; or abandonment. This failure to act holds true for both physical and emotional neglect.

4. **Emotional abuse:** An act of commission or omission that includes rejecting, isolating, terrorizing, ignoring, or corrupting a child. Examples of emotional abuse are confinement; verbal abuse; withholding sleep, food, or shelter; exposing a child to domestic violence; allowing a child to engage in substance abuse or criminal activity; refusing to provide psychological care; and other inattention that results in harm or potential harm to a child. An important component of emotional or psychological abuse is that it must be sustained and repetitive.

From English, 1998.

protect (National Institute of Mental Health, 1977). Thus neglect needs to be addressed along with physical assault.

Figure 15-6 illustrates the relative rates of various forms of maltreatment in the United States in 1996 (U.S. Bureau of the Census, 1998). Approximately 52 percent of the cases involved neglect, and 24 percent, physical abuse.

In general, sexual abuse refers to sexual experiences that occur between youth and older persons or to the sexual exploitation of the young such as in pornographic film. The extent of the problem is difficult to estimate, but most experts agree that it is underreported. This observation is suggested by adults' retrospective reports of their childhood experiences and by the increase in the reporting of sexual abuse in both the United States and Canada (Green, 1993; Wolfe, 1998). Statistics suggest that sexual abuse occurs in about 12 percent of substantiated child maltreatment (U.S. Bureau of the Census, 1998). Abuse of girls is more common than of boys (Finkelhor, 1994; Trickett, McBride-Chang, & Putman, 1994). This finding may, in part, be due to the fact that the data are based on cases in which the perpetrator is a caregiver; however, boys are more likely to be sexually abused by nonfamily members. Of considerable concern is the possibility that sexual abuse occurs in day-care settings. Although reports of such occurrences are frightening, it is important to remember that young children are more likely to be sexually abused at home (Kelly, Brant, & Waterman, 1993; Schroeder & Gordon, 1991).

The definition of emotional (or psychological) maltreatment is probably the most difficult and controversial. Societal and community standards always come into play in judging "abusive" behaviors and "harmful" outcomes (Barnett, Manly, & Cicchetti, 1991; Belsky, 1991; Sternberg & Lamb, 1991). Different standards for both appropriate parenting practices and valued outcomes are particularly at issue when psychological maltreatment is considered (Azar, Ferraro, & Breton, 1998; McGee & Wolfe, 1991). Emotional maltreatment is defined as persistent and extreme actions or neglect that thwart the child's basic emotional needs and that are damaging to the behavioral, cognitive, affective, or physical functioning of the child (Brassard, Germaine, & Hart, 1987; Cicchetti & Lynch, 1995). Emotional maltreatment is seen increasingly as part of all abuse and neglect (Garbarino, 1991; Hart & Brassard, 1991). Thus thinking in terms of physical/sexual abuse alone does not capture the broad nature of the problem.

FACTORS CONTRIBUTING TO MALTREATMENT

Contemporary efforts to conceptualize maltreatment recognize complex, multiple, and interrelated determinants of the problem (Azar et al.,

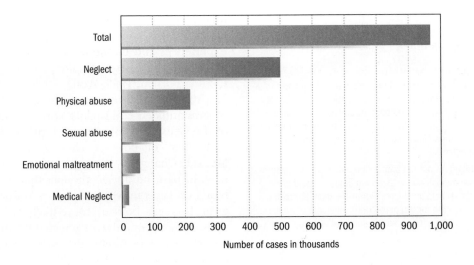

FIGURE 15-6 Child abuse and neglect cases for 1996.
Note: More than one type of maltreatment may be substantiated per child. Therefore, items add up to more than the total shown.
Adapted from U.S. Bureau of the Census, *Statistical Abstract of the United States: 1998* (118th ed.). Washington, DC, 1998.

1998; Belsky, 1993; Cicchetti & Lynch, 1995; Okun, Parker, & Levendosky, 1994). The following factors contribute to maltreatment.

■ Characteristics of the abusing parent

■ Characteristics of the child

■ Parenting practices

■ Parent-child interactional processes

■ Social-cultural influences

The latter category includes both the immediate social environment (e.g., employment, extended family, social network) and larger societal-cultural context (e.g., poverty, societal tolerance for violence). It is impossible even to enumerate all of the influences that have been examined. Ongoing research continues to examine the factors leading to different forms of maltreatment, and the multiple pathways to any specific type of maltreatment. Here we highlight only some of the key findings.

For the most part, parents or parent surrogates are the perpetrators of abuse. Parents who began their families at a younger age, many in their teens, are often the perpetrators (Connelly & Straus, 1992). This finding may be understood, at least in part, within the context of parenting skills. The most pervasive disturbance seen in maltreating parents is a variety of deficits in parenting skills (Azar & Bober, 1999). Maltreating parents tend to engage in fewer positive interactions with their child, and less interaction overall; to use more coercive and negative discipline techniques; and to use explanations less when disciplining their child. These parents also exhibit negative attitudes toward parenting, limited child-rearing knowledge, inappropriate expectations regarding developmentally suitable behavior, lower tolerance for common demanding behavior such as infant crying, and misattributions of the child's motivation for misbehaving.

Several other characteristics of abusive parents have been noted, including difficulties in managing stress, difficulty in inhibiting impulsive behavior, social isolation from family and friends, more emotional symptoms and mood changes, and more physical health problems. High rates of substance abuse have also been reported. These factors are part of the complex influences that contribute to the development of abusive and neglectful interactions.

Intergenerational transmission of maltreatment has been posited. In a review of the literature, Kaufman and Zigler (1987) found that abuse is more common in the backgrounds of abusing parents. However, they also found that many parents who had not been abused became abusive and that some who had been abused did not. They estimate that on the basis of all forms of maltreatment, between 25 and 30 percent of maltreated children repeat the cycle as adults—a number far less than is popularly perceived. It is generally agreed that the majority of maltreated children do not perpetuate the intergenerational cycle. It has been suggested that rather than abuse being transmitted across generations, a set of parenting responses, skill deficits, and "scripts" for parenting and interpersonal relations is transmitted. This process places the next generation at risk for disturbances in parenting, and those who are exposed to additional risk factors are placed in danger of perpetuating abuse (Azar & Bober, 1999).

Characteristics of the youngster may increase the likelihood of being the target of maltreatment. Research suggests that children and adolescents at highest risk for abuse are those who display behavioral and physical problems or interpersonal styles that adversely interact with parental characteristics and family stress (Bonner et al., 1992). Age of the child also plays a role. For example, infants who cry frequently, or whose cry is particularly irritating, may trigger attempts to silence them, whereas adolescents whose behavior is perceived as rebellious may trigger psychological maltreatment or physical assaults.

Maltreatment also is influenced by the larger social context. A relationship between socioeconomic disadvantage and abuse and neglect has been described (English, 1998). It is important to recognize, however, that the majority of families who experience such deprivation do not maltreat their offspring. Although it is hard to isolate the specific causal factors, reduced resources, stress, and other problems that are associated with socioeconomic disadvantage put the family and child at increased risk. It has been suggested that neglect, in particular, is related to low SES. It is also possible that poverty and maltreatment are related because of other factors (Azar & Bober, 1999). For example, poor interpersonal and problem-solving skills in parents may lead to both economic disadvantage and problematic parenting, including maltreatment. Cultural factors may also play a role. Korbin et al. (1998), for example, found that impoverishment had a lesser impact on maltreatment in African-American neighborhoods than in European-American neighborhoods. This differential effect of poverty seems to have been mediated by the perceived quality of social connectedness found in the two kinds of neighborhoods. A sense of community, resources, and extended family may serve as protective factors against maltreatment.

CONSEQUENCES OF MALTREATMENT

With regard to the consequences of maltreatment for the child, no single pattern of emotional or behavioral difficulties has been found. Rather, youngsters can experience health-related difficulties (e.g., physical injury, sexually transmitted diseases) and can manifest appreciable impairments in all early developmental domains and in a variety of areas of later adjustment (Azar et al., 1998; English, 1998; Shields, Cicchetti, & Ryan, 1994; Wolfe & Birt, 1995). Difficulties include increased aggression, poor peer relationships, insecure attachments, impaired social-cognitive abilities, anxiety, depression, speech and language deficiencies, and poor grades and achievement test scores. Thus the impact of abuse is best viewed as undermining a variety of normal developmental processes (Cicchetti & Lynch, 1995; Azar & Bober, 1999). While this is certainly a disheartening picture, it should be acknowledged that some maltreated children develop as competent individuals and that youngsters can be resilient even in the face of maltreatment. Individual protective and environmental protective factors deserve research attention.

TREATMENT

Interventions for maltreatment have been primarily parent and family centered, with less attention paid to child-focused treatments. Given the combination of factors that contributes to the development of maltreatment, effective intervention needs to address many domains (individual, familial, community and societal) and thus to include multiple components (Azar & Wolfe, 1998; Krugman, 1993). As we gain more precise understanding about the different types of maltreatment, we will be better able to shape treatments to fit specific needs (Crittenden, Claussen, & Sugarman, 1994; Manly, Cicchetti, & Barnett, 1994).

Guidelines for appropriate treatment are unavailable, since adequate empirical data are lacking. However, interventions based on a social learning (cognitive-behavioral) approach and on self-help groups show promise (Azar et al., 1998; Azar & Wolfe, 1998). Interventions with maltreating families are likely to involve multiple components. Treatments address improving parenting skills, stress management and anger control training, communications skill training, problem-solving training, and cognitive restructuring (e.g., modifying interpretations of children's behavior). Self-help groups, such as Parents Anonymous, are low cost and may be helpful in building support systems for parents.

Educational efforts are part of the preventive approach to the problem of maltreatment. In addition to promoting public awareness, these efforts seek to decrease the rates of child maltreatment. Earlier we noted that the incidence of reported maltreatment has risen. The question can be raised as to whether this rise represents an actual increase in maltreatment or a greater sensitivity to the problem. It would be encouraging if the latter were the case. Perhaps educational efforts have increased public awareness and rejection of abusive behavior. Cultural values, such as tolerance for violence and neglect as well as rigid reluctance to intrude on family autonomy, are part of the context in which abusive and neglectful relationships develop. To the extent that families are being harmed by these values, change is appropriate.

MENTAL HEALTH AND FOSTER CARE SERVICES FOR YOUTH

So far in this chapter we have discussed efforts to prevent behavioral disorder and concerns about the changing family and the maltreatment of youth. We now turn to a brief discussion of two systems of delivery of services to youth: mental health and foster care services.

MENTAL HEALTH SERVICES

Over the years, many studies of mental health services have been conducted. It is widely agreed that children and adolescents are underserved (Kazdin, 1993a,b). Fewer than one-third of needy youth receive services (Weist, 1997). Particularly underserved are specific groups such as those of minority background and those with physical handicaps.

Funding. Analyses of mental health needs have recognized a lack of adequate funding. To various degrees, funding is provided by federal and state governments, third-party (health insurance) companies, and clients themselves. State governments carry a relatively heavy burden for financing services. The health care system is in a state of flux, however, with regard to managed care and insurance companies. At the present time, the skyrocketing of health care costs adversely affects both middle- and lower-class families.

Kinds of services offered. Mental health services for youth early emphasized a community approach (Pumariega & Glover, 1998). Child guidance clinics provided interdisciplinary and low-cost services to children and adolescents and their families. Services subsequently became more hospital-based, and guidance and mental health clinics experienced lack of funding and support. Hospital and residential care increased during the 1970s and 1980s, partly because of increased third-party payment. All the while there was a dramatic increase in the population of poor minority children who needed but could not obtain mental health services. Many of these children went into the child welfare system when their parents were unable to care for them, and many were placed into residential and detention facilities. This dire situation and growing medical costs resulted in a call for publicly funded community-based services. Knitzer's (1982) book *Unclaimed Children* was particularly influential in attracting attention to the problems.

Today's services are delivered in various settings, including mental health clinics, psychiatric or full service hospitals, residential centers, private professional practices, child welfare and juvenile agencies, and schools. The dominant setting is the community mental health clinic (Weist, 1997). In addition to continuing concerns about the quality and availability of services, services have also been criticized for being fragmented (e.g., Illback, 1994). Because behavioral dysfunctions are multifactorial, services often must have several components. To take a relatively uncomplicated hypothetical case, a child displaying Attention Deficit Hyperactivity Disorder may require a psychologist to plan and monitor a behavior modification program and to work with parents, school personnel to coordinate an academic program, and a psychiatrist for medication evaluation. In more complex cases, still other services are needed. However, services have not been well coordinated.

In recognition of the several problems in the mental health system, the federal government instituted the Child and Adolescent Service System Program (CASSP). By providing leadership and funding to the states, CASSP has encouraged a comprehensive model of care, interagency collaboration, parental involvement, and sensitivity to the needs of minority groups (Pumariega & Glover, 1998). Other aspects of the model include treatment in the least restrictive environment, early identification of problems and intervention, and smooth transition into adult care systems when necessary. This continuum of care approach is being instituted and is being evaluated (e.g., Bickman, 1997; Saxe & Cross, 1997). Some progress is being made in improving services, but much remains to be done.

Some professionals believe that the school can play an important role in delivery of services to the 40 million enrolled young people and their families (Weist, 1997). Traditional mental health services in schools are largely limited to children enrolled in special education and a relatively small number involved in interventions with school psychologists. Yet the school setting has clear advantages. It is accessible to all students, contact can be frequent, and the stigma of mental health consultation can be avoided. Thus a movement exists to expand services and to include the entire range from prevention to treatment to posttreatment monitoring. Several models have been proposed.

One proposal calls for a restructuring of the traditional school support services that would increase coordination and involve other components such as crisis intervention, social skills training, and support to students in transition. Another proposal sets up partnerships between schools and community mental health agencies, which can variously expand school services. Many schools now have general health centers, and mental health services can be readily embedded in these. Also relevant to mental health services is the proposal for "full-service schools," in which the school is the primary neighborhood institution for promoting child and family development (Holtzman, 1997). This is a comprehensive model that incorporates educational, health, and mental health goals within the framework of community-based participation and decision making. It is being evaluated in ethnically different neighborhoods in four cities in Texas, as the School of the Future Project.

Finally, with regard to youth services, there is a need both to continue to evaluate services and to disseminate information about effective services. There is ample documentation of the overall efficacy of psychological, behavioral, and educational treatments (Lipsey & Wilson, 1993). Furthermore, it is clear that treatment for young people is effective for a variety of disorders in a variety of settings (Kazdin 1993a; Johnson, Rasbury, & Siegel, 1997). Benefits can accrue from prevention programs as well. However, families need specific information about the availability, effectiveness, and costs of care (e.g., Newman & Tejeda, 1996).

FOSTER CARE

One of the components of the child welfare systems about which concern has been expressed is foster care. Approximately half a million youth are now in the foster care system in the United States (Shealy, 1995). Although it is ordinarily preferable for children and adolescents to remain with their families, substitute care is not always avoidable. Substitute placement occurs voluntarily when families are unable to care for their offspring or when children are involuntarily removed from their homes because of neglect, abuse, abandonment, or some emergency.

Several concerns have been expressed about foster care (Lewit, 1993; Tuma, 1989). A fundamental question, of course, is whether it might be reduced by better support of families. There is also a need for more complete data about substitute care and for stronger monitoring of the quality of care. In addition, although foster care has often been intended as temporary, many youth remain in care for long periods of time, some until they reach the legal age to be independent. In the meanwhile, they are often moved from placement to placement. In an effort to reduce such "drift," the federal government enacted laws mandating a plan for each child to be returned to the biological parents, be adopted, or be permanently placed with a foster family (Rosenfeld et al., 1997). The initial success of the mandate did not hold up. The number of children in substitute care rose by an alarming 69 percent between 1982 and 1992.

Although there are probably many reasons for the rise in substitute care, it appears that increased parental drug abuse, HIV, poverty, and homelessness are important factors. Many children entering foster care today have lived in disorganized families, been traumatized, have special developmental and behavioral problems, and require special medical and educational care. Foster parents often do not receive the support and training that are needed to facilitate development of these youth.

In discussing foster care, Rosenfeld and colleagues (1997) have noted the following new developments:

■ Many more foster children are placed in the homes of relatives than in past times, largely because of the lack of other alternatives. This kind of placement has both advantages (e.g., connection with birth families and culture) and disadvantages (e.g., less likelihood of receiving health care).

■ Variations of group and family care are being tried. For example, children may be placed in group homes while therapeutic visits with their families are scheduled to determine whether out-of-home placement can be avoided.

■ "Treatment foster care" programs have been created to help children with psychological problems. The foster parents understand prior to placement that the child requires mental health services, and a link is forged with community mental health services.

One of the more optimistic findings is that treatment foster care can improve children's functioning, although long-term follow-up data are needed (Reddy & Pfeiffer, 1997). Nevertheless, the needs of children in foster care are substantial, and the foster care system is inadequately funded and understaffed. Most individuals working in the system are well intentioned and caring; however, increased resources, innovative problem solving, and a greater commitment to improving substitute care are sorely needed

YOUTH IN THE GLOBAL SOCIETY

As we turn our attention to the international scene, one striking fact is that mass transportation and communication are making the functional world smaller day by day. The lives of youth are already being strongly influenced by this phenomenon, and the impact will become even more pervasive throughout the twenty-first century.

ADAPTING TO DIVERSITY

An obvious implication of the shrinking world is the increased need to deal well with others of different color, facial appearance, dress, and custom.

It is estimated that at least 5,000 ethnocultural groups exist around the world (Marsella, 1998). The challenge of adapting to ethnic and racial differences is an age-old one, of course. In the United States, which is enormously heterogeneous, the issue has long been of concern. Prejudice and fears too often have had adverse effects on peoples of various groups—Native Americans, African-Americans, Irish, Poles, Jews, and Catholics, to name a few. Being of "minority" status is a risk factor for children in that it is linked to stress and reduced quality of life and opportunity (e.g., Albee, 1986; Kvernmo & Hyerdahl, 1998).

We continue today to grapple with this issue, as exemplified in controversy about bilingualism in schools and immigration. Although change undoubtedly must be gradual, a reasonable goal is not only to increase tolerance for those who are different from us but also to recognize that heterogeneity can be enormously enriching. Psychologists have written of the need for psychology to become more sensitive to the diversity of the U.S. population and more strongly to recognize and prize worldwide diversity (Hall, 1997; Marsella, 1998).

THIRD WORLD POVERTY

Although poverty in the United States is rightly of concern, the effects of being poor are dramatically worse in the developing countries with regard to death rates, disease, and lack of opportunity. The link between poverty and bodily and psychological development is observed in various measures. For example, in developing countries, the prevalence of iron-deficiency anemia for children up to four years of age is about 51 percent (Pollitt, 1994). These children consistently score lower on a variety of developmental and cognitive tests. Research from several countries also indicates the effects of poor diet and that early supplements of high calorie, high protein foods can enhance mental and motor development in high-risk populations.

EXPOSURE TO ARMED OR SOCIOPOLITICAL CONFLICT

Exposure to armed conflict or to threatening sociopolitical environments influences the development of a significant minority of young people throughout the world (Jensen & Shaw, 1993; Zivcic, 1993). The character of these conflicts varies and brings different kinds of impacts. In recent limited conflicts, more civilians have been killed than military personnel (e.g., in Croatia). Youth are also living in situations in which the threat of war is low to moderate but is long-lasting (e.g., Ireland). Cambodian youth suffered extensive hardships and violence during the Pol Pot regime and subsequently lived in refugee camps for extended periods of time (Mollica et al., 1997; Savin et al., 1996). In addition to direct traumatic experiences and bodily threats to the self and loved ones, these situations can be characterized by uncertainty, separation from family and community, inadequate nutrition, lack of shelter, control by the "enemy," and the like. It is not surprising that the relatively limited number of studies conducted on the effects of these situations indicate heightened emotional symptoms. Depression, anxiety, somatic complaints, social withdrawal, and attention problems have been reported.

One way to view armed conflict is as a trauma that can result in Posttraumatic Stress Disorder. Among others, Savin and colleagues (1996) reported symptoms of PTSD in 18- to 25-year-olds that appeared connected to war trauma they had experienced during childhood. (Depression in this group, in contrast, appeared more strongly linked to the conditions in which they lived in refugee camps.) Researchers have noted that Posttraumatic Stress Disorder may not well apply to situations in which low threat is long-lasting. In this case, people may be able to generate coping mechanisms over time (e.g., Sloan, Adiri, & Arian, 1998). In fact, although psychological upset is widely associated with actual or threatened armed conflict, many children and adolescents show remarkable adaptation. Outcome depends on specific experiences, as well as on individual, family, and community variables. For example, negative outcome is lower when armed conflict is viewed as necessary by the community and when other social support is present.

The more we understand about such mediators, the better the chance of alleviating emotional adversity. Nevertheless, few would dispute the opinion that war "must be regarded with abhorrence in terms of its terrible human toll in human suffering, especially on its most innocent bystanders—children and adolescents" (Jensen & Shaw, 1993, p. 697).

INTERNATIONAL COOPERATION

An important outgrowth of closer communication among the peoples of the world is increased international efforts to solve problems and to optimize living conditions. Over the last decades, world attention has been drawn to promoting the healthy development of youth, as exemplified in the activities of the United Nations. In 1990 the World Summit for Children was convened to promote universal rights for survival, protection, and optimal development (UNICEF, 1991). The United Nations declared 1979 as the International Year of the Child, and subsequently an official statement was drafted on the rights of children. This document, the U.N. Convention on the Rights of the Child, was ratified by a large number of countries and was put into effect in 1989 (Murphy-Berman & Weisz, 1996). Although the United States helped draft the document, it has been reluctant to ratify it on the basis that it may conflict with political and social traditions or Constitutional rights. This problem is an example of the complexity of working internationally to better the lives of children.

The Convention cites, among other rights, the rights of children to a family environment, an adequate standard of living, education, freedom of religion, and self-expression, as well as rights to be free from specific harms such as abuse, torture, and exploitation. The United Nations collects data on youth, on which it bases recommendations; for example, the girl child has been singled out as especially needy. Data collected around the world, and particularly in developing countries, point to many inequalities suffered by females. In developing countries, girls have less food, less adequate health care, and fewer educational opportunities. Early maternity has adverse effects on nutrition, health, and educational and occupational status. Gender bias is reflected by a disproportionate preference for sons and selective abortion of females fetuses.

In other areas, concerned professionals and other citizens are increasingly addressing global issues such as poverty, high birth rates, violence, infant mortality, environmental pollution and destruction, and the lack of medical and mental health services. Since all of these can have dramatic influence on the development of children and adolescents, international cooperation holds some promise of improving the lives of young people.

SUMMARY

■ The care received by children and adolescents reflects not only what is known about development but also the social, political, and economic conditions in which they live. Present-day concerns for the young recognize that they are shaped by a broad spectrum of influences.

■ Prevention of behavioral disorders has been conceptualized as primary, secondary, and tertiary. It is most commonly viewed as intervention that occurs prior to the onset of full-blown disorder. Promotion of competence and wellness that goes beyond reduction of disorder is arguably a part of prevention. Known risk and protective factors provide a basis for prevention.

■ Many effective prevention programs now exist. They vary in their goals, methods, and settings. Examples are mother-infant programs for low birth weight infants, preschool interventions for economically disadvantaged and disabled children, the Rochester Primary Mental Health Project for children at risk for school maladjustment, and the School Transitional Environmental Project that protects students from potential adverse effects of school transitions.

■ Concerns about the impact of family transitions on youth are uppermost in the minds of many people. Much attention is given to the possible adverse effects of maternal employment. Few differences have been found between the children of employed and unemployed women, and many factors influence child outcome.

■ Employment of women has led to increased nonparental child care of various forms. The effects of such care on children likely depend on the quality of care. The effects of self-care by "latchkey" children depend on several factors.

■ Increases in single parenting families are also of concern. Children in these families are at risk developmentally, probably in part because of poverty.

■ Studies of the impact of divorce on youth indicate adverse effects in several areas of functioning, although the effects are small in magnitude. Children's adjustment to the transitions of parental divorce and remarriage depends on interactions between many influences. Preexisting characteristics of the parents and the child, gender of the child, ethnicity, age of the child, economic changes, and other variables may be involved in complex ways.

■ Research on abuse of children and adolescents shows that it occurs in diverse forms and is linked to characteristics of the abused and the abuser, parenting practices, parent-child interaction, and social-cultural influences. Abuse can lead to many kinds of behavioral disturbances. Intervention is usually parent and family centered.

■ There is a consensus that mental health services for youth are underfunded, inadequate, and fragmented. The federally sponsored CASSP encourages integrated, comprehensive services. A movement is under way to extend mental health services in the schools.

■ About half a million children are in foster care. They tend to stay in this system for years and frequently "drift" from placement to placement. Many of these youth require mental health services, and treatment foster care has been established to help meet their needs.

■ As we look to the global society of the twenty-first century, several challenges to the development of young people are evident. International cooperation to improve the lives of youth is reflected in the United Nations declaration of the rights of all young people.

GLOSSARY

ABA′ (reversal) research design Single-subject quasi-experimental design in which the relevant behavior is measured during a baseline period (A), manipulation (B), and a period in which the manipulation is removed (A′). The reintroduction of the manipulation (B′) is added when treatment is the goal.

Accommodation In Piagetian theory, the process of adapting one's mental schemas of the world to fit with new experiences.

Acute onset The sudden (rather than gradual) onset of a disorder.

Adaptive behavior scales Psychological instruments that measure an individual's ability to perform in the everyday environment, for example, to wash one's hair, interact socially, and communicate. Used mostly for evaluation of retarded or severely disturbed persons.

Adoption studies In genetic research, the comparison of adopted children with their biological and their adoptive families to determine hereditary and environmental influences on characteristics.

Affect The conscious, subjective aspect of an emotion.

Agoraphobia Excessive anxiety about being in a situation where escape might be difficult or embarrassing.

Anaclitic depression A period of withdrawal and sadness in very young children in reaction to prolonged separation from their parents.

Anoxia Lack of oxygen.

Antisocial behavior A pattern of behavior that violates widely held social norms and brings harm to others (e.g., stealing, lying).

Aphasia A general term referring to language disturbances not caused by general intellectual deficiency. *Developmental aphasia* refers to language disorders in childhood.

Assimilation In Piagetian theory, the process of taking in or interpreting new information according to existing mental schemas of the world.

Attachment A strong socioemotional bond between individuals. Usually discussed in terms of the child-parent or child-caretaker relationship, attachment is generally viewed as having a strong influence on a child's development.

Attention The focusing or concentration of mental energy on an object or event. *Selective attention* refers to focusing on a stimulus and not being distracted by other stimuli. *Sustained attention* refers to maintaining concentration on a stimulus over time.

Attribution (attributional style) The way an individual thinks about or explains actions and outcomes; for example, a child's attributing his or her school failure to lack of innate intelligence.

Authoritative parenting Style of parenting in which parents set rules and expectations for their children, follow through with consequences, and simultaneously are warm, accepting, and considerate of their children's needs. This style is thought to be associated with positive development in children.

Autoimmune disorder A condition in which the body's immune system attacks it's own healthy tissue.

Autonomic nervous system A part of the nervous system that consists of ganglia along the spinal cord and nerves to peripheral organs (e.g., glands and blood vessels). It regulates functions usually considered involuntary, such as the operation of smooth muscles and glands. The system controls physiological changes associated with the expression of emotion.

Baseline The measured rate of a behavior before an intervention is introduced. Baseline rates of the behavior can then be compared to rates during and following the intervention.

Behavior modification An approach to the treatment of behavior disorders that is based primarily on learning principles. Also referred to as *behavior therapy*.

Binge A relatively brief episode of excessive consumption (e.g., of food) over which the individual feels no control.

Biofeedback Procedures by which the individual is provided immediate information (feedback) about some aspect of physiological functioning (e.g., muscle tension, skin temperature). It is assumed that the individual can come to control bodily functioning through such feedback.

Case study Descriptive method of research in which an individual case is described. The case study can be informative but cannot be generalized to other persons or situations with confidence.

Central nervous system In humans, the brain and spinal cord. (*See* autonomic nervous system)

Child guidance movement An early to mid-20th century effort in the U.S. to treat and prevent childhood mental disorders. Importance was given to influences of family and wider social systems on the child.

Chromosome A threadlike structure in the cell nucleus that contains the genetic code. With the exception of the ova and sperm, human cells possess 23 pairs, 22 pairs of autosomes and 1 pair of sex chromosomes. The ova and sperm possess 23 single chromosomes.

Chromosome abnormalities Abnormalities in the number and/or structure of the chromosome complement that often lead to fetal death or anomalies in development.

Classical conditioning A form of learning, also referred to as Pavlovian conditioning. An individual comes to respond to a stimulus (conditioned stimulus or CS) that did not previously elicit a response. Classical conditioning occurs when a CS is paired with another stimulus (the unconditioned stimulus, or UCS) that does elicit the desired response (unconditioned response, or UCR). When this response is elicited by the conditioned stimulus alone it is called a conditioned response (CR).

Classificatory variable In research methodology, attributes of subjects (e.g., age, sex, diagnosis) that are investigated in some way. Classificatory variables are sometimes erroneously taken for independent variables. (*See* mixed research design)

Clinical significance The degree to which research findings are meaningful regarding real-life applications.

Clinical utility A criterion for judging the adequacy of a classification system, diagnosis, or assessment instrument. Judgments are based on how fully the observed phenomena are described and on how useful the descriptions are.

Coercion A process in which a noxious or aversive behavior of one person (e.g., aggression by a child) is rewarded by another person (e.g., a parent). Often applied to the development of conduct disordered behavior.

Cognitive strategies Information processing and memory strategies; for example, rehearsing and categorizing information.

Cohort A particular age group of participants in a cross-sectional or longitudinal research study. A cohort may differ in life experiences and values from an age group born and raised during a different era.

Comorbidity A term used when individuals meet the criteria for more than one disorder (e.g., Attention Deficit Hyperactivity Disorder and Conduct Disorder). (*See* co-occurrence)

Compulsions Behaviors the individual feels compelled to repeat over and over again, even though they appear to have no rational basis.

Computerized tomography (CT scan) A procedure to directly assess abnormalities of the brain such as blood clots or tumors. Also sometimes referred to as computerized axial tomography or CAT scan.

Concordant In genetic research, refers to individuals who are similar in particular attributes, for example, concordant for hair color or activity level.

Conditioned stimulus (CS) A neutral stimulus, which through repeated pairings with a stimulus (unconditioned stimulus) that already elicits a particular response, comes to elicit a similar response (conditioned response).

Contingency management Procedures that seek to modify behavior by altering the causal relationship between stimulus and response events, for example, between a behavior and its reinforcer.

Continuous performance test (CPT) A method to evaluate sustained attention and impulsivity. The individual must identify a target stimulus when it appears in a series of stimuli consecutively projected on a screen. Errors are made by not reacting to the target stimulus or by reacting to nontarget stimuli.

Control group In an experiment, a group of subjects treated differently than subjects who receive the experimental manipulation and later compared with them. The purpose of control groups is to insure that the results of the experiment can be attributed to the manipulation rather than to other variables.

Co-occurrence A term used when individuals experience the problems (symptoms) associated with more than one disorder (e.g., anxiety and depression). (*See* comorbidity)

Correlation coefficient A number obtained through statistical analysis that reflects the presence or absence of a correlation, the strength of a correlation, and the direction (positive or negative) of a correlation. Pearson *r* is a commonly used coefficient. (*See* positive and negative correlation)

Correlational research A research strategy aimed at establishing whether two or more variables covary, or are associated. (*See* positive correlation and negative correlation.) The establishment of a correlation permits prediction of one variable from the other, but does not establish a causal relationship.

Covert behaviors Behaviors that are not readily observeable. When describing antisocial behaviors this term refers to behaviors that are concealed, such as lying, stealing, and truancy. (*See* overt behaviors)

Critical period A relatively limited period of development during which an organism may be particularly sensitive to specific influences.

Cross-sectional research A research strategy that observes and compares different groups of subjects at one point in time. It is a highly practical way to gather certain kinds of information.

Defense mechanisms In psychoanalytic theory, psychological processes that distort or deny reality so as to control anxiety. Examples are repression, projection, reaction formation.

Deinstitutionalization The movement to place/treat people with disorders at home or in various community settings rather than in institutions.

Delinquency A legal term that refers to an illegal act by a person under 18. Such behavior may be illegal for an adult as well, such as theft, or may only be illegal when committed by a juvenile, for example, truancy.

Delusion An idea or belief that is contrary to reality and is not widely accepted in the culture (e.g., delusions of grandeur or persecution).

Dependent variable In the experimental method of research, the measure of behavior that may be influenced by the manipulation (independent variable).

Development Change in structure and function that occurs over time in living organisms. Typically viewed as change from the simple to the complex, development is the result of transactions among several variables.

Developmental level The level at which an individual is functioning with regard to physical, intellectual, or socioemotional characteristics.

Developmental psychopathology The study of behavioral disorders within the context of developmental influences.

Developmental quotient (DQ) A measure of performance on infant tests of development, paralleling the intelligence quotient (IQ) derived from intelligence tests for older children.

Developmental vs. deficit controversy Theoretical dispute about atypical functioning, especially about mental retardation. The developmental view argues that retarded persons function intellectually in the same ways as do the nonretarded, but that they develop more slowly and perhaps reach a ceiling. The difference view maintains that the intellective processes of retarded persons are qualitatively different than normal processes.

Diathesis A predisposition toward a disease or disorder.

Differential reinforcement of other behaviors (DRO) In behavior modification, refers to applying relatively more reinforcement to desirable behaviors that are incompatible with specific undesirable behaviors.

Difficult temperament Tendency of an individual to display negative mood, intense reactions to stimuli, irritability, and the like. Difficult temperament is a risk factor for behavior problems.

Discordant In genetic research, refers to individuals who are dissimilar in particular attributes, for example, discordant in hair color or activity level.

Discrete trial learning Method of modifying behavior or teaching in which the clinician or teacher presents specific tasks or material in small steps, provides clear directives or prompts, and applies consequences. The setting is structured for learning. (*See* incidental learning)

Discrimination The process by which an individual comes to learn that a particular stimulus, but not others, signals that a certain response is likely to be followed by a particular consequence.

Diversion programs An approach to delinquency that attempts to intervene by providing services (e.g., education, vocational training) that will *divert* delinquent youth away from the juvenile justice system.

Dizygotic twins Twins resulting from two independent unions of ova and sperm that occur at approximately the same time. Dizygotic twins are genetically no more alike than are nontwin siblings.

DNA Deoxyribonucleic acid. The chemical carrier of the genetic code that is found in the chromosomes. The spiral-shaped DNA molecule is composed of sugar, phosphates, and nucleotides. The nucleotides carry the hereditary information that directs protein synthesis.

Dyslexia General term referring to reading disorder not due to general intellectual deficiency.

Echolalia The repetition of the speech of others, either immediately or delayed in time. A pathological speech pattern commonly found in autism and psychoses.

Ego According to psychoanalytic theory, this is the structure of the mind that operates predominantly at the conscious level. It mediates between instinctual urges and reality and is responsible for decision making.

Electroencephalograph (EEG) A recording of the electrical activity of the brain.

Empirical The process of verification or proof by accumulating information or data through observation or experiment (in contrast to reliance on impression or theory).

Epidemiology The study of the occurrence and distribution of a disorder within a specific population. Seeks to understand risk and etiology.

Equifinality The concept that diverse factors or paths can result in the same or similar outcomes.

Etiology The cause or origin of a disease or behavior disorder.

Eugenics Efforts to improve human characteristics through systematic control of reproduction and thus genetics.

Executive functions A term that refers to the ability to select, monitor, evaluate, and revise strategies employed in information processing and memory.

Experimental research A research strategy that can establish causal relationships between variables. Subjects are treated by the independent variable to determine possible effects on the dependent variable. Comparison groups are included to control for extraneous influences and the procedures are carefully controlled by the researchers.

External validity In research, refers to the degree to which findings of an investigation can be generalized to other populations and situations.

Externalizing disorders Behavioral disorders in which the problems exhibited seem directed at others; for example, aggression and lying.

Extinction A weakening of a learned response that is produced when reinforcement that followed the response no longer occurs.

Factor analysis A statistical procedure that correlates each item with every other item, and then groups correlated items into factors.

Fraternal twins See dizygotic twins.

Gene The smallest unit of the chromosome that transmits genetic information.

Generalization The process by which a response is made to a new stimulus that is different but similar to the stimulus present during learning.

Generalized imitation The tendency to imitate across persons, situations, and time.

Genotype The complement of genes that a person inherits; the genetic endowment.

Goodness-of-fit Concept that considers the degree to which an individual's attributes or behaviors match or fit the attributes or demands of the individual's environment. Goodness-of-fit has implications for development.

Hallucination A false perception (e.g., hearing a noise, seeing an object) that occurs in the absence of any apparent environmental stimulation.

Heritability The degree to which genetic influences account for variations in an attribute among individuals in a population.

Heterotypic continuity The continuity of a disorder over time in which the form of the problem behaviors change over time with development. (Contrasts with homotypic continuity.)

Hypothesis In science, a proposition or "educated guess" put forth for evaluation by some scientific method.

Id According to psychoanalytic theory this is developmentally the earliest of the structures of the mind—it is present at birth. The source of all psychic energy, the Id operates entirely at the unconscious level, seeking immediate gratification of all instinctual urges (the pleasure principle).

Identical twins *See* monozygotic twins.

Impulsivity The tendency to act quickly without reflection. Hyperactive children are viewed as impulsive.

Incidence The number or percentage of new cases of a disorder in a given population in a given time period. (*See* prevalence)

Incidental learning Method of modifying behavior or teaching in informal, natural settings. This method takes advantage of the everyday context; for example, by teaching tasks relevant to what the child is engaging in at the moment. Learning principles, such as reinforcement contingencies, are typically employed in this "loose" setting.

Inclusion Term used to refer to the idea that all children with handicaps can best be educated in regular classrooms and thus should be included in regular classrooms. (*See* Regular Education Initiative)

Independent variable In the experimental method of research, the variable manipulated by the researcher.

Individual Education Plan (IEP) Detailed educational plan legally mandated for each person being served by special education.

Information processing Complex mental processes by which the organism attends to, perceives, interprets, and stores information. (*See* attention, memory, executive functions, metamemory, cognitive strategies)

Informed consent In research or treatment, the ethical and legal guideline that potential participants be reasonably informed about the research or treatment as a basis for their willingness to participate.

Intelligence quotient (IQ), deviation A standard score derived from statistical procedures that reflects the direction and degree to which an individual's performance on an intelligence test deviates from the average score of the individual's age group.

Intelligence quotient (IQ), ratio The ratio of mental age (MA), derived from performance on tests of intelligence, to chronological age (CA), multiplied by 100. $IQ = MA/CA \times 100$.

Interactional model of development The view that development is the result of the interplay of organismic and environmental variables. (*See* transactional model of development)

Internalizing disorders The large category of disorders—many of which were traditionally referred to as neuroses—in which the problems exhibited seem directed more at the self than at others; for example, fears, depression, and withdrawal.

Internal validity In research, refers to the degree to which findings can be attributed to certain factors. Frequently concerns the degree to which a result of an *experiment* can be attributed to the experimental manipulation (the independent variable), rather than to extraneous factors.

Interrater reliability The extent to which different raters agree on a particular diagnosis or measurement.

In vivo A term referring to the natural context in which behavior occurs. For example, in vivo treatment is delivered in the setting in which the behavior problem occurs (e.g., the home rather than the clinic).

Joint attention interactions Behaviors, such as pointing and eye contact, that simultaneously focus the attention of two or more people on the same object or situation, presumably for sharing an experience.

Learned helplessness Passivity and a sense of lack of control over one's environment that is learned through experiences where one's behavior was ineffective in controlling events.

Least restrictive environment A term that refers to the idea that handicapped individuals have a right to be educated with and to live with the nonhandicapped to the extent that is maximally feasible. (*See* Public Law 94–142)

Longitudinal research A research strategy that observes the same subjects over a relatively long period of time, measuring behavior at certain points. It is particularly helpful in tracing developmental change.

Magnetic resonance imaging (MRI) A procedure that allows one to directly assess abnormalities in the brain.

Mainstreaming The placing of handicapped individuals into the least restrictive environments in which they are capable of functioning. More specifically, the placement of handicapped children in regular, rather than special classes. (*See* Public Law 94–142)

Masked depression This term refers to cases in which a child's depression is "masked" by other problems such as hyperactivity or delinquency. These "depressive equivalents" are thought to be manifestations of the underlying depression.

Matching Familiar Figures Test (MFFT) A method to evaluate impulsivity. The individual is shown a standard picture and additional stimuli, all of which except one vary from the standard. The individual must select a match for the standard. Errors in matching and relatively fast selection indicate impulsivity.

Maturation Changes that occur in individuals relatively independent of the environment provided that basic conditions are satisfied. For example, most humans will walk, given normal physical capacity, nourishment, and opportunity for movement.

Maturational lag A slowness or falling behind in development; often implies a lag in brain or nervous system development.

Meiosis The specialized maturational process that results in the ova and sperm containing half (23) of the number of chromosomes found in other cells.

Memory Complex process by which perceived information can be recalled in some way. According to a widely-held model, information is first taken in by a sensory register, is passed to short-term storage, and then to long-term storage.

Mental age (MA) The score corresponding to the chronological age (CA) of children whose intellectual test performance the examinee equals. For the average child, MA = CA.

Mental hygiene movement An effort organized in the United States early in the 20th century to bring effective, humane treatment to the mentally ill and to prevent mental disorders. Closely associated with the child guidance movement.

Metacognition The understanding of one's own information processing system. (*See* executive functions)

Metamemory The understanding of the working of one's memory or the strategies used to facilitate memory. (*See* executive functions)

Migraine headache A severe form of headache caused by sustained dilation of the extracranial arteries.

Minimal brain dysfunction (MBD) The assumption that the central nervous system or brain is functioning in a pathological way to a degree that is not clearly detectable. MBD is hypothesized as a cause of hyperactivity and learning disabilities, as well as other behavior disorders.

Mixed research design A research design in which subjects are assigned into groups on the basis of some attribute (i.e., a classificatory variable such as age), and then an experimental manipulation is applied. In interpretation of results, care must be taken not to view the classificatory variable as an independent variable.

Monozygotic twins Twins resulting from one union of an ovum and sperm. The single zygote divides early into two, with the new zygotes having identical genes (and thus being of the same sex).

Morphology In language, the study of word formation.

Multifinality The concept that a factor may lead to different outcomes. For example, child abuse may result in different kinds of behavior problems.

Multiple baseline research design Single subject experimental designs in which a manipulation is made and multiple behaviors or subjects are measured over time.

Mutation Spontaneous change in the genes that can be transmitted to the next generation. One of the genetic mechanisms that accounts for variation in species and individuals.

Nature vs. nurture controversy The continuing debate about the relative influence of innate and experiential factors on the shaping of the individual. Also known as the maturation vs. learning and heredity vs. environment controversy.

Negative corrrelation When two (or more) variables are negatively correlated they co-vary such that high scores on one variable are associated with low scores on the other, and vice versa.

Negative reinforcement The process whereby the probability of a response increases because the response was followed by the removal of an aversive stimulus.

Neuropsychological assessment The use of psychological tests and behavioral measures to *indirectly* evaluate the functioning of the nervous system. Performance on these measures is known or presumed to reflect specific aspects of the functioning of the brain.

Neurosis A traditional term employed to describe any of a group of nonpsychotic disorders that are characterized by unusual levels of anxiety and associated problems. Phobias, obsessions, and compulsions are examples of disorders in this category.

Neurotransmitter A chemical that carries the nerve impulse from one neuron across the synaptic space to another neuron. Examples are serotonin, dopamine, and norepinephrine.

Nonnormative development influences The effects on development that stem from events that are not necessarily unusual in themselves but that occur to only some individuals, perhaps at unpredictable times. Examples are serious injury in childhood and premature death of a parent. These influences may be especially stressful. (*See* normative developmental influences).

Nonshared environment A term derived from genetic research which describes that portion of environmental influences on an attribute that is experienced by one family member but not other members.

Normal distribution (curve) The bell-shaped theoretical distribution or probability curve that describes the way in which many attributes (e.g., height, intelligence) are assumed to occur in the population. Extreme values of the attribute occur with less frequency than middle values of the attribute.

Normalization Assumption that the goal of treatment of behavior disorders should be behaviors that are as normal as possible, and that this goal should be reached by methods as culturally normal as possible. (*See* mainstreaming and least restrictive environment)

Normative developmental influences The effects on development that stem from events that happen to most individuals in some more-or-less predictable way, for example, at the same age or to those of the same generation. (*See* nonnormative developmental influences).

Norms Data based on information gathered from a segment of the population that represents the entire population. Norms serve as standards to evaluate individual development or functioning.

Nuclear family A family unit consisting of the father, mother, and children.

Observational learning The learning that occurs through viewing the behavior of others. Modeled behavior can be presented in live or symbolic form.

Obsessions Recurring and intrusive irrational thoughts over which the individual feels no control.

Operant conditioning Learning processes by which responses are acquired, maintained, or eliminated as a function of consequences (e.g., reinforcement, punishment).

Operational criteria (definition) A specified set of observable operations that are measurable and allow one to define some concept. For example, maternal deprivation might be defined by measuring the amount of time the child is separated from its mother.

Overlearning The procedure whereby learning trials are continued beyond the point at which the child has completed the stated criteria. This is intended to increase the likelihood that the new behavior will be maintained.

Overt behaviors Behaviors that are readily observable. When describing antisocial behaviors this term refers to behaviors that are confrontational such as physical aggression, temper tantrums, and defiance. (*See* covert behaviors)

Paradigm The set of assumptions and conceptions shared by a group of scientists that is used in collecting data and interpreting the phenomena of interest.

Paradoxical drug effect An effect of a drug that contradicts the expected effect. An example is the quieting of hyperactivity by stimulant medications.

Partial correlation statistical procedure A statistical procedure that aids in the interpretation of a demonstrated correlation by removing the effects of one or more specific variables.

Participant modeling A treatment method in which observation of a model is followed by the observer joining the model in gradual approximations of the desired behavior.

Pedigree analysis A research method that examines the pattern of distribution of a disorder, as well as the genetic makeup, in an extended family in order to assist in making inferences regarding the contribution of genetics to that disorder.

Perceptual-motor training Largely outdated approach to rectify learning disabilities that is based on the assumption that perceptual and motor functioning have gone awry or have developed abnormally. Training emphasizes exercises in sensory reception and motor responses.

Perinatal The period at or around the time of birth.

Perspective *See* paradigm.

Phenotype The observable attributes of an individual that result from genetic endowment, developmental processes, and the transactions of these.

Phobia Anxiety about, and avoidance of, some object or situation that is judged to be an excessive, overly persistent, unadaptive, or inappropriate fear.

Phonological awareness The understanding that spoken words can be segmented into sounds (for example, that "cat" has three sounds) and that sounds are represented by letters or combinations of letters of the alphabet.

Phonology Refers to the sounds of a language or the study of speech sounds.

Pica The habitual eating of substances usually considered inedible such as dirt, paper, and hair.

Placebo A treatment—psychological or chemical—that alters a person's behavior because he or she expects that change will occur. Placebos are often employed as control treatments to evaluate whether a treatment being tested is effective for reasons other than the person's belief in it.

Polygenic inheritance Inheritance of a characteristic that is influenced by many genes rather than a single one.

Positive correlation When two (or more) variables are positively correlated they co-vary with each other such that high scores on one variable are associated with high scores on the other variable, and low scores on the one variable are associated with low scores on the other.

Positive reinforcement The process whereby the probability of a response increases because the response is followed by a positive stimulus.

Positron emission tomography (PET scan) A procedure to directly assess activity in different parts of the brain.

Pragmatics (of language) The use of speech and gesture in a communicative way, considering the social context. Pragmatic skills include using appropriate gestures and language style.

Predictive validity The extent to which predictions about future behavior can be made by knowing an individual's diagnosis or performance on some test.

Premorbid adjustment The psychological, social, and academic/vocational adjustment of a person prior to onset of the symptoms of a disorder or its diagnosis.

Prenatal The period of development that occurs during pregnancy.

Prevalence The number or percentage of cases of a disorder in a population at a given time. Lifetime prevalence is the number or percentage of cases of a disorder that is experienced at any time during life. (*See* incidence)

Primary prevention The prevention of disorders in the population by methods that preclude their occurrence. Examples are parent education in child management and prevention of poverty.

Proband The designated individual whose relatives are assessed to determine if an attribute occurs in other members of that family.

Projection A defense mechanism whereby the ego protects against unacceptable thoughts or impulses by attributing them to another person or some object.

Projective tests Psychological tests which present ambiguous stimuli to the person. The subject's response is presumed to reflect unconscious thoughts and feelings that are unacceptable to the ego and therefore cannot be expressed directly.

Pronoun reversal Deviant speech pattern in which speakers refer to themselves as "you" or "she" or "he" and refer to others as "I" or "me." Often found in autism.

Prospective research designs Designs that identify subjects and then follow them over time. (*See* retrospective research designs)

Protective factors Variables that lessen the effects of risk; sometimes referred to as resiliencies.

Psychoactive drugs Chemical substances that influence psychological processes (e.g., behavior, thinking, emotions) by their influence on nervous system functioning. Examples are stimulants and tranquilizers.

Psychogenesis The view that development of a particular disorder is due to psychological influence.

Psychosis A general term for severe mental disorder that affects thinking, the emotions, and other psychological systems. The hallmark of a psychosis is disturbed contact with reality.

Public Law 94–142 The federal *Education for all Handicapped Children Act of 1975*, that sets guidelines for the rights of handicapped children to appropriate education. Now entitled *The Individuals with Disabilities Education Act*, it assures public education and services in the least restrictive environment, parental decision making, and assistance to the states.

Public Law 99–457 An amendment to the federal Public Law 94–142 that mandates the evaluation and special care of children from birth to three years of age.

Punishment A process whereby a response is followed by either an unpleasant stimulus or the removal of a pleasant stimulus, thereby decreasing the frequency of that response.

Qualitative research A research approach that assumes that events are best understood when they are observed in context and from a personal frame of reference. The methods employed include in-depth interviews, memoirs, and participant observation (observers are participants in the situation or event). Can be contrasted with quantitative research that places greater value on objective, controlled methods, such as the experiment.

Random assignment In research, the assignment of individuals to different groups in such a way that each individual has an equal chance of being assigned to any group. Such chance assignment helps make the groups comparable on factors that might influence the findings.

Recidivism The return to a previous undesirable pattern. The juvenile delinquent who again commits a crime after completing a treatment program illustrates recidivism.

Reflexes Automatic, unlearned responses to specific stimulation. Examples are the sucking and coughing reflexes. Reflexes are considered relatively simple acts, some of which give way to voluntary, learned responses.

Regular Education Initiative (REI) Controversial proposal that learning handicapped children be educated in regular classrooms rather than special education classrooms.

Reinforcement A process whereby a stimulus that occurs contingent on a particular behavior results in an increase in the likelihood of that behavior. (*See* positive reinforcement and negative reinforcement)

Relapse The reoccurrence of a problem after it has been successfully treated.

Reliability The degree to which an observation is consistently made. The term can be applied to a test or other measurement or to a system of classification. (*See* test-retest reliability and interrater reliability)

Repression According to psychoanalytic theory, the most basic defense mechanism. Thoughts or impulses unacceptable to the ego are forced back into the unconscious.

Resilience The ability to overcome risk factors, to function adaptively despite negative circumstances.

Respite care Brief alternative care provided to disabled persons in order to lighten the burdens of care carried by the primary caretakers.

Response prevention A behavioral treatment procedure in which the person is not allowed to engage in, or is discouraged from engaging in, a compulsive ritual or avoidant behavior.

Retrospective research designs Designs that utilize information about past events; follow-back designs. (*See* prospective research designs)

Risk The degree to which variables (risk factors) operate to increase the chance of behavior problems. (*See* protective factors)

Rumination The voluntary regurgitation of food by infants.

Savant abilities Specific and remarkable cognitive abilities (e.g., memory, arithmetical) observed in individuals who are otherwise intellectually handicapped.

Schema Mental concepts or constructions of the world. The development of complex schemas is central to Piaget's theory of cognitive growth.

School phobia An extreme reluctance to go to school which is frequently accompanied by somatic complaints. The term *school refusal* is preferred by some clinicians, since an actual fear of school may not be present.

Scientific method An empirical approach to understanding phenomena. The scientific approach involves systematic observation, measurement and testing of relationships, and explanations of phenomena.

Secondary prevention The prevention of disorders in the population by shortening the duration of existing cases through early diagnosis and treatment, especially of at-risk populations.

Self-injurious behavior Repetitious action that damages the self physically, such as head banging, scratching the self, and pulling one's own hair. Observed especially in autism and mental retardation, but occurs in a small percentage of young, normal children.

Self-monitoring A procedure in which the individual observes and records his or her own behaviors or thoughts and the circumstances under which they occur.

Self-stimulatory behavior Sensory-motor behavior that serves as stimulation for the person. Often refers to a pathological process, for example, as when an autistic child repetitiously flaps his or her hands.

Semantics The study of the meanings in language.

Separation anxiety Childhood anxiety regarding separation from the mother or other major attachment figures.

Sequential research designs Various designs that combine the longitudinal and cross-sectional research strategies to maximize the strengths of these methods.

Shared environment A term derived from genetic research which describes that portion of environmental influences on an attribute that is experienced by two or more family members. (*See* nonshared environment)

Single-subject experiments Various experimental research designs employed with a single (or a few) subject(s), in which a manipulation is made and measurements are taken across time periods. (*See* ABA' and multiple baseline designs)

Socioeconomic status (SES) Classification of people according to social class. Indices of SES include monetary level, amount of education, and occupational level. Many factors vary with SES, such as medical care and child-rearing practices.

Somatogenesis The view that development of a particular disorder is due to biological—rather than psychosocial—causes.

Stage theories of development Explanations of development that postulate that growth occurs in a recognizable order of noncontinuous stages or steps, which are qualitatively different from each other. Examples: Piaget's cognitive theory and Freud's psychosexual theory.

Statistical significance In research, refers to a low probability that the findings are merely chance occurrences. By tradition a finding is statistically significant when there is a 5 percent or less probability that it occurred by chance ($p \leq .05$).

Stereotypy A repetitive action or movement, such as hand flapping or incessantly lining up objects in rows.

Stop-Signal task A method to evaluate behavioral inhibition. The individual must press a button when a target stimulus comes on a screen but must withhold this response when a special signal also comes on.

Stress A situation or event that brings strain to the individual. Considered a risk factor for behavioral and physical health.

Superego The third of Freud's three structures of the mind. It is the conscience or self-critical part of the individual that reflects society's morals and standards as they have been learned from parents and others.

Sympathetic nervous system A part of the autonomic nervous system which, among other things, accelerates heart rate, increases blood glucose, inhibits intestinal activity, and in general seems to prepare the organism for stress or activity.

Syndrome A group of behaviors or symptoms which are known or thought to be likely to occur together in a particular disorder.

Syntax The aspect of grammar that deals with the way words are put together to form phrases, clauses, and sentences.

Systematic desensitization A behavioral treatment of anxiety. The client visualizes a hierarchy of scenes, each of which elicits more anxiety than the previous scene. These visualizations are paired with relaxation until they no longer produce anxiety.

Systematic direct observation Observation of specific behaviors of an individual or group of individuals in a particular setting, with the use of a specific observational code or instrument.

Temperament A variety of socioemotional behaviors viewed as relatively stable attributes of individuals, such as activity level and social responsiveness.

Teratogens Conditions or agents that tend to cause developmental malformations, defects, or death of the fetus.

Tertiary prevention The prevention of disorders in the population by reducing problems residual to disorders. An example is support groups for persons who are returning to the community after hospitalization for mental disorders.

Test-retest reliability The degree to which a test or diagnostic system yields the same result when applied to the same individuals at different times.

The Individuals with Disabilities Education Act (IDEA) The federal mandate that sets guidelines for the rights of handicapped individuals to appropriate education. Originally titled the Education for all Handicapped Children's Act (*See* Public Law 94–142)

Theory An integrated set of propositions that explains phenomena and guides research.

Theory of mind The ability to infer mental states (e.g., beliefs, knowledge) in others or the self.

Time-out Behavior modification technique in which an individual displaying an undesirable behavior is removed from the immediate environment, usually by placement into an isolated room. Conceptually time-out is viewed as elimination of positive reinforcement or as punishment.

Token economy A behavioral treatment procedure developed from operant conditioning principles. A set of behaviors that earn or cost reward points, given in the form of some scrip, such as poker chips, is set up. These tokens can then be exchanged for prizes, activities, or privileges.

Transactional model of development The view that development is the result of the continuous interplay of organismic and environmental variables. It is conceptually similar to the interactional model of development but it emphasizes the ongoing, mutual influences of factors.

Treatment foster care A thrust to alleviate and treat the behavioral problems of children in foster care by preparing and working with foster parents and linking the child to the community mental health system.

Twin study A type of research investigation frequently employed to examine the effects of hereditary and environmental variables. Pairs of genetically-identical monozygotic twins and dizygotic twins, which share on average half their genes, are examined to determine whether the former are more alike than the latter.

Unconditioned stimulus A stimulus which elicits a particular response prior to any conditioning trails. The loud noise that causes an infant to startle is an example of an unconditioned stimulus.

Validity A term used in several different ways, all of which address issues of correctness, meaningfulness, and relevancy. (*See* internal validity, external validity, predictive validity)

Zygote The cell mass formed by the joining of an ovum and sperm; the fertilized egg.

REFERENCES

AACAP. (1997). Practice parameters for the assessment and treatment of children and adolescents with anxiety disorders. *Journal of the American Academy of Child and Adolescent Psychiatry, 36,* 69S–84S.

AACAP. (1998a). Practice parameters for the assessment and treatment of children and adolescents with obsessive-compulsive disorder. *Journal of the American Academy of Child and Adolescent Psychiatry, 37,* 27S–45S.

AACAP. (1998b). Practice parameters for the assessment and treatment of children and adolescents with posttraumatic stress disorder. *Journal of the American Academy of Child and Adolescent Psychiatry, 37,* 4S–26S.

Abidin, R. R. (1995). *Parenting Stress Index: Professional manual* (3rd ed.). Odessa, FL: Psychological Assessment Resources.

Abikoff, H., & Hechtman, L. (1996). Multimodal therapy and stimulants in the treatment of children with ADHD. In E. D. Hibbs & P. Jensen (Eds.), *Psychosocial treatment for child and adolescent disorders: Empirically based approaches.* Washington, DC: American Psychological Association.

Ablon, S. L. (1996). The therapeutic action of play. *Journal of the American Academy of Child and Adolescent Psychiatry, 35,* 545–547.

Abramson, L. Y., Metalsky, G. I., & Alloy, L. B. (1989). Hopelessness depression: A theory-based subtype of depression. *Psychological Bulletin, 96,* 358–372.

Abramson, L. Y., Seligman, M. E. P., & Teasdale, J. D. (1978). Learned helplessness in humans: Critique and reformulation. *Journal of Abnormal Psychology, 87,* 49–74.

Achenbach, T. M. (1974, 1982). *Developmental psychopathology.* New York: Wiley.

Achenbach, T. M. (1985). *Assessment and taxonomy of child and adolescent psychopathology.* Beverly Hills: Sage.

Achenbach, T. M. (1990). Conceptualizations of developmental psychopathology. In M. Lewis & S. M. Miller (Eds.), *Handbook of developmental psychopathology.* New York: Plenum.

Achenbach, T. M. (1991a). *Integrative guide for the 1991 CBCL/4-18, YSR and TRF profiles.* Burlington, VT: University of Vermont Department of Psychiatry.

Achenbach, T. M. (1991b). *Manual for the Child Behavior Checklist/4-18 and 1991 profile.* Burlington, VT: University of Vermont Department of Psychiatry.

Achenbach, T. M. (1991c). *Manual for the Teachers Report Form and 1991 profile.* Burlington, VT: University of Vermont Department of Psychiatry.

Achenbach, T. M. (1991d). *Manual for the Youth Self-Report and 1991 profile.* Burlington, VT: University of Vermont Department of Psychiatry.

Achenbach, T. M. (1993). *Empirically based taxonomy: How to use syndromes and profile types derived from the CBCL/4-18, TRF, and YSR.* Burlington, VT: University of Vermont Department of Psychiatry.

Achenbach, T. M. (1998). Diagnosis, assessment, taxonomy and case formulations. In T. H. Ollendick & Hersen, M. (Eds.), *Handbook of child psychopathology* (3rd ed.). New York: Plenum Press.

Achenbach, T. M., & Howell, C. T. (1993). Are American children's problems getting worse? A 13-year comparison. *Journal of the American Academy of Child and Adolescent Psychiatry, 32,* 1145–1154.

Achenbach, T. M., Howell, C. T., McConaughy, S. H., & Stanger, C. (1995a). Six-year predictors of problems in a national sample of children and youth: I. Cross-informant syndromes. *Journal of the American Academy of Child and Adolescent Psychiatry, 34,* 336–347.

Achenbach, T. M., Howell, C. T., McConaughy, S. H., & Stanger, C. (1995b). Six-year predictors of problems in a national sample of children and youth: II. Signs of disturbance. *Journal of the American Academy of Child and Adolescent Psychiatry, 34,* 488–498.

Achenbach, T. M., Howell, C. T., Quay, H. C., & Conners, C. K. (1991). National survey of problems and competencies among four- to sixteen-year-olds. *Monographs of the Society for Research in Child Development, 56* (3, Serial No. 225).

Achenbach, T. M., McConaughy, S. H., & Howell, C. T. (1987). Child/adolescent behavioral and emotional problems: Implications of cross-informant correlations for situational specificity. *Psychological Bulletin, 101,* 213–232.

Achenbach, T. M., Phares, V., Howell, C. T., Ruah, V. A., & Nurcombe, B. (1990). Seven-year outcome of the Vermont Intervention Program for low-birth-weight infants. *Child Development, 61,* 1672–1681.

Adams, M., Kutcher, S., Antoniw, E., & Bird, D. (1996). Diagnostic utility of endocrine and neuroimaging screening tests in first-onset adolescent schizophrenia. *Journal of the American Academy of Child and Adolescent Psychiatry, 35,* 67–73.

Adelman, H. S. (1989). Beyond the learning mystique: An interactional perspective on learning disabilities. *Journal of Learning Disabilities, 22,* 301–304; 328.

Adelman, H. S. (1996). Appreciating the classification dilemma. In W. Stainback & S. Stainback (Eds.), *Controversial issues confronting special education: Divergent perspectives* (2nd ed.). Boston: Allyn and Bacon.

Adrien, J. L., Lenoir, P., Martineau, J., Perrot, A., Hameury, L., Larmande, C., & Sauvage, D. (1993). Blind ratings of early symptoms of autism based upon home movies. *Journal of the American Academy of Child and Adolescent Psychiatry, 32,* 617–626.

Adrien, J. L., Ornitz, E., Barthelemy, C., Sauvage, D., & Lelord, G. (1987). The presence or absense of certain behaviors associated with infantile autism in severely retarded autistic and nonaustistic retarded children and very young normal children. *Journal of Autism and Developmental Disorders, 17,* 407–416.

Ainbinder, J. G., Blanchard, L. W., Singer, G. H. S., Sullivan, M. E., Powers, L. K., Marquis, J. G., & Santelli, B. (1998). A qualitative study of Parent to Parent support for parents of children with special needs. *Journal of Pediatric Psychology, 23,* 99–109.

Alanen, Y. (1960). Some thoughts on schizophrenia and ego development in the light of family investigations. *Archives of General Psychiatry, 3,* 650–656.

Albano, A. M., & Barlow, D. H. (1996). Cognitive behavioral group treatment for adolescent social phobia. In E. D. Hibbs & P. S. Jensen (Eds.), *Psychosocial treatment research of child and adolescent disorders.* Washington, DC: American Psychological Association Press.

Albano, A. M., Chorpita, B. F., & Barlow, D. H. (1996). Childhood anxiety disorders. In E. J. Mash & R. A. Barkley (Eds.), *Child psychopathology.* New York: Guilford Press.

Albee, G. W. (1986).Toward a just society. Lessons from observations on the primary prevention of psychopathology. *American Psychologist, 41,* 891–898.

Albee, G. W. (1996). Revolutions and counterrevolutions in prevention. *American Psychologist, 51,* 1130–1133.

Alessi, N. E., Robbins, D. R., & Dilsaver, S. C. (1987). Panic and depressive disorders among psychiatrically hospitalized adolescents. *Psychiatry Research, 20,* 275–283.

Alexander, A. B. (1980). The treatment of psychosomatic disorders. In B. B. Lahey & A. E. Kazdin (Eds.), *Advances in clinical child psychology,* Vol. 3. New York: Plenum.

Alexander, F. (1950). *Psychosomatic medicine.* New York: W. W. Norton and Co.

Alexander, J. F. (1973). Defensive and supportive communications in normal and deviant families. *Journal of Consulting and Clinical Psychology, 40,* 223–231.

Alexander, J. F., Barton, C., Schiavo, R. S., & Parsons, B. V. (1976). Systems-behavioral intervention with families of delinquents: Therapist characteristics, family behavior, and outcome. *Journal of Consulting and Clinical Psychology, 44,* 656–664.

Alexander, J. F., Holtzworth-Munroe, A., & Jameson, P. B. (1994). The process and outcome of marital and family therapy research: Review and evaluation. In A. E. Bergin & S. L. Garfield (Eds.), *Handbook of psychotherapy and behavior change* (4th ed.). New York: John Wiley & Sons.

Alexander, J. F., & Parsons, B. V. (1973). Short-term behavioral intervention with delinquent families: Impact on family process and recidivism. *Journal of Abnormal Psychology, 81,* 219–225.

Alexander, J. F., & Parsons, B. V. (1982). *Functional family therapy: Principles and procedures.* Carmel, CA: Brooks/Cole.

Alexander, J. F., Waldron, H. B., Barton, C., & Mas, C. H. (1989). The minimizing of blaming attributions and behaviors in delinquent families. *Journal of Consulting and Clinical Psychology, 57,* 19–24.

Algozzine, B. (1977). The emotionally disturbed child: Disturbed or disturbing? *Journal of Abnormal Child Psychology, 5,* 205–211.

Allen, A. J., Leonard, H. L., & Swedo, S. E. (1995a). A new infection-triggered, autoimmune subtype of pediatric OCD and Tourette's syndrome. *Journal of the American Academy of Child and Adolescent Psychiatry, 34,* 307–311.

Allen, A. J., Leonard, H. L., & Swedo, S. E. (1995b). Current knowledge of medications for the treatment of childhood anxiety disorders. *Journal of the American Academy of Child and Adolescent Psychiatry, 34,* 976–986.

Allen, J. S., & Drabman, R. S. (1991). Attributions of children with learning disabilities who are treated with psychostimulants. *Learning Disability Quarterly, 14,* 75–79.

Allen, K., Hart, B., Buell, J., Harris, F., & Wolf, M. (1964). Effects of social reinforcement on isolated behavior of a nursery school child. *Child Development, 35,* 511–518.

Alloy, L. B., Lipman, A. J., & Abramson, L. Y. (1992). Attributional style as a vulnerability factor for depression. *Cognitive Therapy and Research, 16,* 391–407.

Altman, H., & Collins, M., & Mundy, P. (1997). Subclinical hallucinations and delusions in nonpsychotic adolescents. *Journal of Child Psychology and Psychiatry, 38,* 413–420.

Aman, C. J., Roberts, R. J., & Pennington, B. F. (1998). A neuropsychological examination of the underlying deficit in attention deficit hyperactivity disorder: Frontal lobe versus right parietal lobe theories. *Developmental Psychology, 34,* 956–969.

Aman, M. G., Hammer, D., & Rojahn, J. (1993). Mental retardation. In T. H. Ollendick & M. Hersen (Eds.), *Handbook of child and adolescent assessment*. Boston: Allyn and Bacon.

Aman, M. G., & Kern, R. A. (1989). Review of fenfluramine in the treatment of the developmental disabilities. *Journal of the American Academy of Child and Adolescent Psychiatry, 28,* 549–565.

Amato, P. R., & Keith, B. (1991). Parental divorce and the well-being of children: A metaanalysis. *Psychological Bulletin, 110,* 26–46.

American Academy of Child and Adolescent Psychiatry (1998). Practice parameters for the assessment and treatment of children and adolescents with depressive disorders. *Journal of the American Academy of Child and Adolescent Psychiatry, 37,* 63S–83S.

American Psychiatric Association (1952, 1968, 1980, 1987, 1994). *Diagnostic and statistical manual of mental disorders*. Washington, DC: American Psychiatric Association.

American Psychiatric Association (1993). Practice guidelines for eating disorders. *American Journal of Psychiatry, 150,* 207–228.

American Sleep Disorders Association, Diagnostic Classification Steering Committee. (1990). *The international classification of sleep disorders: Diagnostic and coding manual*. Rochester, MN: American Sleep Disorders Association.

Anastasi, A., & Urbina, S. (1997). *Psychological testing*. Upper Saddle River, NJ: Prentice Hall.

Anastopoulos, A. D., & Barkley, R. A. (1992). Attention-deficit hyperactivity disorder. In C. E. Walker & M. C. Roberts (Eds.), *Handbook of clinical child psychology*. NY: John Wiley.

Anastopoulos, A. D., Smith, J. M., & Wien, E. E. (1998). Counseling and training parents. In R. A. Barkley, *Attention-deficit hyperactivity disorder*. New York: Guilford Press.

Anders, T. F., & Eiben, L. A. (1997). Pediatric sleep disorders: A review of the past 10 years. *Journal of the American Academy of Child and Adolescent Psychiatry, 36,* 9–20.

Anderson, G. M., & Hoshino, Y. (1997). Neurochemical studies of autism. In D. J. Cohen & F. R. Volkmar (Eds.), *Handbook of autism and pervasive developmental disorders*. New York: John Wiley.

Anderson, J. C. (1994). Epidemiology. In T. H. Ollendick, N. J. King, & W. Yule (Eds.), *International handbook of phobic and anxiety disorders in children and adolescents*. New York: Plenum Press.

Anderson, J. C., & McGee, R. (1994). Comorbidity of depression in children and adolescents. In W. M. Reynolds & H. F. Johnston (Eds.), *Handbook of depression in children and adolescents*. New York: Plenum Press.

Anderson, J. C., Williams, S., McGee, R., & Silva, P. A. (1987). DSM-III disorders in preadolescent children: Prevalence in a large sample from the general population. *Archives of General Psychiatry, 44,* 69–76.

Anderson, K. E., Lytton, H., & Romney, D. M. (1986). Mothers interactions with normal and conduct-disordered boys: Who affects whom? *Developmental Psychology, 22,* 604–609.

Andrasik, F., & Attansio, V. (1985). Biofeedback in pediatrics: Current status and appraisal. In M. L. Wolraich & D. K. Routh (Eds.), *Advances in developmental and behavioral pediatrics*, Vol. 6, Greenwich, CT: JAI.

Andrasik, F., Blake, D. D., & McCarran, M. S. (1986). A biobehavioral analysis of pediatric headache. In N. A. Krasnegor, J. D. Arasteh, & M. F. Cataldo (Eds.), *Child health behavior: A behavioral pediatrics perspective*. New York: Wiley.

Angold, A., & Rutter, M. (1992). Effects of age and pubertal stratus on depression in a large clinical sample. *Development and Psychopathology, 4,* 5–28.

Anthony, E. J. (1970). Behavior disorders. In P. H. Mussen (Ed.), *Carmichael's manual of child psychology*, Vol. II. New York: John Wiley.

Anthony, E. J. (1981). The psychiatric evaluation of the anxious child: Case record summarized from the clinic records. In E. J. Anthony & D. C. Gilpin (Eds.), *Three further clinical faces of childhood*. New York: S P Medical & Scientific Books.

Aoki, C., & Siekevitz, P. (1988). Plasticity in brain development. *Scientific American, 259,* 56–64.

Aristimuno, G. G., Foster, T. A., Voors, A. W., Srinivasan, S. R., & Berenson, G. S. (1984). Influence of persistent obesity in children on cardiovascular risk factors: The Bogalusa Heart Study. *Circulation, 69,* 895–904.

Armbruster, P. & Kazdin, A. E. (1994). Attrition in child psychotherapy. In T. H. Ollendick & R. J. Prinz (Eds.), *Advances in clinical child psychology*. New York: Plenum Press.

Armistead, L., Forehand, R., Steele, R., & Kotchick, B. (1998). Pediatric AIDS. In T. H. Ollendick & M. Hersen (Eds.), *Handbook of child psychopathology* (3rd ed.). New York: Plenum Press.

Arnold, L. E. and colleagues (1995). Ethical issues in biological psychiatric research with children and adolescents. *Journal of the American Academy of Child and Adolescent Psychiatry, 34,* 929–939.

Asarnow, J. R. (1994). Childhood-onset schizophrenia. *Journal of Child Psychology and Psychiatry, 35,* 1345–1371.

Asarnow, J. R., & Asarnow, R. F. (1996). Childhood-onset schizophrenia. In E. J. Mash & R. A. Barkley (Eds.), *Child psychopathology*. New York: Guilford Press.

Asarnow, J. R., Goldstein, M. J., & Ben-Meir, S. (1988). Parental communication deviance in childhood onset schizophrenia spectrum and depressive disorders. *Journal of Child Psychology and Psychiatry, 29,* 825–838.

Asarnow, R. F., Tanguay, P.E., Bott, L., & Freeman, B. J. (1987). Patterns of intellectual functioning in non-retarded autistic and schizophrenic children. *Journal of Child Psychology and Psychiatry, 28,* 273–280.

Asendorpf, J. B. (1993). Abnormal shyness in children. *Journal of Child Psychology and Psychiatry, 34,* 1069–1081.

Atkinson, L., Scott, B., Chrisholm, V., Blackwell, J., Dickens, S., Tam, F., & Goldberg, S. (1995). Cognitive coping, affective distress, and maternal sensitivity: Mothers of children with Down syndrome. *Developmental Psychology, 31,* 668–676.

Atkinson, R. C., & Shriffin, R. M. (1968). Human memory: A proposed system and its control processes. In K. W. Spence & J. T. Spence (Eds.), *The psychology of learning and motivation.* New York: Academic press.

Attie, I., & Brooks-Gunn, J. (1995). The development of eating regulation across the life span. In D. Cicchetti & D. J. Cohen (Eds.), *Developmental psychopathology* (Vol. 2: *Risk, disorder, and adaptation*). New York: John Wiley.

Attwood, A., Frith, U., & Hermelin, B. (1988). The understanding and use of interpersonal gestures by autistic and Down's Syndrome children. *Journal of Autism and Developmental Disorders, 18,* 241–257.

August, G. J., & Garfinkel, B. D. (1989). Behavioral and cognitive subtypes of ADHD. *Journal of the American Academy of Child and Adolescent Psychiatry, 28,* 739–748.

August, G. J., & Garfinkel, B. D. (1993). The nosology of attention-deficit hyperactivity disorder. *Journal of the American Academy of Child and Adolescent Psychiatry, 32,* 155–165.

Axline, V. M. (1947). *Play therapy.* Boston: Houghton Mifflin.

Azar, S. T., & Bober, S. L. (1999). Children of abusive parents. In W. K. Silverman & T. H. Ollendick (Eds.), *Development issues in the clinical treatment of children.* Boston: Allyn & Bacon.

Azar, S. T., Ferraro, M. H., & Breton, S. J. (1998). Intrafamilial child maltreatment. In T. H. Ollendick & M. Hersen (Eds.), *Handbook of child psychopathology* (3rd ed.). New York: Plenum Press.

Azar, S. T., & Wolfe, D. A. (1998). Child physical abuse and neglect. In E. J. Mash & R. A. Barkely (Eds.), *Treatment of childhood disorders* (2nd ed.). New York: Guilford Press.

Bahr, H. M. (1988). Family change and the mystique of the traditional family. In L. A. Bond & B. M. Wagner (Eds.), *Families in transition: Primary prevention programs that work.* Newbury Park, CA: Sage.

Bailey, A., Le Couteur, A., Gottesman, I., Bolton, P., Simonoff, E., Yuzda, E., & Rutter, M. (1995). Autism as a strongly genetic disorder: Evidence from a British twin study. *Psychological Medicine, 25,* 63–78.

Bailey, A., Phillips, W., & Rutter, M. (1996). Autism: Towards an integration of clinical, genetic, neuropsychological, and neurobiological perspectives. *Journal of Child Psychology and Psychiatry, 37,* 89–126.

Bailey, G. W. (1989). Current perspectives on substance abuse in youth. *Journal of the American Academy of Child and Adolescent Psychiatry, 28,* 151–162.

Baker, E. T., Wang, M. C., & Walberg, H. J. (December 1994/January 1995). *Educational Leadership, 52,* 33–35.

Baker, L., & Cantwell, D. P. (1989). Specific language and learning disorders. In T. H. Ollendick & M. Hersen (Eds.). *Handbook of child psychopathology.* New York: Plenum.

Baker, L., & Cantwell, D. P. (1991). The development of speech and language. In M. Lewis (Ed.), *Child and adolescent psychiatry: A comprehensive textbook.* Baltimore: Williams & Wilkins.

Baker, P., Piven, J., & Sato, Y. (1998). Autism and tuberous sclerosis complex: Prevalence and clinical features. *Journal of Autism and Developmental Disorders, 28,* 279–286.

Bakwin, H. (1971). Enuresis in twins. *American Journal of Diseases in Childhood, 121,* 222–225.

Bandura, A. (1965). Influence of models' reinforcement contingencies on the acquisition of imitative responses. *Journal of Personality and Social Psychology, 1,* 589–595.

Bandura, A. (1977). *Social learning theory.* Englewood Cliffs, NJ: Prentice Hall.

Bandura, A., & Menlove, F. L. (1968). Factors determining vicarious extinction of avoidance behavior through symbolic modeling. *Journal of Personality and Social Psychology, 8,* 99–108.

Barkley, R. A. (1981). Hyperactivity. In E. J. Mash & L. G. Terdal (Eds.), *Behavioral assessment of childhood disorders.* New York: Guilford Press.

Barkley, R. A. (1989). Attention deficit-hyperactivity disorder. In E. J. Mash and R. A. Barkley (Eds.), *Treatment of childhood disorders.* New York, Guilford.

Barkley, R. A. (1990). *Attention-deficit hyperactivity disorder.* New York: Guilford.

Barkley, R. A. (1996). Attention-deficit/hyperactivity disorder. In E. J. Mash & R. A. Barkley (Eds.), *Child psychopathology. New York: Guilford Press.*

Barkley, R. A. (1997). Attention-deficit/hyperactivity disorder. In E. J. Mash & L. G. Terdal (Eds.), *Assessment of childhood disorders.* New York: Guilford Press.

Barkley, R. A. (1998a). *Attention-deficit/hyperactivity disorder.* New York: Guilford Press.

Barkley, R. A. (1998b). Attention-deficit/hyperactivity disorder. In E. J. Mash & R. A. Barkley (Eds.), *Treatment of childhood disorders.* New York: Guilford Press.

Barkley, R. A., Anastopoulos, A. D., Guevremont, D. C., & Fletcher, K. E. (1992). Adolescents with attention deficit hyperactivity disorder: Mother-adolescent interactions, family beliefs and conflicts, and maternal psychopathology. *Journal of Abnormal Child Psychology, 20,* 263–287.

Barlow, D. H., & Hersen, M. (1984). *Single case experimental designs: Strategies for studying behavior change.* Elmsford, NY: Pergamon.

Barnes, G. G. (1994). Family therapy. In M. Rutter, E. Taylor, & L. Hersov (Eds.), *Child and adolescent psychiatry. Modern approaches.* Cambridge, MA: Blackwell Scientific.

Barnett, D., Manly, J. T., & Cicchetti, D. (1991). Continuing toward an operational definition of psychological maltreatment. *Development and Psychopathology, 3,* 19–30.

Barnett, W., & Spitzer, M. (1994). Pathological fire-setting 1951–1991: A review. *Medicine Science and the Law, 34,* 4–20.

Baron–Cohen, S. (1988). Social and pragmatic deficits in autism: Cognitive or affective? *Journal of Autism and Developmental Disorders, 18,* 379–397.

Baron–Cohen, S. (1993). From attention-goal psychology to belief-desire psychology: the development of a theory of mind, and its dysfunction. In S. Baron-Cohen, H. Tager-Flusberg, & D. J. Cohen (Eds.), *Understanding other minds.* New York: Oxford Press.

Baron-Cohen, S., Jolliffe, T., Mortimore, C., & Robertson, M. (1997). Another advanced test of theory of mind: Evidence from very high functioning adults with autism or Asperger syndrome. *Journal of Child Psychology and Psychiatry, 38,* 813–822.

Baron-Cohen, S., & Swettenham, J. (1997). Theory of mind in autism: Its relationship to executive functions and central coherence. In D. J. Cohen & F. R. Volkmar (Eds.), *Handbook of autism and pervasive developmental disorders.* New York: John Wiley.

Barrett, P. M., Dadds, M. R., & Rapee, R. M. (1996). Family treatment of childhood anxiety: A controlled trial. *Journal of Consulting and Clinical Psychology, 64,* 333–342.

Barrios, B. A., & Hartmann, D. P. (1997). Fears and anxieties. In E. J. Mash & L. G. Terdal (Eds.), *Assessment of childhood disorders* (3rd ed.). New York: Guilford Press.

Barrios, B. A., & O'Dell, S. L. (1998). Fears and anxieties. In E. J. Mash & R. A. Barkley (Eds.), *Treatment of childhood disorders* (2nd ed.). New York: Guilford Press.

Barton, C., Alexander, J. F., Waldron, H., Turner, C. W., & Warburton, J. (1985). Generalizing treatment effects of functional family therapy: Three replications. *The American Journal of Family Therapy, 13,* 16–26.

Bashir, A. S., & Scavuzzo, A. (1992). Children with language disorders: Natural history and academic success. *Journal of Learning Disabilities, 25,* 53–65.

Bates, J. E. (1987). Temperament in infancy. In J. D. Osofsky (Ed.), *Handbook of infant development.* New York: Wiley.

Bauer, D. H. (1976). An exploratory study of developmental changes in children's fears. *Journal of Child Psychology and Psychiatry, 17,* 69–74.

Bauer, R. H. (1987). Control processes as a way of understanding, diagnosing, and remediating learning disabilities. In H. L. Swanson (Ed.), *Memory and learning disabilities: Suppl. 2. Advances in learning and behavioral disabilities.* Greenwich, CT: JAI Press.

Bauer, R. H., & Newman, D. R. (1991). Allocation of study time and recall by learning disabled and nondisabled children of different ages. *Journal of Experimental Child Psychology, 52,* 11–21.

Bauermeister, J. J., Bird, H. R., Canino, G., Rubio-Stipec, M., Bravo, M., & Alegria, M. (1995). Dimensions of attention deficit hyperactivity disorder: Findings from teacher and parent reports in a community sample. *Journal of Clinical Child Psychology, 24,* 264–271.

Baumeister, A. A. (1987). Mental retardation: Some conceptions and dilemmas. *American Psychologist, 42,* 796–800.

Bayley, N. (1969, 1993). *Bayley Scales of Infant Development: Birth to two years.* San Antonio, TX: Psychological Corporation.

Beals, J., Piasecki, J. Nelson, S., Jones, M., Keane, E., Dauphinais, Red Shirt, R., Sack, W. H., & Manson, S. M. (1997). Psychiatric disorder among American Indian adolescents: Prevalence in Northern Plains youth. *Journal of the American Academy of Child and Adolescent Psychiatry, 36,* 1252–1259.

Beardslee, W. R., Keller, M. B., Seifer, R., Lavorie, P. W., Staley, J., Podorefsky, D., & Shera, D. (1996). Prediction of adolescent affective disorder: Effects of prior parenteral affective disorders and child psychopathology. *Journal of the American Academy of Child and Adolescent Psychiatry, 35,* 279–288.

Beardslee, W. R., & Podorefsky, D. (1988). Resilient adolescents whose parents have serious affective and other psychiatric disorders: Importance of self-understanding and relationships. *American Journal of Psychiatry, 145,* 63–69.

Beardslee, W. R., Versage, E. M., & Gladstone, T. R. G. (1998). Children of affectively ill parents: A review of the past 10 years. *Journal of the American Academy of Child and Adolescent Psychiatry, 37,* 1134–1141.

Beck, A. T. (1967). *Depression: Clinical, experimental, and theoretical aspects.* New York: Harper & Row.

Beck, A. T. (1976). *Cognitive theory and emotional disorders.* New York: International Universities Press.

Beck, A. T. (1993). Cognitive therapy: Past, present, and future. *Journal of Consulting and Clinical Psychology, 61,* 194–198.

Beck, A. T., Ward, C. H., Mendelson, M., Mock, J. E., & Erbaugh, J. K. (1962). Reliability of psychiatric diagnosis: II. A study of consistency of clinical judgements and ratings. *American Journal of Psychiatry, 119,* 351–357.

Beelmann, A., Pfingsten, U., & Losel, F. (1994). Effects of training social competence in children: A meta-analysis of recent evaluation studies. *Journal of Clinical Child Psychology, 23,* 260–271.

Beidel, D. C., & Randall, J. (1994). Social phobia. In T. H. Ollendick, N. J. King, & W. Yule (Eds.), *International handbook of phobic and anxiety disorders in children and adolescents* (pp. 111–130). New York: Plenum Press.

Beidel, D. C., Silverman, W. K., & Hammond-Laurence, K. (1996). Overanxious disorder: Subsyndromal state or specific disorder? A comparison of clinic and community samples. *Journal of Clinical Child Psychology, 25,* 25–32.

Beidel, D. C., & Turner, S. M. (1997). At risk for anxiety: I. Psychopathology in the offspring of anxious parents. *Journal of the American Academy of Child and Adolescent Psychiatry, 36,* 918–924.

Beidel, D. C., Turner, S. M., & Morris, T. L. (1995). A new inventory to assess childhood social anxiety and phobia: The Social Phobia and Anxiety Inventory for Children. *Psychological Assessment, 7,* 73–79.

Beilen, H. (1992). Piaget's enduring contribution to developmental psychology. *Developmental Psychology, 28,* 191–204.

Beirne-Smith, M., Ittenbach, R. F., & Patton, J. R. (1998). *Mental retardation.* Upper Saddle River, NJ: Prentice Hall.

Beitchman, J. H., Cantwell, D. P., Forness, S. R., Kavale, K. A., & Kauffman, J. M. (1997). Practice parameters for the assessment and treatment of children and adolescents with language and learning disorders. *Journal of the American Academy of Child and Adolescent Psychiatry, 37(10 Supplement),* 46S–62S.

Beitchman, J. H., Wilson, B., Brownlie, E. B., Walters, H., Inglis, A., & Lancee, W. (1996). Long-term consistency in speech/language profiles: II. behavioral, emotional, and social outcomes. *Journal of the American Academy of Child and Adolescent Psychiatry, 35,* 815–825.

Beitchman, J. H., & Young, A. R. (1997). Learning disorders with a special emphasis on reading disorders: A review of the past 10 years. *Journal of the American Academy of Child and Adolescent Psychiatry, 36,* 1020–1032.

Bell, K. E., & Stein, D. M. (1992). Behavioral treatments for pica: A review of empirical studies. *International Journal of Eating Disorders, 11,* 377–389.

Bell, R. (1985). *Holy anorexia.* Chicago: University of Chicago Press.

Bell-Dolan, D. J. (1995). Social cue interpretation of anxious children. *Journal of Clinical Child Psychology, 24,* 2–10.

Bell-Dolan, D. J., Last, C. G., & Strauss, C. C. (1990). Symptoms of anxiety disorders in normal children. *Journal of the American Academy of Child and Adolescent Psychiatry, 29,* 759–765.

Bell-Dolan, D. J., Reaven, N. M., & Peterson, L. (1993). Depression and social functioning: A multidimensional study of the linkages. *Journal of Clinical Child Psychology, 22,* 306–315.

Bellack, A. S., & Mueser, K. T. (1993). Psychosocial treatments for schizophrenia. *Schizophrenia Bulletin, 19,* 317–336.

Bellak, L. (1993). *The T.A.T., C.A.T., and S.A.T. in clinical use* (5th ed.). Boston: Allyn & Bacon.

Bellak, L., & Bellak, S. (1949). *The Children's Apperception Test.* New York: C.P.S. Company.

Belsky, J. (1991). Psychological maltreatment: Definitional limitations and unstated assumptions. *Development and Psychopathology, 3,* 31–36.

Belsky, J. (1993). Etiology of child maltreatment: A developmental-ecological analysis. *Psychological Bulletin, 114,* 413–434.

Bemporad, J. (1991). Psychoanalysis and psychodynamic therapy. In J. M. Weiner (Ed.), *Textbook of child and adolescent psychiatry.* Washington, DC: American Psychiatric Press.

Bemporad, J. R. (1978). Encopresis. In B. B. Wolman, J. Egan, & A. O. Ross (Eds.), Handbook of treatments in childhood and adolescence. Englewood Cliffs, NJ: Prentice Hall.

Bendersky, M., & Lewis, M. (1994). Environmental risk, biological risk, and developmental outcome. *Developmental Psychology, 30,* 484–494.

Benedict, R. (1934a). Anthropology and the abnormal. *Journal of General Psychology, 10,* 59–82.

Benedict, R. (1934b). *Patterns of culture.* Boston: Houghton-Mifflin.

Bennett, D. S. (1994). Depression among children with chronic medical problems: A meta-analysis. *Journal of Pediatric Psychology, 19,* 149–169.

Berg, I., & Jackson, A. (1985). Teenage school refusers grow up: A follow-up study of 168 subjects ten years on average after inpatient treatment. *British Journal of Psychiatry, 147,* 366–370.

Berger, J. (1990). Interactions between parents and their infants with Down syndrome. In D. Cicchetti & M. Beeghly (Eds.), *Children with Down syndrome.* New York: Cambridge University Press.

Berger, M., & Yule, W. (1985). IQ tests and assessment. In A. M. Clarke, A. D. B. Clarke, & J. M. Berg (Eds.), *Mental deficiency. The changing outlook.* New York: The Free Press.

Berkman M. (1997). The legal rights of children with disabilities to education and developmental services. In D. J. Cohen & F. R. Volkmar (Eds.), *Handbook of autism and pervasive developmental disorders.* New York: John Wiley.

Bernstein, G. A., Borchardt, C. M., & Perwien, A. R. (1996). Anxiety disorders in children and adolescents: A review of the past 10 years. *Journal of the American Academy of Child and Adolescent Psychiatry, 35,* 1110–1119.

Bertagnoli, M. W., & Borchardt, C. M. (1990). A review of ECT for children and adolescents. *Journal of the American Academy of Child and Adolescent Psychiatry, 29,* 302–307.

Bettelheim, B. (1967a). *The empty fortress.* New York: Free Press.

Bettelheim, B. (1967b, Feb. 12). Where self begins. *New York Times.*

Bettes, B. A., & Walker, E. (1987). Positive and negative symptoms in psychotic and other psychiatrically disturbed children. *Journal of Child Psychology and Psychiatry, 28,* 555–568.

Bickman, L. (1997). Resolving issues raised by the Fort Bragg evaluation: New directions for mental health services research. *American Psychologist, 52,* 562–565.

Biederman, J., Faraone, S., Mick, E., Moore, P., & Lelon, E. (1996). Child Behavior Checklist findings further support comorbidity between ADHD and major depression in a referred sample. *Journal of the American Academy of Child and Adolescent Psychiatry, 35,* 734–742.

Biederman, J., Faraone, S. V., Milberger, S., Jetton, J. G., Chen, L., Mick, E., Greene, R. W., & Russell, R. L. (1996). Is childhood oppositional defiant disorder a precursor to adolescent conduct disorder? Findings from a four-year follow-up study of children with ADHD. *Journal of the American Academy of Child and Adolescent Psychiatry, 35,* 1193–1204.

Biederman, J., Rosenbaum, J. F., Bolduc-Murphy, E. A., Faraone, S. V., Chaloff, J., Hirshfeld, D. R., & Kagan, J. (1993). A 3-year follow-up of children with and without behavioral inhibition. *Journal of the American Academy of Child and Adolescent Psychiatry, 32,* 814–821.

Bierman, K. L. (1989). Improving the peer relationships of rejected children. In B. B. Lahey & A. E. Kazdin (Eds.), *Advances in clinical child psychology.* Vol. 12. New York: Plenum Press.

Bierman, K., & Furman, W. (1984). The effects of social skills training and peer involvement on the social adjustment of preadolescents. *Child Development, 55,* 151–162.

Bierman, K. L., & Schwartz, L. A. (1986). Clinical child interviews: Approaches and developmental considerations. *Journal of Child and Adolescent Psychotherapy, 3,* 267–278.

Bierman, K. L., & Welsh, J. A. (1997). Social relationship deficits. In E. J. Mash & L. G. Terdal (Eds.), *Assessment of childhood disorders* (3rd ed.). New York: Guilford Press.

Bifulco, A., Harris, T., & Brown, G. (1992). Mourning or early inadequate care? Reexamining the relationship of maternal loss in childhood with adult depression and anxiety. *Development and Psychopathology, 4,* 433–449.

Bigler, E. D. (1987). Acquired cerebral trauma. *Journal of Learning Disabilities, 20,* 455–457.

Bijou, S. W., Peterson, R. F., Harris, F. R., Allen, K. E., & Johnston, M. S. (1969). Methodology for experimental studies of young children in natural settings. *The Psychological Record, 19,* 177–210.

Biller, H. B. (1993). *Fathers and families. Paternal factors in child development.* Westport, CT: Auburn House.

Billings, A. G., Moos, R. H., Miller, J. J., & Gotlieb, J. E. (1987). Psychosocial adaptation in juvenile rheumatic disease: A controlled evaulation. *Health Psychology, 6,* 343–359.

Birch, S. H., & Ladd, G. W. (1998). Children's interpersonal behavior and the teacher-child relationship. *Developmental Psychology, 34,* 934–946.

Bird, H. R. (1996). Epidemiology of childhood disorders in a cross-cultural context. *Journal of Child Psychology and Psychiatry, 37,* 35–50.

Birmaher, B., Ryan, N. D., Williamson, D. E., Brent, D. A., & Kaufman, J. (1996b). Childhood and adolescent depression: A review of the past 10 years. Part II. *Journal of the American Academy of Child and Adolescent Psychiatry, 35,* 1575–1583.

Birmaher, B., Ryan, N. D., Williamson, D. E., Brent, D. A., Kaufman, J., Dahl, R. E., Perel, J., & Nelson, B. (1996a). Childhood and adolescent depression: A review of the past 10 years. Part I. *Journal of the American Academy of Child and Adolescent Psychiatry, 35,* 1427–1439.

Bishop, D. V. M. (1992a). The biological basis of specific language impairment. In P. Fletcher & D. Hall (Eds.), *Specific speech and language disorders in children: Correlates, characteristics and outcome.* San Diego, CA: Singular Publishing Group.

Bishop, D. V. M. (1992b). The underlying nature of specific language impairment. *Journal of Child Psychology and Psychiatry. 33,* 3–66.

Bishop, D. V. M., North, T., & Donlan, C. (1996). Nonword repetition as a behavioural marker for inherited language: Evidence from a twin study. *Journal of Child Psychology and Psychiatry, 37,* 391–404.

Bjorklund, D. F., & Green, B. L. (1992). The adaptive nature of cognitive immaturity. *American Psychologist, 47,* 46–54.

Blacher, J. (1984). Sequential stages of parental adjustment to the birth of a child with handicaps: Fact or artifact? *Mental Retardation, 22,* 55–68.

Black, B., & Uhde, T. W. (1995). Psychiatric characteristics of children with selective mutism: A pilot study. *Journal of the American Academy of Child and Adolescent Psychiatry, 34,* 847–856.

Blagg, N., & Yule, W. (1994). School refusal. In T. H. Ollendick, N. J. King, & W. Yule (Eds.), *International handbook of phobic and anxiety disorders in children and adolescents* (pp. 169–186). New York: Plenum Press.

Blount, R. L., Landolf-Fritsche, B., Powers, S. W., & Sturges, J. W. (1991). Differences between high and low coping children and between parent and staff behaviors during painful medical procedures. *Journal of Pediatric Psychology, 16,* 795–809.

Boivin, M., & Hymel, S. (1997). Peer experiences and social self-perceptions: A sequential model. *Developmental Psychology, 33,* 135–145.

Bolton, P. F., et al. (1997). Obstetric complications in autism: Consequences or causes of the condition? *Journal of the American Academy of Child and Adolescent Psychiatry, 36,* 272–281.

Bonner, B. L., Kaufman, K. L., Harbeck, C., & Brassard, M. R. (1992). Child maltreatment. In C. E. Walker & M. C. Roberts (Eds.), *Handbook of clinical child psychology.* New York: Wiley.

Bootzin, R. R., & Chambers, M. J. (1990). Childhood sleep disorders. In A. M. Gross & R. S. Drabman (Eds.), *Handbook of clinical behavioral pediatrics.* New York: Plenum.

Borden, M. C., & Ollendick, T. H. (1992). The development and differentiation of social subtypes in autism. In B. B. Lahey & A. E. Kazdin (Ed.), *Advances in clinical child psychology.* New York: Plenum.

Borduin, C. M. (1994). Innovative models of treatment and service delivery in the juvenile justice system. *Journal of Clinical Child Psychology, 23 (Suppl.),* 19–25.

Borkovec, T. D. (1970). Autonomic reactivity to sensory stimulation in psychopathic, neurotic and normal delinquents. *Journal of Consulting and Clinical Psychology, 35,* 217–222.

Borkowski, J. G., & Cavanaugh, J. C. (1979). Maintenance and generalization of skills and strategies by the retarded. In N. R. Ellis (Ed.), *Handbook of mental deficiency.* Hillsdale, NJ: Erlbaum.

Borkowski, J. G., Johnston, M. B., & Reid, M. K. (1987). Metacognition, motivation, and controlled performance. In S. J. Ceci (Ed.), *Handbook of cognitive, social, and neuropsychologial aspects of learning disabilities.* Hillsdale, NJ: Erlbaum.

Bornstein, M., Bellack, A., & Hersen, M. (1977). Social skills training for unassertive children: A multiple baseline analysis. *Journal of Applied Behavior Analysis, 10,* 183–195.

Bostanis, B., Smith, B., Chung, M. C., & Corbett, J. (1994). Early detection of childhood autism: A review of screening instruments and rating scales. *Child: Care, Health, and Development, 20,* 165–177.

Botuck, S., & Winsberg, B. G. (1991). Effects of respite on mothers of school-age and adult children with severe disabilities. *Mental Retardation, 29,* 43–47.

Boucher, J., Lewis, V., & Collis, G. (1998). Familiar face and voice matching and recognition in children with autism. *Journal of Child Psychology and Psychiatry, 39,* 171–182.

Bowlby, J. (1960). Grief and mourning in infancy and early childhood. *Psychoanalytic Study of the Child, 15,* 9–52.

Boyce, G. C., &Barnett, W. S. (1993). Siblings of persons with mental retardation. In Z. Stoneman & P. W. Berman (Eds.), *The effects of mental retardation, disability, and illness on sibling relationships. Research issues and challenges.* Baltimore: Paul H. Brookes Pub.

Braddock, D., & Heller, T. (1985). The closure of mental retardation institutions I: Trends in the United States. *Mental Retardation, 23,* 168–176.

Bradley, L. J., & Meredith, R. C. (1991). Interpersonal development: A study with children classified as educable mentally retarded. *Education and Training in Mental Retardation, 26,* 130–141.

Bradley, R. H., & Whiteside-Mansell, L. (1997). Children in poverty. In R. T. Ammerman & M. Hersen (Eds.), *Handbook of prevention and treatment with children and adolescents.* New York: John Wiley.

Bradley, R. H., Whiteside, L., Mundfrom, D. J., Casey, P. H., Kelleher, K. J., & Pope, S. K. (1994). Contributions of early interventions and early caregiving experiences to resilience in low-birthweight, premature children living in poverty. *Journal of Clinical Child Psychology, 23,* 425–434.

Bradley, S. J., & Hood, J. (1993). Psychiatrically referred adolescents with panic attacks: Presenting symptoms, stressors, and comorbidity. *Journal of the American Academy of Child and Adolescent Psychiatry, 32,* 826–829.

Brassard, M. R., Germain, R., & Hart, S. N. (Eds.). (1987). *Psychological maltreatment of children and youth.* New York: Plenum Press.

Braungart-Rieker, J., Rende, R. D., Plomin, R., DeFries, J. C., & Fulker, D. W. (1995). Genetic mediation of longitudinal associations between family environment and childhood behavior problems. *Development and Psychopathology, 7,* 233–245.

Bray, N. W., Fletcher, K. L., & Turner, L. A. (1997). Cognitive competencies and strategy use in individuals with mental retardation. In W. E. MacLean (Ed.), *Ellis' handbook of mental deficiency, psychological theory and research.* Mahwah, NJ: Lawrence Erlbaum.

Bregman, J. D. (1991). Current developments in the understanding of mental retardation: Part II. Psychopathology. *Journal of the American Academy of Child and Adolescent Psychiatry, 30,* 861–872.

Bregman, J. D., & Gerdtz, J. (1997). Behavioral interventions. In D. J. Cohen & F. R. Volkmar (Eds.), *Handbook of autism and pervasive developmental disorders.* New York: John Wiley.

Bregman, J. D., & Hodapp, R. M. (1991). Current developments in the understanding of mental retardation: Part I. Biological and phenomenological perspectives. *Journal of the American Academy of Child and Adolescent Psychiatry, 30,* 707–719.

Brestan, E. V., & Eyberg, S. M. (1998). Effective psychosocial treatments of conduct-disordered children and adolescents: 29 years, 82 studies, and 5,272 kids. *Journal of Clinical Child Psychology, 27,* 180–189.

Briggs, K., Hubbs-Tait, L., Culp, R. E., & Morse, A. S. (1994). Sexual abuse label: Adults' expectations for children. *The American Journal of Family Therapy, 22,* 304–314.

Broman, S., Nichols P. L., Shaughnessy P., & Kennedy, W. (1987). *Retardation in young children: A developmental study of cognitive deficit.* Hillsdale, NJ: Erlbaum.

Bromley, B. E., & Blacher, J. (1991). Parental reasons for out-of-home placement of children with severe handicaps. *Mental Retardation, 29,* 275–280.

Bronfenbrenner, U. (1986). Ecology of the family as a context for human development: Research perspectives. *Developmental Psychology, 22,* 723–742.

Bronfenbrenner, U. (1989). Ecological systems theory. In R. Vasta (Ed.), *Annals of child development* (Vol. 6: *Six theories of child development: Revised formulations and current issues*). London: JAI Press.

Brooks-Gunn, J. (1993). Why do adolescents have difficulty adhering to health regimes? In N. A. Krasnegor, L. Epstein, S. B. Johnson, & S. Yaffe (Eds.), *Developmental aspects of health compliance behavior.* Hillsdale, NJ: Lawrence Earlbaum Associates.

Brooks-Gunn, J., & Duncan, G. J. (1997). The effects of poverty on children. *The Future of Children, 7(2),* 55–71.

Brown, D., Simmons, V., & Methvin, J. (1986). *Oregon Project Curriculum for Visually Impaired and Blind Preschool Children.* Eugene, OR: Jackson County Education Service District.

Brown, R. T., Doepke, K. J., & Kaslow, N. J. (1993). *Clinical Psychology Review, 13,* 119–132.

Brown, R. T., Madan-Swain, A., Walco, G. A., Cherrick, I., Ievers, C. E., Conte, P. M., Vega, R., Bell, B., & Lauer, S. J. (1998). Cognitive and academic late effects among children previously treated for acute lymphocytic leukemia receiving chemotherapy as CNS prophylaxis. *Journal of Pediatric Psychology, 23,* 333–340.

Brownell, C. A. (1986). Convergent developments: Cognitive-developmental correlates of growth in infant/toddler peer skills. *Child Development, 57,* 275–286.

Bruch, H. (1973). *Eating disorders: Obesity, anorexia nervosa, and the person within.* New York: Basic Books.

Bruch, H. (1979). *The golden cage: The enigma of anorexia nervosa.* New York: Vintage Books.

Bruch, H. (1986). Anorexia nervosa: The therapeutic task. In K. D. Brownell & J. P. Foreyt (Eds.), *Handbook of eating disorders: Physiology, psychology, and treatment of obesity, anorexia, and bulimia.* New York: Basic Books.

Bruininks, R. H., Hauber, F. A., & Kudla, M. J. (1980). National survey of community residential facilities: A profile of facilities and residents in 1977. *American Journal of Mental Deficiency, 84,* 470–478.

Brumberg, J. J. (1986). "Fasting girls": Reflections on writing the history of anorexia nervosa. In A. B. Smuts & J. W. Hagen (Eds.), History and research in child development. *Monographs of the Society for Research in Child Development, 50*(4–5, Serial No. 211).

Bryan, T. (1991). Selection of subjects in research on learning disabilities: A view from the social side. *Learning Disability Quarterly, 14,* 297–302.

Bryan, T. (1997). Assessing the personal and social status of students with learning disabilities. *Learning Disabilities Research & Practice, 12,* 63–76.

Bryan, T. H., & Bryan, J. H. (1975, 1986). *Understanding learning disabilities.* Palo Alto, CA: Mayfield.

Bryant, K. (1977). Speech and language development. In M. J. Krajicek & A. I. Tearney (Eds.), *Detection of developmental problems in children.* Baltimore: University Park Press.

Bryant-Waugh, R., & Lask, B. (1995). Eating disorders in children. *Journal of Child Psychology and Psychiatry, 36,* 191–202.

Bryson, S. E. (1997). Epidemiology of autism: Overview and issues outstanding. In D. J. Cohen & F. R. Volkmar (Eds.), *Handbook of autism and pervasive developmental disorders.* New York: John Wiley.

Bryson, S. E., Smith, I. M., & Eastwood, D. (1988). Obstetrical suboptimality in autistic children. *Journal of the American Academy of Child and Adolescent Psychiatry, 27,* 418–422.

Buchanan, R. W., Buckley, P. F., Tamminga, C. A., & Schulz, S. C. (1998). Schizophrenia research: A biennium of progress. *Schizophrenia Bulletin, 24,* 501–518.

Buck, J. N. (1992). *House-Tree-Person projective drawing technique (H-T-P): Manual and interpretive guide* (Revised by W. L. Warren). Los Angeles: Western Psychological Services.

Budd, K. S., & Chugh, C. S. (1998). Common feeding problems in young children. In T. H. Ollendick & R. J. Prinz (Eds.), *Advances in clinical child psychology* (Vol. 20). New York: Plenum Press.

Buitelaar, J. K., Willemsen-Swinkels, S., Van Engelend, H. (1998). Letters to the editor. Naltrexone in children with autism. *Journal of the American Academy of Child and Adolescent Psychiatry, 37,* 800–801.

Bullock, M., & Russell, J. A. (1986). Concepts of emotion in developmental psychology. In C. E. Izard & P. B. Read (Eds.), *Measuring emotions in infants and children,* Vol. 2. New York: Cambridge University Press.

Burack, J. A. (1990). Differentiating mental retardation: The two-group approach and beyond. In R. M. Hodapp, J. A. Burack, & E. Zigler (Eds.)., *Issues in the developmental approach to mental retardation.* New York: Cambridge University Press.

Burack, J. A., Enns, J. T., Stauder, J. E. A., Mottron, L., & Randolph, B. (1997). In D. J. Cohen & F. R. Volkmar (Eds.), *Handbook of autism and pervasive developmental disorders.* New York: John Wiley.

Burack, J. A., Root, R., & Zigler, E. (1997). Inclusive education for students with autism: Reviewing ideological, empirical, and community considerations. In D. J. Cohen and F. R. Volkmar (Eds.), *Handbook of autism and pervasive developmental disorders.* New York: John Wiley.

Burack, J. A., & Volkmar, F. R. (1992). Development of low- and high-functioning autistic children. *Journal of Child Psychology and Psychiatry, 33,* 607–616.

Burchard, J., & Clark, R. (1990). The role of individualized care in a service delivery system for children and adolescents with severely maladjusted behavior. *Journal of Mental Health Administration, 17,* 48–60.

Burns, R. C., & Kaufman, S. H. (1970). *Kinetic Family Drawing (K-F-D) research and applications.* New York: Bruner/Mazel.

Butler, L., Miezitis, S., Friedman, R., & Cole, E. (1980). The effect of two school-based intervention programs on depressive symptoms in preadolescents. *American Educational Research Journal, 17,* 111–119.

Butzlaff, R. L., & Hooley, J. M. (1998). Expressed emotion and psychiatric relapse. *Archives of general psychiatry, 55,* 547–552.

Cambor, R. L., & Millman, R. B. (1996). Alcohol and drug abuse in adolescents. In M. Lewis (Ed.), *Child and adolescent psychiatry: A comprehensive textbook.* Baltimore: Williams & Wilkins.

Camp, B. W., Blom, G. E., Herbert, R., & Van Doornick, W. J. (1977). "Think aloud": A program for developing self-control in young aggressive boys. *Journal of Abnormal Child Psychology, 5,* 157–169.

Campaigne, B. N., Morrison, J. A., Schumann, B. C., Faulkner, F., Lakatos, E. Sprecher, D., & Schreiber, G. B. (1994). Indexes of obesity and comparisons with previous national survey data in 9- and 10-year-old black and white girls: The National Heart, Lung, and Blood Institute Growth and Health Survey. *Journal of Pediatrics, 124,* 675–680.

Campbell, D. T., & Stanley, J. C. (1963). *Experimental and quasi-experimental designs for research.* Chicago: Rand McNally.

Campbell, F. A., & Ramey, C. T. (1994). Effects of early intervention on intellectual and academic achievement: A follow-up study of children from low-income families. *Child Development, 65,* 684–698.

Campbell, M. (1988). Annotation. Fenfluramine treatment of autism. *Journal of Child Psychology and Psychiatry, 29,* 1–10.

Campbell, M., Anderson, L. T., Small, A. M., Adams, P., Gonzalez, N. M., & Ernst, M. (1993). Naltrexone in autistic children: Behavioral symptoms and attentional learning. *Journal of the American Academy of Child and Adolescent Psychiatry, 32,* 1283–1291.

Campbell, M., Armenteros, J. L., Maone, R. P., Adams, P. B., Eisenberg, Z. W., & Overall, J. E. (1997). Neuroleptic-related dyskinesias in autistic children: A prospective longitudinal study. *Journal of the American Academy of Child and Adolescent Psychiatry, 36,* 835–843.

Campbell, M., & Cueva, J. E. (1995). Psychopharmacology in child and adolescent psychiatry: A review of the past seven years. Part I. *Journal of the American Academy of Child and Adolescent Psychiatry, 34,* 1124–1132.

Campbell, M., Schopler, E., Cueva, J. E., & Hallin, A. (1996). Treatment of autistic disorder. *American Academy of Child and Adolescent Psychiatry, 35,* 134–143.

Campbell, S. (1998). Developmental perspectives. In T. H. Ollendick & M. Hersen (Eds.), *Handbook of child psychopathology.* New York: Plenum Press.

Campbell, S. B. (1987). Parent-referred problem three-year-olds: Developmental changes in symptoms. *Journal of Child Psychology and Psychiatry, 28,* 835–845.

Campbell, S. B. (1990). The socialization and social development of hyperactive children. In M. Lewis & S. M. Miller (Eds.). *Handbook of developmental psychopathology.* NY: Plenum.

Campbell, S. B. (1995). Behavior problems in preschool children: A review of recent research. *Journal of Child Psychology and Psychiatry, 36,* 113–149.

Campbell, S. B. (1997). Behavior problems in preschool children. Developmental and family issues. In T. H. Ollendick & R. J. Prinz (Eds.), *Advances in clinical child psychology* (Vol. 19). New York: Plenum Press.

Candy-Gibbs, S. E., Sharp, K. C., & Petrun, C. J. (1985). The effects of age, object, and cultural/religious background on children's concepts of death. *Omega Journal of Death and Dying, 15,* 329–346.

Cannon, T. D., Kaprio, J., Lonnqvist, J., Huttunen, M., & Koskenyuo, M. (1998). The genetic epidemiology of schizophrenia in a Finnish twin cohort. *Archives of General Psychiatry, 55,* 67–74.

Cannon, T. D., Mednick, S. A., Parnas, J., Schulsinger, F., Praestholm, J., & Vestergaad, A. (1993). Developmental brain abnormalities in the offspring of schizophrenic mothers. *Archives of General Psychiatry, 50,* 551–564.

Cannon, T. D., Zorilla, L. E., Shtasel, D., Gur, R. E., Gur, R. C., Marco, E. J., Moberg, P., & Price, A. (1994). Neuropsychological functioning in siblings discordant for schizophrenia and healthy volunteers. *Archives of General Psychiatry, 51,* 651–661.

Cantor, S. (1988). *Childhood schizophrenia.* New York: Guilford.

Cantor, S., & Kestenbaum, C. (1986). Psychotherapy with schizophrenic children. *Journal of the American Academy of Child Psychiatry, 25,* 623–630.

Cantwell, D. P. (1980). The diagnostic process and diagnostic classification in child psychiatry: DSM-III. *Journal of the American Academy of Child Psychiatry, 19,* 345–355.

Cantwell, D. P. (1996). Classification of child and adolescent psychopathology. *Journal of Child Psychology and Psychiatry, 37,* 3–12.

Cantwell, D. P., & Rutter, M. (1994). Classification: Conceptual issues and substantive findings. In M. Rutter, E. Taylor, & L. Hersov (Eds.), *Child and adolescent psychiatry. Modern approaches.* Boston: Blackwell Scientific.

Capaldi, D. M. (1992). The co-occurrence of conduct problems and depressive symptoms in early adolescent boys: II. A 2-year follow-up at Grade 8. *Development and Psychopathology, 4,* 125–144.

Capaldi, D. M., & Patterson, G. R. (1991). The relation of parental transition to boys' adjustment problems: I. A. linear hypothesis, and II. Mothers at risk for transitions and unskilled parenting. *Developmental Psychology, 27,* 489–504.

Caplan, G. (1964). *The principles of preventive psychiatry.* New York: Basic Books.

Caplan, M., & Douglas, V. (1969). Incidence of parental loss in children with depressed mood. *Journal of Child Psychology and Psychiatry, 10,* 225–232.

Caplan, R. (1994). Thought disorder in childhood. *Journal of the American Academy of Child and Adolescent Psychiatry, 33,* 605–615.

Caplan, R., Guthrie, D., & Komo, S. (1996). Conversational repair in schizophrenic and normal children. *Journal of the American Academy of Child and Adolescent Psychiatry, 35,* 941–949.

Carlson, E. A., Jacobvitz, D., & Sroufe, L. A. (1995). A developmental investigation of inattentiveness and hyperactivity. *Child Development, 66,* 37–54.

Carlson, G. A., & Cantwell, D. P. (1980). Unmasking masked depression in children and adolescents. *American Journal of Psychiatry, 137,* 445–449.

Carnine, D. W., & Kameenui, E. J. (1990). The general education intitiative and children with special needs: A false dilemma in the face of true problems. *Journal of Learning Disabilities, 23,* 141–144, 148.

Carpenter, P. J. (1992). Perceived control as a predictor of distress in children undergoing invasive medical procedures. *Journal of Pediatric Psychology, 17,* 757–773.

Carr, J. (1994). Long term outcome for people with Down's syndrome. *Journal of Child Psychology and Psychiatry, 35,* 425–439.

Casaer, P. (1993). Old and new facts about perinatal brain development. *Journal of Child Psychology and Psychiatry, 34,* 101–109.

Casey, B. J., Castellanos, F. X., Giedd, J. N., Marsh, W. L., Hamburger, S. D., Schubert, A. B., Vauss, Y. C., Vaituzis, A. C., Dickstein, D. P., Sarfatti, S. E., & Rapoport, J. L. (1997). Implication of right frontostriatal circuity in response inhibition and Attention-deficit/Hyperactivity Disorder. *Journal of the American Academy of Child and Adolescent Psychiatry, 36,* 374–383.

Caspi, A., Elder, G. H. Jr., & Bem, D. J. (1987). Moving against the world: Life-course patterns of explosive children. *Developmental Psychology, 23,* 308–313.

Caspi, A., Elder, G. H., Jr., & Bem, D. J. (1988). Moving away from the world: Life-course patterns of shy children. *Developmental Psychology, 24,* 824–831.

Caspi, A., & Moffitt, T. E. (1995). The continuity of maladaptive behavior: From description to understanding in the study of antisocial behavior. In D. Cicchetti & D. J. Cohen (Eds.), *Developmental psychopathology.* (Vol 2: *Risk, disorder, and adaptation*). New York: John Wiley & Sons.

Chamberlain, P., & Reid, J. B. (1987). Parent observation and report of child symptoms. *Behavioral Assessment, 9,* 97–109.

Chandola, C. A., Robling, M. R., Peters, T. J., Melville-Thomas, G., & McGuffin, P. (1992). Pre- and perinatal factors and the risk of subsequent referral for hyperactivity. *Journal of Child Psychology and Psychiatry, 33,* 1077–1090.

Charlop, M. H., Schreibman, L., Kurtz, P. F. (1991). Childhood autism. In T. R. Kratochwill & R. J. Morris (Eds.), *The practice of child therapy.* Boston: Allyn and Bacon.

Charman, T., Swettenham, J., Baron-Cohen, S., Cox, A., Baird, G., & Drew, A. (1997). Infants with autism: An investigation of empathy, pretend play, joint attention, and imitation. *Developmental Psychology, 33,* 781–789.

Chassin, L., Curran, P. J., Hussong, A. M., & Colder, C. R. (1996). The relation of parental alcoholism to adolescent substance use: A longitudinal follow-up study. *Journal of Abnormal Psychology, 105,* 70–80.

Chatoor, I., Conley, C., & Dickson, L. (1988). Food refusal after an incident of choking: A posttraumatic eating disorder. *Journal of the American Academy of Child and Adolescent Psychiatry, 27,* 105–110.

Chess, S. (1988). Child and adolescent psychiatry come of age: A fifty year perspective. *Journal of the Amercan Academy of Child and Adolescent Psychiatry, 27,* 1–7.

Chess, S., & Thomas, A. (1972). Differences in outcome with early intervention in children with behavior disorders. In M. Roff, L. Robins, & M. Pollack (Eds.), *Life history research in psychopathology,* Vol. 2. Minneapolis: University of Minnesota Press.

Chess, S., & Thomas, A. (1977). Temperamental individuality from childhood to adolescence. *Journal of American Academy of Child Psychiatry, 16,* 218–226.

Childress, A. C., Brewerton, T. D., Hodges, E. L., & Jarrell, M. P. (1993). The Kids' Eating Disorders Survey (KEDS): A study of middle school students. *Journal of the American Academy of Child and Adolescent Psychiatry, 32,* 843–850.

Chinn, P. C., & Hughes, S. (1987). Representation of minority students in special education classes. *Remedial and Special Education, 8,* 41–46.

Chorpita, B. F., & Barlow, D. H. (1998). The development of anxiety: The role of control in the early environment. *Psychological Bulletin, 124,* 3–21.

Christophersen, E. R., & Edwards, K. J. (1992). Treatment of elimination disorders: State of the art 1991. *Applied and Preventive Psychology, 1,* 15–22.

Cicchetti, D. (1984). The emergence of developmental psychopathology. *Child Development, 55,* 1–7.

Cicchetti, D. (1989). Developmental psychology: Some thoughts on its evolution. *Development and Psychopathology, 1,* 1–3.

Cicchetti, D. (1994). Advances and challenges in the study of the sequelae of child maltreatment. *Development and Psychopathology, 6,* 1–4.

Cicchetti, D., & Cohen, D. J. (1995). Perspectives on developmental psychopathology. In D. Cichetti & D. J. Cohen (Eds.), *Developmental psychopathology.* New York: John Wiley.

Cicchetti, D., & Lynch, M. (1995). Failures in the expectable environment and their impact on individual development: The case of child maltreatment. In D. Cicchetti & D. J. Cohen (Eds.), *Developmental psychopathology: Risk, disorder, and adaptation* (Vol. 2). New York: John Wiley & Sons.

Cicchetti, D., & Olsen, K. (1990). The developmental psychopathology of child maltreatment. In M. Lewis & S. M. Miller (Eds.), *Handbook of developmental psychopathology.* New York: Plenum Press.

Cicchetti, D., & Schneider-Rosen, K. (1986). An organizational approach to childhood depression. In M. Rutter, C. Izard, & P. Read (Eds.), *Depression in young people: Clinical and developmental perspectives.* New York: Guilford.

Cicchetti, D., & Toth, S. L. (1998). The development of depression in children and adolescents. *American Psychologist, 53,* 221–241.

Cicchetti, D., Toth, S., & Bush, M. (1988). Developmental psychopathology and incompetence in childhood: Suggestions for intervention. In B. B. Lahey & A. E. Kazdin (Eds.), *Advances in clinical child psychology,* Vol. 11. New York: Plenum.

Clarizio, H. F. (1994). Assessment of depression in children and adolescents by parents, teachers, and peers. In W. M. Reynolds and H. F. Johnston (Eds.), *Handbook of depression in children and adolescents.* New York: Plenum Press.

Clark, A. F., & Lewis, S. W. (1998). Treatment of schizophrenia in childhood and adolescence. *Journal of Child Psychology and Psychiatry, 39,* 1071–1082.

Clark, D. B., Smith, M. G., Neighbors, B. D., Skerlec, L. M., & Randall, J. (1994). Anxiety disorders in adolescence: Characteristics, prevalence, and comorbidities. *Clinical Psychology Review, 14,* 113–137.

Clark, L. A., & Watson, D. (1991). Tripartite model of anxiety and depression: Psychometric evidence and taxonomic implications. *Journal of Abnormal Psychology, 100,* 316–336.

Clarke, A. D. B., & Clarke, A. M. (1984). Constancy and change in the growth of human characteristics. *Journal of Child Psychology and Psychiatry, 25,* 191–210.

Clarke, A. M., & Clarke, A. D. B. (1985) Criteria and classification. In A. M. Clarke, A. D. B. Clarke & J. M. Berg (Eds.), *Mental deficiency. The changing outlook.* New York: The Free Press.

Clarke, G. N., Hawkins, W., Murphy, M., Sheeber, L. B., Lewinsohn, P. M., & Seeley, J. R. (1995). Targeted prevention of unipolar depressive disorder in an at-risk sample of high-school adolescents: A randomized trial of a group cognitive intervention. *Journal of the American Academy of Child and Adolescent Psychiatry, 34,* 312–321.

Clarke-Stewart, A. (1992). *Daycare* (2nd ed.), Cambridge, MA: Harvard University Press.

Cobham, V. E., Dadds, M. R., & Spence, S. H. (1998). The role of parental anxiety in the treatment of childhood anxiety. *Journal of Consulting and Clinical Psychology, 66,* 893–905.

Cohen, N. J. (1996). Unsuspected language impairments in psychiatrically disturbed children: Developmental conditions and associated conditions. In J. H. Beitchman, N. J. Cohen, M. M. Konstantareas, & R. Tannock (Eds.), *Language, learning, and behavior disorders.* New York: Cambridge University Press.

Cohen, P., Cohen, J., & Brook, J. (1993a). An epidemiological study of disorders in late childhood and adolescence -II. Persistence of disorders. *Journal of Child Psychology and Psychiatry, 34,* 869–877.

Cohen, P., Cohen, J., Kasen, S., Velez, C. N., Hartmark, C., Johnson, J., Rojas, M., Brook, J., & Streuning, E. L. (1993b). An epidemiological study of disorders in late childhood and adolescence-I. Age- and gender-specific prevalence. *Journal of Child Psychology and Psychiatry, 34,* 851–867.

Cohen-Tovee, E. M. (1993). Depressed mood and concern with weight and shape in normal young women. *International Journal of Eating Disorders, 14,* 223–227.

Coie, J. D., Belding, M., & Underwood, M. (1988). Aggression and peer rejection in childhood. In B. B. Lahey & A. E. Kazdin (Eds.), *Advances in clinical child psychology,* Vol. 11. *New York: Plenum.*

Coie, J. D., Watt, N. F., West, S. G., Hawkins, J. D., Asarnow, J. R., Markman, H. J., Ramey, S. L., Shure, M. B., & Long. B. (1993). The science of prevention: A conceptual framework and some directions for a national research program. *American Psychologist, 48,* 1013–1022.

Coles, G. S. (1989). Excerpts from The Learning Mystique: A Critical Look at "Learning Disabilities." *Journal of Learning Disabilities, 22,* 267–273, 277.

Collins, E. (1991). Body figure perceptions and preferences among preadolescent children. *International Journal of Eating Disorders, 10,* 199–208.

Collins, W. A., & Russell, G. (1991). Mother-child and father-child relationships in middle childhood and adolescence: A developmental analysis. *Development Review, 11,* 99–136.

Compas, B. E. (1997). Depression in children and adolescents. In E. J. Mash & L. G. Terdal (Eds.), *Assessment of childhood disorders* (3rd ed.). New York: Guilford Press.

Compas, B. E., Ey, S., & Grant, K. E. (1993). Taxonomy, assessment, and diagnosis of depression during adolescence. *Psychological Bulletin, 14,* 323–344.

Compas, B. E., Haaga, D. A. F., Keefe, F. J., Leitenberg, H., & Williams, D. A. (1998). Sampling of empirically supported psychological treatments from health psychology: Smoking, chronic pain, cancer, and bulimia nervosa. *Journal of Consulting and Clinical Psychology, 66,* 89–112.

Compas, B. E., Hinden, B. R., & Gerhardt, C. (1995). Adolescent development: Pathways and processes of risk and resilience. *Annual Review of Psychology, 46,* 265–293.

Compas, B. E., Oppedisano, G., Connor, J. K., Gerhardt, C. A., Hinden, B. R., Achenbach, T. M., & Hammen, C. (1997). Gender differences in depressive symptoms in adolescence: Comparison of national samples of clinically referred and nonreferred youths. *Journal of Consulting and Clinical Psychology, 65,* 617–626.

Conduct Problems Prevention Research Group (1992). A developmental and clinical model for the prevention of conduct disorder: The FAST Track Program. *Development and Psychopathology, 4,* 509–527.

Conger, J., & Keane, S. (1981). Social skills intervention in the treatment of isolated or withdrawn children. *Psychological Bulletin, 90,* 478–495.

Connell, J. P. (1985). A new multidimensional measure of children's perceptions of control. *Child Development, 56,* 1018–1041.

Connelly, C. D., & Straus, M. A. (1992). Mother's age and risk for physical abuse. *Child Abuse & Neglect, 16,* 709–718.

Conners, C. K. (1980). Artificial colors in the diet and disruptive behavior. In R. M. Knights & D. J. Bakker (Eds.). *Treatment of hyperactive and learning disabled children.* Baltimore: University Park Press.

Conners, C. K., Siltarenios, G., Parker, J. D. A., & Epstein, J. N. (1998a). Revision and restandardization of the Conners Teacher Rating Scale (CTRS-R): Factor structure, reliability, and criterion validity. *Journal of Abnormal Child Psychology, 26,* 279–291.

Conners, C. K., Sitarenios, G., Parker, J. D. A., & Epstein, J. N. (1998b). The revised Conners' Parent Rating Scale (CPRS-R): Factor structure, reliability, and criterion validity. *Journal of Abnormal Child Psychology, 26,* 257–268.

Connors, M. E. (1996). Developmental vulnerabilities for eating disorders. In L. Smolk, M. P., Levine, & R. Striegel-Moore (Eds.), *The developmental psychopathology of eating disorders: Implications for research, prevention, and treatment.* Mahwah, NJ: Lawrence Erlbaum.

Coplan, R. J., Rubin, K. H., Fox, N. A., Calkins, S. D., & Stewart, S. L. (1994). Being alone, playing alone, and acting alone: Distinguishing among reticence and passive and active solitude in young children. *Child Development, 65,* 129–137.

Corkum, V., & Moore, C. (1998). The origins of joint visual attention in infants. *Developmental Psychology, 34,* 28–38.

Corley, D. L., Gevirtz, R., Nideffer, R., & Cummins, L. (1987). Prevention of post-infectious asthma in children by reducing self-inoculatory behavior. *Journal of Pediatric Psychology, 12,* 519–531.

Corsaro, W. A., & Eder, D. (1990). Children's peer cultures. *Annual Review of Sociology, 16,* 197–220.

Costello, E. J. (1989). Developments in child psychiatric epidemiology. *Journal of the American Academy of Child and Adolescent Psychiatry, 28,* 836–841.

Costello, E. J. (1990). Child psychiatric epidemiology. In B. B. Lahey & A. E. Kazdin (Eds.), *Advances in clinical child psychology.* Vol. 14. New York: Plenum.

Costello, E. J., & Angold, A. (1995a). Developmental epidemiology. In D. Cicchetti & D. J. Cohen (Eds.), *Developmental Psychopathology.* New York: John Wiley.

Costello, E. J., & Angold, A. (1995b). Epidemiology. In J. S. March (Ed.), *Anxiety disorders in children and adolescents.* New York: Guilford Press.

Costello, E. J., Burns, B. J., Angold, A., & Leaf, P. J. (1993). How can epidemiology improve mental health services of children and adolescents? *Journal of the American Academy of Child and Adolescent Psychiatry, 32,* 1106–1117.

Cotler, S. (1986). Epidemiology and outcome. In J. M. Reisman (Ed.), *Behavior disorders in infants, children, and adolescents.* New York: Random House.

Courchesne, E., Townsend, J., Akshoomoff, N. A., Saitoh, O., Yeung-Courchesne, R., Lincoln, A. J., James, H. E., Hass, R. H., Schreibman, L., & Lau, L. (1994). Impairment in shifting attention in autistic and cerebellar patients. *Behavioral Neuroscience, 108,* 848–865.

Cowen, E. L. (1991). In pursuit of wellness. *American Psychologist, 46,* 404–408.

Cowen, E. L. (1994). The enhancement of psychological wellness: Challenges and opportunities. *American Journal of Community Psychology, 22,* 149–179.

Cowen, E. L. (1995). The enhancement of psychological wellness: Challenges and opportunity. *American Journal of Community Psychology, 22,* 149–179.

Cowen, E. L. (1997). On the semantics and operations of primary prevention and wellness enhancement (or will the real primary prevention please stand up?) *American Journal of Community Psychology, 25,* 245–255.

Cowen, E. L., Gesten, E. L., & Wilson, A. B. (1979). The Primary Mental Health Project (PMHP): Evaluation of current program effectiveness. *American Journal of Community Psychology, 3,* 293–303.

Cowen, E. L., & Hightower, A. D. (1989a). The Primary Mental Health Project: Alternatives in school based preventive interventions. In T. B. Gutkin & C. R. Reynolds (Eds.), *Handbook of school psychology,* 2nd ed. New York: Wiley.

Cowen, E. L., & Hightower, A. D. (1989b). The Primary Mental Health Projects: Thirty years after. In R. E. Hess, & J. DeLeon (Eds.), *Prevention in human services,* Vol. 6, No. 2, New York: Haworth.

Cowen, E. L., & Hightower, A. D. (1990). The Primary Mental Health Project: Alternative approaches in school-based prevention interventions. In R. E. Hess (Ed.), *Prevention in human services.* New York: Haworth Press.

Cowen, E., Pederson, A., Babigian, H. Izo, L., & Trost, N. (1973). Long term follow-up of early detected vulnerable children. *Journal of Consulting and Clinical Psychology, 41,* 438–446.

Cowen, E. L., Trost, M. A., Lorion, R. P., Dorr, D., Izzo, L. D., & Issacson, R. V. (1975). *New ways in school mental health: Early detection and prevention of school maladaptation.* New York: Human Sciences Press.

Cowen, E. L., Work, W. C., Wyman, P. A., & Jarrell, D. D. (1994). Relationship between retrospective parent reports of developmental milestones and school adjustment at ages 10 to 12 years. *Journal of the American Academy of Child and Adolescent Psychiatry, 33,* 400–406.

Cowen, E. L., Wyman, P. A., Work, W. C., & Parker, G. R. (1990). The Rochester Child Resilience Project: Overview and summary of first year findings. *Development and Psychopathology, 2,* 193–212.

Cowen, E. L., Zax, M., Izzo, L. D., & Trost, M. A. (1966). Prevention of emotional disorders in the school setting: A further investigation. *Journal of Consulting Psychology, 30,* 381–387.

Cox, A., & Rutter, M. (1985). Diagnostic appraisal and interviewing. In M. Rutter & L. Hersov (Eds.), *Child and adolescent psychiatry: Modern approaches.* Oxford: Blackwell Scientific Publications.

Cozby, P. C., Worden, P. E., & Kee, D. W. (1989). *Research methods in human development.* Mountain View, CA: Mayfield.

Craig, E. M., & McCarver, R. B. (1984). Community placement and adjustment of deinstitutionalized clients: Issues and findings. In N. R. Ellis & N. W. Bray (Eds.), *International review of research in mental retardation.* New York: Academic Press.

Cravens, H. (1992). A scientific project locked in time: The Terman genetic studies of genius, 1920s–1950s. *American Psychologist, 47,* 183–189.

Creer, T. L. (1982). Asthma. *Journal of Consulting and Clinical Psychology, 50,* 912–921.

Creer, T. L. (1991). The application of behavioral procedures to childhood asthma: Current and future perspectives. *Patient Education and Counseling, 17,* 9–22.

Creer, T. L. (1998). Childhood asthma. In T. H. Ollendick & M. Hersen (Eds.), *Handbook of child psychopathology* (3rd ed.). New York: Plenum Press.

Crick, N. R. (1997). Engagement in gender normative versus nonnormative forms of aggression: Links to social-psychological adjustment. *Developmental Psychology, 33,* 610–617.

Crick, N. R., Casas, J. F., & Mosher, M. (1997). Relational and overt aggression in preschool. *Developmental Psychology, 33,* 579–588.

Crick, N. R. & Dodge, K. A. (1994). A review and reformulation of social information-processing mechanisms in children's social adjustment. *Psychological Bulletin, 115,* 74–101.

Crick, N. R., & Grotpeter, J. K. (1995). Relational aggression, gender, and social-psychological adjustment. *Child Development, 66,* 710–722.

Crick, N. R., & Grotpeter, J. K. (1996). Children's treatment by peers: Victims of relational and overt aggression. *Development and Psychopathology, 8,* 367–380.

Crijnen, A. A. M., Achenbach, T. M., & Verhulst, F. C. (1997). Comparisons of problems reported by parents of children in 12 cultures: Total problems, externalizing and internalizing. *American Academy of Child and Adolescent Psychiatry, 36,* 1269–1277.

Crisp, A. H. (1984). The psychopathology of anorexia nervosa: Getting the 'heat' out of the system. In A. J. Stunkard & E. Stellar (Eds.), *Eating and its disorders.* New York: Raven Press.

Crittenden, P. M., Claussen, A. H., & Sugarman, D. B. (1994). Dimensions of child maltreatment and their relationship to adolescent adjustment. *Development and Psychopathology, 6,* 145–164.

Crnic, K. A. (1988). Mental retardation. In E. J. Mash & L. G. Terdal (Eds.), *Behavioral assessment of childhood disorders. Selected core problems.* New York: Guilford.

Crockenberg, S. B. (1988). Infant irritability, mother responsiveness, and social support influences on the security of infant-mother attachment. In E. M. Hetherington & R. G. Parke (Eds.), *Contemporary readings in child psychology.* New York: McGraw Hill.

Cronbach, L. J. (1975). Five decades of public controversy over mental testing. *American Psychologist, 30,* 1–14.

Culbertson, J. L. (1998). Learning disabilities. In T. H. Ollendick & M. Hersen (Eds.), *Handbook of child psychopathology.* New York: Plenum Press.

Cummings, E. M., & Davies, P. T. (1994). Maternal depression and child development. *Journal of Child Psychology and Psychiatry, 35,* 73–112.

Cuskelly, M., & Dadds, M. (1992). Behavioural problems in children with Down's syndrome and their siblings. *Journal of Child Psychology and Psychiatry, 33,* 749–761.

Cytryn, L., & Lourie, R. S. (1980). Mental retardation. In H. I. Kaplan, A. M. Freedman, & B. J. Sadock (Eds.), *Comprehensive textbook of psychiatry/III,* Vol. 3. Baltimore: Williams & Wilkins.

Cytryn, L., & McKnew, D. (1974). Factors influencing the changing clinical expression of the depressive process in children. *American Journal of Psychiatry, 131,* 879–881.

DaCosta, M., & Halmi, K. A. (1992). Classifications of anorexia nervosa: Question of subtypes. *International Journal of Eating Disorders, 11,* 305–313.

Dadds, M. R., Barrett, P. M., Rapee, R. M., & Ryan, S. (1996). Family process and child anxiety and aggression: An observational analysis. *Journal of Abnormal Child Psychology, 24,* 715–734.

Dadds, M. R., Rapee, R. M., Barrett, P. M. (1994). Behavioral observation. In T. H. Ollendick, N. J. King, & W. Yule (Eds.), *International handbook of phobic and anxiety disorders in children and adolescents* (pp. 349–364). New York: Plenum Press.

Dadds, M. R., Sanders, M. R., Morrison, M., & Rebgetz, M. (1992). Childhood depression and conduct disorder: II. An analysis of family interaction patterns in the home. *Journal of Abnormal Psychology, 101,* 505–513.

Dahlquist, L. M. (1992). Coping with aversive medical treatments. In A. M. La Greca, L. J. Siegel, J. L. Wallander, & C. E. Walker (Eds.). *Stress and coping in child health.* New York: Guilford.

Dahlquist, L., Power, T., & Carlson, L. (1995). Physician and parent behavior during invasive cancer procedures: A multidimensional assessment. *Journal of Pediatric Psychology, 20,* 477–490.

Danforth, J. S., & Drabman, R. S. (1990). Community living skills. In J. L. Matson (Ed.), *Handbook of behavior modification with the mentally retarded.* New York: Plenum.

Dangel, R. F., & Polster, R. A. (1984). *Parent training: Foundations of research and practice.* New York: Guilford.

Daniels, D., Moos, R. H., Billings, A. G., & Miller, J. J. (1987). Psychosocial risk and resistance factors among children with chronic illness, healthy siblings, and healthy controls. *Journal of Abnormal Child Psychology, 15,* 295–308.

Dare, C., & Eisler, I. (1995). Family therapy and eating disorders. In K. D. Brownell & C. G. Fairburn (Eds.), *Eating disorders and obesity: A comprehensive handbook.* New York: Guilford Press.

Dare, C., & Eisler, I. (1997). Family therapy for anorexia nervosa. In D. M. Garner & P. E. Garfinkel (Eds.), *Handbook of treatment for eating disorders (2nd ed.). New York: Guilford Press.*

Dare, C., Le Grange, D. L., Eisler, I., & Rutherford, J. (1994). Redefining the psychosomatic family: Family process of 26 eating disorder families. *International Journal of Eating Disorders, 16,* 211–226.

Daugherty, T. K., & Shapiro, S. K. (1994). Behavior checklists and rating forms. In T. H. Ollendick, N. J. King, & W. Yule (Eds.), *International handbook of phobic and anxiety disorders in children and adolescents* (pp. 331–348). New York: Plenum Press.

Davidson, W. S., & Basta, J. (1989). Diversion from the juvenile justice system: Research evidence and a discussion of issues. In B. B. Lahey & A. E. Kazdin (Eds.), *Advances in clinical child psychology,* Vol. 12, New York: Plenum.

Davies, P. T., & Cummings, E. M. (1994). Marital conflict and child adjustment: An emotional security hypothesis. *Psychological Bulletin, 116,* 387–411.

Davies, R. R., & Rogers, E. S. (1985). Social skills training with persons who are mentally retarded. *Mental Retardation, 23,* 186–196.

Davison, G. C. & Neale, J. M. (1978, 1982, 1990, 1994, 1996, 1998). *Abnormal psychology.* New York: Wiley.

Dawson, G., & Castelloe, P. (1992). Autism. In C. E. Walker & M. C. Roberts (Eds.), *Handbook of clinical child psychology.* New York: Wiley.

Dawson, G., Frey, K., Panagiotides, H., Osterling, J., & Hessl, D. (1997). Infants of depressed mothers exhibit atypical frontal brain activity: A replication and extension of previous findings. *Journal of Child Psychology and Psychiatry, 38,* 179–186.

de Groot, A., Koot, H. M., & Verhulst, F. C. (1996). Cross-cultural generalizability of the Youth Self-Report and Teacher's Report Form cross-informant syndromes. *Journal of Abnormal Child Psychology, 24,* 651–664.

DE Hann, E., Hoogduin, K. A. L., Buitelaar, J. K., & Keijsers, G. P. J. (1998). Behavior therapy versus clomipramine for the treatment of obsessive-compulsive disorder in children and adolescents. *Journal of the American Academy of Child and Adolescent Psychiatry, 37,* 1022–1029.

Deater-Deckard, K., Reiss, D., Hetherington, E. M., & Plomin, R. (1997). Dimensions and disorders of adolescent adjustment. A quantitative genetic analysis of unselected samples and selected extremes. *Journal of Child Psychology and Psychiatry, 38,* 515–525.

DeFries, J. C., & Gillis, J. J. (1993). Genetics of reading disability. In R. Plomin & G. E. McClearn (Eds.), *Nature, nurture & psychology.* Washington, DC: American Psychological Association.

DeFries, J. C., & Light, J. G. (1996). Twin studies of reading disability. In J. H. Beitchman, N. J. Cohen, M. M. Konstantareas, & R. Tannock (Eds.), *Language, learning, and behavior disorders.* New York: Cambridge University Press.

Dekovic, M., & Janssens, A. M. (1992). Parents' child-rearing style and child's sociometric status. *Developmental Psychology, 28,* 925–932.

DeKraai, M. B., & Sales, B. (1991). Legal issues in the conduct of child therapy. In T. R. Kratochwill & R. J. Morris (Eds.), *The practice of child therapy.* Boston: Allyn and Bacon.

Delamater, A. M. (1986). Psychological aspects of diabetes mellitus in children. In B. B. Lahey & A. E. Kazdin (Eds.), *Advances in clinical child psychology,* Vol. 9, New York: Plenum.

Delamater, A. M., Bubb, J., Davis, S. G., Smith, J. A., Schmidt, L., White, N. H., & Santiago, J. V. (1990). Randomized prospective study of self-management training with newly diagnosed diabetic children. *Diabetes Care, 13,* 492–498.

Delamater, A. M., & Lahey, B. B. (1983). Physiological correlates of conduct problems and anxiety in hyperactive and learning-disabled children. *Journal of Abnormal Child Psychology, 11,* 85–100.

Delfini, L. F. Bernal, M. E., & Rosen, P. M. (1976). Comparison of deviant and normal boys in home settings. In E. J. Mash, L. A. Hammerlynck, & L. C. Handy (Eds.), *Behavior modification and families.* New York: Brunner/Mazel.

DeMyer-Gapin, S., & Scott, T. J. (1977). Effects of stimulus novelty on stimulation-seeking in anti-social and neurotic children. *Journal of Abnormal Psychology, 86,* 96–98.

DeStefano, L., & Thompson, D. S. (1990). Adaptive behavior: The construct and its measurement. In C. R. Reynolds & R. W. Kamphaus (Eds.), *Handbook of psychological & educational assessment of children. Personality, behavior, and context.* New York: Guilford.

Detterman, D. K., & Thompson, L. A. (1997). What is so special about special education? *American Psychologist, 52,* 1082–1090.

Deutsch, C. K., Matthysse, S., Swanson, J. M., & Farkas, L. G. (1990). Genetic latent structure analysis of dysmorphology in attention deficit disorder. *Journal of the American Academy of Child and Adolescent Psychiatry, 29,* 189–194.

Dietz, W. H. (1988). Metabolic aspects of dieting. In N. A. Krasnegor, G. D. Grave, & N. Kretchmer (Eds.), *Childhood obesity: A biobehavioral perspective.* Caldwell, NJ: The Telford Press.

Dietz, W. H. (1995). Childhood obesity: Prevalence and effects. In K. D. Brownell & C. G. Fairburn (Eds.), *Eating disorders and obesity: A comprehensive handbook.* New York: Guilford Press.

Dietz, W. H., Jr., & Gortmaker, S. L. (1985). Do we fatten our children at the television set? Obesity and television viewing in children and adolescents. *Pediatrics, 75,* 807–812.

Dishion, T. J., French, D. C., & Patterson, G. R. (1995). The development and ecology of antisocial behavior. In D. Cicchetti & D. J. Cohen (Eds.), *Developmental psychopathology* (Vol. 2: *Risk, disorder and adaptation*). New York: John Wiley & Sons.

Dissanayake, C., & Crossley, S. A. (1996). Proximity and sociable behaviours in autism: Evidence for attachment. *Journal of Child Psychology and Psychiatry, 37,* 149–156.

Dodge, K. A. (1989). Problems in social relationships. In E. J. Mash & R. A. Bakley (Eds.), *Treatment of childhood disorders.* New York: Guilford.

Dodge, K. A. (1991). The structure and function of reactive and proactive aggression. In D. Pepler & K. Rubin (Eds.), *The development and treatment of childhood aggression.* Hillsdale, NJ: Earlbaum.

Dodge, K. A., Lochman, J. E., Harnish, J. D., Bates, J. E., & Pettit, G. S. (1997). Reactive and proactive aggression in school children and psychiatrically impaired chronically assaultive youth. *Journal of Abnormal Psychology, 106,* 37–51.

Dodge, K. A., & Somberg, D. R. (1987). Hostile attributional biases among aggressive boys are exacerbated under conditions of threats to self. *Child Development, 58,* 213–224.

Doleys, D. M. (1989). Enuresis and encopresis. In T. H. Ollendick & M. Hersen (Eds.), *Handbook of child psychopathology,* 2nd ed. New York: Plenum.

Dolgin, M. J., & Jay, S. M. (1989). Pain management in children. In E. J. Mash & R. A. Barkley (Eds.), *Treatment of childhood disorders.* New York: Guilford.

Dollinger, S. J. (1986). Childhood sleep disturbances. In B. B. Lahey & A. E. Kazdin (Eds.), *Advances in clinical child psychology,* Vol. 9. New York: Plenum.

Douglas, J. (1975). Early hospital admissions and later disturbances of behaviour and learning. *Developmental Medicine and Child Neurology, 17,* 456–480.

Douglas, V. I. (1983). Attentional and cognitive problems. In M. Rutter (Ed.), *Developmental neuropsychiatry.* New York: Guilford.

Douglas, V. I. (1988). Cognitive deficits in children with attention deficit disorder with hyperactivity. In L. M. Bloomingdale & J. Sergeant (Eds.), *Attention deficit disorder: Criteria, cognition, intervention.* Elmsford, New York: Pergamon Press.

Downey, G. & Coyne, J. C. (1990). Children of depressed parents: An integrative review. *Psychological Bulletin, 108,* 50–76.

Drotar, D. (1981). Psychological perspectives in chronic childhood illness. *Journal of Pediatric Psychology, 6,* 211–228.

Drotar, D. (1994). Psychological research with pediatric conditions: If we specialize can we generalize? *Journal of Pediatric Psychology, 19,* 403–414.

Dubas, J. S., Graber, J. A., & Petersen, A. C. (1991). The effects of pubertal development on achievement during adolescence. *American Journal of Education, 99,* 444–460.

Dubow, E. F. Huesmann, L. R., & Eron, R. D. (1987). Childhood correlates of adult ego development. *Child Developement, 58,* 859–869.

Dubow, E. F., & Ippolito, M. F. (1994). Effects of poverty and quality of the home environment on changes in the academic and behavioral adjustment of elementary school-age children. *Journal of Clinical Child Psychology, 23,* 401–412.

Dulcan, M. K. (1989). Attention deficit disorders. In C. G. Last & M. Hersen (Eds.), *Handbook of child psychiatric diagnosis.* New York: Wiley.

Dumas, J. E., LaFreniere, P. J., Serketich, W. J. (1995). "Balance of power": A transactional analysis of control in mother-child dyads involving socially competent, aggressive, and anxious children. *Journal of Abnormal Psychology, 104,* 104–113.

Dummitt, E. S. III & Klein, R. G. (1994). Panic disorder. In T. H. Ollendick, N. J. King, & Yule, W. (Eds.), *International handbook of anxiety disorders in children and adolescents.* New York: Plenum.

Dummit, E. S., Klein, R. G., Tancer, N. K., Asche, B., Martin, J., & Fairbanks, J. A. (1997). Systematic assessment of 50 children with selective mutism. *Journal of the American Academy of Child and Adolescent Psychiatry, 36,* 653–660.

Dunbar-Jacob, J. (1993). Contributions to patient adherence: Is it time to share the blame? *Health Psychology, 12,* 91–92.

Dunn, J. (1988). Annotation. Sibling influences on childhood development. *Journal of Child Psychology and Psychiatry, 29,* 119–127.

Dunn, J. (1996). Children's relationships: Bridging the divide between cognitive and social development. *Journal of Child Psychology and Psychiatry, 37,* 507–518.

Dunn, J., & McGuire, S. (1992). Sibling and peer relationships in childhood. *Journal of Child Psychology and Psychiatry, 33,* 67–105.

Dunn, L. M. (1968). Special education for the mildly retarded—is much of it justifiable? *Exceptional Children, 35,* 5–22.

Dunn, L. M., & Markwardt, F. C. (1970). *The Peabody Individual Achievement Test.* Circle Pines, MN: American Guidance Service.

DuPaul, G. J., Barkley, R. A., & Connor, D. F. (1998). Stimulants. In R. A. Barkley (Ed.), *Attention-deficit hyperactivity disorder.* Guilford Press.

DuPaul, G. J., Guevrement, D. C., & Barkley, R. A. (1991). Attention-deficit hyperactivity disorder. In T. R. Kratochwill & R. J. Morris (Eds.), *The practice of child therapy.* Boston: Allyn and Bacon.

Durand, V. M. (1990). *Severe behavior problems. A functional communication training approach.* New York: Guilford.

Durand, V. M. (1993a). Functional assessment and functional analysis. In M. D. Smith (Ed.), *Behavior modification for exceptional children and youth.* Baltimore: Andover Medical Press.

Durand, V. M. (1993b). Functional communication training using assistive devices: Effects on challenging behavior and affect. *Augmentative Alternative Communication, 9,* 168–176.

Durand, V. M. (In press). New directions in educational programming for students with autism. In D. Zager (Ed.), *Autism: Identification, education, and treatment.* Hillsdale, NJ: Lawrence Erlbaum.

Durand, V. M., & Carr, E. G. (1985). Self-injurious behavior: Motivating conditions and guidelines for treatment. *School Psychology Review, 14,* 171–176.

Durand, V. M. & Carr, E. G. (1988). Autism. In V. B. Van Hasselt, P. S. Strain, & M. Hersen (Eds.), *Handbook of developmental and physical disabilities.* New York: Pergammon Press.

Durand, V. M., & Carr, E. G. (1991). Functional communication training to reduce challenging behavior:

Maintenance and application in new settings. *Journal of Applied Behavior Analysis, 24,* 251–264.

Durand, V. M., & Carr, E. G. (1992). An analysis of maintenance following functional communication training. *Journal of Applied Behavior Analysis, 25,* 777–794.

Durand, V. M., & Crimmins, D. B. (1988). Identifying the variables maintaining self-injurious behavior. *Journal of Autism and Developmental Disorders, 18,* 99–117.

Durand, V. M., & Mindell, J. A. (1990). Behavioral treatment of multiple childhood sleep disorders: Effects on child and family. *Behavior Modification, 14,* 37–49.

Durand, V. M., Mindell, J., Mapstone, E., & Gernet-Dott, P. (1998). Sleep problems. In T. S. Watson & F. M. Gresham (Eds.), *Handbook of child behavior therapy.* New York: Plenum Press.

Durlak, J. A. (1997). Primary prevention programs in schools. In T. H. Ollendick & R. J. Prinz (Eds.), *Advances in clinical child psychology* (Vol. 19). New York: Plenum Press.

Durlak, J. A., & Wells, A. M. (1997). Primary prevention mental health programs for children and adolescents: A meta-analytic review. *American Journal of Community Psychology, 25,* 115–152.

Dykens, E. M., & Cohen, D. J. (1996). Effects of Special Olympics International on social competence in persons with mental retardation. *Journal of the American Academy of Child and Adolescent Psychiatry, 35,* 223–229.

Dykens, E. M., & Volkmar, F. R. (1997). Medical conditions associated with autism. In D. J. Cohen & F. R. Volkmar (Eds.), *Handbook of autism and pervasive developmental disorders.* New York: John Wiley.

Eagly, A. H., Ashmore, R. D., Makhijani, M. G., & Kennedy, L. C. (1991). What is beautiful is good but . . . ; A meta-analytic review of research on the physical attractiveness stereotype. *Psychological Bulletin, 110,* 109–128.

Earls, F. (1994). Oppositional-defiant and conduct disorders. In M. Rutter, E. Taylor, & L. Hersov (Eds.). *Child and adolescent psychiatry: Modern approaches.* 3rd ed. London: Blackwell Scientific Publications.

Earls, F., & Jung, K. G. (1987). Temperament and home environment characteristics as causal factors in the early development of childhood psychopathology. *Journal of the American Academy of Child and Adolescent Psychiatry, 26,* 491–498.

Eaves, L. J., Silberg, J. L., Meyer, J. M., Maes, H. H., Simonoff, E., Pickles, A., Rutter, M., Neale, M. C., Reynolds, C. A., Erickson, M. T., Heath, A. C., Loeber, R., Truett K. R., & Hewitt, J. K. (1997). Genetics and developmental psychopathology: 2. The main effects of genes and environment on behavioral problems in the Virginia Twin Study of Adolescent Behavioral Development. *Journal of Child Psychology and Psychiatry, 38,* 965–980.

Eccles, J. S., Midgley, C., Wigfield, A., Buchanan, C. M., Reuman, D., Flanagan, C., & MacIver, D. (1993). Development during adolescence: The impact of stage-environment fit on young adolescents' experiences in schools and in families. *American Psychologist, 48,* 90–101.

Edelbrock, C., & Costello, A. J., Dulcan, M. K., Kalas, R., & Conover, N.C. (1985). Age differences in the realiability of the psychiatric interview of the child. *Child Development, 56,* 265–275.

Edelbrock, C., & Rancurello, M. D. (1985). Childhood hyperactivity: An overview of rating scales and their applications. *Clinical Psychology Review, 5,* 429–445.

Edelbrock, C., Rende, R., Plomin, R., & Thompson, L. A. (1995). A twin study of competence and problem behavior in childhood and early adolescence. *Journal of Child Psychology and Psychiatry, 36,* 775–785.

Eggers, C. (1978). Course and prognosis of childhood schizophrenia. *Journal of Autism and Childhood Schizophrenia, 8,* 21–36.

Eggers, C. & Bunk, D. (1997). The longterm course of childhood-onset schizophrenia: A 42-year followup. *Schizophrenia Bulletin, 23,* 105–117.

Eisenberg, L., Baker, B. L., & Blacher, J. (1998). Siblings with children with mental retardation living at home or in residential placement. *Journal of Child Psychology and Psychiatry, 39,* 355–363.

Eiser, C. (1994). The eleventh Jack Tizard Memorial Lecture. Making sense of chronic disease. *Journal of Child Psychology and Psychiatry, 35,* 1373–1389.

Eiser, C. (1998). Long-term consequences of childhood cancer. *Journal of Child Psychology and Psychiatry, 39,* 621–633.

Eiser, C., Havermans, T., Pancer, M., & Eiser, J. R. (1992). Adjustment to chronic disease in relation to age and gender: Mother's and father's reports of their children's behavior. *Journal of Pediatric Psychology, 17,* 261–275.

Ekstein, R., Friedman, S., & Carruth, E. (1972). The psychoanalytic treatment of childhood schizophrenia. In B. B. Wolman (Ed.), *Manual of child psychology.* New York: McGraw Hill.

Eley, T. C. (1997). General genes: A new theme in developmental psychopathology. *Current Directions in Psychological Science, 6,* 90–95.

Elias, G., Hayes, A., & Broerse, J. (1988). Aspects of structure and content of maternal talk with infants. *Journal of Child Psychology and Psychiatry, 29,* 523–531.

Elliot, C. H., Jay, S. M., & Woody, P. (1987). An observational scale for measuring children's distress during painful medical procedures. *Journal of Pediatric Psychology, 12,* 543–551.

Elliot, D. S., Huizinga, D., & Ageton, S. S. (1985). *Explaining delinquency and drug use.* Beverly Hills, CA: Sage.

Ellis, E. F. (1988). Asthma: Current therapeutic approach. *Pediatric Clinics of North America, 35,* 1041–1052.

Ely, M. (1991). *Doing qualitative research: Circles within circles.* New York: The Falmer Press.

Emerson, E. B. (1985). Evaluating the impact of deinstitutionalization on the lives of mentally retarded people. *American Journal of Mental Deficiency, 90,* 277–288.

Emery, R. E., & Forehand, R. (1994). Parental divorce and children's well-being: A focus on resilience. In R. J. Haggerty, L. R. Sherrod, N. Garmezy, & Rutter, M. (Eds.), *Stress, risk, and resilience in children and adolescents.* Cambridge, England: Cambridge University Press.

Emery, R. E., & Kitzmann, K. M. (1995). The child in the family: Disruptions in family functions. In D. Cicchetti & D. J. Cohen (Eds.), *Developmental psychopathology: Risk, disorder, and adaptation* (Vol. 2). New York: John Wiley & sons.

Empey, L. T. (1978). *American delinquency.* Homewood, IL: Dorsey.

Emslie, G. J., Weinberg, W. A., Kennard, B. D., & Kowatch, R. A. (1994). Neurobiological aspects of depression in children and adolescents. In W. M. Reynolds & H. F. Johnston (Eds.), *Handbook of depression in children and adolescents.* New York: Plenum.

English, D. J. (1998). The extent and consequences of child maltreatment. *The Future of Children, 8(1),* 39–53.

Epstein, L. H., Valoski, A. M., Vara, L. S., McCurley, J., Wisniewski, L., Kalarchian, M. A., Klein, K. R., & Schrager, L. R. (1995). Effects of decreasing sedentary behavior and increasing activity on weight change in obese children. *Health Psychology, 14,* 109–115.

Erickson, M. T. (1987). *Behavior disorders of children and adolescents.* Englewood Cliffs, NJ: Prentice Hall.

Erlenmeyer-Kimling, L., Cornblatt, B. A., Bassett, A. S., Moldin, S. O., Hilldorf-Adamo, U., & Roberts. S. (1990). High-risk children in adolescence and young adulthood: Course of global adjustment. In L. N. Robins & M. Rutter (Eds.), *Straight and devious pathways from childhood to adulthood.* New York: Cambridge University Press.

Evans, J. A., & Hammerton, J. L. (1985). Chromosomal anomalies. In A. M. Clarke, A. D. B. Clarke, & J. M. Berg (Eds.), *Mental deficiency. The changing outlook.* New York: The Free Press.

Evans, R. B., & Koelsch, W. A. (1985). Psychoanalysis arrives in America. *American Psychologist, 40,* 942–948.

Exner, J. E., Jr., & Weiner, I. B. (1995). *The Rorschach: A comprehensive system* (Vol. 3: Assessment of children and adolescents) (2nd ed.). New York: Wiley.

Eyberg, S. M. (1992). Parent and teacher behavior inventories for the assessment of conduct problem behaviors in children. In L. VandeCreek, S. Knapp, & T. L. Jackson (Eds.), *Innovations in clinical practice: A source book* (Vol. 11). Sarasota, FL: Professional Resource Exchange.

Eyberg, S. M., Bessmer, J., Newcomb, K., Edwards, D., & Robinson, E. (1994). *Dyadic Parent-Child Interaction Coding System II: A manual.* Unpublished manuscript, University of Florida.

Fagan, T. K. (1992). Compulsory schooling, child study, clinical psychology, and special education: Origins of school psychology. *American Psychologist, 47,* 236–243.

Fairburn, C. G. (1985). Cognitive-behavioral treatment for bulimia. In D. M. Garner & P. E. Garfinkel (Eds.), *Handbook of psychotherapy for anorexia nervosa and bulimia.* New York: Guilford.

Fairburn, C. G. (1995). Physiology of anorexia nervosa. In K. D. Brownell & C. G. Fairburn (Eds.), *Eating disorders and obesity: A comprehensive handbook.* New York: Guilford Press.

Fairburn, C. G. (1997). Eating disorders. In D. M. Clark & C. G. Fairburn (Eds.), *Science and practice of cognitive behaviour therapy.* Oxford: Oxford University Press.

Fairburn, C. G., Welch, S. L., Doll, H. A., Davies, B. A., & O'Connor, M. E. (1997). Risk factors for bulimia nervosa: A community-based case-control study. *Archives of General Psychiatry, 54,* 509–517.

Fairburn, C. G. & Wilson, G. T. (1993). Binge eating: Definition and classification. In C. G. Fairburn & G. T. Wilson (Eds.), *Binge eating: Nature, assessment, and treatment.* New York: Guilford.

Faraone, S. V., Biederman, J., Kiely, K. (1996). Cognitive functioning, learning disability, and school failure in attention deficit hyperactivity disorder: A family study perspective. In J. H. Beitchman, N. J. Cohen, M. M. Konstantareas, & R. Tannock (Eds.), *Language, learning, and behavior disorders.* New York: Cambridge University Press.

Faraone, S., Biederman, J., Mennin, D., Russell, R., Tsuang, M. T. (1998). Familial subtypes of attention deficit hyperactivity disorder: A follow-up study of children from antisocial-ADHD families. *Journal of Child Psychology and Psychiatry, 39,* 1045–1053.

Farrington, D. P. (1986). Stepping stones to adult criminal careers. In D. Olweus, J. Block, & M. R. Yarrow (Eds.), *Development of antisocial behavior and prosocial behavior.* New York: Academic Press.

Farrington, D. P. (1987). Early precursors of frequent offending. In J. Q. Wilson & G. C. Loury (Eds.), *From children to citizens: Vol. III. Families, schools, and delinquency prevention.* New York: Springer-Verlag.

Farrington, D. P. (1991). Longitudinal research strategies: Advantages, problems, and prospects. *Journal of the American Academy of Child and Adolescent Psychiatry, 30,* 369–374.

Farrington, D. P. (1995). The development of offending and antisocial behaviour from childhood: Key findings from the Cambridge Study in Delinquent Development. *Journal of Child Psychology and Psychiatry, 36,* 929–964.

Federal Interagency Forum on Child and Family Statistics. (1998). *America's children: Key national indicators of well-being.* Washington, DC: U.S. Government Printing Office.

Felner, R. D., & Adan, A. M. (1988). The School Transition Environment Project: An ecological intervention and evaluation. In R. H. Price, E. L. Cowen, R. P. Lorion, & J. Ramos-McKay (Eds.), *Fourteen ounces of prevention: A casebook for practioners.* Washington, DC: American Psychological Association.

Felner, R., Brand, S., Adam, A. A., Mulhall, P. F., Flowers, N., Sartain, B., & DuBois, B. L. (1993). Restructuring the ecology of the school as an approach to prevention during school transitions: Longitudinal follow-up and extensions of the School Transition Environment Project (STEP). *Prevention and Human Services, 10,* 103–136.

Ferguson, L. R. (1978). The competence and freedom of children to make choices regarding participation in research: A statement. *Journal of Social Issues, 34,* 114–121.

Fergusson, D. M., & Horwood, L. J. (1996). The role of adolescent peer affiliations in the continuity between childhood behavioral adjustment and juvenile offending. *Journal of Abnormal Child Psychology, 24,* 205–221.

Fergusson, D. M., & Horwood, L. J. (1998). Early conduct problems and later life opportunities. *Journal of Child Psychology and Psychiatry, 39,* 1097–1108.

Fergusson, D. M., Horwood, L. J., & Lloyd, M. (1991). Confirmatory factor models of attention deficit and conduct disorder. *Journal of Child Psychology and Psychiatry, 32,* 257–274.

Fergusson, D. M., Horwood, L. J., & Lynskey, M. T. (1993). Early dentine lead levels and subsequent cognitive and behavioural development. *Journal of Child Psychology and Psychiatry, 34,* 215–227.

Fergusson, D. M., Horwood, L. J., & Lynskey, M. T. (1995). The stability of disruptive childhood behaviors. *Journal of Abnormal Child Psychology, 23,* 379–396.

Fergusson, D. M., & Lynskey, M. T. (1995). Childhood circumstances, adolescent adjustment, and suicide attempts in a New Zealand birth cohort. *Journal of the American Academy of Child and Adolescent Psychiatry, 34,* 612–622.

Fergusson, D. M., & Lynskey, M. T. (1997). Early reading difficulties and later conduct problems. *Journal of Child Psychology and Psychiatry, 38,* 899–907.

Fergusson, D. M., Lynskey, M. T., & Horwood, L. J. (1996). Factors associated with continuity and changes in disruptive behavior patterns between childhood and adolescence. *Journal of Abnormal Child Psychology, 24,* 533–553.

Fergusson, D. M., Lynskey, M. T., & Horwood, L. J. (1997). Attentional difficulties in middle childhood and psychosocial outcomes in young adulthood. *Journal of Child Psychology and Psychiatry, 38,* 633–644.

Ferrari, M. (1990). Developmental issues in behavioral pediatrics. In A. M. Gross & R. S. Drabman (Eds.), *Handbook of clinical behavioral pediatrics.* New York: Plenum.

Ferster, C. B. (1961). Positive reinforcement and behavorial deficits of autistic children. *Child Development, 32,* 437–456.

Ferster, C. B. (1966). The repertiore of the autistic child in relation to principles of reinforcement. In L. Gottschalk & A. H. Averback (Eds.), *Methods of research of psychotherapy.* New York: Appleton-Century-Crofts.

Ferster, C. B. (1974). Behavioral approaches to depression. In R. J. Friedman & M. M. Katz (Eds.), *The psychology of depression: Contemporary theory and research.* Washington, DC: Winston.

Field, T. (1992). Infants of depressed mothers. *Development and Psychopathology, 4,* 49–66.

Fiese, B. H., & Bickman, N. L. (1998). Qualitative inquiry: An overview for pediatric psychology. *Journal of Pediatric Psychology, 23,* 79–86.

Fine, R. (1985). Anna Freud. *American Psychologist, 40,* 230–232.

Finkelhor, D. (1994). The international epidemiology of child sexual abuse. *Child Abuse & Neglect, 18,* 409–417.

Finkelstein, H. (1988). The long term effects of early parent death: A review. *Journal of Clinical Psychology, 44,* 3–9.

Fireman, G., & Koplewicz, H. S. (1992). Short-term treatment of children with encopresis. *Journal of Psychotherapy Practice and Research, 1,* 64–71.

Fischer, M., Barkley, R. A., Fletcher, K. E., & Smallish, L. (1993). The adolescent outcome of hyperactive children: Predictors of psychiatric, academic, social, and emotional adjustment. *Journal of the American Academy of Child and Adolescent Psychiatry, 32,* 324–332.

Fixsen, D. L., Wolf, M. M., & Phillips, E. L. (1973). Achievement place: a teaching-family model of community-based group homes for youth in trouble. In L. Hammerlynck, L. Handy, and E. Mash (Eds.), *Behavior change: Methodology, concepts and practice.* Champaign, IL: Research Press.

Flament, M. F., Whitaker, A., Rapoport, J. L., Davies, M., Berg, C. Z., Kalikow, K., Sceery, W., & Shafer, D. (1988). Obsessive compulsive disorder in adolescence: An epidemiological study. *Journal of the American Academy of Child and Adolescent Psychiatry, 27,* 764–771.

Flavell, J. H. (1963). *The developmental psychology of Jean Piaget.* New York: Van Nostrand.

Fleming, J. E., Offord, D. R., & Boyle, M. H. (1989). Prevalence of childhood and adolescent depression in the community: Ontario Child Health Study. *British Journal of Psychiatry, 155,* 647–654.

Fletcher, J. M., & Taylor, H. G. (1997). Children with brain injury. In E. J. Mash & L. G. Terdal (Eds.), *Assessment of childhood disorders* (3rd ed.). New York: Guilford Press.

Fletcher, J. M., Shaywitz, S. E., Shankweiler, D., Katz, L., Liberman, A. Y., Steuben, K. K., Francis, D. J., Fowler, A. F., & Shaywitz, B. A. (1994). Cognitive profiles of reading disability: Comparisons of discrepancy and low achievement definitions. *Journal of Educational Psychology, 86,* 6–23.

Flicek, M. (1992). Social status of boys with both academic problems and attention-deficit hyperactivity disorder. *Journal of Abnormal Child Psychology, 20,* 353–366.

Flint, J. (1996). Behavioural phenotypes: A window into the biology of behaviour. *Journal of Child Psychology and Psychiatry, 37,* 355–367.

Flisher, A. J. (1999). Mood disorder in suicidal children and adolescents: Recent developments. *Journal of Child Psychology and Psychiatry, 40,* 315–324.

Flynt, S. W., Wood, T. A., & Scott, R. L. (1992). Social support of mothers of children with mental retardation. *Mental Retardation, 30,* 233–236.

Follette, W. C., & Houts, A. C. (1996). Models of scientific progress and the role of theory in taxonomy development: A case study of DSM. *Journal of Consulting and Clinical Psychology, 64,* 1120–1132.

Folstein, S., & Rutter, M. (1978). A twin study of individuals with infantile autism. In M. Rutter & E. Schopler (Eds.), *Autism: A reappraisal of concepts and treatment.* New York: Plenum.

Fombonne, E., du Mazaubrun, C., Cans, C., & Grandjean, H. (1997). Autism and associated medical disorders in a French epidemiological survey. *Journal of the American Academy of Child and Adolescent Psychiatry, 36,* 1561–1569.

Forehand, R., Furey, W. M., & McMahon, R. J. (1984). The role of maternal distress in a parent training program to modify child non-compliance. *Behavioral Psychotherapy, 12,* 93–108.

Forehand, R., King, H. E., Peed, S., & Yoder, P. (1975). Mother-child interactions: Comparisons of a non-compliant clinic group and a non-clinic group. *Behaviour Research and Therapy, 13,* 79–84.

Forehand, R., & McMahon, R. J. (1981). *Helping the noncompliant child: A clinician's guide to parent training.* New York: Guilford.

Forehand, R., Wells, K. C., & Griest, D. L. (1980). An examination of the social validity of a parent training program. *Behavior Therapy, 11,* 488–502.

Forehand, R., Wierson, M., Frame, C. L., Kemptom, T., & Armistead, L. (1991). Juvenile firesetting: A unique syndrome or an advanced level of antisocial behavior? *Behaviour Research and Therapy, 29,* 125–128.

Foreyt, J. P. & Goodrick, G. K. (1993). Obesity in children. In R. T. Ammerman & M. Hersen (Eds.), *Handbook of behavior therapy with children and adults: A developmental and longitudinal perspective.* Boston: Allyn & Bacon.

Foreyt, J. P., & McGavin, J. K. (1989). Anorexia nervosa and bulimia nervosa. In E. J. Mash & R. A. Barkley (Eds.), *Treatment of childhood behavior disorders.* New York: Guilford.

Forsyth, J. P., & Chorpita, B. F. (1997). Unearthing the nonassociative origins of fears and phobias: A rejoinder. *Journal of Behaviour Research and Therapy, 28,* 297–305.

Foster, G. G., & Salvia, J. (1977). Teacher response to the label of learning disabled as a function of demand characteristics. *Exceptional Children, 43,* 533–534.

Foster, S. L., & Robin, A. L. (1997). Family conflict and communication in adolescence. In E. J. Mash & L. G. Terdal (Eds.). *Assessment of childhood disorders* (3rd ed.). New York: Guilford Press.

Fowles, D. C. (1992). Schizophrenia: Diathesis-stress revisited. *Annual Review of Psychology, 43,* 303–336.

Frankel, F., Myatt, R., Cantwell, D. P., & Feinberg, D. T. (1997). Parent-assisted transfer of children's social skills training: Effects on children with and without attention-deficit hyperactivity disorder. *Journal of the American Academy of Child and Adolescent Psychiatry, 36,* 1056–1064.

Frankel, M. S. (1978). Social, legal, and political responses to ethical issues in the use of children as experimental subjects. *Journal of Social Issues, 34,* 101–113.

Fredericksen, N. (1986). Toward a broader conception of human intelligence. *American Psychologist, 41,* 445–452.

Freeman, E. H., Feingold, B. F., Schlesinger, K., & Gorman, F. J. (1964). Psychological variables in allergic disorders: A review. *Psychosomatic Medicine, 26,* 543–575.

Fremouw, W., Seime, R., & Damer, D. (1993). Behavioral treatment. In V. B. Van Haselt & M. Hersen (Eds.), *Handbook of behavior therapy and pharmacotherapy for children: A comparative analysis.* Boston: Allyn & Bacon.

French, D. C. (1988). Heterogeneity of peer-rejected boys: Aggressive and nonaggressive subtypes. *Child Development, 59,* 976–985.

French, D. C. (1990). Heterogeneity of peer-rejected girls. *Child Development, 59,* 976–985.

French, T. M., & Alexander, F. (1941). Psychogenic factors in bronchial asthma. *Psychosomatic Medicine Monograph, 4,* 2–94.

Freud, A. (1946). *The psycho-analytical treatment of children.* London: Imago.

Freud, S. (1949). *An outline of psycho-analysis.* Translated and newly edited by J. Strachey. New York: W. W. Norton and Co.

Freud, S. (1953). Analysis of a phobia in a five-year-old boy (1909). *Standard Edition.* Vol. 10. Ed. and trans. James Strachey, London: The Hogarth Press.

Frick, P. J. (1994). Family dysfunction and the disruptive disorders: A review of recent empirical findings. In T. H. Ollendick & Prinz, R. J. (Eds.), *Advances in clinical child psychology.* Vol. 16. New York: Plenum Press.

Frick, P. J. (1998). Conduct disorders. In T. H. Ollendick & Hersen, M. (Eds.), *Handbook of child psychopathology* (3rd ed.). New York: Plenum Press.

Frick, P. J., Van Horn, Y., Lahey, B. B., Christ, M. A. G., Loeber, R., Hart, E. A., Tannenbaum, L. & Hanson, K. (1993). Oppositional defiant disorder and conduct disorder: A metal-analytic review of factor analyses and cross-validation in a clinic sample. *Clinical Psychology Review, 13,* 319–340.

Friedman, A. G., Latham, S. A., & Dahlquist, L. M. (1998). Childhood cancer. In T. H. Ollendick & M. Hersen (Eds.), *Handbook of child psychopathology* (3rd ed.). New York: Plenum Press.

Friedman, A. G., & Mulhern, R. K. (1992). Psychological aspects of childhood cancer. In B. B. Lahey & A. E. Kazdin (Eds.), *Advances in clinical child psychology,* Vol. 14. New York: Plenum Press.

Fuller, B., Holloway, S. D., & Liang, X. (1996). Family selection of child-care centers: The influence of household support, ethnicity, and parental practices. *Child Development, 67,* 3320–3337.

Furman, W., Rahe, D., & Hartup, W. (1979). Rehabilitation of socially withdrawn peschool children through mixed-age and same-age socialization. *Child Development, 50,* 915–922.

Furstenberg, F. F., Jr., Brooks-Gunn, J., & Chase-Lansdale, L. (1989). Teenage pregnancy and childbearing. *American Psychologist, 44,* 313–320.

Gadow, K. D. (1992). Pediatric psychopharmacology: A review of recent research. *Journal of Child Psychology and Psychiatry, 33,* 153–195.

Gadow, K. D., & Pomeroy, J. C. (1991). An overview of psychopharmacotherapy for children and adolescents. In T. R. Kratochwill & R. J. Morris (Eds.), *The practice of child therapy.* Boston: Allyn and Bacon.

Galaburda, A. M. (1989). Learning disability: Biological, societal, or both? A response to Gerald Coles, *Journal of Learning Disabilities, 22,* 278–282: 286.

Garbarino, J. (1991). Not all bad developmental outcomes are the result of child abuse. *Development and Psychopathology, 3,* 45–50.

Garcia, J. (1981). The logic and limits of mental aptitude testing. *American Psychologist, 36,* 1172–1180.

Garland, E. J., & Smith, D. H. (1991). Simultaneous prepubertal onset of panic disorder, night terrors, and somnambulism. *Journal of the American Academy of Child and Adolescent Psychiatry, 30,* 553–555.

Garmezy, N. (1994). Foreword. In C. A. Nelson, (Ed.), *Threats to optimal development: Integrating biological, psychological, and social risk factors. The Minnesota symposium on child psychology.* Vol. 27. Hillsdale, NJ: Erlbaum.

Garmezy, N., & Masten, A. S. (1994). Chronic adversities. In M. Rutter, E. Taylor, & L. Hersov (Eds.), *Child and adolescent psychiatry. Modern approaches.* Cambridge, MA: Blackwell Scientific.

Garn, S. M., & Clark, D. C. (1976). Trends in fatness and the origins of obesity: Ad hoc committee to review the ten-state nutrition survey. *Pediatrics, 57,* 443–456.

Garn, S. M., LaVelle, M., Rosenberg, K. R., & Hawthorne, V. M. (1986). Maturational timing as a factor in female fatness and obesity. *The American Journal of Clinical Nutrition, 43,* 879–883.

Garner, D. M., & Bemis, K. M. (1985). Cognitive therapy for anorexia nervosa. In D. M. Garner & P. E. Garfinkel (Eds.), *Handbook of psychotherapy for anorexia and bulimia.* New York: Guilford.

Garner, D. M., Vitousek, K. M., & Pike, K. M. (1997). Cognitive-behavioral therapy for anorexia nervosa. In D. M. Garner & P. E. Garfinkel (Eds.), *Handbook of treatment for eating disorders* (2nd ed). New York: Guilford Press.

Gath, A. (1985). Chromosomal abnormalities. In M. Rutter & L. Hersov (Eds.), *Child and adolescent psychiatry: Modern approaches,* 2nd ed. Oxford: Blackwell Scientific Publications.

Gathercole, S. E. (1998). The development of memory. *Journal of Child Psychology and Psychiatry, 39,* 3–27.

Gaub, M., & Carlson, C. L. (1997). Gender difference in ADHD: A meta-analysis and critical review. *Journal of the American Academy of Child and Adolescent Psychiatry, 36,* 1035–1045.

Ge, X., Conger, R. D., Lorenz, F. O., Shanahan, M., & Elder, G. H. (1995). Mutual influences in parent and adolescent psychological distress. *Developmental Psychology, 31,* 406–419.

Gerard, M. W. (1939). Enuresis: A study in etiology. *American Journal of Orthopsychiatry, 9,* 48–58.

Gergen, P. J., Mullally, D. I. & Evans, R. (1988). National survey of prevalence of asthma among children in the United States, 1976 to 1980. *Pediatrics, 81,* 1–7.

Gerrity, K. M., Jones, F. A., & Self, P. A. (1983). Developmental psychology for the clinical child psychologist. In C. E. Walker and M. C. Roberts (Eds.), *Handbook of clinical child psychology.* New York: Wiley.

Gershon, E. S., & Rieder, R. O. (1992, Sept.) Major disorders of mind and brain. *Scientific American,* 127–133.

Gesten, E. L. (1976). A Health Resources Inventory: The development of a measure of the personal and social competence of primary grade children. *Journal of Consulting and Clinical Psychology, 44,* 775–786.

Giaconia, R. M., Reinherz, H. Z., Silverman, A. B., Pakiz, B., Frost, A. K., & Cohen, E. (1994). Ages of onset of psychiatric disorders in a community population of older adolescents. *Journal of the American Academy of Child and Adolescent Psychiatry, 33,* 706–717.

Gilbert, S., & Thompson, J. K. (1996). Feminist explanations of the development of eating disorders: Common themes, research findings, and methodological issues. *Clinical Psychology: Science and Practice, 3,* 183–202.

Gillberg, C. (1997). Practitioner review: Physical investigations in mental retardation. *Journal of Child Psychology and Psychiatry, 38,* 889–897.

Gillberg, C. L. (1992). The Emmanuel Miller Memorial Lecture 1991. Autism and autistic-like conditions: Subclasses among disorders of empathy. *Journal of Child Psychology and Psychiatry, 33,* 813–842.

Gillberg, C., & Coleman, M. (1966). Autism and medical disorders: A review of the literature. *Developmental Medicine and Child Neurology, 38,* 181–202.

Gillberg, C., Ehlers, S., Schaumann, H., Jakobsson, G., Dahlgren, S. O., Lindblom, R., Bagenholm, A., Tjuus, T., & Blidner, E. (1990). Autism under age 3 years: A clinical study of 28 cases referred for autistic symptoms in infancy. *Journal of Child Psychology and Psychiatry, 31,* 921–934.

Gillberg, I. C., Hellgren, L., & Gillberg, C. (1993). Psychotic disorders diagnosed in adolescence. Outcome at age 30 years. *Journal of Child Psychology and Psychiatry, 34,* 1173–1185.

Gillham, J. E., Reivich, K. J., Jaycox, L. H., & Seligman, M. E. P. (1995). Prevention of depressive symptoms in school children: A two-year follow-up. *Psychological Science, 6,* 343–351.

Gillin, J. C., Duncan, W., Pettigrew, K. D., Frankel, B., & Synder, F. (1979). Successful separation of depressed, normal and insomniac subjects by EEG sleep data. *Archives of General Psychiatry, 36,* 85–90.

Ginsburg, G. S., La Greca, A. M. & Silverman, W. K. (1998). Social anxiety in children with anxiety disorders: Relation with social and emotional functioning. *Journal of Abnormal Psychology, 26,* 175–185.

Gjone, H., & Stevenson, J. (1997a). A longitudinal twin study of temperament and behavior problems: Common genetic or environmental influences? *Journal of the American Academy of Child and Adolescent Psychiatry, 36,* 1448–1456.

Gjone, H., & Stevenson, J. (1997b). The association between internalizing and externalizing behavior in childhood and early adolescence: Genetic or environment common influences? *Journal of Abnormal Child Psychology, 25,* 277–286.

Gladstone, T. R. G., & Kaslow, N. J. (1995). Depression and attributions in children and adolescents: A meta-analytic review. *Journal of Abnormal Child Psychology, 23,* 597–606.

Glantz, L. H. (1996). Conducting research with children: Legal and ethical issues. *Journal of the American Academy of Child and Adolescent Psychiatry, 35,* 1283–1291.

Glidden, L. M. (1985). Semantic processing, semantic memory, and recall. In N. R. Ellis & N. W. Bray (Eds.), *International Review of Research in Mental Retardation,* Vol. 13. New York: Academic Press.

Glueck, S., & Glueck, E. T. (1968). *Delinquents and nondelinquents in perspective.* Cambridge, MA: Harvard University Press.

Goddard, H. H. (1912). *The Kallikak family.* New York: Macmillan.

Goenjian, A. K., Yehuda, R., Pynoos, R. S., Steinberg, A. M., Tashjian, M., Yang, R. K., Najarian, L. M., Fairbanks, L. A. (1996). Basal cortisol, dexamethasone suppression of cortisol, and MHPG in adolescents after the 1988 earthquake in Armenia. *American Journal of Psychiatry, 153,* 929–934.

Golden, C. J., Purisch, A. D., & Hammeke, T. A. (1985). *Luria-Nebraska Neuropsychological Battery: Forms I and II manual.* Los Angeles: Western Psychological Services.

Goldfarb, W. (1970). Childhood psychosis. In P. H. Mussen (Ed.), *Carmichael's manual of child psychology, Vol. 2.* New York: Wiley.

Gooding, D. C., & Iacono, W. G. (1995). Schizophrenia through the lens of a developmental psychopathology perspective. In D. Cicchetti & D. J. Cohen (Eds.), *Developmental Psychology* (Vol. 2). New York: John Wiley Interscience.

Goodman, R., & Stevenson, J. (1989). A twin study of hyperactivity-II. The aetiological role of genes, family relationships and perinatal adversity. *Journal of Child Psychology and Psychiatry, 30,* 691–709.

Goodyer, I. M., & Cooper, P. (1993). A community study of depression in adolescent girls: II. The clinical features of identified disorder. *British Journal of Psychiatry, 163,* 374–380.

Gortmaker, S. L., Dietz, W. H., Jr., Sobol, A. M., & Wehler, C. A. (1987). Increasing pediatric obesity in the United States. *American Journal of Diseases in Children, 141,* 535–540.

Gortmaker, S. L., & Sappenfield, W. (1984). Chronic childhood disorders: Prevalence and impact. *Pediatric Clinics of North America, 31,* 3–18.

Gottesman, I. I. (1993). Origins of schizophrenia: Past as prologue. In R. Plomin & G. E. McClearn (Eds.), *Nature and nurture & psychology.* Washington, DC: American Psychological Association.

Gottfried, A. E., & Gottfried, A. W. (1988). Maternal employment and children's development. An integration of longitudinal findings with implications for social policy. In A. E. Gottfried and A. W. Gottfried (Eds.), *Maternal employment and children's development.* New York: Plenum.

Gottman, J., Gonso, J., & Schuler, P. (1976). Teaching social skills to isolated children. *Journal of Abnormal Child Psychology, 4,* 170–185.

Gould, J. S. (1981). *The mismeasure of man.* New York: W. W. Norton.

Gould, M. S., Shaffer, D., & Kaplan, D. (1985). The characteristics of dropouts from a child psychiatric clinic. *Journal of the American Academy of Child Psychiatry, 24,* 316–328.

Gowers, S. G., Crisp, A. H., Joughin, N., & Bhat, A. (1991). Premenarcheal anorexia nervosa. *Journal of Child Psychology and Psychiatry, 32,* 515–524.

Graber, J. A., Lewinsohn, P. M., Seeley, J. R., & Brooks-Gunn, J. (1997). Is psychopathology associated with the timing of pubertal development? *Journal of the Academy of Child and Adolescent Psychiatry, 36,* 1768–1776.

Grace, W. J., & Graham, D. T. (1952). Relationship of specific attitudes and emotions to certain bodily diseases. *Psychosomatic Medicine, 14,* 243–251.

Grandin, T. (1997). A personal perspective on autism. In D. J. Cohen & F. R. Volkmar (Eds.), *Handbook of autism and pervasive developmental disorders.* New York: John Wiley.

Grannel de Aldaz, E., Vivas, E., Gelfand, D. M., & Feldman, L. (1984). Estimating the prevalence of school refusal and school-related fears: A Venezuelan sample. *Journal of Nervous and Mental Disease, 172,* 722–729.

Gray, J. A. (1985). Issues in the neuropsychology of anxiety. In A. H. Tuma & J. D. Maser (Eds.), *Anxiety and the anxiety disorders.* Hillsdale, NJ: Lawrence Earlbaum.

Gray, J. A. (1987). *The psychology of fear and stress.* New York: Cambridge University Press.

Graziano, A. M., DeGiovanni, I. S., & Garcia, K. A. (1979). Behavioral treatment of children's fears: A review. *Psychological Bulletin, 86,* 804–830.

Graziano, A. M., & Mooney, K. C. (1982). Behavioral treatment of "nightfears" in children: Maintenance of improvement at $2\frac{1}{2}$ to 3-year follow-up. *Journal of Consulting and Clinical Psychology, 50,* 598–599.

Green, A. H. (1993). Child sexual abuse: Immediate and long-term effects and intervention. *Journal of the American Academy of Child and Adolescent Psychiatry, 32,* 890–902.

Green, W. H., Padron-Gayol, M., Hardesty, A. S., & Bassiri, M. (1992). Schizophrenia with childhood onset: A phenomenological study of 38 cases. *Journal of the American Academy of Child and Adolescent Psychiatry, 31,* 968–976.

Greenberg, M. T., & Crnic, K. A. (1988). Longitudinal predictors of developmental status and social interaction in premature and full-term infants at age two. *Child Development, 59,* 554–570.

Greenberger, E., & Goldberg, W. A. (1989). Work, parenting, and the socialization of children. *Developmental Psychology, 25,* 22–35.

Greenberger, E., O'Neil, R., & Nagel, S. K. (1994). Linking workplace and homeplace: Relations between the nature of adults' work and their parenting behavior. *Developmental Psychology, 30,* 990–1002.

Greene, R. W. (1995). Students with ADHD in school classrooms: Teacher factors related to compatibility, assessment, and intervention. *School Psychology Review, 24,* 81–93.

Greene, R. W., Biederman, J., Faraone, S., Ouellette, C. A., Penn, C., & Griffin, S. N. (1996). Toward a new psychometric definition of social disability in children with attention-deficit hyperactivity disorder. *Journal of the American Academy of Child and Adolescent Psychiatry, 35,* 571–578.

Greenhill, L. L. (1991). Attention-deficit hyperactivity disorder. In J. M. Wiener (Ed.), *Textbook of child & adolescent psychiatry.* Washington, DC: American Psychiatric Press.

Greenough, W. T., Black, J. E., & Wallace, C. S. (1987). Experience and brain development. *Child Development, 58,* 539–559.

Greenspan, S., & Love, P. F. (1997). Social intelligence and developmental disorder: Mental retardation, learning disabilities, and autism. In W. E. MacLean (Ed.), *Ellis' handbook of mental deficiency, psychological theory and research.* Mahwah, NJ: Lawrence Erlbaum.

Greenwood, C. R., et al. (1992). Out of the laboratory and into the community. 26 years of applied behavior analysis at the Juniper Gardens Children's Project. *American Psychologist, 47,* 1464–1474.

Greenwood, C. R., Hart, B., Walker, D., & Risley, T. (1994). The opportunity to respond and academic performance revisited: A behavioral theory of developmental retardation and its prevention. In R. Gardner et al. (Eds.), *Behavior analysis in education: Focus on measurably superior instruction.* Pacific Grove, CA: Brooks/Cole.

Gresham, F. M., & Elliott, S. N. (1989). Social skills deficits as a primary learning disability. *Journal of Learning Disabilities, 22,* 120–124.

Griest, D. L., Forehand, R., Rogers, T., Breiner, J., Furey, W. & Williams, C. A. (1982). Effects of parent enhancement therapy on the treatment outcome and generalization of a parent training program. *Behaviour Research and Therapy, 20,* 429–436.

Griffin, B. S., & Griffin, C. T. (1978). *Juvenile delinquency in perspective.* New York: Harper & Row.

Grinder, R. E. (1967). *A history of genetic psychology*. New York: John Wiley.

Grolnick, W. S., & Ryan, R. M. (1990). Self-perceptions, motivation and adjustment in children with learning disabilities: A multiple group comparison study. *Journal of Learning Disabilities, 23*, 177–183.

Gross, A. M. (1990). Behavioral management of the child with diabetes. In A. M. Gross & R. S. Drabman (Eds.), *Handbook of clinical behavioral pediatrics*. New York: Plenum.

Gross, A. M., & Drabman, R. S. (1990). Clinical behavioral pediatrics: An introduction. In A. M. Gross & R. S. Drabman (Eds.), *Handbook of clinical behavioral pediatrics*. New York: Plenum.

Gross, A. M., Heimann, L., Shapiro, R., & Schultz, R. (1983). Social skills training and hemoglobin A_{ic} levels in children with diabetes. *Behavior Modification, 7*, 151–184.

Gross, M. D., Tofanelli, R. A., Butzirus, S. M., & Snodgrass E. W. (1987). The effects of diets rich in and free from additives on the behavior of children with hyperkinetic and learning disorders. *Journal of the American Academy of Child and Adolescent Psychiatry, 26*, 53–55.

Grossman, H. J. (1983). *Classification in mental retardation*. Washington, DC: American Association on Mental Deficiency.

Grusec, J. E. (1992). Social learning theory and developmental psychology: The legacies of Robert Sears and Albert Bandura. *Developmental Psychology, 28*, 776–786.

Grych, J. H., & Fincham, F. D. (1999). Children of single parents and divorce. In W. K. Silverman & T. H. Ollendick (Eds.), *Developmental issues in the clinical treatment of children*. Boston: Allyn and Bacon.

Guidubaldi, J., & Perry, J. D. (1985). Divorce and mental health sequelae for children: A two-year follow-up of a nationwide sample. *Journal of the American Academy of Child Psychiatry, 24*, 531–537.

Guillen, E. O., & Barr, S. I. (1994). Nutrition, dieting, and fitness messages in a magazine for adolescent women, 1970–1990. *Journal of Adolescent Health, 15*, 464–472.

Gunn, P., & Berry, P. (1990). Financial costs for home-reared children with Down syndrome: An Australian perspective. In W. I. Fraser (Ed.), *Key issues in mental retardation*. New York: Routledge.

Gur, R. E., Cowell, P., Turetsky, B. I., Gallacher, F., Cannon, T., Bilker, W., & Gur, R. C. (1998). A follow-up magnetic resonance imaging study of schizophrenia. *Archives of General Psychiatry, 55*, 145–152.

Guralnick, M. J. (1998). Effectiveness of early intervention for vulnerable children: A developmental perspective. *American Journal on Mental Retardation, 102*, 319–345.

Habermas, T. (1992). Further evidence on early case descriptions of anorexia nervosa and bulimia nervosa. *International Journal of Eating Disorders, 11*, 351–359.

Hafner, A. J., Quast, W., & Shea, M. J. (1975). The adult adjustment of one thousand psychiatric patients: Initial findings from a twenty-five year follow-up. In R. O. Wirt, G. Winokur, & M. Roff (Eds.), *Life history in psychopathology*, Vol. 4, Minneapolis: University of Minnesota Press.

Hall, C. C. I. (1997). Cultural malpractice: The growing obsolescence of psychology with the changing U.S. population. *American Psychologist, 52*, 642–651.

Hallahan, D. P., & Kauffman, J. M. (1978). *Exceptional children: Introduction to special education*. Englewood Cliffs, NJ: Prentice Hall.

Halmi, K. A. (1985). Eating disorders. In H. I. Kaplan & B. J. Sadock (Eds.), *Comprehensive textbook of psychiatry*, 4th ed. Baltimore: Williams & Wilkins.

Hamlett, K. W., Pellegrini, D. S., & Katz, K. S. (1992). Childhood chronic illness is a family stressor. *Journal of Pediatric Psychology, 17*, 33–47.

Hammen, C. (1990). Cognitive approaches to depression in children: Current findings and new directions. In B. Lahey, and A. Kazdin (Eds.), *Advances in clinical child psychology* (Vol. 13). New York: Plenum.

Hammen, C. (1992). Cognitive, life stress, and interpersonal approaches to a developmental psychopathology model of depression. *Development and Psychopathology, 4*, 189–206.

Hammen, C., Burge, D., Burney, E., & Adrian, C. (1990). Longitudinal study of diagnosis in children of women with unipolar and bipolar affective disorders. *Archives of General Psychiatry, 47*, 1112–1117.

Hammen, C., Rudolph, K., Weisz, J., Rao, U., & Burge, D. (1999). The context of depression in clinic-referred youth: Neglected areas in treatment. *Journal of the American Academy of Child and Adolescent Psychiatry, 38*, 64–71.

Hammill, D. D. (1993). A brief look at the learning disabilities movement in the United States. *Journal of Learning Disabilities, 26*, 295–310.

Handen, B. L. (1997). Mental retardation. In E. J. Mash & L. G. Terdal (Eds.), *Assessment of childhood disorders*. New York: Guilford Press.

Handen, B. L. (1998). Mental retardation. In E. J. Mash & L. G. Terdal (Eds.), *Treatment of childhood disorders*. New York: Guilford Press.

Hankin, B. L., Abramson, L. Y., Moffitt, T. E., Silva, P. A., McGee, R., & Angell, K. E. (1998). Development of depression from preadolescence to young adulthood: Emerging gender differences in a 10-year longitudinal study. *Journal of Abnormal Psychology, 107*, 128–140.

Hanna, G. L. (1995). Demographic and clinical features of obsessive-compulsive disorder in children and adolescents. *Journal of the American Academy of Child and Adolescent Psychiatry, 34,* 19–27.

Hansen, C., Weiss, D., & Last, C. G. (1999). ADHD boys in young adulthood: Psychosocial adjustment. *Journal of the American Academy of Child and Adolescent Psychiatry, 38,* 165–171.

Happe, F. G. E. (1994a). Annotation: Current psychological theories of autism: The "theory of mind" account and rival theories. *Journal of Child Psychology and Psychiatry, 35,* 215–229.

Happe, F. G. E. (1994b). Wechsler IQ profile and theory of mind in autism: a research note. *Journal of Child Psychology and Psychiatry, 35,* 1461–1471.

Happe, F. G. E. (1996). Studying weak central coherence at low levels: Children with autism do not succumb to visual illusions. *Journal of Child Psychology and Psychiatry, 37,* 873–878.

Harbeck-Weber, C., & Peterson, L. (1996). Health-related disorders. In E. J. Mash & R. A. Barkley (Eds.), *Child Psychopathology.* New York: Guilford Press.

Harcourt Brace Education Measurement. (1997). *The Stanford Achievement Test, Ninth Edition.* San Antonio: Harcourt Brace Education Measurement.

Harkavy, J., Johnson, S. B., Silverstein, J., Spillar, R., McCallum, M., & Rosenbloom, A. (1983). Who learns what at a diabetes summer camp. *Journal of Pediatric Psychology, 8,* 143–153.

Harley, J. P., & Matthews, C. G. (1980). Food additives and hyperactivity in children: Experimental investigations. In R. M. Knights and D. J. Bakker (Eds.), *Treatment of hyperactive and learning disordered children.* Baltimore: University Park Press.

Harrington, R., Rutter, M., & Fombonne, E. (1996). Developmental pathways in depression: Multiple meanings, antecedents, and endpoints. *Development and Psychopathology, 8,* 601–616.

Harrington, R., Rutter, M., Weissman, M., Fudge, H., Groothues, C., Bredenkamp, D., Pickles, A., Rende, R., & Wickramaratne, P. (1997). Psychiatric disorders in the relatives of depressed probands: I. Comparison of prepubertal, adolescent and early adult onset cases. *Journal of Affective Disorders, 42,* 9–22.

Harris, P. L. (1994). The child's understanding of emotion: Developmental change and the family environment. *Journal of Child Psychology and Psychiatry, 35,* 3–28.

Harris, S. L. (1979). DSM-III—Its implications for children. *Child Behavior Therapy, 1,* 37–46.

Harrison, J. E., & Bolton, P. F. (1997). Tuberous sclerosis. *Journal of Child Psychology and Psychiatry, 38,* 603–614.

Harrison, S. I., & McDermott, J. K. (1972). *Childhood psychopathology.* New York: International Univ. Press.

Hart, B., & Risley, T. R. (1992). American parenting of language-learning children: Persisting differences in family-child interactions observed in natural home environment. *Developmental Psychology, 28,* 1096–1105.

Hart, S. N., & Brassard, M. R. (1991). Psychological maltreatment: Progress achieved. *Development and Psychopathology, 3,* 61–70.

Harter, S. (1985). *Manual for the Self-Perception Profile for Children.* Denver, CO: University of Denver.

Hartung, C. M., & Widiger, T. A. (1998). Gender differences in the diagnosis of mental disorders: Conclusions and controversies of the DSM-IV. *Psychological Bulletin, 123,* 260–278.

Hartup, W. W. (1970). Peer interaction and social organization. In P. H. Mussen (Ed.), *Carmicheal's manual of child psychology.* New York: Wiley.

Hartup, W. W. (1983). Peer relations. In P. H. Mussen (Ed.), *Handbook of child psychology,* Vol. IV, New York: Wiley.

Hartup, W. W. (1989). Social relationships and their developmental significance. *American Psychologist, 44,* 120–126.

Hartup, W. W. (1996). The company they keep: Friendships and their developmental significance. *Child Development, 67,* 1–13.

Harvey, E. (1999). Short-term and long-term effects of early parental employment on children of the National Longitudinal Survey of Youth. *Developmental Psychology, 35,* 445–459.

Hathaway, W., Dooling-Litfin, J. D., & Edwards, G. (1998). Integrating the results of an evaluation: Eight clinical cases. In R. A. Barkley (Ed.), *Attention-deficit hyperactivity disorder.* New York: Guilford Press.

Haywood, H. C., Meyers, C. E., & Switzky, H. N. (1982). Mental retardation. In M. R. Rosenzweig & L. W. Porter (Eds.), *Annual review of psychology.* Palto Alto, CA: Annual Reviews Inc.

Heavey, C. L., Adelman, H. S., Nelson, P., & Smith, D. C. (1989). Learning problems, anger, preceived control, and misbehavior. *Journal of Learning Disabilities, 22,* 47–50.

Hechtman, L. (1991). Developmental, neurobiological, and psychosocial aspects of hyperactivity, impulsivity, and inattention. In M. Lewis (Ed.), *Child and adolescent psychiatry. A comprehensive textbook.* Baltimore: Williams & Wilkins.

Heebink, D. M., & Halmi, K. A. (1995). Psychopharmacology in adolescents with eating disorders. In H. C. Steinhausen (Ed.), *Eating disorders in adolescence: Anorexia and bulimia nervosa.* Berlin: Walter de Gruyter.

Heller, K. (1996). Coming of age of prevention science: Comments on the 1994 National Institute of Mental Health–Institute of Medicine prevention reports. *American Psychologist, 51,* 1123–1127.

Helms, J. E. (1992). Why is there no study of cultural equivalence in standardized cognitive ability testing? *American Psychologist, 47,* 1083–1101.

Hendren, R. L., & Berenson, C. K. (1996). Eating disorders. In J. M. Weiner (Ed.), *Diagnosis and psychopharmacology of childhood and adolescent disorders.* New York: John Wiley.

Henggeler, S. W. (1994). A consensus: Conclusions of the APA Task Force Report on Innovative Models of Mental Health Services for children, Adolescents, and Their Families. *Journal of Clinical Child Psychology, 23 (Suppl.),* 3–6.

Henggeler, S. W., & Borduin, C. M. (1990). *Family therapy and beyond: A multisystemic approach to treating the behavior problems of children and adolescents.* Pacific Grove, CA: Brooks/Cole.

Henggeler, S. W., Melton, G. B., & Smith, L. A. (1992). Family preservation using multisystemic therapy: An effective alternative to incarcerating serious juvenile offenders. *Journal of Consulting and Clinical Psychology, 60,* 953–961.

Henggeler, S. W., Schoenwald, S. K. Borduin, C. M., Rowland, M. D., & Cunningham, P. B. (1998). *Multisystemic treatment of antisocial behavior in children and adolescents.* New York: Guilford Press.

Henin, A., & Kendall, P. C. (1997). Obsessive-compulsive disorder in childhood and adolescence. In T. H. Ollendick & R. J. Prinz (Eds.), *Advances in clinical child psychology* (Vol. 19). New York: Plenum Press.

Hermelin, B., & O'Connor, N. (1970). *Psychological experiments with autistic children.* London: Pergamon.

Hernandez, D. J. (1994). Children's changing access to resources: A historical perspective. *Social Policy Report: Society for Research in Child Development, 8(1),* 1–23.

Hersov, L. A. (1960). Persistent non-atendance at school. *Journal of Child Psychology and Psychiatry, 1,* 130–136.

Hertzler, A. A. (1983a). Children's food patterns—A review. I. Food preferences and feeding problems. *Journal of the American Dietetic Association, 83,* 551–554.

Hertzler, A. A. (1983b). Children's food patterns—A review. II. Family and group behavior. *Journal of the American Dietetic Association,* 555–560.

Hetherington, E. M., Bridges, M., Insabella, G. (1998). What matters? What does not? Five perspectives on the association between marital transitions and children's adjustment. *American Psychologist, 53,* 167–184.

Hetherington, E. M., Stanley-Hagan, M., & Anderson, E. R. (1989). Marital transitions: A child's perspective. *American Psychologist, 44,* 303–312.

Hewitt, J. K., Silberg, J. L., Rutter, M., Simonoff, E., Meyer, J. M., Maes, H., Pickles, A., Neale, M. C., Loeber, R., Erickson, M. T., Kendler, K. S., Heath, A. C., Truett, K. R., Reynolds, C. A., & Eaves, L. J. (1997). Genetics and developmental psychopathology: 1. Phenotypic assessment in the Virginia Twin Study of Adolescent Behavioral Development. *Journal of Child Psychology and Psychiatry, 38,* 943–963.

Hightower, A. D., & Braden, J. (1991). Prevention. In T. R. Kratochwill & R. J. Morris (Eds.), *The practice of child therapy* (2nd ed.). New York: Pergamon Press.

Hightower, A. D., Cowen, E. L., Spinell, A. P., Lotyczewski, B. S., Guare, J. C., Rohrbeck, C. A., & Brown, L. P. (1987). The Child Rating Scale: The development and psychometric refinement of a socioemotional self-rating scale for young children. *School Psychology Review, 16,* 239–255.

Hinshaw, S. P. (1998). Is ADHD and impairing condition in childhood and adolescence? Chapter prepared for NIH Consensus Development Conference on Attention-Deficit Hyperactivity Disorder (ADHD): Diagnosis and Treatment. Bethesda, MD.

Hinshaw, S. P., & Erhardt, D. (1993). Behavioral treatment. In V. B. Van Hasselt & M. Hersen (Ed.), *Handbook of behavior therapy and pharmacotherapy for children: A comparative analysis.* Boston: Allyn and Bacon.

Hinshaw, S. P., Hanker, B., Whalen, C. K., Erhardt, D., & Dunnington, R. E. (1989). Aggressive, prosocial, and nonsocial behavior in hyperactive boys: Dose effects of methylphenidate in naturalistic settings. *Journal of Consulting and Clinical Psychology, 57,* 636–643.

Hinshaw, S. P., Klein, R. G., & Abikoff, H. (1998). Childhood attention deficit hyperactivity disorder: Nonpharmacological and combination treatments. In P. E. Nathan & J. E. Gorman (Eds.), *A guide to treatments that work.* New York: Oxford University Press.

Hinshaw, S. P., Lahey, B. B., & Hart, E. L. (1993). Issues of taxonomy and comorbidity in the development of conduct disorder. *Development and Psychopathology, 5,* 31–49.

Hinshelwood, J. (1917). *Congenital word-blindness.* London: H. K. Lewis.

Hoagwood, K., Jensen, P. S., & Fisher, C. B. (Eds.). (1996). *Ethical tissues in mental health research with children and adolescents.* Mahwah, NJ: Lawrence Erlbaum.

Hobbs, N. (1975). *The futures of children.* San Francisco: Jossey-Bass.

Hobson, P. (1993). Understanding persons: The role of affect. In S. Baron-Cohen, H. Tager-Flusberg, & D. J. Cohen (Eds.), *Understanding other minds.* New York: Oxford Press.

Hobson, R. P., & Lee, A. (1998). Hello and goodbye: A study of social engagement in autism. *Journal of Autism and Pervasive Developmental Disorders, 28,* 117–127.

Hockfield, S., & Lombroso, P. J. (1998). Development of the cerebral cortex: IX. Cortical development and experience: I. *Journal of the American Academy of Child and Adolescent Psychiatry, 37,* 992–993.

Hocutt, A. M. (1996). Effectiveness of special education: Is placement the critical factor? *The Future Of Children, 6,* 77–102.

Hodapp, R. M., Burack, J. A., & Zigler, E. (1990). Summing up and going forward: New directions in the developmental approach to mental retardation. In R. M. Hodapp, J. A. Burack, & E. Zigler (Eds.), *Issues in the developmental approach to mental retardation.* New York: Cambridge University Press.

Hodapp, R. M., & Zigler, E. (1997). New issues in the developmental approach to mental retardation. In W. E. MacLean (Ed.), *Ellis' handbook of mental deficiency, psychological theory and research.* Mahwah, NJ: Lawrence Erlbaum.

Hodges, K. (1994). Evaluation of depression in children and adolescents using diagnostic clinical interviews. In W. M. Reynolds and H. F. Johnston (Eds.), *Handbook of depression in children and adolescents.* New York: Plenum Press.

Hodges, K., Cool, J., & McKnew, D. (1989). Test-retest reliability of a clinical research interview for children: The Child Assessment Schedule (CAS). *Psychological Assessment, 1,* 317–322.

Hoffman, L. W. (1989). Effects of maternal employment in the two-parent family. *American Psychologist, 44,* 283–292.

Hogan, D. M. (1998). The psychological development and welfare of children of opiate and cocaine users: Review and research needs. *Journal of Child Psychology and Psychiatry, 39,* 609–620.

Holden, E. W., Deichmann, M. M., & Levy, J. D. (1999). Empirically supported treatment in pediatric psychology: Recurrent pediatric headache. *Journal of Pediatric Psychology, 24,* 91–109.

Holmes, L. B. (1978). Genetic counseling for the older pregnant woman: New data and questions. *New England Journal of Medicine, 298,* 1419–1421.

Holtzman, W. H. (1997). Community psychology in full-service schools in different cultures. *American Psychologist, 52,* 381–389.

Hoover, H. D., Heironymous, A. N., Frisbie, D. A., & Dunbar, S. B. (1996). *The Iowa Tests of Basic Skills, Forms K, L, and M.* Itasca, IL: Riverside Publishing Company.

Hops, H. (1995). Age- and gender-specific effects of parental depression: A commentary. *Developmental Psychology, 31,* 428–431.

Hops, H., Biglan, A., Sherman, L., Arthur, J., Friedman, L., & Osteen, V. (1987). Home observations of family interactions of depressed women. *Journal of Consulting and Clinical Psychology, 55,* 341–346.

Hops, H., Davis, B., & Longoria, N. (1995). Methodological issues in direct observation: Illustrations with the Living in Familial Environments (LIFE) coding system. *Journal of Clinical Child Psychology, 24,* 193–203.

Hops, H., & Greenwood, C. R. (1988). Social skill deficits. In E. J. Mash & L. C. Terdal (Eds.), *Behavioral assessment of childhood disorders,* 2nd ed. New York: Guilford.

Horne, J. (1992). Sleep and its disorders in children. *Journal of Child Psychology and Psychiatry, 33,* 473–487.

Horowitz, F. D. (1992). John B. Watson's legacy: Learning and environment. *Developmental Psychology, 28,* 360–367.

Houts, A. C., Berman, J. S., & Abramson, H. (1994). Effectiveness of psychological and pharmacological treatments for nocturnal enuresis. *Journal of Consulting and Clinical Psychology, 62,* 737–745.

Houts, A. C., Liebert, R. M., & Padawar, W. (1983). A delivery system for the treatment of primary enuresis. *Journal of Abnormal Child Psychology, 11,* 513–520.

Houts, A. C., Mellon, M. W., & Whelan, J. P. (1988). Use of dietary fiber and stimulus control to treat retentive encopresis: A multiple baseline investigation. *Journal of Pediatric Psychology, 13,* 435–445.

Houts, A. C., Peterson, J. K., & Whelan, J. P. (1986). Prevention of relapse in full-spectrum home training for primary enuresis: A component analysis. *Behavior Therapy, 17,* 462–469.

Howlin, P. (1994). Special education treatment. In M. Rutter, E. Taylor, & L. Hersov (Eds.), *Child and adolescent psychiatry. Modern approaches.* Cambridge MA: Blackwell Scientific.

Howlin, P. (1998). Pyschological and educational treatments for autism. *Journal of Child Psychology and Psychiatry, 39,* 307–322.

Howlin, P., Davies, M., & Udwin, O. (1998). Cognitive functioning in adults with Williams syndrome. *Journal of Child Psychology and Psychiatry, 39,* 183–189.

Hudziak, J. J., Heath, A. C., Madden, P. F., Reich, W., Bucholz, K. K., Slutske, W., Bierut, L. J., Neuman, R. J., & Todd, R. D. (1998). Latent class and factor analysis of DSM-IV ADHD: A twin study of female adolescents. *Journal of the American Academy of Child & Adolescent Psychiatry, 37,* 848–857.

Huesmann, L. R., Eron, L. D., Lefkowitz, M. M., & Walder, L. O. (1984). Stability of aggression over time and generations. *Developmental Psychology, 20,* 1120–1134.

Hughes, C. A., & Smith, J. O. (1990). Cognitive and academic performance of college students with learning disabilities: A synthesis of the literature. *Learning Disability Quarterly, 13,* 66–79.

Huizinga, D., Loeber, R., & Thornberry, T. P. (1993). *Public Health Reports, 108 (Supp. 1),* 90–96.

Hulme, C., & Roodenrys, S. (1995). Verbal working memory development and its disorders. *Journal of Child Psychology and Psychiatry, 36,* 373–398.

Humphrey, L. L. (1989). Observed family interaction among subtypes of eating disorders using structured analysis of social behavior. *Journal of Consulting and Clinical Psychology, 57,* 206–214.

Humphreys, L., Forehand, R., McMahon, R., & Roberts, M. (1978). Parent behavorial training to modify child noncompliance: Effects on untreated siblings. *Journal of Behavior Therapy and Experimental Psychiatry, 9*, 235–238.

Huntington's Disease Collaborative Research Group (1993). A novel gene containing a trinucleotide repeat that is expanded and unstable on Huntington's disease chromsomes. *Cell, 72*, 971–983.

Huse, D. M., Branes, L. A., Colligan, R. C., Nelson, R. A., & Palumbo, P. J. (1982). The challenge of obesity in childhood: I. Incidence, prevalence, and staging. *Mayo Clinic Proceedings, 57*, 279–284.

Hussong, A. M., Curran, P. J., & Chassin, L. (1998). Pathways of risk for accelerated heavy alcohol use among adolescent children of alcoholic parents. *Journal of Abnormal Child Psychology, 26*, 453–466.

Huttenlocher, P. R. (1994). Synaptogenesis, synapse elimination, and neural plasticity in human cerebral cortex. In C. A. Nelson (Ed.), *Threats to optimal development: Integrating biological, psychological, and social risk factors*. Hillsdale, NJ: Lawrence Erlbaum Associates.

Hynd, G. W., Marshall, R., & Gonzalez, J. (1991). Learning disabilities and presumed central nervous system dysfunction. *Learning Disability Quarterly, 14*, 283–296.

Hynd, G. W., & Semrud-Clikeman, M. (1989a). Dyslexia and brain morphology. *Psychological Bulletin, 106*, 447–482.

Hynd, G. W., & Semrud-Clikeman, M. (1989b). Dyslexia and neurodevelopmental pathology: Relationships to cognition, intelligence, and reading skill acquisition. *Journal of Learning Disabilities, 22*, 205–218.

Ialongo, N. S., Horn, W. F., Pascoe, J. M., Greenberg, G., Packard, T., Lopez, M., Wagner, A., & Puttler, L. (1993). The effects of a multimodal intervention with attention-deficit hyperactivity disorder children: A 9-month follow-up. *Journal of the American Academy of Child and Adolescent Psychiatry, 32*, 182–189.

Iannotti, R. J. & Bush, P. J. (1993). Toward a developmental theory of compliance. In N. A. Krasnegor, L. Epstein, S. B. Johnson, & S. Yaffe (Eds.), *Developmental aspects of health compliance behavior*. Hillsdale, NJ: Lawrence Earlbaum Associates.

Illback, R. J. (1994). Poverty and crisis in children's services: The need for services integration. *Journal of Clinical Child Psychology, 23*, 413–424.

Inderbitzen, H. M. (1994). Adolescent peer social competence: A critical review of assessment methodologies and instruments. In T. H. Ollendick & R. J. Prinz, *Advances in Clinical Child Psychology, 16*. New York: Plenum.

Ireys, H. T., Werthamer-Larsson, L. A., Kolodner, K. B., & Gross, S. S. (1994). Mental health of young adults with chronic illness: The mediating effect of perceived impact. *Journal of Pediatric Psychology, 19*, 205–222.

Israel, A. C. (1988). Parental and family influences in the etiology and treatment of childhood obesity. In N. A. Krasnegor, G. D. Grave, & N. Kretchmer (Eds.), *Childhood obesity: A biobehavioral perspective*. Caldwell, NJ: The Telford Press.

Israel, A. C. (1990). Childhood obesity. In A. S. Bellack, M. Hersen, & A. E. Kazdin (Eds.), *International handbook of behavoir modification and therapy*. New York: Plenum.

Israel, A. C., Guile, C. A., Baker, J. E., & Silverman, W. K. (1994). An evaluation of enhanced self-regulation training in the treatment of childhood obesity. *Journal of Pediatric Psychology, 19*, 737–749.

Israel, A. C., Pravder, M. D., & Knights, S. (1980). A peer-administered program for changing the classroom behavior of disruptive children. *Behavioural Analysis and Modification, 4*, 224–238.

Israel, A. C., & Shapiro, L. S. (1985). Behavior problems of obese children enrolling in a weight reduction program. *Journal of Pediatric Psychology, 10*, 449–460.

Israel, A. C., Silverman, W. K., & Solotar, L. C. (1986). An investigation of family influences on initial weight status, attrition, and treatment outcome in a childhood obesity program. *Behavior Therapy, 17*, 131–143.

Israel, A. C., & Solotar, L. C. (1988). Obesity. In M. Hersen, & C. G. Last (eds.), *Child behavior therapy casebook*. New York: Plenum.

Israel, A. C., Stolmaker, L., & Andrian, C. A. G. (1985). The effects of training parents in general child management skills in a behavioral weight loss program for children. *Behavior Therapy, 16*, 169–180.

Israel, A. C., & Zimand, E. (1989). Obestiy. In M. Hersen (Ed.), *Innovations in child behavior therapy*. New York: Springer.

Ivanova, M. Y. (1998). *Dysregulation of the hypothalamic-pituitary-adrenocortical system in childhood and adolescent major depression: Evidence for biological correlates?* Unpublished manuscript, University at Albany, State University of New York, Psychology Department.

Iwata, B. A., Dorsey, M. F., Slifer, K. J., Bauman, K. E., & Richman, G. S. (1994). Toward a functional analysis of self-injury. *Journal of Applied Behavior Analysis, 27*, 197–209.

Izard, C. E. (1994). Innate and universal facial expressions: Evidence from developmental and cross-cultural research. *Psychological Bulletin, 115*, 288–299.

Jacob, R. G., O'Leary, K. D., & Rosenblad, C. (1978). Formal and informal classroom settings: Effects on hyperactivity, *Journal of Abnormal Child Psychology, 6*, 47–59.

Jacobsen, L. K., & Rapoport, J. L. (1998). Research update: Childhood-onset schizophrenia: Implications of clinical and neurobiological research. *Journal of Child Psychology and Psychiatry, 39,* 101–113.

Jacobson, J. W., & Mulick, J. A. (1996). *Manual on diagnosis and professional practice in mental retardation.* Washington, DC: American Psychological Association.

James, E. M., Reynolds, C. R. & Dunbar, J. (1994). Self-report instruments. In T. H. Ollendick, N. J. King, & W. Yule (Eds.), *International handbook of phobic and anxiety disorders in children and adolescents* (pp. 317–330). New York: Plenum Press.

Janicke, D. M., & Finney, J. W. (1999). Empirically supported treatments in pediatric psychology: Recurrent abdominal pain. *Journal of Pediatric Psychology, 24,* 115–127.

Jastak, S., & Wilkinson, G. S. (1984). *Wide Range Achievement Test—Revised.* Wilmington, DE: Jastak Associates.

Jay, S. M. (1988). Invasive medical procedures: Psychological intervention and assessment. In D. K. Routh (Ed.), *Handbook of pediatric psychology,* New York: Guilford.

Jay, S. M., Elliot, C. H., Katz, E., & Siegel, S. E. (1987). Cognitive behavioral and pharmacologic intervention for children's distress during painful medical procedures. *Journal of Consulting and Clinical Psychology, 55,* 860–865.

Jay, S. M., Elliot, C. H., Ozolins, M., Olson, R., & Pruitt, S. (1985). Behavoiral management of children's distress during painful medical procedures. *Behavior Research and Therapy, 23,* 513–520.

Jay, S. M., Elliot, C. H., Woody, P. D., & Siegel, S. (1991). An investigation of cognitive-behavioral therapy combined with oral valium for children undergoing painful medical procedures. *Health Psychology, 10,* 317–322.

Jaycox, L. H., Reivich, K. J., Gillham, J. E., & Seligman, M. E. P. (1994). Prevention of depressive symptoms in school children. *Behaviour Research and Therapy, 32,* 801–816.

Jeffrey, D. B., Lemnitzer, N. B., Hess, J. M., Hickey, J. S., McLellarn, R. W., & Stroud, J. (1979). *Children's responses to television food advertising: Experimental evidence of actual food consumption.* Paper presented at a meeting of the American Psychological Association, New York City, September.

Jennings, K. D., Connors, R. E., & Stegman, E. E. (1988). Does a physical handicap alter the development of mastery motivation during the preschool years? *Journal of Child and Adolescent Psychiatry, 27,* 312–317.

Jensen, A. R. (1969). How much can we boost IQ and scholastic achievement? *Harvard Educational Review, 39,* 1–123.

Jensen, P. S., Bloedau, L., Degroot, J., Ussery, T., & Davis, H. (1990). Children at risk I: Risk factors and child symptomatology. *Journal of the American Academy of Child and Adolescent Psychiatry, 29,* 51–59.

Jensen, P. S., Martin, B. A., Cantwell, D. P. (1997). Comorbidity in ADHD: Implications for research, practice, and DSM-IV. *Journal of the Academy of Child and Adolescent Psychiatry, 36,* 1065–1075.

Jensen, P.S. & Shaw, J. (1993). Children as victims of war: Current knowledge and future research needs. *Journal of the American Academy of Child and Adolescent Psychiatry, 32,* 697–708.

Jersild, A. T., & Holmes, F. B. (1935). Children's fears. *Child Development Monograph,* No. 20.

Jessor, R., & Jessor, S. L. (1977). *Problem behavior and psychosocial development.* New York: Academic Press.

Jockin, V., McGue, M., & Lykken, D. T. (1996). Personality and divorce: A genetic analysis. *Journal of Personality and Social Psychology, 71,* 288–299.

Johnson, J. H., Rasbury, W. C., & Siegel, L. J. (1997). *Approaches to child treatment: Introduction to theory, research, and practice* (2nd ed.). Boston: Allyn and Bacon.

Johnson, S. B. (1984). *Test of Diabetes Knowledge Revised—2.* Gainsville: University of Florida, Department of Psychiatry.

Johnson, S. B. (1988). Chronic illness and pain. In E. J. Mash & L. G. Terdal (Eds.), *Behavioral assessment of childhood disorders,* 2nd ed. New York: Guilford.

Johnson, S. B. (1993). Chronic diseases of childhood: Assessing compliance with complex medical regimens. In N. A. Krasnegor, L. Epstein, S. B. Johnson, & S. Yaffe (Eds.), *Developmental aspects of health compliance behavior.* Hillsdale, NJ: Lawrence Earlbaum Associates.

Johnson, S. B. (1995). Managing insulin-dependent diabetes mellitus in adolescence: A developmental perspective. In J. Wallander & L. Siegel (Eds.), *Adolescent health problems: Behavioral perspectives.* New York: Guilford Press.

Johnson, S. B. (1998). Juvenile diabetes. In T. H. Ollendick & M. Hersen (Eds.), *Handbook of child psychopathology* (3rd ed.). New York: Plenum Press.

Johnson, S. B., & Rodrigue, J. R. (1997). Health-related disorders. In E. J. Mash & L. G. Terdal (Eds.), *Assessment of childhood disorders* (3rd ed.). New York: Guilford Press.

Johnson, S. B., Silverstein, J., Rosenbloom, A., Carter, R., & Cunningham, W. (1986). Assessing daily management in childhood diabetes. *Health Psychology, 5,* 545–564.

Johnson-Martin, N., Jens, K., Attermeier, S., & Hacker, B. (1990). *The Carolina Curriculum for Preschoolers with Special Needs.* Baltimore: Paul H. Brookes.

Johnston, C., & Ohan, J. L. (1999). Externalizing disorders. In W. K. Silverman & T. H. Ollendick (Eds.), *Developmental issues in the clinical treatment of children.* Boston: Allyn and Bacon.

Johnston, H. F., & Fruehling, J. J. (1994). Pharmacotherapy for depression in children and adolescents. In W. M. Reynolds and H. F. Johnston (Eds.), *Handbook of depression in children and adolescents.* New York: Plenum Press.

Joliffe, T., & Baron-Cohen, S. (1997). Are people with autism and Asperger syndrome faster than normal on the Embedded Figures Test? *Journal of Child Psychology and Psychiatry, 38,* 527–534.

Jones, M. C. (1924). A laboratory study of fear: The case of Peter, *Pedagogical Seminary, 31,* 308–315.

Jouriles, E. N., Murphy, C. M., & O'Leary, K. D. (1989). Interspousal aggression, marital discord, and child problems. *Journal of Consulting and Clinical Psychology, 57,* 453–455.

Joyce, K., Singer, M., & Isralowitz, R. (1983). Impact of respite care on parents' perceptions of quality of life. *Mental Retardation, 21,* 153–156.

Kaffman, K., & Elizur, E. (1977). Infants who become enuretics: A longitudinal study of 161 Kibbutz children. *Monographs of the Society for Research in Child Development, 42,* (4,Serial No. 170).

Kagan, J. (1997). Temperament and the reactions to unfamiliarity. *Child Development, 68,* 139–143.

Kagan, J., Arcus, D., & Snidman, N. (1993). The idea of temperament: Where do we go from here? In R. Plomin & G. E. McClearn (Eds.), *Nature, nurture & psychology.* Washington, DC: American Psychological Association.

Kagan, J., Reznick, J. S., & Snidman, N. (1990). The temperamental qualities of inhibition and lack of inhibition. In M. Lewis & S. M. Miller (Eds.), *Handbook of developmental psychopathology.* New York: Plenum Press.

Kalnins, I. V., Churchill, M. P., & Terry, G. E. (1980). Concurrent stresses in families with a leukemic child. *Journal of Pediatric Psychology, 5,* 81–92.

Kamin, L. J. (1974). *The science and politics of IQ.* Potomac, MD: Erlbaum

Kamphaus, R. W. (1993). *Clinical assessment of children's intelligence.* Boston: Allyn & Bacon.

Kamphaus, R. W., & Frick, P. J. (1996). *Clinical assessment of child and adolescent personality and behavior.* Boston: Allyn and bacon.

Kandel, D. B. (1982). Epidemiological and psychosocial perspectives on adolescent drug use. *Journal of the American Academy of Child Psychiatry, 21,* 328–347.

Kandel, D., & Yamaguchi, K. (1993). From beer to crack: Developmental patterns of drug involvement. *American Journal of Public Health, 83,* 851–855.

Kanfer, F. H., Karoly, P., & Newman, A. (1975). Reduction of children's fear of the dark by competence-related and situational threat-related verbal cues. *Journal of Consulting and Clinical Psychology, 43,* 251–258.

Kanner, L. (1943). Autistic disturbances of affective contact, *Nervous Child, 2,* 217–250.

Kanner, L. (1972). *Child psychiatry,* 4th ed. Springfield, IL: Chas. C. Thomas.

Kanner, L. (1973). *Childhood psychoses: Initial studies and new insights.* Washington, DC: V. H. Winston & Sons.

Kanner, L., & Eisenberg, L. (1956). Early infantile autism, 1943–1955. *American Journal of Orthopsychiatry, 26,* 55–65.

Kaplan, R. M. (1985). The controversy related to the use of psychological tests. In B. Wolman (Ed.), *Handbook of intelligence.* New York: Wiley.

Karoly, P., & Bay, R. C. (1990). Diabetes self-care goals and their relation to children's metabolic control. *Journal of Pediatric Psychology, 15,* 83–95.

Kashani, J. H., Daniel, A. E., Dandoy, A. C., & Holcomb, W. R. (1992). Family violence: Impact on children. *Journal of the American Academy of Child and Adolescent Psychiatry, 31,* 181–189.

Kashani, J. H., & Orvaschel, H. (1990). A community study of anxiety in children and adolescents. *American Journal of Psychiatry, 147,* 313–318.

Kaslow, N. J., Brown, R. T., & Mee, L. (1994). Cognitive and behavioral correlates of childhood depression: A developmental perspective. In W. M. Reynolds and H. F. Johnston (Eds.), *Handbook of depression in children and adolescents.* New York: Plenum Press.

Kaslow, N. J., Deering, C. G., & Racusin, G. R. (1994). Depressed children and their families. *Clinical Psychology Review, 14,* 39–59.

Kaslow, N. J., & Racusin, G. R. (1990). Childhood depression: Current status and future directions. In A. S. Bellack, M. Hersen, & A. E. Kazdin (Eds.), *International handbook of behavior modification and therapy,* 2nd ed. New York: Plenum.

Kaslow, N. J., Rehm, L. P., & Siegel, A. W. (1984). Social-cognitive and cognitive correlates of depression in children. *Journal of Abnormal Child Psychology, 12,* 605–620.

Kaslow, N. J., & Thompson, M. P. (1998). Applying the criteria for empirically supported treatments to studies of psychosocial interventions for child and adolescent depression. *Journal of Clinical Child Psychology, 27,* 146–155.

Kassebaum, N. L. (1994). Head Start: Only the best for America's childrens. *American Psychologist, 49,* 123–126.

Kataria, S., Swanson, M. S., & Trevathon, G. E. (1987). Persistence of sleep disturbances in preschool children. *Behavioral Pediatrics, 110,* 642–646.

Katz, L. J., & Slomka, G. T. (1990). Achievement Testing. In G. Goldstein & M. Hersen (Eds.), *Handbook of psychological assessment.* 2nd ed. New York: Pergamon.

Kauffman, J. M., Gerber, M. M., & Semmel, M. I. (1988). Arguable assumptions underlying the regular education initiative. *Journal of Learning Disabilities, 21,* 6–11.

Kaufman, A. S., & Kaufman, N. L. (1983). *Administration and scoring manual for the Kaufman Assessment Battery for Children.* Circle Pines, MN: American Guidance Service.

Kaufman, A. S., & Kaufman, N. L. (1993). Kaufman Adolescent and Adult Intelligence Test: Manual. Circle Pines, MN: American Guidance Service.

Kaufman, J., Birmaher, B., Brent, D., Rao, U., Flynn, C., Moreci, P., Williamson, D., & Ryan N. (1997). Schedule for Affective Disorders and Schizophrenia for School-age Children–Present and Lifetime Version (K-SDAS-PL): Initial reliability and validity data. *Journal of the American Academy of Child and Adolescent Psychiatry, 36,* 980–988.

Kaufman, J., & Zigler, E. (1987). Do abused children become abusive parents? *American Journal of Orthopsychiatry, 57,* 186–192.

Kaye, W. H. (1995). Neurotransmitters and anorexia nervosa. In K. D. Brownell & C. G. Fairburn (Eds.), *Eating disorders and obesity: A comprehensive handbook.* New York: Guilford Press.

Kaye, W. H., & Weltzin, T. E. (1991). Neurochemistry of bulimia nervosa. *Journal of Clinical Psychiatry, 52,* 617–622.

Kazak, A. E., Biancamaria, P. Boyer, B. A., Himelstein, B., Brophy, P., Waibel, M. K., Blackall, G. F., Daller, R., & Johnson, K. (1996). A randomized controlled prospective outcome study of a psychological and pharmacological intervention protocol for procedural distress in pediatric leukemia. *Journal of Pediatric Psychology, 21,* 615–631.

Kazdin, A. E. (1985). *Treatment of antisocial behavior in children and adolescents.* Homewood, IL: Dorsey.

Kazdin, A. E. (1987). Treatment of antisocial behavior in children: Current status and future directions. *Psychological Bulletin, 102,* 187–203.

Kazdin, A. E. (1989a). Conduct and oppositional disorders. In C. G. Last & M. Hersen (Eds.), *Handbook of psychiatric diagnosis.* New York: Wiley.

Kazdin, A. E. (1989b). Identifying depression in children: A comparison of alternative selection criteria. *Journal of Abnormal Child Psychology, 17,* 437–454.

Kazdin, A. E. (1993a). Adolescent mental health. Prevention and treatment programs. *American Psychologist, 48,* 127–141.

Kazdin, A. E. (1993b). Psychotherapy for children and adolescents. Current progress and future research directions. *American Psychologist, 48,* 644–657.

Kazdin, A. E. (1993c). Treatment of conduct disorder: Progress and directions in psychotherapy research. *Development and Psychopathology, 5,* 277–310.

Kazdin, A. E. (1994). Informant variability in the assessment of childhood depression. In W. M. Reynolds and H. F. Johnston (Eds.), *Handbook of depression in children and adolescents.* New York: Plenum Press.

Kazdin, A. E. (1995a). *Conduct disorders in childhood and adolescence* (2nd ed.). Thousand Oaks, CA: Sage.

Kazdin, A. E. (1995b). Child, parent, and family dysfunction as predictors of outcome in cognitive-behavioral treatment of antisocial children. *Behaviour Research and Therapy, 33,* 271–281.

Kazdin, A. E. (1997). Practitioner review: Psychosocial treatments for conduct disorder in children. *Journal of Child Psychology and Psychiatry, 38,* 161–178.

Kazdin, A. E., Esveldt-Dawson, K., Sherick, R. B., & Colbus, D. (1985). Assessment of overt behavior and childhood depression among psychiatrically disturbed children. *Journal of Consulting and Clinical Psychology, 53,* 201–210.

Kazdin, A. E., Holland, L., Crowley, M. & Breton, S. (1997). Barriers to Treatment Participation Scale: Evaluation and validation in the context of child outpatient treatment. *Journal of Child Psychology and Psychiatry, 38,* 1051–1062.

Kazdin, A. E., Kolko, D. J. (1986). Parent psychopathology and family functioning among childhood firesetters. *Journal of Abnormal Child Psychology, 14,* 315–329.

Kazdin, A. E., & Marciano, P. L. (1998). Childhood and adolescent depression. In E. J. Mash & R. A. Barkley (Eds.), *Treatment of childhood disorders* (2nd ed.). New York: Guilford Press.

Kazdin, A. E., Rodgers, A., & Colbus, D. (1986). The Hopelessnes Scale for Children: Psychometric characteristics and concurrent validity. *Journal of Consulting and Clinical Psychology, 54,* 241–245.

Kazdin, A. E., Siegel, T. C., & Bass, D. (1992). Cognitive problem-solving skills training and parent management training in the treatment of antisocial behavior in children. *Journal of Consulting and Clinical Psychology, 60,* 733–747.

Kearney, C. A., Albano, A. M., Eisen, A. R., Allan, W. D., & Barlow, D. H. (1997). The phenomenology of panic disorder in youngsters: An empirical study of a clinical sample. *Journal of Anxiety Disorders, 11,* 49–62.

Kearney, C. A., Eisen, A., & Silverman, W. K. (1995). The legend and myth of school phobia. *School Psychology Quarterly, 10,* 65–85.

Kearney, C. A., & Silverman, W. K. (1992). Let's not push the "panic button": A critical analysis of panic and panic disorder in adolescents. *Clinical Psychology Review, 12,* 293–305.

Kearney, C. A., & Silverman, W. K. (1996). The Evolution and reconciliation of taxonomic strategies for school refusal behavior. *Clinical Psychology: Science and Practice, 3,* 339–354.

Kearney, C. A., & Silverman, W. K. (1998). A critical review of pharmacotherapy for youth with anxiety disorders: Things are not as they seem. *Journal of Anxiety Disorders, 12,* 83–102.

Keenan, K., Loeber, R., Zhang, Q., Stouthamer-Loeber, M., & Van Kammen, W. (1995). The influence of deviant peers on the development of boys' disruptive and delinquent behavior: A temporal analysis. *Development and Psychopathology, 7,* 715–726.

Keenan, K., & Shaw, D. (1997). Developmental and social influences on young girls' early problem behavior. *Psychological Bulletin, 121,* 95–113.

Kell, R. S., Kliewer, W., Erickson, M. T., & Ohene-Frempong, K. (1998). Psychological adjustment of adolescents with sickle cell disease: Relations with demographic, medical, and family competence variables. *Journal of Pediatric Psychology, 23,* 301–312.

Keller, M. B., Lavori, P. W., Wunder, J., Beardslee, W. R., Schwartz, C. E., & Roth, J. (1992). Chronic course of anxiety disorders in children and adolescents. Journal of the *American Academy of Child and Adolescent Psychiatry, 31,* 595–599.

Kellerman, J. (1980). Rapid treatment of nocturnal anxiety in children. *Journal of Behavior Therapy and Experimental Psychiatry, 11,* 9–11.

Kelly, M. L., & Heffer, R. W. (1990). Eating disorders: Food refusal and failure to thrive. In A. M. Gross & R. S. Drabman (Eds.), *Handbook of clinical behavioral pediatrics.* New York: Plenum.

Kelly, S. J., Brant, R., & Waterman, J. (1993). Sexual abuse of children in day care centers. *Child Abuse & Neglect, 17,* 71–89.

Kempe, C. H., Silverman, F. N., Steele, B. B., Droegemueller, W., & Silver, H. K. (1962). The battered child syndrome. *Journal of the American Medical Association, 181,* 17–24.

Kemph, J. P. (1987). Hallucinations in psychotic children. *Journal of the American Academy of Child and Adolescent Psychiatry, 26,* 556–559.

Kendall, P. C. (1991). Guiding theory for therapy with children and adolescents. In P. C. Kendall (Ed.), *Child and adolescent therapy: Cognitive-behavioral procedures.* New York: Guilford.

Kendall, P. C. (1993). Cognitive-behavioral therapies with youth: Guiding theory, current status, and emerging developments. *Journal of Consulting and Clinical Psychology, 61,* 235–247.

Kendall, P. C. (1994). Treating anxiety disorders in children: Results of a randomized clinical trial. *Journal of Consulting and Clinical Psychology, 62,* 100–110.

Kendall, P. C., & Panichelli-Mindel, S. M. (1995). Cognitive-behavioral treatments. *Journal of Abnormal Child Psychology, 23,* 107–124.

Kendall, P. C., Panichelli-Mindel, S. M., Sugarman, A., & Callahan, S. A. (1997). Exposure to child anxiety: Theory, research, and practice. *Clinical Psychology: Science and Practice, 4,* 29–39.

Kendall, P. C., & Southam-Gerow, M. A. (1996). Long-term follow-up of a cognitive-behavioral therapy for anxiety-disordered youth. *Journal of Consulting and Clinical Psychology, 64,* 724–730.

Kendall, P. C., Stark, K. D., & Adams, T. (1990). Cognitive deficit or cognitive distortion in childhood depression. *Journal of Abnormal Child Psychology, 18,* 255–270.

Kendler, K. S., Neale, M. C., Kessler, R. C., Heath, A. C., & Eaves, L. J. (1992a). A population-based twin study of major depression in women: The impact of varying definitions of illness. *Archives of General Psychiatry, 49,* 257–266.

Kendler, K. S., Neale, M. C., Kessler, R. C., Heath, A. C., & Eaves, L. J. (1992b). The genetic epidemiology of phobias in women: The interrelationship of agoraphobia, social phobia, situational phobia, and simple phobia. *Archives of General Psychiatry, 49,* 273–281.

Kendler, K. S., Walters, E. E., Neale, M. C., Kessler, R. C., Heath, A. C., & Eaves, L. J. (1995). The structure of the genetic and environmental risk factors for six major psychiatric disorders in women. *Archives of General Psychiatry, 52,* 374–383.

Kennedy, W. A. (1965). School phobia: Rapid treatment of 50 cases. *Journal of Abnormal Psychology, 70,* 285–289.

Keogh, B. (1988). Improving services for problem learners: Rethinking and restructuring. *Journal of Learning Disabilities, 21,* 19–22.

Kerns, K. A., Klepac, L., & Cole, A. K. (1996). Peer relationships and preadolescents' perceptions of security in the child-mother relationship. *Developmental Psychology, 32,* 457–466.

Kerr, M., Lambert, W. W., Stattin, H., & Klackenberg-Larsson, I. (1994). Stability of inhibition in a Swedish longitudinal sample. *Child Development, 65,* 138–146.

Kerr, M., Tremblay, R. E., Pagani, L., & Vitaro, F. (1997). Boys' behavioral inhibition and the risk of later delinquency. *Archives of General Psychiatry, 54,* 809–816.

Kerwin, M. E., & Berkowitz, R. I. (1996). Feeding and eating disorders: Ingestive problems of infancy, childhood, and adolescence. *School Psychology Review, 25,* 316–328.

Kessler, J. W. (1966, 1988). *Psychopathology of childhood.* Englewood Cliffs, NJ: Prentice Hall.

Kiernan, C. (1985). Behaviour modification. In A. M. Clarke, A. D. B. Clarke, & J. M. Berg (Eds.), *Mental deficiency. The changing outlook.* New York: The Free Press.

Killen, J. D., Hayward, C., Wilson, D. M., Taylor, C. B., Hammer, L. D., Litt, I., Simmonds, B., & Haydel, F. (1994a). Factors associated with eating disorder symptoms in a community sample of 6th and 7th grade girls. *International Journal of Eating Disorders, 15,* 357–367.

Killen, J. D., Taylor, B., Hayward, C., Haydel, K. F., Wilson, D. M., Hammer, L., Kraemer, H., Blair-Greiner, A., & Strachowski, D. (1996). Weight concerns influence the development of eating disorders: A 4-year prospective study. *Journal of Consulting and Clinical Psychology, 64,* 936–940.

Killen, J. D., Taylor, C. B., Hayward, C., Wilson, D. M., Haydel, K. F., Hammer, L. D., Simmonds, B., Robinson, T. N., Litt, I., Varady, A., & Kraemer, H. (1994b). Pursuit of thinness and onset of eating disorder symptoms in a community sample of adolescent girls: A three-year prospective analysis. *International Journal of Eating Disorders, 16,* 227–238.

King, B. H., State, M. W., Shah, B., Davanzo, P., & Dykens, E. (1997). Mental Retardation: A review of the past 10 years. Part I. *Journal of the American Academy of Child and Adolescent Psychiatry, 36,* 1656–1663.

King, N. (1994). Physiological assessment. In T. H. Ollendick, N. J. King, & W. Yule (Eds.), *International handbook of phobic and anxiety disorders in children and adolescents* (pp. 365–396). New York: Plenum Press.

King, N. J. (1993). Simple and social phobias. In T. H. Ollendick & R. J. Prinz (Eds.), *Advances in clinical child psychology,* Vol. 15. (pp. 305–341). New York: Plenum Press.

King, N. J., Clowes-Hollins, V., & Ollendick, T. H. (1997). The etiology of childhood dog phobia. *Behaviour Research and Therapy, 35,* 77.

King, N. J., Mietz, L. T., & Ollendick, T. H. (1995). Psychopathology and cognition in adolescents experiencing severe test anxiety. *Journal of Clinical Child Psychology, 24,* 49–54.

King, N. J., & Ollendick, T. H. (1997). Treatment of childhood phobias. *Journal of Child Psychology and Psychiatry, 38,* 389–400.

King N. J., Ollendick, T. H., & Gullone, E. (1990). School-related fears of children and adolescents. *Australian Journal of Education, 34,* 99–112

King, N. J., Ollendick, T. H., Mattis, S. G., Yang, B., & Tonge, B. (1997). Nonclinical panic attacks in adolescents: Prevalence, symptomatology, and associated features. *Behaviour Change, 13,* 171–183.

King, N. J., Ollier, K., Iacuone, R., Schuster, S., Bays, K., Gullone, E., & Ollendick, T. H. (1989). Fears of children and adolescents: A cross-sectional Australian study using the Revised-Fear Survey Schedule for Children. *Journal of Child Psychology and Psychiatry, 30,* 775–784.

King, R. A., & Noshpitz, J. D. (1991). *Pathways of growth: Essentials of child psychiatry,* Vol. 2. New York: John Wiley & Sons.

King, R. A., Pfeffer, C., Gammon, G. D., & Cohen, D. J. (1992). Suicidality of childhood and adolescence: Review of the literature and proposal for establishment of a DSM-IV category. In B. B. Lahey & A. E. Kazdin (Eds.), *Advances in clinical child psychology,* Vol. 14, New York: Plenum.

Kirby, F. D., & Toler, H. C. (1970). Modification of preschool isolate behavior: A case study. *Journal of Applied Behavior Analysis, 3,* 309–314.

Kirigin, K. A., Braukmann, C. J., Atwater, J. D., & Wolf, M. M. (1982). An evaluation of Teaching-Family (Achievement Place) group homes for juvenile offenders. *Journal of Applied Behavior Analysis, 15,* 1–16.

Kirk, S. A., & Gallagher, J. J. (1989). *Educating exceptional children.* Boston: Houghton Mifflin.

Kirkpatrick, D. R. (1984). Age, gender, and patterns of common intense fears among adults. *Behaviour Research and Therapy, 22,* 141–150.

Klein, D. F., Mannuzza, S., Chapman, T., & Fyer, A. (1992). Child panic revised. *Journal of the American Academy of Child and Adolescent Psychiatry, 31,* 112–113.

Klein, D. N. Riso, L. P., Donaldson, S. K. Shwartz, J. E., Anderson, R. L., Ouimette, P. C., Lizardi, H., & Aronson, T. A. (1995). Family study of early-onset dysthymia: Mood and personality disorders in relatives of outpatients with dysthymia and episodic major depression and normal controls. *Archives of General Psychiatry, 52,* 487–496.

Klein, M. (1932). *The psycho-analysis of children.* London: Hogarth Press.

Klein, N. C., Alexander, J. F., & Parsons, B. V. (1977). Impact of family systems intervention on recidivism and sibling delinquency: A model of primary prevention and program evaluation. *Journal of Consulting and Clinical Psychology, 45,* 469–474.

Klesges, R. C., & Hanson, C. L. (1988). Determining the environmental causes and correlates of childhood obesity: methodological issues and future research directions. In N. A. Krasnegor, G. D. Grave, & N. Kretchmer (Eds.), *Childhood obesity: A biobehavioral perspective.* Caldwell, NJ: The Telford Press.

Kliewer, C., & Biklen, D. (1996). Labeling: Who wants to be called retarded? In W. Stainback & S. Stainback (Eds.), *Controversial issues confronting special education: Divergent perspectives* (2nd ed.). Boston: Allyn and Bacon.

Klin, A., & Cohen, D. J. (1997). Ethical issues in research and treatment. In D. J. Cohen & F. R. Volkmar (Eds.), *Handbook of autism and pervasive developmental disorders.* New York: John Wiley.

Klinger, L. G., & Dawson, G. (1996). Autistic disorder. In E. J. Mash & R. A. Barkley (Eds.), *Child psychopathology.* New York: Guilford Press.

Klinnert, M. D., Mrazek, P. J., & Mrazek, D. A. (1994). Early asthma onset: The interaction between family stressors and adaptive parenting. *Psychiatry: Interpersonal and Biological Processes, 57,* 51–61.

Knitzer, J. (1982). *Unclaimed children: The failure of public responsibility to children and adolescents in need of mental health services.* Washington, DC: Children's Defense Fund.

Knoff, H. M. (1998). Review of the Children's Apperception Test (1991 Revision). In J. C. Impara & B. S. Plake (Eds.), *The thirteenth mental measurement yearbook.* Lincoln: The University of Nebraska–Lincoln.

Koegel, R. L., Camarata, S., Koegel, L. K., Ban-Tall, A., & Smith, A. E. (1998). Increasing speech intelligibility in children with autism. *Journal of Autism and Developmental Disorders, 28,* 241–251.

Koegel, R. L., O'Dell, M. C., & Koegel, L. K. (1987). A natural language teaching paradigm for nonverbal autistic children. *Journal of Autism and Developmental Disorders, 17,* 187–200.

Kog, E., & Vandereycken, W. (1985). Family charcteristics of anorexia nervosa and bulimia: A review of the research literature. *Clinical Psychology Review, 5,* 159–180.

Kolko, D. (1987). Simplified inpatient treatment of nocturnal enuresis in psychiatrically disturbed children. *Behavior Therapy, 18,* 99–112.

Kolko, D. J. (1985). Juvenile firesetting: A review and methodological critique. *Clinical Psychology Review, 5,* 345–376.

Kolko, D. J. (1989). Fire setting and pyromania. In C. Last & M. Hersen (Eds.), *Handbook of child psychiatric diagnosis.* New York: Wiley.

Kolko, D. J., & Kazdin, A. E. (1986). A conceptualization of firesetting in children and adolescents. *Journal of Abnormal Child Psychology, 14,* 49–61.

Kolko, D. J., Kazdin, A. E., & Meyer, E. C. (1985). Aggression and psychopathology in childhood firesetters: Parent and child reports. *Journal of Consulting and Clinical Psychology, 53,* 377–385.

Kolmen, B. K., Feldman, H. M., Handen, B. L., & Janosky, J. E. (1997). Naltrexone in young autistic children: Replication study and learning measures. *Journal of the American Academy of Child and Adolescent Psychiatry, 36,* 1570–1578.

Kolmen, B. K., Feldman, H. M., Handen, B. L., & Janosky, J. E. (1998). Letters to the editor: Naltrexone in children with autism. *Journal of the American Academy of Child and Adolescent Psychiatry, 37,* 801–802.

Kolvin, I. (1971). Psychoses in childhood—a comparative study. In M. Rutter (Ed.), *Infantile autism: Concepts, characteristics, and treatments.* London: Churchill-Livingstone.

Konidaris, J. B. (1997). A sibling's perspective on autism. In D. J. Cohen & F. R. Volkmar (Eds.), *Handbook of autism and developmental disorders.* New York: John Wiley.

Koocher, G. P. (1980). Pediatric cancer: Psychosocial problems and the high costs of helping. *Journal of Clinical Child Psychology, 9,* 2–5.

Koocher, G. P., & Sallan, S. E. (1978). Pediatric oncology. In P. R. Magrab (Ed.), *Psychological management of pediatric problems,* Vol. 1. Baltimore: University Park Press.

Kopp, C. B. (1994). Trends and directions in studies of developmental risk. In C. A. Nelson (Ed.), *Threats to optimal development: Integrating biological, psychological, and social risk factors. The Minnesota symposium on child psychology. Vol. 27.* Hillsdale, NJ: Erlbaum.

Kopp, C. B., & Kaler, S. R. (1989). Risk in infancy: Origins and implications. *American Psychologist, 44,* 224–230.

Koppitz, E. M. (1984). *Psychological evaluation of human figure drawings by middle school pupils.* Orlando, FL: Grune & Stratton.

Korbin, J. E., Coulton, C. J., Chard, S., Platt-Houston, C., & Su, M. (1998). Impoverishment and child maltreatment in African American and European American neighborhoods. *Development and Psychopathology, 10,* 215–233.

Kotses, H., Glaus, K. D., Crawford, P. L., Edwards, J. E., & Scherr, M. S. (1976). Operant reduction of frontalis EMG activity in the treatment of asthma in children. *Journal of Psychosomatic Research, 10,* 453–459.

Kovacs, M. (1992). *Children's Depression Inventory.* North Tonawanda, NY: Multi-Health Systems.

Kovacs, M. (1996). Presentation and course of Major Depressive Disorder during childhood and later years of the life span. *Journal of the American Academy of Child and Adolescent Psychiatry, 35,* 705–715.

Kovacs, M. (1997). Depressive disorders in childhood: An impressionistic landscape. *Journal of Child Psychology and Psychiatry, 38,* 287–298.

Kovacs, M., Devlin, B., Pollack, M., Richards, C., & Mukerji, P. (1997). A controlled family history study of childhood-onset depressive disorder. *Archives of General Psychiatry, 54,* 613–623.

Kovacs, M., Feinberg, T. L., Crouse-Novak, M. A., Paulauskas, S. L., & Finkelstein, R. (1984). Depressive disorders in childhood: I. A longitudinal prospective study of characteristics and recovery. *Archives of General Psychiatry, 41,* 229–237.

Kovacs, M., & Gatsonis, C. (1994). Secular trends in age of onset of major depressive disorder in a clinical sample of children. *Journal of Psychiatric Research, 28,* 319–329.

Kovacs, M., Goldston, D., & Gatsonis, C. (1993). Suicidal behaviors and childhood-onset depressive disorders: A longitudinal investigation. *Journal of the American Academy of Child and Adolescent Psychiatry, 32,* 8–20.

Kraemer, S. (1987). Working with parents: Casework or psychotherapy? *Journal of Child Psychology and Psychiatry, 28,* 207–213.

Krahn, G. L., Hohn, M. F., & Kime, C. (1995). Incorporating qualitative approaches into clinical child psychology research. *Journal of Clinical Child Psychology, 24,* 204–213.

Krasnegor, N. A., Epstein, L., Johnson, S. B., & Yaffe, S. J. (1993). (Eds.) *Developmental aspects of health compliance behavior.* Hillsdale, NJ: Lawrence Earlbaum Associates.

Krasnegor, N. A., Grave, G. D., & Kretchmer, N. (Eds.) (1988). *Childhood obesity: A biobehavioral perspective.* Caldwell, NJ: The Telford Press.

Kratochwill, T. R., & Levin, J. R. (1992). *Single-case research design and analysis.* Hillsdale, NJ: Lawrence Erlbaum.

Krausz, M., & Muller-Thomsen, T. (1993). Schizophrenia with onset in adolescence: An 11-year followup. *Schizophrenia Bulletin, 19,* 831–841.

Krug, D. A., Arick, J., & Almond, P. (1978). *Autism Screening Instrument For Educational Planning.* Portland, OR: ASIEP Education.

Krugman, R. D. (1993). Universal home visiting: A recommendation from the U.S. Advisory Board on Child Abuse and Neglect. *The Future of Children, 3 (3),* 184–191.

Kuhn, T. S. (1962). *The structure of scientific revolutions.* Chicago: University of Chicago Press.

Kuhnley, E. J., Hendren, R. L., & Quinlan, D. M. (1982). Firesetting by children. *Journal of the American Academy of Child Psychiatry, 21,* 560–563.

Kumra, S., Herion, D., Jacobsen, L. K., Briguglia, S., & Grothe, D. (1997). Case study: Risperidone-induced hepatotoxicity in pediatric patients. *Journal of the American Academy of Child and Adolescent Psychiatry, 36,* 701–705.

Kumra, S., Jacobsen, L. K., Lenane, M., Smith, A., Lee, P., Malanga, C. J., Karp, B. I., Hamburger, S., & Rapoport, J. L. (1998). Case series: Spectrum of neuroleptic-induced movement disorders and extrapyramidal side effects in childhood-onset schizophrenia. *Journal of the American Academy of Child and Adolescent Psychiatry, 37,* 221–227.

Kuperman, S., Gaffney, G. R., Hamdan-Allen, G., Preston, D. F., & Venkatesh, L. (1990). Neuroimaging in child and adolescent psychiatry. *Journal of the American Academy of Child and Adolescent Psychiatry, 19,* 159–172.

Kupersmidt, J. B., & Patterson, C. J. (1991). Childhood peer rejection, aggression, withdrawal, and perceived competence as predictors of self-reported behavior problems in preadolescence. *Journal of Abnormal Child Psychology, 19,* 427–449.

Kupfer, D. J., & Reynolds, C. F. (1992). Sleep and affective disorders. In E. S. Paykel (Ed.), *Handbook of affective disorders* (2nd ed.). New York: Guilford Press.

Kvernmo, S., & Heyerdahl, S. (1998). Influence of ethnic factors on behavior problems in indigenous Sami and majority Norwegian adolescents. *Journal of the American Academy of Child and Adolescent Psychiatry, 37,* 743–751.

Labbé, E. E., (1998). Pediatric headache. In T. H. Ollendick & M. Hersen (Eds.), *Handbook of child psychopathology* (3rd ed.). New York: Plenum Press.

Ladd, G. (1981). Social skills and peer acceptance: Effects of a social learning method for training verbal social skills. *Child Development, 52,* 171–178.

LaGreca, A. M. (1987). Diabetes in adolescence: Issues in coping and management. *Newsletter of the Society of Pediatric Psychology, 11,* 13–18.

LaGreca, A. M. (1993). Social skills training with children: Where do we go from here. *Journal of Clinical Child Psychology, 22,* 288–298.

LaGreca, A., & Santogrossi, D. (1980). Social skills training with elementary school students: A behavioral group approach. *Journal of Consulting and Clinical Psychology, 48,* 220–228.

LaGreca, A. M., Siegel, L. J., Wallander, J. L., & Walker, C. E. (Eds.). (1992). *Stress and coping in child health.* New York: Guilford.

LaGreca, A. M., Silverman, W. K., Vernberg, E. M., & Prinstein, M. J. (1996). Symptoms of posttraumatic stress in children after Hurricane Andrew: A prospective study. *Journal of Consulting and Clinical Psychology, 64,* 712–723.

LaGreca, A. M., Silverman, W. K., & Wasserstein, S. B. (1998). Children's predisaster functioning as a predictor of posttraumatic stress following Hurricane Andres. *Journal of Consulting and Clinical Psychology, 66,* 883–892.

LaGreca, A. M., & Stone, W. L. (1993). Social anxiety scale for children-revised: Factor structure and concurrent validity. *Journal of Clinical Child Psychology, 22,* 17–27.

Lahey, B. B., Applegate, B., McBurnett, K., Biederman, J., Greenhill, L., Hynd, G. W., Barkley, R. A., Newcorn, J., Jensen, P., Richters, J., Garfinkel, B., Kerdyk, L., Frick, P. J., Ollendick, T., Perez, D., Hart, E. L., Waldman, I., & Shaffer, D. (1994). DSM-IV field trials for attention deficit hyperactivity disorder in children and adolescents. *American Journal of Psychiatry, 151,* 1673–1685.

Lahey, B. B., & Carlson, C. L. (1991). Validity of the diagnostic category of attention deficit disorder without hyperactivity: A review of the literature. *Journal of Learning Disabilities, 24,* 110–120.

Lahey, B. B., Hartdagen, S. E., Frick, P. J., McBurnett, K., Conner, R., & Hynd, G. W. (1988). Psychopathology and antisocial behavior in the parents of children with conduct disorder and hyperactivity. *Jour-*

nal of the American Academy of Child and Adolescent Psychiatry, 29, 620–626.

Lahey, B. B., Pelham, W. E., Stein, M. A., Loney, J., Trapani, C., Nugent, K., Kipp, H., Schmidt, E., Lee, S., Cale, M., Gold, E., Hartung, C. M., Willcutt, E., & Baumann, B. (1998). Validity of DSM-IV Attention-deficit/Hyperactivity Disorder for younger children. *Journal of the American Academy of Child and Adolescent Psychiatry, 37,* 695–702.

Lainhart, J. E., Piven, J., Wzorek, M., Landa, R., Santangelo, S. L., Coon, H., & Folstein, S. E. (1997). Macrocephaly in children and adults with autism. *Journal of the American Academy of Child and Adolescent Psychiatry, 36,* 282–290.

Lambert, N. M. (1988). Adolescent outcomes for hyperactive children: Perspectives on general and specific patterns of childhood risk for adolescent educational, social, and mental health problems. *American Psychologist, 43,* 786–799.

Lambert, N., Leland, H., & Nihara, K. (1993). *AAMR Adaptive Behavior Scales–School.* Austin, TX: PRO-ED.

Landesman, S. (1990). Institutionalization revisited: Expanding views on early and cumulative life experiences. In M. Lewis & S. M. Miller (Eds.), *Handbook of developmental psychopathology.* New York: Plenum.

Landry, S. H., & Chapieski, M. L. (1989). Joint attention and infant toy exploration: Effects of Down Syndrome and prematurity. *Child Development, 60,* 103–118.

Landsman, M. S. (1994). Comment. Needed: Metaphors for the prevention model of mental health. *American Psychologist, 49,* 1086–1087.

Lang, P. J. (1984). Cognition in emotion: Concept and action. In C. E. Izard, J. Kagan, R. B. Zajonc (Eds.), *Emotions, cognition, and behavior.* New York. Cambridge University Press.

Langer, D. H. (1985). Children's legal rights as research subjects. *Journal of the American Academy of Child Psychiatry, 24,* 653–662.

Lapouse, R., & Monk, M. (1958). An epidemiologic study of behavior characteristics in children. *American Journal of Public Health, 48,* 1134–1144.

Lapouse, R., & Monk, M. A. (1959). Fears and worries in a representative sample of children. *American Journal of Orthopsychiatry, 29,* 803–818.

Lask, B. & Bryant-Waugh, R. (1992). Early-onset anorexia nervosa and related eating disorders. *Journal of Child Psychology and Psychiatry, 33,* 281–300.

Last, C. G. (1988). Separation anxiety. In M. Hersen & C. G. Last (Eds.), *Child behavior therapy casebook.* New York: Plenum Press.

Last, C. G., Hersen, M., Kazdin, A. E., Orvaschel, H., & Perrin, S. (1991). Anxiety disorders in children and their families. *Archives of General Psychiatry, 48,* 928–934.

Last, C. G., Perrin, S., Hersen, M., & Kazdin, A. E. (1992). DSM-III-R anxiety disorders in children: So-

ciodemographic and clinical characteristics. *Journal of the American Academy of Child and Adolescent Psychiatry, 31,* 1070–1076.

Last, C. G., Perrin, S., Hersen, M., & Kazdin, A. E. (1996). A prospective study of childhood anxiety disorders. *Journal of the American Academy of Child and Adolescent Psychiatry, 35,* 1502–1510.

Last, C. G., & Strauss, C. C. (1989). Panic disorder in children and adolescents. *Journal of Anxiety Disorders, 3,* 87–95.

Last, C. G., & Strauss, C. C. (1990). School refusal in anxiety-disordered children and adolescents. *Journal of the American Academy of Child and Adolescent Psychiatry, 29,* 31–35.

Last, C. G., Strauss, C. C., & Francis, G. (1987). Comorbidity among childhood anxiety disorders. *Journal of Nervous and Mental Disease, 175,* 726–730.

Lavigne, J. V. & Faier-Routman, J. (1993). Correlates of psychological adjustment to pediatric physical disorders: A meta-analytic review and comparison with existing models. *Developmental and Behavioral Pediatrics, 14,* 117–123.

Laws, G. (1998). The use of nonword repetition as a test of phonological memory in children with Down syndrome. *Journal of Child Psychology and Psychiatry, 39,* 1119–1130.

Lazarus, A., & Abramavitz, A. (1962). The use of emotive imagery in the treatment of children's phobia. *Journal of Mental Science, 108,* 191–192.

Le Couteur, A., Bailey, A., Goode, S., Pickles, A., Robertson, S., Gottesman, I., & Rutter, M. (1996). A broader phenotype of autism: The clinical spectrum in twins. *Journal of Child Psychology and Psychiatry, 37,* 785–802.

Leaf, P. J., et al. (1996). Mental health service use in the community and schools: Results from the four-community MECA Study. *Journal of the Academy of Child and Adolescent Psychiatry, 35,* 889–897.

Leckman, J. F., Peterson, B. S., Anderson, G. M., Arnsten, F. T., Pauls, D. L., & Cohen, D. J. (1997). Pathogenesis of Tourette's Syndrome. *Journal of Child Psychology and Psychiatry, 38,* 119–142.

Lefkowitz, M. (1977). Discussion of Dr. Gittelman-Klein's chapter. In J. G. Schulterbrandt & A. Raskin (Eds.), *Depression in childhood: Diagnosis, treatment, and conceptual models.* New York: Raven Press, 1977.

Lefkowitz, M., & Burton, N. (1978). Childhood depression: A critique of the concept. *Psychological Bulletin, 85* (4), 716–726.

Lefkowitz, M., & Tesiny, E. (1980). Assessment of childhood depression. *Journal of Consulting and Clinical Psychology, 48,* 43–50.

Leibel, R. L., & Hirsch, J. (1995). The molecular biology of obesity. In K. D. Brownell & C. G. Fairburn (Eds.), *Eating disorders and obesity: A comprehensive handbook.* New York: Guilford Press.

Leitenberg, H., Yost, L. W., & Carroll-Wilson, M. (1986). Negative cognitive errors in children: Questionnaire development, normative data, and comparisons between children with and without self-reported symptoms of depression, low self-esteem, and evaluation anxiety. *Journal of Consulting and Clinical Psychology, 54,* 528–536.

Lemanek, K. L. (1994). Research on pediatric chronic illness: New directions and recurrent confounds. *Journal of Pediatric Psychology, 19,* 143–148.

Lemert, E. M. (1971). *Instead of court: Diversion in juvenile justice.* Rockville, MD: National Institute of Mental Health.

Lemery, K. S., Goldsmith, H. H., Klinnert, M. D., & Mrazek, D. A. (1999). Developmental models of infant and child temperament. *Developmental Psychology, 35,* 189–204.

Lenane, M. C., Swedo, S. E., Leonard, H. L., Pauls, D. L., Sceery, W., & Rapoport, J. L. (1990). Psychiatric disorders in first degree relatives of children and adolescents with obsessive compulsive disorder. *Journal of the American Academy of Child and Adolescent Psychiatry, 29,* 407–412.

Leonard, H. L., Goldberger, E. L., Rapoport, J. L., Cheslow, D. L., & Swedo, S. E. (1990). Childhood rituals: Normal development or obsessive-compulsive symptoms? *Journal of the American Academy of Child and Adolescent Psychiatry, 29,* 17–23.

Leonard, H. L., Swedo, S. E., Allen, A. J., & Rapoport, J. L. (1994). Obsessive-compulsive disorder. In T. H. Ollendick, N. J. King, & Yule, W. (Eds.), *International handbook of anxiety disorders in children and adolescents.* New York: Plenum.

Leonard, H. L., Swedo, S. E., Lenane, M. C., Rettew, D. C., Hamburger, S. D., Bartko, J. J., & Rapoport, J. L. (1993). A two to seven year follow-up study of 54 obsessive compulsive children and adolescents. *Archives of General Psychiatry, 50,* 429–439.

Lerner, J. W. (1989). Educational interventions in learning disabilities. *Journal of the American Academy of Child and Adolescent Psychiatry, 28,* 326–331.

Lerner, R. M. (1987). The concept of plasticity in development. In J. J. Gallagher and C. T. Ramey (Eds.), *The malleability of children.* Baltimore: Brookes Publishing.

Leung, P. W. L., & Connolly, K. J. (1996). Distractibility in hyperactive and conduct-disordered children. *Journal of Child Psychology and Psychiatry, 37,* 305–312.

Leung, P. W. L., Ho, T. P., Luk, S. L., Taylor, E., Bacon-Shone, J., & Lieh Mak, F. (1996). Separation and comorbidity of hyperactivity and conduct disturbance in Chinese schoolboys. *Journal of Child Psychology and Psychiatry, 37,* 841–853.

Levine, M. P., Smolak, L., Moodey, A. F., Shuman, M. D., & Hessen L. D. (1994). Normative developmental challenges and dieting and eating disturbances in middle school girls. *International Journal of Eating Disorders, 15,* 11–20.

Levine, M., Smolak, L., & Streigel-Moore, R. (1996). Conclusions, implications, and future directions. In L. Smolk, M. P., Levine, & R. Streigel-Moore (Eds.), *The developmental psychopathology of eating disorders: Implications for research, prevention, and treatment.* Mahwah, NJ: Lawrence Erlbaum.

Levine, R. J. (1991). Respect for children as research subjects. In M. Lewis (Ed.), *Child and adolescent psychiatry. A comprehensive textbook.* Baltimore: Williams & Wilkins.

Levitt, M. J., Guacci-Franco, N., & Levitt, J. L. (1993). Convoys of social support in childhood and early adolescence: Structure and function. *Developmental Psychology, 29,* 811–818.

Levy, S. R., Jurkovic, G. L., & Spiro, A. (1995). A multisystems analysis of adolescent suicide attempters. *Journal of Abnormal Child Psychology, 23,* 221–234.

Levy, S., Zoltak, B., & Saelens, T. (1988). A comparison of obstetrical records of autistic and nonautistic referrals for psychoeducational evaluations. *Journal of Autism and Developmental Disorders, 18,* 573–581.

Lewinsohn, P. (1974). A behavioral approach to depression. In R. J. Friedman & M. M. Katz (Eds.), *The psychology of depression: Contemporary theory and research.* Washington, DC: Winston.

Lewinsohn, P. M., Clarke, G. N., Hops, H., & Andrews, J. (1990). Cognitive behavioral treatment for depressed adolescents. *Behavior Therapy, 21,* 385–402.

Lewinsohn, P. M., Clarke, G. N., Seeley, J. R., & Rohde, P. (1994). Major depression in community adolescents: Age at onset, episode duration, and time to recurrence. *Journal of the American Academy of Child and Adolescent Psychiatry, 33,* 809–818.

Lewinsohn, P. M., Hops, H., Roberts, R. E., Seeley, J. R., & Andrews, J. A. (1993a). Adolescent psychopathology: I. Prevalence and incidence of depression and other DSM-III-R disorders in high school students. *Journal of Abnormal Psychology, 102,* 133–144.

Lewinsohn, P. M., Klein, D. N., & Seeley, J. R. (1995). Bipolar disorders in a community sample of older adolescents: Prevalence, phenomenology, comorbidity, and course. *Journal of the American Academy of Child and Adolescent Psychiatry, 34,* 454–463.

Lewinsohn, P. M., Rohde, P., Klein, D. N., & Seeley, J. R. (1999). Natural course of adolescent Major Depressive Disorder: I. Continuity into young adulthood. *Journal of the American Academy of Child and Adolescent Psychiatry, 38,* 56–63.

Lewinsohn, P. M., Rohde, P., & Seeley, J. R. (1995). Adolescent psychopathology: III. The clinical consequences of comorbidity. *Journal of the American Academy of Child and Adolescent Psychiatry, 34,* 510–519.

Lewinsohn, P. M., Rohde, P., & Seeley, J. R. (1996). Adolescent suicidal ideation and attempts: Prevalence, risk factors, and clinical implications. *Clinical Psychology: Science and Practice, 3,* 25–46.

Lewinsohn, P. M., Rohde, P., & Seeley, J. R. (1998). Major Depressive Disorder in older adolescents: Prevalence, risk factors, and clinical implications. *Clinical Psychology Review, 18,* 765–794.

Lewinsohn, P. M., Rohde, P., Seeley, J. R., & Fischer, S. A. (1993b). Age-cohort changes in the lifetime occurrence of depression and other mental disorders. *Journal of Abnormal Psychology, 102,* 110–120.

Lewis, S. (1974). A comparison of behavior therapy techniques in the reductio of fearful avoidance behavior. *Behavior Therapy, 5,* 648–655.

Lewit, E. M. (1993). Children in foster care. *The Future of Children. Home Visiting, 3,* 192–200.

Liaw, F. & Brooks-Gunn, J. (1994). Cumulative familial risk and low-birthweight children's cognitive and behavioral development. *Journal of Clinical Child Psychology, 23,* 360–372.

Licht, B. G., & Kistner, J. A. (1986). Motivational problems of learning-disabled children: Individual differences and their implications for treatment. In J. K. Torgesen & B. Y. L. Wong (Eds.), *Psychological and educational perspectives on learning disabilities.* New York: Academic Press.

Lillienfeld, S. O., Waldman, I. D., & Israel, A. C. (1994). A critical examination of the use of the term and concept of comorbidity in psychopathology research. *Clinical Psychology: Science and Practice, 1,* 71–83.

Lilly, M. S. (Ed.). (1979a). *Children with exceptional needs: A survey of special education.* New York: Holt, Rinehart and Winston.

Lilly, M. S. (1979b). Special education. Emerging issues. In M. S. Lilly (Ed.), *Children with exceptional needs.* New York: Holt, Rinehart and Winston.

Lilly, M. S. (1979c). Special education. Historical and traditional perspectives. In M. S. Lilly (Ed.), *Children with exceptional needs.* New York: Holt, Rinehart and Winston.

Link, The (Spring–Summer 1995). Policies and position statements on inclusive schools. Charleston, WV: Appalachia Education Laboratory.

Linscheid, T. R. (1978). Disturbances of eating and feeding. In P. R. Magrab (Ed.), *Psychological management of pediatric problems, Vol. 1: Early life conditions and chronic diseases.* Baltimore: University Park Press.

Lipsey, M. W., & Wilson, D. B. (1993). The efficacy of psychological, educational, and behavioral treatment. *American Psychologist, 48,* 1181–1209.

Little, T. D., & Lopez, D. F. (1997). Regularities in the development of children's causality beliefs about school performance across six sociocultural contexts. *Developmental Psychology, 33,* 165–175.

Lobitz, G. K., & Johnson, S. M. (1975). Deviant and normal children. *Journal of Abnormal Child Psychology, 3,* 353–374.

Lockwood, K. A., Bell, T. S., & Colegrove, R. W., Jr. (1999). Long-term effects of cranial radiation therapy on attention functioning in survivors of childhood leukemia. *Journal of Pediatric Psychology, 24,* 55–66.

Loeber, R. (1988). Natural histories of conduct problems, delinquency, and associated substance use: Evidence for developmental progressions. In B. B. Lahey & A. E. Kazdin (Eds.), *Advances in clinical child psychology,* Vol. 11. New York: Plenum.

Loeber, R., & Hay, D. F. (1994). Developmental approaches to aggression and conduct problems. In M. Rutter & D. F. Hay (Eds.), Development through life: A handbook for clinicians. Malden, MA: Blackwell Scientific.

Loeber, R., & Kennan, K. (1994). Interaction between conduct disorder and its comorbid conditions: Effects of age and gender. *Clinical Psychology Review, 14,* 497–523.

Loeber, R., Green, S. M., Keenan, K., & Lahey, B. (1995). Which boys will fare worse? Early predictors of the onset of conduct disorder in a six-year longitudinal study. *Journal of the American Academy of Child and Adolescent Psychiatry, 34,* 499–509.

Loeber, R., & Schmaling, K. B. (1985) Empirical evidence for overt and covert patterns of antisocial conduct problems: A meta-analysis. *Journal of Abnormal Child Psychology, 13,* 337–354.

Loeber, R., & Stouthamer-Loeber, M. (1998). Development of juvenile aggression and violence: Some common misconceptions and controversies. *American Psychologist, 53,* 242–259.

Loeber, R., Wung, P., Keenan, K., Giroux, B., Stouthamer-Loeber, M., Van Kammen, W. B., & Maughan, B. (1993). Developmental pathways in disruptive child behavior. *Development and Psychopathology, 5,* 103–133.

Lombroso, P. J., Pauls, D. L., & Leckman, J. F. (1994). Genetic mechanisms in childhood psychiatric disorders. *Journal of the American Academy of Child and Adolescent Psychiatry, 33,* 921–938.

Lord, C., & Paul, R. (1997). Language and communication in autism. In D. J. Cohen & F. R. Volkmar (Eds.), *Handbook of autism and pervasive developmental disorders.* New York: John Wiley.

Lord, C., & Rutter, M. (1994). Autism and pervasive developmental disorders. In M. Rutter, E. Taylor & L. Hersov (Eds.), *Child and adolescent psychiatry. Modern approaches.* Boston: Blackwell Scientific.

Lord, C., Rutter, M., Goode, S., Heemsbergen, J., Jordan, H., Mawhood, L., & Schopler, E. (1989). Autism Diagnostic Observation Schedule: A standardized observation of communicative and social behavior. *Journal of Autism and Developmental Disorders, 19,* 185–212.

Lord, C., & Schopler, E. (1989). Stability of assessment results of autistic and non-autistic language-impaired children from preschool years to early school age. *Journal of Child Psychology and Psychiatry, 30,* 575–590.

Lord, J., & Pedlar, A. (1991). Life in the community: Four years after the closure of an institution. *Mental Retardation, 29,* 213–221.

Lorion, R. P., Cowen, E. L., & Caldwell, R. A. (1974). Problem types of children referred to a school based mental health program: Identification and outcome. *Journal of Consulting and Clinical Psychology, 42,* 491–496.

Losier, B. J., McGrath, P. J., & Klein, R. M. (1996). Error patterns on the continuous performance test in non-medicated and medicated samples of children with and without ADHD: A meta-analytic review. *Journal of Child Psychology and Psychiatry, 37,* 971–987.

Lotter, V. (1966). Epidemiology of autistic conditions in young children. I. Prevalence. *Social Psychiatry, 1,* 124–137.

Lotter, V. (1974). Factors related to outcome in autistic children. *Journal of Autism and Childhood Schizophrenia, 4,* 263–277.

Lovaas, O. I. (1987). Behavioral treatment and normal educational and intellectual functioning in young autistic children. *Journal of Consulting and Clinical Psychology, 55,* 3–9.

Lovaas, O. I., & Newsom, C. D. (1976). Behavior modification with psychotic children. In H. Leitenberg (Ed.), *Handbook of behavior modification and behavior therapy.* Englewood Cliffs, NJ: Prentice Hall.

Lovaas, O. I., & Smith, T. (1988). Intensive behavioral treatment for young autistic children. In B. B. Lahey & A. E. Kazdin (Eds.), *Advances in clinical child psychology,* Vol. 2. New York: Plenum.

Lovaas, O. I., Young, D. B., & Newsom, C. D. (1978). Childhood psychosis: Behavioral treatment. In B. B. Wolman (Ed.), *Handbook of treatment of mental disorders in childhood and adolescence.* Englewood Cliffs, NJ: Prentice Hall.

Loveland, K. A., & Tunali-Kotoski, B. (1997). The school-age child with autism. In D. J. Cohen, & F. R. Volkmar (Eds.). *Handbook of pervasive and developmental disorders.* New York: John Wiley.

Lovibond, S. H. (1964). *Conditioning and enuresis.* Oxford: Pergamon.

Lovko, A. M., & Ullman, D. G. (1989). Research on the adjustment of latchkey children: Role of background/demographic and latchkey situation variables. *Journal of Clinical Child Psychology, 18,* 16–24.

Lucas, A. R., & Holub, M. I. (1995). The incidence of anorexia nervosa in adolescent residents of Rochester, Minnesota, during a 50-year period. In H. C. Steinhausen (Ed.), *Eating disorders in adolescence: Anorexia and bulimia nervosa.* Berlin: Walter de Gruyter.

Luckasson, R., et al. (1992). *Mental retardation: Definition, classification, and systems of supports.* Washington, DC: American Association on Mental Retardation.

Luthar, S. S. (1993). Methodological and conceptual issues in research on childhood resilience. *Journal of Child Psychology and Psychiatry, 34,* 441–453.

Luxenberg, J. S., Swedo, S. E., Flament, M. F., Friedland, R., Rapoport, J. L., & Rapoport, S. I. (1988). Neuroanatomical abnormalities in obsessive-compulsive disorder detected with quantitative x-ray computed tomography. *American Journal of Psychiatry, 145,* 1089–1093.

Lynskey, M. T., & Fergusson, D. M. (1995). Childhood conduct problems, attention deficit behaviors, and adolescent alcohol, tobacco, and illicit drug use. *Journal of Abnormal Child Psychology, 23,* 281–302.

Lynskey, M. T., Fergusson, D. M., & Horwood, L. J. (1998). The origins of the correlations between tobacco, alcohol, and cannabis use during adolescence. *Journal of Child Psychology and Psychiatry, 39,* 995–1005.

Lyon, G. R. (1996a). Learning disabilities. In E. J. Mash & R. A. Barkley (Eds.), *Child psychopathology.* New York: Guilford Press.

Lyon, G. R. (1996b). Learning disabilities. *The Future of Children, 6,* 54–76.

Lyon, G. R., & Cutting, L. E. (1998). Learning disabilities. In E. J. Mash & R. A. Barkley (Eds.), *Treatment of childhood disorders.* New York: Guilford Press.

Lyon, G. R., & Moats, L. C. (1988). Critical issues in the instruction of the learning disabled. *Journal of Consulting and Clinical Psychology, 56,* 830–835.

Lyons-Ruth, K., Zeanah, C. H., & Benoit, D. (1996). Disorder and risk for disorder during infancy and toddlerhood. In E. J. Mash & R. A. Barkley (Eds.), *Child psychopathology.* New York: Guilford Press.

Lytton, H., & Romney, D. M. (1991). Parents' differential socialization of boys and girls: A meta-analysis. *Psychological Bulletin, 109,* 267–296.

Maccini, P., & Hughes, C. A. (1997). Mathematics interventions for adolescents with learning disabilities. *Learning Disabilities Research and Practice, 12,* 168–176.

Maccoby, E. E. (1992). The role of parents in the socialization of children: An historic overview. *Developmental Psychology, 28,* 1006–1017.

Maccoby, E. E., & Martin, J. A. (1983). Socialization in the context of the family: Parent-child interaction. In P. H. Mussen (Ed.), *Handbook of child psychology,* Vol. IV. New York: Wiley

Mace, F. C., Vollmer, T. R., Progar, P. R., & Mace, A. B. (1998). Assessment and treatment of self-injury. In T. S. Watson & F. M. Gresham (Eds.), *Handbook of child behavior therapy.* New York: Plenum Press.

MacFarlane, J. W., Allen, L., & Honzik, M. P. (1954). *A developmental study of the behavior problems of normal children between 21 months and 14 years.* Berkeley: University of California Press.

Machover, K. (1949). *Personality projection in the drawing of the human figure.* Springfield, IL: Chas. C. Thomas.

MacLean, W. E., Perrin, J. M., Gortmaker, S., & Pierre, C. B. (1992). Psychological adjustment of children with asthma: Effects of illness severity and recent stressful life events. *Journal of Pediatric Psychology, 17,* 159–171.

MacMillan, D. L. (1982). *Mental retardation in school and society,* 2nd ed. Boston: Little-Brown.

MacMillan, D. L., & Kavale, K. A. (1986). Educational intervention. In H. C. Quay & J. S. Werry (Eds.), *Psychopathological disorders of childhood,* 3rd ed. New York: Wiley.

MacMillan, D. L., Keogh, B. K., & Jones, R. L. (1986). Special educational research on mildly handicapped learners. In M. C. Wittrock (Ed.), *Handbook of research on teaching.* New York: Macmillan.

MacMillan, D. L., & Reschly, D. J. (1997). Issues of definition and classification. In W. E. MacLean, Jr. (Ed.), *Ellis' handbook of mental deficiency, psychological theory and research.* Mahwah, NJ: Lawrence Erlbaum.

Magnuson, E. (1983). Child abuse: The ultimate betrayal. *Time* (Sept. 5), pp. 16–18.

Mahoney, M. J. (1993). Introduction to special section: Theoretical developments in the cognitive psychotherapies. *Journal of Consulting and Clinical Psychology, 61,* 187–193.

Mahoney, W. J., Szatmari, P., MacLean, J. E., Bryson, S. E., Bartolucci, G., Walter, S. D., Jones, M. B., & Zwaigenbaum, L. (1998). Reliability and accuracy of differentiating pervasive developmental disorder subtypes. *Journal of the American Academy of Child and Adolescent Psychiatry, 37,* 278–285.

Maier, S. F., Watkins, L. R., & Fleshner, M. (1994). Psychoneuroimmunology: The interface between behavior, brain, and immunity. *American Psychologist, 49,* 1004–1017.

Main, M. (1996). Introduction to the special section on attachment and psychopathology: 2. Overview of the field of attachment. *Journal of Consulting and Clinical Psychology, 64,* 237–243.

Malatesta, C. Z., Grigoryev, P., Lamb, K., Albin, M., & Culver, C. (1986). Emotion socialization and expressive development in preterm and full-term infants. *Child Development, 57,* 316–330.

Malcarne, V. L., & Ingram, R. E. (1994). Cognition and negative affectivity. In T. H. Ollendick & R. J. Prinz, (Eds.), *Advances in clinical child psychology,* Vol. 16. New York: Plenum.

Malik, N. M., & Furman, W. (1993). Practitioner review: Problems in children's peer relations: What can the clinician do. *Journal of Child Psychology and Psychiatry, 34,* 1303–1326.

Malmquist, C. P. (1977). Childhood depression: A clinical and behavioral prespective. In J. G. Schulterbrandt & A. Raskin (Eds.), *Depression in childhood: Diagnosis, treatment, and conceptual models.* New York: Raven Press.

Malo, J., & Tremblay, R. E. (1997). The impact of paternal alcoholism and maternal social position on boys' school adjustment, pubertal maturation and sexual behavior: A test of two competing hypotheses. *Journal of Child Psychology and Psychiatry, 38,* 187–197.

Maloney, J. (December 1994/January 1995). A call for placement options. *Educational Leadership, 52,* 25.

Manly, J. T., Cicchetti, D., & Barnett, D. (1994). The impact of subtype, frequency, chronicity, and severity of child maltreatment on social competence and behavior problems. *Development and Psychopathology, 6,* 121–144.

Mann, V. A., & Brady, S. (1988). Reading disability: The role of language deficiencies. *Journal of Consulting and Clinical Psychology, 56,* 811–816.

Manne, S. L., Bakeman, R., Jacobsen, P., & Redd, W. H. (1993). Children's coping during invasive medical procedures. *Behavior Therapy, 24,* 143–158.

Mannuzza, S., Klein, R. G., Bessler, A., Malloy, P., & LaPadula, M. (1993). Adult outcome of hyperactive boys. *Archives of General Psychiatry, 50,* 565–576.

Mannuzza, S., Klein, R. G., Bessler, A., Malloy, P., & LaPadula, M. (1998). Adult psychiatric status of hyperactive boys grown up. *American Journal of Psychiatry, 155,* 493–498.

March, J. S., & Albano, A. M. (1998). New developments in assessing pediatric anxiety disorders. In T. H. Ollendick & R. J. Prinz (Eds.), *Advances in clinical child psychology* (Vol. 20). New York: Plenum Press.

March, J. S., & Leonard, H. L. (1996). Obsessive-compulsiver disorder in children and adolescents: A review of the past 10 years. *Journal of the American Academy of Child and Adolescent Psychiatry, 35,* 1265–1273.

March, J. S., & Mulle, K. (1998). *OCD in children and adolescents: A cognitive-behavioral treatment manual.* New York: Guilford Press.

March, J. S., Parker, J. D. A., Sullivan, K., Stallings, P., & Conners, C. K. (1997). The multidimensional anxiety scale for children (MASC): Factor structure, reliability and validity. *Journal of the American Academy of Child and Adolescent Psychiatry 36,* 554–565.

Marchetti, A. G., & Campbell, V. A. (1990). Social skills. In J. L. Matson (Ed.), *Handbook of behavior modification with the mentally retarded.* New York: Plenum.

Marchi, M. & Cohen, P. (1990). Early childhood eating behaviors and adolescent eating disorders. *Journal of the American Academy of Child and Adolescent Psychiatry, 29,* 112–117.

Marcus, J., Hans, S. L., Auerbach. J. G., & Auerbach, A. G. (1993). Children at risk for schizophrenia: The

Jerusalem Infant Development Study. *Archives of General Psychiatry, 50,* 797–809.

Margalit, M. (1989). Academic competence and social adjustment of boys with learning disabilities and boys with behavior disorders. *Journal of Learning Disabilities, 22,* 41–45.

Marsella, A. J. (1998). Toward a "global-community psychology": Meeting the needs of a changing world. *American Psychologist, 53,* 1282–1291.

Marteau, T., Johnston, M., Baum, J. D., & Bloch, S. (1987). Goals of treatment in diabetes: A comparison of doctors and parents of children with diabetes. *Journal of Behavioral Medicine, 10,* 33–48.

Martin, E. W., Martin, R., & Terman, D. L. (1996). The legislative and litigation history of special education. *The Future Of Children, 6,* 25–39.

Masek, B. J., & Hoag, N. L. (1990). Headache, In A. M. Gross & R. S. Drabman (Eds.), *Handbook of clinical behavioral pediatrics.* New York: Plenum.

Mash, E. J., & Dozois, D. J. A. (1996). Child psychopathology: A developmental-systems perspective. In E. J. Mash & R. A. Barkley (Eds.), *Child psychopathology. New York: Guilford Press.*

Masten, A. S., & Coatsworth, J. D. (1998). The development of competence in favorable and unfavorable environments: Lessons from research on successful children. *American Psychologist, 53,* 205–220.

Matarazzo, J. D. (1990). Psychological assessment versus psychological testing: Validation from Binet to the school, clinic, and courtroom. *American Psychologist, 45,* 999–1017.

Matarazzo, J. D. (1992). Psychological testing and assessment in the 21st century. *American Psychologist, 47,* 1007–1018.

Matson, J. L., & Coe, D. A. (1991). Mentally retarded children. In T. R. Kratochwill & R. J. Morris (Eds.), *The practice of child therapy.* Boston: Allyn and Bacon.

Mattis, S., French, J. H., & Rapin, I. (1975). Dyslexia in children and young adults: The independent neuropsychological syndromes. *Developmental Medicine and Child Neurology, 17,* 150–163.

Mattis, S. G., & Ollendick, T. H. (1997). Panic disorder in children and adolescents: A developmental analysis. In T. H. Ollendick & R. J. Prinz (Eds.), *Advances in clinical child psychology,* (Vol. 19). New York: Plenum Press.

Maughan, B. (1995). Long-term outcomes of developmental reading problems. *Journal of Child Psychology and Psychiatry, 36,* 357–371.

Maughan, B., & Rutter, M. (1998). Continuities and discontinuities in antisocial behavior from childhood to adult life. In T. H. Ollendick & R. J. Prinz (Eds.), *Advances in clinical child psychology* (Vol. 20). New York: Plenum Press.

Maughan, B. & Yule, W. (1994). Reading and other learning disabilities. In M. Rutter, E. Taylor, &

L. Hersov (Eds.), *Child and adolescent psychiatry. Modern approaches.* Cambridge, MA: Blackwell Scientific.

Max, J. E., Arndt, S., Castillo, C. S., Bukura, H., Robin, D. A., Lindgren, S. D., Smith, W. L., Sato, Y., & Mattheis, P. J. (1998). Attention-deficit hyperactivity symptomatology after traumatic brain injury: A prospective study. *Journal of the American Academy of Child and Adolescent Psychiatry, 37,* 841–847.

Mayes, S. D. (1992). Rumination disorder: Diagnosis, complications, mediating variables, and treatment. In B. B. Lahey & A. E. Kazdin (Eds.), *Advances in clinical child psychology,* Vol. 14. New York: Plenum.

Mazze, R. S., Lucido, D., & Shannon, H. (1984). Psychological and social correlates of glycemic control. *Diabetes Care, 7,* 360–366.

McAlpine, C., & Singh, N. N. (1986). Pica in institutionalized mentally retarded persons. *Journal of Mental Deficiency Research, 30,* 171–178.

McArdle, P., O'Brien, G., & Kolvin, I. (1995). Hyperactivity: prevalence and relationship with conduct disorder. *Journal of Child Psychology and Psychiatry, 36,* 279–303.

McArthur, D. S., & Roberts, G. E. (1982). *Roberts Apperception Test for Children: Manual.* Los Angeles: Western Psychological Services.

McCall, R. B., Applebaum, M. I., & Hogarty, P. S. (1973). Developmental changes in mental performance. *Monographs of the Society for Research in Child Development, 38* (Whole No. 150).

McClellan, J., & Werry, J. (1994/1997). Practice parameters for the assessment and treatment of children and adolescents with schizophrenia. *Journal of the American Academy of Child and Adolescent Psychiatry, 33,* 616–635.

McDermott, J. (1991). The effects of ethnicity on child and adolescent development. In M. Lewis (Ed.), *Child and adolescent psychiatry. A comprehensive textbook.* Baltimore: Williams & Wilkins.

McDougle, C. J. (1997). Psychopharmacology. In D. J. Cohen & F. R. Volkmar (Eds.), *Handbook of autism and pervasive developmental disorders.* New York: John Wiley.

McEachin, J. J., Smith, T., & Lovaas, O. I. (1993). Long-term outcome for children with autism who received early intensive behavioral treatment. *American Journal on Mental Retardation, 97,* 359–372.

McEvoy, R. E., Rogers, S. J., & Pennington, B. F. (1993). Executive functions and social communication deficits in young autistic children. *Journal of Child Psychology and Psychiatry, 34,* 563–578.

McFadyen-Ketchum, S. A., & Dodge, K. A. (1998). Problems in social relationships. In E. J. Mash & R. A. Barkley (Eds.), *Treatment of childhood disorders* (2nd ed.). New York: Guilford Press.

McGee, R. A., & Wolfe, D. A. (1991). Psychological maltreatment: Toward an operational definition. *Development and Psychopathology, 3,* 3–18.

McGee, R., Feehan, M., Williams, S., & Anderson, J. (1992). DSM-III disorders from age 11 to age 15 years. *Journal of the American Academy of Child and Adolescent Psychiatry, 31,* 50–59.

McGee, R., Feehan, M., Williams, S., Partridge, F., Silva, P. A., & Kelly, J. (1990). DSM-III disorders in a large sample of adolescents. *Journal of the American Academy of Child and Adolescent Psychiatry, 29,* 611–619.

McGee, R., Partridge, F., Williams, S., & Silva, P. A. (1991). A twelve-year follow-up of preschool hyperactive children. *Journal of the American Academy of Child and Adolescent Psychiatry, 30,* 224–232.

McGee, R., & Share, D. L. (1988). Attention deficit disorder-hyperactivity and academic failure: Which comes first and what should be treated? *Journal of the American Academy of Child and Adolescent Psychiatry, 27,* 318–325.

McGrew, K. S., Bruininks, R. H., & Thurlow, M. L. (1992). Relationship between measures of adaptive functioning and community adjustment for adults with mental retardation. *Exceptional Children, 58,* 517–529.

McGue, M., Bouchard, T. J., Iacono, W. G., & Lykken, D. T. (1993). Behavioral genetics of cognitive ability: A life-span perspective. In R. Plomin & G. E. McClearn (Eds.), *Nature, nurture & psychology.* Washington, DC: American Psychological Association.

McGue, M., & Lykken, D. T. (1992). Genetic influence on risk of divorce. *Psychological Science, 6,* 368–373.

McKenna, K., Gordon, C. T., Lenane, M., Kaysen, D., Fahey, K., & Rapoport, J. L. (1994). Looking for childhood-onset schizophrenia: The first 71 cases screened. *Journal of the American Academy of Child and Adolescent Psychiatry, 33,* 636–644.

McLanahan, S., & Sandefur, G. (1994). *Growing up with a single parent: What hurts, what helps?* Cambridge, MA: Harvard University Press.

McLean, J., & Ching, A. (1973). Follow-up study of relationships between family situation and bronchial asthma in children. *Journal of the American Academy of Child Psychiatry, 10,* 142–161.

McLoyd, V. C. (1990). The impact of economic hardship on black families and children: Psychological distress, parenting, and socioemotional development. *Child Development, 61,* 311–346.

McLoyd, V. C. (1998). Socioeconomic disadvantage and child development. *American Psychologist, 53,* 185–204.

McMahon, R. J., & Estes, A. M. (1997). Conduct problems. In E. J. Mash & L. G. Terdal (Eds.), *Assessment of childhood disorders* (3rd ed.). New York: Guilford Press.

McMahon, R. J., & Forehand, R. (1988). Conduct disorders. In E. J. Mash & L. G. Terdal (Eds.), *Behavioral assessment of childhood disorders,* 2nd ed. New York: Guilford.

McMahon, R. J., & Wells, K. C. (1989). Conduct disorders. In E. J. Mash & R. A. Barkley (Eds.), *Treatment of childhood disorders.* New York: Guilford.

McMahon, R. J., & Wells, K. C. (1998). Conduct problems. In E. J. Mash & R. A. Barkley (Eds.), *Treatment of childhood disorders* (2nd ed.). New York: Guilford Press.

McReynolds, P. (1987). Lightner Whitmer: Little-known founder of clinical psychology. *American Psychologist, 42,* 849–858.

Mednick, S. A., Machon, R. A., Huttunen, M. O., & Bonnett, D. (1988). Fetal viral infection and adult schizophrenia. *Archives of General Psychiatry, 45,* 189–192.

Mednick, S. A., & Schulsinger, F. (1968). Some premorbid characteristics related to breakdown in children with schizophrenic mothers. In D. Rosenthal and S. S. Kety (Eds.), *The transmission of schizophrenia.* Elmsford, NY: Pergamon Press.

Meichenbaum, D. (1993). Changing conceptions of cognitive behavior modification: Retrospect and prospect. *Journal of Consulting and Clinical Psychology, 61,* 202–204.

Meichenbaum, D. H., & Goodman, J. (1971). Training impulsive children to talk to themselves: A means of developing self-control. *Journal of Abnormal Psychology, 77,* 115–126.

Melamed, B. G., & Siegel, L. J. (1975). Reduction of anxiety in children facing hospitalization and surgery by use of filmed modeling. *Journal of Consulting and Clinical Psychology, 43,* 511–521.

Melamed, B. G., & Siegel, L. J. (1980). *Behavioral medicine: Practical applications in health care.* New York: Springer.

Melbin, T. & Vuille, J. C. (1989). Further evidence of an association between psychosocial problems and increase in relative weight between 7 and 10 years of age. *Acta Paediatrica Scandinavica, 78,* 576–580.

Mellin, L. M., Irwin, C. E., & Scully, S. (1992), Prevalence of disordered eating in girls: A survey of middle-class children. *Journal of the American Dietetic Association, 92,* 851–853.

Melnick, S. M., & Hinshaw, S. P. (1996). What they want and what they get: The social goals of boys with ADHD and comparison boys. *Journal of Abnormal Child Psychology, 24,* 169–185.

Melton, G. B. (1996). The child's right to a family environment: Why children's rights and family values are compatible. *American Psychologist, 51,* 1234–1238.

Mercer, C. D., King-Sears, P., & Mercer, A. R. (1990). Learning disabilities definitions and criteria used by state education departments. *Learning Disability Quarterly, 13,* 141–152.

Mesibov, G. B. (1992). Letters to the editors. Response to Thompson and McEvoy. *Journal of Autism and Developmental Disorders, 22,* 672–673.

Mesibov, G. B., & Handlan, S. (1997). Adolescents and adults with autism. In D. J. Cohen & F. R. Volkmar (Eds.), *Handbook of autism and pervasive developmental disorders.* New York: John Wiley.

Mesibov, G. B., Schroeder, C. S., & Wesson, L. (1977). Parental concerns about their children. *Journal of Pediatric Psychology, 2,* 13–17.

Mesibov, G., B., & Van Bourgondien, M. E. (1992). Autism. In S. R. Hooper, G. W. Hynd, & R. E. Mattison (Eds.), *Developmental disorders. Diagnostic criteria and clinical assessment.* Hillsdale, NJ: Erlbaum.

Meyer, N. E., Dyck, D. G., & Petrinack, R. J. (1989). Cognitive appraisal and attributional correlates of depressive symptoms in children. *Journal of Abnormal Child Psychology, 17,* 325–336.

Milberger, S., Biederman, J., Faraone, S. V., Chen, L., & Jones, J. (1996). Is maternal smoking during pregnancy a risk factor for attention deficit hyperactivity disorder in children? *American Journal of Psychiatry, 153,* 1138–1142.

Milberger, S., Biederman, J., Faraone, S. V., Chen, L., & Jones, J. (1997). ADHD is associated with early initiation of cigarette smoking in children and adolescents. *Journal of the American Academy of Child and Adolescent Psychiatry, 36,* 37–44.

Milich, R. (1994). The response of children with ADHD to failure: If at first you don't succeed, do you try, try again? *School Psychology Review, 23,* 11–28.

Milich, R., & Lorch, E. P. (1994). Television viewing methodology to understand cognitive processing of ADHD children. In T. H. Ollendick & R. J. Prinz (Eds.), *Advances in clinical child psychology.* New York: Plenum Press.

Milich, R., McAninch, C. B., & Harris, M. J. (1992). Effects of stigmatizing information on children's peer relations: Believing is seeing. *School Psychology Review, 21,* 400–409.

Miller, B. D. & Wood, B. L. (1991). Childhood asthma in interaction with family, school, and peer systems: A developmental model for primary care. *Journal of Asthma, 28,* 405–414.

Miller, B. D. & Wood, B. L. (1994). Psychophysiologic reactivity in asthmatic children: A cholinergically mediated confluence of pathways. *Journal of the American Academy of Child and Adolescent Psychiatry, 33,* 1236–1245.

Miller, L. C., Barrett, C. L., & Hampe, E. (1974). Phobias of childhood in a prescientific era. In A. Davids (Ed.), *Child personality and psychopathology: Current topics,* Vol. 1. New York: John Wiley.

Miller, L. C., Barrett, C. L., Hampe, E., & Noble, H. (1972). Comparison of reciprocal inhibition psychotherapy and waiting list control for phobic children. *Journal of Abnormal Psychology, 79,* 269–279.

Miller, N. E. (1969). Learning of visceral and glandular responses. *Science, 163,* 434–445.

Miller, S. L., & Tallal, P. (1995). A behavioral neuroscience approach to developmental language disorders: Evidence for a rapid temporal processing deficit. In D. Cicchetti & D. J. Cohen (Eds.), *Developmental psychopathology.* Vol. 2. New York: John Wiley.

Millican, F. K., & Lourie, R. S. (1970). The child with pica and his family. In E. J. Anthony and C. Koupernik (Eds.), *The child in his family,* Vol. 1. New York: Wiley-Interscience.

Minde, K., Faucon, A., & Faulkner, S. (1994). Sleep problems in toddlers: Effects of treatment on their daytime behavior. *Journal of the American Academy of Child and Adolescent Psychiatry, 33,* 1114–1121.

Minde, K., Popiel, K., Leos, N., Falkner, S., Parker, K., & Handley-Derry, M. (1993). The evaluation and treatment of sleep disturbances in young children. *Journal of Child Psychology and Psychiatry, 34,* 521–533.

Mindell, J. A. (1993). Sleep disorders in children. *Health Psychology, 12,* 151–162.

Minshew, N. J., Sweeney, J. A., & Bauman, M. L. (1997). Neurological aspects of autism. In D. J. Cohen & F. R. Volkmar (Eds.), *Handbook of autism and pervasive developmental disorders.* New York: John Wiley.

Minuchin, S., Rosman, B. L., & Baker, L. (1978). *Psychosomatic Families: Anorexia nervosa in context.* Cambridge, MA: Harvard University Press.

Mirkin, M. P. (1990). Eating disorders: A feminist family therapy perspective. In M. P. Mirkin (Ed.), *The social and political contexts of family therapy.* Boston: Allyn & Bacon.

Mishler, E. G., & Waxler, N. E. (1965). Family interactional processes and schizophrenia: A review of current theories. *Merrill-Palmer Quarterly, 11,* 269–315.

Mitchell, J. E., & Eckert, E. D. (1987). Scope and significance of eating disorders. *Journal of Consulting and Clinical Psychology, 55,* 628–634.

Moffitt, T. E. (1993a). Adolescence-limited and life-course-persistent antisocial behavior: A developmental taxonomy. *Psychological Review, 100,* 674–701.

Moffitt, T. E. (1993b). The neuropsychology of conduct disorder. *Development and Psychopathology, 5,* 135–152.

Moise, F. N., & Petrides, G. (1996). Case study: Electroconvulsive therapy in adolescents. *Journal of the American Academy of Child and Adolescent Psychiatry, 35,* 312–318.

Mojtabai, R., Nicholson, R. A., & Carpenter, B. N. (1998). Role of psychosocial treatments in management of schizophrenia: A meta-analytic review of controlled outcome studies. *Schizophrenia Bulletin, 24,* 569–587.

Mollica, R. F., Poole, C., Son, L., Murray, C. C., & Tor, S. (1997). Effects of war trauma on Cambodia refugee adolescents' functional health and mental health status. *Journal of the American Academy of Child and Adolescent Psychiatry, 36,* 1098–1106.

Montague, C. T., Farooqui, I. S., Whitehead, J. P., et al. (1997). Congenital leptin deficiency is associated with severe early-onset obesity in humans. *Nature, 387,* 903–907.

Moore, D. R., & Arthur, J. L. (1989). Juvenile delinquency. In T. H. Ollendick & M. Hersen (Eds.), *Handbook of child psychopathology,* 2nd ed. New York: Plenum.

Moos, R. H., & Moos, B. S. (1986). *Family Environment Scale Manual* (2nd ed.). Palo Alto, CA: Consulting Psychologists Press.

Morgan, R. K. (1999). *Case studies in child and adolescent psychopathology.* Upper Saddle River, NJ: Prentice Hall.

Morrell, R. (1998). Project Follow Through: Still ignored. *American Psychologist, 53,* 318.

Morris, R. D. (1988). Classification of learning disabilities: Old problems and new approaches. *Journal of Consulting and Clinical Psychology, 56,* 789–794.

Morris, R. J., & Kratochwill, T. R. (1983). *Treating children's fears and phobias: A behavioral approach.* Elsmford, NY: Pergamon Press.

Morris, S., Alexander, J. F., & Waldron, H. (1988). Functional family therapy: Issues in clinical practice. In I. R. H. Falloon (Ed.), *Handbook of behavioral family therapy.* New York: Guilford.

Morrison, D. N., McGee, R., & Stanton, W. R. (1992). Sleep problems in adolescence. *Journal of the American Academy of Child and Adolescent Psychiatry, 31,* 94–99.

Morrow-Bradley, C., & Elliot, R. (1986). Utilization of psychotherapy research by practicing psychotherapists. *American Psychologist, 41,* 188–197.

Morvitz, E., & Motta, R. W. (1992). Predictors of self-esteem: The roles of parent-child perceptions, achievement, and class placement. *Journal of Learning Disabilities, 25,* 72–80.

Mowrer, O. H., & Mowrer, W. M. (1938). Enuresis: A method for its study and treatment. *American Journal of Orthopsychiatry, 8,* 436–459.

Mulick, J. A. (1994, Nov./Dec.). The non-science of facilitated communication. *Psychological Science Agenda, 7,* 8–9.

Muller, C. (1995). Maternal employment, parent involvement, and mathematics achievement among adolescents. *Journal of Marriage and the Family, 57,* 85–100.

Mulvey, E. P., Arthur, M. W., & Reppucci, N. D. (1993). The prevention and treatment of juvenile delinquency: A review of the research. *Clinical Psychology Review, 13,* 133–167.

Mundy, P. (1993). Normal versus high functioning status in children with autism. *American Journal on Mental Retardation, 97,* 381–384.

Mundy, P., & Adreon, D. (1994). Commentary. Facilitated communication: Attitude, effect, and theory. *Journal of Pediatric Psychology, 19,* 677–680.

Munoz, R. F., Mrazek, P. J., & Haggerty, R. J. (1996). Institute of Medicine report on prevention of mental disorders: Summary and commentary. *American Psychologist 51,* 1116–1122.

Murphy, D. A., Greenstein, J. J., & Pelham, W. E. (1993). Pharmacological treatment. In V. B. VanHasselt & M. Hersen (Eds.), *Handbook of behavior therapy and pharmacotherapy for children: a comparative analysis.* Boston: Allyn and Bacon.

Murphy, L. M. B., Thompson, R. J., Jr., & Morris, M. A. (1997). Adherence behavior among adolescents with type I insulin-dependent diabetes mellitus: The role of cognitive appraisal processes. *Journal of Pediatric Psychology, 22,* 811–825.

Murphy-Berman, V., & Weisz, V. (1996). U. N. Convention of the Rights of the Child: Current challenges. *American Psychologist, 51,* 1231–1233.

Murray, H. A. (1943). *Thematic Apperception Test.* Cambridge, MA: Harvard University Press.

Murray, L. (1992). The impact of postnatal depression on infant development. *Journal of Child Psychology and Psychiatry, 33,* 543–561.

Myers, C. E., Nihira, K., & Zetlin, A. (1979). The measurement of adaptive behavior. In N. R. Ellis (Ed.), *Handbook of mental deficiency.* Hillsdale, NJ: Erlbaum.

Nader, K., Pynoos, R. S., Fairbanks, L. & Frederick, C. (1991). Childhood PTSD reactions one year after a sniper attack. *American Journal of Psychiatry, 147,* 1526–1530.

Nathan, P. E. (1994). DSM-IV: Empirical, accessible, not yet ideal. *Journal of Clinical Psychology, 50,* 103–110.

National Center for Child Abuse and Neglect. (1993). *National child abuse and neglect data system: Working paper 2-1991 Summary data component.* Washington, DC: U.S. Government Printing Office.

National Center for Health Statistics. (1998). *Health, United States, 1998 With Socioeconomic Status and Health Chartbook.* Hyattsville, MD: Author.

National Insitute of Mental Health (1977). *Child abuse and neglect programs: Practice and theory.* Washington, DC: U.S. Government Printing Office.

National Institute of Drug Abuse (1992). National Household Survey on Drug Abuse. *Statistical Abstract of the United States 1992* (112th ed.), U.S. Department of Commerce, Bureau of the Census.

National Institutes of Health. (1997). *Highlights of the expert panel Report 2: Guidelines for the diagnosis and man-*

agement of asthma (NIH publication No. 97-4051 A). Washington, DC: U.S. Department of Health and Human Services.

Nelson, C. A., & Bloom, F. E. (1997). Child development and neuroscience. *Child Development, 68,* 970–987.

Neuman, R. J., Todd, R. D., Heath, A. C., Reich, W., Hudzick, J. J., Bucholz, K. K., Madden, P. A. F., Begleiter, H., Porjesz, B., Kuperman, S., Hesselbruck, V., & Reich, T. (1999). Evaluation of ADHD typology in three contrasting samples: A latent class approach. *Journal of the American Academy of Child and Adolescent Psychiatry, 38,* 25–33.

Newacheck, P. W. & Taylor, W. R. (1992). Childhood chronic illness: Prevalence, severity and impact. *American Journal of Public Health, 82,* 364–371.

Newcomb, A. F., & Bagwell, C. L. (1995). Children's friendship relations: A meta-analytic review. *Psychological Bulletin, 117,* 306–347.

Newcomb, A. F., Bukowski, W. M., Pattee, L. (1993). Children's peer relations: A meta-analytic review of popular, rejected, neglected, controversial, and average sociometric status. *Psychological Bulletin, 113,* 99–128.

Newman, F. L., & Tejeda, M. J. (1996). The need for research that is designed to support decisions in the delivery of mental health services. *American Psychologist, 51,* 1040–1049.

Newsom, C. (1998). Autistic disorder. In E. J. Mash & R. A. Barkley (Eds.), *Treatment of childhood disorders.* New York: Guilford Press.

Newsom, C., & Hovanitz, C. A. (1997). Autistic disorder. In E. J. Mash & L. G. Terdal (Eds.), *Assessment of childhood disorders.* New York: Guilford Press.

Newsom, C., Hovanitz, C., & Rincover, A. (1988). Autism. In E. J. Mash and L. G. Terdal (Eds.), *Behavioral assessment of childhood disorders. Selected core problems.* New York: Guilford.

Nicolson, R., Awad, G., & Sloman, L. (1998). An open trial of risperidone in young autistic children. *Journal of the American Academy of Child and Adolescent Psychiatry, 37,* 372–376.

Nietzel, M. T., Bernstein, D. A., & Milich, R. (1994). *Introduction to clinical psychology.* (4th ed.). Englewood Cliffs, NJ: Prentice Hall.

Nigg, J. T., & Hinshaw, S. P. (1998). Parent personality traits and psychopathology associated with antisocial behaviors in childhood attention-deficit hyperactive disorder. *Journal of Child Psychology and Psychiatry, 39,* 145–159.

Nihira, K., Leland, H., & Lambert, N. (1993). *AAMR Adaptive Behavior Scales—Residential and Community.* Austin, TX: Pro-ed.

Ninio, A., & Rinott, N. (1988). Fathers' involvement in the care of their infants and their attributions of cognitive competence to infants. *Child Development, 59,* 652–663.

Nolen-Hoeksema, S. N., & Girgus, J. S. (1994). The emergence of gender differences in depression during adolescence. *Psychological Bulletin, 115,* 424–443.

Nolen-Hoeksema, S. N., Mumme, D., Wolfson, A., & Guskin, K. (1995). Helplessness in children of depressed and nondepressed mothers. *Developmental Psychology, 31,* 377–387.

Nolen-Hoeksema, S., Girgus, J. S., & Seligman, M. E. P. (1992). Predictors and consequences of childhood depressive symptoms: A 5-year longitudinal study. *Journal of Abnormal Psychology, 101,* 405–422.

Noll, R. B., Bukowski, W. M., Davies, W. H., Koontz, K., & Kulkarni, R. (1993). Adjustment in the peer system of adolescents with cancer: A two-year study *Journal of Pediatric Psychology, 18,* 351–364.

Nottelmann, E. D., & Jensen, P. S. (1995a). Bipolar affective disorders in children and adolescents: Introduction. *Journal of the American Academy of Child and Adolescent Psychiatry, 34,* 705–708.

Nottelmann, E. D., & Jensen, P. S. (1995b). Comorbidity of disorders in children and adolescents: Developmental perspectives. In T. H. Ollendick, & R. J. Prinz (Eds.), *Advances in clinical child psychology* (Vol. 17). New York: Plenum Press.

Nowakowski, R. S. (1987). Basic concepts of CNS development. *Child Development, 58,* 568–595.

Nurcombe, B. (1994). The validity of the diagnosis of major depression in childhood and adolescence. In W. M. Reynolds and H. F. Johnston (Eds.), *Handbook of depression in children and adolescents.* New York: Plenum Press.

O'Brien, M. (1996). Child-rearing difficulties reported by parents of infants and toddlers. *Journal of Pediatric Psychology, 21,* 433–446.

O'Connor, N., & Hermelin, B. (1990). The recognition failure and graphic success of idot-savant artists. *Journal of Child Psychology and Psychiatry, 31,* 203–215.

O'Connor, R. D. (1969). Modification of social withdrawal through symbolic modeling. *Journal of Applied Behavior Analysis, 2,* 15–22.

O'Connor, R. D. (1972). The relative efficacy of modeling, shaping, and combined procedures. *Journal of Abnormal Psychology, 79,* 327–334.

O'Connor, T. G., McGuire, S., Reiss, D., Hetherington, E. M., & Plomin, R. (1998). Co-occurrence of depressive symptoms and antisocial behavior in adolescence: A common genetic liability. *Journal of Abnormal Psychology, 107,* 27–37.

O'Leary, K. D., & Emery, R. E. (1985). Marital discord and child behavior problems. In M. D. Levine & P. Satz (Eds.), *Developmental variation and dysfunction.* New York: Academic Press.

O'Leary, K. D., & Wilson, G. T. (1987). *Behavior therapy: Application and outcome,* 2nd ed. Englewood Cliffs, NJ: Prentice Hall.

Ochoa, S. H., & Palmer, D. J. (1995). A meta-analysis of peer rating of sociometric studies with learning disabled students. *Journal of Special Education, 29,* 1–19.

Oden, S., & Asher, S. (1977). Coaching children in skills for friendship making. *Child Development, 48,* 495–506.

Odom, S. L., & Strain, P. S. (1984). Peer-mediated approaches to promoting children's social interaction: A review. *American Journal of Orthopsychiatry, 54,* 544–557.

Offord, D. R., Boyle, M. H., Szatmari, P., Rae Grant, J. I., Links, P. S., Cadman, D. T., Byles, J. A., Crawford, J. W., Blum, H. M., Byrne, C., Thomas, H., & Woodward, C. A. (1987). Ontario Child Health Study: II. Six-month prevalence of disorder and rates of service utilization. *Archives of General Psychiatry, 44,* 832–836.

Offord, D. R., & Fleming, J. E. (1991). Epidemiology. In M. Lewis (Ed.), *Child and adolescent psychiatry. A comprehensive textbook.* Baltimore: Williams & Wilkins.

Ohman, A., & Hultman, C. M. (1998). Electrodermal activity and obstetric complications in schizophrenia. *Journal of Abnormal Psychology, 107,* 228–237.

Okun, A., Parker, G., & Levendosky, A. A. (1994). Distinct and interactive contributions of physical abuse, socioeconomic disadvantage, and negative life events to children's social, cognitive and affective adjustment. *Development and Psychopathology, 6,* 77–98.

Olds, D. L., & Kitzman, H. (1993). Review of research on home visiting for pregnant women and parents of young children. *Home Visiting, 3,* 53–92.

Ollendick, T. H. (1983). Reliability and validity of the Revised Fear Survey Schedule for Children (FSSC-R). *Behaviour Research and Therapy, 21,* 685–692.

Ollendick, T. H. (1998). Panic disorder in children and adolescents: New developments, new directions. *Journal of Clinical Child Psychology, 27,* 234–245.

Ollendick, T. H., & King, N. J. (1991). Origins of childhood fears: An evaluation of Rachman's theory of fear acquisition. *Behaviour Research and Therapy, 29,* 117–123.

Ollendick, T. H., & King, N. J. (1998). Empirically supported treatments for children with phobic and anxiety disorders: Current status. *Journal of Clinical Child Psychology, 27,* 156–167.

Ollendick, T. H., King, N. J., & Frary, R. B. (1989). Fears in children and adolescents: Reliability and generalizability across gender, age and nationality. *Behaviour Research and Therapy, 27,* 19–26.

Ollendick, T. H., King, N. L., & Hamilton, D. I. (1991). Origins of childhood fears: An evaluation of Rachman's theory of fear acquisition. *Behaviour Research and Therapy, 29,* 117–123.

Ollendick, T. H., Mattis, S. G., & King, N. J. (1994). Panic in children and adolescents: A review. *Journal of Child Psychology and Psychiatry, 35,* 113–134.

Ollendick, T. H., & Mayer, J. A. (1984). School phobia. In S. M. Turner (Ed.), *Behavioral treatment of anxiety disorders.* New York: Plenum.

Olweus, D. (1979). Stability of aggressive reaction patterns in males: A review. *Psychological Bulletin, 86,* 852–875.

Olweus, D. (1993). *Bullying at school: What we know and what we can do.* Cambridge, MA: Blackwell.

Olweus, D. (1994). Bullying at school: Basic facts and effects of a school based intervention program. *Journal of Child Psychology and Psychiatry, 35,* 1171–1190.

Ondersma, S. J., & Walker, E. (1998). Elimination disorders. In T. H. Ollendick & M. Hersen (Eds.), *Handbook of child psychopathology* (3rd ed.). New York: Plenum Press.

Oosterlaan, J., Logan, G. D., & Sergeant, J. A. (1998). Response inhibition in AD/HD, CD, comorbid AD/HD+CD, anxious, and control children: A meta-analysis of studies with the Stop task. *Journal of Child Psychology and Psychiatry, 39,* 411–425.

Orleans, C. T., & Barnett, L. R. (1984). Bulimarexia: Guidelines for behavioral assessment and treatment. In R. C. Hawkins, W. J. Fremouw, & P. F. Clement (Eds.), *The binge-purge syndrome: Diagnosis, treatment, and research.* New York: Springer.

Ornitz, E. M. (1985). Neurophysiology of infantile autism. *Journal of the American Academy of Child Psychiatry, 24,* 251–262.

Orris, J. B. (1969). Visual monitoring performance in three subgroups of male delinquents. *Journal of Abnormal Psychology, 74,* 227–229.

Orton, S. T. (1937). *Reading, writing, and speech problems in children.* New York: W. W. Norton and Co.

Osborne, A. G. (1992). Legal standards for an appropriate education in the post-Rowley era. *Exceptional Child, 58,* 488–494.

Oshima-Takane, Y., & Benaroya, S. (1989). An alternative view of pronominal errors in autistic children. *Journal of Autism and Developmental Disorders, 19,* 73–85.

Öst, L. (1987). Age of onset in different phobias. *Journal of Abnormal Psychology, 96,* 123–145.

Osterhaus, S. O. L., Passchier, J., vander Helm-Hylkema, H., de Jong, K. T., Orlebeke, J. F., de Grauw, A. J. C., & Dekker, P. H. (1993). Effects of behavioral psychophysiological treatment on school children with migraine in a nonclinical setting: Predictors and process variables. *Journal of Pediatric Psychology, 18,* 697–715.

Ozonoff, S. (1997). Casual mechanisms of autism: Unifying perspectives from an information-processing framework. In D. J. Cohen & F. R. Volkmar (Eds.),

Handbook of autism and pervasive developmental disorders. New York: John Wiley.

Ozonoff, S., & Cathcart, K. (1998). Effectiveness of a home program intervention for young children with autism. *Journal of Autism and Developmental Disorder, 28,* 25–32.

Ozonoff, S., Pennington, B. F., & Rogers, S. J. (1991). Executive functions deficits in high-functioning autistic individuals: relationship to theory of mind. *Journal of Child Psychology and Psychiatry, 32,* 1081–1105.

Page, P., Verstraete, D. G., Robb, J. R., & Etzwiler, D. D. (1981). Patient recall of self-care recommendations in diabetes. *Diabetes Care, 4,* 95–98.

Palinscar, A. S., & Brown, A. L. (1986). Interactive teaching to promote indepenent learning from text. *The Reading Teacher, 39,* 771–777.

Park, K. A., & Waters, E. (1989). Security of attachment and preschool friendships. *Child Development, 60,* 1076–1081.

Parke, R. D., & Ladd, G. W. (1992). *Family-peer relationships: Modes of linkage.* Hillsdale, NJ: Earlbaum.

Parker, J. G., & Asher, S. R. (1987). Peer relations and later personal adjustment: Are low-accepted children at risk? *Psychological Bulletin, 102,* 357–389.

Parker, J. G., Rubin, K. H., Price, J. M., & DeRosier, M. E. (1995). Peer relationships, child development, and adjustment: A developmental psychopathology perspective. In D. Cicchetti & D. Cohen (Eds.), *Developmental psychopathology* (Vol. 2: *Risk, disorder and adaptation*). New York: Wiley.

Parnas, J., Cannon. T. D., Jacobsen, B., Schulsinger, H., Schulsinger, F., & Mednick, S. A. (1993). Lifetime DSM-III-R diagnostic outcomes in the offspring of schizophrenic mothers. *Archives of General Psychiatry, 50,* 707–714.

Parsons, B. V., & Alexander, J. F. (1973). Short-term family intervention: A therapy outcome study. *Journal of Consulting and Clinical Psychology, 41,* 195–201.

Paschall, M. J., & Hubbard, M. L. (1998). Effects of neighborhood and family stressors on African American male adolescents' self-worth and propensity for violent behavior. *Journal of Consulting and Clinical Psychology, 66,* 825–831.

Patterson, G. R. (1975). *Families.* Champaign, IL: Research Press.

Patterson, G. R. (1976a). *Living with children: New methods for parents and teachers,* rev. ed. Champaign, IL: Research Press.

Patterson, G. R. (1976b). The aggressive child: Victim and architect of a coercive system. In L. A. Hamerlynck, L. C. Handy, & E. J. Mash (Eds.), *Behavior modification and families.* New York: Brunner/Mazel.

Patterson, G. R. (1982). *Coercive family process: A social learning approach,* Vol. 3. Eugene, OR: Castalia.

Patterson, G. R. (1986). Performance models for antisocial boys. *American Psychologist, 41,* 432–444.

Patterson, G. R., Chamberlain, P., & Reid, J. B. (1982). A comparative evaluation of a parent-training program. *Behavior Therapy, 13,* 638–650.

Patterson, G. R., DeBaryshe, B. D., & Ramsey, E. (1989). A developmental perspective on antisocial behavior. *American Psychologist, 44,* 329–335.

Patterson, G. R., Littman, R. A., & Bricker, W. (1967). Assertive behavior in children: A step toward a theory of aggression. *Monographs of the Society for Research in Child Development, 32* (Serial No. 113).

Patterson, G. R., Reid, J. B., & Dishion, T. J. (1992). *Antisocial boys.* Eugene, OR: Castalia Publishing Company.

Patterson, G. R., Reid, J. B., Jones, R. R., & Conger, R. E. (1975). *A social learning approach to family intervention,* Vol. 1. Eugene, OR: Castalia.

Patton, G. C., Carlin, J. B., Shao, Q., Hibbert, M. E., Rosier, M., Selzer, R., & Bowes, G. (1997). Adolescent dieting: Healthy weight control or borderline eating disorder. *Journal of Child Psychology and Psychiatry, 38,* 299–306.

Patton, J. R., Beirne-Smith, M., & Payne, J. S. (1990). *Mental retardation.* New York: Macmillan.

Pearl, R., Donahue, M., & Bryan, T. (1986). Social relationships of learning-disabled children. In J. K. Torgesen & B. Y. L. Wong (Eds.), *Psychological and educational perspectives on learning disabilities.* New York: Academic Press.

Pelham, W. E., Wheeler, T., & Chronis, A. (1998). Empirically supported psychosocial treatments for attention deficit hyperactivity disorder. *Journal of Clinical Child Psychology, 27,* 190–205.

Pennington, B. F., & Bennetto, L. (1993). Main effects or transactions in the neuropsychology of conduct disorder? Commentary on "The neuropsychology of conduct disorder." *Development and Psychopathology, 5,* 153–164.

Pennington, B. F., Groisser, D., & Welsh, M. C. (1993). Contrasting cognitive deficits in attention deficit hyperactivity disorder versus reading disability. *Developmental Psychology, 29,* 511–523.

Pennington, B. F., & Ozonoff, S. (1996). Executive functions and developmental psychopathology. *Journal of Child Psychology and Psychiatry, 37,* 51–87.

Pennington, B. F., & Welsh, M. (1997). Neuropsychology and developmental psychopathology. In D. Cicchetti & D. J. Cohen (Eds.), *Developmental Psychopathology.* New York: John Wiley.

Perlman, M. D., & Kaufman, A. S. (1990). Assessment of Child Intelligence. In G. Goldstein & M. Hersen (Eds.), *Handbook of psychological assessment* (2nd ed.). New York: Pergamon.

Perner, J., Frith, U., Leslie, A. M., & Leekam, S. R. (1989). Exploration of the autistic child's theory of mind: Knowledge, belief, and communication. *Child Development, 60,* 689–700.

Perrin, E. C., & Perrin, J. M. (1983). Clinician's assessments of children's understanding of illness. *American Journal of Disease in Children, 137,* 874–878.

Perry, A., Bryson, S., & Bebko, J. (1998). Brief report: Degree of facilitator influence in Facilitated Communication as a function of facilitator characteristics, attitudes, belief. *Journal of Autism and Developmental Disorders, 28,* 87–90.

Persson-Blennow, I., & McNeil, T. (1988). Frequencies and stability of temperament types in childhood. *Journal of the American Academy of Child and Adolescent Psychiatry, 27,* 619–622.

Peshkin, M. M. (1959). Intractable asthma of childhood: Rehabilitation at the institutional level with a follow-up of 150 cases. *International Archives of Allergy, 15,* 91–101.

Petersen, G. A. (1982). Cognitive development in infancy. In B. B. Wolman (Ed.), *Handbook of developmental psychology.* Englewood Cliffs, NJ: Prentice Hall.

Peterson, B. S. (1995). Neuroimaging in child and adolescent neuropsychiatric disorders. *Journal of the American Academy of Child and Adolescent Psychiatry, 34,* 1560–1576.

Peterson, L. (1989). Latchkey children's preparation for self-care: Overestimated, underrehearsed, and unsafe. *Journal of Clinical Child Psychology, 18,* 36–43.

Peterson, L., Farmer, J., Harbeck, C., & Chaney, J. (1990). Preparing children for hospitalization and threatening medical procedures. In A. M. Gross & R. S. Drabman (Eds.), *Handbook of clinical behavioral pediatrics.* New York: Plenum.

Peterson, L., & Magrab, P. (1989). Introduction to the special section: Children on their own. *Journal of Clinical Child Psychology, 18,* 2–7.

Peterson, L. J., & Mori, L. (1988). Preparation for hospitalization. In D. K. Routh (Ed.), *Handbook of pediatric psychology.* New York: Guilford.

Peterson, L., Schultheis, K., Ridley-Johnson, R., Miller, D. J., & Tracy, K. (1984). Comparison of three modeling procedures on the presurgical and postsurgical reactions of children. *Behavior Therapy, 15,* 197–203.

Pfefferbaum, B. (1997). Posttraumatic stress disorder in children: A review of the past 10 years. *Journal of the American Academy of Child and Adolescent Psychiatry, 36,* 1503–1511.

Pfiffner, L. J., & Barkley, R. A. (1998). Treatment of ADHD in school settings. In R. A. Barkley (Ed.), *Attention-deficit hyperactivity disorder.* New York: Guilford Press.

Phares, V. (1992). Where's Poppa?: The relative lack of attention to the role of fathers in child and adolescent psychopathology. *American Psychologist, 47,* 656–664.

Phelps, L., Andrea, R., Rizzo, F. G., Johnston, L., & Main, C. M. (1993). Prevalence of self-induced vomiting and laxative-medication abuse among female adolescents: A longitudinal study. *International Journal of Eating Disorders, 14,* 375–378.

Phillips, E. L. (1968). Achievement Place: Token reinforcement procedures in a home-style rehabilitation setting for 'pre-delinquent' boys. *Journal of Applied Behavior Analysis, 1,* 213–223.

Pick, H. L. (1989). Motor development: The control of action. *Developmental Psychology, 25,* 867–870.

Pierce, C. M. (1985). Encopresis. In H. I. Kaplan & B. J. Sadock (Eds.), *Comprehensive textbook of psychiatry/IV.* Baltimore: Williams & Wilkins.

Pierce, J. W. & Wardle, J. (1993). Self-esteem, parental appraisal and body size in children. *Journal of Child Psychology and Psychiatry, 34,* 1125–1136.

Pike, A., & Plomin, R. (1996). Importance of non-shared environmental factors for childhood and adolescent psychopathology. *Journal of the American Academy of Child and Adolescent Psychiatry, 35,* 560–570.

Pike, K. M. (1998). Long-term course of anorexia nervosa: Response, relapse, remission, and recovery. *Clinical Psychology Review, 18,* 447–475.

Pike, K. M., & Rodin, J. (1991). Mothers, daughters, and disordered eating. *Journal of Abnormal Psychology, 100,* 198–204.

Pillow, D. R., Pelham, W. E., Hoza, B., Molina, B. S. G., & Stultz, C. H. (1998). Confirmatory factor analyses examining attention deficit hyperactivity disorder symptoms and other childhood disruptive behaviors. *Journal of Abnormal Child Psychology, 26,* 293–309.

Pirke, K. M., & Platte, P. (1995). Neurobiology of eating disorders in adolescence. In H. C. Steinhausen (Ed.), *Eating disorders in adolescence: Anorexia and bulimia nervosa.* Berlin: Walter de Gruyter.

Piven, J., Arndt, S., Bailey, J., & Andreasen, N. (1996a). Regional brain enlargement in autism: A magnetic resonance imaging study. *Journal of the American Academy of Child and Adolescent Psychiatry, 35,* 530–536.

Piven, J., Harper, J. Palmer, P., & Arndt, S. (1996b). Course of behavioral change in autism: a retrospective study of high-IQ adolescents and adults. *Journal of the American Academy of Child and Adolescent Psychiatry, 35,* 523–529.

Piven, J., & Palmer, P. (1997). Cognitive deficits in parents from multiple-incidence autism families. *Journal of Child Psychology and Psychiatry, 38,* 1011–1022.

Piven, J., Simon, J., Chase, G., Wzorek, M., Landa, R., Gayle, J., & Folstein, S. (1993). The etiology of autism: Pre-, peri-, and neonatal factors. *Journal of the American Academy of Child and Adolescent Psychiatry, 32,* 1256–1263.

Plaisted, K., O'Riordan, M. O., & Baron-Cohen S. (1998). Enhanced visual search for a conjunctive target in a autism: A research note. *Journal of Child Psychology and Psychiatry, 39,* 777–783.

Pliszka, S. R., McCracken, J. T., & Maas, J. W. (1996). Catecholamines in attention-deficit hyperactivity disorder: Current perspectives. *Journal of the American Academy of Child and Adolescent Psychiatry, 35,* 264–272.

Plomin, R. (1994). Genetic research and identification of environmental influences. *Journal of Child Psychology and Psychiatry, 35,* 817–834.

Plomin, R. (1995). Genetics and children's experiences in the family. *Journal of Child Psychology and Psychiatry, 36,* 33–68.

Plomin, R., Chipuer, H. M., & Neiderhiser, J. M. (1994). Behavioral genetic evidence for the importance of nonshared environment. In E. M. Hetherington, D. Reiss, & R. Plomin, (Eds.) *Separate social worlds of siblings: The impact of nonshared environment on development.* Hillsdale, NJ: Erlbaum.

Plomin, R., DeFries, J. C., & McClearn, G. E. (1990). *Behavioral genetics: A primer,* 2nd ed. New York: W. H. Freeman and Company.

Plomin, R., & Rutter, M. (1998). Child development, molecular genetics, and what to do with genes once they are found. *Child Development, 69,* 1223–1242.

Poling, A., Gadow, K. D., & Cleary, J. (1991). *Drug therapy for behavior disorders: An introduction.* New York: Pergamon.

Pollitt, E. (1994). Poverty and child development: Relevance of research in developing countries to the U.S. *Child Development, 65,* 283–295.

Pollock, J. I. (1994). Night-waking at five years of age: predictors and prognosis. *Journal of Child Psychology and Psychiatry, 35,* 699–708.

Polloway, E. A., Patten, J. R., Smith, J. D., & Roderique, T. W. (1991). Issues in program design for elementary students with mild retardation: Emphasis on curriculum development. *Education and Training in Mental Retardation, 26,* 144–150.

Pope, A. W., Bierman, K. L., & Mumma, G. H. (1987). Peer relations of hyperactive and aggressive boys. Paper presented at the Annual Meeting of the Society for Behavioral Pediatrics, April 27, Anaheim, CA.

Pope, H. G., Mangweth, B., Negrao, A. B., Hudson, J. I., & Cordas, T. A. (1994). Child sexual abuse and bulimia nervosa: A comparison of American, Austrian, and Brazilian women. *American Journal of Psychiatry, 151,* 732–737.

Popper, C. W., & Gherardi, P. C. (1996). Anxiety disorders. In J. M. Wiener (Ed.), *Diagnosis and psychopharmacology of childhood and adolescent disorders.* New York: John Wiley & Sons.

Porrino, L. J., Rapoport, J. L., Behar, D., Sceery, W., Ismond, D. R., & Bunney, W. E. (1983). A naturalistic assessment of the motor activity of hyperactive boys: I. Comparison with normal controls. *Archives of General Psychiatry, 40,* 681–687.

Porter, J. P. (1996). Regulatory considerations in research involving children and adolescents with mental disorders. In K. Hoagwood, P. S. Jensen, & C. B. Fisher (Eds.), *Ethical issues in mental health research with children and adolescents.* Mahwah, NJ: Lawrence Erlbaum.

Potter, H. W. (1972). Mental retardation in historical perspective. In S. I. Harrison & J. F. McDermott (Eds.), *Childhood psychopathology.* New York: International Universities Press.

Powers, S. W. (1999). Empirically supported treatments in pediatric psychology: Procedure-related pain. *Journal of Pediatric Psychology, 24,* 131–145.

Powers, S. W., Blount, R. L., Bachanas, P. J., Cotter, M. W., & Swan, S. C. (1993). Helping preschool leukemia patients and their parents cope during injections. *Journal of Pediatric Psychology, 18,* 681–695.

Powers, S. W., & Roberts, M. W. (1995). Simulation training with parents of oppositional children: Preliminary findings. *Journal of Clinical Child Psychology, 24,* 89–97.

Poznanski, E. O., & Mokros, H. B. (1994). Phenomenology and epidemiology of mood disorders in children and adolescents. In W. M. Reynolds and H. F. Johnston (Eds.), *Handbook of depression in children and adolescents.* New York: Plenum Press.

Pressley, M., & Levin, J. R. (1987). Elaborative learning strategies for the inefficient learner. In S. J. Ceci (Ed.), *Handbook of cognitive, social and neuropsychological aspects of learning disabilities.* Hillsdale, NJ: Erlbaum.

Price, R. A. (1995). The search for obesity genes. In D. B. Allison & F. X. Pi-Sunyer (Eds.), *Obesity treatment: Establishing goals, improving outcomes, and reviewing the research agenda.* New York: Plenum Press.

Pring, L., & Hermelin, B. (1993). Bottle, tulip, and wineglass: semantic and structural picture processing by savant artists. *Journal of Child Psychology and Psychiatry, 34,* 1365–1385.

Pring, L., Hermelin, B., & Heavey, L. (1995). Savants, segments, art, and autism. *Journal of Child Psychology and Psychiatry, 36,* 1065–1076.

Prinz, R. J., & Riddle, D. B. (1986). Associations between nutrition and behavior in five-year-old children. *Nutrition Reviews, 44*(Suppl.), 151–157.

Prior, M. (1986). Developing concepts of childhood autism: The influence of experimental cognitive research. In S. Chess & A. Thomas (Eds.), *Annual progress in child psychiatry and child development, 1985.* New York: Brunner/Mazel.

Prior, M. (1992). Childhood temperament. *Journal of Child Psychology and Psychiatry, 33,* 249–279.

Prior, M., & Werry, J. S. (1986). Autism, schizophrenia, and allied disorders. In H. C. Quay and J. S. Werry

(Eds.), *Psychopathological disorders of childhood*. New York: Wiley.

Prugh, D. G., Staub, E. M., Sands, H. H., Kirschbaum, R. M., & Lenihan, E. A. (1953). A study of the emotional reactions of children and families to hospitalization and illness. *American Journal of Orthopsychiatry, 23*, 70–106.

Public Interest. Self-injury 'consensus' stirs strife, not accord. (1989, June). *APA Monitor*.

Puig-Antich, J. (1983). Neuroendocrine and sleep correlates of prepubertal major depressive disorder: Current status of the evidence. In D. P. Cantwell & G. A. Carlson (Eds.), *Affective disorders in childhood and adolescence: An update*. New York: Spectrum.

Puig-Antich, J. (1986). Psychobiological markers: Effects of age and puberty. In M. Rutter, C. E. Izard, & P. B. Read (Eds.), *Depression in young people: Developmental and clinical perspectives*. New York: Guilford.

Puig-Antich, J., Goetz, D., Davies, M., Kaplan, T., Davies, S., Ostrow, L., Asnis, L., Toomey, J., Iyengar, S., & Ryan, N. (1989). A controlled family history study of prepubertal major depressive disorder. *Archives of General Psychiatry, 46*, 406–418.

Pumariega, A. J., & Glover, S. (1998). New developments in service delivery research for children, adolescents, and their families. In T. H. Ollendick & R. J. Prinz (Eds.), *Advances in clinical child psychology* (Vol. 20). New York: Plenum Press.

Purcell, K., Brady, K., Chai, H., Muser, J., Molk, L., Gordon, N., & Means, J. (1969). The effect on asthma in children of experimental separation from the family. *Psychosomatic Medicine, 31*, 144–164.

Putallaz, M., & Dunn, S. E. (1990). The importance of peer relations. In M. Lewis & S. M. Miller, *Handbook of developmental psychopathology*. New York: Plenum.

Pynoos, R. S., Frederick, C., Nader, K., Arroyo, W., Steinberg, A., Eth, S., Nunez, F., & Fairbanks, L. (1987). Life threat and posttraumatic stress in school-age children. *Archives of General Psychiatry, 44*, 1057–1063.

Quay, H. C. (1986a). Classification. In H. C. Quay & J. S. Werry (Eds.), *Psychopathological disorders of childhood*, 3rd ed. New York: Wiley.

Quay, H. C. (1986b). Conduct disorders. In H. C. Quay & J. S. Werry (Eds.), *Psychopathological disorders of childhood*, 3rd ed. New York: Wiley.

Quay, H. C. (1993). The psychobiology of undersocialized aggressive conduct disorder: A theoretical perspective. *Development and Psychopathology, 5*, 165–180.

Quay, H. C. (1997). Inhibition and attention deficit hyperactivity disorder. *Journal of Abnormal Child Psychology, 25*, 7–13.

Quay, H. C., & Peterson, D. R. (1983). *Interim manual for the Revised Behavior Problem Checklist*. Coral Gables, Fl.: University of Miami.

Quine, L., & Rutter, D. R. (1994). First diagnosis of severe mental and physical disability: A study of doctor-parent communication. *Journal of Child Psychology and Psychiatry, 35*, 1273–1287.

Rachman, S. J. (1977). The conditioning theory of fear-acquisition: A critical examination. *Behaviour Research and Therapy, 15*, 375–387.

Raine, A., & Venables, P. H. (1984). Tonic heart rate level, social class and antisocial behaviour in adolescents. *Biological Psychology, 18*, 123–132.

Rainer, J. D. (1980). Genetics and psychiatry. In H. I. Kaplan, A. M. Freedman, & B. J. Sadock (Eds.), *Comprehensive textbook of psychiatry/III*, Vol. 3. Baltimore: Williams & Wilkins.

Rait, D. S., Ostroff, J. S., Smith, K., Cella, D. F., Tan, C., & Lesko, L. M. (1992). Lives in a balance—perceived family functioning and the psychosocial adjustment of adolescent cancer survivors. *Family Process, 31*, 383–397.

Rakic, P. & Lombroso, P. J. (1998). Development of the cerebral cortex: I. Forming the cortical structure. *Journal of the American Academy of Child and Adolescent Psychiatry, 37*, 116–117.

Ramey, C. T., & Campbell, F. A. (1984). Preventive education for high-risk children: Cognitive consequences of the Carolina Abecedarian Project. *American Journal of Mental Deficiency, 88*, 515–523.

Ramey, C. T., & Campbell, F. A. (1987). The Carolina Abecedarian Project: An educational experiment concerning human malleability. In J. J. Gallagher & C. T. Ramey (Eds.), *The malleability of children*. Baltimore: Paul Brookes.

Ramey, C. T., & Ramey, S. L. (1998). Early intervention and early experience. *American Psychologist, 53*, 109–120.

Rao, U., Dahl, D., Ryan, N. D., Birmaher, B., Williamson, D. E., Giles, D. E., Rao, R., Kaufman, J., & Nelson, B. (1996). The relationship between longitudinal clinical course and sleep and cortisol changes in adolescent depression. *Biological Psychiatry, 40*, 474–483.

Rapee, R. M., Barrett, P. M., Dadds, M. R., & Evans, L. (1994). Reliability of the DSM-III-R childhood anxiety disorders using structured interview: Interrater and parent-child agreement. *Journal of the American Academy of Child and Adolescent Psychiatry, 33*, 984–992.

Rapoport, J. L. (1989). The biology of obsessions and compulsions. *Scientific American, 260*, 83–89.

Rapoport, J. L, & Ismond, D. R. (1996). *DSM-IV training guide for diagnosis of childhood disorders*. New York: Brunner/Mazel.

Rapport, M. D. (1993). Attention deficit hyperactivity disorder. In T. H. Ollendick & M. Hersen (Eds.), *Handbook of child and adolescent assessment*. Boston: Allyn and Bacon.

Rapport, M. D., Denney, C., DuPaul, G. J., & Gardner, M. J. (1994). Attention deficit disorder and methylphenidate: Normalization rates, clinical effectiveness, and response prediction in 76 children. *Journal of the American Academy of Child and Adolescent Psychiatry, 33,* 882–893.

Rauh, V. A., Achenbach, T. M., Nurcombe, B., Howell, C. T., & Teti, D. M. (1988). Minimizing adverse effects of low birthweight: Four-year results of an early intervention program. *Child Development, 59,* 544–553.

Reddy, L. A., & Pfeiffer, S. I. (1997). Effectiveness of treatment foster care with children and adolescents: A review of outcome studies. *American Journal of the American Academy of Child and Adolescent Psychiatry, 36,* 581–588.

Rehm, L. P. (1977). A self-control model of depression. *Behavior Therapy, 8,* 787–804.

Reid, J. B. (Ed.) (1978). *A social learning approach to family intervention* (Vol. 2: *Observations in home settings*). Eugene, OR: Castalia.

Reitan, R. M., & Wolfson, D. (1993). *The Halstead-Reitan Neuropsychological Test Battery: Theory and clinical interpretation* (2nd ed.). Tucson: Neuropsychology Press.

Rende, R. D., Plomin, R., Reiss, D., & Hetherington, E. M. (1993). Genetic and environmental influences on depressive symptomatology in adolescence: Individual differences and extreme scores. *Journal of Child Psychology and Psychiatry, 34,* 1387–1398.

Renne, C. M., & Creer, T. L. (1985). Asthmatic children and their families. In M. Wolraich & D. Routh (Eds.). *Advances in developmental and behavioral pediatrics,* Vol. 6. Greenwich, CT: JAI.

Renouf, A. G., & Kovacs, M. (1994). Concordance between mothers' reports and children's self-reports of depressive symptoms: A longitudinal study. *Journal of the American Academy of Child & Adolescent Psychiatry, 33,* 208–216.

Reschly, D. J. (1992). Mental retardation: Conceptual foundations, definitional criteria, and diagnostic operations. In S. R. Hooper, G. W. Hynd, & R. W. Mattison (Eds.), *Assessment and diagnosis of child and adolescent psychiatric disorders, Vol. II. Developmental disorders.* Hillsdale, NJ: Erlbaum.

Reschley, D. J. (1996). Identification and assessment of students with disabilities. *The Future of Children, 6,* 40–53.

Rettew, D. C., Swedo, S. E., Leonard, H. L., Lenane, M. C., & Rapoport, J. L. (1992). Obsessions and compulsions across time in 79 children and adolescents with obsessive compulsive disorder. *Journal of the American Academy of Child and Adolescent Psychology, 31,* 1050–1056.

Rey, J. M. (1993). Oppositional defiant disorder. *American Journal of Psychiatry, 150,* 1769–1778.

Reynolds, C. R., & Kamphaus, R. W. (1992). *The Behavior Assessment System for Children.* Circle Pines, MN: American Guidance Service.

Reynolds, C. R., & Richmond, B. O. (1978). What I think and feel: A revised measure of children's manifest anxiety. *Journal of Abnormal Child Psychology, 6,* 271–280.

Reynolds, C. R., & Richmond, B. O. (1985). *Revised Children's Manifest Anxiety Scale.* Los Angeles: Western Psychological Service.

Reynolds, W. M. (1987). *Reynolds Adolescent Depression Scale: Professional Manual.* Odessa, FL: Psychological Assessment Resources.

Reynolds, W. M. (1989). *Reynolds Child Depression Scale:* Odessa, FL: Psychological Assessment Resources.

Reynolds, W. M. (1993). Self-report methodology. In T. H. Ollendick & M. Hersen (Eds.), *Handbook of child and adolescent assessment.* Boston: Allyn & Bacon.

Reynolds, W. M. (1994). Assessment of depression in children and adolescents by self-report questionnaires. In W. M. Reynolds and H. F. Johnston (Eds.), *Handbook of depression in children and adolescents.* New York: Plenum Press.

Reynolds, W. M., & Johnston, H. F. (1994). The nature and study of depression in children and adolescents. In W. M. Reynolds and H. F. Johnston (Eds.), *Handbook of depression in children and adolescents.* New York: Plenum Press.

Richardson, S. A., Koller, H., & Katz, M. (1985). Relationship of upbringing to later behavior disturbance of mildly mentally retarded young people. *American Journal of Mental Deficiency, 90,* 1–8.

Richters, J. E. (1992). Depressed mothers as informants about their children: A critical review of the evidence for distortion. *Psychological Bulletin, 112,* 485–499.

Richters, J. E. and colleagues (1995). NIMH collaborative multisite multimodal treatment study of children with ADHD: I. Background and rationale. *Journal of the American Academy of Child and Adolescent Psychiatry, 34,* 987–1000.

Riddle, M. A., Scahill, L., King, R., Hardin, M. T., Towbin, K. E., Ort, S. I., Leckman, J. F., & Cohen, D. J. (1992). Obsessive compulsive disorder in children and adolescents: Phenomenology and family history. *Journal of the American Academy of Child and Adolescent Psychology, 29,* 766–772.

Rie, H. E. (1971). Historical perspectives of concepts of child psychopathology. In H. E. Rie (Ed.), *Perspectives in child psychopathology.* New York: Aldine-Atherton.

Riess, D., & Price, R. H. (1996). National research agenda for prevention research: The National Institute of Mental Health Report. *American Psychologist, 51,* 1109–1115.

Riley, D. A. (1997). Using local research to change 100 communities for children and families. *American Psychologist, 52,* 424–433.

Rispens, J., & van Yperen, T. A. (1997). How specific are "Specific Developmental Disorders"? The relevance of the concept of specific developmental disorders for the classification of childhood developmental disorders. *Journal of Child Psychology* and *Psychiatry, 38,* 351–363.

Ritter, D. R. (1989). Social competence and problem behavior of adolescent girls with learning disabilities. *Journal of Learning Disabilities, 22,* 460–461.

Roach, M. A., Barratt, M. S., Miller, J. F., & Leavitt, L. A. (1998). The structure of mother-child play: Young children with Down syndrome and typically developing children. *Developmental Psychology, 34,* 77–87.

Roberts, M. A. (1990). A behavioral observation method for differentiating hyperactive and aggressive boys. *Journal of Abnormal Child Psychology, 18,* 131–142.

Roberts, M. C. (1995). *Handbook of pediatric psychology* (2nd ed.). New York: Plenum Press.

Roberts, M. C., & Lyman, R. D. (1990). The psychologist as a pediatric consultant: Inpatient and outpatient. In A. M. Gross & R. S. Drabman (Eds.), *Handbook of clinical behavioral pediatrics.* New York: Plenum.

Roberts, M. C. & Wallander, J. L. (1992). Family issues in pediatric psychology: An overview. In M. C. Roberts & J. L. Wallander (Eds.). *Family issues in pediatric psychology.* Hillsdale, NJ: Erlbaum.

Robin, A. L., & Foster, S. L. (1989). *Negotiating parent-adolescent conflict: A behavioral family systems approach.* New York: Guilford.

Robin, A. L., Gilroy, M., & Dennis, A. B. (1998). Treatment of eating disorders in children and adolescents. *Clinical Psychology Review, 18,* 421–446.

Robin, A. L., Koepke, T., & Moye, A. (1990). Multidimensional assessment of parent-adolescent relations. *Psychological Assessment, 2,* 451–459.

Robins, L. N. (1978). Sturdy childhood predictors of adult antisocial behavior: Replication from longitudinal studies. *Psychological Medicine, 8,* 611–622.

Robins, L. N., Murphy, G. E., Woodruff, R. A., Jr., & King, L. J. (1971). The adult psychiatric status of black school boys. *Archives of General Psychiatry, 24,* 338–345.

Robins, P. M. (1992). A comparison of behavioral and attentional functioning in children diagnosed as hyperactive or learning disabled. *Journal of Abnormal Child Psychology, 20,* 65–82.

Robinson, N. M., & Robinson, H. B. (1976). *The mentally retarded child.* New York: McGraw-Hill.

Roff, J. D., & Wirt, R. D. (1984). Childhood aggression and social adjustment as antecedants of delinquency. *Journal of Abnormal Child Psychology, 12,* 111–126.

Roff, M. (1961). Childhood social interactions and young adult bad conduct. *Journal of Abnormal and Social Psychology, 63,* 333–337.

Roff, M., Sells, S., & Golden, M. (1972). *Social adjustment and personality development in children.* Minneapolis: University of Minnesota Press.

Rogers, S. (1998). Empirically supported comprehensive treatments for young children with autism. *Journal of Clinical Child Psychology, 27,* 168–179.

Rojahn, J., Tasse, M. J., & Morin, D. (1998). Self-injurious behavior and stereotypes. In T. H. Ollendick & M. Hersen (Eds.), *Handbook of child psychopathology.* New York: Plenum Press.

Rolland-Cachera, M. F., Deheeger, M., Guilloud-Bataille, M., Avons, P., Patois, E., & Sempe, M. (1987). Tracking the development of adiposity from one month of age to adulthood. *Annals of Human Biology, 14,* 219–229.

Rosenfeld, A. A., Pilowsky, D. J., Fine, P., Thorpe, M., Fein, E., Simms, M. D., Halfon, N., Irwin, M., Alfaro, J., Saletsky, R., & Nickman, S. (1997). Foster care: An update. *Journal of the American Academy of Child and Adolescent Psychiatry, 36,* 448–458.

Rosenthal, D. (1975). Heredity in criminality. *Criminal Justice and Behavior, 2,* 3–21.

Rosenthal, T. L. (1984). Some organizing hints for communicating applied information. In B. Gholson & T. L. Rosenthal (Eds.), *Applications of cognitive-developmental theory.* Orlando, FL: Academic Press.

Ross, A. O. (1972). The clinical child psychologist. In B. J. Wolman (Ed.), *Manual of child psychopathology.* New York: McGraw-Hill.

Ross, C. K., Lavigne, J. V., Hayford, J. R., Berry, S. L., Sinacore, J. M., & Pachman, L. M. (1993). Psychological factors affecting reported pain in juvenile rheumatoid arthritis. *Journal of Pediatric Psychology, 18,* 561–573.

Ross, D. M. (1988). Aversive treatment procedures: The school-age child's view. *Newsletter of the Society of Pediatric Psychology, 12,* 3–6.

Rossen, M., Klima, E. S., Bellugi, U., Bihrle, A., & Jones, W. (1996). Interaction between language and cognition: Evidence from Williams syndrome. In J. H. Beitchman, N. J. Cohen, M. M. Konstantareas, & R. Tannock (Eds.), *Language, learning, and behavior disorders.* New York: Cambridge University Press.

Rourke, B. P. (1988). Socioemotional disturbances of learning disabled children. *Journal of Consulting and Clinical Psychology, 56,* 801–810.

Rourke, B. P. (1989). Coles's learning mystique: The good, the bad, and the irrelevant. *Journal of Learning Disabilities, 22,* 275–277.

Rourke, B. P., & Fuerst, D. R. (1995). Cognitive processing, academic achievement, and psychological functioning: A neurodevelopmental perspective. In

D. Cicchetti & D. J. Cohen (Eds.), *Developmental psychopathology*. New York: John Wiley.

Routh, D. K. (1994a). Commentary: Facilitated communication as unwitting ventriloquism. *Journal of Pediatric Psychology, 19,* 673–675.

Routh, D. K. (1994b). Impact of poverty on children, youth, and families: Introduction to the special issue. *Journal of Clinical Child Psychology, 23,* 346–348.

Routh, D. K., Schroeder, C. S., & Koocher, G. P. (1983). Psychology and primary health care for children. *American Psychologist, 38,* 95–98.

Rowe, D. C., & Kandel, D. (1997). In the eye of the beholder? Parental ratings of externalizing and internalizing symptoms. *Journal of Abnormal Child Psychology, 25,* 265–275.

Rubin, K. H. (1994). From family to peer group—relations between relationships systems. *Social Development, 3,* iii–viii.

Rubin, K. H., Fein, G. G., & Vandenberg, B. (1983). Play. In P. H. Mussen (Ed.), *Handbook of child psychology: Vol. 4, Socialization, personality, and social behavior.* New York: Wiley.

Rubin, K. H., Stewart, S. L., & Coplan, R. J. (1995). Social withdrawal in childhood. In T. H. Ollendick and R. Prinz (Eds.), *Advances in clinical child psychology,* Vol. 17. New York: Plenum.

Rumsey, J. M., Rapoport, J. L., & Sceery, W. R. (1985). Autistic children as adults: Psychiatric, social, and behavioral outcomes. *Journal of the American Academy of Child Psychiatry, 24,* 465–473.

Rusby, J. C., Estes, A., & Dishion, T. (1991). *The Interpersonal Process Code (IPC).* Unpublished manuscript. Oregon Social Learning Center, Eugene.

Russ, S. W. (1995). Play psychotherapy research: State of the science. In T. H. Ollendick & R. J. Prinz (Eds.), *Advances in clinical child psychology. Vol. 17.* New York: Plenum.

Russell, A. T., Bott, L., & Sammons, C. (1989). The phenomenology of schizophrenia occurring in childhood. *Journal of the American Academy of Child and Adolescent Psychiatry, 28,* 399–407.

Russell, P. A., Hosie, J. A., Gray, C. D., Scott, C., Hunter, N., Banks, S. J., & Macaulay, M. C. (1998). The development of theory of mind in deaf children. *Journal of Child Psychology and Psychiatry, 39,* 903–910.

Russo, M. F., & Beidel, D. C. (1994). Comorbidity of childhood anxiety and externalizing disorders: Prevalence, associated characteristics, and validation issues. *Clinical Psychology Review, 14,* 199–221.

Russo, M. F., Loeber, R., Lahey, B. B., & Keenan, K. (1994). Oppositional defiant and conduct disorders: Validation of the DSM-III-R and an alternative diagnostic option. *Journal of Clinical Child Psychology, 23,* 56–68.

Rutter, M. (1978). Diagnosis and definition. In M. Rutter and E. Schopler (Eds.), *Autism: A reappraisal of concepts and treatments.* New York: Plenum.

Rutter, M. (1983). School effects on pupils progress: Research findings and policy implications. *Child Development, 54,* 1–29.

Rutter, M. (1987). Psychosocial resilience and protective mechanisms. *American Journal of Orthopsychiatry, 57,* 316–331.

Rutter, M. (1989a). Isle of Wight revisited: Twenty-five years of child psychiatric epidemiology. *Journal of the American Academy of Child and Adolescent Psychiatry, 28,* 633–653.

Rutter, M. (1989b). Pathways from childhood to adult life. *Journal of Child Psychology and Psychiatry, 30,* 23–51.

Rutter, M. (1998). Routes from research to clinical practice in child psychiatry: Retrospect and prospect. *Journal of Child Psychology and Psychiatry, 39,* 805–816.

Rutter, M., Bailey, A., Bolton, P., & Le Couteur, A. (1993). Autism: Syndrome definition and possible genetic mechanisms. In R. Plomin & G. E. McClearn (Eds.), *Nature, nurture & psychology.* Washington DC: American Psychological Association.

Rutter, M., Bailey, A., Bolton, P., & Le Courteur, A. (1994). Autism and known medical conditions: Myth and substance. *Journal of Child Psychology and Psychiatry, 35,* 311–322.

Rutter, M., Bailey, A., Simonoff, E., & Pickles, A. (1997). Genetic influences and autism. In D. J. Cohen & F. R. Volkmar (Eds.), *Handbook of autism and pervasive developmental disorders.* New York: John Wiley.

Rutter, M., Garmezy, N. (1983). Developmental psychopathology. In P. H. Mussen (Ed.), *Handbook of child psychology,* Vol. IV. New York: Wiley.

Rutter, M., & Giller, H. (1984). *Juvenile delinquency: Trends and perspectives.* New York: Guilford.

Rutter, M., Graham, P., & Yule, W. (1970). *A neuropsychiatric study in childhood.* Clinics in Developmental Medicine, Nos. 35/36. London: Heinemann.

Rutter, M., Macdonald, H., Le Couteur, A., Harrington, R., Bolton, P., & Baily, A. (1990). Genetic factors in child psychiatric disorders—II. Empirical Findings. *Journal of Child Psychology and Psychiatry, 31,* 39–83.

Rutter, M., Mayhood, L., & Howlin, P. (1992). Language delay and social development. In P. Fletcher & D. Hall (Eds.), *Specific speech and language disorders in children.* San Diego, CA: Singular Publishing Group.

Rutter, M., and Schopler, E. (1987). Autism and pervasive developmental disorders: Concepts and diagnostic issues. *Journal of Autism and Developmental Disorders, 17,* 159–186.

Rutter, M., Silberg, J., O'Connor, T., & Simonoff, E. (1999). Genetics and child psychiatry: II Empirical research findings. *Journal of Child Psychology and Psychiatry, 40,* 19–55.

Rutter, M., Tizard, J., & Whitmore, K. (Eds). (1970). *Education, health, and behavior.* London: Longmans.

Ryan, N. D., Puig-Antich, J., Ambrosini, P., Ravinovich, H., Robinson, D., Neilson, B., Iyenhar, S., & Toomey, J. (1987). The clinical picture of major depression in children and adolescents. *Archives of General Psychiatry, 44,* 854–861.

Sahley, T. L., & Panksepp, J. (1987). Brain opiods and autism: An updated analysis of possible linkages. *Journal of Autism and Developmental Disorders, 17,* 201–216.

St. Pierre, R. G., & Layzer, J. I. (1998). Improving the life chances of children in poverty: Assumptions and what we have learned. *Social Policy Report. Society for Research in Child Development.* Vol. XII (4).

Saler, L., & Skolnick, N. (1992). Childhood parental death and depression in adulthood: Roles of surviving parent and family environment. *American Journal of Orthopsychiatry, 62,* 504–516.

Sameroff, A. J. (1990). Neo-environmental perspectives on developmental theory. In R. M. Hodapp, J. A. Burack, & E. Zigler (Eds.), *Issues in the developmental approach to mental retardation.* New York: Cambridge University Press.

Sameroff, A. J., & Chandler, M. J. (1975). Reproductive risk and the continuum of caretaking casualty. In F. D. Horowitz (Ed.), *Review of child development research.* Vol. 4, Chicago: University of Chicago Press.

Sanson, A., Smart, D., Prior, M., & Oberklaid, F. (1993). Precursors of hyperactivity and aggression. *Journal of the American Academy of Child and Adolescent Psychiatry, 32,* 1207–1216.

Santostefano, S. (1978). *A biodevelopmental approach to clinical child psychology.* New York: Wiley-Interscience.

Saris, W. J. M. (1995). Metabolic effects of exercise in overweight individuals. In K. D. Brownell & C. G. Fairburn (Eds.), *Eating disorders and obesity: A comprehensive handbook.* New York: Guilford Press.

Satterfield, J. H. (1994). Prediction of antisocial behavior in ADHD. Letters to the editor. *Journal of the American Academy of Child and Adolescent Psychiatry, 34,* 398–400.

Satterfield, J. H., Satterfield, B. T., & Schell, A. M. (1987). Therapeutic interventions to prevent delinquency in hyperactive boys. *Journal of the American Academy of Child and Adolescent Psychiatry, 26,* 56–64.

Sattler, J. M. (1988). *Assessment of children,* 3rd ed. San Diego: Jerome M. Sattler, Publisher.

Satz, P., & Fletcher, J. M. (1988). Early identification of learning disabled children: An old problem revisited. *Journal of Consulting and Clinical Psychology, 56,* 824–829.

Savin, D., Sack, W. H., Clarke, G. N., Meas, N., & Richart, I. (1996). The Khmer Adolescent Project: III. A study of trauma from Thailand's Site II refugee camp. *Journal of the American Academy of Child and Adolescent Psychiatry, 35,* 384–391.

Saxe, L., & Cross, T. P. (1997). Interpreting the Fort Bragg Children's Mental Health Demonstration Project: The cup is half full. *American Psychologist. 52,* 553–556.

Saxe, L., Cross, T., & Silverman, N. (1988). Children's mental health. *American Psychologist, 43,* 800–807.

Saylor, C. F., Powell, P., & Swenson, C. (1992). Hurricane Hugo blows down the broccoli: Preschoolers' post-disaster play and adjustment. *Child Psychiatry and Human Development, 22,* 139–149.

Scarr, S. (1982). Testing for children: Assessment and the many determinants of intellectual competence. In S. Chess & A. Thomas (Eds.), *Annual Progress In Child Psychiatry and Child Development 1982.* New York: Brunner/Mazel.

Scarr, S. (1998). American child care today. *American Psychologist, 53,* 95–108.

Scarr, S., Phillips, D., & McCartney, K. (1989). Working mothers and their families. *American Psychologist, 44,* 1402–1409.

Scarr, S., Phillips, D., & McCartney, K. (1990). Facts, fantasies, and the future of child care in the United States, *Psychological Science, 1,* 26–35.

Schachar, R. (1991). Childhood hyperactivity. *Journal of Child Psychology and Psychiatry, 32, 155–191.*

Schachar, R., & Logan, D. L. (1990). Impulsivity and inhibitory control in normal development and childhood psychopathology. *Developmental Psychology, 26,* 710–720.

Schacht, T., & Nathan, P. E. (1977). But is it good for psychologists? Appraisal and status of DSM-III. *American Psychologist, 32,* 1017–1025.

Schafer, L. C., Glasgow, R. E., & McCaul, K. D. (1982). Increasing the adherence of diabetic adolescents. *Journal of Behavioral Medicine, 5,* 353–362.

Schaughency, E., McGee, R., Raja, S. N., Feehan, M., & Silva, P. A. (1994). Self-reported inattention, impulsivity, and hyperactivity at ages 15 and 18 years in the general population. *Journal of the American Academy of Child and Adolescent Psychiatry, 33,* 173–184.

Scheerenberger, R. C. (1983, 1987). *A history of mental retardation.* Baltimore: Brookes Publishing Co.

Schlicker, S. A., Borra, S. T., & Regan, C. (1994). The weight and fitness status of United States children. *Nutrition Reviews, 52,* 11–17.

Schmidt, K., Solanto, M. V., & Bridger, W. H. (1985). Electrodermal activity of undersocialized aggressive children: A pilot study. *Journal of Child Psychology and Psychiatry, 26,* 653–660.

Schneider, B. H. (1992). Didactic methods for enhancing children's peer relations: A quantitative review. *Clinical Psychology Review, 12,* 363–382.

Schopler, E. (1994). Behavioral priorities for autism and related developmental disorders. In E. Schopler & G. B. Mesibov (Eds.), *Behavioral issues in autism.* New York: Plenum.

Schopler, E. (1997). Implementation of TEACCH philosophy. In D. J. Cohen & F. R. Volkmar (Eds.), *Handbook of autism and pervasive developmental disorders.* New York: John Wiley.

Schopler, E., Reichler, R. J., DeVellis, R. F., & Daly K. (1980). Toward objective classification of childhood autism: Childhood Autism Rating Scale (CARS). *Journal of Autism and Developmental Disorders, 10,* 91–103.

Schopler, E., Reichler, R. J., & Renner, B. R. (1988). *The Childhood Autism Rating Scale (CARS).* Los Angeles: Western Psychological Services.

Schopler, E., Short, A., & Mesibov, G. (1989). Relation of behavioral treatment to "normal functioning": Comment on Lovaas. *Journal of Consulting and Clinical Psychology, 57,* 162–164.

Schothorst, P. F., & van Engeland, H. (1996). Long-term behavioural sequelae of prematurity. *Journal of the American Academy of Child and Adolescent Psychiatry, 35,* 175–183.

Schreibman, L. (1997). Theoretical perspectives on behavioral intervention for individuals with autism. In D. J. Cohen & F. R. Volkmar (Eds.), *Handbook of autism and pervasive developmental disorders.* New York: John Wiley.

Schreibman, L., & Charlop-Christy, M. J. (1998). Autistic disorder. In T. H. Ollendick & M. Hersen (Eds.), *Handbook of child psychopathology.* New York: Plenum Press.

Schroeder, C. S. & Gordon, B. N. (1991). *Assessment and treatment of childhood problems: A clinician's guide.* New York: Guilford.

Schroeder, P. (1989). Toward a national family policy. *American Psychologist, 44,* 1410–1413.

Schulte-Korne, G., Deimel, W., Muller, K., Gutenbrunner, C., & Remschmidt, H. (1996). Familial aggregation of spelling disability. *Journal of Child Psychology and Psychiatry, 37,* 817–822.

Schulz, S. C., Findling, R. L., Wise, A., Friedman, L., & Kenny, J. (1998). Child and adolescent schizophrenia. *The Psychiatric Clinics of North America, 21,* 43–56.

Schwartz, D., Dodge, K. A., & Coie, J. D. (1993). The emergence of chronic peer victimization in boys' play groups. *Child Development, 64,* 1755–1772.

Schwartz, D., Dodge, K. A., Coie, J. D., Hubbard, J. A., Cillessen, A. H. N., Lemerise, E. A., & Bateman, H. (1998). Social-cognitive and behavioral correlates of aggression and victimization in boys' play groups. *Journal of Abnormal Child Psychology, 26,* 431–440.

Schwartz, J. A. J., Gladstone, T. R. G., & Kaslow, N. J. (1998). Depressive disorders. In T. H. Ollendick & M. Hersen (Eds.), *Handbook of child psychopathology* (3rd ed.). New York: Plenum Press.

Scott, K. C., & Carran, D. T. (1987). The epidemiology and prevention of mental retardation. *American Psychologist, 42,* 801–804.

Scott, S. (1994). Mental retardation. In M. Rutter, E. Taylor, & L. Hersov (Eds.), *Child and adolescent psychiatry. Modern approaches.* Cambridge, MA: Blackwell.

Scotti, J. R., Morris, T. L., McNeil, C. B., & Hawkins, R. P. (1996). DSM-IV and disorders of childhood and adolescence: Can structural criteria be functional? *Journal of Consulting and Clinical Psychology, 64,* 1177–1191.

Sears, R. R. (1975). *Your ancients revisited: A history of child development.* Chicago: University of Chicago Press.

Seiffge-Krenke, I. (1998). The highly structured climate in families of adolescents with diabetes: Functional or dysfunctional for metabolic control? *Journal of Pediatric Psychology, 23,* 313–322.

Seligman, M. P., & Peterson, C. (1986). A learned helplessness perspective on childhood depression: Theory and research. In M. Rutter, C. E. Izard, & P. B. Read (Eds.), *Depression in young people: Developmental and clinical perspectives.* New York: Guilford.

Seligman, R., Gleser, G., Rauh, J., & Harris L. (1974). The effect of earlier parental loss in adolescence. *Archives of General Psychiatry, 31,* 475–479.

Selye, H. (1956). *The stress of life.* New York: McGraw-Hill.

Semrud-Clikeman, M., Filipek, P. A., Biederman, J., Steingard, R., Kennedy, D., Renshaw, P., & Bekken, K. (1994). Attention-deficit hyperactivity disorder: Magnetic resonance imaging morphometric analysis of the corpus callosum. *Journal of the American Academy of Child and Adolescent Psychiatry, 33,* 875–881.

Semrud-Clikeman, M., & Hynd, G. W. (1990). Right hemispheric dysfunction in nonverbal learning disabilities: Social, academic, and adaptive functioning in adults and children. *Psychological Bulletin, 107,* 196–209.

Semrud-Clikeman, M., & Hynd, G. W. (1992). Developmental arithmetic disorder. In S. R. Hooper, G. W. Hynd, & R. E. Mattison (Eds.), *Developmental disorders: Diagnostic criteria and clinical assessment.* Hillsdale, NJ: Erlbaum.

Senf, G. M. (1986). LD research in sociological and scientific perspective. In J. K. Torgesen & B. Y. L. Wong (Eds.), *Psychological and educational perspectives on learning disabilities.* New York: Academic Press.

Serbin, L. A., Peters, P. L., McAffer, V. J., & Schwartzman, A. E. (1991). Childhood aggression and withdrawal as predictors of adolescent pregnancy, early parenthood, and environmental risk for the next generation. *Canadian Journal of Behavioural Science 23*, 318–331.

Shaffer, D., Campbell, M., Cantwell, D., Bradley, S., Carlson, G., Cohen, D., Denckla, M., Frances, A., Garfinkel, B., Klein, R., Pincus, H., Spitzer, R. L., Volkmar, F., & Widiger, T. (1989). Child and adolescent psychiatric disorders in DSM-IV: Issues facing the work group. *Journal of the American Academy of Child and Adolescent Psychiatry, 28*, 830–835.

Shaffer, D., Fisher, P., Dulcan, M. K., Davies, M., Piacentini, J., Schwab-Stone, M. E., Lahey, B. B., Bourdon, K., Jensen, P. S., Bird, H. R., Canino, G., & Regier, D. A. (1996). The NIMH Diagnostic Interview Schedule for Children Version 2.3 (DISC-2.3): Description, acceptability, prevalence rates, and performance in the MECA study. *Journal of the American Academy of Child and Adolescent Psychiatry, 35*, 865–877.

Shaffer, D., Garland, A., Gould, M., Fisher, P., & Trautman, P. (1988). Preventing teenage suicide: A critical review. *Journal of the American Academy of Child and Adolescent Psychiatry, 27*, 675–687.

Shaffer, D., & Waslick, B. D. (1996). Elimination and sleep disorders. In J. M. Wiener (Ed.), *Diagnosis and psychopharmacology of childhood and adolescent disorders.* New York: John Wiley.

Shah, A., & Frith, U. (1993). Why do autistic individuals show superior performance on the block design task? *Journal of Child Psychology and Psychiatry, 34*, 1351–1364.

Shapiro, S., Newcomb, M., & Loeb, T. B. (1997). Fear of fat, disregulated-restrained eating, and body-esteem: Prevalence and gender differences among eight- to ten-year-old children. *Journal of Clinical Psychology, 26*, 358–365.

Shapiro, T., & Esman, A. (1992). Psychoanalysis and child and adolescent psychiatry. *Journal of the American Academy of Child and Adolescent Psychiatry, 31*, 6–13.

Sharp, W. S., Walter, J. M., Marsh, W. L., Ritchie, G. F., Hamburger, S. D., & Castellanos, F. X. (1999). ADHD in girls: Clinical comparability of a research sample. *Journal of the American Academy of Child and Adolescent Psychiatry, 38*, 40–47.

Shaywitz, S. E., Fletcher, J. M., & Shaywitz, B. A. (1996). A conceptual model and definition of dyslexia: Findings emerging from the Connecticut Longitudinal Study. In J. H. Beitchman, N. J. Cohen, M. M. Konstantareas, & R. Tannock (Eds.), *Language, learning, and behavior disorders.* New York: Cambridge University Press.

Shaywitz, S. E., Shaywitz, B. A., Pugh, K. R., Fulbright, R. K., Constable, R. T., Mencl, W. E., Shankweiler, D. P., Liberman, A. M., Skudlarski, P., Fletcher, J. M., Katz, L., Marchione, K. E., Lacadie, C., Gatenby, C., & Gore, J. C. (1998). Functional disruption in the organization of the brain for reading in dyslexia. *Proceedings of the National Academy of Sciences, 95*, 2636–2641.

Shealy, C. N. (1995). From Boys Town to Oliver Twist: Separating facts from fiction in welfare reform and out-of-home placement of children and youth. *American Psychologist, 50*, 565–580.

Shields, A. M., Cicchetti, D., & Ryan, R. M. (1994). The development of emotional and behavioral self-regulation and social competence among maltreated school-age children. *Development and Psychopathology, 6*, 57–76.

Shisslak, C. M., Crago, M., & Estes, L. S. (1995). The spectrum of eating disturbances. *International Journal of Eating Disorders, 18*, 209–219.

Siegel, B. (1997). Coping with the diagnosis of autism. In D. J. Cohen & F. R. Volkmar (Eds.). *Handbook of autism and pervasive developmental disorders.* New York: John Wiley.

Siegel, L. S. (1989). IQ is irrelevant to the definition of learning disabilities. *Journal of Learning Disabilities, 22*, 469–478, 486.

Siegel, O. (1982). Personality development in adolescence. In B. B. Wolman (Ed.), *Handbook of developmental psychology.* Englewood Cliffs, NJ: Prentice Hall.

Siegler, R. S. (1992). The other Alfred Binet. *Developmental Psychology, 28*, 179–190.

Siervogel, R. M. (1988). Genetic and familial factors in human obesity. In N. A. Krasnegor, G. D. Grave, & N. Kretchmer (Eds.), *Childhood obesity: A biobehavioral perspective.* Caldwell, NJ: The Telford Press.

Sigman, M. (1998). Change and continuity in the development of children with autism. *Journal of Child Psychology and Psychiatry, 39*, 817–828.

Sigman, M., Dissanayake, C., Arbelle, S., & Ruskin, E. (1997). Cognition and emotion in adolescents with autism. In D. J. Cohen & F. R. Volkmar (Eds.), *Handbook of autism and pervasive developmental disorders.* New York: John Wiley.

Silberg, J., Rutler, M., Meyer, J., Maes, H., Hewitt, J., Simonoff, E., Pickles, A., Loeber, R., & Eaves, L. (1996). Genetic and environmental influences on the covariation between hyperactivity and conduct disturbance in juvenile twins. *Journal of Child Psychology and Psychiatry, 37*, 803–816.

Silva, P. A., Hughes, P., Williams, S., & Faed, J. M. (1988). Blood lead, intelligence, reading attainment, and behaviour in eleven year old children in Dunedin, New Zealand. *Journal of Child Psychology and Psychiatry, 29*, 43–52.

Silver, L. B. (1987). The "magic cure": A review of the current controversial approaches for treating learning disabilities. *Journal of Learning Disabilities, 20*, 498–504.

Silver, L. B. (1989). Learning disabilities. Introduction. *Journal of the American Academy of Child and Adolescent Psychiatry, 28*, 309–313.

Silver, L. B. (1991). Developmental learning disorders. In M. Lewis (Ed.), *Child and adolescent psychiatry: A comprehensive textbook.* Baltimore: Williams & Wilkins.

Silverman, W. K. (1993). DSM and classification of anxiety disorders in children and adults. In C. G. Last (Ed.), *Anxiety across the lifespan: A developmental perspective.* New York: Springer.

Silverman, W. K. (1994). Structured diagnostic interviews. In T. H. Ollendick, N. J. King, & W. Yule (Eds.), *International handbook of phobic and anxiety disorders in children and adolescents* (pp. 293–316). New York: Plenum Press.

Silverman, W. K., & Ginsburg, G. S. (1998). Anxiety disorders. In T. H. Ollendick & M. Hersen (Eds.), *Handbook of child psychopathology* (3rd ed.). New York: Plenum.

Silverstein, A. B. (1982). Note on the constancy of the IQ. *American Journal of Mental Deficiency, 87,* 227–228.

Silverstein, L. B. (1991). Transforming the debate about child care and maternal employment. *American Psychologist, 46,* 1025–1032.

Simon, E. W., Toll, D. M., & Whitehair, P. M. (1994). A naturalistic approach to the validation of facilitated communication. *Journal of Autism and Developmental Disorders, 24,* 647–657.

Simonoff, E., Bolton, P., & Rutter, M. (1996). Mental retardation: Genetic findings, clinical implications and research agenda. *Journal of Child Psychology and Psychiatry, 37,* 259–280.

Singer, L., Arendt, R., Farkas, K., Minnes, S., Huang, J., & Yamashita, T. (1997). Relationship of prenatal cocaine exposure and maternal postpartum psychological distress to child development outcome. *Development and Psychopathology, 9,* 473–489.

Singh, N. N., Oswald, D. P., & Ellis, C. R. (1998). Mental retardation. In T. H. Ollendick & M. Hersen (Eds.), *Handbook of child psychopathology.* New York: Plenum Press.

Siperstein, G. N., & Bak, J. J. (1985). Effects of social behavior on children's attitudes toward their mildly and moderately mentally retarded peers. *American Journal of Mental Deficiency, 90,* 319–327.

Skinner, B. F. (1948). *Walden two.* London: Macmillan.

Skinner, B. F. (1953). *Science and human behavior.* New York: Macmillan.

Skinner, B. F. (1968). *The technology of teaching.* New York: Appleton-Century-Crofts.

Skrzypek, G. J. (1969). Effect of perceptual isolation and arousal on anxiety, complexity preference, and novelty preference in psychopathic and neurotic delinquents. *Journal of Abnormal Psychology, 74,* 321–329.

Slentz, K., Close, D., Benz, M., & Taylor, V. (1982). *Community Living Assessment and Teaching System (CLATS): Self-care curriculum.* Omro, WI: Conover.

Sloan, M., Adiri, M., & Arian, A. (1998). Adverse political events and adjustment: Two cross-cultural studies. *Journal of the American Academy of Child and Adolescent Psychiatry, 37,* 1058–1069.

Slomkowski, C., Klein, R., & Mannuzza, S. (1995). Is self-esteem an important outcome in hyperactive children? *Journal of Abnormal Child Psychology, 23,* 303–315.

Sloper, P., Knussen, C., Turner, S., & Cunningham, C. (1991). Factors related to stress and satisfaction with life in families of children with Down's syndrome. *Journal of Child Psychology and Psychiatry, 32,* 655–676.

Smith, G. T., & Goldman, M. S. (1994). Alcohol expectancy theory and the identification of high risk adolescents. *Journal of Research on Adolescence, 4,* 229–248.

Smith, G. T., Goldman, M. S., Greenbaum, P. E., and Christiansen, B. A. (1995). Expectancy for social facilitation from drinking: The divergent paths of high-expectancy and low-expectancy adolescents. *Journal of Abnormal Psychology, 104,* 32–40.

Smith, J. & Prior, M. (1995). Temperament and stress resilience in school-age children: A within-families study. *Journal of the American Academy of Child and Adolescent Psychiatry, 34,* 168–179.

Smith, P. K. (1988). Children's play and its role in early development: A re-evaluation of the "play ethos." In A. D. Pellegrini (Ed.), *Psychological bases for early education.* New York: Wiley.

Smith, S. D., Pennington, B. E., Kimberling, W. J., & Ing, P. S. (1990). Familial dyslexia. Use of genetic linkage data to define subtypes. *Journal of the American Academy of Child and Adolescent Psychiatry, 29,* 204–213.

Smith, S. L. (1970). School refusal with anxiety: A review of 60 cases. *Canadian Psychiatric Association Journal, 15,* 257–264.

Smith, T. (1999, Spring). Outcome of early intervention for children with autism. *Clinical Psychology: Science and Practice, 6,* 33–49.

Snow, M. E., Hertzig, M. E., & Shapiro, T. (1987). Rate of development in young autistic children. *Journal of the American Academy of Child and Adolescent Psychiatry, 26,* 834–835.

Snowling, M. J. (1991). Developmental reading disorders. *Journal of Child Psychology and Psychiatry, 32,* 49–77.

Sonuga-Barke, E. J. S. (1994). On dysfunction and function in psychological theories of childhood disorder. *Journal of Child Psychology and Psychiatry, 35,* 801–815.

Sonuga-Barke, E. J. S. (1998). Categorical models of childhood disorder: A conceptual and empirical analysis. *Journal of Child Psychology and Psychiatry, 39,* 115–133.

Sonuga-Barke, E. J. S., Houlberg, K., & Hall, M. (1994). When is "impulsiveness" not impulsive? The case of hyperactive children's cognitive style. *Journal of Child Psychology and Psychiatry, 35,* 1247–1253.

Sparrow, S. S., Balla, D., & Cicchetti, D. V. (1984). *Vineland Adaptive Behavior Scales.* Circle Pines, MN: American Guidance Service.

Spence, S. H. (1994). Cognitive therapy with children and adolescents: from theory to practice. *Journal of Child Psychology and Psychiatry, 35,* 1191–1228.

Spielberger, C. D. (1973). *Manual for the State-Trait Anxiety Inventory for Children.* Palo Alto, CA: Consulting Psychologists Press.

Spirito, A., Stark, L. J., & Tyc, V. L. (1994). Stressors and coping strategies described during hospitalization by chronically ill children. *Journal of Clinical Child Psychology, 23,* 314–322.

Spitz, R. A. (1946). Anaclitic depression. In *The psychoanalytic study of the child,* Vol. 2. New York: International Universities Press.

Spock, B. M., & Rothenberg, M. (1992). *Dr. Spock's baby and child care.* New York: Pocket Books.

Spreen, O. (1988). Prognosis of learning disability. *Journal of Consulting and Clinical Psychology, 56,* 836–842.

Spring, B., Chiodo, J., & Bowen, D. J. (1987). Carbohyrates, tryptophan, and behavior: A methodological review. *Psychological Bulletin, 102,* 234–256.

Sroufe, L. A. (1986). Appraisal: Bowlby's contribution to psychoanalytic theory and developmental psychology; attachment; separation; loss. *Journal of Child Psychology and Psychiatry, 27,* 841–849.

Sroufe, L. A. (1997). Psychopathology as an outcome of development. *Development and Psychopathology, 9,* 251–268.

Sroufe, L. A., & Fleeson, J. (1986). Attachment and the construction of relationships. In W. W. Hartup & Z. Rubin (Eds.), *Relationships and development.* Hillsdale, NJ: Erlbaum.

Sroufe, L. A., & Rutter, M. (1984). The domain of developmental psychopathology. *Child Development, 55,* 17–29.

Stahl, A. (1991). Beliefs of Jewish-Oriental mothers regarding children who are mentally retarded. *Education and Training in Mental Retardation, 26,* 361–369.

Stanger, C., Achenbach, T. M., & Verhulst, F. C. (1997). Accelerated longitudinal comparisons of aggressive versus delinquent syndromes. *Development and Psychopathology, 9,* 43–58.

Stanger, C., MacDonald, V. V., McConaughy, S. H., & Achenbach, T. M. (1996). Predictors of cross-informant syndromes among children and youths referred for mental health services. *Journal of Abnormal Child Psychology. 24,* 597–614.

Stanley, L. (1980). Treatment of ritualistic behavior in an eight-year-old girl by response prevention: A case report. *Journal of Child Psychology and Psychiatry, 21,* 85–90.

Stanovich, K. E. (1986). Cognitive processes and the reading problems of learning-disabled children: Evaluating the assumption of specificity. In J. K. Torgesen and B. Y. L. Wong (Eds.), *Psychological and educational perspectives on learning disabilities.* New York: Academic Press.

Stanovich, K. E. (1989). Learning disabilities in broader context. *Journal of Learning Disabilities, 22,* 287–291, 297.

Stanovich, K. E. (1991). Conceptual and empirical problems with discrepancy definitions of reading disability. *Learning Disability Quarterly, 14,* 269–280.

Stanovich, K. E. (1994). Does dyslexia exist? *Journal of Child Psychology and Psychiatry, 35,* 579–595.

Stark, K. D., Reynolds, W. M., & Kaslow, N. J. (1987). A comparison of the relative efficacy of self-control therapy and a behavioral problem-solving therapy for depression in children. *Journal of Abnormal Child Psychology, 15,* 91–113.

Stark, K. D., Rouse, L. W., & Kurowski, C. (1994). Psychological treatment approaches for depression in children. In W. M. Reynolds & H. F. Johnston (Eds.), *Handbook of depression in children and adolescents.* New York: Plenum Press.

State, M. W., King, B. H., & Dykens, E. (1997). Mental retardation: A review of the past 10 years. Part II. *Journal of the American Academy of Child and Adolescent Psychiatry, 36,* 1664–1671.

Stattin, H., & Magnusson, D. (1990). *Paths through life: Vol. 2. Pubertal maturation in female development.* Hillsdale, NJ: Erlbaum.

Staub, D., & Peck, C. A. (January 1994/December 1995). What are the outcomes for nondisabled students? *Educational Leadership, 52,* 36–40.

Steffenburg, S., Gillberg, C., Hellgren, L., Andersson, L., Gillberg, I. C., Jakobsson, G., & Bohman, M. (1989). A twin study of autism in Denmark, Finland, Iceland, Norway and Sweden. *Journal of Child Psychology and Psychiatry, 30,* 405–416.

Stein, A., Woolley, H., Cooper, S. D., & Fairburn, C. G. (1994). An observational study of mothers with eating disorders and their infants. *Journal of Child Psychology and Psychiatry, 35,* 733–748.

Steinberg, L., Lamborn, S. D., Darling, N., Mounts, N. S., & Dornbusch, S. M. (1994). Over-time changes in adjustment and competence among adolescents from authoriative, authoritarian, indulgent, and neglectful families. *Child Development, 65,* 754–770.

Steiner, H., & Lock, J. (1998). Anorexia nervosa and bulimia nervosa in children and adolescents: A review of the past 10 years. *Journal of the American*

Academy of Child and Adolescent Psychiatry, 37, 352–359.

Steinhausen, H. C. (1988). Comparative studies of psychosomatic and chronic diseases among children and adolescents. In E. J. Anthony & C. Chiland (Eds.), *The child in his family,* Vol. 8. New York: Wiley.

Steinhausen, H. C. (1997). Outcome of anorexia nervosa in the younger patient. *Journal of Child Psychology and Psychiatry, 38,* 271–276.

Steinhausen, H.-C., Willms, J., & Spohr, H.-L. (1993). Long-term psychopathological and cognitive outcome of children with fetal alcohol syndrome. *Journal of the American Academy of Child and Adolescent Psychiatry, 32,* 990–994.

Sternberg, K. J., & Lamb, M. E. (1991). Can we ignore context in the definition of child maltreatment? *Development and Psychopathology, 3,* 87–92.

Sternberg, R. J., Wagner, R. K., Williams, W. M., & Horvath, J. A. (1995). Testing common sense. *American Psychologist, 50,* 912–927.

Stetsenko, A., Little, T. D., Oettingen, G., & Baltes, P. B. (1995). Agency, control, and means-ends beliefs about performance. *Developmental Psychology, 31,* 285–299.

Stevenson, J. (1996). Developmental changes in the mechanisms linking language disabilities and behavior disorders. In J. H. Beitchman, N. J. Cohen, M. M. Konstantareas, & R. Tannock (Eds.), *Language, learning, and behavior disorders.* New York: Cambridge University Press.

Stevenson, J., & Fredman, G. (1990). The social environmental correlates of reading ability. *Journal of Child Psychology and Psychiatry, 31,* 681–698.

Stevenson, J., Pennington, B. F., Gilger, J. W., DeFries, J. C., & Gillis, J. J. (1993). Hyperactivity and spelling disability: Testing for shared genetic aetiology. *Journal of Child Psychology and Psychiatry, 34,* 1137–1152.

Stewart, R. B., Mobley, L. A., Van Tuyl, S. S., & Salvador, M. A. (1987). The first-born's adjustment to the birth of a sibling: A longitudinal assessment. *Child Development, 58,* 341–355.

Stone, W. L. (1997). Autism in infancy and early childhood. In D. J. Cohen & F. R. Volkmar (Eds.), *Handbook of autism and pervasive developmental disorders.* New York: John Wiley.

Stone, W. L., & LaGreca, A. M. (1990). The social status of children with learning disabilities. A reexamination. *Journal of Learning Disabilities, 23,* 23–37.

Stores, G. (1996). Assessment and treatment of sleep disorders in children and adolescents. *Journal of Child Psychology and Psychiatry, 37,* 907–925.

Stormont-Spurgin, M., & Zentall, S. S. (1995). Contributing factors in the manifestation of aggression in preschoolers with hyperactivity. *Journal of Child Psychology and Psychiatry, 36,* 491–509.

Stothard, S. E., & Hulme, C. (1995). A comparison of phonological skills in children with reading comprehension difficulties and children with decoding difficulties. *Journal of Child Psychology and Psychiatry, 36,* 399–408.

Strauss, A., & Corbin, J. (1990). *Basics of qualitative research.* Newbury Park, CA: Sage.

Strauss, C. C. (1994). Overanxious disorder. In T. H. Ollendick, N. J. King, & W. Yule (Eds.), *International handbook of phobic and anxiety disorders in children and adolescents.* New York: Plenum Press.

Strauss, C. C., & Last, C. G. (1993). Social and simple phobias in children. *Journal of Anxiety Disorders, 7,* 141–152.

Strauss, C. C., Lease, C. A., Last, C. G., & Francis, G. (1988). Overanxious disorder: An examination of developmental differences. *Journal of Abnormal Child Psychology, 16,* 433–443.

Strean, H. S. (1970). *New approaches in child guidance.* Metuchen, NJ: The Scarecrow Press.

Streissguth, A. P., Barr, H. M., Sampson, P. D., Darby, B. L., & Martin, D. C. (1989). IQ at age 4 in relation to maternal alcohol use and smoking during pregnancy. *Developmental Psychology, 25,* 3–11.

Streissguth, A. P., Bookstein, F. L., Sampson, P. D., & Barr, H. M. (1995). Attention: Prenatal alcohol and continuities of vigilance and attentional problems from 4 through 14 years. *Development and Psychopathology, 7,* 419–446.

Streissguth, A. P., Martin, D. C., Barr, H. M., Sandman, B. M., Kirchner, G. L., & Darby, D. L. (1984). Intrauterine alcohol and nicotine exposure: Attention and reaction time in 4-year-old children. *Developmental Psychology, 20,* 533–541.

Strober, M. (1995). Family-genetic perspectives on anorexia nervosa and bulimia nervosa. In K. D. Brownell & C. G. Fairburn (Eds.), *Eating disorders and obesity: A comprehensive handbook.* New York: Guilford Press.

Strober, M., & Humphrey, L. (1987). Familial contributions to the etiology and course of anorexia nervosa and bulimia. *Journal of Consulting and Clinical Psychology, 55,* 654–659.

Stunkard, A. J., & Sobal, J. (1995). Psychosocial consequences of obesity. In K. D. Brownell & C. G. Fairburn (Eds.), *Eating disorders and obesity: A comprehensive handbook.* New York: Guilford Press.

Sullivan, R. C. (1997). Diagnosis autism: Can you handle it! In D. J. Cohen & F. R. Volkmar (Eds.), *Handbook of autism and pervasive developmental disorders.* New York: John Wiley.

Susman, E. J. (1993). Psychological, contextual, and psychobiological interactions: A developmental perspective on conduct disorder. *Development and Psychopathology, 5,* 181–189.

Swanson, H. L. (1987). Information processing theory and learning disabilities. *Journal of Learning Disabilities, 20,* 3–7.

Swanson, J. M., McBurnett, K., Christian, D. L., & Wigal, T. (1995). Stimulant medications and the treatment of children with ADHD. In T. H. Ollendick & R. J. Prinz (Eds.), *Advances in clinical child psychology.* New York: Plenum Press.

Swedo, S. E., Rapoport, J. L., Cheslow, D. L., Leonard, H. L., Ayoub, E. M., Hosier, D. M., & Wald, E. R. (1989b). High prevalence of obsessive-compulsive symptoms in patients with Sydenhams' Chorea. *American Journal of Psychiatry, 146,* 246–249.

Swedo, S. E., Rapoport, J. L., Leonard, H., Lenane, M., & Cheslow, D. (1989c). Obsessive-compulsive disorder in children and adolescents: Clinical phenomenology of 70 consecutive cases. *Archives of General Psychiatry, 46,* 335–341.

Swedo, S. E., Schapiro, M. B., Grady, C. L., Cheslow, D. L., Leonard, H. L., Kumar, A., Friedland, R., Rapoport, S. I., & Rapoport, J. L. (1989a). Cerebral glucose metabolism in childhood-onset obsessive-compulsive disorder. *Archives of General Psychiatry, 46,* 518–523.

Sykes, D. H., Hoy, E. A., Bill, J. M., McClure, B. G., Halliday, H. L., & Reid, M. M. (1997). Behavioural adjustment in school of very low birthweight children. *Journal of Child Psychology and Psychiatry, 38,* 315–325.

Sylva, K. (1994). School influences on children's development. *Journal of Child Psychology and Psychiatry, 35,* 135–170.

Szatmari, P. (1992). The epidemiology of attention-deficit hyperactivity disorders. In G. Weiss (Ed.), *Child and adolescent psychiatry clinics of North America.* Philadelphia: Saunders.

Szatmari, P., Bartolucci, G., Bremner, R., Bond, S., & Rich, S. (1989). A follow-up study of high-functioning autistic children. *Journal of Child Psychology and Psychiatry, 33,* 489–507.

Szatmari, P., Offord, D. R., & Boyle, M. H. (1989). Correlates, associated impairments, and patterns of service utilization of children with attention deficit disorders: Findings from the Ontario Child Health Study. *Journal of Child Psychology and Psychiatry, 30,* 205–217.

Szymanski, L. S., & Crocker, A. C. (1985). Mental retardation. In H. I. Kaplan & B. J. Sadock (Eds.), *Comprehensive textbook of psychiatry/IV.* Baltimore: Williams and Wilkins.

Szymanski, L. S., & Kaplan, L. C. (1991). Mental retardation. In J. M. Wiener (Ed.), *Textbook of child & adolescent psychiatry.* Washington, DC: American Psychiatric Association.

Tager-Flüsberg, H. (1993). What language reveals about the understanding of minds in children with autism. In S. Baron-Cohen, H. Tager-Flusberg, & D. J. Cohen (Eds.), *Understanding other minds.* New York: Oxford.

Tager-Flüsberg, H. (1997). Perspectives on language and communication in autism. In D. J. Cohen & F. R. Volkmar (Eds.), *Handbook of autism and pervasive developmental disorders.* New York: John Wiley.

Takanishi, R., & DeLeon, P. H. (1994). A Head Start for the 21st century. *American Psychologist, 49,* 120–122.

Tanner, J. M. (1970). Physical growth. In P. H. Mussen (Ed.), *Carmichael's manual of child development,* Vol. 1. New York: John Wiley.

Tannock, R. (1998). Attention deficit hyperactivity disorder: Advances in cognitive, neurobiological, and genetic research. *Journal of Child Psychology and Psychiatry, 39,* 65–99.

Tao, K-T. (1992). Hyperactivity and attention deficit disorder syndrome in China. *Journal of the American Academy of Child and Adolescent Psychiatry, 31,* 1165–1166.

Taras, M. E., & Matese, M. (1990). Acquisition of self-help skills. In J. L. Matson (Ed.), *Handbook of behavior modification with the mentally retarded.* New York: Plenum.

Target, M. and Fonagy, P. (1994). The efficacy of psychoanalysis for children: Prediction of outcome in a developmental context. *Journal of the American Academy of Child and Adolescent Psychiatry, 33,* 1134–1144.

Tarnowski, K. J., & Nay, S. M. (1989). Locus of control in children with learning disabilities and hyperactivity: A subgroup analysis. *Journal of Learning Disabilities, 22,* 381–383.

Tarullo, L. B., DeMulder, E. K., Ronsaville, D. S., Brown, E., & Radke-Yarrow, M. (1995). Maternal depression and maternal treatment of siblings as predictors of child psychopathology. *Developmental Psychology, 31,* 395–405.

Taylor, E. (1994). Syndromes of attention deficit and hyperactivity. In M. Rutter, E. Taylor, & L. Hersov (Eds.), *Child and adolescent psychiatry: Modern approaches.* New York: Blackwell Scientific.

Taylor, E. (1995). Dysfunctions of attention. In D. Cicchetti, & D. J. Cohen (Eds.), *Developmental psychopathology.* New York: John Wiley.

Taylor, H. G. (1988a). Learning disabilities. In E. J. Mash & L. G. Terdal (Eds.), *Behavioral assessment of childhood disorders,* 2nd ed. New York: Guilford.

Taylor, H. G. (1988b). Neuropsychological testing: Relevance for assessing children's learning disabilities. *Journal of Consulting and Clinical Psychology, 56,* 795–800.

Taylor, H. G. (1989). Learning disabilities. In E. J. Mash & R. A. Barkley (Eds.), *Treatment of childhood disorders.* New York: Guilford.

Tennant, C. (1988). Parental loss in childhood: Its effects in adult life. *Archives of General Psychiatry, 45,* 1045–1050.

Teodori, J. B. (1993). Neurological assessment. In T. H. Ollendick & M. Hersen (Eds.), *Handbook of child and adolescent assessment.* Boston: Allyn & Bacon.

Terr, L. (1979). Children of Chowchilla. *The Psychoanalytic Study of the Child, 34,* 522–563.

Terr, L. (1983). Chowchilla revisited: The effects of psychic trauma four years after a school-bus kidnapping. *American Journal of Psychiatry, 140,* 1543–1550.

Tesman, J. R., & Hills, A. (1994). Developmental effects of lead exposure in children. *Social Policy Report. Society for Research in Child Development, VIII (3),* 1–16.

Teti, D. M., Messinger, D. S., Gelfand, D. M., & Isabella, R. (1995). Maternal depression and the quality of early attachment: An examination of infants, preschoolers, and their mothers. *Developmental Psychology, 31,* 364–376.

Thapar, A., Gottesman, I. I., Owen, M. J., O'Donovan, M., & McGuffin, P. (1994). The genetics of mental retardation. *British Journal of Psychiatry, 164,* 747–758.

Thapar, A., & McGuffin, P. (1995). Are anxiety symptoms in childhood heritable? *Journal of Child Psychology and Psychiatry, 36,* 439–447.

Thatcher, R. W. (1994). Psychopathology of early frontal lobe damage: Dependence on cycles of development. *Development and Psychopathology, 6,* 565–596.

Thelen, E. (1986). Treadmill-elicited stepping in seven-month-old infants. *Child Development, 57,* 1498–1506.

Thelen, E., & Adolph, K. E. (1992). Arnold L. Gessell: The paradox of nature and nuture. *Developmental Psychology, 28,* 368–380.

Thelen, M. H., Powell, A. L., Lawrence, C., & Kuhnert, M. E. (1992). Eating and body image concerns among children. *Journal of Consulting and Clinical Psychology, 21,* 41–46.

Thienemann, M. & Steiner, H. (1993). Family environment of eating disordered and depressed adolescents. *International Journal of Eating Disorders, 14,* 43–48.

Thomas, A. M., Peterson, L., & Goldstein, D. (1997). Problem solving and diabetes regimen adherence by children and adolescents with IDDM in social pressure situations: A reflection on normal development. *Journal of Pediatric Psychology, 22,* 541–561.

Thompson, J. R., & McEvoy, M. A. (1992). Letters to the editor. Normalization—still relevant today. *Journal of Autism and Developmental Disorders, 22,* 666–671.

Thompson, L. A. (1997). Behavioral genetics and the classification of mental retardation. In W. E., MacLean (Ed.), *Ellis' handbook of mental deficiency, psychological theory and research.* Mahwah, NJ: Lawrence Erlbaum.

Thompson, R. J. Jr., Gustafson, K. E., George, L. K., & Spock, A. (1994). Change over a 12-month period in the psychological adjustment of children and adolescents with cystic fibrosis. *Journal of Pediatric Psychology, 19,* 189–203.

Thomson, G. O. B., Raab, G. M., Hepburn, W. S., Hunter, R., Fulton, M., & Laxen, D. P. H. (1989). Blood-lead levels and children's behaviour—results from the Edinburgh Lead Study. *Journal of Child Psychology and Psychiatry, 30,* 515–528.

Thorndike, E. L. (1905). *The elements of psychology.* New York: Seiler.

Thorndike, R. L., Hagen, E. P., & Sattler, J. M. (1986). *Stanford-Binet Intelligence Scale,* 4th ed. Chicago: Riverside.

Thurber, C. A., & Sigman, M. D. (1998). Preliminary models of risk and protective factors for childhood homesickness: Review and empirical synthesis. *Child Development, 69,* 903–934.

Tienari, P., Lahti, I., Sorri, A., Naarala, M., Moring, J., Kaleva, M., Wahlberg, K-E., & Wynne, L. C. (1990). Adopted-away offspring of schizophrenics and controls: The Finnish adoptive family study of schizophrenia. In L. N. Robins & M. Rutter (Eds.), *Straight and devious pathways from childhood to adulthood.* New York: Cambridge University Press.

Timko, C., Baumgartner, M., Moos, R. H., & Miller, J. III (1993). Parental risk and resistance factors among children with juvenile rheumatic disease: A four-year predictive study. *Journal of Behavioral Medicine, 16,* 571–588.

Timko, C., Stovel, K. W., Moos, R. H., & Miller, J. J. (1992). A longitudinal study of risk and resistance factors among children with juvenile rheumatic disease. *Journal of Clinical Child Psychology, 21,* 132–142.

Tolan, P. H. (1987). Implication of age of onset for delinquency risk. *Journal of Abnormal Child Psychology, 15,* 47–65.

Tolan, P. H., & Thomas, P. (1995). The implications of age of onset for delinquency risk II: Longitudinal data. *Journal of Abnormal Child Psychology, 23,* 157–181.

Tomporowski, P. D., & Tinsley, V. (1997). Attention in mentally retarded persons. In W. E. MacLean (Ed.), *Ellis' Handbook of mental deficiency, psychological theory and research.* Mahwah, NJ: Lawrence Erlbaum.

Tonge, B. (1994). Separation anxiety disorder. In T. H. Ollendick, N. J. King, & W. Yule (Eds.), *International handbook of phobic and anxiety disorders in children and adolescents.* New York: Plenum Press.

Torgersen, S. (1993). Relationship between adult and childhood anxiety disorders: Genetic hypothesis. In C. G. Last (Ed.), *Anxiety across the lifespan: A developmental perspective.* New York: Springer.

Torgesen, J. K. (1986). Learning disabilities theory: Its current state and future prospects. *Journal of Learning Disabilities, 19,* 399–407.

Toro, P. A., Weissberg, R. P., Guare, J., & Liebenstein, N. L. (1990). A comparison of children with and without learning disabilities on social problem-solving skill, school behavior, and family background. *Journal of Learning Disabilities, 23,* 115–120.

Touyz, S. W., & Beumont, P. J. V. (1997). Behavioral treatment to promote weight gain in anorexia nervosa. In D. M. Garner & P. E. Garfinkel (Eds.), *Handbook of treatment for eating disorders* (2nd ed.). New York: Guilford Press.

Treffert, D. A. (1988). The idiot savant: A review of the syndrome. *American Journal of Psychiatry, 145,* 563–572.

Tremblay, G. C., & Israel, A. C. (1998). Children's adjustment to parental death. *Clinical Psychology: Science and Practice, 5,* 424–438.

Tremblay, G. C., & Peterson, L. (1999). Prevention of childhood injury: Clinical and public policy issues. *Clinical Psychology Review, 19,* 415–434.

Trickett, P. K., McBride-Chang, C., & Putnam, F. W. (1994). The classroom performance and behavior of sexually abused females. *Development and Psychopathology, 6,* 183–194.

Tryphonas, H. (1979). Factors possibly implicated in hyperactivity. In R. L. Trites (Ed.), *Hyperactivity in children.* Baltimore: University Park Press.

Tsai, L. Y. & Ghaziuddin, M. (1991). Autistic disorder. In J. M. Wiener (Ed.), *Textbook of child & adolescent psychiatry.* Washington, DC: American Psychiatric Press.

Tuddenham, R. D. (1962). The nature and measurement of intelligence. In L. Postman (Ed.), *Psychology in the making.* New York: Knopf.

Tuma, J. M. (1982). Pediatric psychology: Conceptualization and definition. In J. M. Tuma (Ed.), *Handbook for the practice of pediatric psychology.* New York: Wiley.

Tuma, J. M. (1989). Mental health services for children: The state of the art. *American Psychologist, 44,* 188–199.

Tuma, J. M., & Pratt, J. M. (1982). Clinical child psychology practice and training: A survey. *Journal of Clinical Child Psychology, 11,* 27–34.

Turkington, C. (1992, Dec.). Ruling opens door—a crack—to IQ-testing some black kids. *The APA Monitor, 23,* 28–29.

Turnure, J. E. (1985). Communication and cues in the functional cognition of the mentally retarded. In N. R. Ellis & N. W. Bray (Eds.), *International Review of Research in Mental Retardation, Vol. 13.* New York: Academic Press.

U.S. Bureau of the Census (1998). *Statistical Abstract of the United States: 1998* (118th ed.). Washington, DC: U.S. Government Printing Office.

U.S. Office of Education. (1977). Definition and criteria for defining students as learning disabled. *Federal Register,* 42:250, p. 65083. Washington, DC: U.S. Government Printing Office.

Udwin, O. (1993). Annotation: Children's reactions to traumatic events. *Journal of Child Psychology and Psychiatry, 34,* 115–127.

Ullmann, C. A. (1957). Teachers, peers, and tests as predictors of adjustment. *Journal of Educational Psychology, 48,* 257–267.

Ullmann, L. P., & Krasner, L. (1975). *A psychological approach to abnormal behavior,* 2nd ed. Englewood Cliffs, NJ: Prentice Hall.

UNICEF (1991). *The girl child.* NY: United Nations Children's Fund Programme Publications.

Valla, J. P., Bergeron, L., Gaudet, N., Reydellet, C., & Harris, T. O. (1994). An empirical comparison between the DSM and psychodynamic approaches for assessment of child disorders in children attending outpatient clinics. *Journal of Child Psychology and Psychiatry, 35,* 1409–1418.

Valone, K., Goldstein, M. J., & Norton, J. P. (1984). Parental expressed emotion and psychophysiological reactivity in an adolescent sample at risk for schizophrenia spectrum disorder. *Journal of Abnormal Psychology, 93,* 448–457.

Van Acker, R. (1997). Rett's syndrome: A pervasive developmental disorder. In D. J. Cohen & F. R. Volkmar (Eds.), *Handbook of autism and pervasive developmental disorders.* New York: John Wiley.

van Balkom, A. J. L. M., van Oppen, P., Vermeulen, A. W. A., van Dyck, R., Nauta, M. C. E., & Vorst, H. C. M. (1994). A metaanalysis on the treatment of obsessive compulsive disorder: A comparison of antidepressants, behavior, and cognitive therapy. *Clinical Psychology Review, 14,* 359–381.

van der Meere, J., & Sergeant, J. (1988). Focused attention in pervasively hyperactive children. *Journal of Abnormal Child Psychology, 16,* 627–639.

van der Meere, J., Wekking, E., & Sergeant, J. (1991). Sustained attention and pervasive hyperactivity. *Journal of Child Psychology and Psychiatry, 32,* 275–284.

Vandereycken, W. (1995). The families of patients with an eating disorder. In K. D. Brownell & C. G. Fairburn (Eds.), *Eating disorders and obesity: A comprehensive handbook.* New York: Guilford Press.

Varni, J. W., Katz, E. R., Colegrove, J. R., & Dolgin, M. (1996). Family functioning predictors of adjustment of children with newly diagnosed cancer: A prospective analysis. *Journal of Child Psychology and Psychiatry, 37,* 321–328.

Varni, J. W., Katz, E. R., & Waldron, S. A. (1993). Cognitive-behavioral treatment interventions in childhood cancer. *The Clinical Psychologist, 46,* 192–197.

Vasey, M. W. (1995). Social anxiety disorders. In A. R. Eisen, C. A. Kearney, & C. A. Schaefer (Eds.), *Clinical handbook of anxiety disorders in children and adolescents.* Northvale, NJ: Jason Aronson.

Vellutino, F. R. (1979). *Dyslexia. Theory and research.* Cambridge MA: MIT Press.

Vellutino, F. R. (1987). Dyslexia, *Scientific American, 256,* 34–41.

Venter, A., Lord, C., & Schopler, E. (1992). A follow-up study of high-functioning autistic children. *Journal of Child Psychology and Psychiatry, 33,* 489–507.

Verhulst, F. C., & Koot, H. M. (1991). Longitudinal research in child and adolescent psychiatry. *Journal of the American Academy of Child and Adolescent Psychiatry, 30,* 361–368.

Verhulst, F. C., & Koot, H. M. (1992). *Child psychiatric epidemiology.* Newbury Park, CA: Sage.

Verhulst, F. C., & van der Ende, J. (1997). Factors associated with mental health service use in the community. *Journal of the American Academy of Child and Adolescent Psychiatry, 36,* 901–909.

Vernberg, E. M., & Vogel, J. M. (1993). Interventions with children after disasters. *Journal of Clinical Child Psychology, 22,* 485–498.

Vernberg, E., Beery, S. H., Ewell, K. K., & Absender, D. A. (1993). Parents' use of friendship facilitation strategies and the formation of friendships in early adolescence: A prospective study. *Journal of Family Psychology, 7,* 356–369.

Vernick, J., & Karon, M. (1965). Who's afraid of death on a leukemia ward? *American Journal of Diseases of Children, 109,* 393–397.

Vogel, J. M., & Vernberg, E. M. (1993). Children's psychological responses to disasters. *Journal of Clinical Child Psychology, 22,* 464–484.

Volkmar, F. R. (1987). Annotation. Diagnostic issues in the pervasive developmental disorders. *Journal of Child Psychology and Psychiatry, 28,* 365–369.

Volkmar, F. R. (1991). Childhood schizophrenia. In M. Lewis (Ed.), *Child and adolescent psychiatry. A comprehensive textbook.* Baltimore: Williams and Wilkins.

Volkmar, F. R. (1996). Childhood and adolescent psychosis: A review of the past 10 years. *Journal of the American Academy of Child and Adolescent Psychiatry, 35,* 843–851.

Volkmar, F. R., Becker, D. F., King, R. A., & McGlashan, T. H. (1995). Psychotic processes. In D. Cicchetti & D. J. Cohen (Eds.), *Developmental psychopathology.* New York: John Wiley.

Volkmar, F. R., Carter, A., Grossman, J., & Klin, A. (1997a). Social development in autism. In D. J. Cohen & F. R. Volkmar (Eds.), *Handbook of autism and pervasive developmental disorders.* New York: John Wiley.

Volkmar, F. R., Cicchetti, D. V., Dykens, E., Sparrow, S. S., Leckman, J. F., & Cohen, D. J. (1988). An evaluation of the Autism Behavior Checklist. *Journal of Autism and Developmental Disorders, 18,* 81–97.

Volkmar, F. R., Klin, A., & Cohen, D. J. (1997b). Diagnosis and classification of autism and related conditions: Consensus and issues. In D. J. Cohen & F. R. Volkmar (Eds.), *Handbook of autism and pervasive developmental disorders.* New York: John Wiley.

Volkmar, F. R., Sparrow, S. S., Goudreau, D., Cicchetti, D. V., Paul, R., & Cohen, D. J. (1987). Social deficits in autism. An operational approach using the Vineland Adaptive Behavior Scales. *Journal of the American Academy of Child and Adolescent Psychiatry, 26,* 156–161.

Vostanis, B., Smith, B., Chung, M. C., & Corbett, J. (1994). Early detection of childhood autism: A review of screening instruments and rating scales. *Child: Care, Health, and Development, 20,* 165–177.

Wagner, B. M. (1997). Family risk factors for child and adolescent suicidal behavior. *Psychological Bulletin, 121,* 246–298.

Wagner, M. M., & Blackorby, J. (1996). Transition from high school to work or college: How special education students fare. *The Future of Children, 6,* 103–120.

Wagner, W. G., Smith D., & Norris, W. R. (1988). The psychological adjustment of enuretic children: A comparison of two types. *Journal of Pediatric Psychology, 13,* 33–38.

Wahler, R. G., & Dumas, J. E. (1984). Changing the observational coding styles of insular and noninsular mothers: A step towards maintenance of parent training effects. In R. F. Dangel & R. A. Polster (Eds.), *Parent training: Foundations of research and practice.* New York: Guilford.

Wahler, R. G., & Dumas, J. E. (1989). Attentional problems in dysfunctional mother-child interactions: An interbehavioral model. *Psychological Bulletin, 105,* 116–130.

Wakschiag, L. S., & Leventhal, B. L. (1996). Consultation with young autistic children and their families. *Journal of the American Academy of Child and Adolescent Psychiatry, 35,* 963–965.

Walco, G. A., Sterling, C. N., Conte, P. M., & Engel, R. G. (1999). Empirically supported treatments in pediatric psychology: Disease-related pain. *Journal of Pediatric Psychology, 24,* 155–167.

Waldman, I. D., Lillienfeld, S. O., & Lahey, B. B. (1995). Toward construct validity in the childhood disruptive behavior disorders: Classification and diagnosis in DSM-IV and beyond. In T. H. Ollendick & R. J. Prinz, (Eds.), *Advances in clinical child psychology.* Vol. 17. New York: Plenum Press.

Walker, C. E., Kenning, M., & Faust-Companile, J. (1989). Enuresis and encopresis. In E. J. Mash & R. A. Barkley (Eds.), *Treatment of childhood behavior disorders.* New York: Guilford.

Walker, H., Greenwood, C., Hops, H., & Todd, N. (1979). Differential effects of reinforcing topographic components of social interaction. *Behavior Modification, 3,* 291–321.

Wallander, J. L., & Varni, J. W. (1998). Effects of pediatric chronic physical disorders on child and family adjustment. *Journal of Child Psychology and Psychiatry, 39,* 29–46.

Wallerstein, J. S. (1991). The long-term effects of divorce on children: A review. *Journal of the American Academy of Child and Adolescent Psychiatry, 30,* 349–360.

Walsh, B. T. (1995). Pharmacotherapy of eating disorders. In K. D. Brownell & C. G. Fairburn (Eds.), *Eating disorders and obesity: A comprehensive handbook.* New York: Guilford Press.

Warren, S. L., Huston, L., Egeland, B., & Sroufe, L. A. (1997). Child and adolescent anxiety disorders and early attachment. *Journal of the American Academy of Child and Adolescent Psychiatry, 36,* 637–644.

Waterhouse, L., & Fein, D. (1997). Perspectives on social impairment. In D. J. Cohen & F. R. Volkmar (Eds.), *Handbook of autism and pervasive developmental disorders.* New York: John Wiley.

Watkins, C. E., Campbell, V. L., Nieberding, R., & Hallmark, R. (1995). Contemporary practice of psychological assessment by clinical psychologists. *Professional Psychology: Research and Practice, 26,* 54–60.

Watkins, J. M., Asarnow, R. F., & Tanguay, P. E. (1988). Symptom development in childhood onset schizophrenia. *Journal of Child Psychology and Psychiatry, 29,* 865–878.

Watson, J. B. (1913). Psychology as the behaviorist views it. *Psychological Review, 20,* 158–177.

Watson, J. B. (1930). *Behaviorism.* New York: Norton.

Watson, J. B., & Rayner, R. (1920). Conditioned emotional reactions. *Journal of Experimental Psychology, 3,* 1–14.

Webster-Stratton, C. (1984). Randomized trial of two parent-training programs for families with conduct-disordered children. *Journal of Consulting and Clinical Psychology, 52,* 666–678.

Webster-Stratton, C. (1985). Predictors of treatment outcome in parent training for conduct-disordered children. *Behavior Therapy, 16,* 223–243.

Webster-Stratton, C. (1990). Enhancing the effectiveness of self-administered videotape parent training for families with conduct-problem children. *Journal of Abnormal Child Psychology, 18,* 479–492.

Webster-Stratton, C. (1994). Advancing videotape parent training: A comparison study, *Journal of Consulting and Clinical Psychology, 62,* 583–593.

Webster-Stratton, C. (1996). Early intervention with videotape modeling: Programs for families of children with Oppositional Defiant Disorder or Conduct Disorder. In E. S. Hibbs & P. S. Jensen (Eds.), *Psychosocial treatments for child and adolescent disorders: Empirically based strategies for clinical practice.* Washington, DC: American Psychological Association.

Webster-Stratton, C., Hollinsworth, T., & Kolpacoff, M. (1989). The long-term effectiveness and clinical significance of three cost-effective training programs for families with conduct-problem children. *Journal of Consulting and Clinical Psychology, 57,* 550–553.

Webster-Stratton, C., & Spitzer, A. (1991). Development, reliability, and validity of the Daily Telephone Discipline Interview. *Behavioral Assessment, 13,* 221–239.

Webster-Stratton, C., & Spitzer, A. (1996). Parenting of young children with conduct problems: New insights using qualitative methods. In T. H. Ollendick & R. J. Prinz (Eds.), *Advances in clinical child psychology* (Vol 18). New York: Plenum Press.

Wechsler, D. (1989). *Wechsler Preschool and Primary Scale of Intelligence—Revised (WPPSI-R).* San Antonio, TX: The Psychological Corporation.

Wechsler, D. (1991). *Manual for the Wechsler Intelligence Scale for Children—Third Edition (WISC-III).* San Antonio, TX: The Psychological Corporation.

Weinberg, M. K., Tronick, E. Z., Cohn, J. F., & Olson, K. L. (1999). Gender differences in emotional expressivity and self-regulation during early infancy. *Developmental Psychology, 35,* 175–188.

Weinberger, D. R. (1987). Implications of normal brain development for the pathogenesis of schizophrenia. *Archives of General Psychiatry, 44,* 660–669.

Weinberger, D. R. (1994). Biological basis of schizophrenia: Structural/functional considerations relevant to potential for antipsychotic drug response. *Journal of Clinical Psychiatry Monograph, 12:2,* 4–8.

Weinrott, M. R., Jones, R. R., & Howard, J. R. (1982). Cost-effectiveness of teaching family programs for delinquents: Results of a national evaulation. *Evaluation review, 6,* 173–201.

Weiss, G. (1991). Attention deficit hyperactivity disorder. In M. Lewis (Ed.), *Child and adolescent psychiatry. A comprehensive textbook.* Baltimore: Williams & Wilkins.

Weiss, G., & Hechtman, L. T. (1986). *Hyperactive children grown up.* New York: Guilford.

Weiss, K. B., Gergen, P. J., Hodgson, T. A. (1992). An economic evaluation of asthma in the United States. *New England Journal of Medicine, 326,* 862–866.

Weissberg, R. P., Cowen, E. L., Lotyczewski, B. S., & Gesten, E. L. (1983). The primary mental health project: Seven consecutive years of program outcome research. *Journal of Consulting and Clinical Psychology, 51,* 100–107.

Weissman, M. M., Kidd, K. K., & Prusoff, B. A. (1982). Variability in rates of affective disorders in relatives of depressed and normal probands. *Archives of General Psychiatry, 39,* 1397–1403.

Weissman, M. M., Warner, V., Wichramaratne, P., & Prusoff, B. A. (1988). Onset of major depression in adolescence and early adulthood: Findings from a family study of children. *Journal of Affective Disorders, 15,* 269–277.

Weissman, M. M., Warner, V., Wickramarante, P., Moreau, D., & Olfson, M. (1997). Offspring of depressed parents: 10 years later. *Archives of General Psychiatry, 54,* 932–940.

Weist, M. D. (1997). Expanded school mental health services: A national movement in progress. In T. H. Ollendick & R. J. Prinz (Eds.), *Advances in clinical child psychology* (Vol. 19). New York: Plenum Press.

Weist, M. D., Finney, J. W., Barnard, M. U., Davis, C. D., & Ollendick, T. H. (1993). Empirical selection of psychosocial treatment targets for children and adolescents with diabetes. *Journal of Pediatric Psychology, 18,* 11–28.

Weisz, J. R., Chaiyasit, W., Weiss, B., Eastman, K. L., & Jackson, E. W. (1995). A multimethod study of problem behavior among Thai and American children in school: Teacher reports versus direct observations. *Child Development, 66,* 402–415.

Weisz, J. R., Suwanlet, S., Chaiyasit, W., Weiss, B., Walter, B. R., & Anderson, W. W. (1998). Thai and American perspectives on over- and undercontrolled child behavior problems: Exploring the threshold model among parents, teachers, and psychologists. *Journal of Consulting and Clinical Psychology, 56,* 601–609.

Weisz, J. R., Thurber, C. A., Sweeney, L., Proffitt, V. D., & LeGagnoux, G. L. (1997). Brief treatment of mild-to-moderate child depression using primary and secondary control enhancement training. *Journal of Consulting and Clinical Psychology, 65,* 703–707.

Weithorn, L. A. (1987). Informed consent for prevention research involving children: Legal and ethical issues. In J. A. Steinberg & M. M. Silverman (Eds.), *Preventing mental disorders.* Rockvill, MD: U.S. Department of Health and Human Services.

Wellman, H. M. (1993). Early understanding of mind: The normal case. In S. Baron-Cohen, H. Tager-Flusberg, & D. J. Cohen (Eds.), *Understanding other minds.* New York: Oxford Press.

Wells, K. (1987). Annotation. Scientific issues in the conduct of case studies. *Journal of Child Psychology and Psychiatry, 28,* 783–790.

Wells, K. C., Forehand, R., & Griest, D. L. (1980). Generality of treatment effects from treated to untreated behaviors resulting from a parent training program. *Journal of Clinical Child Psychology, 9,* 217–219.

Wender, P. H., Kety, S. S., Rosenthal, D., Schulsinger, F., Ortmann, J., & Lunde, I. (1986). Psychiatric disorders in the biological and adoptive families of adopted individuals with affective disorders. *Archives of General Psychiatry, 43,* 923–929.

Werner, E. E., & Smith, R. S. (1982). *Vulnerable but invincible.* New York: McGraw-Hill.

Werry, J. S. (1986). Physical illness, symptoms and allied disorders. In H. C. Quay & J. S. Werry (Eds.), *Psychopathological disorders of childhood,* 3rd ed. New York: Wiley.

Werry, J. S. (1992). Child and adolescent (early onset) schizophrenia: A review in light of DSM-III-R. *Journal of Autism and Developmental Disorders, 22,* 601–624.

Werry, J. S. (1994). Diagnostic and classification issues. In T. H. Ollendick, N. J. King, & W. Yule (Eds.), *International handbook of phobic and anxiety disorders in children and adolescents.* New York: Plenum.

Werry, J. S., & Aman, M. G. (1999). *Practitioner's guide to psychoactive drugs for children and adolescents* (2nd ed.). New York: Plenum Medical Book Company.

Wertlieb, D., Hauser, S. T., & Jacobson, A. M. (1986). Adaptation to diabetes: Behavior symptoms and family context. *Journal of Pediatric Psychology, 11,* 463–479.

West, D. J. (1982). *Delinquency: Its roots, careers, and prospects.* London: Heinemann.

West, D. J. (1985). Delinquency. In M. Rutter & L. Hersov (Eds.), *Child and adolescent psychiatry: Modern approaches,* 2nd ed. Oxford: Blackwell Scientific Publications.

West, M. O., & Prinz, R. J. (1987). Parental alcoholism and childhood psychopathology. *Psychological Bulletin, 102,* 204–218.

West, S. G., Sandler, I., Pillow, D. R., Baca, L., & Gersten, J. C. (1991). The use of structural equation modeling in generative research: Toward the design of a preventative intervention for bereaved children. *American Journal of Community Psychology, 19,* 459–480.

Whalen, C. K. (1989). Attention deficit and hyperactivity disorders. In T. H. Ollendick & M. Hersen (Eds.), *Handbook of child psychopathology.* New York: Plenum.

Whalen, C. K., & Henker, B. (1985). The social worlds of hyperactive (ADDH) children. *Clinical Psychology Review, 5,* 447–448.

Whalen, C. K., & Henker, B. (1998). Attention-deficit/hyperactivity disorders. In T. H. Ollendick & M. Hersen (Eds.), *Handbook of child psychopathology.* New York: Plenum Press.

Whitaker, A., Johnson, J., Shaffer, D., Rappoport, J., Kalikow, K., Walsh, B. T., Davies, M., Braiman, S., & Dolinsky, A. (1990). Uncommon troubles in young people: Prevalence estimates of selected psychiatric disorders in a nonreferred adolescent population. *Archives of General Psychiatry, 47,* 487–496.

White, J. L., Moffitt, T. E., & Silva, P. A. (1989). A prospective replication of the protective effects of IQ in subjects at high risk for juvenile delinquency. *Journal of Consulting and Clinical Psychology, 57,* 719–724.

White, K. J., & Kistner, J. (1992). The influence of teacher feedback on young children's peer preferences and perceptions. *Developmental Psychology, 28,* 933–940.

White, S. H. (1992). G. Stanley Hall: From philosophy to developmental psychology. *Developmental Psychology, 28,* 25–34.

Whitehill, M., DeMyer-Gapin, S., & Scott, T. J. (1976). Stimulation-seeking in antisocial pre-adolescent children. *Journal of Abnormal Psychology, 85,* 101–104.

Whitehurst, G. J. (1982). Language development. In B. B. Wolman (Ed.), *Handbook of developmental psychology.* Englewood Cliffs, NJ: Prentice Hall.

Whitehurst, G. J., & Fischel, J. E. (1994). Early developmental language delay: What, if anything, should the clinician do about it? *Journal of Child Psychology and Psychiatry, 35,* 613–648.

Whitehurst, G. J., & Valdez-Menchaca, M. C. (1988). What is the role of reinforcement in early language acquisition? *Child Development, 59,* 430–440.

Whitman, T. L., Hantula, D. A., & Spence, B. H. (1990). Current issues in behavior modification with mentally retarded persons. In J. L. Matson (Ed.), *Handbook of behavior modification with the mentally retarded.* New York: Plenum.

Whitman, T. L., O'Callaghan, M., & Sommer, K. (1997). Emotion and retardation. In W. E. MacLean (Ed.), *Ellis' handbook of mental deficiency, psychological theory and research.* Mahwah, NJ: Lawrence Erlbaum.

Widiger, T. A., Frances, A. J., Pincus, H. A., Davis, W. W., & First, M. B. (1991). Toward an empirical classification for DSM-IV. *Journal of Abnormal Psychology, 100,* 280–288.

Wiebe, D. J., Alderfer, M. A., Palmer, S. C., Lindsay, R., & Jarrett, L. (1994). Behavioral self-regulation in adolescents with type I diabetes: Negative affectivity and blood glucose symptom perception. *Journal of Consulting and Clinical Psychology, 62,* 1204–1212.

Wilfley, D. E., & Rodin, J. (1995). Cultural influences on eating disorders. In K. D. Brownell & C. G. Fairburn (Eds.), *Eating disorders and obesity: A comprehensive handbook.* New York: Guilford Press.

Williams, B. R., Ponesse, J. S., Schachar, R. K., Logan, G. D., & Tannock, R. (1999). Development of inhibitory control across the life span. *Developmental Psychology, 35,* 205–213.

Williams, C. D. (1959). The elimination of tantrum behavior by extinction procedures: Case report. *Journal of Abnormal and Social Psychology, 59,* 269.

Williams, S., & McGee, R. (1996). Reading in childhood and mental health in early adulthood. In J. H. Beitchman, N. J. Cohen, M. M. Konstantareas, & R. Tannock (Eds.), *Language learning, and behavior disorders.* New York: Cambridge University Press.

Williamson, D. A., Baker, J. D., & Cubic, B. A. (1993). Advances in pediatric headache research. In T. H. Ollendick & R. J. Prinz (Eds.) *Advances in clinical child psycholog.* Vol. 15. New York: Plenum Press.

Williamson, D. A., Bentz, B. G., & Rabalais, J. Y. (1998). Eating disorders. In T. H. Ollendick & M. Hersen (Eds.), *Handbook of child psychopathology* (3rd ed.). New York: Plenum Press.

Williamson, D. A., Head, S. B., & Baker, J. D. (1993). Behavioral treatment. In V. B. Van Hassel & M. Hersen (Eds.), *Handbook of behavior therapy and pharmacotherapy for children: A comparative analysis.* Boston: Allyn and Bacon.

Willner, A. C., Braukmann, G. J., Kirigin, K. A., & Wolf, M. M. (1978). Achievement Place: A community model for youths in trouble. In D. Marholin (Ed.), *Child behavior therapy.* New York: Gardner.

Wills, T. A., & Filer, M. (1996). Stress-coping model of adolescent substance use. In T. H. Ollendick & R. J. Prinz (Eds.), *Advances in clinical child psychology* (Vol. 18). New York: Plenum Press.

Wilsher, C. (1991). Is medicinal treatment of dyslexia advisable? In M. Snowling & M. Thomson (Eds.), *Dyslexia: Integrating theory and practice.* London: Whurr Publishers.

Wilson, C. C., & Haynes, S. N. (1985). Sleep disorders. In P. H. Bornstein & A. E. Kazdin (Eds.), *Handbook of clinical behavior therapy with children.* Homewood, IL: Dorsey.

Wilson, G. T., & Fairburn, C. G. (1993). Cognitive treatments for eating disorders. *Journal of Consulting and Clinical Psychology, 61,* 261–269.

Wilson, G. T., Fairburn, C. G., & Agras, W. S. (1997). Cognitive-behavioral therapy for bulimia nervosa. In D. M. Garner & P. E. Garfinkel (Eds.), *Handbook of treatment for eating disorders.* 2nd ed. New York: Guilford Press.

Wilson, G. T., Heffernan, K., & Black, C. M. D. (1996). Eating disorders. In E. J. Mash & R. A. Barkley (Eds.), *Child psychopathology,* New York: Guilford Press.

Wilson, R. S., & Matheny, A. P. (1986). Behavior-genetics research in infant temperament: The Louisville Twin Study. In R. Plomin & J. Dunn (Eds.), *The study of temperament: Changes, continuities and challenges.* Hillsdale, NJ: Erlbaum.

Wilson, S. R., Mitchell, J. H., Rolnick, S. & Fish, L. (1993). Effective and ineffective management behaviors of parents of infants and young children with asthma. *Journal of Pediatric Psychology, 18,* 63–81.

Windle, M. (1990). A longitudinal study of antisocial behaviors in early adolescence as predictors of late adolescent substance use: Gender and ethnic group differences. *Journal of Abnormal Psychology, 99,* 86–91.

Winett, R. A. (1995). A framework for health promotion and disease prevention programs. *American Psychologist, 50,* 341–350.

Wing, L. (1997). Syndromes of autism and atypical development. In D. J. Cohen & F. R. Volkmar (Eds.), *Handbook of autism and pervasive developmental disorders.* New York: John Wiley.

Wolf, L., Fisman, S., Ellison, D., & Freeman, T. (1998). Effect of sibling perception of differential parental treatment in sibling dyads with one disabled child. *Journal of the American Academy of Child and Adolescent Psychiatry, 37,* 1317–1325.

Wolf, M. M., Braukmann, C. J., & Ramp, K. A. (1987). Serious delinquent behavior as part of a significantly handicapping condition: Cures and supportive environments. *Journal of Applied Behavior Analysis, 20,* 347–359.

Wolfe, V. V. (1998). Child sexual abuse. In E. J. Mash & R. A. Barkley, (Eds.), *Treatment of childhood disorders* (2nd ed.). New York: Guilford Press.

Wolfe, V. V., & Birt, J. (1995). The psychological sequelae of child sexual abuse. In T. H. Ollendick & R. J. Prinz (Eds.), *Advances in clinical child psychology.* Vol. 17. New York: Plenum Press.

Wolfensberger, W. (1980). *The principle of normalization in human services.* Toronto: National Institute on Mental Retardation.

Wolman, B. B. (1972). Psychoanalytic theory of infantile development. In B. B. Wolman (Ed.), *Handbook of child psychoanalysis: Research theory and practice.* New York: Van Nostrand Reinhold.

Wolraich, M., Wilson, D. B., & White, J. W. (1995). The effect of sugar on behavior or cognition in children. *Journal of the American Medical Association, 274,* 1617–1621.

Wong, B. Y. L., Butler, D. L., Ficzere, S. A., & Kuperis, S. (1997). Teaching adolescents with learning disabilities and low achievers to plan, write, and revise compare-and-contrast essays. *Learning Disabilities Research & Practice, 12,* 2–15.

Wood, B. L. (1994). One articulation of the structural family therapy model: A biobehavioral family model of chronic illness in children. *Journal of Family Therapy, 16,* 53–72.

Wood, B., Watkins, J. B., Boyle, J. T., Noguiera, J., Aimand, E., & Carrol, L. (1989). The "psychosomatic family" model: An empirical analysis. *Family Process, 28,* 399–417.

Wood, M., & Valdez-Menchaca, M. C. (1996). The effect of a diagnostic label of language delay on adults' perceptions of preschool children. *Journal of Learning Disabilities, 29,* 582–588.

Woodard, L., Taylor, E., & Dowdney, L. (1998). The parenting and family functioning of children with hyperactivity. *Journal of Child Psychology and Psychiatry, 39,* 161–169.

Woodcock, R. W., & Johnson, M. B. (1978). *Woodcock-Johnson Psycho-Educational Battery.* Allen, TX: DLM/teaching Resources.

Woodcock, R. W., Mather, N. & Barnes, E. K. (1987). *Woodcock Mastery Tests-Revised: Examiner's Manual, Forms G and H.* Circle Pines, MN: American Guidance Service.

Woodhead, M. (1988). When psychology informs public policy. The case of early childhood intervention. *American Psychologist, 43,* 443–454.

Woodward, W. M. (1979). Piaget's theory and the study of mental retardation. In N. R. Ellis (Ed.), *Handbook of mental deficiency.* Hillsdale, NJ: Erlbaum.

World Health Organization (1992). *International classification of diseases: Tenth revision.* Chapter V. Mental and behavioural disorders. Diagnostic criteria for research. Geneva: Author.

Wright, H. F. (1960). Observational child study. In P. H. Mussen (Ed.), *Handbook of research methods in child development.* New York: John Wiley.

Wright, L. (1977). Conceptualizing and defining psychosomatic disorders. *American Psychologist, 32,* 625–628.

Wysocki, T. (1993). Associations among teen-parent relationships, metabolic control, and adjustment to diabetes in adolescents. *Journal of Pediatric Psychology, 18,* 441–452.

Yates, A. (1989). Curent perspectives on the eating disorders: I. History, psychological and biological aspects. *Journal of the American Academy of Child and Adolescent Psychiatry, 28,* 813–828.

Yates, A. (1990). Current perspectives on the eating disorders: II. Treatment, outcome, and research directions. *Journal of the American Academy of Child and Adolescent Psychiatry, 29,* 1–9.

Yirimya, N., Erel, O., Shaked, M., & Solomonica-Levi, D. (1998). Meta-analysis comparing theory of mind abilities in individuals with autism, individuals with mental retardation, and normally developing individuals. *Psychological Bulletin, 124,* 283–307.

Young, M. H., Brennan, L. C., Baker, R. D., & Baker, S. S. (1996). Functional encopresis. In R. S. Feldman (Ed.), *The psychology of adversity.* Amherst: University of Massachusetts Press.

Youngblade, L. M., & Belsky, J. (1992). Parent-child antecedents of five-year olds' close friendships: A longitudinal analysis. *Developmental Psychology, 28,* 700–714.

Ysseldyke, J. E., Thurlow, M. L., Christenson, S. L., & Muyskens, P. (1991). Classroom and home learning differences between students labeled as educable mentally retarded and their peers. *Education and Training in Mental Retardation, 26,* 3–17.

Yule, W. (1994). Posttraumatic stress disorder. In T. H. Ollendick, N. J. King, & W. Yule (Eds.), *International handbook of phobic and anxiety disorders in children and adolescents* (pp. 223–240). New York: Plenum Press.

Yule, W., Udwin, O., & Murdoch, K. (1990). The "Jupiter" sinking: Effects on children's fears, depression and anxiety. *Journal of Child Psychology and Psychiatry, 31,* 1051–1061.

Zametkin, A. J., Ernst, M., & Silver, R. (1998). Laboratory and diagnostic testing in child and adolescent psychiatry: A review of the past 10 years. *Journal of the American Academy of Child and Adolescent Psychiatry, 37,* 464–472.

Zametkin, A. J., & Rapoport, J. L. (1986). The pathophysiology of attention deficit disorder with hyperactivity: A review. In B. B. Lahey & A. E. Kazdin (Eds.), *Advance in clinical child psychology.* Vol. 9. New York: Plenum.

Zax, M., & Cowen, E. L. (1967). Early identification and prevention of emotional disturbance in a public school. In E. L. Cowen, E. A. Gardner, & M. Zax (Eds.), *Emergent approaches to mental health problems.* New York: Appleton-Century-Crofts.

Zeanah, C. H., Anders, T. F., Seifer, R., & Stern, D. N. (1989). Implications of research on infant development for psychodynamic theory and practice. *Journal of the American Academy of Child and Adolescent Psychiatry, 28,* 657–668.

Zero to Three/National Center for Clinical Infant Programs (1995). *Diagnostic classification: 0–3.* Arlington, VA: Author.

Zigler, E., Balla, D., & Hodapp, R. (1984). On the definition and classification of mental retardation. *American Journal of Mental Deficiency, 89,* 215–230.

Zigler, E., & Styfco, S. J. (1993). Using research and theory to justify and inform Head Start expansion. *Social Policy Report. Society for Research In Child Development. VII, Number 2.*

Zivcic, I. (1993). Emotional reactions of children to war stress in Croatia. *Journal of the American Academy of Child and Adolescent Psychiatry, 32,* 709–713.

Zoccolillo, M. (1992). Co-occurrence of conduct disorder and its adult outcomes with depressive and anxiety disorders: A review. *Journal of the American Academy of Child and Adolescent Psychiatry, 31,* 547–556.

CREDITS

CHAPTER 1

Page 4 Fig.1-1 Weisz, J. R. Suwanlet, S., Chaiyasit, W., Weiss, B., Walter, B., R., & Anderson, W. W. (1998). Thai and American perspectives on over- and undercontrolled child behavior problems: Exploring the threshold model among parents, teachers, and psychologists. *Journal of Consulting and Clinical Psychology, 56*, 601–609. Copyright American Psychological Association.

7 Fig. 1–2 Data from Verhulst and Koot, 1992.

9 Table 1-1 Adapted from Hartung, C. M., & Widiger, T. A. (1998). Gender differences in the diagnosis of mental disorders: Conclusions and controversies of the DSM-IV. *Psychological Bulletin, 123*, 260–278.

CHAPTER 2

Page 26 Table 2-3 Based on Bryant, 1977; Whitehurst, 1982.

30 Table 2-5 Adapted from Lyon-Ruth, K., Zeanah, C. H., & Benoit, D. (1996). Disorder and risk for disorder during infancy and toddlerhood. In E.J. Mash & R. A. Barkley (Eds.), *Child psychopathology.* NY: Guilford.

31 Figure 2-2 Adapted from Maccoby, E. E. & Martin, J. A. (1983). Socialization in the context of the family: Parent-child interaction. In P. H. Mussen (Ed.), *Handbook of Child Psychology*, vol. IV. NY: Wiley.

34 Figure 2-3 U.S. Bureau of the Census, Statistical Abstract of the United States: 1998 (118th Ed.). Washington, DC, 1998.

38 Table 2-6 Based in part on Coie et al., 1993.

40 Table 2-7 Adapted from Masten, A.S. & Coatsworth, J.D. (1998). The development of competence in favorable and unfavorable environments: Lessons from research on successful children. *American Psychologist, 53*, 205–220.

41 Table 2-8 Adapted from Masten, A.S. & Coatsworth, J.D. (1998). The development of competence in favorable and unfavorable environments: Lessons from research on successful children. *American Psychologist, 53*, 205–220.

41 Table 2-9 Adapted from Rutter, 1987.

43 Figure 2-4 With permission from the *Annual Review of Psychology*, Volume 46, © 1995, by Annual Reviews, www.AnnualReviews.org

44 Figure 2-5 Adapted from Achenbach,T.M. (1990). Conceptualization of developmental psychopathology. In M. Lewis & S. M. Miller (Eds.), *Handbook of Developmental Psychopathology*, NY: Plenum Publishing Corporation. Reprinted by permission.

CHAPTER 4

74 Table 4-1 Adapted from Dadds, M.R., Sanders, M.R., Morrison, M., Roberz, M. (1992). Childhood depression and conduct disorder: II. An analysis of family interaction patterns in the home. *Journal of Abnormal Child Psychology, 101*, 505–513, NY: Plenum Publishing Corporation. Reprinted by permission.

78 Figure 4-1 From Ramey and Campbell, 1984.

80 Figure 4-4 Adapted from Koegal, O'Dell, and Koegal, 1987. *Journal of Autism and Developmental Disorders, 17*, 187–200, NY: Plenum Publishing Corporation. Reprinted by permission.

CHAPTER 5

94 Table 5-1 Reprinted with permission from the Diagnostic and Statistical Manual of Mental Disorders, Fourth Edition. Copyright 1994 American Psychiatric Association.

98 Table 5-2 Adapted from Achenbach, T.M. (1991). Integrative guide for the 1991 CBCL/4-18, YSR and TRF profiles. Burlington, VT: University of Vermont, Department of Psychiatry.

107 Figure 5-4 From Achenbach et al., 1991. By permission of author.

CHAPTER 6

Page 115 Table 6-1 Copyright by T. M. Achenbach. Reproduced by Permission.

117 Figure 6-1–Reprinted from *Journal of Child Psychology and Psychiatry, 30*, King, N. J., Ollier, K., Iacuone, R., Schuster, S., Bays, K., Gullone, E., & Ollendick, T. H., "Fears of children and adolescents: A cross-sectional Australian study using the Revised-Fear Survey Schedule for Children," 775–784. Copyright 1989 with kind permission from Elsevier Science Ltd., The Boulevard, Langford Lane, Kilington OX5 1GB, UK.

118 Table 6-2 Reprinted from *Behavior Research and Therapy, 27*, Ollendick, T. H., King, N. J., & Frary, R. B., Fears in children and adolescents: Reliability and generalizability across gender, age, and nationality, 19–26. Copyright 1989, with kind permission from Elsevier Science Ltd., The Boulevard, Langford Lane, Kilington OX5 1GB, UK.

119 Figure 6-2 Adapted from Öst, 1987.

121 Table 6-3 By permission of author Annette M. LaGreca.

123 Table 6-4 Reprinted with permission from the Diagnostic and Statistical Manual of Mental Disorders, Fourth Edition. Copyright 1994, American Psychiatric Association.

125 Table 6-5 Reprinted with permission from the Diagnostic and Statistical Manual of Mental Disorders, Fourth Edition. Copyright 1994, American Psychiatric Association.

126 Table 6-6 Adapted from Strauss, C.C., Lease, C.A., Last, C.G., & Francis, G. (1998). Overanxious disorder: An examination of developmental differences. *Journal of Abnormal Child Psychology, 16*, 433–443, NY: Plenum Publishing Corporation. Reprinted by permission.

127 Table 6-7 Reprinted with permission from the Diagnostic and Statistical Manual of Mental Disorders, Fourth Edition. Copyright 1994, American Psychiatric Association.

130 Table 6-8 Reprinted with permission from the Diagnostic and Statistical Manual of Mental Disorders, Fourth Edition. Copyright 1994, American Psychiatric Association.

131 Figure 6-3 Reprinted from LaGreca, A.M., Silverman, W.K., & Wasserman, S.B. (1998). Children's predisaster functioning as a predictor of posttraumatic stress following Hurricane Andrew. *Journal of Consulting and Clinical Psychology, 66*, 883–892. Copyright American Psychological Association.

132 Table 6-9 Reprinted with permission from the Diagnostic and Statistical Manual of Mental Disorders, Fourth Edition. Copyright 1994, American Psychiatric Association.

134 Table 6-10 Adapted from The biology of obsessions and compulsions. Rapoport, J.L. Copyright © (1989) by Scientific American, Inc. All right reserved.

CHAPTER 7

Page 150 Table 7-1 Adapted from Kazdin, A. E. (1989). Identifying depression in children: A comparison of alternative selection criteria. *Journal of Abnormal Child Psychology, 17*, 437–454, NY: Plenum Publishing Corporation. Reprinted by permission.

151 Table 7-2 Reprinted with permission from the Diagnostic and Statistical Manual of Mental Disorders, Fourth Edition. Copyright 1994, American Psychiatric Association.

151 Table 7-3 Reprinted with permission from the Diagnostic and Statistical Manual of Mental Disorders, Fourth Edition. Copyright 1994, American Psychiatric Association.

154 Figure 7-1 From Hankin, B. L., Abramson, L. Y., Moffitt, T. E., Silva, P. A., McGee, R., & Angell, K. E. (1998). Development of depression from preadolescence to young adulthood: Emerging gender differences in a 10 year longitudinal study. *Journal of Abnormal Psychology, 107*, 128–140. Copyright American Psychological Association.

155 Figure 7-2 From Lewinsohn, P. M., Rhode, P., Seeley, J. R., & Fischer, S. A. (1993). Age cohort changes in the lifetime occurrence of depression and other mental disorders. *Journal of Abnormal Psychology, 102*, 110–120. Copyright American Psychological Association.

162 Table 7-4 Adapted from Weissman, M. M., Warner, V., Wickramarante, P., Moreau, D., & Olfson, M. (1997). Offspring of depressed parents: 10 years later. *Archives of General Psychiatry, 54*, 932–940,

162 Table 7-5 Adapted from Beardslee, W. R., Keller, M. B., Seifer, R., Lavorie, P. W., Staley, J., Podorefsky, D., & Shera, D. (1996).

164 Figure 7-3 Adapted from Murray, 1992.

167 Figure 7-4 Adapted from Lewinsohn, P. M., Rohde, P., & Seeley, J. R. (1996). Adolescent suicidal ideation and attempts: Prevalence, risk factors, and clinical implications. *Clinical Psychology: Science and Practice, 3*, 25–46. Copyright American Psychological Association.

168 Table 7-6 Adapted from Lefkowitz, M., & Testiny, E. (1980). Assessment of childhood depression. *Journal of Consulting and Clinical Psychology, 48*, 43–50. By American Psychological Association.

170 Figure 7-5 From Weisz, J. R., Thurber, C. A., Sweeney, L., Proffitt, V. D., & LeGagnoux, G. L. (1997). Brief treatment of mild-to-moderate child depression using primary and secondary control enhancement training. *Journal of Consulting and Clinical Psychology, 65*, 703–707. Copyright American Psychological Association.

171 Figure 7-6 Adapted from Lewinsohn, P.M., et.al. (1990).

173 Table 7-7 Adapted from Kupersmidt and Patterson, 1991.

175 Figure 7-7 Adapted from Kupersmidt, J. B., & Patterson, C. J. (1991). Childhood peer rejection, aggression, withdrawal, and perceived competence as predictors of self-reported behavior problems in preadolescence. *Journal of Abnormal Child Psychology, 19*, 427–449. NY: Plenum Publishing Corporation. Reprinted by permission.

CHAPTER 8

Page 184 Table 8-1 Adapted from Achenbach (1993). By permission of author.

185 Figure 8-1 Adapted from Stranger, C., Achenbach, T. M., & Verhulst, F. C. (1997). Accelerated longitudinal comparisons of agressive versus delinquent syndromes. *Develoment and Psychopathology, 9*, 43–58.

186 Figure 8-2 From Frick, P. J. (1998). Conduct disorders. In T. H. Ollendick & Hersen, M. (Eds.), *Handbook of Child Psychopathology* (3rd Edition), NY: Plenum Publishing Corporation. Reprinted by permission.

186 Table 8-2 Reprinted with permission from the *Diagnostic and Statistical Manual of Mental Disorders, Fourth Edition.* Copyright 1994, American Psychiatric Association.

187 Table 8-3 Reprinted with permission from the *Diagnostic and Statistical Manual of Mental Disorders, Fourth Edition.* Copyright 1994, American Psychiatric Association.

192 Figure 8-3 Adapted from Lynskey, M. T., Fergusson, D. M., & Horwood, L. J.(1998). The origins of the correlations between tobacco, alcohol, and cannabis use during adolescence. *Journal of Child Psychology and Psychiatry, 39*, 995–1005.

193 Table 8-4 Source: U.S. Bureau of the Census, Statistical Abstract of the United States, 1994 (118 edition). Washington, DC, 1994.

196 Figure 8-4 From Moffitt, T. E. (1993a). Adolescence-limited and life-course-persistent antisocial behavior: A developmental taxonomy. *Psychological Review, 100*, 674–701. Copyright American Psychological Association.

197 Figure 8-5 From Loeber, R., & Hay, D. F. (1994). Developmental approaches to aggression and conduct problems. In M. Rutter & D. F. Hay (Eds.), Development through life: A handbook for clinicians. Malden, MA: Blackwell Scientific. Copyright by Blackwell Scientific. Reprinted with Permission.

198 Figure 8-6 From Dishion, T. J., French, D. C. & Patterson, G. R. (1995). The development and ecology of antisocial behavior. In D. Cicchetti and D. J. Cohen (Eds.), *Developmental psychopathology. Vol.2: Risk, disorder, & adaptation.* New York: John Wiley & Sons.

202 Figure 8-7 From Patterson, G. R., Reid, J. B., & Dishion, T. J. (1992). Reprinted by permission from Castalia Publishing Co.

203 Figure 8-8 From Patterson, G. R., DeBaryshe, B. D., & Ramsey, E. (1989). A developmental perspective on antisocial behavior. *American Psychologist, 44*, 329–335. Copyright American Psychological Association.

206 Figure 8-9 From Dodge and Somberg (1987), Child Development, 58, 213–224. Copyright by The Society for Research in Child Development, Inc. by Permission.

210 Figure 8-10 From Dishion, T. J., French, D. C. & Patterson, G. R. (1995). The development and ecology of antisocial behavior. In D. Cicchetti and D. J. Cohen (Eds.), *Developmental psychopathology. Vol.2: Risk, disorder, & adaptation.* New York: John Wiley & Sons.

217 Figure 8-11 From Henggeler, S. W., Schoenwald, S. K. Borduin, C. M., Rowland, M. D., & Cunningham, P. B. (1998). *Multisystemic treatment of antisocial behavior in children and adolescents.* New York: Guilford.

218 Figure 8-12 Adapted from Henggeler, Melton, and Smith, 1992.

CHAPTER 9

Page 222 Table 9-1 Reprinted with permission from the Diagnostic and Statistical Manual of Mental Disorders, Fourth Edition. Copyright 1994 American Psychiatric Association.

225 Figure 9-1 Adapted from Porrino, L. J., Rapoport, J. L., Behar, D., Sceery, W., Ismond, D. R., & Bunney, W. E. (1983). A naturalistic assessment of the motor activity of hyperactive boys: I. Comparison with normal controls. *Archives of General Psychiatry, 40*, 681–687. Copyright 1983, American Medical Association. Reprinted by permission.

231 Figure 9-2 From Barkley, R. A. (1997). Attention-deficit/ hyperactivity disorder. In E. J. Mash & L. G. Terdal (Eds.). *Assessment of childhood disorders.* NY: Guilford Press.

233 Figure 9-4 Adapted from Milberger, S., Biederman, J., Faraone, S. V., Chen, L., & Jones, J. (1997). ADHD is associated with early initiation of cigarette smoking in children and adolescents. *Journal of the American Academy of Child and Adolescent Psychiatry, 36*, 37–44.

236 Figure 9-5 Adapted with Permission from an illustration by Carol Donner from Youdin, M. B. H. & Riederer, P. (1997), Understanding Parkinson's Disease, *Scientific American, 276*, 52–59.

243 Table 9-3 Copyright by Guilford Press, 1981. Reprinted with permission from R. Barkley, Hyperactivity. In E. Marsh & L. Terdal (Eds.), *Behavioral Assessment of Childhood Disorders.* New York: Guilford Press, 1981.

244 Table 9-4 Copyright by Guilford Press, 1981. Reprinted with permission from R. Barkley, Hyperactivity. In E. Marsh & L. Terdal (Eds.), *Behavioral Assessment of Childhood Disorders.* New York: Guilford Press, 1981.

245 Table 9-5 Adapted from Conners, C. K., Sitarenios, G., Parker, J. D. A., & Epstein, J. N. (1998), The revised Conners Parental Rating Scale (CPRS-R): Factor structure, reliability, and criterion validity. *Journal of Abnormal Child Psychology, 26*, 257–268.

247 Figure 9-6 Adapted from Rapport, M. D., Denney, C., DuPaul, G. J., & Gardner, M. J. (1994). Attention deficit disorder and methylphenidate: Nomalization rates, clinical effectiveness, and response prediciton in 76 children. *Journal of the American Academy of Child and Adolescent Psychiatry, 33*, 882–893.

250 Table 9-7 Based iin part on DuPaul, Guevrement, and Barkley, 1991.

CHAPTER 10

Page 255 Figure 10-1 From *Mental Retardation: Definition, Classification, and Systems of Support*, 9th Ed. AAMR, 1992, p.10.

256 Table 10-1 From *Mental Retardation: Definition, Classification, and Systems of Support*, 9th Ed. AAMR, 1992.

258 Table 10-2 Based on APA (1994) and Singh et al. (1998).

265 Figure 10-3 Courtesy of the March of Dimes Birth Defects Foundation.

266 Table 10-4 Based on Cytryn and Lourie, 1980.

267 Figure 10-4 Adapted from Rossen, M., Klima, E. S., Bellugi, U, Bihrle, A., & Jones, W. (1996). Interaction between language and cognition: Evidence from Williams syndrome. In J. H. Beitchman, N. J. Cohen, M. M. Konstantareas, & R. Tannock (Eds.), *Language, learning, and behavior disorders.* NY: Cambridge University Press.

273 Figure 10-5 Adapted from Atkinson and Shiffrin, 1968, and Swanson, 1987.

277 Table 10-5 Adapted from Bromley and Blacher, 1991.

284 Table 10-7 Adapted from Szymanski, L. S. and Kaplan, L. C. (1991). Mental Retardation. In J. M. Weiner (Ed.), *Textbook of Child and Adolescent Psychiatry*. American Psyciatric Association, Copyright 1991.

286 Table 10-8 From Patton, Beirne, and Payne, 1993. Beirne-Smith, Ittenbach, & Patton, 1998.

CHAPTER 11

295 Table 11-2 Reprinted with permission from the Diagnostic and Statistical Manual of Mental Disorders, Fourth Edition. Copyright 1994 American Psychiatric Association.

298 Table 11-4 Reprinted with permission from the Diagnostic and Statistical Manual of Mental Disorders, Fourth Edition. Copyright 1994 American Psychiatric Association.

301 Figure 11-1 From Taylor, 1988a. Permission to reprint by Guilford Press. Copyright 1988 by Guilford Press.

302 Figure 11-2 Wong, B. Y. L. et al. (1998). Teaching adolescents with learning disabilities and low archivers to plan, write, and revise compare-and-contrast essays. *Learning Disabilities Research & Practice, 12*, 2-15.

302 Figure 11-3 From Taylor, 1988a, Permission to reprint by Guilford Press. Copyright 1988 by Guilford Press.

305 Figure 11-4 Data from Stone and LaGreca, 1990.

309 Figure 11-6 Adapted from Morris & Maiston (1998): *Psychology*. Prentice Hall, Upper Saddle River, NJ.

313 Figure 11-8 Adapted from Taylor, H.G. (1998). Learning disabilities. In E. J. Mash & L. G. Terdal (Eds.), *Behavioral Assessment of childhood disorders, 2/E*. New York: Guilford.

316 Table 11-5 Adapted from Reschley, D. J. (1996). Identification & assessment of students with disabilities. *The Future of Children, 6*, 40-53.

CHAPTER 12

Page 322 Table 12-1 Reprinted with permission from the Diagnostic and Statistical Manual of Mental Disorders, Fourth Edition. Copyright 1994 American Psychiatric Association.

323 Figure 12-1 Adapted from Dissanayake, C. & Crossley, S. A. (1996). Proximity and sociable behaviours in autism: Evidence for attachment. *Journal of Child Psychology and Psychiatry, 37*, 149-156.

329 Table 12-2 Based on Wellman, 1993.

336 Table 12-3 Reprinted with permission from the Diagnostic and Statistical Manual of Mental Disorders, Fourth Edition. Copyright 1994 American Psychiatric Association. Based also on Van Acker (1997), Volkmar, Klin, & Cohen (1997).

338 Table 12-4 Adapted from Newsom, Hovanitz, and Rincover, 1988.

342 Figure 12-2 Adapted from Newsom, C. (1998). Autistic disorder. In E. J. Mash & R. A. Barkley (Eds.), *Treatment of childhood disorders*. NY: Guilford Press.

344 Figure 12-3 Adapted from Durand, V. M. & Carr, E. G. (1991). Functional communications training to reduce challenging behavior: Maintenance and application in new settings. *Journal of Applied Behavior Analysis, 24*, 251-264. Copyright JABA. By permission.

345 Table 12-5 Based on Schopler, 1997.

345 Table 12-6 Adapted from Lovaas, 1987.

347 Table 12-7 Reprinted with permission from the Diagnostic and Statistical Manual of Mental Disorders, Fourth Edition. Copyright 1994 American Psychiatric Association.

349 Table 12-8 Adapted from Green et al., 1992, Russell et al., 1989, and Volkmar et al., 1991.

350 Table 12-9 From A. T. Russell, L. Bott, and C. Sammons, The phenomenology of schizophrenia occurring in childhood, Journal of the American Academy of Child and Adolescent Psychiatry, 28 (3), 399-407, 1989. © by the American Academy of Child and Adolescent Psychiatry.

351 Table 12-10 Adapted from Green, W.H., et.al. (1992). Schizophrenia with childhood onset: A phenomenological study of 38 cases. *Journal of American Academy of Child and Adolescent Psychiatry, 31*, 968-976.

CHAPTER 13

Page 363 Figure 13-1 Adapted from Israel and Shapiro, 1985.

365 Figure 13-2 From Israel, A. C., Guile, C. A., Baker, J. E., & Silverman, W. K. (1994). An evaluation of enhanced self-regulation training in the treatment of childhood obesity, *Journal of Pediatric Psychology, 19*, 737-749. Reprinted by permission from Plenum Publishing Corporation.

367 Table 13-1 Reprinted with permission from the Diagnostic and Statistical Manual of Mental Disorders, Fourth Edition. Copyright 1994, American Psychiatric Association.

367 Table 13-2 Reprinted with permission from the Diagnostic and Statistical Manual of Mental Disorders, Fourth Edition. Copyright 1994, American Psychiatric Association.

369 Table 13-3 Adapted from Childress, et.al. (1993). The Kids'Eating Disorders Survey (KEDS): A study of middle school students. *Journal of the American Academy of Child & Adolescent Psychiatry, 32*, 843-850.

371 Figure 13-3 Adapted from Collins, E. Body figure perceptions and preferences among preadolescent children. *International Journal of Eating Disorders.* Copyright 1991. Reprinted by permission of John Wiley & Sons, Inc.

379 Table 13-4 Adapted from Houts, Berman, and Abramson, 1994.

382 Figure 13-5 Adapted from Stores, G. (1996). Assessment and treatment of sleep disorders in children and adolescents. *Journal of Child Psychology and Psychiatry, 37*, 907-925.

386 Table 13-5 Adapted from Wilson and Haynes, 1985.

CHAPTER 14

393 Figure 14-2 Reprinted by permission of the publisher from article by K. Purcell et al., *Psychosomatic Medicine, 31*, 144-164. Copyright © 1969 by the American Psychosomatic Society, Inc.

396 Figure 14-3 From Wallander, J. L. and Varni, J. W. (1998). Effects of pediatric chronic physical disorders on child and family adjustment. *Journal of Child Psychology and Psychiatry, 39*, 29-46.

401 Table 14-1 Adapted from Karoly and Bay, 1990.

402 Table 14-2 Adapted from Suzanne Bennett Johnson (1984). Test of Diabetes Knowledge, Revised-3. Gainesville: University of Florida. Health Sciences Center.

403 Table 14-3 Adapted from Thomas, Peterson, and Goldstein, 1997.

406 Figure 14-4 Adapted from Osterhaus et al., 1993.

410 Table 14-4 Adapted from Dahlquist, 1992.

CHAPTER 15

419 Table 15-1 Adapted from Durlak, J. A. and Wells, A. M. (1997). Primary prevention mental health programs for children and adolescents: A meta-analytic review. *American Journal of Community Psychology, 25*, 115-152.

420 Figure 15-2 McLoyd, V. C. (1998). Socioeconomic disadvantage and child development. *American Psychologist, 53*, 185-204. Copyright American Psychological Association.

421 Figure 15-3 From Achenbach, T. M. (1990). Conceptualizations of developmental psychopathology. In M. Lewis & S. M. Miller (Eds.), *Handbook of developmental psychopathology*. New York: Plenum.

426 Table 15-2 Adapted from U.S. Bureau of the Census, Statistical Abstract of the United States: 1998 (118th edition). Washington , DC, 1998.

428 Figure 15-4 Adapted from U.S. Bureau of the Census, Statistical Abstract of the United States: 1998 (118th edition). Washington , DC, 1998.

431 Figure 15-5 From Hetherington, E. M., Bridges, M., and Insabella, G. M., (1998). What matters? What does not? Five perspectives on the association between marital transitions and children's adjustment. *American Psychologist, 53*, 167-184. Copyright American Psychological Association.

433 Table 15-3 From English, D. J. (1998). The extent and consequences of child maltreatment. *The Future of Children, 8(1)*, 39-53. A publication of the Center for the Future of Children, The David and Lucile Packard Foundation.

434 Figure 15-6 Adapted from U.S. Bureau of the Census, Statistical Abstract of the United States: 1998 (118th edition). Washington , DC, 1998.

Name Index

Chugh, C.S., 359–360
Churchill, M.P., 395
Cicchetti, D., 19, 20, 43, 149, 163, 174, 279, 432, 433–434, 435, 436
Clarizio, H.F., 168
Clark, A.F., 356
Clark, D.B., 121, 124, 126, 128
Clark, D.C., 362
Clark, G.N., 171
Clark, L.A., 113
Clark, R., 217
Clarke, A.D.B., 254, 259, 261
Clarke, A.M., 254, 259, 261
Clarke-Stewart, A., 426
Claussen, A.H., 436
Cleary, J., 68
Clowes-Hollins, V., 137
Coatsworth, J.D., 40, 41
Cobham, V.E., 142–143
Coe, D.A, 271, 282
Cohen, D.J., 19, 43, 274, 321, 336, 338, 339, 346, 433–434, 435
Cohen, J., 126, 153
Cohen, N.J., 296
Cohen, P., 114, 125–126, 126–127, 153, 369
Cohen-Towee, E.M., 369
Coie, J.D., 38, 204, 207
Colbus, D., 168
Colegrove, R.W., Jr., 400
Coleman, M., 332
Coles, G.S., 311
Collins, E., 370, 371
Collins, M., 355–356
Collins, W.A., 30
Collis, G., 327
Compas, B.E., 35, 42–43, 43, 147, 152, 153, 167, 374, 375
Conduct Problems Prevention Research Group, 211–212, 218
Conger, J., 177
Conley, C., 2
Connell, J.P., 107, 168
Connelly, C.D., 434
Conners, C.K., 106, 107, 239, 245
Conners, R.E., 25
Connolly, K.J., 223
Connor, D.F., 247
Connors, M.E., 367
Cool, J., 103
Cooper, P., 151
Coplan, R.J., 174, 176
Corbin, J., 81–82
Corkum, V., 324
Corley, D.L., 391
Corsaro, W.A., 32
Costello, E.J., 6, 7, 10, 11, 85, 86, 87, 118, 125, 193, 416
Cotler, S., 7
Courchesne, E., 329
Cover Jones, M., 59
Cowen, E.L., 174, 418, 423–424, 424–425

Cox, A., 103–104
Coyne, J.C., 163
Cozby, P.C., 88
Crago, M., 368
Craig, E.M., 287
Cravens, H., 83, 261
Creer, T.L., 389, 390, 391, 392, 393
Crick, N.R., 199, 205
Crijnen, A.A.M., 7
Crimmins, D.B., 343
Crisp, A.H., 370
Crittenden, P.M., 436
Crnic, K.A., 35, 259, 269, 419
Crockenberg, S.B., 30
Crocker, A.C., 284
Cronbach, L.J., 422
Cross, T., 437
Crossley, S.A., 323
Cubic, B.A., 404–405
Cueva, J.E., 247
Culbertson, J.L., 299, 302, 304, 306
Cummings, E.M., 162, 163, 203
Cunningham, P.B., 217
Curran, P.J., 192
Cuskelly, M., 276
Cutting, L.E., 314, 315
Cytryn, L., 148, 266, 284

D

DaCosta, M., 366–367
Dadds, M.R., 73–74, 137, 138–139, 142–143, 163, 276
Dahlquist, L.M., 395, 409, 410
Dainer, D., 375
Danforth, J.D., 282
Dangel, R.F., 67
Daniels, D., 395
Dare, C., 372, 374
Daugherty, T.K., 113
Davidson, W.S., 216
Davies, M., 267
Davies, P.T., 162, 163, 203
Davies, R.R., 274
Davis, B., 106
Davison, G.C., 81
Davison, G.C., 357
Dawson, G., 109, 321, 322, 324–325, 326, 327, 331, 333–334, 340
Deater-Deckard, K., 208
DeBaryshe, B.D., 194, 199
Deering, C.G., 162, 164
DeFries, J.C., 269, 308
DeGiovanni, I.S., 116
deGroot, Koot, Verhulst, (1996), 99
De Haan, E., 144
Deichmann, M.M., 405
Dekovic, M., 33
DeKraai, M.B., 17
Delamater, A.M., 209, 401–402
DeLeon, P.H., 7
De Leon, P.H., 423

Delfini, L.F., 200
DeMyer-Gapin, S., 209
Denney, C., 246
Dennis, A.B., 373
DeStefano, L., 280
Detterman, D.K., 278, 286
Deutsch, C.K., 237–238
Dickson, L., 2
Dietz, W.H., 362, 363–364
Dilsaver, S.C., 128
Dishion, T., 211
Dishion, T.J., 189, 198, 200, 202, 210
Dissanayake, C., 323
Dobow, Huesmann, Eron, (1987), 31
Dodge, K.A., 176–177, 177, 205–206, 206, 207
Doepke, K.J., 398
Doleys, D.M., 376, 377, 378, 380
Dolgin, M.J., 413
Doll, E., 279
Dollinger, S.J., 385, 386
Donahue, M., 304
Donlan, C., 297, 308
Dooling-Liftin, J.D., 225–226, 229
Douglas, J., 411
Douglas, V.I., 159, 223, 230
Downey, G., 163
Dozois, D.J.A., 3, 6, 8
Drabman, R.S., 282, 307, 359
Drotar, D., 389, 395
Dubas, J.S., 25
Dubow, E.F., 419
Dulcan, M.K., 226
Dumas, J.E., 137, 202–203, 204
Dummit, E.S., 51
Dummitt, E.S. III, 120
Dunbar, J., 139
Dunbar-Jacob, J., 404
Duncan, G.J., 429
Dunn, J., 30, 32, 171, 173, 277
Dunn, L.M., 64, 313
Dunn, S.E., 171
DuPaul, G.J., 245, 246, 247, 250
Durand, V.M., 280, 339, 341, 343, 344, 384
Durlak, J.A., 63, 416, 418–419, 425
Dyck, D.G., 161
Dykens, E., 267
Dykens, E.M., 274, 332

E

Eagly, A.H., 25
Earls, F., 9, 193, 195
Eastwood, D., 333
Eaves, L.J., 54, 136, 208
Eccles, J.S., 33, 36
Edelbrock, C., 54, 104, 183
Eder, D., 32
Edwards, G., 225–226, 229
Edwards, K.J., 376, 377, 378, 380
Eggers, C., 350–351